*Major Problems in American
Foreign Relations*

MAJOR PROBLEMS IN AMERICAN HISTORY SERIES

GENERAL EDITOR
THOMAS G. PATERSON

Major Problems in American Foreign Relations
Volume II: Since 1914

DOCUMENTS AND ESSAYS

FOURTH EDITION

EDITED BY
THOMAS G. PATERSON
UNIVERSITY OF CONNECTICUT

DENNIS MERRILL
UNIVERSITY OF MISSOURI-KANSAS CITY

D. C. HEATH AND COMPANY
Lexington, Massachusetts   Toronto

Address editorial correspondence to:
D. C. Heath and Company
125 Spring Street
Lexington, MA 02173

Acquisitions Editor: James Miller
Developmental Editor: Sylvia L. Mallory
Production Editor: Elizabeth Gale
Designer: Jan Shapiro
Production Coordinator: Charles Dutton
Permissions Editor: Margaret Roll

Cover photo: Caricature of United Nations Meeting by Miguel Cavarrubias. Courtesy, The Library of Congress. This caricature was originally published in *Vogue.*

Cover research: Sharon Donahue, Photo Editor

Published simultaneously in Canada.

Printed in the United States of America.

International Standard Book Number: 0-669-35078-8

Library of Congress Catalog Number: 94-77213

10   9   8   7   6   5   4

For
Aaron M. Paterson
Barbara Shaw Merrill

Preface

Newspaper headlines and television reports from around the world bombard Americans every day, reminding us, sometimes to our discomfort, that the United States participates in a global community as never before. In a world made interdependent by instant communications, rapid transportation, economic partnerships, and a shared natural environment, we have discovered that everything from gasoline at the pump to the clothes we buy to the air we breathe carries the "international" tag. We express pride when our habits, styles, and values find favor among foreigners, and grumble when our best intentions go unappreciated. We know that a sizable portion of our tax dollars pays for foreign economic, military, and humanitarian aid, for overseas military and intelligence installations, and for interventions, wars, and covert operations intended to change the behavior of other peoples and governments. News of massacres, famines, and violent uprisings constantly arouse Americans' moral sensibilities. Those of us with strong ties to former homelands collect funds and lobby the U.S. government on behalf of relatives and friends abroad. Terrorist attacks bring foreign ethnic and religious disputes close to Americans. Holidays commemorate foreign events. Families worry about the hundreds of thousands of U.S. military personnel stationed abroad. Town after town in the United States pays tribute through memorial statues and plaques to uniformed men and women who have died in foreign wars and expeditions. So it is that we Americans are deeply intertwined in the affairs of the world—and thus necessarily is our government.

This book explores America's many intersections with the world from the First World War to the end of the Cold War. It shows how Americans from various walks of life participate in the world community. It examines why and how American leaders devised policies to protect, manage, and extend U.S. interests abroad. The documents and essays in *Major Problems in American Foreign Relations* reveal that searching debate—among Americans, among Americans and foreign peoples, and among scholars who study the past—has surrounded most issues. Indeed, Americans have spiritedly debated one another about their place in the world, their wars, their territorial expansion, their overseas commitments, and the status of their principles and power; and with comparable vigor they have debated the people of other nations about the spread of U.S. interests and ideologies. This book captures the reasoning and the passion underlying these debates by probing the factors that influence decisionmakers, the processes by which decisions are made, and the impact of those decisions on the United States and other nations.

Readers familiar with the last edition will notice that we have changed the phrasing in the title from *American Foreign Policy* to *American Foreign Relations*. We did so because this subject has evolved in emphasis, interpretation, and research to encompass the myriad ways in which peoples, cultures, economies, national governments, nongovernmental organizations, regional associations, and international institutions interact. The term *"foreign policy"* seems inadequate to account for these multifaceted intersections because it focuses largely on governmental decisionmaking and on policy itself. *"Diplomacy"* falls short because it refers primarily to negotiations or communications among states or organizations. *"International history"* seems so broad a term that it loses meaning, while at the same time it underplays an appropriate emphasis on an *American* foreign relations. The phrase *"foreign relations"* comes closest to the new emphases because it explains the totality of interactions—economic, cultural, political, military, environmental, and more—among peoples, organizations, states, and systems.

The table of contents of this fourth edition reveals both the thoroughness of our revisions and the fertility of the scholarship in history, political science, and international relations during the last several years. More than half of the selections are new. We have revised every chapter, and through reorganization we added two new chapters—one on the United States and the Arab-Israeli peace process and another on why the Cold War ended. We revised the chapter on Franklin D. Roosevelt and U.S. entry into World War II in order to highlight Japanese-American decisions. We redesigned the chapter on Dwight D. Eisenhower and the 1950s to spotlight the nuclear arms race and nuclear confrontations. In this edition, in both documents and essays, we included more foreign voices and more statements by people of color, so as to illuminate the wide array of participants in foreign relations. And we have given greater attention than before to cultural relations, relations with the Third World, and nuclear issues. Several new maps round out the revisions.

The ending of the Cold War and the gradual declassification of documents in foreign archives—Russian, Cuban, and Chinese, for example—have generated new perspectives and more textured discussion of many topics, including the origins of the Cold War, Sino-American relations, the Korean War, and the Cuban missile crisis. Recently released documents and the evolving scholarship on these questions are represented in this volume.

Like other volumes in this series, *Major Problems in American Foreign Relations* approaches its subject in two ways: first, through primary sources; and second, through the interpretations of scholars. We invite readers to contend with a diversity of viewpoints and approaches on critical issues. Documents introduce each chapter's problem, identify key questions, reveal the flavor of the times, and convey the intensity of debate. Through encounters with documents, students can immerse themselves in the historical moment, shape their own perspectives, and test the explanations of others. The essays demonstrate that different scholars read documents differently, come to quite different conclusions, or choose to focus on different aspects of an issue. Students' interaction with the documents and essays builds an appreciation for the complexity of historical problems, a fascination about historical inquiry, and a recognition that events and personalities once buried in the past carry contemporary meaning for students as both scholars and citizens. Introductions and headnotes in each chapter start this empowering and rewarding process.

Instructors and students who want to continue their study of foreign-relations history are invited to join the Society for Historians of American Foreign Relations

(SHAFR). This organization publishes a superb journal, *Diplomatic History,* and an informative newsletter; offers book, article, and lecture prizes and dissertation research grants; and holds an annual conference where scholars present their views and research results. Dues are very reasonable. For information, contact the SHAFR Business Office, Department of History, Wright State University, Dayton, OH 45435.

We are very pleased to acknowledge the many generous people who have helped us with both volumes of this fourth edition as reviewers, researchers, suppliers of documents and essays, advisers about content, and welcomed catchers of errors. Detailed and constructive written reviews were provided by Jeffrey Kimball, Thomas J. Knock, Robert L. Messer, and Martin Sherwin. We also appreciate the assistance of Lloyd E. Ambrosius, Miriam Biurci, J. Garry Clifford, Richard H. Collin, Gregory E. Dowd, James Goode, Peter L. Hahn, Paul W. Harris, Jane Hunter, Teresa Pelto Johnson, Carla Klausner, Carl Murdock, Brian Murphy, Patrick Peebles, Alan Perry, Kenneth E. Shewmaker, and Martha Lund Smalley. The talented D. C. Heath staff deserves special thanks. Imaginative, thorough, and understanding, Heath's editors shaped this book for the better. We thank history editor James Miller, developmental editor Sylvia Mallory, production editor Elizabeth Gale, and permissions editor Margaret Roll.

We are also grateful to the friends, colleagues, and students who contributed in various ways to the first three editions: Harold Barto, Richard Dean Burns, Bruce Cumings, Joe Decker, Bruce dePyssler, John Dobson, Michael Ebner, Mark Gilderhus, Gerald Gordon, Laura Grant, Kenneth J. Hagan, Gregg Herken, James Hindman, Michael Hunt, Holly Izard, Donald Johnson, Lawrence Kaplan, Ellen Kerley, Warren Kimball, Karen Kupperman, Melvyn Leffler, Douglas Little, Jean Manter, Frederick Marks, James Matray, John Merrill, Jean-Donald Miller, Charles Neu, Stephen Pelz, Carol Petillo, Eileen Rice, Barney J. Rickman III, Rodney Scudder, Harlow Sheidley, Kenneth Shewmaker, Mark Stoler, Harry Stout, William Stueck, John Sylvester, Paul Varg, Marvin Zahniser, and Thomas Zoumaras.

We welcome comments, suggestions, and criticisms from students and instructors so that we can continue to improve this book.

T. G. P.
D. M.

Contents

CHAPTER 3
The International History of the 1920s
Page 77

CHAPTER 4
Franklin D. Roosevelt and the Origins of the Second World War in the Pacific
Page 127

CHAPTER 5
Defeating the Axis, Planning the Peace: The Second World War
Page 185

CHAPTER 6
The Origins of the Cold War
Page 235

CHAPTER 7
Mao's China and the Chances for Sino-American Accommodation
Page 316

CHAPTER 8
The Korean War
Page 366

CHAPTER 9
Dwight D. Eisenhower, John Foster Dulles, and the Nuclear-Arms Race
Page 416

CHAPTER 10
Cuba and the Missile Crisis
Page 460

CHAPTER 11
The Vietnam War
Page 532

CHAPTER 12
Richard M. Nixon, Henry A. Kissinger, the Grand Strategy, and Détente
Page 585

CHAPTER 13
Washington and the Arab-Israeli Peace Process
Page 637

CHAPTER 14
The End of the Cold War
Page 707

Maps

Major Problems in American
Foreign Relations

Approaching the Study of

American Foreign Relations

The study of American foreign relations encompasses several central questions. What are the key characteristics of U.S. foreign relations, and what shaped them? What is the relationship between the nation's domestic setting—ideology, core values, politics, geography, social structure, and economy—and its foreign relations? To what extent does American foreign relations owe its character not to domestic conditions and attitudes but to interaction with the wider world of the international system? Does the United States behave like other powers in international relations, or does the nation exhibit exceptional qualities? What weight should we assign to the several ways in which nations relate to one another in the international system—political, strategic, economic, military, cultural, and others? How is power distributed in the international system? And, as the century winds down, is the United States suffering the decline of its vaunted position?

Most scholars agree that the United States built on a tradition of expansionism to emerge as a prominent, even hegemonic, global power in the twentieth century. But how, and why? Was the expansionist course calculated and coherent, or accidental and haphazard? The historian William Appleman Williams's The Tragedy of American Diplomacy, *first published in 1959, profoundly influenced scholars by citing economic—or "Open Door"—expansionism as the key to understanding U.S. foreign relations. With an accompanying "Open Door" ideology that posited that their domestic welfare depended on access to markets abroad, Americans, argued Williams, exploited overseas economies and sought to remake foreign societies. Coercion of foreign peoples necessarily followed, he concluded, producing a "tragedy"—Americans' violation of their own best principles, especially the right of self-determination. Much of the scholarship of the past few decades has applied the Williams thesis, elaborated on it, amended it, or disputed it, but has never ignored it.*

Related to the many questions about U.S. expansionism and the larger world are others that highlight how policy is made and how the process of decision making itself shapes both the policy and the outcome. How have U.S. leaders gone about deciding to use the nation's power abroad, and has that exercise of power produced the results intended? In this category, scholars explore the role of domestic politics and elections, presidential-congressional relations, the Constitution, bu-reaucracies, interest groups and elites, and individuals whose particular personali-ties mold perceptions and influence decisions.

One way in which to think about the different approaches, presented very briefly in this opening chapter, is to ask how each would explain specific events or relations, such as U.S. entry into the First World War, Japanese-American disputes leading to World War II, the origins of the Cold War, the Korean War, the nuclear arms race, or U.S. participation in the search for Arab-Israeli peace in the Middle East. Does one approach or a combination of approaches carry more explanatory power than others?

The diversity of viewpoints in this introductory chapter affords an opportunity to discover and understand the complexity of major problems in American foreign relations whose legacies persist today.

✵ ESSAYS

In the first essay, Thomas J. McCormick of the University of Wisconsin, Madison, empha-sizes U.S. hegemony or dominance in a capitalist world-system comprising core, periph-ery, and semi-periphery countries. In the twentieth century, the United States has possessed predominant economic and military power and exercised political-ideological leadership, rising to the status of preeminent core country. But McCormick notes that hegemony is "impermanent"; great powers become rentier and warfare states, and decline inevitably sets in. In the second essay, Akira Iriye of Harvard University explores international relations as cultural relations. He makes the case that individuals, peoples, and states interact in the world through dreams, mind-sets, values, and shared memories. Cultural relations—oc-curring through tourist travel, religious missions, academic exchanges, movies, and the like—may produce conflict or consensus. A global consciousness or cultural "order" (for example, agreement on the principle of freedom, faith in capitalism, or the necessity for en-vironmental protection) may coexist with and intersect with economic and strategic orders.

In the third essay, Emily S. Rosenberg of Macalester College contends that gender makes a difference in international relations. All societies, after all, are divided along gen-der lines. What if foreign relations were explained in gender rather than economic or cul-tural terms? For example, Rosenberg emphasizes the gendered language and imagery of international relations that have undergirded U.S. imperialism and wars and American jus-tifications for the dependency status of other nations. Melvyn P. Leffler of the University of Virginia, in the fourth essay, claims that the pursuit of national security—the defense of core values against foreign threats—best explains U.S. behavior abroad. In highlighting the exercise of U.S. power to protect core values, Leffler points not only to the realities of ma-terial interests, territory, and ideology but also to perceptions of foreign threats.

The fifth essay, by Michael J. Hogan of Ohio State University, introduces another ap-proach: corporatism. Some scholars use this term to describe both an ideology of corporate liberalism and an American economic-political system whose goals at home and abroad are political order, social harmony, and economic productivity. The key to the realization of these goals is government's collaboration with interest groups in the private sector—busi-ness, agriculture, and organized labor. Such cooperation, Hogan insists, has guided the mak-ing of American foreign relations, especially since the 1920s. In the sixth selection, J. Garry Clifford of the University of Connecticut explains how bureaucratic politics—the give-and-take bargaining within the U.S. government—shapes the pacing, implementation, and there-fore the outcome of foreign policy. Because of all the tugging and hauling in the policy process, U.S. foreign relations does not always come out as leaders intended. In the final es-say, Richard H. Immerman of Temple University argues that an understanding of psychology is essential to grasping the hows and whys of American foreign relations. The personality of leaders—their motives and emotions, for example—interacts with an event or crisis to produce decision and action. Immerman also explains that stress, dogmatism, and distorted perceptions influence behavior in negotiations. Overall, then, the use of psychological theories helps us to explain key decisions, including those based on errors of judgment.

The World-System, Hegemony, and Decline

THOMAS J. McCORMICK

Since modern history began in the late fifteenth century, the earth's inhabitants have lived in three distinct types of environments: the capitalist world-system (or world economy), the external world (empires), or the minisystems of subsistence communities. For the past five hundred years, the dynamic growth and expansion of the world-system has been at the expense of the other two. The Ottoman Empire of the Turks disappeared, the Russian Empire of the Romanovs and the empire of the Manchus in China collapsed in revolutionary disarray, all victims of their archaic political systems and the inability of their quasi-feudal economies to compete with or alternatively to insulate themselves from the more dynamic and efficient economies of the capitalist world-system. Likewise, the minisystems of Eastern Europe, Ireland, the Americas, Africa, and Asia were, over time and despite great resistance, wrenched away from their subsistence, village agriculture and integrated into a cash nexus and the world market. By the late twentieth century, the remnants of the external world of empires, the Soviet Union and the People's Republic of China, had emerged from the containment and self-isolation of the Cold War and begun to experiment with market economies in place of command (planned) economies. Also by that time, the remaining isolated pockets of subsistence systems had virtually disappeared from the face of the earth. The revolutionary expansion of European capitalism and Mediterranean civilization, begun a half-millennium earlier, seemed about to reach its final, all-encompassing frontier. The world-system and the world itself seemed almost one—one world rather than three.

Throughout its five centuries, capitalism has been an inherently expansionistic type of economy. The key to accumulating capital, enlarging market shares, and maximizing profits has historically been long-distance trade, especially by large capitalists with political connections and economic reserves. That was true of Baltic merchant capitalists in the seventeenth century rerouting their grain ships to the Adriatic to take advantage of local famine and exorbitant prices. It was true of nineteenth-century British industrial capitalists using their superior technology and economies of scale to wipe out hand-crafted textiles in Turkey, India, and China and to enlarge the British share of the world market. It is true today of finance capitalists in New York whose overseas bank loans to newly industrializing countries give a high rate of return no longer possible at home. In short, capitalism as an economic system has always functioned most profitably and most efficiently when its universe of options has been sufficiently large and fluid for capital, goods, services,

From Thomas J. McCormick, *America's Half-Century: United States Foreign Policy in the Cold War*, 1989, pp. 1–7. The Johns Hopkins University Press, Baltimore/London. Reprinted by permission.

and people to move from one place to another in order to secure greater returns, even if that place be both distant and foreign. Moreover, even when capitalism has not functioned efficiently, its spatial expansion into distant empires and subsistence enclaves has fueled its rejuvenation. Periodically, crises of overproduction have resulted from the contradictory instincts of entrepreneurs to keep production high (to enlarge market shares) and wage bills low (to reduce production costs). Historically, however, global expansion of new markets for goods and capital has helped restore demand to the level of supply, raised the rate of profit, and replaced economic depression with economic boom. The long slumps of 1680–1730, 1870–1900, and 1930–50 were all resolved in part by the creation of new economic frontiers: the mercantile empires of the eighteenth century, the new imperialism of the late nineteenth century, and the economic internationalization promoted by American foreign policy in the mid-twentieth century.

During the last decade, a number of academic observers have concluded that capitalism's tendency toward international fluidity eventually produced a configuration that could properly be described as a system, a combination of parts forming a complex, unitary whole. Fernand Braudel and Immanuel Wallerstein, in their epic studies of early European capitalism, concluded that such a system was in place by 1650. Others feel that it was not until the nineteenth century that an integrated global division of labor allowed capitalism to merit characterization as a system.

Studies advancing a world-system analysis (including this study) argue that there are three constants about that world-system, even though the particular forms it takes are always changing. First, there are always implicit geographical boundaries within that system, and they are essentially defined by the spatial limits of the world market economy at any given time. In our contemporary period, the term *free world* is essentially a synonym for the capitalist world-system. Cold War rhetoric may impart a more ideological twist to the phrase, but [State Department official] Nelson Rockefeller's chief aide got at its root in late 1941 when he declared that America was "committed to the fight for freedom of economic life and for freedom of the seas, in a word, the fight for a free world." Second, there is always a center or pole to the system, a dominant city that acts as the coordinating point and clearing house of international capital. Its location has shifted historically from the Mediterranean to Northern Europe to North America (and perhaps yet to Northeast Asia), but there is always a central metropolis, be it London in 1845 or New York in 1945.

Finally, the system consists of three successive zones, each performing a specialized function in a complex, international division of labor. *Core* countries (the First World) own most of the high-tech, high-profit enterprises. The *periphery* (the Third World) specializes in primary production of agricultural commodities and raw materials—they are the "hewers of wood and carriers of water." Between them, the *semiperiphery* (the Second World) performs intermediate functions of transport, local capital mobilization, and less complex, less profitable forms of manufacturing. Historically, there has been some limited mobility of individual nations between zones, including America's own transformation from a semiperipheral country in 1790 to a core country by 1890. Likewise, changing technology continually redefines what constitutes high-, intermediate-, or low-value enterprises. Textiles, steel, and shipbuilding might have been high-value activities in an earlier era but have become low- or intermediate-value in the contemporary age of

electrical equipment. What remains constant are the zones themselves and the specialized (and unequally rewarded) division of labor among them. Hence, in 1988
there is a world-system in which North America, Japan, and Europe constitute the
core and specialize in electronics, capital goods, diversified agriculture, and finance; the less developed countries (LDCs) of Africa, Southeast Asia, and the
Caribbean basin, as the periphery, specialize in nonpetroleum raw materials and
single-crop agriculture; and the newly industrializing countries (NICs), Mexico,
Brazil, South Africa, Israel, Iran, India, China, and those of Eastern Europe and the
Pacific rim, as the semiperiphery, specialize in shipping, petroleum, credit transactions, and consumer goods manufacturing.

The emergence of a capitalist world economy coincided with the emergence
of the modern nation-state as the prevailing political unit of governance, and the
nation-state has both fostered and inhibited the capitalist world economy. On one
hand, nation-states have often provided crucial stimulation of economic growth
and development: their banking, taxation, credit, and internal improvement policies have frequently aided domestic entrepreneurs in accumulating capital and
minimizing risks. On the other hand, those same nation-states have often interfered
with and impeded the fluidity and mobility of capital, goods, and labor across national boundaries. This nationalist bias is caused in part by nation-states being, by
definition, wedded to specific territories and committed to the defense and suste-
nance of their citizens. In part, too, it reflects the uneven pace of capitalist development among countries, and the unequal division of labor and rewards that results
from it. The frequent consequence has been an attempt by "have-not" countries to
overtake "have" countries through nationalistic economic measures, often referred
to as mercantilistic policies in earlier periods and, in our own time, as import-sub-
stitution policies (i.e., substitution of indigenous products for those previously imported). Whatever the cause of this nationalist bias, the resulting farm subsidies,
military spending, protective tariffs, navigation laws, capital controls, and restricted currency convertibility have constituted serious obstacles to a free world
of economic internationalism and interdependence in which capitalism, as a purely
economic system, can realize its maximum efficiency and profitability. So, too,
have the policies of territorial expansion that often accompany economic nationalism interfered, by seeking to monopolize whole regions of the earth for the benefit
of a single national economy. Examples are the British mercantile empire of the
eighteenth century and the Japanese Greater East Asian Co-Prosperity Sphere of
the twentieth. In sum, nation-states have tended to pursue policies of economic autarky—capitalism in one country or one self-contained trading bloc—and such approaches limit the options of capital in pursuit of maximum rewards.

Hegemony historically has operated to soften the contradiction between the
internationalist imperatives of capitalism and the nationalist biases of political nation-states. In the context of the world-system, hegemony means that one nation
possesses such unrivaled supremacy, such predominant influence in economic
power, military might, and political-ideological leadership, that no other power, or
combination of powers, can prevail against it. Economic supremacy is the indispensable base of hegemony, for all other forms of power are possible with it and
no others possible, for very long, without it. Any hegemonic power must, simultaneously, contain the dominant financial center, possess a clear comparative
advantage in a wide range of high-tech, high-profit industries, and function

commercially as both the world's major exporter and its major importer. Beyond mere economic power, it must possess clear military superiority and ideological hegemony as well. By fear or respect, it must be able to exert its political will over the rest of the system and command deference to its principles and policies.

Hegemony and the balance of power have been on opposing sides of the contradiction between economic internationalism and national autarky or self-sufficiency. The balance of power attempts to use the alignment of forces and, if necessary, war, to prevent any one power from achieving such preponderance that it could impose economic internationalism on autarkic-minded nations. A single hegemonic power, however, has a built-in incentive to force other nations to abandon their national capitalism and economic controls and to accept a world of free trade, free capital flows, and free currency convertibility. As the world's dominant economic power, a hegemonic power has the most to gain from such a free world and the most to lose from nationalistic efforts to limit the free movement of capital, goods, and currencies. So the preponderant world power is unequivocally self-interested in using its economic power, as workshop and banker of the free world, to create institutions and ground rules that foster the internationalization of capital. It finds it inherently advantageous to use its political power as ideologue of the world-system to preach the universal virtues of freedom of the seas, free trade, open door policies, comparative advantage, and a specialized division of labor. It finds it necessary to use its military power as global policeman to protect the international system against external antagonists, internal rebellions, and internecine differences: to be judge, jury, and executioner, insuring that the ground rules of internationalism are not impeded by either friend or foe.

Only twice in the history of the capitalist world economy has hegemony triumphed over balance of power as the prevailing structure of the international system. Great Britain functioned as hegemonic center between roughly 1815 and 1870, and the United States did so between roughly 1945 and 1970. . . . In each instance, world war was crucial to the formation of hegemony. It radically redistributed power and wealth in ironic fashion, denying hegemony to a European continental power while bestowing postwar supremacy on its balance of power adversary.

In the first instance, France attempted through its Napoleonic Wars (constituting the first truly world war) to impose its dominance on the Eurasian heartland, the very center of European capitalism. Great Britain attempted to thwart that ambition through its traditional balance of power politics, and it ultimately prevailed. But the wars and attendant revolutions were so long, so destructive, so destabilizing that they temporarily obliterated the old balance of power system and left Great Britain the tacit sovereign of the post-Napoleonic world. In the second instance . . . , Germany, under both the Kaiser and Hitler, attempted to impose its dominance on the same Eurasian heartland, while Anglo-American balance of power diplomacy sought to prevent it. But the ironic consequence of World Wars I and II was, by denying hegemony to the Germans, to make it possible for the Americans to become the acknowledged leaders of the free world. In each case, hegemony made it nearly impossible for other core powers to use war as an instrument of diplomacy against each other—a Pax Britannica for the mid-nineteenth century and a Pax Americana for the mid-twentieth. In each case, hegemony blunted the forces of economic nationalism and facilitated greater global interdependence, enabling a freer and easier *exchange* of goods in the nineteenth century and the multinational *production* of goods in the twentieth.

Hegemony is always impermanent, as Great Britain discovered and the United States is discovering. Indeed, hegemony undermines the very economic supremacy upon which it necessarily must rest. Two related tendencies lead the preponderant power to neglect investment in its civilian research and production and to transform itself into a *rentier* nation and *warfare* state. There is a tendency to overinvest and lend overseas and to live off dividends and interests (renting out one's money, hence *rentier*). It happens because it is easy to do, since the hegemonic power is in a position to secure favorable treatment for its capital throughout the free world. It happens also because it is necessary, since higher wage bills make it more profitable to invest overseas than at home. The higher wage bills themselves are part of the burden of power: the necessity to demonstrate to managers and workers that there are ample economic rewards for supporting an internationalist foreign policy with their votes, tax dollars, and conscription.

The tendency to overinvest abroad is compounded by the tendency to overinvest in military production. Essential to the hegemonic power's capacity to act as global policeman, military research and production receive favored treatment from the government in the form of state-subsidized high profits. The government becomes a more predictable and more profitable customer than private individuals and corporate consumers. The end result is to divert capital from civilian to military production, to the neglect of modernization needs of the domestic industrial plan. This disinvestment, as some term it, erodes over time the economic underpinnings of hegemony and makes it more difficult to compete with other core powers who have avoided the pitfalls of similar disinvestment. Moreover, like a snowball rolling downhill, the problems compound as the hegemon grows aware of its decline. Confronted with declining profitability in the civilian sector, it is likely to stress military spending even more as the easiest way to assure its capitalists of adequate returns—often spending far in excess of any plausible military purposes. Relatedly, it is likely to exploit its continuing function as world policeman to extort special privileges from its competitors: favored treatment for its currency, its trade, and its investments in exchange for continued police protection. In short, it is likely to become even more of a rentier or warfare economy and speed up the very decline it is trying to retard.

International Relations as Cultural Relations

AKIRA IRIYE

Culture in the study of international relations may be defined as the sharing and transmitting of consciousness within and across national boundaries, and the cultural approach as a perspective that pays particular attention to this phenomenon. Theoretically, at least, this emphasis distinguishes the cultural approach from the conceptualizations most commonly used in the field: the power and economic ap-

---

proaches. The concepts of power and economy are as elusive concepts as culture, but in the study of diplomatic affairs one may define power as a nation's ability to defend itself and economy as its production and exchange of goods and services. Culture, in contrast, is the creation and communication of memory, ideology, emotions, life styles, scholarly and artistic works, and other symbols.

Of course, power, economy, and culture may be so defined as to become interchangeable. For instance, national security—a power phenomenon—may be comprehended as an idea or a world view, which is a cultural product; political scientists even use "strategic culture" as a conceptual framework to examine the cultural underpinnings of a given strategy. Economic activities may likewise be examined in terms of the cultural equipment (education, technology, or work ethic) with which those activities are pursued. But there is little to gain by mixing up the three, or by developing an overarching, anthropological definition of culture so broad that it includes every human phenomenon. A loose cultural determinism is no more helpful than power determinism (seeing international affairs only as geopolitical interplays—the "realist" construction) or economic determinism (viewing foreign policy as an expression of certain domestic interests—the "self-interest" school of interpretation).

Rather, it would be useful to start by recognizing the obvious. Nations, like individuals, sometimes use force to protect themselves and often engage in selfish pursuits to enrich themselves but they also develop visions, dreams, and prejudices about themselves and the world that influence their relationships. A good example of this tripartite distinction was a statement Secretary of State James Baker made before the House Foreign Affairs Committee in June 1989 concerning U.S. policy toward China. He noted that human rights were the keystone of the American approach to that country, but that the United States also had to take into consideration geopolitical and economic factors. What Baker implied was that the United States and China related to one another as potential allies (or antagonists) in the regional security system, as trading partners (or competitors), and as ideologically compatible (or conflicting) nations. To reduce these three aspects to a single factor would be too simplistic. U.S.-Chinese relations in 1989 and 1990, for instance, were clearly incompatible ideologically, but that did not prevent the growth of trade between the two countries, and Washington was reluctant to punish Beijing too severely for its transgression of human rights lest China's geopolitical importance in the Asian balance of power be compromised. What this suggests is that the United States, China, and all countries are definable as powers, as economic systems, and as cultures, and that they can behave differently in these various modes. The cultural approach to diplomatic history attempts to take account of this fact by considering nations as cultures when looking at their international affairs.

[The scholar] Leslie White's analysis of "cultural systems" may be useful in this connection. There are, he says, intrasystemic and extrasystemic types of behavior. The former refers to movements and developments within the cultural system and the latter to those between one cultural system and another. Historians of international relations must, then, concern themselves both with the formation and preservation of cultural products within nations and with their interactions with their counterparts elsewhere. Ultimately, moreover, it will be necessary to inquire into the existence (or absence) and transformation of a global cultural system. In other words, the cultural approach consists of three levels of analysis: national, cross-national, and global. Of course, the same would be true of the power or economic approaches. But what is most fascinating, as well as most frustrating, about the cultural approach is that it forces the historian to recognize simultaneously qualitative differences among cultural traditions and vocabularies and determine whether some universal "structures of meaning" (to use [the cultural anthropologist] Clifford Geertz's phrase) might result from direct or indirect contact among the representatives of different cultures. The power and economic approaches, in contrast, start by assuming that there exists an international power or economic system in which national entities behave as essentially interchangeable "actors." The international cultural historian cannot make a similar assumption. He or she must accept the existence of and be well versed in various cultures and also have a vision of the world cultural order. This is a tall order, and a far more challenging task than merely reading documents in one language or applying theoretical vocabularies indiscriminately to all nations. Fortunately, there are excellent works that have responded, at least partially, to this demanding task. They may be divided into three categories, corresponding to the three levels mentioned.

First, a growing body of literature explores the ideological or intellectual underpinnings of a nation's behavior toward others. One could call this the intrasystemic approach. It focuses on what Paul Ricoeur calls the "layer of images and symbols which make up the basic ideals of a nation." Fundamental to this approach is the proposition that a nation consists of people with shared memories, dreams, attitudes, and values. Even when their ideas and aspirations are divided, their self-perception prescribes adherence to some "ethico-mythical nucleus" that defines the boundaries within which they exist. One may say that these "core values" make a nation what it is. By focusing on what [the historian] Bernard Bailyn calls "interior world views—shared attitudes and responses and 'mindsets' "—it will become possible to raise serious questions about a country's behavior and attitudes toward others. For instance, the question of mutual understanding or antagonism among nations cannot be fully examined so long as one focuses exclusively on security or trade issues; one will also have to consider the mind sets of leaders and people across national boundaries. In a sense, one will then be exploring the human qualities, not just the geopolitical or economic realities, that define a country's position in the world. . . .

A second kind of cultural study of diplomatic history [is] the cross-systemic approach. . . . Historians of American foreign relations have fruitfully used this approach to study how individual Americans, mostly on private initiative, have reached across national boundaries to engage in commercial, religious, educational, and other activities overseas. After the United States achieved independence, individual traders, missionaries, scientists, teachers, sailors, and travelers were often the first to establish contact with people in other lands, preceding both consuls and naval officers. What they saw, experienced, and reported home constituted a rich legacy of American foreign relations, and it would be no exaggeration to say that until the beginning of the twentieth century these activities defined the nature of American relations with the rest of the world. . . .

Going beyond individual encounters, it is important to consider how American goods, ideas, and ways of life spread to and influence other societies. Through the export of American goods, the activities of missionaries and educators, and the showing of movies and art works, American culture penetrates other cultures. The phenomenon of cultural transmission and diffusion has been studied more extensively by anthropologists and art historians than by historians, but notable exceptions exist. Among the most successful attempts is Frank Costigliola's *Awkward Dominion* [1984], a study of American economic and cultural influence in Europe during the 1920s. Costigliola documents not only the well-known infiltration of European theaters by Hollywood movies but also more intangible influences such as the spreading of the ideas of efficiency, business rationalism, and capitalist internationalism. The converse phenomenon of foreigners making an impact on American life and thought has been described in such works as H. Stuart Hughes's *The Sea Change* [1975], Laura Fermi's *Illustrious Immigrants* [1971], John Diggins's *Mussolini and Fascism* [1972], and James T. Kloppenberg's *Uncertain Victory* [1986]. Studies of this sort remind us that the cross-systemic approach is a fruitful way of coming to grips with deeper layers of international relations as they are transformed by contact among peoples, their ideas, and their products.

Cultural exchange in the ordinary sense also falls into this category. It refers to programs for sending students abroad and for inviting foreign scholars to the United States, to hosting tours by overseas artistic and musical groups, and to holding international symposiums and the like. The historical significance of such enterprises, as well as less structured activities such as tourism, has not been well researched. But in the long run these exchanges may prove to be of decisive importance in changing the ways peoples view one another. Similarly, only recently have historians begun to turn their attention to the intermingling of people of diverse nationalities in different parts of the world. For example, the occupation of Japan can be seen as a cultural phenomenon as well as a military and political act. The consequences of the massive intermingling of Americans and Japanese are yet to be fully assessed. . . .

The third form of cultural history, what may be termed the global approach, builds on these works and attempts to relate national cultures and their interactions to the larger international system, thereby raising the question of global consciousness: whether there exist worldwide concerns that transcend national boundaries. International affairs take place within a world that is defined geopolitically and economically, but the global approach posits that there may also be a world of shared conceptions, dreams, and problems. Just as historians write about the rise and fall of the great powers or the emergence and erosion of a world economic system, they should also ask whether there may develop global cultural trends and countertrends. It is often said, for instance, that contemporary Japan is a global power economically but is isolated culturally. But to speak of cultural isolation assumes that there is an international cultural order in terms of which a nation is judged to be isolated. . . .

Certainly, recent events in China and Eastern Europe and in Indonesia and Brazil, no less than in the United States and Western Europe, would seem to suggest that freedom, human rights, health care, the protection of the environment, and the like know no national boundaries, and that it is never possible to study these issues merely in national or even regional frameworks. The world, it would appear, is fast transforming itself culturally, even faster than it is changing geopolitically or economically. It is the responsibility of historians everywhere to chronicle this striking phenomenon. . . .

It seems possible to go a step farther and anticipate that at the end of the twentieth century, if these trends continue, cultural questions will become increasingly important. In fact, they may already have come to overshadow purely economic issues. After all, economic competition entails work habits, rates of domestic consumption and saving, levels of spending on basic research, and standards of education. These are cultural matters. But beyond such obvious areas, there seems to have been an accelerating tempo of cross-national population movements through tourism, multinational business enterprises, educational exchanges, and, above all, democratization movements symbolized by the razing of the Berlin Wall. At the same time, nations of the world have begun in earnest to cooperate in such matters as the control of drug abuse, the search for a cure for AIDS, the battle against terrorism, the protection of endangered species, and the creation of a global telecommunications network. Under such circumstances, culture may become as crucial a concept of international affairs as security and trade. Historians would seem to have an obligation to recognize this trend and to reexamine the past with the new perspective in mind.

The Gender Difference

EMILY S. ROSENBERG

Walking the borders of power is not an easy task. Walter LaFeber, in a similar call for developing a peripheral perspective, pointed out one obvious difficulty: "It is a problem," he wrote, "to try to act as an outsider when one lives at the center of the system." But there is, after all, no single system of power that arranges international affairs. Centers and peripheries will shift depending on the field of reference: Different systems of power can be framed along lines of nation-states, of economics, of class, of culture, of religion, of gender, of race, and so forth. Most of us are both insiders and outsiders, depending upon which structures of power we wish to analyze. A peripheral vantage is not only a geographic location but can be a habit of mind and a scholarly approach that can be nurtured by an awareness of our own positions as insiders or as outsiders or as would-be mediators on the margins of both. A peripheral view comes less from where we stand than from the critical questions we frame and who we choose to hear. . . .

In nearly every society, social systems and cultural discourse divide sharply along lines of gender, a situation that undermines many universalized formulations based solely on male experience. Feminism, as one kind of peripheral vision, has forced particularistic examinations of much historical discourse. Just as feminist historians revealed the blind spots of male-dominated histories by asking questions such as "was the Renaissance a renaissance for women," so feminist scholarship has similarly challenged some of the language and categories of male-dominated analyses of global issues.

For example, what has development (or underdevelopment) meant for women? Using gender as a framework, an entire subfield of development studies has emerged in the last decade. Most theorists of development and modernization, as well as most theorists of underdevelopment associated with the dependency school, previously neglected women. In terms of global production, however, women have provided most of the agricultural labor, the reproductive tasks, and the goods and services offered in the informal sector. Labor demands upon the time of women have frequently been more intense than those upon men. If the divisions of labor by gender have, historically, provided fundamental organizing principles for most economic systems, how can gender be omitted from economic calculation or historical analysis of economic trends?

As scholars have begun looking at national development through the lens of gender difference, it has become clear that rapid changes in land-use patterns, technology, agricultural practices, communications, sanitation, availability of factory work, and the like have affected practices of "men's work" and "women's work" in substantially different ways. In a number of pathbreaking early studies on the impact of development efforts, liberal feminists charged that particular programs had, by omitting any consideration of women's work, often failed entirely or resulted in greater exploitation of women. Radical feminists, who viewed most development programs as tools of economic domination anyway, often found evidence of further subordination of women, especially where male-run international markets supplanted localized, often women-controlled, systems of production and exchange. Despite different emphases and interpretations, works on historic shifts in the global economy that consider gender-related divisions of labor have begun to transform the meaning of development. Thus, development (or underdevelopment), like other abstractions, needs to be grounded in a specific time, place, and cultural condition.

Many other international phenomena besides development may affect men and women differently, making gender a relevant category of analysis. Examination of gendered overtones of so much foreign policy language and symbolism can provide fresh, provocative insights into the wellsprings of policy formulation and public legitimation. In some historical contexts, for example, cultural definitions of masculinity and bellicose assertions of national power appear to be linked. There have likewise been historical ties between feminism and pacifism.

Ideas about natural hierarchies and dependence that are embedded in general imagery at the turn of the twentieth century, for example, were part of a pervasive cultural milieu that supported foreign policies of domination. The subtle psychological and discursive linkages between attitudes regarding gender, race, and foreign policy have received recent attention in cultural studies such as Michael Paul Rogin's *Ronald Reagan, the Movie* [1987] and Richard Drinnon's *Facing West* [1980]. Women, nonwhite races, and tropical countries often were accorded the same kinds of symbolic characterization from white, male policymakers: emotional, irrational, irresponsible, unbusinesslike, unstable, childlike. These naturally dependent peoples could be expected to exhibit the same kinds of natural responses to patriarchal tutelage. They were assumed, if behaving properly, to be loving, grateful, happy, and appreciative of paternal protection. Concepts of dependency, both in the domestic family order and in the international order, reinforced and helped legitimate each other.

At particular times in the United States's relations with weaker nations, gendered imagery helped convert stories about foreign affairs into mythic tales, often with the form and structure of popular romance novels. Romantic formulas helped articulate and justify policies of dependence, portraying a courtship in which the disorganized but alluring (feminine) tropics ultimately succumbed to the outward thrust of manly organizers of civilization. Gendered imagery abounds in popular portrayals of international relationships: the noisy and muscular parting of Mother Earth in Panama; the fiery engines of progress that penetrated virgin land in the American West and then in Latin America; the North American financial advisers who continually proclaimed the man-sized jobs they were undertaking in financially insolvent countries. [The historian] Michael Hunt observes that when North Americans "saw themselves acting benevolently, they liked to picture the Latino as a white maiden passively awaiting salvation or seduction." Annexationist rhetoric during the Mexican War thus sought to bring the "Spanish maid" into the Yankee's "valiant arms"; in 1898, Cuba frequently became encoded as an alluring damsel in distress.

These kinds of gendered images did not make arguments justifying creation of zones of dependence; but, as powerful rhetorical devices, they *exemplified* the presumed naturalness of the hierarchical arrangements and helped to make arguments unnecessary. Mythical, transhistorical narratives embedded in metaphorical images, as [the historian] Richard Slotkin has argued in a different context, transcended policy argumentation, persuading by symbolic association.

A growing body of literature explores the connections between gender, ideology, and war. Outbursts of a bellicose rhetoric about manliness in foreign relations seem historically related to domestic feminist challenges to male power. Similarly, although gender systems have often bent when men were away fighting, the nationalism and violence of war may ultimately have worked to constrict women's boundaries. During World War II, despite new employment opportunities for women, for example, the broader exaltation of family (reinforced by images of the nation as a family) and of male bonding in an environment of danger and violence may have ultimately widened the gulf between social constructions of male and female.

During the Cold War period, the wartime symbols of gender difference persisted, narrowing opportunities for women while simultaneously suffusing the discourse in which foreign relations were often expressed. Cold War containment, Elaine Tyler May's *Homeward Bound* [1988] suggests, structurally dovetailed with the "containment" of women in the domestic sphere. Richard J. Barnet [in *Roots of War,* 1971] and Carol Cohen [in a *Signs* article, 1987] have elaborated how defense intellectuals of the period had, above all, to be tough and manly in their recommendations; feminine symbolism became a code for weakness, defeat, and even treason. The Vietnam War, argues Susan Jeffords [in *The Remasculinization of America,* 1989], was part of an effort to "remasculinize" American culture. . . .

The discourse of twentieth-century international relations, then, is packed with terms and images that represented gender differences. Sensitivity to how such divisions encoded power relationships of all kinds can prompt new analytical questions and different histories than those that would emerge from supposedly gender-blind examination. . . .

National Security, Core Values, and Power

MELVYN P. LEFFLER

National security policy encompasses the decisions and actions deemed imperative to protect domestic core values from external threats. The national security approach provides an overall interpretative framework for studying foreign policy, because it forces historians to analyze the foreign as well as the domestic factors shaping policy. If the inputs from both sources are faithfully studied, a great divide in the study of American diplomatic history might be overcome. Realist historians believe that diplomatic behavior responds (or should respond) mainly to the distribution of power in the international system; most revisionist and corporatist scholars assume that domestic economic forces and social structures are of overwhelming importance. A synthesis would include study of the dynamic interaction between the two sources of foreign policy behavior. By relating foreign threats to internal core values, the national security approach facilitates such assessment.

It does more. The national security approach acknowledges that power plays a key role in the behavior of nations and the functioning of the international system. Proponents of that approach believe that a nation's power depends on its political stability, social cohesion, and economic productivity as well as the number of its troops, tanks, planes, ships, missiles, and nuclear warheads. It recognizes that an overarching synthesis must integrate questions of political economy, military policy, and defense strategy. It assumes that fears of foreign threats are a consequence of both real dangers in the external environment and ideological precepts, cultural symbols, and mistaken images. . . .

In studying the systemic sources of foreign policy behavior, the national security approach demands that analysts distinguish between realities and perceptions. This task, as simple as it sounds, is fraught with difficulty because it is often harder for historians to agree on what constituted an actual danger than on what was a perceived threat. For example, the very different interpretations of American diplomacy in the 1920s and 1930s between "realists" on the one hand and "revisionists" or "corporatists" on the other hand rests in part on whether or not there were real threats to American security during the interwar years. If there were no real threats before the middle or late 1930s, then contemporary proponents of arms limitation treaties, arbitration agreements, and nonaggression pacts might be viewed as functional pragmatists seeking to create a viable liberal capitalist international order rather than as naive idealists disregarding the realities of an inherently unstable and ominous balance of power.

Perceptions of events abroad are themselves greatly influenced by the core values of the perceiver. The national security approach demands that as much attention be focused on how the American government determines its core values as on how it perceives external dangers. The term *core values* is used here rather than *vital interests* because the latter implies something more material and tangible than is appropriate for a national security imperative. The United States has rarely de-

Text by Melvyn P. Leffler from *Explaining the History of American Foreign Relations* edited by Michael J. Hogan and Thomas G. Paterson, pp. 202–203, 204, 205, 206, 212. Copyright © 1991 Cambridge University Press. Reprinted with the permission of the publisher.

fined its core values in narrowly economic or territorial terms. Core values usually *fuse* material self-interest with more fundamental goals like the defense of the state's organizing ideology, such as liberal capitalism, the protection of its political institutions, and the safeguarding of its physical base or territorial integrity. [The historian] N. Gordon Levin, Jr., has beautifully described how, when faced with unrestricted German submarine warfare, Woodrow Wilson fused ideological, economic, and geopolitical considerations. Together these factors became core values and influenced his decisions for war, for intervention, and for the assumption of political obligations abroad. . . .

The protection and pursuit of core values requires the exercise of power. Power is the capacity to achieve intended results. Power may be an end in itself as well as a means toward an end. In the twentieth century, power (including military power) derives primarily from economic capabilities. Power stems from the scale, vigor, and productivity of one's internal economy and its access to or control over other countries' industrial infrastructure, skilled manpower, and raw materials. Power is relative.

The chief characteristic of twentieth-century American foreign policy has been the willingness and capacity of the United States to develop and exert its power beyond its nineteenth-century range to influence the economic, political, and military affairs of Europe and Asia. This trend has manifested itself in the evolution of the Open Door policy, in the aid to the Allies in both world wars, in the wielding of American financial leverage, in the assumption of strategic obligations, in the deployment of troops overseas, in the provision of economic and military assistance, in the undertaking of covert operations, in the huge expenditures on armaments, and in the growth of the American multinational corporation. The national security approach helps to make sense out of these developments. Alterations in the distribution of power, changes in the international system, and developments in technology influence the perception of threat and the definition of core values and impel American officials to exercise power in varying ways. . . .

Preponderance and hegemony, as Paul Kennedy [*The Rise and Fall of the Great Powers,* 1987] and Robert Gilpin [*War and Change,* 1981] have written, confer advantages and impose costs. If threats are exaggerated and commitments overextended, if one's credibility is vested in the achievement of too many goals, one's relative power will erode and one's core values may become imperiled. There is an ominous dynamic influencing the behavioral patterns of great powers. Whether or not the United States will succumb to it will depend on whether groups, bureaucracies, and individual policymakers can find a means of restoring a viable equilibrium among threats, core values, and the exercise of power.

Corporatism and Capitalism

MICHAEL J. HOGAN

Historians of the New School use the terms corporatism, corporate liberalism, neocapitalism, and associationalism more or less interchangeably to describe a political-economic system that is characterized by certain organizational forms, by a

---

Michael J. Hogan, "Corporatism: A Positive Appraisal," *Diplomatic History,* X (Fall 1986), 363–367. Reprinted by permission of Scholarly Resources Inc.

certain ideology, and by a certain trend in the development of public policy. Organizationally, corporatism refers to a system that is founded on officially recognized economic or functional groups, including organized labor, business, and agriculture. In such a system, institutional regulating, coordinating, and planning mechanisms integrate these groups into an organic whole; elites in the private and public sectors collaborate to guarantee order, progress, and stability; and this collaboration creates a pattern of interpenetration and power sharing that makes it difficult to determine where one sector leaves off and the other begins. [The historian] Ellis W. Hawley defines corporatism primarily in these terms. His definition parallels [the scholar] Philippe Schmitter's "ideal-type" corporatism, and his work on the 1920s, which traces what [the historian] Robert Wiebe called "the search for order" in modern history, sheds new light on the process by which American leaders have sought to adapt the liberal institutions of an earlier day to the imperatives of an organized capitalism. Influenced by the work of neo-institutional and neo-organizational historians, Hawley has called our attention to the emergence of an administrative state with limited but important responsibilities, the concurrent appearance of organized units of private economic power, the collaborative systems that fused these units into concerts of group action and self-government, and the administrative networks that link private governments and public authorities.

Other New School historians have focused on the ideology that corporate liberals used to explain and rationalize the institutional and organizational adaptations described by Hawley. They have identified a body of liberal thought that envisioned a "middle way" between the older laissez-faire system of classical theory and the paternalistic statism of an Orwellian nightmare. According to the most recent of these accounts, the spokesmen of corporate liberalism favored positive programs, including those administered by government, to tame the business cycle, nurture growth, and protect elements of the population that did not yet share in the material benefits of modern capitalism. But they also sought to contain the state by entrusting much of the responsibility for public policy to semiautonomous agencies of economic coordination and control, to supposedly nonpartisan experts from the private sector, and to corporative systems of economic planning, voluntary regulation, and social welfare. Aside from depoliticizing divisive issues and "privatizing" public power in the name of private enterprise and democracy, these strategies would help to discipline the selfish pursuit of individual and group interests. They would weld ostensibly competing private groups into an organic unit and thus maximize the chances for political stability and for an economic growth in which all could share. The idea of growth, what [the historian] Charles S. Maier calls "productionism," formed another component of the ideology of corporatism. Corporate liberals perceived growth as both a goal in its own right and as the key to social harmony, the survival of private enterprise, and the preservation of political democracy. By focusing on growth, it was possible to define a common political and economic agenda for different private groups, thus widening the area of collaboration between them while shrinking the area of competition. And by generating growth it was possible to avoid the dangerous social divisions, the battles over redistribution, and the excessive expansion of state power that might otherwise result from economic stagnation and retrenchment.

Generating growth, however, required more than a common commitment to productionism and particular organizational adaptations. It also required appropriate public programs, especially in such areas as fiscal, monetary, and budgetary policy, international economic policy, and labor policy broadly defined to include measures of social welfare. Corporate liberals have differed among themselves over the nature of these policies, and their recommendations have changed over time. Nevertheless, the general direction of corporatist thinking remained consistent with what American historians would identify as "progressive," and then "liberal," opinion in the public and private sectors. Works that might be fitted into the New School thus talk of an *evolving* corporate liberalism. They tend to view the modern American experience as a single process, but they do not deny the reality of historical change. Indeed, they are particularly interested in the liberal policy innovations growing out of the New Deal, and at least some have linked these changes to interrelated transformations in the structure of American industry and politics.

This is the case with Thomas Ferguson and other historians who have sought to explain the rise and fall of the "System of '96," by which they mean the political alignment that took shape in the United States at the end of the nineteenth century. The Republican party presided over this system, organizing a dominant political coalition centered on a nearly homogeneous community of business and banking leaders. By the 1920s, however, the business community had split into capital-intensive and labor-intensive blocs. Ferguson notes how each bloc adopted different positions on labor and trade policy, a list that later would include fiscal, monetary, and budgetary policy as well.

On the labor question, capital-intensive firms adopted a conciliatory approach similar to the one urged by Republican progressives like Herbert Hoover, out of which came support for employee representation schemes, corporate programs of welfare capitalism, and the eight-hour day in the steel industry. Labor-intensive firms remained wedded to the antilabor policies of an earlier age. Unable to afford the high wages, better benefits, and improved working conditions that it would take to buy a more malleable and cooperative work force, they resorted to the "big stick" in dealing with labor strikes, launched a crusade for the "Open Shop," and applauded the use of antilabor court injunctions by the Justice Department. The same firms also belonged to the nationalist wing of the business community and the Republican party. Fearful of more efficient producers abroad, they sought to shelter the home market behind a wall of restrictions and generally complained about reducing war debts and raising taxes in order to underwrite the recovery of foreign competitors. Their position set them at odds with the capital-intensive firms for whom the world was an oyster to be enjoyed without penalty in the home market. These latter firms had emerged as world leaders in their industries. And, together with their partners among the great international investment houses, they led the campaign to reduce war debts, eliminate trade restrictions, and organize an Open Door world economy.

These divisions help to account for many of the inconsistencies that typified domestic and foreign policy during the Republican Ascendancy. They arose from underlying changes in the industrial structure and resulted in a political stalemate that persisted into the 1930's, when the gradual convergence of progressive opinion in the public and private sectors finally led to a major realignment. But out of this realignment came the dominant coalition, the so-called New Deal coalition, that would set the political agenda under Democratic and Republican administrations alike over the next forty years. The New Deal coalition included at its core the capital-intensive bloc of firms and their allies in the investment community, the leading trade unions, and the major farm associations. Each of these groups stood to gain from policies that buttressed the private sector, promoted overseas expansion, fostered social welfare, or facilitated labor's collaboration in a tripartite partnership with government and business. Their alliance enabled the New Deal to overcome domestic opposition, eliminate some of the earlier contradictions in public policy, and take the nation farther down the road to a corporative political economy than Republican progressives had been able to go in the 1920s. Hoover's concept of countercyclical stabilization now gave way to Keynesian strategies of demand management, welfare capitalism and company unionism to the welfare state and the Wagner Act, and "independent internationalism" to multilateralism.

As the last transformation suggests, the search for order in the United States had an international counterpart. Corporate liberals saw parallels between national policies of economic autarky and the unbridled pursuit of self-interest at home, between state trading and paternalistic government, and between international rivalries and domestic social divisions. From their point of view, moreover, these international dangers could be eliminated by restructuring the world system along lines similar to the corporative order that was emerging in the United States. To the open and competitive system envisioned in classical theory—one founded on the principles of specialization, comparative advantage, stable currencies, and fixed exchanges—corporate liberals would append new mechanisms of economic planning, new institutions of coordination and control, and new partnerships between public and private elites in the collective administration of world trade and development. These were to be the bricks and mortar in an international edifice that Hoover and progressive Republicans started to build in the 1920s, and that Cold War liberals later would seek to protect by adding military alliances and other collective security arrangements. In the final design as drawn after World War II, multinational frameworks would limit competitive nationalisms; market forces and institutional coordinators would integrate economies; and economic, as well as military integration, would help to deter aggressors, clear a path to stable growth, and forge a prosperous community of free nations.

The corporatist synthesis, then, can be used to analyze modern American efforts to organize a neo-capitalist system at home and to reorganize the international system along similar lines; to link both efforts to underlying transformations in the structure of American industry and politics; to explain the innovations in public policy that resulted; and to describe the ideology articulated to legitimize both policy innovations and organizational adaptations.

Bureaucratic Politics and Policy Outcomes

J. GARRY CLIFFORD

In the mid-1960s, when members of the Harvard Faculty Study Group on Bureaucracy, Politics, and Policy began to write their scholarly tomes, their sometime col-

Text by J. Garry Clifford from *Explaining the History of American Foreign Relations* edited by Michael J. Hogan and Thomas G. Paterson, pp. 141–145, 147–150. Copyright © 1991 Cambridge University Press. Reprinted with the permission of the publisher.

league in the mathematics department, the folk singer Tom Lehrer, inadvertently gave song to what came to be called the "bureaucratic politics" approach to the study of U.S. foreign policy. In his ballad about a certain German émigré rocket scientist, Lehrer wrote: "Once the rockets are up / Who cares where they come down? / That's not my department! / Said Wernher von Braun." Lehrer's ditty, by suggesting that government is a complex, compartmentalized machine and that those running the machine do not always intend what will result, anticipated the language of bureaucratic politics. The dark humor also hinted that the perspective might sometimes excuse as much as it explains about the foreign policy of the United States.

The formal academic version of bureaucratic politics came a few years later with the publication in 1971 of Graham T. Allison's *Essence of Decision*. Building on works by Warner R. Schilling, Roger Hilsman, Richard E. Neustadt, and other political scientists who emphasized internal bargaining within the foreign policy process, and adding insights from organizational theorists like James G. March and Herbert A. Simon, Allison examined the Cuban missile crisis to refute the traditional assumption that foreign policy is produced by the purposeful acts of unified national governments. Allison argued that instead of resembling the behavior of a "rational actor," the Kennedy administration's behavior during the crisis was best explained as "outcomes" of the standard operating procedures followed by separate organizations (the navy's blockade, the Central Intelligence Agency's U-2 overflights, and the air force's scenarios for a surgical air strike) and as a result of compromise and competition among hawks and doves seeking to advance individual and organizational versions of the national interest. . . .

The Allisonian message holds that U.S. foreign policy has become increasingly political and cumbersome with the growth of bureaucracy after World War II. Diversity and conflict permeate the policy process. There is no single "maker" of foreign policy. Policy flows instead from an amalgam of large organizations and political actors who differ substantially on any particular issue and who compete to advance their own personal and organizational interests as they try to influence decisions. The president, while powerful, is not omnipotent; he is one chief among many. Even when a direct presidential decision is reached, the game does not end because decisions are often ignored or reversed. Jimmy Carter may have thought he had killed the B-1 bomber, but a decade later the weapon was still being produced and its utility still being debated. Because organizations rely on routines and plans derived from experience with familiar problems, those standard routines usually form the basis for options furnished the president. Ask an organization to do what it has not done previously, and it will usually do what the U.S. military did in Vietnam: It will follow existing doctrines and procedures, modifying them only slightly in deference to different conditions.

Final decisions are also "political resultants," the product of compromise and bargaining among the various participants. As Allison puts it, policies are *resultants* in the sense that what happens is not chosen . . . but rather results from compromise, conflict, and confusion of officials with diverse interests and unequal influence; *political* in the sense [of] . . . bargaining along regularized channels among individual members of government." Similarly, once a decision is made, considerable slippage can occur in implementing it. What follows is hostage to standard operating procedures and the interests of the implementers. Even when a president personally monitors performance, as John F. Kennedy tried to do with the navy's blockade during the missile crisis, organizational repertoires and hierarchies are so rigid and complex that the president cannot micromanage all that happens. Kennedy's own naval background notwithstanding, he did not know that antisubmarine warfare units were routinely forcing Soviet submarines to the surface, thus precipitating the very confrontations he so painstakingly tried to avoid.

The bureaucratic politics perspective also suggests that intramural struggles over policy can consume so much time and attention that dealing effectively with external realities becomes secondary. Strobe Talbott's extraordinarily well informed accounts of arms control policy during the Carter and Reagan years [*Endgame,* 1979, and *Deadly Gambits,* 1984] confirm the truism that arriving at a consensus among the various players and agencies within the government is more complicated, if not more difficult, than negotiating with the Soviets. Ironically, officials who are finely attuned to the conflict and compartmentalism within the American government often see unitary, purposive behavior on the part of other governments. Recall the rush to judgment about the Soviet shooting down of a Korean airliner in 1983 as compared to the tortured ("rules of engagement") justifications that followed the destruction of an Iranian aircraft by the American naval cruiser *Vincennes* in 1988. . . .

Several criticisms have been leveled at the bureaucratic politics approach. Some critics contend that ideological core values shared by those whom Richard J. Barnet has called "national security managers" weigh more in determining policy than do any differences attributable to bureaucratic position. The axiom "where you stand depends on where you sit" has had less influence, they argue, than the generational mindset of such individuals as Paul Nitze, John J. McCloy, and Clark Clifford, whose participation in the foreign policy establishment spanned decades and cut across bureaucratic and partisan boundaries. Similarly, the perspective underestimates the extent to which the president can dominate the bureaucracy by selecting key players and setting the rules of the game. The Tower Commission report [1987] exposed the flaws of instant bureaucratic analysis when it simplistically blamed the Iran-contra affair on a loose cannon in the White House basement and exonerated a detached president who was allegedly cut out of the policy "loop." The historian must be careful in each case to judge how much of the buck that stops with the president has already been spent by the bureaucracy. . . .

Yet those defects in the bureaucratic politics approach may not hamper historians, who do not need models that predict perfectly. Unlike political scientists, they do not seek to build better theories or to propose more effective management techniques. Because the bureaucratic politics approach emphasizes state-level analysis, it cannot fully answer such cosmic questions as why the United States has opposed revolutions or why East-West issues have predominated over North-South issues. It is better at explaining the timing and mechanics of particular episodes, illuminating proximate as opposed to deeper causes, and showing why outcomes were not what was intended. The bureaucratic details of debacles like Pearl Harbor and the Bay of Pigs invasion are thus better understood than the long-term dynamics of war and peace. . . .

When can the perspective be most helpful? Because organizations function most predictably in a familiar environment, major transformations in the international system (wars and their aftermaths, economic crises, the Sino-Soviet split) require the analyst to study how institutional adjustments in U.S. policies resulted from the changes. Similarly propitious are transitions that bring in new players pledged to reverse the priorities of their predecessors, and particularly those administrations in which the president, deliberately or not, encourages competition and initiative from strong-willed subordinates. Fiascos like the American failure to fend off the attack on Pearl Harbor and the Iran-contra affair not only force agencies to reassess procedures and programs but, even better, often spawn official investigations that provide scholars with abundant evidence for bureaucratic analysis. Budget battles, weapons procurement, coordination of intelligence, war termination, alliance politics—in short, any foreign policy that engages the separate attentions of multiple agencies and agents should alert the historian to the bureaucratic politics perspective.

Consider, for example, the complex dynamics of American entry into World War II. Looking at the period through the lens of bureaucratic politics reveals that FDR may have had more than Congress and public opinion in mind when making his famous remark: "It's a terrible thing to look over your shoulder when you are trying to lead—and to find no one there." The institutional aversion to giving commissioned naval vessels to a foreign power delayed the destroyers-for-bases deal for several weeks in the summer of 1940, and only by getting eight British bases in direct exchange for the destroyers could Roosevelt persuade the chief of naval operations, Admiral Harold Stark, to certify, as required by statute, that these destroyers were no longer essential to national defense. According to navy scuttlebutt, the president threatened to fire Stark if he did not support what virtually every naval officer opposed and the admiral agonized before acquiescing. Similarly, the army's initial opposition to peacetime conscription, FDR's dramatic appointment of Henry L. Stimson and Frank Knox to head the War and Navy departments in June 1940, his firing of Admiral James O. Richardson for his opposition to basing the Pacific fleet at Pearl Harbor, the refusal of the army and navy to mount expeditions to the Azores and Dakar in the spring of 1941, the unvarying strategic advice not to risk war until the armed forces were better prepared—all suggest an environment in which the president had to push hard to get the bureaucracy to accept his policy of supporting the Allies by steps short of war. Even the navy's eagerness to begin Atlantic convoys in the spring of 1941 and the subsequent Army Air Corps strategy of reinforcing the Philippines with B-17s were aimed in part at deploying ships and planes that FDR might otherwise have given to the British and the Russians. . . .

In sum, this essay should be read as a modest plea for greater attention to bureaucratic politics. The perspective can enrich and complement other approaches. By focusing on internal political processes we become aware of the conflict within government before arriving at the cooperative core values posited by the corporatists or the neorealists. In its emphasis on individual values and tugging and hauling by key players, bureaucratic politics makes personality and cognitive processes crucial to understanding who wins and why. Although bureaucratic struggles may be over tactics more than over strategy, over pace rather than direction, those distinctions may matter greatly when the outcome is a divided Berlin and Korea, a second atomic bomb, an ABM [antiballistic missile] system that no one really wanted, or the failure of last-minute efforts to avert war in the Pacific. Too easily dismissed as a primer for managing crises that should be avoided, the bureaucratic politics perspective also warns national security managers that when "governments collide," the machines cannot do what they are not programmed to do. Rather than press "delete" and conceptualize policy only as a rational action, it is incumbent on historians to know how the machines work, their repertoires, the institutional rules of the game, and how the box score is kept. The processes are peculiarly American. The British ambassador Edward Lord Halifax once observed that the foreign policy establishment in Washington was "rather like a disorderly line of beaters out shooting; they do put the rabbits out of the bracken, but they don't come out where you would expect." Historians of American foreign relations need to identify the beaters and follow them into the bureaucratic forest because the game is much bigger than rabbit.

Psychology, Personality, and Leadership

RICHARD H. IMMERMAN

Was Richard M. Nixon mad when he assumed responsibility for U.S. foreign policy? The attention paid to his personality, particularly after the Watergate break-in, suggests that many people believed him to be so, or close to it. In one context Nixon evidently preferred it that way: Although he possessed no secret plan to end the war in Vietnam, he intended to persuade Hanoi that it must either agree to a quick peace or, according to [Nixon's White House assistant] H. R. Haldeman, face the consequences of a madman cocking the trigger on the American nuclear shotgun. "They'll believe any threat of force Nixon makes because it's Nixon," the president reportedly confided to his White House chief of staff. "I want the North Vietnamese to believe I've reached the point where I might do *anything* to stop the war. We'll just slip the word to them [that we] can't restrain him when he's angry . . . and Ho Chi Minh himself will be in Paris in two days, begging for peace."

Whether Nixon sincerely sought to portray himself as a madman, was mad to think he could, or was just plain mad cannot be determined from the available evidence. What is more, because Haldeman was reconstructing from memory a conversation that occurred some ten years earlier, he could have distorted the president's words or manufactured the incident to serve his own purposes. Yet Haldeman alleges the conversation did take place, and it is plausible. It is also instructive.

Accounts such as Haldeman's invite us to consider and explore the relationship between psychology and the history of American foreign relations. On the other hand, the episode speaks directly to the influence of a policymaker's personality on his policies. Nixon need not have been mad for his predispositions, attributes, identifications, and emotions to have affected his strategies and tactics, not only toward Vietnam but toward the Middle East, Chile, Bangladesh—everywhere. On the other hand, regardless of the condition of Nixon's mind, he wanted the North Vietnamese to *think* he was mad. This objective suggests another dimension of psychology that bears on foreign relations: cognitive psychology. Here we are concerned with perceptions, beliefs, the encoding and retrieval of information, memory, and other mental processes. Based on his assumptions about the North Vietnamese, Nixon wanted to send a particular signal that he expected to be interpreted in a particular way. Cognitive theories hold that this tactic was vulnerable to error.

Skeptics may judge Nixon and his alleged madman theory too atypical to serve as normative illustrations. Granted that the incident was unusual, the characterization does not negate the argument that psychology is integral to the study of diplomatic history in general. Quite the contrary. Because highly abnormal or unpredictable behavior such as that of Nixon or Woodrow Wilson is not easily explained by situational variables, it is the most accurate barometer of the saliency of personality factors. Personality disorders, moreover, can most readily become consequential. The suitability of a psychological approach, however, is not limited to when individuals appear to act irrationally or erratically.

The history of American foreign relations is punctuated with fascinating individuals: Benjamin Franklin, Thomas Jefferson, John Quincy Adams, William H. Seward, Theodore and Franklin D. Roosevelt, George F. Kennan, James V. Forrestal, John Foster Dulles, John F. Kennedy, Lyndon B. Johnson, Ronald Reagan—the list is endless. Their personalities alone did not determine policy—environmental and situational variables are always influential and frequently decisive. But predispositions, attributes, motives, affects (or emotions), and other elements that constitute personality, broadly defined, played a role. A secretary of state less self-confident, audacious, or stubborn than John Quincy Adams might have failed to orchestrate the transcontinental treaty of 1819 with Spain or might have settled for a joint Anglo-American declaration of policy toward the Western Hemisphere instead of the Monroe Doctrine. The impact of Ronald Reagan's personality on his administration's foreign relations was palpable if ambiguous. At a minimum, psychological variables serve as mediators between the environment and human activity. Behavior, therefore, is the product of the *interaction* between the individual and the situation in which he finds himself.

An individual's cognitions, the processes by which he perceives and evaluates his physical and social environment, likewise contribute to his conclusions and recommendations. How else, for example, does he interpret the data he collects on the threat posed by an adversary or assess the potential for a diplomatic initiative? What are the bases for inferences about the normally and oftentimes deliberately ambiguous behavior of others? It has become almost axiomatic that the assimilation and interpretation of information, the grist for the policymaking mill, does not occur in a contextual vacuum. Decision makers frequently rely on the "lessons of history," drawing analogies with historical precedents in order to define a situation or identify a phenomenon. Psychological theories can help to explain how and why decision makers act in this manner, and in the process they can provide clues for locating errors in judgment or perception. They can also alert us to conditions, such as stress or anxiety, that can affect the deliberations and their outcomes.

The very nature of psychology leads us to associate it with abnormal behavior, distorted perceptions, compromised processes, and the like. For explanatory purposes, therefore, its value would seem to be limited to extraordinary situations, such as Wilson's monumental struggle for the League of Nations. Actually, psychology's relationship to foreign policy is so pervasive as to be unexceptional. Deterrence, brinkmanship, credibility, commitment, risk, threat—these and many more conventional entries in the historian's lexicon are essentially psychological concepts. Central to each are perceptions, fears, wants, values, and parallel mental phenomena. The "psychology of foreign relations" has become more pronounced in the nuclear age as the function, perhaps the raison d'être, of these weapons has been progressively divorced from the military sphere and associated with diplomatic and political solutions. To illustrate, as defined by [the political scientist] Richard Ned Lebow, deterrence "consists of manipulating another actor's assessment of his interests and seeks to prevent any specified behavior by convincing the actor who may contemplate it that its costs exceed any possible gain." The psychological implications are evident. Lebow might have added that experimental evidence suggests that a decision as to what policy best serves the national interest may depend on how decision makers frame their discussions. For example, individuals are more likely to accept greater risks if they perceive the potential outcome as a loss than if they perceive it as a gain.

Conclusions from experiments, of course, do not necessarily generate universal certainties, nor do they generally take into account cultural or temporal differences. When the historian looks at the failures of U.S. policy in Vietnam or the postures of both Washington and Moscow during the Cuban missile crisis, however, the psychological literature on risks and the framing of decisions can prove illuminating. So can the concept of a security dilemma, which is likewise rooted in psychology. The foundation of the security dilemma is the generalization that efforts to increase the security of one nation frequently decrease the security of another. Consider all the historical analyses that emphasize the failure of antagonists to distinguish between offensive and defensive weapons and postures and that show how such spirals of misunderstanding and misperceptions fed tensions and conflict. Indeed, much of the literature on the origins of the Cold War accents this phenomenon. To quote John Lewis Gaddis as an example, "It seems likely that Washington policymakers mistook Stalin's determination to ensure Russian security through spheres of influence for a renewed effort to spread communism outside the borders of the Soviet Union."

Scarcely an element of international relations is devoid of one, two, or several psychological components. What analysis of negotiations, for example, can overlook the psychology of the different actors? Success or failure at the bargaining table depends largely on the chips one holds and usually on domestic factors as well. But outcomes can also turn on the ability of one participant to "read" or even mislead another, the flexibility of the respective personalities, comparative risk-taking tendencies, and parallel attributes and styles. Statesmen adopt negotiating strategies, as a rule, in light of the predicted response they will generate. Carrots and sticks, or sugar and vinegar, are psychological ploys. . . .

Notwithstanding the obstacles to using a psychoanalytic approach, the influence of personality on policies must not and need not be overlooked. The literature on political psychology has indicated that there is a correlation between a policymaker's *observable* personality traits and his behavior. Some analysts have gone so far as to postulate relationships among these traits to produce typologies that generate predictions about styles and policies. I find this approach dangerously reductionist, yet certain finite relationships appear plausible. Evidence suggests, for example, that individuals confident in their ability to control events tend toward more activism in foreign affairs and that extroverts advocate better relations with Communists than do introverts. Although the documentation remains inconclusive, an analysis of such contrasts between Johnson's and Kennedy's personalities as their respective power needs and differing styles of dealing with subordinates raises the possibility that, had Kennedy lived, the American experience in Vietnam would have been different. Even if such unprovable counterfactuals are dismissed as useless, the argument that one's character traits can affect one's decisions remains compelling. An archivally based examination of Johnson's Vietnam policy presents credible evidence that his attributes, including his propensity for the "we-they" thinking and his passionately personal identification with the cause of the United States, manifested themselves in a diminished capacity to assess information and advice.

Dogmatism, mental complexity or flexibility, and similar attributes likewise affect policymaking and state conduct. They are also elements of the individual's overall personality, but they lead us to focus on cognitive psychology. Because the objective of cognitive psychology is to explain how individuals perceive and interpret their environment, it is concerned also with misunderstandings and miscommunications, and its utility for students of international relations is palpable. The two theories of cognitive psychology that are probably most valuable for historians are attribution and schema theory. According to attribution theorists, individuals function like "naive scientists." We explain others' behavior by looking for clues, cumulative evidence; this is a rational process (unless the perceiver's emotions interfere). Schema theorists contend that our ability to assimilate information is limited; as a consequence we are "cognitive misers." We categorize the knowledge we have into schemata, mental or cognitive structures that fit the knowledge into a pattern. In other words, we have preconceived notions, beliefs about how social objects and phenomena relate to one another.

Intricately tied to the concept of schemata is the theory of heuristics. These shortcuts to rationality allow individuals to reduce complicated problem-solving tasks to simple judgments; they are strategies for managing information overload. Typical is the *representative* heuristic, by which people evaluate the extent to which the characteristics of a person, country, or political system—any object—are representative of a category of that same object: Egypt's Gamal Abdel Nasser is another Adolf Hitler. Guatemala's Jacobo Arbenz must be a Communist. If it looks like a duck and acts like a duck, it is a duck. In the *availability* heuristic, we draw inferences based on whatever pattern or frame of reference is most available and therefore most easily comes to mind. A military man such as General Lucius D. Clay is more likely to interpret the Berlin blockade as the first shot in a Soviet offensive than is an official in the State Department.

These theories help to explain how individuals make sense out of the complex world in which they live. They also help to explain why individuals make frequent errors of judgment and inference. Attached to each theory, or explanation for how we perceive and diagnose, are a series of "biases" or common mistakes: We may tend, for example, to overestimate the influence of personal dispositions on behavior and to underestimate the influence of situational influences. Or we may be more influenced by vivid, concrete data than that which is pallid and abstract; a nonevent (the dog that did not bark in the dark; the Soviet intervention that did not occur) may be overlooked altogether. Or because we know our own motives and intentions, we may assume others know them as well. Or we do not always distinguish between the inferences we draw from the data we receive and the data itself. Or we overlook base rate statistics and overestimate the size of the sample we use to generate a heuristic category. There are many other biases, but the point is clear.

Most fundamentally, cognitive psychologists uniformly agree that once we have formed a belief we are reluctant to discard or even qualify it. New evidence will be interpreted to conform to our prior beliefs: If it is consistent with them, it will be accepted; if inconsistent or ambiguous, it will be discredited or ignored. This tendency is most pronounced when the belief is deeply felt and deeply held. . . .

Although cognitive and motivational explanations for behavior are often placed in opposition to one another, they are in fact interrelated. One's beliefs affect one's emotions and vice versa; unmotivated and motivated biases are frequently indistinguishable. Insights drawn from these psychological theories—and my summary is far from exhaustive—can prove illuminating for historians of foreign relations. Anyone who has ever read a State Department situational report, an intelligence estimate, or the memorandums of a National Security Council meeting will profit from an understanding of the normative strategies by which we perceive the world and draw inferences, an awareness of our cognitive shortcomings, and a sensitivity to the possible influence of emotions.

✖ *F U R T H E R   R E A D I N G*

See works mentioned in the essays above.

Richard J. Barnet, *Roots of War* (1972)

Charles Beard and Mary Beard, *The Rise of American Civilization* (1927)

William H. Becker and Samuel F. Wells, eds., *Economics and World Power* (1984)

Barton J. Bernstein, ed., *Towards a New Past* (1968)

J. Garry Clifford and Samuel R. Spencer, Jr., *The First Peacetime Draft* (1986)

Jerald A. Combs, *American Diplomatic History: Two Centuries of Changing Interpretations* (1982)

"Culture, Gender, and Foreign Policy: A Symposium," *Diplomatic History,* 18 (1994), 47–124

Robert Dallek, *The American Style of Foreign Policy* (1983)

Alexander DeConde, ed., *Encyclopedia of American Foreign Policy* (1978)

Arthur A. Ekirch, Jr., *Ideas, Ideals, and American Diplomacy* (1966)

James Fallows, *More Like Us* (1989)

Frances FitzGerald, *America Revised* (1979)

John Lewis Gaddis, "The Corporatist Synthesis: A Skeptical View," *Diplomatic History,* 10 (1986), 357–362

———, "New Conceptual Approaches to the Study of American Foreign Relations," *Diplomatic History,* 14 (1990), 403–425

Lloyd C. Gardner, ed., *Redefining the Past* (1986)

Norman A. Graebner, *Ideas and Diplomacy* (1964)

Gerald K. Haines and J. Samuel Walker, eds., *American Foreign Relations* (1981)

Morton Halperin, *Bureaucratic Politics and Foreign Policy* (1974)

Michael P. Hamilton, ed., *American Character and Foreign Policy* (1986)

Ellis W. Hawley, "The Discovery and Study of a 'Corporate Liberalism,' " *Business History Review,* 52 (1978), 309–320

John Higham, "The Cult of the 'American Consensus,' " *Commentary,* 27 (1959), 93–100

———, *History* (1989)

Michael Hogan, *The Marshall Plan* (1987)

———, "Revival and Reform: America's Twentieth-Century Search for a New Economic Order Abroad," *Diplomatic History,* 8 (1984), 287–310

———, ed., "Writing the History of U.S. Foreign Relations: A Symposium," *Diplomatic History,* 14 (1990), 553–605

——— and Thomas G. Paterson, eds., *Explaining the History of American Foreign Relations* (1991)

Michael H. Hunt, *Ideology and U.S. Foreign Policy* (1987)

———, "The Long Crisis in U.S. Diplomatic History: Coming to a Closure," *Diplomatic History,* 16 (1992), 115–140

Akira Iriye, "Culture and Power," *Diplomatic History,* 3 (1979), 115–128

———, "The Internationalization of History," *American Historical Review,* 94 (1989), 1–10

———, *Power and Culture* (1981)

George F. Kennan, *American Diplomacy, 1900–1950* (1951)

Paul Kennedy, *The Rise and Fall of the Great Powers* (1987)

Gabriel Kolko, *The Roots of American Foreign Policy* (1969)

Melvyn P. Leffler, *A Preponderance of Power* (1992)

William E. Leuchtenburg, "The Pertinence of Political History," *Journal of American History,* 73 (1986), 585–600

Walter Lippmann, *U.S. Foreign Policy: Shield of the Republic* (1943)

Thomas J. McCormick, "Drift or Mastery?" *Reviews in American History,* 10 (1982), 318–330

Charles S. Maier, "Marking Time: The Historiography of International Relations," in Michael Kamman, ed., *The Past Before Us* (1980)

Hans J. Morgenthau, *In Defense of the National Interest* (1951)

Charles E. Neu, "The Rise of the National Security Bureaucracy," in Louis Galambos, ed., *The New American State* (1987)

Richard E. Neustadt, *Presidential Power* (1990)

——— and Ernest R. May, *Thinking in Time* (1986)

Frank Ninkovich, "Interests and Discourse in Diplomatic History," *Diplomatic History,* 13 (1989), 135–161

Peter Novick, *That Noble Dream: The "Objectivity" Question and the American Historical Profession* (1988)

Thomas G. Paterson, ed., "Symposium: Explaining the History of American Foreign Relations," *Journal of American History,* 77 (1990), 93–182

Stephen E. Pelz, "A Taxonomy for American Diplomatic History," *Journal of Interdisciplinary History,* 19 (1988), 259–276

Dexter Perkins, *The Evolution of American Foreign Policy* (1948)

David Potter, *People of Plenty* (1954)

Emily S. Rosenberg, *Spreading the American Dream: American Economic and Cultural Expansion, 1898–1945* (1982)

Arthur M. Schlesinger, Jr., *The Cycles of American History* (1986)

———, *The Imperial Presidency* (1973)

Geoffrey S. Smith, "National Security and Personal Isolation: Sex, Gender, and Disease in Cold-War United States," *International History Review,* 14 (1992), 221–240

"Symposium: Responses to Charles S. Maier, 'Marking Time,' " *Diplomatic History,* 5 (1981), 353–371

Christopher Thorne, *Border Crossings* (1988)

Robert Tucker, *The Radical Left and American Foreign Policy* (1971)

E. L. Tuveson, *Redeemer Nation* (1968)

Theodore H. von Laue, *The World Revolution of Westernization* (1987)

William O. Walker III, "Drug Control and the Issue of Culture in American Foreign Relations," *Diplomatic History,* 12 (1988), 365–382

Immanuel Wallerstein, *The Capitalist World-Economy* (1979)

Albert K. Weinberg, *Manifest Destiny* (1935)

Rubin F. Weston, *Racism in U.S. Imperialism* (1972)

Robert H. Wiebe, *The Search for Order* (1967)

William A. Williams, *The Contours of American History* (1966)

———, *Empire as a Way of Life* (1980)

———, *History as a Way of Learning* (1973)

Special Note: The journal *Diplomatic History,* published by the Society for Historians of American Foreign Relations, regularly presents essays on changing interpretations in and approaches to the field.

CHAPTER

2

Woodrow Wilson,

the First World War,

and the League Fight

In August 1914 Europe descended into war. Now an imperial power and a substantial trader on the high seas, the United States became ensnared in the deadly conflict. Until April 1917, however, President Woodrow Wilson struggled to define policies that would protect U.S. interests and principles, keep the nation out of the war, end the bloodshed, and permit him to shape the terms of the peace settlement and the characteristics of the postwar international system. The president protested violations of U.S. neutral rights, lectured the belligerents to respect international law, appealed for a "peace without victory," and offered to mediate. When his peace advocacy faltered and Germany launched unrestricted submarine warfare, Wilson asked a divided but ultimately obliging Congress for a declaration of war. America's participation in the First World War elevated the nation to great-power status and transformed U.S. foreign relations.

Why did the United States go to war? Historians usually point fingers at the German U-boat, which violated neutral rights, endangered the lives of passengers on ocean liners, and sank American merchant ships. Germany, many have argued, forced the United States into the war. But some scholars of Wilsonian diplomacy have asked: Would Germany have unleashed the submarine if U.S. policy had been different? That is, was the United States truly neutral, or did it side with the British? Did U.S. economic interests, especially the expanded wartime trade and loans, force Wilson's hand? Did U.S. officials favor the British owing to deep-rooted cultural affinities—shared values, language, and political institutions?

Studies of Woodrow Wilson have speculated about the roles of his personality, his religious faith, his interpretation of international law, his penchant for personalizing issues and speaking in exaggerated terms, and his grasp of hard-nosed world politics. Did Wilson act to protect U.S. economic and strategic interests (was he a realist?), or did he decide on war primarily to satisfy his lofty principles about saving humanity (was he an idealist?)? Did he take America to war in order to ensure himself a seat at the postwar peace table? Why did his calls for peace fail? Did

Wilson have viable options other than war? Should the United States have stayed out of the European conflict?

Once the United States became a belligerent, Wilson strove not only to win the war but to shape the postwar peace. He called for a nonvindictive peace treaty and urged creation of an association of nations to deter war. The president's Fourteen Points outlined his plans for shelving balance-of-power politics in favor of disarmament, open diplomacy, Open Door trade, and self-determination. Having tipped the balance in favor of the Allies, the United States helped to force Germany to surrender on November 11, 1918. In January of the following year, Wilson went to the Versailles Palace near Paris to negotiate a peace treaty and a covenant for the League of Nations that he believed would sustain a stable world order. European leaders sneered that Wilson was a dreamer, out of touch with reality, but millions of people on the Continent cheered his arrival and his high-minded appeals for a moral and pacific future.

At home, however, many Americans began to question Wilson's handling of foreign policy, especially after they learned that he had compromised some of his principles in order to win approval for his League. Some critics listened to his lofty rhetoric and wondered if the president had deluded himself into thinking that he was a new messiah. Republican leaders, who had defeated the Democrats in the 1918 congressional elections, calculated that Wilson was politically vulnerable. Supreme nationalists feared that an international organization would undermine American sovereignty—that opting for collective security would snub George Washington's venerable advice to avoid restrictive foreign entanglements. Wilson battled back in an intense national debate, denouncing naysayers as narrow, backward-looking people who did not understand humanity's demand for a new world order. He refused to abandon the collective-security provision of Article 10 of the League covenant. He insisted that the covenant would ensure American prosperity, protect the U.S. national interest, and help the United States to take its rightful place as world leader. Unwilling to compromise with senators who demanded "reservations" (amendments), opposed by "irreconcilables" who would accept no league whatsoever, and laid low by illness, Wilson lost the fight. The Senate rejected the peace treaty and U.S. membership in the League of Nations.

Explanations for this outcome vary widely. Some scholars believe that the personal feud between Wilson and Republican senator Henry Cabot Lodge, chair of the Foreign Relations Committee, doomed Wilson's efforts; that two-party politics took its toll; or that the Wilson administration's trampling on civil liberties at home during the war and the president's abandonment of liberal allies undermined his international cause. Others have emphasized the president's personality—his arrogance, ignorance, self-righteousness, stubbornness. Wilson's deteriorating health, especially his severe stroke in October 1919, has raised the question of whether a healthy, more clear-headed Wilson might have accepted compromise. Finally, some scholars have questioned interpretations built on personality or politics. They have argued that the League fight represented a debate about the very core of American foreign policy: whether the nation would adhere to the tradition of unilateralism or instead embrace collective security.

Other questions look to the future: Did the peace treaty impose such harsh terms on Germany and create such a weak international system that another world war became inevitable? Did it matter that the United States rejected membership in the League? Is Woodrow Wilson responsible for the turmoil of international relations that followed his presidency, including the descent into the Second World War?

✳ D O C U M E N T S

When a German U-boat sank the British liner *Lusitania* on May 7, 1915, killing 1,198, including 128 Americans, President Woodrow Wilson sent a strong note to Berlin. The May 13 warning, the first document, demanded that Germany disavow submarine warfare and respect the right of Americans to sail on the high seas. On April 20, 1916, Secretary of State Robert Lansing and Count Johann-Heinrich Bernstorff, German ambassador to the United States, debated U-boat warfare. This meeting, reported in the second document, came less than a month after the torpedoing of the French ship *Sussex* and helped to produce a German pledge not to attack merchant vessels and liners without warning. The third document is the Zimmermann telegram of January 1917. Sent from Berlin and intended for German diplomats in Mexico City, the message was intercepted by the British and turned over to U.S. officials, who interpreted it as a serious German challenge to U.S. security. On January 22, 1917, Wilson went before the Senate to appeal for a "peace without victory." His remarks are included as the fourth selection. Soon Germany declared unrestricted submarine warfare and Wilson broke diplomatic relations with Berlin. On April 2, after the sinking of several American vessels, the president asked Congress for a declaration of war. His war message, the fifth document, outlines U.S. grievances against Germany. One of the few dissenters in the Senate—the war measure passed, 82 to 6—was Robert M. La Follette of Wisconsin. In his speech of April 4, the sixth document, the great reform politician revealed his fear of an American "war machine."

President Wilson issued his Fourteen Points in a speech on January 8, 1918, reprinted here as the seventh document. Articles 10 through 16 of the Covenant of the League of Nations hammered out at the Paris peace conference in 1919 are included as the eighth document. Wilson explained during his busy western U.S. speaking tour in September 1919 that these provisions would prevent wars. Excerpts from his speeches are featured in the ninth document. Led by Senator Henry Cabot Lodge of Massachusetts, critics worked to add "reservations" to the covenant through a Lodge resolution dated November 19, 1919, the final document. But neither an amended peace treaty (which contained the covenant) nor an unamended treaty passed the Senate.

The First *Lusitania* Note, 1915

The Government of the United States has been apprised that the Imperial German Government considered themselves to be obliged by the extraordinary circumstances of the present war and the measures adopted by their adversaries in seeking to cut Germany off from all commerce, to adopt methods of retaliation which go much beyond the ordinary methods of warfare at sea, in the proclamation of a war zone from which they have warned neutral ships to keep away. This Government has already taken occasion to inform the Imperial German Government that it cannot admit the adoption of such measures or such a warning of danger to operate as in any degree an abbreviation of the rights of American shipmasters or of American citizens bound on lawful errands as passengers on merchant ships of belligerent nationality; and that it must hold the Imperial German Government to a strict accountability for any infringement of those rights, intentional or incidental. It does not understand the Imperial German Government to question those rights. It assumes, on the contrary, that the Imperial Government accept, as of course, the rule that the lives of noncombatants, whether they be of neutral citizenship or citizens of one of the nations at war, can not lawfully or rightfully be put in jeopardy by the capture or destruction of an unarmed merchantman, and recognize also, as all other nations do, the obligation to take the usual precaution of visit and search to ascertain whether a suspected merchantman is in fact of belligerent nationality or is in fact carrying contraband of war under a neutral flag.

The Government of the United States, therefore, desires to call the attention of the Imperial German Government with the utmost earnestness to the fact that the objection to their present method of attack against the trade of their enemies lies in the practical impossibility of employing submarines in the destruction of commerce without disregarding those rules of fairness, reason, justice, and humanity, which all modern opinion regards as imperative. It is practically impossible for the officers of a submarine to visit a merchantman at sea and examine her papers and cargo. It is practically impossible for them to make a prize of her; and, if they can not put a prize crew on board of her, they can not sink her without leaving her crew and all on board of her to the mercy of the sea in her small boats. These facts it is understood the Imperial German Government frankly admit. We are informed that, in the instances of which we have spoken, time enough for even that poor measure of safety was not given, and in at least two of the cases cited, not so much as a warning was received. Manifestly submarines can not be used against merchantmen, as the last few weeks have shown, without an inevitable violation of many sacred principles of justice and humanity.

American citizens act within their indisputable rights in taking their ships and in traveling wherever their legitimate business calls them upon the high seas, and exercise those rights in what should be the well-justified confidence that their lives will not be endangered by acts done in clear violation of universally acknowledged international obligations, and certainly in the confidence that their own Government will sustain them in the exercise of their rights.

Robert Lansing and Johann-Heinrich Bernstorff Debate Submarine Warfare, 1916

L: You will recall that we said in the first *Lusitania* note that we thought it was impossible to use submarines in a really humane way and that later, in our note of July 21, we said that the way submarine warfare had been conducted for the past two months showed that it was possible and therefore we hoped that course would be pursued. Then we had the sinking of the *Arabic* right on top of that, which was another great disaster. Our position is that, if submarine warfare had been conducted in that way, that possibly there would have been no further question raised. But it has not. It has been conducted in the most indiscriminate way and we cannot help but believe that it is ruthless. In those conditions submarine warfare should stop against commercial vessels, unless visit and search is observed.

B: That, of course, is impossible. Germany cannot abandon submarine warfare. No government could come out and say—"We give up the use of submarines." They would have to resign.

L: What possible methods in the use of submarines, that are effective from a belligerent standpoint, can be suggested which will comply with the law?

B: I had always supposed that warning was to be given.

L: We do not consider that the people on board—the non-combatants on board the vessels—are in a place of safety when put into an open boat a hundred miles from land. It might be calm there, but in the two days it would take them to reach land there might be a severe storm. That is one of the grounds of complaint.

B: That, of course, speaking of neutral vessels—

L: The fact that we do not have Americans on these vessels does not remove the menace to American lives. The sinking of neutral vessels shows that Americans cannot travel with safety on neutral vessels even. That is the serious part of it and I do not know how your government can modify submarine warfare and make it effective and at the same time obey the law and the dictates of humanity.

B: Humanity. Of course war is never humane.

L: "Humanity" is a relative expression when used with "war" but the whole tendency in the growth of international law in regard to warfare in the past 125 years has been to relieve non-combatants of needless suffering.

B: Of course I think it would be an ideal state of affairs, but our enemies violate all the rules and you insist on their being applied to Germany.

L: One deals with life; the other with property. . . .

L: There would have to be a complete abandonment first and then if the German Government desires to discuss the matter—

B: I want to do what I can, because I am perfectly convinced they do not want to break; quite apart from the sentimental side I think they do not want a break. A break would prolong the war. It would last for years.

L: We do not any of us want to prolong the war.

B: That is exactly why I want to get out of this present difficulty. From the present state of affairs it looks as if the end is coming and if now there was a break and the United States was brought into the war it would prolong it. It would cause new complications.

L: New complications?

B: New economic difficulties.

L: I think that would be Germany's problem. The only possible course is an abandonment of submarine warfare, whether limited or not would depend on the terms. I would want to see an abandonment first and then possibly a discussion could follow as to how submarine warfare can be conducted within the rules of international law and entire safety of non-combatants, because, of course, in my viewpoint that is the chief question of international law in regard to attacks by belligerents on enemy's commerce.

B: Then I am to understand that you do not recognize the law of retaliation?

L: We do not recognize retaliation when it affects the rights of neutrals.

B: The British retaliate by stopping all commerce to Germany.

L: It is a very different thing. The right to life is an inherent right, which man has from birth; the right of property is a purely legal right.

B: Only in this case, England's methods affect the lives of non-combatants of Germany.

L: Not neutrals.

B: No, but it affects non-combatants.

The Zimmermann Telegram, 1917

We intend to begin on the 1st of February unrestricted submarine warfare. We shall endeavor in spite of this to keep the United States of America neutral. In the event of this not succeeding, we make Mexico a proposal of alliance on the following basis: make war together, make peace together, generous financial support and an understanding on our part that Mexico is to reconquer the lost territory in Texas, New Mexico, and Arizona. The settlement in detail is left to you. You will inform the President of the above most secretly as soon as the outbreak of war with the United States of America is certain and add the suggestion that he should, on his own initiative, invite Japan to immediate adherence and at the same time mediate between Japan and ourselves. Please call the President's attention to the fact that the ruthless employment of our submarines now offers the prospect of compelling England in a few months to make peace.

President Woodrow Wilson's "Peace Without Victory" Speech, 1917

The present war must first be ended; but we owe it to candour and to a just regard for the opinion of mankind to say that, so far as our participation in guarantees of future peace is concerned, it makes a great deal of difference in what way and upon what terms it is ended. The treaties and agreements which bring it to an end must embody terms which will create a peace that is worth guaranteeing and preserving, a peace that will win the approval of mankind, not merely a peace that will serve the several interests and immediate aims of the nations engaged. We shall have no voice in determining what those terms shall be, but we shall, I feel sure, have a voice in determining whether they shall be made lasting or not by the guarantees of a universal covenant; and our judgment upon what is fundamental and essential as a condition precedent to permanency should be spoken now, not afterwards when it may be too late.

No covenant of cooperative peace that does not include the peoples of the New World can suffice to keep the future safe against war; and yet there is only one sort of peace that the peoples of America could join in guaranteeing. The elements of that peace must be elements that engage the confidence and satisfy the principles of the American governments, elements consistent with their political faith and the practical convictions which the peoples of America have once for all embraced and undertaken to defend.

I do not mean to say that any American government would throw any obstacle in the way of any terms of peace the governments now at war might agree upon, or seek to upset them when made, whatever they might be. I only take it for granted that mere terms of peace between the belligerents will not satisfy even the belligerents themselves. Mere agreements may not make peace secure. It will be absolutely necessary that a force be created as a guarantor of the permanency of the settlement so much greater than the force of any nation now engaged or any alliance hitherto formed or projected that no nation, no probable combination of nations could face or withstand it. If the peace presently to be made is to endure, it must be a peace made secure by the organized major force of mankind.

The terms of the immediate peace agreed upon will determine whether it is a peace for which such a guarantee can be secured. The question upon which the whole future peace and policy of the world depends is this: Is the present war a struggle for a just and secure peace, or only for a new balance of power? If it be only a struggle for a new balance of power, who will guarantee, who can guarantee, the stable equilibrium of the new arrangement? Only a tranquil Europe can be a stable Europe. There must be, not a balance of power, but a community of power; not organized rivalries, but an organized common peace.

Fortunately we have received very explicit assurances on this point. The statesmen of both of the groups of nations now arrayed against one another have said, in terms that could not be misinterpreted, that it was no part of the purpose they had in mind to crush their antagonists. But the implications of these assurances may not be equally clear to all,—may not be the same on both sides of the water. I think it will be serviceable if I attempt to set forth what we understand them to be.

They imply, first of all, that it must be a peace without victory. It is not pleasant to say this. I beg that I may be permitted to put my own interpretation upon it and that it may be understood that no other interpretation was in my thought. I am seeking only to face realities and to face them without soft concealments. Victory would mean peace forced upon the loser, a victor's terms imposed upon the vanquished. It would be accepted in humiliation, under duress, at an intolerable sacrifice, and would leave a sting, a resentment, a bitter memory upon which terms of peace would rest, not permanently, but only as upon quicksand. Only a peace between equals can last. Only a peace the very principle of which is equality and a common participation in a common benefit. The right state of mind, the right feeling between nations, is as necessary for a lasting peace as is the just settlement of vexed questions of territory or of racial and national allegiance. . . .

I am proposing, as it were, that the nations should with one accord adopt the doctrine of President Monroe as the doctrine of the world: that no nation should seek to extend its polity over any other nation or people, but that every people should be left free to determine its own polity, its own way of development, unhindered, unthreatened, unafraid, the little along with the great and powerful.

I am proposing that all nations henceforth avoid entangling alliances which would draw them into competitions of power, catch them in a net of intrigue and selfish rivalry, and disturb their own affairs with influences intruded from without. There is no entangling alliance in a concert of power. When all unite to act in the same sense and with the same purpose all act in the common interest and are free to live their own lives under a common protection.

I am proposing government by the consent of the governed; that freedom of the seas which in international conference after conference representatives of the United States have urged with the eloquence of those who are the convinced disciples of liberty; and that moderation of armaments which makes of armies and navies a power for order merely, not an instrument of aggression or of selfish violence.

These are American principles, American policies. We could stand for no others. And they are also the principles and policies of forward looking men and women everywhere, of every modern nation, of every enlightened community. They are the principles of mankind and must prevail.

Wilson's War Message, 1917

On the third of February last I officially laid before you the extraordinary announcement of the Imperial German Government that on and after the first day of February it was its purpose to put aside all restraints of law of humanity and use its submarines to sink every vessel that sought to approach either the ports of Great Britain and Ireland or the western coasts of Europe or any of the ports controlled by the enemies of Germany within the Mediterranean. That had seemed to be the object of the German submarine warfare earlier in the war, but since April of last year the Imperial Government had somewhat restrained the commanders of its undersea craft in conformity with its promise then given to us that passenger boats should not be sunk and that due warning would be given to all other vessels which its submarines might seek to destroy, when no resistance was offered or escape attempted, and care taken that their crews were given at least a fair chance to save their lives in their open boats. The precautions taken were meagre and haphazard enough, as was proved in distressing instance after instance in the progress of the cruel and unmanly business, but a certain degree of restraint was observed. The new policy has swept every restriction aside. Vessels of every kind, whatever their flag, their character, their cargo, their destination, their errand, have been ruthlessly sent to the bottom without warning and without thought of help or mercy for those on board, the vessels of friendly neutrals along with those of belligerents. Even hospital ships and ships carrying relief to the sorely bereaved and stricken people of Belgium, though the latter were provided with safe conduct through the proscribed areas by the German Government itself and were distinguished by unmistakable marks of identity, have been sunk with the same reckless lack of compassion or of principle.

I was for a little while unable to believe that such things would in fact be done by any government that had hitherto subscribed to the humane practices of civilized nations. International law had its origin in the attempt to set up some law which would be respected and observed upon the seas, where no nation had right of dominion where lay the free highways of the world. By painful stage after stage has that law been built up, with meagre enough results, indeed, after all was accomplished that could be accomplished, but always with a clear view, at least of what the heart and conscience of mankind demanded. This minimum of right the German Government has swept aside under the plea of retaliation and necessity and because it had no weapons which it could use at sea except these which it is impossible to employ as it is employing them without throwing to the winds all scruples of humanity or of respect for the understandings that were supposed to underlie the intercourse of the world. I am not now thinking of the loss of property involved, immense and serious as that is, but only of the wanton and wholesale destruction of the lives of noncombatants, men, women, and children, engaged in pursuits which have always, even in the darkest periods of modern history, been deemed innocent and legitimate. Property can be paid for; the lives of peaceful and innocent people cannot be. The present German submarine warfare against commerce is a warfare against mankind.

It is a war against all nations. American ships have been sunk, American lives taken, in ways which it has stirred us very deeply to learn of, but the ships and people of other neutral and friendly nations have been sunk and overwhelmed in the waters in the same way. There has been no discrimination. The challenge is to all mankind. Each nation must decide for itself how it will meet it. The choice we make for ourselves must be made with a moderation of counsel and a temperateness of judgment benefiting our character and our motives as a nation. We must put excited feeling away. Our motive will not be revenge or the victorious assertion of the physical might of the nation, but only the vindication of right, of human right, of which we are only a single champion. . . .

With a profound sense of the solemn and even tragical character of the step I am taking and of the grave responsibilities which it involves, but in unhesitating obedience to what I deem my constitutional duty, I advise that the Congress declare the recent course of the Imperial German Government to be in fact nothing less than war against the government and people of the United States; that it formally accept the status of belligerent which has thus been thrust upon it; and that it take immediate steps not only to put the country in a more thorough state of defense but also to exert all its power and employ all its resources to bring the Government of the German Empire to terms and end the war. . . .

Does not every American feel that assurance has been added to our hope for the future peace of the world by the wonderful and heartening things that have been happening within the last few weeks in Russia? Russia was known by those who knew it best to have been always in fact democratic at heart, in all the vital habits of her thought, in all the intimate relationships of her people that spoke their natural instinct, their habitual attitude towards life. The autocracy that crowned the summit of her political structure, long as it had stood and terrible as was the reality of its power, was not in fact Russian in origin, character, or purpose; and now it has been shaken off and the great, generous Russian people have been added in all their naive majesty and might to the forces that are fighting for freedom in the world, for justice, and for peace. Here is a fit partner for a League of Honour.

One of the things that has served to convince us that the Prussian autocracy was not and could never be our friends is that from the very outset of the present war it has filled our unsuspecting communities and even our offices of government with spies and set criminal intrigues everywhere afoot against our national unity of counsel, our peace within and without, our industries and our commerce. . . . That it means to stir up enemies against us at our very doors the intercepted note to the German Minister at Mexico City is eloquent evidence.

We are accepting this challenge of hostile purpose because we know that in such a government, following such methods, we can never have a friend; and that in the presence of its organized power, always lying in wait to accomplish we know not what purpose, there can be no assured security for the democratic governments of the world. We are now about to accept gauge of battle with its natural foe to liberty and shall, if necessary, spend the whole force of the nation to check and nullify its pretensions and its power. We are glad, now that we see the facts with no veil of false pretense about them, to fight thus for the ultimate peace of the world and for the liberation of its peoples, the German peoples included: for the rights of nations great and small and the privilege of men everywhere to choose their way of life and of obedience. The world must be made safe for democracy. . . .

It is a distressing and oppressive duty, Gentlemen of the Congress, which I have performed in thus addressing you. There are, it may be, many months of fiery trial and sacrifice ahead of us. It is a fearful thing to lead this great peaceful people into war, into the most terrible and disastrous of all wars, civilization itself seeming to be in the balance. But the right is more precious than peace, and we shall fight for the things which we have always carried nearest our hearts—for democracy, for the right of those who submit to authority to have a voice in their own governments, for the rights and liberties of small nations, for a universal dominion of right by such a concert of free peoples as shall bring peace and safety to all nations and make the world itself at last free. To such a task we can dedicate our lives and our fortunes, everything that we are and everything that we have, with the pride of those who know that the day has come when America is privileged to spend her blood and her might for the principles that gave her birth and happiness and the peace which she has treasured. God helping her, she can do no other.

Senator Robert M. La Follette's Dissent, 1917

The poor, sir, who are the ones called upon to rot in the trenches, have no organized power, have no press to voice their will upon this question of peace or war; but, oh, Mr. President, at some time they will be heard. I hope and I believe they will be heard in an orderly and a peaceful way. I think they may be heard from before long. I think, sir, if we take this step, when the people to-day who are staggering under the burden of supporting families at the present prices of the necessaries of the life find those prices multiplied, when they are raised a hundred percent, or 200 percent, as they will be quickly, aye, sir, when beyond that those who pay taxes come to have their taxes doubled and again doubled to pay the interest on the nontaxable bonds held by Morgan and his combinations, which have been issued to meet this war, there will come an awakening; they will have their day and they will be heard. It will be as certain and as inevitable as the return of the tides, and as resistless, too. . . .

Just a word of comment more upon one of the points in the President's address. He says that this is a war "for the things which we have always carried nearest to our hearts—for democracy, for the right of those who submit to authority to have a voice in their own government." In many places throughout the address is this exalted sentiment given expression. . . .

But the President proposes alliance with Great Britain, which, however liberty-loving its people, is a hereditary monarchy, with a hereditary ruler, with a hereditary House of Lords, with a hereditary landed system, with a limited and restricted suffrage for one class and a multiplied suffrage power for another, and with grinding industrial conditions for all the wageworkers. The President has not suggested that we make our support of Great Britain conditional to her granting home rule to Ireland, or Egypt, or India. We rejoice in the establishment of a democracy in Russia, but it will hardly be contended that if Russia was still an autocratic Government, we would not be asked to enter this alliance with her just the same. Italy and the lesser powers of Europe, Japan in the Orient; in fact all of the countries with whom we are to enter into alliance, except France and newly revolutionized Russia, are still of the old order—and it will be generally conceded that no one of them has done as much for its people in the solution of municipal problems and in securing social and industrial reforms as Germany. . . .

Who has registered the knowledge or approval of the American people of the course this Congress is called upon in declaring war upon Germany? Submit the question to the people, you who support it. You who support it dare not do it, for you know that by a vote of more than ten to one the American people as a body would register their declaration against it.

In the sense that this war is being forced upon our people without their knowing why and without their approval, and that wars are usually forced upon all peoples in the same way, there is some truth in the statement; but I venture to say that the response which the German people have made to the demands of this war shows that it has a degree of popular support which the war upon which we are entering has not and never will have among our people. The espionage bills, the conscription bills, and other forcible military measures which we understand are being ground out of the war machine in this country is the complete proof that those responsible for this war fear that it has no popular support and that armies sufficient to satisfy the demand of the entente allies can not be recruited by voluntary enlistments.

The Fourteen Points, 1918

I. Open covenants of peace, openly arrived at, after which there shall be no private international understandings of any kind but diplomacy shall proceed always frankly and in the public view.

II. Absolute freedom of navigation upon the seas, outside territorial waters, alike in peace and in war, except as the seas may be closed in whole or in part by international action for the enforcement of international covenants.

III. The removal, so far as possible, of all economic barriers and the establishment of an equality of trade conditions among all the nations consenting to the peace and associating themselves for its maintenance.

IV. Adequate guarantees given and taken that national armaments will be reduced to the lowest point consistent with domestic safety.

V. A free, open-minded, and absolutely impartial adjustment of all colonial claims, based upon a strict observance of the principle that in determining all such questions of sovereignty the interests of the populations concerned must have equal weight with the equitable claims of the government whose title is to be determined.

VI. The evacuation of all Russian territory and such a settlement of all questions affecting Russia as will secure the best and freest cooperation of the other nations of the world in obtaining for her an unhampered and unembarrassed opportunity for the independent determination of her own political development and national policy and assure her of a sincere welcome into the society of free nations under institutions of her own choosing; and, more than a welcome, assistance also of every kind that she may need and may herself desire. The treatment accorded Russia by her sister nations in the months to come will be the acid test of their good will, of their comprehension of her needs as distinguished from their own interests, and of their intelligent and unselfish sympathy.

VII. Belgium, the whole world will agree, must be evacuated and restored, without any attempt to limit the sovereignty which she enjoys in common with all other free nations. No other single act will serve as this will serve to restore confidence among the nations in the laws which they have themselves set and determined for the government of their relations with one another. Without this healing act the whole structure and validity of international law is forever impaired.

VIII. All French territory should be freed and the invaded portions restored, and the wrong done to France by Prussia in 1871 in the matter of Alsace-Lorraine, which has unsettled the peace of the world for nearly fifty years, should be righted, in order that peace may once more be made secure in the interest of all.

IX. A readjustment of the frontiers of Italy should be effected along clearly recognizable lines of nationality.

X. The peoples of Austria-Hungary, whose place among the nations we wish to see safeguarded and assured, should be accorded the freest opportunity of autonomous development.

XI. Rumania, Serbia, and Montenegro should be evacuated; occupied territories restored; Serbia accorded free and secure access to the sea; and the relations of the several Balkan states to one another determined by friendly consul along historically established lines of allegiance and nationality; and international guarantees of the political and economic independence and territorial integrity of the several Balkan states should be entered into.

XII. The Turkish portions of the present Ottoman Empire should be assured a secure sovereignty, but the other nationalities which are now under Turkish rule should be assured an undoubted security of life and an absolutely unmolested opportunity of autonomous development, and the Dardanelles should be permanently opened as a free passage to the ships and commerce of all nations under international guarantees.

XIII. An independent Polish state should be erected which should include the territories inhabited by indisputably Polish populations, which should be assured a free and secure access to the sea, and whose political and economic independence and territorial integrity should be guaranteed by international covenant.

XIV. A general association of nations must be formed under specific covenants for the purpose of affording mutual guarantees of political independence and territorial integrity to great and small states alike.

Articles 10 Through 16 of the League Covenant, 1919

Article 10. The Members of the League undertake to respect and preserve as against external aggression the territorial integrity and existing political independence of all Members of the League. In case of any such aggression or in case of any threat or danger of such aggression the Council shall advise upon the means by which this obligation shall be fulfilled.

Article 11. Any war or threat of war, whether immediately affecting any of the Members of the League or not, is hereby declared a matter of concern to the whole League, and the League shall take any action that may be deemed wise and effectual to safeguard the peace of nations. . . .

It is also declared to be the friendly right of each Member of the League to bring to the attention of the Assembly or of the Council any circumstance whatever affecting international relations which threatens to disturb international peace or the good understanding between nations upon which peace depends.

Article 12.   The Members of the League agree that if there should arise between them any dispute likely to lead to a rupture, they will submit the matter either to arbitration or to inquiry by the Council, and they agree in no case to resort to war until three months after the award by the arbitrators or the report by the Council.

In any case under this Article the award of the arbitrators shall be made within a reasonable time, and the report of the Council shall be made within six months after the submission of the dispute.

Article 13.   The Members of the League agree that whenever any dispute shall arise between them which they recognise to be suitable for submission to arbitration and which cannot be satisfactorily settled by diplomacy, they will submit the whole subject-matter to arbitration. . . .

Article 14.   The Council shall formulate and submit to the Members of the League for adoption plans for the establishment of a Permanent Court of International Justice. The Court shall be competent to hear and determine any dispute of an international character which the parties thereto submit to it. The Court may also give an advisory opinion upon any dispute or question referred to it by the Council or by the Assembly.

Article 15.   If there should arise between Members of the League any dispute likely to lead to a rupture, which is not submitted to arbitration in accordance with Article 13, the Members of the League agree that they will submit the matter to the Council. . . .

Article 16.   Should any Member of the League resort to war in disregard of its covenants under Articles 12, 13 or 15, it shall *ipso facto* be deemed to have committed an act of war against all other Members of the League, which hereby undertake immediately to subject it to the severance of all trade or financial relations, the prohibition of all intercourse between their nationals and the nationals of the covenant-breaking State, and the prevention of all financial, commercial or personal intercourse between the nationals of the covenant-breaking State and the nationals of any other State, whether a Member of the League or not.

It shall be the duty of the Council in such case to recommend to the several Governments concerned what effective military, naval or air force the Members of the League shall severally contribute to the armed forces to be used to protect the covenants of the League.

Wilson Defends the Peace Treaty and League, 1919

Indianapolis, Indiana, September 4

You have heard a great deal about Article X of the Covenant of the League of Nations. Article X speaks the conscience of the world. Article X is the article which goes to the heart of this whole bad business, for that article says that the members of this League—and that is intended to be all the great nations of the world—engage to respect and to preserve against all external aggression the territorial integrity and political independence of the nations concerned. That promise is necessary in order to prevent this sort of war from recurring, and we are absolutely discredited if we fought this war and then neglect the essential safeguard against it.

You have heard it said, my fellow citizens, that we are robbed of some degree of our sovereign independence of choice by articles of that sort. Every man who makes a choice to respect the rights of his neighbors deprives himself of absolute sovereignty, but he does it by promising never to do wrong, and I cannot, for one, see anything that robs me of any inherent right that I ought to retain when I promise that I will do right.

We engage in the first sentence of Article X to respect and preserve from external aggression the territorial integrity and the existing political independence, not only of the other member states, but of all states. And if any member of the League of Nations disregards that promise, then what happens? The Council of the League advises what should be done to enforce the respect for that Covenant on the part of the nation attempting to violate it, and there is no compulsion upon us to take that advice except the compulsion of our good conscience and judgment. So that it is perfectly evident that if, in the judgment of the people of the United States, the Council adjudged wrong and that this was not an occasion for the use of force, there would be no necessity on the part of the Congress of the United States to vote the use of force. But there could be no advice of the Council on any such subject without a unanimous vote, and the unanimous vote would include our own, and if we accepted the advice we would be accepting our own advice. . . . There is in that Covenant not one note of surrender of the independent judgment of the government of the United States, but an expression of it, because that independent judgment would have to join with the judgment of the rest.

But when is that judgment going to be expressed, my fellow citizens? Only after it is evident that every other resource has failed, and I want to call your attention to the central machinery of the League of Nations. If any member of that League, or any nation not a member, refuses to submit the question at issue either to arbitration or to discussion by the Council, there ensues automatically by the engagements of this Covenant an absolute economic boycott. There will be no trade with that nation by any member of the League. There will be no interchange of communication by post or telegraph. There will be no travel to or from that nation. Its borders will be closed. No citizen or any other state will be allowed to enter it, and no one of its citizens will be allowed to leave it. It will be hermetically sealed by the united action of the most powerful nations in the world. And if this economic boycott bears with unequal weight, the members of the League agree to support one another and to relieve one another in any exceptional disadvantages that may arise out of it.

And I want you to realize that this war was won not only by the armies of the world, but it was won by economic means as well. Without the economic means, the war would have been much longer continued. What happened was that Germany was shut off from the economic resources of the rest of the globe, and she could not stand it. A nation that is boycotted is a nation that is in sight of surrender. Apply this economic, peaceful, silent, deadly remedy, and there will be no need for force. It is a terrible remedy. It does not cost a life outside the nation boycotted, but it brings a pressure upon that nation which, in my judgment, no modern nation could resist. . . .

I therefore want to call your attention, if you will turn to it when you go home, to Article XI, following Article X, of the Covenant of the League of Nations. That Article XI, let me say, is the favorite article in the treaty, so far as I am concerned. It says that every matter which is likely to affect the peace of the world is everybody's business, and that it shall be the friendly right of any nation to call attention in the League to anything that is likely to affect the peace of the world or the good understanding between nations, upon which the peace of the world depends, whether that matter immediately concerns the nation drawing attention to it or not. . . .

There is not an oppressed people in the world which cannot henceforth get a hearing at that forum, and you know, my fellow citizens, what a hearing will mean if the cause of those people is just. The one thing which those who have reason to dread, have most reason to dread, is publicity and discussion, because if you are challenged to give a reason why you are doing a wrong that it has to be an exceedingly good reason, and if you give a bad reason you confess judgment, and the opinion of mankind goes against you.

St. Louis, Missouri, September 5

[T]here can hereafter be no secret treaties. There were nations represented around that board—I mean the board at which the Commission on the League of Nations sat, where fourteen nations were represented—there were nations represented around that board who had entered into many a secret treaty and understanding, and they made not the least objection to promising that hereafter no secret treaty should have any validity whatever. The provision of the Covenant is that every treaty or international understanding shall be "registered," I believe the word is, with the General Secretary of the League, that the General Secretary shall publish it in full just so soon as it is possible for him to publish it, and that no treaty shall be valid which is not thus registered. It is like our arrangements with regard to mortgages on real estate, that until they are registered nobody else need pay any attention to them. So with the treaties. Until they are registered in this office of the League, nobody, not even the parties themselves, can insist upon their execution. You have cleared the deck thereby of the most dangerous thing and the most embarrassing thing that has hitherto existed in international politics.

Sioux Falls, South Dakota, September 8

I cannot understand the psychology of men who are resisting it [the treaty]. I cannot understand what they are afraid of, unless it is that they know physical force and do not understand moral force. Moral force is a great deal more powerful than physical. Govern the sentiments of mankind and you govern mankind. Govern their fears, govern their hopes, determine their fortunes, get them together in concerted masses, and the whole thing sways like a team. Once get them suspecting one another, once get them antagonizing one another, and society itself goes to pieces. We are trying to make a society instead of a set of barbarians out of the governments of the world. . . .

America can stay out, but I want to call you to witness that the peace of the world cannot be established without America. America is necessary to the peace of the world. And reverse the proposition: the peace and good will of the world are necessary to America. Disappoint the world, center its suspicion upon you, make it feel that you are hot and jealous rivals of the other nations, and do you think you are going to do as much business with them as you would otherwise do?

I do not like to put the thing on that plane, my fellow countrymen, but if you want to talk business, I can talk business. If you want to put it on the low plane of how much money you can make, you can make more money out of friendly traders than out of hostile traders. You can make more money out of men who trust you than out of men who fear you.

San Francisco, California, September 17

The Monroe Doctrine means that, if any outside power, any power outside this hemisphere, tries to impose its will upon any portion of the western hemisphere, the United States is at liberty to act independently and alone in repelling the aggression; that it does not have to wait for the action of the League of Nations; that it does not have to wait for anything but the action of its own administration and its own Congress. This is the first time in the history of international diplomacy that any great nation has acknowledged the validity of the Monroe Doctrine. And now, for the first time, all the great fighting powers of the world except Germany, which for the time being has ceased to be a great fighting power, acknowledge the validity of the Monroe Doctrine and accept it as part of the international practice of the world.

But they [critics] are nervous about domestic questions. They say, "It is intolerable to think that the League of Nations should interfere with domestic questions." And, whenever they begin to specify, they speak of the question of immigration, of the question of naturalization, of the question of the tariff. My fellow citizens, no competent or authoritative student of international law would dream of maintaining that these were anything but exclusively domestic questions. And the Covenant of the League expressly provides that the League can take no action whatever about matters which are in the practice of international law regarded as domestic questions.

San Francisco, California, September 18

In order that we may not forget, I have brought with me the figures as to what this war meant to the world. This is a body of businessmen, and you will understand these figures. They are too big for the imagination of men who do not handle big things. Here is the cost of the war in money, exclusive of what we loaned one another, the direct costs of the war: Great Britain and her Dominions, $38,000,000,000; France, $26,000,000,000; the United States, $22,000,000,000 (this is the direct cost of our operations); Russia, $18,000,000,000; Italy, $13,000,000,000; and the total, including Belgium, Japan, and other countries, $123,000,000,000. This is what it cost the Central Powers: Germany, $39,000,000,000, the biggest single item; Austria-Hungary, $21,000,000,000; Turkey and Bulgaria, $3,000,000,000—a total of $63,000,000,000. And the grand total of direct war costs is thus $186,000,000,000—almost the capital of the world.

The expenditures of the United States were at the rate of $1,000,000 an hour for two years, including nighttime with daytime. That is the biggest advertising item I have ever heard of!

The record of dead during the war is as follows: Russia lost in dead 1,700,000 men—poor Russia, that got nothing but terror and despair out of it all; Germany lost 1,600,000 men; France, 1,385,000 men; Great Britain, 900,000 men; Austria, 800,000 men; Italy, 364,000 men; the United States, 50,300 in dead—a total for all the belligerents of 7,450,300 men—just about seven and a half million men killed because we could not have arbitration and discussion, because the world had never had the courage to propose the conciliatory methods which some of us are now doubting whether we ought to accept.

San Diego, California, September 19

But it is feared that our delegates will be outvoted, because I am constantly hearing it said that the British Empire has six votes and we have one. I am perfectly content to have only one vote when the one counts six, and that is exactly the arrangement under the League. But let us examine that matter a little more particularly. Besides the vote of Great Britain herself, the other five votes are the votes of Canada, of South Africa, of Australia and New Zealand, and of India. We ourselves were champions and advocates of giving a vote to Panama, of giving a vote to Cuba— both of them under the direction and directorate of the United States. And if a vote was given to Panama and to Cuba, could it reasonably be denied to the great Dominion of Canada? Could it be denied to that republic in South Africa, that is now living under a nation which did, indeed, overcome it at one time, but which did not dare retain its government in its hands, but turned it over to the very men whom it had fought? Could it be denied to Australia, that independent republic in the Pacific, which has led the world in so many liberal reforms? Could we deny it to New Zealand? Could we deny it to the hundreds of millions who live in India?

But, having given the six votes, what are the facts? The League can take no active step without the unanimous vote of all the nations represented on the Council, added to a vote of the majority in the Assembly itself. These six votes are in the Assembly, not in the Council. The Assembly is not a voting body, except upon a limited number of questions. And whenever those questions are questions of action, the affirmative votes of every nation represented on the Council is needed, and the United States is represented on the Council.

Salt Lake City, Utah, September 23

I am not going to stop, my fellow citizens, to discuss the Shantung provision [which shifted control of the area from Germany to Japan] in all its aspects, but what I want to call your attention to is that, just so soon as this Covenant is signed, rather ratified, every nation in the world will have the right to speak out for China. I want to say very frankly, and I ought to add that representatives of these great nations themselves admit, that Great Britain, France, and the other powers which have insisted upon similar concessions in China will be put in a position where they will have to reconsider.

This is the only way to serve and redeem China, unless it be you want to start a war for the purpose. At the beginning of the war, during the war, Great Britain and France engaged by solemn treaty with Japan that, if she would come in the war and continue in the war, she could have, provided she in the meantime took it by force of arms, what Germany had in China. Those are treaties already in force. They are not waiting for ratification. France and England cannot withdraw from those obligations. And it will serve China not one iota if we should dissent from the Shantung arrangement. But, being parties to that arrangement, we can insist, if it is necessary to insist, upon the promise of Japan—the promise which the other governments have not matched—that she will return to China immediately all sovereign rights within the province of Shantung. Under the operations of Article XI and of Article X, it will be impossible for any nation to make any further inroads either upon the territorial integrity or the political independence of China.

Denver, Colorado, September 25

And consequently it means disarmament. Think of the economic burden and the restriction of liberty in professional and mechanical lines in the maintenance of great armies, not only in the United States, but in Germany, Italy, France, and Great Britain. If the United States should stand off, we would have to have the biggest army in the world. There would be nobody else to take care of our fortunes. We would have to look out for ourselves.

When I hear gentlemen say, "We will be independent, and we are able to look out for ourselves," I say, consult your fellow citizens. It will have to mean universal conscription, taxes such as we have never seen, concentration of authority in the governmental activities and for the uses of these terrible instruments.

You cannot conduct a war or command an army by a debating society. You cannot determine the war in community centers. The commander in chief is going to have to have a staff like the German staff. You will have to center it in the commander in chief of the army and navy. America will never consent to any such thing.

The Lodge Reservations, 1919

1. . . . In case of notice of withdrawal from the league of nations, as provided in said article [Article 1], the United States shall be the sole judge as to whether all its international obligations . . . have been fulfilled, and notice of withdrawal . . . may be given by a concurrent resolution of the Congress of the United States.

2. The United States assumes no obligation to preserve the territorial integrity or political independence of any other country . . . under the provisions of article 10, or to employ the military or naval forces of the United States under any article of the treaty for any purpose, unless in any particular case the Congress, which . . . has the sole power to declare war . . . shall . . . so provide.

3. No mandate shall be accepted by the United States under article 22 . . . except by action of the Congress of the United States.

4. The United States reserves to itself exclusively the right to decide what questions are within its domestic jurisdiction. . . .

5. The United States will not submit to arbitration or to inquiry by the assembly or by the council of the league of nations . . . any questions which in the judgment of the United States depend upon or relate to . . . the Monroe doctrine; said doctrine is to be interpreted by the United States alone and is . . . wholly outside the jurisdiction of said league of nations. . . .

6. The United States withholds its assent to articles 156, 157, and 158 [Shantung clauses]. . . .

7. The Congress of the United States will provide by law for the appointment of the representatives of the United States in the assembly and the council of the league of nations, and may in its discretion provide for the participation of the United States in any commission. . . . No person shall represent the United States under either said league of nations or the treaty of peace . . . except with the approval of the Senate of the United States. . . .

9. The United States shall not be obligated to contribute to any expenses of the league of nations . . . unless and until an appropriation of funds . . . shall have been made by the Congress of the United States.

10. If the United States shall at any time adopt any plan for the limitation of armaments proposed by the council of the league . . . it reserves the right to increase such armaments without the consent of the council whenever the United States is threatened with invasion or engaged in war. . . .

14. The United States assumes no obligation to be bound by any election, decision, report, or finding of the council or assembly in which any member of the league and its self-governing dominions, colonies, or parts of empire, in the aggregate have cast more than one vote.

✖ ESSAYS

In the first essay, Wilson's major biographer, Arthur S. Link of Princeton University, praises the president for a "higher realism" and defends him against critics who have argued that excessive idealism blinded Wilson. Link raises questions about the meaning of realism, and he exonerates Wilson from responsibility for the tumult of international relations that followed Wilson's presidency. In the second essay, the Dutch scholar Jan Wilhelm Schulte-Nordholt disputes Link's flattering portrayal. While admiring Woodrow Wilson's commitment to peace, Schulte-Nordholt depicts a strong-willed dreamer who lost touch with reality. What drove Wilson was the belief that only he and the United States could provide an appropriate model for world peace. Unlike Link, Schulte-Nordholt concludes that Wilson failed to understand the complexities of world politics and spoke in abstract language about goals that had little chance of success because they "skipped over historical problems." At Paris, Wilson's imagination collided with reality, and the Versailles negotiators manipulated the president, who conceded much in order to save the League. The flawed peace, Schulte-Nordholt observes, helped to sow the seeds of the Second World War. The last essay, by Thomas J. Knock of Southern Methodist University, places Wilson in his intellectual-political milieu in the early twentieth century—a left-of-center progressive internationalism. Treating this body of ideas with respect, Knock probes the sources of Wilson's commitment to a league for peace. Knock argues that Wilson ultimately lost the support of both conservative and progressive internationalists (for different reasons). Wilson failed to achieve a Wilsonian league not because of poor health or an uncompromising personality but because the support of the progressive internationalists that he needed for victory eroded in the face of strong forces of reaction at home and abroad during the era of the First World War.

Wilson's Higher Realism

ARTHUR S. LINK

Europeans on the whole still view Wilson very much as many of them viewed him forty years ago at the end of the Paris Peace Conference and the great struggle in the United States over ratification of the Treaty of Versailles. This European image is, I think it is fair to say, one of a well-intentioned idealist, a man good by ordinary Christian standards, but essentially a destructive force in modern history because he was a visionary, unrealistic, provincial, and ignorant of European problems, and zealous and messianic in conceit but devoid of either practical knowledge or the humility to follow others better informed than he. I do not think that this is an essentially unfair statement of the European point of view. It was, of course, the image held by John Maynard Keynes, Georges Clemenceau, and most of the thoughtful European public at the end of the Peace Conference. It is the view still largely held by English, French, and German scholars alike, if for different reasons.

I have felt impelled to my subject not only by . . . forceful reminders of the strong survival of the old European image of President Wilson, but also . . . in our own country . . . [by a] school of historical critics, and by their work in constructing an image of President Wilson that is remarkably like the older European one. Calling themselves realists, and drawing their inspiration from the distinguished diplomat-historian, George Kennan, and the Austrian-trained authority in international relations, Hans J. Morgenthau, . . . these new American critics have found Wilson wanting because he did not think in terms of strategy, bases, and armed power, but dwelt too much in ethereal realms.

Are the old European and new American critics right, I have asked myself over and over during the past few years: is this the image that I also see, the Wilson that I know? Were the Austrians right in thinking that his irresponsible preaching of a slogan, "self-determination," was primarily responsible for the destruction of the Hapsburg Empire? Were the Germans right in holding him responsible for what they regarded as the monstrous betrayal of Versailles? Were the French right in thinking that he prevented the imposition of the only kind of peace settlement upon Germany that could endure? Were the English and new American critics near the truth when they portrayed him as a tragic figure irrelevant in the modern world?

I must confess that I have sometimes been tempted to agree. No one who has ever given any serious attention to President Wilson's life could fail to agree that he was *primarily* a Christian idealist. By this I mean a man who almost always

"The Higher Realism of Woodrow Wilson" by Arthur S. Link from *Journal of Presbyterian History*, XLI (March 1963), pp. 1–13. Reprinted by permission of the Presbyterian Historical Society.

tended to judge policies on a basis of whether they were right by Christian standards, not whether they brought immediate material or strategic advantage. I mean also a man whose foreign policies were motivated by the assumption that a nation as much as an individual should live according to the law of Christian love, and by a positive repudiation of the assumptions of the classical "realists" about international behavior.

No one who has given serious study to Wilson's career, moreover, could fail to agree that there is at least an appearance of reality about the old European and new American image. Wilson was not merely an idealist, but a crusading idealist. An orator of enormous eloquence and power, he was also a phrasemaker who more than once fell victim to the magic of his own words. In international relations, he did not give undue weight to material forces or base his policies upon the assumption that nations must always act selfishly. At times, he did seem to give the appearance of believing that he was a kind of messiah divinely appointed to deliver Europe from the cruel tyranny of history.

I have myself made all these criticisms and others more elaborately in my own writings. But they have never really satisfied me and do not satisfy me now. I do not think that they add up to a historical image that is accurate. Indeed, I cannot escape the conclusion that they altogether miss the main point and meaning of President Wilson's career.

The point, in my opinion, and the theme of this paper, is that among all the major statesmen and thoughtful critics of his age, President Wilson was in fact the supreme realist, and that because this is true, what he stood for and fought to accomplish has large meaning for our own generation.

This is, to be sure, a very broad, perhaps even an audacious, statement, one that does not mean very much unless we are careful to define our terms. A realist, I take it, is one who faces life and its situations without illusions, in short, one who can see realities or truth through the fog of delusion that normally shrouds the earth-bound individual. If the European and American critics of President Wilson who thought mainly in strategic and material terms, who measured national power by army divisions and naval bases, and the like, if *they* were realists, then President Wilson was a realist of a different sort. Sheerly for purposes of convenience, let us call his view of the national and international situations with which he had to cope a "higher realism," higher because more perceptive, more in accord with ultimate reality, more likely to win the long-run moral approval of societies professing allegiance to the common western, humane, Christian traditions. . . .

I am sure that in talking about Wilson's "higher realism" in meeting domestic challenges, I have simply been saying things and making judgments with which virtually every historian of the United States would readily agree. It is precisely this "higher realism" that has entitled Wilson to rank, by the agreement of American historians, among the four or five most successful Presidents in our history. In talking about Wilson's policies and contributions in the realm of foreign affairs, I am, I know, on more controversial ground. Wilson was magnificently prepared for leadership in internal affairs by long study of American history and institutions. He had little if any preparation for leadership in the world at large; indeed, at the outset of his tenure in the White House he had no serious interest in foreign affairs. At the outset and later he made mistakes that still seriously impair his record. Even so,

I cannot but conclude that President Wilson on the whole showed the same kind of wisdom and long-range vision and understanding—in short, "higher realism"—in his third career as international statesman as he had already revealed in his first two careers at home.

This, I know, is a big statement, and I would like to preface it with a few generalizations about Wilson's thought and character as a diplomat in order to lay foundations for some later observations.

The first is the most obvious and the one with which most historians would agree, namely, that President Wilson was, as I have already said, above all an idealist in the conduct of foreign affairs, one who subordinated immediate goals and material interests to what he considered to be superior ethical standards and moral purposes. His idealism was perhaps best revealed in his thinking about the purposes that the United States should serve in the world. The mission of America, he said over and over and sincerely believed, was not a mission of aggrandizement of material power but one of service to mankind. It was a mission of peace, of sacrifice, of leading the nations into a new international community organized to achieve right ends.

Second, all of Wilson's thinking about international relations was conditioned, in general, by a loathing for war and, in particular, by a conviction that physical force should never be used to achieve selfish and material aims.

Third, Wilson was actually in many ways "realistic," even by conventional standards, in his thinking about and methods in the conduct of foreign relations. For example, he used armed force in the classic way to achieve certain diplomatic objectives in Mexico and the Caribbean. He understood the meaning of the term "balance of power." He was keenly aware of the relevance of material interests and had few illusions about the fundamental bases of international behavior. It is, one must say, the sheerest nonsense to talk about him as an impractical idealist and visionary.

Fourth, while admitting that there were times when a nation had no recourse but to use armed force in international disputes, and while using force himself on behalf of the American government on certain occasions, President Wilson never permitted war's neuroses and fascinations either to derange his reason or to obscure the political objectives for which force was being used. Hence he was never the victim of that greatest twentieth-century delusion, that it is necessary to win wars even at the risk of losing everything for which wars are fought.

This is a very imperfect characterization of the thought and character of Wilson the diplomatist, but it may help us to understand his policies during the greatest tragedy of the modern epoch and the event that raised the gravest challenges to his leadership—the First World War. It was for Wilson a period with three distinct stages: the period of American neutrality, from August 1914 to April 1917; the period of American belligerency, from April 1917 to November 1918; and the period of peacemaking, from November 1918 to June 1919. The challenges of each period were different, but he met them all, on the whole, with the same "higher realism" that had characterized his leadership at home.

His policies during the first period can best be briefly described by saying that from the outbreak of the war in Europe to the beginning of the German unlimited submarine campaign in early 1917, President Wilson tried as hard as any man could have done to be neutral, to make the necessary accommodations to the exercise of belligerent power, and to engage in stern defense of American rights only when they could not, because fundamental human principles were involved, be compromised.

Some of the recent American "realists" have joined the older English and French critics in charging Wilson with impractical idealism precisely because he did follow such a course—because he did not rally the American people to preparation for what they have said was an inevitable participation; because he conducted long and patient negotiations to avoid a break with Germany; because he did not undertake large and early measures of assistance to the Allies and thus help to shorten the duration of Europe's agony; because he refused throughout the period of American neutrality even to align the American people and their government morally on the Allied side.

Looking back upon the final outcome, as we are entitled to do, we well might wonder who the true realists were during this period: so-called realists, or President Wilson, who in an almost uncanny way kept himself immune from the emotional hysterias and passions that seized other men; who believed that the causes of the war were so complex and remote that it was impossible to assess the blame; who, overborne by the tragedy of the event, fought desperately to preserve American neutrality so that he could perform the healing task of reconciliation once the nations of Europe had come to some sense; who believed that an enduring peace could come only through a "peace without victory," a "peace between equals"? Who were the deluded men who had lost sight of reality? The European leaders who thought that they could win decisive victories on the battlefields and on or under the seas, and who thought that they could impose their nations' wills upon other great peoples? Or Wilson, who thought that they were momentarily mad?

The climactic confrontation, the supreme reckoning between so-called realists and the alleged impractical idealist, came, once the United States had been forced into the conflict and Germany was defeated. It did not occur earlier, because the British and French leaders had refused to permit it to occur before the Armistice was safely signed. But it could not then be long postponed, for the Allied leaders had matured their plans, and President Wilson had meanwhile formed a peace program of his own and announced it to the world in the Fourteen Points address and other speeches.

There is no need to review the turbulent events of the Paris Peace Conference here. They are familiar enough, to begin with; but a detailed account of them now would obscure my larger purpose—to look back upon the Paris settlement and, while looking back, to attempt to see who the true realists were.

The supreme task of the victors at Paris in 1919 was, obviously, to work out a peace settlement and reconstruct an international order that could endure. It had to be a peace that could survive the ebbing of passions and hatreds that consumed Europe in 1919. It had to be a peace that could survive because it could command the approval of the German people. Above all, it had to be the kind of settlement that would endure because it could retain the long-run support of the American and English peoples, even of the French people. The necessity of constructing this kind of settlement was, as we can now see clearly, the supreme reality of peacemaking in 1919. We must, therefore, judge men and measures at the Paris Conference according to whether they met this test or not.

By this criterion I do not see how any fair historian can but conclude that the so-called realists at Paris—the dedicated if cynical [Georges] Clemenceau, concerned only about the destruction of the ancient foe and the future security of France; the well-intentioned [David] Lloyd George, who had given so many hostages to war passions at home and to the Commonwealths that he was no longer a free man; and the Italians, [Sidney] Sonnino and [Vittorio] Orlando, eager only for spoils—how could they be called anything other than sublime irrationalists and dreamers? Theirs was a dream, a nightmare, of unreality. Given the task of reconstructing Europe and preventing a future war, they would have responded by attempting to perpetuate the division of Europe and by making a new war almost inevitable.

On the other side and standing usually in solitary if splendid isolation was the alleged impractical idealist fighting for the only kind of settlement that had any chance of survival—for a peace of reconciliation, for disarmament by victors as well as vanquished, against annexations and indemnities, and for a new international organization that would include former enemy states as active members from the beginning. Over and over he warned that this was the only kind of peace that would prove acceptable to the American people in the short run and to the moral opinion of the world in the long run, in short, the only kind of settlement that could endure. It should require little reference to events that followed the Paris Conference to demonstrate the "higher realism" of President Wilson's views.

If proof is needed on specific points, one could cite, for example, Wilson's point of view on the problem of reparations. Over and over he insisted, and with a steadfast consistency, that reparations should be compensation for specific willful damage only, not indemnity; that the Germans should not be saddled with a debt that was heavier than they could carry; and that there should be a time limit to the obligation that the German nation should be forced to assume. What the Allied leaders demanded and finally obtained is well known. . . . What the realistic solution of this problem was is now too obvious for comment. Or, as a second example, one might cite Wilson's attitude toward the Russian Revolution—how he saw the deeply rooted causes of that cataclysm and the futility of any western effort to suppress it by military force; and how the realism of his attitude contrasted with the egregious folly of so-called realists who thought that it lay within their power to change the course of Russian history.

The result of the clash between European so-called realism and Wilsonian so-called idealism was of course the Treaty of Versailles, that compromise that violated the terms of the agreement by which the Germans had stopped fighting and made a mockery of some of the principal planks in the American President's peace program. Why, it is fair to ask, did President Wilson permit such a peace to be made and sign the treaty embodying it? The answer, I submit, is that it was "higher realism" that drove him to this difficult decision. Having won, at least partially, many of the things for which he had been fighting, he had to give as well as to take, for he could not impose his will entirely upon his colleagues. He signed the Versailles Treaty in the conviction that the passage of time and the Treaty's new creation, the League of Nations, would almost certainly operate to rectify what he knew were the grievous mistakes of the Peace Conference. He signed the Versailles Treaty, in short, because he believed that it was the best settlement possible in the circumstances of 1919.

What President Wilson hoped would occur did of course in large part take place during the 1920s and early 1930s, even though alleged realists in the United States combined with authentic visionaries to repudiate Wilson's work and prevent their government from playing the role of mediating leadership within the League of Nations of which Wilson had dreamed. The great tragedy of the postwar period was not that the Versailles Treaty was imperfect. It was that the forces of reconciliation could not operate rapidly enough without American leadership in the League, that France and Great Britain had neither the will nor the strength to defend the Treaty alone during the 1930s and, above all, that the German people submitted to demonic forces that promised a speedy rectification of all the injustices of Versailles. But this is precisely what President Wilson, in another flash of "higher realism," predicted would occur if the so-called realists, both in the United States and in Europe, continued to have their way.

That is the age-old question, whether the so-called realists or the higher realists shall have their way in determination of national and international policies. President Wilson survives as a more powerful force in history than when he lived because he gave us the supreme demonstration in the twentieth century of higher realism in statesmanship.

This, obviously, was no accident. Woodrow Wilson's "higher realism" was the product of insight and wisdom informed by active Christian faith. He was not, fundamentally, a moralist, as he so often seemed to be, but a man who lived in faith, trying to be guided by the Holy Spirit in meeting the complex problems of a changing nation and world. Using one of his own metaphors, we can say that the light of Heaven gleamed upon his sword. His precepts and ideals will be relevant so long as democracy endures, so long as men seek after a new international community organized for peace and the advancement of mankind.

The Peace Advocate Out of Touch with Reality

JAN WILHELM SCHULTE-NORDHOLT

We are in many respects Woodrow Wilson's heirs. That is why it is of great importance to us to make out what kind of man he was, how he came to his exalted and advanced ideas, and why in the end he failed. That is my purpose. . . . I want to examine more closely the life of a man who sought a solution to problems that are still ours, and who was therefore the first great advocate of world peace. He was, as it were, a whole peace movement all by himself.

From *Woodrow Wilson: A Life For Peace* by Jan W. Schulte-Nordholt, trans./ed. by Rowen, Herbert. Copyright © 1991 Jan Wilhelm Schulte-Nordholt and Meulenhoff Informatief, Amsterdam, The Netherlands. Reprinted by permission of University of California Press, 1991.

I almost wrote "apostle of peace," but this phrase is too strong. It makes it seem that I had at least to some extent a work of hagiography in mind. Far from it! History is about people, their dreams and their failures. It would be all too easy to paint Woodrow Wilson as the great prophet who was always wiser than his fellow men. The purpose of a biography ought not to be to turn a human being into a figure of puppetry; to change the metaphor, to press him into flat uniformity. Was Wilson a prophet, an idealist, a dissembler, a practical man, a revolutionary reformer? He was to some small extent all of these. Like most great men, indeed like most people, Wilson was a bundle of contradictions. That is what makes him so fascinating. He was many things: a scholar driven by deep feelings; a poet who found his vocation in politics; a Christian consumed by his need for recognition; a lonely man who thought he understood mankind; a practical man who became fossilized in all too lofty dreams; a reasonable man full of turbulent passions. It is this paradoxical personality that I have tried to respect, . . . the irritating, moving grandeur of a self-willed man who played an immense role in history and whose importance has become extraordinarily great in our own times, even though he failed so wretchedly. That is why his life story is a dramatic tale, almost a Greek tragedy, with a catharsis at the end that still drains and raises our emotions. . . .

The outbreak of the war [in 1914] affected the president deeply. It shocked his sensitive nature. We read for example in a letter to [his assistant Edward] House in August: "I feel the burden of the thing almost intolerably from day to day." Two months later he wrote in the same vein but at greater length to Walter Page, the ambassador in London:

> The whole thing is vivid in my mind, painfully vivid, and has been almost ever since the struggle began. I think my thought and imagination contain the picture and perceive its significance from every point of view. I have to force myself not to dwell upon it to avoid the sort of numbness that comes from deep apprehension and dwelling upon elements too vast to be yet comprehended or in any way controlled by counsel.

Here we see once again in Wilson the tension between feeling and detachment.

This only emphasizes the importance of the question of how neutral he really was or wanted to be. His first personal reactions were emotionally favorable to the Allies. He was, after all, imbued with English values and ideals. The French ambassador to Washington, Jules Jusserand, wondered what "the great doctrinaire" in the White House was thinking, but the president soon gave his answer, as it were, to the English ambassador, Sir Cecil Spring-Rice. Spring-Rice informed Sir Edward Grey, the English foreign secretary, that Wilson had admitted to him that everything he held dear was now at stake. The president, he added, spoke with deep emotion. The ambassador, who knew the man he was dealing with, quoted a few lines from Wordsworth's sonnets about English freedom written during the Napoleonic wars. He knew them by heart, Wilson said with tears in his eyes. (Spring-Rice, as it happened, was also playing up to Grey, who, like Wilson, was passionately fond of Wordsworth.)

In his personal feelings Wilson was not in the slightest neutral. House heard him inveigh against everything German—government and people and what he called abstract German philosophy, which lacked spirituality! But he was quite able to separate his personal opinions and his official duties. In the first place, he understood that neutrality was necessary, that the American people were totally set against intervention. But he was also moved by the great goal that he had glimpsed since the beginning of the war, a possibility that fitted his character like a glove. It makes its appearance in his call for neutrality, for he did not merely issue a scrupulously formal official declaration, as any other president would have done. He did more, accompanying this declaration with a personal call to the people to remain truly neutral in thought and words. America, he reminded them, was composed of many peoples and too great sympathy for one or the other side could bring division among them.

Unity was even more necessary for another reason as well. This was the grand ideal that he now made public officially for the first time and which henceforth would inspire him and more and more involve him in international complications. America, he announced, was chosen to mediate, as only America could, just because it was neutral. He spoke in an exalted, religious tone, as he liked to do on so many other occasions. It was as if the war at last made possible things that all his life he had dreamed of—his country as the model and the very leader of the whole world, and himself called and chosen as the leader of his country and the maker of the future. . . .

One thing led to another. The arms shipments [to the Allies] led to loans. [William Jennings] Bryan, the pacifist-minded secretary of state, doubted that this flow of funds, which went almost entirely to the Entente, was really neutral. In good biblical fashion, he saw money as the root of all evil. Was it not written in Scripture that where one's treasure was, one's heart was too? He was able to convince Wilson that steps had to be taken against these loans, and American bankers were therefore warned on August 15, 1914, that such credits were "inconsistent with the true spirit of neutrality." But such a splendid position could not be maintained in the long run. Arms deliveries continued to grow, and the American economy could not do without them. In the spring of 1915 Bryan's idealistic approach was abandoned and one loan after another was floated in the United States. When America entered the war in 1917, the loans to the Allies had risen to more than two billion dollars, while those to the Central Powers amounted to no more than $27,000,000.

Although it is not correct to say that America went to war to protect its interests, it must be added that it was not fully neutral either. The majority of the people were favorable to the Allies, and so was their government. Wilson himself tried to be neutral, but his closest collaborators very soon were of the opinion that it was to America's interest that the Allies win the war. Furthermore, the majority of the Republican opposition in Congress was very pro-English, especially the old, influential, and experienced elite from New England. . . .

War brings all international agreements into question, for war is unpredictable and full of surprises, always different from what anyone could have imagined. This was never so painfully evident as in the question of submarine warfare, since submarines were a weapon without equal, but operated effectively only by surprise. A multitude of notes discussed and debated the question of their surprise attacks. What was the status of the fine agreements about merchant ships in wartime? The answer was clear: a warship might halt, search, seize, and even sink a merchantman, but only after prior warning and giving civilian travelers the opportunity to leave safely. But a submarine that adhered to such rules would of course become defenseless and useless.

When the war broke out, German ships were swept off the seas, Germany was blockaded, and the Germans desperately turned to the submarine as a means of breaking the Allied stranglehold. The initial successes of the U-boats in the autumn of 1914 brought a sudden resurgence of hope, and the German military command slowly realized what a powerful weapon it had in its hands. On February 4, 1915, the German government published an official declaration putting a blockade around the British islands: in a zone around Great Britain, all enemy ships, including merchant vessels, would be attacked without warning. Neutral ships were advised to avoid these regions, since the Allied ships could always be disguised with neutral flags.

It was a risky weapon, the most blatant violation of international standards of conduct. The Germans were aware of that difficulty, but war seldom leaves intact much of standards and morality. The German fleet commander, Admiral Friedrich von Ingenohl, had his argument ready. Since England disregarded international law by its hunger blockade, Germany had the right to act without regard to the treaty agreements. More important than the moral question, however, was whether the weapon was as effective as the Kaiser's admirals wanted to believe. From the beginning the question had to be faced of how America would react to such drastic measures of naval warfare. . . .

The submarine weapon made it much more difficult for the United States, like all nonbelligerents, to remain neutral. Neutrality became a dilemma as never before. Was it neutral to waive fundamental rights of free navigation? Wasn't this itself a serious breach of international law, a grave derogation of morality in a world where morality seemed more and more on the wane?

Wilson, a man of principle, protested, but in so doing he reduced his chances for mediation. A sharp note was sent to Berlin, declaring that the policy set forth in the German note was "so unprecedented in naval warfare that this Government is reluctant to believe that the Imperial Government of Germany in this case contemplates it as possible." The American government would hold the German government fully responsible for the consequences. This seemed like plain talk, but what would happen if American rights were really challenged could not be foreseen. It was nonetheless probable that once such a stand on principle was taken, a conflict would result. . . .

Wherever the inspiration for the phrase ["peace without victory"] came from, the address that the president made to the Senate on January 22 [1917] was genuine Wilson from beginning to end. It was a plea, splendid, grandiose, and vague, for America's involvement in a future world order. That order—an organization of the peoples with its own force—had to come, he said. The question was, what kind of force? This was and remained the point of difficulty. For Wilson, the moralist who knew that without human inspiration and dedication the finest promises are empty, had in mind a "force" that was greater than the force of any country or alliance, which was "the organized major force of mankind." The nations must come to an agreement and then the old system of the "balance of power" would give way to a "community of power." And that could happen only if there was true reconciliation, upon the basis of a "peace without victory," a peace among equals.

That did not bring pleasure to everyone's ears, he realized. But he had to say it, for his intention was "only to face realities and to face them without soft concealments." Dreamers want so much to be taken for realists!

"Peace without victory." At stake were the peoples. Nothing could be brought to pass in the world if the peoples did not believe in it. It was not the governments but the peoples who had to be brought together. Behind this lay a great American principle: "the consent of the governed." It was this principle that made America the model for the world. America was what the other nations still had to become, a land that, in Wordsworth's words, was made "great and free" by its soul. In the name of the United States he spoke to the whole world. He was defending, he said, American principles, and so he sought to disarm the criticism from the far right. His solution for world peace was not denial of the Monroe Doctrine but its application to the whole world. It was the best means to avoid for all time the "entangling alliances" against which George Washington had warned: "There is no entangling alliance in a concert of power." What he proposed, "consent of the governed," freedom of the seas, arms limitation, were the true American principles. He concluded:

> These are American principles, American policies. We could stand for no others. And they are also the principles and policies of forward looking men and women everywhere, of every modern nation, of every enlightened community. They are the principles of mankind and must prevail.

That was the purest essence of Woodrow Wilson. He spoke in the name of the United States of America, the unique and superior country, as he himself liked to call it, forward-looking and in the lead in the service of mankind. All liberal-thinking people everywhere, in Europe and in America, rejoiced at his words. But conservatives (must we call them the realists?) on both sides of the ocean shook their heads over such empty phrases. Among the first of these, as we know, were persons in Wilson's own backyard, his closest advisers. [Secretary of State Robert] Lansing had warned against the term "peace without victory." What did it really mean? And, most of all, how would these words be taken in the Allied countries? But, Lansing tells us, Wilson did not want to listen. "I did not argue the matter, especially as I knew his fondness for phrasemaking and was sure that it would be useless to attempt to dissuade him." . . .

As was to be expected, Lodge surpassed all the others in his hostility to Wilson. In an angry speech to the Senate he wielded the full resources of his logic to tear apart the arguments of his enemy. What did it mean to say that America had no interest in the peace terms but only in the peace? How can men be required to wage war not to win, so that all their sacrifices were in vain, "a criminal and hideous futility"? How could the Monroe Doctrine be given worldwide application when it had nothing to do with the rights of small or great nations as such but applied only to the Western Hemisphere? How could the "organized major force of mankind" be applied? Voluntarily, or automatically, or compulsorily? When the idea of a league was broached two years earlier, he had been greatly attracted to it, but the more he thought about it, the more problems he saw. It could not be made effective by "high-sounding phrases, which fall so agreeably upon the ear, when there is no thought behind it." Does it mean that the small nations can, by majority vote, involve the large nations in war? "Are we prepared to commit ourselves to a purely general proposition without knowing where we are going or what is to be demanded of us, except that we shall be compelled to furnish our quota of military and naval forces to the service of a league in which we shall have but one voice?" A league for peace meant readiness to wage war against any country that did not obey its decisions. What if it decided that Japan and China should have the right of migration anywhere, and Canada, Australia, and New Zealand declined to accept the decision? Or California, for that matter?

The points made by Lodge were fundamental, which is why I present them at such length. Already at this time, in January 1917, the lines of division were drawn which would define the great debate and the great tragedy of 1919. On one side stood the idealist, on the other the realist, and on both sides more than personal animosity was involved. Furthermore, a political alliance was beginning to take shape that slackened during the war years but operated with full force in 1919; it brought together the Republican isolationists from the West, who were also idealists, for the most part from the Progressive camp, and the Republican internationalist realists, [Senator William] Borah on the one side and Lodge on the other. It was an alliance that would bring disaster to Wilson, but in 1917 he could not foresee that. . . .

Wilson shrank from taking the final step [after the German decision in late January 1917 to launch unrestricted submarine warfare], not out of fear, not out of unsullied pacifism, but because his whole conception of mediating between the belligerents (and thereby saving white civilization) would be shattered. This was the principal reason for his hesitation. And so he talked during these weeks in almost pacifist terms about war and imperialism, spoke out in anger against the support for war from right-wing circles, which he described as "Junkerthum trying to creep in under the cover of the patriotic feeling of the moment." . . .

[The journalist] Walter Lippmann, who looked at him with cool rationality and was among those bitterly disappointed with him after 1919, draws for us nonetheless a portrait of Wilson in his book *Men of Destiny,* showing the orator of light learning about darkness. He gazed in March 1917, says Lippmann, "in the bottomless pit." He was "an anguished prophet," full of compassion and doubt, a man who experienced the tragedy of his time and therefore was able, with overwrought absoluteness, to see the league of nations as the only justification of his action.

With this as his justification he went into the war, not out of economic interest, not because of the violation of the neutral rights of the United States, although these played a part, but in order to bring about genuine peace. Only if America took part could it have a voice in the peace. Mediation through participation would be more effective than neutrality, he now believed. To a delegation of pacifists led by Jane Addams, he said on February 28 that "as head of a nation participating in the war, the President of the United States would have a seat at the Peace Table, but that if he remained the representative of a neutral country he could at best only 'call through a crack in the door.' " Personal ambition and general interest concurred in what we may call a mission. The man and his times seemed to fit each other like the two halves of a piece of fruit. . . .

Of all the impressive sermons that Wilson preached to his people and to the world, none became so famous as his "Fourteen Points" speech of January 8, 1918. It attained a breadth and depth, in space and in time, greater than that of all the others. Not that it is his finest address; there are others, such as the "peace without victory" speech of a year earlier and the declaration of war of April 1917, which are more splendid in rhetoric and wider in vision. But this time Wilson was more practical, adding as it were deed to words; he developed a practical program that was of importance for the whole world. . . .

All in all, the Fourteen Points seemed practical and responsible. How lightly they skipped over historical problems would only become evident in Paris. But there was also a fourteenth point, a panacea for all the shortcomings now and later, a League of Nations: "A special association of nations must be formed under specific covenants for the purpose of affording mutual guarantees of political independence and territorial integrity to great and small states alike." This short sentence carried a heavy burden, too heavy as it turned out. In these few words the future world peace was settled, totally and permanently. For Wilson everything revolved around it; he did not see the difficulties and he did not want to see them, and this would in the end bring his downfall. . . .

In general Wilson's principles more and more broke loose from reality and lived their own lives. Self-determination was one such principle. During the war it became one of the major foundations of Wilson's new world order. We shall never subject another people, he had said back in 1915, "because we believe, we passionately believe, in the right of every people to choose their own allegiance and be free of masters altogether."

Only very slowly, as the reality of Europe began to come closer, did he discover the dangerous consequences of the principle. In the discussion with Spring-Rice on January 3 . . . , he wondered whether it was in fact possible to apply it consistently. The example of the threatening dismemberment of Austria-Hungary was probably in his thoughts when he said: "Pushed to its extreme, the principle would mean the disruption of existing governments to an undefinable extent. Logic was a good and powerful thing but apart from the consideration of existing circumstances might well lead to very dangerous results." The Englishman must have heard this with satisfaction, for the British Empire was not about to grant self-determination to all its peoples.

Later, in Paris, many began to realize the difficulties and dangers in this splendid principle. Lansing hit the nail on the head in a confidential memorandum, in which he wondered what self-determination would mean for the Irish, Indians, Egyptians, and South African Boers. What would happen with the Muslims in Syria and Palestine, and how did that fit in with the idea of Zionism, to which Wilson was very sympathetic. "The phrase is simply loaded with dynamite. It will raise hopes which can never be realized." It was the dream of an idealist, he said, and it is clear whom Lansing really had in mind.

As Wilson himself came to see, he had to be very cautious in Paris when trying to put his great principles into practice. He acknowledged that when he had first spoken of self-determination he had not realized that there were so many peoples who would claim it as their right. . . .

Wilson did not underestimate the devastation in Europe, but he retained his nineteenth-century American optimism. His whole existence was tied up with it; he could not live without hope. He clung to the idea of a grand radical cure, to a mystical faith in the mankind of the future, who were purified by events and repented. He had to represent that mankind; he had to make a new peace.

That is why he had to go to Paris [after the German surrender in late 1918]. . . . He was overwhelmed by his mission. His Czech colleague Thomas Masaryk, who understood him well ("now, we were both professors") warned him about the European statesmen: "But he wouldn't listen, for he was too filled with his plan for a League of Nations to take obstacles into account." . . .

Wilson's triumphal tour of Europe took him from Paris to London and then to Rome. Everywhere he was greeted as a savior, as the "Redeemer of Humanity" (*Redentore dell' Humanità*) and "God of Peace" (*Dio di Pace*), in the words of the Italian banners. He spent weeks indulging in this pomp and circumstance, immersed in a sea of flags and songs, carried along by beautiful words that promised so much for the future. Justice! Peace! When we hear Wilson speak in these first weeks, everything is radiant. Sometimes a harsh sound breaks through, as when he replies to [Raymond] Poincaré, the president of France, who wants no reconciliation with the foe, that there exist "eternal principles of right and justice" which bring with them "the certainty of just punishment." But for the most part his outlook is peaceful. He speaks of the peoples who form "the organized moral force of men throughout the world," of the tide of good will: "There is a great tide running in the hearts of men. The hearts of men have never beaten so singularly in unison before. Men have never been so conscious of this brotherhood."

In these speeches Wilson rose high, very high, above the bustle of daily life. In Manchester:

> For, after all, though we boast of the material sides of our civilization, they are merely meant to support the spiritual side. We are not men because we have skill of hand, but we are men because we have elevation of spirit. It is in the spirit that we live and not in the task of the day.

And, that same evening:

> There is a great voice of humanity abroad in the world just now to which he who cannot hear is deaf. We are not obeying the mandates of parties or of politics. We are obeying the mandates of humanity.

What words these are! House, who remained behind in Paris, was moved by them, but [Stephen] Bonsal, his secretary, heard them more skeptically. There were millions of people, he thought, who would not listen to the promises of the great crusader from over the sea, although they had welcomed him with such rejoicing a few weeks earlier.

Bonsal may have felt that the tide was beginning to turn and that enthusiasm was collapsing. Alas, there was in fact no moral tide that carried all with it. There was rather a divided Europe in which the peoples were driven at least as much by muddled feelings of rage and revenge as by lofty thoughts of right and reason. Wilson himself had experienced the impact of such vindictiveness during the off-year elections in the United States, and it was at least as prevalent in Europe. [French premier Georges] Clemenceau told the Chamber of Deputies at the end of December that he disagreed with Wilson, although he had, he said, the greatest admiration for the American president's "noble candor" (which was changed in the parliamentary journal to "noble grandeur"); he thereupon won a vote of confidence by a majority of 380 to 134. [British prime minister] Lloyd George triumphed equally convincingly in elections for the House of Commons just before Christmas. His coalition of Liberals and Tories, in which the latter were dominant, ran on an electoral program of hate and revenge against Germany with slogans like "Hang the Kaiser" and "Make Germany Pay," received no less than 526 of the 707 seats. It was not Lloyd George himself but the navy minister Sir Eric Geddes who uttered the notorious words, "We shall squeeze the German lemons until the pips squeak."

Wilson's moral majority therefore existed only in his poetic imagination. He was totally out of touch with reality. The Europeans did not know what to make of his fine words. They asked themselves whether he actually meant what he said. "I am one of the few people who think him honest," said Lloyd George to his friends. But he too was exasperated when the president blew his own horn loudly and gave no sign that he understood the sacrifices England had made: "Not a word of generous appreciation issued from his lips." Wilson, the American, could not establish an accepted character and place in Europe. The Europeans thought he was American, with his smooth, streamlined face, showing no emotion behind his shining glasses. . . .

In a word, the European leaders did not like Woodrow Wilson. From the start there was tension between them. Clemenceau, an old hand in politics, was not the man to come under the influence of Wilson's lofty words. He knew the United States; he had lived there just after the Civil War, spoke English well, and had married an American woman. He had no high opinion of American idealism, as was evident in the witticisms he made at Wilson's expense. God had needed only ten commandments, but Wilson fourteen, he jibed. That was a superficial play on numbers, but there was real bite in his jest that Wilson talked like Jesus Christ but acted like Lloyd George. Years before, in May 1916, he had been sharply critical of Wilson's speech before the League to Enforce Peace: "If the Creator needed seven days to organize a couple of creatures of which the first born instinctively tore each other apart, Mr. Wilson, in one sovereign word, is going to create men such as never have been seen, whose first need will be love and universal harmony." And, in reaction to the "peace without victory" speech, he wrote: "Never before has any political assembly heard so fine a sermon on what human beings might be capable of accomplishing if only they weren't human." In brief, this was classic realism confronting classic idealism. No wonder that Theodore Roosevelt admired Clemenceau, even writing to him, "Oh Lord, how I wish you were President of the United States." Clemenceau believed in France and in nothing else. France must be protected against German aggression, once and for all, and that could be done only by power, not by a superparliament such as Wilson, who did not know what Europe wanted. . . .

Wilson believed in his League of Nations as a remedy for all troubles, a miraculous cure that would work precisely because it was so entwined with the peace treaty itself. The treaty might not be perfect, he said in April, but with the League of Nations as an integral part of the treaty, there was a mechanism to improve its operation.

But actually it worked the other way round, a fact that Wilson completely missed. The delegates of the Allied countries exploited his League of Nations proposal to extract concessions from him; the peace turned out very badly because he repeatedly made compromises in order to save his beloved plan, carrying it through the bustling debates to safe harbor. . . . "The fact is," wrote the deeply disappointed [diplomat Henry] White in May, "that the League of Nations, in which he had been more deeply interested than anything else from the beginning, believing it to be the best if not the only means of avoiding war in the future, has been played to the limit by France and Japan in extracting concessions from him; to a certain extent by the British too, and the Treaty as it stands is the result." . . .

The history of the Versailles peace has called forth a welter of difficult questions. Was it too harsh, a *Diktatfrieden* that automatically elicited a reaction of re-vanche? Or was it, on the contrary, too mild a settlement, enabling the old forces in Germany to continue? In any case, is there a direct causal link between 1919 and 1933? Does the guilt for the disastrous consequences lie with the men who, in Paris, laid down the rules for the future? These are all questions that in their nature cannot be given a conclusive or logically satisfactory answer. But they are also questions that cannot be evaded. If this peace were not accepted, Wilson said many times on his swing through the West in the fall, there would be another war in twenty years. . . .

How horribly right he proved to be! What he predicted came about just as he said. But was he himself guiltless? Hadn't he written the whole scenario for that future? The defeat [of Germany] was a humiliation, not intended as such by him in his noble naïveté, but nonetheless felt as such by the vanquished. Humiliation led to dreams of revenge; the seeds of a new war were put into the soil. Of course, they would only grow when the climate was favorable, when events, primarily the Great Depression that began in 1929, permitted. But beyond question the seeds were planted by the peace of Versailles. Obviously, too, we must add at once that the world of 1919 was far too frightful in its confusion to be straightened out by talks between four heads of state. The problems were overwhelming and the fail-ure of the Big Four was almost inevitable. . . .

Historians, in their quest for consistency, have to fit Wilson into some pattern, if need be, one that takes time into account. This provides a way out: in the long run, in the future (but with what a frightful intermezzo!), Wilson would be right. This is the way Arthur Link, Wilson's outstanding biographer, approaches the question. For him, Wilson's vision might seem foolish at first sight, because it clashed with reality, but there is in fact a "higher realism." This adds a wider di-mension to the problem of Wilson; his deeds then must be judged within the per-spective of the future. In it his deeds accord with his words; if they were failures in the short run, all is reconciled in the perspective of a better future. It is a quite Wilsonian idea, paralleling the way Wilson himself saw the League of Nations as the panacea for all temporary compromises.

But is it possible to separate today and tomorrow from each other in this way? Is this how the relationship between realism and idealism actually works? What is the value of a prophet in politics? These are the questions we constantly encounter. There is a deep tragedy within them. Let me repeat: Wilson himself saw and warned that if there was not a just peace, there would be war again in twenty years. Does it follow from this that he personally shared in the responsibility for the hor-rors that would break out two decades later? Link's reply is that he did not. At Ver-sailles there was the familiar tension between the ideal and reality, but it is inher-ent in all human striving. One can only ask why Wilson failed. There are more than enough reasons. After the armistice he had no means to compel France and

England; he had been weakened in his own country by the elections; he had formidable opponents in Clemenceau, Lloyd George, [Italian prime minister] Orlando, and [Italian foreign minister Sidney] Sonnino; his ideal of "open covenants" was frustrated. And yet, Link maintains, he gained a reasonable peace that worked and created a new international order. He snaps at the critics:

> It is time to stop perpetuating the myth that the Paris settlement made inevitable the rise to power of Mussolini, the Japanese militarists, and Hitler, and hence the Second World War. That war was primarily the result of the Great Depression.

All the same, questions persist. If the war that came in twenty years was not the consequence of a bad peace, or if it wasn't such a bad peace after all, was Wilson's forecast just a stab in the dark? But then why reproach the others who opposed him?

Wilson's Battle for the League: Progressive Internationalists Confront the Forces of Reaction

THOMAS J. KNOCK

As the historian Frederick Jackson Turner once remarked, the age of reform in the United States was "also the age of socialistic inquiry." Indeed, by 1912, the Socialist Party of America and its quadrennial standard-bearer, Eugene Debs, had attained respectability and legitimacy. The party's membership exceeded 115,000, and some 1,200 socialists held public office in 340 municipalities and twenty-four states. As many as three million Americans read socialist newspapers on a regular basis. Julius Wayland's *Appeal to Reason,* with 760,000 weekly subscribers, ranked among the most widely read publications in the world.

The general cast of the four-way presidential campaign of 1912 also lent credence to Turner's observation. Notwithstanding the conservatism of the incumbent, William Howard Taft, the impact of progressivism on the two main parties, in tandem with the success of the Socialist party, caused a certain blurring of traditional political lines. To millions of citizens, a vote for either Woodrow Wilson, the progressive Democrat, Theodore Roosevelt, the insurgent "Bull Moose" who bolted the Republicans to form the Progressive party, or Debs, the Socialist, amounted to a protest against the status quo of industrial America. And that protest, from top to bottom, sanctioned an unfolding communion between liberals and socialists practically unique in American history.

In this new age of progressive reform and socialistic inquiry, it would be Woodrow Wilson's opportunity and challenge to reconcile and shape domestic and foreign concerns in ways that no previous chief executive had ever contemplated. From the start of his tenure, Wilson regularly sought the counsel and support not only of progressives within and outside the Democratic party, but also of individuals of relatively pronounced leftist tendencies. Although its development and consequences have rarely been scrutinized, Wilson's communion with the Ameri-

This is an original essay written for this volume based on *To End All Wars: Woodrow Wilson and the Quest for a New World Order* (New York: Oxford University Press, 1992).

can left, as well as with the liberal-left, exerted a profound impact on his diplomacy and, especially, the League of Nations movement. Organizations such as the Woman's Peace party, the American Union Against Militarism, and various elements of the Socialist party, moreover, made up the most intellectually vital part of the historically crucial, left-of-center coalition that elected Wilson to a second term in 1916. These groups were at once the advance guard of the so-called New Diplomacy in the United States and the impassioned proponents of an Americanized version of social democracy. From this heady welter emanated most of the salient components of Wilson's blueprint for a new world order as well as a program for social and economic justice at home.

In August 1914, no one living on the planet could imagine a spectacle as violent and complicated as the one into which humanity was about to be plunged. In September, during the first Battle of the Marne, the Allies and the Central Powers together suffered more than a million casualties. By the end of 1914, France, alone, counted 900,000 dead, wounded, or missing. In all, some ten million people— mainly Europeans but also hundreds of thousands of Asians and Americans— would go to their deaths as a result of the Great War. To the vast majority of Americans during the otherwise quiet summer of 1914, the outbreak of such a titanic struggle came "as lightning out of a clear sky," as one editorialist wrote. With the country's nearly unanimous approval, President Wilson established a policy of neutrality toward all of the belligerents.

In the immediate circumstances of the war, Wilson found himself beset by innumerable complex problems—not the least being Great Britain's naval blockade of northern Europe and Germany's submarine warfare against enemy vessels—for which there existed few guiding precedents in American history. Fully grasping the magnitude of Europe's grief, the president soon sketched out, in private, a program for avoiding such catastrophes in the future. This document included proposals to eliminate the production of munitions by private enterprise, to settle international disputes through arbitration, and to provide mutual guarantees (or, collective security) for the protection of the contracting parties.

In all of this, it would be misleading to portray a solitary Wilson contemplating possible solutions to the world crisis. The League of Nations had many authors and the concept was in a constant state of metamorphosis. Wilson's essential contribution was grand synthesis and propagation. At a fairly early stage in the war, a new internationalist movement came into being in the United States. Two divergent aggregations of activists—"progressive internationalists" and "conservative internationalists"—composed this movement. Wilson's relationship with both groups was of fundamental importance.

Feminists, liberals, pacifists, socialists, and reformers of varying kinds filled the ranks of the progressive internationalists. Their leaders included many of the era's authentic heroes and heroines: Jane Addams of Hull House, the poet-journalist John Reed, Max Eastman of the *Masses,* the civil-rights crusader Oswald Garrison Villard, and Lillian Wald of New York's Henry Street Settlement, to name a few. For them the search for a peaceful world order provided a logical common ground. Peace was indispensable to change itself—to the survival of the labor movement, to their campaigns on behalf of women's rights and the abolition of child labor, and to social justice legislation in general. If the war in Europe were permitted to rage on indefinitely, progressive internationalists believed, then the United States could not help but get sucked into it; not only their great causes, but also the very moral fiber of the nation would be destroyed should its resources be diverted from reform to warfare. Thus, their first goal (and one in keeping with Wilson's policy of neutrality) was to bring about a negotiated settlement of the war.

The Woman's Peace party, founded in January 1915, in Washington, D.C., and led by Jane Addams, played a pivotal role in the progressive internationalist movement. Guided by the principle of "the sacredness of human life," the platform of the Woman's Peace party constituted the earliest manifesto on internationalism advanced by any American organization throughout the war. The party's "program for constructive peace" called for an immediate armistice, international agreements to limit armaments and nationalize their manufacture, a reduction of trade barriers, self-determination, machinery for arbitration, and a "Concert of Nations" to supersede the balance-of-power system. The platform also pressed for American mediation of the war. Its authors made sure that the president received all of their recommendations.

The ideas and activities of the Woman's Peace party cut a wide swath. Within a year, it had an active membership of 40,000, while several kindred organizations sprang up and adopted its platform. On numerous occasions, Addams and her associates met with Wilson at the White House. Although they sometimes found him evasive, his consistent example of restraint during the early submarine crises with Germany made him something of a hero in their eyes. For his part, the president was deeply impressed with the "program for constructive peace." Addams's personal record of an interview in July 1915 is particularly enlightening: "He drew out the papers I had given him, and they seem[ed] to have been much handled and read. 'You see I have studied these resolutions,' he said, 'I consider them by far the best formulation which up to the moment has been put out by any body.' " The fact of the matter was that the Woman's Peace party had furnished Wilson with a pioneering synthesis of the New Diplomacy during the critical year in which his own thinking acquired a definite shape.

The Socialist Party of America, too, devised a momentous program for a "democratic peace" and motivated a sizeable constituency to think about foreign policy in new ways. In May 1915, the party adopted and published a "Manifesto on Disarmament and World Peace." Read by millions, this analysis of the political and economic causes of the war contained statements on disarmament, self-determination, and the establishment of an international parliament to replace secret diplomacy. The Socialist party was arguably second only to the Woman's Peace party in its impact upon both radicals and reformers during the progressive internationalist movement's formative stage.

In January 1916, Wilson welcomed to the Oval Office Morris Hillquit, the primary architect of the "Manifesto"; James H. Maurer, president of the Pennsylvania State Federation of Labor; and Meyer London, a Socialist member of the House of Representatives. According to Hillquit's account, their host looked tired and preoccupied when they arrived but became animated once their conversation about the Socialist declaration got under way. Hillquit was somewhat surprised when Wilson, in confidence, "informed us that he had had a similar plan under consideration" and also "hinted at the possibility of a direct offer of mediation by . . . the United States." The meeting proved to be more encouraging and productive than they might have hoped. "[H]is sympathies were entirely with us," Hillquit told the *Appeal to Reason.* As the committee rose to take its leave, however, Maurer said, "Your promises sound good, Mr. President, but the trouble with you is that you are surrounded by capitalist and militarist interests who want the war to continue; and I fear you will succumb to their influence." Placing a hand on Maurer's shoulder, Wilson replied, "If the truth be known, I am more often accused of being influenced by radical and pacifist elements than by the capitalist and militarist interest."

The question of which elements of the polity exerted the greatest influence on Wilson became especially relevant in light of the ongoing public debate over the state of the nation's military strength. Many progressive internationalists regarded the reactionary opponents of domestic reform and the advocates of militarism and imperialism as twins born of the same womb; they watched with alarm as the champions of "preparedness" mounted what they viewed as an insidious offensive to thwart social and economic progress at home, as well as disarmament and the repudiation of war as an instrument of foreign policy. In response to the preparedness movement, liberal reformers and leading socialists joined forces to establish the American Union Against Militarism (AUAM). Within months, the AUAM had branches in every major city in the country. When, in the wake of the *Lusitania* disaster, Wilson introduced legislation to increase substantially the size of the army and navy, it appeared that he had surrendered to the enemy. Then, too, a competing, conservative vision of internationalism was vying for national attention.

The program of the conservative internationalists was different in both subtle and conclusive ways. It was developed by the organizers of the League to Enforce Peace (LEP), founded in June 1915, and led by former president William Howard Taft and other Republicans prominent in the field of international law. Within two years, they had established four thousand branches in forty-seven states. The LEP's platform, "Warrant from History," called for American participation in a world parliament, which would assemble periodically to make appropriate changes to international law and employ arbitration and conciliation procedures to settle certain kinds of disputes. While more or less endorsing the general principle of collective security, most conservative internationalists also believed that the United States should build up its military complex and reserve the right to undertake independent coercive action whenever the "national interest" was threatened. Unlike progressive internationalists, the LEP did not concern itself with self-determination or advocate disarmament or even a military standoff in Europe. These internationalists were openly pro-Allied; in fact, the slogan, "The LEP does *not* seek to end the present war," appeared on their letterhead in the autumn of 1916.

Throughout that year, Wilson met and corresponded with representatives of both wings of the new internationalist movement. In May 1916, for example, he delivered an important address before a gathering of the LEP, the occasion for his first public affirmation on behalf of American membership in some kind of postwar peacekeeping organization. Yet Wilson's sympathies lay decidedly with the progressive internationalists. Two weeks earlier, for the first time, he had articulated to persons other than his absolute confidants his ideas for a "family of nations," during a lengthy White House colloquy with leaders of the AUAM.

The AUAM stood neither for "peace at any price" nor against "sane and reasonable" military preparedness, Lillian Wald explained to the president; but they were anxious about those agents of militarism who were "frankly hostile to our institutions of democracy." Wilson contended that his preparedness program conformed to his interlocutors' criteria—that it would provide adequate security "without changing the spirit of the country" and that one of his motives for it was to achieve a league of nations. "[I]f the world undertakes, as we all hope it will undertake, a joint effort to keep the peace, it will expect us to play our proportional part," he said. "Surely that is not a militaristic ideal. That is a very practical, possible ideal." During the exchange, Amos Pinchot, a journalist of the liberal-left, expounded on the dangers of militarism and of profiteers and politicians who cloaked their purposes in cheap appeals to patriotism. Pinchot asserted that the United States itself held the potential to become the most aggressive nation on earth should its enormous economic strength be diverted to armaments. "I quite see your point," Wilson replied. "It might very easily, unless some check was placed upon it by some international arrangement."

In making a case for stronger national defense to the AUAM, Wilson scored political as well as intellectual points with doubting progressive internationalists who represented liberal and socialist constituencies of key importance. According to Max Eastman's account in the *Masses,* the president had "referred to the [AUAM] as though he were a member of it," and the delegation came away convinced that he "sincerely hates his preparedness policies." The connection Wilson made between preparedness and "the idea of world-federation and the international enforcement of peace," Eastman went on, placed him "far above and beyond" his peers, especially Theodore Roosevelt.

Wilson could not have made a truly plausible case for a new diplomacy and a league—nor would he have been continued in office—if, at the same time, he had not been willing and able to move plainly to the left of center in American politics. Indeed, the array of social justice legislation he pushed through Congress on the eve of his reelection campaign gave legitimacy to his aspirations in foreign affairs like nothing else could have. Wilson could boast of a number of accomplishments for his first two years in office: the Underwood Tariff, the Clayton Antitrust Act, the Federal Reserve System, and the Federal Trade Commission. Then, as his polestar moved comparatively leftward with the approach of the 1916 campaign, he put two "radicals" (Louis D. Brandeis and John Hessin Clarke) on the Supreme Court. Over the protests of conservatives in and out of Congress, he secured passage of the Adamson Act, which established the eight-hour day for railroad workers, and the Keating-Owen bill, which imposed restrictions on child labor. Finally, he had defused the conservatives' appeal to jingoism with his "moderate" preparedness program, which, in conjunction with the Revenue Act of 1916, yielded the first real tax on wealth in American history. It was no mere coincidence that progressive internationalists cheered him on in these endeavors and that conservative internationalists lined up as his vehement domestic critics. On the one hand, Taft and Charles Evans Hughes, the Republican presidential nominee, condemned the Brandeis appointment and the Adamson Act. On the other hand, both Jane Addams, the reformer, and John Reed, the radical, declared that it was fairly impossible to have improved upon Wilson's record on behalf of children and railroad workers.

But this was only the half of it. As the complement to his advanced progressivism, Wilson also made American membership in a league of nations one of the cardinal themes of his campaign, a theme that complemented the Democratic chant, "He Kept Us Out Of War!" His utterances on the league exerted a significant impact on the outcome. Max Eastman predicted that Wilson would win reelection because "he has attacked the problem of eliminating war, and he has not succumbed to the epidemic of militarism." Indeed, his speeches on the league constituted "the most important step that any President of the United States has taken towards civilizing the world since Lincoln." Herbert Croly, the influential editor of the *New Republic,* threw his support to Wilson not only on the grounds of the president's domestic record but also because he had "committed himself and his party to a revolutionary doctrine": American participation in a postwar league of nations.

Wilson had prevailed in 1912 mainly because the Republicans were divided between Roosevelt and Taft. By 1916, Roosevelt had consummated a rapprochement with the party's conservative chieftains and abandoned his Progressive followers. On the surface, it appeared that Wilson was fated to a one-term presidency. As things turned out, however, Wilson had deprived the Republicans of any completely serviceable issue. From child labor and preparedness to the European war, he had made the causes of advanced progressivism, peace, and, especially, internationalism his own. On election day, large numbers of Socialists and former Bull Moose Progressives swelled the normal Democratic vote for president. By a narrow margin, Wilson managed a stunning upset over Hughes.

The proposed League of Nations had already begun to take on a vexatious partisan dimension, owing in part to the failure of conservative internationalists to have secured even a vague endorsement of the proposition in the Republican party platform. (Roosevelt would not hear of it, and Taft deferred to his wishes.) Moreover as the contest heated up, contempt for Wilson among Republicans and conservative internationalists grew apace. In beating the drum for Hughes, Roosevelt became the administration's most wrathful critic (and the country's most obstreperous pro-Allied extremist). Taft referred to Wilson as "a ruthless hypocrite . . . who has no convictions that he would not barter at once for votes." But what the LEP president did not realize was that his party had, in essence, handed the issue of the league, like a gift, to Wilson and the Democrats.

In any event, the election returns suggested that Wilson and the progressive internationalists had not merely checked the reactionaries; they had presided over the creation of a left-of-center coalition that seemed to hold the balance of political power in the United States. Precisely what all of this portended for future domestic struggles could hardly be predicted. As for foreign policy, the deeper meaning of their victory was unmistakable. "[T]he President we reelected has raised a flag that no other president has thought or perhaps dared to raise," Amos Pinchot submitted. "It is the flag of internationalism."

American neutrality was a fragile thing. Wilson had always shared the conviction of fellow peace seekers that the best way to keep the country out of the war was to try to bring about a negotiated settlement. Twice, to that end, in 1915 and 1916, he had sent his personal emissary, Colonel Edward M. House, to Europe for direct parlays with the heads of all the belligerent governments. These appeals had proved futile. Now, fortified by reconfirmation at the polls, he decided on a bold stroke. In a climactic attempt to end the war, he went before the Senate on January

22, 1917, and called for "peace without victory." In this address, Wilson drew together the strands of progressive internationalist thought and launched a penetrating critique of European imperialism, militarism, and balance-of-power politics—the root causes of the war, he said. In their stead, he held out the promise of a "community of nations"—a new world order sustained by procedures for the arbitration of disputes between nations, a dramatic reduction of armaments, self-determination, and collective security. The chief instrumentality of this sweeping program was to be a league of nations. Thus, Wilson began his ascent to a position of central importance in the history of international relations in the twentieth century.

Responses to the address varied. The governments of both warring coalitions, still praying for decisive victory in the field, either ignored it or received it with contempt. Many pro-Allied Republicans, such as Senator Henry Cabot Lodge of Massachusetts, heaped scorn upon the very notion of "peace without victory" and wondered exactly what membership in a league might entail. Nonetheless, Wilson's manifesto met with an unprecedented outpouring of praise from progressive groups at home and abroad. When it was read aloud to the annual conference of the British Labour party, the delegates stood and cheered his name for five minutes. The AUAM hailed him for having rendered "a service to all humanity which it is impossible to exaggerate" and stated that Wilson's words were "destined to an immortality as glorious as that of the Gettysburg Address." These were stirring, if highly anxious, days indeed for American liberals and socialists.

One week later, Germany announced the resumption of unrestricted submarine warfare against all flags. After three American ships were sunk without warning, public opinion shifted markedly. On March 20, the cabinet unanimously recommended full-fledged belligerency. Wilson, too, had concluded that after some thirty months of neutrality, war had "thus been thrust upon" the United States. "But," the secretary of interior recorded in his diary, "he goes unwillingly."

In his address to Congress on April 2, 1917, the president explained why neutrality no longer seemed tenable and outlined the measures necessary for getting the country on a war footing. He then turned to more transcendent matters. His goals were the same as when he had addressed the Senate in January; he said, "The world must be made safe for democracy. Its peace must be planted upon the tested foundations of political liberty. We have no selfish ends to serve. We desire no conquest, no dominion. We seek no indemnities for ourselves, no material compensation for the sacrifices we shall freely make." He implied that Americans would be fighting to establish some degree of "peace without victory," or, as he put it, "for a universal dominion of right by such a concert of free nations as shall bring peace and safety to all nations and the world itself at last free"—a program now attainable apparently only through the crucible of war.

Wilson never wavered in his fundamental aim though the obstacles in his path were enormous. As the brilliant young radical, Randolph Bourne, asked of all prowar liberals and socialists in a famous essay, "If the war is too strong for you to prevent, how is it going to be weak enough for you to control and mould to your liberal purposes?" Indeed, Wilson had to cope not only with an indeterminate measure of opposition clustered in the Senate but also with the antagonism of the Allies themselves, who all but refused to embrace his ideas for a fair and democratic peace. Then, just as the United States entered the war, Russia, staggering under the relentless blows of the German army, was seized by revolutionary upheaval. By the end of 1917, the Bolshevik leaders, V. I. Lenin and Leon Trotsky, pulled their ravaged nation out of the war. They thereupon issued proclamations on behalf of a democratic peace based on self-determination and summoned the peoples of Europe to demand that their governments—the Allies and the Central Powers alike—repudiate plans for conquest.

In the circumstances, Wilson really had no choice but to respond to the Bolshevik challenge. In his Fourteen Points Address, of January 8, 1918, the most celebrated speech of his presidency, he reiterated much of the anti-imperialist "peace without victory" formula and once again made the League of Nations the capstone. In answer to Lenin's entreaty to stop the war, he argued that German autocracy and militarism must be crushed so that humanity could set about the task of creating a new and better world. Wilson's endeavor to remove the suspicions hanging over the Allied cause and rally doubters to see the war through to the bitter end succeeded magnificently. The popular approbation that greeted the Fourteen Points in both Europe and America approached phenomenal proportions. (Even Lenin hailed the address as "a great step ahead towards the peace of the world.") But as before, the Allied governments declined to endorse or comment on Wilson's progressive war aims.

At home, Wilson's own immediate priorities inexorably shifted toward the exigencies of war mobilization. And, in part owing to stinging Republican criticism of "peace without victory" and, later, the Fourteen Points as the basis for the postwar settlement, he refused to discuss his plans for the League in any concrete detail throughout the period of American belligerency. He also neglected to lay essential political groundwork for it at home. By the autumn of 1918, important segments among both conservative and progressive internationalists had grown disenchanted with Wilson, albeit for entirely different reasons.

This development would prove to be as unfortunate as the partisan opposition led by the president's arch-nemeses, Theodore Roosevelt and Henry Cabot Lodge. For example, Wilson grievously offended Taft by frustrating the wartime efforts of the LEP and other conservative internationalists, who wanted to make formal plans for the League of Nations in cooperation with the British government. (There were, of course, serious ideological differences between his and Taft's conception of the League, but Wilson might have found a way to use the Republican-dominated LEP to defuse some of the incipient senatorial criticism.)

Perhaps just as consequential, Wilson failed to nurture the left-of-center coalition of 1916, a dynamic political force that, had it remained intact, might have made it possible for him to secure and validate American leadership in a peacekeeping organization intended to serve progressive purposes. But he began to lose his grip on his former base of support as a tidal wave of anti-German hysteria and superpatriotism swept over the country in 1917–1918. Like a giant wrecking machine, "One Hundred Percent Americanism," as it was known, had the potential to batter the progressive wing of the American internationalist movement to ruins. In every part of the United States, acts of political repression and violence (sanctioned by federal legislation) were committed against German-Americans as well as pacifists and radicals. Only at risk of life or limb did antiwar dissenters express their views in public. For example, for speaking out against American participation in the war, Eugene Debs was sentenced to ten years in prison. The postmaster general denied second-class mailing privileges to such publications as the *Milwaukee Leader,* the *Appeal to Reason,* and the *Masses,* virtually shutting them down. The majority of progressive internationalists steadfastly supported the war effort, but they could not abide these kinds of violations of basic First Amendment rights, for which, ultimately, they held Wilson responsible. And so, because he acquiesced in the suppression of civil liberties, Wilson himself contributed to a gradual unraveling of his coalition.

The circumstances in which the war ended compounded the larger problem. By September 1918, the combined might of the Allied and American armies had pushed the enemy back toward Belgium. On October 6, German Chancellor Max von Baden appealed to Wilson to take steps for the restoration of peace based on the Fourteen Points. The armistice was signed on November 11. Meanwhile, a midterm congressional election more important than most presidential elections in American history had taken place. Against the Wilsonian peace plan, the Republicans launched a fiercely partisan, ultraconservative campaign. This time around, endorsements on behalf of the administration by leading progressives outside the Democratic party hardly matched those of the 1916 contest. Even so, the centralization of the wartime economy and the core of Wilson's foreign policy placed him far enough to the left to make all Democrats vulnerable to Republican charges that they were "un-American." Most historians maintain that Wilson committed the worst blunder of his presidency in countering the attacks: He asked the public for a vote of confidence—an ostensibly partisan appeal to sustain the Democrats' control of Congress. When the Republicans won majorities of forty-five in the House and two in the Senate, they could claim that the president, who planned to attend the Paris Peace Conference personally, had been repudiated. The Republicans also thereby gained control over congressional committees, including the Senate Foreign Relations Committee, which would be chaired by Lodge.

Yet despite these political setbacks, the Fourteen Points had acquired the status of sacred text among the war-weary peoples of Europe, and "Wilson" was becoming something more than the name of a president. Italian soldiers placed his picture in their barracks. An old woman said she heard that in America "there was a great saint who is going to make peace for us." Romain Rolland, the French Nobel laureate, pronounced him the greatest "moral authority" in the world. The whole world seemed to come to a halt to honor Wilson when he arrived in Europe. Into the streets and piazzas of Paris, London, Rome, and Milan, millions of people turned out to hail "the Moses from Across the Atlantic." Tributes of such historic proportions transcended mere pageantry and alarmed the Allied prime ministers. An articulate expression of mass political opinion, the demonstrations strengthened the hand of "the Savior of Humanity" during the early stages of the conference and helped to ensure the inclusion of the Covenant of the League as an integral part of the treaty of peace.

Whereas he could not have prevailed without the massive outpouring of public support, Wilson still had to pay a heavy price for the League. If he was adored by the "common people," the statesmen of Europe—David Lloyd George, Georges Clemenceau, and Vittorio Orlando—held grave reservations about a Wilsonian peace. They were also keen students of American politics. Fully aware of the arithmetic of the Senate, they used their acceptance of the covenant as a lever to gain concessions on other vital and contentious issues.

For instance, Wilson was compelled to swallow a less-than-satisfactory compromise on the disposition of captured enemy colonies, which the Allies (in particular, Australia and South Africa) coveted for themselves. Clemenceau, on threat of withdrawal of his certification of the League, demanded for France military occupation of the Rhineland; Orlando claimed for Italy the Yugoslav port city of Fiume; and the Japanese insisted on retaining exploitative economic privileges in China's Shantung province. On several occasions, Wilson was able to moderate the more extreme Allied demands and uphold at least the spirit of the Fourteen Points. But, then, on verge of physical collapse, he permitted the Allies to impose upon Germany a huge reparations burden and, on top of everything else, a "war-guilt" clause—saddling it with the moral responsibility for allegedly having started the war. Wilson tried to take comfort in the hope that, once the "war psychosis" had receded, the League would be in position to arbitrate and rectify the injustices contained in the peace treaty itself. After six long months of often acrimonious deliberations, however, the signing of that document in the Hall of Mirrors at Versailles, on June 28, 1919, was at best a fleeting triumph for the exhausted president.

By the time Wilson returned to the United States in the summer of 1919, thirty-two state legislatures and thirty-three governors had endorsed the covenant. According to a *Literary Digest* poll, the vast majority of nearly 1,400 newspaper editors, including a majority of Republican editors, advocated American membership in some kind of league. Had a national referendum been held at just that moment, the country almost certainly would have joined. The reasons for its failure to do so are still debated by historians. To begin, Wilson had already lost the active support of most left-wing progressives, not to mention that of the socialists. Many liberals, too, shook their heads in dismay upon reading the Versailles settlement. They believed that, regardless of his motives, he had forsaken the Fourteen Points; that he had conceded too much to the Allies in the territorial compromises; and that vindictiveness, not righteousness, had ruled at the Paris conclave. In short, they feared that the League of Nations would be bound to uphold an unjust peace.

The great debate also coincided with the opening phase of the Red Scare, an even more hysterical and pervasive manifestation of "One Hundred Percent Americanism" whose focus had shifted from the German menace to the threat of bolshevism. Deterioration of civil liberties continued to discourage many progressive internationalists from giving Wilson's crusade their full devotion, and they implored him to issue a blanket amnesty to all those who still suffered political repression and imprisonment. Such a dramatic gesture of goodwill would revitalize the coalition of 1916 and, as one of them contended, inspirit "a force great and militant enough to crush the opposition to the League." At length, however, Wilson deferred to the objections of his red-baiting attorney general, A. Mitchell Palmer. While the president's conservative detractors never doubted the "bolshevik" purposes behind his internationalism, John Spargo, a widely respected prowar socialist, reluctantly concluded, "The administration has become reactionary and deserves no support from any of us." Thus, Wilson's political base beyond his own party had badly eroded.

In the Senate on one hand sheer partisanship motivated much of the opposition. Until the autumn of 1918, Wilson had been the most uniformly successful (if controversial) president since Lincoln. What would become of the Republican party, a friend asked Senator Lodge, if Wilson got his League and the Democrats could boast of "the greatest constructive reform in history"? On the other hand, many of the senatorial objections were grounded in ideological principles. Most Republicans acknowledged that the United States should cooperate with the Allies and play its part in upholding the peace settlement; but they also believed that Wilson had consigned too many vital national interests to the will of an international authority. (At one point, Wilson had frankly admitted, "Some of our sovereignty would be surrendered.") The Republicans found Article X of the covenant particularly troubling. It obliged contracting nations to "preserve as against external aggression the territorial integrity and political independence of all Members of the League." Thus, at least on paper, the United States might be required to take part in some far-flung military intervention in which it had no compelling interest; at the same time, the United States apparently would be prevented from using its military power unilaterally whenever it wanted to. Although during the peace conference he had responded to early criticisms and amended the covenant—to provide for withdrawal from the League and nominally to exempt the Monroe Doctrine and domestic matters (such as immigration) from its jurisdiction—Wilson had not done enough to assuage the anxieties of the majority of Republicans.

Then, too, a small but sturdy knot of senators known as the "irreconcilables" flat-out opposed the League in any form. Not all of the fifteen or so irreconcilables were partisans or reactionaries (though most, like Albert Fall, were); several of them, including Robert La Follette and George Norris, were bona-fide progressives who based their opposition on convictions similar to those of many liberals and socialists. Irreconcilable or no, only a few of Wilson's opponents were strict isolationists. No one had cut through to the crux of the debate with more discernment than Gilbert M. Hitchcock of Nebraska, the Democratic leader in the Senate, when he observed, "Internationalism has come, and we must choose what form the internationalism is to take." The *Appeal to Reason,* though disillusioned with the president and highly dubious of his labors, was harsher: Republicans feared Wilson's League because it placed restrictions on "America's armed forces . . . [and] the commercial and territorial greed of American capitalists." The Lodge crowd hardly advocated isolationism, but rather "the internationalism of unrestrained plunder and competition."

By summer's end, the Senate Foreign Relations Committee, dominated by Republicans and irreconcilables and with Lodge at the helm, had formulated forty-six amendments as the conditions for ratification; by autumn, these had evolved into formal reservations—curiously, fourteen in number. The most controversial one pertained to Article X of the covenant: "The United States assumes no obligation to preserve the territorial integrity or political independence of any country . . . unless in any particular case the Congress . . . by act or joint resolution [shall] so provide." Reservation V addressed the equally important corollary to the collective security provision—that is, the restrictions that League membership would also presumably impose against independent coercive action by any single power. It declared that the United States would not submit to arbitration questions or disputes that related in any way to the Monroe Doctrine, or accede to judgments arrived at thereto, without the express consent of the Congress. Other reservations raised doubts about financial contributions to the League, membership in the International Labour Organization, and whether the United States would comply with disarmament (one of the elementary tenets of progressive internationalism).

Meanwhile, Wilson held a series of White House meetings with groups of Republicans known as "mild reservationists" and tried to persuade them to ratify the treaty as it was written. In fact, there was very little difference between their views and those of the senators called "strong reservationists." Hence, none of these conferences changed anyone's mind. Then, against the advice of his personal physician and the pleading of the First Lady, Wilson determined that he must take his case directly to the American people and let them know what was at stake. For three weeks in September 1919, he traveled ten thousand miles by train throughout the Middle and Far West, making some forty speeches to hundreds of thousands of people.

Wilson appealed to his audiences on the intellectual and the emotional level both. Despite the importance of Article X, he told them, military sanctions probably would not have to come into play very often—in part because of the deterrent manifest within the threat of collective force, in part because of the cooling-off provisions in the arbitration features of the League, and in part because disarmament, which he heavily emphasized, would help to eliminate most potential problems from the start. He also addressed the question of sovereignty, as it related to the Senate's concern over arbitration and the hindrance to unilateral action that League membership implied: "The only way in which you can have impartial determinations in this world is by consenting to something you do not want to do." And the obvious corollary was to agree to refrain from doing something that you *want* to do, for there might be times "when we lose in court [and] we will take our medicine."

But there could be no truly effective League without America's participation. Should Americans turn their backs, he said, they would have to live forever with a gun in their hands. And they could not go in grudgingly or on a conditional basis. The "Lodge Reservations" would utterly "change the entire meaning of the Treaty." If the League were thus crippled, he would feel obliged to stand "in mortification and shame" before the boys who went across the seas to fight and say to them, " 'You are betrayed. You fought for something that you did not get.' " And there would come, "sometime, in the vengeful providence of God, another struggle in which, not a few hundred thousand fine men from America would have to die, but as many millions as are necessary to accomplish the final freedom of the peoples of the world."

As the crowds grew larger and the cheers louder, Wilson looked more haggard and worn out at the end of each day. His facial muscles twitched. Headaches so excruciating that he could hardly see recurred. To keep from coughing all night, he slept propped up in a chair. At last, his doctor called a halt to the tour and rushed him back to Washington. Two days later, on October 2, he suffered a stroke that nearly killed him and permanently paralyzed the left side of his body. From that point onward, Wilson was but a fragile husk of his former self, a tragic recluse in the White House, shielded by his wife and doctor.

The Senate roll was called three times, in November 1919 and March 1920. But whether on a motion to ratify the treaty unconditionally or with the fourteen Lodge reservations attached to it, the vote always fell short of a two-thirds majority. In November 1920, Warren G. Harding, the Republican presidential candidate, won a landslide victory over the Democrat, James M. Cox. The Republicans were only too happy to interpret the returns as the "great and solemn referendum" that Wilson had earlier said he had wanted for his covenant. "So far as the United States is concerned," Lodge now declared, "that League is dead."

In surveying the ruins, many historians have cited the president's stroke as the primary factor behind the outcome. A healthy Wilson, they argue, surely would have grasped the situation and strived to find a middle ground on the question of reservations. Other historians have maintained that his refusal to compromise was consistent with his personality throughout his life, that he would never have yielded to the Republicans (especially to Lodge), regardless of the state of his health. Although there is merit in both of these interpretations—the stroke and Wilson's personality are of obvious relevance—neither provides a complete explanation. They do not take adequate account of the evolution of the League idea, the ideological gulf that had always separated progressive and conservative internationalism, or the domestic political conditions that had taken shape long before the treaty was in the Senate.

In a very real sense, Wilsonian, or progressive, internationalism had begun at home, as part of the reform impulse in the "age of socialistic inquiry." By the touchstone of Wilson's advanced reform legislation and his synthesis of the tenets of the New Diplomacy, progressive internationalists had been able to define the terms of the debate and claim title to the League until 1917–1918—that is, until "One Hundred Percent Americanism" released uncontrollable forces that overwhelmed them. Wilson contributed to this turn of events by losing sight of the relationship between politics and foreign policy—by refusing to acknowledge his administration's culpability in the wartime reaction and by declining to take any action to combat it. The results of the 1918 midterm elections were the first tangible sign of the erosion of the domestic foundation and depletion of the political environment essential to both ratification on Wilson's terms and American leadership in a progressive, as opposed to a conservative, league movement.

Thus the die was cast, but not alone for the reasons conventionally cited in the literature—including Wilson's physical collapse, though this misfortune surely worsened the ensuing political gridlock. On one level, the ratification fight represents no more (and no less) than a dénouement to a sequence of events set in motion at the birth of the progressive and conservative internationalist movements and in the forging of Wilson's victory coalition of 1916. The circumstances surrounding the dissolution of progressive internationalism—in particular, the wartime repression and Wilson's failure to rekindle the coalition just as the bitter parliamentary contest was getting under way—at length sealed the fate of a *Wilsonian* league.

Yet if the stroke made him less amenable to compromise, Wilson was no less alert (and legitimately so) to the all-out assault on progressive internationalism that the Republican reservations embodied. "The imperialist wants no League of Nations," he wrote in a published letter just before the Senate rendered its final verdict, "but if . . . there is to be one, he is interested to secure one suited for his own purposes." International security involved not only responsibilities but also restraints, or "a renunciation of wrong-doing on the part of powerful nations." For Wilson, Article X constituted, as ever, "a bulwark, the only bulwark . . . against the forces of imperialism and reaction." And so, if he permitted the United States to go in under the Lodge reservations, the meaning of the League would no longer be in doubt; it would become a Lodgian league, an imperialist league, a reactionary league. Perhaps no league would be better than one that would "venture to take part in reviving the old order." In the end, despite their scorn for him, the "stern covenanter" still possessed the soul of a progressive internationalist.

Ray Stannard Baker, his sympathetic biographer, once commented on Wilson's fate: "He can escape no responsibility & must go to his punishment not only for his own mistakes and weaknesses of temperament but for the greed and selfishness of the world." Whatever the central cause of his historic failure, Wilson's conservative and partisan adversaries earnestly believed that his was a dangerously radical vision, a new world order alien to their own understanding of how the world worked. His severest critics among progressive internationalists believed he had not done enough to rally the people to his side and resist the forces of reaction—either in America or at the Paris Peace Conference. Wilson's response to them was a cry of anguish. "What more could I have done?" he asked historian William E. Dodd shortly before leaving the presidency. "I had to negotiate with my back to the wall. Men thought I had all power. Would to God I had had such power." His voice choking with emotion, he added, "The 'great' people at home wrote and wired every day that they were against me."

On all counts, and no doubt for all concerned, it had been, as Dodd himself concluded, "one long wilderness of despair and betrayal, even by good men."

✖ *FURTHER READING*

Lloyd Ambrosius, *Wilsonian Statecraft* (1991)

———, *Woodrow Wilson and the American Diplomatic Tradition: The League Fight in Perspective* (1987)

———, "Woodrow Wilson and the Quest for Orderly Progress," in Norman A. Graebner, ed., *Traditions and Values: American Diplomacy, 1865–1945* (1985), pp. 73–100

Thomas A. Bailey, *Woodrow Wilson and the Great Betrayal* (1945)

———, *Woodrow Wilson and the Lost Peace* (1944)

John M. Blum, *The Progressive Presidents* (1980)

Edward H. Buehrig, ed., *Wilson's Foreign Policy in Historical Perspective* (1957)

Frederick S. Calhoun, *Power and Principle: Armed Intervention in Wilsonian Foreign Policy* (1986)

John W. Chambers III, *The Tyranny of Change: America in the Progressive Era, 1890–1920* (1992)

Kendrick A. Clements, *The Presidency of Woodrow Wilson* (1992)

———, *Woodrow Wilson: World Statesman* (1987)

G. R. Conyne, *Woodrow Wilson: British Perspectives* (1992)

John W. Coogan, *The End of Neutrality: The United States, Britain, and Maritime Rights, 1899–1915* (1981)

John M. Cooper, Jr., *The Warrior and the Priest: Woodrow Wilson and Theodore Roosevelt* (1983)

——— and Charles E. Neu, eds., *The Wilson Era* (1991)

Charles DeBenedetti, *Origins of the Modern American Peace Movement, 1915–1929* (1978)

Patrick Devlin, *Too Proud to Fight* (1975)

Richard R. Doerries, *Imperial Challenge: Ambassador Count von Bernstorff and German-American Relations, 1908–1917* (1989)

Robert H. Ferrell, *Woodrow Wilson and World War I* (1985)

Lloyd C. Gardner, *Safe for Democracy* (1984)

Hans W. Gatske, *Germany and the United States* (1980)

Alexander L. George and Juliette George, *Woodrow Wilson and Colonel House: A Personality Study* (1956)

———, "Woodrow Wilson and Colonel House: A Reply to Weinstein, Anderson, and Link," *Political Science Quarterly*, 96 (1981–1982), 641–665

Ross Gregory, *The Origins of American Intervention in the First World War* (1971)

Herbert Hoover, *The Ordeal of Woodrow Wilson* (1958)

George F. Kennan, *American Diplomacy, 1900–1950* (1951)

Thomas J. Knock, *To End All Wars: Woodrow Wilson and the Quest for a New World Order* (1992)

Antony Lentin, *Lloyd George, Woodrow Wilson, and the Guilt of Germany* (1985)

N. Gordon Levin, *Woodrow Wilson and World Politics* (1968)

Arthur S. Link, *Wilson*, 5 vols. (1947–1965)

———, *Woodrow Wilson: Revolution, War, and Peace* (1979)

———, ed., *Woodrow Wilson and a Revolutionary World* (1982)

David W. McFadden, *Alternative Paths: Soviets and Americans, 1917–1920* (1993)

Herbert F. Margulies, *The Mild Reservationists and the League of Nations Controversy in the Senate* (1989)

Ernest R. May, *The World War and American Isolation, 1914–1917* (1959)

Arno Mayer, *Politics and Diplomacy of Peacemaking* (1967)

Charles E. Neu, "The Search for Woodrow Wilson," *Reviews in American History*, 10 (1982), 223–228

Robert E. Osgood, *Ideals and Self-Interest in American Foreign Relations* (1953)

Bert E. Park, *Ailing, Aging, Addicted: Studies of Compromised Leadership* (1993)

Stuart I. Rochester, *American Liberal Disillusionment in the Wake of World War I* (1977)

Klaus Schwabe, *Woodrow Wilson, Revolutionary Germany, and Peacemaking, 1918–1919* (1985)

Ralph A. Stone, *The Irreconcilables* (1970)

Roland N. Stromberg, *Collective Security and American Foreign Policy* (1963)

Marc Trachtenburg, *Reparations in World Politics* (1980)

Barbara Tuchman, *The Zimmermann Telegram* (1958)

Arthur Walworth, *Wilson and His Peacemakers* (1986)

Edwin A. Weinstein, *Woodrow Wilson: A Medical and Psychological Biography* (1981)

———, James W. Anderson, and Arthur S. Link, "Woodrow Wilson's Political Personality," *Political Science Quarterly*, 93 (1978–1979), 585–598

William C. Widenor, *Henry Cabot Lodge and the Search for an American Foreign Policy* (1980)

The International History

of the 1920s

The transition from war to peace proved rough. The embittering experiences of the First World War and the Versailles peacemaking left postwar leaders with a daunting international agenda. Throughout the 1920s they worked diligently to devise plans and prescriptions that could stabilize economies and currencies, energize foreign trade and investment, facilitate payment of foreign debts and reparations, curb political extremism, reduce armaments, tame national rivalries, protect imperial interests, and prevent war. Central to the decade's contentions were the questions of how to contain yet restore Germany, whose economic health was so essential to European stability; how to reassure a skeptical France about its security as Germany revitalized itself; how to manage great-power competition in East Asia, especially how to persuade Japan to respect Western interests and China's sovereignty; and how to contain radical Soviet Russia yet integrate it into the international community.

As the 1930s opened, however, devastating events demonstrated that the quest for a peaceful world order and balance of power had failed. The Great Depression began to cripple the world economy, debts and reparations went unpaid, and trade wars broke out. Militarists in hobbled Germany and vulnerable Japan vowed destruction of the Versailles settlement and nonaggression pacts, and the League of Nations continued to struggle to define its role in world affairs. As fervent nationalism drove countries away from the once-high hopes of Wilsonian internationalism, a second world war seemed possible.

Americans reacted in many different ways to the upheaval of international relations in the 1920s. Some preferred that the country stay out of Europe and let the Old World alone contend with its self-made miseries. This so-called isolationist opinion drew on the disillusioning experience of the First World War, which fed thoughts that the United States could not provide answers to generations-long European questions. Other Americans argued that the United States simply could not retreat from worldwide responsibilities, because trade, immigration, debts, investments, colonies, and overseas allies and bases (especially in Latin America) inevitably thrust it into the maelstrom and demanded the unilateral use of power to stem threats to U.S. interests. One scholar has called such thinking "independent internationalism."

At the same time, American pacifists and internationalists intent on reviving Wilsonianism advocated multilateral agreements on disarmament and the outlawry of war and urged U.S. participation in the World Court. Business and banking expansionists, eager to maintain American supremacy in the increasingly interdependent world economy, pressed receptive Republican administrations to trumpet the "Open Door" policy and encourage private experts to craft workable debts and reparations plans. Americans who claimed that the Caribbean and Central America constituted North America's "backyard" advocated continued U.S. hegemony in Latin America, preferably through economic rather than military penetration.

As Americans participated actively in the world economy, many proudly observed that their culture gained influence abroad as other peoples became attracted to U.S. goods, productivity, movies, and technology. Although some foreigners applauded the United States as a model for the future, others rejected Americanism and Americanization as threats to national tradition and identity.

Historians continue to debate what to call U.S. foreign relations in the 1920s: isolationist, unilateralist, internationalist, expansionist, corporatist? U.S. leaders worked for peaceful change through economic reconstruction and cultural influence, but the United States, clearly the era's giant, did not succeed in establishing a stable world order. Did it fail for want of serious trying? Did it fall short because of troubles endemic to the international system—national rivalries and the legacy of Versailles, for example—that were impervious to outside solution? Was the reason for failure the U.S. government's and the American people's naive belief that appeals to principle and signatures on unenforceable agreements rather than applications of power would set things right? Did America's absence from the League of Nations matter? Did the United States let down its guard in the 1920s, refusing to maintain a strong military that might have deterred disturbers of peace? Did the United States pay too much attention to economic and financial remedies, ignoring critical political questions like the balance of power and strategic commitments?

Did Washington too often refrain from direct, effective participation in problem solving and instead let the private sector handle crises? Did failure to build a stable world order stem from selfishness on the part of private interests that too narrowly served themselves for short-term gain (making questionable loans, for example) instead of building a durable international structure? Was failure rooted in contradictory U.S. policies such as the Open Door abroad and protectionist tariffs at home? Just how wisely did American leaders address international issues? What more should they and could they have done? Put another way, did American leaders prudently understand the limits of U.S. power, avoiding overcommitment and misapplication? Or did they—and other international leaders—squander opportunities to avert the calamities that ultimately brought on the Second World War?

Many of these questions are applicable to almost any period of international history. Here they are tested in the pivotal decade of the 1920s.

✖ DOCUMENTS

In the first document, dated November 12, 1921, Secretary of State Charles Evans Hughes addresses the Washington Conference on naval disarmament. In making the case that arms reductions would permit public funds to be more wisely applied to economic rehabilitation and growth, Hughes boldly asks the major powers to scrap great numbers of warships. The

Five-Power Treaty of 1922 did just that. The second document, a *Chicago Tribune* editorial of November 13, 1921, expresses what many Americans believed after the First World War: that Europe was hopelessly entrapped in rivalries and that the United States ought to stay clear until the continent set its house in order. In the third document, a speech before the American Historical Association on December 29, 1922, Secretary Hughes identifies German reconstruction and the reparations issue as keys to European stability and recommends the mobilization of private experts to devise solutions. Hughes's proposals came to fruition in the Dawes Plan of 1924, which set a schedule for German reparations payments and provided for private American loans to alleviate Germany's economic plight.

The fourth document is a selection from the prolific Argentine anti-imperialist writer Manuel Ugarte, who identifies the United States as a "New Rome" that annexes wealth rather than territory, manipulates native politics, and creates a detrimental dependency among Latin Americans. The fifth selection, Edward G. Lowry's article "Trade Follows the Film" (*Saturday Evening Post,* November 7, 1925), reveals the link between economic and cultural expansion in the 1920s as American-made movies penetrated world markets. Secretary of Commerce Herbert Hoover, an ardent economic expansionist, establishes the value of foreign trade to the U.S. economy and dismisses critics of America's protective tariffs in the sixth document, a speech of March 16, 1926. The seventh selection is the antiwar Kellogg-Briand Pact, signed by the United States and most of the world's nations in August 1928. One of the signers was Soviet Russia, a nation that the United States still refused to recognize even though U.S. businesses invested in and traded with the communist nation. In the last document, Republican senator William E. Borah of Idaho, chair of the Foreign Relations Committee, appeals for U.S. recognition in a speech of March 3, 1931. Recognition finally came in 1933.

Secretary of State Charles Evans Hughes on Naval Disarmament, 1921

We not only have the lessons of the past to guide us, not only do we have the reaction from the disillusioning experiences of war, but we must meet the challenge of imperative economic demands. What was convenient or highly desirable before is now a matter of vital necessity. If there is to be economic rehabilitation, if the longings for reasonable progress are not to be denied, if we are to be spared the uprisings of peoples made desperate in the desire to shake off burdens no longer endurable, competition in armament must stop. The present opportunity not only derives its advantage from a general appreciation of this fact, but the power to deal with the exigency now rests with a small group of nations, represented here, who have every reason to desire peace and to promote amity. . . . Is it not plain that the time has passed for mere resolutions that the responsible Powers should examine the question of limitation of armament? We can no longer content ourselves with investigations, with statistics, with reports, with the circumlocution of inquiry. The essential facts are sufficiently known. The time has come, and this Conference has been called, not for general resolutions or mutual advice, but for action. . . .

It is apparent that this can not be accomplished without serious sacrifices. Enormous sums have been expended upon ships under construction and building programs which are now under way can not be given up without heavy loss. Yet if the present construction of capital ships goes forward other ships will inevitably be built to rival them and this will lead to still others. Thus the race will continue so long as ability to continue lasts. The effort to escape sacrifices is futile. We must face them or yield our purpose. . . .

In making the present proposal the United States is most solicitous to deal with the question upon an entirely reasonable and practicable basis, to the end that the just interests of all shall be adequately guarded and that national security and defense shall be maintained. Four general principles have been applied:

1. That all capital-ship building programs, either actual or projected, should be abandoned;
2. That further reduction should be made through the scrapping of certain of the older ships;
3. That in general regard should be had to the existing naval strength of the Powers concerned;
4. That the capital ship tonnage should be used as the measurement of strength for navies and a proportionate allowance of auxiliary combatant craft prescribed.

The principle features of the proposed agreement are as follows:

Capital Ships

United States.   The United States is now completing its program of 1916 calling for 10 new battleships and 6 battle cruisers. One battleship has been completed. The others are in various stages of construction; in some cases from 60 to over 80 per cent of the construction has been done. On these 15 capital ships now being built over $330,000,000 have been spent. Still, the United States is willing in the interest of an immediate limitation of naval armament to scrap all these ships.

The United States proposes, if this plan is accepted—

1. To scrap all capital ships now under construction. This includes 6 battle cruisers and 7 battleships on the ways and in course of building, and 2 battleships launched.

The total number of new capital ships thus to be scrapped is 15. The total tonnage of the new capital ships when completed would be 618,000 tons.

2. To scrap all of the older battleships up to, but not including, the *Delaware* and *North Dakota.* The number of these old battleships to be scrapped is 15. Their total tonnage is 227,740 tons.

Thus the number of capital ships to be scrapped by the United States, if this plan is accepted, is 30, with an aggregate tonnage (including that of ships in construction, if completed) of 845,740 tons.

Great Britain.   The plan contemplates that Great Britain and Japan shall take action which is fairly commensurate with this action on the part of the United States.

It is proposed that Great Britain—

1. Shall stop further construction of the 4 new Hoods, the new capital ships not laid down but upon which money has been spent. These 4 ships, if completed, would have tonnage displacement of 172,000 tons.
2. Shall, in addition, scrap her pre-dreadnaughts, second line battleships, and first line battleships up to, but not including, the *King George V* class.

These, with certain pre-dreadnaughts which it is understood have already been scrapped, would amount to 19 capital ships and a tonnage reduction of 411,375 tons.

The total tonnage of ships thus to be scrapped by Great Britain (including the tonnage of the 4 Hoods, if completed) would be 583,375 tons.

Japan. It is proposed that Japan

1. Shall abandon her program of ships not yet laid down, viz., the *Kii, Owari, No. 7* and *No. 8* battleships, and *Nos. 5, 6, 7,* and *8,* battle cruisers.

It should be observed that this does not involve the stopping of construction, as the construction of none of these ships has been begun.

2. Shall scrap 3 capital ships (the *Mutsu* launched, the *Tosa,* and *Kago* in course of building) and 4 battle cruisers (the *Amagi* and *Akagi* in course of building, and the *Atoga* and *Takao* not yet laid down, but for which certain material has been assembled).

The total number of new capital ships to be scrapped under this paragraph is seven. The total tonnage of these new capital ships when completed would be 289,100 tons.

3. Shall scrap all pre-dreadnaughts and battleships of the second line. This would include the scrapping of all ships up to, but not including, the *Settsu*; that is, the scrapping of 10 older ships, with a total tonnage of 159,828 tons.

The total reduction of tonnage on vessels existing, laid down, or for which material has been assembled (taking the tonnage of the new ships when completed), would be 448,928 tons.

Thus, under this plan there would be immediately destroyed, of the navies of the three Powers, 66 capital fighting ships, built and building, with a total tonnage of 1,878,043.

It is proposed that it should be agreed by the United States, Great Britain, and Japan that their navies, with respect to capital ships, within three months after the making of the agreement shall consist of certain ships designated in the proposal and numbering for the United States 18, for Great Britain 22, for Japan 10. . . .

With the acceptance of this plan the burden of meeting the demands of competition in naval armament will be lifted. Enormous sums will be released to aid the progress of civilization. At the same time the proper demands of national defense will be adequately met and the nations will have ample opportunity during the naval holiday of 10 years to consider their future course. Preparation for offensive naval war will stop now.

The Isolationist *Chicago Tribune* Denounces
Europe's Folly, 1921

It is natural that pacifists and excited humanitarians should stress the evil consequences of the world war at this time. It is equally natural that foreign statesmen
and public agencies should join them in keeping this phase of the European situation [of famine and insurrections] before us. It gives a tremendous momentum to
the pacifist propaganda, and it relieves the governments and peoples of Europe of a
large part of their responsibility for the present condition of their affairs.

But the American mind should clear itself on this point. No one will deny that
the war is responsible directly for a vast wastage of life and property. But what
needs recognition and emphasis at this moment . . . is that had common sense and
self-control governed the policies of the governments and the sentiments of the
peoples of Europe their affairs would not be tottering now on the rim of chaos.

On the contrary, were there wisdom and courage in the statesmanship of Europe, were there the same selfless devotion in chancelleries and parliaments as was
exhibited on the battlefield, Europe would have been today well on the way to recovery.

The expenditures of the war and the intensification of long existing animosities and jealousies undoubtedly have complicated the problems of statecraft and of
government. Undoubtedly the temporary depletion of man power and the temporary exhaustion of body and spirit among the war worn peoples were a burden
which recovery has had to assume. Undoubtedly the wastage of wealth and diversion of productive agencies were a handicap to expeditious restoration.

But that these are chiefly responsible for the present state of Europe we do not
admit and the future judgment of history, we are confident, will deny.

It is chiefly the folly which has been persistently demonstrated by governments and people since the war that is responsible for Europe's condition today. It
is because the moment hostilities ceased and the enemy was disarmed, victors and
vanquished turned their backs on the healing and constructive principles they had
solemnly asserted from time to time when matters were going against them at the
battle front, that the European nations almost without exception have been going
down hill. There never in history has been a more perfect illustration of the ancient
sarcasm: "When the devil is sick, the devil a monk would be; when the devil is
well, the devil a monk is he."

If we wish to know why Europe is in the present state, we cannot do better
than to draw a parallel between the assertions of purpose and principle of the allies
and "associated" powers in 1916, '17, and '18, and what has actually happened
since Nov. 11, 1918.

The war was a gigantic folly and waste. No one will deny that. But it was not
so foolish nor so wasteful as the peace which has followed it. The European governments, those who come at our invitation and those who remain away, would
have us believe they are mere victims of the war. They say nothing of what the war
did for them. We might remind them that they profited as well as lost by the war.

Chicago Tribune, November 13, 1921.

Many of them were freed from age long tyranny. They got rid of kaisers and saber clattering aristocracies. They were given freedom, and their present state shows how little they have known how to profit by it. They have been given new territories and new resources, and they have shown how little they deserve their good fortune. The last three years in Europe have been given not to sane efforts to heal wounds, remove hostilities, develop cooperation for the common economic restoration which is essential to the life of each. On the contrary, they have been marked by new wars and destruction, by new animosities and rivalries, by a refusal to face facts, make necessary sacrifices and compromises for financial and economic recovery, by greedy grabbing of territory and new adventures in the very imperialism which brought about the war.

It is well for Americans and their representatives to keep this in mind. The appeal to America's disinterestedness is unfairly fortified by the assumption that Europe is the innocent victim of one egotist's or one nation's ruthless ambition. We can take due account of the disastrous effects of the Prussian effort at dominance, but that should not overshadow the stubborn errors which began over again on the very threshold of peace, and which have made the peace more destructive than the war. When the European governments and peoples are ready to make a real peace, which cannot arrive until they give over the policies and attitudes that produced the world war, America will then not fail to give generous aid. But America would be foolish to contribute to the support of present methods or give any encouragement to the spirit which now prevails in the old world.

Debts and German Reparations: Hughes Calls on Private Experts for Help, 1922

The economic conditions in Europe give us the greatest concern. They have long received the earnest consideration of the administration. It is idle to say that we are not interested in these problems, for we are deeply interested from an economic standpoint, as our credits and markets are involved, and from a humanitarian standpoint, as the heart of the American people goes out to those who are in distress. We cannot dispose of these problems by calling them European, for they are world problems and we cannot escape the injurious consequences of a failure to settle them.

They are, however, European problems in the sense that they cannot be solved without the consent of European Governments. We cannot consent for them. The key to the settlement is in their hands, not in ours.

The crux of the European situation lies in the settlement of reparations. There will be no adjustments of other needs, however pressing, until a definite and accepted basis for the discharge of reparation claims has been fixed. It is futile to attempt to erect any economic structure in Europe until the foundation is laid.

How can the United States help in this matter? We are not seeking reparations. We are, indeed, asking for the reimbursement of the costs of our army of occupation; and with good reason, for we have maintained our army in Europe at the request of the Allies and of Germany, and under an agreement that its cost with like army costs should be a first charge upon the amounts paid by Germany. Others have been paid and we have not been paid.

But we are not seeking general reparations. We are bearing our own burden and through our loans a large part of Europe's burden in addition. No demands of ours stand in the way of a proper settlement of the reparations question.

Of course we hold the obligations of European Governments and there has been much discussion abroad and here with respect to them. There has been a persistent attempt ever since the Armistice to link up the debts owing to our Government with reparations or with projects of cancellation. This attempt was resisted in a determined manner under the former administration and under the present administration. The matter is plain enough from our standpoint. The capacity of Germany to pay is not at all affected by any indebtedness of any of the Allies to us. That indebtedness does not diminish Germany's capacity, and its removal would not increase her capacity. For example, if France had been able to finance her part in the war without borrowing at all from us, that is, by taxation and internal loans, the problem of what Germany could pay would be exactly the same. Moreover, so far as the debtors to the United States are concerned, they have unsettled credit balances, and their condition and capacity to pay cannot be properly determined until the amount that can be realized on these credits for reparations has been determined. . . .

We have no desire to see Germany relieved of her responsibility for the war or of her just obligations to make reparation for the injuries due to her aggression. There is not the slightest desire that France shall lose any part of her just claim. On the other hand, we do not wish to see a prostrate Germany. There can be no economic recuperation in Europe unless Germany recuperates. There will be no permanent peace unless economic satisfactions are enjoyed. There must be hope, and industry must have promise of reward if there is to be prosperity. We should view with disfavor measures which instead of producing reparations would threaten disaster.

Some of our own people have suggested that the United States should assume the role of arbiter. There is one sufficient answer to this suggestion, and that is that we have not been asked to assume the role of arbiter. There could be no such arbitrament unless it were invited, and it would be an extraordinary and unprecedented thing for us to ask for such an invitation.

I do not think that we should endeavor to take such a burden of responsibility. We have quite enough to bear without drawing to ourselves all the ill-feeling which would result from disappointed hopes and a settlement which would be viewed as forced upon nations by this country which at the same time is demanding the payment of the debts owing to it. . . .

Why should they [statesmen] not invite men of the highest authority in finance in their respective countries—men of such prestige, experience and honor that their agreement upon the amount to be paid, and upon a financial plan for working out the payments, would be accepted throughout the world as the most authoritative expression obtainable? Governments need not bind themselves in advance to accept the recommendations, but they can at least make possible such an inquiry with their approval, and free the men who may represent their country in such a commission from any responsibility to Foreign Offices and from any duty to obey political instructions. In other words, they may invite an answer to this difficult and pressing question from men of such standing and in such circumstances of freedom as will ensure a reply prompted only by knowledge and conscience. I have no doubt that distinguished Americans would be willing to serve in such a commission.

Manuel Ugarte Identifies the United States as the "New Rome," 1923

The flexibility of North American imperialism in its external activities, and the diverse forms which it adopts according to circumstances, the racial composition and the social conditions of the peoples upon which its action is exercised, is one of the most significant phenomena of this century from the point of view of political science. Never in all history has such an irresistible or marvellously concerted force been developed as that which the United States are bringing to bear upon the peoples which are geographically or politically within its reach in the south of the Continent or on the shores of the sea. . . . At times imperious, at other times suave, in certain cases apparently disinterested, in others implacable in its greed, pondering like a chess-player who foresees every possible move, with a breadth of vision embracing many centuries, better-informed and more resolute than any, without fits of passion, without forgetfulness, without fine sensibilities, without fear, carrying out a world activity in which everything is foreseen—North American imperialism is the most perfect instrument of domination which has been known throughout the ages.

By adding to what we may call the scientific legacy of past imperialisms the initiative born of its own inspiration and surroundings, this great nation has subverted every principle in the sphere of politics just as it had already transformed them in the sphere of material progress. Even the European powers, when confronted with North American diplomacy, are like a rapier pitted against a revolver. In the order of ideas with which we are dealing, Washington has modified the whole perspective. The first conquerors, with their elementary type of mind, annexed the inhabitants in the guise of slaves. Those who came afterwards annexed territories without inhabitants. The United States . . . inaugurated the system of annexing wealth, apart from inhabitants or territories, disdaining outward shows in order to arrive at the essentials of domination without a dead-weight of areas to administrate and multitudes to govern. The interplay of internal forces in the life of a community is of small importance to them; still less the external form under which domination has to be exercised, provided that the result offers the maximum of influence, benefits and authority, and the minimum of risks, commitments or cares.

Thus there has arisen within their spheres of influence an infinite variety of forms and shades. The new imperialism, far from applying a formula or a panacea, has founded a system of special diagnosis for every case, taking into account the area of the region, its geographical situation, the density of its population, its origin, predominating racial composition, level of civilisation, customs, neighbours, whatever may favour or hinder resistance, whatever may induce assimilation or alienation by reason of affinities or differences of race, whatever has to be brought

---

From Manuel Ugarte, *The Destiny of a Continent*, Catherine A. Phillips (tr.), with an introduction by J. Fred Rippy (ed.) (New York: Knopf, 1925), pp. 139–148.

about with a view to future contingencies. The higher motives of force or healthy activity which give direction to expansionist energy, watch particularly over the racial purity of the group and reject every addition which is not identical with it. To annex peoples is to modify the composition of one's own blood, and the invader who does not desire to be diluted, but to perpetuate himself, avoids as far as possible any impairing or enfeebling of the superiority which he claims.

Imperialist policy might with no effort have doubled or tripled in recent years the official area of its territories, but it saw the danger of adding to its original community great masses of different origin. . . .

That species of action which makes itself felt in the form of financial pressure, international tutelage, and political censorship admits of every advantage with no risk. In the development of these tactics imperialist policy has given evidence of that incomparable dexterity which is admired even by its victims. In the financial sphere its tendency is to control the markets to the exclusion of all competition, to take upon itself the regulation of any production to which it attaches any value, and to lead the small nations on to contract debts which afterwards provoke conflicts, give rise to claims, and prepare the way for interference favourable to the extension of its virtual sovereignty. In the sphere of external policy it appoints itself the defender of these peoples, obliging the world to accept its intervention in treating with them, and drawing them as satellites into its orbit. In the internal order it encourages the diffusion of whatever increases its prestige, forwards the ambitions of those men who favour its influence, and opposes the spread of all influences of a different nature, blocking the way peremptorily to those who, from a superior sagacity or patriotism, try to maintain their nationality unimpaired.

It is in this last sphere of action that we can best observe the commanding ability of imperialism. Its subtle intrusion into the private affairs of each people has always in consecrated phrase invoked peace, progress, civilisation, and culture; but its motives, procedure, and results have frequently been a complete negation of these premises.

It is obvious that the point of departure and the fulcrum on which to rest the lever is the unceasing political effervescence of our peoples. But the use which has been made of this circumstance is so prodigious that it seems incredible. Profiting by the clash of factions, and by the trend of men's ambition, taking advantage of the instability of governments in these unruly and impressionable democracies, it has created within each country a higher power, sometimes hidden, sometimes apparent, which confuses, enmeshes, combines, weaves and unweaves events, bringing about solutions favourable to its interests. Here it foments tyrannies, there it supports attempts at revolution, always constituting itself the conciliator or the arbiter, and indefatigably pressing events in the direction of the two ends which it sets before it: first in the moral order, to increase anarchy, so as to bring discredit upon the country; and second, in the political order, to get rid of national representatives who are refractory to the dominant influence, till they meet with a weak or not very enlightened man who, out of inexperience or impatience, will make himself the accomplice of its domination. . . .

The greatest triumph of this system has consisted in the fact that it has come to be a cause of success within our own life. As the source of expedients in our civil struggles, as the dispenser of favours in official life, it has driven not only those who are impatient, but even the most incorruptible and upright to the utmost limit of what can be granted without abdication. In this manner it has proceeded to create subconsciously, in the countries it has "manipulated," a peculiar state of mind, which admits the collaboration in its civil struggles of forces not arising from their own surroundings, and allows an element of foreign life and interest to enter into every national act or project. . . .

When we consider the work of imperialism in America as a whole, it is impossible to refrain from a certain admiration for the magnitude of its effort and the clearness of its conceptions. Never in all history has such subtlety been seen, combined with such a capacity for sustained action. It is evident, I repeat, that from the Spanish-American point of view we have to do with a policy which we ought all to work together to check. A good number of us have been writing and speaking in this sense without intermission for long years. But if we are to stem the advance, our most urgent task is to arrive at a full knowledge of the truth, and to give up vain speech-making. Every strong people extends its ambitions as far as its arms can reach, and every weak people lasts just so long as its energy for defending itself endures. In sacrificing doctrines in order to favour its present and future greatness, the new Rome believes itself to be accomplishing a duty, since it is thus preparing that world dominion for which it considers itself to be set apart. By developing to its full volume and protecting itself against these risks, Latin America would preserve its personality.

"Trade Follows the Film," 1925

The sun, it now appears, never sets on the British Empire and the American motion picture. It is a droll companionship, and one which is beginning to evoke comment and provoke inquiry in exalted quarters in foreign parts. The world at large has become so accustomed to seeing the British Empire take this daily promenade in the sun alone that it now lifts its eyebrows and regards the scene with what the fictionists of another day used to call mixed emotions.

In the British the spectacle calls forth a touch of asperity. The French are puzzled and ask, "Is it an amour?" The Germans have begun to dig in and erect barriers. All of them are in varying degrees alarmed by the portent. They are just a teeny bit afraid of this gay, laughing, amusing hussy who parades the whole wide world with such assurance and to such applause from the diverse races and breeds of men.

When this note of apprehension began first to be heard the motion-picture makers here were rather puzzled. They wondered, when they discovered that they and their product could be considered abroad in the light of a peril or a menace. They knew that their whole intent and aim was to please everybody. It is by successful adherence to this rule that they have grown so great. At first they did not understand this viewing with alarm to which they and their output were subjected. But as the stirrings of uneasiness abroad became more manifest and more coherent

Edward G. Lowry, "Trade Follows the Film," *Saturday Evening Post,* 198 (November 7, 1925), 12–13, 151, 158.

the truth came out. It is not the quality of the pictures, it is not the movie as an amusement, that has caused the pother and commotion among the foreigners. They are not concerned with the art of the pale heroes, the calcimined comics or the lovely heroines with the mascara in their eyelashes. None of these things in the least matters. What does concern is the discovery, made abroad before it was made here, that the pictures have become a factor in international trade. They are making the United States the best-known and most widely advertised country to the very remotest habitations of man on the globe.

Our pictures are doing for us what the Prince of Wales so frankly and so capably is doing for the British. International trade is, of course, based on good will. The Prince for some years now has been going about all over the world promoting good will for his countrymen and subjects. Incidentally he has helped trade. Everybody remembers when he was last in New York he set a vogue for blue shirts with soft collars, for a style of hat that blossomed in the shop windows even before he departed, and for gray flannels. Every day what he wore was chronicled in the newspapers, and the youth who set store by styles were quick to copy him. The same thing, it is fair to suppose, happened in the colonies and in South America. The heir apparent did something to introduce and popularize English clothes, shoes, hats, pipes and what not.

Happily, or unhappily—just as you choose—we have no royal family to do that sort of thing for us. But now the word comes from abroad, from many quarters and in increasing volume, that the movie stars and their associates, and the happy and handsome environment in which they are displayed in the films are creating and stimulating a demand for American wares. We now hear that the old saying that trade follows the flag is archaic and out of joint.

"Trade follows the film" is the cry from overseas. It is the discovery of this new factor in international relationships that has caused the flutter. When the movies were simply an amusement and a relaxation and a form of entertainment for the millions, they could be laughed at by the sophisticates as examples of crude American taste, and no harm was done. But once it became clear that the films directly influenced the currents of trade—that from Spain, the Near East, Chile, the Argentine and Brazil were coming demands for American office furniture, shoes, hardware, clothing and types of California bungalows "like those we see in the movies," then the pictures became a menace and a peril to the foreign trader. His pocketbook touched, he became aroused and began to appeal to his government.

The Prince of Wales himself, as a promoter of trade and good will for his people, was among the earliest to declare and disclose the potency of our pictures as a competitor in securing foreign trade. As long ago as 1923 the Prince was saying in a speech before the British National Film League that the importance of the film industry deserved attention. There was the imperial aspect, he urged. Trade followed the film, he said, and films were a real aid both to the development of imperial trade and the work of individual firms. The film helped to bring together nations speaking different languages. It had no one language of its own, but could convey its ideas in all languages. And so on to the extent of nearly a column in the *London Morning Post,* in which the speech was reported. The same newspaper, commenting on the Prince's outgiving, said: "If the United States abolished its diplomatic and consular services, kept its ships in harbor and its tourists at home, and retired from the world's markets, its citizens, its problems, its towns and countryside, its roads, motor cars, counting houses and saloons would still be familiar in the uttermost corners of the world. . . . The film is to America what the flag was once to Britain. By its means Uncle Sam may hope some day, if he be not checked in time, to Americanize the world." . . .

Hear these other witnesses for a moment before we go on: Douglas Miller, one of the commercial attachés in Berlin, reports to Secretary Hoover: "No one has yet been able to estimate the large amount of advertising for American goods that has come through the motion pictures and the stage. The amusement world of Germany now gets its tone from across the Atlantic. American styles as seen on the film, American tunes brought over by traveling jazz bands—all cannot fail to have a marked influence on the German habit of mind. A stranger, taking an evening stroll down the chief promenade of Berlin's new rich, cannot fail to notice the American touch in the clothing of many persons, in the advertising in shop windows and in the type of entertainment offered to the public." . . .

A recent issue of *Brazilian Business,* issued by the American Chamber of Commerce for Brazil, said: "One of the representatives of an American film company in Brazil has had many proofs of the trade-producing possibilities of celluloid drama. Not so long ago he threw a sport picture on the local screens, the punch being put over by means of half a dozen high-powered racing cars. Some time later the representative of an American car told the film man that before the picture appeared his agents were selling five or six cars a month. After its appearance the office began closing orders for four or five cars a day." . . .

Here is an extract from an official report from a European country now on file at Washington:

Mr. ——————— told me that films are very effective agents for developing trade. One illustration of this, he suggested, was seen in the demand for clothes modeled on those worn by American heroes in pictures shown in this country. This demand, he said, had caused makers of clothing here to make their product more on American lines than formerly. Also our language has become affected, he added. Even such Americanisms as "Gee!" are becoming part of popular conversation, and all owing to the subtitles on the films made in America.

An American firm manufacturing sewing machines was surprised to receive a number of orders from Java and Sumatra. There were no agents of the firm out there, but inquiries disclosed that an American film showing one of the characters sewing on one of the firm's machines had brought a small flow of orders to the factory. . . .

For whatever may be said about our movies, the stubborn fact stands up that millions of all sorts of people all over the world like them and are willing to pay habitually and constantly to see them. Neither in Germany, England, France, Italy nor Scandinavia can they make pictures with such a universal appeal. I will not be put in the light of a defender or champion of the quality of the American movie; I am not a fan. But their world dominance is an incontestable fact. They are popular, they are affecting trade, they are coloring the minds and changing the desires of foreign peoples, they are the most vivid and potent projection—however distorted—of life in the United States that foreigners receive. The stay-at-homes abroad get their conception of us from our pictures. Whether that condition is or is not deplorable, it is a proved fact.

Now what is the secret of this great popularity and success? It is built on a firm economic basis. For that, the motion-picture industry can take no credit. Lady

Luck dealt our producers a hand all aces. The great domestic market afforded in the United States makes it possible to have $1,000,000 superfeatures. Here we have 40 per cent of all the motion-picture theaters in the world. The average weekly attendance at these theaters in the United States is something more than 50,000,000. This great throng pays admissions of about $500,000,000 annually. That is the solid-rock basis on which the American producer has built his world-wide dominion.

With this great supporting, pleasure-loving, money-spending public at home he can afford to experiment, to develop, to lavish expenditures on his productions. If he only just breaks even on a $1,000,000 picture at home, he is still in a comfortable position, for he can count on his export for a profit. It is this domestic market, which no foreign producer has, that gives our industry its solid base. The figures prove it. In 1913, 32,000,000 linear feet of film were exported. In 1928, 200,000,000 feet were sent abroad. On the other hand, only 425 foreign pictures were sent here in 1922, and of these only six were sold and exhibited. The number of imported films has increased in the past three years, but the proportion of imports to exports remains about the same. The foreign and the domestic fan are as one in preferring the American picture to all others.

Now what quality is inherent in the American picture that causes every sort of foreigner—English, German, French, Italian, South American, Central European and Asiatic—to prefer it to his own? What is it in the American picture that has made it a trade and political factor? There is no definite answer, but the industry offers suggestions and possible explanations. One of these, made to me, is this:

> There is no laughter in the European films. They lack gayety, light-heartedness, sprightliness. They do not portray happiness. There is not in them anywhere any sense of irresponsible children at play. These lacking qualities are supplied in almost every American film. Our pictures show people having fun. They reflect freedom, prosperity, happiness, a higher standard of living in clothing, houses, interiors, motor cars—all the material appurtenances of good living.
>
> The European intelligentzia criticize the happy endings of our stories as bad art. But to peoples recovering from the shock of war, and whose financial, economic and social problems are not yet solved, these happy pictures are beacon lights of hope. They seem to show the way to peace, prosperity and happiness. They make the spectators forget their cares and worries and anxieties. They bring relaxation and give entertainment. They are an escape from the daily routine of work. They open a fresh new world of play where there are no class restrictions or the inertia that comes of despair. That is why American pictures are popular abroad. I think, too, we know more of what can be done with the camera.

It may be that that is the true reason. We are at that particular period of our history and growth that gives us happiness in youth and strength and wealth. We are an extraordinarily fortunate and blessed people. Not all of us realize it. But the rest of the world does and is constantly reminded of it by our movies. It has awakened desires in them for some of the things we possess. That is what has made the movie a factor in trade and in our international relationships. That is why trade begins to follow the film.

And it all began as a five-cent peep show. An astonishing evolution, isn't it?

Secretary of Commerce Herbert Hoover Extols
U.S. Foreign Trade, 1926

Foreign trade has become a vital part of the whole modern economic system. The war brought into high relief the utter dependence of the life of nations upon it. The major strategy of war is to crush the enemy by depriving him of it. In peace time our exports and imports are the margins upon which our well-being depends. The export of our surplus enables us to use in full our resources and energy. The creation of a wider range of customers to each production unit gives to that unit greater stability in production and greater security to the workers.

And we may quite well view our exports from the other side of the trade balance sheet. They enable us to purchase and import those goods and raw materials which we can not produce ourselves. We could probably get along as a nation if we had to suppress the 7 to 10 per cent of our production which goes to export, but our standard of living and much of the joy of living is absolutely dependent upon certain import commodities. We could not carry on our material civilization without some of the fibers, rubber, and some metals. Without diamonds we would not be able to get satisfactorily engaged to marry. The prosperity of our people in many ways can be measured by the volume of imports. . . .

The Government can chart the channels of foreign trade and keep them open. It can assist American firms in advancing their goods. In the improvement of all the foreign services the Department of Commerce has made great progress in the past five years, and it has been developed into organizing in internal cooperation and consultation with our industries and our merchants. I can refer to the success of that service without egotism, for it has been the work of Doctor [Julius] Klein and his assistants [of the Bureau of Foreign and Domestic Commerce]. Some indication of the degree of their success is shown by the increased demand upon the services of the bureau they direct. The requests of merchants, manufacturers, and farm cooperatives for information and assistance have grown from some 15,000 inquiries per month four years ago to a total of 170,000 inquiries per month during the past year, a total of over 2,040,000 during the year.

I believe the effect of the efforts of the department [of Commerce] in establishment of standards, elimination of waste, and the provision of wider information has been to expand the possibilities of foreign trade to many concerns not hitherto able to extend into this field. One of the interesting and encouraging facts is the rapid increase in the number of small concerns participating in export business. The surprisingly large number of inquiries now being received by the department from such firms amply proves that the virtues of high quality, specialized production, good service, precise export technique, and farsighted policy are by no means monopolized by big corporations. Literally thousands of small dealers and manufacturers, whose commodities have a strong specialty appeal and meet a definite need, are now successfully cultivating overseas markets. Foreign trade is thus becoming a national asset in the fullest sense of the word. . . .

I do not wish to be understood as saying that we are going to obtain our share of these increases without effort and without competition. What I wish to get clear is that, in the large view, our exports are not based on the destruction of our competitors but on insistence that we shall participate with them in the growth of world demand. . . .

Without entering upon any partisan discussion of the protective tariff, which I, of course, support, there is one phase of the tariff which I believe experience shows has less effect upon the volume of international movement of commodities than had at one time been assumed.

As a result of the hardships suffered by many people of both combatant and neutral nations during the war, there came to all nations a deep resolution, in so far as the resources of their countries permitted, to produce as far as possible their essential commodities. The struggle to overcome post-war unemployment has added to this impulse. The result is that 52 of the 70 nations of the world, including almost every important trading nation, increased their tariffs after the war. It might seem that these widespread protective policies would tend to localize industry and thus decrease the total volume of international trade. But it certainly appears that internal economic and social currents which make for prosperity or depression in a nation have a much larger effect upon the total volume of imports than the tariffs and thus more largely affect world trade as a whole. In our case, far from our present tariff diminishing our total imports, they have increased about 35 per cent since the higher tariff came into effect. This has also been the case with other nations which have progressed in internal economy. In any event our experience surely indicates that in considering the broad future of our trade we can dismiss the fear that our increased tariff would so diminish our total imports as to destroy the ability of other nations to buy from us.

The most commonly remarked revolution in our foreign economic relations is our shift from a debtor to a creditor nation upon a gigantic scale. It is the father of much speculative discussion as to its future effect upon our merchandise trade. Alarm has been repeatedly raised that repayment of the war debts must necessitate the increase of imports of competitive goods in order to provide for these payments—to the damage of our industry and workmen. These ideas are out of perspective. Our war debt when settled upon our own views of the capacity to pay will yield about $300,000,000 per annum, although as yet the actual payments are much less than this. The private foreign loans and investments to-day require repayments in principal and interest of about $600,000,000 annually, or nearly twice the war debt. I have heard of no suggestion that interest and repayment of these private debts will bring the disaster attributed to the war debt. The question is of importance, however, as to how this $800,000,000 or $900,000,000 of annual payments may affect our merchandise movement. There is a compensating factor in American trade relations unique to our country which has a large bearing upon this question—that is, the vast dimension of our invisible exports in the form of tourist expenditure, emigrants' remittances, and other forms of American expenditure abroad. These items in 1925 amounted to about $900,000,000, or about $100,000,000 more than our incoming payments on debts of all kinds. In other words, at this stage of calculation the balance of trade should be in our favor by about $100,000,000. But beyond this we are making, and shall long continue to make, loans abroad. For the last four years these loans have averaged nearly $700,000,000 a year, and in fact the merchandise balance in our favor has been running just about this amount.

Now the summation and purpose of all these words is the conclusion that there is no disastrous shift in our imports and exports of merchandise in prospect from debt causes. . . .

By contributing to peace and economic stability, by the loan of our surplus savings abroad for productive purposes, by the spread of inventions over the world, we can contribute to the elevation of standards of living in foreign countries and the demand for all goods.

The Kellogg-Briand Pact Outlaws War, 1928

Article 1.   The high contracting parties solemnly declare in the names of their respective peoples that they condemn recourse to war for the solution of international controversies, and renounce it as an instrument of national policy in their relations with one another.

Article 2.   The high contracting parties agree that the settlement or solution of all disputes or conflicts of whatever nature or of whatever origin they may be, which may arise among them, shall never be sought except by pacific means.

Senator William E. Borah Urges Recognition of Soviet Russia, 1931

As we all know, Russia occupies about one-sixth of the earth's surface; she has a population of about 150,000,000; at the present rate of increase her population will number 300,000,000 in 35 years. Russia has a radio station 650 miles north of the Arctic Circle. Her southern boundary is upon a parallel with Richmond, Va. Her timber lands are more extensive than were the timber lands of the United States 60 years ago. Her cotton lands are more extensive than the cotton lands of the United States. Her wheat lands are equal in area to the wheat lands of the United States and Canada combined. This is the government and these are the people which our Government officially does not know exist.

I can see no real peace in Europe until the Russian problem is settled. It is my belief there can be no disarmament of any moment, particularly land disarmament, until Russia is brought into the family of nations and amicable relations and clear understanding with all other powers are established; that there can be no economic health or stability in Europe, or the world, so long as this gigantic power, stupendous and incalculable in her natural wealth and her man power, is writhing and struggling to escape her thralldom; and this will last so long as she is treated as an outlaw and denied an opportunity to enjoy the ordinary methods of credit and trade. I feel that all efforts toward peace and better understanding among the nations must be indefinitely retarded so long as one-sixth of the earth's surface, occupied by the third largest population in the world, is estranged and afraid.

The great question is: How can the problem be solved? My contention is that friendly relations between nations springing out of a tolerant practice of the usual amenities of friendly powers will heal rapidly the wounds left by the revolution, dissipate the fears—which are the basis of armaments—and harmonize the conflicting economic policies of the world.

I realize that there are serious problems connected with Russia and our relationship to Russia, but it is my feeling that these problems can better be dealt with if the ordinary relations between nations are established between Russia and all other governments. I do not feel that we can ever deal with Russia satisfactorily to ourselves or to Russia under the present program.

Mr. President [president pro tempore of the Senate], the present Government of Russia has been in existence now for 12 years. That Government is in complete control of Russia. There is no other government disputing its authority; there is no other government or organized force contending with it or assuming to contend with it for authority in Russia. . . .

It has maintained that control under most extraordinary circumstances and most adverse conditions. It has resisted invasion from without and revolution from within. I do not know of any government in Europe which has maintained its existence under more trying and difficult circumstances or under greater or more severe attacks than has the Russian Government. . . .

It has been said, and is constantly repeated, that the peasantry of Russia, constituting 85 per cent of the Russian people, are opposed to the Russian Government; that they are held in subjection and in control through sheer force; and that, if they had their way, they would overthrow the Russian Government.

I have no doubt that the peasantry of Russia are individualistic. I have no doubt that they are opposed to the communistic theory in a large measure, if not by a large majority. They evidenced that fact in 1921 when they compelled Lenin to modify his views with reference to communism. I apprehend that if they were entirely free to exercise their choice they would greatly modify, if not entirely change, the Russian form of government. Let that be conceded. But, Mr. President, as between the Russian Government as it now exists and has existed since it was organized 12 years ago and what the peasantry see in the future in case this Government is destroyed, the peasantry undoubtedly are for this Government. They feel that if the present Government is overthrown the old régime will be restored, that the peasantry will be separated from the land, that the old estates will be reestablished. . . .

When I think of Russia, therefore, and seek to determine a proper course to be pursued by this Government toward Russia, I do not think primarily of Lenin and Trotsky and Stalin, although they have been and some still are outstanding figures in that moving drama. I think of the 150,000,000 men, women, and children who are moved by the same passions and governed by the same virtues as other peoples. Thinking of them and their interests, and the United States and our interests, I seek to determine what our policy should be. These people are struggling in their own way and under the most adverse circumstances to work out their own salvation. It is for their aid and for their interests that I would act, and by which I would be governed. I can understand how one could loathe and abhor an individual leader, but I do not know how one could hate, or even be indifferent to, the welfare of a whole people. How can a whole people encompass within their wrath another people? These people are endeavoring to put behind them for all time their everlasting peonage and degradation. They are traveling through fire in devious paths and over bloody roads. But they are striving to be an independent and powerful people.

These people want freedom. They want security against old oppression. They may not see clearly, but they are reaching for better things and a better life. . . .

Mr. President, when I was discussing the recognition of Russia eight years ago a learned and able Secretary of State [Hughes] took the position that there was nothing in Russia to recognize, or about which we should be concerned. He referred to Russia as an economic vacuum. On one occasion he used language as follows:

> It is manifest to this Government that in existing circumstances there is no assurance for the development of trade, as the supplies which Russia might now be able to obtain would be wholly inadequate to meet her needs and no lasting good can result so long as the present causes of progressive impoverishment continue to operate. It is only in the productivity of Russia that there is any hope for the Russian people, and it is idle to expect resumption of trade until the economic bases of production are securely established.

Mr. President, the gravest concern of the economic world to-day, and of the capitalistic nations of the world, is how to take care of that "economic vacuum," what to do with the vast exports coming out of Russia. The greatest economic disturbance in the world to-day arises out of the productive power as it is rapidly increasing in Russia. It is dangerous to prophesy concerning 150,000,000 people when devoted and consecrated to a definite object. What seemed an impossibility has become a startling reality. Russia is no longer an economic vacuum, she is a vast economic power creating concern in every capitalistic nation on the globe.

Our exports to Russia have increased about 214 per cent over the pre-war exports. Our imports from Russia are something like 24 per cent less than before the war. For the first six months of 1930, the Soviet Government spent nearly $7 in this country for every dollar's worth of goods they sold to us.

According to the report of the United States Chamber of Commerce for January–June, 1930, the Soviet Government was the sixth best foreign customer of the United States during that period.

According to the Department of Commerce Reports, August 25, 1930, the first half of 1930 gave Russia the first place as a purchaser of our agricultural machinery.

The Commerce Reports, April 28, 1930, showed that the Soviet Union was our third largest foreign customer for American industrial machinery. . . .

There are now something over 40 American corporations doing business in Russia and helping in a substantial way the Russians to work out their industrial revolution. There are over 2,000 experts from the United States employed as technical experts and as employees of American corporations. Those corporations extend credit running over four and five years. The Russian régime now owes America something over $175,000,000—that is, American corporations and individuals. All over Russia there are important enterprises conducted and directed by American engineers and American business men.

The result of the policy now obtaining with reference to Russia is to dedicate Russia to exploitation by powerful business interests and to withhold any advantage which might accrue to the ordinary business man in dealing with Russia. For instance, the Standard Oil Co. of New York and the Vacuum Oil Co. are dealing with Russia and have been for some time. They purchased from the soviet oil industry under various contracts oil products valued at $10,000,000 yearly. When Mr. Hughes was Secretary of State he declared that Russia was an economic vacuum and that it was dangerous to make contracts or undertake to do business in Russia. After he became attorney for the Standard Oil Co. upon his retirement his client felt perfectly safe, apparently, in making contracts in Russia. . . .

Mr. President, the International General Electric Co. sold technical apparatus and supplies to Russia valued at $25,000,000 over a period of six years. The International Harvester Co. have sold farm machinery valued at $20,000,000 during the past four years. The United States Steel Corporation have purchased soviet manganese ore valued at millions of dollars during the past six years. The Bethlehem Steel Corporation have purchased soviet manganese ore valued at millions of dollars during the past six years.

The Radio Corporation of America have sold soviet organizations $1,000,000 worth of commodities. The Ford Motor Co. have received orders from the soviet organization covering tens of millions of dollars. The du Pont de Nemours Co. have large contracts with the Soviet Government. The Westinghouse Electric Co. have sold considerable apparatus to the Soviet Government. . . .

So the large business interests are carrying on business with Russia, possibly under some disadvantages, but not under controlling disadvantages, while the smaller business man is precluded practically from carrying on business under present conditions. . . .

I have listened over the radio to and read discussions on Russia much of late, and I have been interested in some of the reasons for inveighing against Russia; some of the arguments which are advanced as to why we should refuse to recognize Russia or to even trade with Russia. It is urged in the first place that Russia is governed by a cruel dictator, that only a few ruthless rulers hold control. Suppose that is true. When has Russia been governed by other than a dictator? When have other than a few ruthless rulers had control of Russia? What kind of government did Russia have before the present Government? How many people participated in the rule of Russia then? Who complained of the old dictatorship? Did we not recognize the old Russian Government? Did we not do business with the old Russian Government? Did we have societies and organizations inveighing against the old Russian Government? . . .

Further, it is contended that Russia is antireligious. There is no doubt that the leaders of Russia, or some of the most important leaders, are antireligious. But how much of religion, of real religion, was in Russia when a vile, lascivious pervert like Rasputin could dominate and direct the religious affairs, as well as the civic affairs of Russia? How much of religion, save now and then an isolated and devoted follower of the Savior, existed in Russia when the Russian court was infested and dominated by this miserable, slimy creature who was not only a disgrace and a challenge to religion, but who was a disgrace to the most ordinary rules of decency, who had sunk to the dead level of total depravity? And what religious leaders in this country protested against recognizing the old régime while these conditions prevailed? And what religious leaders in this country would now like to return to such conditions as prevailed under the old régime?

It is also claimed that she has repudiated her debts and confiscated property. She did repudiate her debts and confiscate property. She has stood ready for eight years to pay her debts. She is willing to meet the United States at any time upon a basis of equality to compensate for the damages of confiscation if the United States will consider the damages of invasion. It is claimed also that Russia does not respect her contracts and her agreements. I have here upon my desk a list of some three or four hundred firms who have been, and still are, doing business in Russia. Has anyone heard of any violation of contract with these men? These firms have extended credit, they have made heavy contracts. Is not the very fact that they continue to do business with Russia a better evidence of Russia's keeping her contracts than the testimony of escapes and convicts and criminals and heated agitators? Russia has kept her contracts with our business men, and I have been advised by a number of these business men that she has kept her contracts most carefully and meticulously.

Mr. President, the three great and, I believe, imperishable instincts of the human race are religion, family, and property—something to believe, something to love, something to possess. Let us admit that those who now govern and dominate Russia, not the people of Russia, stand against them all. We stand for them all. Let us admit that it is an irreconcilable conflict. Let us concede that those who govern Russia, not the people of Russia, would uproot and destroy them all. Let us admit that they would summon them all to the bar of public opinion and would exile them from human affairs, if they had the power. We would foster and strengthen them all. Our whole civilization is built around them. But how deep and strong is our faith? Do we fear that capitalism will fall, will cave in, if brought in contact with communism? Are we afraid of the contest? My belief is that the closer the contact, the more certainly will communism be modified and ultimately disappear. In such a contest we have not only the experience of all time behind us, but we have the support of one of the most dominant and irresistible of human passions—the desire for property. Do we believe in our institutions? Do we doubt the intelligence and character of our own people? Are we fearful lest the family as an institution, around which our whole fabric of society has been constructed, will break in pieces if brought to the test by that cruel absurdity which would make the family hearthstone the casual meeting place of social derelicts? Is our religion of that feeble sort that we dare not meet face to face those who have said in their hearts there is no God? For my part, I have no fear. . . .

But let me assume I am in error in the belief that our Government and our people are secure against communism. What are we going to do about it? The American people are neither blind nor deaf nor dumb. They read, they see, they hear, they know what is going on. They know all about the communistic creed. Our newspapers and magazines tell of the teachings and the preachings of the Russian leaders. You can not put an embargo upon news or ideas in these days. The people do their own reading and their own thinking. I am glad it is so. The restlessness and the discontent in this country springs not at all from Russian literature or Russian teachings. We stand or fall not by what Russia does, but by what we do right here in our own country. We are slow about cleaning up our cities and making property safe and human life secure. We have failed to give work to those who are hungry and who would like to work. We have been unable to cleanse our system of corruption. We have tolerated a system which compels honest and clean business men to pay tribute to crooks and criminals for the protection which their government fails to give. These are the things which cause restlessness and discontent and discouragement among our own people. It is not Russian literature which is disturbing our people or which we need fear. It is not that which is happening in Russia nor what Russia is proposing that is bringing doubt and worry to our own people. It is the conditions here in our own land. These are the things which challenge the attention and arouse the anxiety of the American people.

Capitalism should turn its eyes inwardly and take an account of its own internal affairs. Capitalism must turn its eyes inwardly and take into consideration and solve its own internal problems. If we do not solve them, God only knows what will happen. If we do solve them, communism and all antagonistic "isms" will prove impotent in their tasks. We have in this country from five to seven million men and women unemployed, seeking something to do. What has communism to do with that, and what is our solution? . . . I am not in the least disturbed about communism of itself. I am, I confess, disturbed about the unsolved problems of capitalism. And I am most equally disturbed over the fact that the time which we ought to devote to solving these questions and to bringing about conditions which would help to solve them, are devoted to attacking some other theory and agitating against some other government. The time to stop building smoke screens ought to be near at hand.

✖ *E S S A Y S*

In the first essay, Norman A. Graebner, long a professor at the University of Virginia, criticizes Americans and U.S. foreign policy in the 1920s for retreating from world leadership. A self-defined "realist," Graebner claims that Americans' embrace of both isolationism and internationalism left the United States incapable of using its great power to thwart aggression and sustain peace. In the second essay, John Braeman of the University of Nebraska, Lincoln, disputes Graebner's interpretation, arguing instead that the United States sustained adequate military power, kept the nation secure, and protected its interests abroad. Braeman wonders what more the United States should have done, given the many obstacles to a more vigorous foreign policy—not only domestic reluctance to engage in foreign ventures but also the intractability of foreign crises that would likely have arisen regardless of the U.S. posture. In the last essay, Frank Costigliola of the University of Rhode Island agrees with Braeman that, although the United States contributed to international problems, there was little that Washington could have done to stem the world's descent into chaos because neither Europeans nor Americans would have tolerated massive U.S. intervention. Rather than treating the 1920s as an interlude between disasters, Costigliola sees the decade as a time of relative peace and prosperity. One of his contributions to our understanding of the 1920s is the spotlighting of another dimension of foreign relations that Americans considered a success and that calls into question the label "isolationist"—cultural expansion in the form of the "Americanization" of Europe through Hollywood films and other cultural exports.

Oblivious to Reality:
The Extremes of American Isolationism and Internationalism

NORMAN A. GRAEBNER

During the critical months of debate and decision which followed the Versailles Conference, the United States deserted its wartime commitment to remake the world in its own image and retreated instead to the confines of its immediate interests. For this violent counterrevolution in the nation's outlook [Woodrow] Wilson, its primary victim, was in some measure responsible. The American involvement in the Great War has demonstrated again that the United States could not and would not escape any major European struggle that threatened the balance of power or ventured onto the Atlantic. That involvement demonstrated, furthermore, that the United States could not influence European politics with policies that avoided direct and sizeable commitments of American economic and military power to the affairs of the continent. On the other hand, Wilson's failure at Versailles to eliminate from international relations the traditional reliance on national interest and force made it clear that the world's leading nations had less interest in his idealism than in the remarkable capacity of the United States to wage total war. Thus sound American policy, in the future as in the past, would avoid the extreme goals of either attempting to escape all obligations abroad or defending the interests of oppressed humanity everywhere. Rather such policy would be directed at the definition and protection of a wide variety of specific historic and geographic interests in competition with nations which would pursue traditional interests of their own with whatever means came to hand.

Unfortunately Wilson's concepts and personality so dominated the American scene that they drove American policies toward the extremes against which the nation's experience had warned. In his wartime effort to transform world politics in accordance with his principles of peaceful change and self-determination, Wilson had warred with such remarkable success on the guiding traditions of national interest and balance of power that he succeeded in eliminating them almost completely from the main currents of American political thought. Only with difficulty would the nation ever again agree on the goals and assumptions which should underlie its policies abroad. At the same time Wilson's failure to restructure world politics created the foundations for a pervading postwar isolationism. The nation could measure Wilson's success by his standards alone, and by those standards he had failed. If few Americans pondered the consequences of a possible German victory, it was because the country's wartime leadership had not formulated American interventionist policy in terms of protecting the traditional balance of power. By ignoring the limited, but precise, gains that lay within the nation's capabilities, Wilson managed to transform a successful, and perhaps essential, national effort

Text by Norman A. Graebner "America's Twentieth-Century Search for World Order" in *The National War College Forum*, Winter 1970, pp. 36–39. Reprinted with the permission of the author.

into failure. For those, in short, who accepted his assumptions of an American world role, as well as for those who rejected them totally, Wilson failed to establish the bases of a sound national response to the challenges of the future.

Unable to discover any demonstrable gain from their wartime efforts, millions of Americans emerged from the European involvement determined to prevent its repetition. Europe, the isolationists agreed, had demonstrated again the hopelessness of her politics, the bitterness of her diplomacy. Her troubles, whatever their nature, were not the concern of the United States and thus no legitimate cause for American involvement. Never again, warned the *New Republic,* should the American people become embroiled in a system of European alliances. "We ask only to live our own life in our own way," declared California's Senator, Hiram Johnson, in March, 1922, "in friendship and sympathy with all, in alliance with none." Much of the postwar cynicism toward the war focused on Britain, the nation allegedly responsible for undermining American neutrality. The powerful newspaper publisher, William Randolph Hearst, reminded his readers that Britain had often been the target of American patriotism. American isolationism, as it demolished the country's wartime pro-Allied sentiment, gained the support of those Irish and German minorities which had resented Wilson's decision to underwrite the British cause.

Isolationism took additional strength from the rebirth of nationalism with its conviction of national superiority and its faith in the country's ability to protect itself from attack. Proud of their nation's wealth and achievements, which they attributed to hard work and the relative perfection of their institutions, the spokesmen of "America first" expressed their reluctance to share again their prosperity and good fortune with peoples less deserving. What compounded this determination to preserve their favored position was the widespread notion that Europe, still engaged in petty quarrels and turmoil, was untrustworthy and corrupt. Why take responsibility for the security of the greedy and ungrateful people of Europe? For a rich and supposedly self-sufficient country what mattered was less the welfare of Europe than the quality and direction of American life. Sinclair Lewis captured the spirit of postwar America when his George Babbitt informed the Zenith Real Estate Board that the real American was "the ideal type to which the entire world must tend if there's to be a decent, well-balanced, go-ahead future for this little old planet!" A country in pursuit of nineteenth-century values could find easy intellectual and emotional rewards in contemplating the superiority of its civilization and the security afforded by both its industrial power and the existence of surrounding oceans.

Isolationism, in rejecting the importance of events abroad, could scarcely form the basis for policies that would sustain the essentials of the Versailles settlement. But internationalism, as embodied in the Wilsonian tradition, was as oblivious to political reality as was isolationism. Both were strangers to the conservative tradition of American diplomacy [the matching of ends and means and an understanding of power]. Both denied that the United States need be concerned with any specific political or military configuration in Europe or Asia. Whereas isolationism limited the nation's interests to the Western Hemisphere, internationalism assumed that American interests were universal—wherever mankind was oppressed or threatened by aggression. Isolationists preached that events outside the hemisphere were inconsequential; internationalists insisted not only that they mattered but also that the United States, in its role as a world leader, could not renounce its obligation to engage in policies of cooperation. In practice, however, the internationalists would control the world environment, not with the traditional devices of diplomacy or force, but by confronting aggressors with a combination of international law, signed agreements, and world opinion. Every program fostered by American internationalists throughout the twenties—membership in the League of Nations or the World Court, the resort to arbitration and conciliation, collective security, naval disarmament, or the outlawry of war—denied the need of any precise definition of either the ends or the means of national policy. What mattered in world politics was the limitation of change to peaceful means. Thus in the hands of the internationalists the concepts of peace and peaceful change became the bulwark of the *status quo,* for change limited to general agreement could alter the international order only on questions of little or no consequence.

Isolationism and internationalism had more in common than the conflicting rhetoric of the twenties would suggest. Americans—even the isolationists—had no desire to escape the world of commerce and investment. Businessmen, isolationists and internationalists alike, demanded that their government sustain their privileged economic position everywhere on the globe. And because a stable world environment would best serve the needs of Americans, many citizens insisted that the country accept the moral responsibility for the peace, provided that the responsibility entail no specific obligation for the defense of any foreign country or region. These limited, and generally conflicting, objectives established the bounds of popular national policy. The successive Republican administrations of the twenties, in their perennial support of American business interests abroad, satisfied the demands of nationalists who believed in "America First." The repeated involvements of the United States in the cause of peace delighted those internationalists who believed that the nation should serve, not merely the needs of its own citizens, but the needs of humanity everywhere. United States policies varied from narrow nationalism to limited internationalism, all designed to serve the specific interests of trade and investment as well as the general interest in peace.

In the roseate years of the late twenties the great democracies—the creators of Versailles—shared an illusion that the decade of peace reflected the triumph of their moral and intellectual leadership. So often had officials and editors of the English-speaking countries insisted that power had been eliminated from international relations that they began to believe it. Because war would bring disaster, they could scarcely believe that any nation would resort to war in the face of reason or an outraged world opinion. Unfortunately the peace of the twenties was no demonstration of either a general acceptance of the Versailles settlement (symbolic of the *status quo*) or even the universal rejection of force. What sustained the assumption that all wars had been fought and all issues resolved was the predominance of Western power which permitted the spokesmen of the democracies to manage the game of international politics so effortlessly that they were quite unconscious of the role which power had played in their success. Thus peace rested primarily on the weakness of those nations whose governments had already made clear their dissatisfaction with the Versailles Treaty. Any collapse of the Western monopoly of power would witness the almost immediate return of force to international life.

So precarious was the world's peace structure that an armed clash outside Mukden, Manchuria, in September 1931, could threaten it with disaster. For it quickly became apparent that Japanese officials in Manchuria were determined to exploit the crisis occasioned by the alleged destruction of tracks along the South Manchurian Railway by altering the regions political status. In part, the ensuing Japanese assault on Manchuria was defensive, for Chinese nationalism and anti-foreignism endangered Japan's special privileges in Manchuria, which included the right to station troops along the South Manchurian Railway. So successful had been Japanese investments and industrial leadership in developing the Manchurian economy that by 1931 almost thirty million people, overwhelmingly Chinese, lived in the three Eastern Japanese–occupied provinces. The large Chinese migration into Manchuria evolved into a massive effort to drive out the Japanese. For Japan, however, Manchuria had become a region of vital necessity. The Japanese islands had only limited arable land, no mineral resources, and a population increasing at the rate of a million each year. Korea and Formosa had failed to satisfy the Japanese requirements for land and resources. But Manchuria, with its abundant natural riches, promised at last to supply the food and raw materials necessary for Japan's economic existence. Rather than withdraw from the mainland under Chinese pressure, the Japanese preferred to convert Manchuria into a Japanese dependency.

What troubled official Washington in the Japanese conquest of Manchuria were not this nation's vital interests. Nelson T. Johnson, the American minister in China, observed as early as March 1931, that a possible Japanese possession of Manchuria need not embroil the United States in war. With this judgment the Hoover administration agreed. But if the United States had little interest in the disposition of Manchuria's resources, it had a profound interest in the Far Eastern peace structure embodied in the Nine Power Pact and the Kellogg-Briand Pact. In signing these documents Japan had joined other nations in agreeing to limit its ambitions to what it might achieve through peaceful means alone. In a cabinet meeting on October 9, 1931, Secretary of State Henry L. Stimson warned the President against getting into a humiliating position in case Japan refused to honor her own signatures on the paper treaties. But Stimson recorded in his diary the essential character of United States policy in the Far East:

> The question of the "scraps of paper" is a pretty crucial one. We have nothing but "scraps of paper." This fight has come on in the worst part of the world for peace treaties. The peace treaties of modern Europe made out by the Western nations of the world no more fit the three great races of Russia, Japan, and China, who are meeting in Manchuria, than, as I put it to the Cabinet, a stovepipe hat would fit an African savage. Nevertheless they are parties to these treaties and the whole world looks on to see whether the treaties are good for anything or not, and if we lie down and treat them like scraps of paper nothing will happen, and in the future the peace movement will receive a blow that it will not recover from for a long time.

Thus Hoover and Stimson refused from the outset to accept any new arrangement in the Far East which resulted from the Japanese resort to force. At stake in Manchuria was the credibility of the whole system of collective security based on the force of world opinion as well as on the influence and prestige of the League of Nations. Johnson warned the administration in a letter of November, 1931, "The fate of Manchuria is of secondary importance compared with the fate of the League." Throughout the crisis, however, the United States attached its policy to the Kellogg Pact and the Nine Power Treaty, not to the League of Nations, and thereby limited its response to reminding the Japanese of their obligation to uphold the provisions of the two treaties. But what if such moral pressure failed to control Japan? The democracies would then face the ultimate choice of witnessing the collapse of the Versailles settlement or sustaining the world they favored with a resort to superior force.

Powerful, Secure, and Involved:
What More Should the United States Have Done?

JOHN BRAEMAN

Since Pearl Harbor, American foreign policy during the Harding-Coolidge-Hoover years has received a largely negative appraisal from historians. In the aftermath of World War II, the adherents of Wilsonian internationalism dominated the writing of American diplomatic history. The crux of their indictment of the Republican administrations of the twenties was that this country's refusal to participate in collective-security arrangements for upholding the peace was responsible for the breakdown of international order in the years that followed. If the United States had joined the League of Nations, or at the minimum cooperated with the peace-loving nations, Britain, France, and, until the illusions of the wartime alliance collapsed, the Soviet Union, against would-be or actual aggressors, the Second World War could have been avoided. Although this view has continued to have its champions, the hardening of Cold War tensions—and the accompanying disillusionment with the efficacy of the United Nations—spurred a major counterattack upon what [the scholar-diplomat] George F. Kennan has termed the "legalistic-moralistic approach to international problems." With the emergence of the so-called realist school came a different—though no more positive—evaluation of the role played by the United States during the age of normalcy.

The dominant intellectual figure in the post–World War II realist movement was University of Chicago political scientist Hans J. Morgenthau. Morgenthau's starting point was a complex of assumptions about the behavior of nations and, more fundamentally, about human nature, which were in striking contrast to the nineteenth-century liberal faith in the existence of an inherent harmony of interests that underlay the Wilsonian vision of collective security.

"The primordial social fact," he postulated in *Scientific Man vs. Power Politics,* "is conflict, actual or potential. . . ." Or as he put the matter more bluntly still in his now-classic *Politics Among Nations,* "the struggle for power is universal in time and space and is an undeniable fact of experience." Within most nations, he acknowledged, there existed a community of interests and values that tended to reduce the intensity of conflict. But the international arena was different. "The his-

From "Power and Diplomacy: The 1920s Reappraised," *The Review of Politics,* 44 (July 1982). Reprinted with the permission of the editor of *The Review of Politics,* Notre Dame, Indiana 46556. Pp. 342–355, 358–366, 369.

tory of the nations active in international politics shows them continuously preparing for, actively involved in, or recovering from organized violence in the form of war." In such an anarchical world, force remained the ultimate arbiter. Thus, whatever the long-term goals of a nation, "Power is always the immediate aim." And given this country's geopolitical situation, he defined as the American national interest "to preserve the unique position of the United States as a predominant power without rival" in the Western Hemisphere and "the maintenance of the balance of power" in Europe and Asia.

The trouble was, runs the realist indictment, few Americans in the age of normalcy grasped those truths. [The political scientist] Robert E. Osgood lamented that the post–World War I revulsion against Wilsonian utopianism had fostered a no less dangerous set of illusions: a millennialist hope for "peace by incantation," "a blind aversion to war and the instruments of war as absolute evils abstracted from the conflicts of power and national self-interest which lead to war," and, thus, a refusal to accept "the uses of force and the threat of force as indispensable instruments of national policy." [The historian] Robert H. Ferrell placed much of the responsibility for this situation upon the organized peace movement, which was in the 1920's at the zenith of its influence; more still upon an "immature" and "appallingly naive" public. But the elite was as much at fault as the man in the street. [The historian] Betty Glad penned a damning portrait of Secretary of State Charles Evans Hughes, the chief architect of American foreign policies in the 1920's, belaboring his "evasion of the role of power in international politics." [The scholar-diplomat] Herbert Feis blamed the ineffectiveness of American "dollar diplomacy" during the Harding-Coolidge-Hoover administrations upon "the hazy, lazy faith"—shared by the public, business leaders, and government policymakers—that trade, loans, and investments would automatically promote world peace without backing "the dollar with our diplomacy and, if essential, by arms." "Far from coordinating force and diplomacy," [the historian] J. Chalmers Vinson summed up, "the American statesmen and people set the two up as incompatible." The dominant ethos was rather that peace could, and would, be maintained, "by persuasion and example rather than force."

Military historians deplored the lack of machinery for civilian-military consultation in formulating foreign policies, the resulting widening gap between goals and capabilities, and the flight from "reality" in the services' own strategic planning. The United States's refusal to assume a share of the burdens of economic reconstruction, its aloofness from foreign political involvements, and what [the historian] Edward W. Bennett has stigmatized as its "indifference to, or even revulsion from, the principle of the balance of power" were blamed for undercutting the Versailles settlement in Europe. Even heavier fire was directed against this country's Far Eastern policies. A minority of the postwar realists questioned the wisdom of American hostility to Japanese ambitions. . . . But the preponderant view among the post–Pearl Habor generation of historians was that the fault lay in this country's failure to maintain sufficient military strength to meet the Japanese challenge. Popular hostility to naval spending, congressional economizing, and the naval limitations agreements undercut the deterrent power of the navy. And when Japan in Manchuria launched the first major direct attack upon the world order, the United States responded with no more than words.

There is no question that the political and intellectual atmosphere in the United States during the twenties opposed large-scale military and naval expenditures. But a nation's military capability cannot be measured by any absolute standard. Even in the narrow sense of armed forces-in-being, what matters is their relative size and efficiency vis-à-vis those of potential enemies. And in the larger sense, a nation's "military potential" depends upon a number of factors: its geographical vulnerability; the kind of war to be fought; and most importantly, as World War I had demonstrated, its technological and economic capacity. Perhaps the most salient feature of the Republican era was this country's overwhelming superiority in the economic sphere. In the late 1920's, the United States produced an output of manufactures larger than that of the other six major powers—Great Britain, Germany, France, the Soviet Union, Italy, and Japan—combined. The extent to which a nation translates its available resources into mobilized strength is a political decision. That decision, as [the scholar] Klaus Knorr has pointed out, reflects a "cost-gain calculation" of the advantages and disadvantages anticipated from the maintenance of military strength at different levels. "The desirability of ready combat strength depends, first, on the importance of the prevailing goals for the achievement of which military power is a means and, secondly, on the prevailing assumptions about the amount of military resources necessary to achieve these goals." If such variables are taken into account, substantial evidence exists for a reappraisal of the conventional wisdom about American policies during the Harding-Coolidge-Hoover years.

In the first place, the extent of pacifist influence upon American policy during the 1920's should not be exaggerated. Although the organized peace groups mobilized impressive shows of public support on such issues as naval disarmament and outlawing war, the military services could, and did, rally the backing of veterans' organizations, patriotic societies, and special interest groups. Viewing the world as a competitive arena in which each nation pursued its self-interest, the increasingly influential professional careermen in the State Department had no illusions that moral force did, or could, regulate international relations. And their thinly veiled hostility toward those peace enthusiasts who hoped for a radical transformation of the international order was shared by their politically responsible superiors. Nor was there any lack of consultation with the services on matters involving national security; even Hoover, the most pacifist-minded of the chief executives of the era, took pains to do so. The crux of the services' grievance was that their advice was not always followed when purely military considerations conflicted with larger policy goals. Most important, the Republican administrations remained committed to the basic principles of military and naval policy that had been formulated during the preceding two decades: "a strong Navy and battle fleet, second to none, as a first line of defense capable of dominating the western Atlantic and the eastern Pacific"; "a small Regular Army devoted primarily to the preservation and increase of military knowledge, the training of civilian components, and the preparation of plans for future wars"; and "a strong civilian industrial economy capable of conversion to war production in an emergency."

Post–World War I army planning was based upon an "insurance" concept of preparedness resting upon a small professional force capable of emergency defense, while providing the nucleus for the mobilization and training of a mass "citizen" army. Funding limitations did keep the army's enlisted strength in the latter twenties and early thirties to 118,750 men—a far cry from the 280,000 maximum envisaged by the National Defense Act of 1920 and below the 165,000 figure estimated by the General Staff as required for carrying out the army's responsibilities. But even in the midst of the depression, appropriations were more than double the pre–World War I level. And while during the years of prosperity recruiters found difficulty in attracting and retaining high-caliber enlistees, the impact of hard times allowed the army to upgrade its standards. The officer corps remained at approximately twice the prewar level, thus providing the cadre that was able to lead the vastly expanded army of World War II. This pool of potential leaders was reinforced by the continuation of Citizens' Military Training Camps and the expansion of the Reserve Officers' Training Corps in the colleges. . . .

Nor was there any threat on the European side warranting a larger American buildup. The military establishments of all the major European powers—except for the Soviet Union—suffered during the twenties from popular suspicion, stringent budgetary limitations, and a loss of self-confidence that bordered upon defeatism. From 1919 until its abrogation in 1932, British military policy was shaped by the "Ten Year Rule" that the Empire would not become involved in a major war during the next decade. Given this assumption, the strength of pacifist sentiment, and the country's near-desperate need for financial retrenchment, the British army was cut back to a level barely capable of handling its routine peacetime responsibilities. Although France as of 1933 had 450,000 officers and men under arms—with plans to mobilize within two weeks sufficient reserves to raise the total to a million—Paris' anxiety over Germany's superior population and industry, and its potential military superiority, bred a state-of-siege mentality. The Treaty of Versailles had bound the German army by a network of restrictions down to the equipping and arming of units. Despite the growing evasion of these limitations after mid-decade, the *Reichswehr* in the years before Hitler did not envisage the possibility of mobilizing more than a maximum 300,000-man force in the event of war and doubted their ability to equip even that many. The Soviet Union was probably the most formidable military power on the continent. In the late twenties, its regular army numbered 562,000 men, and starting in 1931 a large-scale program of expansion and reequipment was launched under a leadership committed to an offensive strategy based on mobility, maneuver, and mechanization. But the USSR's technological and industrial backwardness, its continuing internal problems, and its leaders' obsession with the threat of "capitalist encirclement" made the avoidance of war the keystone of Soviet policy.

Similarly exaggerated are the charges, made then and since, that American policymakers were blind to the revolutionary potentialities of air power. The Army Reorganization Act of 4 June 1920 provided formal recognition of the Air Service as a combatant arm, while the Air Force Act of 1926 provided for a new assistant secretary of war to deal with aviation matters, added an air section to each of the General Staff divisions, and authorized a five-year program of expansion in personnel and equipment. Insufficient money prevented achievement of the authorized 1800-plane force. But appropriations did rise sharply, with the result that by 1933 the Air Corps boasted 1619 planes, of which over 1100 were regarded as first-line craft. While balking at granting the air arm full autonomy as an independent service, the General Staff in its contingency war planning from 1923 on envisaged establishment of a consolidated air strike force under a single commander directly responsible to Army General Headquarters. By the early 1930's, army officialdom was gradually moving toward acceptance of this organizational setup for peacetime. Although the most vocal champion of the supremacy of air power, Brigadier General "Billy" Mitchell, was forced out of the service, his ideas about the airplane as primarily an offensive weapon whose function was to destroy the enemy's industrial base had come to permeate Air Corps' thinking. If the air power enthusiasts failed to achieve all their goals, the reasons were not simply old-guard obstruction and congressional parsimony. The major obstacles were the limits of the existing technology, substantive differences over strategy and tactics, and the absence of any immediate threat. "Despite popular legend," World War II Air Corps chief H. H. "Hap" Arnold acknowledged, "we could not have had any real air power much sooner than we got it."

The same factors retarded air power development abroad. In structure and theory, Britain was in advance of the United States. An independent Royal Air Force and Air Ministry had been established in World War I, and the air staff's doctrine of the deterrent role of strategic bombing directed against an enemy's industrial base was accepted as official government policy. Yet financial stringency prevented full implementation of the 52-squadron Home Defense Force program authorized in 1923. Thus, in 1930, the RAF had 770 front-line aircraft compared to France's 1300, Italy's 1100, and the United States's 900. By the spring of 1932, Britain's first-line air strength had slipped to fifth place, behind France, the Soviet Union, the United States, and Italy. Although the world leader in number of aircraft, the French air force remained until 1933 a branch of the army, which envisaged for air power no more than a limited auxiliary role in support of ground forces. Notwithstanding an impressive short-run showing in the 1920's, Italy lacked the resource base to remain a major air power. Despite the increasing momentum of German secret air rearmament after 1926, the *Reichswehr* had by the spring of 1932 only 228 aircraft—with a goal of 274 for the following year—of which 192 were converted civilian planes. Probably no government of the time was more air conscious than the Soviet, which rapidly expanded the size of the Red Air Force to roughly 2200 planes by the end of 1932. But the Soviets continued to lag behind the Western powers in technology and training. And given the domination of the air force by the Red Army, major emphasis was placed upon providing tactical support for ground campaigns.

Most important, aviation technology still left the oceans as safe defenses. Even the head of the Air Service acknowledged in the fall of 1925 that the United States was not in any immediate danger of air attack. Eight years later, a board headed by Major General Hugh A. Drum, the army's deputy chief of staff—pointing to the difficulties attending the flight of the highly rated Italian bombers to the Chicago World Fair—reaffirmed that this country need not fear attack by land-based planes. As late as 1935, Britain's top heavy bomber, the Hawker "Hendon," could carry 1,500 pounds of bombs for no more than a thousand miles round trip. Despite the enthusiasm of *Reichswehr* air planners from the early twenties for a long-range strategic bomber, the first steps toward implementing its development were not undertaken until late 1933, and Germany would remain without an operational heavy bomber at the beginning of World War II. Rather than lagging behind, the United States was in the forefront of long-range bomber development. The landmark breakthrough came in 1931 with the appearance of the Martin B-10, an all-metal monoplane that was the first of the modern bombers. In July 1933 the Air Corps Materiel Division began work on the plans for what would become the B-17 Flying Fortress. And what would prove decisive in the long run, the growth of civilian aviation and the aircraft industry—stimulated by the Air Mail Act of 1925, the Air Commerce Act of 1926, Charles Lindbergh's 1927 transatlantic flight, and the Air Corps's policy of encouraging private manufacturers to build up their design and engineering staffs through placing orders for experimental prototypes— gave the United States an industrial and technological infrastructure in the aeronautics field that no rival could match.

The most controversial issue involved the state of the navy. Whereas the army command acquiesced without major protest in civilian decisions about funding and manpower levels, most naval officers made no secret of their unhappiness. Their anger was first roused by the restrictions placed upon capital ships by the Five Power Treaty of the Washington Conference of 1921–1922: a ten-year ban upon new construction; maximum tonnage quotas; and a 5:5:3 ratio for the United States, Britain, and Japan. Their anxieties about the navy's deterrent capability were heightened by the agreement reached at the London Conference of 1930. That pact continued the holiday in capital ship construction until 1936 and reduced further the tonnage allowances; fixed tonnage quotas for heavy cruisers, light cruisers, destroyers, and submarines; and provided for a 10:10:7 ratio in the first three categories with parity in submarines. Domestic political realities were an important factor in the American government's championship of naval limitation. The struggle over the naval appropriations bill of 1921 demonstrated the resistance to implementing the Wilson administration's planned building program. But the key point, and what made the agreements possible, was that similar forces were at work in this country's two major sea rivals. In Britain, the mood of pacificism and the demand for financial retrenchment joined to exert tremendous pressure for major cutbacks in naval expenditures. Similarly, the balance of political forces in Japan up until the Great Depression worked in favor of a policy of accommodation with the United States: the backlash against military interventionism spurred by the unsuccessful Siberian invasion; the growing influence of the political parties; the acceptance by the civilian decision-making elite that Japan's interests in China were primarily economic; the financial burdens of a naval arms race; Japan's dependence on this country for vital raw materials; and the sense of security given the existing favorable power balance in the western Pacific.

Qualitatively, the agreements were, as [the historian] William R. Braisted has suggested, "a service to the Navy" by requiring the service to make the most efficient use of its available resources. The reduced capital ship tonnage required by the Five Power Treaty allowed the navy to eliminate overaged and obsoletely equipped vessels. With new construction halted, the navy concentrated upon an extensive program of modernization of its remaining battleships. The installation of new engines and the conversion from coal to oil increased speed and range; new electrical power systems were developed; improvements in the elevating mechanism of turreted guns resulted in increased firing power; and the substitution of plastics and aluminum for heavier materials allowed improved armor while keeping within the tonnage limitations. Naval researchers made important advances in radio communications, in radar, and in radio-controlled torpedoes. And despite their reputed obsession with the battleship, naval planners in the 1920's were committed to the construction and maintenance of a balanced fleet. Most of the eighteen of the 8-inch gunned cruisers the navy had in 1941 were authorized between 1922 and 1933. As for light cruisers, the ten *Omaha* class commissioned between 1923 and 1925 were regarded by foreign sources as the finest of their type in the world. The large number of destroyers—349—built or building at the end of World War I precluded the construction of additional vessels until the existing ships reached overage classification twelve years after their commissioning. But starting in 1931–1932, Congress authorized the beginning of an extensive replacement program that would be continued by the Roosevelt administration. When the test came after Pearl Harbor, the American treaty-era ships proved "effective if not optimal military units, capable of performing their fundamentally defensive strategic function."

Similarly impressive were the innovations in strategy. In line with its assigned mission of capturing Japanese bases in Micronesia in support of the fleet in the western Pacific, the Marine Corps during the twenties worked out the basic principles of amphibious assault doctrine, gave increased emphasis in its training, course work, and maneuvers to landing operations, and worked out techniques of air support for such landings. The navy's most glaring weakness was in submarines. But the Naval Research Laboratory worked to improve submarine technology; submarine officers engaged in an ongoing study of design and tactics; and the London Conference's restrictions on tonnage forced a rethinking of submarine design to maximize cruising distance and torpedo power. Probably most significant for the future was the progress achieved in naval aviation. Despite its ponderousness and slowness, the airplane carrier *Langley*—a converted old fleet collier commissioned in 1922—proved invaluable for training and experimental purposes. When commissioned in 1927, the *Saratoga* and *Lexington* were the finest carriers afloat. Although the undersized *Ranger* proved a misstep, the navy in 1933 gained congressional authorization for the *Yorktown* and *Enterprise*. At the same time, a group of younger aviation-oriented officers pioneered in formulating the concept of the carrier as an independent striking force. By contrast, British carrier development lagged because of the Royal Air Force's preoccupation with long-range, land-based strategic bombers. And though more active than the British in this area, the Japanese continued to view the carrier as an auxiliary in support of the main battle fleet. This country's fleet aircraft, Rear Admiral Ernest J. King, chief of the Bureau of Aeronautics, reported in 1934, "have reached a degree of efficiency not equaled by any other power." . . .

The most important single factor shaping, and delimiting, United States foreign policymaking in the Republican era was this country's overwhelming sense of security. While favoring the expansion of overseas trade and investment, American officials were not willing to incur excessive costs and risk in their pursuit. Washington was most activist in backing American business abroad when such action coincided with its larger strategic and political goals: the World War I–inspired desire for American control over petroleum reserves, cables, and banking facilities in Latin America; defense of the traditional Open Door policy in China; and access to the oil of the Middle East and Dutch East Indies because of the feared depletion of American reserves. Where such political and strategic objectives were not at stake, State Department support for private interests was limited to routine calls for equal opportunities for American firms. Exports and overseas investments represented no more than a minor factor in the total national economy. The country remained self-sufficient in most mineral resources; by the latter 1920's even the anxieties over oil supplies had largely faded. The third world, as we now call it, remained under colonial rule; most of the underdeveloped countries that were independent, far from resisting, welcomed American investment from a wish to play this country off against more immediately threatening powers, to tap new sources of revenue, or to promote economic growth.

American strategic planning for Latin America up to the late thirties envisaged United States interests almost exclusively in terms of the Caribbean region as this country's "soft underbelly." Although plans were drawn up for intervention in each of the South American countries, these were more conceptual and intellectual exercises than operational realities. Even with regard to the Caribbean area, the absence of any meaningful danger from Europe after World War I led American policymakers to inaugurate a shift away from military intervention in favor of other methods of promoting order and stability. When temporary intervention was required to safeguard American lives and property, the forces at the disposal of the navy's Special Squadron were sufficient for the purpose. Only in Nicaragua was there significant resistance—and the *Sandinistas* were more a political embarrassment than a military threat. Nor was there—except for Mexico—any effective challenge to American primacy south of the border from the larger Latin American countries. Developments during and after World War I had strengthened the bonds of Latin American economic dependency upon this country. Notwithstanding the strain of anti-Americanism among Latin American intellectuals, most local elites welcomed the Yankee dollar. Apart from Argentina, the South American republics deferred to American leadership in political matters. The 1920's did witness major frictions with Mexico, partly because of the threat to American property rights from Mexican revolutionary nationalism, partly because of the Mexican government's anticlerical campaign. But, despite rumors to the contrary, American officials never seriously contemplated using force. And a judicious mixture of pragmatic official and unofficial diplomacy with economic pressure brought a resolution of the differences on terms satisfactory to Washington.

Despite the popular distrust of Old World entanglements, the Republican administrations of the age of normalcy were not indifferent to, nor aloof from, European problems. On the contrary, the establishment of a peaceful and prosperous Europe ranked high upon their list of priorities. American negotiators disregarded congressional guidelines to scale down substantially the Allied war debts. Convinced of the adverse political and economic effects of excessive reparations, Washington simultaneously labored to work out a "realistic" solution based upon Germany's capacity to pay. After the failure of his efforts to forestall the French occupation of the Ruhr, Secretary of State Charles Evans Hughes took the lead in arranging for the Dawes Plan settlement of the deadlock. The Federal Reserve—encouraged and supported by the Treasury—cooperated with the European central banks to achieve currency stabilization. Although the United States took no formal part in the security arrangements reached at Locarno, American officials exerted behind-the-scenes pressure in favor of the accord by warning that continued American loans depended upon the return of political stability. In contrast with the later ridicule of the naiveté of outlawing war, the Kellogg-Briand treaty was hailed by contemporaries as the harbinger of a larger role by the United States in world affairs, while influential elements in this country saw in the pact an opening wedge for American cooperation with collective action against aggressors.

The question is not the fact of United States involvement in European affairs, but its extent. The promotion of European recovery did take a secondary place in the calculations of American officialdom to what was regarded as more important priorities, such as tariff protection for the home market and reducing the burden on American taxpayers. Nor did support for European political stability extend to a willingness to make binding diplomatic or military commitments. Yet, even leaving aside the domestic political constraints upon American decision-makers, what more *should* the United States have done? American political and business leaders remained confident—and here Herbert Hoover was simply the most articulate spokesman of a widely shared optimism—that the United States could prosper economically, regardless of what happened in Europe. Diplomatic and military commitments meant in the context of the time support for France against Germany. Although regarding a strong France as indispensable for a European balance of power, Washington did not accept Paris' definition of what constituted French security. American officials were convinced that the French hard line on reparations, their refusal to meet Germany's legitimate grievances, and their efforts to keep Germany down were self-defeating by undermining the possibility of a prosperous, satisfied, republican Germany. Thus, they worried that any commitments on this country's part would strengthen French intransigence. Nor were they alone in this view. Their British counterparts were no more willing to underwrite the *status quo*.

If from the vantage point of the Second World War, the failure to back up France appears misguided, was that the wisest course in the 1920's? Despite the Treaty of Versailles, Germany remained potentially the most powerful nation in Europe. Nothing short of the massing of overwhelming military force could have kept Germany in a permanently inferior status. The disastrous results of Hitler's rise to power showed the validity of the American view that future European peace depended upon the success of the Weimar Republic. More immediately relevant, American policies appeared to have been successful. The influx of American loans that followed adoption of the Dawes Plan, and the achievement of currency stabilization, led to a spurt of economic growth and a new mood of optimism in Europe. The resulting prosperity contributed to muting the social conflicts that had wracked the domestic politics of the European nations in the first half of the decade. American leaders shared the contemporary optimism about the Locarno settlement as the dawn of a new era of cooperation and peace. With the benefit of hindsight, historians have emphasized the fragility of the "spirit of Locarno." While the historian can only speculate about what might have been, there is no difficulty in imagining a better Europe in the 1930's were it not for the devastating impact of the Great Depression. In the context of the time, the pact did establish, as [the scholar] William J. Newman has persuasively argued, "a viable and stable balance . . . which held considerable promise of diplomatic and international stability in Europe."

When this structure began to crumble under the impact of the Great Depression, the Hoover administration was not blind to the dangers. In the face of the German financial crisis in the spring of 1931, the President moved boldly to forestall the threatened collapse of the Central European banking and financial structure with his moratorium, while simultaneously working behind the scenes to promote a new debt-reparations settlement. By 1932, he had become sufficiently alarmed at the deadlock at the Geneva Disarmament Conference to take new initiatives that went far toward meeting the French demand for security guarantees. Reversing its long-standing position, Washington endorsed a system of international supervision and control as part of any new arms limitation agreement. Although Hoover continued to balk at making commitments in advance—even if no more than a formal consultative pact—American officials repeatedly assured the Western Europeans that this country would not interfere with collective action against aggressors. That Hoover's efforts to unravel the debt-reparations tangle proved a failure was due as much to the intransigence of the European powers as to domestic political impediments. The administration's decision not to go further in meeting French security anxieties reflected in part popular and congressional hostility to involvement in European power rivalries, partly the chief executive's own fear that such involvement might entangle the United States in responsibilities and dangers, such as in Eastern Europe, not commensurate with its interests.

Limited interest similarly shaped United States policy in the Far East. Although firms with a large economic stake in China, such as Standard Oil, were not without political muscle, this country's trade with and investment in China were relatively minor—and substantially below trade with and investment in Japan. Nor did American bankers, despite State Department urgings, show any enthusiasm for loans to China. American interests in China were primarily ideological, or, to put the matter more bluntly, sentimental. Captivated by the image of this country as the protector and friend of China, a vocal body of American opinion spearheaded by the missionary lobby indulged in fanciful visions of the United States as the mentor to China's evolution into a modern liberal democracy. Responsible government officials had a more realistic grasp of the rampant confusion and chaos in China, and were painfully aware of this country's limited ability to shape events in the Celestial Empire to its liking. Taking as axiomatic their duty to protect the lives, property, and rights of American citizens abroad, American diplomats kept up a drumfire of protests when those were threatened. Wishing to maintain a show of the flag, the State Department overruled the army's wish to withdraw the tiny force stationed in China. But the major thrust of American policy toward China during the twenties was toward accommodation with Chinese nationalism. The Hoover administration even accepted in principle, and entered into negotiations for, the gradual relinquishment of the keystone of the so-called unequal treaty system, the right of extraterritoriality.

Those historians who fault American policymakers for failing to take a firmer stand against Japan fail to ask what was the alternative to the attempt at a *modus vivendi* inaugurated by Secretary of State Charles Evans Hughes. China was a weak reed; Russia in the aftermath of the war was in temporary eclipse as a Far

Eastern power; and Britain, painfully aware of its vulnerability in Asia, was anxious to avoid provoking the Japanese. American efforts first under Taft and then under Wilson to resist Japanese ambitions in China had antagonized the Japanese without any substantive gain for the United States. Most importantly, Hughes did not think the Open Door a sufficiently vital interest for the United States to be worth fighting for. Even if he had, the public and their representatives in Congress were not willing to make the military and naval expenditures required to deter Japan if she determined to close the door. Given this situation, Hughes achieved at the Washington Conference a diplomatic triumph that gained for the United States the abrogation of the long-suspect Anglo-Japanese Alliance, Japan's formal withdrawal of Group V of the Twenty-One Demands, and its pledge to respect the Open Door and China's independence and territorial integrity. And until 1931, Tokyo remained committed to the "Washington system" of peaceful economic expansion in China and cooperation with the Anglo-American powers.

The United States was not without blame for the breakdown of Japanese adherence to the "Washington system." The Japanese exclusion provision of the 1924 immigration act contributed to undercutting the pro-Western moderates, as did this country's unilateral support for Chinese nationalism. But more important were forces beyond Washington's control: the continued strength of traditional attitudes and values antagonistic to the new "cooperative diplomacy"; the shifting balance of power on the Asiatic mainland with the rise of Chinese nationalism and the reemergence of Russia as a Far Eastern power; and Japan's worsening economic difficulties. Would a stronger United States navy have deterred the invasion of Manchuria? The militants who precipitated the crisis were not moved by a feeling of strength but rather by a sense of weakness: by anxieties about Japan's isolation in the world; by fear that the London naval agreement of 1930 jeopardized Japanese supremacy in the western Pacific; and by alarm over Chiang Kai-shek's growing pressure on the Japanese position in Manchuria. When a broad cross section of Japanese opinion forced the government in Tokyo to sanction the actions taken by the soldiers in the field, what could the United States do? As [the historian] Christopher Thorne has brilliantly shown, given the Japanese domestic political situation and Japan's preponderant military power in the area, "there was little that the United States, Britain and France, singly or even together, could do to make the Japanese surrender over Manchuria . . . without accepting a high risk of extensive costs." . . .

The basic flaw in the realist indictment of American foreign and military policies during the so-called age of normalcy is a case of confusing the 1920's with the 1930's. The years after 1933 did witness an extraordinary rapid shift in the world balance of power. That shift was due partly to the accelerating pace of technological innovation, but more to the differing willingness by the major powers to allocate resources to arms. If the United States was ill-prepared to meet the resulting challenges, the fault lay with the men in charge when those changes took place. In the context of 1921–1933, however, American policies were neither naive nor unwise. Perhaps at no time in its history—before or since—has the United States been more secure. Nor did his Republican successors have Wilson's messianic zeal to create a new global order. "The foreign policy of small nations is often determined for them," the British scholar A. E. Campbell has pointed out, "but in a nation complex, powerful, and unusually secure the assessment of the national interest can only rest on a general conception of the world situation. . . . Politically conscious men will have such a conception at the back of their minds, if not always at the forefront, and against that conception they will test the importance or unimportance for their nation of specific world events, and so the need for government action." Thus, what must be kept in mind about the years after World War I is that "the United States possessed a unique combination of great power and an isolated position."

U.S. Cultural Expansion in an Era of Systemic Upheaval

FRANK COSTIGLIOLA

The United States emerged from the Great War as the world's leading nation. With its economic superiority, cultural vigor, and demonstrated military potential, America enjoyed influence in virtually every European corner, in the Old World's chancelleries, countinghouses, and even coffeehouses. This influence gave the United States important, but not unlimited, power in Europe. . . .

In the quarter-century following the Great Crash, many historians wrote the 1920s off as a decade of amusing antics, precarious prosperity, and isolationist diplomacy. One example of such an approach is Frederick Lewis Allen's *Only Yesterday,* published in the midst of the Depression, which poked fun at a silly decade of flat-chested flappers, narrow-minded businessmen, and tight-fisted diplomats. All this, Allen suggested, especially when mixed with bathtub gin, had to end in a crash. Though his focus was broad, Allen denigrated the achievements of the 1920s.

However historians evaluate the years 1919–33, they must come to grips with the period's central force: political, economic, and cultural upheaval. That systemic instability has often blinded historians to the real accomplishments of the era. Much of the recent historical literature performs a valuable corrective by considering the decade on its own terms, as a period of relative peace and prosperity. These works remind us that most Americans and Europeans of the 1920s believed they could avoid the catastrophes of war and depression. To disparage the 1920s as a period of "false" prosperity and peace because those happy conditions did not endure is to distort history. Certainly the economic and political collapse in the Great Depression evidenced a terrible failure. Yet it is impossible to show how the disaster could have been avoided. By 1929 it was probably beyond the power of the United States to save the international order short of massive intervention—something neither Americans nor Europeans would have tolerated. Moreover, the dissolution of post–World War II prosperity should make us more humble and sympathetic in our criticism of those who were unable to preserve post–World War I prosperity.

And yet we cannot forget how short the post–World War I economic expansion was, lasting only from 1924 to 1929. In Europe the pinch began in 1928. Basic economic conditions change from era to era, but certainly this prosperity was fleeting when compared to the pre–World War I or the post–World War II years. Similarly, the relative international political stability achieved in 1924–25 collapsed by 1931–32, as compared to much longer eras of relative political constancy in Europe before 1914 and after 1948. Finally, there was cultural turbulence in Europe and America during the 1919–33 period. This change was sometimes more subtle than that in the political and economic realms and did not fall neatly within specific dates, but it affected how people—leaders and lesser folk—worked, played, created, thought, and spoke.

Thus, in the areas of politics, economics, and culture the period 1919–33 exhibited dramatic upheaval. Although change is endemic to all historical eras, 1919–33 was a particularly unstable period in American-European affairs.

In the political realm, instability emerged from the Versailles, St. Germain, and Trianon treaties which made up the 1919 peace settlement. The key point was that these treaties *were* an international issue, an object of debate and struggle that ended only with the outbreak of war in 1939. The treaties imposed a settlement that the defeated nations—Germany, Austria, and Hungary—did not accept and that three of the four main victors—the United States, Great Britain, and Italy—soon saw as at least partially unwise and unsatisfactory. In opposition to the defeated nations, which wanted to overthrow the treaties, France and its eastern allies—Poland, Czechoslovakia, and Rumania—sought to preserve the 1919 settlement.

American pressures and sympathies, both official and unofficial, lay toward moderate treaty revision. Most Americans opposed a total overthrow of Versailles. They did not want to see Germany free of all fetters, nor did they appreciate any change, political, economic or social, that was drastic and destabilizing. Yet the peace treaties were too harsh, many Americans believed, and hampered integration of the defeated powers, particularly Germany, into a stable, prosperous, and peaceful Europe. Although the United States refused to form political alliances with Europeans after 1919, it consistently favored slow, moderate peace treaty revision that would ease the burdens on Germany. In the reparations conferences of 1924 and 1929, the unofficial American representatives who dominated the proceedings substantially transformed reparations from a club with which to beat Germany to a contractual debt owed by Germany. In 1924, at American and British insistence, France reluctantly relinquished its right under Versailles to march into Germany in case of reparations default. Americans encouraged Europeans to accept Germany into the Locarno Pacts and the League of Nations. In 1931, President Herbert Hoover and Secretary of State Henry L. Stimson went so far as to urge the French to pressure their Polish ally to revise the Polish corridor in Germany's favor.

Americans strongly favored European disarmament. Hence in the 1920s they sympathized with a largely disarmed Germany and suspected highly armed France. But when in 1932 the Germans pressed for the right to rearm, in violation of Versailles, America backed French opposition.

This American solution of peaceful change, of moderate Versailles revision, fit with the Progressive reform tradition such policymakers as Herbert Hoover and Charles E. Hughes carried with them into the postwar years. Like the Progressives of the previous decade, makers of American foreign policy in the 1920s sought stability and order through slow reform that would give repressed groups (workers in the 1910s, Germans in the 1920s) a stake in the improved, fairer system.

American leaders opposed sudden overthrow of the peace treaties just as they opposed socialist revolution at home or anywhere else. Taken in its widest context, the policy of peaceful change was part of America's effort throughout the twentieth century to combat revolutionary upheaval with moderate reform. Pacifying and rebuilding Germany was integral to containing the Bolshevik revolution. Bolshevik Russia presented both a symbolic and a substantive threat to the peaceful change alternative. Most American leaders viewed the Soviet Union as revolution incarnate, despite Moscow's caution and conservatism. If Germany's political and economic structure collapsed, its people, Americans feared, might in desperation forge a Russian alliance to overthrow both Versailles and capitalism. Their very opposition to revolution led Hoover, Hughes, and other American leaders to combat the French policy of rigidly enforcing Versailles, which would only build up pressures for change until they exploded in revolutionary upheaval.

This emphasis on stability meant, however, that when presented with the stark choice of rigid order or drastic change, Americans generally chose the former. For example, when confronted in 1932 with Germany's more insistent revisionary demands, Washington officials tilted from Berlin to Paris. This conservative bias in the peaceful change policy paralleled Americans' reaction to European domestic upheavals. Here again Americans preferred the middle road of democratic capitalism. Yet when faced with the options of revolutionary socialism or fascist order, Americans consistently picked the latter. The United States maintained cordial relations with Benito Mussolini, funding Italy's war debt on favorable terms, allowing private bankers to make large loans, and cooperating closely in 1931 on disarmament and political issues. Similarly, United States representatives welcomed a right-wing takeover in Bulgaria in 1923. In contrast to the good relations with Fascist Italy, the United States refused to recognize Soviet Russia, forbade long-term loans, and awaited the Communists' fall. Until Adolf Hitler came to power in January 1933, the United States government feared the Nazis as a revolutionary force, finding parallels between Hitler and Lenin rather than between Hitler and Mussolini. Nevertheless, despite this readiness to swing to the right, Americans preferred the middle solution of orderly moderation, as the Progressives defined their position, whether in Europe's domestic or foreign policy matters.

Confronted with disorder in the European and world economies, the United States responded with a solution parallel to the political answer of peaceful change. Orderly growth in the international capitalist economy, Americans believed, would reduce political tensions and the threat of revolution while expanding markets and investment opportunities for United States business. Although the United States carefully measured its political entanglements in Europe, its economic involvement was broad and deep. In the 1920s, moreover, economics and business enjoyed enormous popular prestige in both America and Europe. For reasons of conviction and of expedience, the United States government approached basically political questions such as reparations from an economic or business perspective. This economic emphasis was particularly suited to American policy's decentralized implementation and to its goal of a prosperous Europe. By 1923–24, government officials, central bankers, and top private businessmen forged a loose alliance. Although tactical differences often separated these leaders, they usually cooperated enough to present Europeans with a united front on war debt, loan, and other issues.

Before the crash, Americans pressed the Europeans to adopt the international gold standard, reduce government expenditures, and fund war debts and reparations. This financial program, the Yankees believed, would lay the foundation for Europe's recovery and reestablish an orderly flow of goods and capital. Responding to American and internal pressures, most European governments adopted the gold standard in the 1920s. This move boosted both international business and the power of America's huge gold reserve, but also burdened the world economy with a rigid monetary system that probably depressed prices. Similar consequences followed from American efforts to impose order upon the chaos of war debts and reparations. Under U.S. prodding, by 1929 the Allies and Germany settled these political debts on a fixed, reduced basis. This helped stabilize the world credit system, but the rigid debt settlements, like the rigid gold standard, proved brittle in the Depression.

Unfortunately America's formulas for orderly change proved unable in the early 1920s to cope with the accelerated pace of German revisionism or the decelerated pace of the world economy. Indeed United States policy may have contributed somewhat to the debacles by reviving Germany and rigidifying the financial structure.

These political and economic relations can only be understood in their cultural context. The term *culture* is here comprehensively defined to include high culture such as literature, painting, and formal music; popular entertainment forms such as jazz, dancing, film, and sports; mundane matters such as household appliances, foods, and gadgets; more abstract concerns such as religion, philosophy, and language; attitudes toward work, play, money, and war; and finally technological innovations that had sociological implications, such as increased emphasis on machines, statistics, and mass assembly-line production.

Europeans interpreted virtually every manifestation of American culture, whether it was music, films, or automobiles, as the product of a society dominated by technology and the machine. America's technological superiority, moreover, made other aspects of its culture more attractive to Europeans. And it was this technological influence that persisted in Europe after the fad for Americans faded in the Great Depression. In virtually every cultural aspect, there was significant interchange between America and Europe during the 1919–33 period, with most, but not all, of the influence flowing eastward.

To war-weary Europe, struggling to cope with the problems of modern mass society, the United States, emerging from the war rich and buoyant, seemed to have the answers. Since the machine civilization was most advanced and apparently most successful in the United States, many European artists, businessmen, and politicians alike looked westward for models. To help Europe deal with the turbulence of modernization, America offered its own institutions and values, or what contemporaries termed *Americanism*.

Americanism meant a pragmatic, optimistic outlook on life; a peaceful, rational compromise of political differences; an efficient, modern way of organizing work that emphasized machines and mass assembly production; rising standards of living with declining class antagonisms; scientific use of statistics and other information; and the predominance of mass society (this meant democratic politics, widespread consumption, and popular entertainment). Many Europeans welcomed Americanism; others railed against it or were ambivalent, but nearly all believed it was in Europe's future.

In 1630, Governor John Winthrop predicted that America would become a model for the world—"a Citty Upon a Hill" with "the eies of all people" upon it. Three hundred years later Paul Claudel, ambassador from France and himself a man of letters, told Americans: "Your movies and talkies have soaked the French mind in American life, methods, and manners. American gasoline and American ideas have circulated throughout France, bringing a new vision of power and a new tempo of life. The place in French life and culture formerly held by Spain and Italy, in the nineteenth century by England, now belongs to America. More and more we are following America." Hans Joachim, a German writer, recalled the powerful influence in the 1920s of the United States as a land and as a symbol: "America was a good idea; it was the land of the future. It was at home in its age . . . we loved it. Long enough had . . . technology appeared only in the forms of tank, mine, shell-gas. . . . In America, it [technology] was at the service of human life. Our interest in elevators, radio towers, and jazz was . . . expressive of the wish to beat the sword into a plowshare. It was against cavalry but for horsepower. . . . It was an attitude that wanted to convert the flame thrower into a vacuum cleaner. . . . Our belief in America demonstrated where we stood." Europeans in the 1920s were entranced by the image of that city upon the hill.

America's cultural influence was both a product of and a contributor to the United States' economic, political, and (in 1917–19) military power in Europe. In 1917–18 the American economy's size and technological superiority made a psychological as well as military impact on Europe. Exhausted Europeans watched as the Americans quickly raised, equipped, and transported across the Atlantic a two-million-man army. Allies and Germans alike marveled at the Yankees' modern, efficient modes of transportation and organization.

The U.S. Committee on Public Information directed propaganda campaigns at war-weary Europeans eager for new, better answers. Other agencies, such as Herbert Hoover's American Relief Administration, made promotion of America and its way of life an integral part of their operation. Hoover made sure that relief recipients understood their food was coming from a beneficent America. When labor-management strife threatened to stop coal production in central Europe, Hoover's men introduced more liberal labor practices coupled with emphasis on increased labor productivity. President Woodrow Wilson was an enormously effective propagandist, even though—like his chief rival, Vladimir Lenin—he excited European expectations which he could not fulfill.

Indeed, the propaganda war between the United States' liberal capitalism and Russia's revolutionary socialism contained not only antagonistic but complementary aspects that prepared the ground for Europe's Americanization in the 1920s. Wilson and Lenin had both told the European masses that the old imperialist regimes with their balance-of-power politics had produced the war and had to be replaced. Both proclaimed a new era of popular sovereignty, mass society, economic growth, and technological improvement. By the early 1920s, most Europeans were disillusioned with both Wilson's and Lenin's millennial visions. Yet

America's enormous economic power and apparent success as a society ensured that many Europeans looking for social solutions, including some of those who had been inspired by Lenin, would turn to the United States for models. Even the Russian Bolsheviks, despite continued hostility toward capitalism, tried to adopt many of America's technological wonders. The United States government ceased propaganda efforts in 1919, but in the ensuing decade private Americans advertised their ideas, institutions, and products in Europe.

Yankee merchandise, films, aviators, artists, entertainers, and above all dollars flooded the Old World, bringing Europeans direct evidence of the United States' position as the leader of Western civilization. Economic and cultural factors intertwined in various ways. In the early twenties, many European currencies depreciated rapidly, in part because of the United States' debt, tariff, and loan policies. This made living in Europe cheap for those with dollars. Alienated by the ascendant business civilization at home, many American artists fled to Europe, seeking high culture and low prices. Some had already acquired a taste for Europe while in the American army. These artists then discovered that many European writers, painters, and architects looked to America's machine- and business-dominated civilization for esthetic themes and inspiration. To the Americans' surprise, many Europeans took such creations as jazz and skyscrapers seriously. Many expatriate artists found in Europe the basis for an American art of which they could be proud. Some of these expatriates, such as Harold Loeb and Matthew Josephson, wrote enthusiastically of Europe's Americanization. Others were more ambivalent about America's cultural influence. But as Malcolm Cowley, chronicler of the generation, explained, consciously or unconsciously they became purveyors in Europe of American products, life-styles, and ideas.

Hollywood films, a world box-office hit, had a more widespread impact. Europeans picked up the mannerisms they saw in Charlie Chaplin or Clara Bow movies and bought the American goods they ogled in the films. Yankee tourists enjoyed less popularity than Hollywood films, but the annual pilgrimage of hundreds of thousands boosted Europe's balance of payments while their demands created an American economy in Paris and other cities. Sometimes the link between culture and economics was a simple exchange, as when Secretary of the Treasury Andrew Mellon and other wealthy Americans made multimillion-dollar purchases of Russian painting masterpieces, sold by the Soviets to pay for desperately needed machinery imports. Both sides ignored their political antagonism to forge one of the economic/cultural bonds that characterized American relations with Europe in the 1920s.

Two elements lay at the source of these cultural interactions: the United States' economic power, which captured European markets and imaginations while financing a flood of tourists and expatriate artists and giving Americans the money to buy what they wanted; and the process of Americanization. Contemporaries used *Americanization* to refer to both the United States' cultural penetration of Europe and the overlapping process of Europe's indigenous modernization. That America became a metaphor and a symbol for modernization testified to the nation's leading position in Western civilization.

In subtle yet important ways, this cultural influence and prestige enhanced the ability of the United States to conduct its political and economic policies in Europe with minimal cost and entanglement. This was especially important after 1919, when the United States government, under both Democratic and Republican administrations, shifted away from direct, official involvement in European politics. The new diplomacy was unofficial rather than official, economic rather than political, limited rather than open-ended, cautious rather than crusading. The respect that many Europeans held for American ideas and methods made such diplomacy easier to implement. At the 1924 Dawes reparations conference, for example, the unofficial American representatives conducted a successful publicity campaign in Europe that presented their plan as a pragmatic and businesslike—that is, an American—solution. Recognizing the importance of prestige (or what they termed moral power), American leaders tried to limit their intervention to instances where it would be successful, thereby enhancing their reputation for effectiveness.

Although Europeans looked to the United States for dollars and for answers, they often resented America and defied its wishes. France, for example, consistently ignored American pleas and pressure for land disarmament and maintained its large army in readiness against Germany. Yet Paris officials never succeeded in obtaining what they most needed for security against Germany, a commitment from Washington. Comprehensive or lasting solutions were not possible without American approval and assistance; French security remained at an impasse.

Just as America's prestige flowered with its impressive performance in World War I and in the 1920s, so did its cultural influence, economic power, and political leverage wilt with the Depression and the dissolution of its economy. European artists became disillusioned with their Americanist dream of permanent prosperity and progress and, with the flow of checks and tourists drying up, most American artists went home. The Depression also revealed flaws in the American reconstruction of the world economy. The United States had stabilized trade and financial relations in ways that both protected American interests and enabled Europe to recover, and Americans confidently believed that the beneficent change of economic growth would make the system work. The gold standard, the political debt settlements, the private loans, and the high U.S. tariff were burdens Europe probably could have borne had prosperity continued. But in hard times the economic structure proved too rigid and too tilted toward American interests. It collapsed.

The economic collapse also crippled the policy of peaceful change. The Depression hit Germany hard, aggravated by Berlin's pursuit of a deflationary policy in the hope of convincing America and the Allies that reparation payments had become impossible. With surging strength, radical parties on the German right and left loudly demanded immediate and wholesale Versailles revision. The right-centrist government of Heinrich Brüning pointed to these pressures and demanded more rapid revision than the French would grant or the Americans thought proper. In late 1931, Hoover and Stimson hoped to satisfy German ambitions with revision of the Polish corridor, but the effort met determined Polish and French resistance. When Brüning was replaced in June 1932 with governments further to the right, the United States moved closer to the French position of Versailles enforcement. In the storm of depression, the American middle road of peaceful change proved impassable.

The Depression exposed the fatal flaws in the American-dominated political, economic, and cultural order. The system depended on continued international prosperity—a precarious prosperity that by the late 1920s required a continuous flow of Wall Street loans. Most American banking and government officials shied away from regulating this vital capital movement, relying instead on the collective wisdom of individual investors. The international economic structure was also weakened by American insistence on rebuilding with policies that stacked most burdens on the eastern shore of the North Atlantic and most benefits on its own.

American policymakers like Hoover, Hughes, Stimson, and [General Electric Company chairman Owen D.] Young had a sophisticated understanding of the uses and limits of national power. They understood that an American answer did *not* exist for every foreign problem, and that although the United States was the most powerful nation in the world, it was not all-powerful and could easily dissipate its strength through fruitless and unnecessary foreign entanglements. Excessive foreign intervention would generate further resentment overseas and division at home. The informal division of policy implementation among governmental officials, semiprivate central bankers, and private businessmen, moreover, provided checks and balance. Yet ironically, this division of power and restraint in its use made impossible the wholesale U.S. intervention in Europe that might have prevented world depression and world war.

The rise of Nazi Germany and Soviet Russia during this turbulent period of a revolutionary century made mock of American attempts to implement policies of peaceful, moderate political reform and orderly, capitalist economic growth. By 1933, only the cultural leg of the triad was left standing at all, and here too both the Nazis and Soviets demonstrated that technological modernization was easily separated from the rest of the Americanization process. America could not control the chaos unloosed in 1914 after all. . . .

After 1917 American culture penetrated Europe in various ways. The American Expeditionary Force prepared the way for post-war cultural exchange by introducing Europeans to jazz and doughboys to the charm of the Old World. The doughboys' machines, their efficiency, energy, and innovativeness, impressed Europeans. Exhausted by the war, disillusioned with their own societies, many Europeans wondered whether they should not adopt the methods of these highly successful Americans. After the war, many former soldiers returned to the Old World as artists, tourists, or businessmen, each in his own way spreading U.S. culture. Along with Herbert Hoover's American Relief Administration, smaller private aid teams initiated Progressive reforms. Hollywood films stimulated demand for America's products while exposing Europeans to its speech, its manners (and mannerisms), and its values. Fads swept Europe as boxers and dance troupes pioneered this cultural and economic frontier.

Yankee popular culture excited many European artists, particularly avant-garde Germans of the *neue Sachlichkeit,* or new objective school, who sought modern cultural models to replace discredited imperial ones. Although many of these artists, like other Europeans, feared domination by the machine, they welcomed Americanism as a way to increase the Old World's economic productivity while resolving its social and ideological conflicts.

America's mass culture seemed democratic and progressive, the wave of the future. Many German leftist artists saw little contradiction in paying simultaneous allegiance to Bolshevism and Americanism. Both creeds preached popular sovereignty, mass culture, and technological development. In the heyday of U.S. influence, such German artists as Bertolt Brecht decided that Americanism, not bolshevism, offered the surer and more comfortable road to progress.

The United States was not only Europe's competitor, creditor, and occasional political mediator, but also the leader of Western civilization; and what happened in America was of intense, often personal interest to many Europeans. They watched closely, and reacted with near-hysterical joy, to [the aviator] Charles Lindbergh's solo flight across the Atlantic and, only a few months later passionately repudiated the Massachusetts trial and execution of Nicola Sacco and Bartolomeo Vanzetti.

America's influence in Europe had great impact also on its own artistic development. American painters, writers, composers, and other artists made pilgrimages to Europe, looking for freedom and esthetic inspiration. There they found many artists fascinated with the technologically dominated culture they had scorned. Moreover, significant numbers of expatriate artists ended up financing their adventures by working for compatriot businessmen and tourists. In the Old World, then, many Yankee artists found both esthetic validation and financial support for developing an indigenous American art.

Just as America's power led Europeans to heed American culture, so too did such prestige or moral power enhance the effectiveness of the United States' unofficial economic diplomacy. Washington officials realized that America's reputation for success and efficiency, coupled with its lack of interest in most European political rivalries, gave the nation a subtle but important moral authority in the Old World.

The State Department valued this asset because it yielded influence abroad with minimal cost or responsibility. Department officials tried to maximize America's moral power by making sure their foreign policy initiatives would succeed. In 1927, the department countered European resentment of U.S. power by using Charles Lindbergh as a goodwill ambassador. Like the AEF [American Expeditionary Force] a decade earlier, Lindbergh riveted Europeans' attention on Yankee boldness and technology, and thus quickened the pace of Americanization. . . .

Tourists constituted the largest and economically most important American group in Europe. The number of United States visitors jumped from roughly 15,000 in 1912 to 251,000 in 1929. In the latter year, American citizens in Europe spent close to $323 million and immigrants visiting home expended an additional $87 million. By the end of the 1920s, foreign travel became possible for middle-class Americans.

Visits to Paris nightclubs and the Louvre seemed a painless answer to America's balance-of-payments dilemma. Tourists' dollars helped Europe pay its debts and the United States maintain its tariff. Herbert Hoover's Commerce Department noted happily that worldwide American tourist expenditures of $770 million in 1927 more than matched $714 million in war and private debt receipts. In addition to the financial dividend, tourism had a beneficial "political effect," American officials told the Germans, "leading to a normal resumption of relations" between the two nations.

The flood of travelers generated resentment as well as dollars. Always the tourists' favorite, France in 1926 attracted foreigners who picked up bargains as the franc fell. Americans commonly asked waiters and shopkeepers "How much is that in real money?" A few even papered their train compartments or luggage with franc notes. Such insensitivity aggravated tensions over the war debt, and in July Paris erupted in several antiforeign, and especially anti-American demonstrations. Both French and American officials tried to calm emotions. Calvin Coolidge balanced a rebuke of "bumptious" tourists with a warning that badly treated Americans would stay home. But probably the majority of visitors had pleasant tours that never made newspaper headlines—in any case, France remained the number one American tourist attraction in Europe.

In 1929, the combined expenditure of American tourists and residents in France totaled over $137 million, creating an American economy in Paris. In the French capital one could be born in the American hospital, attend one of several American schools and churches, belong to the American Legion, the YMCA, the Cornell, Harvard, or American Women's Club; read one of three Parisian-American newspapers, in a favorite café or at the American Library; sip whiskey in the many American bars, drink milk delivered by American milkmen, eat sweet corn and ice cream produced by local Americans; go to hockey games, boxing matches, and other imported sport events; receive care from American dentists and doctors and be buried by an American undertaker. With fewer United States tourists or permanent residents, Berlin still supported an American church, student association, newspaper and, intermittently, chapters of the American Medical Association, Daughters of the American Revolution, and the Harvard Club. . . .

During the Great War, Hollywood invaded European and other world markets. YMCA representatives entertained Allied troops with American films, and the "movie habit" caught on among civilians and soldiers. In the 1920s, American films were an international box-office hit. Assured of the domestic market, which netted 60 percent of total world film revenue, Hollywood produced extravaganzas with which Europeans could not compete. By 1925, United States films made up 95 percent of the total shown in Britain, 60 percent of the total in Germany, 70 percent in France, 65 percent in Italy, and 95 percent in Australia and New Zealand. In Germany, the number of cinemas increased by 35 percent from 1920 to 1929, while the production dropped from 646 films to 175 films. Americans owned three-fourths of the most fashionable movie theatres in France. Hollywood's profits depended on foreign screenings, since domestic revenues covered only production costs, and frequently not even that.

"Trade follows the film," Americans and Europeans agreed. Greek appliance wholesalers and Brazilian furniture dealers found that their customers demanded goods like those pictured in the American movies. Although direct correlation between films and trade was hard to prove, Congress, parsimonious in most matters, established a Motion Picture Section in the Bureau of Foreign and Domestic Commerce in 1926. Bureau chief Julius Klein and his officials attested that United States films "stimulat[ed] the desire to own and use such garments, furnishing, utensils, and scientific innovations as are depicted on the screen." Will H. Hays, Hollywood czar, boasted of the power of these "silent salesmen of American goods."

American films not only sold United States goods, but, many Europeans feared, threatened independent national identity. "America has colonized us through the cinema," one Frenchman complained. Another French critic testified to the secularization of John Winthrop's city upon the hill: "Formerly US preachers . . . deluged the world with pious brochures; their more cheerful offspring, who pursue the same ends, inundate it with blonde movie stars; whether as missionaries loaded with bibles or producers well supplied with films, the Americans are equally devoted to spreading the American way of life." Charles Pomaret, a member of the Chamber of Deputies, remarked that Europeans had become "galley-slaves" to American finance and culture—appropriately, an image taken from the Hollywood hit *Ben-Hur.* British groups worried that the many Hollywood films shown throughout the empire led to "American domination in the development of national character or characteristics." After a concerned speech by the Prince of Wales, the London *Morning Post* warned: "The film is to America what the flag was once to Britain. By its means Uncle Sam may hope some day, if he be not checked in time, to Americanize the world."

After 1925, Britain, Germany, and France tried to check the trend. Governments enacted measures to limit the number of imported Hollywood films and encourage domestic production. This policy diminished but did not eliminate Hollywood's dominance in Europe. Required by law to produce domestic films if they wanted to import the popular American ones, German and other European producers responded with "quota quickies," often subgrade efforts produced only to meet the letter of the law. American filmmakers circumvented the restrictions by investing in Europe, especially Germany. They imported European directors and performers and remained preeminent in world film exports. The State and Commerce departments vigorously supported Hollywood's diplomacy. In the late twenties film exporters faced a new danger, with talkies. How could they screen English-language movies in polyglot Europe? Hollywood responded with multi-language production. In collaboration with a Berlin company, Paramount filmed *The Blue Angel* in English and German versions. In France, Paramount worked on an assembly-line basis: sixty-six features in twelve languages for the first year. Dubbed sound tracks helped, and by 1931 United States films had regained all but 10 percent of their 1927 market in England and Germany.

Hollywood films were a hit in Europe because they projected modern culture in a vivid and attractive light. Film embodied the era's emphasis on mechanical, simultaneous, and concentrated production. The message was mass entertainment. As Adolf Behne, a German avant-gardist, recognized, "Film is . . . democratic. . . . This ha[s] been recognized by the German masses, which flock to see Charlie Chaplin films." As the industry's global leaders, Hollywood producers had budgets large enough to pay for the casts of thousands and other spectacular effects calculated to please those masses. Finally, the films portrayed an image of life in fabulous America, the giant of the contemporary world and the pioneer of Europe's own future.

From Switzerland to the Soviet Union, Europeans acknowledged America's cultural leadership. "Mrs. Lenin," Anna Louise Strong reported from Moscow, "wants . . . American ideas on education through doing; manuals about . . . various things." Jean-Paul Sartre reflected, "Skyscrapers . . . were the architecture of the future, just as the cinema was the art and jazz the music of the future." André Siegfried, a French sociologist, concluded that America had replaced Europe as "the driving force of the world." . . .

What happened in America affected the whole world. The United States had become John Winthrop's city upon the hill, though not for the religious reasons that he had expected, and Europeans could not avert their gaze. Whether they welcomed the prospect or dreaded it, most Europeans believed that American civilization portrayed the future course of their own societies. The United States was the metropolis, the hub of the modern cultural system, and Europe now figured as a satellite.

✖ *FURTHER READING*

Selig Adler, *The Isolationist Impulse* (1957)

Derek H. Aldcroft, *From Versailles to Wall Street, 1919–1929* (1977)

Harriet Hyman Alonso, *The Women's Peace Union and the Outlawry of War, 1921–1942* (1989)

Leroy Ashby, *The Spearless Leader: Senator Borah and the Progressive Movement in the 1920s* (1972)

John Braeman, "American Foreign Policy in the Age of Normalcy: Three Historiographical Traditions," *Amerikastudian/American Studies,* 26 (1981), 125–158

Joseph Brandes, *Herbert Hoover and Economic Diplomacy* (1962)

Thomas Buckley, *The United States and the Washington Conference, 1921–1922* (1970)

———— and Edwin B. Strong, *American Foreign and National Security Policies, 1914–1945* (1987)

Kathleen Burk, "The Lineaments of Foreign Policy: The United States and a 'New World Order,' 1919–39," *Journal of American Studies,* 26 (1992), 377–391

Bruce J. Calder, *The Impact of Intervention* (1984) (Dominican Republic)

Warren I. Cohen, *Empire Without Tears* (1987)

Frank Costigliola, "The United States and the Reconstruction of Germany in the 1920s," *Business History Review,* 50 (1976), 477–502

Charles DeBenedetti, *Origins of the Modern American Peace Movement, 1915–1929* (1978)

Roger Dingman, *Power in the Pacific: The Origins of Naval Arms Limitations, 1914–1922* (1976)

Justus D. Doenecke, *When the Wicked Rise: American Opinion-Makers and the Manchurian Crisis of 1931–1933* (1984)

L. Ethan Ellis, *Republican Foreign Policy, 1921–1933* (1968)

Martin L. Fausold, *The Presidency of Herbert C. Hoover* (1985)

Herbert Feis, *The Diplomacy of the Dollar* (1950)

Robert H. Ferrell, *American Diplomacy in the Great Depression* (1957)

————, *Frank B. Kellogg and Henry L. Stimson* (1963)

————, *Peace in Their Time* (1952)

Peter Filene, *Americans and the Soviet Experiment, 1917–1933* (1967)

Betty Glad, *Charles Evans Hughes and the Illusions of Innocence* (1966)

Norman A. Graebner, *Ideas and Diplomacy* (1964)

Kenneth J. Grieb, *The Latin American Policy of Warren G. Harding* (1976)

Ellis W. Hawley, ed., *Herbert Hoover, Secretary of Commerce, 1921–1928* (1981)

Michael J. Hogan, *Informal Entente: The Private Structure of Cooperation in Anglo-American Economic Diplomacy* (1977)

Jon Jacobson, "Is There a New International History of the 1920s?" *American Historical Review,* 88 (1983), 617–645

Harold Josephson, *James T. Shotwell and the Rise of Internationalism in America* (1976)

William Kamman, *A Search for Stability: United States Diplomacy Toward Nicaragua, 1925–1933* (1968)

Robert G. Kaufman, *Arms Control in the Pre-Nuclear Era: The United States and Naval Limitation Between the Two World Wars* (1990)

Bruce Kent, *The Spoils of War* (1989) (reparations)

Michael L. Kreen, *U. S. Policy Toward Economic Nationalism in Latin America, 1917–1929* (1990)

Walter LaFeber, *Inevitable Revolutions* (1993) (Central America)

Melvyn P. Leffler, *The Elusive Quest: America's Pursuit of European Stability and French Security, 1919–1933* (1979)

———, "1921–1932: Expansionist Impulses and Domestic Constraints," in William H. Becker and Samuel F. Wells, Jr., eds., *Economics and World Power* (1984), pp. 225–275

———, "Political Isolationism, Economic Expansionism, or Diplomatic Realism? American Policy toward Western Europe, 1921–1933," *Perspectives in American History,* 8 (1974), 413–461

Clifford R. Lovin, "Herbert Hoover, Internationalist, 1919–1923," *Prologue,* 20 (1988), 249–267

Richard Lowitt, *George W. Norris: The Persistence of a Progressive, 1913–1933* (1971)

Brian McKercher, ed., *Anglo-American Relations in the 1920s* (1991)

———, "Reaching for the Brass Ring: The Recent Historiography of Interwar American Foreign Relations," *Diplomatic History,* 15 (1991), 565–598

———, "Wealth, Power, and the New International Order: Britain and the American Challenge in the 1920s," *Diplomatic History,* 12 (1988), 411–441

Charles S. Maier, *Recasting Bourgeois Europe* (1975)

Sally Marks, *The Illusion of Peace: International Relations, 1918–1933* (1976)

Elting E. Morison, *Turmoil and Tradition* (1960)

Robert K. Murray, *The Harding Era* (1969)

Carl Parrini, *Heir to Empire* (1969)

Louis A. Pérez, Jr., *Cuba Under the Platt Amendment, 1902–1934* (1986)

Stephen J. Randall, *United States Foreign Oil Policy, 1919–1948* (1986)

Emily S. Rosenberg, *Spreading the American Dream* (1982)

——— and Norman L. Rosenberg, "The Public-Private Dynamic in United States Foreign Financial Advising, 1898–1929," *Journal of American History,* 74 (1987), 59–82

Thomas J. Saunders, *Hollywood in Berlin: American Cinema and Weimar Germany* (1994)

Stephen A. Schuker, *American "Reparations" to Germany, 1919–33* (1988)

———, *The End of French Predominance in Europe: The Financial Crisis of 1924 and the Adoption of the Dawes Plan* (1976)

Robert D. Schulzinger, *The Making of the Diplomatic Mind: The Training, Outlook, and Style of United States Foreign Service Officers, 1908–1931* (1975)

Michael S. Sherry, *The Rise of American Air Power* (1987)

Robert F. Smith, "Republican Policy and Pax Americana, 1921–1932," in William Appleman Williams, ed., *From Colony to Empire* (1972), pp. 253–292

George Soule, *Prosperity Decade* (1947)

Marc Trachtenberg, *Reparation in World Politics* (1980)

Christine A. White, *British and American Commercial Relations with Soviet Russia, 1918–1924* (1992)

William Appleman Williams, "The Legend of Isolationism in the 1920s," *Science and Society,* 18 (1954), 1–20

John Hoff Wilson, *American Business and Foreign Policy, 1920–1933* (1971)

———, *Herbert Hoover* (1975)

———, *Ideology and Economics: U.S. Relations with the Soviet Union, 1918–1933* (1974)

———, "A Reevaluation of Herbert Hoover's Foreign Policy," in Martin L. Fausold and George T. Mazuzan, eds., *The Hoover Presidency: A Reappraisal* (1974), pp. 164–186

Franklin D. Roosevelt
and the Origins of
the Second World War
in the Pacific

German and Japanese aggression in the 1930s presented Americans once again with questions of war and peace, neutrality or alliance. The United States protested this aggression—witness the strongly worded Stimson Doctrine after Japan invaded Manchuria in 1931—but Americans sought to avoid entanglement in the cascading crises that engulfed Europe and Asia. Congress passed neutrality acts, and President Franklin D. Roosevelt publicly endorsed the United States' neutral stance. Recalling the horrors of World War I and beset by a terrible economic depression at home, many Americans embraced "isolationism," or what one historian has called "independent internationalism." After the outbreak of full-scale war in Europe in September 1939, Roosevelt and the nation gradually moved toward an interventionist posture, repealing the arms embargo and in 1941 sending Britain and the Soviet Union Lend-Lease supplies. When war came for the United States, however, it occurred six thousand miles away from Europe, in Asia.

For most of the twentieth century, the United States had opposed Japanese expansion into China. When the Japanese sought access to vital raw materials and markets to relieve their economic stress in the 1930s, taking Manchuria and renaming it Manchukuo, Americans viewed Japanese imperialism as a violation of the Open Door and a threat to world order. Later in the decade, as the Sino-Japanese war intensified, the United States gradually expanded its navy, granted loans to China, and did not invoke the neutrality acts—thereby permitting China to buy armaments from the United States. Yet Washington protested Japanese aggression in a manner designed not to provoke war with the Empire of the Sun. Certain that America's strategic priorities lay across the Atlantic in Europe, the Roosevelt administration hoped to avoid a two-front war.

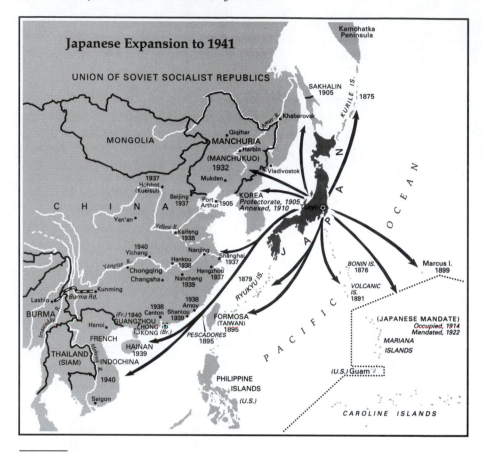

From *American Foreign Relations*, 4/e by Thomas G. Paterson, et al., p. 180. Copyright © 1995 by
D. C. Heath and Company.

*Following conclusion of the Tripartite Pact among Japan, Germany, and Italy
in September 1940 and Japan's acquisition of bases in French Indochina, the administration embargoed shipments of scrap iron and steel to the island nation. The
crisis in the Pacific reached a critical juncture when Japanese troops, in July 1941,
occupied French Indochina. In response, the Roosevelt administration froze Japanese assets in the United States, thereby denying Japan essential petroleum shipments. Tokyo and Washington exchanged proposals and counterproposals for the
rest of the year, but to no avail. On December 7, in a surprise attack, Japanese pilots bombed the U.S. naval base at Pearl Harbor in the Hawaiian Islands. The
United States declared war on Japan, and Germany declared war on the United
States. Americans braced once again for world war.*

*Historians have grappled with weighty questions in explaining America's
road to war. What at root caused the deterioration in U.S.-Japanese relations? Was
the economic downturn of the 1930s the culprit? Were cultural differences a major
source of conflict? Did Japan's aggressive nationalism and economic exclusiveness*

*pose an unacceptable threat to the international system? Why did Japan's defini-
tion of a "new order" alarm other nations? Did the United States push Japan toward war? Was Japanese-American conflict unavoidable? Did conflict have to
escalate into war? Or could different policies toward Japanese expansionism have
produced a different outcome? Why did the Roosevelt administration bow to "appeasement" sentiment in dealing with Germany but adopt a more confrontational
stance toward Japan? What was the relationship between events in Europe and
events in Asia? Was the issue of China solvable, and why was the United States so
concerned about the fate of China? Could war have been delayed? How important
was timing?*

*Almost all historians of this subject have studied Franklin D. Roosevelt as deci-
sionmaker, probing his ideas, leadership, and choices, and the results of his policies. Did FDR have a coherent strategy for coping with aggression in Europe and
Asia, or did he deal with issues haphazardly? Was he in command of the making
of foreign policy, or did he leave crucial decisions to subordinates, who complicated
his diplomacy or pressed Japan harder than the president intended? What roles
did the State Department and Secretary of State Cordell Hull play? What advice did
military officials offer? Did bureaucratic infighting confuse matters? To what extent did public opinion influence policy?*

*Finally, although most historians reject any notion of a Rooseveltian conspir-
acy, questions of this nature persist: Did Roosevelt, eager to enter the European conflict, devise policies toward Japan that guaranteed entry into war through the
Asian "back door"? Did the president deliberately set up Pearl Harbor for disaster?
Or did American leaders simply err in not alerting the base to possible attack?*

✖ D O C U M E N T S

The first document, the Stimson Doctrine of January 7, 1932, was issued by Secretary of
State Henry L. Stimson after the Japanese overran Manchuria. Stimson's policy of nonrecognition guided the United States for the rest of the 1930s. U.S. pressure on Tokyo escalated following a clash between Japanese and Chinese troops at the Marco Polo bridge,
south of Beijing, in July 1937, and Japan's full-fledged invasion of China. In obvious reference to what Japan's leaders called the "China Incident," President Franklin D. Roosevelt
told a Chicago audience on October 5, 1937 that aggressors should be "quarantined" (the
second selection). Although FDR offered no concrete policies, the administration in the
following months began to send modest amounts of aid to China.

The third document, an official Japanese statement of November 3, 1938, following a
string of military victories in China, proclaimed the establishment of a "new order" in East
Asia. Japan's bold actions sparked debate among American policymakers over how best to
halt and reverse the aggression. On November 14, 1938, Stanley K. Hornbeck, a senior adviser on Asian affairs in the State Department, urged the United States to develop a diplomatic "war plan" to punish and deter the Japanese (the fourth document). An outspoken
hawk, Hornbeck called for economic measures, including the abrogation of the 1911 U.S.-
Japan commercial treaty. U.S. ambassador to Japan Joseph C. Grew disagreed. In a memorandum to Secretary of State Cordell Hull on December 1, 1939, the fifth document, he
predicted that sanctions would only alienate Japanese leaders and provoke further conquest.

A high-level meeting in Tokyo on July 10, 1941 conducted by Foreign Minister
Yosuke Matsuoka, heard his adviser, Yoshie Saito, analyze the divisive issues in U.S.-

Japanese relations and, specifically, Secretary Hull's proposal for a Sino-Japanese settlement. Saito's comments are reprinted in the sixth document. On July 25, 1941, following Japan's invasion of French Indochina, the Roosevelt administration froze Japanese assets. The seventh document, "Guidelines for Implementing National Policies," formally adopted at a Japanese leaders' conference in the presence of the emperor on September 6, set a deadline of early October for the conclusion of a diplomatic agreement with the United States. After that time military preparations would commence. The eighth document, the American proposals to Japan dated November 29, 1941, sought to roll back Japanese expansion and revive the Open Door principle. The Japanese position paper (the ninth selection), handed to Hull on December 7, 1941, as the Rising Sun's warriors descended on Pearl Harbor, outlined Japan's case against the United States and for mastery of China. The final document is Roosevelt's war message to Congress, delivered on December 8, 1941.

The Stimson Doctrine, 1932

With the recent [Japanese] military operations about Chinchow, the last remaining administrative authority of the Government of the Chinese Republic in South Manchuria, as it existed prior to September 18th, 1931, has been destroyed. The American Government continues confident that the work of the neutral commission recently authorized by the Council of the League of Nations will facilitate an ultimate solution of the difficulties now existing between China and Japan. But in view of the present situation and of its own rights and obligations therein, the American Government deems it to be its duty to notify both the Imperial Japanese Government and the Government of the Chinese Republic that it cannot admit the legality of any situation *de facto* nor does it intend to recognize any treaty or agreement entered into between those Governments, or agents thereof which may impair the treaty rights of the United States or its citizens in China, including those which relate to the sovereignty, the independence, or the territorial administrative integrity of the Republic of China, or to the international policy relative to China, commonly known as the open door policy; and that it does not intend to recognize any situation, treaty or agreement which may be brought about by means contrary to the covenants and obligations of the Pact of Paris of August 27, 1928, to which Treaty both China and Japan, as well as the United States, are parties.

President Franklin D. Roosevelt's "Quarantine" Speech, 1937

Some fifteen years ago the hopes of mankind for a continuing era of international peace were raised to great heights when more than sixty nations solemnly pledged themselves not to resort to arms in furtherance of their national aims and policies. The high aspirations expressed in the Briand-Kellogg Peace Pact and the hopes for peace thus raised have of late given way to a haunting fear of calamity. The present reign of terror and international lawlessness began a few years ago.

It began through unjustified interference in the internal affairs of other nations or the invasion of alien territory in violation of treaties; and has now reached a stage where the very foundations of civilization are seriously threatened. The landmarks and traditions which have marked the progress of civilization toward a condition of law, order and justice are being wiped away.

Without a declaration of war and without warning or justification of any kind, civilians, including vast numbers of women and children, are being ruthlessly murdered with bombs from the air. In times of so-called peace, ships are being attacked and sunk by submarines without cause or notice. Nations are fomenting and taking sides in civil warfare in nations that have never done them any harm. Nations claiming freedom for themselves deny it to others.

Innocent peoples, innocent nations, are being cruelly sacrificed to a greed for power and supremacy which is devoid of all sense of justice and humane considerations. . . .

The peace-loving nations must make a concerted effort in opposition to those violations of treaties and those ignorings of humane instincts which today are creating a state of international anarchy and instability from which there is no escape through mere isolation or neutrality.

Those who cherish their freedom and recognize and respect the equal right of their neighbors to be free and live in peace must work together for the triumph of law and moral principles in order that peace, justice and confidence may prevail in the world. There must be a return to a belief in the pledged word, in the value of a signed treaty. There must be recognition of the fact that national morality is as vital as private morality. . . .

There is a solidarity and interdependence about the modern world, both technically and morally, which makes it impossible for any nation completely to isolate itself from economic and political upheavals in the rest of the world, especially when such upheavals appear to be spreading and not declining. There can be no stability or peace either within nations or between nations except under laws and moral standards adhered to by all. International anarchy destroys every foundation for peace. It jeopardizes either the immediate or the future security of every nation, large or small. It is, therefore, a matter of vital interest and concern to the people of the United States that the sanctity of international treaties and the maintenance of international morality be restored.

The overwhelming majority of the peoples and nations of the world today want to live in peace. They seek the removal of barriers against trade. They want to exert themselves in industry, in agriculture and in business, that they may increase their wealth through the production of wealth-producing goods rather than striving to produce military planes and bombs and machine guns and cannon for the destruction of human lives and useful property.

In those nations of the world which seem to be piling armament on armament for purposes of aggression, and those other nations which fear acts of aggression against them and their security, a very high proportion of their national income is being spent directly for armaments. It runs from thirty to as high as fifty percent. We are fortunate. The proportion that we in the United States spend is far less— eleven or twelve percent.

How happy we are that the circumstances of the moment permit us to put our money into bridges and boulevards, dams and reforestation, the conservation of our soil and many other kinds of useful works rather than into huge standing armies and vast supplies of implements of war.

I am compelled and you are compelled, nevertheless, to look ahead. The peace, the freedom and the security of ninety percent of the population of the world is being jeopardized by the remaining ten percent who are threatening a breakdown of all international order and law. Surely the ninety percent who want to live in peace under law and in accordance with moral standards that have received almost universal acceptance through the centuries, can and must find some way to make their will prevail.

The situation is definitely of universal concern. The questions involved relate not merely to violations of specific provisions of particular treaties; they are questions of war and of peace, of international law and especially of principles of humanity. It is true that they involve definite violations of agreements, and especially of the Covenant of the League of Nations, the Briand-Kellogg Pact and the Nine Power Treaty. But they also involve problems of world economy, world security and world humanity.

It is true that the moral consciousness of the world must recognize the importance of removing injustices and well-founded grievances; but at the same time it must be aroused to the cardinal necessity of honoring sanctity of treaties, of respecting the rights and liberties of others and of putting an end to acts of international aggression.

It seems to be unfortunately true that the epidemic of world lawlessness is spreading.

When an epidemic of physical disease starts to spread, the community approves and joins in a quarantine of the patients in order to protect the health of the community against the spread of the disease.

It is my determination to pursue a policy of peace. It is my determination to adopt every practicable measure to avoid involvement in war. It ought to be inconceivable that in this modern era, and in the face of experience, any nation could be so foolish and ruthless as to run the risk of plunging the whole world into war by invading and violating, in contravention of solemn treaties, the territory of other nations that have done them no real harm and are too weak to protect themselves adequately. Yet the peace of the world and the welfare and security of every nation, including our own, is today being threatened by that very thing.

Japan's Vision of a "New Order" in Asia, 1938

By the august virtue of His Majesty, our naval and military forces have captured Canton and the three cities of Wuhan; and all the vital areas of China have thus fallen into our hands. The Kuomintang Government exists no longer except as a mere local régime. However, so long as it persists in its anti-Japanese and pro-communist policy our country will not lay down its arms—never until that régime is crushed.

What Japan seeks is the establishment of a new order which will insure the permanent stability of East Asia. In this lies the ultimate purpose of our present military campaign.

This new order has for its foundation a tripartite relationship of mutual aid and co-ordination between Japan, Manchoukuo [the name Japan gave to Manchuria in February 1932], and China in political, economic, cultural and other fields. Its object is to secure international justice, to perfect the joint defence against Communism, and to create a new culture and realize a close economic cohesion throughout East Asia. This indeed is the way to contribute toward the stabilization of East Asia and the progress of the world.

What Japan desires of China is that that country will share in the task of bringing about this new order in East Asia. She confidently expects that the people of China will fully comprehend her true intentions and that they will respond to the call of Japan for their co-operation. Even the participation of the Kuomintang Government would not be rejected, if, repudiating the policy which has guided it in the past and remolding its personnel, so as to translate its re-birth into fact, it were to come forward to join in the establishment of the new order.

Japan is confident that other Powers will on their part correctly appreciate her aims and policy and adapt their attitude to the new conditions prevailing in East Asia. For the cordiality hitherto manifested by the nations which are in sympathy with us, Japan wishes to express her profound gratitude.

The establishment of a new order in East Asia is in complete conformity with the very spirit in which the Empire was founded; to achieve such a task is the exalted responsibility with which our present generation is entrusted. It is, therefore, imperative to carry out all necessary internal reforms, and with a full development of the aggregate national strength, material as well as moral, fulfill at all costs this duty incumbent upon our nation.

Such the Government declare to be the immutable policy and determination of Japan.

Stanley K. Hornbeck Urges Economic Sanctions Against Japan, 1938

It is an important interest of the United States that Japan not gain control of China. It therefore would be to our interest that Chinese resistance to Japan's effort to gain that control continue. The Japanese nation today is animated by concepts and is pursuing objectives which are in conflict with the concepts and the legitimate objectives of the people of the United States. The Japanese are embarked upon a program of predatory imperialism. Unless the Japanese march is halted by the Chinese or by some other nation, the time will come when Japan and the United States will be face to face and definitely opposed to each other in the international political arena. It is desirable that the development of such a situation be prevented. It therefore is desirable that the United States act toward the preventing of such a development.

The American Government should formulate and adopt a program of action (a diplomatic "war plan") toward averting an armed conflict between the United States and Japan. In the conducting of our relations with Japan and with China we should not take haphazard and unrelated steps. Such action as we may take in the realm of use of words should be related to action which we may plan to take in the realm of material pressures (positive or negative, or both). It should be our objective to have Japan's predatory march halted. Our course of action should, therefore, be a course in opposition to that march. That march will be halted only by the power of resistance of material obstacles and material pressures. Any nation which definitely opposes that march should be prepared in last analysis to use, if it prove necessary, armed force. The Chinese have already found resort to armed force necessary. China's resistance may possibly be overcome by Japanese armed force. Resistance which may be made by other countries may in the long run have to take the form of armed force. This country, therefore, in formulating its course of action should make it its business to be prepared if necessary to use armed force.

The American Government has during recent years been opposing Japan by use of words (appeal to principles, to rules of law, to provisions of treaties, etc.). Our Department of State may be able to get the better of the Japanese Foreign Office—though even that is not certain—in the field of argumentation, but victories on our part in that field will not halt the forward march of Japan's military machine. The fact is that unless the United States expects and intends to use weapons stronger than those of argument, continuance on our part along that line is almost certain to lead to the development of a situation in which this country will have either to accept a diplomatic defeat or find itself forced to resort to arms. The more we talk and the longer we refrain from resort to some substantial measures of positive (material) pressure toward preventing the Japanese from taking or destroying our rights, titles and interests in the Far East, the more likely will it be that resort by us to such measures at some future time—if and when—will be replied to by the Japanese with resort to armed force against us, which would, in turn, compel us to respond with armed force.

The most practicable course for us to follow would be that of giving assistance to the Chinese and withholding those things which are of assistance to the Japanese, toward prolonging and strengthening China's resistance and curtailing Japan's ability to continue military operations against China. If and when, however, we commit ourselves to that line of action, we should do so wholeheartedly and with determination. We should not take some one step without expecting, intending and being able to take further steps, many further steps, in the same direction. Such steps should include a combination of diplomatic, economic and potential military pressures. If this Government wishes to embark upon such a course, it should be prepared to consider seriously the taking of such steps as denunciation of the U.S.-Japan Commercial Treaty of 1911, repeal of the Neutrality Act, retaliatory tariff measures against Japan, placing of embargoes upon trade and shipping between Japan and the United States, [and] disposal of our naval resources in such manner as to indicate to the Japanese Government and nation that we "mean business."

Ambassador Joseph C. Grew Warns Against Economic Sanctions, 1939

The United States is solemnly (to use that somewhat overworked Wilsonian term) committed to uphold the principles of the Nine Power Treaty, primarily to uphold the territorial and administrative integrity of China and the Open Door. Therein lies the point of principle.

On the other side of the picture, nothing in international affairs can be more mathematically certain (if anything in international affairs is ever certain) than that

Japan is not going to respect the territorial and administrative integrity of China, now or in future, has not the slightest intention of doing so and could be brought to do so only by complete defeat. Observance in practice of the Open Door is and will continue to be a matter of degree governed by expediency, not by principle. Herein lies the point of realism.

Given the situation now existing in Europe, there does not now appear on the horizon the possibility of such a defeat being inflicted by any nation or by any set of circumstances, military, social, economic or financial. There may be temporary setbacks or a stalemate in the military field or even, over a course of time, under increasing Chinese pressure, what the military experts call "strategic withdrawal to previously prepared positions," in other words, withdrawal into North China the control of which was the primary purpose of the so-called "China Incident"; there may be financial and economic difficulties and depression; a pulling in of the belt; perhaps serious hardships; there may be increasing social unrest at home; but of an overwhelming debacle there is little present outlook.

We have already drawn the Department's [of State] attention to the beginning of an inflationary movement in this country, and in a despatch now under preparation there will be discussed the further development of this movement as reflected in slower absorption of government bonds, a large increase in the paper currency, and mounting commodity prices, along with far-reaching measures designed to control prices. Attempts to control the supply and demand of rice are causing wide agrarian unrest. It is our opinion, however, that even if worse came to worst there is realization that Japan has irrevocably committed herself to the continental adventure and is determined to see it through. The majority opinion in the Embassy, which I myself share, does not believe that an American embargo, even if it covered all American exportation and importation to and from Japan, would bring about such a debacle as would cause the Japanese to relinquish their program in China.

Statisticians have proved to their own satisfaction, and will continue so to prove, that Japan can be defeated by economic pressure from without. But the statisticians generally fail to include psychological factors in their estimates. Japan is a nation of hardy warriors still inculcated with the samurai do-or-die spirit which has by tradition and inheritance become ingrained in the race. The Japanese throughout their history have faced periodic cataclysms brought about by nature and by man: earthquakes, hurricanes, floods, epidemics, the blighting of crops, and almost constant wars within and without the country. By long experience they are inured to hardships and they are inured to regimentation. Every former difficulty has been overcome. Estimates based on statistics alone may well mislead.

During the months since my return from the United States I have carefully and thoroughly studied opinion in Japan, including opinion in the Government, the army, the influential elements in civil life, the business world and the masses, and on one issue that opinion can definitely be said to be unanimous: the so-called "new order in East Asia" has come to stay. That term is open to wide interpretation, but the minimum conception of the term envisages permanent Japanese control of Manchuria, Inner Mongolia, and North China. In the army and among certain elements of the Government and the public the conception is very much broader; those elements would exert Japanese control throughout all of China, or as much of China as can now or in future be grasped and held, including the treaty ports and the international settlements and concessions. Control in Manchuria is already crystallized through the puppet state of "Manchukuo"; control in Inner Mongolia is a problem for the future. It is hoped and expected here that control of North and Central China will be exercised by setting up the two regimes under Wang Kehmin and Wang Ching-wei. These plans of course envisage long-term and probably permanent Japanese garrisons to compel subserviency to Japanese interests. It would be difficult to find any Japanese who visualizes "the new order in East Asia" as less far-reaching than the foregoing minimum conception. . . .

To await the hoped-for discrediting in Japan of the Japanese army and the Japanese military system is to await the millenium. The Japanese army is no protuberance like the tail of a dog which might be cut off to prevent the tail from wagging the dog: it is inextricably bound up with the fabric of the entire nation; its ramifications are far too deep for any effective amputation, or any effective withering through discredit. Certainly there are plenty of Japanese who dislike the army's methods; there is plenty of restiveness at the wholesale impressment of the able-bodied young men to fight in China, of the death and crippling of many, and of the restrictions and handicaps in every-day life entailed by the expenses of the campaign. But that the army can be discredited in the eyes of the people to a degree where its power and prestige will become so effectively undermined as to deprive the army of its control or at least of its preponderant influence in shaping national policy is an hypothesis which I believe no one intimately conversant with Japan and the Japanese would for a moment entertain. . . .

So here we find ourselves squarely faced with a problem which, from all present indications, is to be permanently with us: the problem of principle versus realism. What are we going to do about it? . . .

Granting a priori that this is our determined position, it appears that two general courses, neither of which involves compromise with principle, are open, each of them susceptible of modification as developments might require.

One course envisages complete intransigence. Unless and until Japan reorientates her policy and actions, both as regards her commitments under the Nine Power Treaty (until modified by orderly processes) and her respect of American rights and interests in China, we would refuse to negotiate a new treaty of commerce and navigation and would, if public demand in the United States calls for it, impose an embargo next winter.

This course would set Japanese-American relations moving on a downward slope to a point from which it would be difficult to bring them back to normal for a long time to come; a treatyless situation, with its attending handicaps to Japanese trade, would start the movement; the imposition of an embargo would greatly accelerate it.

The other course, after endeavoring to consider the situation and outlook from all angles, I believe is in our own interests now and, so far as we can foresee the future, the wiser one to follow. We would say to Japan: "The United States concedes no right and recognizes no compromise with respect to the provisions and principles of the Nine Power Treaty. We, however, desire so far as feasible to maintain good relations with Japan. We await progressive implementation of your assurances that American rights and interests in China will be respected, not only in negative ways, such as cessation of the bombings of American property, indignities to

American citizens and the more flagrant interferences with American business and trade, but also in positive ways through the presentation progressively of concrete evidence that American commercial, cultural and other rights and interests are not to be crowded out of China by Japanese measures as hitherto has appeared patently to be intentional. As soon as some definite start is made in presenting concrete evidence to the foregoing effect, we, for our part, with a view to facilitating the efforts of the Government in Tokyo to further such a program, will enter into negotiations for a new treaty of commerce and navigation and concurrently for a *modus vivendi* of limited duration to tide over a treatyless situation, it being clearly understood that the ratification of such a treaty will depend upon future developments, namely, the progressive implementation of such a program. In the meantime, also depending upon developments, we will endeavor to hold in abeyance the question of imposing an embargo against Japan. Such an effort will obviously depend upon American public opinion and public demand which, in turn, will depend in large measure upon the character of the concrete evidence presented by the Japanese Government that the desired program is being faithfully carried out. As for the Nine Power Treaty, we shall meanwhile confidently await a favorable moment for a reconsideration of the provisions of that treaty through orderly processes.

Within the next two months we are coming to a crisis in Japanese-American relations, to a possible parting of the ways. One way points straight down hill. A treatyless situation plus an embargo would exasperate the Japanese to a point where anything could happen, even serious incidents which could inflame the American people beyond endurance and which might call for war. The Japanese are so constituted and are just now in such a mood and temper that sanctions, far from intimidating, would almost certainly bring retaliation which, in turn, would lead to counterretaliation. Japan would not stop to weigh ultimate consequences. It would be all very well to say that Japan had brought our action on her own head, that the United States can get along without Japanese friendship and that the dignity and power of the United States cannot tolerate compromise, but such an attitude would be lacking in any constructive element. I think that our dignity and our power in themselves counsel moderation, forbearance and the use of every reasonable means of conciliation without the sacrifice of principle. . . .

It is axiomatic to say that good relations between the United States and Japan are in our own interests. No purely altruistic motives are involved. In our own interests, particularly our commercial and cultural interests, we should approach this problem from a realistic and constructive standpoint. Not only on Japan's future action but on our own future action too will depend the question whether our relations with Japan are susceptible of improvement or whether they are to go straight down hill. There is no use whatever in quibbling about this, no use in refusing to face facts. The bombings of our property, the personal indignities and interferences, and some of the more flagrant violations of our commercial rights can be stemmed, but unless we are prepared to fight for it, the Open Door, as we conceive it, is not going to be kept open. We have the choice of losing everything or of saving something from the wreckage, while opening the way to a potential building up of our relations with Japan. Whatever course we elect to take should be adopted only after reaching a perfectly clear perception of where the alternative courses will lead, and then of most carefully weighing the pros and cons between them.

Japanese Officials on China
and U.S. Pressure, July 1941

Saito: I have studied the present [U.S.] proposal, and find many reasons, to be explained shortly, why it is unacceptable.

The present world, divided into those who are for the maintenance of the status quo and those who are for its destruction, the democracies and the totalitarian states, is in the midst of a war. [Secretary of State Cordell] Hull's reply is for the status quo and for democracy. It is obvious that America sent it after consultation with Britain and China. Thus I think the countries that are for the status quo are getting together to put pressure on Japan. On the matter of Sino-Japanese negotiations, the United States hopes to make us negotiate on the basis of conditions existing prior to the China Incident. In this proposal the phrase "Chinese Government" is used. I think this tricky wording is tantamount to saying that we should renounce the basic treaty between Japan and China. Cancelling our recognition of the Nanking Government would mean reviving the moribund Chungking Government. We must consider and study this phrase "Chinese Government."

The Americans think that Manchuria should revert to China. This proposal says, in effect, that Japan and China should negotiate after Japan has renounced the joint declaration made by Japan, Manchukuo, and China. If we begin negotiations by doing this at a time when Chungking is trying to regain lost territory, it is certain that from the very beginning things would go against us.

This proposal does not recognize the stationing of troops [in China] to maintain peace and order; it seeks the unconditional withdrawal of all troops. The stationing of troops to maintain peace and order is a most important element in our national policy. If we withdrew our troops unconditionally, the Chinese Communists, the Nationalists, the Nanking Government, and Chungking would fight, causing greater disorder. If this happened, Britain and the United States would intervene. Accordingly, the unconditional withdrawal of troops will deadlock our negotiations with the United States.

The proposal does not recognize the stationing of troops as a defense against Communism. Whereas the Japanese draft tries to recognize the treaties that have been concluded to date, the United States proposal tries to invalidate them. That the United States does not recognize the stationing of troops as a defense against Communism is indicated in Hull's Statement.

Japan aims at complete cooperation between Japan and China. By contrast, the United States is advocating nondiscriminatory treatment. This makes it impossible to establish a New Order in East Asia. Britain and the United States have continued to aid Chiang until the present time; and they are planning to obtain an advantageous position in China in the future. When an overall peace comes to China, the influence of American "dollars," which are backed by 80 per cent of the world's gold supply, will spread all over China, working from today's special position. America's intention is to bring about peace between Japan and China by means of

From *Japan's Decision for War: Records of the 1941 Policy Conferences,* 94–97, edited and translated by Nobutaka Ike, with the permission of the publishers, Stanford University Press. ©1967 by the Board of Trustees of the Leland Stanford Junior University.

an agreement between Japan and the United States, and then to let Japan and China negotiate directly within the limits thus set. This procedure will transfer leadership in East Asia to the United States. It will interfere with the implementation of an independent policy by our Empire. It will give the United States the right to have a say in the China Problem.

The attitudes of Japan and the United States toward European war differ greatly. Stated another way, we can only suppose that they mean to enter the war but are telling us to keep quiet. The United States has interpreted her right of self-defense very broadly. She has also practically said that Japan should renounce the Tripartite Pact. We must naturally reject such ideas.

As for trade between Japan and America, America plans to limit it to the pre-Incident level. In short, a maintain-the-status-quo mentality is evident. Moreover, the proposal talks about ordinary commercial transactions, but in the future we must increase trade in vital materials, such as steel and scrap iron; and by keeping trade at the pre-Incident level the United States will be legally preventing the development of Japan's foreign trade. That is, this action will interfere with Japan's future economic development, and the United States will freely control the markets of the Far East. The fact that the Americans have eliminated the word "Southwest" from "Southwest Pacific" is evidence that they are also greatly concerned with the North Pacific. They say "normal trade relations"; but Japan has in mind not only trade, but also mining and industry. The United States, by talking about "trade relations," is clearly limiting Japan's demands.

On the question of Japanese emigration to the United States, the previous draft stated that Japan would be treated the same as other countries; but this statement has been eliminated in the present draft.

We made a proposal regarding the independence of the Philippines; but the American proposal simply states that the Philippines has not yet developed to the point of independence.

Hull's "Oral Statement" contains especially outrageous language. For instance, it says, "We have no intention of considering the stationing of troops a defense against Communism." Or again: "There are differences of opinion within the Japanese Government. I understand that there are Cabinet members who say Japan should ally herself with the Axis and fight side-by-side with Hitler. We cannot make an agreement with a Japanese Government of that kind. If you want to facilitate an improvement in Japanese-American relations, you had better change your Cabinet." His attitude is one of contempt for Japan. I have been in the foreign service for a long time. This language is not the kind one would use toward a country of equal standing: it expresses an attitude one would take toward a protectorate or a possession. These words are inexcusable.

Matsuoka: In general, I am in agreement with Adviser Saito's report; but I would like to state one or two thoughts.

First of all, Hull's "Statement" is outrageous. Never has such a thing occurred since Japan opened diplomatic relations with other countries. [Ambassador Kichisaburo] Nomura and I are good friends, but it is inexcusable for him to transmit such an outrageous statement. I was truly amazed that he would listen without protest to a demand that Japan, a great world power, change her Cabinet. I sent a message to him right away, saying: "You should not have transmitted such a statement. Was there not some misunderstanding? Inform me of the circumstances at the time." But I have not yet received an answer from him.

Second, we cannot dissolve the Tripartite Pact.

Third, acceptance of the American proposal would threaten the establishment of a Greater East Asia Co-prosperity Sphere, and this would be a very grave matter.

Fourth, I think that Britain and the United States are trying to meddle in the settlement of the Sino-Japanese problem in one way or another. I am unhappy that among our people there are those who believe it would be better to achieve peace through the mediation of a third party, even though we have fought for four years trying to secure the leadership of East Asia. Such people use as a precedent the times when we sought the aid of third parties, including the United States, in the peace negotiations during the Sino-Japanese and Russo-Japanese wars; but they forget the position that the Empire occupies thirty years later.

Japan's Minimum Demands, September 1941

In view of the increasingly critical situation, especially the aggressive plans being carried out by America, England, Holland and other countries, the situation in Soviet Russia and the Empire's latent potentialities, the Japanese Government will proceed as follows in carrying out its plans for the southern territories. . . .

1. Determined not to be deterred by the possibility of being involved in a war with America (and England and Holland) in order to secure our national existence, we will proceed with war preparations so that they be completed approximately toward the end of October.
2. At the same time, we will endeavor by every possible diplomatic means to have our demands agreed to by America and England. Japan's minimum demands in these negotiations with America (and England), together with the Empire's maximum concessions, are embodied in the attached document [Annex Document].
3. If by the early part of October there is no reasonable hope of having our demands agreed to in the diplomatic negotiations mentioned above, we will immediately make up our minds to get ready for war against America (and England and Holland).

Policies with reference to countries other than those in the southern territories will be carried out in harmony with the plans already laid. Special effort will be made to prevent America and Soviet Russia from forming a united front against Japan.

Annex Document

I. Japan's Minimum Demands in Her Negotiations with America (and England)

1. America and England shall not intervene in or obstruct a settlement by Japan of the China Incident.

(a) They will not interfere with Japan's plan to settle the China Incident in harmony with the Sino-Japanese Basic Agreement and the Japan-China-Manchoukuo Tripartite Declaration.

(b) America and England will close the Burma Route and offer the Chiang Regime neither military, political nor economic assistance. . . .

Commercial operations in China on the part of America and England may also be guaranteed, in so far as they are purely commercial.

2. America and England will take no action in the Far East which offers a threat to the defense of the Empire.

(a) America and England will not establish military bases in [Thailand], the Netherlands East Indies, China or Far Eastern Soviet Russia.

(b) Their Far Eastern military forces will not be increased over their present strength.

Note: Any demands for the liquidation of Japan's special relations with French Indo-China based on the Japanese-French Agreement will not be considered.

3. America and England will cooperate with Japan in her attempt to obtain needed raw materials.

(a) America and England will restore trade relations with Japan and furnish her with the raw materials she needs from the British and American territories in the Southwest Pacific.

(b) America and England will assist Japan to establish close economic relations with [Thailand] and the Netherlands East Indies.

II. Maximum Concessions by Japan

It is first understood that our minimum demands as listed under I above will be agreed to.

1. Japan will not use French Indo-China as a base for operations against any neighboring countries with the exception of China.

Note: In case any questions are asked concerning Japan's attitude towards Soviet Russia, the answer is to be that as long as Soviet Russia faithfully carries out the Neutrality Pact and does not violate the spirit of the agreement by, for instance, threatening Japan or Manchuria, Japan will not take any military action.

2. Japan is prepared to withdraw her troops from French Indo-China as soon as a just peace is established in the Far East.

3. Japan is prepared to guarantee the neutrality of the Philippine Islands.

American Proposals to Japan, November 1941

Section I   Draft Mutual Declaration of Policy

The Government of the United States and the Government of Japan both being solicitous for the peace of the Pacific affirm that their national policies are directed toward lasting and extensive peace throughout the Pacific area, that they have no territorial designs in that area, that they have no intention of threatening other countries or of using military force aggressively against any neighboring nation, and that, accordingly, in their national policies they will actively support and give practical application to the following fundamental principles upon which their relations with each other and with all other governments are based:

1. The principle of inviolability of territorial integrity and sovereignty of each and all nations.
2. The principle of non-interference in the internal affairs of other countries.
3. The principle of equality, including equality of commercial opportunity and treatment.
4. The principle of reliance upon international cooperation and conciliation for the prevention and pacific settlement of controversies and for improvement of international conditions by peaceful methods and processes.

The Government of Japan and the Government of the United States have agreed that toward eliminating chronic political instability, preventing recurrent economic collapse, and providing a basis for peace, they will actively support and practically apply the following principles in their economic relations with each other and with other nations and peoples:

1. The principle of non-discrimination in international commercial relations.
2. The principle of international economic cooperation and abolition of extreme nationalism as expressed in excessive trade restrictions.
3. The principle of non-discriminatory access by all nations to raw material supplies.
4. The principle of full protection of the interests of consuming countries and populations as regards the operation of international commodity agreements.
5. The principle of establishment of such institutions and arrangements of international finance as may lend aid to the essential enterprises and the continuous development of all countries and may permit payments through processes of trade consonant with the welfare of all countries.

Section II   Steps to Be Taken by the Government of the United States and by the Government of Japan

The Government of the United States and the Government of Japan propose to take steps as follows:

1. The Government of the United States and the Government of Japan will endeavor to conclude a multilateral non-aggression pact among the British Empire, China, Japan, the Netherlands, the Soviet Union, Thailand and the United States.
2. Both Governments will endeavor to conclude among the American, British, Chinese, Japanese, the Netherland and Thai Governments an agreement whereunder each of the Governments would pledge itself to respect the territorial integrity of French Indochina and, in the event that there should develop a threat to the territorial integrity of Indochina, to enter into immediate

consultation with a view to taking such measures as may be deemed necessary and advisable to meet the threat in question. Such agreement would provide also that each of the Governments party to the agreement would not seek or accept preferential treatment in its trade or economic relations with Indochina and would use its influence to obtain for each of the signatories equality of treatment in trade and commerce with French Indochina.

3.   The Government of Japan will withdraw all military, naval, air and police forces from China and from Indochina.

4.   The Government of the United States and the Government of Japan will not support—militarily, politically, economically—any government or regime in China other than the National Government of the Republic of China with capital temporarily at Chungking.

5.   Both Governments will give up all extraterritorial rights in China, including rights and interests in and with regard to international settlements and concessions, and rights under the Boxer Protocol of 1901.

   Both Governments will endeavor to obtain the agreement of the British and other governments to give up extraterritorial rights in China, including rights in international settlements and in concessions and under the Boxer Protocol of 1901.

6.   The Government of the United States and the Government of Japan will enter into negotiations for the conclusion between the United States and Japan of a trade agreement, based upon reciprocal most-favored-nation treatment and reduction of trade barriers by both countries, including an undertaking by the United States to bind raw silk on the free list.

7.   The Government of the United States and the Government of Japan will, respectively, remove the freezing restrictions on Japanese funds in the United States and on American funds in Japan.

8.   Both Governments will agree upon a plan for the stabilization of the dollar-yen rate, with the allocation of funds adequate for this purpose, half to be supplied by Japan and half by the United States.

9.   Both Governments will agree that no agreement which either has concluded with any third power or powers shall be interpreted by it in such a way as to conflict with the fundamental purpose of this agreement, the establishment and preservation of peace throughout the Pacific area.

10. Both Governments will use their influence to cause other governments to adhere to and to give practical application to the basic political and economic principles set forth in this agreement.

The Japanese Position, Presented on December 7, 1941

Ever since the China Affair broke out owing to the failure on the part of China to comprehend Japan's true intentions, the Japanese Government has striven for the restoration of peace and it has consistently exerted its best efforts to prevent the extension of war-like disturbances. It was also to that end that in September last year Japan concluded the Tripartite Pact with Germany and Italy.

However, both the United States and Great Britain have resorted to every possible measure to assist the Chungking regime so as to obstruct the establishment of a general peace between Japan and China, interfering with Japan's constructive endeavors toward the stabilization of East Asia. Exerting pressure on the Netherlands East Indies, or menacing French Indo-China, they have attempted to frustrate Japan's aspiration to the ideal of common prosperity in cooperation with these regions. Furthermore, when Japan in accordance with its protocol with France took measures of joint defence of French Indo-China, both American and British Governments willfully misinterpreting it as a threat to their own possessions, and inducing the Netherlands Government to follow suit, they enforced the assets freezing order, thus severing economic relations with Japan. While manifesting thus an obviously hostile attitude, these countries have strengthened their military preparations perfecting an encirclement of Japan, and have brought about a situation which endangers the very existence of the Empire. . . .

From the beginning of the present negotiation the Japanese Government has always maintained an attitude of fairness and moderation, and did its best to reach a settlement, for which it made all possible concessions often in spite of great difficulties. As for the China question which constituted an important subject of the negotiation, the Japanese Government showed a most conciliatory attitude. As for the principle of non-discrimination in international commerce, advocated by the American Government, the Japanese Government expressed its desire to see the said principle applied throughout the world, and declared that along with the actual practice of this principle in the world, the Japanese Government would endeavor to apply the same in the Pacific Area including China, and made it clear that Japan had no intention of excluding from China economic activities of third powers pursued on an equitable basis. Furthermore, as regards the question of withdrawing troops from French Indo-China, the Japanese Government even volunteered, as mentioned above, to carry out an immediate evacuation of troops from Southern French Indo-China as a measure of easing the situation.

It is presumed that the spirit of conciliation exhibited to the utmost degree by the Japanese Government in all these matters is fully appreciated by the American Government.

On the other hand, the American Government, always holding fast to theories in disregard of realities, and refusing to yield an inch on its impractical principles, caused undue delay in the negotiation. It is difficult to understand this attitude of the American Government and the Japanese Government desires to call the attention of the American Government especially to the following points:

1. The American Government advocates in the name of world peace those principles favorable to it and urges upon the Japanese Government the acceptance thereof. The peace of the world may be brought about only by discovering a mutually acceptable formula through recognition of the reality of the situation and mutual appreciation of one another's position. An attitude such as ignores realities and imposes one's selfish views upon others will scarcely serve the purpose of facilitating the consummation of negotiations.

    Of the various principles put forward by the American Government as a basis of the Japanese-American Agreement, there are some which the Japanese Government is ready to accept in principle, but in view of the world's actual conditions, it seems only a utopian ideal on the part of the American Government to attempt to force their immediate adoption.

Again, the proposal to conclude a multilateral non-aggression pact between Japan, United States, Great Britain, China, the Soviet Union, the Netherlands and Thailand, which is patterned after the old concept of collective security, is far removed from the realities of East Asia.

2. The American proposal contained a stipulation which states—"Both Governments will agree that no agreement, which either has concluded with any third power or powers, shall be interpreted by it in such a way as to conflict with the fundamental purpose of this agreement, the establishment and preservation of peace throughout the Pacific area." It is presumed that the above provision has been proposed with a view to restrain Japan from fulfilling its obligations under the Tripartite Pact when the United States participates in the War in Europe, and, as such, it cannot be accepted by the Japanese Government.

   The American Government, obsessed with its own views and opinions, may be said to be scheming for the extension of the war. While it seeks, on the one hand, to secure its rear by stabilizing the Pacific Area, it is engaged, on the other hand, in aiding Great Britain and preparing to attack, in the name of self-defense, Germany and Italy, two Powers that are striving to establish a new order in Europe. Such a policy is totally at variance with the many principles upon which the American Government proposes to found the stability of the Pacific Area through peaceful means.

3. Whereas the American Government, under the principles it rigidly upholds, objects to settle international issues through military pressure, it is exercising in conjunction with Great Britain and other nations pressure by economic power. Recourse to such pressure as a means of dealing with international relations should be condemned as it is at times more inhumane than military pressure.

4. It is impossible not to reach the conclusion that the American Government desires to maintain and strengthen, in coalition with Great Britain and other Powers, its dominant position it has hitherto occupied not only in China but in other areas of East Asia. It is a fact of history that the countries of East Asia for the past hundred years or more have been compelled to observe the *status quo* under the Anglo-American policy of imperialistic exploitation and to sacrifice themselves to the prosperity of the two nations. The Japanese Government cannot tolerate the perpetuation of such a situation since it directly runs counter to Japan's fundamental policy to enable all nations to enjoy each its proper place in the world.

   The stipulation proposed by the American Government relative to French Indo-China is a good exemplification of the above-mentioned American policy. Thus six countries,—Japan, the United States, Great Britain, the Netherlands, China and Thailand,—excepting France, should undertake among themselves to respect the territorial integrity and sovereignty of French Indo-China and equality of treatment in trade and commerce would be tantamount to placing the territory under the joint guarantee of the Governments of those six countries. Apart from the fact that such a proposal totally ignores the position of France, it is unacceptable to the Japanese Government in that such an arrangement cannot be considered as an extension to French Indo-China of a system similar to the Nine Power Treaty structure which is the chief factor responsible for the present predicament of East Asia.

5. All the items demanded of Japan by the American Government regarding China such as wholesale evacuation of troops or unconditional application of the principle of non-discrimination in international commerce ignored the actual conditions of China, and are calculated to destroy Japan's position as the stabilizing factor of East Asia. The attitude of the American Government in demanding Japan not to support militarily, politically or economically any regime other than the regime at Chungking, disregarding thereby the existence of the Nanking Government, shatters the very basis of the present negotiation. This demand of the American Government falling, as it does, in line with its above-mentioned refusal to cease from aiding the Chungking regime, demonstrates clearly the intention of the American Government to obstruct the restoration of normal relations between Japan and China and the return of peace to East Asia.

In brief, the American proposal contains certain acceptable items such as those concerning commerce, including the conclusion of a trade agreement, mutual removal of the freezing restrictions and stabilization of yen and dollar exchange, or the abolition of extra-territorial rights in China. On the other hand, however, the proposal in question ignores Japan's sacrifices in the four years of the China Affair, menaces the Empire's existence itself and disparages its honour and prestige. Therefore, viewed in its entirety, the Japanese Government regrets that it cannot accept the proposal as a basis of negotiations.

Roosevelt's War Message, 1941

Yesterday, December 7, 1941—a date which will live in infamy—the United States of America was suddenly and deliberately attacked by naval and air forces of the Empire of Japan.

The United States was at peace with that Nation and, at the solicitation of Japan, was still in conversation with its Government and its Emperor looking toward the maintenance of peace in the Pacific. Indeed, one hour after Japanese air squadrons had commenced bombing in Oahu, the Japanese Ambassador to the United States and his colleague delivered to the Secretary of State a formal reply to a recent American message. While this reply stated that it seemed useless to continue the existing diplomatic negotiations, it contained no threat or hint of war or armed attack.

It will be recorded that the distance of Hawaii from Japan makes it obvious that the attack was deliberately planned many days or even weeks ago. During the intervening time the Japanese Government has deliberately sought to deceive the United States by false statements and expressions of hope for continued peace.

The attack yesterday on the Hawaiian Islands has caused severe damage to American naval and military forces. Very many American lives have been lost. In addition American ships have been reported torpedoed on the high seas between San Francisco and Honolulu.

Yesterday the Japanese Government also launched an attack against Malaya.

Last night Japanese forces attacked Hong Kong.

Last night Japanese forces attacked Guam.

Last night Japanese forces attacked the Philippine Islands.

Last night the Japanese attacked Wake Island.

This morning the Japanese attacked Midway Island.

Japan has, therefore, undertaken a surprise offensive extending throughout the Pacific area. The facts of yesterday speak for themselves. The people of the United States have already formed their opinions and well understand the implications to the very life and safety of our Nation.

As Commander-in-Chief of the Army and Navy I have directed that all measures be taken for our defense.

Always will we remember the character of the onslaught against us.

No matter how long it may take us to overcome this premeditated invasion, the American people in their righteous might will win through to absolute victory.

I believe I interpret the will of the Congress and of the people when I assert that we will not only defend ourselves to the uttermost but will make very certain that this form of treachery shall never endanger us again.

Hostilities exist. There is no blinking at the fact that our people, our territory, and our interests are in grave danger.

With confidence in our armed forces—with the unbounded determination of our people—we will gain the inevitable triumph—so help us God.

I ask that the Congress declare that since the unprovoked and dastardly attack by Japan on Sunday, December seventh, a state of war has existed between the United States and the Japanese Empire.

✹ *E S S A Y S*

In the first essay, Akira Iriye of Harvard University places the origins of the Pacific war in the context of the global crisis of the 1930s. Economic chaos and militant nationalism put Japan on an expansionist course that challenged the structure or "system" of international relations established at the Washington Conference in 1921–1922. Iriye suggests that, although President Roosevelt sought to delay war with Japan, he ultimately had little choice but to join the international community to block aggression. Depicting Japan as relentlessly expansionistic, Iriye emphasizes the role of uncompromising military leaders who launched a poorly conceived and unwinnable war rather than submit to other powers' pressure. In the second essay, Hosoya Chihiro of the International University of Japan holds Roosevelt's hardline advisers responsible for provoking the Pacific war. Stanley K. Hornbeck and other hardliners, Hosoya argues, miscalculated badly in believing that economic sanctions would deter Japan. As Ambassador Joseph C. Grew had predicted, these restrictive measures simply emboldened the hardliners in the Tokyo government to initiate a war that could have been avoided. Hornbeck misread Japanese psychology, concluding quite wrongly that the Japanese would never dare to attack the United States. In the last essay in this chapter, Waldo Heinrichs of San Diego State University seeks to understand why, in mid-1941, at a time when U.S. strategy emphasized defeating Germany in Europe, the Roosevelt administration took hardline steps that intensified Japanese-U.S. hostility and set both nations on a war path. Heinrichs introduces the "Russian factor." That is, eager to keep a struggling and occupied Soviet Russia in the war against Hitler's Germany, Roosevelt chose policies calculated to influence Japanese leaders, should they decide for war, to move southward rather than northward into the Soviet Union.

Clash of Systems: The International Community Confronts Japanese Aggression

AKIRA IRIYE

On 18 September 1931, a small number of Japanese and Chinese soldiers clashed outside of Fengtien (Mukden) in southern Manchuria—an event which soon developed into what was to be a long, drawn-out, intermittent war between China and Japan. Over ten years later, on 7 December 1941, Japanese air, naval, and land forces attacked American, British, and Dutch possessions throughout Asia and the Pacific. It marked the beginning of Japan's war against the combined forces of China, America, Britain, the Netherlands and, ultimately, France and the Soviet Union.

How did a war between two Asian countries develop into one in which a single nation was pitted against a multinational coalition? Clearly, from Japan's perspective the development signalled a failure to prevent the formation of such a coalition; on the other hand, for China it was a culmination of its efforts to create an international force to isolate and punish Japan. Why did the Western powers, which stood by while Japanese forces overran Manchuria in 1931, end up by coming to China's assistance ten years later even at the risk of war with Japan? . . .

Japan had not always been an international loner. On the contrary, the country's leadership and national opinion had emphasized the cardinal importance of establishing Japan as a respected member of the community of advanced powers. And in the 1920s it had enjoyed such a status. The treaties it signed during the Washington Conference (1921–22) symbolized it. In one—the naval disarmament treaty—Japan was recognized as one of the three foremost powers; together with the United States and Britain, the nation would seek to maintain an arms equilibrium in the world and contribute to stabilizing the Asian-Pacific region. Another treaty, signed by these three plus France, provided for a mechanism whereby they would consult with one another whenever the stability was threatened. Most important, the nine-power treaty (signed by Japan, the United States, Britain, France, Italy, Belgium, the Netherlands, Portugal, and China) established the principle of international co-operation in China. Eight signatories were to co-operate with respect to the ninth, China, to uphold the latter's independence and integrity, maintain the principle of equal opportunity, and to provide an environment for the development of a stable government. Japan was a full-fledged member of the new treaty regime, which historians have called the Washington Conference system. Since much of the story of the 1930s revolves around Japan's challenge to these treaties, it is well at the outset to examine what was involved in the regime.

The term "the Washington Conference system," or "the Washington system" for short, was not in current use in the 1920s, nor was it subsequently recognized as a well-defined legal concept. None the less, immediately after the conference there was much talk of "the spirit of the Washington Conference," and a country's

From Akira Iriye, *The Origins of the Second World War in Asia and the Pacific,* Longman, 1987, pp. 1–7, 14, 18–19, 41, 46, 65–68, 70–71, 78–79, 113, 119–122, 140–141, 143, 146–150, 158–160, 165–166, 170–173, 175–177, 180–181, 184–185. Reprinted by permission of Longman Group Ltd.

behaviour in Asia tended to be judged in terms of whether it furthered or under-mined that spirit. As such it connoted more a state of mind than an explicit mecha-nism; it expressed the powers' willingness to co-operate with one another in maintaining stability in the region and assisting China's gradual transformation as a modern state. It was viewed as an alternative to their unilateral policies or exclu-sive alliances and *ententes* aimed at particularistic objectives. Instead, the Wash-ington system indicated a concept of multinational consultation and co-operation in the interest of regional stability. By the same token, this spirit was essentially gradualist and reformist, not radical or revolutionary. It was opposed to a rapid and wholesale transformation of Asian international relations, such as was being advo-cated by the Communist International and by an increasing number of Chinese na-tionalists. Rather, the Washington powers would stress an evolutionary process of change so as to ensure peace, order, and stability. . . .

Moreover, there was an economic system that underlay the structure. All the Washington signatories were linked to one another through their acceptance of the gold standard. More precisely called "the gold exchange standard," the mechanism called upon nations to accept gold as the medium of international economic trans-actions, to link their currencies to gold, and to maintain the principle of currency convertibility. Through such devices, it was believed that commercial activities across national boundaries would be carried out smoothly for the benefit of all. The gold-currency nations accounted for the bulk of the world's trade and invest-ment, so that the Washington system was synonymous with and sustained by the gold regime. Since the majority of these countries were advanced capitalist economies, it is possible to characterize the Washington Conference system as capitalist internationalism, or even as a new form of imperialism. . . .

Till the late 1920s, the system worked by and large to bring order and stability to the Asian-Pacific region. There were few overtly unilateral acts by a Washing-ton signatory, and the powers continued their mutual consultation as they sought to revise the old treaties with China. The latter, on its part, had come steadily to seek to realize its aspirations in co-operation with, rather than defiance of, the Washing-ton powers. To be sure, Chinese Nationalists were initially adamantly opposed to the Washington Conference treaties, viewing them as a device for perpetuating foreign control. However, with their military and political successes, they emerged as the new leaders of the country, and with them there came a willingness to mod-ify some of the radical rhetoric. After 1928, when they established a central gov-ernment in Nanking under Chiang Kai-shek, they had to concentrate on domestic unification and economic development, tasks which necessitated foreign capital and technology, as well as a respite in international crises that would drain re-sources away from much-needed projects at home. . . .

The United States, Britain, Japan and others one by one recognized the Nanking regime, signed new treaties for tariff revision, and began negotiations for an ultimate abrogation of extra-territoriality, the traditional symbol of China's second-class status. Although these negotiations dragged on, by 1931 differences between China and the powers had narrowed considerably, so that a full restoration of jurisdictional authority to Chinese courts seemed to be a matter of time. It was at that juncture that the Japanese army struck, not only to oppose further concessions to Chinese nationalism, but ultimately to redefine the international system itself. . . .

The precise timing for [the Japanese] action was a matter of some deliberation. But in many ways the year 1931 appeared the right moment. For one thing, the government's commitment to the existing international order had begun to encounter widespread domestic opposition. In 1930 Japan under the cabinet of Hamaguchi Osachi had signed a new naval disarmament treaty in London. The treaty covered "auxiliary craft" such as light cruisers and submarines which had been excluded from the provisions of the Washington naval treaty, and limited the total sizes of these ships that Japan, Britain, and the United States were allowed to possess. The new treaty established the allowable tonnages in the ratio of 6.975 for Japan and 10 for the other two. This was a higher ratio for Japan than the 6 to 10 formula for capital ships adopted by the Washington treaty, but it split the Japanese navy. Those who supported the government's acceptance of the new ratio (the "treaty faction") confronted the adamant opposition of the "fleet faction," determined to wage a public campaign against the treaty. The latter made it a constitutional issue, accusing the civilian government of having violated the emperor's "right of supreme command," according to which the military presumably had direct access to the emperor as his advisers on command problems. Although no such case had been made after the Washington Conference, now the naval activists believed the public would be more receptive to this type of argument.

They judged the public mood and political climate of the country quite accurately. In 1925 Japan had instituted a universal manhood suffrage, and the political parties had become sensitive to changing moods and diverse interests of the population. Although the bulk of the newly enfranchised public may have understood or cared little for international affairs, it appears that it paid attention to and was fascinated by the kind of argument put forth by the navy's anti-government minority and its sympathizers. This receptivity reflected the economic situation, for the coming of the age of mass politics coincided with the world economic crisis that began with the Wall Street crash of October 1929. Although its effects in Japan were not as severe as those in the United States or Germany, in 1930 Japanese unemployment reached 1 million, while farm prices (particularly rice and silks) fell to the lowest point in years. Tenant farmers, unable to make their rent payments, sold their daughters into prostitution, and their sons were encouraged to move to Korea or Manchuria. Particularly hard-hit was Japan's export trade. . . .

Such background explains the timing of 1931, why that year must have seemed particularly auspicious for those who had chafed under what they considered undue constraints of foreign policy and domestic politics over a legitimate assertion of national rights. A group of Kwantung Army officers, led by Ishiwara Kanji and Itagaki Seishirō, judged that the moment was ripe for bold action. Unless it were taken, they feared that the powers would continue to give in to China's demands, and Japan's position become more and more untenable. The thing to do, they reasoned, was not to seek to preserve Japanese interests within the existing system of co-operation with the Western powers, but to act unilaterally and entrench Japanese power once and for all in Manchuria. . . .

The League [of Nations] invoked the 1928 [Kellogg-Briand] pact to denounce Japan's violation of its spirit. . . . China was now clearly a victim of lawlessness, and by the same token a champion of international law and order, whereas Japan was put in the position of having to defend aggressive military action. For the first time, the United States became actively involved by sending Consul-General Prentis Gilbert to attend the Council meetings. It was symbolic that America was thus identifying itself with the League and what it stood for, thus explicitly joining China's new cause. The result was a Council resolution, with Japan alone opposing, to call on the Japanese army to return to the position it had held prior to 18 September. This resolution, voted on in late October [1931], marked a clear beginning of Japan's ostracization in the world community. It is surprising how fast Japan's international position was collapsing. Already in early November, high officials in Washington were considering sanctions. Although nothing came of this, the willingness of President Herbert Hoover, Secretary of State [Henry] Stimson, Secretary of War Patrick J. Hurley, and others even to contemplate sanctions against Japan indicates that in their view the latter was clearly undermining the postwar framework of international affairs. . . .

This did not mean, however, that there was an anti-Japanese coalition forming in the world that would support China's struggle against Japan. This remained the goal of Chinese leaders. . . . It is interesting to note that by 1932 "the spirit of the Washington Conference" had become a Chinese way of reminding the powers of their obligation to punish Japan; as a Kuomintang declaration noted in March, China was fighting for the principle that treaties must be observed, for otherwise there would be no peace in the world. A meeting of concerned citizens issued a statement in April that the Washington Conference had established peace in the Asian-Pacific region which, however, was again being threatened, and there was a danger that the crisis could lead to a second world war. The most important thing now was to coalesce nations which "preserve justice and treat China equally."

Despite such hopes, the powers would not go beyond criticizing Japan. . . . Both Washington and London were satisfied with these steps, somehow hoping that ultimately the Japanese would see the light and mend their ways. In the meantime, neither the United States nor Britain was prepared to employ anti-Japanese sanctions to help China. . . .

The outbreak of war between China and Japan in July 1937 [also] came at a critical moment in the orientation of Japanese policy. For some months civilian officials and military leaders had been divided between those who wanted to return to some modified version of the Washington system and those who preferred to push for an alternative—albeit loosely defined—order of Asian-Pacific affairs. Chinese-Japanese skirmishes outside of Peking on 7 July added fuel to the debate, and the internal discord continued until the government decided on seeking a "new order in East Asia" by expanding the hostilities. Such action compelled other countries to take a stand, to redefine once again their respective positions not only towards the war but towards the whole issue of Asian-Pacific order. Unless they opted to adopt a policy of indifference and passivity, which became more and more untenable because of the increasing gravity of the European situation, they would either have to intervene by force in order to check Japanese aggression in China, or they could try to reason with the belligerents, including the aggressors, to persuade them to put an end to the fighting and to re-establish order and stability. This latter approach, the equivalent of the "appeasement" strategy pursued energetically in Europe, was, however, never seriously tried in Asia. Instead, the Western powers and the Soviet Union were willing, for at least two years after July 1937, to consider collective and individual measures short of war to punish Japan and assist China. The result was that by September 1939, when a European war broke out, Japan found itself more isolated than ever, even more so than Germany. Why the West was prepared to appease Germany but not Japan is an interesting question, one that is ultimately linked to the issue of the survival of the Washington system. . . .

When, on 6 October [1937], the [League of Nations] Assembly denounced Japan and called for a nine-power conference, the Roosevelt administration quickly concurred, joining in the condemnation of Japan's violation of the peace and of Chinese independence. Moreover, on just the preceding day, Roosevelt had delivered an important speech in Chicago—the "quarantine address"—indicating America's interest in acting together with other countries to "quarantine" those that were "creating a state of international anarchy and instability." He did not specify which these countries were, but it was clear to his listeners at home and abroad that he had in mind Germany, Italy, and Japan. (He had privately branded them "bandit nations," in view of what Germany had done in Spain, Italy in Ethiopia, and Japan in China.) Although vague, it was not difficult to see the implications of the speech. The United States, after several years of relative passivity and lack of interest in identifying with an international structure, was once again showing signs of willingness to act together with other nations to "preserve peace.". . .

[During 1938] there was no equivalent to the European appeasement, nothing comparable [in Asian-Pacific affairs] to the Munich conference taking place. Reasons for this contrast are not as simple as might at first appear. After all, Britain, France, and even the United States were fearful of, and at the same time had to be prepared for, another European war, and would not have wanted to provoke a serious crisis in Asia. The Japanese were enlarging their fighting on the continent, and if any outside pressure was needed to check it, it was the Soviet Union which was providing it. Western democracies might have decided that the time was opportune to induce Japan to negotiate for a settlement of the Chinese war. Without some international agreement in Asia, Munich alone would not have ensured global stability for, after all, the Versailles system had been complemented by the Washington structure, so that its resilience would hinge on what happened to the latter.

That neither London nor Washington was much interested in an Asian Munich, in the wake of the fateful conference, suggests several underlying assumptions on their part. First, the Western governments may have considered chances for an Asian appeasement much more problematical than one in Europe. Second, related to this must have been a tacit assumption that China was not quite the same thing as Austria or Czechoslovakia. Japan could not have used the German argument for a racial *Anschluss*. Japanese military action was much more of a transparent aggression. Third, at the same time, the democracies may have believed that the Asian war was less likely to develop into a world war than the European crisis brought about by Hitler's revanchism. Fourth, they may have reasoned that the Soviet Union would be more successful in checking Japanese than German expansionism, and therefore that an appeasement strategy in Asia would have to involve it as a principal actor; but the latter had not abandoned its popular front policy and would have vehemently opposed any appeasement of Fascist nations at that time. In fact, Munich impressed [Marshal Josef] Stalin as an attempt by the West to mollify Germany, which had the effect of weakening their resolve to stand firm towards Hitler. The Soviet leader would in time respond to this turn of events by approaching Hitler himself for an understanding. But this was in the future, and for the moment the Soviet Union's adamant opposition to an international settlement in Europe made it certain that it would likewise object to an Asian Munich.

A combination of all these factors resulted in the West's lack of initiative to appease Japan in late 1938. But one should also add another significant difference between Europe and Asia. The United States was more prepared to be involved in the latter region. Opinion polls indicated that the American people were far more willing to take a stand on the Chinese-Japanese War than on any European issue at that time. With an overwhelming majority (consistently three-quarters or more of those polled) expressing their sympathy for China, the Roosevelt administration, even if it had wanted to, would have found it virtually impossible to approach Japan for some kind of agreement, unless it included the latter's withdrawal from China, an unrealistic goal. Moreover, the public was becoming alarmed over the fact, which newspapers and magazines began stressing, that American trade with Japan, especially export of arms, was growing. An inference could readily be drawn that the United States was supplying Japan with munitions which the latter used to fight against China. Japan's dependence on American scrap iron and steel was particularly noticeable, and these items could easily be pictured as being turned into tanks and aircraft for use in China. This was an appalling revelation, and a movement to stop shipments of raw materials and arms to Japan began to be organized throughout the United States. It was supported even by some isolationists, such as Senators Gerald P. Nye and George W. Norris, in sharp contrast to the much more cautious and cynical stand they took regarding European issues. . . .

The only conceivable Asian appeasement, under the circumstances, would have been one in which Japan came together with the Western powers for a stable Asian order on the basis of the status quo *ante bellum* and the respect for China's integrity and the Open Door. In other words, just as some in the West imagined that Munich would reintegrate Germany into a resuscitated, albeit modified, Versailles system, so Asian appeasement would have to mean a reconstructed Washington treaty system. The powers, to be sure, might have been willing to forgo consideration of Manchuria for the time being, but at least they would have insisted on a return to the situation prevailing before July 1937. Japan, furthermore, would have had to accept, in principle at least, the concept of economic internationalism. . . .

On 3 November [1937], Prime Minister [Fumimaro] Konoe issued a public statement, defining the basic national objective as the construction of "a new order for ensuring permanent stability in East Asia." This, the statement asserted, was the joint goal of Japan, Manchukuo, and China; all three must co-operate politically, economically, and culturally so as to "establish international justice, carry out a common defence against communism, create a new culture, and bring about an economic combination" in East Asia. . . .

In other words, the treaties and principles cited by the United States government were no longer valid and would not be accepted as such by the Japanese. One could date Japan's formal rejection of the Washington system from this point. The Konoe statement . . . showed that Japan, after long hesitation, finally crossed the bridge of no return. Although . . . Japanese officials would later equivocate and even try to conciliate Americans by speaking of their co-operation in Asia and the Pacific, as far as Washington was concerned an irrevocable decision had been made by the Japanese leadership, and no reconciliation could now be effected unless these statements were explicitly repudiated. . . .

It was around this time that some key officials in Washington began contemplating specific measures to sanction Japan. Rather than vaguely formulated contingency plans for naval action which Roosevelt had favoured, these officials were thinking of economic pressure. They were particularly interested in two ideas: the abrogation of the existing treaty of commerce with Japan, and the offer of loans to China. The first began to be urged by some officials as an effective way of sanctioning Japan. The 1911 treaty of commerce and navigation had regulated trade between the two countries, and to abrogate it would mean depriving the trade of American legal protection. It would place Japanese import from and export to the United States at the mercy of the latter. This would be a drastic but necessary step, according to its advocates, now that the Japanese had explicitly repudiated the Washington treaties. The second suggestion was less dramatic: the United States might offer China loans so as to enable it to keep resisting Japan. Secretary of the Treasury Henry Morgenthau emerged as the spokesman for this alternative, pleading with Roosevelt for an initial $25 million loan to China. The "future of democracy, the future of civilization," he declared, "are at stake." Supporting Morgenthau, Stanley K. Hornbeck, adviser to Secretary of State [Cordell] Hull on Asian affairs, argued, "Unless the Japanese march is halted by the Chinese or by some other nation, the time will come when Japan and the United States will be face to face and definitely opposed to each other in the international political arena." Such a perception was shared by an increasing number of officials in Washington. But they disagreed among themselves as to specific action America should now take. Hull thought all these proposals were premature and would unnecessarily irritate Japan, but Roosevelt at least approved the loan scheme, and thus the first of what would amount to billions of dollars of credit was offered to the Chinese at the end of the year. . . .

On 26 July [1939], Washington notified Japan that it intended to abrogate the 1911 treaty of commerce and navigation between the two countries. According to the terms of the treaty, abrogation would take effect in six months after notification, namely January 1940. . . .

By August 1939, then, Japan's international position had seriously deteriorated. It was becoming more and more difficult to avoid complications with third powers while the nation tried to conclude the war with China, and the attempt to take advantage of the European situation for enhancing Japanese power in Asia was not working. In the growingly desperate situation, some in Tokyo, notably War Minister Itagaki [Seishirō], strongly argued that the best way out of the impasse was to conclude an alliance with Germany as quickly as possible, even accepting the latter's terms. Japan would then at least have one reliable ally, whereas otherwise it would be totally alone in the world. . . .

The Axis alliance, consummated among Germany, Italy, and Japan in September 1940, was to have been Japan's trump card in implementing its vision of a new Asian order directed against the Anglo-American nations. It would augment

Japan's potential power by tying the nation's destiny to German military accomplishments in Europe, and to Soviet neutrality in Asia, and thereby expel Anglo-American influence from Asia. Time was soon to show, however, that this influence, if anything, grew steadily during the months following the formation of the alliance so that, by mid-1941, the Japanese would feel even more insecure than before. They would find themselves surrounded by the ABCD powers—America, Britain, China, and the Dutch East Indies. Rarely did a diplomatic initiative end in a more complete fiasco. . . .

Given [the Axis alliance], one thing that the Chinese could count on was the unswerving position of the United States and Britain *vis-à-vis* Japan. They would have been heartened if they had known that in early October Prime Minister [Winston] Churchill confided that nothing compared "with the importance of the British Empire and the United States being co-belligerents." He believed that American entry into the war against the Axis powers would be "fully conformable with British interests." Plans were made for staff talks both in Asia and in Washington among British, American, and Dutch officials for a joint strategy against Japan. It is true that at this stage neither London nor Washington was envisaging full strategic co-ordination with Chinese forces, but the implications were clear; the coming together of Germany and Japan, and even possibly of the Soviet Union and Japan, was only confirming the solidarity of America and Britain, so that the Chinese would find themselves part of a coalition just as the Japanese were trying to establish a global alliance of their own. The Chinese-Japanese War was turning into a conflict between two groups of nations. . . .

The only issue at the end of 1940 was one of strategic priorities. Granted that America was involved in a global struggle against the Axis powers, it needed to establish a sense of where to place its emphasis in the immediate future. Assuming that it could not do everything all at once, the government in Washington would have to decide the most effective ways of implementing the aid policy. Here all-out aid to the British home isles took precedence. Whatever London asked, Washington would provide. China came next. After the reopening of the Burma Road, shipments from America, and smaller amounts from Britain, were resumed. An agreement with Chungking for a loan of $100 million, announced on 30 November, was the most massive given China by the United States. The funds were to be used at Chiang Kai-shek's discretion. Equally important, the United States would provide him with fifty pursuit planes, and American citizens would be allowed to serve in China as aviators and aviation instructors. The planes and aviators would be assigned to a volunteer air force which Colonel Claire Chennault would create in Chungking. The air force, officially called the American Volunteer Group but popularly known as the Flying Tigers, would be in place in the autumn of 1941.

America's top military strategists, however, were unwilling to go much further at this time. They all shared Roosevelt's perception that the nation was engaged in a quasi-war, and that it must be prepared for a real war as well. But they were not yet ready to fight a two-front war, against both Germany and Japan. Although ultimately the nation would have to fight them both, the strategists at this time generally agreed with Admiral Harold R. Stark, chief of naval operations, and General George C. Marshall, army chief of staff, that the United States should first concentrate on the Atlantic theatre. Defeat of Germany would take all the nation's resources and manpower, which should not be diverted to a Pacific war with Japan. The United States should not be on the defensive in that part of the world at least until the situation definitely improved in Europe. . . .

War across the Pacific was not inevitable. At least as of June 1941, both Tokyo and Washington were intent upon avoiding such an eventuality. But whereas the Japanese thought war could be avoided if only the United States desisted from assisting Britain against Germany and intervening in Asia, American officials were fast establishing a global system of collective security to push back Germany and Japan to earlier positions. Given the success of American strategy, Japan's only hope, if it were to persist in its Asian scheme, lay in establishing an impregnable empire so as to withstand the pressures of the United States and its allies.

Developments in the summer of 1941 confirmed these two trends. On one hand, the German invasion of the Soviet Union, commenced on 22 June, had the effect of adding the latter to the global American-led coalition. On the other, Japan's decision to take advantage of the German-Russian War by invading southern Indo-China was designed to prepare the nation for an ultimate confrontation with the ABCD powers. Under these circumstances, only a break-up of that partnership or Japan's reversal of southern expansionism could have prevented a Pacific war.

Hitler's decision to nullify the Soviet non-aggression pact and invade Russian territory at once weakened Japan's and strengthened America's respective positions. It signalled the bankruptcy of Tokyo's grand strategy, coalescing Japan, Germany, Italy, and the Soviet Union as revisionist powers against the Anglo-American nations. Overnight the scheme broke into pieces, forcing the Japanese leadership to consider alternatives. Prime Minister Konoe understood that Germany's invasion of the Soviet Union would push the latter to seek the assistance of Britain and the United States, thus in effect adding the country to the Anglo-American coalition. . . .

The question, of course, was what was to be done. One drastic alternative would have been for Japan to recognize frankly the failure of its pro-German policy and, as Konoe said, reorient Japanese policy to effect a *rapprochement* with the United States. He reasoned that the Axis pact had outlived its usefulness; now that it had revealed its utter bankruptcy, Japan should release itself from it and seek an accommodation with the United States. As the prime minister wrote to [Foreign Minister] Matsuoka [Yōsuke] in early July, Japan could never afford to go to war with both America and the Soviet Union; the two powers must be prevented from establishing a close relationship, and in the meantime Japan must have a continued supply of raw materials. All such aims necessitated a readjustment of Japanese relations with America. That would require that Japan make concessions in China and South-East Asia, but Konoe believed such concessions would be worth an improved relationship with the United States. In essence he was arguing for a return to an earlier pattern of Japanese foreign policy in which economic and political ties to America had been of fundamental importance. . . .

This was too drastic a scheme to be acceptable to Japan's military, or to Matsuoka. For them, to go back to the framework of co-operation with the United States would be incompatible with the Axis alliance and entail giving up the scheme for establishing an Asian co-prosperity sphere. They were right, of course, and Konoe was asking them to reorient their thinking so as to accommodate the drastic turn of events overseas. From the military's point of view, however, such reorientation was tantamount to yielding to American pressure and giving up the war in China as hopeless. They could not do so without risking loss of prestige and their privileged position in domestic affairs. Some army strategists, moreover, judged that the world was finally becoming divided into two fighting camps, with Japan, Germany, and Italy on one side and the United States, Britain, the Soviet Union, and China on the other. In such a situation, it was too late for Japan to change sides, it was argued; what the nation must do was to consider the most appropriate strategy for the impending global war. . . .

Between 26 June and 2 July, [Japan's top leaders debated] the next steps Japan was to take, and the result of their deliberations was the crucial policy document ("Outlines of fundamental national policy") adopted at a meeting in the presence of the emperor, held on 2 July. According to the memorandum, Japan was to "construct the Great East Asian Co-prosperity Sphere regardless of the changes in the world situation." More specifically, Japan would concentrate on the settlement of the Chinese war, prepare for southern expansion, and try to solve the "northern problem." In other words, both southern and northern strategies were to be pursued simultaneously; which came first would depend on circumstances, particularly the course of the European war. However, greater specificity was given to [a] southern advance when the document referred to a 25 June decision by the liaison conference that had called for the stationing of Japanese troops in southern Indo-China. The 2 July memorandum stated that such action was part of the preparedness against the United States and Britain.

In other words, the policy that emerged from the deliberations of late June and early July combined a determination to extend Japanese control to southern Indo-China with, at the same time, preparing for war against the United States, Britain, and the Soviet Union. Since Japan was already fighting a war with China, what was visualized was the possibility of a war with four powers, plus probably Indo-China and the Dutch East Indies. This sort of development was the very thing the Japanese had sought to avoid, and apparently they still believed it could be prevented by acting with lightning speed to entrench Japanese power in southern Indo-China. If that could be carried out without incurring foreign intervention, then Japan would have successfully enlarged its empire and be in a better position to fight an all-front war, should it become necessary.

In retrospect, there was faulty logic behind such a decision. Since all parties in Japan were agreed on the imperative of preventing a war against the combined force of its potential enemies, in particular America, Britain, and the Soviet Union, every effort should have been made to establish clear-cut priorities and concentrate on preparedness against one enemy at a time. . . .

The last ten days of July were crucial in determining the future of Japanese-American relations. Already on 21 July, Under-Secretary of State Sumner Welles warned the Japanese that their occupation of Indo-China would be incompatible with the negotiations going on between the two countries. Through "Magic," the code-breaking device that had now become operational, American officials had known of Japan's intention to occupy southern Indo-China, an action which they believed would seriously affect the situation in South-East Asia and must be resisted. American policy after the German invasion of the Soviet Union a month earlier had been quite forceful and clear-cut. The United States welcomed the new development, Roosevelt agreeing with Churchill that, in the latter's words, "Any man or state who fights on against Nazidom will have our aid." The government in Washington immediately started planning for extending lend-lease aid to the Soviet Union, and in the meantime Roosevelt released part of the latter's assets, frozen after the latter's invasion of Finland in late 1939. "If the Russians could hold the Germans until October 1," he said, "that would be of great value in defeating Hitler." In that connection, the president wanted to discourage any Japanese attack on the Soviet Union, warning Prime Minister Konoe in a personal message on 4 July that any such action would jeopardize the negotiations in Washington and undermine the peace in the Pacific.

The United States, in short, was already seeing itself as being tied to the Soviet Union in the European war. It could help the latter by shipping aid goods and by frustrating Japanese attempts to take advantage of the German assault to attack the Soviet Union from the rear. In that connection, Japan's southern advance would be welcome inasmuch as it might divert resources from the north and make less likely an impending Japanese war with the Soviet Union. Instead of acquiescing in Japanese occupation of Indo-China, however, the Roosevelt administration decided to throw obstacles in its way, thus in effect choking off Japan from both northern and southern options. The main instrument was to be economic, in particular the freezing of Japanese assets in the United States. Just as the United States was unfreezing Soviet assets to enable the latter to fight Germany, it would make it impossible for Japan to obtain funds with which to purchase goods in America, especially much-needed oil. A total cessation of exports to Japan was not visualized, however. What Roosevelt, Hull, Welles, and others had in mind was that henceforth Japan would require an export licence whenever it wanted to buy American commodities. Moreover, some small quantities of low-octane gasoline could still be sold to Japan so as not to provide the latter with an excuse for going into the Dutch East Indies. Nevertheless, the intent of such measures was unmistakable. The United States would take steps to deter Japan both from attacking the Soviet Union and occupying Indo-China. Such warning was explicitly communicated to Tokyo so as to leave little room for doubt about America's serious intentions. . . .

Konoe should have taken such warning seriously, but he was too weak to stop the momentum. On 14 July Japan had presented a note to the [French] Vichy regime, demanding the right to station troops in southern Indo-China, and five days later the new foreign minister, Toyoda [Teijirō], gave Vichy the deadline of 23 July. Regardless of Vichy's response, the supreme command was determined to carry out the invasion, and plans were completed for the dispatch of necessary troops on 24 July. Vichy's acceptance came on the 23rd, and thus a "peaceful" landing on the Indo-China coast was accomplished between 28 and 30 July. In retaliation, on 25 July the United States ordered the freezing of Japanese assets. The following day, Britain and the Philippines followed suit, and on 27 July New Zealand and the Netherlands did likewise. The ABCD encirclement of Japan was virtually complete. . . .

America's stiff measures had at least one effect on Japanese policy. The supreme command in Tokyo became less and less sanguine about the prospect of waging a successful campaign against the Soviet Union. Given the deteriorating condition of Japanese-American relations, the nation would have to be prepared for a grave crisis in South-East Asia which could lead to war against the ABCD powers. Under the circumstances, even the die-hard exponents of the northern strategy began showing signs of hesitancy, the more so as the German assault on the Soviet Union was not proceeding as smoothly as had at first been antici-pated. . . .

Between 2 July and 9 August, then, a crucial reversal of Japanese strategy had taken place. From preparedness for an impending offensive against the Soviet Union, the supreme command reverted to a more passive stance in the north. Six-teen divisions would still be mobilized, but they would not be engaged in any ac-tion for the time being. Henceforth, Japanese strategy would focus on a possible conflict with the ABCD powers. In this sense, 9 August may be taken as the point of no return as far as Japanese-American relations were concerned.

The United States contributed to that turn of events by instituting a *de facto* embargo on oil. The freezing of Japanese assets, announced on 25 July, had been followed by a week of intensive work by State department, Treasury, and other of-ficials to set up a machinery for implementing the order. The idea, which Roo-sevelt approved, was to let the Japanese apply for export licences which would then be examined on a case-by-case basis and necessary funds released from blocked Japanese monies to purchase the goods. Oil, too, would be dealt with in this fashion. But the processing of applications for licences and release of funds took time, and the matter was overseen by Dean Acheson, assistant secretary of state, who refused to release funds, intent upon punishing Japan for its southern expansionism. The result was that Japan never got any oil after 25 July, a fact that even Roosevelt did not find out till early September. But the Japanese were under no illusion about the matter. They now realized that a total oil embargo was being put into effect. Japanese strategy would now have to take that development into consideration. . . .

During the second half of August, [Roosevelt and Konoe] continued to ex-change messages, and there was much talk of a possible summit conference. This was because both sides, for different reasons, clearly wanted to avoid a showdown. The Japanese would not go so far as to embrace the entire principles of the Atlantic Charter, viewing them as a unilateral list of America's traditional beliefs with little regard for other countries' special needs. As the Japanese government noted in a message transmitted to Washington on 28 August, certain nations such as the United States that were endowed with superior economic and geographical advan-tages should be more understanding of other countries and co-operate with the lat-ter in a more equitable distribution of material resources. Japan, in other words, was struggling for its needs and for security, an objective it was finding more and more difficult to accomplish because of the ABCD encirclement. Nevertheless, de-spite such differences, Konoe believed a compromise settlement was possible. Be-cause of the lateness of the hour, he believed a personal meeting with Roosevelt alone would defuse the crisis atmosphere and might conceivably lead to a more stable relationship across the Pacific.

President Roosevelt, on his part, was interested in the idea of a summit meeting with Konoe, but not necessarily because he believed a long-lasting settlement of the crisis could be achieved. For him it would be unthinkable to give up the basic principles, but at least a meeting with Konoe would give time for the United States armed forces to be better prepared for a possible war. The president's enthusiasm, however, was not reciprocated by Hull, who believed no summit meeting would be useful until some fundamental issues had been discussed beforehand. Moreover, he was worried lest the meeting affect the solidarity of the ABCD *entente* and drive China out of desperation to the Japanese. If the Chinese should feel they were being betrayed by the Americans, such an outcome would not be unthinkable, Hull believed, and could even lead to releasing Japanese forces out of China for use southward. . . .

Given Chinese sensitivity about any sign of the weakening of the ABCD *entente,* the American government had to tread very cautiously in considering a summit meeting between Roosevelt and Konoe. Nevertheless, the United States might have gone through with the meeting if the Japanese side had been solidly behind Konoe and willing to modify significantly its policy in Asia. Such was not the case, and in the final analysis the aborting of the summit conference must be attributed to the unwillingness of Japan to change course.

For it was during the crucial weeks of late August and early September 1941 that the Japanese leadership finally decided on war. Even as Konoe and his supporters were trying desperately to avert a crisis with the United States through his meeting with President Roosevelt, the supreme command's army and navy sections began a series of intensive discussions to arrive at a consensual decision concerning the timing and scale of preparedness for war against the ABD powers. . . . [T]he navy had believed that war preparedness could be undertaken without a national decision for war, whereas the army believed a definite commitment to go to war was needed before mobilization of necessary forces could be implemented. After daily meetings, the two sides finally reached a compromise at the beginning of September. It was to the effect that Japan should complete war preparedness by late October and decide on war against the ABD powers if no diplomatic settlement had been arrived at by the first part of the month. In other words, war preparedness would be followed by a decision for war, but in the meantime diplomatic efforts would be continued to see if war could be avoided. The army's and the navy's viewpoints were neatly balanced in the compromise. The formula was written into a document, "Guidelines for implementing national policies," which was formally adopted at a leaders' conference in the presence of the emperor on 6 September.

That document may be regarded as a virtual declaration of war by Japan. It clearly implied that war would come unless a peaceful settlement could be worked out with the United States and Britain. In an appendix [annex] to the document the minimal terms acceptable to Japan were spelled out; if those terms were not met, then war would come. Japan would insist, first, that the Anglo-American powers desist from extending military and economic aid to the Chiang Kai-shek regime; second, that they refrain from establishing military facilities within Thailand, the Dutch East Indies, China, or the Far Eastern provinces of the Soviet Union and from augmenting their forces beyond their existing strength; and, third, that they provide Japan with resources needed for its existence by restoring trade relations and offering friendly co-operation with Japan as the latter undertook to collaborate economically with Thailand and the Dutch East Indies. In return for such concessions on the part of the United States and Britain, Japan would be willing to promise not to undertake further military expansion in Asia and to withdraw its troops from Indo-China "upon the establishment of a just peace in East Asia." Furthermore, it would be prepared to guarantee Philippine neutrality and refrain from hostile action against the Soviet Union so long as the latter observed the neutrality treaty.

The 6 September guidelines were interpreted by some, the emperor and the prime minister for example, as sanctioning one last effort to negotiate with the United States in order to avoid war. The emperor emphasized this point both at the meeting of the top leaders held on that day, and also at his prior conferences with Konoe, [General] Sugiyama, and [Admiral] Nagano [Osami]. The emperor's approval of the guidelines may, therefore, have been intended as a way to encourage further diplomatic endeavours. For the military, however, the decisions clearly signalled war. . . .

[Japan's] terms were clearly unacceptable to America. Although the language was somewhat modified, the American side was unimpressed when they were transmitted on 23 September. At a meeting with [Ambassador] Nomura [Kichisaburō] on 2 October, Hull bluntly told the ambassador that he saw little point in holding a summit conference. . . . China was the crucial question. Without further concessions on Japan's part on this point, it was extremely unlikely that any agreement could be reached with the United States—a contingency that could only mean war. If war were to be avoided, therefore, the Konoe cabinet would have somehow to persuade the army to commit itself to withdrawing from China, an impossible demand at this late hour. Thus the Japanese army seized on Hull's 2 October message as a virtual rejection of the peace efforts and pressed Konoe to give up the idea of a summit conference. . . .

On 14 October, [war minister] Tōjō [Hideki] made an impassioned speech at a cabinet meeting against making concessions on the troop withdrawal question. If Japan should submit to American pressure, he said, the fruits of the war with China would be nullified, the existence of Manchukuo jeopardized, and colonial control over Korea itself endangered. It would signal the nation's return to "Little Japan before the Manchurian incident." That was the crux of the matter. The army refused to return to the situation existing in the 1920s, something the United States was insisting upon. The question of Japanese troops in China had come to symbolize this conflict. There could be no compromise on that issue. Tōjō reminded the other cabinet members that the 6 September decisions still stood, and that according to them the nation was to have decided on war if no diplomatic settlement had been achieved by early October. Military mobilization had been going on in accordance with the guidelines, and it could not now be stopped unless agreement were reached with Washington concerning the troops question.

Here, in stark simplicity, was the moment of decision forced upon the cabinet by the war minister. Tōjō was correct in saying that if war was not to be the decision, then the 6 September guidelines would have to be revised. Since the cabinet had been responsible for those guidelines, it was accountable for not having carried out those policies. Thus the only thing left was for the entire cabinet, including Konoe, to resign. The prime minister understood the logic. If war were to be avoided, then a new cabinet would have to start afresh, unencumbered by the 6 September decisions. Konoe, too, had his logic. For him, the most important thing was to avoid war with the United States, and all decisions, including those of 6 September, must be the means towards that end. He recognized that Japan had no chance of winning an American war and did not understand why the army insisted on it. He was acutely aware that no power, not even Germany, could be counted upon to come to Japan's aid in its struggle against the ABCD combination. There was no point in going into a war which the nation was bound to lose. But he, too, realized that if peace at any cost were to be sought, a new cabinet would have to be organized. All such developments led inevitably to the cabinet's resignation on 16 October. With it the idea of a conference with President Roosevelt, on the realization of which Konoe had pinned his hopes for peace, also evaporated. . . .

[Japan's military] strategy was now in its final stages of refinement. It consisted of several important components. First, there would be undertaken a simultaneous attack on Hawaii and South-East Asia (in particular, Singapore and the Philippines). The navy air force would strike at the United States fleet in Pearl Harbor, while at the same moment the army would bombard Malaya and the Philippines, to be followed a few hours later by the landing of troops on these latter areas. These initial assaults, followed by military action in the East Indies, were expected to establish Japan's initial supremacy in South-East Asia and the south-western Pacific within four to eight months. After the successful completion of the "southern strategy," Japan would consolidate its initial gains, secure crucial strategic bases, obtain mineral resources, and prepare for a long-range conflict with the enemy. That was the second component of the emerging strategy. It was assumed that even though the British colonies and the Dutch East Indies might succumb to Japan, the United States never would, so that Japan would have to be prepared for a drawn-out conflict with America, primarily a naval confrontation in the Pacific. That confrontation would last for years, but it should be possible for Japan to maintain at least a status quo in the western Pacific once it established its supremacy in South-East Asia and the south-western Pacific. Third, the war in China would continue, but if Japan should successfully occupy and control Singapore, Hong Kong, Burma, and other areas adjoining China, the latter would find it progressively more difficult to obtain outside assistance. Fourth, although not much could be expected from the German ally, Japan should obtain the latter's co-operation in the war; presumably, Germany as well as Italy would declare war against the United States, and could possibly assist in disrupting the flow of American merchant shipping. But more crucial would be German military successes against Britain and, it was hoped, against the Soviet Union. Japan would have to make sure that Germany would not enter into a separate peace with Britain, which would enable the latter to concentrate on the Asian situation. . . .

Optimism doomed the Japanese strategy at its inception. It was flawed in two critical areas. One, it underestimated the capacity and determination of the United States and Britain to launch a speedy counter-attack after the expected initial disasters. Second, it overestimated German power, assuming that Germany could continue to immobilize Britain in Europe and might even crush the Soviet Union.

Most fundamental was Japan's lack of experience in fighting a multinational war. The First World War had not really been its war, and its participation had been actually limited to seizing German spheres of influence in China and the Pacific; it had essentially been a bilateral war, just like the first Sino-Japanese War and the Russo-Japanese War. Now, for the first time, the nation was having to face a conflict with a multiple number of enemy countries. . . .

What should be the absolute minimal conditions Japan could accept to maintain a peace with the United States? Much time was spent on defining those terms. Here [Foreign Minister] Tōjō [Shigenori] came up with a two-pronged approach. The first (Plan A) was to arrive at a comprehensive settlement of the major issues with the United States. Japan, according to the policy approved by the liaison conference on 1 November, would agree to withdraw its forces from most areas of China within two years of the establishment of a truce, concentrating them in certain parts of north China, Mongolia, Sinkiang, and Hainan Island. They would stay in those areas for up to twenty-five years. Once the war with China was settled, all Japanese troops would be withdrawn from Indo-China. Japan would also accept the principle of non-discrimination in trade in the Pacific and in China if the same principle were applied throughout the world. This was in response to Hull's fundamental principles; the Japanese were in effect saying that the problem of commercial opportunity in China should not be treated in isolation from the rest of the world. It was a rather tame response and reflected a reluctance to make a firm commitment on China before the settlement of the war. As for the Axis alliance, Japan would act "in accordance with its own decisions"—an indirect way of saying that the German pact would not be applicable to the United States unless the latter attacked Germany first.

These terms still indicated a determination to retain Japan's special position in China and the rest of Asia that it had sought to establish by force. As Prime Minister Tōjō explained at the crucial 5 November meeting of the Japanese leaders in the presence of the emperor, Japan could never go back to the "constraints" of the nine-power treaty, which was what Hull's four principles signified. Since the nation had tried to free itself from these constraints by going to war in Manchuria and China, it made no sense to return to the situation existing before 1931. Because the United States appeared adamant on this point, there was little expectation in Tokyo that an agreement could be reached under Plan A. As Foreign Minister Tōjō stated frankly, there was too little time to negotiate a basic understanding on China. Since, however, every effort must be maintained to avoid war if at all possible, Japan was to present a second set of conditions (Plan B) to the United States as the absolute minimum acceptable terms. They would not try for a comprehensive agreement on China, and instead seek to prevent further deterioration of Japanese-American relations. Specifically, Japan would pledge not to advance militarily beyond French Indo-China; the two nations would co-operate in the Dutch East Indies so as to procure the resources they needed; the United States would restore its trade with Japan by lifting the freezing of Japanese assets and providing Japan with the oil it required; and the United States would not obstruct the attempts by Japan and China for peace. If an agreement could be reached on the basis of these terms, Japan would be willing to evacuate southern Indo-China and ultimately the entire peninsula. . . .

The Japanese recognized that . . . there really was little chance that the United States would give up its support of China or agree to the loosening of the ABCD *entente*. Thus virtually all who participated in the 5 November conference resigned themselves to the possibility of war against the ABCD powers. But they also realized that such a war would be an extremely difficult one to wage. Prior to meeting on 5 November, the top military leaders had conferred with the emperor on a number of occasions to apprise him of the crucial decisions that were being made. They all assumed that war would come in early December. Admiral Nagano expressed confidence that through a lightning attack on the enemy, Japan would be able to score initial victories and establish strategic bases in the south-western Pacific; however, he reiterated his earlier scepticism about Japan's chances in a prolonged war. Much would depend on the state of national mobilization as well as world conditions, he said. Japan's only hope, he went on, would lie in the possibility of British defeat through the severing of its oceanic routes by Japan and the landing of German troops on the home isles. Even so, Japan was disadvantaged in that it would never be possible to attack the United States at its source. General Sugiyama was more optimistic; he asserted that the initial southern strategy should enable the nation to establish a position of impregnability, from which to continue the war against American and British forces. At the same time, he cautioned that the United States would force the Soviet Union to offer its Asian territory for use as airfields and submarine bases, and the latter would find it impossible to resist the pressure. Thus, Sugiyama said, there was a possibility that the Soviet Union too might enter the war, especially if it became prolonged.

Given such realistic estimates, why should Japan decide on war? Prime Minister Tōjō concluded that it was now the only alternative. If the nation should simply persevere, within two years America's position would become even more strengthened as it would have extended its air power to the Pacific, whereas Japan would have exhausted its oil stock. It would then be too late to undertake a southern strategy to obtain petroleum. In China, in the meantime, American-supported movements against the Japanese forces of occupation would intensify, and even the Soviet Union might be emboldened to help China. In other words, inaction would make matters worse in two years, whereas the military were saying that at least for that duration the war would go well for the nation. Japan would have a southern empire for two years, and although the China war might still not be settled within the time span, the situation could not be worse than the certain deterioration caused by passivity. It was some such thinking that persuaded Japan's top leaders to make the fatal decision for war, on 5 November 1941.

What the discussion revealed was lack of a long-range vision. Nobody knew how the war would go after the initial successes, still less how the ABCD nations would act in two years' time. But all agreed that the continuation of the existing situation was intolerable. It would, as Tōjō declared, relegate Japan to the status of a third-rate nation, since the nation would become more and more subject to American power and will. It would be better to resist this power as much as possible and see how things developed. It was believed that Japan would suffer in a United States–dominated world order, whereas if it challenged that order, the way might be opened for an alternative arrangement of international affairs. . . .

Given such developments, the relationship between Japan and the United States was reaching an impasse. Only a comprehensive understanding would prevent their total rupture, but no comprehensive understanding could be worked out in the short span of time that Tokyo and Washington had available to make the effort. This became painfully evident in the second half of November, when negotiators in Washington made one last attempt to see if Japan's Plan B could be salvaged. That plan, in contrast to Plan A, proposed to set aside the China issue and aimed at restoring the status quo of June 1941, but for that very reason it had little chance of success. American officials, nevertheless, were willing to consider a temporary arrangement so as to postpone a showdown. Aware, through "Magic" intercepts, that the Japanese would strike unless an agreement had been reached by 1 December, and desirous of putting off a war for at least several months, they drafted a counter-proposal, the so-called *modus vivendi*. A product of high-level deliberations in Washington, the proposal would call for Japanese withdrawal of troops from southern Indo-China, keeping a limited number (25,000) in northern Indo-China, in return for resumption of American shipments of oil to Japan. That was to be a three-month experiment, far from the comprehensive settlement that was needed. Even so, had the British, Chinese, and Dutch governments endorsed the plan, it would have been presented to the Japanese negotiators in Washington, now headed by Kurusu Saburō, special envoy hastily dispatched from Tokyo. Quite predictably, however, the Chinese took strong exception, and from London [Winston S.] Churchill cabled his support of the Chinese stance. After all, the maintenance of the ABCD *entente* was at stake, and the United States could not unilaterally deal with Japan. The decision not to submit the *modus vivendi* proposal, then, was added evidence that the ABCD *entente* could not be broken up to placate Japan, even for three months.

If the ABCD *entente* could not be broken up, there was little point in negotiations between Japan and the United States. . . . In the short span of time that they had available—from the middle to the end of November—it was impossible either for Japan or the United States to reorient its position. Hull's 26 November note, in which he reiterated the basic principles on which America had insisted, confirmed this state of affairs. Japanese officials in Washington and Tokyo took the Hull note as an indication of the wide cleavage between the two countries, and they were of course right. However, they were off the mark when they viewed the note as an ultimatum. It merely restated the position that the United States would stand with China, Britain, and the Dutch, and would invite Japan to join them in re-establishing order in the Asian-Pacific region. If Japan refused to do so, then no compromise could be achieved.

From that point onward, what was left to the United States was not to negotiate further with Japan but to strengthen the ABCD partnership. On 1 December, President Roosevelt assured Lord Halifax, the British ambassador, that in the event of a Japanese attack on British or Dutch possessions in Asia, "we should obviously all be together." In other words, the United States would come to their assistance, so that there would be war between Japan and the ABCD powers together. Japan would get what it had been planning for. In the subsequent days, Roosevelt reiterated the commitment, explicitly stating that America's support meant "armed support," and that the ABCD powers should act together in issuing parallel warnings to Japan not to attack Thailand, Malaya, or the Indies. China, in the meantime, would continue to receive full American support. The ABCD alliance had now come into being in all but name. . . .

Postwar history was to show that the two nations [Japan and the United States] shared much in common and could co-operate for their mutual benefit. That framework of mutuality and co-operation had been the pattern through most of modern history, and reached a peak during the 1920s. Somehow, however, the framework—the Washington Conference system—had been eroded and a sense of rivalry and conflict had replaced that of friendly co-existence. In the long history of Japanese-American relations, however, the crisis and war of the late 1930s and the 1940s were but a brief interlude.

The story, however, must be put in the larger context of international relations, for Japanese-American relations were never purely bilateral ones. In the 1920s, they were the main proponents, together with Britain, of the Washington system, and during the first half of the 1930s there was little actual crisis across the Pacific as Japan managed to act forcefully in China without incurring the combined opposition of other nations. From the mid-1930s, however, there grew progressively a realignment of powers so that China no longer had to fight alone against Japanese aggression. One after another outside powers' help was obtained, and by the end of the decade there had emerged a loose coalition of the United States, Britain, the Netherlands, France, and the Soviet Union, all desirous of checking Japanese advance. In a sense this was a modified Washington system, shorn of Japan but with the addition of Russia. To counter the trend, Japan tried to detach the Soviet Union from the *entente* and enter into a solid alliance with Germany and Italy. The hope was to form an alternative alignment, consisting of Japan, Germany, Italy, and the Soviet Union to oppose the first. The attempt failed, and the result was that Japan found itself more than ever isolated, "encircled" as it was said. In the end it was an encircled Japan pitting itself against a fortified coalition. That enhanced the feeling of insecurity and crisis on the part of the Japanese. The only way out of isolation would have been to go back to the Washington Conference system, but this appeared difficult now that China and the Soviet Union were more closely involved in that system. Seeing no way out of the dilemma except through a gamble for an alternative system of Asian-Pacific affairs, Japan struck. It was, as the government declared, a struggle for a new order and for national survival. The two aims were closely linked. But the war was to demonstrate that survival within the old framework would have been just as plausible.

Miscalculation and Economic Sanctions: U.S. Hardliners Ensure War with Japan

HOSOYA CHIHIRO

Hard-liners in the U.S. government such as Stanley Hornbeck, Cordell Hull, Henry Stimson, and Henry Morgenthau, who favored economic sanctions against Japan in the years immediately preceding the Japanese attack on Pearl Harbor, seriously

---

"Miscalculations in Deterrent Policy: U.S.-Japanese Relations, 1938–1941," by Hosoya Chihiro, in Hilary Conroy and Harry Wray, eds. *Pearl Harbor Reexamined: Prologue to the Pacific War,* pp. 51–58, 59–61, 62, Copyright 1990. Reprinted by permission of The University of Hawaii Press.

miscalculated the impact of such a policy on Japan. Instead of deterring the Japanese from pursuing an expansionist policy, these economic sanctions exacerbated U.S.-Japanese relations, encouraged Japan's southward expansion, and provoked Japanese hard-liners to risk war with the United States. The advocates of the hard-line policy toward Japan misunderstood the psychology of the Japanese, particularly the middle levels of the military, the Japanese decision-making process, and Japanese economic realities. They also rode roughshod over the prudent proposals of the soft-liners in the U.S. State Department such as the director of the Far Eastern Division, Maxwell Hamilton, and Ambassador Joseph Grew in Japan.

The demand of the hard-liners for economic sanctions against Japan played into the hands of the ultranationalists in the Japanese government. The latter argued that the imposition of economic sanctions by the United States necessitated risk and expansion by Japan. In such a climate Japanese moderates found it impossible to counsel caution and accommodation. Their counterparts in the U.S. government similarly learned that they were no match for those who foolishly believed that Japan would not dare attack the United States and that economic reprisals would so cripple Japan that she would acquiesce to American pressures.

After the Marco Polo Bridge Incident of July 7, 1937, Japan adopted an increasingly aggressive course in China. After the *Panay* incident on December 12 [in which Japanese planes attacked a U.S. gunboat, the *Panay*, on China's Yangtze River], the Japanese occupation forces there increasingly interfered with U.S. economic interests. These actions stiffened the American attitude and led to diplomatic protests. When these actions had limited effect on the Japanese military, hard-liners in the U.S. government favored an imposition of economic sanctions against Japan. They believed that Japan's economic dependence on the United States gave them a decided advantage in restraining Japanese expansion. Hence they counseled strong, punitive economic actions against Japan such as prohibiting the importing and exporting of selected goods, suspending credit, restricting monetary exchange, and even imposing a total economic boycott. The legal obstacle confronting them was the 1911 U.S.-Japanese Treaty of Commerce and Navigation.

The first official to advocate the abrogation of this treaty was Hornbeck in a memorandum of July 19, 1938. Initially, he had few supporters. The mood in Washington, D.C., changed, however, when the Japanese government announced on November 3, 1938, a "New Order in East Asia" and Foreign Minister Arita Hachirō stated on November 18 that the large-scale involvement of Japan in China could not help violating U.S. economic interests and that pre-war standards and principles would need to be altered to fit the present and future conditions in Asia. These Japanese actions were taken to be a violation of the Nine-Power Treaty. They created a majority opinion within the State Department that was favorable to an abrogation of the U.S.-Japanese Treaty of Commerce and Navigation. In a curiously argued report issued on December 5, Francis Sayre, assistant secretary of state, maintained correctly that full-scale economic reprisals against Japan posed the serious danger of a military conflict and would create widespread domestic economic disturbances. Paradoxically, however, he went on to maintain that the commercial treaty should be abolished and that steps should be taken to end the granting of credits and loans.

In rapid succession the U.S. government announced on January 14, 1939, a "moral embargo" on airplanes and parts and on February 7, 1939, a cessation of credit to Japan. However, soft-liners in the State Department, represented by Grew and Hamilton, argued that a moderate policy would lead to a revival of the moderate faction (Shidehara diplomacy) in Japan and would also blunt the efforts of the hard-liners who were advocating a strengthened coalition with Nazi Germany. These moderate arguments temporarily bore fruit. Further study by the State Department led to a decision to hand Japan an *aide memoire* proposing a new commercial treaty that would exclude articles five and fourteen [which guaranteed most-favored-nation treatment with respect to tariffs and prohibited export/import restrictions] in the existing treaty. Such a move would be a less severe shock to Japan but would still make it possible to impose embargoes and discriminatory duties.

Unfortunately, on April 27, before the *aide memoire* could be submitted to Japan, the chairman of the Foreign Relations Committee, Key Pitman, submitted a resolution to the Senate that scuttled the State Department's plans. This resolution gave the president the "power to effect an embargo and limit credits against a country which infringes the Nine-Power Treaty and injures American lives and interests." Hamilton feared that the planned revision of the commercial treaty would appear to be connected to the Senate bill and would produce too strong an impression concerning U.S. policy toward Japan. As a result the State Department decided in May to postpone the *aide memoire.*

The hard-line faction in the State Department, led by Hornbeck, could not prevail in 1938 and 1939 because the moderates were supported at that time by the [U.S.] military. The military leaders did not feel the country was sufficiently ready for a conflict with Japan. A Hornbeck memorandum to Sayre on December 29, 1938, argued a position that would be repeated incessantly until the Pearl Harbor attack, namely that a strong U.S. stand of "comprehensive and thoroughgoing program of measures of material pressure" could prevent military conflict and lead to a revision in Japanese policy. Hornbeck's view was echoed in the Senate and by the general populace. A Gallup poll survey showed 66 percent in favor of a boycott on Japanese goods and 78 percent in favor of an embargo on weapons and munitions to Japan. When Japan blockaded the Tientsin settlement in June over Britain's refusal to return four accused Chinese to the Japanese and news circulated of Japan's intention to remove English interests from China, an aroused American public opinion strengthened the hard-line faction's stand on Japanese policy. On July 26, 1939, President Roosevelt announced that the treaty of commerce would be void after January 26, 1940. Hull and Sayre believed that the U.S. ability to impose economic sanctions thereafter would have a "sobering effect" on Japan because of her economic dependence on America.

In Japan Foreign Minister Arita [Hachirō] was more optimistic about the American announcement than were those from the anxious economic circles engaged in trade with the United States or the pro-Anglo-American groups. Arita assessed the American move as largely political, "first in order to settle the question of its rights and interests in China, and second as a gesture in connection with the coming elections this fall." Although he thought a solution could be found, a document developed by the foreign office, which reflected the more hard-line approach of its middle-level officials, opposed a passive "wait and see policy." Instead, the document demanded that Japan should "denounce the unfriendly attitude of the U.S. Government" and appeal to the American public and isolationist faction there.

The hard-liners in Japan suffered a temporary setback when the Nazis signed a non-aggression pact with the Soviet Union. The Hiranuma cabinet fell in late August, and the new Prime Minister, Abe Nobuyuki, by his own volition as well as orders from the emperor, sought to improve U.S.-Japanese relations. Documents developed on October 4 and October 20 by, respectively, the foreign office (based on an army plan) and the Japanese navy argued for bettering U.S.-Japanese relations through the favorable treatment of U.S. interests in China and U.S. citizens residing there. The navy document also advocated holding a U.S.-Japanese conference in Tokyo to conclude a new commercial treaty or at least to obtain a "generalized, temporary agreement even if it fails to affirm specifically the principle of non-discriminatory treatment." It called for avoiding discussion of the Nine-Power Treaty, opening the Yangtze and Canton rivers, compensating U.S. interests in China, and moderating restrictions on U.S. cultural work. Here was an opportunity for the U.S. government to improve U.S.-Japanese relations, but the Japanese conciliatory attitude did not bear fruit because of miscalculations by the hard-liners in the U.S. government.

On the surface, it appeared that these conciliatory Japanese decisions confirmed the thesis of the U.S. hard-liners that a tough approach against Japan would be effective. But two points mitigate against acceptance of this view. First, the German-Soviet non-aggression pact had frightened many Japanese. Second, the same navy document mentioned above also incorporated a hard-line policy. It warned that non-diplomatic measures might have to be adopted against the United States to counter U.S. pressure. The argument was that if Japan were to advance southward or to make more rapid war preparations, Japan would have to enter into arrangements with other countries to obtain necessary raw materials. Furthermore, the document claimed that the alleged tendency of U.S. foreign policy to change rapidly forced Japan to accelerate her war preparations to meet all contingencies.

As a result of the Abe government's effort to improve relations with the United States, Japanese concessions were made at the Tokyo conference in meetings of November 4 and December 18, 1939. The Japanese promised that talks about concessions to U.S. citizens for losses sustained in China through Japanese bombings, settlement problems, and taxes and currency problems would prove satisfactory to the United States and that the Yangtze and Canton rivers would be opened in two months. In return the Japanese wanted mutual concessions and negotiations for the concluding of a new commercial treaty of *modus vivendi*. On December 22 the Japanese ambassador to the United States, Horinouchi Kensuke, presented the details of the *modus vivendi* to Hull. It called for: (1) the principle of the most-favored-nation treatment for commerce, navigation, and tariffs; (2) freedom of entry, travel, and residence where the purpose was that of trade; (3) the handling of taxes, duties, and commissions, direct or indirect, on the basis of non-discrimination or the most-favored-nation principle.

Diametrically opposite reactions to Abe's efforts to improve U.S.-Japanese relations occurred within the U.S. government. Ambassador Grew consistently called for a conciliatory policy. In support of the *modus vivendi* proposed by Japan he said the following in a strongly worded telegram to Washington on December 18, 1939:

> The simple fact is that we are here dealing not with a unified Japan but with a Japanese Government which is endeavoring courageously, even with only gradual success, to fight against a recalcitrant Japanese Army, a battle which happens to be our own battle. . . . If we now rebuff the Government we shall not be serving to discredit the Japanese Army but rather to furnish the Army with powerful arguments to be used in its own support. I am convinced that we are in a position either to direct American-Japanese relations into a progressively healthy channel or to accelerate their movement straight down hill.

The strong reaction of the hard-liners to the *modus vivendi* was demonstrated repeatedly over the next two years. In a memorandum issued the next day Hornbeck argued:

> In my opinion adoption as a major premise of the thought that the "civilian" element in the Japanese nation, may gain an ascendancy over the "military" element and, having done so, would alter the objectives of Japanese policy can lead to nothing but confusion and error in reasoning. . . . Practically the whole of the Japanese population believes in and is enthusiastic over the policy of expansion and aggrandisement of the Japanese empire.

He urged policymakers to believe that the Japanese were insincere; within them "there is a change neither of attitude nor of heart." He and Grew were far apart in their assessments. Grew, however, had been on the Japanese scene for almost a decade; Hornbeck did not know Japan and was strongly pro-Chinese.

Secretary Hull became increasingly sympathetic to Hornbeck's view. Although he did not support the hard-line faction's argument (stated in a December 11, 1939, memorandum to Roosevelt) to impose duties on Japanese commerce upon the termination of the commerce treaty, he refused to heed Grew's advice to implement a new treaty or a *modus vivendi* (December 20). The consequent failure of the Tokyo conference was the final straw that brought about the collapse of the Abe cabinet. The new cabinet headed by Admiral Yonai Mitsumasa and Foreign Minister Arita submitted the same proposal with no new approaches. That effort failed, and the Treaty of Commerce and Navigation lapsed on January 26, 1940.

Despite the Japanese awareness that a lapse of the treaty did not mean an automatic levy of discriminatory tariffs or restrictions on Japanese products, the psychological impact was profound. Immediately, the foreign office concluded that they "must end as quickly as possible the present high level of economic dependence on the U.S. and press on for a policy to establish an economic system which would not be endangered by the U.S. attitude." When the Nazi Blitzkrieg defeated Norway, the Netherlands, Belgium, Luxemburg, and France between April and June, 1940, many Japanese feared that Japan "might miss the bus." They saw an opportunity by a quick southward movement to obtain oil and other materials from the Dutch East Indies and to prevent the transport of war supplies to Chiang Kai-shek from French Indochina.

All factions in the U.S. government were opposed to a Japanese southern advance and an alliance with Germany, but they differed on how to prevent these possibilities. Grew wanted the United States to break the deadlock with Japan by discussing a new commercial treaty and by extending credit to Japan for non-military supplies. At a meeting of Hull, Hamilton, and Hornbeck on May 24, the latter feared that American concessions would be perceived as a sign of weakness and would encourage new Japanese aggression. He opposed any new moves. In May and June, however, Hull seemed to have adopted a more conciliatory attitude. He even allowed the opening of conferences by Grew with Foreign Minister Arita to discuss the promotion of trade and the strengthening of relations between the two countries. These talks failed because Grew had to assert that the *sine qua non* for improved U.S.-Japanese relations was non-interference in U.S. interests and the halting of the use of force in effecting national policy. Foreign Minister Arita was just as adamant that the obstacle to that goal was the lack of a commercial treaty. Grew, at least, sought to initiate talks in support of a *modus vivendi* from Washington, but by July Hull was no longer interested. He may have been interested in these talks in May and June only because of the altered condition in Europe and Hornbeck's advice that such talks might stall the feared Japanese advance southward.

The failure of the Grew-Arita talks contributed to the fall of the Yonai cabinet and to the creation of a more aggressive cabinet led by Konoe Fumimaro with Matsuoka Yōsuke as foreign minister. It was recognized that such a cabinet would be more favorable to both a southern advance and a coalition with Italy and Germany. When Japan closed the Burma Road, Hornbeck advocated either immediate export restrictions on aviation gasoline or the implementation of a full-scale embargo on exports. The rationale was that these actions would "retard or prevent new adventuring."

In the meantime the U.S. government took a number of steps beyond diplomatic action. It ordered the continued stationing of the fleet in Hawaii on May 4 to deter a Japanese attack on the Dutch Indies and also passed the National Defense Act, which gave the president power to license the export of arms, munitions, raw materials, airplane parts, optical instruments, and other items. Scrap iron and petroleum were omitted because, as Hamilton put it, "such restrictions or prohibition would tend to impel Japan towards moving into the Dutch East Indies. . . ."

The appointment of Henry Stimson as secretary of war also hardened the U.S. position. Stimson had been advocating a strong policy of economic sanctions against Japan since the Manchurian Incident of 1931. He was very close to the Secretary of the Treasury Morgenthau and to Hornbeck and other hard-liners. From hindsight we can see that he and Hornbeck suffered from the same two misconceptions: (1) that Japan would never dare wage war against the United States despite American actions against her, and (2) that Japan's southern advance would prove unlikely because of her deeper involvement in the Chinese quicksand. Stimson argued to prohibit the export of munitions and war materials to Japan as well as imports from Japan. At a dinner party at the British embassy on July 18 he said, "The only way to treat Japan is not to give in to her on anything."

The soft-liners fought an ever-losing battle. A conference requested by President Roosevelt to discuss Morgenthau's proposed moratorium on petroleum was held in late July. It included Morgenthau, the secretaries of the army and navy, and Acting Secretary of State Sumner Welles. Although Welles argued vigorously for

Hull against Morgenthau regarding a proposed export licensing system for products including petroleum and scrap iron, he was able to achieve only a small compromise on July 26. The compromise on petroleum limited export restrictions to aviation motor fuel and lubricants; scrap iron restrictions were limited to Number 1 heavy melting iron and steel scrap. Stimson was elated and wrote in his diary: "We have won . . . a long battle, which we have been waging against Japan for about four years." In fact, however, given developments in Japan, they had not won at all.

The severe economic sanctions deeply shocked citizens in every quarter of Japan. The army's general staff argued strongly on August 2 for strengthening the southern expansion policy. The first section of the navy's general staff on August 1 drew up "A Study Relating to Policy Towards French Indo-China" that echoed the army's response to the economic sanctions imposed by the United States. The conviction of the Japanese military that a "U.S. imposition of complete embargo" would make the "use of military forces toward the south . . . a matter of life and death" was confirmed by the navy's general staff toward the end of August. Such a policy also received unanimous support at a round-table conference of the middle-echelon officers of the army and navy. Although the minister for naval affairs, Yoshida Zengo, opposed the use of force in the event of a complete embargo, the middle-echelon officers of the Japanese army and navy did not. . . .

The enforcement of U.S. economic sanctions had stiffened the attitude of the middle-echelon officers and provoked them to execute the plan for a southern advance. Their action, however, escalated things further. Far from learning anything from the results of their hard-line action, the American proponents of this approach now demanded more economic sanctions to halt Japanese aggression.

Successive pieces of information regarding Japan's new demands toward Indochina and the Dutch Indies reached the U.S. government in the first two weeks of August. On August 15 Morgenthau again stressed to Hornbeck the need for a full embargo on oil to Japan. Both were convinced that such an embargo would prevent Japan from any resolute action such as occupying the Dutch East Indies. On the next day, Hornbeck told representatives of the Dutch East Indies oil companies not to submit to Japanese pressure, especially to the demand for a large quantity of aviation gasoline.

On September 6, when the Japanese troops caused an incident on the Indochina border, the U.S. cabinet witnessed a sharp exchange of words between Morgenthau and Stimson on the one hand and Hull on the other concerning the question of an embargo on petroleum. Hornbeck on September 11 stressed to Stimson the need for a more active policy of restraining Japanese actions and promoting friendly relations with the Soviet Union. On September 19, after hearing about the latest Japanese ultimatum regarding Indochina, the American cabinet met again to examine the question of a complete embargo on aviation gasoline. Although Hull feared that an oil embargo would incite Japan to attack the Dutch East Indies, Stimson and Morgenthau demanded a complete embargo on oil. State Department opposition limited economic sanctions to a prohibition on the export of all grades of scrap iron.

On October 5, Foreign Minister Matsuoka expressed his displeasure to Ambassador Grew at this U.S. action. He stated that "such embargoes would intensely anger the Japanese people." On October 8, Ambassador Horinouchi, in a hand-delivered note to Hull, heatedly protested restrictions that he claimed constituted a "virtual embargo" and an "unfriendly act" that "may cause future relations between the United States and Japan to become 'unpredictable.' "

In Japan the hard-liners now made their own miscalculations. On September 27 the Tripartite Pact between Japan, Germany, and Italy was signed. Matsuoka expected that the strengthening of the Axis would enhance Japan's position. He believed the pact would frustrate the U.S. intention to intervene in a Japanese southern advance and would lessen the possibility of the outbreak of war with the United States.

The U.S. reaction was completely contrary to what Matsuoka had divined. According to a U.S. public opinion survey of late September, the attitude toward Japan had worsened. The number of Americans favoring strong action against Japan had greatly increased. A cabinet meeting on October 4 led to the consensus that the United States would not yield one inch to Japanese intimidation. A navy squadron was proposed for sailing to the Dutch East Indies or Singapore. Furthermore, Roosevelt stated on October 12 that the United States would not be intimidated. The Tripartite Pact had failed dismally to produce the impact the Japanese hard-liners had predicted. Instead, it had exacerbated relations with the United States. Middle-echelon army officers intensified their cry for an acceleration of southern expansion. Even before the enactment of the Tripartite Pact, Japan had demanded permission to move troops into southern Indochina and did so on July 28.

The Japanese pressures on Indochina led the U.S. government on July 25 to freeze Japanese assets in the United States and to impose an embargo against Japan. The lines were drawn. Hull wrote: "Nothing will stop them except force. . . . The point is how long we can maneuver the situation until the military matter in Europe is brought to a conclusion." From hindsight it is curious why Hull stated such an objective but pursued policies that played into the hands of Japanese hard-liners and contributed to their escalated aggression.

Middle-echelon officers in the Japanese navy were resolved to go to war because of the oil embargo. They were anxious about the existing supply of oil turning the Japanese navy into a "scarecrow navy." A secret war diary of the army general staff noted on August 1 that the "atmosphere of the inevitability of war with England and the U.S. had gradually deepened" and on August 2 "the Military Affairs Section of the Ministry of War proposed an Imperial Conference to determine to go to war with England and the United States." Simultaneously, Ambassador Grew was in a state of despair as a result of the oil embargo. He wrote, "The vicious circle of reprisals and counter reprisals is on. The obvious conclusion is eventual war."

Thus, the American hard-liners' policy of first proposing and then imposing economic sanctions to deter a Japanese southern advance and war failed badly. To understand how it produced the opposite effect it is necessary to consider two miscalculations about the Japanese made by the hard-line faction of the U.S. government. One was that Japan would seek to avoid war with the United States at all costs. The other assumption followed from the first, namely that Japan would inevitably submit to unbending American resolution. However, economic pressure did not restrain Japan from a southern advance. Instead it accelerated a Japanese southern policy even at the risk of possible war with the United States.

Why had the hard-liners miscalculated? First, their predictions of Japan's reactions were based on an analysis of Japan's upper-level policymakers. They lacked an understanding of the important role played by the middle-echelon military officers in the making of Japanese foreign policy. This middle-echelon group was more adventurous, more contemptuous of compromise, and more militaristic.

Second, the hard-liners were prone to making false analogies from the past. For example, Hornbeck argued that the exaggerated gestures of men such as Matsuoka in the past actually reflected a lack of Japanese resolve to wage war. . . .

Third, the hard-line faction concluded that, in light of the disparity in strength between Japan and the United States, Japanese decision makers could not rationally decide on war. In this regard they made the mistake of applying to the Japanese in unaltered form the western model of decision making based upon rational behavior. Lack of knowledge about the psychology of the Japanese people and especially of the middle-echelon military officers in the period immediately preceding the war led the hard-line faction to miscalculate Japanese psychology. That psychology was marked by a predisposition to making crucial decisions in the face of extremely great, even illogical, risks—as was expressed in Tōjō Hideki's often quoted statement that "sometimes a man has to jump with his eyes closed, from the temple of Kiyomizu into the ravine below." This predisposition was also characterized by an absolute abhorrence of submission. They would choose "death rather than humiliation." Grew understood that mentality. He wrote, "Japan is a nation of hard warriors, still inculcated with the samurai do-or-die spirit which has by tradition and inheritance become ingrained in the race." He was correct in warning the decision makers at home not to miscalculate the peculiarities in the Japanese mode of action. Had his advice been followed the Pacific War might very well have been avoided. Grew was prudent. The same thing could not be said for the hard-liners.

Roosevelt's Global Perspective:
The Russian Factor in Japanese-American Relations

WALDO HEINRICHS

Despite all we know about the road to Pearl Harbor, it is still hard to fathom why the United States brought matters to a head with Japan in July–August 1941 when it was supposedly pursuing a strategy of concentration against Germany and strict defense in the Pacific. In particular, it is difficult to understand why the United States imposed a total embargo on the shipment of petroleum products to Japan when officials from the president on down recognized that such an act might propel Japan into a grab for Dutch East Indies oil, the very southern advance the United States hoped to prevent. The various explanations at hand—sentimentalism

From Waldo Heinrichs, "The Russian Factor in Japanese-American Relations, 1941," in Hilary Conroy and Harry Wray, eds. *Pearl Harbor Reexamined: Prologue to the Pacific War,* 1990, pp. 163–174. Reprinted by permission of The University of Hawaii Press.

over China, naive hopes about the deterrent capacity of air power in the Philippines, a coup by hawkish bureaucrats while the president was at the Atlantic Conference, chaotic decision making in the Roosevelt administration—simply do not alone or together provide satisfying answers.

Perhaps we are looking in the wrong direction. It is true that East Asia–Pacific policy had its own parameters, as did Atlantic-European policy, and that American policies East and West tended to be the reciprocals of one another. Yet this was not the only framework of policy. The great question for world leaders in the first half of 1941 was whether Hitler would attack the Soviet Union, and the great question in the latter half was whether he would succeed. This was the central dynamic of world politics from which hung in large measure the strategic decisions of Japan, Great Britain, and the United States, not to mention the USSR, which had its own East-West reciprocals, standing as it did between Germany and Japan.

A chain of reciprocals encircled the globe, and every link was relevant to Roosevelt and his advisers; their framework of policy was truly worldwide by 1941. So we may hypothesize that the German-Soviet conflict had a direct bearing on Japanese-American relations. Within this wider canvas we may find better answers to nagging questions.

A decisive change—one needing greater emphasis—occurred in American foreign and strategic policy in mid-1941. It occurred at the time of, and partly as a result of, the Atlantic Conference between Churchill and Roosevelt but was not bounded by the time frame or agenda of that conference.

From January until well into July of 1941 Roosevelt's policy had been extremely cautious and hesitant. Fear of encouraging isolationist sentiment during the Lend-Lease debate was undoubtedly one factor. So was a scarcity of military resources. The U.S. Atlantic Fleet simply did not have the ships and readiness to make an important contribution to the Battle of the Atlantic before mid-summer. Japan's threat of southward advance, reinforced by the Soviet-Japanese neutrality treaty, delayed the transfer of reinforcements from the Pacific Fleet to the Atlantic.

What most worried Roosevelt, however, was uncertainty about Hitler's intentions. The United States did not, as we thought was the case, receive an unambiguous warning early in 1941 of the forthcoming German attack on the Soviet Union. In these months an invasion of England remained the most likely possibility. From April on German troop movements to the East made a decisive outcome of Soviet-German tensions seem inevitable, but the overwhelming belief was that the German concentration was for the purpose of intimidation, that Hitler would finally present an ultimatum demanding concessions, and that Stalin would bow. The German blitz in the Balkans in April and the seizure of Crete in May pointed the way to Suez and the Middle East, and at all times intelligence flowed into Washington, which was especially sensitive on the score, of a possible German southwestern drive through Spain and Gibraltar to northwestern Africa and Dakar.

Roosevelt and his advisers were truly uncertain about which set of reports to believe until early June. No possible vector of German advance seemed sure enough to build policy on, and so the tendency was to guard against the worst case and protect the Atlantic. After a year of devastating events, a German attack on Russia looked too good to be true. Even if an attack occurred, the war was not expected to last longer than four to eight weeks, allowing time for further campaigning that year. The aura of German power before the Russian campaign was little short of overwhelming.

Beginning with the Japanese acquisition of bases in southern Indochina at the end of July, American policy changed dramatically. It is hard to imagine how Roosevelt could have avoided some demonstration of firmness in the face of this latest Japanese move, obviously penultimate to an attack on Malaya and the Dutch East Indies and taken despite American warnings and mounting trade curbs stopping just short of oil. What is difficult to account for solely in an East Asian or any other regional context is the sweeping nature and boldness of his moves. He ordered a suspension of petroleum exports to Japan before leaving for the Atlantic Conference and converted it into an embargo upon his return. At the conference he established that no significant secret agreements yet existed between Britain and the USSR and worked out with [Winston S.] Churchill a set of war aims that were congruent with American Wilsonian values and that formed a basis for risking or waging war. He agreed to undertake an escort of convoys in the western Atlantic. He ordered maximum assistance to the Soviet Union before winter set in and pushed for a conference in Moscow to arrange for further deliveries in amounts acceptable to the Soviets. He agreed to Churchill's plea for a warning to Japan that any further move would lead to war, and he gave it, although in diluted form. Finally, he began reinforcement of the Philippines, especially with air power.

The assertion that Roosevelt temporarily suspended oil exports contradicts the conclusion of well-accepted, independent studies of the question and requires an explanation. [The historians] Jonathan Utley and Irvine Anderson have been most helpful in showing the extent to which shipments of petroleum products had already been virtually halted by various means such as the withdrawal of tankers and a ban on shipment of oil in drums. They contend that despite Roosevelt's declared intent of permitting the shipment of some kinds and amounts of petroleum products, Dean Acheson and other second-level officials managed to discover bureaucratic devices to shut the tap completely while the president was away at the Atlantic Conference.

On the point of presidential knowledge and intent, I disagree. Declarations to the contrary notwithstanding, Roosevelt left for the Atlantic Conference determined to withhold further shipments of oil until he had discussed this and related questions with Churchill. Sumner Welles, acting secretary of state and long-time confidant of Roosevelt, told Assistant Secretary [Dean] Acheson on July 29 that the "happiest solution" would be to withhold action on Japanese applications for dollars to buy oil for the "next week or so." Evidence suggests that the time frame he meant was in fact two weeks, or not far short of the time during which Welles and the president would be at the Atlantic Conference.

It is difficult to imagine Welles not speaking for Roosevelt or Acheson acting without authorization on so sensitive an issue. Acting on orders fits with Acheson's account in his memoirs and with his discontent at his own performance eight years earlier when, as undersecretary of the treasury, he had refused to sign an order legalizing the devaluation of the dollar and had been fired for it. The lesson he drew and undoubtedly applied on this his second chance was that an assistant to the president must be "very alert and watchful" of the president's position and interests, indeed "twice as much as your own." Acheson was under orders to stall and found ways to comply.

The president was temporizing but moving in a direction he knew entailed great risk. Why would he do so just when he was about to enter into the Battle of the Atlantic? Surely the logic of Plan Dog and Rainbow 5, of concentration against Germany and defense in the Pacific, would argue against so severe an oil policy.

We begin to understand Roosevelt's intent if we consider an event that coincided with the Japanese move into southern Indochina and war at least as significant: a pause in the German advance on Moscow beginning July 19 and lasting into mid-August, occasioned by the need for resupply and a disagreement among Hitler and his generals about a strategy for the next stage. While Roosevelt was considering what to do about Japan he was seeing the first evidence that the Soviet Union might, after all, survive the German onslaught until winter and so into 1942. The press reported "Nazi drives halted," "blitzkrieg braked." On July 29 the *Washington Post* described the German invasion timetable as "completely upset." The same day Hanson Baldwin, under a headline, "Winter Looms as Red Ally," wrote: "The future history of the world is being written in the struggling melee of tanks and planes and men on the 2,000 mile front." Diplomatic reports reinforced the emerging optimism. The American embassy in Berlin learned that German plans were awry due to the discovery of a second Soviet defense line of more than 100 fresh divisions east of the so-called Stalin Line. The general feeling in Germany now was that the war would go into another winter. At his conference with Churchill, Roosevelt heard [presidential assistant] Harry Hopkins' encouraging report of his meeting with Stalin.

From the depths of despair, morale bounded higher than circumstances at the moment justified, but even the possibility of Russian survival made all the difference. The reversal of fortunes from as late as March 1941 when an alignment of the Axis with the Soviet Union seemed quite possible was near miraculous. A coalition of the United States, Great Britain, and the Soviet Union had the power to defeat Germany. This was the time to get Hitler, said Treasury Secretary Henry Morgenthau. "We will never have a better chance. . . . [W]e can't count on the good Lord and just plain dumb luck forever." Roosevelt began pressing his aides to allocate and speed shipments of arms to the Soviet Union in the strongest possible way, as a matter of vital national safety.

Support for the Soviet Union and the grand coalition to defeat Hitler had serious implications for American East Asian policy. The question before the Japanese government in the wake of the German attack was whether to join Germany, as requested, in attacking the Soviet Union or to pursue its southward advance. The decision of the Imperial Conference of July 2 was to move into southern Indochina but to prepare in the north and to attack if circumstances favored it, that is, if the Germans were clearly winning and the Soviets transferred enough of their Far Eastern forces to the western front. Preparing in the north meant mobilizing 850,000 men, causing an inflow of troops carefully monitored by American consuls in Manchuria. It was difficult to decide whether Japan would go north or south, or when and under what conditions, but an attack on Russia became a distinct possibility.

Opposite were thirty tough, experienced Soviet divisions, three cavalry brigades, sixteen tank brigades, and 2,000 tanks and aircraft. A great deal depended on whether a crisis in the west would compel Stalin to withdraw these forces. American leaders undoubtedly asked themselves what conditions would provide Stalin with sufficient assurance about Siberia to withdraw enough of these forces to survive in the west. Foreign Minister V. M. Molotov sought an American warning that the United States would come to Russia's assistance if it were attacked by Japan. Roosevelt was not prepared to offer such a commitment, to join the war and send an army to the Russian front, as invited, to provide more than token aid in 1941. What could he do to help?

To do nothing regarding Japan would not only leave the resources of southeast Asia and Britain's connections to Australia and New Zealand at Japan's mercy but would offer no discouragement to a Japanese attack on the Soviet rear. To pursue diplomacy might prevent or delay a southward advance, but any agreement at China's expense was likely to weaken China's will to resist and permit further redeployment of Japanese forces north or south or both. Furthermore, any evidence of American appeasement was likely to undermine American credibility and reliability in the eyes of the anti-Hitler coalition. Any security Japan might gain in the south by an agreement with the United States could well encourage Japan to strike northward. Any assurance of American petroleum supplies, a probable requirement of agreement, would provide the wherewithal. Even reducing allocations to Japan's peacetime levels would allow the import of more than five million barrels of crude oil and nearly half a million barrels of gasoline in the remainder of 1941.

Roosevelt could also apply maximum pressure: not a drop of oil. Let Japan's oil supplies dry up and its capacity for military operations anywhere shrink. Seek closer collaboration with the British, Dutch, and Australians and provide further assistance to the Chinese. Reinforce the Philippines, especially with long-range bombers capable of raiding Japanese cities. Create such uncertainty and concern among Japanese decision makers regarding the south and relations with America that they did not dare go north. This was a line of argument advanced by an officer in the Far Eastern division of the State Department a few days after the German attack on the Soviet Union.

Containment was Roosevelt's preferred way of dealing with Japanese aggression. Victory in any struggle between the two nations, he wrote in 1923, was bound to lie with the United States, which had vast economic superiority. In 1937 he had commented approvingly on a suggestion by the U.S. Asiatic Fleet commander, Admiral Harry Yarnell, that the way to fight Japan was to form a common front with Britain, France, the Netherlands, and the Soviet Union to cut off all trade with Japan, simply attacking Japanese commerce from distant encircling bases, while China tied down Japanese troops. The result would be the "strangulation" of Japan without the cost of huge armies or Jutland-style naval battles.

Containment on this order, of course, remained only an idea as the threat of Hitler supervened and conceivable Asian partners fell by the wayside, weakened or turned in other directions. Now, however, the British-American alignment with the Soviet Union, even if only implicit as far as Japan was concerned, the growing possibility of establishing a British Eastern Fleet, and the availability of B-17 bombers and their success in flying the longest hop to Hawaii in a possible ferry route to the Philippines revived the idea of containment.

July was a wonderful clarifying month for Roosevelt and his advisers. Hitler's attack on the Soviet Union together with the first evidence of the Russians' ability to sustain resistance made it conceivable, realistic, and calculable to marshal forces sufficient to defeat Nazi Germany. On July 9 the president ordered the services to estimate how much total production would be required to defeat the nation's potential enemies.

The incalculable component of this global scheme was Japan. The Soviet-German war had intensified Japanese expansionism, opportunism, and unpredictability. Whether Japan went north or south—and who could tell which?—it threatened to upset the improving balance of forces. This careening expansionism must be stopped. Japan must be boxed in, contained, immobilized. Embargo, coalition diplomacy, military aid, demonstrations of firmness, and air and naval deployments would, it was hoped, keep Japan within bounds. The risks of war would increase, but the risks of inaction, in the global calculus, seemed greater. Roosevelt could see the whole picture now. He was forceful, impatient of delay, pressing upon events, so different from the reserved, withdrawn president of the spring.

Let no one mistake the severity of American policy toward Japan. Acheson reported to Welles upon the latter's return from the Atlantic Conference that none of Japan's applications for funds had been approved. No countervailing directive came down; Roosevelt had promised Churchill to maintain his economic measures in full force, and he did. Utley and Anderson have shown that Acheson and his colleagues, by insisting that the Japanese pay from sequestered funds before dollars could be unblocked and by other devices, managed to bring trade to a halt without any formal order. They could point out, Acheson explained with relish to a British diplomat, that the Japanese had "imposed [an] embargo upon themselves by their lack of loyalty" to the American order to freeze their dollars.

Roosevelt's dilution of the war warning was not a weakening but a means of delay. The Japanese suggestion of a leaders' meeting provided too good an opportunity of stringing out talks while reinforcement of the Philippines proceeded and the de facto embargo took hold. Careful examination of the American documents and negotiating position reveals not a whit of evidence that Roosevelt or Hull intended compromise or summit. Somewhat like Acheson and his trade officials, the Far Eastern officers of the State Department questioned, compared, and criticized Japanese terms, asking always for further clarification and explanation without registering progress or impasse. The object was, as Roosevelt had told Churchill, to gain a delay of thirty to sixty days. Upon the fall of the Konoe cabinet in October he wrote Churchill that he had gained "two months of respite in the Far East."

Before meeting Churchill at the Atlantic Conference, Roosevelt met with his military advisers and authorized sending thirty-six B-17's to the Philippines. "That was a distinct change of policy," General H. H. Arnold later reminisced. "It was the start of a thought to give General MacArthur weapons for offensive operations." As General George Marshall, chief of staff, explained, these planes would act as a "serious deterrent" to Japan, especially in the winter months that were suitable for high altitude bombing.

After the Atlantic Conference, from the middle of August through September, news from the Russian front was dismal; the Germans besieged Leningrad and encircled Kiev, capturing two-thirds of a million Soviet troops. The Ukraine and Odessa were lost, the Crimea cut off, the crossings of the Dnieper seized. Beyond lay the riches of the Donetz Basin and the Caucasus. Every major city of European Russia except, for the moment, Moscow, was imperiled. Stalin admitted in a letter to Churchill that the Soviet Union was in "mortal menace" and would be defeated or rendered useless as an ally unless the British mounted a second front in the Balkans or France and provided large quantities of aluminum, aircraft, and tanks. The Soviet ambassador, in conveying the message, Churchill informed Roosevelt, used language implying a separate peace if Soviet demands could not be met.

A second front was out of the question, but Roosevelt and Churchill were determined to do what they could by way of supply. They hastened a conference in Moscow and cobbled together a commitment of 500 tanks per month, which meant stretching out the equipping of the U.S. Third, Fourth, and Fifth Armored Divisions and fifteen independent tank battalions, and postponing the activation of the Sixth Armored Division. They also promised 1,800 planes. Roosevelt supplied the three largest U.S. troop transports to take a British division to Basra, Iraq, from where it might reinforce the Russians in the Caucasus or, in case they collapsed, defend against a German thrust from that direction.

On September 5, the day Roosevelt received Stalin's message, besides approving arrangements for the first escort of convoys and the Basra transports, the president saw Hull, who converted Acheson's undercover stalling tactics into a de facto embargo. On that same day nine B-17's departed from Hawaii for the Philippines, and twenty-seven more received orders to depart in October. As Churchill had informed Stalin on August 28, Roosevelt "seemed disposed . . . to take a strong line against further Japanese aggression whether in the South or in the Northwest Pacific." General [George C.] Marshall urged the president to authorize a buildup of air power in the Philippines to restrain Japan "from advance into Malaysia or Eastern Siberia." On September 12, when the first nine B-17's arrived safely, the army ordered thirty-five more across in December, totaling seventy, together with dive bombers, more fighters, and command, air warning, reconnaisance, ordnance, and engineering units for the air force as well as tanks, antiaircraft, and artillery. About this time, according to the British ambassador Lord Halifax, Roosevelt sent a verbal message to [Josef] Stalin (possibly through Averell Harriman) advising that in case of an acute crisis in the west he should withdraw his troops from Siberia and not worry about what the Japanese did, because any incursion could be corrected later. Support for the Soviet Union correlated with a stiffening policy toward Japan.

In October a powerful, concentrated German assault on Moscow made the Russian situation even more precarious. The question returned of how to get Japan "off Russia's back," as one diplomat put it. An army intelligence estimate of October 2 warned against any agreement with Japan that would permit Japan to withdraw the bulk of its army from China. Any liberation of Japanese forces "for action against Russia's rear in Siberia would be foolhardy." The Army War Plans Division advised a continuation of existing pressures "with a view to rendering Japan incapable of offensive operations against Russia or against possessions of the associated powers in the Far East."

The fall of the Konoe cabinet on October 16 and the appointment of General Tōjō as premier increased fears of Japanese aggression. Some signs pointed south, but the balance of opinion in October, including the president's, was that Japan would strike to the north. With the embargo now complete, with persistent warnings already given to Japan against an attack to the north as well as to the south, the only further means of pressure was to strengthen American military power in the region. With the president's approval the army had increased the number of B-17's planned for the Philippines to 170. The dispatch of these aircraft, however, was scheduled over many months, and the force would not be complete until October 1942. On October 16, 1941, in the wake of the fall of the Konoe cabinet and after an emergency meeting of the president and his military advisers, the dispatch of the bombers was accelerated so that 165 would arrive by March 1942. Now also for the first time the army committed an additional ground combat unit, an infantry regiment, and another tank battalion, an antiaircraft regiment, and a field artillery brigade. The navy dispatched Submarine Squadron Two, twelve newly commissioned boats, pushing the Asiatic Fleet's submarine force to twenty-nine, the largest in the navy.

As the establishment of American air power in East Asia progressed, the American military leadership warmed to the idea. The Army War Plans Division argued that "strong offensive air forces" in the Philippines, prepared to operate from British and Dutch bases, would provide a crucial deterrent to Japanese expansion southward. Deterring a Japanese attack on Siberia would be American, British, and Dutch forces in Japan's rear, as well as the possibility of American entry into the war and the use of Russian bases for bombardment of Japan's cities.

Secretary of War Henry Stimson was enthusiastic about the capability of the B-17's to deter an attack on Singapore. He was skeptical about northward deterrence but nevertheless advised the president that Vladivostock was crucial for the supply of Russian troops because the Archangel route was in jeopardy from the German advance and the Persian corridor was undeveloped. He presented an exciting picture of these long-range bombers sweeping from the Philippines across Japan to Soviet bases on the Kamchatka Peninsula and onward to Alaska and back, after the fashion of the German Condors shuttling between bases in western France and Norway.

General Marshall showed unaccustomed enthusiasm in describing the new possibilities. In a phone conversation he pointed out that the B-17's could operate from Australia, New Britain, Singapore, and the Dutch East Indies, "possibly even Vladivostock." They could cover the whole area of possible Japanese operations and "exercise a more determining influence on the course of events right now than anything else." This force, he said, "practically backs the Japanese off and would certainly stop them on the Malaysian thing. It probably would make them feel they didn't dare take the Siberian thing and I think it has a better than 50 percent chance of forcing them to practically drop the Axis." By acting quickly the United States might give Japan "a complete pause."

Similar thinking was occurring in London. The fall of the Konoe cabinet and what Foreign Minister Anthony Eden described as the "Russian defeats," and the

Admiralty as "the deterioration of the Russian situation," precipitated a decision pressed by Churchill and Eden to send H.M.S. *Prince of Wales* with the new carrier *Indomitable* to join the battlecruiser *Repulse* in the Indian Ocean. "The firmer your attitude and ours," Churchill wrote Roosevelt, "the less chance of their taking the plunge."

In early November it appeared that the threat to the survival of Russia had passed, and a change occurred. The German offensive against Moscow bogged down in bad weather at the end of October. Winter seemed to have finally arrived. Optimism about Russia's ability to survive reemerged. Now the Soviet problem could be disengaged from Japanese-American relations. This was fortunate, too, because evidence was now accumulating about a Japanese attack to the south. Plan Dog thinking revived, and the president and Hull seriously attempted to reach a temporary accommodation with the Japanese that would permit the completion of the reinforcement of the Philippines. This foundered on Chinese and British objections, and the road then led directly to Pearl Harbor. Confidence that the Russian campaign was over for the winter lasted only briefly. The German offensive resumed on November 15, and by November 25, the day the *modus vivendi* project was cancelled, Moscow was imperiled. The Red Army was said to be fighting "one of the most critical battles of its history." The Russian situation looked "awful" to Roosevelt; Moscow, he said, was "falling." The time called for solidarity and steadfastness. Critical in the final defense of Moscow and the Russian counteroffensive launched December 4 were the Siberian troops withdrawn from the Far East.

It was not a case of Roosevelt's saving Moscow. Stalin withdrew half his Far Eastern forces on information gathered in October by his spy Richard Sorge in the German embassy in Tokyo that the Japanese were headed south not north. The Japanese decided on August 9, at the time of the Atlantic Conference and before Roosevelt had settled on a full-scale embargo, not to attack Siberia unless the Soviets collapsed. The embargo did not contain; it precipitated a decision to attack southward. Only a small portion of the air-power deterrent arrived in time and was soon wiped out. Submarine Squadron Two's torpedoes did not work. The *Indomitable* went on reef in Jamaica, the *Prince of Wales* and *Repulse* to the bottom of the South China Sea. Fallacies about air power, confusion between deterrence (the B-17's) and coercion (the embargo), gross underestimation of Japanese military capability and desperate determination, and racist notions of firmness in dealing with Asians: all these errors occurred.

Yet what other reasonable courses lay open to Roosevelt and his advisers? Was serious negotiation possible with a Japanese government that was so opportunistic, unpredictable, and given to force? What would be the consequences of negotiation in light of information available to the American government, which by no means ruled out an attack northward? Circumstances can outpace men's ability to avoid war.

However one judges the wisdom of the containment of Japan, the Russian factor goes a long way toward answering the questions raised here. Roosevelt engaged in an oil embargo to immobilize Japan and prevent any attack north or south. This entailed a risk—more than he knew—of an attack southward but less of a risk than a Japanese attack northward because the survival of the Soviet Union was crucial to a victory over Germany. Roosevelt rejected negotiation with Japan except to gain time because any measure of stability Japan might secure in the south might encourage an attack northward. It pays to think beyond Plan Dog and the Atlantic-Pacific options and to see the problem the way FDR saw it, in a global perspective.

FURTHER READING

Patrick Abbazia, *Mr. Roosevelt's Navy* (1975)

Frederick Adams, *Economic Diplomacy* (1976)

Selig Adler, *The Isolationist Impulse* (1957)

Irvine H. Anderson, *The Standard-Vacuum Oil Company and United States East Asia Policy* (1975)

Michael Barnhart, *Japan Prepares for Total War* (1987)

Charles A. Beard, *President Roosevelt and the Coming of the War, 1941* (1948)

Michael Beschloss, *Kennedy and Roosevelt* (1980)

Dorothy Borg, *The United States and the Far Eastern Crisis of 1933–1938* (1964)

———and Shumpei Okamoto, eds., *Pearl Harbor as History* (1973)

Russell D. Buhite, *Nelson T. Johnson and American Policy Toward China* (1968)

James M. Burns, *The Lion and the Fox* (1956)

Richard D. Burns and Edward M. Bennett, eds., *Diplomats in Crisis* (1974)

Robert J. C. Butow, *The John Doe Associates* (1974)

———, *Tojo and the Coming of the War* (1961)

Mark Chadwin, *The Hawks of World War II* (1968)

J. Garry Clifford and Samuel R. Spencer, Jr., *The First Peacetime Draft* (1986)

Warren I. Cohen, *America's Response to China* (1990)

Wayne S. Cole, *America First: The Battle Against Intervention, 1940–1941* (1953)

———, *Charles A. Lindbergh and the Battle Against Intervention in World War II* (1974)

———, *Roosevelt and the Isolationists, 1932–1945* (1983)

———, *Senator Gerald P. Nye and American Foreign Relations* (1962)

James V. Compton, *The Swastica and the Eagle* (1967)

James Crowley, *Japan's Quest for Autonomy* (1966)

David H. Culbert, *News for Everyman* (1976) (radio and foreign affairs)

Robert Dallek, *Franklin D. Roosevelt and American Foreign Policy* (1979)

Kenneth R. Davis, *FDR* (1993)

Roger Dingman, *Power in the Pacific* (1976)

Robert A. Divine, *The Illusion of Neutrality* (1962)

———, *The Reluctant Belligerant* (1979)

———, *Roosevelt and World War II* (1969)

Justus D. Doenecke and John E. Wilz, *From Isolation to War* (1991)

Jean-Baptiste Duroselle, *From Wilson to Roosevelt* (1963)

Herbert Feis, *The Road to Pearl Harbor* (1950)

Frank Freidel, *Franklin D. Roosevelt: A Rendezvous with Destiny* (1990)

Lloyd Gardner, *Economic Aspects of New Deal Diplomacy* (1964)

Martin Gilbert, *Winston S. Churchill: Finest Hour, 1939–1941* (1983)

John M. Haight, Jr., *American Aid to France, 1938–1940* (1970)

Patrick Hearden, *Roosevelt Confronts Hitler* (1987)

Waldo H. Heinrichs, Jr., *American Ambassador* (1966) (Joseph Grew)

———, *Threshold of War* (1988)

Saburō Ienaga, *The Pacific War* (1978)

Akira Iriye, *Across the Pacific* (1967)

————, *After Imperialism* (1969)

———— and Warren Cohen, eds., *American, Chinese, and Japanese Perspectives on Wartime Asia, 1931–1949* (1990)

Manfred Jonas, *Isolationism in America* (1966)

Kenneth P. Jones, *U.S. Diplomats in Europe, 1919–1941* (1981)

Thomas C. Kennedy, *Charles A. Beard and American Foreign Policy* (1975)

Warren F. Kimball, *The Most Unsordid Act: Lend-Lease, 1939–1941* (1969)

Charles P. Kindleberger, *The World in Depression, 1929–1939* (1973)

William E. Kinsella, Jr., *Leadership in Isolation* (1978)

William L. Langer and S. E. Gleason, *The Challenge to Isolation, 1937–1940* (1952)

————, *The Undeclared War, 1940–1941* (1953)

William E. Leuchtenburg, *Franklin D. Roosevelt and the New Deal* (1963)

Robert D. Love, ed., *Pearl Harbor Revisited* (1994)

Mark A. Lowenthal, *Leadership and Indecision* (1988) (war planning)

Thomas R. Maddux, *Years of Estrangement* (1980) (Soviet Union)

Frederick W. Marks III, *Wind over Sand* (1988) (FDR)

Gorden Martel, ed., *The Origins of the Second World War Reconsidered* (1986)

Martin V. Melosi, *The Shadow of Pearl Harbor* (1977)

James W. Morley, ed., *Deterrent Diplomacy* (1976)

————, ed., *The Fateful Choice* (1979) (Japan and Southeast Asia)

Charles Neu, *The Troubled Encounter* (1975)

William L. Neumann, *America Encounters Japan* (1963)

Arnold Offner, *American Appeasement* (1969)

————, *The Origins of the Second World War* (1975)

Stephen Pelz, *Race to Pearl Harbor* (1974)

Gordon W. Prange, *At Dawn We Slept: The Untold Story of Pearl Harbor* (1981)

————, *Pearl Harbor* (1986)

Julius Pratt, *Cordell Hull* (1964)

Willard Range, *Franklin D. Roosevelt's World Order* (1959)

David Reynolds, *The Creation of the Anglo-American Alliance, 1937–41* (1982)

Bruce Russett, *No Clear and Present Danger* (1972)

Michael Schaller, *The U.S. Crusade in China, 1938–1945* (1978)

David F. Schmitz, *The United States and Fascist Italy, 1922–1940* (1988)

Paul W. Schroeder, *Axis Alliance and Japanese-American Relations, 1941* (1958)

Raymond Sontag, *A Broken World, 1919–1939* (1971)

Richard Steele, *Propaganda in an Open Society* (1985) (FDR and media)

Youli Sun, *China and the Origins of the Pacific War* (1993)

Charles C. Tansill, *Back Door to War* (1952)

James C. Thomson, Jr., et al., *Sentimental Imperialists* (1981)

John Toland, *Infamy: Pearl Harbor and Its Aftermath* (1982)

Jonathan G. Utley, *Going to War with Japan, 1937–1941* (1985)

Cornelis A. Van Minnen and John F. Sears, eds., *FDR and His Contemporaries* (1992) (foreign views)

Paul A. Varg, *The Closing of the Door* (1973)

D. C. Watt, *How War Came* (1989)

Lawrence Wittner, *Rebels Against War* (1984)

Roberta Wohlstetter, *Pearl Harbor: Warning and Decision* (1962)

CHAPTER
5

Defeating the Axis,
Planning the Peace:
The Second World War

After American entry into the Second World War, Great Britain, the United States, and the Soviet Union formed the fifty-nation Grand Alliance, which in time would force the Axis to surrender. Through extensive correspondence and summit meetings, the Allied leaders Winston S. Churchill, Franklin D. Roosevelt, and Josef Stalin not only plotted military strategy to defeat Germany, Italy, and Japan but also shaped plans for the postwar era. Big Three decisions about war and peace, and the upending results of the war, transformed the international system: Power shifted from some states to others, wartime destruction battered economies, decolonization eroded traditional empires, social divisions widened, political stability in both defeated and victorious nations fractured, new world organizations emerged, and the atomic bomb terrified all. Soon after defeating the Axis, the Grand Alliance broke apart, already having generated the sources of a new conflict—the Cold War.

Although the Allies cooperated sufficiently to win the war, they bickered a great deal over both war strategy and the postwar structure of international relations Legacies of distrust from hostile prewar relations and opposing ideologies impeded harmony. Allied goals also differed: Britain sought to resurrect its empire, to blunt Soviet expansion, and to direct European affairs; the Soviet Union coveted the Baltic states and friendly communist governments in Eastern Europe; the United States eyed new influence, especially in Asia and the Pacific, worked for the Open Door in trade, and looked to great-power postwar control through what Roosevelt called the "Four Policemen," with the United States, of course, ranking first among these international sheriffs.

The Allies exchanged sharp views during the war on the opening of a second, or western, military front. They squabbled over the location of new military campaigns and the timely availability of U.S. supplies under the U.S. Lend-Lease program. They suspected each other of flirting with separate peaces. They jockeyed for political position in the countries liberated from Nazi and Japanese control, such as

Poland and China. The Allies, moreover, debated the colonial question—should France return to imperial rule in Indochina, for example? They also created the United Nations Organization, the World Bank, the International Monetary Fund, and the United Nations Relief and Rehabilitation Administration. Then they competed for influence in the new bodies, in the process shattering unity. All the while, three bold individuals of exceptional power—Churchill, Roosevelt, and Stalin—alternately clashed and cooperated, nipped and purred, in extraordinary episodes of personal diplomacy.

The foreign policy of President Franklin D. Roosevelt stands at the center of any discussion on the Grand Alliance. Some scholars treat his record favorably, emphasizing his grasp of power realities, his understanding of both the limits and the opportunities of power, his deft handling of Churchill and Stalin to keep the alliance together, his highminded desire to free colonies, and his skill in negotiating the unique complexities of conducting a global war. After all, the Allies did achieve the impressive feat of smashing powerful enemies, and they did sketch promising plans for the future. In the eventual faltering of those plans, the responsibility perhaps lies with Roosevelt's successors. Some historians argue, furthermore, that the United States used the opportunity of war to weaken the British Empire, to expand American interests, including overseas bases and new markets and economic holdings, and to thwart a rising political left. Under Roosevelt's leadership, then, the United States deliberately developed and protected a larger American sphere of influence while offering to honor the spheres of other great powers. Without recognized spheres, some defenders of Roosevelt suggest, the world would have descended into even deeper chaos than that it in fact did.

Roosevelt's management of wartime and postwar issues has also drawn considerable criticism. Some writers believe that the president made military decisions without adequately considering their long-term political impact. Some critics hold Roosevelt responsible for the postwar Soviet domination of Eastern Europe, faulting him for not using American power to blunt Stalin's aggressive push into neighboring nations. The president's negotiations at summit conferences have particularly sparked debate, in large part because many of the agreements did not hold and because, in the case of the Yalta Conference, Roosevelt's deteriorating health raises questions about his performance. Critics, too, challenge his spheres-of-influence approach to world politics, noting that it trampled on weak or small nations. Some conclude that Roosevelt said much about decolonization but did little. Others charge that the president, fearing a rebirth of isolationism, did not prepare the American people for the global role they would have to play and the compromises they would be called on to accept after the war. Even more, some claim, Roosevelt deceived people and ignored his advisers, holding his cards close to the vest, arrogantly thinking that he would fix everything in the long run. But for him, there was no long run; he died in April 1945, before the war ended. Thus is prompted a perennial question in history: What if he had lived?

✖ D O C U M E N T S

President Franklin D. Roosevelt spoke frequently during the Second World War about ending European empires and granting independence to colonial peoples, particularly in Asia and especially in French Indochina. Several Roosevelt statements on the colonial issue compose the first document: an August 10, 1941, discussion with Prime Minister Winston S. Churchill at the "Atlantic Charter" Conference (as reported by FDR's son Elliott Roosevelt); a November 28, 1943, exchange with Marshal Josef Stalin at the Teheran Conference (from Department of State records); a January 24, 1944, memorandum to Secretary of State Cordell Hull; a February 23, 1945, press conference comment; and a March 15, 1945, conversation with Charles Taussig, a State Department official who kept notes.

The timing of the opening of a second front in Europe troubled Allied relations until June 6, 1944, when British, American, and Canadian troops crossed the English Channel to attack German forces in France. Until that time, bearing the brunt of the European war, the Soviets pressed for action. In the second document, a U.S. report on the Washington, D.C., meeting of May 30, 1942, between Roosevelt and Soviet foreign minister V. M. Molotov, FDR promised a second front before year's end. But delays set in. Stalin's letter of June 24, 1943, to Churchill reveals the embittered Soviet premier's impatience. A Soviet record, it is reprinted here as the third document. At the Allied conference held at Teheran, Iran, Roosevelt and Stalin discussed the president's concept of "Four Policemen." The American record of the Roosevelt-Stalin meeting on November 29, 1943, is reprinted as the fourth document. Allied interest in spheres of influence is illustrated by the fifth document—the Churchill-Stalin percentages agreement, which delineated British and Soviet roles in liberated nations. This account of the Moscow meeting of October 1944 is drawn from Churchill's memoirs.

The next two documents—agreements struck at the Yalta Conference of February 4–11, 1945—demonstrate a high degree of Allied compromise and unity on many issues as the Big Three neared victory over Germany. In the eighth document, a letter dated April 5, 1945, Roosevelt chided Stalin for charging that U.S. officials were negotiating with German authorities in Switzerland behind Soviet backs. Just before Roosevelt's death, in response to Churchill's warnings about Soviet manipulation of Polish politics, the president wrote the prime minister a reassuring letter of April 11, 1945, reprinted here as the final document.

President Franklin D. Roosevelt on the Colonial Issue, 1941–1945

"Atlantic Charter" Conference, August 10, 1941

Father [FDR] started it.

"Of course," he remarked, with a sly sort of assurance, "of course, after the war, one of the preconditions of any lasting peace will have to be the greatest possible freedom of trade."

He paused. The P.M.'s [Churchill's] head was lowered; he was watching Father steadily, from under one eyebrow.

"No artificial barriers," Father pursued. "As few favored economic agreements as possible. Opportunities for expansion. Markets open for healthy competition." His eye wandered innocently around the room.

Churchill shifted in his armchair. "The British Empire trade agreements," he began heavily, "are—"

Father broke in. "Yes. Those Empire trade agreements are a case in point. It's because of them that the people of India and Africa, of all the colonial Near East and Far East, are still as backward as they are."

Elliott Roosevelt, *As He Saw It* (New York: Duell, Sloan and Pearce, 1946).

Churchill's neck reddened and he crouched forward. "Mr. President, England does not propose for a moment to lose its favored position among the British Dominions. The trade that has made England great shall continue, and under conditions prescribed by England's ministers."

"You see," said Father slowly, "it is along in here somewhere that there is likely to be some disagreement between you, Winston, and me.

"I am firmly of the belief that if we are to arrive at a stable peace it must involve the development of backward countries. Backward peoples. How can this be done? It can't be done, obviously, by eighteenth-century methods. Now—"

"Who's talking eighteenth-century methods?"

"Whichever of your ministers recommends a policy which takes wealth in raw materials out of a colonial country, but which returns nothing to the people of that country in consideration. *Twentieth*-century methods involve bringing industry to these colonies. *Twentieth*-century methods include increasing the wealth of a people by increasing their standard of living, by educating them, by bringing them sanitation—by making sure that they get a return for the raw wealth of their community."

Around the room, all of us were leaning forward attentively. [Harry] Hopkins [a major FDR adviser] was grinning. Commander [C. R.] Thompson, Churchill's aide, was looking glum and alarmed. The P.M. himself was beginning to look apoplectic.

"You mentioned India," he growled.

"Yes. I can't believe that we can fight a war against fascist slavery, and at the same time not work to free people all over the world from a backward colonial policy."

"What about the Philippines?"

"I'm glad you mentioned them. They get their independence, you know, in 1946. And they've gotten modern sanitation, modern education; their rate of illiteracy has gone steadily down. . . ."

"There can be no tampering with the Empire's economic agreements."

"They're artificial. . . ."

"They're the foundation of our greatness."

"The peace," said Father firmly, "cannot include any continued despotism. The structure of the peace demands and will get equality of peoples. Equality of peoples involves the utmost freedom of competitive trade. . . ."

It was after two in the morning when finally the British party said their good nights. I helped Father into his cabin, and sat down to smoke a last cigarette with him.

Father grunted. "A real old Tory, isn't he? A real old Tory, of the old school."

"I thought for a minute he was going to bust, Pop."

"Oh," he smiled, "I'll be able to work with him. Don't worry about that. We'll get along famously."

"So long as you keep off the subject of India."

"Mmm, I don't know. I think we'll even talk some more about India, before we're through. *And* Burma. *And* Java. *And* Indo-China. *And* Indonesia. *And* all the African colonies. *And* Egypt and Palestine. We'll talk about 'em all."

Teheran Conference, November 28, 1943

The President [FDR] said that Mr. Churchill was of the opinion that France would be very quickly reconstructed as a strong nation, but he did not personally share this view since he felt that many years of honest labor would be necessary before France would be re-established. He said the first necessity for the French, not only for the Government but the people as well, was to become honest citizens.

Marshal [Josef] Stalin agreed and went on to say that he did not propose to have the Allies shed blood to restore Indochina, for example, to the old French colonial rule. He said that the recent events in the Lebanon [where the French ended their mandate] made public service the first step toward the independence of people who had formerly been colonial subjects. He said that in the war against Japan, in his opinion, that in addition to military missions, it was necessary to fight the Japanese in the political sphere as well, particularly in view of the fact that the Japanese had granted the least nominal independence to certain colonial areas. He repeated that France should not get back Indochina and that the French must pay for their criminal collaboration with Germany.

The President said he was 100% in agreement with Marshal Stalin and remarked that after 100 years of French rule in Indochina, the inhabitants were worse off than they had been before. . . .

The President continued on the subject of colonial possessions, but he felt it would be better not to discuss the question of India with Mr. Churchill, since the latter had no solution of that question, and merely proposed to defer the entire question to the end of the war.

Marshal Stalin agreed that this was a sore spot with the British.

Memorandum to Cordell Hull, January 24, 1944

I saw Halifax [Lord Halifax, British ambassador to the United States] last week and told him quite frankly that it was perfectly true that I had, for over a year, expressed the opinion that Indo-China should not go back to France but that it should be administered by an international trusteeship. France has had the country—thirty million inhabitants for nearly one hundred years, and the people are worse off than they were at the beginning.

As a matter of interest, I am wholeheartedly supported in this view by Generalissimo Chiang Kai-shek [of China] and by Marshal Stalin. I see no reason to play in with the British Foreign Office in this matter. The only reason they seem to oppose it is that they fear the effect it would have on their own possessions and those of the Dutch. They have never liked the idea of trusteeship because it is, in some instances, aimed at future independence. This is true in the case of Indo-China.

Each case must, of course, stand on its own feet, but the case of Indo-China is perfectly clear. France has milked it for one hundred years. The people of Indo-China are entitled to something better than that.

Press Conference, February 23, 1945

With the Indo-Chinese, there is a feeling they ought to be independent but are not ready for it. I suggested at the time [1943], to Chiang, that Indo-China be set up under a trusteeship—have a Frenchman, one or two Indo-Chinese, and a Chinese and a Russian because they are on the coast, and maybe a Filipino and an American—to educate them for self-government. It took fifty years for us to do it in the Philippines.

Stalin liked the idea. China liked the idea. The British don't like it. It might bust up their empire, because if the Indo-Chinese were to work together and eventually get their independence, the Burmese might do the same thing to England. The French have talked about how they expect to recapture Indo-China, but they haven't got any shipping to do it with. It would only get the British mad. Chiang would go along. Stalin would go along. As for the British, it would only make the British mad. Better to keep quiet just now.

Conversation with Charles Taussig, March 15, 1945

The President [FDR] said he was concerned about the brown people in the East. He said that there are 1,100,000,000 brown people. In many Eastern countries, they are ruled by a handful of whites and they resent it. Our goal must be to help them achieve independence—1,100,000,000 potential enemies are dangerous. He said he included the 450,000,000 Chinese in that. He then added, Churchill doesn't understand this.

The President said he thought we might have some difficulties with France in the matter of colonies. I said that I thought that was quite probable and it was also probable the British would use France as a "stalking horse."

I asked the President if he had changed his ideas on French Indo-China as he had expressed them to us at the luncheon with [British secretary of state for the colonies Oliver] Stanley. He said no he had not changed his ideas; that French Indo-China and New Caledonia should be taken from France and put under a trusteeship. The President hesitated a moment and then said—well if we can get the proper pledge from France to assume for herself the obligations of a trustee, then I would agree to France retaining these colonies with the proviso that independence was the ultimate goal. I asked the President if he would settle for self-government. He said no. I asked him if he would settle for dominion status. He said no—it must be independence. He said that is to be the policy and you can quote me in the State Department.

Roosevelt's Promise of a Second Front, 1942

Mr. [V. M.] Molotov . . . remarked that, though the problem of the second front was both military and political, it was predominantly political. There was an essential difference between the situation in 1942 and what it might be in 1943. In 1942 Hitler was the master of all Europe save a few minor countries. He was the chief enemy of everyone. To be sure, as was devoutly to be hoped, the Russians might hold and fight on all through 1942. But it was only right to look at the darker side of the picture. On the basis of his continental dominance, Hitler might throw in such reinforcements in manpower and material that the Red Army might *not* be able to hold out against the Nazis. Such a development would produce a serious situation which we must face. The Soviet front would become secondary, the Red Army would be weakened, and Hitler's strength would be correspondingly greater, since he would have at his disposal not only more troops, but also the foodstuffs and raw materials of the Ukraine and the oil-wells of the Caucasus. In such circumstances the outlook would be much less favorable for all hands, and he would not pretend that such developments were all outside the range of possibility. The war would thus become tougher and longer. The merit of a new front in 1942 depended on the prospects of Hitler's further advantage, hence the establishment of such a front should not be postponed. The decisive element in the whole problem lay in the question, when are the prospects better for the United Nations: in 1942 or in 1943.

Amplifying his remarks, Mr. Molotov observed that the forces on the Soviet front were large, and, objectively speaking, the balance in quantity of men, aviation, and mechanized equipment was slightly in Hitler's favor. Nevertheless, the Russians were reasonably certain they could hold out. This was the most optimistic prospect, and the Soviet morale was as yet unimpaired. But the main danger lay in the probability that Hitler would try to deal the Soviet Union a mighty crushing blow. If, then, Great Britain and the United States, as allies, were to create a new front and to draw off 40 German divisions from the Soviet front, the ratio of strength would be so altered that the Soviets could either beat Hitler this year or insure beyond question his ultimate defeat.

Mr. Molotov therefore put this question frankly: could we undertake such offensive action as would draw off 40 German divisions which would be, to tell the truth, distinctly second-rate outfits? If the answer should be in the affirmative, the war would be decided in 1942. If negative, the Soviets would fight on alone, doing their best, and no man would expect more from them than that. He had not, Mr. Molotov added, received any positive answer in London. Mr. [Winston] Churchill had proposed that he should return through London on his homeward journey from Washington, and had promised Mr. Molotov a more concrete answer on his second visit. Mr. Molotov admitted he realized that the British would have to bear the brunt of the action if a second front were created, but he also was cognizant of the role the United States plays and what influence this country exerts in questions of major strategy. Without in any way minimizing the risks entailed by a second front action this summer, Mr. Molotov declared his government wanted to know in frank terms what position we take on the question of a second front, and whether we were prepared to establish one. He requested a straight answer.

The difficulties, Mr. Molotov urged, would not be any less in 1943. The chances of success were actually better at present while the Russians still have a solid front. "If you postpone your decision," he said, "you will have eventually to bear the brunt of the war, and if Hitler becomes the undisputed master of the continent, next year will unquestionably be tougher than this one."

The President then put to General [George C.] Marshall the query whether developments were clear enough so that we could say to Mr. Stalin that we are preparing a second front. "Yes," replied the General. The President then authorized

Mr. Molotov to inform Mr. Stalin that we expect the formation of a second front this year.

Josef Stalin's Impatience over a Second Front, 1943

From your [Winston Churchill's] messages of last year and this I gained the conviction that you and the President [FDR] were fully aware of the difficulties of organising such an operation and were preparing the invasion accordingly, with due regard to the difficulties and the necessary exertion of forces and means. Even last year you told me that a large-scale invasion of Europe by Anglo-American troops would be effected in 1943. In the Aide-Memoire handed to V. M. Molotov on June 10, 1942, you wrote:

> Finally, and most important of all, we are concentrating our maximum effort on the organization and preparation of a large-scale invasion of the Continent of Europe by British and American forces in 1943. We are setting no limit to the scope and objectives of this campaign, which will be carried out in the first instance by over a million men, British and American, with air forces of appropriate strength.

Early this year you twice informed me, on your own behalf and on behalf of the President, of decisions concerning an Anglo-American invasion of Western Europe intended to "divert strong German land and air forces from the Russian front." You had set yourself the task of bringing Germany to her knees as early as 1943, and named September as the latest date for the invasion.

In your message of January 26 you wrote:

> We have been in conference with our military advisers and have decided on the operations which are to be undertaken by the American and British forces in the first nine months of 1943. We wish to inform you of our intentions at once. We believe that these operations together with your powerful offensive, may well bring Germany to her knees in 1943.

In your next message, which I received on February 12, you wrote, specifying the date of the invasion of Western Europe, decided on by you and the President:

> We are also pushing preparations to the limit of our resources for a cross-Channel operation in August, in which British and United States units would participate. Here again, shipping and assault-landing craft will be the limiting factors. If the operation is delayed by the weather or other reasons, it will be prepared with stronger forces for September.

Last February, when you wrote to me about those plans and the date for invading Western Europe, the difficulties of that operation were greater than they are now. Since then the Germans have suffered more than one defeat: they were pushed back by our troops in the South, where they suffered appreciable loss; they were beaten in North Africa and expelled by the Anglo-American troops; in submarine warfare, too, the Germans found themselves in a bigger predicament than ever, while Anglo-American superiority increased substantially; it is also known that the Americans and British have won air superiority in Europe and that their navies and mercantile marines have grown in power.

It follows that the conditions for opening a second front in Western Europe during 1943, far from deteriorating, have, indeed, greatly improved.

That being so, the Soviet Government could not have imagined that the British and U.S. Governments would revise the decision to invade Western Europe, which they had adopted early this year. In fact, the Soviet Government was fully entitled to expect the Anglo-American decision would be carried out, that appropriate preparations were under way and that the second front in Western Europe would at last be opened in 1943. . . .

So when you now declare: "I cannot see how a great British defeat and slaughter would aid the Soviet armies," is it not clear that a statement of this kind in relation to the Soviet Union is utterly groundless and directly contradicts your previous and responsible decisions, listed above, about extensive and vigorous measures by the British and Americans to organise the invasion this year, measures on which the complete success of the operation should hinge.

I shall not enlarge on the fact that this [ir?]responsible decision, revoking your previous decisions on the invasion of Western Europe, was reached by you and the President without Soviet participation and without inviting its representatives to the Washington conference, although you cannot but be aware that the Soviet Union's role in the war against Germany and its interest in the problems of the second front are great enough.

There is no need to say that the Soviet Government cannot become reconciled to this disregard of vital Soviet interests in the war against the common enemy.

You say that you "quite understand" my disappointment. I must tell you that the point here is not just the disappointment of the Soviet Government, but the preservation of its confidence in its Allies, a confidence which is being subjected to severe stress. One should not forget that it is a question of saving millions of lives in the occupied areas of Western Europe and Russia and of reducing the enormous sacrifices of the Soviet armies, compared with which the sacrifices of the Anglo-American armies are insignificant.

Roosevelt and Stalin on the "Four Policemen," at the Teheran Conference, 1943

The President then said the question of a post-war organization to preserve peace had not been fully explained and dealt with and he would like to discuss with the Marshal the prospect of some organization based on the United Nations.

The President then outlined the following general plan:

1. There would be a large organization composed of some 35 members of the United Nations which would meet periodically at different places, discuss and make recommendations to a smaller body.

Marshal Stalin inquired whether this organization was to be world-wide or European, to which the President replied, world-wide.

The President continued that there would be set up an executive committee composed of the Soviet Union, the United States, United Kingdom and China, together with two additional European states, one South American, one Near East, one Far Eastern country, and one British Dominion. He mentioned that Mr.

Churchill did not like this proposal for the reason that the British Empire only had two votes. This Executive Committee would deal with all non-military questions such as agriculture, food, health, and economic questions, as well as the setting up of an International Committee. This Committee would likewise meet in various places.

Marshal Stalin inquired whether this body would have the right to make decisions binding on the nations of the world.

The President replied, yes and no. It could make recommendations for settling disputes with the hope that the nations concerned would be guided thereby, but that, for example, he did not believe the Congress of the United States would accept as binding a decision of such a body. The President then turned to the third organization which he termed "The Four Policemen," namely, the Soviet Union, United States, Great Britain, and China. This organization would have the power to deal immediately with any threat to the peace and any sudden emergency which requires this action. He went on to say that in 1935, when Italy attacked Ethiopia, the only machinery in existence was the League of Nations. He personally had begged France to close the Suez Canal, but they instead referred it to the League which disputed the question and in the end did nothing. The result was that the Italian Armies went through the Suez Canal and destroyed Ethiopia. The President pointed out that had the machinery of the Four Policemen, which he had in mind, been in existence, it would have been possible to close the Suez Canal. The President then summarized briefly the idea that he had in mind.

Marshal Stalin said that he did not think that the small nations of Europe would like the organization composed of the Four Policemen. He said, for example, that a European state would probably resent China having the right to apply certain machinery to it. And in any event, he did not think China would be very powerful at the end of the war. He suggested as a possible alternative, the creation of a European or a Far Eastern Committee and a European or a Worldwide organization. He said that in the European Commission there would be the United States, Great Britain, the Soviet Union and possibly one other European state.

The President said that the idea just expressed by Marshal Stalin was somewhat similar to Mr. Churchill's idea of a Regional Committee, one for Europe, one for the Far East, and one for the Americas. Mr. Churchill had also suggested that the United States be a member of the European Commission, but he doubted if the United States Congress would agree to the United States' participation in an exclusively European Committee which might be able to force the dispatch of American troops to Europe.

The President added that it would take a terrible crisis such as at present before Congress would ever agree to that step.

Marshal Stalin pointed out that the world organization suggested by the President, and in particular the Four Policemen, might also require the sending of American troops to Europe.

The President pointed out that he had only envisaged the sending of American planes and ships to Europe, and that England and the Soviet Union would have to handle the land armies in the event of any future threat to the peace. He went on to say that if the Japanese had not attacked the United States, he doubted very much if it would have been possible to send any American forces to Europe. The President added that he saw two methods of dealing with possible threats to the peace. In one case if the threat arose from a revolution or developments in a small country, it might be possible to apply the quarantine method, closing the frontiers of the countries in question and imposing embargoes. In the second case, if the threat was more serious, the four powers, acting as policemen, would send an ultimatum to the nation in question and if refused, [it] would result in the immediate bombardment and possible invasion of that country. . . .

Marshal Stalin then stated he still was dubious about the question of Chinese participation.

The President replied that he had insisted on the participation of China in the 4 Power Declaration at Moscow not because he did not realize the weakness of China at present, but he was thinking further into the future and that after all China was a nation of 400 million people, and it was better to have them as friends rather than as a potential source of trouble.

The Churchill-Stalin Percentages Deal, 1944

The moment was apt for business, so I [Churchill] said, "Let us settle about our affairs in the Balkans. Your armies are in Rumania and Bulgaria. We have interests, missions, and agents there. Don't let us get at cross-purposes in small ways. So far as Britain and Russia are concerned, how would it do for you to have ninety per cent predominance in Rumania, for us to have ninety per cent of the say in Greece, and go fifty-fifty about Yugoslavia?" While this was being translated I wrote out on a half-sheet of paper:

Rumania	
Russia	90%
The others	10%
Greece	
Great Britain	90%
(in accord with U.S.A.)	
Russia	10%
Yugoslavia	50–50%
Hungary	50–50%
Bulgaria	
Russia	75%
The others	25%

I pushed this across to Stalin, who had by then heard the translation. There was a slight pause. Then he took his blue pencil and made a large tick upon it, and passed it back to us. It was all settled in no more time than it takes to set down.

Of course, we had long and anxiously considered our point, and were only dealing with immediate war-time arrangements. All larger questions were reserved on both sides for what we then hoped would be a peace table when the war was won.

After this there was a long silence. The pencilled paper lay in the centre of the table. At length I said, "Might it not be thought rather cynical if it seemed we had disposed of these issues, so fateful to millions of people, in such an offhand manner? Let us burn the paper." "No, you keep it," said Stalin.

The Yalta Protocol of Proceedings, 1945

I. World Organization

It was decided:

1. that a United Nations Conference on the proposed world organization should be summoned for Wednesday, 25th April, 1945, and should be held in the United States of America.
2. the Nations to be invited to this Conference should be:
   a. the United Nations as they existed on the 8th February, 1945; and
   b. such of the Associated Nations as have declared war on the common enemy by 1st March, 1945. (For this purpose by the term "Associated Nations" was meant the eight Associated Nations and Turkey). When the Conference on World Organization is held, the delegates of the United Kingdom and United States of America will support a proposal to admit to original membership two Soviet Socialist Republics, i.e. the Ukraine and White Russia.
3. that the United States Government on behalf of the Three Powers should consult the Government of China and the French Provisional Government in regard to decisions taken at the present Conference concerning the proposed World Organization.
4. that the text of the invitation to be issued to all the nations which would take part in the United Nations Conference should be as follows:

Invitation

The Government of the United States of America, on behalf of itself and of the Governments of the United Kingdom, the Union of Soviet Socialist Republics, and the Republic of China and the Provisional Government of the French Republic, invite the Government of ——————— to send representatives to a Conference of the United Nations to be held on 25th April, 1945, or soon thereafter, at San Francisco in the United States of America to prepare a Charter for a General International Organization for the maintenance of international peace and security.

The above named governments suggest that the Conference consider as affording a basis for such a Charter the Proposals for the Establishment of a General International Organization, which were made public last October as a result of the Dumbarton Oaks Conference, and which have now been supplemented by the following provisions for Section C of Chapter VI:

C. Voting
1. Each member of the Security Council should have one vote.
2. Decisions of the Security Council on procedural matters should be made by an affirmative vote of seven members.

3. Decisions of the Security Council on all other matters should be made by an affirmative vote of seven members including the concurring votes of the permanent members; provided that, in decisions under Chapter VIII, Section A, and under the second sentence of paragraph 1 of Chapter VIII, Section C, a party to a dispute should abstain from voting.

Further information as to arrangements will be transmitted subsequently.

In the event that the Government of ————— desires in advance of the Conference to present views or comments concerning the proposals, the Government of the United States of America will be pleased to transmit such views and comments to the other participating Governments.

Territorial Trusteeship.   It was agreed that the five Nations which will have permanent seats on the Security Council should consult each other prior to the United Nations Conference on the question of territorial trusteeship.

The acceptance of this recommendation is subject to its being made clear that territorial trusteeship will only apply to (a) existing mandates of the League of Nations; (b) territories detached from the enemy as a result of the present war; (c) any other territory which might voluntarily be placed under trusteeship; and (d) no discussion of actual territories is contemplated at the forthcoming United Nations Conference or in the preliminary consultations, and it will be a matter for subsequent agreement which territories within the above categories will be placed under trusteeship.

II. Declaration on Liberated Europe

The following declaration has been approved:

The Premier of the Union of Soviet Socialist Republics, the Prime Minister of the United Kingdom and the President of the United States of America have consulted with each other in the common interests of the peoples of their countries and those of liberated Europe. They jointly declare their mutual agreement to concert during the temporary period of instability in liberated Europe the policies of their three governments in assisting the peoples of the former Axis satellite states of Europe to solve by democratic means their pressing political and economic problems.

The establishment of order in Europe and the rebuilding of national economic life must be achieved by processes which will enable the liberated peoples to destroy the last vestiges of Nazism and Fascism and to create democratic institutions of their own choice. This is a principle of the Atlantic Charter—the right of all peoples to choose the form of government under which they will live—the restoration of sovereign rights and self-government to those peoples who have been forcibly deprived of them by the aggressor nations.

To foster the conditions in which the liberated peoples may exercise these rights, the three governments will jointly assist the people in any European liberated state or former Axis satellite state in Europe where in their judgment conditions require (a) to establish conditions of internal peace; (b) to carry out emergency measures for the relief of distressed peoples; (c) to form interim governmental authorities broadly representative of all democratic elements in the population and pledged to the earliest possible establishment through free elections of governments responsible to the will of the people; and (d) to facilitate where necessary the holding of such elections.

The three governments will consult the other United Nations and provisional authorities or other governments in Europe when matters of direct interest to them are under consideration.

When, in the opinion of the three governments, conditions in any European liberated state or any former Axis satellite state in Europe make such action necessary, they will immediately consult together on the measures necessary to discharge the joint responsibilities set forth in this declaration.

By this declaration we reaffirm our faith in the principles of the Atlantic Charter, our pledges in the Declaration by the United Nations, and our determination to build in cooperation with other peace-loving nations world order under law, dedicated to peace, security, freedom and general well-being of all mankind.

In issuing this declaration, the Three Powers express the hope that the Provisional Government of the French Republic may be associated with them in the procedure suggested.

III. Dismemberment of Germany

It was agreed that Article 12 (a) of the Surrender Terms for Germany should be amended as follows:

> The United Kingdom, the United States of America and the Union of Soviet Socialist Republics shall possess supreme authority with respect to Germany. In the exercise of such authority they will take such steps, including the complete disarmament demilitarization and dismemberment of Germany as they deem requisite for future peace and security. . . .

IV. Zone of Occupation for the French and Control Council for Germany

It was agreed that a zone in Germany, to be occupied by the French Forces, should be allocated to France. This zone would be formed out of the British and American zones and its extent would be settled by the British and Americans in consultation with the French Provisional Government.

It was also agreed that the French Provisional Government should be invited to become a member of the Allied Control Council of Germany.

V. Reparation

The heads of the three governments agreed as follows:

1. Germany must pay in kind for the losses caused by her to the Allied nations in the course of the war. Reparations are to be received in the first instance by those countries which have borne the main burden of the war, have suffered the heaviest losses and have organized victory over the enemy.
2. Reparation in kind to be exacted from Germany in three following forms:
   a. Removals within 2 years from the surrender of Germany or the cessation of organized resistance from the national wealth of Germany located on the territory of Germany herself as well as outside her territory (equipment, machine-tools, ships, rolling stock, German investments abroad, shares of industrial, transport and other enterprises in Germany etc.), these removals

to be carried out chiefly for purpose of destroying the war potential of Germany.

    b. Annual deliveries of goods from current production for a period to be fixed.

    c. Use of German labor.

3. For the working out on the above principles of a detailed plan for exaction of reparation from Germany, an Allied Reparation Commission will be set up in Moscow. It will consist of three representatives—one from the Union of Soviet Socialist Republics, one from the United Kingdom and one from the United States of America.

4. With regard to the fixing of the total sum of the reparation as well as the distribution of it among the countries which suffered from the German aggression the Soviet and American delegations agreed as follows:

> The Moscow Reparation Commission should take in its initial studies as a basis for discussion the suggestion of the Soviet Government that the total sum of the reparation in accordance with the points (a) and (b) of the paragraph 2 should be 20 billion dollars and that 50% of it should go to the Union of Soviet Socialist Republics.

The British delegation was of the opinion that pending consideration of the reparation question by the Moscow Reparation Commission no figures of reparation should be mentioned.

The above Soviet-American proposal has been passed to the Moscow Reparation Commission as one of the proposals to be considered by the Commission.

VI. Major War Criminals

The Conference agreed that the question of the major war criminals should be the subject of enquiry by the three Foreign Secretaries for report in due course after the close of the Conference.

VII. Poland

The following Declaration on Poland was agreed by the Conference:

> A new situation has been created in Poland as a result of her complete liberation by the Red Army. This calls for the establishment of a Polish Provisional Government which can be more broadly based than was possible before the recent liberation of [the] Western part of Poland. The Provisional Government which is now functioning in Poland should therefore be reorganized on a broader democratic basis with the inclusion of democratic leaders from Poland itself and from Poles abroad. This new Government should then be called the Polish Provisional Government of National Unity.
>
>   M. Molotov, Mr. Harriman and Sir A. Clark Kerr are authorized as a commission to consult in the first instance in Moscow with members of the present Provisional Government and with other Polish democratic leaders from within Poland and from abroad, with a view to the reorganization of the present Government along the above lines. This Polish Provisional Government of National Unity shall be pledged to the holding of free and unfettered elections as soon as possible on the basis of universal suffrage and secret ballot. In these elections all democratic and anti-Nazi parties shall have the right to take part and to put forward candidates.

When a Polish Provisional Government of National Unity has been properly formed in conformity with the above, the Government of the U.S.S.R., which now maintains diplomatic relations with the present Provisional Government of Poland, and the Government of the United Kingdom and the Government of the United States of America will establish diplomatic relations with the new Polish Provisional Government of National Unity, and will exchange Ambassadors by whose reports the respective Governments will be kept informed about the situation in Poland.

The three Heads of Government consider that the Eastern frontier of Poland should follow the Curzon Line with digressions from it in some regions of five to eight kilometers in favor of Poland. They recognize that Poland must receive substantial accession of territory in the North and West. They feel that the opinion of the new Polish Provisional Government of National Unity should be sought in due course on the extent of these accessions and that the final delimitation of the Western frontier of Poland should therefore await the Peace Conference.

[Following this declaration, but omitted here for reasons of space, are brief statements on Yugoslavia, the Italo-Yugoslav frontier and Italo-Austrian frontier, Yugoslav-Bulgarian relations, Southeastern Europe, Iran, meetings of the three foreign secretaries, and the Montreux Convention and the Straits.]

The Yalta Agreement on Soviet Entry into the War Against Japan, 1945

The leaders of the three Great Powers—the Soviet Union, the United States of America and Great Britain—have agreed that in two or three months after Germany has surrendered and the war in Europe has terminated the Soviet Union shall enter into the war against Japan on the side of the Allies on condition that:

1. The *status quo* in Outer-Mongolia (The Mongolian People's Republic) shall be preserved;
2. The former rights of Russia violated by the treacherous attack of Japan in 1904 shall be restored, viz:
   a. the southern part of Sakhalin as well as all the islands adjacent to it shall be returned to the Soviet Union,
   b. the commercial port of Dairen shall be internationalized, the preeminent interests of the Soviet Union in this port being safeguarded and the lease of Port Arthur as a naval base of the USSR restored,
   c. the Chinese-Eastern Railroad and the South-Manchurian Railroad which provides an outlet to Dairen shall be jointly operated by the establishment of a joint Soviet-Chinese Company; it being understood that the preeminent interests of the Soviet Union shall be safeguarded and that China shall retain full sovereignty in Manchuria;
3. The Kurile islands shall be handed over to the Soviet Union.

It is understood, that the agreement concerning Outer-Mongolia and the ports and railroads referred to above will require concurrence of Generalissimo Chiang Kai-shek. The President will take measures in order to obtain this concurrence on advice from Marshal Stalin.

The Heads of the three Great Powers have agreed that these claims of the Soviet Union shall be unquestionably fulfilled after Japan has been defeated.

For its part the Soviet Union expresses its readiness to conclude with the National Government of China a Pact of friendship and alliance between the USSR and China in order to render assistance to China with its armed forces for the purpose of liberating China from the Japanese yoke.

Roosevelt's Anger with Stalin, 1945

I have received with astonishment your message of April 3 containing an allegation that arrangements which were made between Field Marshals [Harold] Alexander and [Albert] Kesselring at Berne [Switzerland] "permitted the Anglo-American troops to advance to the East and the Anglo-Americans promised in return to ease for the Germans the peace terms."

In my previous messages to you in regard to the attempts made in Berne to arrange a conference to discuss a surrender of the German army in Italy I have told you that: (1) No negotiations were held in Berne, (2) The meeting had no political implications whatever, (3) In any surrender of the enemy army in Italy there would be no violation of our agreed principle of unconditional surrender, (4) Soviet officers would be welcomed at any meeting that might be arranged to discuss surrender.

For the advantage of our common war effort against Germany, which today gives excellent promise of an early success in a disintegration of the German armies, I must continue to assume that you have the same high confidence in my truthfulness and reliability that I have always had in yours.

I have also a full appreciation of the effect your gallant army has had in making possible a crossing of the Rhine by the forces under General [Dwight D.] Eisenhower and the effect that your forces will have hereafter on the eventual collapse of the German resistance to our combined attacks.

I have complete confidence in General Eisenhower and know that he certainly would inform me before entering into any agreement with the Germans. He is instructed to demand and will demand unconditional surrender of enemy troops that may be defeated on his front. Our advances on the Western Front are due to military action. Their speed has been attributable mainly to the terrific impact of our air power resulting in destruction of German communications, and to the fact that Eisenhower was able to cripple the bulk of the German forces on the Western Front while they were still west of the Rhine.

I am certain that there were no negotiations in Berne at any time and I feel that your information to that effect must have come from German sources which have made persistent efforts to create dissension between us in order to escape in some measure responsibility for their war crimes. If that was [General Karl] Wolff's purpose in Berne, your message proves that he has had some success.

With a confidence in your belief in my personal reliability and in my determination to bring about, together with you, an unconditional surrender of the Nazis, it is astonishing that a belief seems to have reached the Soviet Government that I have entered into an agreement with the enemy without first obtaining your full agreement.

Finally I would say this, it would be one of the great tragedies of history if at the very moment of the victory, now within our grasp, such distrust, such lack of faith should prejudice the entire undertaking after the colossal losses of life, material and treasure involved.

Frankly I cannot avoid a feeling of bitter resentment toward your informers, whoever they are, for such vile misrepresentations of my actions or those of my trusted subordinates.

Roosevelt's Last Letter to Churchill, 1945

I would minimize the general Soviet problem as much as possible because these problems, in one form or another, seem to arise every day and most of them straighten out as in the case of the Berne meeting.

We must be firm, however, and our course thus far is correct.

 *E S S A Y S*

In the first essay, a positive assessment of Roosevelt's wartime diplomacy, the historian Gary R. Hess of Bowling Green University depicts the president as a "practical idealist" who understood the uses of American power, articulated clear objectives consistent with the United States' ideals, provided the effective leadership necessary for victory in the Second World War, and charted a sensible peace for the future. The second essay, in contrast, attempts to deflate Roosevelt's reputation as an adept manager of Allied relations. Frederick W. Marks III, who has also written studies of Theodore Roosevelt and John Foster Dulles, diplomats whom he admires, argues that Franklin D. Roosevelt badly misjudged his ability to charm Stalin and failed to apply U.S. bargaining power to contain the Soviets. Conceding too much to the Soviets, Roosevelt created a one-sided relationship that only whetted Stalin's appetite for more. In the last essay, the historian Lloyd C. Gardner of Rutgers University explores Allied relations over the colonial question, especially the future of French Indochina (Vietnam, Laos, Cambodia). Gardner documents Roosevelt's "dream" to dismantle empires. But Gardner finds Roosevelt fuzzy-minded on the subject. The president talked about a United Nations trusteeship but never drew up precise plans, and in the end, after British and French resistance to decolonization, he backed off, leaving the pressing question unresolved at the time of his death.

Roosevelt's Practical Idealism and the Successful Management of the Alliance

GARY R. HESS

"War," the German military theoretician, Karl von Clausewitz, wrote in the early nineteenth century, "is nothing but a continuation of politics by different means." As that quotation underscores, a nation engages in war not as an end in itself, but to achieve political objectives. Nations are usually driven to war by a belief that vital

From *The United States at War, 1941–1945* by Gary R. Hess, pp. 103–126. The American History Series, © 1986 by Harlan Davidson, Inc. Reprinted by permission.

interests cannot be attained through peaceful means. Hence, during World War II the United States had objectives in Europe and Asia that it believed would be realized upon the defeat of the Axis powers.

The strength of the enemy, of course, necessitated the military alliance with Great Britain, the Soviet Union, China, and the other Allied nations; and each of the other powers brought their own long-term objectives into the alliance. In the Declaration of the United Nations that was signed on January 1, 1942, the members of the Allied coalition agreed on their common purpose of defeating the Axis powers and creating a postwar world based on the principles of political freedom, economic cooperation, self-determination, and disarmament. Yet beyond that fundamental agreement, the Allied powers, especially in the relationship among the Big Three, constantly differed over military strategy and the postwar settlement. The United States, Great Britain, and the Soviet Union each brought into the alliance immediate and long-term objectives reflecting their histories, traditions, ideologies, and wartime experiences. The relationship among the major powers revealed constant points of difference, but in that respect, the World War II Allies were by no means unique. Writing in the late eighteenth century, the French diplomat, Comte de Segur, observed that alliances were "marriages followed promptly by divorce," for while a common enemy "momentarily unites, a constant jealousy separates."

Roosevelt set forth the American postwar objectives. In general, his vision looked to the preservation of the wartime alliance. The nations that fought together against the Axis were to cooperate in the preservation of international peace. To Roosevelt the "constant jealousy" or points of divergence among the Allies had to be minimized so this alliance would not be a "marriage followed promptly by divorce." Roosevelt's postwar objectives, broadly stated, can be summarized as envisioning (1) an expanded role for the United States in world affairs, (2) Soviet-American cooperation to help preserve peace, (3) China's emergence as a strong force for peace in Asia, and (4) the gradual demise of colonial empires leading eventually to independent states in Asia and Africa.

A "strong" president who had provided decisive leadership on domestic issues and foreign policy, Roosevelt, in the midst of a global war, became an even more dominant figure. Distrustful of the State Department and disdainful of Cordell Hull who served as secretary of state until late 1944, Roosevelt largely relied on his own instincts, a few close advisers, and a variety of special emissaries to help him define and implement the major elements of his foreign policy. (While Roosevelt frequently ignored the State Department, its leaders in Washington and its diplomatic personnel abroad generally shared Roosevelt's vision of the postwar world; the Department engaged extensively in postwar planning that provided the President with much useful information as he strove for the realization of his objectives.)

Roosevelt worked diligently to preserve the inherently fragile wartime coalition and to achieve his postwar goals. He corresponded frequently with Prime Minister Winston Churchill and Premier Josef Stalin. In addition, he met on several occasions with Churchill and twice undertook long trips to meet with both Churchill and Stalin. At the first Big Three Conference held at Teheran, Iran, in November 1943, an expectant and buoyant atmosphere prevailed because the

Allies had gained military ascendancy in Europe and the Pacific. At the conference, the British and Americans finally promised to launch the cross-Channel invasion of German-occupied France the following spring, thus satisfying longstanding Russian demand for a "second front," in western Europe. For his part Stalin reaffirmed that following the defeat of Germany the Soviet Union would help the United States in the struggle against Japan. Beyond those military agreements, the Teheran Conference produced no important concrete results, but it did provide an opportunity for discussing postwar plans in a candid and forthright manner. Altogether, the conference led to much optimism that the Big Three would work together in the postwar world. Such expectations had been somewhat modified by the time of the second Big Three Conference, which was held at Yalta in the Soviet Union in February 1945. By that time Germany was on the verge of defeat and differences had developed between Russia and the Western Allies over the postwar status of eastern Europe (especially Poland) and the treatment of Germany. Circumstances required compromise which, Roosevelt believed, still provided the basis for a peaceful world.

Roosevelt's wartime diplomacy has been criticized from two perspectives. First, some contemporaries and scholars have argued that Roosevelt was too idealistic; that is, his objectives lacked a firm definition of American interests and reflected a misunderstanding of the behavior of other nations. Such criticisms of Roosevelt began during the late stages of the war and continued in the postwar period, especially when the United States encountered serious difficulties with the Soviet Union and China. In view of subsequent Cold War tensions with the Russians, some historians have maintained that Roosevelt's efforts to promote Soviet-American friendship were naive. He has been criticized for failing to understand the seriousness of Soviet-American differences and for relying too heavily on personal diplomacy to resolve problems. From this perspective Roosevelt's negotiations with Stalin are seen as futile; in particular, the agreements reached at the Yalta Conference of February 1945 are seen as evidence of a trusting Roosevelt being deceived by Stalin with the result that the United States tacitly sanctioned Russian control over eastern Europe. Likewise, Roosevelt's hope for promoting a strong China under the leadership of Chiang Kai-shek [Jiang Jieshi] has seemed in retrospect to be ill-considered in view of the deep divisions within China between Chiang's government and the communists led by Mao Tse-tung [Mao Zedong], and the ineffectiveness of Chiang's armies in fighting against the Japanese.

On the other hand, some contemporaries and scholars have criticized Roosevelt for failing to use American power and influence to achieve his ideals. From this perspective Roosevelt was not too idealistic; rather, his objectives would have been worthwhile and obtainable had he exercised American power effectively. Roosevelt is seen as impeding Soviet-American friendship by delaying the cross-Channel invasion. His plan for a strong China was undermined by the absence of military aid for the war in China caused by the priority given to the island campaign against Japan. And, finally, the Roosevelt commitment to ending colonialism was weakened by his failures to support nationalist movements, especially in India. According to his biographer, James MacGregor Burns, Roosevelt did not coordinate means and objectives:

So the more he preached his lofty ends and practiced his limited means, the more he . . . widened the gap between popular expectations and actual possibilities. Not only did this derangement of ends and means lead to crushed hopes, disillusion, and cynicism at home, but it helped sow the seeds of the Cold War during World War II, as the Kremlin contrasted Roosevelt's coalition rhetoric with his Atlantic First strategy and falsely suspected a bourgeois conspiracy to destroy Soviet Communism; and the Indians and Chinese contrasted Roosevelt's anticolonial words with his military concessions to colonial powers, and falsely inferred that he was an imperialist at heart and a hypocrite to boot.

But perhaps Roosevelt was neither naive nor indifferent to power. Roosevelt's leadership was realistic in the sense of its being firmly grounded on American interests and American capabilities. He recognized the forces that undermined his objectives and adjusted his plans accordingly. Roosevelt was aware of the inconsistency between rhetoric and practice, but his ability to translate plans into actions was limited by the diverse pressures of the wartime alliance and the vast demands on American resources. On close examination Roosevelt emerges as a thoughtful, calculating, well-informed leader whose efforts reflected American national interests and the potential, as well as the limits, of American power. Roosevelt himself summarized the character of his leadership when he wrote that, "I dream dreams, but am, at the same time, an intensely practical person." Roosevelt the practical idealist can be seen in the ways in which he endeavored to realize his four major objectives.

Roosevelt's commitment to an expanded role for the United States in international affairs resulted from his fear that the nation would retreat, as it had following World War I, from substantial responsibility for preserving world peace. To keep America vigilant, Roosevelt supported a new organization designed to replace the League of Nations. During the war various groups in the United States worked diligently to enlist popular and official backing for such an international organization, and the American public responded enthusiastically to this movement. American failure to join the League of Nations after World War I, many Americans believed, had led directly to World War II. The mistakes of the past should not be repeated. World War II offered Americans a second chance to prove their commitment to international peace. Support for a new international organization increased steadily, so that by early 1945 fully 90 percent of the American public favored inclusion in a world body. Eight out of ten Americans approved the use of force by the new organization in order to keep the peace. Recognizing the existence of widespread support among the public and in Congress for both a new international organization and unequivocal American participation in the forum, Roosevelt championed this movement and worked for the establishment of the desired organization. While the conference at San Francisco that formally established the United Nations met after his death, Roosevelt, especially in his negotiations with Stalin and Churchill at the Yalta Conference, had set forth clearly the American objectives for the new international body.

Roosevelt diverged from the public view of the United Nations on one important point. Most Americans assumed that the new organization would be based on the equality of nations, and that all members would participate in the preservation of international peace. They foresaw an organization which, like its predecessor the League of Nations, would rely on a system of collective security where all members would cooperate, economically and militarily, against aggressive nations. This idealistic vision had much appeal, for Americans tended to abhor suggestions of reliance on concepts such as the balance of power and spheres of influence, since those practices accepted the inequality of nations and seemed to have led to conflict in the past. Roosevelt appeared to share such views; indeed, when he addressed Congress after the Yalta Conference, he spoke of a postwar world free of power politics:

> It ought to spell the end of the system of unilateral action, the exclusive alliances, the spheres of influence, the balances of power, and all the other expedients that have been tried for centuries—and have always failed. We propose to substitute for all these, a universal organization in which all peace-loving nations will finally have a chance to join.

Roosevelt actually believed that international stability could only be achieved by strength and cooperation among the major powers; he considered collective security to be impractical. During the early part of the war, he spoke privately of the "four policemen"—the United States, the Soviet Union, Great Britain, and China—as principally responsible for the preservation of world peace. Each of the "policemen" was to be dominant in its area of the world (sphere of influence). As circumstances required, the four would cooperate to preserve international stability.

Roosevelt's concept of the postwar world assumed, not the end, but the continuation of power politics. As the plans for the United Nations progressed, Roosevelt's four-policemen concept took form in the Security Council; its permanent members (the four policemen plus France) were to be responsible for international peace. "Though the Four Policemen disappeared in substance," [the historian] Robert Divine observes, "the grant of veto power to the permanent members of the Security Council continued Roosevelt's insistence on great-power control over the enforcement of peace."

How can Roosevelt's public promotion of a United Nations based on collective security and his personal commitment to big-power domination be reconciled? His support of the United Nations rested on the belief that it was necessary to involve the United States permanently in world affairs. Big-power control, [the historian] Robert Dallek writes, was "obscure[d] . . . through a United Nations organization which would satisfy widespread demand in the United States for new idealistic or universalist arrangements for assuring the peace." Hence, membership in the United Nations capitalized on popular enthusiasm and was part of Roosevelt's strategy to ensure a permanent American involvement in world affairs.

The importance Roosevelt attached to big-power domination of the postwar world explains his determined efforts to cooperate with the Soviet Union and enhance China's status. Those two nations, in Roosevelt's thinking, were vital to a stable world order.

Among Roosevelt's most monumental challenges was to promote long-term Soviet-American cooperation. The mutual need to defeat Hitler created the "strange alliance" between the world's preeminent capitalist and communist nations. The Soviet and American governments had long distrusted one another; in Moscow, leaders recalled the Western hostility toward the communist revolution of 1917 and the prolonged period of American nonrecognition of the Soviet government (until 1933 the United States did not extend diplomatic recognition). In Washington, officials could not ignore many aspects of Soviet rule: the efforts to promote communist revolutions internationally, the totalitarian character of the Soviet government which was vividly evident during the brutal purges of Stalin's political opponents in the late 1930s, Stalin's deal with the Germans (the Nazi-Soviet Non-Aggression Pact of August 1939) which facilitated Hitler's invasion of Poland, and the parallel Russian takeover of the Baltic states and its aggression against Finland.

Roosevelt shared the nation's disgust over much of what had occurred in Russia since 1917, but circumstances forced cooperation. "I can't take communism," he once wrote, "but to cross this bridge I would hold hands with the Devil." To build cooperation Roosevelt relied heavily on personal diplomacy, believing that through discussions and negotiations directly with Stalin, the Americans and Soviets could reach understandings. Following their first meeting at the Teheran Conference, Roosevelt reported that he had found in Stalin a man "something like me . . . a realist."

Roosevelt's aspirations for Soviet-American friendship found wide support among the American public. In a dramatic reversal of prewar sentiments, Americans came to look very favorably upon the Russian people and even the dictatorial government of Josef Stalin. Americans admired Russian resistance to the German invasion and appreciated in particular the rigors of the Battle of Stalingrad. When they were asked to characterize the Russian people by selecting from a list of twenty-five adjectives, Americans responded "hard-working" (61 percent) and "brave" (48 percent); few persons associated negative attributes with the Russians. On several occasions when public opinion polls asked which nation—Britain, China, the United States, or the Soviet Union—was contributing the most to winning the war, Americans always ranked either their own country or the Soviet Union first and the other second, and, in all cases, both were seen as contributing far more than China or Britain. Respect for the Soviet contribution was especially strong during the critical winter of 1942–1943 when Americans, despite their own offensives in north Africa and the Pacific, rallied around the Russians fighting the Battle of Stalingrad. Popular interest in that struggle has been described by the [historian] Ralph Levering:

> This, it was sensed even then, was the crucial battle of the war, and millions of attentive Americans followed the shifting tides in the streets of the city and on the Volga plain as they would follow a "crucial" televised football game. The hesitant American advances on small Pacific islands were as nothing compared with the epic quality of this struggle.

When the American public was asked in 1943 what *people,* not armies, were working hardest to win the war, they placed the Russians first (48 percent), themselves next (26 percent) and the British a distant third (13 percent).

The press, radio, and motion pictures reinforced these attitudes by consistently portraying the Soviet Union in positive terms. Several popular movies dramatized the fighting on the Eastern Front. The book *Mission to Moscow,* written by former Russian ambassador Joseph Davies, and the motion picture based on it presented Soviet leaders as men of honesty and integrity. Wendell Willkie, the Republican candidate for president in 1940, wrote the best-selling *One World* which spoke glowingly of Stalin and other Soviet leaders, and of the economic and social progress the Russian people had made under their communist government. *Life* and *Time* magazines—perhaps the most influential journals of the era—extolled Russian virtues. *Time* named Stalin its "Man of the Year" in 1943. A special issue of *Life,* featuring a smiling Stalin on the cover, was devoted entirely to the Soviet Union. From the several pro-Russian articles and pages of photographs, Americans learned that Lenin, the leader of the communist revolution of 1917, was "perhaps the greatest man of modern times" and that Stalin and his fellow leaders were "tough, loyal, capable administrators . . . 'Men of Good Will.'" *Life* concluded that the Russians were "one hell of a people" who "look like Americans, dress like Americans and think like Americans."

This identification with the Russians encouraged Americans to believe that the wartime alliance would lead to postwar cooperation. Repeatedly, public opinion polls revealed American confidence that the Russians could be trusted after the war. As a result Roosevelt enjoyed strong popular backing for his efforts to build Soviet-American cooperation. The public, however, was only dimly aware of the seriousness of points of Soviet-American disagreement.

Roosevelt assumed that he and his fellow realist, Stalin, could resolve their differences. And to a large extent they succeeded. Perhaps the most vexing issue was the future status of eastern Europe. The Soviets sought recognition of their dominance over that region which twice within the previous thirty years had been the path for a devastating German invasion of Russian territory. Soviet security, Stalin reiterated in messages to British and American officials, demanded friendly governments along Russia's western frontier. For the British and Americans, such claims posed great problems. The British had gone to war in 1939 to uphold Polish sovereignty; they were not prepared to see German control replaced by that of the Soviet Union. London was the headquarters of the Polish government-in-exile that had fled Warsaw at the time of the German invasion in 1939. Both British and American governments, as well as public opinion in those countries, held to the ideal of the self-determination of peoples. In the Atlantic Charter, Roosevelt and Churchill had pledged to oppose "territorial changes that do not accord with the freely expressed wishes of the peoples concerned" and to have "sovereign rights and self-government restored to those who have been forcibly deprived of them."

Yet Roosevelt recognized that increased Soviet influence in eastern Europe could not be denied; indeed, he assumed that the Russians would function as the "policemen" of that area. The question confronting the president was how to reconcile Russian influence with the concept of self-determination. Roosevelt delayed forthright negotiations on eastern Europe—especially the thorny subject of Poland—and permitted military developments to resolve the issues. Thus Roosevelt, in meetings with Stalin at the Teheran Conference, tacitly acknowledged Russian demands as reasonable, but urged that the eastern European question be handled by the Russians in ways that would not alienate world opinion. He pointedly observed that six to seven million American voters were of Polish descent and he could not risk losing their support by appearing to sanction the loss of their ancestral homeland's sovereignty.

By the time of the Big Three meeting at Yalta, the future of Poland had been substantially determined. In early 1944 Russian armies crossed into Polish territory and, as they pushed the Germans to the west, established a provisional government headed by Polish communists and headquartered at Lublin. This Committee of National Liberation became the vehicle for establishing Russian control over Poland. The British and the Polish government-in-exile protested bitterly but to no avail. Hence, when the Polish question was discussed at Yalta, Churchill and Roosevelt faced the fact of a functioning pro-Soviet government supported by the Russian army. Meeting with congressional leaders prior to his departure to Yalta, Roosevelt forthrightly acknowledged that spheres of influence were a reality the United States had to accept; he observed "that the Russians had the power in Eastern Europe, that it was obviously impossible to have a break with them and that, therefore, the only practical course was to use what influence we had to ameliorate the situation."

The Yalta Conference offered Roosevelt a compromise that under the circumstances provided the West with as much influence as it could possibly attain in Poland. Stalin agreed to the broadening of the Lublin government to include representatives of the government-in-exile and other important groups, and to the holding of timely free and democratic elections. Regarding the remainder of eastern Europe (where Russian armies by that time were well entrenched), the Big Three agreed to the Declaration on Liberated Europe. Like the Polish settlement, the declaration provided for participation of all political groups in provisional governments to be followed by free, democratic elections. While the agreements failed to provide any international guarantees for their implementation, they did, at least, place some moral obligation on the Soviet Union to act with restraint in their sphere. "For all intents and purposes," Dallek concludes, "[Roosevelt] conceded that Eastern Europe was a Soviet sphere of influence."

Clearly, Roosevelt regarded that concession as inevitable, given the Soviet military position and the need for continued Soviet cooperation. The settlements on eastern Europe were, simply, the best he could get. Roosevelt's chief concern, [the historian] John Gaddis maintains, "was cosmetic: to put the best possible face on a bad situation in order to make palatable to the American public the postwar expansion of Soviet influence."

Moreover, Roosevelt's acquiescence was made within the atmosphere of give-and-take on a number of questions, which included Soviet concessions to the interests of the United States. At Yalta Stalin promised to enter the war against Japan within three months of the end of the conflict in Europe; to Americans who anticipated that an invasion of the main Japanese islands would result in very substantial casualties, Russian support in the final campaign against the Japanese leader was considered a high priority. Also, the Soviet leader accepted the bases of American plans for a new international organization.

While Roosevelt worked throughout the war to reach understandings with the Soviet Union, his actions were not naive. A certain skepticism about the Russians was evident in his decision to withhold from them information about the development of the atomic bomb. Roosevelt did enter into secret confidences with

Churchill about full postwar Anglo-American coordination in the development of atomic energy for military and commercial purposes. Excluding the Soviet Union from such understandings (while their agents in the United States were generally aware of the top-secret development of the bomb) was hardly reassuring to Stalin. This American policy led the Soviets to question the depth of the Roosevelt commitment to postwar alliance. From the perspective of Moscow, America's atomic monopoly appeared to be hostile to the Soviet Union. Whether Roosevelt meant to create that impression is unclear, but after the Yalta conference he became increasingly dubious about the prospects for Soviet-American cooperation. "We can't do business with Stalin," an exasperated Roosevelt exclaimed in late March, but in his last communiqué to Churchill, he wrote, "I would minimize the general Soviet problem as much as possible. . . . Most of [the problems] straighten out. . . . We must be firm, however, and our course thus far is correct."

Roosevelt was committed to aiding China so that it would be in a position to assume a prominent role in postwar Asia. The defeat of Japan would leave a power vacuum in Asia and the Pacific that a resurgent China, friendly with the United States, would help to fill. To raise China's international status during the war, the United States ended its longstanding, unequal treaty relationship with China and its policy of excluding Chinese immigrants. More important, Roosevelt insisted on treating China as a power equal to the Big Three. While he urged that Britain and the Soviet Union accord such recognition to the Chinese, neither Churchill nor Stalin shared American expectations for China. To make his point, Roosevelt, while en route to the first Big Three meeting at Teheran, arranged to confer with Chiang Kai-shek at Cairo. (A reluctant Churchill was also in attendance.) And China, again at American insistence, was given one of the permanent seats on the security council of the newly formed United Nations.

Although the United States treated China as a major power, the Chinese had not yet earned such status. Chinese armies had been unable to prevent Japanese conquest of most of northern and coastal China, which included the major centers of population in the country. The Chinese were badly divided politically, and the Kuomintang government, headed by Chiang Kai-shek, was steadily losing support. The Kuomintang faced much internal opposition, principally from the communist movement headed by Mao Tse-tung. During the war, the Communists increased their strength and appeal, especially among the rural peasantry. To Chiang the Communists were a danger far greater than the Japanese; the United States, he assumed, would eventually defeat Japan. Hence, at a time when the United States was directing its resources to the battle against Japan, its principal Asian ally was preoccupied with preparing for the final showdown in a prolonged internal struggle against the Communists.

American diplomatic and military personnel in wartime China recognized the significance of these developments. They came to deplore the massive corruption and inefficiency of the Kuomintang. That regime became increasingly repressive and appeared as brutal as the fascist nations against which the Allies were fighting. Conversely, the communist movement seemed to be progressive, as it introduced long-needed land reform programs in those rural areas under its control. Moreover, the communist forces were fighting against the Japanese. Few astute observers of the Chinese situation doubted that the future of the country rested with the Communists, not with the discredited Kuomintang.

These shortcomings of the Chinese war effort received scant attention in America, for the public generally identified closely with the Chinese and with the government of Chiang Kai-shek in the struggle against the hated Japanese. Under the influence of wartime propaganda, Americans rather uncritically expected that China was progressing toward democracy and major power status. When Americans were asked in 1942 which of twenty-five adjectives best described the Chinese, the predominant responses were "hard-working" (69 percent), "honest" (52 percent), and "brave" (48 percent). (Less than 5 percent attributed negative features—such as "cruel, warlike, treacherous"—to the Chinese; those were, however, the predominant characteristics given to the Japanese.)

Wartime news and information, motion pictures and propaganda glorified the heroic Chinese people. A series of popular films, including *The Battle of China, Inside Fighting China, Ravaged Earth, Burma Convoy, A Yank on the Burma Road, China Girl,* and *God Is My Co-Pilot,* dramatized the common American and Chinese cause against the Japanese. When Mrs. Chiang Kai-shek visited the United States in 1943, she was enthusiastically received. After her emotional plea to Congress for more American support, "tough-guys melted," according to *Time,* and one congressman said, "God-damnit, I never saw anything like it." Madame Chiang had me on the verge of bursting into tears."' In this atmosphere, [the historian] Harold Isaacs notes, "a sympathetic image of the Chinese rose now to a unique pinnacle in a mass of American minds." The contrast between popular perceptions and realities could hardly have been sharper.

Despite the image of the Chinese struggle with the Japanese, the immediate challenge for the United States was to encourage Chinese political stability and military concentration on fighting against Japan. The Americans sent General Joseph Stilwell to serve as chief of staff of the Kuomintang Army. Stilwell's plans to improve Chinese military prowess failed completely when Stilwell and Chiang came to despise one another. To the American general, Chiang was a petty dictator (in the privacy of his diary, Stilwell contemptuously described Chiang as "Peanut"). Stilwell's demands for reform threatened Chiang, who eventually demanded that Roosevelt recall Stilwell.

In addition to the Stilwell mission, the United States provided important air support for the Chinese, principally through the "hump" supply flights across the Himalayas from bases in India. Yet the Chinese always regarded American help as insufficient, and contrasted the low volume of supplies they were receiving with the flow of American supplies to the Soviet Union, Great Britain, and other Allies.

Why didn't the United States provide what Chiang demanded? Might that support have enabled him to fight more effectively against the Japanese? The failure to meet his demands resulted, in part, from the fact that the China theater always had had a low priority in the allocation of American resources. The Europe-first strategy dictated that the needs of European allies would receive primary consideration. And within the Pacific theater, China's needs were secondary to the island campaign. Moreover, the United States considered assistance as its most effective lever in forcing Chiang to fight more actively against the Japanese;

increasing levels of support came to depend upon Chinese demonstration of willingness to fight the enemy. The Kuomintang, however, always insisted that American support had to come first—only then could its armies fight effectively. "While the Americans refused to contribute more aid until the Chinese stepped up their war effort," [the historian] Warren Cohen writes, "the Chinese refused to step up their effort until they received more aid. At no time during the war was the circle broken."

American efforts to encourage political change led to similar frustrations. Whenever American officials warned Chiang of his declining popularity or urged Kuomintang reforms to counter communist appeal, the Chinese leader refused to accept responsibility for his domestic problems. Rather, Chiang blamed the United States, charging that its policies were undermining his position.

For two and a half years after Pearl Harbor, Roosevelt and other officials promoted China's international status and encouraged military and political changes by the Kuomintang, but by late 1944, American patience was largely exhausted. By that time it had become evident that Chiang's followers would not undertake any major offensive against the Japanese. A special mission to China headed by Vice-President Henry Wallace in the spring of 1944 failed to change Chiang's attitudes toward his country's problems. And Roosevelt in the fall of 1944 reluctantly acquiesced to Chiang's demand for Stilwell's recall.

Roosevelt's enthusiasm for Chiang waned, but he still tried to ensure the emergence of a strong postwar China. Always the realist, Roosevelt adjusted his means as circumstances changed. In late 1944 and early 1945 he directed American policy toward fostering a coalition government for China in which the communists would join with the Kuomintang. Given the deep-seated antagonism between those two groups, forming a coalition was an unwieldy task that eventually proved impossible. But at the time a coalition seemed the only solution to China's internal divisions. (An important impetus for coalition was the number of Americans who had established a rapport with the communist movement through its leaders Mao Tse-tung and Chou En-lai; Mao and Chou in turn had considerable faith in the United States.)

Besides cultivating a Kuomintang-communist coalition, Roosevelt also worked to make certain that the Soviet Union would become a partner in America's plans for postwar Asia. At the Yalta Conference Roosevelt agreed to Stalin's demand for special concessions in China (particularly privileges in the province of Manchuria, an area of historic Russian interest). An allowance was considered necessary to help assure Soviet participation in the war against Japan. This concession was an affront to Chinese sovereignty. "To dispose of Chinese territory without China's prior consent," Cohen observes, "was hardly calculated to make the Chinese rejoice." Yet Roosevelt also secured an important concession from Stalin which benefitted Chiang's government: the Russian leader agreed to enter into a treaty of friendship and alliance with the Kuomintang. The effects of this arrangement were to enhance Chiang's status and to commit, at least implicitly, the Soviets to the objective of working for a coalition government in China. As he endeavored to salvage American expectations of China, Roosevelt recognized the difficulties confronting the United States in that endeavor. At the Yalta Conference he remarked to Stalin that, "for some time we have been trying to keep China alive." And in the end the promotion of a coalition government and involvement of the Soviet Union seemed the most feasible means of stabilizing the Chinese situation.

Roosevelt's visions of China failed to appreciate the rapidity of political change there that led, shortly after World War II, to communist ascendancy in the renewed civil war. For as Chiang was discredited, defeated, and forced from the mainland, the United States—as his benefactor—suffered an immense loss of prestige. Roosevelt and later American leaders failed to recognize that the United States could not solve the internal problems of other lands. The China problem defied American solutions. The Chinese had to determine their own destiny.

Roosevelt's final objective—promotion of the self-determination of colonial peoples—dealt with the future of Asia and Africa. Western empires largely covered the area stretching from Southeast Asia to the Middle East and nearly all of the African continent. Parts of those empires had been disrupted by the war, in particular by the German-Italian encroachment in north Africa and the Japanese conquest of Southeast Asia.

The American government assumed that World War II would mark the beginning of the end of Western imperialism. Under Secretary of State Sumner Welles expressed American sentiments when he stated:

> If the war is in fact a war for the liberation of peoples, it must assure the sovereign equality of peoples throughout the world. . . . Our victory must bring in its train the liberation of all peoples. . . . The age of imperialism is ended. . . . The principles of the Atlantic Charter must be guaranteed to the world as a whole—in all oceans and in all continents.

This strong sense of anticolonialism led the State Department, in its extensive planning for the postwar world, to anticipate that the imperial powers would be called upon to train their colonial peoples in self-government leading eventually to independence. The American record in the Philippine Islands was advanced as the model for other imperial powers. After acquiring the Philippines, the United States had introduced substantial economic, social, and educational reforms; it also had provided for progressively greater self-government. Proud of its record in the Philippines, the United States expected that the British, French, Dutch, and Belgians would follow similar policies toward their colonial possessions.

This immodest American plan meant overhauling the imperial system. Henceforth, imperial powers would have to accept "international accountability" for their actions; they would be expected to educate subject peoples in self-government. Such expectations were bitterly resented by the European imperial powers who were also America's wartime allies. The British, French, and Dutch had always looked upon their empires as possessions; the home government designed and implemented colonial policies in terms of their own national interests. American ideals of local self-determination were not shared by the European powers. Thus American anticolonialism triggered vigorous criticism, especially from the British who held the largest empire and who, throughout the war, were in the best position to speak on behalf of imperial interests. The question of the future of the imperial system exemplified the "constant jealousies" that can undermine wartime alliances.

The focus of the imperialism issue was Southeast Asia. Japan controlled this vast region that included the colonies of Britain (Malaya, Burma); France (French Indochina, that is, the present nations of Vietnam, Laos, Cambodia); the Netherlands (Netherlands East Indies, that is, the present nation of Indonesia); and, of course, the United States (the Philippines). The British, French, and Dutch assumed that, at the end of the war, they would re-establish the old imperial order. The critical question was: Would it be a return to "business as usual" or would there be a commitment to self-government?

Among the countries of Southeast Asia, Roosevelt took a strong personal interest in the future of French Indochina. In fact, he undertook to assure that the French would not re-establish control over their former colony. By promoting international administration in the form of a "trusteeship," Roosevelt attempted to provide for training in self-government leading to eventual independence. Why did Roosevelt champion the cause of Indochina? First, he had little regard for the French whom, he believed, had forfeited any claim to treatment as a major world power. France had been weak and ineffectual in the face of German aggression in 1940 and Japanese pressure on Indochina in 1940–1941. Moreover, in Roosevelt's opinion the French were the worst of the imperial powers; he repeatedly said they had shamelessly exploited the peoples of Indochina. Denial of French claims to Indochina was Roosevelt's way of punishing the French and of signalling their demise as a world power. Roosevelt's distaste for the French was intensified by his personal antagonism toward General Charles de Gaulle, the leader of the Free French. (This sentiment was not one-sided; de Gaulle also despised Roosevelt.)

Roosevelt also meant to make certain that the principle of anticolonialism would be achieved in at least one European-held colony. Unlikely to overcome British opposition to American anticolonial ideals, Roosevelt seized upon Indochina as an opportunity to prove that the war marked the "end of imperialism." An international trusteeship for Indochina would serve as a stimulus for the advancement of colonial peoples generally.

These American objectives for the colonial areas became the source of the most serious wartime tensions between the United States and Britain. In no other issue did the Americans and their closest ally find reconciliation of interest as intractable as in discussions of the future of Southeast Asia. "The differences between the two major Allies were indeed real and extensive enough," [the historian] Christopher Thorne argues, "but they could at least have been clarified and faced more squarely. As it was, Southeast Asia remained an area where Anglo-American relations, so successful in many ways, were extremely poor."

As the war approached its end, America had to modify its plans for Southeast Asia. Since the region was not vital in the American plan to defeat Japan, the United States exercised little military influence in Southeast Asia (except, of course, for the Philippines). Accordingly, responsibility for military operations was given to a British command. As happened in other areas of the world, military occupation led to political domination. The British re-established their control in Burma and Malaya, assisted the French to retake Indochina, and helped the Dutch to regain the East Indies. As reality overcame idealism, the United States had to compromise with its western European allies to assure postwar cooperation. In the end the Americans agreed to a vague provision in the Charter of the United Nations which exhorted imperial powers to train subject peoples in self-government. Deferring to the British and other imperial powers, the United States rejected an alternative plan advanced by the Soviet Union which called for full national independence and self-determination in all colonial areas. Thus, by the end of the war the United States had retreated considerably from its earlier "end of imperialism" goal.

Yet in the long run Roosevelt's efforts against colonialism were prophetic. As the European imperial powers tried to resume "business as usual" in Southeast Asia, they found that the war had brought fundamental changes heralding the true end of imperialism. Four years of Japanese administration had stimulated nationalist movements. The peoples of Southeast Asia sought their independence and rejected the imperial pretensions of the European powers; within a few more years most of Southeast Asia had gained that independence. Two decades after the end of World War II, virtually all of Asia and Africa was free from European domination.

The United States, as the nation that championed self-determination throughout the greater part of the war, contributed to this irrepressible nationalism. While the European imperial powers may have gained some short-term advantages at the end of the war, in overview, it was the American vision for colonial areas which was realized. For his role in bringing about self-determination, Roosevelt remains—decades after his death—a widely known and inspiring leader among peoples of Asia and Africa.

Franklin Delano Roosevelt died on April 12, 1945, just as the Allies were on the threshold of victory. Throughout the last weeks of the war and into the immediate postwar era, Harry S Truman, who succeeded to the presidency, endeavored to follow Roosevelt's policies. While Roosevelt's objectives were not fully achieved, his diplomatic leadership during the war represented perhaps the most effective expression of American interests and ideals that the circumstances permitted. Those who criticize his actions must present feasible alternatives. Was it possible for the United States to "get tough" with the Soviet Union over eastern Europe at a time when Russian influence was firmly established there? Was it possible for the United States to alter the political situation in China? However much Americans disliked European colonialism, how could the United States force its allies to recognize the inevitability of independence in Asia? Politics is, after all, the art of the *possible.*

The Pupil Roosevelt Concedes Too Much
to His Teacher Stalin

FREDERICK W. MARKS III

Roosevelt would have done well to bear in mind his own analogy: that one cannot stroke a tiger into a kitten. The smiles, jests, and territorial concessions which he felt would be disarming served merely to whet Russia's appetite for more. They

---

From *Wind Over Sand: The Diplomacy of Franklin Roosevelt* by Frederick W. Marks III, pp. 169–177, 178–179, 201–202, 216. Copyright © 1988 by the University of Georgia Press, Athens, Georgia. Reprinted by permission of the publisher.

did not alter the way a great power sought to do business. Neither did they alter the kind of business it sought to do.

There were weaknesses at nearly every point along the line of Roosevelt's thought. If he felt that Russia could be made amenable, he also assumed that Britain would remain America's chief commercial rival and that postwar France would be unable to raise a finger. Especially did he bank on the idea that China would survive the war as a strong and viable nation. According to much of the advice he received at the time, there were no real communists in China and Chiang's domestic feuding came down to a simple matter of personalities. By knocking heads together, by pressing Chiang for social democratic reform and insisting on coalition government, China would coalesce and find herself. Needless to say, on each of these counts Churchill knew Roosevelt to be mistaken, but there was no way the English leader could prevail upon his opposite number. When the truth finally began to dawn in Washington, pundits were to speak of a "Cold War." But again, London knew differently. America's Cold War was nothing but a continuation of Britain's age-old struggle to contain the power of the czars. International life had changed but little.

Stalin, whose name means steel, was nothing if not worldly wise. The only thing he had in common with FDR was a scourge of physical illness that left his face pock-marked and one arm several inches shorter than the other. Far removed from the sheltered groves of Dutchess County, New York, he had endured a drunken father's beatings. As a revolutionary verging on the criminal, he had taken a pseudonym, "Koba," which to the people of his native Georgia meant Robin Hood, and he went on to brave the censure of polite society. Having survived a brutal power struggle and achieved mastery in a world of Oriental intrigue, he knew how to dissemble. He could make men crawl. Thus when Roosevelt approached him in 1933 seeking his friendship, he instinctively held back. A decade later, he announced himself the champion of religious liberty and dissolved the Comintern, giving credence to liberal theories of communist evolution. At Teheran, where butter would not melt in his mouth, he expressed a preference for [Juho Kusti] Paasikivi as Finnish president even though the latter was a democrat rather than a communist. The Red Army, he insisted, would return home with a new ideology, and the USSR would then chart a postwar course between communism and capitalism. There would be private ownership, he assured Roosevelt, along with freedom of worship. The time had come, he added, to change the name of the Soviet Union back to Russia. And no sooner were these words spoken than the Soviet ambassador was reported at a Washington banquet going by the title of "Russian Ambassador." This was Stalin.

As for the outstanding questions central to any study of World War II, there are several which may be succinctly stated. First, did Roosevelt, during the Big Three Conference at Teheran in late November of 1943, have to offer so much in return for Moscow's continued support against Germany and her pledge to join the war against Japan? In addition to promising Stalin a second military front in Europe, Roosevelt acquiesced in a Soviet protectorate over Mongolia, against Chiang's wishes, as well as Soviet acquisition of the Kurile Islands and the southern half of Sakhalin Island. He violated another solemn engagement to Chiang Kai-shek at the same conference when he bestowed his official blessing upon the internationalization of Dairen and the cession of Port Arthur to the Soviet Union as a naval base on long-term lease. Dairen and Port Arthur were among China's most vital ports. Finally, he agreed unilaterally, again in violation of the spirit of his understanding with Chiang, to a half-interest for Russia in the operation of Manchurian railways, with Soviet interests throughout the area to be recognized as "preeminent." Other questions follow along a similar line. During the Big Three Conference at Yalta in February 1945, Roosevelt obtained a modicum of Soviet cooperation regarding the structure of the United Nations. In return, he threw American support to the communist-sponsored Lublin government of Poland, broadened to include various noncommunist elements, but communist nevertheless. Was this a wise bargain? Did the president have to reject, out of hand, Churchill's plea for practical safeguards to ensure the outcome of "free elections" as promised for eastern Europe? And did he have to side with Stalin against Churchill on miscellaneous questions regarding reparations, industry, and labor in postwar Germany?

Few will deny that there were many tactics Roosevelt might have used to contain communist expansion in eastern Europe and the Far East, although how successful they would have been will continue to be a matter for speculation. Some have argued that Russia's postwar gains were inevitable and even morally justifiable given her enormous sacrifice in human life, estimated at twenty million (approximately ten times the figure for all the rest of the Allied forces). To be sure, there is an element of truth in this argument. Few things in history are inevitable, and Stalin did carry weight at the conference table. The specter of a separate peace between Russia and Germany could never be laid. Moreover, Stalin proved masterful in the use of veiled threats. No Western leader was ever permitted to forget that Moscow had engaged 270 German divisions as compared with only 90 for Washington and London combined. Roosevelt needed Stalin's cooperation and he needed it badly since his goal was to win the war at minimum cost to his country while securing the unconditional surrender of Germany and Japan. Nevertheless, had he operated on a different set of assumptions, his strategy and prospects would also have been different. The crux of the issue is simple: *he never grasped the need* for an alternative approach. He believed that the Soviet Union would exhaust itself against Germany and, in association with a cooperative West, evolve gradually toward capitalism and democracy. The Russian empire was too cumbersome, he felt, to absorb additional territory, and he was convinced that by charming Stalin he could lead him gently along the path to postwar unity. "I think I can personally handle Stalin better than either your Foreign Office or my State Department," he confided to Churchill. "Stalin hates the guts of all your top people. He thinks he likes me better, and I hope he will continue to do so."

Had FDR glimpsed the true contours of power in a world aborning, he might have given more support to Mao Tse-tung or backed Chiang with less reserve. It was his to decide which would be more important in negotiating with Stalin, the United Nations charter or the composition of eastern European government. He might have accepted [Charles] de Gaulle's advice that Polish interests dictated an Anglo-American demand for access to Baltic ports in return for Soviet access to terminals in the North Sea. Furthermore, had he assumed, as Eden and the Red Chinese did, that Russia had a natural interest in entering the war against Japan, he might have yielded far less in exchange. Never was he the absolute prisoner of events.

On the one hand, Stalin derived powerful leverage from his option to grant or withhold aid against Japan. Atomic warfare, still in the experimental stage, offered little assurance of instantaneous surrender, particularly given the depth of Japanese commitment, and Roosevelt's military advisers were as one in stressing the importance of Moscow's aid. On the other hand, it is clear that Roosevelt gave away much of his hand in a game whose rules he did not comprehend. He did not have to *volunteer* to hand over such prizes as Dairen and the Kurile Islands. He need not have offered Stalin a free gift of Allied merchant vessels, along with captured enemy warships. Admiral [Ernest J.] King said he could not believe the Allies were in a position to demand Italian men of war, yet the president insisted on letting the USSR have one-third of these vessels as a token of goodwill. Ultimately, Stalin was granted one battleship, one cruiser, and eight destroyers. Britain supplied thirteen warships from the Royal Navy, and the United States turned over one of its cruisers, the USS *Milwaukee*. Roosevelt also volunteered to make part of the Anglo-American merchant fleet available to Stalin after the war.

Possibilities abound. FDR might have baited his line with the promise of a credit or loan for Soviet postwar rehabilitation, as recommended by [Ambassador to the Soviet Union W. Averell] Harriman and [Secretary of the Treasury Henry] Morgenthau. He might have been more stringent on conditions for the continuation of Lend-Lease. He did not have to announce his intention of withdrawing from Europe at the end of the war, particularly when a contrary policy had the support of public opinion, as well as of powerful political leaders and top military advisers. By the fall of 1944, the Joint Chiefs of Staff had reversed their opposition to an occupation policy, and Senators [Arthur] Vandenberg and [Wallace] White were agreed that stationing American occupation forces in Germany for a prolonged period would "not be at all difficult"; there would be "less difficulty . . . on this point than on almost any other" because it could be done by volunteers, of whom there would be many. There was no reason why Roosevelt had to rule out American spy activity in Russia, just as it fell within his province to file a much stronger protest on the Soviet takeover of Romania. In addition, his armies might have rolled on into Berlin and Prague as Churchill advised. At Teheran, he allowed Stalin to persuade him to put less effort into an underbelly invasion of Europe and more into the battle for France. Again, the decision can scarcely have been predetermined since it was FDR, not an Englishman, who in late 1943 proposed a landing at the head of the Adriatic, followed by a thrust to the east in conjunction with Soviet forces. General [Dwight D.] Eisenhower did not object at the time, and neither Churchill nor anyone else assumed that the underbelly approach would preclude a cross-Channel invasion, always the darling of American strategists. To lengthen the list of alternatives, Roosevelt might have sided with Churchill on the value of Germany and France as potential makeweights against Soviet power. He might have bargained on questions affecting the partition of Germany, the sum of reparations to be exacted, or the question of a fair trial for prisoners of war.

Above all, he might have given the Polish government in exile more of an opportunity to survive. When Russian armies were about to enter Warsaw and pro-

Western underground forces rose to attack retreating Nazi units, Stalin ordered his troops to halt on the Vistula River. There they stayed until German gunners had all but annihilated the prospective leadership of a democratic Poland. Churchill proposed an airlift to relieve the embattled patriots, but Stalin refused to permit American or British planes to land at nearby airfields. When Churchill insisted that Roosevelt go ahead with or without Soviet permission, the president could not be budged. He declined even to write Stalin a note of protest. As it happened, a detailed American plan for the United Nations was under consideration at Dumbarton Oaks, and what FDR wanted was Soviet support on voting procedure along with assembly membership and location of the organization in New York City. This, rather than Poland, was the apple of his eye. Hopkins put it bluntly when he said, "We cannot take a chance of having that bitched up." In essence this was the American position. But it was to no avail. A crafty Stalin withheld his assurances even as he swallowed Warsaw. Cooperation on the United Nations would still be his to grant or withhold when it came time to muster support for the Soviet-sponsored Lublin government.

At Teheran, in November of 1943, FDR sat silent when he was not actively undermining the case for Polish territorial integrity. Later, Averell Harriman, who at the time was serving as American ambassador to the Soviet Union, would assure Poland's foreign minister that FDR had not agreed to any revision of prewar Polish boundaries. In fact, the president had told Stalin that he had no objection to a new frontier for Poland because he was interested in the Poles and Balts for only one reason: their impact on the election campaign of 1944. According to the official record of the Teheran Conference:

> He [Roosevelt]said personally he agreed with the view of Marshal Stalin as to the necessity of the restoration of a Polish state but would like to see the Eastern border moved further to the west and the Western border moved to the River Oder. He hoped, however, that the Marshal would understand that for political reasons outlined above, he could not participate in any decision here in Teheran or even next winter on this subject . . . the President went on to say that there were a number of persons of Lithuanian, Latvian, and Estonian origin, in that order, in the United States. He said he fully realized the three Baltic Republics had in history and again more recently been a part of Russia and added jokingly that when the Soviet armies reoccupied these areas, he did not intend to go to war with the Soviet Union on this point.

None of this is to suggest that Churchill, in contrast with Roosevelt, was exactly unswerving in his support for the Poles. One could not expect someone in the position of British prime minister to be as much concerned over the future of Warsaw as he would be over that of Calcutta, Hong Kong, Athens, or even Paris. Full well did he know that Soviet support at the bargaining table might prove invaluable in a test of wills with Roosevelt. Some have gone so far as to suggest that Churchill traded on the future of Poland for that of France. One suspects, however, that the problem went deeper. Doubtless, he shared something of the attitude of Permanent Under-Secretary of State Sir Alec Cadogan, in whose eyes the Polish people were "suicidal" and to whom [Stanislaw] Mikolajczyk [leader of the London Poles] seemed "unconstructive—like all Poles." At the Moscow Conference of 1944, the king's first minister exchanged Polish jokes with Stalin and intimated that his country took less interest in the status of Poland than in that of other parts of the world. The previous year, when the Soviet leader proposed at Teheran to move Polish borders westward, Churchill signified his assent by moving three match sticks across the table. He also found it opportune, at both Teheran and Yalta, to criticize the Polish national character.

Nevertheless, if the Polish people were ever represented in the counsels of the Big Three, they found their voice in Winston Churchill rather than in Franklin Roosevelt. Ultimately, the difference between London and Washington came down to a question of diplomatic judgment. Churchill concluded that while it might be futile to contest the Polish boundary issue, one must nevertheless fight for a pro-Western government in Warsaw. Roosevelt, on the other hand, demonstrated scant concern about the future of Poland because he never shared Churchill's suspicion of the Soviet Union. Churchill insisted on a total scrapping of the Lublin puppet government; FDR was content with a broadening. The former urged strong representations against Lublin while the latter sent weak ones accompanied by a slur against the London Poles. Where Churchill wanted to insist on Western observers, Roosevelt again demurred. When Mikolajczyk asked that Western troops be sent to Poland to prevent Russian reprisals, Roosevelt not only declined to send troops but proposed a political cease-fire, which could only help Russia. Churchill nudged him to intervene personally, but he preferred to let the ambassadors handle it. Exasperated, the prime minister opened fire: "Poland has lost her frontier. Is she now to lose her freedom? . . . We are in the presence of a great failure." Roosevelt, who diagnosed the problem as one of semantics, could not even be brought to the point of prodding Stalin.

Perhaps it is suggestive that Roosevelt never appointed an ambassador to the London Poles once [Anthony] Biddle resigned in the aftermath of Teheran. Before this, he sided with Stalin on the hotly contested question of responsibility for the Katyn Forest Massacre, telling him that the London Poles must learn to act "with more common sense." After Teheran, from 1 December 1943 until August 1945, the United States continued in the same posture, with Roosevelt counseling Mikolajczyk to trust Stalin and pressing him to replace anti-Soviet cabinet members with neutrals or communist sympathizers. Secretly, he sent two pro-Soviet American Poles to Moscow against the advice of Hull and [Edward R.] Stettinius, and in the months after Teheran he rejected two requests by Mikolajczyk and four by Ambassador Jan Ciechanowski for a personal meeting. When he did see the Polish prime minister in June of 1944, he promised he would help him establish his claim to Lvov, Tarnopol, and the oil fields of eastern Galicia. In truth, Poland might well have done without such help as it consisted in Roosevelt's telling Stalin that Polish demands were not to be regarded as demands but merely as suggestions for Soviet consideration. Mikolajczyk promptly resigned.

Without question, Stalin held a strong hand. His armies were on the ground. Nevertheless, nothing about the shape of postwar Polish politics had been foreordained. There was more than empty pride in Mikolajczyk's charge that "we were sacrificed by our allies." Nowhere was it written that twenty thousand pro-Western Polish patriots had to die in the Warsaw Uprising. Roosevelt did not have to boost Soviet hopes at Teheran by conceding that Polish affairs were "of special concern" to Stalin. Nor did he have to remain silent when Churchill depicted Poles as the type of people who would never be satisfied. He need not have repeated to Stalin at Yalta what he had already told him, that his only interest in Poland was to appear "in some way involved with the question of freedom of elections." And he did not have to characterize Poles as a "quarrelsome people not only at home but also abroad." By stressing that his principal interest lay in six million Polish-American voters and alleging that in some years there had not really been any Polish government, he was sinking saber teeth into the future of eastern Europe. It is strange to read the minutes of the plenary meetings at Yalta and to discover that Stalin, of all people, was the only one to volunteer anything complimentary on the subject of Poland or its people.

FDR made Stalin's work relatively easy. In the face of American willingness to grant unconditional Lend-Lease, Stalin responded with condescension: he was "willing to accept" it. When Admiral William H. Standley, Roosevelt's ambassador to Moscow, spoke out against unconditional aid, the president dismissed him with a curt reminder that his mission had but one purpose: "full and friendly cooperation" with the Soviet Union. Again and again, Roosevelt described himself as "deeply appreciative" and "thrilled" at Soviet cooperation, and eventually the United States would succeed in shipping some four hundred thousand trucks, two million tons of petroleum products, four million tons of food, two thousand locomotives, and ten thousand flatcars, along with vast quantities of clothing. All to the Soviet Union.

When roving envoy Joseph Davies journeyed to Moscow to convey a presidential apology for Standley's behavior, Stalin listened in stony silence, doodling on a piece of paper. Davies then appealed for a personal meeting between the Soviet and American chiefs and, denigrating Churchill, reassured his listener that there would be no American objection to a new Polish border as long as it was postponed so as not to inflame American opinion before the next election. . . .

On meeting Stalin [at Teheran in 1943], Roosevelt was the first to speak: "I'm glad to see you. I have tried for a long time to bring this about." There were numerous jokes at Churchill's expense; indeed, FDR refused to meet individually with the Briton the way he did with the Russian. He took delight, he said, in welcoming the Soviets as a new member of the international family circle. Later, on his return home, he assured the American people that judging from his talks with Marshal Stalin, they would "get along very well with him and the Russian people—very well indeed." It was a lesson similar to [Senator Samuel] McReynolds's lesson of 1933, one not quickly unlearned, especially when FDR drove it deeper into the national consciousness as part of his Third Inaugural Address a month later: "We have learned the simple truth, as Emerson said, that 'the only way to have a friend is to be one.' "

By the end of the year, Stalin had extended his power beyond anything dreamed of by the czars and given Americans a succession of lessons in the art of statecraft. To Hopkins, he termed it a mistake to believe that just because a state was small, it was necessarily innocent. To Davies, who hoped that a top-level meeting between Soviet and American leaders would resolve all outstanding problems, Stalin replied that he was not so sure. [Maxim] Litvinov instructed Ambassador [William] Bullitt in like manner: there was no such thing as "really friendly" relations between nations. When FDR took the liberty of calling Stalin "Uncle

Joe," the reaction proved unexpectedly frigid. Always, it seemed, one man spoke as teacher while the other listened as pupil. On one occasion, when Roosevelt suggested that India needed reform from the bottom up, Stalin remarked that in a land with so many tiers of culture and no interchange between the castes, this would invite revolutionary chaos. The Soviet chairman also favored restoration of the monarchy in Yugoslavia. On another occasion, when Roosevelt called Hitler mad, Stalin again corrected him, pointing out that whatever one might think of Hitler's methods or his level of cultural and political sophistication, there was no ground for judging him mentally unbalanced. Only a very able man could have succeeded in unifying the German people. Finally, as if to make the picture complete, FDR advocated a peace imposed by "four policemen" only to be reminded by the Soviet leader of the feelings of smaller nations. Realistically, Stalin predicted that China, one of the prospective four, would not be powerful enough in the aftermath of the war to assume such responsibility.

Of Roosevelt's relationship with Chiang Kai-shek there is only one thing to be said. It was nearly the reverse of what has been observed in the case of Stalin. FDR made practically no effort to assuage Chiang's fears or to cater to him personally. In the epic battle for China, he extended remarkably little material or moral aid, and such sacrifices as were made by the United States tended to undermine Chiang politically. Intentionally or not, great blows were leveled against the prestige of Nationalist China as Roosevelt broke one promise after another. . . .

Having come this far in our analysis, we are free to go a step further and address the knotty question of what Winston Churchill really thought of his distant cousin, Franklin Roosevelt. In Churchill's widely read war memoirs, America's chief executive appears noble, far-seeing, and valiant; he is a man of knowledge and experience who possessed "commanding gifts." Each of the six volumes, moreover, contains at least one special term of endearment. It may also be recalled that Churchill was selected by Parliament to deliver a fitting eulogy on the death of FDR and that on this particular occasion the president was lauded for his upright and generous disposition: he was a man of "clear vision and vigour upon perplexing and complicated matters," in fact "the greatest American friend we have ever known" and "the greatest champion of freedom who has ever brought help and comfort from the New World to the Old."

Such encomiums must, of course, be evaluated within the context of their immediate background as well as against a body of countervailing evidence. Even if it were not apparent that Churchill leaned heavily upon his American connection, there are other grounds for questioning the genuineness of his regard for Roosevelt. Nearly all his praise is contained in the memoirs, which, according to Halifax, were askew in certain places and designed to make a record. Maurice Ashley, after four years as Churchill's research assistant, commented on his employer's "extraordinary gift for irony." And surely there is more than a touch of sarcasm in Churchill's offhand comment that Lend-Lease increased British supplies by about 20 percent so that "we were actually able to wage war as if we were a nation of fifty-eight millions instead of forty-eight." Britain, in other words, sacrificed the flower of her youth while Washington stood by and furnished ammunition. In like vein, nothing could be more devastatingly suggestive than Churchill's choice of an epithet for Lend-Lease when he pronounced it "the most unsordid act." He alone could have given such verisimilitude to a token vote of thanks. The record did not show it at the time, indeed it is no more than faintly visible today, but Churchill was woefully angry, disappointed, and let down by America's two-and-a-half-year refusal to come into the war.

Additional terms such as "evil" and "wicked" were most often code words signifying a departure from conventional wisdom. Thus when one reads that Argentina, one of Britain's most valued trading partners, chose "to dally with evil," one can be fairly certain the author is speaking with tongue in cheek. Of another of FDR's antagonists, Churchill says, "It is fashionable at the present time to dwell on the vices of General [Francisco] Franco [of Spain], and I am, therefore, glad to place on record this testimony to the duplicity and ingratitude of his dealings with Hitler and Mussolini. I shall presently record even greater services which these evil qualities in General Franco rendered to the Allied cause." The prime minister had no love for Hitler, yet one cannot fail to detect a perverse note of respect when he calls him a "bad man." It is likewise as an ardent defender of the British imperial record in India that he must be read when he indicts Japan for "torturing China by her wicked invasions and subjugations." His contempt for America's China policy is barely concealed in the remark that "although the Generalissimo and his wife are now regarded as wicked and corrupt reactionaries by many of their former admirers, I am glad to keep this [photograph of Churchill, FDR, and Chiang] as a souvenir." Neither is he endorsing the presidential standard when he reflects on American behavior toward India: "States which have no overseas colonies or possessions are capable of rising to moods of great elevation and detachment about the affairs of those who have."

[Foreign Secretary Anthony] Eden stated flatly that Churchill "had to play the courtier" and that if he had ever aired his real opinion he would have described the president as a charming country gentleman without any businesslike method for dealing with serious situations. In de Gaulle's judgment, Churchill "bitterly resented" the "tone of supremacy" which FDR adopted toward him, while the prime minister's physician relates that his patient was most reticent when it came to criticizing Roosevelt. Nowhere is it recorded that Churchill ever uttered a word of praise in private. . . .

A number of individuals, including Australian Prime Minister Robert Menzies, marveled at the way Roosevelt, after singling Hitler out as a threat to world freedom, acted with imagination and persistence to convert strict neutrality into benevolent neutrality and thence into all aid short of war. On balance, however, the respect that Roosevelt might have earned as president of the United States simply did not materialize. Nothing is more misleading than the eulogies that poured from foreign chancelleries in 1945, when few failed to see the benefit, if not the necessity, of cultivating the party of Roosevelt. Within two years, veteran diplomat George Kennan would be moved to declare that world opinion toward the United States was "at worst hostile and at best resentful." Thoughtful Americans might well have wondered at the time, reading Kennan's dour appraisal, how their nation's standing could have fallen off so precipitately. But the more one sees of FDR, in particular his image in the eyes of the world, the more one is inclined to take Kennan at his word. America's reputation did not fall suddenly, however. It had been in semi-eclipse for more than a decade.

Backing Off the Colonial Issue

LLOYD C. GARDNER

"Did I ever tell you the story of French Indochina?" asked the president. It was March of 1944, the eve of the Allied invasion of Europe, a moment when all things seemed possible—or, maybe, simply inevitable. Either way Franklin Roosevelt liked to muse aloud about postwar changes. "A year or so ago when Churchill was over here," the president told Vice-President Henry A. Wallace, "I called his attention to the fact that the French had renounced their claims to Indochina in favor of the Japs six months before the United States was attacked by the Japs."

For three presidents—Roosevelt, Truman, Eisenhower—that was the most obvious fact about colonialism. It was on its way out. By their inability to defend Indochina, contended Roosevelt, the French had forfeited any claims to sovereignty there. Now it was up to America—up to Roosevelt—to oversee the transition to colonial independence. American leaders felt enthusiastic about the challenge, and confident they could take the lead in such a vast endeavor, in part because after World War II there would be no one else to do it, and in part because they all believed the United States could count on the goodwill of Asian and African peoples. . . .

In Roosevelt's day, policymakers . . . were not yet looking over their shoulders at what Moscow had planned for the "third world." The Soviet menace played some part in official thinking, especially, of course, as the war came to an end in Europe. Pre–Cold War concern not to alienate a potential ally while relations with Russia remained a question mark would later develop into a fixation, but it was secondary to the threat of postwar chaos caused by inept attempts to retake the colonies by shortsighted European leaders seeking a lost glory.

However presumptuous such a perspective seems today, it was the basis for FDR's various suggestions for dealing with problem areas like Indochina. Some critics would say Mr. Roosevelt took too much to heart the quip about small minds and a foolish consistency. FDR had no fear of hobgoblins, so he was as inconsistent as he liked. After all, he could hardly predict what the situation would be at war's end, what could be done immediately and what would simply have to be anticipated without a precise plan. So he *was* fuzzy-minded. He might, as he told Wallace he had, try to line up China and Russia against Churchill on taking Indochina away from France. And he might, as he did on occasion, make public promises that France would be restored to all its greatness after the war, which meant retaining its overseas territory. There was no telling what he might say.

Beneath this free-floating style was a firm commitment to an American role expanded far beyond past definitions of national security. The biggest change from prewar years was not that FDR or his aides might juggle hard-nosed strategic concerns with self-flattering moral pronouncements about the evils of colonialism—all nations and leaders entertain themselves that way—but that they vowed not to be denied a voice, the major voice, in the settlement of any issue of concern.

Indochina claimed less attention than most other wartime issues. But it seemed obvious to Roosevelt and other policymakers that the French colony could not be left alone to fend for itself. It had to be part of something bigger. The only question was what. When he first shocked Prime Minister Winston Churchill with his proposal to place the colony under a trusteeship, adding that he had already consulted Russia and China without telling Churchill, he got the negative reaction he expected. "Well," he remembered telling the nettled British leader, "we are three to one against you on this. You had better come across and we will make it unanimous." When the prime minister still demurred, saying he had to consult the cabinet, Roosevelt chided: "The trouble with you is that you are thinking that Burma might want to be independent, that the Straits Settlements might want to be independent, or the Dutch East Indies might want to be independent after they have gone through an apprenticeship under a trusteeship."

Roosevelt seemed to relish such encounters, more, perhaps, in the retelling, when they became embellished into morality plays. This behavior confirmed a vision of America's benevolent postwar role, of the United States as history's agent, endowed not only with a superior political and economic system, but also with a superior moral system. Whatever Americans did, therefore, whether they talked about transforming the war into a crusade against colonialism, or only about defeating the Axis, it could hardly be surprising that America's European allies believed, as one British observer put it, that America was "on the verge of a great expansionist movement," without having thought through very carefully where it wanted to go.

The problem for the prewar colonial powers thus became how to manage Roosevelt's dream so that the least damage was done to British and French interests, while obtaining the most from America's postwar position as a superpower. "Our main reason for favoring the restoration of Indo-China to France," read a British Foreign Office conclusion near the end of the war, "is that we see danger to our own Far Eastern colonies in President Roosevelt's idea that restoration depends upon the United Nations (or rather the United States) satisfying themselves that the French record in Indo-China justifies the restoration of French authority." . . .

French Indochina proved a good example of the moral concern Americans felt about colonialism's heritage, while at the same time illustrating the largely abstract nature of thinking about colonial issues in general. "Indo-China should not go back to France," Roosevelt admonished Secretary of State Cordell Hull in mid-October 1944. "France has had the country—thirty million inhabitants—for nearly one hundred years, and the people are worse off than they were at the beginning. . . . The people of Indo-China are entitled to something better than that." . . .

Colonialism touched upon everything else. Indeed, if the later domino theory ever had any validity, it was probably during World War II. World War II was no sooner begun than its protagonists realized that in truth they were fighting many overlapping wars; traditional struggles raged in the same geographic areas where shadowy wars of national independence were being fought out, and ideology permeated the thinking of many in the anti-Fascist grand alliance, just as it did on another level in the villages of Southeast Asia. Above all, there was the sense that this time the victors, as well as the vanquished, would be held accountable before the world. The feeling was present everywhere, from the street corner to the summit.

Throughout the war Roosevelt dealt with French Indochina through several "screens." He seldom talked directly with French authorities, but instead preferred to send "messages," as Admiral [William] Leahy had done during his tenure as ambassador to Vichy. This situation did not change when the Free French put forward their appeals for recognition as the rightful government of France and ruler of the French empire. Roosevelt simply turned Free French entreaties aside as premature. He always spoke as if the real obstacle to his program for Indochina were the British. French views simply didn't count. Repeating his Indochina "story" to another group of advisers, the president explained how he had assured Churchill that China had no designs to succeed the French. He wanted to encourage the prime minister to believe that Big Four management could work, but, Roosevelt added, "we are still going to have a tough time with the British on this issue."

There were places in the world, Roosevelt told British chargé Sir Ronald Campbell, who came to see him at Hyde Park in early August of 1942, such as Korea, Malaya, and the Dutch East Indies, where the people "were simply not ready to manage their own affairs." For Korea the trustees might be China, the United States, and Russia. In any event, Korea could not be left to itself, nor to Russia and China alone.

As for Malaya, the trustees might be China, the United States, and Great Britain. The Netherlands would have to be included for the East Indies, he supposed. "The poor dears thought they should have them back for themselves in the same conditions as before, but he doubted whether this was possible." As he envisioned the postwar situation, the trusteeship would be on the lines of ordinary trusteeships in private life, with a stipulated term, say ten years, and with provisions for a further extension of ten years.

When Campbell asked about details of this machinery, the president "waved my question aside." At that point Sir Ronald thought it best to say nothing more and seek guidance from London. Additional Roosevelt musings convinced the Foreign Office that the president was off on a tear, stimulating his advisers to say outrageous things that would store up trouble for the future. . . .

Roosevelt arrived at Casablanca at the end of January 1943, ready to celebrate the Anglo-American victory in North Africa. The first awkward corner of the war had been turned. German armies had been beaten; Hitler's mythical supermen, who devastated enemies with their blitzkrieg, were exposed as ordinary humans who bled and died.

The president had invited Stalin to be present, indeed, had importuned him to come, so that together they might do battle with Churchill's advisers on military strategy. FDR did not want to be trapped in a Mediterranean imbroglio, where, it could be charged, America's future role was to help John Bull regain his imperial territories and prestige. It was time to start thinking in earnest about the postwar "facts of life."

Without Stalin's presence, FDR would lose this battle. Whether the Russian's vote would have made any difference may be doubted, but the next campaign, it was decided, should be the invasion of Sicily, then Italy. To compensate for the loss, and out of concern for Stalin's reaction to the decision, Roosevelt summoned newspaper reporters to tell them "unconditional surrender" on all fronts was the Allied aim, not the particular interests of any one of them.

Searching for ways to make the point clear, Roosevelt settled on a familiar topic: the end of empire. Empire was not on the agenda at Casablanca, but in peripheral discussions, at dinner, for example, with the sultan of Morocco, Roosevelt entertained those present by disparaging colonial regimes. On other occasions, he belittled Free French leader Charles de Gaulle's pretensions, and stripped France of nearly all its prewar possessions to provide for setting up an Anglo-American police force at strategic points around the world.

Roosevelt thus picked up where he had left off in Washington at the beginning of 1942. If he wanted to draw Churchill into a debate on colonialism, he was to be disappointed; the prime minister knew better than to fight on the grounds Roosevelt chose. A British observer recorded that at the outset of the Casablanca Conference, he had privately "christened the two personalities the Emperor of the East and the Emperor of the West, and indeed it was rather like a meeting of the later period of the Roman Empire."

Surrounding the Emperor of the West in his villa were military advisers—who had always had their own suspicions of British political "imperial" motives in urging the North African campaign. To them, the president stated that he did not feel bound by any promises made to the French. Looking mildly reproachful, he told his diplomatic representative in the area, Robert Murphy, that he, Murphy, had overdone things a bit in promises to guarantee France the return of "every part of her empire." "That was the first indication to me," recalled the ambassador, "that Roosevelt was planning to encourage extensive reductions in the French empire, but it was apparent at Casablanca that this project was much on his mind."

Roosevelt was to meet Charles de Gaulle at this conference, an assignment necessary to unite Free French forces—but not one he looked forward to with much relish. He prepared for this confrontation by scarcely disguised attempts to put de Gaulle on notice that the Emperor of the West, and not the Emperor of the East, called the shots. This piece of diplomatic business was accomplished at a dinner with the sultan of Morocco, then a protectorate of the French. With Churchill seated nearby, Roosevelt launched into a discussion of his sympathy for colonial aspirations for independence, and suggested to the sultan that he hoped to see postwar economic cooperation between the United States and Morocco.

This table talk was reported, of course, to de Gaulle, who had been summoned to appear at the conference against his will, under actual threat of Allied abandonment. In sharp contrast to his wooing of the sultan, Roosevelt would not recognize General de Gaulle as the leader of a provisional French government in exile. The president had made it plain he regarded France as having ceased to exist, and until the liberation of metropolitan France no French authority could be recognized. Harold Macmillan, Churchill's chief diplomatic adviser in North Africa, who was also present at the dinner for the sultan, concluded that the prime minister had ample reason for his "sulkiness" beyond the absence of his usual liquid refreshments. "The President talked a great deal about colonial aspirations towards independence and the approaching end of 'imperialism.' All this was equally embarrassing to the British and to the French."

More was to come. In de Gaulle's presence, Roosevelt described France's present state as like a "child" in need of trustees. And without Churchill's knowledge, the president attempted to promote de Gaulle's chief rival, General Henri Giraud, to a superior position in the Free French movement. He did this, it has been convincingly argued, because de Gaulle had served notice he would not accept "a secondary role for France after the war."

Returning to Washington, Roosevelt unveiled his personal sketches for the United Nations. Once again, France was left out. The postwar security organization was to consist of three bodies: a general assembly of all members, an executive committee of the Big Four, and an advisory council elected on a regional basis to meet from time to time with the Big Four to resolve crisis issues. The assembly, suggested Roosevelt, would meet once a year to let "the smaller powers . . . blow off steam." The executive committee, on the other hand, would "take all the more important decisions and wield police powers of the United Nations."

Within this framework he imagined that some mechanism—still undefined—could be devised to solve the colonial problem. The Big Four executive committee that Roosevelt had put at the center, for example, he often spoke about as having special regional responsibilities. Sometimes he called them the Four Policemen. But if that were so, how would the demands of the colonial areas for genuine independence fare against what was shaping up as a traditional spheres of influence arrangement?

Russia had already indicated it wanted no one bothering too much about what it did in the Baltic states. And China was known to have its own ambitions, especially in regard to Hong Kong and Indochina, which it wanted to classify as "lost territories." Roosevelt professed not to be troubled in conversations with the British ambassador, Lord Halifax, who had been invited to the unveiling.

As Halifax watched in astonishment, Roosevelt redrew prewar maps, not as Wilson had done in Europe, but all around the globe. French Indochina would be placed under trusteeship, he said. When the ambassador asked who would administer the former colony, FDR ignored the question, and continued scratching out other pieces of the French empire, including the Marquesas and Tuamotu Islands—to be used as United Nations bases, he said—and strong points in North and West Africa, Dakar and Bizerta.

He had decided, Roosevelt at last explained, that the United States should "act as policeman" for the United Nations at Dakar, and Great Britain likewise at Bizerta. In reply to this breathtaking recital, Halifax could only manage to wonder if perhaps the president was not being "very hard on the French." Yes, that was so, admitted Roosevelt, but then "France would no doubt require assistance for which consideration might be the placing of certain parts of her territory at the disposal of the United Nations." . . .

At the Cairo and Teheran conferences, the president discussed Indochina with Chiang and Premier Joseph Stalin. In the first conference, Roosevelt continued his efforts, without much consultation of the British, to insure that China received its full due. The communiqué from Cairo stressed that China must have all its lost territories restored. It did not, however, mention the territories Japan had taken from the Western powers. Instead, FDR proposed to "negotiate" about those. According to the Chinese record of his conversation with Chiang, Roosevelt began with an invitation, readily accepted, for China to "participate on an equal footing in the machinery of the Big Four Group and in all its decisions." Then he proposed that China and the United States "should reach a mutual understanding on the future status of Korea, Indo-China and other colonial areas as well as Thailand." Chiang replied that the two nations should help Indochina achieve independence. "The President expressed his agreement."

His initial meeting with Stalin a few days later at Teheran began on the same plane, with outstretched hands of greetings for the first nation to be invited to join the Grand Alliance chartered by Roosevelt and Churchill. "I am glad to see you. I have tried for a long time to bring this about." In this case, however, it was the Russian who first brought up Indochina, saying that he did not propose to shed Allied blood to restore French rule. FDR said he was in "100%" agreement. France had had the colony for a hundred years, and the inhabitants were worse off than they had been. Chiang Kai-shek had assured him, he went on, that China harbored no designs on Indochina. But the generalissimo had also said that the people there were not ready for independence. Roosevelt also agreed with that, suggesting a parallel with the Philippines. The best solution, Roosevelt and Stalin concluded, would be for an international trusteeship.

They did not tell Prime Minister Churchill what had been "decided" about Indochina at this intimate little session, but from Stalin's jibes at France, he may have suspected the worst. At dinner, the Soviet ruler declared the entire French ruling class was rotten to the core, and that it would be not only "unjust but dangerous to leave in French hands any important strategic points after the war," or indeed to restore its empire. Roosevelt chimed in. He "agreed in part," he began, with the marshal's opinion, and mentioned Dakar and New Caledonia as vital strong points. The latter he now identified as a threat to Australia and New Zealand.

Churchill responded in remarkably subdued tones, not to the accusations against France, but only to say that his country had no desire for new territory. Since the Big Four would have to be responsible for the future peace of the world, he conceded that it was obvious that certain strategic points would have to be under their control.

At dinner alone with Churchill, Roosevelt tried to reassure the prime minister that whatever harsh things were said about France and the colonial issue could be, should be, interpreted as crisis management. The French, he now added, must not be allowed to let the world down a second time. "Therefore Indo-China should *not* be returned to them; Dakar (in French West Africa) should be under American protection; Bizerta under British, and so on. There is no need to abolish French sovereignty in these places; the French flag can fly, 'But if Great Britain and America are to police the world, they must have the right to select the police stations. Dakar can be a French-owned station, with an American sergeant; Bizerta the same.'"

Although Roosevelt once claimed to have spoken to Churchill at least twenty-five times about Indochina—and the prime minister confirmed, if not the exact number, then the frequency of these expressions—both men preferred to save their most dramatic statements for third parties. Immediately following the Cairo and Teheran meetings, Roosevelt received a group of diplomats, including representatives from Turkey, Egypt, Persia (Iran), China, the Soviet Union, and Great Britain. To London's dismay, the president went on record before this group of outsiders—in effect telling all the world—to say that he had been "working very hard" to prevent Indochina's return to France. "At recent meetings it has been decided," he went on in a reference to his discussions with Churchill and Stalin, "that peace must be kept by force. There was no other way and world policemen would be necessary who would need certain places from which to exercise their function without bringing up [the] question of changes in sovereignty." . . .

Yet Roosevelt still deferred a decision: "In regard to this Indochina matter," he instructed Cordell Hull [in October 1944], "it is my judgment that we should do nothing in regard to resistance groups or in any other way in relation to Indochina. You might bring it up to me a little later when things are a little clearer."

They never were.

With both Churchill and Roosevelt willing to wait until things were a "little clearer," their advisers had no alternative but to sit tight and hope for the best. One of the most difficult assessments to make, in this regard, concerns the shifting domestic political climates within the two leading Western powers. Roosevelt's New Deal coalition held firm for electoral occasions through 1944, but the influx of the famous "dollar-a-year men" into key policy-making positions altered the tone and some of the substance of internal debates. The presence of many such new faces in the wartime Roosevelt administration probably gave encouragement to the more conservative voices in foreign policy making, such as Secretaries of State Hull and Stettinius. But it is difficult to say that the influx of conservatives really tipped the balance, when one finds [one of FDR's liberal advisers] Harry Hopkins arguing for full reintegration of France, with all that implied for FDR's trusteeship plan, early in 1945.

There is also other evidence to consider. Roosevelt's antipathies toward France, perhaps as much as any other factor, account for the harsh tones he used about French colonialism. These reached their highest levels in the general time frame of the Casablanca Conference. Yet an old diplomat with long-standing access to the White House, Norman Davis, reported to a postwar planning committee that the president was changing his mind about certain ideas such as his view that France should be disarmed. After Casablanca, the president had "received a thesis concerning what would happen if Russia was not fully cooperative and France and Germany were both disarmed. Europe in this case would be impotent against aggression. It was thus necessary to have France a strong power as part of our own security."

Combined with other factors, this concern no doubt began to weigh on FDR in the last months of 1944 and early 1945. In the Far East there was China's "decline"; in Europe, the growing evidence of a postwar contest for political control of the liberated nations. . . .

At the end of 1944, frustration and division characterized the various echelons of policy-making in the State Department and the Foreign Office. But still no word came from on high in either capital. M. E. Dening, [Admiral Lord Louis] Mountbatten's political adviser, issued a dark prophecy that the unrest evident in liberated Europe would soon spread to Asia. "On our side there is a sense of frustration and resentment, and on the American a spirit of ruthless go-getting, coupled with a conviction of our Far Eastern bankruptcy." If the "problems of empire" he saw looming over the horizon were not solved "before the reaction and ill temper following upon a long and strenuous war begin to manifest themselves . . . all discontents will come to the surface . . . and hostile elements will not be lacking beyond our borders who will seek to take advantage of the situation to undermine our whole position in the Far East."

Had Dening sat in unobserved in a corner somewhere at Washington policy sessions, on the other hand, he would have been surprised at the disarray reigning there as well. State Department policymakers were sharply divided, more sharply than ever, between WE (Western European experts) and SEA (Asian specialists) over what to do about dependent territories in Asia. Those who worked closely with Southeast Asian problems warned that American troops would be largely responsible for driving out the Japanese, and Washington would, therefore, be held largely responsible also "for the postwar treatment accorded those areas." It was easy enough to stand back and criticize the European empires, but how would Americans react to the assignment of providing even temporary civil government for peoples of different races? The American experience in the Caribbean area offered little comfort to those worried about getting off to a good start in postwar Asia. . . .

The longer he delayed, the less likely Roosevelt would have any options. The president was under siege, whether from SEAC [South East Asia Command] or the more obscure offices of the State Department. His personal strength rapidly failing after nearly twelve momentous years in the White House, FDR could concentrate on only the biggest issues. Meanwhile his chief adviser at the forthcoming Yalta Conference, Harry Hopkins, was telling Secretary of State Edward R. Stettinius, Secretary of War Henry L. Stimson, and Secretary of the Navy James V. Forrestal that a review of "our entire French approach" was overdue. In certain instances, Hopkins went on, "we had held back," only to change our position in the end anyway under British pressure. "This had resulted in the French feeling that we were opposing their regrowth." The group nodded their agreement: "With the British position what it is . . . our policy of deferring a decision on Indo-China until some general peace settlement would probably be doomed."

When Roosevelt met with Ambassador Halifax, the change was apparent. If it was absolutely necessary to use some Frenchmen for "sabotage work" to disrupt Japanese communications, "we had better tell Mountbatten to do it and ask no questions." One reason for the secrecy, he warned Halifax, nevertheless, was that "he did not want to appear to be committed to anything that would seem to prejudice political decisions about Indo-China in a sense favorable to restoration of French status quo ante." If he were quoted, FDR added, he would disown everything. This was most unsatisfactory, concluded the ambassador, because while it seemed to permit Mountbatten to go ahead, it did not settle the main question. Most important, it did not permit him to get the word to American military commanders. It was indeed most unsatisfactory, almost a trap.

Roosevelt had his own ideas about what to do next. At Yalta he let his advisers in on part of the secret, without implying he had approved any British schemes. Any action that damaged the Japanese in Indochina was "satisfactory to him." "He had no objection to any *U.S. action* [emphasis added] which it was considered desirable to take in Indochina as long as it did not involve any alignments with the French." But there was no meeting with Churchill [on the issue]. . . . Instead, FDR took his case to Stalin privately, and in a curiously nostalgic session linked his original 1942 plan for a three-power (Russia, China, the United States) Korean trusteeship with his continuing interest in seeing Indochina put under international control. The British did not approve, he said, because of the danger to Burma. Stalin agreed that Indochina "was a very important area."

Encouraged once more, the president told the Russian leader that the Indochinese were people of "small stature . . . and were not warlike." General de Gaulle had asked for ships to transport his troops to Indochina, said Roosevelt. When Stalin asked where the general would get the troops, he answered that de Gaulle "said he was going to find the troops when the President could find the ships, but the President added that up to the present he had been unable to find the ships."

It may be that Roosevelt imagined that he had disarmed Stalin, and enlisted him in a stabilizing effort for postwar Asia. The president had seen his hopes for China go aglimmering, and in fact confided during this tête-à-tête that he had for some time "been trying to keep China alive." His references to the Indochinese people—with their suggestions that he understood them best, à la Woodrow Wilson's old view of Mexico—coupled with his self-assumed role as China's spokesman at Yalta, and the offer of a share of responsibility in Korea, point to a gambler's inclination to envision Russia as a potential ally, a silent backer as it were, in a chancy, last-ditch scheme to keep France from sneaking back into Indochina.

If so, it was a piece of self-deception. He could no longer maneuver effectively between the various rocks and shoals that confronted him on this final journey to secure a postwar settlement among the great powers. The trusteeship plan as finally presented at Yalta, the day after his private talk with Stalin, provided for placing under the United Nations only those territories taken from the defeated Axis powers, or those "voluntarily" put under international control by the colonial powers. Though the plan involved only pinpoints of territory, Roosevelt had another reason to alter his original ideas for a trusteeship system—the U.S. Navy's insistence that nothing hamper its administration of former Japanese mandated islands in the Pacific. Pinpoints of territory, it developed, could move tons of principle, with the right leverage.

At Yalta, Admiral Leahy, now Roosevelt's chief of staff, sensed perfectly what had happened. He had heard the president talk about his interest in having Hong Kong returned to Chinese sovereignty during preparations for the Yalta meeting. At the conference, however, Roosevelt proceeded to agree to a Russian demand that another nominally Chinese port be opened to them. Leahy recalled that he leaned over and said, "Mr. President, you are going to lose out on Hong Kong if you agree to give the Russians half of Dairen." Roosevelt shook his head. "Well, Bill, I can't help it."

After Yalta the president told reporters that the French had talked about recapturing Indochina, "but they haven't got any shipping to do it with." Still, plans for a trusteeship would only "make the British mad. Better to keep quiet just now." . . .

Roosevelt was a powerful conjurer. Long after he had left the stage, the impression lingered that he had never abandoned his determination to liberate colonial peoples, but had been outmaneuvered by the wily Europeans. Sometimes, unfortunately, this made self-deception all the easier. Roosevelt may not have believed in the dream—or all of it, anyway—but his curious discussion with Stalin at Yalta, when he might have said nothing and let the issue drop, suggested that even when none of the pieces had fallen into place, he still held out a hope that an atmosphere could be created that would help move things along to a more decent world order than had prevailed before the war.

Confidence had given way to ambiguity. Roosevelt had "dreamed up" a magical trusteeship system that would at one and the same time protect and advance American interests, remove the onus of colonialism from the Allied cause, maintain big-power unity in keeping the peace, adjust legitimate demands for independence, yet avoid the chaos of violent revolution. In a sudden gust at Roosevelt's death, the pieces all flew apart. What survived out of the confused ending to World War II colonial policy could not have been foreseen by Roosevelt; nor could it be said that he would have disavowed what his successors did in his name. . . .

Roosevelt had not been pushed off the colonial issue. In the end he had backed off, avoiding a confrontation that involved too many uncertainties. During the war it had been easy to believe, as he once told an ambassador, he could change "all that" by turning over his hand. By the time he discovered that was not so, and that it was not at all certain *anything* America could do would head off the incipient armed struggles in colonial areas, Roosevelt had no time left.

✖ *F U R T H E R   R E A D I N G*

Stephen E. Ambrose, *Eisenhower and Berlin, 1945* (1967)
———, *Rise to Globalism* (1993)
Robert Beitzell, *The Uneasy Alliance* (1972)
Edward M. Bennett, *Franklin D. Roosevelt and the Search for Victory* (1990)
Robert Blake and Wm. Roger Louis, eds., *Churchill* (1993)
Richard Breitman and Alan M. Kraut, *American Refugee Policy and European Jewry, 1933–1945* (1987)
Douglas Brinkley and David Facey-Crowther, eds., *The Atlantic Charter* (1994)
A. Russell Buchanan, *The United States and World War II* (1964)
Russell Buhite, *Decisions at Yalta* (1986)
James M. Burns, *Roosevelt: The Soldier of Freedom* (1970)
Thomas M. Campbell, *Masquerade Peace: America's UN Policy, 1944–1945* (1973)
Diane Shaver Clemens, *Yalta* (1970)
Wayne S. Cole, *Roosevelt and the Isolationists, 1932–1945* (1983)
Kenneth R. Crispell and Carlos F. Gomez, *Hidden Illness in the White House* (1988)
R. D. Cuff and J. L. Granatstein, *Canadian-American Relations in Wartime* (1975)
Robert Dallek, *Franklin D. Roosevelt and American Foreign Policy, 1933–1945* (1979)
Kenneth R. Davis, *FDR* (1993)
Robert A. Divine, *Roosevelt and World War II* (1969)
———, *Second Chance* (1967)
John W. Dower, *War Without Mercy* (1986)
Robin Edmonds, *The Big Three* (1991)
Herbert Feis, *Between War and Peace* (1960)
———, *Churchill, Roosevelt, Stalin* (1957)
Robert H. Ferrell, *Ill-Advised* (1992)
Frank Freidel, *Franklin D. Roosevelt* (1990)
Lloyd C. Gardner, *Spheres of Influence* (1993)

Martin Gilbert, *Winston S. Churchill* (1986)
Gary R. Hess, *America Encounters India, 1941–1947* (1971)
———, *The United States' Emergence as a Southeast Asian Power, 1940–1950* (1987)
Robert C. Hilderbrand, *Dumbarton Oaks* (1990)
Julian C. Hurstfield, *America and the French Nation, 1939–1945* (1986)
Akira Iriye, *Power and Culture* (1981)
Warren Kimball, *The Juggler* (1991)
Richard H. Kohn, ed., "The Scholarship on World War II," *Journal of Military History,* 55
    (1991), 365–393
Gabriel Kolko, *The Politics of War* (1968)
Eric Larrabee, *Commander in Chief* (1987)
Michael Leigh, *Mobilizing Consent* (1976) (public opinion)
Ralph B. Levering, *American Opinion and the Russian Alliance* (1976)
Wm. R. Louis, *Imperialism at Bay* (1978) (decolonization)
Richard Lukas, *The Strange Alliance* (1978) (Poland)
William H. McNeill, *America, Britain, and Russia* (1953)
Vojtech Mastny, *Russia's Road to the Cold War* (1979)
Steven M. Miner, *Between Churchill and Stalin* (1988)
Samuel Eliot Morison, *Strategy and Compromise* (1958)
William L. Neumann, *After Victory* (1967)
Robert Nisbet, *Roosevelt and Stalin* (1988)
Raymond G. O'Connor, *Diplomacy for Victory* (1971) (unconditional surrender)
William O'Neill, *A Democracy at War* (1993)
Forrest C. Pogue, *George C. Marshall* (1963–1987)
David Reynolds et al., eds., *Allies at War* (1994)
———, *Churchill and Roosevelt at War* (1994)
Keith Sainsbury, *The Turning Point* (1985)
John Sbrega, *Anglo-American Relations and Colonialism in East Asia* (1983)
Michael Schaller, *The U.S. Crusade in China, 1938–1945* (1978)
Michael S. Sherry, *Preparing for the Next War* (1977)
———, *The Rise of American Air Power* (1987)
Gaddis Smith, *American Diplomacy During the Second World War, 1941–1945* (1985)
John L. Snell, *Illusion or Necessity* (1963)
———, ed., *The Meaning of Yalta* (1956)
Ronald H. Spector, *Eagle Against the Sun* (1984)
Mark A. Stoler, "A Half Century of Conflict: Interpretations of U.S. World War II Diplo-
    macy," *Diplomatic History, 18 (1994), 375–403*
———, *George Marshall* (1989)
———, *The Politics of the Second Front* (1977)
Kenneth W. Thompson, *Winston Churchill's World View* (1983)
Christopher Thorne, *Allies of a Kind* (1978)
———, *The Issue of War* (1985)
Adam Ulam, *Expansion and Coexistence* (1974) (Soviet foreign policy)
Gerhard L. Weinberg, *A World at Arms* (1994)
Randall Woods, *A Changing of the Guard* (1990)
Llewellyn Woodward, *British Foreign Policy in the Second World War* (1970–1971)
David S. Wyman, *The Abandonment of the Jews* (1984)

CHAPTER
6

The Origins of the Cold War

The Grand Alliance collapsed soon after the Second World War. Strife had developed during the war itself, and the scramble for postwar position accentuated differences of power, interests, and ideology, especially between the United States and the Soviet Union. As they defined their postwar goals, each side in the unfolding contest drew different lessons from the 1930s and pushed aside the plans devised at the Yalta and Potsdam conferences near the end of the war.

While Soviet leaders came to see the United States as an expansionist power seeking world supremacy, threatening USSR security, and manipulating weaker states, U.S. leaders increasingly read the Soviet Union as a bullying aggressor bent on grabbing territory, subjugating neighbors, and disturbing the postwar peace through subversion. The Kremlin charged the United States with trying to encircle the Soviet Union; Washington claimed that it was only seeking to contain the Soviet Union. Each side saw offense when the other saw defense. Fearful about the future, the adversaries competed to build and enlarge spheres of influence, to attract allies, to improve military capabilities, and to gain economic advantage. Shortly after the Second World War, a new, long global war that would endure for more than four decades began—the Cold War.

Poland, Germany, Iran, Czechoslovakia, Greece, China, Korea, and many other nations became the diplomatic and military battlegrounds for the Cold War by midcentury. The Soviet Union and the United States never sent their troops into battle directly against one another. Instead, they started an expensive arms race, cultivated and at times intimidated client states, constructed overseas bases and intelligence posts, intervened in civil wars, launched covert operations, constructed rival alliance systems, sponsored exclusionist economic relationships and foreign-aid programs, and initiated propaganda campaigns in which they charged one another with conspiracy. Soon such designations as "West" and "East" and "Third World" (nonaligned nations in the developing world) reflected global divisions.

The end of the Cold War in the late 1980s and early 1990s, and the question of who won or lost it, are treated in the last chapter in this book. Here we strive to understand why and how the Cold War began. The scholarship on this subject is in transition because post–Cold War Russian, Eastern European, Chinese, and other archives are beginning to open for the first time, providing a limited amount of new documentation and stimulating new or revised perspectives. The traditional view that the Cold War was all the Soviet Union's fault, the revisionist view that both the United States and the Soviet Union caused it and that U.S. expansionism stands as a major catalyst, and the postrevisionist view that the USSR was primarily responsible for disrupting international relations and prompting the United States to build a global empire—all these views will necessarily be tested anew.

Three sets of questions have guided and will continue to guide scholars as they explore the sources of the Cold War. First is the international context: Was postwar conflict inevitable because of the wrenching changes wrought in the international system by the Second World War? How was power redistributed in that system, and which nation held the most? What restraints and opportunities did the state of the world present to the United States and the Soviet Union? Which of the two was more responsible for the Cold War—or must they share responsibility? And why did a conflict that began largely in Europe spread to the rest of the world?

The second set of questions studies the national context of the Soviet Union and the United States: What drove them to become international activists? Power? Security interests? Economic needs? Ideology? Lessons from the past? To what extent did domestic politics or governmental organization shape their policies? Especially in the case of the United States, to what extent did public opinion contribute to the deepening antagonisms? Why did Americans ultimately see the Soviets as an unparalleled menace? Because of Moscow's influence in Eastern Europe, because of communist ideology, because of Stalinist authoritarianism, because of the economic and social instability in Europe that communists might exploit? Because the Soviet Union stood as the one major obstacle to a U.S.-ordered and U.S.-centered postwar world? Or because the USSR had the potential, in a disorderly world, to shut off the United States from overseas bases, from raw materials such as oil, and from lucrative markets? For their part, why did Soviet leaders think the worst of the United States? Which historical legacies and immediate issues influenced Soviet interpretations and behavior? Why did Moscow come to believe that the United States practiced a reprehensible atomic diplomacy and dollar diplomacy? Finally, did the Cold War evolve because the two sides simply misunderstood one another, or rather because they understood each other very well, including their quite different national interests?

The third set of questions addresses the role of individuals, whose personalities, political ambitions, and styles of diplomacy influenced their nation's foreign relations. The personal imprints of President Harry S. Truman and Premier Josef Stalin stand out. Individual leaders usually define their nation's needs and goals, shape ideologies, decide whether to negotiate, and play politics with foreign policy. Some leaders are wise and patient, others shallow and impatient; some understand nuance and gray areas, others see extreme blacks and whites; some decisionmakers are driven blindly by ideology, entrenched interests, or ignorance, while others are more knowledgeable, practical, and flexible. In an accounting of the origins of the Cold War, how much weight should scholars give to Truman and Stalin as compared to systemic and national sources of conflict? More precisely, to ask a counterfactual question in the case of the United States, would Franklin D. Roosevelt have handled Soviet-American relations differently?

To end with an overarching question: Was the Cold War inevitable, or were there viable alternatives to the long war?

✖ D O C U M E N T S

As the Second World War neared its end, President Harry S. Truman sent a special representative to Moscow to explain U.S. policies to Josef Stalin and reduce growing tensions. Harry Hopkins, who had served for years as an adviser to President Franklin D. Roosevelt,

Changes in Europe After World War II

Territorial Changes After World War II

Notes: — The United States, British, and French Zones of Germany merged in 1949 as the Federal Republic of Germany.

— The Russian Zone of Germany became the German Democratic Republic in 1949.

— The four zones of Austria merged in 1955 to become the Federal Republic of Austria.

already knew the Soviet premier, and Stalin apparently trusted him. On May 27, 1945, as the first document reveals, they talked frankly about two rancorous issues: the abrupt American termination of Lend-Lease aid to the Soviet Union, and the USSR's manipulation of Polish politics.

On June 11, 1945, a group of scientists in Chicago who had been secretly developing an atomic bomb petitioned Secretary of War Henry L. Stimson to recognize the importance of future international (especially Soviet) agreement to prevent nuclear warfare. Headed by Jerome Franck, the scientists' committee recommended against a surprise atomic attack on Japan and instead advocated a noncombatant use of the bomb on an island or in a desert, with international observers. But President Truman and his advisers rejected the Franck Committee's advice, presented as the second document. On September 11, 1945, Stimson sent Truman a memorandum in which the secretary of war argued that "the problem" of the atomic bomb "dominated" Soviet-American relations. Stimson now urged that the United States approach the Soviet Union to discuss controls in order to reduce distrust, as the third selection indicates.

The next document, written by George F. Kennan, is his "long telegram" sent to Washington on February 22, 1946, from his post as attaché in the U.S. embassy in Moscow. Kennan pessimistically speculated on the motivations for Soviet behavior. His critique proved persuasive among Truman officials, and Kennan went on to serve as head of the State Department's Policy Planning Staff, where he helped to establish "containment" as U.S. Cold War doctrine. The fifth selection is former British Prime Minister Winston S. Churchill's "iron curtain" speech of March 5, 1946, delivered in Fulton, Missouri, with an approving President Truman present. Secretary of Commerce Henry A. Wallace disapproved the trend toward an American "get tough" policy and appealed to Truman to seek accommodation, not confrontation, with the Soviets. Wallace's memorandum of July 1946 is printed below as the sixth document. When Wallace went public with his criticisms in September, Truman fired him from the cabinet. On September 27, 1946, Nikolai Novikov, Soviet ambassador to the United States, sent his own long telegram to his superiors in Moscow. Included as the seventh document, Novikov's report described the United States as an expansionist power bent on world supremacy.

On March 12, 1947, the president addressed Congress to announce the "Truman Doctrine," or containment doctrine, in conjunction with a request for aid to Greece and Turkey. Much of the significant speech is reprinted here as the eighth document. The Marshall Plan for European reconstruction soon followed. Suggested by Secretary of State George C. Marshall in June 1947, the aid program took form in the Economic Cooperation Act of 1948, which the president signed on April 3; the introduction to this legislation is included as the ninth document. An excerpt from National Security Council Paper No. 68 (NSC-68), dated April 7, 1950, is reprinted as the last document. Requested by the president, this alarmist report represented high-level American thinking about the Cold War and argued the need for a large military buildup on the eve of the Korean War.

Harry Hopkins and Josef Stalin
Discuss Lend-Lease and Poland, 1945

Marshal Stalin said he would not attempt to use Soviet public opinion as a screen but would speak of the feeling that had been created in Soviet government circles as a result of recent moves on the part of the United States Government. He said these circles felt a certain alarm in regard to the attitude of the United States Government. It was their impression that the American attitude towards the Soviet Union had perceptibly cooled once it became obvious that Germany was defeated, and that it was as though the Americans were saying that the Russians were no longer needed. He said he would give the following examples: . . .

[1] 3. The attitude of the United States Government towards the Polish question. He said that at Yalta it had been agreed that the existing government was to be reconstructed and that anyone with common sense could see that this meant that the present government was to form the basis of the new. He said no other understanding of the Yalta Agreement was possible. Despite the fact that they were simple people the Russians should not be regarded as fools which was a mistake the West frequently made, nor were they blind and could quite well see what was going on before their eyes. It is true that the Russians are patient in the interests of a common cause but that their patience has its limits.

[2] 4. The manner in which Lend Lease had been curtailed. He said that if the United States was unable to supply the Soviet Union further under Lend Lease that was one thing but that the manner in which it had been done had been unfortunate and even brutal. For example, certain ships had been unloaded and while it was true that this order had been cancelled the whole manner in which it had been done had caused concern to the Soviet Government. If the refusal to continue Lend Lease was designed as pressure on the Russians in order to soften them up then it was a fundamental mistake. He said he must tell Mr. [Harry] Hopkins frankly that [if] the Russians were approached frankly on a friendly basis much could be done but that reprisals in any form would bring about the exact opposite effect. . . .

Mr. Hopkins replied that what disturbed him most about Marshal's statement was the revelation that he believed that the United States would use Lend Lease as a means of showing our displeasure with the Soviet Union. He wished to assure the Marshal that however unfortunate an impression this question had caused in the mind of the Soviet Government he must believe that there was no attempt or desire on the part of the United States to use it as a pressure weapon. He said the United States is a strong power and does not go in for those methods. Furthermore, we have no conflict of immediate interests with the Soviet Union and would have no reason to adopt such practices. . . .

Mr. Hopkins concluded the discussion of Lend Lease by stating that he thought it would be a great tragedy if the greatest achievement in cooperation which the Soviet Union and the United States had on the whole worked out together on the basis of Lend Lease were to end on an unsatisfactory note. He said he wished to add that we had never believed that our Lend Lease help had been the chief factor in the Soviet defeat of Hitler on the eastern front. That this had been done by the heroism and blood of the Russian army. . . .

Mr. Hopkins then said with the Marshal's permission he would like to review the position of the United States in regard to Poland. He said first of all he wished to assure the Marshal that he had no thought or indeed any right to attempt to settle the Polish problem during his visit here in Moscow, nor was he intending to hide behind American public opinion in presenting the position of the United States.

Marshal Stalin said he was afraid that his remark concerning Soviet public opinion has cut Mr. Hopkins to the quick and that he has not meant to imply that

Mr. Hopkins was hiding behind the screen of American public opinion. In fact he knew Mr. Hopkins to be an honest and frank man.

Mr. Hopkins said that he wished to state this position as clearly and as forcibly as he knew how. He said the question of Poland per se was not so important as the fact that it had become a symbol of our ability to work out problems with the Soviet Union. He said that we had no special interests in Poland and no special desire to see any particular kind of government. That we would accept any government in Poland which was desired by the Polish people and was at the same time friendly to the Soviet Government. He said that the people and Government of the United States felt that this was a problem which should be worked out jointly between the United States, the Soviet Union and Great Britain and that we felt that the Polish people should be given the right to free elections to choose their own government and their own system and that Poland should genuinely be independent. The Government and people of the United States were disturbed because the preliminary steps towards the reestablishment of Poland appeared to have been taken unilaterally by the Soviet Union together with the present Warsaw Government and that in fact the United States was completely excluded. . . .

Marshal Stalin replied that he wished Mr. Hopkins would take into consideration the following factors: He said it may seem strange although it appeared to be recognized in United States circles and Churchill in his speeches also recognized it, that the Soviet Government should wish for a friendly Poland. In the course of twenty-five years the Germans had twice invaded Russia via Poland. Neither the British nor American people had experienced such German invasions which were a horrible thing to endure and the results of which were not easily forgotten. He said these German invasions were not warfare but were like the incursions of the Huns. He said that Germany had been able to do this because Poland had been regarded as a part of the cordon sanitaire around the Soviet Union and that previous European policy had been that Polish Governments must be hostile to Russia. In these circumstances either Poland had been too weak to oppose Germany or had let the Germans come through. Thus Poland had served as a corridor for the German attacks on Russia. He said Poland's weakness and hostility had been a great source of weakness to the Soviet Union and had permitted the Germans to do what they wished in the East and also in the West since the two were mixed together. It is therefore in Russia's vital interest that Poland should be both strong and friendly. He said there was no intention on the part of the Soviet Union to interfere in Poland's internal affairs, that Poland would live under the parliamentary system which is like Czechoslovakia, Belgium and Holland and that any talk of an intention to Sovietize Poland was stupid. . . . Mr. Hopkins had spoken of Russian unilateral action in Poland and United States opinion concerning it. It was true that Russia had taken such unilateral action but they had been compelled to. He said the Soviet Government had recognized the Warsaw Government and concluded a treaty with it at a time when their Allies did not recognize this government. These were admittedly unilateral acts which would have been much better left undone but the fact was they had not met with any understanding on the part of their Allies. The need for these actions has arisen out of the presence of Soviet troops in Poland and it would have been impossible to have waited until such time as the Allies had come to an agreement on Poland. The logic of the war against Germany demanded that the Soviet rear be assured and the Lublin Commit-

tee had been of great assistance to the Red Army at all times and it was for this reason that these actions had been taken by the Soviet Government. He said it was
contrary to the Soviet policy to set up [a] Soviet administration on foreign soil
since this would look like occupation and be resented by the local inhabitants. It
was for this reason that some Polish administration had to be established in Poland
and this could be done only with those who had helped the Red Army. He said he
wished to emphasize that these steps had not been taken with any desire to eliminate or exclude Russia's Allies. He must point out however that Soviet action in
Poland had been more successful than British action in Greece and at no time had
they been compelled to undertake the measures which they had done in Greece.
Stalin then turned to his suggestion for the solution of the Polish problem.

Marshal Stalin said that he felt that we should examine the composition of the
future Government of National Unity. He said there were eighteen or twenty min-
istries in the present Polish Government and that four or five of these portfolios
could be given representatives of other Polish groups taken from the list submitted
by Great Britain and the United States (Molotov whispered to Stalin who then said
he meant four and not five posts in the government). He said he thought the Warsaw Poles would not accept more than four ministers from other democratic
groups. He added that if this appears a suitable basis we could then proceed to consider what persons should be selected for these posts. He said of course that they
would have to be friendly to the U.S.S.R. and to the Allies. He added that [Stanis-
law] Mikolajczyk [leader of the London Poles] had been suggested and he thought
he was acceptable and that the question was now who else. He inquired of Mr.
Hopkins whether possibly Professor [Oscar] Lange [a Polish American] might be
willing to join the government.

Mr. Hopkins said he doubted whether Professor Lange, who was an American
citizen, could be induced to give up his American citizenship for this purpose but
that of course was only a private opinion.

Marshal Stalin then said it might be wise to ask some of the Warsaw leaders to
come to Moscow now and to hear what they had to say and to learn more of what
had been decided. He added that if we are able to settle the composition of the new
government he felt that no differences remained since we were all agreed on the
free and unfettered elections and that no one intended to interfere with the Polish
people.

The Franck Committee Predicts a Nuclear-Arms Race
If the Atomic Bomb Is Dropped on Japan, 1945

The way in which the nuclear weapons, now secretly developed in this country,
will first be revealed to the world appears of great, perhaps fateful importance.

One possible way—which may particularly appeal to those who consider
the nuclear bombs primarily as a secret weapon developed to help win the present
war—is to use it without warning on an appropriately selected object in Japan. It is
doubtful whether the first available bombs, of comparatively low efficiency and
small in size, will be sufficient to break the will or ability of Japan to resist, especially given the fact that the major cities like Tokyo, Nagoya, Osaka and Kobe already will largely be reduced to ashes by the slower process of ordinary aerial

bombing. Certain and perhaps important tactical results undoubtedly can be achieved, but we nevertheless think that the question of the use of the very first available atomic bombs in the Japanese war should be weighed very carefully, not only by military authority, but by the highest political leadership of this country. If we consider international agreement on total prevention of nuclear warfare as the paramount objective, and believe that it can be achieved, this kind of introduction of atomic weapons to the world may easily destroy all our chances of success. Russia, and even allied countries which bear less mistrust of our ways and intentions, as well as neutral countries, will be deeply shocked. It will be very difficult to persuade the world that a nation which was capable of secretly preparing and suddenly releasing a weapon, as indiscriminate as the rocket bomb and a thousand times more destructive, is to be trusted in its proclaimed desire of having such weapons abolished by international agreement. . . .

Thus, from the "optimistic" point of view—looking forward to an international agreement on prevention of nuclear warfare—the military advantages and the saving of American lives, achieved by the sudden use of atomic bombs against Japan, may be outweighed by the ensuing loss of confidence and wave of horror and repulsion, sweeping over the rest of the world, and perhaps dividing even the public opinion at home.

From this point of view a demonstration of the new weapon may best be made before the eyes of representatives of all United Nations, on the desert or a barren island. The best possible atmosphere for the achievement of an international agreement could be achieved if America would be able to say to the world, "You see what weapon we had but did not use. We are ready to renounce its use in the future and to join other nations in working out adequate supervision of the use of this nuclear weapon."

This may sound fantastic, but then in nuclear weapons we have something entirely new in the order of magnitude of destructive power, and if we want to capitalize fully on the advantage which its possession gives us, we must use new and imaginative methods. After such a demonstration the weapon could be used against Japan if a sanction of the United Nations (and of the public opinion at home) could be obtained, perhaps after a preliminary ultimatum to Japan to surrender or at least to evacuate a certain region as an alternative to the total destruction of this target.

It must be stressed that if one takes a pessimistic point of view and discounts the possibilities of an effective international control of nuclear weapons, then the advisability of an early use of nuclear bombs against Japan becomes even more doubtful—quite independently of any humanitarian considerations. If no international agreement is concluded immediately after the first demonstration, this will mean a flying start of an unlimited armaments race.

Henry L. Stimson's Appeal
for Atomic Talks with the Soviets, 1945

In many quarters it [atomic bomb] has been interpreted as a substantial offset to the growth of Russian influence on the continent. We can be certain that the Soviet Government has sensed this tendency and the temptation will be strong for the

Soviet political and military leaders to acquire this weapon in the shortest possible time. Britain in effect already has the status of a partner with us in the development of this weapon. Accordingly, unless the Soviets are voluntarily invited into the partnership upon a basis of cooperation and trust, we are going to maintain the Anglo-Saxon bloc over against the Soviet in the possession of this weapon. Such a condition will almost certainly stimulate feverish activity on the part of the Soviet toward the development of this bomb in what will in effect be a secret armament race of a rather desperate character. There is evidence to indicate that such activity may have already commenced.

If we feel, as I assume we must, that civilization demands that some day we shall arrive at a satisfactory international arrangement respecting the control of this new force, the question then is how long we can afford to enjoy our momentary superiority in the hope of achieving our immediate peace council objectives.

Whether Russia gets control of the necessary secrets of production in a minimum of say four years or a maximum of twenty years is not nearly as important to the world and civilization as to make sure that when they do get it they are willing and co-operative partners among the peace-loving nations of the world. It is true if we approach them now, as I would propose, we may be gambling on their good faith and risk their getting into production of bombs a little sooner than they would otherwise.

To put the matter concisely, I consider the problem of our satisfactory relations with Russia as not merely connected with but as virtually dominated by the problem of the atomic bomb. Except for the problem of the control of that bomb, those relations, while vitally important, might not be immediately pressing. The establishment of relations of mutual confidence between her and us could afford to await the slow progress of time. But with the discovery of the bomb, they became immediately emergent. Those relations may be perhaps irretrievably embittered by the way in which we approach the solution of the bomb with Russia. For if we fail to approach them now and merely continue to negotiate with them, having this weapon rather ostentatiously on our hip, their suspicions and their distrust of our purposes and motives will increase. It will inspire them to greater efforts in an all-out effort to solve the problem. If the solution is achieved in that spirit, it is much less likely that we will ever get the kind of covenant we may desperately need in the future. This risk is, I believe, greater than the other, inasmuch as our objective must be to get the best kind of international bargain we can—one that has some chance of being kept and saving civilization not for five or for twenty years, but forever.

The chief lesson I have learned in a long life is that the only way you can make a man trustworthy is to trust him; and the surest way to make him untrustworthy is to distrust him and show your distrust.

If the atomic bomb were merely another though more devastating military weapon to be assimilated into our pattern of international relations, it would be one thing. We could then follow the old custom of secrecy and nationalistic military superiority relying on international caution to prescribe the future use of the weapon as we did with gas. But I think the bomb instead constitutes merely a first step in a new control by man over the forces of nature too revolutionary and dangerous to fit into the old concepts. I think it really caps the climax of the race between man's growing technical power for destructiveness and his psychological power of self-control and group control—his moral power. If so, our method of approach to the Russians is a question of the most vital importance in the evolution of human progress. . . .

My idea of an approach to the Soviets would be a direct proposal after discussion with the British that we would be prepared in effect to enter an arrangement with the Russians, the general purpose of which would be to control and limit the use of the atomic bomb as an instrument of war and so far as possible to direct and encourage the development of atomic power for peaceful and humanitarian purposes. Such an approach might more specifically lead to the proposal that we would stop work on the further improvement in, or manufacture of, the bomb as a military weapon, provided the Russians and the British would agree to do likewise. It might also provide that we would be willing to impound what bombs we now have in the United States provided the Russians and the British would agree with us that in no event will they or we use a bomb as an instrument of war unless all three Governments agree to that use. We might also consider including in the arrangement a covenant with the U.K. and the Soviets providing for the exchange of benefits of future developments whereby atomic energy may be applied on a mutually satisfactory basis for commercial or humanitarian purposes. . . .

I emphasize perhaps beyond all other considerations the importance of taking this action with Russia as a proposal of the United States—backed by Great Britain but peculiarly the proposal of the United States. Action of any international group of nations, including many small nations who have not demonstrated their potential power or responsibility in this war would not, in my opinion, be taken seriously by the Soviets. The loose debates which would surround such proposal, if put before a conference of nations, would provoke but scant favor from the Soviet. As I say, I think this is the most important point in the program.

After the nations which have won this war have agreed to it, there will be ample time to introduce France and China into the covenants and finally to incorporate the agreement into the scheme of the United Nations. The use of this bomb has been accepted by the world as the result of the initiative and productive capacity of the United States, and I think this factor is a most potent lever toward having our proposals accepted by the Soviets, whereas I am most skeptical of obtaining any tangible results by way of any international debate. I urge this method as the most realistic means of accomplishing this vitally important step in the history of the world.

George F. Kennan's "Long Telegram," 1946

At bottom of Kremlin's neurotic view of world affairs is traditional and instinctive Russian sense of insecurity. Originally, this was insecurity of a peaceful agricultural people trying to live on vast exposed plain in neighborhood of fierce nomadic peoples. To this was added, as Russia came into contact with economically advanced West, fear of more competent, more powerful, more highly organized societies in that area. But this latter type of insecurity was one which afflicted rather Russian rulers than Russian people; for Russian rulers have invariably sensed that their rule was relatively archaic in form, fragile and artificial in its psychological foundation, unable to stand comparison or contact with political systems of Western countries. For this reason they have always feared foreign penetration, feared direct contact between Western world and their own, feared what would happen if Russians learned truth about world without or if foreigners learned truth about world within. And they had learned to seek security only in patient but deadly struggle for total destruction of rival power, never in compacts and compromises with it.

It was no coincidence that Marxism, which had smouldered ineffectively for half a century in Western Europe, caught hold and blazed for first time in Russia. Only in this land which had never known a friendly neighbor or indeed any tolerant equilibrium of separate powers, either internal or international, could a doctrine thrive which viewed economic conflicts of society as insoluble by peaceful means. After establishment of Bolshevist regime, Marxist dogma, rendered even more truculent and intolerant by Lenin's interpretation, became a perfect vehicle for sense of insecurity with which Bolsheviks, even more than previous Russian rulers, were afflicted. In this dogma, with its basic altruism of purpose, they found justification for their instinctive fear of outside world, for the dictatorship without which they did not know how to rule, for cruelties they did not dare not to inflict, for sacrifices they felt bound to demand. In the name of Marxism they sacrificed every single ethical value in their methods and tactics. Today they cannot dispense with it. It is fig leaf of their moral and intellectual respectability. Without it they would stand before history, at best, as only the last of that long succession of cruel and wasteful Russian rulers who have relentlessly forced country on to ever new heights of military power in order to guarantee external security of their internally weak regimes. This is why Soviet purposes must always be solemnly clothed in trappings of Marxism, and why no one should underrate importance of dogma in Soviet affairs. Thus Soviet leaders are driven [by?] necessities of their own past and present position to put forward a dogma which [apparent omission] outside world as evil, hostile and menacing, but as bearing within itself germs of creeping disease and destined to be wracked with growing internal convulsions until it is given final *coup de grace* by rising power of socialism and yields to new and better world. This thesis provides justification for the increase of military and police power of Russian state, for that isolation of Russian population from outside world, and for that fluid and constant pressure to extend limits of Russian police power which are together the natural and instinctive urges of Russian rulers. Basically this is only the steady advance of uneasy Russian nationalism, a centuries old movement in which conceptions of offense and defense are inextricably confused. But in new guise of international Marxism, with its honeyed promises to a desperate and war torn outside world, it is more dangerous and insidious than ever before.

It should not be thought from above that Soviet party line is necessarily disingenuous and insincere on part of all those who put it forward. Many of them are too ignorant of outside world and mentally too dependent to question [apparent omission] self-hypnotism, and who have no difficulty making themselves believe what they find it comforting and convenient to believe. Finally we have the unsolved mystery as to who, if anyone, in this great land actually receives accurate and unbiased information about outside world. In atmosphere of oriental secretiveness and conspiracy which pervades this Government, possibilities for distorting or poisoning sources and currents of information are infinite. The very disrespect of Russians for objective truth—indeed, their disbelief in its existence—leads them to view all stated facts as instruments for furtherance of one ulterior purpose or another. There is good reason to suspect that this Government is actually a conspiracy within a conspiracy; and I for one am reluctant to believe that Stalin himself receives anything like an objective picture of outside world. Here there is ample scope for the type of subtle intrigue at which Russians are past masters. Inability of foreign governments to place their case squarely before Russian policy makers—extent to which they are delivered up in their relations with Russia to good graces of obscure and unknown advisers who they never see and cannot influence—this to my mind is most disquieting feature of diplomacy in Moscow, and one which Western statesmen would do well to keep in mind if they would understand nature of difficulties encountered here. . . .

In summary, we have here a political force committed fanatically to the belief that with US there can be no permanent *modus vivendi,* that it is desirable and necessary that the internal harmony of our society be disrupted, our traditional way of life be destroyed, the international authority of our state be broken, if Soviet power is to be secure. This political force has complete power of disposition over energies of one of world's greatest peoples and resources of world's richest national territory, and is borne along by deep and powerful currents of Russian nationalism. In addition, it has an elaborate and far flung apparatus for exertion of its influence in other countries, an apparatus of amazing flexibility and versatility, managed by people whose experience and skill in underground methods are presumably without parallel in history. Finally, it is seemingly inaccessible to considerations of reality in its basic reactions. For it, the vast fund of objective fact about human society is not, as with us, the measure against which outlook is constantly being tested and re-formed, but a grab bag from which individual items are selected arbitrarily and tendenciously to bolster an outlook already preconceived. This is admittedly not a pleasant picture. Problem of how to cope with this force [is] undoubtedly greatest task our diplomacy has ever faced and probably greatest it will ever have to face. It should be point of departure from which our political general staff work at present juncture should proceed. It should be approached with same thoroughness and care as solution of major strategic problem in war, and if necessary, with no smaller outlay in planning effort. I cannot attempt to suggest all answers here. But I would like to record my conviction that problem is within our power to solve—and that without recourse to any general military conflict. And in support of this conviction there are certain observations of a more encouraging nature I should like to make:

1. Soviet power, unlike that of Hitlerite Germany, is neither schematic nor adventuristic. It does not work by fixed plans. It does not take unnecessary risks. Impervious to logic of reason, and it is highly sensitive to logic of force. For this reason it can easily withdraw—and usually does—when strong resistance is encountered at any point. Thus, if the adversary has sufficient force and makes clear his readiness to use it, he rarely has to do so. If situations are properly handled there need be no prestige-engaging showdowns.

2. Gauged against Western World as a whole, Soviets are still by far the weaker force. Thus, their success will really depend on degree of cohesion, firmness and vigor which Western World can muster. And this is factor which it is within our power to influence.

3. Success of Soviet system, as form of internal power, is not yet finally proven. It has yet to be demonstrated that it can survive supreme test of successive transfer of power from one individual or group to another. Lenin's death was first such transfer, and its effects wracked Soviet state for 15 years. After Stalin's death or retirement will be second. But even this will not be final test. Soviet internal system will now be subjected, by virtue of recent territorial expansions, to series of additional strains which once proved severe tax on Tsardom. We here are convinced that never since termination of civil war have mass of Russian people been emotionally farther removed from doctrines of Communist Party than they are today. In Russia, party has now become a great and—for the moment—highly successful apparatus of dictatorial administration, but it has ceased to be a source of emotional inspiration. Thus, internal soundness and permanence of movement need not yet be regarded as assured.

4. All Soviet propaganda beyond Soviet security sphere is basically negative and destructive. It should therefore be relatively easy to combat it by any intelligent and really constructive program.

Winston S. Churchill's "Iron Curtain" Speech, 1946

The United States stands at this time at the pinnacle of world power. It is a solemn moment for the American democracy. With primacy in power is also joined an awe-inspiring accountability to the future. As you look around you, you feel not only the sense of duty done but also feel anxiety lest you fall below the level of achievement. Opportunity is here now, clear and shining, for both our countries. To reject it or ignore it or fritter it away will bring upon us all the long reproaches of the after-time. It is necessary that constancy of mind, persistency of purpose, and the grand simplicity of decision shall guide and rule the conduct of the English speaking peoples in peace as they did in war. . . .

Would a special relationship between the United States and the British Commonwealth be inconsistent with our overriding loyalties to the world organization? I reply that on the contrary, it is probably the only means by which that organization will achieve its full stature and strength. . . .

A shadow has fallen upon the scenes so lately lighted by the Allied victory. Nobody knows what Soviet Russia and its Communist international organization intends to do in the immediate future, or what are the limits, if any, to their expansive and proselytizing tendencies. I have a strong admiration and regard for the valiant Russian people and for my wartime comrade, Marshal Stalin. There is sympathy and good will in Britain—and I doubt not here also—toward the peoples of all the Russias and a resolve to persevere through many differences and rebuffs in establishing lasting friendships.

We understand the Russian need to be secure on her western frontiers from all renewal of German aggression. We welcome her to her rightful place among the

leading nations of the world. Above all, we welcome constant, frequent, and growing contacts between Russian people and our own people on both sides of the Atlantic. It is my duty, however, to place before you certain facts about the present
position in Europe.

From Stettin in the Baltic to Trieste in the Adriatic, an iron curtain has descended across the continent. Behind that line lie all the capitals of the ancient
states of Central and Eastern Europe. Warsaw, Berlin, Prague, Vienna, Budapest,
Belgrade, Bucharest, and Sofia, all these famous cities and the populations around
them lie in the Soviet sphere and all are subject, in one form or another, not only to
Soviet influence but to a very high and increasing measure of control from
Moscow. Athens alone, with its immortal glories, is free to decide its future at an
election under British, American, and French observation.

The Russian-dominated Polish government has been encouraged to make
enormous and wrongful inroads upon Germany, and mass expulsions of millions of
Germans on a scale grievous and undreamed of are now taking place. The Communist parties, which were very small in all these eastern states of Europe, have been
raised to preeminence and power far beyond their numbers and are seeking everywhere to obtain totalitarian control. Police governments are prevailing in nearly
every case, and so far, except in Czechoslovakia, there is no true democracy.

Turkey and Persia are both profoundly alarmed and disturbed at the claims
which are made upon them and at the pressure being exerted by the Moscow government. An attempt is being made by the Russians in Berlin to build up a quasi-
Communist party in their zone of occupied Germany by showing special favors to
groups of left-wing German leaders. At the end of the fighting last June, the American and British Armies withdrew westward, in accordance with an earlier agreement, to a depth at some points of 150 miles on a front of nearly 400 miles, to
allow the Russians to occupy this vast expanse of territory which the Western
democracies had conquered.

If now the Soviet government tries, by separate action, to build up a pro-Communist Germany in their areas, this will cause new serious difficulties in the
British and American zones, and will give the defeated Germans the power of
putting themselves up to auction between the Soviets and the Western democracies. Whatever conclusions may be drawn from these facts—and facts they are—
this is certainly not the liberated Europe we fought to build up. Nor is it one which
contains the essentials of permanent peace.

In front of the iron curtain which lies across Europe are other causes for anxiety. In Italy the Communist party is seriously hampered by having to support the
Communist-trained Marshall Tito's claims to former Italian territory at the head of
the Adriatic. Nevertheless, the future of Italy hangs in the balance. Again, one cannot imagine a regenerated Europe without a strong France. . . .

However, in a great number of countries, far from the Russian frontiers
and throughout the world, Communist fifth columns are established and work
in complete unity and absolute obedience to the directions they receive from
the Communist center. Except in the British Commonwealth, and in the United
States, where communism is in its infancy, the Communist parties or fifth columns
constitute a growing challenge and peril to Christian civilization. These are

somber facts for anyone to have to recite on the morrow of a victory gained by so much splendid comradeship in arms and in the cause of freedom and democracy, and we should be most unwise not to face them squarely while time remains.

The outlook is also anxious in the Far East and especially in Manchuria. The agreement which was made at Yalta, to which I was a party, was extremely favorable to Soviet Russia, but it was made at a time when no one could say that the German war might not extend all through the summer and autumn of 1945 and when the Japanese war was expected to last for a further eighteen months from the end of the German war. In this country you are all so well informed about the Far East and such devoted friends of China that I do not need to expatiate on the situation there. . . .

Our difficulties and dangers will not be removed by closing our eyes to them; they will not be removed by mere waiting to see what happens; nor will they be relieved by a policy of appeasement. What is needed is a settlement, and the longer this is delayed, the more difficult it will be and the greater our dangers will become. From what I have seen of our Russian friends and allies during the war, I am convinced that there is nothing they admire so much as strength, and there is nothing for which they have less respect than for military weakness. For that reason the old doctrine of a balance of power is unsound. We cannot afford, if we can help it, to work on narrow margins, offering temptations to a trial of strength. If the Western democracies stand together in strict adherence to the principles of the United Nations Charter, their influence for furthering these principles will be immense and no one is likely to molest them. If, however, they become divided or falter in their duty, and if these all-important years are allowed to slip away, then indeed catastrophe may overwhelm us all.

Henry A. Wallace Questions the "Get Tough" Policy, 1946

How do American actions since V-J Day appear to other nations? I mean by actions the concrete things like $13 billion for the War and Navy Departments, the Bikini tests of the atomic bomb and continued production of bombs, the plan to arm Latin America with our weapons, production of B-29s and planned production of B-36s, and the effort to secure air bases spread over half the globe from which the other half of the globe can be bombed. I cannot but feel that these actions must make it look to the rest of the world as if we were only paying lip service to peace at the conference table. These facts rather make it appear either (1) that we are preparing ourselves to win the war which we regard as inevitable or (2) that we are trying to build up a predominance of force to intimidate the rest of mankind. How would it look to us if Russia had the atomic bomb and we did not, if Russia had ten thousand-mile bombers and air bases within a thousand miles of our coast lines and we did not?

Henry A. Wallace, "The Path to Peace with Russia," *New Republic,* 115 (1946), 401–406.

Some of the military men and self-styled "realists" are saying: "What's wrong with trying to build up a predominance of force? The only way to preserve peace is for this country to be so well armed that no one will dare attack us. We know that America will never start a war."

The flaw in this policy is simply that it will not work. In a world of atomic bombs and other revolutionary new weapons, such as radioactive poison gases and biological warfare, a peace maintained by a predominance of force is no longer possible.

Why is this so? The reasons are clear:

First. Atomic warfare is cheap and easy compared with old-fashioned war. Within a very few years several countries can have atomic bombs and other atomic weapons. Compared with the cost of large armies and the manufacture of old-fashioned weapons, atomic bombs cost very little and require only a relatively small part of a nation's production plant and labor force.

Second. So far as winning a war is concerned, having more bombs—even many more bombs—than the other fellow is no longer a decisive advantage. If another nation had enough bombs to eliminate all of our principal cities and our heavy industry, it wouldn't help us very much if we had ten times as many bombs as we needed to do the same to them.

Third. The most important, the very fact that several nations have atomic bombs will inevitably result in a neurotic, fear-ridden, itching-trigger psychology in all the peoples of the world, and because of our wealth and vulnerability we would be among the most seriously affected. Atomic war will not require vast and time-consuming preparations, the mobilization of large armies, the conversion of a large proportion of a country's industrial plants to the manufacture of weapons. In a world armed with atomic weapons, some incident will lead to the use of those weapons. . . .

There is, however, a fatal defect in the Moscow statement, in the Acheson report, and in the American [Baruch] plan recently presented to the United Nations Atomic Energy Commission. That defect is the scheme, as it is generally understood, of arriving at international agreements by "easy stages," of requiring other nations to enter into binding commitments not to conduct research into the military uses of atomic energy and to disclose their uranium and thorium resources while the United States retains the right to withhold its technical knowledge of atomic energy until the international control and inspection system is working to our satisfaction. In other words, we are telling the Russians that if they are "good boys" we may eventually turn over our knowledge of atomic energy to them and to the other nations. But there is no objective standard of what will qualify them as being "good" nor any specified time for sharing our knowledge. . . .

Insistence on our part that the game must be played our way will only lead to a deadlock. The Russians will redouble their efforts to manufacture bombs, and they may also decide to expand their "security zone" in a serious way. Up to now, despite all our outcries against it, their efforts to develop a security zone in Eastern Europe and in the Middle East are small change from the point of view of military power as compared with our air bases in Greenland, Okinawa and many other places thousands of miles from our shores. We may feel very self-righteous if we refuse to budge on our plan and the Russians refuse to accept it, but that means only one thing—the atomic armament race is on in deadly earnest.

I am convinced therefore that if we are to achieve our hopes of negotiating a treaty which will result in effective international atomic disarmament we must abandon the impractical form of the "step-by-step" idea which was presented to the United Nations Atomic Energy Commission. We must be prepared to reach an agreement which will commit us to disclosing information and destroying our bombs at a specific time or on terms of specified actions by other countries, rather than at our unfettered discretion. If we are willing to negotiate on this basis, I believe the Russians will also negotiate seriously with a view to reaching an agreement. . . .

Our basic distrust of the Russians, which has been greatly intensified in recent months by the playing up of conflict in the press, stems from differences in political and economic organizations. For the first time in our history defeatists among us have raised the fear of another system as a successful rival to democracy and free enterprise in other countries and perhaps even our own. I am convinced that we can meet that challenge as we have in the past by demonstrating that economic abundance can be achieved without sacrificing personal, political and religious liberties. We cannot meet it, as Hitler tried to, by an anti-Comintern alliance.

It is perhaps too easy to forget that despite the deep-seated differences in our culture and intensive anti-Russian propaganda of some twenty-five years' standing, the American people reversed their attitudes during the crisis of war. Today, under the pressure of seemingly insoluble international problems and continuing deadlocks, the tide of American public opinion is again turning against Russia. In this reaction lies one of the dangers to which this letter is addressed.

I should list the factors which make for Russian distrust of the United States and of the Western world as follows: The first is Russian history, which we must take into account because it is the setting in which Russians see all actions and policies of the rest of the world. Russian history for over a thousand years has been a succession of attempts, often unsuccessful, to resist invasion and conquest—by the Mongols, the Turks, the Swedes, the Germans and the Poles. The scant thirty years of the existence of the Soviet government has in Russian eyes been a continuation of their historical struggle for national existence. The first four years of the new regime, from 1917 through 1921, were spent in resisting attempts at destruction by the Japanese, British and French, with some American assistance, and by the several White Russian armies encouraged and financed by the Western powers. Then, in 1941, the Soviet state was almost conquered by the Germans after a period during which the Western European powers had apparently acquiesced in the rearming of Germany in the belief that the Nazis would seek to expand eastward rather than westward. The Russians, therefore, obviously see themselves as fighting for their existence in a hostile world.

Second, it follows that to the Russians all of the defense and security measures of the Western powers seem to have an aggressive intent. Our actions to expand our military security system—such steps as extending the Monroe Doctrine to include the arming of the Western Hemisphere nations, our present monopoly of the atomic bomb, our interest in outlying bases and our general support of the British Empire—appear to them as going far beyond the requirements of defense. I think we might feel the same if the United States were the only capitalistic country in the world and the principal socialistic countries were creating a level of armed strength far exceeding anything in their previous history. From the Russian point of view, also, the granting of a loan to Britain and the lack of tangible results on their request to borrow for rehabilitation purposes may be regarded as another evidence of strengthening of an anti-Soviet bloc.

Finally, our resistance to her attempts to obtain warm water ports and her own security system in the form of "friendly" neighboring states seems, from the Russian point of view, to clinch the case. After twenty-five years of isolation and after having achieved the status of a major power, Russia believes that she is entitled to recognition of her new status. Our interest in establishing democracy in Eastern Europe, where democracy by and large has never existed, seems to her an attempt to reestablish the encirclement of unfriendly neighbors which was created after the last war and which might serve as a springboard of still another effort to destroy her.

If this analysis is correct, and there is ample evidence to support it, the action to improve the situation is clearly indicated. The fundamental objective of such action should be to allay any reasonable Russian grounds for fear, suspicions and distrust. We must recognize that the world has changed and that today there can be no "one world" unless the United States and Russia can find some way of living together. For example, most of us are firmly convinced of the soundness of our position when we suggest the internationalization and defortification of the Danube or of the Dardanelles, but we would be horrified and angered by any Russian counterproposal that would involve also the internationalizing and disarming of Suez or Panama. We must recognize that to the Russians these seem to be identical situations.

We should ascertain from a fresh point of view what Russia believes to be essential to her own security as a prerequisite to the writing of the peace and to cooperation in the construction of a world order. We should be prepared to judge her requirements against the background of what we ourselves and the British have insisted upon as essential to our respective security. We should be prepared, even at the expense of risking epithets of appeasement to agree to reasonable Russian guarantees of security. . . .

It is of the greatest importance that we should discuss with the Russians in a friendly way their long-range economic problems and the future of our cooperation in matters of trade. The reconstruction program of the USSR and the plans for the full development of the Soviet Union offers tremendous opportunities for American goods and American technicians.

American products, especially machines of all kinds, are well established in the Soviet Union. For example, American equipment, practices and methods are standard in coal mining, iron and steel, oil and nonferrous metals.

Nor would this trade be one-sided. Although the Soviet Union has been an excellent credit risk in the past, eventually the goods and services exported from this country must be paid for by the Russians by exports to us and to other countries. Russian products which are either definitely needed or which are noncompetitive in this country are various nonferrous metal ores, furs, linen products, lumber products, vegetable drugs, paper and pulp and native handicrafts. . . .

Many of the problems relating to the countries bordering on Russia could more readily be solved once an atmosphere of mutual trust and confidence is established and some form of economic arrangements is worked out with Russia. These problems also might be helped by discussions of an economic nature. Russian economic penetration of the Danube area, for example, might be countered by concrete proposals for economic collaboration in the development of the resources of this area, rather than by insisting that the Russians should cease their unilateral penetration and offering no solution to the present economic chaos there.

This proposal admittedly calls for a shift in some of our thinking about international matters. It is imperative that we make this shift. We have little time to lose. Our postwar actions have not yet been adjusted to the lessons to be gained from experience of Allied cooperation during the war and the facts of the atomic age.

It is certainly desirable that, as far as possible, we achieve unity on the home front with respect to our international relations; but unity on the basis of building up conflict abroad would prove to be not only unsound but disastrous. I think there is some reason to fear that in our earnest efforts to achieve bipartisan unity in this country we may have given away too much to isolationism masquerading as tough realism in international affairs.

Soviet Ambassador Nikolai Novikov
Identifies a U.S. Drive for World Supremacy, 1946

The foreign policy of the United States, which reflects the imperialist tendencies of American monopolistic capital, is characterized in the postwar period by a striving for world supremacy. This is the real meaning of the many statements by President Truman and other representatives of American ruling circles: that the United States has the right to lead the world. All the forces of American diplomacy— the army, the air force, the navy, industry and science—are enlisted in the service of this foreign policy. For this purpose broad plans for expansion have been developed and are being implemented through diplomacy and the establishment of a system of naval and air bases stretching far beyond the boundaries of the United States, through the arms race, and through the creation of ever newer types of weapons. . . .

Europe has come out of the war with a completely dislocated economy, and the economic devastation that occurred in the course of the war cannot be overcome in a short time. All of the countries of Europe and Asia are experiencing a colossal need for consumer goods, industrial and transportation equipment, etc. Such a situation provides American monopolistic capital with prospects for enormous shipments of goods and the importation of capital into these countries—a circumstance that would permit it to infiltrate their national economies.

From *Origins of the Cold War: The Novikov, Kennan and Roberts "Long Telegram" of 1946*, Kenneth M. Jensen, editor, Washington: United States Institute of Peace, 1991. Translated by Kenneth M. Jensen and John Glad.

Such a development would mean serious strengthening of the economic position of the United States in the whole world and would be a stage on the road to world domination by the United States.

On the other hand, we have seen a failure of calculations on the part of U.S. circles which assumed that the Soviet Union would be destroyed in the war or would come out of it so weakened that it would be forced to go begging to the United States for economic assistance. Had that happened, they would have been able to dictate conditions permitting the United States to carry out its expansion in Europe and Asia without hindrance from the USSR.

In actuality, despite all of the economic difficulties of the postwar period connected with the enormous losses inflicted by the war and the German fascist occupation, the Soviet Union continues to remain economically independent of the outside world and is rebuilding its national economy with its own forces.

At the same time the USSR's international position is currently stronger than it was in the prewar period. Thanks to the historical victories of Soviet weapons, the Soviet armed forces are located on the territory of Germany and other formerly hostile countries, thus guaranteeing that these countries will not be used again for an attack on the USSR. In formerly hostile countries, such as Bulgaria, Finland, Hungary, and Romania, democratic reconstruction has established regimes that have undertaken to strengthen and maintain friendly relations with the Soviet Union. In the Slavic countries that were liberated by the Red Army or with its assistance—Poland, Czechoslovakia, and Yugoslavia—democratic regimes have also been established that maintain relations with the Soviet Union on the basis of agreements on friendship and mutual assistance.

The enormous relative weight of the USSR in international affairs in general and in the European countries in particular, the independence of its foreign policy, and the economic and political assistance that it provides to neighboring countries, both allies and former enemies, has led to the growth of the political influence of the Soviet Union in these countries and to the further strengthening of democratic tendencies in them.

Such a situation in Eastern and Southeastern Europe cannot help but be regarded by the American imperialists as an obstacle in the path of the expansionist policy of the United States.

The foreign policy of the United States is not determined at present by the circles in the Democratic party that (as was the case during Roosevelt's lifetime) strive to strengthen the cooperation of the three great powers that constituted the basis of the anti-Hitler coalition during the war. The ascendance to power of President Truman, a politically unstable person but with certain conservative tendencies, and the subsequent appointment of [James F.] Byrnes as Secretary of State meant a strengthening of the influence on U.S. foreign policy of the most reactionary circles of the Democratic party. The constantly increasing reactionary nature of the foreign policy course of the United States, which consequently approached the policy advocated by the Republican party, laid the groundwork for close cooperation in this field between the far right wing of the Democratic party and the Republican party. . . .

At the same time, there has been a decline in the influence on foreign policy of those who follow Roosevelt's course for cooperation among peace-loving countries. Such persons in the government, in Congress, and in the leadership of the Democratic party are being pushed farther and farther into the background. The contradictions in the field of foreign policy existing between the followers of [Henry] Wallace and [Claude] Pepper, on the one hand, and the adherents of the reactionary "bi-partisan" policy, on the other, were manifested with great clarity recently in the speech by Wallace that led to his resignation from the post of Secretary of Commerce. Wallace's resignation means the victory of the reactionary course that Byrnes is conducting in cooperation with [Senator Arthur] Vandenberg and [Senator Robert] Taft.

Obvious indications of the U.S. effort to establish world dominance are also to be found in the increase in military potential in peacetime and in the establishment of a large number of naval air bases both in the United States and beyond its borders.

In the summer of 1946, for the first time in the history of the country, Congress passed a law on the establishment of a peacetime army, not on a volunteer basis but on the basis of universal military service. The size of the army, which is supposed to amount to about one million persons as of July 1, 1947, was also increased significantly. The size of the navy at the conclusion of the war decreased quite insignificantly in comparison with wartime. At the present time, the American navy occupies first place in the world, leaving England's navy far behind, to say nothing of those of other countries.

Expenditures on the army and navy have risen colossally, amounting to 13 billion dollars according to the budget for 1946–47 (about 40 percent of the total budget of 36 billion dollars). This is more than ten times greater than corresponding expenditures in the budget for 1938, which did not amount to even one billion dollars.

Along with maintaining a large army, navy, and air force, the budget provides that these enormous amounts also will be spent on establishing a very extensive system of naval and air bases in the Atlantic and Pacific oceans. According to existing official plans, in the course of the next few years 228 bases, points of support, and radio stations are to be constructed in the Atlantic Ocean and 258 in the Pacific. . . .

The establishment of American bases on the islands that are often 10,000 to 12,000 kilometers from the territory of the United States and are on the other side of the Atlantic and Pacific oceans clearly indicates the offensive nature of the strategic concepts of the commands of the U.S. army and navy. This interpretation is also confirmed by the fact that the American navy is intensively studying the naval approaches to the boundaries of Europe. For this purpose, American naval vessels in the course of 1946 visited the ports of Norway, Denmark, Sweden, Turkey, and Greece. In addition, the American navy is constantly operating in the Mediterranean Sea.

All of these facts show clearly that a decisive role in the realization of plans for world dominance by the United States is played by its armed forces.

One of the stages in the achievement of dominance over the world by the United States is its understanding with England concerning the partial division of the world on the basis of mutual concessions. The basic lines of the secret agreement between the United States and England regarding the division of the world consist, as shown by facts, in their agreement on the inclusion of Japan and China in the sphere of influence of the United States in the Far East, while the United States, for its part, has agreed not to hinder England either in resolving the Indian problem or in strengthening its influence in Siam and Indonesia.

In connection with this division, the United States at the present time is in control of China and Japan without any interference from England. . . .

In recent years American capital has penetrated very intensively into the economy of the Near Eastern countries, in particular into the oil industry. At present there are American oil concessions in all of the Near Eastern countries that have oil deposits (Iraq, Bahrain, Kuwait, Egypt, and Saudi Arabia). American capital, which made its first appearance in the oil industry of the Near East only in 1927, now controls about 42 percent of all proven reserves in the Near East, excluding Iran. Of the total proven reserves of 26.8 billion barrels, over 11 billion barrels are owned by U.S. concessions. Striving to ensure further development of their concessions in different countries (which are often very large—Saudi Arabia, for example), the American oil companies plan to build a trans-Arabian pipeline to transport oil from the American concession in Saudi Arabia and in other countries on the southeastern shore of the Mediterranean Sea to ports in Palestine and Egypt.

In expanding in the Near East, American capital has English capital as its greatest and most stubborn competitor. The fierce competition between them is the chief factor preventing England and the United States from reaching an understanding on the division of spheres of influence in the Near East, a division that can occur only at the expense of direct British interests in this region. . . .

It must be kept in mind, however, that incidents such as the visit by the American battleship *Missouri* to the Black Sea straits, the visit of the American fleet to Greece, and the great interest that U.S. diplomacy displays in the problem of the straits have a double meaning. On the one hand, they indicate that the United States has decided to consolidate its position in the Mediterranean basin to support its interests in the countries of the Near East and that it has selected the navy as the tool for this policy. On the other hand, these incidents constitute a political and military demonstration against the Soviet Union. The strengthening of U.S. positions in the Near East and the establishment of conditions for basing the American navy at one or more points on the Mediterranean Sea (Trieste, Palestine, Greece, Turkey) will therefore signify the emergence of a new threat to the security of the southern regions of the Soviet Union.

Relations between the United States and England are determined by two basic circumstances. On the one hand, the United States regards England as its greatest potential competitor; on the other hand, England constitutes a possible ally for the United States. Division of certain regions of the globe into spheres of influence of the United States and England would create the opportunity, if not for preventing competition between them, which is impossible, then at least of reducing it. At the same time, such a division facilitates the achievement of economic and political cooperation between them. . . .

The current relations between England and the United States, despite the temporary attainment of agreements on very important questions, are plagued with great internal contradictions and cannot be lasting.

The economic assistance from the United States conceals within itself a danger for England in many respects. First of all, in accepting the [U.S.] loan, England finds herself in a certain financial dependence on the United States from which it will not be easy to free herself. Second, it should be kept in mind that the conditions created by the loan for the penetration by American capital of the British Empire can entail serious political consequences. The countries included in the British Empire or dependent on it may—under economic pressure from powerful American capital—reorient themselves toward the United States, following in this respect the example of Canada, which more and more is moving away from the influence of England and orienting itself toward the United States. The strengthening of American positions in the Far East could stimulate a similar process in Australia and New Zealand. In the Arabic countries of the Near East, which are striving to emancipate themselves from the British Empire, there are groups within the ruling circles that would not be averse to working out a deal with the United States. It is quite possible that the Near East will become a center of Anglo-American contradictions that will explode the agreements now reached between the United States and England.

The "hard-line" policy with regard to the USSR announced by [Secretary of State James F.] Byrnes after the rapprochement of the reactionary Democrats with the Republicans is at present the main obstacle on the road to cooperation of the Great Powers. It consists mainly of the fact that in the postwar period the United States no longer follows a policy of strengthening cooperation among the Big Three (or Four) but rather has striven to undermine the unity of these countries. The objective has been to impose the will of other countries on the Soviet Union. This is precisely the tenor of the policy of certain countries, which is being carried out with the blessing of the United States, to undermine or completely abolish the principle of the veto in the Security Council of the United Nations. This would give the United States opportunities to form among the Great Powers narrow groupings and blocs directed primarily against the Soviet Union, and thus to split the United Nations. Rejection of the veto by the Great Powers would transform the United Nations into an Anglo-Saxon domain in which the United States would play the leading role.

The present policy of the American government with regard to the USSR is also directed at limiting or dislodging the influence of the Soviet Union from neighboring countries. In implementing this policy in former enemy or Allied countries adjacent to the USSR, the United States attempts, at various international conferences or directly in these countries themselves, to support reactionary forces with the purpose of creating obstacles to the process of democratization of these countries. In so doing, it also attempts to secure positions for the penetration of American capital into their economies. . . .

One of the most important elements in the general policy of the United States, which is directed toward limiting the international role of the USSR in the postwar world, is the policy with regard to Germany. In Germany, the United States is taking measures to strengthen reactionary forces for the purpose of opposing democratic reconstruction. Furthermore, it displays special insistence on accompanying this policy with completely inadequate measures for the demilitarization of Germany.

The American occupation policy does not have the objective of eliminating the remnants of German Fascism and rebuilding German political life on a democratic basis, so that Germany might cease to exist as an aggressive force. The United States is not taking measures to eliminate the monopolistic associations of German industrialists on which German Fascism depended in preparing aggression and waging war. Neither is any agrarian reform being conducted to eliminate large landholders, who were also a reliable support for the Hitlerites. Instead, the United States is considering the possibility of terminating the Allied occupation of German territory before the main tasks of the occupation—the demilitarization and democratization of Germany—have been implemented. This would create the prerequisites for the revival of an imperialist Germany, which the United States plans to use in a future war on its side. One cannot help seeing that such a policy has clearly outlined anti-Soviet edge and constitutes a serious danger to the cause of peace.

The numerous and extremely hostile statements by American government, political, and military figures with regard to the Soviet Union and its foreign policy are very characteristic of the current relationship between the ruling circles of the United States and the USSR. These statements are echoed in an even more unrestrained tone by the overwhelming majority of the American press organs. Talk about a "third war," meaning a war against the Soviet Union, and even a direct call for this war—with the threat of using the atomic bomb—such is the content of the statements on relations with the Soviet Union by reactionaries at public meetings and in the press. At the present time, preaching war against the Soviet Union is not a monopoly of the far-right, yellow American press represented by the newspaper associations of Hearst and McCormick. This anti-Soviet campaign also has been joined by the "reputable" and "respectable" organs of the conservative press, such as the *New York Times* and *New York Herald Tribune*. Indicative in this respect are the numerous articles by Walter Lippmann in which he almost undisguisedly calls on the United States to launch a strike against the Soviet Union in the most vulnerable areas of the south and southeast of the USSR.

The basic goal of this anti-Soviet campaign of American "public opinion" is to exert political pressure on the Soviet Union and compel it to make concessions. Another, no less important goal of the campaign is the attempt to create an atmosphere of war psychosis among the masses, who are weary of war, thus making it easier for the U.S. government to carry out measures for the maintenance of high military potential. It was in this very atmosphere that the law on universal military service in peacetime was passed by Congress, that the huge military budget was adopted, and that plans are being worked out for the construction of an extensive system of naval and air bases.

Of course, all of these measures for maintaining a high military potential are not goals in themselves. They are only intended to prepare the conditions for winning world supremacy in a new war, the date for which, to be sure, cannot be determined now by anyone, but which is contemplated by the most bellicose circles of American imperialism.

Careful note should be taken of the fact that the preparation by the United States for a future war is being conducted with the prospect of war against the

Soviet Union, which in the eyes of American imperialists is the main obstacle in the path of the United States to world domination. This is indicated by facts such as the tactical training of the American army for war with the Soviet Union as the future opponent, the siting of American strategic bases in regions from which it is possible to launch strikes on Soviet territory, intensified training and strengthening of Arctic regions as close approaches to the USSR, and attempts to prepare Germany and Japan to use those countries in a war against the USSR.

The Truman Doctrine, 1947

The gravity of the situation which confronts the world today necessitates my appearance before a joint session of the Congress.

The foreign policy and the national security of this country are involved.

One aspect of the present situation, which I present to you at this time for your consideration and decision, concerns Greece and Turkey.

The United States has received from the Greek Government an urgent appeal for financial and economic assistance. Preliminary reports from the American Economic Mission now in Greece and reports from the American Ambassador in Greece corroborate the statement of the Greek Government that assistance is imperative if Greece is to survive as a free nation. . . .

The British Government has informed us that, owing to its own difficulties, it can no longer extend financial or economic aid to Turkey.

As in the case of Greece, if Turkey is to have the assistance it needs, the United States must supply it. We are the only country able to provide that help.

I am fully aware of the broad implications involved if the United States extends assistance to Greece and Turkey, and I shall discuss these implications with you at this time.

One of the primary objectives of the foreign policy of the United States is the creation of conditions in which we and other nations will be able to work out a way of life free from coercion. This was a fundamental issue in the war with Germany and Japan. Our victory was won over countries which sought to impose their will, and their way of life, upon other nations.

To ensure the peaceful development of nations, free from coercion, the United States has taken a leading part in establishing the United Nations. The United Nations is designed to make possible lasting freedom and independence for all its members. We shall not realize our objectives, however, unless we are willing to help free peoples to maintain their free institutions and their national integrity against aggressive movements that seek to impose upon them totalitarian regimes. This is no more than a frank recognition that totalitarian regimes imposed upon free peoples, by direct or indirect aggression, undermine the foundations of international peace and hence the security of the United States.

The peoples of a number of countries of the world have recently had totalitarian regimes forced upon them against their will. The Government of the United States has made frequent protests against coercion and intimidation, in violation of the Yalta agreement, in Poland, Rumania, and Bulgaria. I must also state that in a number of other countries there have been similar developments.

At the present moment in world history nearly every nation must choose between alternative ways of life. The choice is too often not a free one.

One way of life is based upon the will of the majority, and is distinguished by free institutions, representative government, free elections, guarantees of individual liberty, freedom of speech and religion, and freedom from political oppression.

The second way of life is based upon the will of a minority forcibly imposed upon the majority. It relies upon terror and oppression, a controlled press and radio, fixed elections, and the suppression of personal freedoms.

I believe that it must be the policy of the United States to support free peoples who are resisting attempted subjugation by armed minorities or by outside pressures.

I believe that we must assist free peoples to work out their own destinies in their own way.

I believe that our help should be primarily through economic and financial aid which is essential to economic stability and orderly political processes.

The world is not static, and the *status quo* is not sacred. But we cannot allow changes in the *status quo* in violation of the Charter of the United Nations by such methods as coercion, or by such subterfuges as political infiltration. In helping free and independent nations to maintain their freedom, the United States will be giving effect to the principles of the Charter of the United Nations.

It is necessary only to glance at a map to realize that the survival and integrity of the Greek nation are of grave importance in a much wider situation. If Greece should fall under the control of an armed minority, the effect upon its neighbor, Turkey, would be immediate and serious. Confusion and disorder might well spread throughout the entire Middle East.

Moreover, the disappearance of Greece as an independent state would have a profound effect upon those countries in Europe whose peoples are struggling against great difficulties to maintain their freedoms and their independence while they repair the damages of war.

It would be an unspeakable tragedy if these countries, which have struggled so long against overwhelming odds, should lose that victory for which they sacrificed so much. Collapse of free institutions and loss of independence would be disastrous not only for them but for the world. Discouragement and possibly failure would quickly be the lot of neighboring peoples striving to maintain their freedom and independence.

Should we fail to aid Greece and Turkey in this fateful hour, the effect will be far reaching to the West as well as to the East.

We must take immediate and resolute action.

I therefore ask the Congress to provide authority for assistance to Greece and Turkey in the amount of $400,000,000 for the period ending June 30, 1948. In requesting these funds, I have taken into consideration the maximum amount of relief assistance which would be furnished to Greece out of the $350,000,000 which I recently requested that the Congress authorize for the prevention of starvation and suffering in countries devastated by the war.

In addition to funds, I ask the Congress to authorize the detail of American civilian and military personnel to Greece and Turkey, at the request of those countries, to assist in the tasks of reconstruction, and for the purpose of supervising the use of such financial and material assistance as may be furnished. I recommend that authority also be provided for the instruction and training of selected Greek and Turkish personnel. . . .

This is a serious course upon which we embark.

I would not recommend it except that the alternative is much more serious. The United States contributed $341,000,000,000 toward winning World War II. This is an investment in world freedom and world peace.

The assistance that I am recommending for Greece and Turkey amounts to little more than 1/10 of 1 percent of this investment. It is only common sense that we should safeguard this investment and make sure that it was not in vain.

The seeds of totalitarian regimes are nurtured by misery and want. They spread and grow in the evil soil of poverty and strife. They reach their full growth when the hope of a people for a better life has died.

We must keep that hope alive.

The free peoples of the world look to us for support in maintaining their freedoms.

If we falter in our leadership, we may endanger the peace of the world—and we shall surely endanger the welfare of this Nation.

Great responsibilities have been placed upon us by the swift movement of events.

I am confident that the Congress will face these responsibilities squarely.

The Marshall Plan (Economic Cooperation Act of 1948)

Recognizing the intimate economic and other relationships between the United States and the nations of Europe, and recognizing that disruption following in the wake of war is not contained by national frontiers, the Congress finds that the existing situation in Europe endangers the establishment of a lasting peace, the general welfare and national interest of the United States, and the attainment of the objectives of the United Nations. The restoration or maintenance in European countries of principles of individual liberty, free institutions, and genuine independence rests largely upon the establishment of sound economic conditions, stable international economic relationships, and the achievement by the countries of Europe of a healthy economy independent of extraordinary outside assistance. The accomplishment of these objectives calls for a plan of European recovery, open to all such nations which cooperate in such plan, based upon a strong production effort, the expansion of foreign trade, the creation and maintenance of internal financial stability, and the development of economic cooperation, including all possible steps to establish and maintain equitable rates of exchange and to bring about the progressive elimination of trade barriers. Mindful of the advantages which the United States has enjoyed through the existence of a large domestic market with no internal trade barriers, and believing that similar advantages can accrue to the countries of Europe, it is declared to be the policy of the people of the United States to encourage these countries through a joint organization to exert sustained common efforts as set forth in the report of the Committee of European Economic

Cooperation signed at Paris on September 22, 1947, which will speedily achieve that economic cooperation in Europe which is essential for lasting peace and prosperity. It is further declared to be the policy of the people of the United States to sustain and strengthen principles of individual liberty, free institutions, and genuine independence in Europe through assistance to those countries of Europe which participate in a joint recovery program based upon self-help and mutual cooperation: *Provided,* That no assistance to the participating countries herein contemplated shall seriously impair the economic stability of the United States. It is further declared to be the policy of the United States that continuity of assistance provided by the United States should, at all times, be dependent upon continuity of cooperation among countries participating in the program.

National Security Council
Paper No. 68 (NSC-68), 1950

Within the past thirty-five years the world has experienced two global wars of tremendous violence. It has witnessed two revolutions—the Russian and the Chinese—of extreme scope and intensity. It has also seen the collapse of five empires—the Ottoman, the Austro-Hungarian, German, Italian, and Japanese—and the drastic decline of two major imperial systems, the British and the French. During the span of one generation, the international distribution of power has been fundamentally altered. For several centuries it had proved impossible for any one nation to gain such preponderant strength that a coalition of other nations could not in time face it with greater strength. The international scene was marked by recurring periods of violence and war, but a system of sovereign and independent states was maintained, over which no state was able to achieve hegemony.

Two complex sets of factors have now basically altered this historical distribution of power. First, the defeat of Germany and Japan and the decline of the British and French Empires have interacted with the development of the United States and the Soviet Union in such a way that power has increasingly gravitated to these two centers. Second, the Soviet Union, unlike previous aspirants to hegemony, is animated by a new fanatic faith, antithetical to our own, and seeks to impose its absolute authority over the rest of the world. Conflict has, therefore, become endemic and is waged, on the part of the Soviet Union, by violent or nonviolent methods in accordance with the dictates of expediency. With the development of increasingly terrifying weapons of mass destruction, every individual faces the ever-present possibility of annihilation should the conflict enter the phase of total war. . . .

Our overall policy at the present time may be described as one designed to foster a world environment in which the American system can survive and flourish. It therefore rejects the concept of isolation and affirms the necessity of our positive participation in the world community.

This broad intention embraces two subsidiary policies. One is a policy which we would probably pursue even if there were no Soviet threat. It is a policy of attempting to develop a healthy international community. The other is the policy of "containing" the Soviet system. These two policies are closely interrelated and interact on one another. Nevertheless, the distinction between them is basically valid and contributes to a clearer understanding of what we are trying to do. . . .

As for the policy of "containment," it is one which seeks by all means short of war to (1) block further expansion of Soviet power, (2) expose the falsities of Soviet pretentions, (3) induce a retraction of the Kremlin's control and influence and (4) in general, so foster the seeds of destruction within the Soviet system that the Kremlin is brought at least to the point of modifying its behavior to conform to generally accepted international standards.

It was and continues to be cardinal in this policy that we possess superior overall power in ourselves or in dependable combination with other like-minded nations. One of the most important ingredients of power is military strength. In the concept of "containment," the maintenance of a strong military posture is deemed to be essential for two reasons: (1) as an ultimate guarantee of our national security and (2) as an indispensable backdrop to the conduct of the policy of "containment." Without superior aggregate military strength, in being and readily mobilizable, a policy of "containment"—which is in effect a policy of calculated and gradual coercion—is no more than a policy of bluff.

At the same time, it is essential to the successful conduct of a policy of "containment" that we always leave open the possibility of negotiation with the U.S.S.R. A diplomatic freeze—and we are in one now—tends to defeat the very purposes of "containment" because it raises tensions at the same time that it makes Soviet retractions and adjustments in the direction of moderated behavior more difficult. It also tends to inhibit our initiative and deprives us of opportunities for maintaining a moral ascendancy in our struggle with the Soviet system.

In "containment" it is desirable to exert pressure in a fashion which will avoid so far as possible directly challenging Soviet prestige, to keep open the possibility for the U.S.S.R. to retreat before pressure with a minimum loss of face and to secure political advantage from the failure of the Kremlin to yield or take advantage of the openings we leave it.

We have failed to implement adequately these two fundamental aspects of "containment." In the face of obviously mounting Soviet military strength ours has declined relatively. Partly as a byproduct of this, but also for other reasons, we now find ourselves at a diplomatic impasse with the Soviet Union, with the Kremlin growing bolder, with both of us holding on grimly to what we have and with ourselves facing difficult decisions. . . .

It is apparent from the preceding sections that the integrity and vitality of our system is in greater jeopardy than ever before in our history. Even if there were no Soviet Union we would face the great problem of the free society, accentuated many fold in this industrial age, of reconciling order, security, the need for participation, with the requirements of freedom. . . .

It is quite clear from Soviet theory and practice that the Kremlin seeks to bring the free world under its dominion by the methods of the cold war. The preferred technique is to subvert by infiltration and intimidation. Every institution of our society is an instrument which it is sought to stultify and turn against our purposes. Those that touch most closely our material and moral strength are obviously the prime targets, labor unions, civic enterprises, schools, churches, and all media for influencing opinion. . . .

At the same time the Soviet Union is seeking to create overwhelming military force, in order to back up infiltration with intimidation. In the only terms in which it understands strength, it is seeking to demonstrate to the free world that force and the will to use it are on the side of the Kremlin, that those who lack it are decadent and doomed. In local incidents it threatens and encroaches both for the sake of local gains and to increase anxiety and defeatism in all the free world.

The possession of atomic weapons at each of the opposite poles of power, and the inability (for different reasons) of either side to place any trust in the other, puts a premium on a surprise attack against us. It equally puts a premium on a more violent and ruthless prosecution of its design by cold war, especially if the Kremlin is sufficiently objective to realize the improbability of our prosecuting a preventive war. It also puts a premium on piecemeal aggression against others, counting on our unwillingness to engage in atomic war unless we are directly attacked. . . .

A more rapid build-up of political, economic, and military strength and thereby of confidence in the free world than is now contemplated is the only course which is consistent with progress toward achieving our fundamental purpose. The frustration of the Kremlin design requires the free world to develop a successfully functioning political and economic system and a vigorous political offensive against the Soviet Union. These, in turn, require an adequate military shield under which they can develop. It is necessary to have the military power to deter, if possible, Soviet expansion, and to defeat, if necessary, aggressive Soviet or Soviet-directed actions of a limited or total character. The potential strength of the free world is great; its ability to develop these military capabilities and its will to resist Soviet expansion will be determined by the wisdom and will with which it undertakes to meet its political and economic problems. . . .

Our position as the center of power in the free world places a heavy responsibility upon the United States for leadership. We must organize and enlist the energies and resources of the free world in a positive program for peace which will frustrate the Kremlin design for world domination by creating a situation in the free world to which the Kremlin will be compelled to adjust. Without such a cooperative effort, led by the United States, we will have to make gradual withdrawals under pressure until we discover one day that we have sacrificed positions of vital interest.

It is imperative that this trend be reversed by a much more rapid and concerted build-up of the actual strength of both the United States and the other nations of the free world. The analysis shows that this will be costly and will involve significant domestic financial and economic adjustments.

✖ *E S S A Y S*

In the opening essay, Barton J. Bernstein, a professor of history at Stanford University, analyzes the Roosevelt and Truman administrations' thinking about the atomic bomb's place both as a weapon to defeat Japan and as a lever to pry diplomatic concessions from the

Soviet Union. Bernstein agrees with most other historians that Truman ordered the use of the atomic bomb against Japanese civilians primarily to end the war quickly and to save American lives. But Bernstein also explores the bomb as a diplomatic "bonus" that American leaders believed would enhance U.S. bargaining power in the Cold War, and he explains the detrimental effects of the bomb and atomic diplomacy on Soviet-American relations.

The second essay, an example of recent Russian scholarship in the aftermath of the Cold War's demise, in some ways resembles what in American scholarship has been called "traditionalist"—that is, blaming the Cold War on the Soviet Union and Josef Stalin. The authors, Vladislav Zubok and Constantine Pleshakov, are affiliated with the Institute for the U.S.A. and Canada, Russian Academy of Sciences, Moscow. Examining Stalin's mindset and ambitions, the authors find an arrogance and single-mindedness that proved immutable to outside influence. Determined to follow an aggressive course, Stalin miscalculated the Western response and closed out opportunities to prevent the Cold War.

The last essay is drawn from the conclusion of Melvyn P. Leffler's *A Preponderance of Power* (1992). A professor of history at the University of Virginia, Leffler posits that, although the postwar United States was more powerful than any other nation, its leaders grew apprehensive about several international conditions that they feared the Soviets might exploit to America's detriment. U.S. leaders, in Leffler's view, wisely understood American strengths and Soviet weaknesses. They prudently acted to prevent worst-case scenarios in the "industrial core areas." But they foolishly magnified the importance of the Third World ("the periphery"). Leffler also argues that Truman officials exaggerated Soviet behavior. He suggests, finally, why Moscow could not accept postwar American priorities and why U.S. officials could not take chances in the conflict-ridden international system.

Secrets and Threats: Atomic Diplomacy and Soviet-American Antagonism

BARTON J. BERNSTEIN

Ever since the publication in 1965 of Gar Alperovitz's *Atomic Diplomacy,* scholars and laymen have developed a new interest in the relationship of the atomic bomb to wartime and postwar diplomacy and to the origins of the Cold War. This bold book revived and sometimes recast old themes and thereby sparked renewed interest in questions that once seemed settled: Why was the atomic bomb dropped on Japan? Why weren't other alternatives vigorously pursued? How did the bomb influence American policy before and after Hiroshima? Did the dropping of the bomb and postwar American atomic policies contribute to the cold war?

Unfortunately many studies of these questions have focused exclusively on the Truman period and thereby neglected the Roosevelt administration, which bequeathed to Truman a legacy of assumptions, options, and fears. Acting on the assumption that the bomb was a legitimate weapon, Roosevelt initially defined the relationship of American diplomacy and the atomic bomb. He decided to build the bomb, to establish a partnership on atomic energy with Britain, to bar the Soviet

From "Roosevelt, Truman and the Atomic Bomb, 1941–1945: A Reinterpretation" by Barton J. Bernstein from *Political Science Quarterly* 90 (Spring 1975), pp. 23–24, 30–32, 34–43, 44–54, 57–69. Reprinted by permission of the publisher.

Union from knowledge of the project, and to block any effort at international control of atomic energy. These policies constituted Truman's inheritance—one he neither wished to abandon nor could easily escape. He was restricted politically, psychologically, and institutionally from critically reassessing this legacy.

Like Roosevelt, Truman assumed that the bomb was a legitimate weapon and also understood that it could serve as a bargaining lever, a military counterweight, a threat, or a combat weapon in dealing with the Soviet Union in the postwar world. In addition to speeding the end of the war, the combat use of the bomb, the Truman administration understood, offered the United States great advantages in the postwar world. Policy makers assumed that use of the bomb would help shape the world in a desirable mold: The bomb would impress the Soviets and make them more tractable. Contrary to some contentions, this consideration about the postwar world was not the controlling reason why the United States used the bomb. Rather, it was an additional reason reinforcing an earlier analysis. Ending the war speedily was the primary purpose; impressing the Soviet Union was secondary. This secondary aim did constitute a subtle deterrent to reconsidering combat use of the bomb and to searching for alternative means of ending the war. Had the use of the bomb threatened to impair, rather than advance, American aims for the postwar peace, policy makers would have been likely to reassess their assumptions and perhaps to choose other alternatives. . . .

Running through the tangled skein of America's wartime policy on atomic energy is the persistent evidence of concern about the Soviet Union. Roosevelt knew that the Soviets were gathering information about the bomb project, and on September 9, 1943, Henry L. Stimson, the secretary of war, informed the president that spies "are already getting information about vital secrets and sending them to Russia." In late December 1944, at two sessions, they again discussed these issues. On December 31, Roosevelt told Stimson that he, too, was worried about how much the Soviets might know about the project, and they briefly discussed trading information for substantial concessions. As Stimson later summarized the conversation in his diary:

> I told him . . . that I knew they [Russia] were spying on our work but that they had not yet gotten any real knowledge of it and that, while I was troubled by the possible effect of keeping from them even now that work, I believed that it was essential not to take them into our confidence until we were sure to get a real quid pro quo from our frankness. I said I had no illusions as to the possibility of keeping permanently such a secret but that I did think that it was not yet time to share it with Russia. He said he thought he agreed with me.

They did not discuss the specific nature of the concessions, and perhaps Stimson and the president would not have agreed on how to use the bomb as a bargaining lever and what to demand from the Soviet Union. Whatever their unexplored differences on these issues, they did agree to continue for a period the same policy: exclusion of the Soviets. "It was quite clear," recorded General Leslie Groves, commanding general of the Manhattan Project, "that no one present was interested in bringing Russia into the picture, at least at this time." It is less clear why Roosevelt and Stimson, faced with the realization that the Soviet Union knew about the American research, still did not want formally to notify the Soviets about the bomb project. There is no direct evidence on this subject, but probably they feared that formal disclosure would lead to explicit Soviet inquiries and then to demands for participation that American leaders were not prepared to handle. As long as the United States technically kept the project secret, the Soviets could never raise issues about the bomb without admitting their espionage.

On March 15, 1945, at their last meeting together, Stimson and Roosevelt again discussed atomic energy. Roosevelt acknowledged that he would have to choose between (1) continuing the policy of secrecy and the Anglo-American partnership that barred the Soviets or (2) moving to international control with a sharing of information. Under Roosevelt, there was no further resolution of these issues. When he died in April, American policy had not advanced beyond the point where it had been in December.

Had Roosevelt lived, perhaps he would ultimately have reversed the policy of secrecy and decided to move toward international control in return for *quid pro quo*—perhaps on Eastern Europe which he had "ceded" at Yalta to the Soviet Union. Any consideration of what "might have happened" is, of course, a matter of speculation, since the evidence is skimpy and oblique on what Roosevelt might have done. What is clear is that he had maintained the strategy of excluding the Soviets from knowledge of the bomb and of reserving the options of using it in the future as a bargaining lever, threat, military counterweight, or even a weapon against the Soviets.

It was not that he lacked opportunities to reverse his policy. He did not want to change policy—at least not up to April. At Yalta, in February, for example, Roosevelt might have approached Stalin on the bomb, but the president neither discussed this subject nor the loan that the Soviets wanted, and thereby he simply kept open the options for the future of using economic leverage and the bomb to secure concessions. His position, then, made possible the future strategy of "atomic diplomacy"—of using the bomb as an implied or explicit threat to influence negotiations and to compel concessions from the Soviets. Would he have practiced "atomic diplomacy"? Probably. But that answer is speculative and rests principally upon the theory that he would not have wasted the options he was jealously guarding.

Roosevelt and his advisers had more clearly defined another issue: the combat use of the bomb. From the inception of the project, when it was directed primarily against Germany, they usually assumed, and most policy makers never questioned, that the bomb was a legitimate weapon to be used in combat. This assumption was phrased as policy on a number of occasions. In October 1942, for example, Stimson had directed Groves that the mission is "to produce [the bomb] at the earliest possible date so as to bring the war to a conclusion." Any time "that a single day could be saved," the general should save that day. In 1944, policy makers were also talking comfortably about "*after* S-1 [the bomb] is used." "At no time," Stimson later wrote, "did I ever hear it suggested by the President, or by any other responsible member of the government, that atomic energy should not be used in war." . . .

When Harry S Truman became president on April 12, 1945, he was only dimly aware of the existence of the Manhattan Project and unaware that it was an atomic-bomb project. Left uninformed of foreign affairs and generally ignored by

Roosevelt in the three months since the inaugural, the new president inherited a set of policies and a group of advisers from his predecessor. While Truman was legally free to reverse Roosevelt's foreign policies and to choose new advisers on foreign policy, in fact he was quite restricted for personal and political reasons. Because Truman was following a very prestigious president whom he, like a great many Americans, loved and admired, the new president was not free psychologically or politically to strike out on a clearly new course. Only a bolder man, with more self-confidence, might have tried critically to assess the legacy and to act independently. But Truman lacked the confidence and the incentive. When, in fact, he did modify policy—for example, on Eastern Europe—he still believed sincerely, as some advisers told him, that he was adhering to his predecessor's agreements and wishes. When seeking counsel on foreign affairs, he usually did not choose new advisers but simply drew more heavily upon those members of Roosevelt's staff who were more anti-Soviet and relied less upon those who were more friendly to the Soviet Union. Even in this strategy, he believed that he was adhering to the policies of his predecessor, who, in his last weeks, Truman stressed, had become more suspicious of Stalin, more distressed by Soviet action in Eastern Europe, and more committed to resisting Soviet encroachments.

In the case of the international-diplomatic policy on the bomb, Truman was even more restricted by Roosevelt's decisions, for the new president inherited a set of reasonably clear wartime policies. Because Roosevelt had already decided to exclude the Soviets from a partnership on the bomb, his successor could not *comfortably* reverse this policy during the war—unless the late president's advisers pleaded for such a reversal or claimed that he had been about to change his policy. They did neither. Consider, then, the massive personal and political deterrents that blocked Truman from even reassessing this legacy. What price might he have paid at home if Americans learned later that he had reversed Roosevelt's policy and had launched a bold new departure of sharing with the Soviets a great weapon that cost the United States $2 billion? Truman, in fact, was careful to follow Roosevelt's strategy of concealing from Congress even the dimensions of the secret partnership on atomic energy with Britain.

Truman, depending as he did upon Roosevelt's advisers, could not easily reassess the prevailing assumption that the bomb was a legitimate weapon to be used in combat against Japan. Truman lacked the will and the incentive to reexamine this assumption, and his dependence upon Roosevelt's advisers and the momentum of the project confirmed this tendency. Only one close adviser, Admiral William Leahy, may have later challenged the use of the bomb, but he was an old "war horse," an expert on explosives of another era, who had often proclaimed that the bomb would not work, that the scientists were duping the administration, and that they were squandering $2 billion. His counsel could not outweigh the continuing legacy of assumptions and commitments, of advisers and advice, that Truman had inherited from Roosevelt. It was a subtle legacy, one that infiltrated decisions and shaped actions, so that Truman accepted it as part of his unquestioned inheritance. For Truman, the question would never be how openly to challenge this legacy, only how to fulfill it, how to remain true to it.

During his first weeks in office, Truman learned about the project from Stimson and from James F. Byrnes, Roosevelt's former director of the Office of War

Mobilization and Reconversion who was to become Truman's secretary of state. Byrnes, despite his recent suspicions that the project might be a scientific boondoggle, told Truman, in the president's words, that "the bomb might well put us in a position to dictate our own terms at the end of the war." On April 25, Stimson discussed issues about the bomb more fully with Truman, especially the "political aspects of the S-1 [atomic bomb's] performance." The bomb, the secretary of war explained in a substantial memorandum, would probably be ready in four months and "would be the most terrible weapon ever known in human history [for it] . . . could destroy a whole city." In the future, he warned, other nations would be able to make atomic bombs, thereby endangering the peace and threatening the world. The bomb could be either a threat to or a guarantor of peace. "[I]n the light of our present position with reference to this weapon, the question of sharing it with other nations and, if so shared, upon what terms, becomes a primary question of our foreign relations," Stimson lectured the president. If "the problem of the proper use of this weapon can be solved, we would have the opportunity to bring the world into a pattern in which the peace of the world and our civilization can be saved."

The entire discussion, judging from Stimson's daily record and Groves's memorandum, assumed that the bomb was a legitimate weapon and that it would be used against Japan. The questions they discussed were not *whether* to use the bomb, but its relationship to the Soviet Union and the need to establish postwar atomic policies. Neither Stimson nor Truman sought then to resolve these outstanding issues, and Truman agreed to his secretary's proposal for the establishment of a high-level committee to recommend "action to the executive and legislative branches of our government when secrecy is no longer in full effect." At no time did they conclude that the committee would also consider the issue of whether to use the bomb as a combat weapon. For policy makers, that was not a question; it was an operating assumption.

Nor did Stimson, in his own charge to the Interim Committee, ever *raise* this issue. Throughout the committee's meetings, as various members later noted, all operated on the assumption that the bomb would be used against Japan. They talked, for example, about drafting public statements that would be issued after the bomb's use. They did not discuss *whether* but how to use it. Only one member ultimately endorsed an explicit advance warning to Japan, and none was prepared to suggest that the administration should take any serious risks to avoid using the bomb. At lunch between the two formal meetings on May 31, some members, perhaps only at one table, briefly discussed the possibility of a noncombat demonstration as a warning to Japan but rejected the tactic on the grounds that the bomb might not explode and the failure might stiffen Japanese resistance, or that Japan might move prisoners of war to the target area.

What impact would the bomb have on Japan? At the May 31 meeting, the Interim Committee, joined by its four-member scientific advisory panel discussed this question. Some felt, according to the minutes, that "an atomic bomb on an arsenal would not be much different in effect" from present bombing attacks. J. Robert Oppenheimer, the eminent physicist and member of the scientific panel, expecting that the bomb would have an explosive force of between 2,000 and 20,000 tons of TNT, stressed its visual effects ("a brilliant luminescence which would run to a height of 10,000 to 20,000 feet") and its deadly power ("dangerous to life for a radius of at least two-thirds of a mile"). Oppenheimer's predictions did not answer the question. There were too many unknowns—about the bomb and Japan. According to the official minutes, Stimson concluded, with unanimous support: "that we could not concentrate on a civilian area; but we should seek to make a profound psychological impression on as many of the inhabitants as possible." At [the scientist James B.] Conant's suggestion, "the Secretary agreed that the most desirable target would be a vital war plant employing a large number of workers and closely surrounded by workers' houses." ("I felt," Stimson later explained, "that to extract a genuine surrender from the Emperor and his military advisers, they must be administered a tremendous shock . . . proof of our power to destroy the empire.") The Interim Committee ruled out the strategy of several atomic strikes at one time, for, according to Groves, the United States would lose the benefit of additional knowledge from each successive bombing, would have to rush in assembling bombs and court error, and also would risk the possibility that multiple nuclear attacks "would not be sufficiently distinct from our regular Air Force bombing program."

Two weeks later, after the Franck Committee recommended a noncombat demonstration, Stimson's assistant submitted this proposal to the four-member scientific advisory panel for advice. The panel promptly rejected the Franck Committee proposal: "we can propose no technical demonstration likely to bring an end to the war; we see no acceptable alternative to direct military use." Had the four scientists known that an invasion was not scheduled until November, or had they even offered their judgment after the unexpectedly impressive Alamogordo test on July 16, perhaps they would have given different counsel. But in June, they were not sure that the bomb explosion would be so dramatic, and, like many others in government, they were wary of pushing for a change in tactics if they might be held responsible for the failure of those tactics—especially if that failure could mean the loss of American lives.

A few days after the panel's report, the issue of giving Japan an advance warning about the bomb was raised at a White House meeting with the president, the military chiefs, and the civilian secretaries. On June 18, after they agreed upon a two-stage invasion of Japan, beginning on about November 1, Assistant Secretary of War John J. McCloy became clearly troubled by the omission of the bomb from the discussion and planning. When Truman invited him to speak, the assistant secretary argued that the bomb would make the invasion unnecessary. Why not warn the emperor that the United States had the bomb and would use it unless Japan surrendered? "McCloy's suggestion had appeal," the official history of the AEC [Atomic Energy Commission] later recorded, "but a strong objection developed" to warning Japan in advance, "which no one could refute—there was no assurance the bomb would work." Presumably, like the Interim Committee, they too feared that a warning, followed by a "dud," might stiffen Japan's morale. There was no reason, policy makers concluded, to take this risk.

Though the Interim Committee and high administration officials found no reason not to use the bomb against Japan, many were concerned about the bomb's impact, and its later value, in Soviet-American relations. "[I]t was already apparent," Stimson later wrote, "that the critical questions in American policy toward atomic energy would be directly connected with Soviet Russia." At a few meetings of the Interim Committee, for example, members discussed informing the Soviets of the bomb before its use against Japan. When the issue first arose, [the scientist Vannevar] Bush and Conant estimated that the Soviet Union could develop the bomb in about four years and argued for informing the Soviets before combat use as a preliminary to moving toward international control and thereby avoiding a postwar nuclear arms race. Conant and Bush had been promoting this strategy since the preceding September. Even though Roosevelt had cast them to the side in 1943, when he cemented the Anglo-American alliance, the two scientist-administrators had not abandoned hope for their notions. They even circulated to the Interim Committee one of their memoranda on the subject. But at the meetings of May 18 and 31 they again met defeat. General Groves, assuming that America was far more advanced technologically and scientifically and also that the Soviet Union lacked uranium, argued that the Soviets could not build a bomb for about twenty years. He contributed to the appealing "myth" of the atomic secret—that there was a secret and it would long remain America's monopoly. James Byrnes, with special authority as secretary of state–designate and Truman's representative on the committee, accepted Groves's analysis and argued for maintaining the policy of secrecy—which the committee endorsed. Byrnes was apparently very pleased, and Stimson agreed, as he told Truman on June 6, "There should be no revelation to Russia or anyone else of our work on S-1 [the atomic bomb] until the first bomb has been laid successfully on Japan."

At a later meeting on June 21, the Interim Committee, including Byrnes, reversed itself. Yielding to the pleas of Bush and Conant, who were strengthened by the scientific panel's recommendations, the Interim Committee advised Truman to inform the Soviets about the bomb before using it in combat. Like the Franck Committee, the Interim Committee concluded (as the minutes record):

> In the hope of securing effective future control and in view of the fact that general information concerning the project would be made public shortly after the [Potsdam] conference, the Committee *agreed* that there would be considerable advantage, if suitable opportunity arose, in having the President advise the Russians that we were working on this weapon with every prospect of success and that we expected to use it against Japan.
>
> The president might say further that he hoped this matter might be discussed some time in the future in terms of insuring that the weapon would become an aid to peace.

Because of this recommendation, and perhaps also because of the continuing prodding of Bush and Conant, Stimson reversed his own position. He concluded that if the United States dropped the bomb on Japan without first informing the Soviet Union, that act might gravely strain Soviet-American relations. Explaining the committee's position to Truman, Stimson proposed that if the President "thought that Stalin was on good terms with him" at the forthcoming Potsdam conference, he would inform Stalin that the United States had developed the bomb, planned to use it against Japan, knew the Soviets were working on the bomb, and looked forward to discussing international control later. This approach left open the option of "atomic diplomacy."

The issues of the bomb and the Soviet Union had already intruded in other ways upon policy and planning. Awaiting the bomb, Truman had postponed the Potsdam conference, delayed negotiations with Russia, and hoped that atomic energy would pry some concessions from Russia. Truman explained in late May to Joseph Davies, an advocate of Soviet-American friendship, and in early June to Stimson that he was delaying the forthcoming Potsdam conference until the Alamogordo test, when he would know whether the United States had a workable atomic bomb—what Stimson repeatedly called the "mastercard." Truman also told some associates that he was delaying because he wanted to work out budget matters, but it is unlikely that the budget was the controlling reason. Certainly, there was no reason that he should have told Davies, who, unlike Stimson, was not counseling delay of the conference, that he was waiting for the bomb. Stimson's counsel of caution, offered on May 15, had apparently triumphed: it would be "a terrible thing to gamble with such high stakes in diplomacy without having your master card in your hand. . . . Over [the] tangled wave of problems the S-1 secret would be dominant." This was not the counsel for a "delayed showdown," as some have wrongly argued, but for no showdown and for delaying some negotiations until the bomb test so that policy makers could determine whether they would have to make concessions to the Soviet Union.

For the administration, the atomic bomb, if it worked, had great potential value. It could reduce the importance of early Soviet entry into the war and make American concessions unnecessary. It could also be a lever for extracting concessions from the Soviet Union. On June 6, for example, Stimson discussed with Truman "quid pro quos which should be established for our taking them [Russia] into [a nuclear] partnership. He [Truman] said that he had been thinking of the same things that I was thinking of, namely the settlement of the Polish, Rumanian, Yugoslavian, and Manchurian problems." There is no evidence that they were planning explicitly to threaten the Soviets to gain these concessions, but, obviously, they realized that the Soviets would regard an American nuclear monopoly as threatening and would yield on some issues in order to terminate that monopoly and thereby reduce, or eliminate, the threat. Neither Stimson nor Truman discussed brandishing the bomb or using it explicitly as a threat to compel concessions. "Atomic diplomacy," as a conception, advanced no further than the notion of possibly trading in the future an atomic partnership, which was still undefined, for Soviet concessions.

For policy makers, the atomic weapons scheduled for combat use against Japan were intimately connected with the problem of Russia. In recent years some historians have focused on this relationship and raised troubling questions: Did the bomb, for policy makers, constitute an alternative to Soviet intervention in the Pacific war? Did they delay or even try to prevent Soviet entry because the bomb made it unnecessary? If so, did they do this in order to use the bomb? Was the bomb dropped on Japan primarily to influence Russia? Did the bomb influence American policy at Potsdam?

At Yalta, Roosevelt had granted the Soviet Union concessions in China in order to secure Soviet entry into the Pacific war, which Stalin promised, within two to three months after V-E Day (May 8). Stalin made it clear that Soviet entry would await a Sino-Soviet pact ratifying these concessions. At the time of Yalta, American military planners were counting on a Soviet attack in Manchuria to pin down the Kwantung army there and hence stop Japan from shifting these forces to her homeland to meet an American invasion.

But by April, war conditions changed and military planners revised their analysis: Japan no longer controlled the seas and therefore could not shift her army, so Soviet entry was not essential. In May, the State Department asked Stimson whether Soviet participation "at the earliest possible moment" was so necessary that the United States should abide by the Far East section of the Yalta agreement. Stimson concluded that the Soviets would enter the war for their own reasons, at their schedule, and with little regard to any American action, that the Yalta concessions would be largely within the grasp of Soviet military power, and that Soviet assistance would be useful, but not essential, if an American invasion was necessary. If there is an invasion, "Russian entry," he wrote, "will have a profound military effect in that almost certainly it will materially shorten the war and thus save American lives." But if the bomb worked, he implied in other discussions, then an invasion would probably not be necessary and Soviet help would be less important. As a result, he urged a delay in settling matters with Russia on the Far East until after the Alamogordo test, and the President apparently followed this counsel. . . .

Truman claimed that he went to Potsdam to secure Soviet entry and that he never changed his position. The first part of that claim is correct, but the second part is dubious, for Truman did nothing substantive at Potsdam to encourage Soviet intervention and much to delay or prevent it. The successful test at Alamogordo emphasized to policy makers that prompt Soviet entry was no longer necessary and that the United States might even be able to end the war without Soviet entry. After the unexpectedly glowing report of the test, Truman wanted to know whether Marshall considered Soviet entry necessary. "Marshall felt," Stimson recorded, "that now with our new weapon we would not need the assistance of the Russians to conquer Japan." "The bomb as a merely probable weapon had seemed a weak reed on which to rely, but the bomb as a colossal reality was very different," Stimson later explained. From Potsdam on July 23, Churchill cabled London: "It is quite clear that the United States do not at the present time desire Russian participation in the war against Japan." The bomb had eliminated the importance of Russia's prompt entry, since the planned American invasion no longer seemed necessary. Invasion and the bomb were the likely alternatives. As a result, Truman had no reason to offer concessions to secure early Soviet entry.

Could the United States keep the Soviet Union out of the war? Did policy makers try to do this? In mid-July Soviet troops were stationed on the Manchurian border and would soon be ready to intervene. Marshall concluded that even if Japan surrendered on American terms before Soviet entry, Russia could still march into Manchuria and take virtually whatever she wanted there in the surrender terms. Truman, if he believed Marshall's analysis, had nothing to gain politically from deterring Soviet entry, unless he feared, as did Stimson, that the Soviets might try to reach the Japanese homeland and put in a "claim to occupy and help rule it." Perhaps Truman followed the counsel of Stimson and Byrnes, who, for slightly different reasons, were eager to restrain the Soviets.

Byrnes, unlike Stimson, was sometimes naively optimistic. Part of the time he hoped to keep the Soviet Union out of the war, and not simply delay her entry, in order to protect China. On July 28, he explained to Secretary of the Navy James

Forrestal (in Forrestal's words): "Byrnes said he was most anxious to get the Japanese affair over with before the Russians got in, with particular reference to Dairen and Port Arthur." These were the areas that both Stimson and Marshall acknowledged the Soviets could seize. Walter Brown, the friend who accompanied the secretary to Potsdam, recorded in his diary notes for July 20 Byrnes's strategy: "JFB determined to outmaneuver Stalin on China. Hopes Soong [the Chinese foreign minister] will stand firm and then Russians will not go in war. Then he feels Japan will surrender before Russia goes to war and this will save China." On July 24, four days later, Brown noted that Byrnes was linking the bomb and Japan's surrender but was less optimistic about excluding Russia: "JFB still hoping for time, believing after atomic bombing Japan will surrender and Russia will not get in so much on the kill, thereby [not] being in a position to press for claims against China."

Byrnes purposely impeded Sino-Soviet negotiations in order to *prevent* the Soviets from entering the war. Did Truman support Byrnes for the *same* reasons?—as Byrnes claimed later and as Truman obliquely denied. Perhaps. But, more likely, Truman supported his secretary's strategy for a different reason: the early entry of the Soviets was no longer important and, therefore, Truman did not want Chiang to make the required concessions, which would later weaken Chiang's government. In addition, Truman *may* have concluded that Russia's delayed entry would weaken her possible claims for a role in the postwar occupation government in Japan.

Why didn't Truman invite Stalin to sign the Potsdam Proclamation of July 26 calling for Japan's surrender? Some analysts argued later that this omission was part of a devious strategy: that Truman wanted to use the bomb and feared that Stalin's signature, tantamount to a declaration of war, might catapult Japan to surrender, thereby making a nuclear attack impossible. The major difficulty with this interpretation is that it exaggerates occasional, sometimes ambiguous, statements about the *possible* impact of Soviet entry and ignores the fact that this possible shock was not a persistent or important theme in American planning. Truman did not exclude the Soviets from the Proclamation in order to use the bomb. The skimpy, often oblique evidence *suggests* a more plausible explanation and a less devious pattern: he wanted to avoid requesting favors from the Soviets. As a result, he did not try this one possible, but not very likely, way of ending the war without using atomic weapons.

At Potsdam, on July 24, Truman told Stalin casually that the United States had developed "a new weapon of unusual destructive force" for use against Japan but did not specify an atomic weapon. Why didn't Truman explicitly inform Stalin about the atomic bomb? Was Truman, as some have suggested, afraid that the news would prompt Stalin to hasten Soviet intervention and therefore end the war and make combat use of the bomb impossible? Did Truman simply want to delay Soviet entry and did he, like Byrnes, fear that his news would have the opposite effect? Did Truman think that the destruction wrought by the bomb would not impress the Soviets as forcefully if they were informed in advance? Why did Truman reject the counsel of the Interim Committee, of Stimson, and even of Churchill, who, after the flowing news of the Alamogordo test, "was not worried about giving the Russians information on the matter but was rather inclined to use it as an argument in our favor in the negotiations"?

Many of these questions cannot be definitively answered on the basis of the presently available evidence, but there is enough evidence to refute one popular interpretation: that Truman's tactic was part of an elaborate strategy to prevent or retard Soviet entry *in order* to delay Japan's surrender and *thereby* make combat use of the bomb possible. That interpretation claims too much. Only the first part can be supported by some, albeit indirect, evidence: that he was probably seeking to delay or prevent Soviet entry. Byrnes later said that he feared that Stalin would order an immediate Soviet declaration of war if he realized the importance of this "new weapon"—advice Truman dubiously claimed he never received. Truman was not trying to postpone Japan's surrender *in order* to use the bomb. In addition to the reasonable theory that he was seeking to prevent or retard Soviet entry, there are two other plausible, complementary interpretations of Truman's behavior. First, he believed, as had some of his advisers earlier, that a combat demonstration would be more impressive to Russia without an advance warning and therefore he concealed the news. Second, he was also ill-prepared to discuss atomic energy with Stalin, for the president had not made a decision about postwar atomic policy and how to exploit the bomb, and probably did not want to be pressed by Stalin about sharing nuclear secrets. Perhaps all three theories collectively explained Truman's evasive tactics.

Even without explicit disclosure, the bomb strengthened American policy at Potsdam. The Alamogordo test stiffened Truman's resolve, as Churchill told Stimson after the meeting of the Big Three on July 22: "Truman was evidently much fortified . . . and . . . he stood up to the Russians in a most emphatic and decisive manner, telling them as to certain demands that they absolutely could not have." Probably, also, the bomb explains why Truman pushed more forcefully at Potsdam for the Soviets to open up Eastern Europe. It is less clear whether the bomb changed the substance of American policy at Potsdam. Probably Byrnes endorsed a reparations policy allowing the division of Germany because the bomb replaced Germany as a potential counterweight to possible Soviet expansion.

Not only did the bomb strengthen American resolve in dealing with the Soviets, but Stimson and Truman linked the bomb and the Soviet Union in another way: the selection of targets for atomic attacks. Kyoto, a city of religious shrines, was originally on the list, but Stimson removed it, with Truman's approval. Truman "was particularly emphatic in agreeing with my suggestion," Stimson wrote, because

> the bitterness . . . caused by such a wanton act might make it impossible during the long post war period to reconcile the Japanese to us in that area rather than to the Russians. It might thus, I pointed out, be the means of preventing what our policy demanded, namely, a sympathetic Japan to the United States in case there should be any aggression by Russia in Manchuria.

Scholars and laymen have criticized the combat use of the atomic bomb. They have contended, among other points, that the bombs were not necessary to end the war, that the administration knew or should have known this, that the administration knew that Japan was on the verge of defeat and *therefore* close to surrender, and that the administration was either short-sighted or had other controlling international-political motives (besides ending the war) for using the bomb. These varying contentions usually focus on the alleged failure of the United States to pursue five alternatives, individually or in combination, in order to achieve Japanese surrender before using the bomb: (1) awaiting Soviet entry, a declaration of war, or a public statement of intent (already discussed); (2) providing a warning and/or a noncombat demonstration (already discussed); (3) redefining unconditional surrender to guarantee the Imperial institution; (4) pursuing Japan's "peace feelers"; or (5) relying upon conventional warfare for a longer period. These contentions assume that policy makers were trying, or should have tried, to avoid using atomic bombs—precisely what they were not trying to do. . . .

There were powerful reasons why the fifth alternative—the use of conventional weapons for a longer period *before* using atomic bombs—seemed undesirable to policy makers. The loss of American lives, while perhaps not great, would have been unconscionable and politically risky. How could policy makers have justified to themselves or to other Americans delaying the use of this great weapon and squandering American lives? Consider the potential political cost at home. In contrast, few Americans were then troubled by the mass killing of enemy citizens, especially if they were yellow. The firebombings of Tokyo, of other Japanese cities, and even of Dresden had produced few cries of outrage in the United States. There was no evidence that most citizens would care that the atomic bomb was as lethal as the raids on Dresden or Tokyo. It was unlikely that there would be popular support for relying upon conventional warfare and not using the atomic bomb. For citizens and policy makers, there were few, if any, moral restraints on what weapons were acceptable in war.

Nor were there any powerful advocates within the high councils of the administration who wanted to delay or not use the bomb and rely instead upon conventional warfare—a naval blockade, continued aerial bombings, or both. The advocates of conventional warfare were not powerful, and they did not directly oppose the use of the bomb. Admiral Ernest L. King, chief of Naval Operations, did believe that the invasion and the atomic bomb were not the only alternative tactics likely to achieve unconditional surrender. A naval blockade, he insisted, would be successful. The army, however, he complained, had little faith in sea power and, hence, Truman did not accept his proposal. Leahy had serious doubts about using the bomb, but as an old explosives expert who had long claimed that the bomb would never work, he carried little weight on this matter. Surprisingly, perhaps, he did not forcefully press his doubts on the president. Had Marshall plumped for the strategy of stepping up conventional warfare and delaying or not using the bomb, he might have been able to compel a reassessment. He had the respect and admiration of the president and could command attention for his views. But Marshall had no incentive to avoid the use of the bomb, prolong the war, and expend American lives. For him, nuclear weapons and invasion were likely alternatives, and he wanted to avoid invasion. If the bomb was used as quickly as possible, the invasion might be unnecessary and American lives would be saved.

For policy makers, the danger was not simply the loss of a few hundred American lives *prior* to the slightly delayed use of the bombs if the United States relied upon conventional warfare for a few more weeks. Rather the risk was that, if the nuclear attacks were even slightly delayed, the scheduled invasion of Kyushu, with perhaps 30,000 casualties in the first month, would be necessary. After the war, it became fashionable to assume that policy makers clearly foresaw and comfortably expected that an atomic bomb or two would shock Japan into a speedy surrender. But the evidence does not support this view. "The abrupt surrender of Japan came more or less as a surprise," Henry H. Arnold, commanding general of the air force, later explained. Policy makers were planning, if necessary, to drop at least three atomic bombs in August, with the last on about August 24, and more in September. Before Hiroshima, only occasionally did some policy makers imply (but never state explicitly) that one bomb or a few bombs might shock Japan into a prompt surrender: capitulation within a few days or weeks. Usually they were less optimistic, sometimes even pessimistic. They often assumed that the war might drag on after the nuclear attacks. Faced with this prospect, policy makers were unprepared to take risks and delay using the bombs. So unsure was Truman of the likelihood of a speedy surrender after the first atomic attack that he left domestic officials unprepared for the surrender and thereby seriously weakened his stabilization program and lost political support at home. Because policy makers feared that the attack on Hiroshima might not speedily end the war, they continued conventional bombing and also dropped the second bomb. Their aim was to end the war without a costly invasion of Kyushu. According to their analysis, atomic weapons, if employed promptly and combined with conventional attacks, were likely to achieve that goal. Delay was unconscionable, as Stimson later explained.

There have been criticisms of the administration for failing to pursue two other alleged opportunities: (1) redefining the unconditional surrender demands before Hiroshima to guarantee the Imperial institution; (2) responding to Japan's "peace feelers," which stressed the need for this guarantee. Byrnes and apparently Truman, however, were fearful at times that concessions might strengthen, not weaken, the Japanese military and thereby prolong, not shorten, the war. Some critics imply that Byrnes and Truman were not sincere in presenting this analysis and that they rejected concessions consciously in order to use the bomb. That is incorrect. Other critics believe that these policy makers were sincere but disagree with their assessment—especially since some intelligence studies implied the need for concessions on peace terms to shorten the war. Probably the administration was wrong, and these latter critics right, but either policy involved risks and some were very unattractive to Truman.

Truman, as a new president, was not comfortable in openly challenging Roosevelt's policy of unconditional surrender and modifying the terms. That was risky. It could fail and politically injure him at home. Demanding unconditional surrender meant fewer risks at home and, according to his most trusted advisers at times, fewer risks in ending the war speedily. Had his most powerful and trusted advisers pushed for a change in policy, perhaps he might have found reason and will to modify Roosevelt's policy well before Hiroshima. But most of Truman's closest advisers first counseled delay and then some moved into opposition. As a result, he too shifted from delay to opposition. At Potsdam, when Stimson pushed unsuccessfully for providing the guarantee in the proclamation, Truman refused but told Stimson that he would carefully watch Japan's reactions on this issue and implied that he would yield if it seemed to be the only impediment to surrender. After August 10, when Japan made the guarantee the only additional condition, Truman yielded on the issue. He deemed it a tactical problem, not a substantive one. But even then, Byrnes was wary of offering this concession, despite evidence that it would probably end the war promptly—precisely what he wanted in order to forestall Soviet gains in the Far East. . . .

Let us look at the remaining, but connected, alternative—pursuing Japan's "peace feelers." Japan's so-called peace feelers were primarily a series of messages from the foreign minister to his nation's ambassador in Moscow, who was asked to investigate the possibility of having the Soviets serve as intermediaries in negotiating a peace. American intelligence intercepted and decoded all the messages. Most, if not all, were sent on to Potsdam, where Truman and Byrnes had access to them. Both men showed little interest in them, and may not even have read all of them, apparently because the proposed concessions were insufficient to meet American demands and because Truman and Byrnes had already decided that the peace party in Japan could not succeed until American attacks—including atomic bombs—crushed the military's hopes. The intercepted and decoded messages fell short of American expectations. Not only did Japan's foreign minister want to retain the Imperial institution, which was acceptable to some policy makers, but he also wanted a peace that would maintain his nation's "honor and existence," a phrase that remained vague. As late as July 27, the day after the Potsdam Proclamation, when Japan's foreign minister was planning a special peace mission to Russia, he was still unwilling or unable to present a "concrete proposal" for negotiations. What emerges from his decoded correspondence is a willingness by some elements in Japan's government to move toward peace, their fear of opposition from the military, and their inability to be specific about terms. Strangely, perhaps, though they feared that Stalin might be on the verge of entering the war, they never approached the United States directly to negotiate a peace settlement. For Truman and Byrnes, Japan was near defeat but not near surrender when the three powers issued the Potsdam Proclamation on July 26. When Japan's premier seemed to reject it, the president and secretary of state could find confirmation for their belief that the peace party could not triumph in Japan without more American "aid"—including nuclear attacks.

Given the later difficulties of Japan's peace party, even after the atomic bombings, after Soviet entry, and after more large-scale conventional bombings, top American policy makers could find evidence in the ambiguous record for their assessment that Japan's leaders were not ready to surrender before Hiroshima. More troubling were American policy makers' wartime convictions that any concessions or pursuit of unsure "peace feelers" might stiffen resistance. Most American leaders were fearful of softening demands. War had bred an attitude that any efforts at compromise might indicate to the enemy America's flaccidity of spirit and weakness of will. Toughness, for most policy makers, seemed to promise success.

Looking back upon these years, Americans may well lament the unwillingness of their leaders to make some concessions at this time and to rely upon negotiations before using the bombs. That lament, however, is logically separable from the unfounded charges that policy makers consciously avoided the "peace feelers" *because* they wanted to drop the bombs in order to intimidate the Soviets. It is true that American leaders did not cast policy in order to avoid using the atomic bombs. Given their analysis, they had no reason to avoid using these weapons. As a result, their analysis provokes ethical revulsion among many critics, who believe that policy makers should have been reluctant to use atomic weapons and should have sought, perhaps even at some cost in American lives, to avoid using them.

Truman inherited the assumption that the bomb was a legitimate weapon to use to end the war. No policy maker ever effectively challenged this conception. If the combat use of the bomb deeply troubled policy makers morally or politically, they might have been likely to reconsider their assumption and to search ardently for other alternatives. But they were generally inured to the mass killing of civilians and much preferred to sacrifice the lives of Japanese civilians to those of American soldiers. As a result, they were committed to using the bomb *as soon as possible* to end the war. "The dominant objective was victory," Stimson later explained. "If victory could be speeded by using the bomb, it should be used; if victory must be delayed in order to use the bomb, it should *not* be used. So far as . . . [I] knew, this general view was fully shared by the President and his associates." The morality of war confirmed the dictates of policy and reinforced the legacy that Truman had inherited. Bureaucratic momentum added weight to that legacy, and the relatively closed structure of decision making served also to inhibit dissent and to ratify the dominant assumption.

Had policy makers concluded that the use of the bomb would impair Soviet-American relations and make the Soviets intransigent, they might have reconsidered their assumption. But their analysis indicated that the use of the bomb would aid, not injure, their efforts to secure concessions from the Soviets. The bomb offered a bonus. The promise of these likely advantages probably constituted a subtle deterrent to any reconsideration of the use of the atomic bomb. Policy makers rejected the competing analysis advanced by the Franck Committee:

> Russia, and even allied countries which bear less mistrust of our ways and intentions, as well as neutral countries, will be deeply shocked. It will be very difficult to persuade the world that a nation which was capable of secretly preparing and suddenly releasing . . . [the bomb] is to be trusted in its proclaimed desire of having such weapons abolished by international agreement.

Instead, policy makers had come to assume that a combat demonstration would advance, not impair, the interests of peace—a position shared by Conant, Oppenheimer, Arthur H. Compton, Nobel laureate and director of the Chicago Metallurgical Laboratory, and Edward Teller, the physicist and future father of the hydrogen bomb. In explaining the thinking of the scientific advisory panel in recommending combat use of the bomb, Oppenheimer later said that one of the two "overriding considerations . . . [was] the effect of our actions on the stability . . . of the postwar world." Stimson's assistant, Harvey H. Bundy, wrote in 1946, that some thought "that unless the bomb were used it would be impossible to persuade the world that the saving of civilization in the future would depend on a proper international control of atomic energy." The bomb, in short, would impress the Soviets.

In addition, there was another possible advantage to using the bomb: retribution against Japan. A few days after Nagasaki, Truman hinted at this theme in a private letter justifying the combat use of the bombs:

> Nobody is more disturbed over the use of Atomic bombs than I am but I was greatly disturbed over the unwarranted attack by the Japanese on Pearl Harbor. The only

language they seem to understand is the one that we have been using to bombard them. When you have to deal with a beast you have to treat him as a beast. It is most regrettable but nevertheless true.

In this letter, one can detect strains of the quest for retribution (the reference to Pearl Harbor), and some might even find subtle strains of racism (Japan was "a beast"). The enemy was a beast and deserved to be destroyed. War, as some critics would stress, dehumanized victors and vanquished, and justified inhumanity in the name of nationalism, of justice, and even humanity.

In assessing the administration's failure to challenge the assumption that the bomb was a legitimate weapon to be used against Japan, we may conclude that Truman found no reason to reconsider, that it would have been difficult for him to challenge the assumption, and that there were also various likely benefits deterring a reassessment. For the administration, in short, there was no reason to avoid using the bomb and many reasons making it feasible and even attractive. The bomb was used primarily to end the war *promptly* and thereby to save American lives. There were other ways to end the war, but none of them seemed as effective. They would not produce victory as promptly and seemed to have greater risks. Even if Russia had not existed, the bombs would have been used in the same way. How could Truman, in the absence of overriding contrary reasons, justify not using the bombs, or even delaying their use, and thereby prolonging the war sacrificing American lives?

Some who have searched for the causes of Truman's decision to use atomic weapons have made the error of assuming that the question was ever open, that the administration ever carefully faced the problem of *whether* to use the bombs. It was not a carefully weighed decision but the implementation of an assumption. The administration devoted thought to how, not whether, to use them. As Churchill later wrote, "the decision whether or not to use the atomic bomb to compel the surrender of Japan was never even an issue."

In examining American policy for the few months after Hiroshima, scholars have disagreed on whether the United States practiced "atomic diplomacy." Simply defined, this term means the use of nuclear weapons as threats or as bargaining levers to secure advantages from the Soviet Union. Since there were no *explicit* threats, some scholars have dubiously disposed of the problem by comfortably declaring that there was no "atomic diplomacy"—which they define too narrowly by excluding *implicit* threats. That is too simple and avoids important issues. A full investigation of the complex problem of atomic diplomacy requires detailed attention to a number of questions: Did the United States threaten, or seem to threaten, the Soviet Union? Did observers think so? How did the Soviets react and how did observers interpret their reactions? . . .

On August 9, the day that Nagasaki was bombed, the president delivered a national address on the Potsdam meeting. The United States, he declared, "would maintain military bases necessary for the complete protection of our interests and of world peace." The secret of the bomb, he promised, would be retained until the world ceased being "lawless." "We must constitute ourselves trustees of this new force—to prevent its misuse, and to turn it into the channels of service to mankind." He also emphasized that the Balkan nations "are not to be the spheres of influence of any one power"—a direct warning to the Soviet Union. Here was the first, albeit muted, statement of atomic diplomacy: the implicit threat that the bomb could roll back Soviet influence from Eastern Europe.

"In many quarters," Stimson lamented in late August and early September, the bomb is "interpreted as a substantial offset to the growth of Russian influence on the continent." He complained that Byrnes was wearing the bomb ostentatiously on his hip and hoping to use the weapon to secure his program at the September Conference of Foreign Ministers in London. "His mind is full of his problems," Stimson wrote in his diary. Byrnes "looks to having the presence of the bomb in his pocket, so to speak, as a great weapon to get through the thing. . . . " Assistant Secretary of War John J. McCloy concluded, after a long discussion with Byrnes, that he "wished to have the implied threat of the bomb in his pocket during the conference . . . [in London]." This evidence is unambiguous as to Byrnes's intent, and it cannot be ignored or interpreted as misleading. Byrnes had no reason to seek to deceive Stimson and McCloy about his hopes and tactics. Byrnes had no incentive to posture with them or to appear militant, since they opposed his vigorous tactics and instead counseled moderation and international control of atomic energy.

How could the United States employ the bomb in dealing with the Soviet Union? Apparently Byrnes had not decided precisely how to exploit the weapon to strengthen position. He did not explicitly threaten the Soviets but apparently assumed that the weapon itself would be a sufficient, though implicit, threat. Even before Hiroshima, Byrnes and others, including Stimson, had assumed that the bomb would impress the Soviet Union with the need for concessions. The bomb, itself, even without any explicit statements, as Conant told Bush, constituted a "threat" to the Soviet Union. Because Byrnes wanted the bomb's power in negotiations and distrusted the Soviets, he opposed Stimson's plea in September for approaching the Soviets promptly and directly on international control of atomic energy. At the same time, he was urging America's scientists to continue their work to build even more powerful nuclear bombs.

At the London Conference, an uneasy Vyacheslav Molotov, the Soviet foreign minister, twitted Byrnes about America's nuclear monopoly and tried uneasily to minimize its importance. Molotov's humor betrayed Soviet fears. On September 13, three days into the conference, "Molotov asks JFB if he has an atomic bomb in his side pocket. 'You don't know Southerners,' Byrnes replied. 'We carry our artillery in our hip pocket. If you don't cut out all this stalling and let us get down to work I am going to pull an atomic bomb out of my hip pocket and let you have it.' " In response to this veiled threat, according to the informal notes, "Molotov laughed as did the interpreter." Byrnes's barb emphasized American power. A few nights later, after a stormy session during the day, Molotov commented once more, with strained jocularity, that Byrnes had two advantages that the Soviet minister could not match—eloquence and the atomic bomb.

In this period, the Soviets never officially admitted great concern or anxiety about America's nuclear monopoly. They never claimed that it actually constituted a threat to their welfare, and they publicly minimized its strategic value. Presumably they adopted these tactics because they did not want to reveal their fears and encourage the United States to continue atomic diplomacy. They even devised stratagems to suggest that they had also developed the bomb. At the London Conference, for example, Molotov contrived a scene where he "accidentally" let slip the statement, "You know we have the atomic bomb," and then was quickly hustled out of the room by an associate. In November, this time in a national address, he implied that the Soviet Union had nuclear weapons. During this period, as later sources made clear, Soviet scientists were rushing to build the bomb.

Though Soviet officials at this time never publicly charged the United States with conducting atomic diplomacy, the Soviet media carried oblique charges. A Soviet columnist contended, for example, "The atomic bomb served as a signal to the incorrigible reactionaries all over the world to launch a lynching campaign against the Soviet Union." After Truman's militant Navy Day address in late October, Moscow radio charged that the United States was keeping the bomb as part of the American program "to pursue power."

On October 19, J. Robert Oppenheimer complained to Henry Wallace about America's nuclear policy and about Byrnes's attitudes. According to Wallace's diary notes, Oppenheimer "says that Secretary Byrnes' attitude on the bomb had been very bad. It seems that Byrnes has felt that we could use the bomb as a pistol to get what we wanted in international diplomacy. Oppenheimer believes that this method will not work." Oppenheimer, who did not attend the London meeting, did not indicate his source. He had served with Byrnes at some Interim Committee meetings and had later communicated with the secretary on at least a few occasions, so perhaps his conclusion was based upon a conference with Byrnes and knowledge of Byrnes's earlier attitudes. Significantly, Wallace, long a foe of Byrnes on foreign policy, did not challenge Oppenheimer's conclusion. Oppenheimer rightly forecast that the Soviets would rush to build the atomic bomb and that the result would be an arms race. The Soviets, Oppenheimer implied, were worried about their security, and his analysis suggested that they were not unreasonable in being uneasy.

Some British and American observers stressed that the bomb frightened the Soviets and injured Soviet-American relations. The bomb "overshadowed" the unsuccessful London Conference, Prime Minister Clement Attlee told Truman in October. Clark Kerr, the British ambassador to the Soviet Union, explained the growing bitterness of the Soviet Union toward the United States in terms of the bomb. "When the bomb seemed to them to become an instrument of . . . [American policy, the reaction was] spleen." Writing from Moscow, the American ambassador, W. Averell Harriman, outlined a similar diagnosis:

> Suddenly the atomic bomb appeared and they recognized that it was an offset to the power of the Red Army. This must have revived their old feeling of insecurity. . . .

The combat use of the bomb against Japan added weight to American demands for freer elections in Eastern Europe and may have helped bring about some Soviet concessions—especially delay of the scheduled election in Bulgaria in August and a broadening of the multiparty ticket there to enlarge the representation of noncommunist groups. When the American public and Congress compelled partial demobilization after the war, the bomb constituted a valued counterweight to the large armies that policy makers mistakenly thought the Soviet Union possessed. The military use of the bomb, policy makers presumably assumed, provided some credibility that the United States might use it again, in still undefined situations against the Soviet Union.

Though the bomb strengthened American policy and partly compensated for reductions in conventional forces, Truman had private doubts about whether he could use atomic weapons against the Soviet Union. On October 5, in talking with Harold Smith, his budget director, the president worried about the international situation and that the United States might be demobilizing too fast. "There are some people in the world who do not seem to understand anything except the number of divisions you have," he complained. Smith replied, "You have the atomic bomb up your sleeve." "Yes," Truman acknowledged, "but I am not sure it can ever be used." He did not explain his thinking, but presumably he meant that, short of a Soviet attack on Western Europe or on the United States, the American people, given the prevailing sentiments of late 1945, would not tolerate dropping atomic bombs on the Soviet Union. Certainly, they would not then countenance the military use of the bomb to roll back the Soviets from Eastern Europe. Few Americans then cared enough about Eastern Europe or were willing to endorse war against the Soviet Union. The bomb, rather than conferring omnipotence on the United States, had a more restricted role: it was a limited threat. Perhaps partly because of popular attitudes, policy makers felt restrained from employing explicit threats. Implicit threats, however, may have seemed equally useful and have allowed more flexibility: Policy makers were not committed publicly to using the bomb as a weapon in future situations.

Did the bomb make a critical difference in shaping the early Cold War? Roosevelt's repeated decisions to bar the Soviets from the nuclear project and Truman's decision to use the bomb in combat without explicitly informing the Soviet Union and inviting her to join in postwar control of atomic energy undoubtedly contributed to the Cold War and helped shape the form that it took. Yet, in view of the great strains in the fragile wartime Soviet-American alliance, historians should not regard America's *wartime* policy on the bomb as *the* cause, but only as one of the causes, of the Cold War. The wartime policy on atomic energy represented one of a number of missed opportunities at achieving limited agreements and at testing the prospects for Soviet-American cooperation on a vital matter.

The atomic bomb, first as prospect and then as reality, did influence American policy. The bomb reduced the incentives for compromise and even stiffened demands by the time of the Potsdam meeting in July 1945 because the weapon gave the United States enhanced power. Without the bomb, policy makers probably would have been more conciliatory after V-J Day in dealing with the Soviet Union, especially about Eastern Europe. The president certainly would have been unable to try to use atomic diplomacy (implied threats) to push the Soviets out of Eastern Europe. Rather, he might have speedily, though reluctantly, agreed to the dominance of Soviet power and to the closed door in that sector of the world. The bomb, as potential or actual weapon, did *not* alter the administration's conception of an ideal world, but possession of the weapon did strengthen the belief of policy makers in their capacity to move toward establishing their goal: an "open door" world with the Soviets acceding to American demands. This ideal world included free elections, an open economic door, and the reduction of Soviet influence in Eastern Europe. Without the bomb, the Truman administration would not have surrendered these ultimate aims, but policy makers would have had to rely primarily on economic power as a bargaining card to secure concessions from the Soviet Union. And economic power, taken alone, would probably have seemed insufficient—as the record of lend-lease and the Russian loan suggests.

The atomic bomb was the most important weapon in the American arsenal, but its promise proved to be disappointing, for it did not make America omnipotent. It did not allow her to shape the world she desired, perhaps because in 1945–1946 neither policy makers nor most citizens were willing to use the bomb as a weapon to "liberate" Eastern Europe, a section of the world that was not then deemed worth war or the risk of war.

Without the bomb, in summary, American policy after V-J Day would have been more cautious, less demanding, less optimistic. Such restraint would not have prevented the breakdown of the Soviet-American alliance, but probably the cold war would not have taken the form that it did, and an uneasy truce, with less fear and antagonism, might have been possible.

Stalin's Inexorable Aggression

VLADISLAV ZUBOK AND CONSTANTINE PLESHAKOV

First, what was in the minds of Stalin and his closest subordinates in 1945–6 and later, when confrontation became more and more likely? How did they understand Western conduct and motives, and which Western reactions did they miscalculate? Among the cases often mentioned in this regard are the Baruch plan on atomic energy, Churchill's Iron Curtain speech, the Truman Doctrine, the Marshall Plan, and the Berlin blockade.

Second, were there missed opportunities for accommodation with Stalin and his successors? Did the West over-react—or under-react—to Soviet attempts to consolidate their war gains? Several episodes come to mind here: Soviet policies in Iran and Manchuria (1946), Stalin's plans for Eastern Europe (1945–6), the Moscow meeting of foreign ministers (March 1947), Stalin's proposals to reunify Germany (spring 1952) and the Malenkov–Beria peace initiative (spring–summer 1953).

Third, was Soviet conduct in the Cold War a result of the monolithic totalitarian drive, involving ideology and the leader's whims, or was it shaped by diverse forces and interests, for instance party ideologues vs. technocrats, security vs. army, and the like? Some authors believed Stalin chose the wrong policy in 1945–6; others argue that he, and [Nikita] Khrushchev in the years of crises, reacted to domestic challenges.

From Vladislav Zubok and Constantine Pleshakov, "The Soviet Union" in David Reynolds, ed. *The Origins of the Cold War in Europe,* pp. 56–68 and 73–74, 1994. Reprinted by permission of Yale University Press.

Besides, new sources suggest a set of new issues, that had not attracted enough attention from Western historiography, mostly for lack of evidence. Among these issues are:

1. The effectiveness of US and Western actions in the early Cold War. Did they help to curb Soviet expansion, or did they rather contribute to siege mentality, in other words helping to prolong the totalitarian regime and the cold war? How exactly did American policies (containment, psychological warfare, "secret wars" in the third world) affect the Kremlin's conduct?
2. The consequences of the Soviet Union's dual communist/imperial commitments. To what extent were Soviet policies in the Cold War a product of the Kremlin's hegemony in the communist movement? Or were they a reflection of the tyranny of the weak, that is pressures from near-to-collapse satellites like East Germany?
3. The totalitarian state and its policies in the Cold War. Were the Soviets inefficient in the cold war, as in the economy, or had they certain advantages (such as "party," as well as "state," means of foreign policy, superior intelligence and total secrecy, ruthless military administration in satellite countries), that helped them wage it for so long? How comparable were the Cold-War structures in Western democracies and the totalitarian Soviet state?

Before we begin our analysis, however, a few words of definition are required. The Cold War was unique as an international confrontation that was not merely bipolar but also global, in which nuclear weapons played a distinctive role as both the potentially explosive and ultimately stabilizing force. The *Cold War* should be distinguished from the *Cold-War Era*. The former lasted roughly from 1948 to 1962 and was characterized by its intense military fever, culminating in the Cuban missile crisis. What ensued was a prolonged armistice in which, at the same time, both sides extended their tentacles, particularly into Latin America and Africa. But neither Vietnam nor Afghanistan provoked a military stand-off on the scale of Cuba. As for *the roots of the Cold War:* ideologically it stemmed from the 1917 revolution in Russia, geopolitically from the Second World War, which left the USA and USSR in positions of dominance, and technologically from the atomic revolution of 1945.

This triad—Bolshevik revolution, the Second World War, and the nuclear era—was absolutely central for the genesis of the Cold War as the main structural phenomenon in international relations since 1945. Yet structure is not everything: history is about people. And no one was more important in the origins of the Cold War than Josef Vissarionovich Dzugashvili—known to history by his revolutionary pseudonym of "Stalin," man of steel.

Stalin's mind is a riddle. All men are divided by psychology into extroverts and introverts. Extroverts enjoy talking before the crowds; they are the darlings of newspapermen; they leave diaries; they write outspoken books like *Mein Kampf;* never afraid of revealing their real self, they insist on stenographers being present; they freely develop their ideas even before strangers. Introverts are different: they try to destroy every evidence of their earthly ways; their speeches, talks and books are carefully formulated; they always want to sound nice, always in accordance with the norms of morality of a certain group. When they reveal their real self they are like snails, ready any time to withdraw into the shell. They are simultaneously shy and fierce about their ego: shy to reveal it, fierce to protect.

That is why we should not expect too much from the Soviet sources concerning Stalin, the supreme introvert. Could there possibly be solid evidence on the state of Stalin's mind? So, when one comes to the task of analyzing Stalin's mentality, one has no other way but to collect the pieces of evidence from all sides, disbelieving most of them, some of Stalin's remarks included.

Some leaders devote their career to one major axis of ideas. However complicated their life pattern is, it develops around this particular axis. But other leaders are different; they move along several axis. To be more precise by changing the metaphor: some planets in the universe rotate around more than one sun. Stalin's planet was exactly of that kind. It had two suns: the sun of revolution and the sun of empire.

The two ideas—world revolution and empire—did not contradict each other at all. What, after all, was the ideal of communists? A universal state with total domination over the globe, a world without borders; in short, an unprecedented empire. Marxism was imperial by its nature. A true Marxist state must long for an imperial status, otherwise it does not have a *raison d'être*, it is doomed to be a satellite, and its government will be hated by the people. Only the idea of building the empire can arouse people's enthusiasm and provide revolutionaries with a decent task. Numerous apostles of world revolution would become lieutenants of the empire, its backbone. That is why Stalin was successful in bringing the ideas of revolutionary eschatology (death of the old world and birth of the new one) and imperial glory together. Stalin viewed himself not only as a founder of a new—Soviet—empire, but also as an heir of the empire which had seemingly collapsed—the Russian empire.

Self-identification with the great heroes of the past was crucial for Stalin. The heroes he had subconsciously chosen were Lenin and Russian tsars. Self-identification with Lenin was first studied by Robert C. Tucker, who described it as a heroic self-image. Tucker was also the first to identify Stalin as a neurotic. This Lenin fixation demanded acts of revolution, surpassing those of Lenin himself. Karen Horney in her fundamental book [*Neurosis and Human Growth*, 1950] wrote: "The neurotic's self-idealization is an attempt to remedy the damage done by lifting himself in his mind above the crude reality of himself and others." The deeds of self-heroization were enacted in the international arena, where Stalin at last put the theory of world revolution into practice, as well as inside the country.

There was one very important component in Stalin's mind: aversion to everything foreign. His brief stay in Vienna in 1913 (unlike other Bolshevik leaders he never spent much time abroad) became a trauma for him: lonely, isolated, surrounded by a hostile world. Of course Vienna was not the cause; the cause lay in Stalin's soul, because interaction with the outside world demanded a certain openness, a relaxed nature—qualities unknown to Stalin. The trauma of Vienna was very strong. Together with envy towards others (like Lenin, Trotsky and Bukharin), who felt themselves equally free in the tsar's gaol or in a Geneva café, it gave birth to a pronounced inferiority complex. That inferiority should have been displaced; the easiest way was clear—xenophobia. But the xenophobia of Stalin was not that of a prudent tyrant; it was the xenophobia of a neurotic. Stalin was therefore displacing a deep inferiority complex in a primitive and not very effective way. Such displacement only made the inferiority complex deeper and more painful. Only later, on becoming a member of a narrow circle of world leaders, did Stalin succeed in getting rid of it, and then only for a short period of time.

Every person has his own reference group, people whose opinion is important for him. A person usually does not care about everybody ("How can they understand me?"), but there are people whose respect he seeks. For Stalin petty apparatchiks [Communist party secretaries] like [V. M.] Molotov and [L. M.] Kaganovitch did not count; inferior in all senses, they were just puppets in his hands. He looked for his reference group abroad. Only important leaders like Hitler, Roosevelt and Churchill mattered. Of course, Hitler must have intrigued Stalin most of all; he must have felt that they shared a good deal. Who else but Hitler could understand a leader like Stalin? But interaction with Hitler was brief and never personal, notwithstanding the fact that in 1939–40 it had brought the best fruits of expansion one could ever wish for. That said, co-operation with the leaders of Britain and the United States proved to be very satisfactory in the psychological sense. The atmosphere was relatively relaxed; the Big Three behaved as a group with specific relations between the members, with common memories, even with jokes that only they could understand. At last Stalin had found the company of equals. It was an extremely important motive that pushed him towards post-war co-operation. In some sense this motive was the summing up of his "human evolution," with all its complexes. As Karen Horney wrote of the neurotic personality: "Nobody can function, or even live, under such conditions. The individual must make, and does make, automatic attempts at solving these problems, attempts at removing conflicts, allaying tensions, and preventing terrors."

The hypothesis that Stalin was displacing certain complexes, looking for a specific comradeship among the Big Three, does not mean that the relationship among them was ideal. Stalin had his doubts about his partners. In 1944 he told [the Yugoslav emissary] Milovan Djilas, pointing at the map of the Soviet Union: "They will never accept the idea that so great a space should be red, never, never!" Nevertheless Stalin enjoyed redistributing spheres of influence, with Churchill in particular in October 1944, when they were deciding the exact percentage of Moscow's and London's influence in post-war Eastern Europe.

So this psychological motive was pushing Stalin towards accommodation with the West. There were also more practical considerations. After all, the Big Three were engaged in a large-scale redistribution of spheres of influence during the War and afterwards. The process did not go all that smoothly, but in general one is struck by a spirit of mutual understanding in this imperialist circle: liberal Roosevelt, venerable anti-communist Churchill, communist Stalin. An imperialist fraternity was uniting them all, and the West was acknowledging Soviet predominance in Poland, the Baltics, Eastern Europe in general. Was it only the result of the Red Army's strength? No, because the allies had effectively recognized the Soviet conquests of 1940 long before Soviet victory in the War became a certainty.

Stalin knew it and he was prepared to co-operate with the West after the War. Taking into consideration Stalin's dependence upon archetypes, one can suggest that he was influenced by the archetype of the Vienna Congress of 1815, with himself as Alexander I (1801–25) and perhaps Churchill as Metternich? There is at least one piece of evidence that his self-identification with Alexander I as archetype was clear to Stalin himself. When he was asked by [Averell] Harriman whether it felt good that he was dividing Berlin only several years after Germans had been standing at the walls of Moscow, Stalin replied that "Tsar Alexander had reached Paris."

In the speech that is usually regarded in the West as the proclamation of the Cold War on 9 February 1946, Stalin actually proposed a specific model of peaceful coexistence. He said: "It might be possible to avoid military catastrophes, if there were a way of periodically reapportioning raw materials and markets among the countries according to their economic weight—taking concerted and peaceful decisions." He added: "But this is impossible to fulfil in contemporary capitalist conditions of world economic development." This was an awkward reference to Western values, as he understood them. But the American embassy in Moscow overlooked this point. When he spoke about raw materials and markets, he must have meant reapportionment of spheres of influence; but many in Washington regarded his speech as a declaration of Cold War.

Stalin's rape of Eastern Europe preceded the Cold War and, as many argue, triggered it. Stalin did not understand the difference between the swallowing of eastern Poland, the Baltics, and eastern Prussia, on the one hand, and the construction of "friendly" regimes in Poland and Czechoslovakia, on the other. And in terms of moral and international law there really was not any difference. What moral or legal argument underpinned the decision to give eastern Prussia to Stalin? Presumably, to punish Germany and to deprive it of a bridgehead in Eastern Europe. As a result, to Stalin, Western protests against changes in Eastern Europe and other regions seemed just a political game; by approving the earlier Stalin gains, the West lost the moral ground to protest against further expansion of the Soviet empire.

Today most historians speak about lost opportunities in the Cold War. But when one thinks about the real lost opportunities in 1945–8, the probable hypothesis is—the West was not firm enough, it did not check Stalin's imperial expansion.

In categories of "good guys" and "bad guys" Stalin was indisputably a bad guy in the Cold War. But he was also a bad guy during the Second World War and before it—and the good guys had actually encouraged him to go on being bad, for they needed his strength and also found themselves under the evil spell of totalitarianism. Stalin was allowed to feel that he was good when he was occupying eastern Prussia and preserving the lands conquered before the War. Then, suddenly, he became bad, without obvious reasons. He felt betrayed by former allies. But he was not prepared to wage the Cold War (that is, open confrontation without much diplomatic coverage) until 1948. Probably the coup d'état in Czechoslovakia in February of 1948 and the Berlin crisis that began four months later were the first battles of the real Cold War, when no compromise was hoped for, and when Stalin was waiting only for the contradictions in the Western camp to ripen and lead to another war in which, he hoped, imperialism would be buried. According to Molotov, Stalin had constructed a strict logical chain: "The First World War had pulled one country out of the capitalist slavery. The Second World War has created a so-cialist system, and the Third will terminate imperialism once and for all."

His policies in the East displayed the same evolution—from cautious waiting to the promotion of expansion. In 1945–7 Stalin was not in a hurry to support Mao Zedong, the leader of a relatively independent and undoubtedly strong revolution-ary communist movement. As long as there was a possibility of coming to terms with the Americans, he was not going to ruin the fragile balance between the Na-tionalist Guomindang and the Chinese communists. He still preferred official rela-tions with the Guomindang government of Chiang Kai-shek [Jiang Jieshi], though by revolutionary logic he should have denounced Chiang as a puppet of the imperi-alists. Even Chiang's pro-Western policies, of which Stalin was being constantly reminded by his agents in China, did not change his mind. After Stalin's death Mao complained to Pavel Yudin, Soviet Ambassador in Beijing:

> In the last period . . . Stalin also made wrong estimates of the situation in China and of the possibilities of revolutionary development. He continued to believe more in the Guomindang's strength than in the Communist Party [of China]. In 1945 he insisted on peace with Chiang, on the common front with the Guomindang and the creation of a "democratic republic" in China. . . . In 1947 . . . when our troops were winning victo-ries, Stalin insisted on striking a peace with Chiang, because he doubted the strength of the Chinese revolution.

Only in 1948, anticipating trouble in future, did Stalin reluctantly give a firm hand-shake to Mao Zedong.

Here we must ask ourselves a question: how was the Eastern front of the Cold War connected with the Western, in Stalin's eyes? Stalin, as well as most other So-viet leaders, was Eurocentric and, more precisely, German-oriented. His major ambitions and challenges lay westward. In part, this was because his psychological archetypes of glory and national interest were linked with Europe (the Middle East was one notable exception). Just like the Russian empire before, he had not re-garded his vast provinces in Siberia and in the Far East as of extraordinary value. The geopolitical utility of the Far East seemed to Stalin of minor importance. Even if he was eager to take part in Japan's defeat and conquest, he readily relinquished his "right" to occupation in exchange for Western acceptance of Soviet dominance in Romania and Hungary.

Stalin was developing expansion in Europe and adjoining regions with vigour and persistence, unlike in the Far East. Yet, ironically, he had a much more power-ful natural ally in China than in Iran or even Greece. Had Stalin's imperialist aspi-rations been not much influenced by psychological archetypes, he would have used the opportunity to project his influence in the Far East, not in 1948–9 but at least three years earlier. Instead he was prepared to give China, Korea and Japan to the Americans as their share in the post-war division of the world, whereas in Eu-rope he longed to take as much as he could.

It is not true, of course, that geopolitical considerations in the Far East were a matter of total indifference for Stalin in 1945–7. He was influenced by the same imperialist dreams that had pushed Russian tsars; he desired to re-establish spheres of influence lost by Russia under Nicholas II (1894–1917). There were other historical parallels. The Russian empire had turned its attention to the Far East only when the European powers made further expansion in Europe totally impossible. Similarly, Stalin switched his attention and his efforts to the Far East only when American power had stopped his expansion in Europe. Even when the Cold War developed into a global confrontation and then erupted into an open conflagration in Korea, its core, from Stalin's viewpoint, always remained in Europe, not in Asia.

The period from the fall of 1947 to the spring of 1948 was a kind of turning point for Stalin. The sun of world revolution seemed to rise again—as was reflected in the last works of Stalin. There he tried to present a concept of a post-war world. Churchill, wrote Stalin, became a warmonger. He and his friends exhibited "a striking resemblance to Hitler and his friends." Billionaires and millionaires regarded war as a source of profits. "They, these aggressive forces, hold in their hands reactionary governments and guide them."

Stalin expatiated again and again about the general crisis of capitalism. He insisted on the collapse of the world economy: "One should regard the disintegration of the single integral world market as the most important economic result of the Second World War and its economic consequences." He admitted that after the War two prophecies had proved invalid: his own, on a "relative stability of markets during the general crisis of capitalism," and Lenin's conclusion that, despite the crisis, "capitalism in general is growing faster than before."

Stalin seemed not to understand the nature of the epoch in which he was living, especially its major characteristic—bipolarity. He still thought in routine categories of the pre-Cold-War history and was sure that the new war was inevitable. Stalin did not see a future war as a conflict between socialism and capitalism: a repetition of the scenario of 1937–9 seemed more probable in his eyes. He wrote:

> Some comrades make a mistake when they say that "contradictions between the socialist camp and capitalist camp are stronger than contradictions between capitalist countries, that the United States of America has subjugated other capitalist countries enough, stopping them waging wars with each other and weakening each other. . . ." Wouldn't it be wiser to say that capitalist England, and then capitalist France will in the end have to break away from the USA, embrace and venture a conflict with it in order to secure independent policy and of course high profits? . . . To think that . . . [West Germany and Japan] would not try to become independent, to break away from the U.S. "regime" and rush to the road of independent development—means believing in miracles.

He believed Germany would be again a major European power, with Great Britain and France as a poor match. Even earlier, in 1945, he warned Yugoslav communists that the Germans were not "finished":

> No, they will recover, and very quickly. That is a highly developed industrial country with an extremely qualified and numerous working class and technical intelligensia. Give them twelve to fifteen years and they'll be on their feet again. And this is why the unity of the Slavs is important.

He regarded the Cold War as something really emanating from the West, which had ignored his good will; one of a series of confrontations with imperialism which was to be resolved one day in conflict.

It would be a simplification to say that the Cold War was Stalin's choice or his child. He did not want it. He regarded it not as a logical consequence of his politics, but as a deliberate Western policy. He did not consider swallowing one country after another as something really capable of causing the crisis; he took it as his legal share. This process is known in psychology as externalization: "I am not hostile to others; they are doing things to me."

For all its historical roots, then, Stalin's imperialism was not a simple continuation of the Russian imperial tradition. It represented an externalization of his power-hungry ego. Examining a post-war map, Stalin revelled in the new borders of the Soviet Union. "Let's have a look at what has turned out. . . . In the North everything is all right. In the West everything is all right. . . . But here I don't like our borders!"—and Stalin pointed to the region to the south from the Caucasus. In fact, the borders of the tsarist empire and its spheres of influence had been completely restored. The vassal states formed a huge Eurasian belt of which the tsars could not even have dreamt—Eastern Europe and Eastern Asia. It was too much even for Molotov. Although he said in 1975: "It is good that the Russian tsars gained so much land for us. Now it is easier for us to fight capitalism," he regretted Stalin's claims to Turkey; his imperialism was more down-to-earth, that of a book-keeper, not a semi-deity. He admitted: "In the last years Stalin began to get a swelled head."

Stalin's hyper-inflated ego might help explain why sometimes he tried to trangress all the traditional limits of Russian imperialism. Molotov recalled with a certain bewilderment:

> Libya turned out to be necessary for us. Stalin says: "Go ahead, push!" . . . At one of the meetings of the foreign ministers I declared that the national-liberation movement had appeared in Libya. But it is pretty weak, we want to support it and to build our military base there.

Stalin even played with the idea of regaining Alaska from the United States. . . .

To a far greater degree than in any other state . . . the foreign policy of the Soviet Union was the creation of its leader. Central though Stalin's mentality is to our understanding of the Cold War, however, we cannot stop there. In its external policy after 1945 the USSR was acting simultaneously as a "normal" state playing international politics, as the centre of a revolutionary international party, and as an occupying power administering vast new territories. It is the interplay of Stalin's mind with these three sets of systemic imperatives which takes us to the heart of the Soviet Cold War.

There was a popular story among the veterans of the Second World War: when the Red Army met the American forces at the Elbe river, Marshal [Grigori] Zhukov insisted that the Soviets should continue the victorious march further to the West. But Stalin objected. Had he agreed, the Red Army allegedly would have reached the Channel in two weeks.

Stalin had a better chance of achieving predominance in Europe without war, using the multi-tiered foreign policy of a totalitarian great power. On the level of "state" foreign policy, that is relations with the Allies, he made certain commitments at Yalta and Potsdam. He came all the way to please the Americans on the United Nations: the UN Statute, written with direct Soviet participation, was a direct precursor of [Mikhail] Gorbachev's new thinking in international relations. With an obvious Stalin nod, Maxim Litvinov, Molotov's rival and architect of "collective security" in the 1930s, turned out many position papers aimed at the revival of his old designs of collective security.

The "party" level became less prominent in Kremlin foreign policy with Stalin's dissolution of the Comintern in 1943. The Comintern's staff, however, stayed in the International Department of the Central Committee and its branches: the Sovinformburo, the Jewish Anti-Fascist Committee, and a number of secret institutes. This department, together with the department of Agitation of Propaganda, continued to collect information from the communist and "progressive" network abroad. The network's low profile concealed high expectations Stalin had in 1945–6 about communist politics in Western Europe, especially in Italy and France. In a triumphant mood, Stalin told German communists that "there would be two Germanies, despite all the unity of the Allies." In a struggle for his Germany he planned to act through the unified KPD or Communist Party of Germany.

There was a third level of Stalin's foreign policy, dealing with the countries and territories liberated, defeated and/or occupied by the Red Army. Some Politburo members were appointed by Stalin to supervise the countries of the Soviet sphere of influence in Eastern Europe—from Finland (Zhdanov) to Romania (Vyshinsky). From the start a Soviet style of consolidation of new regimes in Eastern Europe implied a special role for native communists: most of them had lived in Moscow since the 1930s and returned in the rearguard of the Red Army under Soviet instructions. Among them were members of the Lublin Polish government, Walter Ulbricht in East Germany, Matyas Rakosi in Hungary, Anna Pauker and Georgiu Dej in Romania, Georgy Dimitrov in Bulgaria, and so on. Stalin, in conversation with Milovan Djilas, a Yugoslav communist, suggested that these countries must be up for socialization, with the help of the Soviet military administration. In fact, this approach was adopted by Soviet military administrators not only in Eastern Europe, but in northern Iran and North Korea. Yet in 1945 Moscow hoped to bring communists to power by parliamentary intrigues: either in alliance with agrarian parties against social democrats, or together with social democrats against the peasant parties. The directives to expel the non-communists and to eliminate the rudiments of parliamentary democracy came two years later.

The relationship between these three levels of Soviet foreign policy depended, largely, on how Stalin assessed the changing international situation. When his regular state diplomacy did not satisfy him, he turned to a party level, increasingly associated with his subordinate Andrei Zhdanov, Secretary and Politburo member. The underlying goals, though, were always, unmistakably imperial. Molotov, a chief engineer of Stalin's foreign policy, put it in historical perspective:

> Stalin used to say that [tsarist] Russia won wars, but could not enjoy the fruits of its victories. Russians are remarkable warriors, but they do not know how to make peace; they are duped, fobbed off. So I think, after this war, we scored a success, we built up the Soviet state. It was my major task . . . so that nobody would dupe us. Here we tried hard and, I believe, results were not bad.

In 1945 and later all three levels were used to create the most favorable correlation of forces, which Stalin judged was crucial for the consolidation of his post-war empire. Initially the interstate, ally-to-ally relations were considered as important as the overtly imperial policies. Stalin agreed to sign the Yalta Declaration on Liberated Europe only because "it was to our advantage to keep intact an alliance with America."

In early 1945 Stalin had a number of reasons to think that the correlation of forces was changing in his favour:

1. American foreign policy was determined by Franklin Roosevelt, who hated British imperialism. He was also prepared to withdraw American forces from Europe in two years and wanted to co-operate with Stalin as one of "global policemen" under the aegis of the United Nations;
2. he believed that the United States could not defeat Japan without the Red Army;
3. Eastern Europe and East Germany were safely locked in the Soviet sphere;
4. in Italy and France communists had marvellous chances to come to power; in the rest of Western Europe the popularity of the Soviet Union was at its peak;
5. many believed that the world role of the United States would be crippled by a serious economic crisis and that America would seek an escape in isolationism;
6. Stalin had the world's best intelligence service and could look at opponents' cards while keeping his hidden.

By early 1947 Stalin was obliged to correct these assessments. The United States did not intend to resume its pre-war role in the world. Roosevelt was replaced by Truman. Imperialist contradictions between America and Britain were buried in an Anglo-Saxon alliance, increasingly dominated by the United States. Roosevelt's line was defeated in domestic politics by what one Soviet diplomat called the "bloc of reactionary Southern Democrats and the old guard of the Republicans." Stalin helped the polarization a great deal by his insistence on bigger reparations from Germany and the dismantling of the Ruhr coal and steel industries, by his claim to have a role in Japan's occupation, by miscellaneous probes around the Soviet periphery (Turkey and the Straits, Iran, Manchuria) and even *démarches* outside the traditional Russian sphere of influence such as in Libya. Litvinov, frustrated and isolated, suggested that the West should be tougher with Stalin and Molotov. His complaints were overheard by the secret police, and must have triggered Stalin's anger and Litvinov's later assassination.

In late 1945 and during 1946 Stalin clearly overplayed his hand. Military triumphs by the Red Army boosted his hubris to classical dimensions. It was at this stage, as Molotov admitted, years later, that Stalin toyed with the plans to retrieve Alaska and get control over the Turkish straits—the dreams of Great Russian imperialists. Most of those plans were clearly not feasible and were not pursued. But they characterised the state of mind and mood in the Kremlin at that time; and they scared many in the West.

Several factors contributed to Stalin's intransigence and arrogance. The atomic bomb placed in doubt the Soviet military role in the defeat of Japan and raised Truman's morale. In Stalin's eyes it shattered the correlation of forces. This conclusion was borne out by the awkward attempts of Secretary of State James Byrnes to practise, momentarily, atomic diplomacy. Stalin instructed Molotov to undercut Byrnes's policy and personal credentials during the Allied negotiations. Consequently, the Soviets behaved as if the atomic bomb had not existed.

The striking contrast between the Soviet economy and the economic might of the United States also, ironically, made Stalin more, not less, arrogant. He refused to negotiate any American credits with strings attached. Participation of the Soviet Union in international economic cooperation and rehabilitation of Europe could reveal Soviet weakness or allow America to put its foot into the Soviet door. The Soviets waited for the world economic crisis to extract from the capitalists what they wanted, on their own terms.

American pragmatic disengagement in Eastern Europe, manifested in the Harriman-Stalin deal in October 1945, along with unexpected American pressure on the Soviets in Iran, must have confirmed Moscow's belief that American foreign policy was dictated by mercenary, traditionally imperialist interests such as Arab oil. This also contributed to Molotov's horse-trading and to the diplomatic impasse.

Finally, the Soviets initially had a clear edge over the Western powers in filling an enormous political vacuum inside the former Third Reich. Soviet military administration in Eastern Germany (SVAG) launched a client party of Socialist Unity (SED), uniting communists with some social-democrats. In 1946, while the Social Democratic Party (SDP) and Christian Democratic Union (CDU) were still weak, SED and its trade unions attempted to win political control over the whole of Berlin and to make inroads into Western zones. The economic situation, especially food, in the Soviet zone was better than in the West. Efficient combination of party and occupation means seemed to guarantee an edge to the Soviets in Germany and could have encouraged Stalin to be self-confident in his conversation with U.S. Secretary of State George Marshall in Moscow in April 1947. "When the partners exhaust each other," he argued, "a moment will come for possible compromises."

The Soviet boycott of the Marshall plan was a turning point towards the Cold War: state diplomacy was virtually buried; not only ideas of co-operation, but even a traditional diplomacy of balancing among powers were all abandoned in favor of bipolar confrontation ("two camps"). Party foreign policy triumphed for a while in Soviet relations with both Western and Eastern Europe. With regard to the latter it dominated even over the common-sense needs of occupation policies. This led to the rise of Andrei Zhdanov and Nikolai Voznesensky and to the eclipse of Molotov, Lavrenti Beria, Georgi Malenkov and Anastas Mikoyan, who had run foreign affairs on a routine basis in 1945–6. Molotov, along with most state agencies that were interested in foreign credits, initially planned to join the European recovery program. Only after he sensed Stalin's mood did he make a U-turn and oppose the participation in the Marshall plan.

Most historians now agree that Stalin miscalculated. Did he expect that both Western and Eastern Europe would knuckle under to his bull-like pressure? Zhdanov and later Molotov presented the Soviet reaction as a great counteroffensive and, in general, a great success. But Khrushchev recalled that after the war the leaders in Moscow had expected that economic chaos in Western Europe would reach "the point of a revolutionary explosion." Intervention by the powerful economy of the United States came as a great evil from two angles: it led to defeats for Western communists and it cushioned a future (and inevitable) economic crisis overseas. The next fear was a reunification of Germany under American hegemony.

Using the Cominform (September 1947) as a tool, Stalin and Zhdanov sent foreign communists to snatch the chestnuts out of the fire for the Soviet Union. They egged on these collaborators ("you underestimate your strength") to frustrate the Marshall plan by fomenting strikes, nationalism and anti-Americanism. The party foreign policy helped the Soviet Union to gain time, amid the post-war demobilization, for the modernization of its armed forces. At the same time Stalin, in a year of hunger and want, widely used "bread-and-butter diplomacy" to win the Polish, German, Czech and even Italian publics over to the communist side.

All the time the Soviet leadership was confident there was no immediate war threat from the United States, as long as Western Europe was in political turmoil. "America may pull on our leg," explained Malenkov to Italian communists, "but war is out of the question now." Zhdanov agreed that "elements of blackmail prevail over the real war preparations." Even though some in the leadership talked about strangulation of the Soviet Union, the war scare came much later, in 1950–1.

The renaissance of Zhdanov was facilitated, in part, by growing crises in state and occupation policies, particularly in Germany. Throughout 1945–6 the negotiations on German government and Germany unity were deadlocked, and a struggle for the German soul was on. Before long the Soviet military administration and various state agencies ran rough-shod over traditional socio-economic structures in the Eastern zone; by February 1947 all military plants were transferred to the Soviet Union; various "techno-science bureaux" pipelined German technology to the East. In March, however, Stalin decided to step up a campaign for restoration of a unified German state: not only to be in better position to press for reparations without Allied interference, but also aiming at German nationalism.

One option was to transform SVAG (Soviet military administration in Germany), "with its orders and peremptory commands, to a more flexible system, closer to civilian government." Another was to introduce a combination of party and occupation means to create a satellite East German regime. During 1947 the entrenched interests of the military and the East German communists coincided with Stalin's growing belief in the latter option. Gradually the military administration, with Stalin's approval, began to increase control over communications between the Eastern and Western zones—a process that eventually escalated into the Berlin blockade in June 1948.

From this time on Stalin over-reacted to Western hostile designs as he perceived them. He did not regard an Anglo-American bloc or American military expansion as immediate threats. But the addition of Western Germany to the bloc changed calculations drastically: it was seen as a force aimed at the re-acquisition of East Germany, in other words against Soviet imperial interests. Probably nothing could have shaken Stalin out of these convictions, especially since all intelligence after the fall of 1947 reported to him tailored conclusions in a single, centralized voice. . . .

Today, when the Cold War has come to an end through and because of the global retreat and disintegration of the Soviet Union, the question remains—could it have been prevented, stopped at some early stage, or directed into less virulent forms? For those who believe that the biggest victors in the Cold War were Germany and Japan, American strategies in 1945–55 now look short-sighted—"prudent, but not wise," to quote US historian Melvyn Leffler. Hence the search for

missed opportunities to make a post-war peace with Stalin and his regime. Our research, however, has left us in doubt that such opportunities were really present.

Some Western decisions and reactions might have been different, more balanced. But they mattered little to Soviet foreign policy, whose logic and politics (a
political scientist would say "micro-level") had their own dynamics. Of the three
dimensions in Soviet foreign policy (the state, the party and the occupational),
the latter two created a powerful momentum towards autarky and aggressive self-
isolation.

Stalin's personal impact on Soviet foreign policy was great, his peculiarly
dual mind-set as "a synthesizer . . . of the revolutionary and the traditional" pushed
him inexorably up and up in the spiral of confrontation with the West. State relations with the West, despite his early hopes, ground to a halt. American economic
might and nuclear monopoly did not make him cautious but, on the contrary, provoked his arrogance and animosity.

With a Preponderance of Power:
America's Wise, Prudent, and Foolish Leaders

MELVYN P. LEFFLER

At the end of World War II, the United States possessed incomparably more power
than any other nation. Aware of this, U.S. officials hoped to sustain the wartime alliance, transform vanquished enemies into democratic and capitalist friends, and
persuade imperial allies in London, Paris, and the Hague to pursue orderly decolonization policies on the periphery. If friends as well as foes could be convinced of
the beneficent character of a liberal capitalist multilateral order, U.S. officials believed that the world would enter a new era of peace and harmony and that the
United States would recover its traditional sense of safety from external threats.
All of this seemed possible because, so long as there was an open world order hos-
pitable to the free flow of capital and goods, no nation could control sufficient resources to jeopardize U.S. security. In fact, quite the opposite was the case.
America's surplus capital, comparative advantage in the production of goods,
abundant supply of raw materials and foodstuffs, and huge domestic market would
lure the world into a U.S.-led orbit. All the United States needed to do was to become the world's financial and economic hegemon. And this role the U.S. government appeared willing to perform, as illustrated by its leadership in creating the
International Monetary Fund and the World Bank, its generous lending and relief
actions, and its self-professed commitment to lower tariffs and to offer most-
favored-nation treatment.

The vision of a cooperative multilateral international order was an attractive
one. Having learned the bitter lessons of the interwar era, the United States would
join the United Nations and play a constructive role in the international economy.
In so doing, policymakers would enhance U.S. security, promote its economic in-

Reprinted from *A Preponderance of Power* by Melvyn P. Leffler, pp. 496–516, with the permission of
the publishers, Stanford University Press. © 1992 by the Board of Trustees of the Leland Stanford Junior University.

terests, and disseminate its ideals while serving the world community and advancing the well-being of all humankind.

It was a wonderful vision, but it was threatened by four interrelated phenomena. First, the presence of Soviet armies in Eastern Europe and Northeast Asia meant the Kremlin might absorb these areas into its own sphere in order to expedite reconstruction and enlarge its long-term military capabilities. Second, the rise of the left in Greece, Italy, France, China, Korea, and other countries meant that Communists might win or seize power, reject the liberal capitalist multilateralism espoused by the United States, and bring their nations into a Soviet orbit. Third, the demoralization and deprivation in postwar Germany and Japan suggested that leaders might arise who would seek to solve their nations' problems through statist practices, neutralist options, or a Soviet alliance. Countries like Germany and Japan with no democratic traditions might easily gravitate eastward. They could be lured by the enormous markets within the Soviet orbit or duped by hopes of regaining territory and national autonomy that the Kremlin might offer to them. And, fourth, the awakening of nationalist impulses in Southeast Asia, the Middle East, and North Africa made these areas susceptible to the appeal of Marxist ideology. The Leninist theory of imperialism explained away their backwardness while the Soviet model of development through a command economy seemed to promise rapid modernization.

The convergence of these four threats conjured up enormous apprehensions in U.S. policymaking circles. No one could dispute that in the heartland of Eurasia a brutal totalitarian state existed with the capacity to take advantage of the manifold opportunities presented by the postwar world. To what extent Stalin would choose to do so was uncertain. The signals he gave were mixed. But if he tried to exploit prevailing circumstances, Soviet Russia might gradually co-opt, either directly or indirectly, enormous industrial infrastructure, natural resources, and skilled labor. The lessons of the 1930's taught that when totalitarian powers had such resources they used them to challenge vital U.S. interests, attack the United States, and wage protracted war. Even if Stalin did not choose such an aggressive course, the United States would have to prepare for it. And as it did so, it would find itself in an unenviable situation. Increasingly, it would have to regiment its own economy in order to compete and deal with the statist regimes in Eurasia; it would have to raise taxes and boost defense expenditures; and it would have to limit dissent lest Communist sympathizers undermine the country's morale and vigor. Faced with an ominous threat in Eurasia, the United States would have to transform its own political economy and its liberal capitalist system. Even if war never came, the specter of Soviet/Communist expansion threatened to transform the American way of life. And if war did come, Soviet domination of Eurasia might afford it the wherewithal to fight to a stalemate, perhaps even to victory. Of course, none of this would happen quickly. U.S. officials were thinking about worst-case developments over a ten-, fifteen-, or twenty-year period.

Faced with these possibilities, the United States shifted tactics. Initially content with the role of financial hegemon, U.S. officials came to believe that they had to offer economic assistance in amounts they had not anticipated; they had to establish linkages with foreign elites in ways they had not envisioned; and they had to incur strategic commitments and assume political-military responsibilities in places they had not contemplated. These new tactics were deemed essential to establish a configuration of power that safeguarded U.S. security and that institutionalized Washington's preponderant influence in the international system.

The United States moved first to integrate Western Europe, West Germany, and Japan into a U.S.-led orbit. The co-optation of these power centers, however, was considered impossible unless revolutionary nationalism on the periphery was thwarted and unless Third World markets and raw materials were linked to the industrial core areas of Eurasia. The accomplishment of all these tasks required considerable risk-taking. Conscious of their superior warmaking potential and atomic monopoly, U.S. officials initially took the attendant risks without augmenting military capabilities. They bet that the Soviets would seek to avoid a military conflict. But after the Soviets detonated their own atomic device and after the Chinese Communists intervened in the Korean War, U.S. officials felt less and less certain about the shadows cast by the existing military strength of the United States.

They came to believe that ever more weapons were necessary to support the risk-taking that inhered in co-opting the industrial core of Eurasia and in integrating its underdeveloped periphery. So long as Europe was vulnerable to Soviet counteraction and so long as there was a possibility that a Soviet preemptive strike might neutralize America's own arsenal and cripple its industrial infrastructure, the appropriate risk-taking could not proceed. So eventually rearmament became the essential prerequisite to America's diplomatic, economic, and political initiatives. As British and French power atrophied in the Third World, U.S. officials also began to assume responsibility for co-opting the periphery. They prepared to use military assistance, covert actions, and mobile forces to influence local situations while they relied on America's strategic arsenal and NATO's [North Atlantic Treaty Organization] growing conventional capabilities to discourage any Soviet counteraction in Western Europe.

Faced with the reality of Soviet domination in Eastern Europe and the prospective growth of Soviet power throughout Eurasia, America's cold war policies took shape. Looking back, we can see that those policies were partly wise, partly prudent, and partly foolish. Given the imponderables policymakers faced in the international system and the uncertainties about Soviet aims, it is their prudence that seems most striking.

Truman administration officials grasped the nature of the Soviet threat. From the outset, [the experts on the Soviet Union] George Kennan and Charles Bohlen believed that the Soviet Union was fundamentally weak and would not engage in premeditated aggression. Notwithstanding Soviet Russia's huge comparative military superiority over other Eurasian countries, either defeated or weakened by World War II, the men in the Kremlin were purported to have an enormous respect for America's superior warmaking capabilities as well as its atomic monopoly. Even if the latter did not intimidate Stalin, as some Soviet experts like Jonathan Haslam and Adam Ulam contend, the Soviet ruler was believed to have a healthy respect for the capacity of the United States to turn out steel, coal, and machines, all of which could be converted in wartime to the manufacture of tanks, planes, ships, munitions, and bombs. It could be assumed that the Russians' awareness of their relative weakness vis-à-vis the United States would encourage them to move cautiously. When faced with U.S. determination, they would back down.

Not only did U.S. officials show a shrewd understanding of Soviet weaknesses, but they also understood Soviet strengths. The Soviet threat resided principally in the Kremlin's capacity to exploit economic vulnerabilities, capitalize on social dislocation, and take advantage of the nascent nationalism that was astir in the Third World. Communist ideology and statist solutions seemed to be alluring not only to peoples in the industrial core who, in a 30-year period, had endured two world wars and a great depression but also to peoples in the Third World who aspired to gain control over their own destiny, excise their colonial masters, and modernize their countries. Policymakers in Washington understood that their principal task was not to deal with Russian military power but to fill the vacuums of power, infuse a spirit of hope, promote economic reconstruction, and champion the principle of self-determination without compromising vital interests. By 1947 they also came to recognize that they would not have the resources to do all these things at the same time. The magnitude of the problems abroad and the intensity of the partisan struggle at home circumscribed available funds and compelled tough choices.

In selecting priorities, Washington policymakers again showed their grasp of economic and geostrategic realities. They understood that they had to turn their attention initially to the industrial core areas of Western Europe. State Department and Pentagon officials agreed that they had to thwart Communist gains and Soviet influence in France and western Germany. Revitalizing the German economy was the key to fostering economic growth and eroding Communist strength in neighboring countries. They recognized that, by providing massive economic aid designed to boost productivity, they might help the West Europeans overcome the payments deficits that encouraged statist solutions, bilateralism, and autarky. They correctly believed that open markets would fuel worldwide economic growth. And though the Marshall Plan demonstrated their willingness to assume the role of hegemon, U.S. policymakers shrewdly understood that it would be self-defeating to dictate solutions. Insisting on self-help and mutual aid, they established linkages with European elites and permitted them considerable flexibility in setting priorities. Europeans had only to rebuff Soviet overtures, resist indigenous Communists, and accept America's hegemonic role in the international economy.

Critical to the success of U.S. reconstruction efforts in the industrial core areas of Eurasia was occupation policy, particularly in Germany and Japan. Here again, U.S. officials wisely recognized that neither the American people nor the Germans or Japanese would be receptive to long and harsh occupation. To the chagrin of America's other wartime allies, reparations were scaled down or canceled, occupation controls lightened, and responsibilities shifted to local administrators. The emphasis on labor reform and industrial decartelization swiftly changed to economic growth, commercial expansion, and conservative fiscal practices. Instead of punishing wartime criminals and instituting progressive social reforms, occupation officials turned more of their attention to forging mutually rewarding linkages with moderate business elites and conservative reformers. The goal was to co-opt German and Japanese power by demonstrating to local elites that their national aspirations could be fulfilled within a U.S.-led orbit. Dean Acheson, Robert Lovett, John McCloy, John Foster Dulles, and their friends believed that the lessons of the Versailles peace treaty and the Weimar years in Germany taught that concessions should be made to moderate leaders before demagogues on the right and left seized on the grievances of the masses to infuse their countries with a virulent nationalism.

Policymakers in Washington also shrewdly understood that the revival of German and Japanese power agitated America's other friends in Europe and Asia, endangered their security, and posed considerable risks to the international community. Once controls were lifted, autonomy restored, and sovereignty returned, no one could really be certain of what would happen. Germany and Japan might become peaceful, stable, democratic, and prosperous participants in the international system, or they might be afflicted with economic woes, social discontent, and political division. They might collaborate with the United States, or they might choose to pursue nationalist goals either alone or in combination with the Kremlin. To reassure America's allies and to maintain leverage over dangerous future scenarios, Acheson extracted promises and commitments from [German chancellor] Konrad Adenauer and [Japanese prime minister] Yoshida Shigeru that they would not pursue independent foreign policies. More important, Truman administration officials decided to retain U.S. (and Allied) forces in Germany and to maintain bases in Japan. Furthermore, they helped to forge the NATO and the Australia–New Zealand–U.S. alliances, both of which were designed not simply to deter the Soviets but also to convince ambivalent allies to go ahead with the risks that accompanied Germany's and Japan's revival.

More than security guarantees were necessary to reassure wartime allies and co-opt former enemies. The Truman administration supported sophisticated supranational institutions that were designed to channel and absorb the energy and talent of the Germans and Japanese into constructive pursuits that bulwarked a U.S.-led anti-Soviet coalition. In Europe, France assumed the initiative in proposing these mechanisms, like the Organization of European Economic Cooperation, the European Coal and Steel Community, and the European Defense Community. French foreign minister Robert Schuman and Jean Monnet hoped to harness German economic and military power for the good of the larger European community. Officials in Washington warmly applauded these efforts. At the same time they worried that, in the long run, these institutions might encourage West Europeans to become a third force or to pursue policies independent of the United States. Consequently, U.S. officials focused more of their own attention on developing NATO as an institutional device to insure U.S. leadership and to preserve cohesion within an Atlantic community that periodically would be afflicted with its own centrifugal forces.

Behind this sophisticated strategy rested the conviction that, if the United States could successfully co-opt the industrial core of Eurasia, it would establish a magnet to attract the Kremlin's satellites westward. Here, too, U.S. policymakers demonstrated a sagacious understanding of the intensity of nationalist feelings in Eastern Europe and of the tenuous nature of Soviet controls. The Truman administration never conceded Eastern Europe to the Russians. For the moment, it was a low priority. But these men understood that they were fashioning strategies for the long run. If they were successful in co-opting the industrial core and integrating that core with the underdeveloped periphery, they would demonstrate the superiority of Western liberal capitalist institutions, create a flourishing international economy, and demonstrate the bankruptcy of Soviet economic as well as political and ideological leadership.

The magnet, however, would only work if the industrial core prospered within the U.S.-led multilateral economy. The geopolitical configurations of power to which contemporary officials attributed such great importance depended on sound economic foundations. Western Europe, western Germany, and Japan would not long accept U.S. leadership if they did not prosper. And the split between the so-called free world and the slave world, which U.S. policies accelerated after 1947, initially made it more difficult for the industrial core areas to prosper if they accepted the multilateral norms of open trade and capital movements that U.S. officials deemed so important. Indeed the division of Europe accentuated the payments problems of European friends because they were cut off from traditional markets and raw materials in Eastern and Central Europe and had to replace them with supplies from the Western Hemisphere and markets in the Third World. Likewise, Mao's [Mao Zedong's] seizure of power and U.S. wariness about Japanese trade with the Chinese mainland underscored the need for the Japanese to find markets and raw materials elsewhere. Policymakers in Washington demonstrated an incisive awareness of these problems. They did not insist that their allies immediately comply with the multilateral rules they championed. While pressing their allies to boost productivity, limit domestic consumption, and welcome the economic benefits that inhered in Germany and Japan's rehabilitation, the Americans did what they could to ease the difficult transition. The United States not only provided the dollars and the security safeguards but also encouraged the development of cheap raw materials and foodstuffs in the Third World and sought to foster the growth of markets abroad and (less successfully) to reduce tariffs at home.

In understanding the nature of the Soviet threat in the early postwar years, in grasping the economic foundations of geopolitical success, in forging ties with moderate elites, in modulating the severity and duration of occupation regimes, in acquiescing to large doses of national autonomy within an overall integrationist strategy, and in supporting supranational mechanisms of control, Truman administration officials manifested sagacity, sensitivity, and wisdom. Of course, none of this would have been possible if the United States did not have the wealth and power to offer economic aid and strategic guarantees. Money and security were of decisive importance to governments and peoples who were wavering in 1946–47 between alternative strategies of development and who were as wary about Germany and Japan as they were about Soviet Russia. But U.S. policymakers' judicious use of power to support farsighted objectives that had the support of people abroad as well as at home was what made them wise.

Prudent officials take calculated risks. Operating on given sets of assumptions and beliefs and with finite information, they seek to advance national interests and avoid worst-case scenarios. For the prudent and powerful men who made U.S. policy in the aftermath of World War II, the worst case involved another totalitarian adversary gaining direct or indirect control of Eurasia and mobilizing its resources against the United States. To avoid this specter, Truman administration officials were willing to accept moderate costs and intermediate dangers if they were reasonably confident that short-term sacrifices could be translated into long-term gains. They were prepared, if necessary, to break with the Kremlin, avoid negotiations, grant financial aid and strategic guarantees to allies, and even run the risk of war so long as they thought that such initiatives would stave off a redistribution of power that would seriously jeopardize U.S. security. Ultimately, their policies were successful, but flawed assumptions and beliefs drove up the costs of their efforts. Of course, this is clearer in retrospect than it was at the time; contemporaries saw great imponderables, felt very vulnerable, and thought they were acting prudently by building situations of strength.

All this became most apparent in late 1946 and early 1947, when Truman administration officials decided they had to seize the initiative in Western Europe, Germany, and Japan notwithstanding the prospective impact of their actions on the Soviet Union. Ever since the war ended, they had determined that Soviet power must not extend beyond the reach of Russian armies of occupation. And although Soviet policies were not uniformly aggressive or expansionist, neither were they conciliatory and reassuring. The Soviet threat loomed ever larger because the prospective termination of U.S. assistance to Europe, the possible withdrawal of U.S. troops from Germany, and the anticipated negotiation of an early peace treaty with Japan portended a huge shift in the balance of domestic forces in those countries as well as in the international configuration of power.

From the perspective of Washington, the situation in Europe seemed especially fraught with peril. Despite impressive figures of macroeconomic growth, the persistent shortages and hardships, coupled with new retrenchment measures, created a volatile situation. On one level, the trend backwards toward bilateralism and regimentation was ominous. More frightening still was the anticipated capacity of Communists to capitalize on the expected economic slowdown and ensuing popular disillusionment. . . .

The prudent men in Washington in 1947 wanted to stymie economic retrogression and Communist political gains. Already they had promised military assistance to Greece, fearing that a Communist victory there would have a bandwagon effect on the rest of Europe. U.S. officials believed that Communist-dominated governments would eagerly sign bilateral accords with the Kremlin and thereby orient their countries eastward. Should this occur, the political and diplomatic influence that might have otherwise emanated from the infusion of U.S. capital and the export of U.S. goods would never materialize. France and other countries might gravitate into the Soviet orbit. And once this occurred, the U.S. capacity to oversee the occupation of Germany would be nullified. The Germans, too, would join the bandwagon heading eastward. Gradually, the Kremlin would gain control, however indirectly, over the industrial core of Western Europe.

Prudent men aware of the wealth and power of the United States could not allow such worst-case scenarios to unfold. Hence, in the spring of 1947, they went on the offensive, proclaiming the Truman Doctrine and announcing the Marshall Plan. They championed increases in Germany's level of industrial production, supported the formation of a German government within the western zones, and promised to guarantee France's frontiers against future threats. These actions were intended to promote U.S. national security by thwarting bilateralism, fostering productivity, co-opting western Germany, and promoting West European integration within a U.S.-led orbit. The United States acted as hegemon: providing the aid, helping to establish the basic guidelines, and offering the security guarantees.

Substantial risks inhered in this course of action. U.S. officials were altogether aware that their initiatives would antagonize the Soviets, intensify the emerging rivalry, and probably culminate in the division of Germany and of Europe. Their intent was *not* to provoke the Kremlin, but they recognized that this result would be the logical consequence of their actions. The Americans were caught in the classic security dilemma whereby the steps deemed essential to promote their own security clashed with the security imperatives of the adversary. The Soviets, seeing Communists excised from the governing coalitions in Western and Southern Europe, fearing a loss of influence in Eastern Europe, and frightened by the specter of German reconstruction under Western auspices, would surely strike back.

Truman administration officials were willing to accept a rupture in the Soviet-U.S. relationship because they were convinced that the dangers of inaction greatly exceeded the risks that inhered in provoking the Soviets. Simply stated, the cold war and the division of Europe were regrettable prospects but not nearly so ominous as the dangers that inhered in economic contraction, autarkical trends, Communist gains, and the prospective erosion of U.S. influence throughout the industrial core of western Eurasia. The Soviet response might be vile, but Soviet capabilities were limited. Soviet actions would be circumscribed if the United States acted with sufficient resolve and imagination. Surprised by the Soviet blockade of Berlin, U.S. officials momentarily feared the possibility of war and wondered whether, in fact, the Soviets would acquiesce to Western initiatives. But Truman and his advisers would not retreat from Berlin, repudiate the London agreements, or abandon their efforts to co-opt German strength. And when Stalin did not interfere with the airlift, U.S. policy triumphed. The diplomatic, economic, and political actions necessary to create a configuration of power compatible with U.S. security interests did provoke the Kremlin, but the shadows cast by U.S. warmaking capabilities and atomic monopoly also deterred the Soviets from escalating to the threshold of full-scale war.

The calculated risk-taking of the prudent men who occupied the highest offices in the Truman administration turned out to be a great success. But some of the assumptions undergirding this risk-taking were not altogether wise. In early 1947, for example, U.S. policymakers not only magnified the negative aspects of the proliferating bilateral agreements but may have also overestimated the adverse economic consequences of the exchange crisis under way.

More significantly, they sometimes exaggerated the capacity and at other times the willingness of indigenous Communists to take their countries into the Soviet orbit. Until the summer of 1947, Communist parties beyond the Soviet sphere usually abided by democratic norms and, while respectful of the Communist motherland, nevertheless operated somewhat independently of Soviet control. Local Communists often feuded among themselves and could not always discern what Stalin wanted them to do (and for good reason, since he probably had not made up his own mind). If they had won majority control by their own means, and if the United States had not threatened them, they would have had little incentive to keep their countries in the Soviet orbit. They would have seen, as did the Yugoslavs, that the Kremlin placed its needs ahead of their own and sought to exploit them. And when they perceived this reality, they would have probably demanded, as did Tito and his comrades, respect and equality. This is because European

Communists outside of Eastern Europe, despite their deference to Moscow's pre-eminent position, also possessed nationalist loyalties. Given their grass-roots support—for example, in France and Italy—and given their distance from Soviet occupation armies, had they won power freely it is not likely that they would have accepted the Kremlin's priorities and ensconced themselves happily in the Soviet orbit, as U.S. officials feared.

But even if local Communists took office and chose to collaborate with the Kremlin, would other countries have joined the bandwagon, as U.S. officials assumed would be the case? Kennan popularized the bandwagon concept and no-body disputed it at the time. But it was based on dubious assumptions. Govern-ments do not fall like dominoes. Seeking national autonomy and security, they are as likely to balance perceived threats as they are inclined to bend with them, so long as there is some prospect of outside assistance. This was clearly illustrated in the reaction of many West European countries to the Czech coup in February 1948. In retrospect, therefore, it seems likely that U.S. officials underestimated the re-siliency of nationalist impulses throughout Western and Southern Europe while they exaggerated the appeal of Soviet communism.

The penchant to overstate the Kremlin's leverage was particularly apparent in the way U.S. policymakers dealt with Germany. They were forever fearful that the Germans would turn eastward, ally with the Soviets, or be co-opted by them. Ger-mans did grow unhappy with the Allied occupation, but their antipathy toward the Russians and toward communism far outmatched any reservations they may have had about the Americans and their reconstruction policies. Particularly after the Berlin blockade, German sentiment against the Soviets hardened. When Germans were asked whether they preferred a West German government or a united Com-munist Germany, the overwhelming majority opted for the former. Even among Social Democrats a significant group of dissenters objected to Kurt Schumacher's affinity for neutralism. Much of this was apparent in 1952, when the majority of West Germans showed little enthusiasm for Stalin's unification proposal. Nor were they interested in trade with the East if it conflicted with U.S. wishes. In short, U.S. analysts wildly exaggerated the prospects of a German-Soviet coalition.

Of course, we do not know what would have happened if the United States had operated according to a different set of beliefs and assumptions and had not seized the initiative in the spring and summer of 1947. Surely, the course of postwar his-tory would have been different. But in what ways? With the power of hindsight we can see that sound foundations for economic recovery had been laid, that the left was neither so united nor so bound to Moscow as previously thought, that the lure of Eastern markets was not so great as assumed, and that the demoralization of conservative elites was not so advanced as U.S. officials thought. Yet without the marginal help offered by the United States, the worst-case scenarios in the minds of prudent men in Washington *might* have unfolded. Although their fears were ex-aggerated, they were not irrational. Their intent was to minimize dangers and take calculated risks. And the risks that inhered in the efforts to thwart indigenous Communists, rebuild Western Europe, and co-opt German and Japanese power seemed much smaller than the risks that existed in trying to work out cooperative solutions with a totalitarian power whose aims were unclear and whose ability to capitalize on systemic vacuums and internal weaknesses appeared substantial.

Theoretically, one could argue that a policy of reassurance might have worked. For example, [the historian] Anders Stephanson has recently suggested that it might have been possible to fashion a German settlement based on reparations from current production. But even the advocates of a strategy of reassurance acknowledge that it is a treacherous and high-risk policy when the overall balance of power is at stake, as it was in Central and Western Europe between 1946 and 1948. Rather than take such risks, rather than seek compromise and accommodation (as Walt Rostow suggested in 1946 and General Lucius Clay advocated in 1947), the men who made the final decisions in Washington decided that it was more prudent to cultivate situations of strength. However nastily the Soviets might respond in the short run, they would bow to power realities in the long run. They would learn to acclimatize themselves to a configuration of power that insured America's preponderance.

But the configuration of power envisioned by U.S. officials was increasingly defined in ways that distorted the importance of the Third World, underestimated the local sources of conflict, and exaggerated the relevance of strategic arms and the conventional military balance in Europe to developments on the periphery. For all their wisdom and prudence, Truman administration officials, like policymakers everywhere, made significant errors.

They attributed excessive value to the Third World. The periphery was important because it contained valuable base sites (for example, in Egypt) and raw materials (for example, in Iran and Saudi Arabia). But far more significantly, the periphery was considered of vital importance because policymakers believed that the industrial core areas of Eurasia might be lured into the Soviet orbit if they were not effectively integrated with markets and resources on the periphery. When the Marshall Plan was launched and the decisions to rehabilitate the German and Japanese economies were made, officials assumed that the advanced industrial countries of Eurasia would need to save dollars by procuring supplies of foodstuffs and raw materials in Africa, the Middle East, and Southeast Asia (rather than in North America). Likewise, they also assumed that the advanced industrial countries would have to earn dollars by competing more effectively in Third World countries and by repatriating profits from overseas investments in those areas. Not surprisingly, when U.S. policymakers became alarmed during 1949 that the Marshall Plan might end before European payments difficulties were solved, and when they realized how resistant Congress was to lowering barriers to foreign foods, they became ever more determined to preserve stability and thwart the rise of revolutionary nationalism on the periphery. Otherwise, Japan, West Germany, and Western Europe might be enticed to look to the Eastern bloc for the markets and raw materials they so desperately needed.

Officials assigned much too much importance to the role of the periphery in solving the payments problems of industrial core areas. Once Japanese and German industrial recovery got under way, these countries developed the capacity to earn dollars to pay for indispensable imports. Despite all the rhetoric about the critical importance of Southeast Asia to Japanese, British, French, and Dutch rehabilitation, there is little reason to think that this area played a decisive role in the economic performance of the advanced industrial core areas. U.S. officials underestimated the latent vitality of European and Japanese industrial producers and the magnitude of trade that would develop between the industrial core countries themselves. By the late 1950's, for example, trade between Japan and Western Europe was growing far more quickly than trade between Japan and Southeast Asia. In fact, neither exports to nor repatriated earnings from any particular country or specific region in the Third World was of decisive importance in solving the dollar-gap problems of industrial core countries, nor nearly so important as America's invisible imports and overseas military expenditures. As it turned out, the underdeveloped periphery was only of marginal importance in sustaining the economic dynamism of advanced industrial core areas, despite the overall importance of export-led growth.

Of course, imports of raw materials and especially of fossil fuels became critical to the economic well-being of European economies and particularly that of Japan. Cheap Middle Eastern oil fueled the economic resurgence of Western Europe and Northeast Asia. But U.S. fears that somehow this area would fall into the clutches of the Kremlin were exaggerated. Revolutionary nationalists like Mohammed Musaddiq had no affinity for the Russians. Nor did the Soviets have the capacity, the need, or the will to purchase and transport Persian Gulf oil. U.S. officials themselves acknowledged these facts. Musaddiq wanted to sell Iranian oil to the West. The problem was that the British did not want to purchase it unless they could be guaranteed an exaggerated price for its nationalization and future control over its marketing. British intransigence, not indigenous revolutionary nationalism or aggressive Soviet probing, endangered access to Persian Gulf oil. And, elsewhere in the Third World, the Eastern bloc showed little desire to purchase raw materials or to invest capital in the modernization of underdeveloped economies.

U.S. officials exaggerated the ability of the Soviet Union to capitalize on the rising tide of nationalism in the Third World and incorrectly assessed the relationships between most Third World Communists and Moscow. Although policymakers in the Truman administration did possess an acute appreciation of the intensity of nationalist feelings in Southeast Asia, the Middle East, and North Africa, they foolishly believed that Communist leaders in these areas had a greater loyalty to Moscow than to their own countries. Nowhere was this more true than in Indochina, where the case for Ho Chi Minh's subservience to the Kremlin was always assumed rather than proved. Ho's popularity was acknowledged, but his initial overtures to the United States were rebuffed and his subsequent struggle against the French won no support. In fact, America's growing indirect embroilment in the war against the Viet Minh was motivated not simply by the exigencies of winning French compliance with U.S. policies in Europe but also by the indiscriminate anticommunism that generally characterized U.S. policy everywhere in the Third World. While sensitive to nationalist impulses, the Truman administration desired orderly decolonization and did not want Third World areas to escape the control of the West. Acheson, for example, urged the French to reform but did not want them to withdraw from Indochina.

The effort to divide Communists from Moscow, the so-called wedge strategy, was pursued belatedly or not at all. Only after Tito broke with the Kremlin did he win any support from the Truman administration. Until the rift became public, U.S. officials had not the slightest notion of the difficulties plaguing Yugoslav-Russian relations. They exaggerated the salience of ideological ties and subordinated the importance of nationalist aspirations among Communist leaders. Of course, after the rupture, U.S. officials pondered the possibilities of a similar rift between Mao and Stalin. Much as they privately grasped the potential for such a break, they did rather little to encourage it. Worse yet, their public speeches and declarations greatly reinforced popular notions about the subservience of all Communists to the whims and commands of the Cominform's leaders in Moscow. The great bulk of available evidence suggests that, elsewhere in the Third World, U.S. officials wanted to isolate, discredit, and eliminate Communist factions rather than maneuver to loosen their alleged ties to Moscow or to convince them of the openness of U.S. policy.

So obsessed were U.S. officials about the Communist threat in Third World areas that they frequently confused revolutionary nationalism and indigenous discontent with externally supported Communist movements. A good example of this was in the Philippines. Inept and corrupt leadership inspired the resurgence and growth of the Huk insurrection in the late 1940's and early 1950's. U.S. officials correctly excoriated the government in Manila for its incompetence and corruption. Yet at the same time policymakers in Washington alleged that the Huks were the stooges of either the Russian or the Chinese Communists. Such accusations were unproven at the time and remain highly dubious to this day. The Huks did not receive aid from the Kremlin. Indeed, neither the Russians nor the Chinese showed much interest in the Huk insurrection. Yet policymakers in Washington assumed the existence of such external support, feared it, and embraced repugnant and repressive regimes in order to counter it.

Throughout the Third World, the United States established linkages with discredited elites who, in the pursuit of their own ends, were willing to work with the Americans (as they had often with the British and French). With regard to the Middle East, for example, U.S. policymakers acknowledged the rising tensions between emerging urban groups and traditional leaders. With equal understanding, analysts recognized the burgeoning unrest in the countryside where demands for agrarian reform were growing. Truman administration officials dwelled on the need for change and then concluded that they must nevertheless work with the very elites who were threatened by such reforms. Fear of upsetting the status quo that comported with Western interests exceeded the desire for progressive change, the consequences of which remained unclear. Increasingly, the Americans felt they could do a better job than the British and the French because they were not handicapped by the colonial image that tarnished their European friends. But as they moved into Third World countries, they found themselves supporting unpopular leaders like Mohammad Reza Pahlavi in Iran and Bao Dai in Vietnam.

Not only did U.S. officials align themselves with leaders of questionable popularity and with groups resistant to progressive change, but they vested these countries and these regimes with importance disproportionate to their true value. As the British and French hold on these areas eroded in the late 1940's, as their payments problems and those of Germany and Japan appeared to be insoluble, and as the U.S. Congress seemed unwilling to open American markets and to disperse additional economic aid, Truman administration officials grudgingly and foolishly concluded that the United States had to become the world's policeman as well as its financial hegemon. This thinking did not simply mean that the United States would increase its mobile forces and covert capabilities. In fact, the enormous increment in strategic weapons in the United States and the substantial buildup of conventional weapons in Europe were largely prompted by concerns with prospective Soviet gains on the periphery. The Soviets, thought [Policy Planning Staff Director] Paul Nitze, wanted to fish in troubled waters. In turn, the United States had to shore up the periphery and counter Soviet probes. If necessary, Washington had to be prepared to dominate the escalatory process and to deter Soviet counteraction against Western Europe. . . .

It is no accident that, subsequently, most of the nuclear alerts occurred over crises in the Third World. During Truman's presidency, U.S. officials rarely, indeed almost never, expected the Kremlin to engage in premeditated aggression in Europe. A Soviet invasion might indeed occur, but most likely as a result of a cycle of action and reaction in which the Russians would misjudge the degree of the Americans' commitment to bolster their own or their allies' interests on the periphery. The Soviets, therefore, had to be convinced that they could not conquer Western Europe, preemptively cripple America's retaliatory capabilities, or fight a global war to a stalemate. Once convinced of these realities, the Kremlin would learn to defer to U.S. leadership in the Third World.

The thinking underlying this strategy was flawed. The relationships of costs to benefits and of costs to risks appear to have been totally out of proportion to the interests that were at stake. A willingness to risk atomic war over the periphery misconstrued the intrinsic value of even the most important of these countries and misjudged the prospective behavior of neighboring states. For if nations tend to balance rather than band, if they tend to respond to outside threats rather than fall like dominoes, as the political scientist Stephen Walt contends, then even the "loss" of northern Iran or all of Iran would not justify the use of atomic weapons. Yet Acheson, Nitze, and their associates talked as if they should be ready to run the risk of an escalatory cycle over much less significant interests—for example, those in Southeast Asia.

Of course, policymakers never intended to use atomic weapons over disputes in these peripheral areas. By multiplying the arsenal and casting huge military shadows, U.S. officials believed they would never have to employ the very military capabilities they sought to deploy. But how large did the arsenal really have to become to have this effect? Was there anything in Soviet behavior to suggest that they would run the risk of global war over interests in the Third World? Stalin was a monstrous person who treated his own people with utter brutality, yet he was anything but a large risk-taker in the international arena. Unfortunately, U.S. officials convinced themselves that the size of the nuclear balance decisively shaped the settlement of political conflicts in the Third World. Yet this assumption itself was a dubious one. Case studies suggest that the balance of strategic weapons rarely influences the outcomes of crisis situations. And, in fact, there is little reason even to think that Soviet risk-taking has been primarily inspired by their growing atomic or nuclear capabilities.

When the crunch came, of course, Truman administration officials themselves never dared to use atomic weapons. They were prudent men. Indeed, overall they were more prudent than wise and more prudent than foolish. So they, too, realized that it would be erroneous to the point of criminality to use atomic weapons over a Third World country. They might threaten their use, as their successors did by triggering a number of nuclear alerts, but it is hard to believe that they would have used them in rebuffing Communist inroads or Soviet gains in any Third World area. [The scholar] John Mueller and [the policymaker and writer] McGeorge Bundy, therefore, are right in arguing that policymakers wasted large sums of money in building up stockpiles of offensive weapons that had little purpose. For prudent men to have attributed so much importance to the periphery, for them to have possessed such exaggerated notions of Soviet capabilities in the Third World, and for them to have invested so heavily in strategic overkill was foolish indeed.

The type of risk-taking in which U.S. officials wanted to engage on the periphery and the magnitude of military capabilities they sought to deploy would have been justified only if the Russians intended to seek world domination. For the most part, Truman administration officials attributed such desires to the Kremlin. And in this respect U.S. policymakers made another significant error. Greatly fearing the appeal of Communist ideology to the war-devastated and disillusioned peoples of industrialized Eurasia and dreading the allure of Soviet propaganda to captive peoples in the colonial world, U.S. officials confused the ideological tenets of Marxist-Leninist thought with the actions and behavior of Soviet leaders in the Kremlin. Policymakers in Washington misconstrued Communist aspirations with Russian intentions and capabilities. Seeing before them a potentially strong totalitarian adversary with an apparently attractive ideology, Truman administration officials refused to acknowledge that their foe, however duplicitous and cruel, had far-reaching security requirements of its own.

Although the documents are still not available to determine the motivations and objectives of Soviet foreign policy, it is clear that Russian behavior was not consistently aggressive. At the end of the war, Soviet leaders must have been sorely tempted to exploit a uniquely favorable position. Their armies dominated Eastern Europe and much of Northeast Asia. Germany and Japan were defeated. Communist partisans were at the peak of their popularity in most of the countries formerly occupied by the Axis powers. And in important parts of the Third World, nationalist leaders were struggling to resist the reimposition of European imperial control or to throw it off. Yet Stalin and his colleagues did not avail themselves of all the opportunities that lay before them. They did consolidate their hold over their immediate periphery in Poland, Romania, and Bulgaria; they did maneuver for greater influence in Germany and request participatory control in Japan; they did probe in Iran and make demands on Turkey; and they did rhetorically support the nationalist struggles of Third World peoples. But the Soviets also demobilized their armies and withdrew from important areas. In 1945 and 1946 they pulled their troops out of northern Norway and Bornholm, Denmark, established acceptable governments in Austria and Finland, allowed free elections in Hungary and Czechoslovakia, discouraged revolutionary action in France, Italy, and Greece, endeavored to maintain acceptable relations with the Chinese Nationalists, and evacuated their forces, however belatedly, from Iran and Manchuria.

Soviet cooperative actions were not disinterested. To the extent that the Russians maintained friendly ties with the Americans (and the British), they could hope to secure loans and reparations and avoid the political and military costs of renewed rivalry with their wartime allies. Most of all, maintenance of the wartime coalition constituted the key to averting the prospective revival of an aggressive Germany and a bellicose Japan. These countries were Russia's traditional enemies.

Germany, in particular, as Michael MccGwire has argued, was seen by Stalin as the foremost security danger to long-term Soviet interests. Through collaborative action with its wartime allies, the Soviet Union might be able to control Germany's resurgence by extracting reparations, regulating its industrial production, and overseeing its political reorientation. On the other hand, a rupture of the grand alliance could undermine the Kremlin's ability to monitor Germany's future position in the international arena. This development could be particularly dangerous if the Americans withdrew politically from Europe, as was expected, and if the Germans escaped from the control of the wartime victors, as they had managed to do after World War I.

Yet much as they might have had incentive to cooperate with the Anglo-Saxons, the Russians could not do so at the expense of their most vital security imperatives. Hence they could not comply with U.S. conditions that they accept popular elections, self-determination, open trade, and the free flow of capital in the countries on their immediate periphery. Nor could they satisfy U.S. demands that they defer reparation payments and provide raw materials and foodstuffs to the western zones of Germany. Free elections would lead to the emergence of hostile governments on Russian borders. Open trade would draw its East European neighbors into a Western orbit. Two German invasions within a generation dictated the essential need for a buffer zone. The Poles could not be trusted; they had collaborated with the Germans during part of the 1930's, joined in the dismemberment of Czechoslovakia in 1938, seized part of Lithuania in 1939, and sought to regain territory that the Kremlin had taken for itself. Nor could the Russians count on the good faith of the Hungarians, Romanians, or Bulgarians, all of whom had collaborated directly or indirectly with the Nazis. And if Stalin had deferred to U.S. policy in Germany, he would have found himself sacrificing Russia's economic and strategic imperatives in order to reduce the burden on the U.S. and British treasuries and to expedite West European recovery. Given the devastation Soviet Russia had endured at the hands of the Nazis and given the uncertainties about Germany's future that prevailed everywhere, it was unreasonable to expect any Russian leader to comply with such priorities.

Soviet actions during 1945 and 1946 were contradictory. The Russians showed some restraint but not enough to allay U.S. fears. In fact, those apprehensions grew for reasons independent of Soviet behavior. The Kremlin had rather little to do with the worsening exchange crisis in Western Europe, the growing insurrections in Greece and China, the popularity of Communist parties in France and Italy, the economic paralysis in western Germany and Japan, and the rise of nationalism in Indochina, Indonesia, Egypt, and India. Yet these phenomena portended a great erosion in the strength of the Western democracies and in the capacity of the United States (and Great Britain) to uphold a balance of power on the Eurasian land mass that was preponderantly favorable to U.S. (and British) interests. So the United States felt the need to take the initiative. The Truman Doctrine, the Marshall Plan, and the London agreements regarding Germany were the decisive steps leading to the collapse of the wartime coalition.

Soviet actions were reactive. The establishment of the Cominform, the strikes and demonstrations in France and Italy, the coup in Czechoslovakia, and the blockade of Berlin were responses to the Western offensive. U.S. and British officials acknowledged this truism at the time. The most standard work on Stalin's U.S. policy, ably written by a decidedly nonrevisionist scholar, accepts this interpretation. The challenging question, therefore, is not whether U.S. actions exacerbated Soviet-U.S. relations but whether they were intelligent responses to the real and perceived dangers that existed at the time, including Stalin's maneuvering, previous Soviet gains, and the portentous developments both in the industrial core and on the periphery.

However one answers this question, and we shall return to it in a moment, it is clear that after 1947–48 the Soviets were on the defensive. They faced profound security dilemmas. At best, the revitalization of the western zones of Germany and the formation of the Federal Republic adumbrated the creation of a viable West European economic community and a formidable Atlantic alliance, spearheaded by the Americans. At worst, the restoration of German strength portended the reestablishment of an independent power in the center of Europe intent on territorial rectification and unification. This threat, as has been described, was no figment of the Russians' imagination. It traumatized the French, deeply worried the British, and perplexed the Americans. Western allies dealt with this possibility through the formation of NATO, the retention of Allied troops in Germany, the establishment of supranational mechanisms of control, and the framing of provisions in the contractual agreements that maintained Western leverage over the Federal Republic's capacity to arrange for Germany's unification. The Russians responded with less imagination and more brutality. Faced at the same time with Tito's defection, Stalin consolidated his hold over repressive regimes in Eastern Europe, established the Council for Mutual Economic Aid, and created the German Democratic Republic.

In Western Europe, Soviet capabilities were limited. The Kremlin tightened its relations with Communist parties and pressed them to obstruct the Marshall Plan. But rather than risk revolutionary action and provocative coups that might lead to war, the Communists sought primarily the right to reenter the coalitions from which they had been excluded. More daringly, the Soviets blockaded Berlin. But again fearing war, they did not challenge the airlift and eventually acquiesced to Western policies in western Germany. Defeated, the Soviets periodically tried to sidetrack the integration of the Federal Republic into the Atlantic community by holding out the lure of unification and neutralization and by talking about peace and coexistence. The United States, Britain, and France parried such initiatives with timely concessions to Adenauer's government and with redoubled efforts to achieve integration. In truth, after the Berlin crisis of 1948–49, it was not too difficult to overcome Soviet overtures because they were halfhearted at best. Stalin could not really take the idea of a unified, neutralized Germany very seriously because it portended a Germany that might cast its future with the West or that might boldly reestablish its own preponderance in Central and Eastern Europe. Faced with Germany's renewal and Western Europe's revitalization, the Kremlin did indeed face the specter of a mighty alliance, a resurgent Germany, and a powerful magnet drawing the Soviets' European satellites westward. While Stalin tightened controls at home and stepped up his ideological campaign abroad, his major hope was in a renewed economic crisis in the West that might undermine America's financial and commercial leadership, trigger renewed autarkic forces, splinter the non-Communist coalitions in France and Italy, and drive western Germany to seek markets in the Soviet sphere.

These contingencies were precisely the ones most feared by Truman administration officials. However secretive, repressive, and inhumane Stalin's rule was inside Russia, it was not so much the internal character of the regime that frightened U.S. officials as its alleged capacity to expand its power abroad. Yet after the 1948–49 German crisis, Soviet behavior in Western Europe was quite cautious. But still, U.S. concerns did not abate. Policymakers remained uncertain whether they could preserve Western cohesion, overcome traditional Franco-German rivalries, sustain economic recovery, and solve the dollar gap. Hence they attributed enormous importance to Soviet atomic weapons and to Communist successes in the periphery. They worried that the existence of Soviet atomic capabilities might dissuade West European governments from going ahead with the risks that inhered in West Germany's rearmament and their own military buildup. The Americans also feared that Mao's victory in China and revolutionary nationalist unrest elsewhere in Asia and the Middle East would undermine the prospects for effectively integrating the industrial core with the Third World periphery. The North Korean attack on South Korea [in 1950] accentuated these apprehensions. But aside from Soviet acquiescence to the North Korean attack, or perhaps because of the U.S. response, Soviet actions on the periphery remained restrained. Throughout Southeast Asia, for example, Soviet policy was cautious. During these years little or no aid was given to the Viet Minh. Nor did the Soviets play an active role in the turbulent affairs of Iran and Egypt. No doubt they hoped to capitalize on the trend of events, but their behavior was circumspect.

The Soviets, of course, did respond to the overall U.S. military buildup that went on during the Korean War. They, too, accelerated efforts to develop a hydrogen bomb, augmented their air/atomic capabilities, and strengthened the military establishments of their satellites in Eastern Europe. But ... the U.S. strategic buildup and the West's rearmament efforts far outpaced that of the Soviet Union during the last years of the Truman administration. A war might arise from miscalculations on the periphery or from an escalatory cycle, but few U.S. analysts thought the Soviets would launch a premeditated attack on Western Europe.

U.S. analysts were right. Stalin preferred to concentrate on his own sphere and on developments inside the Soviet Union. He never concealed his desire to reannex territory lost at the end of World War I and to consolidate the gains obtained in the Molotov-Ribbentrop pact of 1939. These objectives were necessary to isolate his regime behind a security zone in Eastern Europe. But the nature of that zone was not predetermined, nor was the magnitude of the Soviet challenge beyond that zone. Initially, Stalin probed only occasionally beyond the sphere of his occupation armies. His most provocative and heinous foreign policy actions came in the latter part of 1947 and 1948, but they were in response to Western initiatives. As we have seen, the formation of the Cominform, the coup in Czechoslovakia, the purges in Eastern Europe, and the blockade of Berlin were reactions to the Truman Doctrine, the Marshall Plan, and, most important of all, the affirmative program in western Germany.

There is, then, reason to assign as much of the responsibility for the origins of the cold war to the United States as to the Soviet Union. But it would be a mistake

to carry the logic of this argument too far, because neither nation was simply react-
ing to the actions of the other. The causes of the cold war were more complex. The
United States was responding to a matrix of perceived dangers. As ominous as Soviet behavior were the vacuums of power in Germany and Japan, the grass-roots
support for Communist parties in France, Italy, Greece, and China, the stirrings of
revolutionary nationalism in the Third World, and the disruptions of traditional
patterns of commerce and finance. In other words, the cold war was the legacy of
World War II. That conflict deranged the international system, altered the balance
of power in Europe, shattered colonial empires, restructured economic and social
arrangements within nations, and bequeathed a legacy of fear that preordained a
period of unusual anxiety and tension. The national security policies of the Truman
administration were an attempt to apply the lessons and cope with the legacies of
World War II as much as they were an effort to contain the Soviet Union. Yet no
one should deny that the very existence of the Soviet Union, situated in a predominant position in the center of Eurasia, with a totalitarian regime, a rival ideology,
and expansive security interests of its own, cast harrowing shadows and accentuated anxieties. Prudent men with great power and wealth, like those occupying the
highest offices in Washington, could not take chances.

✖ FURTHER READING

Gar Alperovitz, *Atomic Diplomacy* (1965 and 1985)
Stephen Ambrose, *Rise to Globalism* (1993)
Terry H. Anderson, *The United States, Great Britain, and the Cold War* (1981)
Josef Becker and Franz Knipping, eds., *Power in Europe?* (1986)
Barton J. Bernstein, ed., *The Atomic Bomb* (1975)
———, ed., *Politics and Policies of the Truman Administration* (1970)
Michael Boll, *Cold War in the Balkans* (1984)
Paul Boyer, *By the Bomb's Early Light* (1986)
H. W. Brands, *The Devil We Knew* (1993)
———, *Inside the Cold War* (1991) (on Loy Henderson)
Douglas Brinkley, ed., *Dean Acheson and the Making of U.S. Foreign Policy* (1993)
Bulletin of the Atomic Scientists, 41 (1985), entire issue for August
McGeorge Bundy, *Danger and Survival* (1990) (nuclear-arms race)
Robert J. C. Butow, *Japan's Decision to Surrender* (1954)
David Callahan, *Dangerous Capabilities* (1990) (on Paul Nitze)
Committee for the Compilation of Materials on Damage Caused by the Atomic Bombs in
    Hiroshima and Nagasaki, *Hiroshima and Nagasaki* (1981)
Isaac Deutscher, *Stalin* (1967)
Robert J. Donovan, *Conflict and Crisis* (1977)
———, *Tumultuous Years* (1982)
David Ellwood, *Rebuilding Europe* (1992)
Herbert Feis, *The Atomic Bomb and the End of World War II* (1966)
———, *From Trust to Terror* (1970)
Richard Freeland, *The Truman Doctrine and the Origins of McCarthyism* (1971)
John Lewis Gaddis, *The Long Peace* (1987)
———, *Russia, the Soviet Union, and the United States* (1990)
———, *Strategies of Containment* (1982)
———, *The United States and the Origins of the Cold War* (1972)
Lloyd C. Gardner, *Architects of Illusion* (1970)
Richard Gardner, *Sterling-Dollar Diplomacy* (1969)

John Gimbel, *The American Occupation of Germany* (1968)
———, *The Origins of the Marshall Plan* (1976)
———, *Science, Technology, and Reparations* (1990)
James L. Gormly, *The Collapse of the Grand Alliance, 1945–1948* (1987)
Fraser J. Harbutt, *The Iron Curtain* (1986)
John L. Harper, *America and the Reconstruction of Italy* (1986)
Robert M. Hathaway, *Ambiguous Partnership: Britain and America, 1944–1947* (1981)
Gregg Herken, *The Winning Weapon* (1981)
George Herring, *Aid to Russia, 1941–1946* (1973)
James Hershberg, *James B. Conant and the Birth of the Nuclear Age* (1994)
Walter Hixson, *George F. Kennan* (1990)
Michael J. Hogan, *The Marshall Plan* (1987)
David Holloway, *The Soviet Union and the Arms Race* (1984)
John O. Iatrides, *Revolt in Athens* (1972)
———, ed., *Greece in the 1940s* (1981)
Walter Isaacson and Evan Thomas, *The Wise Men* (1986)
Howard Jones, *"A New Kind of War"* (1989)
Lawrence S. Kaplan, *The United States and NATO* (1984)
Gabriel Kolko and Joyce Kolko, *The Limits of Power* (1972)
Bruce Kuklick, *American Reparations Policy and the Division of Germany* (1972)
Bruce Kuniholm, *The Origins of the Cold War in the Near East* (1980)
Walter LaFeber, *America, Russia, and the Cold War* (1993)
Deborah Larson, *Origins of Containment* (1985)
Melvyn P. Leffler, "The American Conception of National Security and the Beginnings of
    the Cold War, 1945–48," *American Historical Review,* 89 (1984), 346–381
Ralph Levering, *The Cold War, 1945–1987* (1988)
Geir Lundestad, *The American "Empire"* (1990)
———, *The American Non-Policy Towards Eastern Europe, 1943–1947* (1975)
Mark H. Lytle, *The Origins of the Iranian-American Alliance, 1941–1953* (1987)
Thomas J. McCormick, *America's Half Century* (1989)
Donald McCoy, *The Presidency of Harry S Truman* (1984)
David McLellan, *Dean Acheson* (1976)
Robert J. McMahon, *The Cold War on the Periphery* (1994) (India and Pakistan)
Robert H. McNeal, *Stalin* (1988)
Michael Mandlebaum, *The Fate of Nations* (1988)
Richard Mayne, *Recovery of Europe* (1973)
Robert L. Messer, *The End of an Alliance* (1982)
Aaron Miller, *Search for Security* (1980) (on Saudi Arabian oil)
James E. Miller, *The United States and Italy, 1940–1950* (1986)
Alan Milward, *The Reconstruction of Western Europe, 1945–51* (1984)
Wilson D. Miscamble, *George F. Kennan and the Making of American Foreign Policy*
    (1992)
David S. Painter, *Oil and the American Century* (1986)
Thomas G. Paterson, ed., *Cold War Critics* (1971)
———, *Meeting the Communist Threat* (1988)
———, *On Every Front: The Making and Unmaking of the Cold War* (1992)
———, *Soviet-American Confrontation* (1973)
——— and Robert J. McMahon, eds., *The Origins of the Cold War* (1991)
William E. Pemberton, *Harry S. Truman* (1989)
Stephen J. Randall, *United States Foreign Oil Policy, 1919–1984* (1985)
Michael Ruddy, *The Cautious Diplomat* (1986) (on Bohlen)
Thomas A. Schwartz, *America's Germany* (1991)
Martin Sherwin, *A World Destroyed* (1975)
Nikolai V. Sivachev and Nikolai N. Yakovlev, *Russia and the United States* (1979)
E. Timothy Smith, *The United States, Italy, and NATO* (1991)
Gaddis Smith, *Dean Acheson* (1972)

Joseph Smith, ed., *The Origins of NATO* (1990)
John Spanier, *American Foreign Policy Since World War II* (1992)
Ronald Steel, *Walter Lippmann and the American Century* (1980)
Mark A. Stoler, *George C. Marshall* (1989)
William Taubman, *Stalin's American Policy* (1982)
Athan G. Theoharis, *The Yalta Myths* (1970)
Hugh Thomas, *Armed Truce* (1987)
Kenneth W. Thompson, *Cold War Theories* (1981)
Adam Ulam, *The Rivals* (1971)
Dimitri Volkogonov, *Stalin* (1991)
J. Samuel Walker, "The Decision to Use the Bomb: A Historiographical Update," *Diplomatic History,* 14 (1993), 97–114
———, *Henry A. Wallace and American Foreign Policy* (1976)
Irwin M. Wall, *The United States and the Making of Postwar France* (1991)
Piotr S. Wandycz, *The United States and Poland* (1980)
Imanuel Wexler, *The Marshall Plan Revisited* (1983)
Lawrence S. Wittner, *American Intervention in Greece, 1943–1949* (1982)
———, *One World or None* (1993) (disarmament movement)
Daniel Yergin, *Shattered Peace* (1977)

CHAPTER
7

Mao's China and the Chances

for Sino-American

Accommodation

The landmark Chinese communist revolution reshaped one of the world's oldest, most populous civilizations, reconfigured Asian foreign relations, and initiated a new phase of the Cold War. The United States intervened substantially in the conflict from 1945 to 1949. About $3 billion in U.S. economic and military aid flowed to the regime of Jiang Jieshi (Chiang Kai-shek), leader of the Guomindang (Kuomintang), or Nationalists. But the corrupt Jiang squandered much of the aid, stubbornly resisted recommendations for reform, and obstructed American mediation between the warring parties. After two decades of civil war, Mao Zedong's (Mao Tse-tung's) communists claimed victory in 1949 and established the People's Republic of China (PRC).

Although many Americans understood that the upheaval grew from indigenous roots and that communists enjoyed considerable popular support within China, U.S. officials snubbed contacts with communist leaders because Washington feared the international consequences of a communist triumph, especially a Sino-Soviet alliance. The United States' failure to block the communist revolution in China emboldened President Harry S. Truman's critics, who believed that he, Secretary of State Dean Acheson, and the China experts in the foreign service had "lost" China. The extremely anticommunist McCarthyites relentlessly pushed this charge, even going so far as to accuse American leaders of communist sympathies.

In this politically electric atmosphere, the Truman administration groped for an appropriate response to revolutionary change. What was the new Chinese government's relationship with the Soviet Union? Would Mao's China emulate Josip Tito's Yugoslavia and reject alignment with Moscow? Or would it become a dangerous member of the Soviet camp in the Cold War? Would the PRC's leaders make good on China's treaty obligations? Would they restart trade and respect foreign investment with the West? Or would Communist party leaders seek a radical restructuring of foreign relations that greatly diminished U.S. interests? Could China's Marxism coexist peacefully with the capitalist world? Could the PRC's sus-

picions of Western imperialism and its ardent nationalism be soothed so as to allow stable relations? How should Washington treat the defeated Guomindang, exiled to the island of Formosa (Taiwan)? What implications did China's revolution have for the rest of East Asia—especially such volatile areas as the Korean peninsula, occupied Japan, and colonial French Indochina? Would China's revolution inspire similar unrest across all of the non-Western world?

The most pressing issue was that of U.S. diplomatic recognition of the People's Republic of China. Whether Truman and Acheson withheld recognition from Mao because of their fear of the domestic political repercussions remains a point of debate among historians. Some scholars suggest instead that the Truman administration had become so inveterately anticommunist that it interpreted Mao's victory as a Soviet thrust into Asia and hence passed up Chinese overtures for negotiations. Others have argued that strong Chinese anti-Americanism made the chances of Sino-American accommodation minimal. Historians agree, however, that the Korean War killed all chances for an accommodation. The origins of American nonrecognition policy, which lasted until 1979, is the subject of this chapter.

✖ D O C U M E N T S

In May and June 1949, the U.S. ambassador in China, John Leighton Stuart, met with Huang Hua, a communist foreign-affairs official. Stuart's two telegrams to Washington, which constitute the first document, reported the conversations and the tender of an "invitation" from Mao Zedong and Zhou Enlai to talk with them. In late May, Zhou Enlai, Mao's chief foreign-policy adviser, indirectly approached the U.S. consulate in Beijing. Consul General O. Edmund Clubb reported this *démarche* to Washington in a June 1 telegram, reprinted in the second document. The State Department's initial answer to the Zhou *démarche* is the third document, followed by President Truman's cool response toward the *démarche*. In the fifth document, an excerpt from Huang Hua's memoir (published in China in 1990), the former Chinese official recalls that it was Stuart who initiated contacts with Chinese leaders, and the United States that abruptly cut off discussions. The new China, he suggests, was willing to consider relations with the United States but insisted that Washington first end its support for Jiang Jieshi.

On July 30, 1949, the Department of State issued a "White Paper"—a huge volume of documents and analysis that defended pre-1949 American policies toward China against charges that the United States had "lost" China. Secretary of State Dean Acheson's public letter transmitting the book to the president is included as the sixth selection. The next document is a speech of August 18 by Mao Zedong. Several weeks earlier, he had announced that China was "leaning to one side"—the Soviet side—in the Cold War. In his August speech, he vented his strong anti-American views, accusing the United States of aggression. In the eighth document, from the memoir of Bo Yibo (first published in China in 1991), the PRC's first finance minister explains the ideological and strategic assumptions behind Mao's decision to "lean to one side" and describes Mao's late 1949 trip to Moscow to sign the Sino-Soviet Treaty of Friendship and Alliance. Although the People's Republic jealously guarded its independence and held out the possibility of relations with all nations, the defense of the revolution, Bo insisted, required friendship with the Soviet Union. In the last document, a speech of January 5, 1950, Senator William Knowland of California, a McCarthyite anticommunist and member of the "China lobby," argues against U.S. recognition of the People's Republic.

U.S. Ambassador John Leighton Stuart on Mao's Overture, 1949

Telegram of May 14, 1949

Huang [Hua] called my residence last evening remaining almost 2 hours. Our conversation was friendly and informal. I refrained from political remarks until he opened way which he did after few personal exchanges. I then spoke earnestly of great desire that peoples of all countries had for peace, including, emphatically, my own, of dangerous situation developing despite this universal popular will; of indescribable horrors of next war; of my conviction that much, but not all, present tension due to misunderstandings, fears, suspicions which could be cleared away by mutual frankness; of fears Americans and other non-Communists had of Marxist-Leninist doctrine, subscribed to by CCP [Chinese Communist party], that world revolution and overthrow of capitalistic governments necessary, thus proclaiming subversive interference or armed invasion as fixed policy. Huang spoke of Chinese people's resentment at American aid to Kmt [Kuomintang, or Nationalist party] and other "mistakes" of US Policy to which I briefly replied.

Huang asked about my plans and I told him of my instructions, adding that I was glad to stay long enough for symbolic purpose of demonstrating American people's interest in welfare of Chinese people as whole; that I wished to maintain friendly relations of past; that being near end of my active life I hoped to be able somewhat to help restore these relations as I knew my Government and people desired; that my aim was unity, peace, truly democratic government and international good will for which Huang knew I had worked all my life in China.

Huang expressed much interest in recognition of Communist China by USA on terms of equality and mutual benefit. I replied that such terms together with accepted international practice with respect to treaties would be only proper basis. He was greatly surprised at my explanation of status of armed forces in China particularly Marines in Shanghai. Our side of story, that is desire to protect American lives during civil disturbances and chaotic conditions brought on by war, appeared never to have occurred to him. He was obviously impressed. I explained question of national government was internal; that Communists themselves at present had none; that it was customary to recognize whatever government clearly had support of people of country and was able and willing to perform its international obligations; that therefore USA and other countries could do nothing but await developments in China. I hinted that most other nations would tend to follow our lead. I explained functions of foreign consulates in maintaining informal relations with *de facto* regional authorities.

Huang expounded upon needs of China for commercial and other relations with foreign countries. He said instructions had been issued to all military units to protect safety and interests of foreigners. Intrusion into my bedroom [by Communist soldiers] was discussed and he promised to do his best in constantly shifting military situation to trace offenders. He explained that first Communist troops in city had not been prepared or properly instructed on treatment of foreigners.

Telegram of June 30, 1949

Huang Hua called on me by appointment June 28. He reported that he had received message from Mao Tse-tung and Chou En-lai assuring me that they would welcome me to Peiping if I wished to visit Yenching University. Background of this suggestion is as follows:

In early June Philip Fugh, in one of his conversations with Huang, asked casually, and not under instructions from me, if it would be possible for me to travel to Peiping to visit my old University as had been my habit in previous years on my birthday and Commencement. At that time Huang made no comment. However, 2 weeks later, June 18 to be precise, in discussing my return to Washington for consultation, Huang himself raised question with Fugh of whether time permitted my making trip to Peiping. Fugh made no commitment, commenting only that he himself had made this suggestion 2 weeks earlier. Neither Fugh nor I followed up this suggestion but apparently Huang did. Present message (almost an invitation) is reply.

Regardless whether initiation of this suggestion is considered [by] Peiping to have come from me or from Communists, I can only regard Huang's message as veiled invitation from Mao and Chou to talk with them while ostensibly visiting Yenching. To accept would undoubtedly be gratifying to them, would give me chance to describe American policy; its anxieties regarding Communism and world revolution; its desires for China's future; and would enable me to carry to Washington most authoritative information regarding CCP intentions. Such trip would be step toward better mutual understanding and should strengthen more liberal anti-Soviet element in CCP. It would provide unique opportunity for American official to talk to top Chinese Communists in informal manner which may not again present itself. It would be imaginative, adventurous indication of US openminded attitude towards changing political trends in China and would probably have beneficial effect on future Sino-American relations.

On negative side, trip to Peiping before my return to US on consultation would undoubtedly start rumors and speculations in China and might conceivably embarrass Department because of American criticism. It would probably be misunderstood by my colleagues in Diplomatic Corps who might feel that US representative was first to break united front policy which we have sponsored toward Communist regime and might prove beginning of trek of chiefs of mission to Peiping on one pretext or another. Trip to Peiping at this time invariably suggests idea of making similar one to Canton [temporary Nationalist capital] before my return to US.

While visiting both capitals might effectively dramatize American interest in Chinese people as a whole, it might also appear as peace-making gesture, unwarranted interference in China's internal affairs, and would probably be misunderstood by Chinese Communists, thus undoing any beneficial effects of visit north. Finally, trip of US Ambassador to Peiping at this time would enhance greatly prestige, national and international, of Chinese Communists and Mao himself and in a sense would be second step on our part (first having been my remaining Nanking) toward recognition of Communist regime.

I received clear impression that Mao, Chou and Huang are very much hoping that I make this trip, whatever their motives. I, of course, gave Huang no answer to Mao's message. . . .

I have made this rather full statement of case for Department's consideration and decision. I am, of course, ready to make journey by either means should Department consider it desirable, and should be grateful for instructions earliest and nature of reply to Huang.

Zhou Enlai's (Chou En-lai's) *Démarche,* 1949

Following message given Assistant Military Attaché [David D.] Barrett May 31 by reliable intermediary, origin being Chou En-lai. Chou desired message be transmitted highest American authorities on top secret level without his name being mentioned, said in fact that if it were attributed him he would positively disavow it. Essential there be no leak his name to outside channels. Chou approved transmittal via Barrett who gave message me to transmit, but wanted name unmentioned even to Barrett. Chou desired what he said be conveyed to British, expressed preference transmittal be through Department.

There were few disagreements in CCP Party [*sic*] during agrarian stage revolution but with arrival at urban stage there have now developed disagreements of serious nature primarily re industrial-commercial policies and questions international relations. There is still no actual split within party but definite separation into liberal and radical wings, with Chou being of liberal, and Liu Shao-chi of radical wing. Chou however said it would be as big [a] mistake to base any policy toward China on idea there would develop major split in party as it was to attempt stop Communism in China by aiding Kmt [Kuomintang or Nationalist party] paraliberal group; feels that country is in such bad shape that most pressing need is reconstruction without regard political theories and that Mao Tse-tung concepts regarding private capital should be effected. Group feels there should have been coalition with Kmt because of party lack necessary knowledge regarding reconstruction, did not favor coalition with elements Ho Ying-chin-Chen Li-fu type but felt that without coalition reconstruction might be so delayed that party would lose support people. Realistic coalition advocated by group failed after big dispute involving most of higher figures in party with exception Mao (Chou was most careful in references to Mao). Coalition having failed, party must make most of bad job and obtain aid from outside. USSR cannot give aid which, therefore, must come from USA or possibly Britain. Chou favors getting help from USA and does not accord Soviet attitude regarding USA. Chou professedly sincere Communist but feels there has developed in USA economy something which is outside Marxist theories and that present American economic situation is, therefore, not susceptible Marxian interpretation. Therefore, Soviet attitude this respect wrong, feels American economy will continue without internal collapse or revolution and that there is no real bar to relations between USA and other governments, different political type. Unequivocally opposed to American aid to Kmt but feels this was given from mistaken motives altruism rather than American viciousness. Feels USA has genuine interest in Chinese people which could become basis friendly relations between two countries.

Chou, speaking for liberal group, felt China should speedily establish *de facto* working relations with foreign governments.

This question will be prime issue in struggle between two wings. Radicals wish alliance with USSR, sort now existing between US and Britain, while liberals regard Soviet international policy as "crazy." Chou feels USSR is risking war which it is unable fight successfully and that good working relations between China and USA would have definite softening effect on party attitude toward Western countries. Chou desires these relations because he feels China desperately needs that outside aid which USSR unable give. Feels China on brink complete economic and physical collapse, by "physical" meaning breakdown physical well-being of people.

Chou feels USA should aid Chinese because: (1) China still not Communist and if Mao's policies are correctly implemented may not be so for long time; (2) democratic China would serve in international sphere as mediator between Western Powers and USSR; (3) China in chaos under any regime would be menace to peace Asia and world. Chou emphasized he spoke solely for certain people personally and not as member party, that he was not in position make formal or informal commitments or proposals. He hoped American authorities would recall wartime contacts with Communists and character and opinions of many whom they knew at that time. He hoped American authorities remembering this would believe there were genuine liberals in party who are concerned with everything connected with welfare Chinese people and "peace in our time" rather than doctrinaire theories. As spokesman for liberal wing he could say that when time came for Communist participation in international affairs his group would work within party for sensible solution impasse between USSR and west and would do its best make USSR discard policies leading to war. . . .

Chou emphasized that despite deficiencies, errors, disagreements, Communists had won military victory and in spite of same drawbacks would win future victory in reconstruction. Chou said Mao Tse-tung stands aside from party disputes using Chou, Liu Shao-chi and other liberals and radicals for specific purposes as he sees fit. Mao is genius in listening arguments various sides, then translating ideas into practical working policies.

Chou per source appeared very nervous and worried.

The State Department's Response
to the *Démarche,* 1949

US has traditionally maintained close and friendly relations with China and has thruout past 100 years Sino-US relations, particularly since end last century, taken lead in efforts obtain internatl respect for Chi territorial and administrative integrity to end that China might develop as stable, united and independent nation. Unique record US relations with China gives clear evidence US had no territorial designs on China and has sought no special privileges or rights which were not granted other fon [foreign] nations; US has sought maintain relations on basis mutual benefit and respect. Basic US objectives and principles remain unchanged.

In present situation US hopes maintain friendly relations with China and continue social, economic and polit relations with that country insofar as these relations based upon principle mutual respect and understanding and principle equality and are to mutual benefit two nations. In absence these basic principles, it can hardly be expected that full benefit Sino-US relations can be attained.

In this connection, US Govt and people are naturally disturbed and seriously concerned over certain recent occurrences which represent significant departure from these principles and some of which, in fact, widely at variance with accepted internatl custom and practice: Repeated bitter propaganda misrepresenting US actions and motives in China and elsewhere in world; arbitrary restrictions on movement and denial communications ConGen [U.S. consul general] Mukden and Commie failure reply to ConGen Peiping repeated representations this matter, including request withdraw ConGen and staff Mukden; and Commie failure take action release two US Marine flyers or reply ConGen Peiping representations this matter.

While we welcome expressions friendly sentiments, he must realize that they cannot be expected bear fruit until they have been translated into deeds capable of convincing American people that Sino-US relations can be placed upon solid basis mutual respect and understanding to benefit both nations.

President Harry S. Truman on the *Démarche*, 1949

I brought the President up to date with respect to the Chou En-lai *Demarche* and read to him the pertinent sections of our reply. He approved this course of action and directs us to be most careful not to indicate any softening toward the Communists but to insist on judging their intentions by their actions.

Huang Hua Recalls His Talks with Stuart (1949), 1990

On the eve of the PLA [People's Liberation Army] crossing of the Yangzi River and liberation of Nanjing, [Ambassador John Leighton] Stuart, by his own wishful thinking, intended to continue exerting influence over the New China's policies in order to maintain American interests in China. He wanted to make use of not only his official position as the representative of the United States and "friend of China," but also of his personal friendship with some democratic elements in China, as well as of his relationship with Yenching University students. On 10 March 1949, Stuart telegraphed the State Department, asking to remain in Nanjing to contact our Party in order to establish "new relations." In his return telegram on 6 April, [Secretary of State Dean] Acheson authorized Stuart to have meetings with our Party's leaders. Acheson instructed him not to say anything definitive, to keep the talks secret, and to avoid any leak of information which might cause reactions from the opposition party in Congress. Therefore, Stuart did not leave Nanjing, though the GMD [Guomindang] Government requested all foreign embassies to move southward to Guangzhou (Canton) with it. On 21 April, our army crossed the Yangzi River. Two days later, Nanjing was liberated. . . .

"Huang Hua Recalls His Talks with Stuart" from *Chinese Historians* 5 (Spring, 1992), pp. 49–56, translated by Li Xiaobing. Reprinted with the permission of Chinese Historians of the United States, Inc.

Right after my arrival in Nanjing, I heard that there were a couple of PLA soldiers who entered Stuart's residence. This had caused some uneasiness among the
remaining foreign diplomats. According to directives from the CCP [Chinese
Communist party] Central Committee, we did not recognize the diplomatic and legal status of any foreign diplomatic organ or personnel of the GMD period. We
considered those remaining ex-diplomats in Nanjing as common foreign residents.
We announced at the same time that we would protect all legal interests and guaranteed the personal safety of foreign residents. We were willing to establish diplomatic relations with all countries on the basis of the principle of equality. . . .

Stuart . . . was eager to set up communications with me immediately. On 6
May 1949, Stuart sent over his secretary, Philip Fugh, to request a meeting with
me. I met Fugh the next day. Fugh began the conversation by defending Stuart. According to Fugh's explanation, Stuart gradually recognized the American misperception of the GMD during the past year and the United States had stopped
assisting Jiang Jieshi. Moreover, Fugh alleged, Stuart was appointed as the Ambassador when he was in China. He did not have much knowledge of diplomacy
and was unfamiliar with the State Department. Moreover, [special American envoy George C.] Marshall had been surrounded by the Nationalists. All of these factors brought about Marshall's failure in mediation [of the Chinese Civil War] and
he was called back to America in 1946. There was no reason to blame Stuart unduly. Before the Nationalists retreated, He Ying-qin [GMD minister of national
defense] had requested that Stuart go to Guangzhou. Stuart, however, decided to
stay in Nanjing. His purpose was to contact the Chinese Communists, an action
which had been approved by Acheson. Stuart was anxiously looking forward to
meeting me. . . .

After receiving the Party leadership's approval, I went to Stuart's residence to
meet him on a personal basis on 13 May. . . .

Stuart showed his willingness to establish new relations with the New China.
He expressed his hope that the new Chinese Government would recruit [noncom-
munist] democratic figures into its administration. Then he said that the United
States had stopped its assistance to Jiang Jieshi, and did not want to interfere in
China's civil war. He suggested that immediately after Shanghai's liberation the
Shanghai branch of the Economic Cooperation Administration transfer its stocks
of grain, cotton, and other goods, which had been used to assist Jiang, to us to help
the recovery of Shanghai's production and reconstruction. My answer was that we
would not accept the grain and cotton (because we would take them from the Guomindang's hands in any case). If the United States announced that it would not interfere in China's internal affairs, it should withdraw its naval vessels and marine
garrisons from Qingdao and other areas in order to avoid any conflict. Stuart
agreed to pass these words on to Washington.

After this meeting, Stuart sent Fugh over to meet me two more times. Fugh
talked about Shanghai's liberation and Stuart's desire to visit Shanghai. He emphasized that Stuart had kept his every word regarding the military issues we had
discussed last time. American warships had withdrawn from Qingdao on 21 May.
Some ships headed to Japan, and the others to other countries. After the PLA
entered Shanghai, American naval vessels would leave Shanghai immediately.
And American naval forces would withdraw from any port immediately after its

liberation by the PLA. Fugh added that General Douglas MacArthur had insisted that American naval vessels not leave Qingdao. The State Department made the final decision for the withdrawal. Henceforth China would no longer be the center of American naval activities. . . .

After asking instructions from the CCP Central Committee, I made another appointment with Stuart and Fugh for the second meeting at the Foreign Affairs Office on 6 June. Stuart mentioned first his plan to travel to Shanghai and go back to the United States. I told him that he could apply to the Foreign Affairs Office as a foreign resident. Then, Stuart said that at the Cairo Conference President Franklin D. Roosevelt had agreed that Taiwan would be placed under China's trusteeship and be returned to China after the signing of the peace treaty with Japan. The Peace Conference with Japan, however, had been delayed for various reasons, especially the misunderstandings between the Soviet Union and the United States. There was no certainty as to when the conference would be scheduled. My answer was that Taiwan had always been part of China's territory historically. During Japan's occupation of Taiwan, the Chinese people never accepted the occupation and never stopped struggling against it. Since Taiwan had been returned to China, the GMD Government had no ground to sell it out, nor should any foreign government make trouble under the excuse of the absence of a peace treaty.

Then we talked about the prospects for Sino-American relations. I told Stuart that if we were to build a new Sino-American relationship, the United States had to stop its assistance to and cut off its relations with the GMD Government. Stuart pointed out that the fact that many foreign diplomats stayed in Nanjing showed their attitude toward the GMD. If the GMD Government were to move again from Guangzhou to another place in the future, he could promise that the American representatives would not follow it. Currently, however, since no new government had been founded, no recognition of a new government for China could take place. Under the circumstance that the GMD and the CCP respectively controlled different parts of China, Stuart continued, the United States did not know what was happening in many areas. So according to international custom the United States could not break off its diplomatic relations with the old regime. If there had been some criticism of America's interference with China's internal affairs in the past, it was better for the United States to adopt a more cautious approach now. Thus the United States had a passive attitude and did not declare its stand on supporting or opposing any of the warring parties. It was thought that this problem could be solved automatically after a democratic government appeared, which was supported by the Chinese people and proved to be willing to and capable of committing itself to international obligations. With regard to America's aid, what was shipped to the GMD currently was what had been approved by Congress last year but was only now being shipped. There was not much aid left to be shipped and no more aid was planned.

I expressed my personal opinion to Stuart that the Chinese Political Consultative Conference could probably be held after the take-over of Guangzhou. The Conference would finalize the foundation of a coalition government. General Li Tao, spokesman of the Chinese People's Liberation Army General Headquarters, had made clear our opposition to any kind of American aid for the GMD. He had also explained our principles for establishing diplomatic relations with all foreign governments. Thus, with regard to their responsibilities, the American Government should clearly cut off its relations with the GMD Government and stop its assistance to Jiang Jieshi. Those steps would prove America's abandonment of its failed policy of interference. Now the United States, however, was still supporting the reactionary government of the GMD in its war against the Chinese people. We were in no position to talk about the issues of establishing diplomatic relations. . . .

On 8 June, Fugh came to see me again. He believed, according to the conclusions reached by his conversations with Stuart, that the United States currently had difficulties in giving any formal answer to the question of its relations with the New China. A new American policy would require Stuart's further efforts after his return to America. Stuart, however, needed to know the opinion of the highest leaders of the CCP, which would strengthen his bargaining position in America. Fugh asked me if I had access to Zhou Enlai, and if I could pass on their words to him. I told him not to worry about that; he could talk about whatever he liked. Fugh stated that Marshall, Acheson, and Stuart belonged to the same group, which knew Zhou Enlai very well. Stuart had received a telegram recently from [Under Secretary of State James] Webb, who hoped that Stuart could go to Peiping to visit Zhou Enlai before his return to the United States. Webb thought Stuart could stop by Yenching University for a visit, where he could get some ideas from the CCP Central Committee. This would make his arguments in America stronger upon his return. Fugh asked me to pass on the message to the CCP leadership. . . .

After this meeting, I reported Stuart's request to the CCP Central Committee. The Central Committee believed that it would be better to contact Stuart through unofficial channels. It was arranged to have Lu Zhiwei, President of Yenching University, write a letter to invite Stuart to visit Yenching. (Stuart travelled back to Yenching every year to celebrate his birthday on 24 June.)

On 27 June, Fugh came to visit me again. He brought with him a letter in English, dated 16 June, from President Lu to Stuart. The letter stated that Lu had had a meeting with Zhou Enlai. Zhou expressed his gratitude for Stuart's greetings. Zhou said that Stuart could expect the CCP authorities' approval of his trip to Peiping if he requested it. Stuart did not understand what Zhou really meant. He hoped that I could clarify it by telegraphing Peiping. I cabled to Comrade Zhou Enlai and received his instructions. On 28 June, I informed Stuart that I had received Peiping's telegram and his trip to Yenching was approved. It was also going to be possible for him to meet Chinese leaders as he had wished. Stuart told me that he was very glad to get this message. Congress, however, would be adjourned by the end of July, Stuart was worried whether he would have enough time to work out something. Moreover, divided factions existed on Capitol Hill; and his trip to Peiping at this moment would bring about criticism and could easily cause problems. He decided to report this to Acheson to let him make the final decision.

On 2 July, Fugh came to visit me. He told me that Acheson had cabled Stuart, ordering him to make a non-stop rush trip back to Washington before 25 July. Acheson had also decided that Stuart should not go to Peiping at that moment in order to avoid criticism at home. After a short stay in America, Stuart was to return to China and then he could go to Peiping. I told Fugh immediately that Peiping had responded to Stuart's request to invite him to visit Yenching. It was Stuart who should decide whether he would go or not. Fugh asked me how to keep in touch after Stuart had returned to America. I replied that we found no need to maintain contact at this point.

On 25 July, Stuart came to see me one more time for his departure papers. Stuart asked my opinions of America's future China policy. I told him that the United States could do nothing at the present stage but give up its errant policy and prove the sincerity of pursuing a true friendship with the Chinese people. The United States, however, had not stopped supporting the Chinese reactionaries in the civil war and was organizing "the Pacific Treaty Organization." The Chinese people would firmly oppose this imperialist policy. Stuart told me: "The U.S. Government will do nothing in the near future. We will wait to see how the situation develops." He added that the civil war in China occurred against the will of the U.S. Government. This was a "methodological mistake." The U.S. Government had not yet offered any support for or agreement with the idea of "the Pacific Treaty Organization." So it disclaimed any responsibility for the idea. Stuart commented on Chairman Mao's speech at the New Political Consultative Conference and on *On People's Democracy*. While the tone of the former seemed flexible and inclusive, that of the latter stressed "lean to one side." Moreover, Stuart asked why American residents in Shanghai were disturbed frequently by our handling of cases concerning foreign residents and labor-management conflicts after the liberation. The Americans there were not sure whether we wanted them to stay in China or not. I responded by stressing that we treated all foreign residents equally. As long as they wanted to stay and observe China's law, we would protect their safety and property. But those who violated the law would be punished. Stuart's question was certainly uncalled for.

In mid-July, Stuart applied to return home by plane. On 2 August, following a designated route, Stuart, accompanied by Fugh and six other people, flew from Nanjing to Okinawa, and then to America. Three days after Stuart's departure from China (5 August), the State Department of the United States published its "White Paper" on Sino-American relations and Secretary of State Acheson's letter to President Truman. Stuart, as Chairman Mao described him later, became "a symbol of the complete failure of the aggressive policy of the United States toward China."

Secretary of State Dean Acheson in the "White Paper," 1949

When peace came the United States was confronted with three possible alternatives in China: (1) it could have pulled out lock, stock and barrel; (2) it could have intervened militarily on a major scale to assist the Nationalists to destroy the Communists; (3) it could, while assisting the Nationalists to assert their authority over as much of China as possible, endeavor to avoid a civil war by working for a compromise between the two sides.

The first alternative would, and I believe American public opinion at the time so felt, have represented an abandonment of our international responsibilities and of our traditional policy of friendship for China before we had made a determined effort to be of assistance. The second alternative policy, while it may look attractive theoretically and in retrospect, was wholly impracticable. The Nationalists had been unable to destroy the Communists during the 10 years before the war. Now after the war the Nationalists were . . . weakened, demoralized, and unpopular. They had quickly dissipated their popular support and prestige in the areas liberated from the Japanese by the conduct of their civil and military officials. The Communists on the other hand were much stronger than they had ever been and were in control of most of North China. Because of the ineffectiveness of the Nationalist forces which was later to be tragically demonstrated, the Communists probably could have been dislodged only by American arms. It is obvious that the American people would not have sanctioned such a colossal commitment of our armies in 1945 or later. We therefore came to the third alternative policy whereunder we faced the facts of the situation and attempted to assist in working out a *modus vivendi* which would avert civil war but nevertheless preserve and even increase the influence of the National Government. . . .

The reasons for the failures of the Chinese National Government appear in some detail in the attached record. They do not stem from any inadequacy of American aid. Our military observers on the spot have reported that the Nationalist armies did not lose a single battle during the crucial year of 1948 through lack of arms or ammunition. The fact was that the decay which our observers had detected in Chungking early in the war had fatally sapped the powers of resistance of the Kuomintang. Its leaders had proved incapable of meeting the crisis confronting them, its troops had lost the will to fight, and its Government had lost popular support. The Communists, on the other hand, through a ruthless discipline and fanatical zeal, attempted to sell themselves as guardians and liberators of the people. The Nationalist armies did not have to be defeated; they disintegrated. History has proved again and again that a regime without faith in itself and an army without morale cannot survive the test of battle. . . .

Fully recognizing that the heads of the Chinese Communist Party were ideologically affiliated with Moscow, our Government nevertheless took the view, in the light of the existing balance of forces in China, that peace could be established only if certain conditions were met. The Kuomintang would have to set its own house in order and both sides would have to make concessions so that the Government of China might become, in fact as well as in name, the Government of all China and so that all parties might function within the constitutional system of the Government. Both internal peace and constitutional development required that the progress should be rapid from one party government with a large opposition party in armed rebellion, to the participation of all parties, including the moderate non-communist elements, in a truly national system of government.

None of these conditions has been realized. The distrust of the leaders of both the Nationalist and Communist Parties for each other proved too deep-seated to permit final agreement, notwithstanding temporary truces and apparently promising negotiations. The Nationalists, furthermore, embarked in 1946 on an overambitious military campaign in the face of warnings by General [George C.] Marshall that it not only would fail but would plunge China into economic chaos and eventually destroy the National Government. General Marshall pointed out that though Nationalist armies could, for a period, capture Communist-held cities, they could not destroy the Communist armies. Thus every Nationalist advance would expose their communications to attack by Communist guerrillas and compel them to retreat or to surrender their armies together with the munitions which the United States has furnished them. No estimate of a military situation has ever been more completely confirmed by the resulting facts.

The historic policy of the United States of friendship and aid toward the people of China was, however, maintained in both peace and war. Since V-J Day, the United States Government has authorized aid to Nationalist China in the form of grants and credits totaling approximately 2 billion dollars, an amount equivalent in value to more than 50 percent of the monetary expenditures of the Chinese Government and of proportionately greater magnitude in relation to the budget of that Government than the United States has provided to any nation of Western Europe since the end of the war. In addition to these grants and credits, their United States Government has sold the Chinese Government large quantities of military and civilian war surplus property with a total procurement cost of over 1 billion dollars, for which the agreed realization to the United States was 232 million dollars. A large proportion of the military supplies furnished the Chinese armies by the United States since V-J Day has, however, fallen into the hands of the Chinese Communists through the military ineptitude of the Nationalist leaders, the defections and surrenders, and the absence among their forces of the will to fight.

It has been urged that relatively small amounts of additional aid—military and economic—to the National Government would have enabled it to destroy communism in China. The most trustworthy military, economic, and political information available to our Government does not bear out this view.

A realistic appraisal of conditions in China, past and present, leads to the conclusion that the only alternative open to the United States was full-scale intervention in behalf of a Government which had lost the confidence of its own troops and its own people. Such intervention would have required the expenditure of even greater sums than have been fruitlessly spent thus far, the command of Nationalist armies by American officers, and the probable participation of American armed forces—land, sea, and air—in the resulting war. Intervention of such a scope and magnitude would have been resented by the mass of the Chinese people, would have diametrically reversed our historic policy, and would have been condemned by the American people.

It must be admitted frankly that the American policy of assisting the Chinese people in resisting domination by any foreign power or powers is now confronted with the gravest difficulties. The heart of China is in Communist hands. The Communist leaders have foresworn their Chinese heritage and have publicly announced their subservience to a foreign power, Russia, which during the last 50 years, under czars and Communists alike, has been most assiduous in its efforts to extend its control in the Far East. In the recent past, attempts at foreign domination have appeared quite clearly to the Chinese people as external aggression and as such have been bitterly and in the long run successfully resisted. Our aid and encouragement have helped them to resist. In this case, however, the foreign domination has been masked behind the facade of a vast crusading movement which apparently has seemed to many Chinese to be wholly indigenous and national. Under these circumstances, our aid has been unavailing.

The unfortunate but inescapable fact is that the ominous result of the civil war in China was beyond the control of the government of the United States. Nothing that this country did or could have done within the reasonable limits of its capabilities could have changed that result; nothing that was left undone by this country has contributed to it. It was the product of internal Chinese forces, forces which this country tried to influence but could not. A decision was arrived at within China, if only a decision by default.

And now it is abundantly clear that we must face the situation as it exists in fact. We will not help the Chinese or ourselves by basing our policy on wishful thinking. We continue to believe that, however tragic may be the immediate future of China and however ruthlessly a major portion of this great people may be exploited by a party in the interest of a foreign imperialism, ultimately the profound civilization and the democratic individualism of China will reassert themselves and she will throw off the foreign yoke. I consider that we should encourage all developments in China which now and in the future work toward this end.

In the immediate future, however, the implementation of our historic policy of friendship for China must be profoundly affected by current developments. It will necessarily be influenced by the degree to which the Chinese people come to recognize that the Communist regime serves not their interests but those of Soviet Russia and the manner in which, having become aware of the facts, they react to this foreign domination. One point, however, is clear. Should the Communist regime lend itself to the aims of Soviet Russian imperialism and attempt to engage in aggression against China's neighbors, we and the other members of the United Nations would be confronted by a situation violative of the principles of the United Nations Charter and threatening international peace and security.

Meanwhile our policy will continue to be based upon our own respect for the Charter, our friendship for China, and our traditional support for the Open Door and for China's independence and administrative and territorial integrity.

Mao Zedong (Mao Tse-tung) on U.S. "Imperialism," 1949

The war to turn China into a U.S. colony, a war in which the United States of America supplies the money and guns and Chiang Kai-shek the men to fight for the United States and slaughter the Chinese people, has been an important component of the U.S. imperialist policy of world-wide aggression since World War II. The U.S. policy of aggression has several targets. The three main targets are Europe, Asia and the Americas. China, the centre of gravity in Asia, is a large country with a population of 475 million; by seizing China, the United States would possess all of Asia. With its Asian front consolidated, U.S. imperialism could concentrate its forces on attacking Europe. U.S. imperialism considers its front in the Americas relatively secure. These are the smug over-all calculations of the U.S. aggressors.

But in the first place, the American people and the peoples of the world do not want war. Secondly, the attention of the United States has largely been absorbed by the awakening of the peoples of Europe, by the rise of the People's Democracies in Eastern Europe, and particularly by the towering presence of the Soviet

Union, this unprecedentedly powerful bulwark of peace bestriding Europe and Asia, and by its strong resistance to the U.S. policy of aggression. Thirdly, and this is most important, the Chinese people have awakened, and the armed forces and the organized strength of the people under the leadership of the Communist Party of China have become more powerful than ever before. Consequently, the ruling clique of U.S. imperialism has been prevented from adopting a policy of direct, large-scale armed attacks on China and instead has adopted a policy of helping Chiang Kai-shek fight the civil war.

U.S. naval, ground and air forces did participate in the war in China. There were U.S. naval bases in Tsingtao, Shanghai and Taiwan. U.S. troops were stationed in Peiping, Tientsin, Tangshan, Chinwangtao, Tsingtao, Shanghai and Nanking. The U.S. air force controlled all of China's air space and took aerial photographs of all China's strategic areas for military maps. At the town of Anping near Peiping, at Chiutai near Changchun, at Tangshan and in the Eastern Shantung Peninsula, U.S. troops and other military personnel clashed with the People's Liberation Army and on several occasions were captured. [Colonel Claire] Chennault's air fleet took an extensive part in the civil war. Besides transporting troops for Chiang Kai-shek, the U.S. air force bombed and sank the cruiser *Chungking*, which had mutinied against the Kuomintang. All these were acts of direct participation in the war, although they fell short of an open declaration of war and were not large in scale, and although the principal method of U.S. aggression was the large-scale supply of money, munitions and advisers to help Chiang Kai-shek fight the civil war.

The use of this method by the United States was determined by the objective situation in China and the rest of the world, and not by any lack of desire on the part of the Truman-Marshall group, the ruling clique of U.S. imperialism, to launch direct aggression against China. Moreover, at the outset of its help to Chiang Kai-shek in fighting the civil war, a crude farce was staged in which the United States appeared as mediator in the conflict between the Kuomintang and the Communist Party; this was an attempt to soften up the Communist Party of China, deceive the Chinese people and thus gain control of all China without fighting. The peace negotiations failed, the deception fell through and the curtain rose on the war.

Liberals or "democratic individualists" who cherish illusions about the United States and have short memories! Please look at Acheson's own words:

> When peace came the United States was confronted with three possible alternatives in China: (1) it could have pulled out lock, stock and barrel; (2) it could have intervened militarily on a major scale to assist the Nationalists to destroy the Communists; (3) it could, while assisting the Nationalists to assert their authority over as much of China as possible, endeavor to avoid a civil war by working for a compromise between the two sides.

Why didn't the United States adopt the first of these policies? Acheson says:

> The first alternative would, and I believe American public opinion at the time felt, have represented an abandonment of our international responsibilities and of our traditional policy of friendship for China before we had made a determined effort to be of assistance.

So that's how things stand: the "international responsibilities" of the United States and its "traditional policy of friendship for China" are nothing but intervention against China. Intervention is called assuming international responsibilities and showing friendship for China; as to non-intervention, it simply won't do. Here Acheson defiles U.S. public opinion; his is the "public opinion" of Wall Street, not the public opinion of the American people.

Why didn't the United States adopt the second of these policies? Acheson says:

> The second alternative policy, while it may look attractive theoretically and in retrospect, was wholly impracticable. The Nationalists had been unable to destroy the Communists during the 10 years before the war. Now after the war the Nationalists were, as indicated above, weakened, demoralized and unpopular. They had quickly dissipated their popular support and prestige in the areas liberated from the Japanese by the conduct of their civil and military officials. The Communists on the other hand were much stronger than they had ever been and were in control of most of North China. Because of the ineffectiveness of the Nationalist forces which was later to be tragically demonstrated, the Communists probably could have been dislodged only by American arms. It is obvious that the American people would not have sanctioned such a colossal commitment of our armies in 1945 or later. We therefore came to the third alternative policy. . . .

What a splendid idea! The United States supplies the money and guns and Chiang Kai-shek the men to fight for the United States and slaughter the Chinese people, to "destroy the Communists" and turn China into a U.S. colony, so that the United States may fulfill its "international responsibilities" and carry out its "traditional policy of friendship for China.". . .

What matter if we have to face some difficulties? Let them blockade us! Let them blockade us for eight or ten years! By that time all of China's problems will have been solved. Will the Chinese cower before difficulties when they are not afraid even of death? Lao Tzu said, "The people fear not death, why threaten them with it?" U.S. imperialism and its running dogs, the Chiang Kai-shek reactionaries, have not only "threatened" us with death but actually put many of us to death. Besides people like Wen Yi-to, they have killed millions of Chinese in the last three years with U.S. carbines, machine-guns, mortars, bazookas, howitzers, tanks and bombs dropped from aeroplanes. This situation is now coming to an end. They have been defeated. It is we who are going in to attack them, not they who are coming out to attack us. They will soon be finished. True, the few problems left to us, such as blockade, unemployment, famine, inflation and rising prices, are difficulties, but we have already begun to breathe more easily than in the past three years. We have come triumphantly through the ordeal of the last three years; why can't we overcome these few difficulties of today? Why can't we live without the United States?

When the People's Liberation Army crossed the Yangtse River, the U.S. colonial government at Nanking fled helter-skelter. Yet His Excellency Ambassador Stuart sat tight, watching wide-eyed, hoping to set up shop under a new signboard and to reap some profit. But what did he see? Apart from the People's Liberation Army marching past, column after column, and the workers, peasants, and students rising in hosts, he saw something else—the Chinese liberals or democratic individualists turning out in force, shouting slogans and talking revolution together with the workers, peasants, soldiers and students. In short, he was left out in the cold, "standing all alone, body and shadow comforting each other." There was nothing more for him to do, and he had to take to the road, his briefcase under his arm.

There are still some intellectuals and other people in China who have muddled ideas and illusions about the United States. Therefore we should explain things to them, win them over, educate them and unite with them, so they will come over to the side of the people and not fall into the snares set by imperialism. But the prestige of U.S. imperialism among the Chinese people is completely bankrupt, and the White Paper is a record of its bankruptcy. Progressives should make good use of the White Paper to educate the Chinese people.

Leighton Stuart has departed and the White Paper has arrived. Very good. Very good. Both events are worth celebrating.

Bo Yibo Remembers the Origins
of China's "Lean to One Side" Policy (1949–1950), 1991

Both to clarify the ambiguous thoughts of some non-party people and to lay the foundation for the new China's foreign policy, Chairman Mao, on June 30, 1949 proclaimed in his article "On People's Democratic Dictatorship":

> Leaning to one side stems from the lessons we have learned from the forty years of Sun Yat-sen and the twenty-eight years of the Communist Party. We are keenly aware that we must lean to one side in order to achieve and consolidate victory. According to the experience of (Sun Yat-sen's) forty years and (our party's) twenty-eight years, the Chinese have either leaned toward imperialism or toward socialism. There has been no exception. To sit on the fence is to go nowhere. There is no third path. We oppose the Jiang Jieshi reactionaries who leaned toward imperialism. We also oppose the illusion of taking a third path. . . . Internationally, we belong to the anti-imperialist front headed by the Soviet Union. We can only seek true friendship from this front, not from the imperialist front.

Why did we propose this diplomatic strategic principle at the time? What was its background and at whom was it directed? What was its long-term significance? In his letter to the comrades in the Party's East China Bureau on July 19, Comrade Deng Xiaoping, who was directing military operations in East China, wrote a brilliant exposition, which can still help us today, especially young comrades, to deepen our understanding of the "leaning to one side" decision. For that purpose, I am quoting his exposition here:

> The purpose of the various plots of imperialism including blockade is to force us to submit to imperialism. Likewise, the aim of our struggle is to force imperialism to give

"Bo Yibo Remembers the Origins of China's 'Lean to One Side' Policy (1949–1950)" from *Chinese Historians* 5 (Spring 1992), pp. 59–62, translated by Zhai Qiang. Reprinted with the permission of Chinese Historians of the United States, Inc.

in to us. Judging by the lessons of the past month, however, we can see that it will not be an easy matter for imperialism to give in to us. In fact, during that period both sides had been testing the water until Britain and the United States decided to institute a blockade. Though for the moment the blockade has exasperated the many difficulties we face, it was nevertheless advantageous for us as well. However, if the blockade lasts too long, it will be very disadvantageous. In order to break the blockade, Chairman Mao stresses that we should quickly occupy Guangdong, Guangxi, Yunnan, Guizhou, Sichuan, Xikang, Qinghai and Ningxia and strive to take the offshore islands and Taiwan as soon as possible. At the same time, we propose a foreign policy of "leaning to one side." The earlier we put this into practice, the better our position will be (Chairman Mao says that this leaning is on our initiative, and is better than being forced to lean to one side in the future). . . .

The newly-established People's Republic of China faced the serious problem of breaking the imperialist blockade. Therefore, it became all the more important to consolidate and develop the friendship and cooperation between the two great countries of China and the Soviet Union. On November 12, Chairman Mao cabled Stalin: "Thank you for inviting me to visit Moscow." On December 16, Chairman Mao reached Moscow, and was given a grand welcoming reception by the Soviet party and government. When Chairman Mao delivered a speech at the party celebrating Stalin's seventieth birthday on December 21, the entire audience rose three times. On December 22, Chairman Mao wrote to the Party Central Committee: "In preparation for the trade agreement with the Soviet Union, we should take the over-all situation into consideration. Of course, the Soviet Union has the priority, but we should also be ready to do business with such countries as Poland, Czechoslovakia, Germany, Britain, Japan and the United States." Chairman Mao also told the Central Committee that he had "already made an appointment with Stalin to have a talk either on the 23rd or on the 24th." Right at this moment (December 24, 1949), Soviet General Advisor to China I. V. Kovalev, who was accompanying Chairman Mao during his trip to the Soviet Union, presented Stalin with a written report, "On Certain Policy and Practical Matters Concerning the CCP Central Committee." This report claimed that within the Chinese Communist Party and among members of the Central Committee there were some people who had been pro-American and anti-Soviet in the past, and now received support from the leadership of the Central committee. . . .

For a period of time after Chairman Mao's arrival in the Soviet Union, the Soviet side did not take the initiative and Chairman Mao stayed in his quarters. This situation might have been the result of Kovalev's report. Chairman Mao lost his temper in front of the Soviet officials in charge of organizing his visit, and he said: "I came to the Soviet Union not just to celebrate Stalin's birthday, but to discuss important matters concerning bilateral relations between the two countries." After learning this, Stalin quickly started negotiations with Chairman Mao and gave him General Advisor Kovalev's report, thus improving mutual understanding, although unresolved suspicions remained.

On January 2, 1950, Chairman Mao sent a telegram to the Party Central Committee: "In the past two days there has been an important development here. Comrade Stalin has agreed to let Comrade Zhou Enlai come to Moscow to sign the new Sino-Soviet Friendship and Alliance Treaty and other agreements regarding loans, trade, and civil aviation.". . .

Subsequently on April 11, Chairman Mao chaired the Sixth Meeting of the Central People's Government Committee. Premier Zhou delivered "The Report on the Sino-Soviet Treaty." The treaty [signed February 14, 1950] was approved at the meeting. In his speech Chairman Mao pointed out: "Under what circumstances did we conclude this treaty? We have defeated one enemy, that is, the reactionary forces at home. We have driven the international reactionary forces out of China. But there are still reactionaries in the world, that is, imperialists outside China. Internally, we still face difficulties. . . . Under these conditions, we need friends. . . . We should solidify our relations and our friendship with the Soviet Union in a legal manner, that is, through a treaty. To solidify the friendship between the Soviet Union and China and to establish an alliance relationship. . . . If imperialists prepare to attack us, we already have help."

Speaking of the great significance of the treaty and agreements, Chairman Mao asserted: "The recently-concluded Sino-Soviet Treaty and agreements have solidified in a legal way the friendship between the two great countries, China and the Soviet Union, and have enabled us to secure a reliable ally. Therefore, we can carry out domestic reconstruction freely, deal with possible imperialist aggression together, and win world peace." In sum, "this action will place the People's Republic in a more advantageous position, enable us to force capitalist countries to submit, and to force foreign countries to recognize China without conditions, . . . making capitalist countries hesitate to take aggressive action."

Senator William Knowland Argues Against Recognition, 1950

Mr. President and Members of the Senate, within the last 90 days two catastrophic events have taken place. These are the Soviet success in atomic development, as announced by the President of the United States on September 23, 1949, and the establishment of a Soviet-recognized Communist regime in China. Only in retrospect will we be able to finally determine which event will have the most far-reaching influence. Both have set off chain reactions that have not yet run their full course.

Fifty years of friendly interest on the part of our people and our Government in a free and independent China and the overwhelming contribution made by our Army, Navy, and Air Force in the Pacific during World War II gave us the power, the prestige, and the opportunity for constructive action no western nation had ever before possessed. We could have pioneered in exporting the ideals that inspired men who loved freedom everywhere following our own breakaway from colonial status.

All this opportunity has been frittered away by a small group of willful men in the Far Eastern Division of the State Department who had the backing of their superiors.

In Europe where the record of Soviet aims was clearly outlined in Poland, Czechoslovakia, Bulgaria, Hungary, Rumania, Latvia, Lithuania, and Estonia we finally stood up to communism in Greece, Turkey, Iran, Berlin, and western Germany. . . .

Communism is destructive of human liberty everywhere in the world. It is no less destructive in China or Korea than it is in Poland, Czechoslovakia, Latvia, Estonia, Lithuania, Hungary, Rumania, or Bulgaria. The pattern may differ slightly. In Poland the opposition leader, Mikolajczyk, was forced to flee; in Bulgaria Petkov was hanged; in Rumania the King was given a 2-hour ultimatum to change the government regardless of the constitution; in Czechoslovakia Masaryk's life was forfeited when it became apparent that coalition with communism would not work.

A Chinese official put it clearly by saying to me recently that there can be no real coalition with a tiger unless you are inside the tiger.

The President's State of the Union message of January 4 was notable for its silence on the question of China. In what we hope will be a free world of freemen does the administration have less concern with human liberty in Asia than it does in Europe? On what basis does the administration write off freemen in China? . . .

In Europe we have had a foreign policy in which the Republicans and the Democrats have contributed to the initiation and formulation of doctrines that are understandable. In the Far East there has been no bipartisan foreign policy. The Republicans in Congress have not been consulted in the moves leading up to the bankrupt policy which now stands revealed in all its sorry detail. . . .

Our long-standing far eastern policy was first compromised at Yalta. We gave to the Soviet Union vital rights in Manchuria which were not ours to give. It was done without the consent or approval of the American Congress or the American people. It was done in violation of the open-door policy of John Hay and of Woodrow Wilson's concept of "open covenants, openly arrived at." The Yalta agreement made Soviet domination of Manchuria and other border provinces inevitable. It made possible Chinese Communist domination of the balance of continental China and has opened the door to bringing the entire continent of Asia, with more than a billion people and vast resources, into the orbit of international communism. Sitting with our American delegation at Yalta was Alger Hiss [a State Department official who in 1948 was accused of conducting espionage for the Soviet Union].

Following VJ-day the representatives of our Department of State persistently tried to get the Government of the Republic of China to form a coalition with the Communists. When they refused we placed an embargo against the shipments of any arms or ammunition to the legal government of the country while during those same months the Soviet army of occupation in Manchuria, as the result of the Yalta agreement, was turning over to the Communist forces large amounts of captured Japanese war stocks.

Like a person with a bad conscience, the State Department on August 6 released the China white paper. All the blame was placed on the National Government, then with its back to the wall. It was apparently issued with the hope that our own sorry part and share of responsibility might be overlooked. . . .

The basic objective the United States should have kept constantly in mind was to preserve a free, independent, united non-Communist China. In the postwar illness of that nation we prescribed that the strychnine of communism be taken. The State Department having contributed greatly to the Chinese disaster, still proclaims that we must follow a hands off policy, or that we must wait for the dust to settle, or we must investigate some more. Are they preparing for a post mortem rather than a consultation? . . .

Like Mr. Chamberlain at Munich, there are some in this country and in Great Britain who believe that by appeasing the Communists they may change their way of life. This is naive, and such a viewpoint is dangerous to the peace of the world and the security of this country. . . .

It is my judgment that history will record the recognition of Communist China as being as great a betrayal of human freedom as was the Pact of Munich. . . .

The question is asked "Can anything be done at this late date?" I believe that it can. While desperate, the situation is not more desperate than it was at the time of Dunkerque or Valley Forge.

First, of course, we need a foreign policy in the Far East. We have none there today. As a basis for such a foreign policy, I suggest the following:

First. That we make clear that we have no intention of recognizing the Communist regime in China at this time nor in the immediate future and that we make known to the powers associated with us that we do not look with favor upon such recognition by others.

It is of course not sufficient merely to delay our own recognition if, with a wink of the eye or tongue in cheek the State Department leaves doubt in the minds of others as to the course of action we may pursue.

Second. That we have a major shakeup in the Far Eastern Division of the State Department. We cannot expect to get inspired leadership for a new policy in the Far East from those who have been receivers of the bankrupt policy we have been following.

Third. Our policy itself, of course, will have to be set by our constitutional officers, the President, his advisers, and the Congress. Once we have a foreign policy there is great need for it to be coordinated in both its economic and defense phases. As coordinator, either Gen. Douglas MacArthur or some other comparable figure should be selected so that in that area of the world the right hand will know what the left is doing.

Fourth. We should give supervised aid to the legal Government of China in the same way we gave it to the legal Governments of Greece and Korea when they were threatened by communism.

ESSAYS

He Di of the Institute of American Studies, Chinese Academy of Social Sciences, in Beijing, China, argues in the first essay that Washington's unbending support for Jiang Jieshi prevented Sino-American accommodation. Although Mao Zedong and others tried to cooperate with the United States during and immediately following the Second World War, and even remained open to informal discussions as late as mid-1949, Marxist ideology and practical national-security concerns drove the Chinese Communist party (CCP) to ally with the Soviet Union. In the second essay, William W. Stueck, Jr., of the University of Georgia probes American thinking and concludes that Dean Acheson's distaste for the new communist regime, rather than domestic political pressures, led the Truman administration to stand by Jiang and reject opportunities to explore relations with the People's Republic of

China. Stueck laments the decision and speculates about what might have come from such discussions. Nancy Bernkopf Tucker of Georgetown University disagrees. She argues in the closing essay that Acheson worked cautiously but steadily to cut the administration's ties to Jiang Jieshi. Acheson strove to position the United States so as to recognize the People's Republic—with the goal of driving a wedge between Chinese and Soviet communists. Domestic opposition to recognition and the outbreak of the Korean War in June 1950 wrecked Acheson's plans.

From Cooperation to Confrontation: Chinese Communist Views on Sino-American Relations

HE DI

In August 1944, Mao Zedong revised an editorial in *Jiefang ribao (Liberation Daily)* entitled "Welcome Our Friends the American Military Observers." Five years later, in August 1949, Mao personally wrote an editorial in *Renmin ribao (People's Daily)* entitled "Farewell, Leighton Stuart." The change of tone from welcome to farewell accurately reflected both the development of the relationship between the Chinese Communist Party (CCP) and the U.S. government over this period of time and the evolution of the former's policy toward the latter.

During these five years, while working for China's independence, territorial unification, and political democracy, the CCP twice sought to cooperate with Washington. Gradually, however, the Party came to regard U.S. policy in China as fundamentally irreconcilable with its own goals and objectives and thus was ultimately compelled to direct its effort from cooperation with Washington to struggle against it. During this process of reassessment and realignment, Mao proposed his theory of confrontation between the two camps and of contending for the intermediate zone and, in light of China's national security interests, made the historic decision to "lean to one side."

The CCP's desire to cooperate with the United States was evident as early as December 1935, even before the Sino-Japanese war. At that time, the Japanese wished to be the sole power controlling China. This ambition both exacerbated existing tensions between Japan and the Western powers and affected the factional alignment among the various contending groups within China. These developments gave the small and weak CCP an opportunity to survive and develop and further relieved the Party's isolation in the world political arena. At the Wayaobao Conference of December 1935, the CCP grasped this opportunity to execute a policy change and, in the spirit of the Seventh Conference of the Comintern, which had called for a worldwide popular front against fascism, established a united front with pro-Western elements within the Kuomintang (KMT) against the Japanese aggressors. To this end, the CCP decided to make the necessary compromises and establish alliance relationships with all countries, political parties, factions, and individuals that opposed the Japanese imperialists and their Chinese puppets. . . .

From He Di, "The Evolution of the Chinese Communist Party's Policy toward the United States, 1944–1949, in Harry Harding and Yuan Ming, eds., *Sino-American Relations, 1945–1955: A Joint Reassessment of a Critical Decade* , pp. 31–47. Copyright 1989 by Scholarly Resources, Inc. Reprinted by permission of Scholarly Resourcs, Inc.

Accordingly, the CCP issued its "Directive on Establishing a United Front against Japan in the Pacific" during the week following Pearl Harbor. The directive pointed out that "the central task of the Party was the formation and the development of an extensive anti-Japanese and anti-fascist united front of all nations around the Pacific Ocean. This united front should be an alliance that includes both the upper classes and the lower classes, and both the government and the people." In this united front, the cooperation of the CCP and the Chinese people with Washington and London was of paramount importance. American and British support was a necessary condition for China's national liberation, just as its internal unity, political and military reforms, and war effort against Japan were essential for the United States and Great Britain to defeat the Japanese. The directive continued: "For this reason, the CCP should sincerely and honestly cooperate with the Americans and the British on various occasions in order to increase the strength of the American and the British forces and improve the situation for China's war effort against Japan." . . .

In Chungking, Zhou Enlai and his colleagues put this new policy into practice. Meeting with American diplomats such as John C. Vincent, John P. Davies, and John S. Service, Zhou in 1942 and 1943 reviewed the achievements of the Eighth Route Army, sketched the extent of the CCP-controlled areas, explained CCP goals and policies, and expressed the Party's willingness to fight under General Joseph Stilwell. He also invited the Roosevelt administration to send official representatives to visit and stay in Yenan. The CCP sought support from the U.S. government and the American people in its efforts to bring about political reform and to prevent the KMT government from attacking CCP-controlled areas. In the summer of 1943, as Washington became more critical of the KMT government and more favorable toward the CCP, the United States adopted a more flexible China policy. President Franklin D. Roosevelt, at the suggestion of various American China hands, three times asked Chiang Kai-shek to allow an observation group to be sent to Yenan.

Finally, on July 22, 1944, the first official American representatives, the U.S. Army Observation Group (known as the Dixie Mission), entered CCP territory. Zhou later described the event as a milestone in the development of CCP-U.S. relations. The Party's Central Committee, in its first major foreign policy document ("Instructions on Diplomatic Work"), heralded the visit as a product of its efforts to develop an international united front and as the beginning of its diplomatic activities. This directive described clearly the guidelines and principles of CCP foreign policy and set forth regulations pertaining to such practical matters as military, political, and cultural exchanges as well as religion. The document also formalized the CCP's draft "Directive on Establishing a United Front against Japan in the Pacific" of December 9, 1941; and finally, it conveyed the CCP's wish to raise what had previously been isolated contacts with the United States to the level of semiofficial cooperation.

The arrival of the Dixie Mission marked the establishment of this semiofficial relationship and the beginning of formal military cooperation. Although the stated purpose of the American visit to Yenan was to collect information and coordinate rescue operations for U.S. airmen, the CCP hoped that this would lead to further military cooperation with, and material assistance from, the United States. "This military cooperation made subsequent cultural, political, and economic cooperation possible," Zhou wrote to Wang Bingnan [a communist foreign-affairs official]. "With this channel established, future contacts will not be difficult. . . . The prospect for subsequent cooperation is boundless.". . .

Concurrent with such military cooperation were CCP efforts for political cooperation. The Party welcomed American involvement in the CCP-KMT negotiations and in effecting a coalition government. Moreover, the CCP believed that a U.S. role was useful to compel the KMT government to enact democratic reforms, consolidate an anti-Japanese united front during the war, and promote democracy in China after the war. For this reason, Mao on several occasions instructed Lin Boqu, a Party negotiator, secretly to deliver CCP proposals to the U.S. embassy and to General Stilwell's headquarters, seek talks with Vice President Henry Wallace to brief the administration on the CCP-KMT negotiations, and try to persuade Wallace to visit Yenan.

After President Roosevelt's personal representative, General Patrick J. Hurley, arrived in China on September 6, 1944, the United States began to involve itself formally in Chinese internal political struggles. After repeated invitations from the CCP, and with Chiang's consent, Hurley arrived in Yenan on November 7. After two days of discussions, he and Mao signed a five-point draft agreement on the question of establishing a coalition government in China and on other issues. The draft agreement was highly commended by the Central Committee. Mao wrote to President Roosevelt that "the spirit of this agreement is what we of the Chinese Communist Party and the Chinese people have been striving for in the anti-Japanese United Front during the past eight years.". . .

The CCP policy of cooperation provided the United States with an opportunity to determine its postwar China policy. Regrettably, U.S. decision makers did not fully understand the political reality of Chinese society and treated their relations with the CCP merely as an expediency. With the success of the U.S. landing operations in the Pacific islands and the smooth development of the atomic bomb—and especially after the October 1944 Moscow Conference of Foreign Ministers when the Soviet Union declared its willingness to attack the Japanese in Northeast China—the value of the China theater declined drastically in American eyes. . . . Under pressure from Chiang, Hurley [who had since been named ambassador] soon abandoned the five-point draft agreement that he had signed with the CCP. Instead, he collaborated with the KMT right wing in inducing and compelling the CCP to relinquish its military forces and abandon its base areas.

Mao was infuriated upon hearing of Hurley's radical change in position. He told Colonel [David D.] Barrett [head of the Dixie Mission] on December 8, 1944, that the five-point draft agreement constituted the maximum concession of the CCP. The Chinese Communists would never give up their military forces and their demand for a coalition government, and they would never trade principles for American military aid. Nevertheless, in the interest of the common war effort against Japan and of maintaining its existing relations with Washington, the CCP chose an attitude of restraint and did not publicize its criticism of Hurley. On December 12, Mao cabled the Party's representative in Chungking, Wang Ruofei, and asked him to tell Hurley that the CCP had no intention of breaking relations with the United States; and, except for basic principles, everything else was negotiable. Meanwhile, Zhou wrote to Hurley that the CCP still hoped to cooperate with the U.S. Army in military affairs. In an attempt further to sound out U.S. policy and to express its willingness to cooperate, the CCP dispatched a letter to Washington, offering to send an unofficial delegation to the United States. The letter indicated that, if necessary, Mao or Zhou personally would go to the White House to meet President Roosevelt.

Hurley's actions destroyed this ray of hope for good relations. Not only did he discontinue American military cooperation with the CCP and purge the U.S. embassy in China of opponents to his policy, but he also returned to Washington to lobby President Roosevelt to redirect China policy to the exclusive support of Chiang. On April 2, 1945, he declared that the administration would support the Chiang government and would not support any "warlords" or "armed political parties." . . .

From April 23 to June 11, 1945, the Party held its Seventh Party Congress to formulate its general line and major policies for the postwar period. Several factors had enormous impact on the outcome of the congress. First, Hurley's actions had reinforced Chiang's wish to fight the Communists, thereby increasing the risk of a civil war. Second, there were widespread reports of the suppression of Communists in Greece by the British forces commanded by General Ronald Scobie. In addition, conflicts between the United States and the Soviet Union began to surface. All these led the CCP to realize that, although the anti-Fascist war was succeeding, "within the camp now fighting fascist aggression there are forces which oppose democracy and oppress other nations, and they will continue to oppress the people in various countries and in the colonies and semi-colonies."

Anticipating the possibility that the United States would attempt to transform China into a semicolonial country headed by the American-controlled KMT, Mao warned the Party that this development would make the Chinese revolution more difficult. He repeatedly used Greece as an example to point out that the CCP should guard against external intervention and prevent a repetition of the Scobie case in China. To avoid such a scenario, he advised the senior ranking cadres of the Party to watch carefully for any possible change in the direction of U.S. intervention in Chinese affairs. Meanwhile, concluding that the Soviet Union and foreign proletariats would not be able to render assistance to the CCP in the foreseeable future, the Party decided to highlight the principle of independence in the international anti-Fascist united front. . . .

On August 8, 1945, the military forces of the Soviet Union marched into Northeast China, putting the last nail in the coffin of Japanese imperialism. In the name of the Far East Command of the Allied Forces, General Douglas MacArthur ordered Japanese troops in China to surrender—but to KMT forces only, not to CCP forces. On August 14, the KMT government and Moscow signed the Sino-Soviet Treaty of Friendship and Alliance, which legitimized the secret protocols of the Yalta agreement concerning China. On August 15, Japan surrendered. Around this time, Chiang invited Mao three times to go to Chungking to negotiate a peaceful settlement between the KMT and the CCP, an idea approved by Joseph Stalin.

Within two weeks, several important ambiguities in the domestic and international situations were clarified. Politically, the KMT attempted to use its position of international legitimacy to mobilize foreign pressure and make the CCP comply with its demands. Militarily, the KMT attempted to expand its territorial control, especially in the Northeast, and to prepare for a civil war against the CCP. Noting the KMT moves, Mao predicted that the war against Japan waged jointly by the CCP and the KMT would turn into a conflict between the two political parties for national unification and that, in the long run, civil war was unavoidable. The timing and scale of such a war would be influenced by a number of factors, however. Given that the United States and the Soviet Union did not want a Chinese civil war, that the Chinese people desired peace, and that the CCP and the KMT needed time for preparations, the outbreak could be postponed and a new period of peaceful cooperation between the CCP and the KMT inaugurated. Based upon such an analysis, the CCP declared that its postwar policy would be "tit-for-tat and to fight for every inch of land." The Party was to be ready to negotiate with the KMT even as it prepared for KMT attacks and expanded its territory in formerly Japanese-occupied areas. . . .

China's plight received much international attention. Within the U.S. State Department (particularly in the Far East Division), opposition grew to Hurley's policies. Hurley found himself in a difficult position, and on November 27 he angrily resigned. On December 15, President Harry S. Truman issued a statement supporting a peaceful settlement between the CCP and the KMT. Truman announced that he would send General George C. Marshall to China as his special representative to help accomplish this end. On December 16, Secretary of State Edward R. Stettinius met in Moscow with the foreign ministers of the Soviet Union and Great Britain. In the declaration of the Moscow Conference, the three governments expressed their hope for peace in China, pledged not to intervene in that country's internal affairs, and announced that all foreign troops would withdraw from China.

Facing this new situation, the CCP concluded that Truman's policy was essentially unchanged in its support of Chiang, but it also recognized that the president's statement demonstrated that his administration would not directly involve itself in China's civil war and would not agree to Chiang's attempt to unify the country by force. The CCP believed that the Truman administration sought a peaceful unification of China—a policy beneficial to the Party's own struggle for peace and democracy—and therefore welcomed this change and the prospect of the Marshall mission.

On December 20, Marshall arrived in China to mediate between the CCP and the KMT. With his help the two political parties reached an armistice agreement. On the same day the Political Consultative Conference convened, and on December 30 it passed five agreements, including the Program of Peaceful Construction of the Country. In effect, this program negated the monopoly of power by the KMT, its system of dictatorship, and its civil war policy. Marshall demonstrated his fairness on the question of the number of KMT troops to be transported to the Northeast and on the settlement of disputes over such strategic points as Chifeng and Buolun. For this he was highly commended by the CCP. In remarks to United Press journalists (his first public speech since the previous October), Mao on February 9, 1946, stated that the success of the conference marked the completion of the preparation of China for democracy. He lavishly praised Marshall's role in stopping the civil war and promoting unity, peace, and democracy. . . .

However, Marshall's [subsequent] actions disappointed the CCP. In April, he agreed to Chiang's request to move two additional armies to the Northeast. At the beginning of May, the United States helped the Generalissimo ship these troops despite the CCP's opposition. Under the condition that Marshall would bring about a cease-fire on the part of the KMT forces, the CCP withdrew from Siping and Changchun, respectively, on May 19 and 23. However, after taking over Changchun, KMT troops continued to move against CCP territories. On the day the KMT entered Changchun, Chiang flew to Shenyang with Marshall's plane to command these maneuvers. These actions made the CCP think that it had been cheated by the United States. Apart from superficial successes, Marshall's mediation had not stopped any activities of the Chinese reactionaries. On the contrary, prodded by much de facto American assistance, they became even more bold and unscrupulous.

On June 14, Secretary of State James F. Byrnes proposed legislation to the Senate for military aid to China. On June 22, Mao voiced a strong protest to Washington, marking the beginning of a new phase of CCP-U.S. relations. Two days later the Central Committee directed its members to mobilize the masses to demand that the U.S. government stop supporting Chiang. It pointed out that the Truman administration's military support for the Generalissimo had become increasingly apparent and that colonial symptoms in the Chiang regime were increasingly prominent. In July, civil war broke out, and on August 10, Marshall and Ambassador [John] Leighton Stuart issued a joint statement admitting the failure of the American mediation effort. . . .

Anger at being cheated combined with humiliation generated from the long period of the CCP's outlawed status became important factors in the formulation of subsequent Party policy towards the United States. In addition, the credibility of the Truman administration dropped to its lowest point in the eyes of the CCP. Summarizing its experience with the U.S. government, Mao said in private: "We made mistakes in our work during the previous period. We have struggled against Chiang Kai-shek for many years and accumulated a good deal of experience. Thus Chiang could not cheat us with any tricks and schemes. It was the first time for us to deal with the U.S. imperialists. We didn't have much experience. As a result we were taken in. With this experience, we won't be cheated again."

After two periods of heightened expectations followed by two disappointments, the CCP was forced to face a KMT backed by the United States. On the world scene, a Soviet-U.S. Cold War confrontation had emerged. The KMT argued that a civil war would lead to a new global conflict between Moscow and Washington. Furthermore, the KMT used the 1945 Sino-Soviet Treaty of Friendship and Alliance to compel the Soviets to make compromises and concessions in China. Stalin worried about the apparent weakness of the CCP, which did not appear to be able to defend itself against a U.S.-backed KMT. He also was unwilling to become involved in a civil war that might divert Soviet forces from the European front. His primary worry was that renewed Chinese civil war would lead to another world upheaval. In order to unify the Party's understanding of the current international and domestic situations, assuage the Soviet fear of involvement, and respond to war propaganda from the KMT and the United States, Mao met with journalists and published many articles in which he systematically analyzed the world situation and proposed the theories of the "intermediate zone" and the "two camps."

Mao argued that the United States and the Soviet Union

> are separated by a vast zone which includes many capitalist, colonial, and semi-colonial countries in Europe, Asia, and Africa. Before the U.S. reactionaries have subjugated these countries, an attack on the Soviet Union is out of the question.

> The practical significance of the anti-Soviet slogans of the United States during the post-war period lay in domestic oppression of the American people and external aggression against countries other than the Soviet Union with "peaceful" means, that is, contending with the Soviet Union for territories of the "intermediate zone."

Mao added that the major contradictions in the world, therefore, were those between the peoples of the intermediate zone and the U.S. government, especially those between China and the United States. Until these problems were solved, the Truman administration could not launch a war directly against the Soviet Union.

The possibility of delaying and preventing the outbreak of another world war depended upon the struggles of peoples against the American imperialist policies in countries within the intermediate zone. Therefore, the compromises between the Soviet Union and the United States, Britain, and France should not lead to the adoption of compromises on the part of the Communist parties in those countries. They should continue their struggles in various forms. Finally, in order to achieve victory over antidemocratic forces made up of U.S. imperialists and the reactionaries of various countries, the American people, together with peoples of other capitalist, colonial, and semicolonial countries, must form a worldwide united front that undoubtedly would receive sympathy and support from the Socialist Soviet Union.

At the end of 1947, noting the formation of two camps headed by the Soviet Union and the United States, Mao adopted [Soviet Politburo official] Andrei Zhdanov's two-camps thesis and for the first time employed the concept of the world anti-imperialist camp and the imperialist camp. He regarded the forces of the Chinese revolution as an important part of the anti-imperialist camp headed by the Soviet Union, and he pointed out that "the anti-imperialist camp headed by the Soviet Union has already been formed."

With this new theory, Mao solved three problems. First, confronted with the war cry from the United States and the KMT and the fear of war among the ranks of the CCP, he pointed out that a new world war was not likely. Second, noting that compromises between the Soviet Union and the United States in Asia, particularly on the question of China, were the result of their contention in Europe, Mao stressed that the CCP should not follow up with its own compromises. Rather, it should dare to overcome various difficulties and carry out an independent struggle. Third, in the light of Stalin's fear that the Chinese civil war might escalate into a global conflict, Mao pointed out that this struggle could only enhance the forces of peace and democracy headed by the Soviet Union and would not cause any problems for the Soviets or lead to a new world war. . . .

In late 1947 and early 1948 the CCP's military posture changed from strategic defense to strategic offense. During this period the CCP noted U.S. hesitation in supporting Chiang as conflicts began to arise between the two erstwhile allies. On March 23, 1948, the Central Committee issued a "Directive on the Tactics of Diplomacy in the Struggle against the United States." It stated that the Party not only should overcome fear in its struggle against American imperialism but it also should avoid radical actions in this struggle. In other words, it should mobilize popular support both at home and abroad to oppose any increase in American support to Chiang. At the same time, the CCP should exploit all disagreements and conflicts within the U.S. ruling classes and between the U.S. government and the KMT regime in order to reduce American assistance to Chiang. The goal was to enable the people to perceive the true intentions of the Truman administration's China policy, and to separate and isolate Washington from Chiang.

By January 1949, after success in three major military campaigns, the CCP's impending victory over the KMT was obvious. With the defeat of Chiang, the contradiction between the CCP and the KMT came to a resolution, while that between New China and the United States became more prominent. The Party believed that the threat from Washington might take the form of direct military intervention as well as indirect intervention through sabotage, espionage, and political infiltration. It regarded its major task during this period to be the prevention of any U.S. intervention or plotting against New China. . . . This policy was . . . spelled out in the Central Committee's "Directive on Diplomacy" and "Supplementary Directives" issued on January 19 and 25, respectively. The Second Plenary Session of the Seventh Party Congress held in March again discussed and reaffirmed this policy, which contained four primary principles.

First, the CCP and the people in its controlled areas should prepare both psychologically and militarily for direct American military intervention in China. Mao pointed out: "When we make war plans, we have always taken into account the possibility that the U.S. Government may send troops to occupy some of the coastal cities and fight us directly. We should continue to prepare for this now so as to avoid being taken by surprise if it really occurs." Such preparation also responded to Soviet fears that the crossing of the Yangtze River by the People's Liberation Army (PLA) would prompt American military intervention. Even if the U.S. government sent troops to China, the CCP was prepared to fight until national independence and unification were realized.

Second, on the question of when to establish diplomatic relations with the United States and other imperialist countries, the CCP had decided on the following policy in the Second Plenary Session of the Seventh Party Congress: "We should not be in a hurry to solve [the problem of recognition by the imperialist countries]; we should not be in a hurry to solve it now and need not be in a hurry to solve it even for a fairly long period after country-wide victory." Indeed, the CCP opted for a completely new start. It would "refuse to recognize the legal status of any foreign diplomatic establishments and personnel of the Kuomintang period, refuse to recognize all the treasonable treaties of the Kuomintang period, abolish all imperialist propaganda agencies in China, [and] take immediate control of foreign trade and reform the customs system." These measures were aimed not only at completely negating the legitimacy of the KMT government and establishing the independent foreign policy of New China but also at eliminating the political influence of the United States and preventing American sabotage from within.

Third, on economic relations the CCP decided to adhere to the principle of separating politics from economic affairs and trade for mutual benefit. Mao said that one should not hesitate when business opportunities came: "We must first of all trade with the socialist and people's democratic countries; at the same time we will also trade with capitalist countries." The purpose was to develop the economy as well as to preempt a U.S. blockade. And fourth, the CCP issued numerous directives to its members to avoid provoking the United States. It forbade anyone from entering foreign diplomatic compounds without authorization; it ordered that the lives and property of Americans and British be protected; and it stipulated severe punishment for violation of these policies. The CCP repeatedly emphasized the necessity of observing discipline and regulations in foreign affairs and of educating cadres and soldiers about diplomacy and the need to avoid impulsive actions against foreigners.

On April 24, 1949, after the KMT government had moved to Canton, the PLA occupied Nanking. The founding of the People's Republic of China was close at hand, and the CCP now applied its new diplomatic principles to the emerging conflict with the United States over the questions of establishing diplomatic relations and avoiding external military intervention. Despite the CCP occupation, Ambassador Stuart remained in Nanking, hoping to find opportunities to contact the Party and explore the possibility of establishing diplomatic relations with New China.

At the Second Plenary of the Seventh Party Congress, the CCP already had discounted the possibility of rapidly establishing diplomatic relations with the United States, when it concluded that "the imperialists, who have been always hostile to the Chinese people, will definitely not be in a hurry to treat us as equals." But when Stuart stayed behind in Nanking, Mao thought that contact with him might allow the CCP some flexibility in future dealings with the United States. Therefore, the Party gave this situation serious consideration. On April 28, in the name of the Central Committee's Military Commission, Mao cabled the General Front Party Committee and certain commanding officers of the PLA East China field army, telling them that both the United States and Great Britain had sought to establish contacts with the CCP. If those two countries could sever their diplomatic relations with the KMT, Mao said, the CCP could consider the question of establishing diplomatic relations with them. . . .

On May 10, the Central Committee cabled the Party's Nanking Committee and East China Bureau detailing its instructions for the meeting between Huang Hua and Ambassador Stuart. It asked Huang to spend more time listening to Stuart and less time talking, so as to explore the U.S. government's intention. It stipulated that Huang should follow the spirit of Li Tao's statement, imply that New China would not reject Philip Fugh's suggestion that Stuart continue to be the American ambassador, and suggest that the U.S. government and the CCP revise the existing commercial treaty between the two countries.

Thus instructed, Huang met Stuart on May 13 and stated that the CCP was willing to establish diplomatic relations with foreign countries and hoped that Washington would recognize the new government. After learning that Stuart wanted to use the occasion of his birthday party at Yenching University in Peking to meet the top leaders of the CCP, Huang responded positively. On June 28 he told Stuart that he would be able to see Mao, Zhou, and other Party chiefs during his stay in Peking. However, Stuart's government did not want to cut off both diplomatic relations and actual support of the KMT government, which contradicted the CCP's terms for establishing diplomatic relations. Consequently, on July 1, Secretary of State Dean Acheson wired President Truman's instruction to Stuart that he should not visit Peking under any circumstances. The ambassador's last effort thus failed, providing further confirmation of the CCP's previous estimate. After this time the Party took a cautious wait-and-see attitude regarding U.S. diplomatic initiatives.

Compared with the Huang-Stuart meeting, the activities of the American military forces in Qingdao might appear to have little importance, but it should be noted that they had a significant impact on the making of CCP foreign policy. The Party had been preparing for the possibility of U.S. military intervention and thus was very sensitive when, at the end of April and the beginning of May 1949, the U.S. Army suddenly increased its activities in Qingdao. The CCP misinterpreted this as a prelude to direct intervention in the Chinese revolution. . . .

On June 30, 1949, Mao announced the policy of "leaning to one side" in his "On the People's Democratic Dictatorship," revealing his strategic concept of New China's role in world affairs for the period following the civil war. We have previously shown that the policy of "leaning to one side" had its own theoretical foundation as well as being grounded in considerations of the CCP's practical self-interest. It thus was a logical development. For a long time, Mao had been stressing the thesis that China's new democratic revolution was a part of the world Socialist revolution initiated by the Soviet Union. . . .

Although the CCP's policy of "leaning to one side" was deeply ingrained in Marxist ideology, even more important practical concerns—for national security and economic construction—made the CCP's pro-Soviet stance a necessity. Policymakers in Washington at the time hoped to use the lure of diplomatic recognition to compel the CCP to drop, or at least to modify, its pro-Soviet policy. Actually establishing diplomatic relations between the United States and New China would not have changed the CCP's "lean to one side" decision. There was simply no alternative under the historical circumstances of the time.

The U.S. government did not leave the CCP much choice. Its long-term course of supporting Chiang had created deep mistrust on the part of the CCP and fostered strong anti-American feelings on the part of the Chinese people. Second, Acheson's policy of "waiting for the dust to settle" (that is, as long as the KMT government did not disintegrate, the Truman administration would not change its existing recognition of that government) generated the Taiwan problem, making it impossible for the CCP to develop normal diplomatic relations with the United States. Third, the buildup of American influence along China's periphery—in French Indochina, the Philippines, South Korea, and, above all, Japan—increased the people's insecurities. The American occupation policy toward Japan had aroused widespread and emotional opposition in China, and the U.S. inclination to back Japan in place of KMT China in its strategic policy in Asia led the CCP to believe that Washington was the main threat to national security. Coupled with the U.S. view that New China was in league with the Soviets, these constraints presented the CCP with no real alternatives. It had no choice but to ally with the Soviet Union. Finally, the Truman administration's economic blockade against China prevented it from acquiring modern technology and investment from the West and compelled it to turn to the Soviet Union and other Socialist countries for support for large-scale construction.

Similarly, the Soviets also gave China little choice, although for opposite reasons. First, they sought to convince CCP leaders that leaning to the side of the Soviet Union was both possible and realistic. Historically, the record of the USSR in the Chinese revolution was much better than that of the United States; and while Soviet support for the CCP had been relatively passive, the CCP regarded this as a problem between two parties sharing the same revolutionary ideals, rather than equating it with U.S. support of the KMT. Pro-Soviet sentiment had been formed and developed within the CCP through ideological education, especially after Stalin admitted his error on the Chinese revolution to CCP leaders in 1949. Second, there was no problem in terms of diplomatic recognition between the two countries; as early as the beginning of 1949, [the Soviet official] A. I. Mikoyan came to China and agreed that his government would accord the CCP diplomatic recognition immediately after the founding of the People's Republic.

Third, the Soviet Union was a powerful force against the United States and Japan in Asia, and the CCP had regarded it as its strategic rear. In light of the Soviet punishment of Yugoslavia and rumors that "Mao Zedong might become a second Tito," the CCP also thought it necessary to clarify its position in order to avoid hostility from Moscow. Finally, the Soviet Union served as a viable political and economic model in the eyes of the CCP and had promised economic and technological assistance during both Mikoyan's visit to China and Liu's [Liu Shao-chi] visit to the Kremlin in July 1949. Once the CCP adopted the Soviet model, it had to "lean to one side." Thus, the combination of a theoretical rationale, historical expediency, and pro-Soviet sentiment among the people led to the formation of the CCP's foreign policy of "leaning to one side."

The foregoing review of the development of the CCP's policy toward the United States prior to the Korean War reveals a number of factors that characterize the making of its foreign policy. First, the Party's foreign policy was a result of its analysis of Marxism and of its understanding of the external world. The CCP had been seeking theoretical guidance for its cause of national independence and unification. Consequently, the writings of Stalin and V. I. Lenin on the subject of revolution in colonial and semicolonial countries and on united front tactics had greatly appealed to CCP foreign policymakers. On some specific questions, especially during the early period, Soviet foreign policy had a significant impact on that of the CCP. However, as the Chinese Party matured politically, such influence gradually decreased. The CCP was not an instrument of Soviet foreign policy. Indeed, one might even say that victory in the war of liberation of the Chinese people was realized in spite of Stalin's will. . . .

Second, the CCP personnel, procedures, and processes involved in policymaking also influenced the course of foreign relations at this time. When certain American and Taiwanese scholars [today] seek to explain the changes of CCP policy toward the United States during this period, they tend excessively to emphasize factional struggle within the Party between pro-United States and pro-Soviet groups. As a result, they are inclined to direct their attention to the specific speeches and behavior of the various CCP leaders and search for subtle differences among them. Actually, in the late 1940s, after the rectification campaign and particularly after the Seventh Party Congress in 1945, the CCP had realized a high degree of unity. Mao had consolidated all power so that within the Party there was no struggle between pro-U.S. and pro-Soviet factions. . . .

Third, and most important, in making its foreign policy the CCP's first priority was to satisfy the requirements of domestic political struggle. Its foreign policy was merely an extension of its domestic policy. The basic objectives of the CCP during the period of new democratic revolution were national independence and the unification of the country. During the war against Japan, the CCP's major goals were to defeat Japan (to realize national independence) and to promote reforms within the KMT government (to realize national unification through united government). After the war, the CCP opposed dictatorship and sought through peaceful consultation to solve the contradictions between itself and the KMT and thereby achieve national reunification.

It was in order to realize this objective that the CCP twice decided to cooperate with the U.S. government. Nevertheless, the United States twice tied itself to a hopeless regime in China. Its policy moved from supporting Chiang to opposing the CCP. This course completely destroyed the basis of cooperation between the CCP and Washington.

The American Failure to Negotiate

WILLIAM W. STUECK, JR.

The issue of political relations with a Chinese Communist regime was closely tied to commercial matters. The Communists might survive a Western economic boycott, but State Department officials believed that the new masters of China would at least temporarily want trade with the capitalist powers. Yet, during late 1948 and early 1949, as the Communists moved into cities of Manchuria and North China in which American consular personnel resided, they refused to acknowledge the official standing of the representatives of foreign governments. Communist leaders also announced their intention to abrogate U.S. treaties with Nationalist China.

American officials deeply resented this attitude. Not only were representatives of the United States accustomed to favored treatment in China, they, as well as top policymakers in Washington, regarded the upholding of treaty obligations as "basic to relations among modern States." This view, together with the belief that, for commercial reasons, the Communists would soon adopt a less extreme course, produced a tough position regarding the formal recognition of Peking. As Ambassador [John Leighton] Stuart put it, "the Communists, rather than nations with well-established tradition[s] and accepted international standards," should be placed "on trial." In early May 1949, [Secretary of State Dean] Acheson decided that the United States should not initiate moves toward recognition, and he instructed American officials to impress upon Western European governments the desirability of developing a "common front" on the issue. Weeks before the secre-

From *The Road to Confrontation: American Policy Toward China and Korea, 1947–1950* by William W. Stueck, Jr. Copyright 1981 The University of North Carolina Press. By permission of the publisher.

tary, responding to political pressures at home, outlined publicly the criteria for establishing political relations, he privately had adopted the Jeffersonian model. A Communist regime would be judged in three areas: its capacity to control the territory it purported to govern, its "ability and willingness . . . to discharge its international obligations," and the "general acquiescence" of the people of the country under its rule.

This attitude led to rejection of an apparent opportunity for an American official to talk directly to Mao and other top men in Peking. Ironically, just after the United States moved to create a united front among the Western powers on the recognition question, Huang Hua, head of the Communist Alien Affairs Bureau in Nanking, approached Ambassador Stuart. On 13 May, the two men talked for nearly two hours. Raising the matter of recognition, Huang expressed much interest in Communist relations with the United States on a basis of "equality and mutual benefit." Stuart outlined the criteria recently established in Washington. The Chinese official then apologized for a recent incident in which Communist soldiers had trespassed on Stuart's living quarters.

Then, at the end of the month, Chou En-lai, a powerful figure in the Chinese Communist Party, made an indirect approach to the American consulate general at Peking through Michael Keon, an Australian journalist employed by the United Press. Chou talked of a division within the Communist camp between a liberal group, of which he was a leader, and a radical faction, headed by Liu Shao-chi. The liberals desired friendly relations with the Western democracies, especially the United States and Great Britain, as a means of obtaining the assistance necessary for economic reconstruction at home. The radicals demurred, desiring a close alliance with the Soviet Union. The State Department authorized O. Edmund Clubb, the consul general at Peking, to respond that Washington hoped for amicable relations with the new China on the basis of "mutual respect" and "equality," but was deeply disturbed by Communist treatment of American representatives in the country and propaganda attacks on the United States. President Truman approved this reply, though he emphasized that Clubb must avoid any indication of a "softening" American attitude toward the Communists. When Clubb sought to transmit the message directly to Chou or his secretary, however, the Communist leader abruptly broke off contact.

In the meantime, Stuart's talks with Huang in Nanking had continued. On 28 June, only days after Chou had squelched his own initiative in Peking, Huang told the ambassador that Mao would welcome him in the northern city if he wished to visit Yenching University. This proposal was a response to a query from Philip Fugh, Stuart's secretary and confidant, regarding the feasibility under present circumstances of the ambassador's annual July pilgrimage to his former school. Stuart immediately cabled Washington for instructions. In the State Department, both [W. Walton] Butterworth and John Paton Davies considered the invitation to be significant, but they feared the domestic reaction if Stuart accepted. They proposed to skirt this problem. The ambassador could stop in Peking after traveling to Mukden to pick up Angus Ward, the American consul general there, who, along with his staff, was being held under house arrest; or Washington could announce that Stuart had gone to Peking to read Communist leaders "the riot act" regarding mistreatment of American diplomats.

On 1 July, however, Acheson wired Stuart and stated that a decision had been reached at the "highest level" against a journey to Peking. Communist attitudes toward American officials in China, of which the Ward case was only the most extreme expression, and toward treaties concluded by the National government, were foremost in reaching this verdict. On 16 June 1949, President Truman had instructed [Under Secretary of State James] Webb to be "most careful not to indicate any softening toward the Communists but to insist on judging their intentions by their actions." A trip by Stuart to Peking also might have disrupted American efforts to unite Western governments on a cautious policy regarding recognition, and, to Acheson, a united front was a prerequisite to applying effective pressure on the Communists. Moreover, the Communists had not yet officially proclaimed themselves the government of China. The United States continued to recognize the National government. A trip to Peking by the American ambassador could not be kept secret, and Stuart was known to be inclined to deviate from instructions. His journey would detract from the already diminished prestige of the Nationalists and bolster the Communists at a time when their capacity to rule China remained uncertain. In a narrow legal sense, talks between the United States and a Chinese party, against the wishes of the recognized government, were inappropriate.

From the standpoint of politics in the United States, the trip would add fuel to the already intense attacks from Capitol Hill on Truman administration China policy. On 24 June, twenty-two Senators, including six Democrats, sent a letter to the President urging him to withhold recognition of the Communists. A week later, on the very day that the proposed Stuart trip to Peking was rejected, Acheson wrote to Senator [Tom] Connally [chair of the Foreign Relations Committee] outlining the previously established criteria for recognition; the secretary assured him he would consult the Foreign Relations Committee before acting on the matter. The North Atlantic Treaty was then before the Senate, and the military assistance program, considered essential to give teeth to the pact, had not yet been sent to Congress. The specter, which had been so pervasive in late 1947 and early 1948, of a China bloc on Capitol Hill withholding support for critical enterprises in Europe, reappeared.

Yet domestic political concerns probably only reinforced Truman's and Acheson's inclination against the Huang overture. Had they believed that a major opportunity was at hand to advance American interests in China, they surely would have moved with less dispatch to stifle it. Certainly they would have explored the possibility of using Clubb at Peking to initiate talks with Communist leaders, a procedure that stood an excellent chance of remaining secret. If revealed to the public, it could be explained away, both to international lawyers and hostile politicians, far more easily than the Stuart trip. In all likelihood, Acheson advised Truman to reject the Huang initiative, and the president, already inclined in that direction, agreed. To them, a more positive response might encourage the Communists to persist in their aggressive behavior toward American officials in China, and undermine administration efforts to maintain a united Western front on recognition.

Both temperamentally and intellectually, Acheson was poorly suited to deal in an astute manner with the Communists. For one thing, he was preoccupied with the European theater. It was there, he felt, that the great issues of international politics would be played out. Furthermore, as Dean Rusk [assistant secretary of state for

Far Eastern affairs in the Truman administration] noted many years later, Acheson never had much respect for Asian peoples. He was a Europeanist not only in American foreign policy, but in culture as well. Finally, he had a passion for order. "In fact, I was always a conservative," he was to declare in 1969: "I sought to meet the Soviet menace and help create some order out of the world. I was seeking stability and never had much use for revolution. As a friend once said, we had plenty of chaos, but not enough to make a world." From this perspective, it was up to Communist China to demonstrate its worthiness to enter into the family of nations. Although the secretary of state was far from inflexible on China policy, neither was he anxious to explore every possible opportunity for constructive relations with the Communists. . . .

Few American decisions toward China in the postwar period were as unfortunate as the outright rejection of the Huang overture. To be sure, much of Communist behavior in preceding months evinced strong hostility toward the United States. Then, on 1 July—and probably unknown to Truman and Acheson at the time of their decision—Mao published an essay, "On People's Democratic Dictatorship," in which he asserted that the United States was the "one great imperialist power" remaining on earth. Because America sought "to enslave the world," he claimed, China must ally itself "with the Soviet Union, with every New Democratic country, and with the proletariat and broad masses in all other countries."

Such statements, however, do not eliminate the possibility that a careful probing of Peking's position in the summer of 1949 could have been useful to the United States. As John M. Cabot, the outspoken American consul general in Shanghai, observed, "Virulent anti-American propaganda is natural in view of our aid to the Nationalists." That aid was ineffectual in sustaining the Nationalists in China, but it added significantly to the anti-Communist resistance there. Even so, Communist leaders expressed interest in relations with the United States. On 15 June, Mao stated in a speech that his regime was

> willing to discuss with any foreign government the establishment of diplomatic relations on the basis of the principles of equality, mutual benefit and mutual respect for territorial integrity and sovereignty, provided it is willing to sever relations with the Chinese reactionaries, stops conspiring with them or helping them and adopts an attitude of genuine, and not hypocritical, friendship toward People's China.

Other evidence existed that the Communists were, as Stuart put it, "far from a Soviet Punch and Judy show." Clearly they were not anxious to eliminate the American presence in China. Throughout 1949, the Communist attitude toward American missionaries encouraged them to remain in China. Some American-owned businesses had similar experiences. Relations between the Peking regime and the Shanghai Power Company, for instance, remained smooth for months after the May 1949 Communist takeover of Shanghai.

Talks with Communist leaders could have served a variety of purposes. They could have been used to protest the treatment of American representatives in China. To avoid conveying a sense of American weakness or desperation, the United States could have held to a firm position on this issue. Top officials in Peking might well have demonstrated flexibility on the matter. It was by no means certain, after all, either then or later, that the harassment of American officials represented a centrally coordinated policy of the Communists or merely the independent acts of local forces.

Acheson could have minimized confusion and resentment among Western European nations by keeping their leaders informed of the proceedings. The mere fact of discussions in Peking need not have detracted from caution and unity on the recognition question. In fact, Peking talks might actually have strengthened Western harmony. It they went poorly, tendencies, already apparent in Great Britain and France, to open relations with the Communists once they formed a government, might have been weakened.

On the other hand, conversations in Peking might have been a basic step toward mutual toleration between Communist China and the West. Washington's failure to pursue discussions diminished such prospects. As Cabot noted, the out-and-out rejection of the Huang overture may "have placed those Communists favoring better relations with the West in an impossible situation." The American response was especially damaging because the ambassador's secretary had initiated the idea of a Stuart visit to Peking. The Communists probably viewed the suggestion as a concrete overture by the United States. When Washington squelched it, therefore, Peking was understandably embarrassed and displeased. Indeed, between July and September 1949 there emerged little new evidence that Communist leaders desired a "working relationship with the United States." Even Chou En-lai made strong anti-American speeches. And Communist officials in Mukden, who on 21 June had notified Ward that transportation facilities would be made available for him and his staff to leave the city, hardened their position toward the American diplomat. Although a variety of considerations may have dictated against Stuart traveling to Peking, Acheson should at least have communicated to the Communists that the United States desired talks but wanted, for the present, to pursue them through Clubb.

Direct contacts between the United States and the Communist Chinese were especially desirable in view of continued American aid to Chiang. In the absence of diplomatic exchanges between Peking and Washington, Communist leaders inevitably saw an American plot behind every Nationalist move. In late June, for example, in an effort to impede Communist efforts to rule China, the Nationalists blockaded Shanghai. The action consisted of both air and naval maneuvers to prevent foreign ships from unloading cargoes there. Although the United States did not approve the move, the Communists soon labeled it as American-inspired. This characterization may have been part of a Communist strategy of exploiting popular resentments against foreigners for the purpose of building unity at home. But past American support for the Nationalists—which continued, albeit at a low level—coupled with Washington's rejection of Peking's overtures, made it just as likely that the Communists truly believed that the United States was responsible for the blockade.

In addition to the possibility that talks would have increased Communist understanding of the American position, they also might have added to the Truman administration's grasp of events in China. Washington's perceptions of the Communists already had suffered from insufficient contact. Although the State Department had tentatively concluded—perhaps in part because of the recent example of Yugoslavia—that, in a positive sense, there was little the United States could or need do to influence Communist relations with the Soviet Union, more extensive knowledge might have led to a different judgment. As *New York Times* correspondent Seymour Topping has noted, even if the Truman administration could not have influenced Mao "to adopt a neutral position in the East-West struggle," conversations with the Communist leader might have "led at least to the establishment of a channel of communication between Peking and Washington." "If Americans had continued to talk to the Chinese Communists," Topping maintains, "many of the misunderstandings and much of the agony in Asia over the next two decades might have been averted." . . .

The administration's top priority was to maintain a united front against early recognition. The American effort faced serious difficulties, for the Labour government in Great Britain, in the face of pressures from commercial interests at home, leaned toward the establishment of relations with the Mao government. India's Prime Minister Jawaharlal Nehru also favored quick action. A succession of other Western European and Asian governments undoubtedly would follow the British and Indian lead. Rather than planning to move with the tide, Acheson summoned his persuasive powers in an attempt to reverse it. He failed in the endeavor; India recognized the People's Republic in December, and Great Britain took the same course a week later. By 18 January 1950, nine more non-Communist regimes had taken similar action.

Acheson's stand enjoyed widespread congressional and public support. Gallup polls of the summer and fall of 1949 indicated that Americans with opinions on the matter—only about 60 percent of those questioned— opposed recognition by more than a two to one margin. In late November, the Committee to Defend America by Aiding Anti-Communist China launched a "nationwide drive" against recognition with a rally at Carnegie Hall in New York. Several members of Congress attended the event. On 29 December, Senator [Tom] Connally, following the overwhelming opinion expressed in letters to him from private citizens, announced his opposition to recognition.

James Reston, Washington correspondent for the *New York Times,* reported that State Department officials conceded in private that the domestic climate alone was delaying American recognition. As earlier, however, this consideration merely reinforced Acheson's inclinations, for Communist China's comportment in international matters genuinely disturbed him. On 24 October 1949, Angus Ward was jailed in Mukden for an alleged assault on a former Chinese servant at the American consulate. The State Department managed to obtain his release a month later, but Communist aggressiveness toward American officials and property in China did not end. On 14 January 1950, the Chinese government seized American consular compounds in Peking. In response to this action, and to the termination two months later of American radio communications with its representatives on the mainland, the United States withdrew completely from China. To the secretary of state, these were only the most overt manifestations of a generally intolerable state of mind that prevailed within the new government. Although he did not desire to slam the door permanently on American recognition, a halt to the "active abuse of us" in Peking was a prerequisite to a reevaluation of his position.

In early 1950, there was little movement on the question. Acheson toyed with the idea of using continued Nationalist air attacks on Shanghai—which often damaged American property—as a pretext for a total break with the Nationalist government, but such a break never occurred. In March, on the eve of Clubb's final departure from Peking, the secretary of state suggested that the consul general seek "an informal discussion with high Commie authorities of outstanding points of friction" between the United States and the new regime. Acheson emphasized, however, that Clubb must avoid " any inference [that] such [a] discussion constituted [a] move toward recognition or is a preliminary to such a move," or that the overture resulted from Communist "pressure" or American "weakness." Concern for American credibility abroad remained a barrier to flexible diplomacy.

In early April, Communist Chinese officials made it clear that termination of United States support for Chiang was a quid pro quo for talks on other issues. For all practical purposes, this exchange closed the matter. Clubb left China before the end of the month. Intent on avoiding any implication that Communist pressure could soften American policy, Acheson held firmly to the view that the Mao regime must submit to generally accepted standards of international conduct before the United States would talk about halting aid to the Nationalists and recognizing Peking. If the domestic political factor was critical, it was so only in an indirect sense: the American failure during 1949 to abandon the Nationalists completely—which was partially a result of pressures at home—influenced the Communist attitude toward the United States which, in turn, shaped the State Department position on relations with the Mao regime.

Another factor early in the fall of 1949 concerned pockets of armed resistance to the Communists in China. Although American officials recognized the probable futility of such activity, they did not want to openly discourage it. The desire remained strong to make the road to power of the Communists as rocky as possible. By mid-November, however, this consideration was no longer a significant impediment to recognition.

Concern for resistance to Communism on China's borders continued to influence Acheson's deliberations. On 16 December, he sent telegrams to his representatives in Southeast Asia requesting their views on the impact of American recognition. In the next two weeks, the secretary received replies from the consul general in Saigon, the chargé in Burma, and the ambassadors to Thailand and the Philippines. All of them emphasized the negative impact early recognition might have on efforts to bolster anti-Communist forces south and east of China's borders. This negative consideration took on decisive weight when combined with the prevailing State Department view that little could be done, in a positive vein, to alter the essentially hostile attitude of the Communists toward the United States.

From a domestic political standpoint, the Truman administration's best opportunity to talk to Peking was in the last months of 1949. The Communist government had been officially established, and the Atlantic Pact and the Military Assistance Plan had passed Congress. Public and congressional opinion did not necessitate a negative policy on recognition. In October, for instance, the State Department's Office of Public Opinion Studies reported that "most observers" in the press, while seeing "little need for haste, . . . expected eventual *de facto* recognition as the most 'realistic' course." Even after the Ward case made headlines in late October, most commentators "did not discount the possibility or desirability of recognition at some time in the future." Most Asian experts in the academic community, most Protestant church organizations, and many businessmen with interests in China favored early recognition. Admittedly, Catholic organizations and much of organized labor disagreed, as did large pluralities of those Americans queried by pollsters. The firmness of much of this opposition, however, especially in the general citizenry, may be doubted. Recognizing Peking would not take money or jobs away from many Americans, nor would it lead directly to physical setbacks to the security of the United States. Surely a public-relations offensive by the administration in favor of recognition would have had some impact.

Furthermore, if the hostility of the Chinese Communists toward the United States was related to American hostility toward them, and if the antagonism of many Americans toward recognition derived in part from Peking's antagonism to the United States, then American overtures to Mao might have led ultimately to a decline of public opposition to relations with the new government. In the absence of American initiatives toward Peking, on the other hand, Communist hostility was virtually certain to continue, as was the tendency of the American public to oppose recognition. In fact, much can be said for the argument that the Truman administration's best chance of overcoming the charge that it had "lost" China rested in the cautious but active pursuit of rapprochement with the Communists.

What were the prospects for rapprochement? Although the hostile acts in Mukden in late October 1949 and in Peking in the following January indicated to many the total hostility of the Communists, it remains uncertain that the incidents reflected decisions by a unified national leadership. One plausible explanation of the Ward affair is that Kao Kang, the pro-Russian head of the Northeastern People's Government, which was seated in Mukden—a government that had been established in late August and that temporarily maintained a degree of autonomy—took the action without prior approval from Peking. Clubb believed that the Soviet Union had instigated Ward's arrest in retaliation for the prosecution in the United States of Valentin Gubichev, a Russian citizen who the Kremlin asserted had diplomatic immunity. The State's Department's Office of European Affairs suspected a direct connection between the Ward case and the October 1949 arrest in the United States of officials in the Soviet-owned Amtorg Trading Corporation for failing to register as foreign agents. Whatever the reasons for Ward's arrest, its occurrence so soon after Clubb had seen evidence that the Communists genuinely desired to establish relations with the United States suggests that powerful forces were pulling in opposite directions within China. Whether or not the United States could have influenced the situation remains a mystery. It is certain, however, that in October 1949 the State Department rejected an opportunity to explore the possibility. . . .

Sino-American talks in Peking in October 1949 would have run into difficulties in two areas: continued American assistance to the Nationalists and the status of treaties between the United States and the Chiang regime. Agreement could have come only through concessions on both sides. The United States undoubtedly would have been expected to end economic and military aid to Taiwan.

Past Sino-American agreements would have needed to be renegotiated. Pressure from the pro-Soviet faction in China and the China bloc in the United States made flexibility difficult for either government.

Nevertheless, an exchange of views might have shown compromise to be possible. For instance, the United States might have offered to end all assistance to the Nationalists after 15 February 1950, the termination date for the commitment of funds through the China Aid Act. The United States might also have agreed to revise old pacts between the two countries, provided that changes were more of form than of substance. In a Sino-American agreement of 1943, the United States had renounced the most blatant privileges in the "unequal treaties" of the nineteenth and early twentieth centuries, but dissatisfaction remained among the Communists in certain areas, including the status of part of the United States consular compound in Peking, which had been seized in 1900 as a barracks for American troops in the foreign intervention against the Boxer Rebellion. A protocol of 1901 had given the United States title to this land, and the agreement of 1943, though calling for an end to all rights received in the earlier pact, provided for the continued American use of property allocated for its diplomatic quarters. It may be wondered here if relatively minor concessions by Washington would have satisfied Communist determination to remove all vestiges of "imperialist" domination. A demonstrated willingness on the part of the United States to discuss the matter might at least have prevented precipitous action such as occurred on 14 January 1950 [when the Chinese government seized American consular compounds in Beijing].

Perhaps the Communists, fearing the Kremlin's reaction, would have shied away from serious talks with the United States. The Soviets maintained a strong, possibly even dominant, presence in Manchuria, and—in the aftermath of Yugoslavia's revolt against Stalin's direction—were particularly sensitive to any Peking flirtations with the West. Walter McConaughy, who during the previous summer had replaced Cabot as consul general at Shanghai, had information that Mao's trip to Moscow was the result of a "strong and rather sudden . . . pressure" from the Kremlin in response to "moves" by Great Britain and other non-Communist nations toward recognition and an impending visit by [Acheson's assistant] Philip Jessup to the western Pacific. On the other hand, McConaughy also reported a "rapidly swelling tide [of] Chinese charges and bitterness re[garding] Soviet greed [and] encroachments" in Manchuria. Had Washington demonstrated greater flexibility toward the new regime, it might have evaluated its options somewhat differently.

But the cold war had so come to dominate Acheson's mentality that common bargaining was unthinkable with a Communist government that repudiated widely accepted standards of international conduct—standards, by the way, that China had had no role in constructing—and showed open allegiance to Moscow. To Acheson, there was little to discuss and nothing to concede. If "keeping a foot in the door" and avoiding the diversion of potential Chinese irredentist sentiments against Russia in the north were of sufficient worth to merit a degree of restraint on the part of the United States, they warranted little in the way of positive effort. And Acheson received little pressure within the administration, from either above or below, to loosen his stance.

Dean Acheson's Plan
for Accommodation and Recognition

NANCY BERNKOPF TUCKER

Scholars examining the second Truman Administration have come to see Dean Acheson as the embodiment of Cold War ideology from 1949 to 1953. Acheson certainly subscribed to a picture of himself manning the gates against a dangerous Communist menace whose threat to the security of the United States was staunched only through his vigilance and determination. His memoir *Present at the Creation* [1969] makes his position on the ramparts clear. During his tenure as Secretary of State the United States imposed the North Atlantic Treaty upon the Marshall Plan, turning it into a military alliance, and mounted an airlift to keep Berlin free. Acheson abjured negotiation with Moscow, demanding that the Western alliance first establish positions of strength to bargain from. Thus Acheson emerged as a potent force for Communist containment across Europe. This stance, however, has misled students of the Secretary's policies to assume a seamless, global application of his outlook. . . .

On 17 November 1949 Acheson . . . arranged a meeting between President Harry S. Truman and a team he had assembled to examine China policy and suggest new directions for the administration. The three men—Philip Jessup, Raymond Fosdick and Everett Case, the latter two consultants from outside the Department—told Truman that the United States should not attempt to overthrow the Communist government in China. Rather, as Acheson anticipated, they advised the President that he must face reality: the Communists would continue to hold sway in Beijing. The only sensible course, therefore, would be to extend diplomatic recognition to them. The main thrust of American policy should be, recorded Acheson, "to attempt to detach [China] from subservience to Moscow and over a period of time encourage those vigorous influences which might modify it." Lest the President miss the message, Acheson followed the group session with a private conversation to emphasize his point. Ultimately the persistent Secretary convinced Truman that the analysis was "correct" and the President conceded that he had learned a great deal.

There existed, then, another Dean Acheson, one who took a moderate, flexible, accommodating stance toward Communist China; who emphasized the pragmatic need to deal with Beijing and divest America of distasteful ties to the corrupt Chinese Nationalist regime; who approved policies that permitted trade with mainland China and kept American diplomats in place after the Communist takeover; who held out against criticism from Congress, the China Lobby, the military and even from within the Department of State. This Acheson emerges clearly if only one examines the actual developments regarding China during his tenure as Secretary and his responses to them, instead of listening to rhetorical flourishes, reading

From Nancy Bernkopf Tucker, "China's Place in the Cold War: The Acheson Plan," in Douglas Brinkley, ed., *Dean Acheson and the Making of U.S. Foreign Policy*, pp. 109–124. Copyright © Douglas Brinkley; reprinted with permission of St. Martin's Press, Incorporated.

later attitudes into an earlier time, or assuming that decisions made for Europe or Japan dictated parallel policies toward China. Acheson saw alternatives for China and pursued them until war in Korea foreclosed his options. . . .

Above all, Acheson must be understood as an Atlanticist. He felt fundamentally indifferent to Asia and lamented the fact that China's collapse required the taking of time from European affairs to try to deal with unfathomable Chinese politics. Compiling his list of urgent international problems at the start of his incumbency in January 1949, Acheson did not include China, although the most decisive battle of the civil war was at that moment destroying the Kuomintang (KMT). He never seriously considered a commitment sufficient to save China from Communist takeover, husbanding America's limited resources for more significant purposes. With his emphasis on European recovery and the creation of NATO [North Atlantic Treaty Organization] even the outbreak of war in Korea became an opportunity to increase military aid to Europe. In the end, although he struggled over questions of how to find a third-force party in preference to either the KMT or CCP [Chinese Communist party], how to compel Chiang Kai-shek to institute reforms, and how to distance Washington from Taipei, he never solved America's China problems. Nor did he come to understand China. In 1950 he participated in the decision to send American forces across the 38th parallel in Korea, despite explicit warnings from Chinese premier Zhou Enlai that this would mean a new, far more costly war.

Acheson's efforts to navigate the shoals of Chinese-American relations suffered attacks by foes in the Defense Department (DOD), the China bloc in Congress, the China Lobby and even a few of his advisers at State. The opposition that these elements mounted to his policies proved constant but ineffectual prior to the Korean War. They fought him on every appropriations measure, every authorization, every policy directive.

The case of National Security Council document 48 [a statement of U.S. policy toward Asia] provides an illustration both of the contest and Acheson's mastery of it. In the autumn of 1949 Secretary of Defense Louis Johnson, long a proponent of Chiang Kai-shek, initiated a National Security Council paper designed to support continued aid for the KMT and a hardline toward the Communists. Although the Joint Chiefs of Staff had repeatedly judged that Taiwan's strategic importance did not justify overt military action, most recently in August during a review of NSC 37/5 [a statement of U.S. policy toward Taiwan], Johnson and the JCS [Joint Chiefs of Staff] tried to force military assistance to the island back into policy through NSC 48. The Far Eastern Bureau of the State Department, however, was horrified by the belligerent tone of the draft paper and its unacceptable policy recommendations. With Acheson's blessing, the staff retained the rhetorical brimstone to keep DOD happy, but changed the policy guidelines to match more moderate views prevalent at State. Acheson then secured Truman's assent even though the President had seemed to encourage Johnson along lines that matched his own characteristic desire for forceful action.

If Acheson actually knew little about China, he believed that he knew quite enough about Chiang Kai-shek and the Kuomintang to justify distaste and a desire to disentangle Washington from its commitment to the Generalissimo. Military disaster and Kuomintang unwillingness and inability to make vital economic and political changes convinced Acheson that America's ally could not win the raging civil war. Rather than send more assistance to be misused or embezzled, Acheson advocated severing ties. On 3 February 1949 the National Security Council called for the suspension of shipments to China and, when Congressional opposition made that politically impossible, Acheson acted instead to slow down transport. He vigorously opposed a $1.5 billion aid package promoted by Senator Pat McCarran (D-NV), appearing in executive session before the Senate Foreign Relations Committee to explain that China was all but lost. And when the issue of new funds under Section 303 of the Mutual Defense Assistance Act arose in the summer of 1949, Acheson managed to maneuver Congress into accepting a provision for using the funds at presidential discretion and in the general area of China—not specifically for Chiang.

Acheson recognized that to sustain his effort at disengagement he would have to explain to the public why America could do no more to help China. As early as November 1948 the State Department discussed publishing a detailed indictment of Chinese Nationalist ineptitude and corruption. In February 1949 Acheson thought about replying to a Congressional round robin letter with an exposé. Deterred in both instances by domestic political considerations, he finally authorized the compilation of a white paper in April. So obvious had the impending fall of the Nationalist regime become that Acheson's fear of accusations that he had pushed Chiang over a precipice carried less weight than the need to prevent new pressures favoring a rescue of Taiwan. The volume, which the Department released in August 1949, told the sad story of Nationalist Chinese ineptitude and decline in 1,054 pages. This work was loudly criticised by members of the so-called China Lobby. But Acheson's contempt for these people lessened his sensitivity to the anger he had generated.

Hesitancy in ending aid or disclosing KMT weakness reflected both the dynamics of American politics and the mythology of American ideals. After the unexpected defeat of Thomas Dewey in 1948, Truman and his administration became targets of increasingly vicious Republican attacks designed to turn the Democrats out of the presidency at any cost in 1952. Among the issues that fueled the onslaught were Communism and China. Acheson had to protect himself and his President from charges that they had been soft on Communists of the Russian, American or Chinese variety. This did not, in his mind, dictate enthusiastic cooperation with the KMT, but it militated against a clean break as well. That seemed especially unnecessary given intelligence estimates and predictions from the American consulate in Taipei that Taiwan would fall to the communists in the summer of 1950. . . .

When Acheson arrived at the State Department in January 1949, he discovered active interest among his subordinates in the Formosan independence movement. By giving it encouragement, the United States could rid itself of Chiang (certainly no democrat), promote self-determination among the Formosans, who had been brutally massacred by the KMT in 1947, and keep a strategically valuable piece of property out of Communist hands. These hopes became policy in NSC 37/2 on 4 February 1949 and Acheson dispatched a trusted lieutenant, Livingston

Merchant, to Taiwan to explore the situation. But Merchant discovered that the independence movement did not have enough strength to contest the grip of Chiang's regime, a judgment confirmed by Economic Cooperation Administration officials in Taiwan.

Acheson, always the pragmatist, abandoned his hopes of saving Taiwan. He rejected alternatives proposed by W. Walton Butterworth for a UN plebiscite and George Kennan for an American military takeover and ouster of Chiang. The Secretary might abhor Communism but he was too much of a realist to believe that America could force democracy upon Taiwan unless the people of the island had the desire and power to support it. Although he castigated the mainland leaders for having "forsworn their Chinese heritage," the Kuomintang/Chiang Kai-shek embodiment of that heritage did not strike Acheson as a better bargain. And so, on 5 January 1950 Harry Truman announced that the United States would not intervene in the Chinese civil war to save Taiwan from Communist attack, and on 12 January Acheson reconfirmed this in a speech to the National Press Club in which he placed Taiwan outside the American defensive perimeter. . . .

Acheson's assumption . . . was that Taiwan would collapse in 1950 and that Washington would, in time, open diplomatic relations with the new regime in Beijing. This certainly was the impression Acheson gave Ernest Bevin, the British Foreign Secretary, in April 1949. "The U.S. henceforth," Acheson averred, "will pursue a more realistic policy respecting China."

Of all the governments with which Acheson dealt, Whitehall commanded his greatest affection and respect, and therefore had the greatest foreign influence on his views of China policy. Throughout 1949 British and American consultations regarding China occurred regularly. The Secretary of State tried to delay British recognition of Beijing in order to maintain a united front for negotiating purposes, and deplored Britain's eager response to Zhou Enlai's October bid for mutually beneficial relations. But Acheson understood the economic impetus behind London's actions, particularly the importance of protecting an otherwise helpless Hong Kong. State Department intelligence research staffers attested to the popularity of accommodation among the British in London and China. There was also considerable evidence that Asian members of the Commonwealth were pressing London for a racially unbiased position that would support the triumph of nationalism in China. . . .

One aspect of the realism Acheson imposed upon American policy involved the issue of trade. The British were not alone in asserting the importance of commercial relations with Beijing. American businessmen hoped to continue their economic intercourse with China and chafed at the idea of losing markets to Englishmen. Moreover, Acheson confronted the problems of Japan's still floundering economy. Japanese businessmen and government officials argued enthusiastically for trade with China, pointing to their traditional ties, a desperate need for raw materials only China could supply cheaply, and the vast China market. If the United States ever hoped to rid itself of the burden of feeding Japan, warned the Department's Office of Intelligence and Research, it must permit Sino-Japanese trade. Southeast Asia offered some alternatives, but the British objected to Japanese competition in that region, and it could not supply all the resources which Japan could hope to obtain from China. . . .

By pursuing a policy of modest trade with China, Acheson hoped to further the development of an independent, even if Communist, regime in Beijing. Building on the experience that the Truman Administration had had with Yugoslavia, Acheson believed that the Communist world was not monolithic. Mao Zedong possessed the same divisive characteristics as Josip Broz Tito [of Yugoslavia], having come to power without Kremlin support, having led a nationalistic resistance against foreign invaders and having nurtured a cult of personality. To examine the parallels the Secretary dispatched John Cabot, whose prior service in Belgrade qualified him to assess Chinese Titoism, as his Consul General to Shanghai. Cabot concluded that conditions in China were even more favorable to the West than they had been in Yugoslavia, particularly if the United States avoided hostile criticism of the regime, trade restrictions and other pressures.

Inherent in the encouragement of Titoism in China were hopes that Sino-Soviet frictions would widen into a significant split. Considerable evidence existed that disputes had already arisen over such things as the [Soviet's] stripping of Manchurian industry during World War II, Stalin's advice against the [CCP] conquest of southern China, and the Soviet–Chiang Kai-shek treaty of 1945. The Chinese bridled at Kremlin efforts to control developments inside China and, as Foreign Service Officer John Melby noted, "We have all seen too many examples of Russian, even official Russian, contempt for the Chinese as Chinese to assume that the Communists have not noticed it too." In addition to Soviet racism there was also Soviet imperialism to contend with. Mao bitterly resented the Kremlin's demands for joint stock companies, mining and industrial concessions, and likened his efforts to secure aid from Stalin to taking "meat out of the tiger's mouth."

Acheson recognized these animosities and hoped to prevent the deflection of righteous anger away from Moscow. His refusal to consider plots to interfere in Taiwan stemmed, as he told the Senate Foreign Relations Committee, from his desire not to allow "historic Chinese xenophobia" to focus on Americans rather than the Russians who were busy provoking it in the north and west. The key, as Acheson reminded the Senators, was not whether the Chinese regime was Communist but that "even if the devil himself runs China, if he is an independent devil that is infinitely better than if he is a stooge of Moscow."

Nevertheless, it proved difficult for Americans to judge reliably whether the Chinese would behave as puppets or patriots. State Department analysts believed that part of their confusion stemmed from the existence of competing factions within the Chinese Communist Party. There was, to be sure, an important group which held a stridently ideological line and looked to the Soviet Union for leadership. But American observers also identified a more flexible coterie around Zhou Enlai which sought better relations with the United States so as to quicken economic recovery as well as to prevent total domination by Moscow. Trusting to this latter view, Acheson ordered American diplomatic personnel to remain in place as the CCP "liberated" China so that moderates in the party could make contact.

And contacts did, in fact, follow. Huang Hua, one of Zhou's experts on Western barbarians, assumed the directorship of the Alien Affairs Office in Nanjing after the CCP captured the Kuomintang capital in May 1949. He immediately initiated conversations with the American Ambassador J. Leighton Stuart, who had been his teacher at Yenching University. Eventually those talks resulted in an invitation for Stuart to visit Beijing and meet with Mao and Zhou. Even when Truman forbade the visit and after Mao made his "lean to one side" speech, Huang reiterated the suggestion for a trip north. Approaches also came from Ye Jianying, Mayor of Beijing, regarding trade treaties. During April 1949, Yao Yilin, the Minister of Industry and Commerce, asked O. Edmund Clubb, the American Consul General in Beijing, about developing economic relations. In June the Mayor of Shanghai, Chen Yi, told an audience of cultural leaders that China would welcome not just trade but also loans and technical assistance. Behind the scenes there were also Chinese Communist representatives in the United States who, having completed their training at major American universities, hoped to expedite Sino-American commercial intercourse.

Possibly as part of this effort to improve relations with the United States, in the spring of 1949 a secret *démarche* passed from Zhou Enlai through an Australian journalist to American officials in Beijing. The authenticity of the opening has subsequently been challenged by some scholars, but at the time the State Department and the White House judged it to be genuine. Zhou made it clear that China needed economic assistance to avoid collapse and launch a program of reconstruction. This would be an enormous effort which the Soviets did not have the wherewithal to support. Thus, Zhou suggested, Washington might facilitate better relations with Beijing by providing the economic and technical aid required. Although Zhou had specified that he wanted no reply, the President authorized an effort to express American interest. Nothing came of that attempt, however, since a spy had leaked word of the *démarche* to Zhou's major opponent, Liu Shaoqi, and Clubb was rebuffed.

Even had the available expertise on China been more plentiful and less cautious, Washington would have had difficulty assessing Chinese Communist intentions. The general noise level in China, given the revolutionary overthrow of the Nationalist regime after years of civil conflict and anti-Japanese war, obscured the significance of discreet events. If some Communist leaders appeared to be reaching out, others exercised their anti-foreign anger in ways that discouraged American observers. Incidents involving Foreign Service Officers and American businessmen occurred in Shanghai and elsewhere. Communist officials closed the Consulate General in Manchuria and put its occupants under house arrest. And Mao declared on 1 July 1949 that the new China would lean to the side of the Soviet Union. But, although Harry Truman thought seriously about implementing a blockade to liberate Angus Ward in Mukden, soberer judgment recognized some justice in Chinese ire, given that an espionage network had, in fact, been operating out of the consulate, and Ward was known to be difficult and belligerent. State Department observers rated the degree of anti-American violence low for a revolutionary situation, and American businessmen generally hoped to remain in China despite problems. Even Mao's clear determination to ally with the Soviet Union (expressed in July and confirmed in a treaty of friendship in February 1950) did not, in Acheson's mind, foreclose Sino-American contacts entirely.

The final blow thwarting Acheson's pragmatism came on 25 June 1950 when North Korean forces crossed the border initiating war. This event pulled the props out from under Acheson's efforts at moderation, calling into question both his own convictions and his ability to defend an unpopular viewpoint against critics. Acheson, the government and the American people understood the attack as Soviet induced. The connivance of the Communist regime in Beijing was assumed. Efforts to see the Communist world as anything other than monolithic could not withstand the North Korean onslaught. If frictions between Moscow and Beijing were clear, it appeared that in extremis the Chinese would subordinate their interests to those of the Soviets. Using the Chinese to constrain Moscow no longer seemed viable. Acheson reacted with anger and dismay, giving way to others who had long anticipated just such an event.

Indeed, two critical decisions would follow from the attack that collided with the earlier moderation displayed by the Secretary of State: dispatch of the Seventh fleet to the Taiwan Straits and crossing of the 38th parallel to reunify Korea. In both cases these acts grew out of unfortunate coincidences of opportunity and domestic political necessity. They betrayed a profound misunderstanding of Communist China, typical of Acheson and much of the administration in Washington. Ultimately, each led to disaster. . . .

Acheson viewed imposition of the Seventh Fleet in the Taiwan Straits as a temporary measure. Once the emergency in Korea passed, so too would the necessity of interfering in the Taiwan situation. Acheson argued that the administration should decline Chiang's offer to send 33,000 soldiers to Korea, recalling their disastrous performance in China. The Secretary welcomed the President's declaration that he would not supply more financial aid since the Nationalists had invested earlier support in American real estate. Acheson persuaded Truman to reject Chiang's pleas (which were supported by the JCS, General Douglas MacArthur, and Defense Secretary Louis Johnson) for a pre-emptive strike against massing Chinese Communist troops along the Fujian coast in July. In September Acheson chastised the American Ambassador in Taipei for giving Nationalist officials false hopes regarding American intentions, and Dean Rusk warned, "We do not wish to make any commitment to Chinese authorities as to how long this relationship will extend into the future."

Acheson, however, learned to his chagrin a lesson he should have absorbed earlier: it was not so easy to disentangle the United States from Chiang's embrace. Beginning with a $14 million military assistance package in August, the bonds of association with the Kuomintang once again tightened around Washington. The general military expansion necessitated and facilitated by the war in Korea made the use of hitherto scarce resources viable in an area which, at least momentarily, did not look as peripheral as it had previously. With the funds available and fighting in progress, Acheson was no longer inclined, nor indeed able, to oppose aid to "Free China."

Not only did Acheson miscalculate his maneuvering room with the Kuomintang, he also misread the capacities and intentions of the Chinese Communists. There might be good American military reasons to take the precaution of placing the Seventh Fleet in the Taiwan Straits, but from Beijing's point of view it was unforgivable. After Acheson's and Truman's statements in January that the United States would stay out of the civil war, this act smacked of duplicity and blatant imperialism. China's meagre amphibious capability could not possibly confront

American might and so, once again, conclusion of its unification drive had to be postponed.

The setback of Taiwan had not yet been fully absorbed when Beijing perceived an even more basic threat to its survival. Washington, rapidly successful in Korea, had to decide where its drive northward would stop. The temptation of pushing to the Yalu [River] and reunifying Korea proved too strong for Acheson and Truman. They did not heed the judgments of Soviet specialists like George Kennan and Charles Bohlen or CIA analysts that the US would be embarking on a lonely and dangerous effort. The 38th parallel was, after all, an artificial construct that had no saliency for an American public which longed for victory over Communism. . . .

Of course, the Secretary [Acheson] proved drastically, tragically wrong. Beijing found the crossing of the 38th parallel intolerable and had tried to make it clear beforehand that that would be the case. During the summer of 1950, Zhou Enlai, through public and private channels, warned that China could not stay out of the conflict if Americans marched to the river. These admonitions were ignored by the Secretary, assuming that the Chinese had neither the strength nor the will to fight in Korea. . . .

Acheson the Cold War warrior recast his view of Chinese affairs as a result of the Korean War. Having argued that the stakes in the East were not sufficiently important to necessitate a major American effort there, the war caught him off-guard and embarrassed him. Suddenly the credibility of American commitments on behalf of the free world appeared to be under assault. North Korea had become a puppet of Moscow's expansionist aims which, thwarted in Europe, must be exercised in Asia. More disturbing, China, which he had pictured as following its own socialist road, demonstrated by its November intervention enough subservience to Moscow to sacrifice its own interests regarding Taiwan. The Secretary had succeeded in distancing Washington from Taipei by convincing his President that the island would fall under the weight of Kuomintang corruption and ineptitude when Beijing attempted its invasion. Although he had acknowledged that Soviet control would be dangerous there, this seemed an unlikely prospect. But the North Korean attack changed everything. Nationalist China quickly reestablished ties with Washington. And although Acheson tried to remain flexible in dealing with China, bloodshed rapidly made that impossible.

✻ *F U R T H E R   R E A D I N G*

Robert M. Blum, *Drawing the Line* (1982)

Robert Boardman, *Britain and the People's Republic of China* (1976)

Dorothy Borg and Waldo Heinrichs, eds., *Uncertain Years: Chinese-American Relations, 1947–1950* (1980)

Russell Buhite, *Patrick J. Hurley and American Foreign Policy* (1973)

——, *Soviet-American Relations in Asia, 1945–1954* (1982)

Gordon H. Chang, *Friends and Enemies* (1990)

Warren I. Cohen, *America's Response to China* (1990)

——, "The United States and China Since 1945," in Warren I. Cohen, ed., *New Frontiers in American East Asian Relations* (1983)

John P. Davies, *Dragon by the Tail* (1972)
John K. Fairbank, *The United States and China* (1979)
Herbert Feis, *The China Tangle,* (1953)
Marc S. Gallicchio, *The Cold War Begins in Asia* (1988)
John Gittings, *The World and China, 1922–1972* (1974)
Akira Iriye, *The Cold War in Asia* (1974)
——— and Warren Cohen, eds., *American, Chinese, and Japanese Perspectives on Wartime Asia, 1931–1949* (1990)
Arnold Xiangze Jiang, *The United States and China* (1988)
E. J. Kahn, *The China Hands* (1972)
Robert C. Keith, *The Diplomacy of Zhou Enlai* (1989)
Ross Koen, *The China Lobby in American Politics* (1974)
Paul G. Lauren, *The China Hands Legacy* (1987)
Ronald L. McGlothlen, *Controlling the Waves: Dean Acheson and U.S. Foreign Policy in Asia* (1993)
Edwin Martin, *Divided Counsel: The Anglo-American Response to Communist Victory in China* (1986)
Ernest R. May, ed., *The Truman Administration and China, 1945–1949* (1975)
Gary May, *China Scapegoat: The Diplomatic Ordeal of John Carter Vincent* (1979)
David Mayers, *Cracking the Monolith: U.S. Policy Against the Sino-Soviet Alliance* (1986)
Robert P. Newman, *Owen Lattimore and the "Loss" of China* (1992)
Thomas G. Paterson, *Meeting the Communist Threat* (1988)
Brian E. Porter, *Britain and the Rise of Communist China* (1967)
James Reardon-Anderson, *Yenan and the Great Powers* (1980)
Michael Schaller, *The U.S. Crusade in China, 1938–1945* (1978)
———, *The United States and China in the Twentieth Century* (1990)
Shaw Yu-Ming, *John Leighton Stuart and Twentieth Century China-America Relations* (1992)
Shuguang Zhang, *Deterrence and Strategic Culture* (1992)
William W. Stueck, Jr., *The Wedemeyer Mission* (1984)
James C. Thomson et al., *Sentimental Imperialists* (1981)
Tang Tsou, *America's Failure in China, 1941–1950* (1963)
Barbara Tuchman, "If Mao Had Come to Washington," *Foreign Affairs,* 51 (1972), 44–64
———, *Stilwell and the American Experience in China, 1911–1945* (1971)
Nancy Bernkopf Tucker, *Patterns in the Dust: Chinese-American Relations and the Recognition Controversy, 1949–1950* (1983)
Paul Varg, *The Closing of the Door: Sino-American Relations, 1936–1947* (1973)
Odd Arne Westad, *Cold War and Revolution* (1993)
H. Bradford Westerfield, *Foreign Policy and Party Politics* (1955)
Donald Zagoria, "Choices in the Postwar World: Containment and China," in Charles Gati, ed., *Caging the Bear* (1974)

The Korean War

Before the outbreak of the Korean War in June 1950, the United States had launched a number of Cold War strategies and programs—the Truman Doctrine, the Marshall Plan, and NATO—and had participated in crises in Iran, Turkey, Greece, Berlin, and elsewhere. Crisis also rocked China, where Mao Zedong's (Mao Tse-tung's) communists unseated Jiang Jieshi's (Chiang Kai-shek's) Nationalists in late 1949 and created the People's Republic of China.

A powerful shock wave hit the United States in August 1949 when the Soviet Union successfully exploded an atomic device, thereby ending America's atomic monopoly. Many Americans jumped to the conclusion that the United States was losing the Cold War. The phenomenon of McCarthyism, driven by an exaggerated fear of communism on the home front, surfaced in early 1950. Then in June of that year, the Korean War erupted. The Truman administration quickly decided to intervene in the conflict—to apply the containment doctrine.

U.S. intervention in Korea had actually begun in 1945, during the closing days of the Second World War, when Washington and Moscow drew a line at the thirty-eighth parallel and occupied the former Japanese colony. The two superpowers had agreed to a temporary division, but Korea soon became contested Cold War territory, an arena where the Soviets and the Americans competed to establish client states. In South Korea the United States threw its support behind the conservative government of Syngman Rhee, and in North Korea the Soviets backed Kim Il Sung's communist regime. Both Korean leaders considered themselves devout nationalists, and each envisioned himself as the head of a unified, independent Korea. As American and Soviet forces pulled back from the peninsula in 1949 and 1950, the two Koreas clashed in frequent border skirmishes and headed for a showdown. War came on June 25, 1950, when 75,000 Soviet-equipped North Korean troops punched through the thirty-eighth parallel and invaded South Korea.

The Korean War significantly altered the Cold War's course. In addition to dispatching U.S. forces to Korea, the Truman administration redoubled its efforts to contain communism around the globe and increasingly relied on military power to do the job. At home the administration raised annual defense expenditures from some $17 billion in 1950 to more than $50 billion in 1953, implementing the military buildup envisioned by the authors of NSC-68. In Europe military aid assumed priority over economic aid as Washington sought to give NATO more muscle. U.S. officials also laid plans for regional defense arrangements in the Middle East and

East Asia. In Southeast Asia the Truman administration increased military assistance to noncommunist forces in French Indochina, thus deepening U.S. intervention in Vietnam's struggle for independence. After battling Chinese troops in Korea, moreover, the United States recoiled from diplomatic recognition of the People's Republic of China. The Korean War of 1950–1953 thus transformed international relations.

Since then, a number of complex questions have challenged historians, and the opening of Soviet, Chinese, and Korean documents has enabled new perspectives. One set of questions centers on the origins of the war. Did the Korean War spring from global, Soviet-engineered communist aggression? Or did its sources lie in a Korean civil war? Which social and political conditions on the Korean peninsula during the months leading up to the North Korean invasion of South Korea contributed to the war's outbreak? Did Soviet leaders plan and order the North Korean attack? Did they give the "green light"? Or did their North Korean allies initiate the conflict? What, exactly, was China's role, and why did it decide to intervene in the fall of 1950? Why did the United Nations take action? Was the military operation to stop North Korean aggression truly an international undertaking—or primarily a U.S. effort?

A second set of questions focuses on decisionmaking in Washington. Why did the Truman administration intervene? Should the United States have intervened? Who made the key decisions in the Truman administration during the height of the crisis? Did President Truman maintain control of policymaking? Or did subordinates, among them General Douglas MacArthur, pursue independent initiatives? What role did Congress and domestic politics play? Did administration officials carefully study the ramifications of U.S. intervention? Or did they rush to simplistic conclusions and make hurried, ill-considered decisions? How thoroughly did administration officials understand Korea's political and cultural context? Did they grasp Chinese intentions? Why did Truman change U.S. war goals—that is, why did he order American troops to cross the thirty-eighth parallel? Did the United States seriously contemplate the use of atomic weapons in Korea, or were American strategists simply dangling the nuclear threat to force diplomatic concessions? Why was General MacArthur fired? Should the United States have conducted a "limited" war, or should the war have been enlarged, as MacArthur advised?

The fighting dragged on until July 1953, when lengthy negotiations finally produced a cease-fire and peace terms that reestablished the status quo that had existed before June 25, 1950. Korea remained a divided nation, each side heavily armed and destined to live in a constant state of readiness and alert. Although Korea had been a limited war, the final casualty rate proved staggering. An estimated 3 million Koreans, nine hundred thousand Chinese, and thirty-five thousand Americans had perished.

✖ *D O C U M E N T S*

On January 12, 1950, Secretary of State Dean Acheson delivered a major speech (the first document) defining the American defense perimeter in Asia, from which he excluded Korea. Critics later charged that Acheson's omission gave the Soviet Union the incentive to use its North Korean allies to attack South Korea. The second document, the first North Korean statement after the war's outbreak in June 1950, blames South Korea for provoking hostilities.

The Korean War, 1950–1953

← United States (United Nations) forces
← North Korean forces

During the opening days of the crisis, President Harry S. Truman met with key advisers at Blair House, a building near the White House. The third document is a record of the June 26, 1950, meeting in which Acheson recommended several important policies, not only for Korea but also for the Philippines, Formosa, and French Indochina. The fourth document, dated August 7, 1950, is a Defense Department memorandum, top secret at the time, that made the case for sending U.S. troops across the thirty-eighth parallel. Truman accepted this advice, and, on September 15, American marines landed at Inchon and began the penetration of North Korea.

Meanwhile, in Beijing, Chinese authorities watched the United States' advance northward with deep concern and decided to launch a counteroffensive. On October 2, 1950, Mao Zedong sent a cable, the fifth document, to Marshal Josef Stalin in Moscow. Describing the danger posed by the American "invaders," Mao informed the Soviet leader of China's decision for war and asked for the U.S.S.R.'s cooperation in the mission. Yet around this same time, at a meeting with Truman on Wake Island on October 15, 1950, General Douglas MacArthur, supremely confident of U.S. power, assured the president that the Chinese would not enter the war. This conversation is reprinted below as the sixth selection. Six weeks later, U.N. and U.S. troops frantically retreated down the Korean peninsula following China's entry into the war.

On November 30, 1950, President Truman told a press conference (an excerpt from which appears here as the seventh document) that the United States had not ruled out the use of atomic weapons in the Korean theater. In the eighth document, a November 28, 1950, speech to the United Nations, People's Republic of China official Wu Xinchnan (Wu Hsiu-ch'uan) explains why China felt compelled to enter the Korean War. Truman summarized American policy in a speech on April 11, 1951 (the ninth selection), shortly after he relieved MacArthur of his command. The last document is MacArthur's rebuttal of April 19, delivered as a speech to Congress.

Secretary of State Dean Acheson on the Defense Perimeter in Asia, 1950

What is the situation in regard to the military security of the Pacific area, and what is our policy in regard to it?

In the first place, the defeat and the disarmament of Japan has placed upon the United States the necessity of assuming the military defense of Japan so long as that is required, both in the interest of our security and in the interests of the security of the entire Pacific area and, in all honor, in the interest of Japanese security. We have American—and there are Australian—troops in Japan. I am not in a position to speak for the Australians, but I can assure you that there is no intention of any sort of abandoning or weakening the defenses of Japan and that whatever arrangements are to be made either through permanent settlement or otherwise, that defense must and shall be maintained.

This defensive perimeter runs along the Aleutians to Japan and then goes to the Ryukyus. We hold important defense positions in the Ryukyu Islands, and those we will continue to hold. In the interest of the population of the Ryukyu Islands, we will at an appropriate time offer to hold these islands under trusteeship of the United Nations. But they are essential parts of the defensive perimeter of the Pacific, and they must and will be held.

The defensive perimeter runs from the Ryukyus to the Philippine Islands. Our relations, our defensive relations with the Philippines are contained in agreements between us. Those agreements are being loyally carried out and will be loyally carried out. Both peoples have learned by bitter experience the vital connections between our mutual defense requirements. We are in no doubt about that, and it is hardly necessary for me to say an attack on the Philippines could not and would not be tolerated by the United States. But I hasten to add that no one perceives the imminence of any such attack.

So far as the military security of other areas in the Pacific is concerned, it must be clear that no person can guarantee these areas against military attack. But it must also be clear that such a guarantee is hardly sensible or necessary within the realm of practical relationship.

Should such an attack occur—one hesitates to say where such an armed attack could come from—the initial reliance must be on the people attacked to resist it and then upon the commitments of the entire civilized world under the Charter of the United Nations which so far has not proved a weak reed to lean on by any people who are determined to protect their independence against outside aggression. But it is a mistake, I think, in considering Pacific and Far Eastern problems to become obsessed with military considerations. Important as they are, there are other problems that press, and these other problems are not capable of solution through military means. These other problems arise out of the susceptibility of many areas, and many countries in the Pacific area, to subversion and penetration. That cannot be stopped by military means. . . .

That leads me to the other thing that I wanted to point out, and that is the limitation of effective American assistance. American assistance can be effective when it is the missing component in a situation which might otherwise be solved. The United States cannot furnish all these components to solve the question. It can not furnish determination, it can not furnish will, and it can not furnish the loyalty of a people to its government. But if the will and if the determination exists and if the people are behind their government, then, and not always then, is there a very good chance. In that situation, American help can be effective and it can lead to an accomplishment which could not otherwise be achieved. . . .

Korea

In Korea, we have taken great steps which have ended our military occupation, and in cooperation with the United Nations, have established an independent and sovereign country recognized by nearly all the rest of the world. We have given that nation great help in getting itself established. We are asking the Congress to continue that help until it is firmly established, and that legislation is now pending before the Congress. The idea that we should scrap all of that, that we should stop half way through the achievement of the establishment of this country, seems to me to be the most utter defeatism and utter madness of our interests in Asia. . . .

So after this survey, what we conclude, I believe, is that there is a new day which has dawned in Asia. It is a day in which the Asian peoples are on their own, and know it, and intend to continue on their own. It is a day in which the old relationships between east and west are gone, relationships which at their worst were exploitation, and which at their best were paternalism. That relationship is over, and the relationship of east and west must now be in the Far East one of mutual respect and mutual helpfulness. We are their friends. Others are their friends. We and those others are willing to help, but we can help only where we are wanted and only where the conditions of help are really sensible and possible. So what we can see is that this new day in Asia, this new day which is dawning, may go on to a glorious noon or it may darken and it may drizzle out. But that decision lies within the countries of Asia and within the power of the Asian people. It is not a decision which a friend or even an enemy from the outside can decide for them.

North Korea Blames South Korea for Starting the War, 1950

Official announcement made by the Home Affairs Bureau of the People's Republic of Korea. The so-called "defense army" of the South Korea puppet regime started a surprise invasion of the north along the whole front of the thirty-eighth parallel line at dawn on the 25th. The enemy, who started the surprise operation, invaded the territory north of the thirty-eighth parallel line one to two kilometers at three points west of Haeju, Kumchon, and Chorwon. The Home Affairs Bureau of the People's Republic of Korea has issued an order to the security army of the People's Republic to repulse the enemy. At this moment, our security army is putting up stiff counter-operations against the enemy. The People's Republic army succeeded in repulsing the enemy force which penetrated into the north at Yangyang. In this connection, the People's Republic of Korea wishes to remind the South Korea puppet regime of the fact that, unless the puppets immediately suspend their adventurous military actions, the People's Republic will be obliged to resort to decisive countermeasures. At the same time the People's Republic entrusted the Home Affairs Bureau to call the attention of the South Korea puppet regime to the fact that the whole responsibility for the grave consequences arising from their reckless venture would squarely rest on the shoulders of the South Korea puppet regime.

President Harry S. Truman and His Advisers at the "Blair House Meeting," June 26, 1950

GENERAL [HOYT S.] VANDENBERG reported that the First Yak [North Korean] plane had been shot down.

THE PRESIDENT remarked that he hoped that it was not the last.

GENERAL VANDENBERG read the text of the orders which had been issued to our Air Forces calling on them to take "aggressive action" against any planes interfering with their mission or operating in a manner unfriendly to the South Korean forces. He indicated, however, that they had been avoiding combat where the direct carrying-out of their mission was not involved.

MR. [DEAN] ACHESON suggested that an all-out order be issued to the Navy and Air Force to waive all restrictions on their operations in Korea and to offer the fullest possible support to the South Korean forces, attacking tanks, guns, columns, etc., of the North Korean forces in order to give a chance to the South Koreans to reform.

THE PRESIDENT said he approved this.

MR. [FRANK] PACE inquired whether this meant action only south of the thirty-eighth parallel.

MR. ACHESON said this was correct. He was making no suggestion for any action across the line.

GENERAL VANDENBERG asked whether this meant also that they should not fly over the line.

MR. ACHESON said they should not.

THE PRESIDENT said this was correct; that no action should be taken north of the thirty-eighth parallel. He added "not yet.". . .

MR. ACHESON said that the second point he wished to bring up was that orders should be issued to the Seventh Fleet to prevent an attack on Formosa.

THE PRESIDENT said he agreed.

MR. ACHESON continued that at the same time the National Government of China should be told to desist from operations against the mainland and that the Seventh Fleet should be ordered to see that those operations would cease.

MR. ACHESON said his third point was an increase in the United States military forces in the Philippines and an acceleration of aid to the Philippines in order that we might have a firm base there.

THE PRESIDENT said he agreed.

MR. ACHESON said his fourth point was that aid to Indochina should be stepped up and that a strong military mission should be sent. . . .

THE PRESIDENT said that he had a letter from the Generalissimo [Jiang Jieshi] about one month (?) ago to the effect that the Generalissimo might step out of the situation if that would help. He said this was a private letter and he had kept it secret. He said that we might want to proceed along those lines in order to get Chinese forces helping us. He thought that the Generalissimo might step out if MacArthur were put in.

MR. ACHESON said that the Generalissimo was unpredictable and that it was possible that he might resist and "throw the ball game." He said that it might be well to do this later.

THE PRESIDENT said that was alright. He himself thought that it was the next step. . . .

MR. ACHESON added in regard to the Formosan situation that he thought it undesirable that we should get mixed up in the question of the Chinese administration of the Island.

THE PRESIDENT said that we were not going to give the Chinese "a nickel" for any purpose whatever. He said that all the money we had given them is now invested in United States real estate. . . .

MR. [JOHN D.] HICKERSON read the draft of the Security Council resolution recommending that UN members render such assistance as was needed to Korea to repel the attack.

THE PRESIDENT said that was right. He said we wanted everyone in on this, including Hong Kong.

GENERAL [OMAR] BRADLEY reported that British Air Marshall Tedder had come to see him, was generally in accord with our taking the firm position, and gave General Bradley a full report of the forces which the British have in that area.

MR. [DEAN] RUSK pointed out that it was possible the Russians would come to the Security Council meeting and cast a veto. In that case we would still take the position that we could act in support of the Charter.

THE PRESIDENT said that was right. He rather wished they would veto. He said we needed to lay a base for our action in Formosa. He said that he would work on the draft of his statement tonight and would talk to the Defense and State Departments in the morning regarding the final text.

MR. RUSK pointed out that it was Mr. [George F.] Kennan's estimate that Formosa would be the next likely spot for a Communist move.

SECRETARY [LOUIS A.] JOHNSON reported that SCAP's [Supreme Commander to the Allied Powers] guess was that the next move would be on Iran. He thought there should be a check on this.

GENERAL [J. LAWTON] COLLINS said that SCAP did not have as much global information as they have in Washington. He and Mr. Pace stated that they have asked for full reports all over the world in regard to any developments, particularly of Soviet preparations.

SECRETARY JOHNSON suggested to Mr. Acheson that it would be advisable to have some talks with the UK regarding possible action in Iran.

MR. ACHESON said he would talk with both the British and French. . . .

MR. ACHESON suggested that the President might wish to get in Senator [Tom] Connally and other members of the Senate and House and tell them what had been decided.

THE PRESIDENT said that he had a meeting scheduled for 10:00 tomorrow morning with the Big Four [congressional leaders] and that he would get in any others that the Secretary thought should be added. He suggested that Secretaries Acheson and Johnson should also be there. . . .

GENERAL COLLINS stated that the military situation in Korea was bad. It was impossible to say how much our air can do. The Korean Chief of Staff has no fight left in him.

MR. ACHESON stated that it was important for us to do something even if the effort were not successful.

MR. JOHNSON said that even if we lose Korea this action would save the situation. He said this action "suits me." He then asked whether any of the military representatives had any objection to the course of action which had been outlined. There was no objection.

GENERAL VANDENBERG, in response to a question that Mr. [Thomas] Finletter, said that he bet a tank would be knocked out before dark.

THE PRESIDENT said he had done everything he could for five years to prevent this kind of situation. Now the situation is here and we must do what we can to meet it. He had been wondering about the mobilization of the National Guard and asked General Bradley if that was necessary now. If it was he must go to Congress and ask for funds. He was merely putting the subject on the table for discussion. He repeated we must do everything we can for the Korean situation—"for the United Nations."

GENERAL BRADLEY said that if we commit our ground forces in Korea we cannot at the same time carry out our other commitments without mobilization. He wondered if it was better to wait now on the question of mobilization of the National Guard. He thought it would be preferable to wait a few days.

THE PRESIDENT said he wished the Joint Chiefs to think about this and to let him know in a few days time. He said "I don't want to go to war."

GENERAL COLLINS stated that if we were going to commit ground forces in Korea we must mobilize.

MR. ACHESON suggested that we should hold mobilization in reserve. . . .

GENERAL COLLINS remarked that if we had had standing orders we could have stopped this. We must consider this problem for the future.

THE PRESIDENT said he agreed.

The Defense Department's Case for Crossing the Thirty-Eighth Parallel to Reunite the Two Koreas, 1950

The following principles form the basis for consideration of U.S. actions:

a. The unification of Korea conforms with Korean aspirations, U.S. policies, and the objectives of the United Nations.

b. The establishment of a free and united Korea and the elimination of the North Korea Communist regime, following unprovoked military aggression, would be a step in reversing the dangerous strategic trend in the Far East of the past twelve months.

c. The thirty-eighth parallel, in and of itself, has no military significance other than such an artificial barrier as would limit if not prevent a military victory.

d. The chief potential limitation on the objective of unifying Korea will be Soviet military countermeasures including the use of Chinese Communist troops, or Soviet diplomatic and political actions in the UN.

e. Consequently, the timing and speed of U.S. politico-military operations are crucial, and call for especially close working relationships.

f. In the long run, a maximum UN effort will be needed in securing peace in Korea and in meeting the acute problems of political and economic reconstruction.

g. The continued functioning of the Republic of Korea, as the only sovereign government in Korea, is indispensable to the re-establishment of the rule of law in Korea and is necessary to the fulfillment of U.S. objectives.

h. Long-range policies in support of independence for Korea conform to the general objectives of the United States in Asia.

In consonance with the above principles and in pursuit of its basic long-range objectives with respect to Korea, the U.S. should take measures to effect:

a. The establishment of a free, independent and stable Korea oriented toward the U.S.

b. The security of Korea against foreign aggression and internal subversion.

c. The reconstruction of Korea in political, economic, and social fields to develop a stable, self-sustaining, and advancing state.

As the basis for realizing these objectives, the United States should take the following series of actions:

a. Statements of Aims

1. At an appropriate time, the President should proclaim that our peace aim is a united, free, and independent Korea, as envisaged by the UN. Such a statement should be supported by a Joint Resolution of Congress.
2. Again at an appropriate time, the U.S. should seek to translate this aim into UN objectives. In view of the possibility that uncoordinated measures would provoke Soviet counter-action, either in the military or diplomatic field or both, the United States should seek UN action in two stages: first, at the 1950 meeting of the General Assembly, the United Nations should immediately endorse the resolutions of 25 and 27 June and 7 July, of the Security Council and seek maximum support for the unified command; second, at a later date, at the moment when the unified command has taken the offensive, the United Nations should re-affirm the basic UN aims in Korea along the lines of the General Assembly Resolution of 14 November 1947.
3. No statement of U.S. general objectives should be made until the unified command has launched offensive military measures to carry out the military objectives listed below. Until such time, great caution and discretion should be taken in public discussion of the thirty-eighth parallel.
4. In the meantime, the U.S. should use all its diplomatic means to forestall any Soviet effort to mediate the conflict on any terms short of the unification of all Korea on a free and representative basis under UN auspices.

b. Military Objectives

1. The unified command should seek to occupy Korea and to defeat North Korean armed forces wherever located north or south of the thirty-eighth parallel.
2. To achieve this objective, the Commanding General of the unified command should pursue military operations in Korea without regard to the thirty-eighth parallel.

Mao Zedong Informs Josef Stalin of China's Decision to Enter the Korean War, 1950

(1) We have decided to send a portion of our troops, under the name of [the Chinese] Volunteers, to Korea, assisting the Korean comrades in fighting the troops of the United States and its running dog Syngman Rhee. We regarded the mission as necessary. If Korea were completely occupied by the Americans and the Korean revolutionary forces were substantially destroyed, the American invaders would be more rampant, and such a situation would be very unfavorable to the whole East.

(2) We realize that since we have decided to send Chinese troops to Korea to fight the Americans, we must first be able to solve the problem, that is, that we are

From *Chinese Historians* 5 (Spring, 1992), pp. 67–68, translated by Li Xiaobing, Wang Xi and Chen Jian. Reprinted with the permission of Chinese Historians of the United States, Inc.

prepared to annihilate the invaders from the United States and from other countries, and to drive them out [of Korea]; second, since Chinese troops will fight American troops in Korea (although we will use the name the Chinese Volunteers), we must be prepared for an American declaration of war on China. We must be prepared for the possible bombardments by American air forces of many Chinese cities and industrial bases, and for attacks by American naval forces on China's coastal areas.

(3) Of the two issues, the first one is whether the Chinese troops would be able to defeat American troops in Korea, thus effectively resolving the Korean problem. If our troops could annihilate American troops in Korea, especially the Eighth Army (a competent veteran U.S. army), the whole situation would become favorable to the revolutionary front and China, even though the second question ([the possibility] that the United States would declare war on China) would still remain as a serious issue. In other words, the Korean problem will end in fact with the defeat of American troops (although the war might not end in name, because the United States would not recognize the victory of Korea for a long period). If this occurs, even though the United States had declared war on China, the ongoing confrontation would not be on a large-scale, nor would it last very long. We consider that the most unfavorable situation would be that the Chinese forces fail to destroy American troops in large numbers in Korea, thus resulting in a stalemate, and that, at the same time, the United States openly declares war on China, which would be detrimental to China's economic reconstruction already under way, and would cause dissatisfaction among the national bourgeoisie and some other sectors of the people (who are absolutely afraid of war).

(4) Under the current situation, we have decided, starting on October 15, to move the twelve divisions, which have been earlier transferred to southern Manchuria, into suitable areas in North Korea (not necessarily close to the thirty-eighth parallel); these troops will only fight the enemy that venture to attack areas north of the thirty-eighth parallel; our troops will employ defensive tactics, while engaging small groups of enemies and learning about the situation in every respect. Meanwhile, our troops will be awaiting the arrival of Soviet weapons and being equipped with those weapons. Only then will our troops, in cooperation with the Korean comrades, launch a counter-offensive to destroy the invading American forces.

(5) According to our information, every U.S. army (two infantry divisions and one mechanized division) is armed with 1500 pieces of artillery of various calibers ranging from 70mm to 240mm, including tank guns and anti-aircraft guns, while each of our armies (three divisions) is equipped with only 36 pieces of artillery. The enemy would control the air while our air force, which has just started its training, will not be able to enter the war with some 300 planes until February 1951. Therefore, at present, we are not assured that our troops will be able to annihilate an entire U.S. army once and for all. But since we have decided to go into the war against the Americans, we should be prepared that, when the U.S. high command musters up one complete army to fight us in a campaign, we should be able to concentrate our forces four times greater than those of the enemy (that is, to use four of our armies to fight against one enemy army) and to marshal firing power one and a half to two times stronger than that of the enemy (that is, to use 2200 to

3000 pieces of artillery of 70mm calibre and upward to deal with the enemy's 1500 pieces of artilleries of the same calibers), so that we can guarantee a complete and thorough destruction of one enemy army.

(6) In addition to the above-mentioned twelve divisions, we are transferring another twenty-four divisions, as the second and third echelons to assist Korea, from south of the Yangzi River and the Shaanxi-Ganshu areas to the Long-hai, Tianjin-Pukuo, and Beijing–Southern Manchuria railways; we expect to gradually employ these divisions next spring and summer in accordance with the situation at the time.

General Douglas MacArthur on the Likelihood of Chinese Intervention, 1950

The President: What are the chances for Chinese or Soviet interference?

General MacArthur: Very little. Had they interfered in the first or second months it would have been decisive. We are no longer fearful of their intervention. We no longer stand hat in hand. The Chinese have 300,000 men in Manchuria. Of these probably not more than 100/125,000 are distributed along the Yalu River. Only 50/60,000 could be gotten across the Yalu River. They have no Air Force. Now that we have bases for our Air Force in Korea, if the Chinese tried to get down to Pyongyang there would be the greatest slaughter.

With the Russians it is a little different. They have an Air Force in Siberia and a fairly good one, with excellent pilots equipped with some jets and B-25 and B-29 planes. They can put 1,000 planes in the air with some 2/300 more from the Fifth and Seventh Soviet Fleets. They are probably no match for our Air Force. The Russians have no ground troops available for North Korea. They would have difficulty in putting troops into the field. It would take six weeks to get a division across and six weeks brings the winter. The only other combination would be Russian air support of Chinese ground troops. Russian air is deployed in a semicircle through Mukden and Harbin, but the coordination between the Russian air and the Chinese ground would be so flimsy that I believe Russian air would bomb the Chinese as often as they would bomb us. Ground support is a very difficult thing to do. Our Marines do it perfectly. They have been trained for it. Our own Air and Ground Forces are not as good as the Marines but they are effective. Between untrained Air and Ground Forces an air umbrella is impossible without a lot of joint training. I believe it just wouldn't work with Chinese Communist ground and Russian air. We are the best.

Truman Discusses the Possible Use of Atomic Weapons in Korea, 1950

Q. Mr. President, will attacks in Manchuria depend on action in the United Nations?

The President. Yes, entirely.

Q. In other words, if the United Nations resolution should authorize General MacArthur to go further than he has, he will—

The President. We will take whatever steps are necessary to meet the military situation, just as we always have.

Q. Will that include the atomic bomb?

The President. That includes every weapon that we have.

Q. Mr. President, you said "every weapon that we have." Does that mean that there is active consideration of the use of the atomic bomb?

The President. There has always been active consideration of its use. I don't want to see it used. It is a terrible weapon, and it should not be used on innocent men, women, and children who have nothing whatever to do with this military aggression. That happens when it is used. . . .

Q. Mr. President, I wonder if we could retrace that reference to the atom bomb? Did we understand you clearly that the use of the atomic bomb is under active consideration?

The President. Always has been. It is one of our weapons.

Q. Does that mean, Mr. President, use against military objectives, or civilian—

The President. It's a matter that the military people will have to decide. I'm not a military authority that passes on those things.

Q. Mr. President, perhaps it would be better if we are allowed to quote your remarks on that directly?

The President. I don't think—I don't think that is necessary.

Q. Mr. President, you said this depends on United Nations action. Does that mean that we wouldn't use the atomic bomb except on a United Nations authorization?

The President. No, it doesn't mean that at all. The action against Communist China depends on the action of the United Nations. The military commander in the field will have charge of the use of the weapons, as he always has.

The Chinese Case for Intervention, 1950

Under the pretext of the Korean civil war, which was of its own making, the United States Government launched armed aggression simultaneously against Korea and Taiwan. From the very outset the United States armed aggression against Korea gravely threatened China's security. Korea is about 5,000 miles away from the boundaries of the United States. To say that the civil war in Korea would affect the security of the United States is a flagrant, deceitful absurdity. But there is only a narrow river between Korea and China. The United States armed aggression in Korea inevitably threatens China's security. That the United States aggression forces in Korea have directly threatened China's security is fully borne out by the facts.

From 27 August to 10 November 1950, the military aircraft of the United States aggression forces in Korea have violated the territorial air of North-East China ninety times; they have conducted reconnaissance activities, strafed and bombed Chinese cities, towns and villages, killed and wounded Chinese peaceful inhabitants and damaged Chinese properties. . . .

Now the United States forces of aggression in Korea are approaching our north-eastern frontiers. The flames of the war of aggression waged by the United

States against Korea are swiftly sweeping towards China. Under such circumstances the United States armed aggression against Korea cannot be regarded as a matter which concerns the Korean people alone. No, decidedly not. The United States aggression against Korea gravely endangers the security of the People's Republic of China. The Korean People's Democratic Republic is a country bound by close ties of friendship to the People's Republic of China. Only a river separates the two countries geographically. The Chinese people cannot afford to stand idly by in the face of this serious situation brought about by the United States Government's aggression against Korea and the dangerous tendency towards the extension of the war. . . .

One of the master-planners of Japanese aggression, Tanaka, once said: to conquer the world, one must first conquer Asia; to conquer Asia, one must first conquer China; to conquer China, one must first conquer Manchuria and Mongolia; to conquer Manchuria and Mongolia, one must first conquer Korea and Taiwan.

Ever since 1895, the course of aggression taken by imperialist Japan has exactly corresponded to the Tanaka plan. In 1895, imperialist Japan invaded Korea and Taiwan. In 1931, imperialist Japan occupied the whole of NorthEast China. In 1937, imperialist Japan launched the war of aggression against the whole of China. In 1941, it started the war aimed at the conquest of the whole of Asia. Naturally, as everyone knows, before it had realized this design, Japanese imperialism collapsed. American imperialism, by its aggression against Taiwan and Korea, in practice plagiarizes Tanaka's memorandum and follows the beaten path of the Japanese imperialist aggressors. The Chinese people are maintaining a sharp vigilance over the progress of American imperialist aggression. They have already acquired the experience and learned the lesson from history as to how to defend themselves from aggression.

American imperialism has taken the place of Japanese imperialism. It is now following the old track of aggression against China and Asia on which Japanese imperialism set forth in 1894–95, only hoping to proceed with greater speed. But after all, 1950 is not 1895; the times have changed, and so have the circumstances. The Chinese people have arisen. The Chinese people who have victoriously overthrown the rule of Japanese imperialism and of American imperialism and its lackey, Chiang Kai-shek on China's mainland, will certainly succeed in driving out the United States aggressors and recover Taiwan and all other territories that belong to China.

Truman Defends U.S. Policy, 1951

In the simplest terms, what we are doing in Korea is this: We are trying to prevent a third world war.

I think most people in this country recognized that fact last June. And they warmly supported the decision of the Government to help the Republic of Korea against the Communist aggressors. Now, many persons, even some who applauded our decision to defend Korea, have forgotten the basic reason for our action.

It is right for us to be in Korea. It was right last June. It is right today.

I want to remind you why this is true.

The Communists in the Kremlin are engaged in a monstrous conspiracy to stamp out freedom all over the world. If they were to succeed, the United States would be numbered among their principal victims. It must be clear to everyone that the United States cannot—and will not—sit idly by and await foreign conquest. The only question is: When is the best time to meet the threat and how?

The best time to meet the threat is in the beginning. It is easier to put out a fire in the beginning when it is small than after it has become a roaring blaze.

And the best way to meet the threat of aggression is for the peace-loving nations to act together. If they don't act together, they are likely to be picked off, one by one.

If they had followed the right policies in the 1930's—if the free countries had acted together, to crush the aggression of the dictators, and if they had acted in the beginning, when the aggression was small—there probably would have been no World War II.

If history has taught us anything, it is that aggression anywhere in the world is a threat to peace everywhere in the world. When that aggression is supported by the cruel and selfish rulers of a powerful nation who are bent on conquest, it becomes a clear and present danger to the security and independence of every free nation.

This is a lesson that most people in this country have learned thoroughly. This is the basic reason why we joined in creating the United Nations. And since the end of World War II we have been putting that lesson into practice—we have been working with other free nations to check the aggressive designs of the Soviet Union before they can result in a third world war.

That is what we did in Greece [in 1947], when that nation was threatened by the aggression of international communism.

The attack against Greece could have led to general war. But this country came to the aid of Greece. The United Nations supported Greek resistance. With our help, the determination and efforts of the Greek people defeated the attack on the spot.

Another big Communist threat to peace was the Berlin blockade. That too could have led to war. But again it was settled because free men would not back down in an emergency.

The aggression against Korea is the boldest and most dangerous move the Communists have yet made.

The attack on Korea was part of a greater plan for conquering all of Asia. . . .

The whole Communist imperialism is back of the attack on peace in the Far East. It was the Soviet Union that trained and equipped the North Koreans for aggression. The Chinese Communists massed 44 well-trained and well-equipped divisions on the Korean frontier. These were the troops they threw into battle when the North Korean Communists were beaten. . . .

So far, by fighting a limited war in Korea, we have prevented aggression from succeeding and bringing on a general war. And the ability of the whole free world to resist Communist aggression has been greatly improved. . . .

Our resolute stand in Korea is helping the forces of freedom now fighting in Indochina and other countries in that part of the world. It has already slowed down the timetable of conquest. . . .

But you may ask: Why can't we take other steps to punish the aggressor? Why don't we bomb Manchuria and China itself? Why don't we assist Chinese Nationalist troops to land on the mainland of China?

If we were to do these things, we would be running a very grave risk of starting a general war. If that were to happen, we would have brought about the exact situation we are trying to prevent.

If we were to do these things, we would become entangled in a vast conflict on the continent of Asia and our task would become immeasurably more difficult all over the world.

What would suit the ambitions of the Kremlin better than for our military forces to be committed to a full-scale war with Red China? . . .

First of all, it is clear that our efforts in Korea can blunt the will of the Chinese Communists to continue the struggle. The United Nations forces have put up a tremendous fight in Korea and have inflicted very heavy casualties on the enemy. Our forces are stronger now than they have been before. These are plain facts which may discourage the Chinese Communists from continuing their attack.

Second, the free world as a whole is growing in military strength every day. In the United States, in Western Europe, and throughout the world, free men are alert to the Soviet threat and are building their defenses. This may discourage the Communist rulers from continuing the war in Korea—and from undertaking new acts of aggression elsewhere. . . .

I believe that we must try to limit the war to Korea for these vital reasons: to make sure that the precious lives of our fighting men are not wasted; to see that the security of our country and the free world is not needlessly jeopardized; and to prevent a third world war.

A number of events have made it evident that General MacArthur did not agree with that policy. I have therefore considered it essential to relieve General MacArthur so that there would be no doubt or confusion as to the real purpose and aim of our policy.

It was with the deepest personal regret that I found myself compelled to take this action. General MacArthur is one of our greatest military commanders. But the cause of world peace is more important than any individual.

MacArthur's "No Substitute for Victory" Speech, 1951

While I was not consulted prior to the President's decision to intervene in the support of the Republic of Korea, that decision from a military standpoint proved a sound one. As I say, a brief and sound one as we hurled back the invaders and decimated his forces. Our victory was complete and our objectives within reach when Red China intervened with numerically superior ground forces. This created a new war and an entirely new situation, a situation not contemplated when our forces were committed against the North Korean invaders, a situation which called for new decisions in the diplomatic sphere to permit the realistic adjustment of military strategy. Such decisions have not been forthcoming.

While no man in his right mind would advocate sending our ground forces into continental China—and such was never given a thought—the new situation did urgently demand a drastic revision of strategic planning if our political aim was to defeat this new enemy as we had defeated the old.

Apart from the military need as I saw it to neutralize sanctuary, protection given to the enemy north of the Yalu, I felt that military necessity in the conduct of the war made necessary:

First, the intensification of our economic blockade against China.

Second, the imposition of a naval blockade against the China coast.

Third, removal of restrictions on air reconnaissance of China's coastal areas and of Manchuria.

Fourth, removal of restrictions on the forces of the Republic of China on Formosa with logistical support to contribute to their effective operation against the Chinese mainland.

For entertaining these views all professionally designed to support our forces committed to Korea and bring hostilities to an end with the least possible delay and at a saving of countless American and Allied lives, I have been severely criticized in lay circles, principally abroad, despite my understanding that from a military standpoint the above views have been fully shared in the past by practically every military leader concerned with the Korean campaign, including our own Joint Chiefs of Staff.

I called for reinforcements, but was informed that reinforcements were not available. I made clear that if not permitted to utilize the friendly Chinese force of some 600,000 men on Formosa; if not permitted to blockade the China coast to prevent the Chinese Reds from getting succor from without; and if there were to be no hope of major reinforcements, the position of the command from the military standpoint forbade victory. We could hold in Korea by constant maneuver and at an approximate area where our supply advantages were in balance with the supply line disadvantages of the enemy, but we could hope at best for only an indecisive campaign, with its terrible and constant attrition upon our forces if the enemy utilized his full military potential. I have constantly called for the new political decisions essential to a solution. Efforts have been made to distort my position. It has been said in effect that I was a warmonger. Nothing could be further from the truth. I know war as few other men now living know it, and nothing to me is more revolting. . . .

But once war is forced upon us, there is no other alternative than to apply every available means to bring it to a swift end. War's very object is victory—not prolonged indecision. In war, indeed, there can be no substitute for victory.

There are some who for varying reasons would appease Red China. They are blind to history's clear lesson. For history teaches with unmistakable emphasis that appeasement but begets new and bloodier war. . . .

The tragedy of Korea is further heightened by the fact that as military action is confined to its territorial limits, it condemns that nation, which it is our purpose to save, to suffer the devastating impact of full naval and air bombardment, while the enemy's sanctuaries are fully protected from such attack and devastation. Of the nations of the world, Korea alone, up to now, is the sole one which has risked its all against communism. . . .

I am closing my 52 years of military service. When I joined the Army even before the turn of the century, it was the fulfillment of all my boyish hopes and dreams. The world has turned over many times since I took the oath on the plain at West Point, and the hopes and dreams have long since vanished. But I since re-member the refrain of one of the most popular barrack ballads of that day which proclaimed most proudly that—

"Old soldiers never die; they just fade away." And like the old soldier of that ballad, I now close my military career and just fade away—an old soldier who tried to do his duty as God gave him the light to see that duty.

✹ E S S A Y S

In the first essay, the journalist Jon Halliday and Professor Bruce Cumings of Northwestern University analyze the origins of the Korean War and the roots of the U.S. intervention. They conclude that the conflict began as a civil war between rival Korean governments, north and south, both of which sought to unify their country following its arbitrary division in 1945. Halliday and Cumings fault the Truman administration for supporting an oppressive political and social hierarchy in South Korea and then leading the United Nations to war to contain a monolithic communist threat that did not exist. In the second essay, James I. Matray of New Mexico State University is less critical than Halliday and Cumings of the decision to defend South Korea, but he questions the wisdom of U.S. policymakers' changing American war aims to unite the two Koreas forcibly by ordering troops across the thirty-eighth parallel and northward toward China. Matray discounts the view that Truman acted because he was pressured by military experts or because he sought to improve his sagging political popularity at home. He instead stresses Truman's quest for a decisive Cold War victory over Soviet communism. In the last essay, Michael H. Hunt of the University of North Carolina, Chapel Hill, uses newly released Chinese sources to explain why China entered the war. Hunt emphasizes that decisionmakers in Beijing, like their counterparts in Washington, operated in an uncertain, crisis-filled atmosphere. According to Hunt, several factors influenced China's chief policymaker Mao Zedong: perceptions of the United States as an imperialist power, concern for China's security, North Korean requests for assistance, mixed signals of support from the Soviet Union, and China's own drive for national unity at home. Most important, Hunt argues, Mao's war aims, like U.S. war objectives, changed unpredictably as the crisis unfolded and as new battlefield and diplomatic challenges arose.

Korea's Civil War and the Roots of U.S. Intervention

JON HALLIDAY AND BRUCE CUMINGS

Korea is one of the oldest nations on earth, with a rich culture, more than a millennium of unity and an indisputable national identity. In 1945, after nearly four decades of harsh Japanese colonial rule, it was divided and denied its independence by outside powers; its people were not consulted. The USA occupied the South between 1945 and 1948, while the Russians occupied the North. Separate

From *Korea: The Unknown War* by Jon Halliday and Bruce Cumings. Copyright © 1988 by Jon Halliday and Bruce Cumings. Reprinted by permission of Pantheon Books, a division of Random House, Inc.

republics emerged on both sides of the thirty-eighth parallel in 1948, each claiming to be the legitimate Korean sovereign, yet Korea was universally recognized as a single nation, and no party in Korea, nor any international body, endorsed the national division.

The question most often asked about the Korean war is "Who started it?" No one asks who started the Vietnam war, or the civil war in China. Yet all these conflicts were the same in essence—a civil war fought between two domestic forces: a revolutionary nationalist movement, which had its roots in tough anti-colonial struggle, and a conservative movement tied to the *status quo,* especially to an unequal land system. What was different in Korea was the form and timing of outside intervention.

Unlike the other two conflicts, that in Korea is treated by many Western commentators as though it were a black hole in outer space, where a war just happened to happen. Because it came at the height of the Cold War, and because of near-complete ignorance of the internal forces playing upon Korean society, an entire literature treats the war as a bolt out of the blue in June 1950, with unknown or irrelevant antecedents. Even today the enemy side, in particular, remains an opaque Never-never-land, undeserving of inquiry. . . .

Just before Koreans heard the voice of Emperor Hirohito, for the first time, broadcasting Japan's surrender and Korea's liberation on 15 August 1945, John J. McCloy of the American War Department directed two young colonels, Dean Rusk and Charles H. Bonesteel, to withdraw to an adjoining room and find a place to divide Korea. Given thirty minutes to do so, they chose the thirty-eighth parallel because, as Dean Rusk told us, it would "place the capital city in the American zone." The Russians, who had begun to fight the Japanese in Korea on 8 August, accepted the division in silence. American forces arrived from Okinawa in early September, and Korea began the most anomalous period in its history since A.D. 668—the era of national division, not yet ended.

Many Americans express surprise when they learn that US involvement with Korea came well before 1950, in a three-year occupation (1945–8) in which Americans operated a full military government. A. M. Rosenthal, former editor and now a regular columnist of *The New York Times,* wrote in 1986 that "the government of Korea" functioned throughout the peninsula in 1945 but was undermined by Americans who stupidly let the Russians come into the North. This is exactly backwards. An ostensible Korean government did exist within a few weeks of Japan's demise; its headquarters was in Seoul, and it was anchored in widespread "people's committees" in the countryside. But this Korean People's Republic (formed on 6 September 1945) was shunned by the Americans. It was the Soviets who "let" the Americans come into the South and who supported the people's committee network. The American preference was for a group of conservative politicians who formed the Korean Democratic Party (KDP) in September 1945, and so the occupation spent much of its first year dismantling the committees in the South, which culminated in a major rebellion in October 1946 that spread over several provinces.

In October 1945 both military commands sponsored welcoming ceremonies for two returned exiles: Syngman Rhee, who later became the first President of the

Republic of Korea (ROK), and Kim Il Sung, subsequently premier of the Democratic People's Republic of Korea (DPRK). Within a few months they were the dominant figures in the two zones. Rhee was a septuagenarian who had lived in the USA for nearly four decades, had a Ph.D. from Princeton and had taken an Austrian wife; a patriot well known for devoting his life to Korean independence, he was also a willful man of legendary obstinacy and strong anti-communist beliefs. Kim Il Sung had begun armed resistance in the Sino-Korean border region shortly after Japan established the puppet state of Manchukuo in 1932 and was fortunate enough to survive a rugged guerrilla war that had killed most of his comrades by 1945. Kim was 33 years old when he returned, and represented a younger generation of revolutionary nationalists filled with contempt for the failure of their fathers and determined to forge a Korea that could resist foreign domination. Although both leaders had the support of a superpower, neither was an easily malleable puppet.

The ROK was not proclaimed until 15 August 1948; nonetheless the Southern political system was built in the first few months of the occupation and did not change substantially until the 1960s. Under American auspices Koreans captured the colonial government and used its extensive and penetrative apparatus to preserve the power and privilege of a traditional land-owning elite, long the ruling class of Korea but now tainted by its associations with the Japanese. The one reliable and effective agency of this restoration and reaction was the Korean National Police (KNP). The effective opposition to this system was very broad and almost wholly on the left; a mass popular resistance from 1945 to 1950 mingled raw peasant protest with organized union activity and, finally, armed guerrilla resistance in the period 1948–50.

Central Intelligence Agency (CIA) analyses in 1948 bear out this picture. South Korean political life was, it said, "dominated by a rivalry between rightists and the remnants of the left-wing people's committees," which it termed a "grassroots independence movement which found expression in the establishment of the people's committees throughout Korea in August 1945," led by "communists" who based their right to rule on the resistance to the Japanese. The leadership of the right, on the other hand,

> is provided by that numerically small class which virtually monopolizes the native wealth and education of the country, . . . Since this class could not have acquired and maintained its favored position under Japanese rule without a certain minimum of "collaboration," it has experienced difficulty in finding acceptable candidates for political office and has been forced to support imported expatriate politicians such as Syngman Rhee and Kim Ku. These, while they have no pro-Japanese taint, are essentially demagogues bent on autocratic rule.

The South did have a police state, and it was an agent of a small class of landlords. But it was more than that, or it could not have survived even to June 1950. The landlord class contained both obtuse reactionaries and vibrant capitalists. Korean capitalism had formidable practitioners, of which Kim Song-su, scion of a wealthy landed family, founder of Korea University, early textile industrialist, leader of the conservatives, was the most formidable. His opportunities had depended on close association with the colonial regime, but his aristocratic dignity had militated against unseemly pro-Japanism. Kim Song-su and people like him laid the foundations for the economic growth of the 1960s and thereafter. . . .

The Korean problem was what we would now call a "North-South" or "Third World" problem, a conflict over how best to overcome the debilities of colonial rule and comparative backwardness. In the Cold War milieu of the time, however, it was always seen by Americans as an East-West problem. The Soviets, we might say, pushed the North-South angle as a way of besting the USA in the East-West conflict on the peninsula. That is, they stayed in the background and let Koreans run the government; they put anti-Japanese resistance leaders out in front; and they supported radical reform of the land system, labour conditions and women's rights—all of which were pushed through by late 1946. By this time northern Korea also held its first elections for people's committees, a controlled affair that offered few choices to the electorate. The Soviets and their Korean allies acted ruthlessly against opponents of these changes, killing some, jailing others, but letting the majority of recalcitrants flee to the South. At the end of 1948 the Soviets withdrew their troops, leaving behind a cadre of military and government advisers and a Korean government under Kim Il Sung. . . .

The Americans could not withdraw their troops so easily because they were worried about the viability of the southern regime, its dictatorial tendencies and its frequent bluster about marching north. Korea had also become more important to American global policy as part of the new policy of containment. Acting Secretary of State Dean Acheson remarked in secret Congressional testimony in early 1947 that the USA had drawn the line in Korea and sought funding for a major programme to turn back communism there, on the model of "Truman Doctrine" aid to Greece and Turkey. Congress and the Pentagon balked at a major commitment to Korea, however, and so Acheson and his advisers took the problem to the United Nations, hoping to contain Korea through collective security.

The United Nations was completely dominated by the USA at the time and agreed to form a committee (the United Nations Temporary Commission on Korea, or UNTCOK) to observe elections in Korea; its members included representatives of the Philippines and Nationalist China, which could be counted on to follow American direction, and representatives from Australia and Canada who, although more recalcitrant once they got a taste of South Korean politics, came from allied governments subject to American influence and pressure. The North Koreans and Soviets opposed the move to the UN and refused to participate in UN activities in Korea.

The UNTCOK-observed elections presaged a separate southern government and thus raised the issue of Korea's permanent division. For that reason virtually all the major politicians and political parties in the South refused to participate— including Kim Ku, a man probably to the right of Rhee. The election went forward nonetheless on a restricted franchise and boycotted by the majority of parties. The outcome, even according to several members of UNTCOK, was a foregone conclusion. The National Police and associated ring-wing auxiliaries organized the voting. On 10 May 1948 the South's first National Assembly was elected, composed mostly of supporters of Rhee or Kim Song-su. After fragmentary observation of 2 per cent of the polling stations, UNTCOK endorsed the poll.

After the ROK was inaugurated, on 15 August, the State Department successfully delayed the final withdrawal of American combat troops until 30 June 1949. It then replaced them with a 500-man Korean Military Advisory Group (KMAG), established an aid mission (known as the Economic Cooperation Administration, or ECA) and pushed big aid bills through Congress to get the Korean economy moving and to equip an army capable of defending South Korea. Meanwhile events world-wide, and especially the communist revolution in China, pushed the USA towards a formal policy of resisting further communist advances in Asia. . . .

The critical background to the Korean War was in the realm . . . of the social and political conflict between left and right throughout the peninsula. This conflict went on at the national level in 1945, and at the provincial and county levels in 1946, as local people's committees fought with their antagonists. The suppression of the massive autumn harvest uprisings in 1946 consolidated state control in the county seats, making the seizure of power by county people's committees unlikely thereafter. Yet villages continued to be isolated from central power, and leftists therefore migrated downwards through the bureaucratic reaches of the system in search of space for organization.

By 1947 most leftists were members of the South Korean Labour Party (SKLP). The party was always indigenous to the South, drawing its members especially from the south-west and south-east, but it was more independent of Northern or Soviet influence in 1947 than after the formation of the Rhee government. Only vague and unreliable evidence existed on Northern or Soviet provision of funding for the party, and American intelligence sources did not believe that the North directed SKLP activity—they thought instead that the two worked towards common goals.

It appears, however, that by mid-1948, if not earlier, the party was under Northern guidance. Intercepted instructions from the North urged members to infiltrate into "all important bureaux" of the Rhee government, secrete food and other supplies for guerrillas in the mountains and "infiltrate into the South Korean Constabulary and begin political attacks aimed at causing dissension and disorder." Up to the Korean war, however, it cannot be said that Southern communists were mere creatures of Kim Il Sung, and there was much conflict between the Northern and Southern parties.

Rhee and his allies formed counter-organizations at the village level to fight the left. Roy Roberts of the Associated Press wrote in August 1947 that US intelligence received each day an average of five police reports "telling of fights in villages, fights between villages, beatings of rightists, beatings of leftists, burning of granaries, attacks on village officials, attacks on police, stoning of political meetings.". . .

One CIA estimate suggested that the total number of guerrillas in the South in early 1949 was somewhere between 3,500 and 6,000, not counting several thousands on Cheju [an island off the southern coast]. Some were armed with rifles, mostly Japanese and American, but many carried just clubs and bamboo spears. Food and other supplies came from foraging, contributions made by villages or the theft of rice stocks. American advisers thought overall strategy was in North Korean hands, passed through the Labour Party's headquarters in Haeju, just across the thirty-eighth parallel. One team of sixty guerrillas was known to have been dispatched from the North, and defectors estimated that another 1,000 or so were undergoing training for missions in the South. . . .

Except in remote and under-populated places, the guerrillas were not able to hold several towns at the same time or to create base areas outside the mountains. They would enter a village at night, call out the population, give speeches and secure food and other supplies. As their situation got more desperate, especially when winter dawned in 1949, they would attack whole villages and lay them waste in search of supplies. Attacks on police stations were the most common sort of activity, both because of widespread hatred for the National Police and because records of leftist families were kept at the stations.

Walter Sullivan of *The New York Times* was almost alone among foreign journalists in seeking out the facts of this guerrilla war. Large parts of South Korea, he wrote in early 1950, "are darkened today by a cloud of terror that is probably unparalleled in the world." In the "hundreds of villages across the guerrilla areas" local village guards "crouch in pyramided straw shelters," and nights "are a long, cold vigil of listening." Guerrillas made brutal assaults on police, and the police took the guerrillas to their home villages and tortured them for information. Then the police shot them, and tied them to trees as an object lesson.

The persistence of the guerrillas, Sullivan wrote, "puzzles many Americans here," as does "the extreme brutality" of the conflict. But Sullivan went on to argue that "there is great divergence of wealth" in the country, with both middle and poor peasants living "a marginal existence." He interviewed ten peasant families; none owned all of its own land, and most were tenants. The landlord took 30 per cent of tenant produce, but additional exactions—government taxes and various contributions—ranged from 48 to 70 per cent of the annual crop.

There was little evidence of Soviet or North Korean support for the Southern guerrillas. In April 1950 the Americans found that the North Koreans had supported guerrillas in Kangwon and along the upper coast of North Kyongsang with weapons and supplies but that "almost 100 per cent of the guerrillas in the Cholla and Kyongsang provinces have been recruited locally." No Soviet weapons had ever been authenticated in South Korea except near the parallel; most guerrillas had Japanese and American arms. Another report found that the guerrillas "apparently receive little more than moral support from North Korea."

The principal source of external involvement in the guerrilla war was, in fact, American. Americans usually perceive an important gap between the withdrawal of US combat forces in June 1949 and the war that came a year later, such that the question becomes: why did the Americans return? But the point is that they never left. American advisers were all over the war zones in the South, constantly shadowing their Korean counterparts and urging them to greater effort. . . .

At the end of September 1949 KMAG chief [Brigadier General William] Roberts said that it was of the "utmost importance" that the guerrillas "be cleared up as soon as possible" and asked that the US Army dispatch more infantry officers to work with the ROK Army. Every division in the ROK Army, he told MacArthur, was being diverted in part or in full from the parallel to the interior and "ordered to exterminate guerrilla bands in their zones."

Roberts later said that 6,000 guerrillas had been killed in the November 1949–March 1950 period, in what he called an "all-out mop-up campaign [that] broke the backbone of the guerrilla movement."

If the Rhee regime had one unqualified success, viewed through the American lens, it was the apparent defeat of the Southern partisans by the spring of 1950. A year before it had appeared that the guerrilla movement would only grow with the passage of time, but the suppression campaign begun in the autumn of 1949 resulted in high body counts and a perception that the guerrillas could no longer mount significant operations when the spring foliage returned in early 1950.

Both Dean Acheson and George Kennan saw the suppression of the internal threat as the litmus test for their support of the Rhee regime: if this worked, so would American-backed containment; if it did not, the regime would be viewed as another Kuomintang, as "little China." Colonel [M. Preston] Goodfellow had told Rhee in late 1948, in the context of a letter in which he referred to his "many opportunities to talk with [Acheson] about Korea," that the guerrillas had to be "cleaned out quickly . . . everyone is watching how Korea handles the communist threat." A weak policy would lose support in Washington; handle the threat well, and "Korea will be held in high esteem."

In May and June 1950 guerrilla incidents tapered off remarkably, reaching in early June a "new low." The last report filed before the war began said that small bands of fifteen to thirty guerrillas still operated in various areas but were generally quiet.

The war that began in June 1950 followed on the guerrilla war and a summer of battles along the thirty-eighth parallel in 1949; this 1949 border fighting is essential to an understanding of what happened a year later. The battles began at Kaesong on 4 May 1949, in an engagement that the South started, lasting about four days and taking an official toll of 400 North Korean and twenty-two South Korean soldiers, as well as upwards of a hundred civilian deaths in Kaesong, according to American and South Korean figures. The South committed six infantry companies and several battalions, and two of the companies defected to the North.

Another important battle occurred on the Sunday morning of the last weekend of June 1949, on the remote Ongjin Peninsula above Seoul on the west coast. After this engagement the United Nations Commission on Korea (UNCOK) sent a delegation to investigate; it arrived courtesy of a South Korean naval vessel and was guided around by ROK Army personnel. United Nations observers remained at Ongjin for a day or so and returned to Seoul on Monday evening; they then filed a report to the UN blaming "northern invaders" for the trouble. It is likely that the North was to blame for this one, but what is remarkable is the utter failure of UN observers to investigate and report upon the many battles started by the South as well.

The worst fighting of 1949 occurred in early August, when North Korean forces attacked ROK Army units occupying a small mountain north of the thirty-eighth parallel. It went on for days, right through an important conference between Syngman Rhee and Chiang Kai-shek. . . .

The point is not that North Korea was an innocent party to this fighting but that both sides were at fault—and, according to several statements by Roberts, the

South started more of the battles than did the North. Also important is the opening of the fighting in the Ongjin and Kaesong areas in many of the 1949 battles, for this is where the war began a year later. . . .

Little was known about North Korea in the 1940s; it was always assumed that the USSR ruled the roost. Recent studies indicate that the main points about North Korea were: first, that it had evolved an indigenous political system in the late 1940s, and its basic structure has not changed substantially; second, that Soviet influence was always in competition with Chinese influence in Korea, and both were in conflict with indigenous political forms and practices; third, the closest comparison with North Korea was Yugoslavia, not the states under complete Soviet hegemony such as East Germany. The DPRK was, and is, a divergent case among established Marxist-Leninist systems, representing a profound reassertion of native Korean political practice—from the superordinate role of the leader, to his self-reliant ideology, to the independent foreign-policy stance. . . .

North Korea was never simply a Soviet satellite in the 1940s but evolved from a coalition regime based on widespread "people's committees" in 1945–6 to a period of relative Soviet dominance in 1947–8, thence in 1949 to important links with China, which in turn provided the DPRK with scope to manoeuvre between the two communist giants. Kim Il Sung was not a handpicked Soviet puppet but organized politically first to establish his leadership, then to isolate and best the communists who had remained in Korea during the colonial period, then to ally with Soviet-aligned Koreans for a time, then to create under his own leadership (in February 1948) a powerful army that welded Koreans who had fought together in Manchuria and China proper with those who remained at home. . . .

In 1946 and 1947 the North Koreans eliminated all non-leftist political opposition with remarkable thoroughness. A couple of "united front" non-communist parties were allowed to exist, but they had no power. The intent was the same as that of the right wing in the South, to squash alternative centres of power. But the Northerners did it much more effectively because of their superior organization and the general weakness of the opposition. Neither North nor South had qualms about using violence towards political ends, but the North tended to be more discriminating, in part because its enemies were numerically small classes and groups, and also because of a political practice, perhaps growing out of the Korean leadership's experience with Chinese communism, of seeking to re-educate and reform political recalcitrants. . . .

The number of Soviet advisers was never very high in the North, even in the military. British sources estimated that Soviet advisers to the central government dropped from 200 in 1946 to only thirty in April 1947, the greatest number of those, predictably, being in the Ministry of the Interior. Soviet Colonel G. K. Plotnikov told us that between 200 and 250 Soviet advisers were left behind after the Red Army pulled out. The South Korean Defence Minister put the number of Soviet military advisers at only 120 before the war, which accords with intelligence estimates after the war began, saying the Soviets used "approximately fifteen advisory officers per [North Korean] division," there being fewer than ten divisions before June 1950. There were only fifteen Soviet advisers to the Korean Air Force. Advisers went down to the battalion level, the Americans liked to say, which sounds impressive. But there were three regiments to each division and three battalions to each regiment. If the total number were around 120, fifteen per division, then a battalion would have had only one or two Soviet advisers. This Soviet presence simply cannot be compared with fully functioning satellites in Eastern Europe, which had thousands of Soviet staff people and advisers.

It has been asserted that the USSR provided North Korea with vast amounts of weaponry just before the war. The North did get a great deal of World War II vintage tanks, artillery and planes, although most of them had been left when Soviet forces departed in 1948. There is little evidence of the shipment of new equipment in 1950. Within weeks of the opening of the fighting in June the CIA reported that the North's equipment "appears to have been obsolete or obsolescent Soviet discards." Hanson Baldwin [a *New York Times* writer] reported at about the same time that the North had nothing beyond World War II vintage equipment. Military historians later concluded that the USSR had been reluctant to equip the North with its newer weaponry, even during the worst periods of the war, let alone before the war. The new Stalin tank, the heavy 152-mm howitzer and other advanced weaponry were never supplied, which "lessened the effectiveness of the North Korean enemy immeasurably." The Soviets also *sold* their weaponry to the North before and through much of the war; they even exacted payment for the large stocks of equipment they left behind in 1948. One glaring difference between the South and North was in air capability, the North having propeller-driven fighters and light bombers. All of these planes were of pre-1945 vintage, however, with no jet aircraft such as the USSR delivered to the Chinese in the spring of 1950.

In late February 1949 Kim Il Sung left Pyongyang for his only official visit to the Soviet Union before the Korean war. When he returned to Korea in March, Kim brought with him an economic and cultural agreement and, intelligence rumour had it, a secret military agreement. We do not know much about what was discussed at these talks. It seems unthinkable that Kim did not discuss the question of unification. In the West it is generally asserted that Stalin colluded with Kim about starting a war. The heavily edited [Nikita] Khruschchev memoirs claim that Kim returned to Moscow once between March 1949 and June 1950 to discuss the matter, although there is no good evidence that this is true. The USSR made the Koreans pay for everything, including a 220-million-rouble loan at 2 per cent interest, which was about what mortgages returned to American banks in 1949—that is, there was profit in it. At this time South Korea was getting more than $100 million a year from the USA, most of it in the form of outright grants. The entire Southern national budget for 1951 was $120 million, with $27 million earmarked for defence, and American aid for the year 1951 was set at $100 million.

Even before the entry of Chinese forces into the Korean war China had an important influence on the North—mainly through tens of thousands of Koreans who fought in the Chinese civil war, establishing a reciprocal call on Chinese assistance later on.

American intelligence paid close attention to troop and *matériel* movements across the Sino-Korean border in early 1947; North Korean military forces had expanded rapidly in late 1946 within Korea, preparing for a spring offensive in Manchuria. Some 30,000 Koreans, under the command of Kim Chaek, reportedly moved into Manchuria during April 1947; by May of that year 15 to 20 per cent of Chinese communist forces in Manchuria were Koreans. From that point onward, until the winter of 1950, American intelligence designated these "Chinese Communist Forces" (CCF) or "CCF Koreans," which made it hard to identify truly Chinese soldiers when they entered the Korean war.

Several intelligence sources put the total for all Koreans in the Chinese Fourth Field Army alone at 145,000; this army, under Lin Biao, was the crack force of the communists, having never lost a battle as it swept southwards from Manchuria. Chinese Nationalist estimates were that 50,000 Koreans fought below the Great Wall. Probably the total number of Koreans who fought in China was about 100,000.

American influence in the South had reached new heights by 1950. British Minister Vyvyan Holt eloquently captured this a few weeks before the war broke out: "Radiating from the huge ten-storeyed Banto Hotel," American influence "penetrates into every branch of administration and is fortified by an immense outpouring of money." Americans kept the government, the Army, the economy, the railways, the airports, the mines and factories going, supplying money, electricity, expertise and psychological succour. American petrol fuelled every motor vehicle in the country. American cultural influence was "exceedingly strong," ranging from scholarships to study in the USA, several strong missionary denominations, "a score of traveling cinemas" and theatres that played mostly American films and the Voice of America, to big-league baseball: America was the "dream-land" to thousands, if not millions, of Koreans.

The ECA and KMAG missions were the biggest of their type in the world. The US Information Service had, according to its own testimony, "one of the most extensive country programs that we are operating anywhere," with nine centres in Korea, parlaying libraries, mobile units, a variety of publications and films. American officials ran Kimpo International Airport and controlled the entry and exit of American citizens. Besides the official presence, private Americans often advised or directed private industry.

KMAG's work in training the South's Army also seemed highly successful. In some exuberant interviews with Marguerite Higgins just before the war Roberts said, "KMAG is a living demonstration of how an intelligent and intensive investment of 500 combat-hardened American men and officers can train 100,000 guys to do the shooting for you." The countryside had been "in a perpetual uproar" until recently, he said, but was now under control, thanks to American advisers "at every level" who "live right there with [the Koreans] . . . and stay with them in battles." Higgins cited rumours that French counter-insurgency officers had arrived to learn about KMAG techniques for "export" to Indochina. In sum, Roberts said, "the American taxpayer has an army that is a fine watchdog over the investments placed in this country and a force that represents the maximum results at minimum cost." He discounted threats about an invasion from the North, saying, "at this point we rather invite it. It will give us target practice.". . .

On 30 May 1950, a few weeks before the war began, the South held its second National Assembly elections. The result was a disastrous loss for the Rhee regime, bringing into the Assembly a strong collection of moderates, several of them associated with Yo Un-hyong's political lineage and most of them hoping for peaceful unification with the North. The Korean Ambassador to the USA, John Chang, informed American officials of a crisis in his regime in early June, prompting John Foster Dulles to decide to visit Korea on his way to see MacArthur in Tokyo.

In Tokyo MacArthur hoped for a change in US policy in the Far East, especially with regard to Taiwan. On Taiwan Chiang hoped the talks with MacArthur would herald a commitment to his regime. In Seoul Rhee hoped for a military alliance with the USA. In Pyongyang Dulles's longstanding pro-Japan position would raise the gravest suspicions.

During Dulles's visit to Seoul Rhee not only pushed for a direct American defence but also advocated an attack on the North. Dulles invited along with him a favourite reporter, William Mathews, editor of the *Arizona Daily Star*. Mathews wrote just after the meeting between Rhee and Dulles: "He is militantly for the unification of Korea. Openly says it must be brought about soon. . . . Rhee pleads justice of going into North country. Thinks it could succeed in a few days . . . if he can do it with our help, he will do it." And Mathews noted that Rhee said he would "do it," "even if it brought on a general war." All this was yet more proof of Rhee's provocative behaviour, but it was no different from his threats to march north made many times before. The Dulles visit was vintage Rhee, but there is little evidence that Dulles was in collusion with him, as the North Koreans have always claimed.

After the Korean war [the historian and former State Department official] Herbert Feis questioned Dean Acheson about Dulles's visit: "Are you sure his presence didn't provoke the attack, Dean? There has been comment about that—I don't think it did. You have no views on the subject?"

Acheson's response was deadpan: "No, I have no views on the subject."

George Kennan then interjected: "There is a comical aspect to this, because the visits of these people over there, and their peering over outposts with binoculars at the Soviet people, I think must have led the Soviets to think that we were on to their plan and caused them considerable perturbation."

"Yes," Acheson said. "Foster up in a bunker with a homburg on—it was a very amusing picture."

It may be, however, that Chinese Nationalists on Taiwan were willing to intrigue with Rhee. From the New Year onwards American and British intelligence agencies predicted that the "last battle" of the Chinese civil war would come in June 1950. In January British Foreign Office sources predicted an invasion of Taiwan "by the end of June." Guy Burgess, interestingly enough, watched this situation closely. In April Burgess said the invasion would come in May/June or September/October. . . .

With all this bubbling activity, the last weekend in June 1950 nonetheless dawned on a torpid, somnolent and very empty Washington. Harry Truman was back home in Independence [Missouri]; Acheson was at his Sandy Spring country farm [in Maryland]; Kennan had disappeared to a remote summer cottage without so much as a telephone; Paul Nitze was away; the Joint Chiefs were occupied elsewhere. Even the United Nations representative, Warren Austin, was not at his post. . . .

Most accounts of the outbreak of fighting in June 1950 give the impression that an attack began all along the parallel at dawn, against an enemy taken completely unawares. But the war began in the same remote locus as much of the 1949 fighting, the Ongjin Peninsula, and, some hours later, spread along the parallel eastwards, to Kaesong, Chunchon and the east coast. As an official American history put it: "On the Ongjin Peninsula, cut off from the rest of South Korea, soldiers of the 17th Regiment stood watch on the quiet summer night of 24–25 June 1950. For more than a week, there had been no serious incident along the thirty-eighth parallel. . . . Then at 0400, with devastating suddenness . . . [artillery and mortar fire] crashed into the ROK lines."

The North's official radio had a different account. On 26 June it said that South Korean forces had begun shelling the Unpa-san area on the Ongjin Peninsula on 23 June at 10 P.M. and had continued until 4 A.M. on 24 June, using howitzers and mortars. A Northern unit was defending Turak Mountain on Ongjin in the early hours of 25 June when it was attacked by the "Fierce Tiger," unit of the ROK's 17th Regiment, which it proceeded to destroy. By 2:30 P.M. on 25 June the unit had advanced as far as Sudong on the Ongjin Peninsula; meanwhile partisans sprang forward to disrupt South Korean police stations and units in Ongjin.

South Korean sources asserted, on the contrary, that elements of the 17th Regiment had counter-attacked and were in possession of Haeju city, the only important point north of the thirty-eighth parallel claimed to have been taken by the South's army. This was announced at 11 o'clock on the morning of 26 June, a timing that would account for numerous newspaper articles saying that elements of the ROK Army had occupied Haeju, which have been used since to support the argument that the South might have attacked first. . . .

MacArthur's command reported through the UN at the end of July that the North attacked at the eastern and western portions of the parallel with reinforced border Constabulary brigades, at Kaesong and Chunchon with a division each (but, interestingly, not at the start) and ran through the Uijongbu corridor with 8,000 to 10,000 troops and fifty tanks—in other words, a total force of about 38,000. Just before the war the North Korean order of battle numbered about 95,000 troops. Thus the initial attacking force was not very large; the KPA had mobilized less than half its forces on 25 June. Arrayed against them were five ROK Army divisions located near Seoul or north of it, some 50,000 troops.

This evidence is compatible both with an unprovoked invasion and with an interpretation linking the summer of 1949 with June 1950—that the North waited until it had the majority of its crack soldiers back from China and then positioned them to take advantage of the first major Southern provocation in June 1950.

The American position has always been that the North Koreans stealthily prepared an attack that was completely unprovoked and that constituted an all-out invasion. On 26 June Kim Il Sung, on the contrary, accused the South of making a "general attack" across the parallel. Rhee had long sought to "provoke" a fratricidal civil war, he said, having incessantly provoked clashes at the front line; in preparing a "northern expedition" he had "even gone so far as to collude with our sworn enemy, Japanese militarism." Some of these charges were true, but the charge of making a general attack across the parallel is false. The possibility that the South opened the fighting on Ongjin, with an eye to seizing Haeju, cannot be discounted, but there is no evidence that it intended a general invasion.

The question pregnant with ideological dynamite, "Who started the Korean war?" is surely the wrong question. No Americans care any more that the South fired first on Fort Sumter in their Civil War; they do still care about slavery and secession. No one asks who started the Vietnam war. Like Vietnam, Korea was a civil and revolutionary war.

Ensuring Korea's Freedom: The Decision to Cross the Thirty-Eighth Parallel

JAMES I. MATRAY

Some scholars have argued that Truman's primary motive for ordering American combat forces across the thirty-eighth parallel was political gain. Popular happiness over Korean reunification would increase sharply the popularity of the Democratic party and lead to a sweep of the 1950 midterm congressional elections. Domestic politics may have been an important consideration, but Truman ultimately decided to cross the thirty-eighth parallel because he believed that the reunification of Korea would inflict a momentous defeat on the strategy of Soviet expansion. Once the United States destroyed the North Korean army, the administration was confident that a united Korea would reject the communist model for national development. In crossing the parallel, Truman sought to guarantee for all Koreans the right of national self-determination.

Truman's decision to cross the thirty-eighth parallel was in large part the outgrowth of past policy. Ever since the Cairo Conference in December 1943, Washington's objective in Korea had been the creation of an independent, united, western-oriented nation that would possess a progressive and democratic government. Following the death of Franklin D. Roosevelt, Truman devised a strategy that appeared to ensure the realization of this goal. If American forces liberated Korea unilaterally, Truman reasoned, then the United States could reconstruct this Asian nation without Soviet interference. Josef Stalin's decision to send the Red Army into Korea before the United States had an opportunity to land troops on the peninsula forced Truman to settle for a line dividing Korea at the thirty-eighth parallel into zones of occupation. The Soviet-American partition of Korea meant that only a diplomatic agreement among the great powers could produce peaceful reunification.

After World War II Truman sought to reunify Korea under a government that reflected the American rather than the Soviet model of political and economic development. At the Moscow Conference in December 1945, the United States and the Soviet Union appeared to agree on an international trusteeship as the best method for resolving the Korean problem. When Stalin refused to accept the American interpretation of the Moscow decision, Truman rejected further negotia-

From James I. Matray, "Truman's Plan for Victory: National Self-Determination and the Thirty-Eighth Parallel Decision in Korea," *Journal of American History*, 66 (September 1979), pp. 314-333. Copyright Organization of American Historians, 1979. Reprinted by permission.

tions and ultimately turned to the policy of containment in an effort to break the deadlock. Truman's strategy for containing Soviet expansion in Korea, in contrast to western Europe, was limited and required only that the United States provide economic aid, technical advice, and small amounts of military assistance. If successful, containment in Korea would foster the emergence of a strong and stable government south of the thirty-eighth parallel closely allied with the United States and capable of self-defense.

American objectives in Korea were, however, far more grandiose, since Truman and his advisors believed that containment would act as a liberating force. Arthur C. Bunce, the American economic advisor in Korea, indicated the nature of Washington's expectations in a revealing letter that expressed his hope that the South Korean leaders "will institute a whole series of necessary reforms which will so appeal to the North Koreans that their army will revolt, kill all the nasty Communists, and create a lovely liberal democracy to the everlasting credit of the U.S.A.!" Once containment registered its first victory for national self-determination in Korea, many American leaders hoped that other Asian nations would reject communism as well and thereby frustrate Stalin's strategy for expansion. . . .

In analyzing [Secretary of State Dean Acheson's] Press Club speech [of January 12, 1950], scholars have pointed to Acheson's exclusion of Korea from America's "defensive perimeter" as evidence of the absence of an American commitment to defend South Korea. This argument has tended, however, to divert attention from Acheson's statement of the actual nature of Truman's Korea policy. Washington believed that it could achieve peace and stability, not only in Korea but elsewhere in Asia, without a positive guarantee of military protection. If Asian nations developed strong democratic institutions and stable economies, Acheson argued, they could withstand communist "subversion and penetration." The United States could best contribute to the growth of stability in Asia through providing economic aid, technical knowledge, and administrative advice. Such a strategy, Acheson stressed, would be particularly successful in Korea, because, in contrast to China, the Republic of Korea not only wanted American aid but would use it effectively. Acheson indicated the importance of Korea to America's strategy when he concluded that "we have a greater opportunity to be effective" in South Korea than anywhere else on the Asian mainland. . . .

Truman and his advisors were totally unprepared for the North Korean invasion of South Korea in June 1950. The logic of containment precluded the possibility that Moscow would revert to open military aggression to further its expansionist aims. During the senate hearings regarding the subsequent dismissal of General Douglas MacArthur, Acheson indicated the nature of the administration's assumptions: "The view was generally held that since the Communists had far from exhausted the potentialities for obtaining their objectives through guerilla and psychological warfare, political pressure and intimidation, such means would probably continue to be used rather than overt military aggression." Acheson explained that the administration recognized that the situation was serious, "but it was not believed that the attack would take place at that time." North Korea's decision to pursue forcible reunification had a decisive impact on Truman's strategy for ending the Korean partition. American economic assistance and military advice alone would not provide sufficient means for resolving the Korean problem on terms advantageous to the United States. Since the Soviet challenge was now essentially military and far more aggressive, Truman concluded that he had to alter his Korea policy accordingly.

American leaders relied heavily on a global interpretation of the Korean conflict in the formulation of subsequent policy alternatives. Dulles spoke for the administration when he exclaimed that "one thing is certain, they [the North Koreans] did not do this purely on their own but as part of the world strategy of international communism." He stressed that South Korea was making tremendous progress toward political freedom and economic stability just prior to the attack. For the Soviet Union, this "promising experiment in democracy" in Asia was a source of embarrassment. Stalin and his cohorts had "found that they could not destroy it by indirect aggression, because the political, economic, and social life of the Republic was so sound that subversive efforts, which had been tried, had failed." The Truman administration reasoned that the very success of containment in Korea forced Moscow to alter its tactics. Since Asians would reject communism if given a free choice, Stalin turned to open military conquest to expand the area of Soviet control.

Stalin's decision to use armed force for the destruction of "wholesome" nations appeared to justify, if not demand, an American willingness to employ its military power to counter the new Soviet strategy. As Dulles explained at the time, "The Korean affair shows that communism cannot be checked merely by building up sound domestic economies." Such an approach had only encouraged military aggression. Washington now feared that Moscow would initiate similar thrusts into such areas as Yugoslavia and Indochina. Perhaps more alarming, if Stalin had attacked South Korea because of its political and economic progress, there was a strong possibility of "Soviet application [of] similar reasoning to Western Europe. . . ." "Since international communism may not be deterred by moral principles backed by *potential* might," Dulles concluded, "we must back those principles with military strength-in-being, and do so quickly."

North Korea's invasion of South Korea also destroyed all basis for continued faith in the power of containment as a liberating force. Soon after the attack, the administration recognized that the United States could achieve reunification of Korea under a desirable government only if American forces crossed the thirty-eighth parallel and eliminated the communist regime by military means. Initially, however, American leaders stated that the objective in Korea was merely to restore the status quo ante bellum. During a meeting on June 27, 1950, George F. Kennan assured the North Atlantic Treaty Organization (NATO) ambassadors that the United States had no intention of pursuing forcible reunification. Two days later, Acheson declared publicly that American efforts in Korea were aimed only at upholding the rule of law in international affairs and preserving the credibility of the United Nations. He stated categorically that military action "is solely for the purpose of restoring the Republic of Korea to its status prior to the invasion from the north and of reestablishing the peace broken by that aggression."

Once the United States had intervened in the Korean conflict with combat troops, certain individuals in the administration began to press for an American commitment to cross the thirty-eighth parallel in pursuit of reunification. Perhaps the most vocal member of this group was John M. Allison, the director of the Office of Northeast Asian Affairs. In a statement dated July 1, 1950, he wrote:

> I understand that there has been some suggestion that in the speech which is being prepared for President Truman to make on the Korean situation should be included a statement to the effect that United States forces and presumably South Korean forces will only attempt to drive the North Koreans back to the thirty-eighth parallel and will not go any further. I most strongly urge that no such statement be included in the speech. In my opinion it would be fatal to what may be left of South Korean morale if such a statement were made. It would also appear to me to be most unrealistic in the present situation. I believe there is ample justification in the last part of the second Resolution of the Security Council for any action which may be deemed appropriate at the time which will contribute to the permanent restoration of peace and stability in that area. I am convinced that there will be no permanent peace and stability in Korea as long as the artificial division at the thirty-eighth parallel continues. I believe the time has come when we must be bold and willing to take even more risks than we have already and, while I certainly would not advocate saying in the speech that we would proceed beyond the thirty-eighth parallel, nevertheless we should not commit ourselves at this time not to do so.

Allison strongly recommended that the United States establish military control over the entire peninsula and then sponsor the free election of a government to rule a reunited Korea.

MacArthur clearly shared Allison's point of view with respect to the thirty-eighth parallel. During the first week of July, American forces were unable to halt the North Korean advance, yet MacArthur was already considering offensive action. On July 4, American military leaders in Tokyo began to discuss the feasibility of an amphibious landing behind enemy lines. MacArthur speculated that the operation could begin as early as July 22. Three days later, he informed Washington of his intention to halt the North Korean advance as soon as possible and then launch a counteroffensive in coordination with an amphibious landing behind enemy lines that would permit the United States to "compose and unite" Korea. . . .

Paul Nitze, head of the Policy Planning Staff, voiced strong opposition to forcible reunification and counseled against crossing the thirty-eighth parallel under any circumstances. The United Nations would never sanction the military conquest of North Korea, while the Soviet Union would perceive such an operation as a clear threat to its national security. Nitze's Policy Planning Staff favored instead an attempt to restrict the conflict to south of the parallel and thereby avoid the dangers involved in pursuing reunification by force: "The risks of bringing on a major conflict with the U.S.S.R. or Communist China, if U.N. military action north of the thirty-eighth parallel is employed in an effort to reach a 'final' settlement in Korea, appear to outweigh the political advantages that might be gained from such further military action." If Washington sought only to repel aggression and restore the status quo, the United States could gain a settlement more quickly and implement it with a smaller number of combat troops. The Policy Planning Staff recognized that a permanent peace would require positive guarantees for the security of South Korea. Such an approach would also entail certain political hazards, since "public and Congressional opinion in the United States might be dissatisfied with any conclusion falling short of what it would consider a 'final' settlement of the problem.". . .

Allison's objections forced the Policy Planning Staff to alter its position paper. The new draft stated plainly that the ultimate objective in Korea was reunification, but stressed that "we have no commitment to use armed force in the effort to bring about Korean independence and unity.". . .

American military leaders initially voiced support for the Kennan-Nitze position. They were quite fearful of widening the war and opposed consideration of offensive action north of the thirty-eighth parallel. On July 21 the Joint Chiefs of Staff (JCS) submitted a policy paper that warned against any "excessive commitment of United States military forces and resources in those areas of operations which would not be decisive." Truman's military advisors were apprehensive that Moscow would exploit American involvement in Korea and stage new acts of aggression in areas of greater strategic importance to the United States. Even if the Soviet Union intervened militarily in support of North Korea, the JCS believed that "the U.S. should prepare to minimize its commitment in Korea and prepare to execute war plans." Events on the Korean battlefield appeared to warrant the adoption of a cautious approach. By July 18 the North Korean army had advanced one hundred miles south of Seoul and seemed to be on the verge of total victory.

Despite the desperate nature of the situation, MacArthur was urging the administration to grant early approval of his plan for an amphibious landing behind enemy lines at Inchon. On July 23 he supplied Washington with the details and expressed confidence that the operation would sever North Korea's "main line of communication and enable us to deliver a decisive and crushing blow." If the United States refused to implement such a plan, MacArthur warned, a costly and prolonged frontal assault would be the only other feasible alternative. It was obvious, however, that the JCS would not grant approval as long as the North Korean offensive continued. As a result, MacArthur traveled to Korea on July 26 and informed the Eighth Army commander Walton H. Walker that he would not tolerate further retreat. This "stand or die" order was evidently effective; battlelines stabilized during the first week of August. MacArthur's army rapidly consolidated its position and on August 7 launched its first counterattack. That same day, MacArthur wrote to former Secretary of War Robert P. Patterson that "in spite of great odds, I am sure that before too long a time has passed we will again be on the winning end."

MacArthur's successful halting of the North Korean military advance had a decisive impact on the administration's attitude toward crossing the thirty-eighth parallel. American leaders who had been reluctant to support forcible reunification now began to reconsider their position. Significantly, the JCS advised Truman on July 31 that the occupation of North Korea was desirable if the Soviet Union did not intervene and "the United States would mobilize sufficient resources to attain the objective and strengthen its military position in all other areas of strategic importance." Improved conditions on the Korean battlefield undoubtedly produced a new sense of optimism among Truman's civilian advisors as well. In all probability, Truman and his advisors decided during the second week of August to cross the thirty-eighth parallel in pursuit of a final settlement to the Korean problem. American actions at the United Nations provide strong support for such a conclusion.

On August 17 Ambassador Warren Austin delivered a pivotal speech to the General Assembly in response to an Indian request for an American statement of peace terms. At the outset Austin reminded his listeners that the United States supported Korea's freedom and independence and would not have intervened in the absence of North Korea's aggression. "The Security Council," he declared, "has set as its first objective the end of the breach of the peace. This objective must be pursued in such a manner that no opportunity is provided for another attempt at invasion." The United Nations had to establish complete individual and political freedom in Korea. The ambassador then proclaimed, "Shall only a part of the country be assured this freedom? I think not." The United Nations had a moral obligation to assist all Koreans in creating a reunited and democratic nation eligible for admission as a member of the international organization.

Having decided to pursue forcible reunification of the Korean peninsula, the Truman administration now turned its attention to formulating plans for the achievement of this objective. Despite its support for military ground operations north of the parallel, the JCS continued to emphasize the need for caution, particularly in regard to MacArthur's Inchon landing project. On August 19 [Army Chief of Staff J. Lawton] Collins and Navy Chief of Staff Forrest Sherman traveled to Tokyo and reminded MacArthur of the serious risks involved in his plan. All those present during the subsequent discussions agreed that Inchon would be an extremely dangerous operation, but MacArthur delivered an extemporaneous speech that by all accounts was a masterful job of persuasion. He convinced his audience that the element of surprise alone guaranteed success. "We shall land at Inchon," MacArthur perorated, "and I shall crush them."

Perhaps the most significant aspect of the conference, however, was that a consensus existed on the need to cross the thirty-eighth parallel. Collins, Sherman, and MacArthur agreed that the United States had to destroy the North Korean army completely or the threat of invasion would remain. Since the Soviet Union had not as yet intervened militarily in Korea, MacArthur expressed confidence that Moscow would not become involved in the future. MacArthur adopted the global perspective and focused attention on the wider importance of total victory in Korea when he argued: "The Oriental follows a winner. If we win, the Chinese will not follow the USSR." Upon their return to Washington, Collins and Sherman informed Truman of MacArthur's plans. The president now instructed his advisors to formulate a detailed course of action for the occupation of North Korea and the reunification of the peninsula.

On August 28 the JCS tentatively approved the Inchon landing project and set September 15 as the target date. The administration simultaneously completed work on its plans for an offensive across the thirty-eighth parallel. On September 1 the JCS submitted a memorandum predicting that the Soviet Union would probably attempt to retain possession of North Korea. Once the United Nations reached the thirty-eighth parallel, Moscow would either call for a ceasefire or intervene militarily "under the guise of . . . maintaining law and order." The JCS then outlined a course of action designed to forestall such an eventuality:

Our objective of unifying Korea, however, can be accomplished if we forestall Soviet action by early entry of United Nations forces into North Korea. Such a maneuver would deny to the Soviets the initiative, deal them a major political rebuff, and, if properly timed, may not necessarily increase the risk of collision with Soviet troops.

For American military leaders, time was of the essence if the United States hoped to reunify Korea without at the same time starting a global war.

American leaders were also concerned that the Soviet Union would apply pressure on the United Nations to accept a compromise settlement in Korea. India had already demonstrated that it would ignore American opposition and respond favorably to such a Soviet proposal. To avoid a possible stalemate at the United Nations, the National Security Council (NSC) recommended that the State Department inaugurate immediate and "vigorous action on the psychological and diplomatic front." The United States had to prevail upon its allies to support postponement at the United Nations of consideration of a compromise settlement. Once MacArthur had launched a successful offensive for reunification, the entire issue would become academic.

American leaders summarized plans for Korean reunification in a NSC report. The document proceeded from the basic assumption that the United Nations, in three previous resolutions, had established as its "political objective" in Korea the achievement of a completely independent and united nation. "If the present United Nations action in Korea can accomplish this political objective without substantial risk of general war with the Soviet Union or Communist China," the paper continued, "it would be in our interest to advocate the pressing of the United Nations action to this conclusion." It would be ill-advised to pursue forcible reunification, however, if it led to global war or sacrificed American support at the United Nations. To reduce the possibility of either occurrence, the report recommended certain precautions. First, MacArthur would offer peace terms to the North Koreans prior to crossing the thirty-eighth parallel. Second, the JCS would instruct MacArthur to permit only Korean forces in the most northern provinces. Finally, the United States should obtain the explicit support of the United Nations for reunification.

The report emphasized that "a clear legal basis" existed for such American "military actions north of the thirty-eighth parallel as are necessary" to compel the North Korean army to withdraw from South Korea. The United Nations resolutions did not, however, authorize the pursuit of the political aim of establishing Rhee's control over the entire peninsula. To counter opposition in the United Nations to offensive action north of the parallel, the paper urged the administration to concentrate on the military disadvantages of merely restoring the status quo ante bellum. If the United Nations permitted North Korea to survive, it would also have to provide sufficient military power on the peninsula to enforce the ceasefire.

The report also advised the administration to expect the outbreak of global war and prepare for such an eventuality. Since American military capabilities remained relatively limited, the JCS should instruct MacArthur to cross the thirty-eighth parallel only if there were no apparent threat or indication of Soviet or Chinese intervention. If Moscow intervened, MacArthur should withdraw to the parallel and notify the United Nations. The international organization would then either increase its military commitment to achieve reunification or condemn the Soviet Union for aggression. If, however, the Chinese intervened, the JCS should instruct

MacArthur to continue military operations "as long as action by UN military forces offers a reasonable chance of successful resistance.". . . .

On September 7, 1950, the JCS informed Truman of its strong support for the NSC recommendations. Thus American leaders abandoned their earlier opposition to crossing the thirty-eighth parallel and now advocated the pursuit of forcible re-unification. Although Kennan and probably Nitze continued to warn against military action north of the parallel, Allison's views now appeared to represent the attitude of most of Truman's diplomatic advisors. During a radio interview on August 27, Ambassador-at-Large Philip C. Jessup emphasized that both the United States and the United Nations were committed to the creation of a free and united Korea. Although it was an entirely United Nations decision, Washington intended to impress upon the international organization that only strong action would deter further aggression and build confidence in the effectiveness of collective security.

Assistant Secretary of State Dean Rusk was perhaps the most influential advocate of crossing the thirty-eighth parallel. In a speech delivered on September 9, he pointed out that the United States was attempting to foster the triumph of national self-determination throughout Asia. Rusk then declared that American leaders "believe that the United Nations must have the opportunity to give effect to its long-standing policy in favor of a free and united Korea. . . . We have tried every other method to build peace—we must now make it clear to any aggressor that aggression carries with it their certain destruction." International security demanded that all nations rely upon peaceful and legal means to settle disputes. Rusk viewed it as imperative that the United Nations punish those governments refusing to follow established rules for proper conduct.

Truman approved the NSC report on September 11 after only minor alterations. MacArthur did not receive a complete copy of the paper until September 22, largely because Truman had just replaced Louis Johnson with George C. Marshall as secretary of defense. The United States was now committed to the pursuit of forcible reunification in Korea as long as military action north of the parallel did not ignite a major war. For Truman and his advisors, success in Korea was a matter of global importance. As State Department official H. Freeman Matthews revealed in a memorandum to the JCS, if the United States reunified Korea militarily, "the resultant defeat to the Soviet Union and to the Communist world will be of momentous significance." It was Washington, then, and not MacArthur, that made the decision to seek the destruction of North Korea. When the general crossed the thirty-eighth parallel, he "was not violating policy but putting it into effect."

Truman was careful not to admit publicly that he had instructed MacArthur to cross the thirty-eighth parallel. At a press conference on September 21, a newsman asked the president if he had reached a decision with respect to military action in North Korea. Truman stated flatly: "No, I have not. That is a matter for the United Nations to decide. That is a United Nations force, and we are one of the many who are interested in that situation. It will be worked out by the United Nations and I will abide by the decision that the United Nations makes." Truman remained fearful that the Soviet Union would be able to mobilize sufficient support at the United Nations for a compromise settlement to block offensive action north of the parallel. It was vital for the United States to avoid any appearance of unilateralism that might undermine its position at the United Nations. Washington could forestall a prolonged debate at the General Assembly if crossing the thirty-eighth parallel appeared to be a matter of military necessity.

American efforts to minimize the possibility of United Nations interference in the military advance north of the thirty-eighth parallel are important in understanding the administration's instructions to MacArthur during the final week of September. Truman and his advisors demonstrated an acute sensitivity to any public reference to the parallel. In a cable to MacArthur on September 29, for example, Secretary Marshall expressed alarm over rumors that the Eighth Army commander had announced his intention to halt at the parallel and await authorization from the United Nations to cross into northern Korea. The secretary of defense then explained the reason for Washington's displeasure: "We want you to feel unhampered tactically and strategically to proceed north of thirty-eighth parallel. Announcement above referred to may precipitate embarrassment in the UN where evident desire is not to be confronted with necessity of a vote on passage, rather to find you have found it militarily necessary to do so." In response, MacArthur assured Marshall that the report was erroneous and the parallel was "not a factor in the mil[itary] employment of our forces." "Unless and until the enemy capitulates," the general emphasized, "I regard all of Korea open for our mil[itary] operations."

MacArthur apparently failed to comprehend the basis for Washington's concern. On October 1 he informed the JCS of his desire to issue a "dramatic" statement announcing his intention to pursue and destroy North Korean forces throughout the peninsula. The proclamation would warn the enemy that "the field of our military operations is limited only by military exigencies and the international boundaries of Korea." The JCS cabled MacArthur immediately that Washington considered "it unwise to issue your statement. In accordance with General Marshall's message . . . we desire that you proceed with your operations without any further explanation or announcement and let action determine the matter." The JCS continued: "Our Government desires to avoid having to make an issue of the thirty-eighth parallel until we have accomplished our mission of defeating the North Korean forces." The Truman administration was probably following the advice of its allies in adopting such an approach. The strategy was successful; on October 7 the United Nations passed a resolution instructing MacArthur to "ensure conditions of stability throughout Korea."

Acheson later insisted that the administration never advocated as a war aim the achievement of an independent and united Korea. Washington's sole objective was to destroy the North Korean army and restore peaceful conditions in the area, which required the crossing of the thirty-eighth parallel. Only the Korean people themselves could realize the "political objective" of a united and democratic government through participation in free elections under the sponsorship of the United Nations. Critics subsequently maintained that Acheson was engaged in a feeble attempt to counter charges that Truman had abandoned reunification as a war aim after Chinese intervention. In reality, the secretary of state's explanation illustrates well the administration's perception of what would soon transpire. . . .

Truman's decision to pursue the complete destruction of North Korea was an extremely dangerous policy in both military and political terms. When the administration reverted to the restoration of the status quo ante bellum as its military objective early in 1951, the Republicans began to denounce Truman for engaging in appeasement. MacArthur also exploited popular dissatisfaction with Truman's apparent retreat. During the MacArthur hearings he stressed that his "mission was to clear out all North Korea, to unify it and to liberalize it." According to MacArthur, Truman placed unwarranted restrictions on his command and thereby prevented the fulfillment of his assignment. The administration found it difficult to counter these charges. General Omar N. Bradley insisted that Washington had never issued orders of a political nature and that MacArthur's sole mission was to destroy the North Korean army. Chinese intervention had forced the United States to abandon this "military objective," but the administration never wavered in its commitment to the creation of a united Korea through free elections. Bradley stressed that the United States had not altered its "political objective" in Korea.

Public criticism of the administration probably would have been even more severe had Truman refused to authorize military action across the parallel. Few Americans raised any words of opposition to MacArthur's offensive into North Korea. In fact, most commentators demanded a "final" settlement in Korea. In one senate speech the Democratic chairman of the Senate Foreign Relations Committee, Tom Connally, called upon the United Nations to reaffirm its commitment to the creation of a united Korea. Republicans were even more enthusiastic about the prospects for victory in Korea. Dulles explained in one private letter that "if we have the power to do otherwise, it would be folly to go back to the division of Korea at the thirty-eighth Parallel." Dulles conveyed his opinion to the administration in a memorandum to Nitze. "If we have the opportunity to obliterate the line as a political division," he reasoned, "certainly we should do so in the interest of 'peace and security in the area.' " Even liberals voiced support for crossing the thirty-eighth parallel and anticipated the establishment of a united, democratic, and reform-minded government in Korea.

In the final analysis, Truman's decision to order American forces across the thirty-eighth parallel was the culmination of America's persistent efforts to resolve the Korean predicament. MacArthur's offensive into North Korea sought to guarantee for all Koreans the right of national self-determination, which had been the primary aim of America's Korea policy since World War II. Truman's decision to cross the parallel was not the product of "military momentum" or "a surge of optimism" following the Inchon landing, since the President had adopted this course of action early in August. The Truman administration turned to military means as a last resort and only after concluding that force alone would ensure Korea's freedom to determine its own destiny.

If the United States had halted at the thirty-eighth parallel, it would have registered a significant victory. The successful defense of South Korea would have secured the interests of the United States by maintaining American international credibility and prestige. Unfortunately, the assumptions underlying American foreign policy prevented the administration from being satisfied with a mere restoration of the status quo. American leaders interpreted the Korean conflict in the larger context of the global Soviet-American competition and believed a decisive victory was within easy grasp.

Yet Truman and his advisors never perceived the American offensive north of the parallel as aggressive and struggled to avoid any indication that the United States intended to force its will on the Korean people. American leaders sought instead to portray the operation as essentially negative and designed only to create conditions in which all Koreans would enjoy, or at least appear to possess, freedom of choice. The election of a united Korean government, rather than the destruction of the North Korean army, would inflict a momentous defeat on the Soviet strategy of expansion. When a united Korea produced economic prosperity, social stability, and the appearance of democracy, Truman believed that the popularity of communism throughout the world would begin to wane. The international community would soon realize that only national self-determination could produce "final" settlements. Crossing the thirty-eighth parallel was then only the prelude to the fulfillment of Truman's plan for victory in Korea and around the globe.

Why China Intervened in the Korean War

MICHAEL H. HUNT

New materials coming out of China complicate and marginally clarify our picture of Beijing's role in the origins of the Korean War and its response to the final months of the fighting. They do not set directly in doubt the older impression that the actual outbreak of the war found the Chinese leadership preoccupied with reconstructing the economy, carrying out land reform in newly liberated areas, and in general consolidating the revolution at home.

There are now, however, some hints that Beijing knew that the North Korean leader Kim Il Sung had some military initiative afoot. Several accounts claim that Mao and Stalin discussed the Korean question during their summit meeting Moscow (December 1949–February 1950) and that Mao exchanged views with Kim during a later meeting in Beijing. Whatever may have been said on these occasions, it is clear that Beijing and Pyongyang worked together in the year before the war to repatriate Korean troops who had fought in the Chinese civil war. Those troops had marched into the Northeast with the Chinese Communist Eighth Route Army at the end of the Pacific War carrying orders to organize Korean residents of the Northeast and to help the Soviet army in the liberation of Korea. . . .

On 25 June 1950, North Korean forces launched an invasion of South Korea, setting off a string of unpleasant surprises for Beijing. The first of these came on 27 June when President Harry S. Truman announced that the United States would not only defend South Korea under the auspices of the United Nations but also "neutralize" the Taiwan Strait by sending the Seventh Fleet to block any communist invasion attempt. Beijing's earliest public response to the American intervention, published on 28 and 29 June, was notably cautious and vague. While deploring American intervention around the world and especially in Asia, Mao, Premier Zhou Enlai, and a *Renmin ribao [People's Daily]* editorial all nonetheless focused their public fire on the American attempt to deny China control of its province of Taiwan.

From Michael H. Hunt, "Beijing and the Korean Crisis, June, 1950–June, 1951," *Political Science Quarterly* 107 (Fall, 1992), pp. 457–474. Reprinted by permission of the publisher.

But the Chinese Communist Party (CCP) began almost at once to prepare against untoward developments in Korea. On 30 June Zhou ordered Chinese military observers to North Korea. On 7 and 10 July the Military Affairs Committee met, and in sessions chaired by Zhou and attended by the army commander-in-chief, Zhu De, and Nie Rongzhen recommended creating a force to defend the border and if necessary cross the Yalu River to help North Korea. Mao at once endorsed the proposal. By early August more than a quarter of a million troops were assembled along the Yalu with Gao Gang, in charge of party and military affairs in the Northeast, bearing responsibility for logistical support. Even so, Beijing's alarm, reflected in public warnings directed against the advance of the United Nations forces, continued to mount. On 5 August Mao personally instructed Gao Gang to have the border forces ready for combat by early September. Told by Gao of the difficulties in completing the preparations, Mao agreed on 18 August to extend the deadline to the end of the month. On 17 September, in the immediate aftermath of the successful American landing at Inchon, the Military Affairs Committee dispatched Chinese officers to Korea to lay the groundwork for possible intervention.

China's growing alarm, reenforced by Soviet and Korean calls for assistance, gave rise to efforts to coordinate policy among the three countries, so at least the new [Chinese] secondary accounts suggest. While some older accounts contend that regular high-level consultations among the three began in early July, the new evidence points to a later date—after the Inchon landing and General Douglas MacArthur's rapid push north created panic in Pyongyang and alarm in Beijing and Moscow. These contacts quickly moved to the highest level, bringing the Chinese fully into inner councils of the war. In late September Stalin raised with Beijing the possibility of Kim Il Sung setting up a government in exile in China, and on 1 October with South Korean forces crossing the thirty-eighth parallel Kim personally followed up with a desperate request for China's help in the war. . . .

The new materials offer some new insights on the decisions that led China to intervene militarily in the conflict. These materials, which include a substantial body of documents, reveal Mao's dominant role. Not surprisingly, however, given the complexity of the man, the rapidly developing crisis confronting him, and the size of the stakes for the CCP, those materials raise fresh, knotty questions about precisely when and exactly why Mao resolved to act.

To clarify the issue of timing it is useful to think of Mao moving along two sometimes intersecting tracks toward a definitive commitment of his forces. Suspiciously, little of either track is evident before Kim's appeal for help on 1 October, even though we know that Mao began to take a hold of strategic planning two months earlier.

One of those tracks led to Moscow. Having announced to his colleagues his own view that China should intervene, Mao on 2 October cabled his decision to Stalin. Chinese troops would enter Korea on 15 October, Mao announced, and there they would assume a defensive posture, letting the enemy forces know that they faced a new situation. Once better prepared and equipped with Soviet arms, those troops could if need be take the offensive. Aside from equipment, Mao wanted from Stalin help in fending off possible American naval and air attacks on Chinese cities and industry. Thus, while indicating that China was ready to shoulder the main burden of saving North Korea, Mao also sought to ensure practical military cooperation from a Soviet leader known for his caution and now perhaps growing reluctant to be drawn directly into a protracted or escalating conflict.

In any case, on 8 October Mao followed up by sending Zhou Enlai to meet with Stalin on Chinese intervention. Zhou, accompanied by Lin Biao (seeking Soviet medical treatment) and perhaps by Ambassador Wang Jiaxiang, travelled to Sochi on the Black Sea for a meeting with Stalin that lasted through the night of 9–10 October. Stalin revealed that he would not provide the air cover Chinese forces operating in Korea would desperately need. The Soviet air force, he explained, needed more time for preparation before being engaged even in the defense of Chinese airspace. Zhou returned to Moscow to cable Mao this disappointing news but also to pass on assurances that the Soviets would immediately begin supplying weaponry for twenty Chinese divisions.

While dealing with Stalin, Mao moved along the second track defined by a string of high-level meetings devoted to discussing the grave crisis facing the new regime. The existing record suggests that Mao's proposal for decisive action elicited doubts that he was not able to dispel either quickly or easily, and indeed that he himself seems at points to have fallen prey to uncertainties. Indeed, as early as 2 October in his cable to Stalin, Mao had identified one set of risks: attacking Chinese troops might fail to destroy American forces in Korea and become entangled in a Sino-American military stand-off that would bring serious collateral damage to China's economic reconstruction and that would deepen the discontent of the Chinese already unsettled by revolution. Mao's colleagues who opposed sending troops or at least wanted to delay intervention also pointed out the military risks and the prospects of a direct, damaging attack on China. They also argued that the new Chinese state needed time to consolidate its political control, wipe out remaining Chinese Nationalist resistance, complete land reform, stabilize the economy, and upgrade the armed forces. They pointed to the burdens intervention would place on a war-weary population. They may also have stressed the uncertain nature of Soviet assistance. The rapidly deteriorating battlefield situation, the delays in getting Chinese troops ready for combat, Stalin's refusal of air support, and in general the gnawing anxieties about the risk China was about to take—all combined to complicate Mao's task and prolong the discussion. . . .

The first of a hurried and tension-filled series of high-level meetings took place on 1 October. The leadership broke away early from the public celebration of the PRC's [People's Republic of China's] first anniversary to discuss Kim Il Sung's urgent request for military assistance. This meeting, held like most of the others to follow within the CCP headquarters compound at Zhongnanhai in Beijing, did not end until dawn.

The middle of the afternoon the next day (2 October) Mao met with Zhu, Li Shaoqi, Zhou, Nie, and Gao (having just flown into the capital), and he announced that troops had to intervene. The only questions were when and under whose command would the intervention take place. The assembled leaders agreed on 15 October as the day for Chinese forces to march. The selection of a commander seems to have been more difficult. Mao indicated that he had considered first Su Yu and then, once the size of the operation grew, Lin Biao. However, both were medically indisposed, and Lin had evidenced anxiety over American military superiority.

Mao suggested Peng Dehuai and won general approval. Mao then dispatched his cable to Stalin, and Zhou called in the Indian ambassador, K. M. Pannikar, to warn that Beijing "has to be concerned" *(yaoguan)* if the Americans crossed the thirty-eighth parallel. . . .

On 8 October, following a series of planning meetings, Mao met again with the enlarged Political Bureau and gave the orders for Chinese forces to prepare to move across the Yalu River and do battle with U.S. troops then crossing the thirty-eighth parallel and threatening Pyongyang. At the same time he cabled his decision to Kim Il Sung and formally named Peng Dehuai the commander of the volunteers. Peng left at once for the Northeast to take up his command. He was accompanied by Gao and Mao Zedong's son, Anying, who was to serve as translator for the Soviet advisers.

The arrival of Zhou Enlai's unsettling report of his interview with Stalin during the afternoon of 10 October set the stage for a second round of consultations in Zhongnanhai. On 11–12 October Mao not only suspended his intervention order but also recalled Peng and Gao to Beijing for another round of discussions. The Political Bureau met on 13 October and stayed in session through the night before coming to a unanimous agreement to send troops to Korea despite the lack of Soviet air support. Mao devoted the 14th to detailed consultation with Peng on the impending military operations.

The 13 October Political Bureau meeting and Mao's discussions with Peng on the 14th produced a consensus in favor of proceeding cautiously and avoiding a direct challenge to the United States. The volunteers were to concentrate their attack on the South Korean "puppet" forces and avoid hitting any but isolated American forces. The volunteers were, moreover, not to make a rapid advance but rather establish a base of operations in the mountainous region north of Pyongyang and Wonsan. If American forces did not advance beyond those two points for six months, then Chinese forces would gain time to prepare for whatever action Beijing might think best at the end of that period. This action, the Political Bureau resolution somewhat vaguely opined, would "produce a change to our advantage." The consensus did not address the possibility that MacArthur might continue his rapid advance, giving the Chinese force no grace period and Beijing no chance for a peaceful resolution of the confrontation. This oversight may have reflected a reluctance to see the crisis in worst-case terms and thus play into the hands of the doubters. Mao now cabled Zhou, still in Moscow, the terms on which China was acting and made clear that the intervening force would consist not of the six divisions that Stalin had urged earlier in the crisis but fifteen divisions together with supporting units (260,000 troops). . . .

He [Mao] now set 19 October for the major crossing of the Yalu. As instructed, the first major body of Chinese troops advanced into Korea late that day, setting in motion the events that would soon bring war with the United States.

Any effort to pin down the exact motive behind Mao's decision to intervene must enter a mind as complicated as the crisis it wrestled with. That effort must also confront the different, though not mutually exclusive, rationales that Mao offered in his effort to neutralize the hesitations or objections that he felt he faced on three distinct fronts. The puzzle for the historian is to judge how much Mao chose his arguments to win support, how much those arguments were keenly felt by him, and how important one was relative to the other.

That Mao's attitude toward China's role in the Korean conflict was complex is amply illustrated by his cable of 2 October to Stalin. He contended that he felt an internationalist duty to rescue the beleaguered Korean revolution and to help maintain revolutionary morale around the world in the face of a counteroffensive launched by American reactionaries. The danger of a revival of reactionary sentiment in China and elsewhere in Asia was equally troubling and called for a decisive response. If China meekly acquiesced while the Americans occupied all of Korea and dealt a heavy blow to the Korean revolution, "then the American aggressors would run even more wild to the detriment of all of East Asia." While giving considerable weight overall to the dangers of appeasement and the opportunities for creating an international environment favorable to revolutionary change, Mao also invoked a narrower, more conventional concern with China's security. He had to act, he argued, to preempt a possible American offensive into China itself.

When Mao shifted from addressing Stalin to his compatriots, especially the petty and national bourgeoisie and intellectuals, another set of concerns—national unity—came to the fore. He and Zhou Enlai made patriotic appeals calculated to calm their fear of war and neutralize their lingering philo-Americanism, which Mao himself had attacked only a year earlier. He now again warned that patriots should not be deceived by American propaganda. He indicated that the war was necessary to defend the vital interests of China against renewed aggression, and he urged "all patriotic industrialists and merchants" to join with the masses in a united front against foreign aggression. Zhou Enlai, playing his accustomed role as spokesman for united front policies, drew on China's past in making a similarly patriotic appeal. In an address to the Chinese People's Consultative Congress on 24 October, he invoked the traditional figure of speech—Korea as lips to China's teeth—to underline the long accepted strategic importance of the peninsula. He compared the line of attack the Americans were following to that of the Japanese, beginning in Korea before moving on to the Northeast and then China as a whole.

Finally, the discussions within the Political Bureau found Mao once more an internationalist, but one now with China decidedly at the center. Joined by Peng Dehuai and other advocates of action in the meetings of 4–5 October, Mao expressed fears of China being thrown on the defensive if it did not now deal the Americans a blow. An unchecked American advance in Korea would draw wavering countries and classes to the side of the United States, strengthen the resolve of reactionaries at home and abroad, and encourage the United States to send troops to other points along China's border.

The final consensus reached at the meeting of 13 October seemed to reflect this combination of concerns. According to Mao's summary of that consensus, military intervention was necessary above all to prevent the enemy from dominating the Yalu River and thus posing a constant threat to the Northeast. But it was also important for guaranteeing the North Koreans a secure base of operations and for denying imperialism a victory that would fan counterrevolutionary sentiments in China and internationally.

Mao's own precise personal goals at this point are difficult to pin down and may not have been entirely clear in his own mind. Indeed, the risks and uncertainties of intervention put a premium on keeping policy flexible with several options left open. His cables to Zhou, sent in the immediate aftermath of the decisive

13 October Political Bureau meeting, reflected this reluctance to be pinned down. Chinese troops might win a decisive battlefield victory that would force the American-led coalition to abandon the peninsula. Even a limited success might send a wake-up call to Washington, making clear China's determination and hence the dangers of a more costly Korean conflict. Once rudely shaken, Washington might reassess its goals in Korea; the pause in Chinese military operations following the initial entry into Korea would give the Americans time to indicate their interest in a peaceful resolution of the conflict. If on the other hand Washington held to its aggressive course, then Chinese troops, by then better prepared for combat, could take the offensive in a renewed test of strength. Mao must have played out in his mind each of these scenarios in the anxious days before the crossing of the Yalu. But they amounted, as he and his Political Bureau colleagues must have realized, to nothing more concrete than the pious hope that an early blow might produce a turn for the better on the peninsula.

These materials are also revealing on Mao's deep involvement in the actual planning and execution of the first three campaigns, beginning in late October and running to early January. The point that deserves stress is that Mao's role here, as in the high-level decision to take a military stand, was central and controlling. For example, through October Mao appears to have focused on the Korean crisis to the exclusion of other pressing issues facing the new government. His preoccupations, even anxieties, are evident in the drumbeat of advice that he showered on the commander of his forces in Korea. For example, one collection has Mao sending out fifty-five telegrams to Peng Dehuai between 21 October and 26 December with no fewer than eighteen going out on the eve of the first offensive and into its first few days (that is, between 21 and 26 October). The concerns reflected in the published telegrams, sometimes numbering two or three a day, range from placement of Chinese units and the line of approach of enemy forces down to the proper location for Peng's own headquarters. . . .

The new materials make strikingly clear that Mao, once deeply and successfully engaged in the Korean conflict, resolved the ambiguities in Chinese war aims in favor of bold, far-reaching goals and without any apparent formal consultation with his Political Bureau colleagues. The resolution came in late November and early December. As Peng's drive south gave increasing promise of a sweeping victory, Mao in effect fell victim to military opportunism. On 4 December he ordered reconnaissance in force against the clearly panicked UN army now retreating across the thirty-eighth parallel into South Korea. The next day Pyongyang fell amid hints that the Americans might altogether abandon Korea. On 13 December he ordered the advance to continue *beyond* the parallel, and he reiterated that position as late as 21 December. Bolstered militarily, Beijing publicly linked peace on the peninsula to the withdrawal of all foreign troops, U.S. disengagement from Taiwan, and a place for China in the UN.

From this high point of optimism, Mao began a retreat toward a more sober appraisal of the military situation and toward more modest goals. He took the first step back on 26 and 29 December when he began to concede the seriousness of the supply and morale problems afflicting his army. Peng was calling for rest for Chinese forces, and Nie claims to have then endorsed the proposal. But Mao insisted for political reasons on launching another offensive. The third offensive thus began on 31 December against the better judgment of Mao's chief military associ- ates in the Korean commitment. A month later (25–29 January) at a Sino-Korean military conference Peng again proposed a rest for his forces, this time in prepara- tion for renewed offensive action in March. (The difficulties of supply and morale were exacerbated and hopes for a rest denied when the Americans launched their own offensive on 25 January.) With his troops exhausted, short on supplies, and harried by the enemy, Mao now at last conceded in early February that he had be- come entangled in a war of attrition and would have to shift to "rotational warfare" whereby Chinese armies would be trained and sent to Korea for a time, and then withdrawn in favor of a fresh force. . . .

By [late May] the fifth major Chinese offensive had ground to a halt, confirm- ing the military stalemate that Mao had perceived earlier and revealing the contin- uing problem of supply and the fragility of Chinese units in the face of a still strong enemy. The Americans, he observed on 26 May, remained determined and confi- dent. He had failed to destroy their will to fight, and he would have to shift to a de- fensive strategy. Mao's own willingness to concede this point and the American approach to the Soviet ambassador to the United Nations on 31 May appears to have signaled to his colleagues that a major reappraisal of the Korean strategy was in order. On 3 June Kim Il Sung held talks with Mao and Zhou, followed in mid- June by high-level CCP discussions. This flurry of activity produced consensus on trying for a negotiated end to the conflict with the thirty-eighth parallel to serve once again as the dividing line between the two Koreas. On 23 June the Soviet UN ambassador publicly proposed talks, and it was immediately endorsed by an edito- rial in *Renmin ribao*. Talks opened in Kaesong on 10 July. . . .

Reflecting back in July 1951, Mao tried to put the developments of the past year in positive terms. "As the ancients said, only by being able to fight is one then able to make peace." But the fighting had already proved more costly than anti- cipated, and Mao would soon discover that the talks were a slow and tortuous process. Two years of deadlock would pass and China's dead and wounded on the battlefield would climb to 360,000 before the military sacrifices that China had made could be translated into a peace agreement.

The new materials add marginally to the impression derived from long avail- able public sources that the Chinese leadership may have been worried but not de- terred by the American nuclear threat. Recent research on the American side demonstrates that the Truman administration engaged in atomic diplomacy, first through Secretary of State Dean Acheson's leak to the *New York Times* in early August 1950, then through Harry Truman's own sensational press conference statement of 30 November, and finally through a warning conveyed by contact in Hong Kong in May 1951. To give these threats substance, Washington kept nu- clear-armed bombers within striking distance of China until late June 1951 and the air force made reconnaissance flights over the Northeast and Shandong to get data for a possible nuclear strike.

Beijing publicly dismissed the nuclear threat. A lightly industrialized and heavily rural, agricultural China was not a particularly fruitful target for nuclear attack. Similarly, in Korea nuclear weapons did not seem useful as an actual tool of land warfare. This tendency to downplay the nuclear threat may have been nei- ther off-handed nor disingenuous. One study contends that the dangers of atomic warfare did at least intrude into the discussions over intervention in October 1950, while another account indicates that Mao in a 5 September 1950 talk to the Council of the Central People's Government raised the atomic threat only to downplay its significance. Even so, the nuclear threat required attention. Mao was concerned enough about popular fears of atomic bombing that he had the wartime mobilization campaign address them. On the off-chance that the United States did attack from the air, the leadership ordered bomb shelters prepared in urban areas, some industrial plants removed from vulnerable urban cities, and civil defense education directed at the civilian population.

Finally, these new materials are suggestive on the pervasive impact of the Korean war on the homefront. Intervention in Korea clearly complicated the tasks of economic reconstruction and drained away scarce resources needed domestically. The constraints the war imposed on reconstruction is evident in the national budget. In 1951, the first full year of the war, defense ate up 46 percent (up from about 38 percent the previous year), and only 30 percent was left for economic development. But already by 1952 the overall military burden had dropped to 32 percent of the total budget, and economic construction had risen to an impressive 52 percent.

The war also provided an opportunity to mobilize the urban population and integrate intellectuals into the new political order. This process, begun on the eve of liberation, had intensified in July 1950, paralleling China's military preparations at each step of the way. As noted above, national unity particularly preoccupied Mao as he made the decision in early October to intervene. The Korean crisis also gave a push to the land reform movement in the newly liberated areas, particularly in the Southeast. After China entered the war, Mao issued orders to accelerate efforts along that vulnerable section of the coast in order to consolidate control and improve defense capabilities.

Perhaps most intriguing of all the domestic ramifications is the way the war intersected with the counterrevolutionary effort. Even before the war began, Beijing had regarded as urgent the suppression of remnant Nationalist forces on the mainland (estimated at 1.5 million in late 1949), spies and covert operations sponsored by Taibei and Washington, and banditry. . . .

According to party sources, the American intervention in Korea and especially the Inchon landing were signals of hope for China's counterrevolutionaries. Active resistance groups, now joined by landlords, secret societies, and unemployed soldiers, thought that better times were just ahead and intensified their resistance. They carried out widely scattered acts of violence extending into the Northeast, the logistical base for Chinese forces in Korea, and stirred up rumors, while intimidating local party cadres. "You're like a frog in a well with no idea of the big picture and still in a mess. The third world war is coming and the Nationalist army will be right back."

The party center responded to this upsurge on 10 October with a directive calling for an end to a counterrevolutionary policy that had been too rightist, accommodating enemies of the new regime, killing too few, suspending the sentences of too many, and letting cases drag on too long. The party center ordered local authorities to step up internal security measures in order to blunt this threat. The first uncertain months of the military contest with the United States seem to have marked the high point of danger, which did not begin to recede until early 1951.

On 24 January Mao offered the judgment that there was no risk of an American invasion (though he did think a Nationalist invasion threat remained). . . .

While our perspective is still one-sided with much work remaining to be done before the scribes can offer a full and genuinely international picture of the Korean War, we do have enough fresh evidence to reconsider our broader understanding of that crisis and especially to relate what we now know about the Chinese side of the war to some of the key points that emerge from the recent studies of American policy.

Mao's leadership style stands in striking contrast to that of Harry Truman, at least in their markedly different relationships with their respective field commanders. Recent treatments of U.S. policy reveal a Truman presidency in crisis, internally divided, under the growing scrutiny of its worried European allies, besieged by domestic critics, and confused by the failure of the Soviets to behave belligerently and the Chinese to take American professions of good will at face value. At the root of these troubles was a president whose involvement in making policy might be described as spasmodic rather than either weak or strong. He hesitated at critical moments to play a decisive role even though the interminable and inconclusive debates among his aides cried out for presidential direction. . . .

Mao's assertive style, his hands-on approach, and the general deference accorded him contrasts with Truman's striking lack of assurance, his episodic involvement in policy making, and the leadership vacuum that MacArthur and others sought to fill more or less constructively. For Mao the close link between politics and warfare was a given, a point that Truman was slow to grasp or at least to act on. Even when Mao withdrew from daily direction of military affairs from January to May, he still provided a guiding hand as Chinese forces adopted the strategy of rotation discussed above.

Miscalculation afflicted both sides. It has long been a commonplace in the historical literature that American leaders were dealing with a dimly imagined Chinese foe on the basis of very limited information and insight. Ignorance and wishful thinking proved especially costly between June and December 1950 when underestimation in Washington and Tokyo of Chinese determination and capacity led to a disastrous military setback and ultimately a costly deadlock on the battlefields of Korea. . . .

The Chinese, we can now see, did little better. The mix of calculations Mao applied to the Korean intervention in October brings to mind nothing so strongly as the outlook in Washington at the very same time. Like the Truman administration, Mao was guided by one part "national security" and another part "new world order." Taken together, the elements that made up China's policy toward Korea were every bit as complicated and unstable as Washington's.

Once engaged in the fighting, Mao himself fell victim to the military opportunism that also characterized U.S. policy, in no small measure because he too suffered from a highly schematic view of the enemy, a view that led him as well to underestimate his foe. Mao believed that a rational calculus guided the American ruling class in its approach to the Korean crisis. Once the high cost of aggression became clear, the imperialists would beat a retreat. Moreover, he believed that the masses in the United States had nothing to gain by fighting in Korea. He could accentuate popular disaffection by killing American troops and releasing American prisoners. Finally, he believed that the links between the United States and its allies were weak. By chewing up South Korean puppet forces and British commonwealth troops, he could destroy their will to fight. Thus beleaguered at home and isolated internationally, Washington would have to abandon Korea or seek a comprehensive solution of East Asian questions with China.

Finally, what is most striking about this crisis viewed from a supranational perspective is that neither side could have read the intentions of the other; hence crisis resolution or management was virtually impossible in the initial stages—down to the spring of 1951. Even had Mao and Truman been clairvoyant, each would have come away from an examination of the mind of the other unimpressed by clarity or vision. Rather, both would have been shocked by the muddle their opposite number was in. This ambiguity that marked the approach of the two sides, in itself a serious impediment to managing the Korean conflict, was further heightened by time lag and perceptual distortions. What limited information one side received about the other side was often outdated when it arrived and mangled in the transmission.

✸ *FURTHER READING*

Frank Baldwin, ed., *Without Parallel* (1975)

Barton J. Bernstein, "The Truman Administration and the Korean War," in Michael Lacey, ed., *The Truman Presidency* (1989), pp. 410–444

Clay Blair, *The Forgotten War* (1988)

Ronald J. Caridi, *The Korean War and American Politics* (1969)

Thomas J. Christensen, "Threats, Assurances, and the Last Chance for Peace: The Lessons of Mao's Korean War Telegrams," *International Security,* 17 (1992), 122–154

Bruce Cumings, ed., *Child of Conflict* (1983)

———, "Korean-American Relations," in Warren I. Cohen, ed., *New Frontiers in American-East Asian Relations* (1983), pp. 239–282

———, *The Origins of the Korean War,* 2 vols. (1981–1990)

Roger Dingman, "Atomic Diplomacy During the Korean War," *International Security,* 13 (1988–1989), 50–91

Charles Dobbs, *The Unwanted Symbol* (1981)

Rosemary J. Foot, "Making Known the Unknown War: Policy Analysis of the Korean Conflict in the Last Decade," *Diplomatic History,* 15 (1991), 411–431

———, *A Substitute for Victory* (1990)

———, *The Wrong War* (1985)

Alexander L. George and Richard Smoke, *Deterrence in American Foreign Policy* (1974)

Sergei N. Goncharov et al., *Uncertain Partners: Stalin, Mao, and the Korean War* (1993)

Joseph Goulden, *Korea* (1982)

Karunaker Gupta, "How Did the Korean War Begin?" *China Quarterly,* 52 (1972), 699–716. Critics' comments in 54 (1973), 354–368

Allen Guttmann, ed., *Korea: Cold War and Limited War* (1972)

Francis H. Heller, ed., *The Korean War* (1977)

Hoa Yufan and Zhai Zhihai, "China's Decision to Enter the Korean War: History Revisited," *China Quarterly,* 121 (1990), 94–114

D. Clayton James, *Refighting the Last War* (1992)

———, *The Years of MacArthur* (1985)

Jian Chen, "China's Changing Aims During the Korean War, 1950–1951," *Journal of East Asian-American Relations,* 1 (1992), 8–41

Burton I. Kaufman, *The Korean War* (1986)

Edward C. Keefer, "President Dwight D. Eisenhower and the End of the Korean War," *Diplomatic History,* 10 (1986), 267–289

Gabriel Kolko and Joyce Kolko, *The Limits of Power* (1972)

Peter Lowe, *The Origins of the Korean War* (1986)

Callum A. MacDonald, *Korea* (1987)

David McLellan, *Dean Acheson* (1976)

James I. Matray, ed., *Historical Dictionary of the Korean War* (1991)

———, *The Reluctant Crusade* (1985)

Ernest R. May, *"Lessons" of the Past* (1973)

John Merrill, *Korea: The Peninsular Origins of the War* (1989)

Yonosuke Nagai and Akira Iriye, eds., *The Origins of the Cold War in Asia* (1977)

Glenn D. Paige, *The Korean Decision* (1968)

———, ed., *1950: Truman's Decision* (1970)

David Rees, *Korea, The Limited War* (1964)

Mark A. Ryan, *Chinese Attitudes Toward Nuclear Weapons: China and the United States During the Korean War* (1989)

Michael Schaller, *Douglas MacArthur: The Far Eastern General* (1989)

Robert R. Simmons, *The Strained Alliance* (1975)

Gaddis Smith, *Dean Acheson* (1972)

John W. Spanier, *The Truman-MacArthur Controversy* (1959)

Russell Spurr, *Enter the Dragon: China's Involvement in the Korean War* (1988)

I. F. Stone, *The Hidden History of the Korean War* (1952)

William Stueck, "The Korean War as International History," *Diplomatic History,* 10 (1986), 291–309

———, *The Road to Confrontation* (1981)

John Tolland, *In Mortal Combat* (1991)

Philip West, "Confronting the West," *Journal of American-East Asian Relations,* 2 (1993), 5–28

———, "Interpreting the Korean War," *American Historical Review,* 94 (1989), 80–96

Allen Whiting, *China Crosses the Yalu* (1960)

John E. Wiltz, "Truman and MacArthur, The Wake Island Meeting," *Military Affairs,* 42 (1978), 169–176

Dwight D. Eisenhower, John Foster Dulles, and the Nuclear-Arms Race

In 1952 Americans elected Dwight D. Eisenhower as president. The popular World War II hero, known to many simply as Ike, named John Foster Dulles as his secretary of state and promised to oppose communism vigorously and to assert American leadership around the globe. Yet in line with his conservative, Republican principles, the president also pledged to keep taxes low and to contain spiraling military costs.

Eisenhower found a way to realize his twin goals in the doctrine of "massive retaliation." Buttressed by America's overwhelming superiority in nuclear arms at the time, Eisenhower and Dulles proclaimed that the United States reserved the right to counter communist aggression wherever it occurred with a swift, decisive nuclear response. Massive retaliation, they hoped, would allow the United States to block aggressive nations, defend its interests, and at the same time cut back on expensive conventional weapons and troops. The "New Look" for the American armed forces, sloganeers concluded, would provide the United States with "more bang for the buck," or, as the Soviets put it, "more rubble for the ruble."

As the Eisenhower administration's policies took shape, the world witnessed an ever accelerating nuclear-arms race. The United States had enjoyed an atomic monopoly until September 1949, when Moscow had detonated its first atomic bomb. The Truman administration had responded by immediately speeding up development of the hydrogen bomb, a nuclear weapon that packed nearly eight hundred times the destructive force of the original atom bomb dropped on Hiroshima, Japan. But the successful test of that awesome weapon on November 1, 1952, was duplicated by the Soviet Union in less than a year's time.

Technological innovations during the 1950s further fueled the arms race. U.S. scientists and military officials engineered more powerful warheads and produced and deployed sophisticated intercontinental jet bombers such as the B-52 to serve as "delivery vehicles." Also in the early 1950s, the U.S. Army began to develop and deploy nuclear weapons for battlefield use. Then, in 1957, the Soviet Union stunned the world when it used a ballistic missile to lift an artificial satellite, Sputnik, *into outer space. The achievement revealed that Moscow had developed the ability to place a nuclear warhead atop a long-range missile and strike targets as far away as the United States. Meanwhile, atmospheric nuclear tests conducted by both sides showered poisonous, radioactive fallout on the earth. When U.S. tests at Bikini atoll in the western Pacific in March 1954 infected unsuspecting Japanese fishermen with radiation poisoning, pressure mounted for a nuclear test ban. Cities and towns rushed to construct shelters for civil defense, but arms-race critics believed that few people would survive a nuclear war. By the time Eisenhower left office in 1961, the two superpowers together possessed more than twenty thousand nuclear and atomic weapons with enough firepower to inflict millions of casualties and incalculable damage.*

Cold War politics during the Eisenhower era heightened tensions. In the Soviet Union, Josef Stalin died, and eventually Premier Nikita Khrushchev took command. Although the new regime in Moscow hinted that it wanted improved relations with the West, the two superpowers continued to quarrel over familiar problems: Korea, Indochina, Berlin, China, and Eastern Europe. At the same time, problems arose in the Third World, where emerging nations were asserting their independence. The Middle East, Asia, Africa, and Latin America became more unsettled, and hence more dangerous, to international stability. The people of the world shuddered during Cold War crises—Korea (1953), the Taiwan Strait (1954 and 1958), and Berlin (1959)—when leaders went to the nuclear brink.

Eisenhower and Khrushchev, however, did participate in summit conferences at Geneva (1955) and Camp David (1959), and they evidently shared a profound unease with reliance on nuclear weapons and with the terrible consequences of nuclear competition. In 1955 the Soviets advanced a proposal for step-by-step nuclear disarmament. Eisenhower countered with a program called Open Skies to allow air surveillance and inspection of nuclear facilities as a first step toward arms control. The concrete results of summit diplomacy, however, proved meager, and the arms race continued to gather frightening momentum. In the United States, a group of antinuclear and peace activists formed the Committee for a Sane Nuclear Policy (SANE) in 1957 to press the United Nations to oversee a cessation in nuclear testing and to initiate disarmament negotiations. Although the critics raised public awareness of nuclear issues, they carried little weight with U.S. and Soviet policymakers. And despite some analysts' conclusion that nuclear arms stabilized international politics, client-state wars, civil wars, and interventions proliferated. To cite but two examples, Khrushchev dispatched troops to Hungary in 1956, and Eisenhower sent troops to Lebanon in 1958.

Several questions inform scholarly study of Eisenhower's doctrine of massive retaliation and the nuclear-arms race. One set of questions centers on the impact of nuclear arms on superpower relations. Would the administration actually have used nuclear weapons against the Soviet Union or China? Or did it assume that the mere threat of nuclear war provided adequate deterrence? Did the Eisenhower-Dulles policy of nuclear retaliation intimidate Moscow and reduce the danger of a superpower confrontation? Or did it lead the Soviets to expand their arsenal, to speed up the arms race, and to increase the likelihood of a showdown? How did Moscow view the arms race? Did Khrushchev seek serious disarmament negotiations? Or did the Soviet political and economic system preclude compromise and peaceful coexistence? Did the growing Soviet strength in nuclear arms, especially the development of the Sputnik *missile, heighten the danger of a surprise, preemptive strike against the United States? Or did American alarmists exaggerate the threat? Did growing Soviet power undermine the massive retaliation strategy be-cause it gave Moscow the capability to retaliate? Could the superpowers fight a lim-ited nuclear war? Or would such a conflict inevitably escalate into a full-fledged Armageddon? Would a winner emerge from a Soviet-American nuclear war? Or would the devastation be so great that neither side could claim victory?*

The impact of the arms race went beyond Soviet-American relations. How did Eisenhower's nuclear saber rattling affect U.S. relations with its allies, many of whom grew alarmed at the arms buildup and feared that they might become the battleground in a nuclear exchange? Would the United States use nuclear weapons in limited wars in the Third World even though such conflicts usually sprang from local conditions rather than Soviet aggression? Would the United States deploy nu-clear weapons or make a nuclear threat over relatively insignificant places—the offshore islands of the Taiwan Strait, for example? Did the Eisenhower adminis-tration's reliance on nuclear deterrence leave it ill prepared for smaller, localized conflicts?

A third set of questions focuses on nuclear policymaking. How did nuclear strategy evolve? Did President Eisenhower play the dominant role in planning and deploying nuclear weapons? Did the hawkish views of Secretary of State Dulles prevail? What advice did the nation's military brass give the president? Did de-fense contractors and military leaders, the "military-industrial complex" as Presi-dent Eisenhower termed it, collude to feed the arms race by lobbying Congress for unnecessarily large defense budgets? Did Democrats exploit the issue of the "missile gap" in the late 1950s for domestic political gain and in doing so contribute to the arms-race momentum? What impact did antinuclear groups such as SANE have on public opinion and policy deliberation?

A major question hung over the era: Why could not American and Soviet lead-ers find a way to halt, slow, or at least control the arms race? Had Cold War poli-tics and the march of technology made them prisoners of a headlong race they could not stop?

✳ D O C U M E N T S

In the opening document, minutes of a National Security Council meeting held on October 7, 1953, members of the Eisenhower administration debate how to balance the nation's need for military defense with budgetary constraints, and they discuss the possible use of nuclear weapons. The second document, tagged NSC 162/2, approved by the president and adopted on October 30, 1953, concluded that the United States should rely on cost-effec-tive nuclear weapons to safeguard its interests. In the third selection, from a speech of Jan-uary 12, 1954, Secretary of State John Foster Dulles announces the policy of "massive retaliation." The fourth document is a letter to the *New York Times* dated March 28, 1954, by Lewis Mumford, a social critic and the author of books on cities, culture, and technol-ogy, including *In the Name of Sanity* (1954), on nuclear weapons. Questioning the rational-ity and the morality of the nuclear-arms race, Mumford urges concerned citizens to press their government to reverse the buildup.

The Eisenhower administration publicly threatened to use nuclear weapons during the Taiwan Strait crisis of late 1954 and early 1955. The fifth selection consists of two parts: a *New York Times* account of Secretary of State John Foster Dulles's press conference on March 15, 1955, in which the secretary discussed the possible use of tactical nuclear weapons to resolve the Taiwan Strait crisis; and an excerpt from a press conference the next day in which President Eisenhower reiterated the nuclear threat. Some of the tensions of the times temporarily dissipated in 1955 when U.S. and Soviet leaders agreed to hold their first summit meeting since World War II. At that conference, held in Geneva in July, President Eisenhower came with an offer that surprised the conferees—his "Open Skies" proposal, calling for mutual aerial inspection of Soviet and American military facilities as a first step toward verifiable arms control. Eisenhower's statement is reprinted as the sixth document. Eisenhower later admitted that he had anticipated Soviet rejection of the intrusive procedures but had nonetheless advanced the proposal to score propaganda points.

Despite a thaw in Cold War tensions following the Geneva Conference, the superpowers' stockpiling and testing of nuclear weapons went on apace. In the seventh selection, an excerpt from his book *Atomic Soldiers* (1980), Howard L. Rosenberg describes the experience of a soldier who participated in nuclear-weapons testing and psychological experiments conducted by the U.S. Army in the Nevada desert in August 1957. On October 4, 1957, the Soviet Union placed its *Sputnik* satellite into outer space, a feat that intensified Cold War fears in the United States and generated charges that Eisenhower's conservative spending policies had caused the country to lag behind in missile and satellite development. The National Security Council met on October 10, 1957, to discuss the political, scientific, and military ramifications of the Soviet achievement. An excerpt of that discussion appears as the eighth selection.

In the ninth document, an excerpt from Nikita Khrushchev's memoirs, the former Soviet premier explains how he came to depend on nuclear-tipped ballistic missiles to implement a Soviet version of massive retaliation. Khrushchev also recalls his conversations with Eisenhower and their mutual lament over how both the Soviet and the American military establishment continuously lobbied for more weapons. Domestic politics also increased the pressures for a buildup. In a speech delivered on February 29, 1960, the tenth document, Democratic senator and presidential hopeful John F. Kennedy charged that the Eisenhower administration's tight-fisted budgets had made the nation vulnerable to Soviet attack. Kennedy's criticism echoed that of others who decried the existence of a missile gap in the Soviets' favor at the end of the Eisenhower era (the "gap" actually favored the United States). The last document is Eisenhower's farewell address of January 17, 1961, whose warning against a "military-industrial complex" aroused wide interest.

The National Security Council Debates
Cold War Defense Costs and Nuclear Weapons, 1953

Mr. [Robert] Cutler [special assistant for national security affairs] first briefed the Council on the historical background of NSC 162 [September 30, 1953]. He then explained the manner in which the present report had been drafted, the important differences which NSC 162 contained, and expressed the hope that the Council would be able in the course of its consideration to resolve these differences of opinion and arrive at an agreed statement of policy. In order to assist in this process, Mr. Cutler said that he had attempted to reduce the statement of these differences in each case to a paragraph and suggested that the Council discuss each of these paragraphs and come to an agreement to resolve the differences.

The first of these differences concerned the nature of the Soviet threat. Side "A," Mr. Cutler pointed out, sees the threat to the United States as the basic Soviet hostility to the United States and the Soviet's formidable military power. While acknowledging a sound U.S. economy is essential, Side "A" believes the United States *must* first meet necessary security costs.

Side "B," on the other hand, sees the threat to the United States as a dual threat—the external threat of Soviet power; the internal threat of weakening our economy and changing our way of life. Side "B" believes the U.S. must strike a proper balance between the risks arising from these two threats. . . .

The Director of the Budget [Joseph Dodge] explained that the basic objection of the Budget and the Treasury to Side "A's" statement as to the nature of the threat was that it ignored the economic threat at the very outset of the report. It chose to do this even though all of us know that it is an objective of Soviet strategy to destroy our capitalist economy by means of economic warfare. Mr. Dodge gave it as his opinion that this was a very successful element of the Soviet strategy although it was not so dangerous as the H-bomb. In sum, Mr. Dodge argued that as the threat to the economy was part and parcel of the Soviet threat, it should be mentioned at the beginning and not relegated to later pages in the report. . . .

Secretary [of the Treasury George] Humphrey said that it was essential to get beyond disagreements in language to divergences of thought which were obviously very deep. Actually the issue of the nature of the threat was the number one problem facing the Administration. . . . The great difficulty, of course, was that we don't really have all the facts we need either on the nature of the Soviet threat or on the nature of the economic threat. On top of this problem was the question of timing. There were plenty of things that you could stand for one year that you might not be able to stand for ten years. Are we going to meet this threat, asked Secretary Humphrey, in the same way that the previous Administration had tried to meet it. To decide on some future D-day and then try desperately and in the shortest possible time to rearm the country to a point which might enable it to meet this threat; or do we propose to consider ways and means of meeting a threat which will be with us over a very long time. It was important to decide this, thought Secretary Humphrey, because over the long haul we could easily be destroyed by either of the two threats, external or internal. If we mean to face this Soviet threat over a long time we must spend less than we are now spending and do less than we are now doing. If, on the other hand, we believe that we must anticipate a Soviet attack in a year's time or that we might be compelled to attack the Soviet Union, then obviously we ought to do and spend more than we are doing and spending now. This, said Secretary Humphrey, seemed to him the essence of the issue.

The Secretary of State [John Foster Dulles] commented that it was not wholly clear to him what adoption of the present report would really decide. If adoption of the paper meant that the United States was going ahead to balance its budget and cut its taxes and that everything else must give way to this objective, he was strongly against it. This would be a decision reached in the dark. With obvious emotion, Secretary Dulles pointed out that as yet the National Security Council had been presented with no precise estimates of the costs to maintain the defense system of the free world coalition. No one knew as yet what this would cost but we certainly couldn't throw the common defense system out the window because we had to balance the budget. Furthermore, continued Secretary Dulles, it seemed significant to him that there was never any talk of making any drastic cuts except in defense expenditures. What about cutting in other areas. Why do we continue spending $2 billion annually for price supports of agriculture. . . .

Both the President and Secretary Humphrey questioned the justice of Secretary Dulles' contention that Side "B" was arguing that the budget must be balanced at whatever cost to the national security programs. They also pointed out that cuts and reductions had been made in other areas than the national security programs. Director Dodge added figures to show that there was no hope of balancing the budget unless cuts were made in appropriations for the national security. . . .

The President . . . reverted to his earlier argument that Side "A" seemed to assume that everything that was necessary for national defense could be accomplished without grave damage to the economy. The Joint Chiefs had gone even further and said that we should do what was necessary even if the result was to change the American way of life. We could lick the whole world, said the President, if we were willing to adopt the system of Adolph Hitler. He wished, said the President, that some of the other members of the Council could see the daily beating which he was taking from exponents of the balanced budget and greater economy. I feel sure, said the President, that I can get what we need for a period of time but if these necessities are to continue over a long period, I am inclined to go along with Secretary Humphrey. The real issue is how long can we afford to do all that Side A feels we must do to meet the threat. . . .

The next point, said Mr. Cutler, related to our policy with regard to the use of special [atomic and nuclear] weapons as set forth in paragraph 38-b, with particular respect to securing the understanding and approval of the use of special weapons by our allies.

The President suggested that securing this approval and understanding of our allies should precede the use of these special weapons, which was not the case in the present text of paragraph 38–b.

Mr. Cutler, however, pointed out that in their written comments the Joint Chiefs had been even firmer in their insistence on the use of these weapons.

The President commented that however that might be, nothing would so upset the whole world as an announcement at this time by the United States of a decision to use these weapons.

Secretary [of Defense Charles] Wilson said he saw the President's point, but that nevertheless the Defense Department must know whether or not to plan for the use of these weapons. Do we intend to use weapons on which we are spending such great sums, or do we not?

The President replied that after all, he had to make the ultimate decision as to the use of these weapons, and if the use of them was dictated by the interests of U.S. security, he would certainly decide to use them.

Admiral [Arthur] Radford said that he was nevertheless still very worried about this problem. Can we, he inquired, use these weapons from bases where the permission of no foreign government is required? Admiral Radford thought it vital that we should be able to make this decision.

The President reiterated his belief that we should issue no statements on this point until we have given our Government officials a chance to convince our friends as to the desirability of using these weapons. So far, however, as war plans were concerned, continued the President, he thought that the JCS [Joint Chiefs of Staff] should count on making use of special weapons in the event of general war. They should not, however, plan to make use of these weapons in minor affairs.

Secretary Dulles repeated his often-expressed view that somehow or other we must manage to remove the taboo from the use of these weapons.

The President pointed out that there were certain places where you would not be able to use these weapons because if you did it would look as though the U.S. were initiating global war. If, however, we actually go into a global war, we would certainly use the weapons.

National Security Council Paper
No. 162/2 (NSC-162/2), 1953

The capability of the USSR to attack the United States with atomic weapons has been continuously growing and will be materially enhanced by hydrogen weapons. The USSR has sufficient bombs and aircraft, using one-way missions, to inflict serious damage on the United States, especially by surprise attack. The USSR soon may have the capability of dealing a crippling blow to our industrial base and our continued ability to prosecute a war. Effective defense could reduce the likelihood and intensity of a hostile attack but not eliminate the chance of a crippling blow. . . .

The USSR does not seem likely deliberately to launch a general war against the United States during the period covered by current estimates (through mid-1955). The uncertain prospects for Soviet victory in a general war, the change in leadership, satellite unrest, and the U.S. capability to retaliate massively, make such a course improbable. Similarly, an attack on NATO [North Atlantic Treaty Organization] countries or other areas which would be almost certain to bring on general war in view of U.S. commitments or intentions would be unlikely. The Soviets will not, however, be deterred by fear of general war from taking the measures they consider necessary to counter Western actions which they view as a serious threat to their security. . . .

Although Soviet fear of atomic reaction should still inhibit local aggression, increasing Soviet atomic capability may tend to diminish the deterrent effect of U.S. atomic power against peripheral Soviet aggression. It may also sharpen the reaction of the USSR to what it considers provocative acts of the United States. If either side should miscalculate the strength of the other's reaction, such local conflicts could grow into general war, even though neither seeks nor desires it. To avoid this, it will in general be desirable for the United States to make clear to the USSR the kind of actions which will be almost certain to lead to this result, recognizing, however, that as general war becomes more devastating for both sides the threat to resort to it becomes less available as a sanction against local aggression. . . .

Within the free world, only the United States can provide and maintain, for a period of years to come, the atomic capability to counterbalance Soviet atomic power. Thus, sufficient atomic weapons and effective means of delivery are indispensable for U.S. security. Moreover, in the face of Soviet atomic power, defense of the continental United States becomes vital to effective security: to protect our striking force, our mobilization base, and our people. Such atomic capability is also a major contribution to the security of our allies, as well as of this country.

The United States cannot, however, meet its defense needs, even at exorbitant cost, without the support of allies. . . .

The United States must maintain a sound economy based on free private enterprise as a basis both for high defense productivity and for the maintenance of its living standards and free institutions. Not only the world position of the United States, but the security of the whole free world, is dependent on the avoidance of recession and on the long-term expansion of the U.S. economy. Threats to its stability or growth, therefore, constitute a danger to the security of the United States and of the coalition which it leads. Expenditures for national security, in fact all federal, state and local governmental expenditures, must be carefully scrutinized with a view to measuring their impact on the national economy.

The economy of the country has a potential for long-term economic growth. Over the years an expanding national income can provide the basis for higher standards of living and for a substantial military program. But economic growth is not automatic and requires fiscal and other policies which will foster and not hamper the potential for long-term growth and which will operate to reduce cyclical fluctuations.

Excessive government spending leads to inflationary deficits or to repressive taxation, or to both. Persistent inflation is a barrier to long-term growth because it undermines confidence in the currency, reduces savings, and makes restrictive economic controls necessary. Repressive taxation weakens the incentives for efficiency, effort, and investment on which economic growth depends. . . .

The requirements for funds to maintain our national security must thus be considered in the light of these dangers to our economic system, including the danger to industrial productivity necessary to support military programs, arising from excessive levels of total Government spending, taxing and borrowing. . . .

In specific situations where a warning appears desirable and feasible as an added deterrent, the United States should make clear to the USSR and Communist China, in general terms or with reference to specific areas as the situation requires, its intention to react with military force against any aggression by Soviet bloc armed forces.

In the event of hostilities, the United States will consider nuclear weapons to be as available for use as other munitions. Where the consent of an ally is required for the use of these weapons from U.S. bases on the territory of such ally, the United States should promptly obtain the advance consent of such ally for such use. The United States should also seek, as and when feasible, the understanding and approval of this policy by free nations.

This policy should not be made public without further consideration by the National Security Council.

Secretary of State John Foster Dulles Explains Massive Retaliation, 1954

The Soviet Communists are planning for what they call "an entire historical era," and we should do the same. They seek, through many types of maneuvers, gradually to divide and weaken the free nations by overextending them in efforts which, as Lenin put it, are "beyond their strength, so that they come to practical bankruptcy." Then, said Lenin, "our victory is assured." Then, said Stalin, will be "the moment for the decisive blow."

In the face of this strategy, measures cannot be judged adequate merely because they ward off an immediate danger. It is essential to do this, but it is also essential to do so without exhausting ourselves.

When the Eisenhower administration applied this test, we felt that some transformations were needed.

It is not sound military strategy permanently to commit U.S. land forces to Asia to a degree that leaves us no strategic reserves.

It is not sound economics, or good foreign policy, to support permanently other countries; for in the long run, that creates as much ill will as good will.

Also, it is not sound to become permanently committed to military expenditures so vast that they lead to "practical bankruptcy." . . .

We need allies and collective security. Our purpose is to make these relations more effective, less costly. This can be done by placing more reliance on deterrent power and less dependence on local defensive power.

This is accepted practice so far as local communities are concerned. We keep locks on our doors, but we do not have an armed guard in every home. We rely principally on a community security system so well equipped to punish any who break in and steal that, in fact, would-be aggressors are generally deterred. That is the modern way of getting maximum protection at a bearable cost.

What the Eisenhower administration seeks is a similar international security system. We want, for ourselves and the other free nations, a maximum deterrent at a bearable cost.

Local defense will always be important. But there is no local defense which alone will contain the mighty landpower of the Communist world. Local defenses must be reinforced by the further deterrent of massive retaliatory power. A potential aggressor must know that he cannot always prescribe battle conditions that suit him. Otherwise, for example, a potential aggressor, who is glutted with manpower, might be tempted to attack in confidence that resistance would be confined to manpower. He might be tempted to attack in places where his superiority was decisive.

The way to deter aggression is for the free community to be willing and able to respond vigorously at places and with means of its own choosing.

So long as our basic policy concepts were unclear, our military leaders could not be selective in building our military power. If an enemy could pick his time and place and method of warfare—and if our policy was to remain the traditional one of meeting aggression by direct and local opposition—then we needed to be ready to fight in the Arctic and in the Tropics; in Asia, the Near East, and in Europe; by sea, by land, and by air; with old weapons and with new weapons. . . .

But before military planning could be changed, the President and his advisers, as represented by the National Security Council, had to take some basic policy decisions. This has been done. The basic decision was to depend primarily upon a great capacity to retaliate, instantly, by means and at places of our choosing. Now the Department of Defense and the Joint Chiefs of Staff can shape our military establishment to fit what is *our* policy, instead of having to try to be ready to meet the enemy's many choices. That permits of a selection of military means instead of a multiplication of means. As a result, it is now possible to get, and share, more basic security at less cost.

Lewis Mumford Protests the Nuclear-Arms Race, 1954

The power of the hydrogen bomb has, it is plain, given pause even to the leaders of our Government. Their very hesitation to give away the facts in itself gives away the facts. Under what mandate, then, do they continue to hold as secret the results we may expect from the use of weapons of extermination—not merely on our own cities and people but on all living organisms; not merely on our present lives but on the lives of countless generations to come?

Are our leaders afraid that when the truth is known our devotion to the perfection of scientific weapons of total destruction and extermination will turn out to be a profoundly irrational one: repulsive to morality, dangerous to national security, inimical to life?

Do they suspect that the American people are still sane enough to halt the blind automatism that continues, in the face of Soviet Russia's equal scientific powers, to produce these fatal weapons?

Do they fear that their fellow-countrymen may well doubt the usefulness of instruments which, under the guise of deterring an aggressor or insuring a cheap victory, might incidentally destroy the whole fabric of civilization and threaten the very existence of the human race?

Our secret weapons of extermination have been produced under conditions that have favored irresponsible censorship and short-sighted political and military judgments. Under the protection of secrecy a succession of fatal errors has been made, primarily as the result (since 1942) of our accepting total extermination as a method of warfare. These errors have been compounded by our counting upon such dehumanized methods to preserve peace and security.

In turn, our very need for secrecy in an abortive effort to monopolize technical and scientific knowledge, has produced pathological symptoms in the whole body politic: fear, suspicion, non-cooperation, hostility to critical judgment, above all delusions of power based on fantasies of unlimited extermination, as the only possible answer to the political threat of Soviet Russia. But demoralized men cannot be counted upon to control such automatic instruments of demoralization.

At a fatal moment our self-induced fears may produce the incalculable and irretrievable holocaust our own weapons have given us reason to dread. Only courage and intelligence of the highest order, backed by open discussion, will give us the strength to turn back from the suicidal path we have blindly followed since 1942.

Are there not enough Americans still possessed of their sanity to call a stop to these irrational decisions, which are automatically bringing us close to a total catastrophe?

From *New York Times*, March 28, 1954.

There are many alternative courses to the policy to which we have committed ourselves, practically without debate. The worst of all these alternatives, submission to Communist totalitarianism, would still be far wiser than the final destruction of civilization.

As for the best of these alternatives, a policy of working firmly toward justice and cooperation, and free intercourse with all other peoples, in the faith that love begets love as surely as hatred begets hatred—would, in all probability, be the one instrument capable of piercing the strong political armor of our present enemies. . . .

In the name of sanity let our Government now pause and seek the counsel of sane men: men who have not participated in the errors we have made and are not committed, out of pride, to defending them. Let us cease all further experiments with even more horrifying weapons of destruction, lest our own self-induced fears further upset our mental balance.

Let us all, as responsible citizens, not the cowed subjects of an all-wise state, weigh the alternatives and canvass new lines of approach to the problems of power and peace.

Dulles and President Dwight D. Eisenhower Threaten to Use Nuclear Weapons: The Taiwan Strait Crisis, 1955

Dulles Statement, March 15, 1955

Secretary of State Dulles expounded today a doctrine of less-than-massive retaliation by the United States anywhere in the world if it became engaged in major military action.

The pattern was based, he said, on the use of small nuclear weapons against military targets rather than city-destroying weapons such as the full-scale hydrogen bomb.

Mr. Dulles said the likelihood of using city-destroying bombs in a war went down as the availability of smaller atomic weapons went up. Unlike the situation in World War II, he said, when mass destruction weapons were used against population centers, the new weapons offer a chance for victory on the battlefield without harming civilians.

Whether the tactical-weapons pattern would fit a Communist Chinese attack on Quemoy [Jinmen] and Matsu [Mazu] Islands, Mr. Dulles indicated, is up to Peiping[Beijing]. . . .

In the event of a big push against Formosa, the United States might well intervene, using sea and air forces equipped with small and precise nuclear weapons, Mr. Dulles said in his first press conference since his return from the Far East on March 6. . . .

"It would seem as though it was quite possible at least that the Chinese Communists do not intend to stop until it is apparent that they are stopped by superior resistance," Mr. Dulles said.

New York Times, March 16, 1955.

The answer to this threat, he asserted, is not to maintain standing forces at every point of possible danger. "Our more effective contribution to the defense of the entire area," Mr. Dulles said, "is by strategic forces with a high degree of striking power by sea and by air. That power is available to be used wherever the occasion arises."

A trace of humor punctuated today's conference when a reporter mentioned that there was "a lot of speculation" about how the United States would react to a Communist assault on the offshore islands [Quemoy and Matsu].

"Really?" Mr. Dulles asked, grinning broadly.

He went on to say that some ambiguity about the United States reaction was inevitable. The situation, he said, is inherently a speculative one because it depends on an unknown quantity—the ultimate intentions of the Communists.

Eisenhower Statement, March 16, 1955

Q. Mr. President, yesterday at his news conference, Secretary of State Dulles indicated that in the event of general war in the Far East, we would probably make use of some tactical small atomic weapons. Would you care to comment on this and, possibly, explain it further?

The President. I wouldn't comment in the sense that I would pretend to foresee the conditions of any particular conflict in which you might engage; but we have been, as you know, active in producing various types of weapons that feature nuclear fission ever since World War II.

Now, in any combat where these things can be used on strictly military targets and for strictly military purposes, I see no reason why they shouldn't be used just exactly as you would use a bullet or anything else.

I believe the great question about these things comes when you begin to get into those areas where you cannot make sure that you are operating merely against military targets. But with that one qualification, I would say, yes, of course they would be used.

Eisenhower Proposes "Open Skies," 1955

Disarmament is one of the most important subjects on our agenda. It is also extremely difficult. In recent years the scientists have discovered methods of making weapons many, many times more destructive—not only of opposing armed forces but also of homes, and industries and lives—than ever known or even imagined before. These same scientific discoveries have made much more complex the problems of limitation and control and reduction of armament.

After our victory as Allies in World War II, my country [the United States] rapidly disarmed. Within a few years our armament was at a very low level. Then events occurred beyond our borders which caused us to realize that we had disarmed too much. For our own security and to safeguard peace we needed greater strength. Therefore we proceeded to rearm and to associate with others in a partnership for peace and for mutual security. . . .

But we know that a mutually dependable system for less armament on the part of all nations would be a better way to safeguard peace and to maintain our security.

It would ease the fears of war in the anxious hearts of people everywhere. It would lighten the burdens upon the backs of the people. It would make it possible for every nation, great and small, developed and less developed, to advance the standards of living of its people, to attain better food, and clothing, and shelter, more of education and larger enjoyment of life.

Therefore the United States government is prepared to enter into a sound and reliable agreement making possible the reduction of armament. . . .

I should address myself for a moment principally to the delegates from the Soviet Union, because our two great countries admittedly possess new and terrible weapons in quantities which do give rise in other parts of the world, or reciprocally, to the fears and dangers of surprise attack.

I propose, therefore, that we take a practical step, that we begin an arrangement, very quickly, as between ourselves—immediately. These steps would include:

To give to each other a complete blueprint of our military establishments, from beginning to end, from one end of our countries to the other, lay out the establishments and provide the blueprints to each other.

Next, to provide within our countries facilities for aerial photography to the other country—we to provide you the facilities within our country, ample facilities for aerial reconnaissance, where you can make all the pictures you choose and take them to your own country to study, you to provide exactly the same facilities for us and we to make these examinations, and by this step to convince the world that we are providing as between ourselves against the possibility of great surprise attack, thus lessening danger and relaxing tension.

Likewise, we will make more easily attainable a comprehensive and effective system of inspection and disarmament, because what I propose, I assure you, would be but a beginning.

Now from my statements I believe you will anticipate my suggestion. It is that we instruct our representatives in the Subcommittee on Disarmament in discharge of their mandate from the United Nations to give priority effort to the study of inspection and reporting. Such a study could well include a step-by-step testing of inspection and reporting methods. . . .

The successful working out of such a system would do much to develop the mutual confidence which will open wide the avenues of progress for all our peoples.

Howard L. Rosenberg's Description of a 1957 Atomic Test in Nevada Witnessed by "Atomic Soldiers," 1980

Corporal Russell Jack Dann felt an uneasiness rumble up from the pit of his stomach as he settled back into a canvas sling along the plane's bulkhead and waited quietly for the pilots to lift C-124 Globemaster's lumbering body skyward. It

From Howard L. Rosenberg, *Atomic Soldiers,* 1980, pp. 5, 101–105, 117. Beacon Press, Boston. Reprinted by permission of the author.

wasn't the usual anxiety that all paratroopers feel before a jump that had the 20-year-old soldier's guts tied in knots but rather the uncertainty of what to expect when he finally faced the atomic bomb he knew was waiting for him on a desolate strip of Nevada desert [near Camp Desert Rock]. . . .

On Monday [August 26, 1957], the troops attended an indoctrination lecture on atomic effects at a nearby Quonset hut that had been converted into a classroom. The steel folding chairs were uncomfortable, but a few of the soldiers still managed to drift off to sleep. The most memorable detail of the nondescript classroom was a large sign hanging above the blackboard at the front of the hut. It read: "Anything you hear here while you are here, leave here when you leave here."

The indoctrination, which had been carefully coordinated by the HumRRO [Human Resources Research Office] team so material in their questionnaire would be covered, began with a film. Dann remembers the film opening with a scene on a street corner. One old codger, sitting under a nearby awning, turned to another and said, "This weather is all screwed up on account of those damn bombs." "Then the narrator would come on," said Dann, "and tell how foolish those people were. They don't understand what the bomb is, the narrator would say, and that there should be no fear at all."

The film was followed by a two-hour lecture on the bomb. The men were told what to expect and briefed on the nature of radiation. . . .

"The first thing you'll see when this bomb goes off is an intense light. Six miles away, the flash will be 100 times as bright as the sun. The blast itself will vaporize the material the bomb is made of and the firing platform or tower will become part of the fireball. As the fireball cools, the mushroom cloud you've heard or read about starts forming. This happens within a couple of seconds after the detonation. Within 10 seconds, the light will have subsided and the shock wave will have passed your position.

"The cloud, containing the fission products, the remnants of the firing platform and dirt and debris, rises high into the air. The heaviest particles and debris will drop right back down on the ground. Beyond about 7,000 feet, the immediate nuclear radiation is virtually harmless.

"As an observer during an atomic test, the position assigned you by the Nevada Test Organization will be one determined to be absolutely safe—even if you should be standing erect at the time the shock wave passes. This distance has also been calculated to be sufficient to protect you from the nuclear radiation. However, the flash of light might be dangerous. Exposure of the unprotected eye could result in a blind spot which might be permanent. This is why you must face away from the flash at the moment of detonation. . . .

"If highly radioactive fallout particles are deposited on or near the surface of your skin, like on your clothes or hair, and stay there for any long period of time, the beta radiation can cause you to lose your hair, discolor your skin or even burn you. This isn't likely to happen, but just in case, you should know about it.

"Beta burns look similar to burns from any other kind of heat, except they usually don't appear until about two weeks later and they take longer to heal. You can reduce the possibility of burns with simple decontamination measures, like bathing and changing clothes.

"Now, I want to debunk some of those horror stories I'm sure you guys have been told," the lecturer continued reassuringly. "It's true you can't see, feel, smell, taste or hear nuclear radiation. But that doesn't mean you have to fear it. Not too many of you can explain electricity I'll bet. But you've all learned to live with it and use it. It's the same with radiation."

After the indoctrination, the HumRRO psychologists handed out their questionnaires once again and asked the soldiers to fill them out. Many of the troopers had slept soundly throughout the lecture. They knew they were being propagandized, or as one soldier put it later, "the Army was just trying to blow smoke up our butts. I wondered if they actually think people are that dumb. Sure they said we'd be completely monitored at all times, but hell, nobody believed them. Nine chances out of ten the monitor was just some PFC assigned to the detail who didn't give a damn. Just a detail, just a job." . . .

The Smoky test [in Nevada] repeated many of the previous exercises. Its primary purpose was to "indoctrinate selected individuals in the effects of atomic weapons and to conduct certain specified troop and material tests of doctrine, tactics, techniques and equipment related to atomic weapons." Yet the Smoky test had another objective, one that ultimately took precedence: the Army was especially interested in actually demonstrating how effective battle groups and pentomic warfare tactics could be. That made public relations equally as important as indoctrination and training.

More reporters, cameramen and television crews were invited to watch the Smoky shot than any other test. Military photographers and combat artists abounded. A film crew was even dispatched to record the event for the Army's "Big Picture," a television series then enjoying wide popularity on the airwaves. And the newsmen were treated royally.

In an after-action report compiled by the Army months after the exercise, the brass hats candidly admitted that the real purpose of Smoky was "to portray to the public the Army at its best employing pentomic organization in operations under atomic warfare conditions." In their zeal to impress the press corps, the Army commanders may have carried their mission a bit too far.

The National Security Council Discusses the Ramifications of *Sputnik,* 1957

Mr. Allen Dulles [director of the Central Intelligence Agency] stated that . . . on October 4 the Soviets had fired their earth satellite from the Tyura Tam range. Its initial path followed the range, crossing approximately over the range's other end at Klyuchi . . . [A]fter the successful orbiting of the earth satellite and after the second circuit of the earth by the satellite, the Soviets announced their achievement. This delay in the announcement was in line with the previous statements of the Soviet Union that they would not announce an attempt to orbit their satellite until they had been assured that the orbiting had been successful. . . .

Mr. Dulles then turned to the world reaction to the Soviet achievement. He first pointed out that Khrushchev had moved all his propaganda guns into place.

The launching of an earth satellite was one of a trilogy of propaganda moves, the other two being the announcement of the successful testing of an ICBM [intercontinental ballistic missile] and the recent test of a large-scale hydrogen bomb at Novaya Zemlya. . . .

Larded in with Khrushchev's propaganda statements had been a number of interesting remarks, such as the one in which Khrushchev consigned military aircraft to museums in the future. With respect to this remark, Mr. Dulles pointed out that U.S. intelligence had not observed as many Soviet heavy bombers on airfields as had been expected. This raised the question as to whether the Soviets are in the process of de-emphasizing the role of the heavy bomber. There had been no clear verdict yet by the intelligence community on this question.

Mr. Dulles thought that there was no doubt that in gearing up all this propaganda of recent days and weeks, the Soviets had had an eye to the situation in the Middle East, and wished to exert the maximum influence they could summon on that situation. Much of the Soviet propaganda comment is following closely the original Soviet boast relating their scientific accomplishments to the effectiveness of the Communist social system. The target for this particular thrust, thought Mr. Dulles, was evidently the underdeveloped nations in the world. . . .

At the conclusion of Mr. Allen Dulles' briefing, Mr. Cutler asked [Deputy Defense] Secretary [Donald] Quarles to speak. Secretary Quarles began by stating that much of what he was going to say would be familiar to the President and other members of the Council. The President quipped that this was indeed the case, and he was beginning to feel somewhat numb on the subject of the earth satellite. Thereafter, Secretary Quarles outlined briefly the development of satellite programs beginning with the period of World War II. . . .

As to the implications of the Soviet achievement, Secretary Quarles said he would not comment on the [C]old [W]ar aspects, since they had been dealt with by the Director of Central Intelligence. Beyond this, it was clear that the Soviets possess a competence in long-range rocketry and in auxiliary fields which is even more advanced than the competence with which we had credited them; although, of course, we had always given them the capability of orbiting an earth satellite. Finally, said Secretary Quarles, the outer space implications of the launching of this satellite were of very great significance, especially in relation to the development of reconnaissance satellites. . . .

Mr. Cutler then called on Dr. [Detlev W.] Bronk [president of the U.S. National Academy of Sciences], who stated initially that there was one thing about which he was very greatly concerned—that is, that we avoid getting our whole scientific community into a race to accomplish everything before the Russians do. He therefore thought we should adhere strictly to our stated earth satellite program and not be deflected from our course merely by the fact that the Russians had been the first to launch an earth satellite.

The President pointed out that all those around the table and others could anticipate before very long being obliged to testify before Congressional committees, to talk to the press, and the like. In the circumstances, he could imagine nothing more important than that anybody so involved should stand firmly by the existing earth satellite program which was, after all, adopted by the Council after due deliberation as a reasonable program. In short, we should answer inquiries by stating that we have a plan—a good plan—and that we are going to stick to it.

Mr. Cutler then called on Secretary [of State Christian] Herter for an appraisal of the foreign policy implications for U.S. security of the successful launching of the Soviet satellite. Secretary Herter initially stated that it was extremely difficult to make such an assessment because there was such a mass of information pouring into the Department of State. While there had been insufficient time to analyze this intake, there were already some indications of the serious effects of the Soviet success which we hope to be able to counteract.

Thereafter, Secretary Herter read selected quotations to illustrate his point, with particular reference to Turkey, Morocco, and the Philippines. He also pointed out the probable repercussions of the Soviet success in the United Nations. The United States may now encounter much greater difficulty in defending its disarmament position.

By and large, continued Secretary Herter, the reaction of our allies had been pretty firm and good, though even the best of them require assurance that we have not been surpassed scientifically and militarily by the USSR. The neutralist countries are chiefly engaged in patting themselves on the back and insisting that the Soviet feat proves the value and the wisdom of the neutralism which these countries have adopted.

Summing up, Secretary Herter described the first foreign policy reactions as "pretty somber." The United States will have to do a great deal to counteract them and, particularly, to confirm the existence of our own real military and scientific strength. . . .

Mr. Cutler then called on Mr. [Arthur] Larson [director of the U.S. Information Agency], who said that he was hesitant to say what he was going to say because he was not sure that he really believed it. He then went on to say that while we could not permit ourselves to be panicked by the Soviet achievement, he did wonder whether our U.S. plans were now adequate with regard to the next great break-through. If we lose repeatedly to the Russians as we have lost with the earth satellite, the accumulated damage would be tremendous. We should accordingly plan, ourselves, to accomplish some of the next great break-throughs first—for example, the achievement of a manned satellite, or getting to the moon. Do we have any such plans, asked Mr. Larson. If not, our people should begin to think about them.

The President replied to Mr. Larson by stating that while he could hardly quarrel with Mr. Larson's conclusions if the Soviets were to win every time, the fact remained that the United States couldn't possibly set up a whole vast scientific program of basic research in areas about which we don't know anything, and then attempt to outdo the Russians in each aspect of such a program. We must, above all, still seek a military posture that the Russians will respect. . . .

Thereafter, the President stressed once again the great political and psychological advantage of the first achievement of an IRBM [intermediate-range ballistic missile] and an ICBM. He noted that from the inception of the ballistic missiles program the Council had agreed that these political and psychological considerations were perhaps even more important than the strictly military considerations.

Soviet Premier Nikita Khrushchev Reflects on the Nuclear-Arms Race, 1970

Even honest people who want to avoid the use of atomic and hydrogen weapons can't ignore the question of how many such arms are available to us in case a global war should break out. That's why we must decide realistically on priorities for the allocation of funds.

When I was the leader of the Party and the Government, I decided that we had to economize drastically in the building of homes, the construction of communal services, and even in the development of agriculture in order to build up our defenses. I even suspended the construction of subways in Kiev, Baku, and Tblisi so that we could redirect those funds into strengthening our defense and attack forces. We also built fewer athletic stadiums, swimming pools, and cultural facilities. I think I was right to concentrate on military spending, even at the expense of all but the most essential investments in other areas. If I hadn't put such a high priority on our military needs, we couldn't have survived. I devoted all my strength to the rearmament of the Soviet Union. It was a challenging and important stage of our lives. . . .

Our potential enemy—our principal, our most powerful, our most dangerous enemy—was so far away from us that we couldn't have reached him with our air force. Only by building up a nuclear missile force could we keep the enemy from unleashing war against us. As life has already confirmed, if we had given the West a chance, war would have been declared while Dulles was alive. But we were the first to launch rockets into space; we exploded the most powerful nuclear devices; we accomplished those feats first, ahead of the United States, England, and France. Our accomplishments and our obvious might had a sobering effect on the aggressive forces in the United States, England, France, and, of course, inside the Bonn [West German] government. They knew that they had lost their chance to strike at us with impunity.

Now that it's the size of our nuclear missile arsenal and not the size of our army that counts, I think the army should be reduced to an absolute minimum. There's no question in my mind that we have indeed reached the stage where that's possible. When I led the Government and had final authority over our military allocations, our theoreticians calculated that we had the nuclear capacity to grind our enemies into dust, and since that time our nuclear capacity has been greatly intensified. During my leadership we accumulated enough weapons to destroy the principal cities of the United States, not to mention our potential enemies in Europe. . . .

I have always been against war, but at the same time I've always realized full well that the fear of nuclear war in a country's leader can paralyze that country's defenses. And if a country's defenses are paralyzed, then war really is inevitable: the enemy is sure to sense your fright and try to take advantage of it. . . .

However, we must also keep in mind the true character of all imperialists, capitalists, monopolists, and militarists who are interested in making money out of the political tension between nations. We must make sure that we don't allow ourselves to get involved in a lot of senseless competition with the West over military spending. If we try to compete with America in any but the most essential areas of military preparedness, we will be doing two harmful things. First, we will be further enriching wealthy aggressive capitalist circles in the United States who use our own military buildups as a pretext for overloading their own country's arms budget. Second, we will be exhausting our material resources without raising the living standard of our people. We must remember that the fewer people we have in the army, the more people we will have available for other, more productive kinds of work. This realization would be a good common point of departure for the progressive forces of the world in their struggle for peaceful coexistence. If one side were to curtail its accumulation of military means, it would be easier for the other side to do the same. We must be prepared to strike back against our enemy, but we must also ask, "Where is the end to this spiraling competition?"

I know from experience that the leaders of the armed forces can be very persistent in claiming their share when it comes time to allocate funds. Every commander has all sorts of very convincing arguments why he should get more than anyone else. Unfortunately there's a tendency for people who run the armed forces to be greedy and self-seeking. They're always ready to throw in your face the slogan "If you try to economize on the country's defenses today, you'll pay in blood when war breaks out tomorrow." I'm not denying that these men have a huge responsibility, and I'm not impugning their moral qualities. But the fact remains that the living standard of the country suffers when the budget is overloaded with allocations to unproductive branches of consumption. And today as yesterday, the most unproductive expenditures are all of those made on the armed forces. That's why I think that military leaders can't be reminded too often that it is the government which must allocate funds, and it is the government which must decide how much the armed forces can spend.

Apparently the control of military spending is a universal problem. I remember a conversation I once had with President Eisenhower when I was a guest at his dacha at Camp David [in September 1959]. We went for walks together and had some useful informal talks. During one of these talks, he asked, "Tell me, Mr. Khrushchev, how did you decide the question of funds for military expenses?" Then, before I had a chance to say anything, he said, "Perhaps first I should tell you how it is with us."

"Well, how is it with you?"

He smiled, and I smiled back at him. I had a feeling what he was going to say. "It's like this. My military leaders come to me and say, 'Mr. President, we need such and such a sum for such and such a program.' I say, 'Sorry, we don't have the funds.' They say, 'We have reliable information that the Soviet Union has already allocated funds for their own such program. Therefore if we don't get the funds we need, we'll fall behind the Soviet Union.' So I give in. That's how they wring money out of me. They keep grabbing for more and I keep giving it to them. Now tell me, how is it with you?"

"It's just the same. Some people from our military department come and say, 'Comrade Khrushchev, look at this! The Americans are developing such and such a system. We could develop the same system, but it would cost such and such.' I tell them there's no money; it's all been allotted already. So they say, 'If we don't get the money we need and if there's a war, then the enemy will have superiority over us.' So we discuss it some more, and I end up by giving them the money they ask for."

"Yes," he said, "that's what I thought. You know, we really should come to some sort of an agreement in order to stop this fruitless, really wasteful rivalry."

"I'd like to do that. Part of my reason for coming here was to see if some sort of an agreement would come out of these meetings and conversations."

But we couldn't agree then, and we can't agree now. I don't know. Maybe it's impossible for us to agree.

Senator John F. Kennedy Presses for More Military Spending to Close the Missile Gap, 1960

Winston Churchill said: "We arm—to parley." We prepare for war—in order to deter war. We depend on the strength of armaments, to enable us to bargain for disarmament. It is my intention, later this week, to make a second address on what positive preparations for disarmament we can make now. We compare our military strength with the Soviets, not to determine whether we should use it, but to determine whether we can persuade them that to use theirs would be futile and disastrous, and to determine whether we can back up our own pledges in Berlin, Formosa, and around the world.

In short, peace, not politics, is at the heart of the current debate—peace, not war, is the objective of our military policy. But peace would have no meaning if the time ever came when the deterrent ratio shifted so heavily in favor of the Soviet Union that they could destroy most of our retaliatory capacity in a single blow. It would then be irrelevant as to whether the Soviets achieved our demise through massive attack, through the threat of such attack, or through nibbling away gradually at our security.

Will such a time come?

The current debate has too often centered on how our retaliatory capacity compares today with that of the Soviets. Our striking force, the President said one week ago Sunday night, is "ample for today—far superior to any other" and large enough to deter any aggressor. But the real issue is not how we stand today but tomorrow—not in 1960 but in 1961, 1962 and particularly 1963 and thereafter. Nineteen hundred and sixty is critical because this is the year that the money must be appropriated—by this session of this Congress—if we are to obtain initial results in subsequent years. . . .

Those who uphold the administration defense budget are right on one count: We cannot be certain that the Soviets will have, during the term of the next administration, the tremendous lead in missile striking power which they give every evidence of building—and we cannot be certain that they will use that lead to threaten or launch an attack upon the United States. Consequently those of us who call for a higher defense budget are taking a chance on spending money unnecessarily. But those who oppose these expenditures are taking a chance on our very survival as a nation. . . .

But I am convinced that every American who can be fully informed as to the facts today would agree to an additional investment in our nation's security now rather than risk his survival, and his children's survival, in the years ahead—in particular, an investment effort designed, first, to make possible an emergency stopgap air alert program, to deter an attack before the missile gap is closed; second, to step up our ultimate missile program that will close the gap when completed. . . .

Whether the missile gap—that everyone agrees now exists—will become critical in 1961, 1962, or 1963—whether during the critical years of the gap the Russian lead will be 2 to 1, 3 to 1, or 5 to 1—whether the gap can be brought to a close—by the availability in quantity of Polaris and Minuteman missiles—in 1964 or in 1965 or ever—on all these questions experts may sincerely differ. I do not challenge the accuracy of our intelligence reports—I do not charge anyone with intentionally misleading the public for purposes of deception. For whichever figures are accurate, the point is that we are facing a gap on which we are gambling with our survival—and this year's defense budget is our last real chance to do something about it. . . .

Unless immediate steps are taken, failure to maintain our relative power of retaliation may in the near future expose the United States to a nuclear missile attack. Until our own mobile solid-fuel missiles are available in sufficient quantities to make it unwise for an enemy to consider an attack we must scrape through with what we can most quickly make available. At the present time there are no Polaris submarines on station ready for an emergency. There are no hardened missile bases. There is no adequate air defense. There is no capacity for an airborne alert in anything like the numbers admittedly needed. . . .

Time is short. This situation should never have been permitted to arise. But if we move now, if we are willing to gamble with our money instead of our survival, we have, I am sure, the wit and resource to maintain the minimum conditions for our survival, for our alliances, and for the active pursuit of peace.

Eisenhower on the "Military-Industrial Complex," 1961

A vital element in keeping the peace is our military establishment. Our arms must be mighty, ready for instant action, so that no potential aggressor may be tempted to risk his own destruction.

Our military organization today bears little relation to that known by any of my predecessors in peacetime, or indeed by the fighting men of World War II or Korea.

Until the latest of our world conflicts, the United States had no armaments industry. American makers of plowshares could, with time and as required, make swords as well. But now we can no longer risk emergency improvisation of national defense; we have been compelled to create a permanent armaments industry of vast proportions. Added to this, three and a half million men and women are directly engaged in the defense establishment. We annually spend on military security more than the net income of all United States corporations.

This conjunction of an immense military establishment and a large arms industry is new in the American experience. The total influence—economic, political, even spiritual—is felt in every city, every State house, every office of the Federal government. We recognize the imperative need for this development. Yet we must not fail to comprehend its grave implications. Our toil, resources and livelihood are all involved; so is the very structure of our society.

In the councils of government, we must guard against the acquisition of unwarranted influence, whether sought or unsought, by the military-industrial complex. The potential for the disastrous rise of misplaced power exists and will persist.

We must never let the weight of this combination endanger our liberties or democratic processes. We should take nothing for granted. Only an alert and knowledgeable citizenry can compel the proper meshing of the huge industrial and military machinery of defense with our peaceful methods and goals, so that security and liberty may prosper together.

Akin to, and largely responsible for the sweeping changes in our industrial-military posture, has been the technological revolution during recent decades.

In this revolution, research has become central; it also becomes more formalized, complex, and costly. A steadily increasing share is conducted for, by, or at the direction of, the Federal government.

Today, the solitary inventor, tinkering in his shop, has been overshadowed by task forces of scientists in laboratories and testing fields. In the same fashion, the free university, historically the fountainhead of free ideas and scientific discovery, has experienced a revolution in the conduct of research. Partly because of the huge costs involved, a government contract becomes virtually a substitute for intellectual curiosity. For every old blackboard there are now hundreds of new electronic computers.

The prospect of domination of the nation's scholars by Federal employment, project allocations, and the power of money is ever present—and is gravely to be regarded.

Yet, in holding scientific research and discovery in respect, as we should, we must also be alert to the equal and opposite danger that public policy could itself become the captive of a scientific-technological elite.

It is the task of statesmanship to mold, to balance, and to integrate these and other forces, new and old, within the principles of our democratic system—ever aiming toward the supreme goals of our free society. . . .

Down the long lane of the history yet to be written America knows that this world of ours, ever growing smaller, must avoid becoming a community of dreadful fear and hate, and be, instead, a proud confederation of mutual trust and respect.

Such a confederation must be one of equals. The weakest must come to the conference table with the same confidence as do we, protected as we are by our moral, economic, and military strength. That table, though scarred by many past frustrations, cannot be abandoned for the certain agony of the battlefield.

Disarmament, with mutual honor and confidence, is a continuing imperative. Together we must learn how to compose differences, not with arms, but with intellect and decent purpose. Because this need is so sharp and apparent I confess that I lay down my official responsibilities in this field with a definite sense of disappointment. As one who has witnessed the horror and the lingering sadness of war—as one who knows that another war could utterly destroy this civilization which has been so slowly and painfully built over thousands of years—I wish I could say tonight that a lasting peace is in sight.

✖ *E S S A Y S*

In the first essay, Robert A. Divine, a professor of history at the University of Texas, Austin, challenges scholars who have portrayed Eisenhower's massive retaliation policy as reckless and belligerent. Divine lauds the strategy for balancing the nation's security needs with budgetary realities. Another advantage to massive retaliation, Divine argues, was that aggressors could not know whether the administration would actually carry it out; it thus allowed the United States to deter aggression without ever having to use nuclear weapons. Divine also stresses Eisenhower's complementing massive retaliation with efforts to control the arms race and to limit nuclear testing.

In the second essay, the historian Gordon H. Chang of Stanford University explores Eisenhower's handling of the Taiwan Strait crisis of 1954–1955. Chang asserts that Eisenhower foolishly extended a commitment to Jiang Jieshi (Chiang Kai-shek) to defend the Jinmen (Quemoy) and Mazu (Matsu) islands off the shore of mainland China against Chinese communist attack. Eisenhower also threatened to use nuclear weapons. Rather than defusing the crisis, Eisenhower's nuclear threat and plans for a naval blockade of China's coast strained the NATO alliance, carried the United States to the nuclear brink over relatively insignificant territories, and spurred China's nuclear program.

The Beauty of Eisenhower's Nuclear Strategy

ROBERT A. DIVINE

Eisenhower's first priority on taking office was to reassess American strategy in the Cold War. The lesson of the Korean War seemed clear to the new President— neither the American people nor the American economy could stand a succession of limited, conventional wars. The public resented the commitment of American troops to battle for anything less than complete victory; the heavy deficits such conflicts incurred would slowly sap the nation's resources. . . .

The search for a new military stance in the Cold War led to Operation Solarium, named for the White House sun room where it was conceived in May 1953. The President appointed separate task forces to examine three broad options available to the United States. The first was containment, the policy inherited from the Truman administration, with its stress on both allies abroad and the readiness of

---

From Robert A. Divine, *Eisenhower and the Cold War* (New York: Oxford University Press, 1981), pp. 33–38, 55, 58–59, 61–65, 111–124, 127–131, 135–136, 146–151, 153. Notes omitted.

the United States to join with them in fighting conventional wars like the one in Korea to stem Communist aggression. A second alternative to be studied was essentially an amalgam of . . . [a] Dulles-Radford [Secretary of State John Foster Dulles and Admiral Arthur Radford] proposal. The United States would draw a line about the world and warn the Soviet Union that any penetration could lead to a nuclear response. The third group was to examine the campaign slogan of liberation [which called for the rollback of Soviet communism in Eastern Europe] to see if the new administration should conduct a program of economic, psychological, and possibly even para-military warfare against the Communist bloc.

The three task forces worked through the summer at the Naval War College and then submitted their recommendations to the National Security Council. By October, the NSC had ruled out the alternative of liberation and had decided to continue the policy of containment with modifications to permit a greater reliance on nuclear retaliation to hold the line against Communist expansion in Third World areas.

At the same time, Eisenhower was seeking ways to cut back the heavy defense budget he had inherited. In May, he replaced the Joint Chiefs of Staff with four new appointees, including Admiral Radford as chairman. In a White House meeting, he instructed them to make a complete survey of the nation's strategic requirements and to take into consideration diplomatic and fiscal factors as well as narrowly military ones. Despite this injunction, the recommendations they made disappointed the President and his chief economizer, Secretary of the Treasury George Humphrey. Balancing reductions made possible by the end of the Korean War against new expenditures occasioned by the Soviet Union's successful test of the hydrogen bomb in August, the Chiefs urged a continuation of both existing force levels and defense spending at approximately $35 billion a year.

In explaining and defending this recommendation, Admiral Radford pointed out that the Chiefs had to plan for every possible contingency, ranging from limited war to general conventional war on up to all-out nuclear war. If, however, the military were to be authorized to rule out conventional warfare and to plan on using nuclear weapons whenever it was technically advantageous to do so, then they could achieve significant reductions in manpower and large cuts in the total defense budget. . . .

Eisenhower accepted the new strategy, and it was incorporated into his administration's statement of basic national security policy, NSC 162/2, adopted on October 30, 1953. After a statement outlining the nature of the Soviet threat to American well-being, NSC 162/2 stipulated the necessity for the United States to maintain "a strong military posture, with emphasis on the capability of inflicting massive retaliatory damage by offensive striking power." Near the end of this review of national strategy, the document stated specifically that "in the event of hostilities, the United States will consider nuclear weapons to be as available for use as other munitions." While in fact the President still retained the ultimate decision on the use of nuclear weapons, his assent to NSC 162/2 amounted at least to a promise to the Joint Chiefs that he would authorize nuclear retaliation in case of overt Communist aggression.

The reliance on strategic power enabled the Eisenhower administration to make a significant reduction in both force levels and defense spending. . . .

The policy [also] reflected Eisenhower's belief that it was necessary to regain the initiative in the Cold War. Instead of waiting for the Communists to probe along the perimeter for weaknesses, Ike preferred to warn them of America's determination to respond, possibly with nuclear weapons. The policy was deliberately ambiguous, designed to make the enemy weigh the danger of a limited challenge turning into a nuclear holocaust. . . .

On the morning of September 3, 1954, Communist batteries on the mainland of China began lobbing artillery shells into the Chinese Nationalist [Jiang Jieshi's] positions on the island of Quemoy. Two American soldiers died in the opening onslaught of what proved to be the severest test yet of the administration's policy of massive retaliation. . . .

The crisis in the Taiwan Strait reached a new peak in mid-January 1955 when the Communists began an attack on the Tachen [Dachen] islands, some two hundred miles northwest of Formosa. Although these islands were not vital to the defense of Taiwan, Eisenhower decided it was time "to draw the line" against further Chinese aggression. In a series of meetings with his national security advisers, the President decided to assist the Nationalists in evacuating the Tachens while strengthening the defenses at Quemoy and Matsu. At the same time, Eisenhower announced that he would ask Congress for a joint resolution authorizing the use of force to protect Formosa and the nearby Pescadores [Penghus]. In his message to Congress, Ike made clear his desire to defend Formosa, and then asked the legislators to grant him authority to include "closely related localities" in the American commitment. The President was deliberately ambiguous about the offshore islands; he wanted to keep the Chinese guessing whether or not the United States in fact would resist an attack on Quemoy and Matsu. . . .

The climax came in March 1955. Returning from a two-week trip to Asia, Secretary of State Dulles told the President on March 10 that the situation in the Formosa Strait was "far more serious" than he had realized. The Communists were bent on conquering Formosa as well as the offshore islands, Dulles reported. "If we defend Quemoy and Matsu," he continued, "we'll have to use atomic weapons." Ike immediately sent an aide to Pearl Harbor to confer with the commander of the Pacific Fleet, and his report was equally pessimistic, predicting a Chinese attack on the islands in late March.

While Eisenhower mulled over this estimate, Dulles went public with his threat of atomic reprisals. In a statement on March 12, the secretary spoke of "new and powerful weapons of precision which can utterly destroy military targets without endangering unrelated civilian centers." Puzzled by such an assertion of a "clean" nuclear strike, one of Dulles's aides checked with the CIA and came back with the estimate that tactical nuclear strikes at Chinese airfields and troop concentrations opposite Quemoy and Matsu would kill between 12 and 14 million Chinese civilians! Despite this report, Dulles told the press on March 15 that the administration was prepared to use tactical atomic weapons in case of war in the Formosa Strait. The next day, a reporter asked Ike to comment, and the President replied affirmatively. "Now, in any combat where these things [tactical atomic weapons] can be used on strictly military targets and for strictly military purposes," Eisenhower declared, "I see no reason why they shouldn't be used just exactly as you would use a bullet or anything else." . . .

Eisenhower moved to quiet the fears at home that his nuclear warning to China had raised. When [press secretary] Jim Hagerty advised him to duck any questions at his March 23 press conference on the sensitive Formosa Strait issue, Ike replied, "Don't worry Jim . . . I'll just confuse them." The President then proceeded to tell the reporter who asked him if he planned to use nuclear weapons to defend Quemoy and Matsu that he could not answer directly, but that nothing in warfare was predictable, and that "every war is going to astonish you in the way it occurred, and in the way it is carried out." A week later, Eisenhower arranged for Hagerty to inform journalists that "the President did not believe war was upon us." . . .

Eisenhower was right. Despite the risk he took in stimulating concern at home, his nuclear threat apparently got through to Peking. On April 23, Foreign Minister Chou En-lai [Zhou Enlai], in Bandung, Indonesia, for a meeting of Third World nations, spoke of Chinese friendship for the American people, said that they "do not want to have a war with the United States of America" and suggested negotiations to "discuss the question of relaxing tension in the Far East and especially the question of relaxing tension in the Taiwan area." The State Department immediately dismissed this proposal out of hand, treating it as purely a propaganda move by China to impress nonaligned nations. But Eisenhower took it seriously, and four days later expressed a willingness to open negotiations "if there seemed to be an opportunity for us to further the easing of tensions." On August 1, 1955, discussions got under way in Geneva between American and Chinese diplomats. Although the Geneva talks failed to resolve the issues of the offshore islands and the fate of Formosa, they provided a face-saving way for China to stop its shelling of Quemoy and thus to end the crisis.

Ever since, most commentators have been critical of Dulles and Eisenhower for taking the nation to the brink of war over the remote offshore islands. The prevailing view is to condemn Dulles for practicing "brinksmanship" and to praise Eisenhower for showing restraint. . . .

In reality, Eisenhower not only determined American policy throughout the crisis, but carried it out to a successful conclusion. He took Dulles's concept of massive retaliation and refined it. Instead of relying on the certainty of nuclear retaliation to frighten America's opponents, as his critics complained, Ike preferred to keep the Communists guessing. He introduced a note of deliberate ambiguity into American policy. He refused to announce publicly whether or not he would commit the United States to oppose an attack on Quemoy and Matsu, and thereby kept the Chinese Communists off balance. When the crisis became most serious, he used a measured nuclear threat to warn the Chinese without insulting them or provoking them into an attack. The beauty of Eisenhower's policy is that to this day no one can be sure whether or not he would have responded militarily to an invasion of the offshore islands, and whether he would have used nuclear weapons. . . .

As soon as he took office [in 1953], Eisenhower [had] searched for some way to bring home the awful realities of the nuclear age to the American people. Responding to the recommendations of a scientific panel headed by Robert Oppenheimer, he asked presidential assistant C. D. Jackson, his specialist in Cold War strategy, to prepare a speech informing the world of the new danger created by the hydrogen bomb. . . .

On December 8 [1953] the President began the speech by reciting the horrors of nuclear war to the United Nations delegates [in the General Assembly]. In somber tones, he described the "awful arithmetic" of the dread weapons, pointing out that atomic bombs had become twenty-five times more powerful than those used in 1945, while "hydrogen weapons are in the range of millions of tons of TNT equivalent." There was no defense against such weapons. A thermonuclear attack would "cause hideous damage" and lead to "the annihilation of the irreplaceable heritage of mankind." But then he began to outline a positive proposal. The nations possessing fissionable material should "begin now and continue to make joint contributions from their stockpiles . . . to an International Atomic Energy Agency." The United Nations should establish this new body, which would use the radioactive material to serve the needs of agriculture, medicine, and "to provide abundant electrical energy in the power-starved areas of the world." The United States "would be proud" to contribute to such a program, but of course the Soviet Union must also participate, the President insisted. The result, he concluded, would mean that "the contributing powers would be dedicating some of their strength to serve the needs rather than the fears of mankind. . . ."

It was a brilliant proposal that met with nearly universal praise. The General Assembly showered him with applause, with even the Communist delegates joining in. The press quickly labeled the new program "atoms for peace." Some cynics dismissed it as a public relations gimmick, while the Russians dragged their feet. But finally in 1957 the United Nations created the International Atomic Energy Agency and the "atoms for peace" program eventually was responsible for spreading the new technology around the world. Unfortunately, the safeguards proved inadequate, and the dissemination of fissionable materials contributed to the proliferation of nuclear weapons. . . .

Unfortunately, the President's words could not halt the technological process. On March 1, 1954, less than six months after his hopeful speech, the AEC [Atomic Energy Commission] detonated America's first deliverable H-bomb at Bikini atoll. The resulting explosion led to an unexpected cloud of deadly radioactivity that forced the United States to evacuate nearly 300 people on nearby islands. Twenty-three Japanese fishermen on board the *Lucky Dragon,* trolling some eighty miles from ground zero, were not so fortunate. Dusted with a silvery ash a few hours later, they wisely washed the unknown substance off their boat, but by the time they returned to Japan, they were all suffering from radioactive poisoning, and several months later one of them would die. Their plight heralded to the world the presence of a new and deadly by-product of the thermonuclear age: fallout. . . .

Worldwide pressure for a [Soviet-American] summit conference had become irresistible by the spring of 1955. . . .

The Russians took two steps to ensure that the conference would take place. The first was an announcement in April that they were now ready to reach an agreement on a peace treaty for Austria, a development they had blocked for nine years. A treaty creating a neutral Austria was quickly signed in May. Then that same month the Soviet delegate to the UN disarmament subcommittee in London suddenly offered a comprehensive plan to control the arms race. Departing from past Russian policy, which had insisted on the abolition of nuclear weapons as the first step toward disarmament, the Soviets now came close to previous Western plans by proposing a sharp reduction in conventional forces and a willingness to accept some form of inspection. There were, to be sure, loopholes in the Soviet offer, notably the restriction of international monitors to fixed inspection posts "at large ports, at railway junctions, on main motor highways and in aerodromes." But for the first time since disarmament talks had begun in 1946, the Russians were at least willing to discuss the Western concept of international control and supervision. . . .

The President's concern for controlling the arms race dominated his preparations for the Geneva Conference. In March he had appointed Harold Stassen as his special assistant on disarmament, charging him with the difficult task of reconciling differences between various branches of the government and using his dogged perseverance to arrive at a consensus in this area. Surprised by the May Soviet disarmament proposal, Eisenhower then asked another presidential assistant, Nelson Rockefeller, who had succeeded C. D. Jackson in directing Cold War strategy, to develop a new American initiative in the arms field. Rockefeller organized a panel of experts at the Quantico Marine Corps base in Virginia and came up with the idea of mutual aerial inspection. Ike was immediately attracted to this new approach, but when Dulles raised objections, he agreed to await developments at the Geneva Conference before deciding whether or not to present it to the Russians. Thus the President ordered Rockefeller and Stassen to stand by in Paris when the conference opened and be ready to join him in Geneva with the new proposal. . . .

After several days of fruitless discussion on the German issue, the President decided to take a gamble. He ordered Harold Stassen and Nelson Rockefeller to join him in Geneva and conferred with them for several hours on the details of the aerial inspection plan. After showing it to Anthony Eden [the recently elected British prime minister], who immediately approved, the President decided to go ahead with what became known as "open skies," though he was still not sure whether to include it in his formal presentation on disarmament or to save it for later in the conference.

The next day, acting on impulse, Eisenhower took off his glasses and began speaking directly to the Soviet leaders as he laid out the open skies concept. The United States, he said, was prepared to exchange military blueprints of all its armed forces for those of the Soviet Union and to permit regular and frequent aerial inspection of its territory in return for similar privileges on the part of the Russians. Speaking mainly from memory, the President concluded his presentation with an earnest appeal: "I do not know how I could convince you of our sincerity in this matter and that we mean you no harm. I only wish that God would give me some means of convincing you of our sincerity and loyalty in making this proposal." As if on cue, a late afternoon thunderstorm broke with a flash of lightning and the lights suddenly went out in the conference room, plunging the gathering into a few seconds of total darkness.

The British and French leaders quickly voiced their approval of open skies; the Russians, obviously caught by surprise, withheld any immediate reaction. [Soviet premier Nicholas] Bulganin promised only to give it careful study, but when Eisenhower told him, "The United States will never take part in an aggressive war," the Soviet Premier immediately responded, "We believe that statement." Khrushchev, however, came up to Eisenhower during cocktails at the end of that day's session and said ominously, "I don't agree with the chairman." According to Ambassador [Charles] Bohlen, who translated Khrushchev's remarks, the Soviet leader went on to ask Eisenhower "whom he was trying to fool?" "In our eyes," Khrushchev continued, "this is a very transparent espionage device. . . . You could hardly expect us to take this seriously." The Russians never formally rejected open skies, but by their inaction, as Bohlen noted, they let it "die of malnutrition."

Most observers have agreed with Khrushchev's evaluation of open skies. [The historian] Peter Lyon called it "a spectacular victory for the Cold Warriors" who practiced psychological warfare. He noted that in discussing the idea with Rockefeller and Stassen, Eisenhower observed that since the Russians already knew the location of most American military bases, "mutual agreements for such overflights would undoubtedly benefit us more than the Russians, because we know very little about their installations." Historian Herbert Parmet agreed, calling the proposal "a grand gesture" and citing the President's remark to an interviewer in 1965: "We knew the Soviets wouldn't accept it. We were sure of that." Yet while it is true that open skies clearly benefited the United States, it is unlikely that Eisenhower was sure it would be rejected. His 1965 remarks reflect rather the desire to take the sting out of the Soviet rebuff. . . . Eisenhower, both in atoms-for-peace and open skies, was breaking away from the previous Western insistence on comprehensive disarmament proposals and searching instead for more limited measures that could break the deadlock and help bring the arms race under some measure of control. . . .

The Geneva Conference failed to achieve the détente that some hoped for. The leaders resolved neither the problem of Germany nor the disarmament stalemate, and the subsequent session of the foreign ministers made no headway. The only positive result was an agreement on cultural exchanges and the phrase "spirit of Geneva," an outgrowth of Eisenhower's optimistic expectations. The real significance of the conference was the evident realization by both sides that nuclear war was unthinkable. . . .

This common understanding of the nuclear danger was in itself a valuable development. Equally important was the emergence at Geneva of Dwight Eisenhower as the world's most eloquent spokesman for peace. Commenting on the impact of Eisenhower's personality—his friendliness and spontaneity, his warmth and naturalness—[the journalist] Robert Donovan concluded, "Eisenhower conveyed a sense of decency and dignity which mocked the picture of his country as an immature nation hell-bent for war.". . .

In the spring of 1957, growing worldwide concern over the danger of fallout created a powerful impulse for a halt to atmospheric testing. [The famous medical missionary] Albert Schweitzer made an eloquent appeal for an end to weapons testing, while Linus Pauling, a Nobel prize winner in chemistry, secured the signatures of over 9000 scientists calling for a test ban. Hearings held before a subcommittee of the Joint Committee on Atomic Energy highlighted the possibility that even the small amount of radiation from tests in the atmosphere could increase the incidence of cancer and cause unknown genetic damage. The AEC, supported by many independent scientists, challenged these assertions, but the fact that no one could be certain as to the exact effects of nuclear fallout on human health and well-being proved unsettling. . . .

The test ban issue came to a head in 1958. The Soviet Union began a series of huge H-bomb tests in February, while the United States planned an extensive series, code-named HARDTACK, for its Pacific proving grounds in the late spring and summer. By mid-March, the administration had learned that the Soviets might declare a voluntary moratorium on further tests when their series was completed. John Foster Dulles feared that such a move would prove embarrassing to the United States, leading to worldwide demands that America follow the Russian lead and cancel HARDTACK. Harold Stassen had resigned as disarmament adviser in February after the administration had rejected his proposal for a two-year suspension of testing; with his chief rival gone, Dulles began to shift his position toward a test ban. Aware of the growing global outcry over fallout and the effective way in which the Soviets could capitalize on it at the end of their current test series, Dulles was now ready to take the initiative. . . .

Just as Dulles had predicted, the Soviets announced a unilateral suspension of nuclear testing on March 31, adding that they would have to reconsider their action if the United States continued its own test program. While the Russians reaped an impressive propaganda victory, the administration went ahead with the HARD-TACK series. The President, however, now received a significant report from his scientific advisers which opened up new possibilities for a test ban agreement. A panel headed by Hans Bethe of Cornell University reported on March 28 that a network of control posts could detect nuclear explosions as small as 2 kilotons. The full scientific advisory committee met in early April and on the basis of the Bethe panel report recommended that the President "stop testing after the HARDTACK series." Since it was now feasible to create an effective inspection system, the committee concluded that a test ban would serve the national interest. The President concurred, and in late April he instructed Dulles to invite Khrushchev to send a team of Soviet technical experts to seek agreement on an inspection system. Without making any explicit promises, the administration was signaling the Russians its intention of entering into a test ban agreement once the inspection problem had been solved.

Khrushchev quickly accepted the American proposal, and delegations of Soviet and American scientists met for six weeks at Geneva in the summer of 1958. By mid-August they had reached agreement on a worldwide network of 180 control posts which they believed would be capable of detecting all nuclear explosions, whether conducted in the atmosphere or underground, greater than 5 kilotons. Aware of this progress, Eisenhower began to discuss the next step with his advisers—the negotiation of a test ban agreement. . . .

On August 22, 1958, the President announced that he had invited the Soviets to attend a conference on October 31 of all nations possessing nuclear weapons to create an international control system and negotiate a test ban treaty. As a sign of good faith, Eisenhower offered to suspend future American testing for one year, provided that the Russians would also refrain from testing during that period. If the negotiations proved successful, the United States was prepared to extend the moratorium for another year. Above all, the President expressed his hope that the test ban negotiations would become a first step toward "more substantial agreements" on nuclear disarmament.

A few days later Khrushchev agreed to enter into the proposed test ban talks, and the two countries now settled on Geneva as the site for the meeting. The Soviets refused to say whether they would join the moratorium on testing after October 31, and for the next two months both the United States and the Soviet Union engaged in a last-minute orgy of nuclear detonations—the AEC conducted nineteen tests while the Russians held fourteen. When the conference opened at Geneva on October 31, Khrushchev had not yet agreed to the voluntary moratorium. The United States detected Russian tests on November 1 and 3, but these were apparently the last in the fall Russian series. For the next three years, there were no additional nuclear tests, to the great relief of those who worried over the effect of fallout on human health. Eisenhower had scored a significant diplomatic victory by taking the initiative in halting nuclear tests in the atmosphere, and thus winning worldwide approval. At the same time, he had done what he had always opposed, agreed to stop testing without a functioning inspection system and without any corresponding Soviet concessions on halting nuclear weapons production. In the minds of his military advisers, he had taken a dangerous gamble with American security; Eisenhower, however, was convinced that he had assumed an acceptable risk in the cause of peace. Less concerned with fallout than with the nuclear arms race itself, he hoped that a test ban treaty would be the first step toward a comprehensive disarmament agreement.

The optimism created by the moratorium on testing and the opening of the Geneva negotiations did not last very long. On November 10, 1958, Nikita Khrushchev renewed the Berlin crisis, quiet since the end of the blockade in 1949, by announcing Soviet intentions of signing a separate peace treaty with East Germany. Such a move would leave the Western-occupied portions of Berlin isolated 110-miles deep within a Communist nation and call into question the occupation rights of the United States and its allies. On November 27 the new Berlin crisis took on ominous proportions when the Russians sent the Western nations a note declaring their intention of signing the feared peace treaty with East Germany within six months if a negotiated solution to the Berlin problem could not be reached. . . .

While the crisis continued to mount, the American people got a glimpse of Eisenhower's policy in his press conference replies to reporters' questions. He ruled out the use of conventional weapons, telling reporters that the United States had no plans "to shoot our way into Berlin" and asserting that "we are certainly not going to fight a ground war in Europe." At the same time, when a reporter asked him if the United States was ready "to use nuclear weapons if necessary to defend free Berlin," Ike replied, "Well, I don't know how you could free anything with nuclear weapons." But then he went on to say that the United States was prepared to meet its "responsibilities with respect to Berlin." Any movement toward "real hostilities," he added, would have to come "from the side of the Soviets." Only then would he make his final response. Thus the President took refuge in ambiguity, just as he had during the Formosa Strait crisis. Aware of the tactical situation in Berlin, he ruled out a ground war, but he left open the possibility of a nuclear conflict, always with the understanding that he would never fire the first shot. Walking a careful line between firmness and conciliation, Eisenhower sought to convince the Russians that the best answer to the Berlin crisis lay in diplomacy, not war.

The tension began to break in March. [British foreign minister] Harold Macmillan journeyed to Russia and came back with word that Khrushchev was willing to call off the May 27 deadline in return for Western agreement for a new summit conference. Macmillan came to the United States in late March to urge Eisenhower to grant this Soviet condition. The President expressed his reluctance to attend a summit conference unless there was substantial progress toward a settlement at a lower level. When Macmillan pleaded with the President, expressing his belief that as few as eight nuclear missiles could wipe out England, Ike finally agreed to a foreign ministers conference with the Soviets, with a summit meeting in the future "as soon as developments justify." Khrushchev quickly accepted this formula, and, while the Russians never formally gave up their May 27 deadline, the agreement to meet at the foreign ministers level in Geneva on May 11 effectively removed the ultimatum. . . .

As the time approached for the summit conference [scheduled for mid-May 1960], the chances for a genuine breakthrough in the Cold War were mixed. The growing optimism over a test ban treaty had to be balanced against the lack of progress toward a Berlin settlement. Khrushchev's rhetoric on the German issue had been getting tougher in the spring of 1960. He renewed his threat to sign a separate peace treaty with East Germany, asserting that such a step would automatically terminate all Western occupation rights in Berlin. He was careful, however, not to set a time limit for this development. On April 20, Undersecretary of State C. Douglas Dillon replied for the United States. Terming the continued partition of Germany a "monstrous" abnormality, Dillon warned the Soviets that the United States would "not negotiate under duress." "No nation," he asserted, "could preserve its faith in collective security if we permitted the courageous people of West Berlin to be sold into slavery." Several days later, the President endorsed Dillon's remarks, telling the press that "we are not going to give up the juridical rights that we have."

The ill-fated U-2 flight of Francis Gary Powers on May 1, 1960, doomed the summit conference before it ever began. The high altitude intelligence overflights of the Soviet Union had begun in mid-1956, the outgrowth of recommendations of a scientific panel headed by James Killian. The Russians were aware of the flights from the outset, tracking the American spy planes with radar. The high altitude at which the U-2 flew placed the planes beyond the range of both Soviet interceptors and surface-to-air missiles. The photographs taken on these flights gave the United States vital information about Soviet military progress, especially in regard to missiles, but Eisenhower had frequently expressed his reservations about them. "Some day one of these machines is going to be caught," he later recalled having told his advisers, "and we're going to have a storm." . . .

An aide informed the President on the afternoon of May 1 that Powers's plane was overdue and presumed missing. The next day the CIA confirmed that the plane had been lost; Eisenhower, who had been assured that the U-2 was equipped to self-destruct in an emergency, assumed that no evidence would survive to link the plane with the United States. . . .

On May 8, Khrushchev stunned the Eisenhower administration and shocked the world by announcing that the Soviet Union had not only shot down the U-2 but captured the pilot alive and the wreckage of his plane intact. . . .

The fate of the Paris summit now hung in the balance. In Moscow, Khrushchev began to suggest that he could not sit down and negotiate with a man who had deliberately violated Soviet air space. At the very least, it seemed appropriate for Eisenhower to announce that the flights would not be continued. In fact, the President ordered the U-2 missions stopped before he left for Paris, but he stubbornly refused to make this vital decision public. Instead he planned to reveal it at the opening of the summit as part of a conciliatory speech stressing American desire to negotiate a Berlin settlement and a test ban treaty.

Eisenhower had miscalculated. When he arrived in Paris, he found that Khrushchev was now demanding that the President apologize for the Powers flight, punish those responsible for it, and promise to end all future overflights of the Soviet Union. . . .

The break-up of the Paris summit [on May 16] ended any chance for easing Cold War tensions in the last year of Eisenhower's presidency. On his return to Moscow, Khrushchev ruled out any further negotiations over Berlin, saying that he preferred to wait until after the American elections so that he could deal with Eisenhower's successor. . . .

The sense of a heightened Cold War troubled Eisenhower as he left office. His fondest wish had been to use his skills to reduce tension and lessen the possibility of a nuclear holocaust. His record, however, was far better than the crises of 1960 would suggest. He had halted the Korean War six months after taking office. In the ensuing seven-and-a-half years he had kept the United States at peace. In the Middle East he had managed to contain the Suez crisis and restore temporary stability to that troubled region; in Asia, he had balanced the somewhat flamboyant rhetoric of his secretary of state with his own restraint and achieved a delicate stand-off between the Nationalists and the Chinese Communists in the Formosa Strait; in Europe, he had stood fast before Khrushchev's threats over Berlin, maintaining the American commitment to that city while avoiding a resort to force. And if he had failed in his most ambitious undertaking, the control of the arms race, at least he had achieved a cessation of nuclear testing, with its potentially deadly fallout, during the last two years of his term.

Eisenhower's Reckless Nuclear Gamble over the Taiwan Strait

GORDON H. CHANG

On September 3, 1954, while Secretary of State Dulles was in Manila making final arrangements for the establishment of the anticommunist military pact known as the Southeast Asia Treaty Organization (SEATO), Chinese Communist coastal batteries opened up on Jinmen [Quemoy], one of the small Nationalist-held islands off the coast of the mainland. Acting Secretary of Defense Robert Anderson

Excerpted from Chapter Four "To the Nuclear Brink," in *Friends and Enemies: The United States, China, and the Soviet Union, 1948–1972* by Gordon H. Chang with the permission of the publishers, Stanford University Press. © 1990 by the Board of Trustees of the Leland Stanford Junior University.

warned President Eisenhower that the intensity of the shelling seemed a prelude to an all-out assault. Over the next nine months the United States, in supporting the Nationalists' stubborn defense of these islands, lurched toward disaster—in Eisenhower's own recollection the crisis almost caused a "split between the United States and nearly all its allies" and seemingly carried the country to the "edge of war." In fact the crisis was even more serious than Eisenhower described. Before tensions finally subsided at the end of April 1955, the United States had come dangerously close to using nuclear weapons against the Chinese mainland. . . .

The situation in the Taiwan Strait continued to deteriorate through 1954, and, then, in Eisenhower's description, took a "turn for the worse" at the start of 1955. Both the Communists and Nationalists now predicted imminent widespread hostilities. On January 10 a hundred planes from the mainland raided the Dachens, and on January 18 Communist forces overwhelmed 1,000 Nationalist guerrillas (and eight American military personnel) on Yijiang Island, just north of the Dachens. The Nationalists counterattacked with air strikes on mainland ports and shipping. The CIA reported that on the morning of January 23 some 20,000 to 30,000 Communist troops embarked from Qingdao for Shanghai, evidently for use against the Dachens in the opinion of the intelligence agency. From Washington's vantage point all-out war for the offshore islands and perhaps Taiwan itself seemed to loom.

Eisenhower concluded that since the Dachens were not reachable from Taiwan's airfields, they were not as defensible militarily as Jinmen and Mazu. Nevertheless, he decided that the United States had to clarify its position. On January 19, in a meeting with [Secretary] Dulles and [Admiral] Radford, the president agreed with their assessment that the remaining offshore islands could not be held without "U.S. interposition." As he wrote in his memoirs, "the time had come to draw the line" over what territories the United States would fight for. Dulles, on Eisenhower's instructions, confidentially informed Nationalist Foreign Minister George K. C. Yeh, then visiting Washington, that the United States would publicly announce its intention to join in the defense of Jinmen if Chiang [Kai-shek (Jiang Jieshi)] would withdraw from the Dachens.

On the next day, January 20, the NSC argued heatedly about the path Eisenhower and Dulles had chosen. On behalf of the president, Dulles reviewed U.S. policy: the United States had obscured its public stand to confuse the enemy. This policy, though, had begun to "backfire." The Communists now seemed convinced the United States would not fight for any of the offshore islands. Dulles recommended that, while continuing to seek a ceasefire through the United Nations, the administration should ask Congress to grant the president the explicit power to commit U.S. forces to the defense of Taiwan and related areas not specifically mentioned in the Mutual Defense Treaty. These "related areas" would include Jinmen, and probably Mazu, so long as the Communists professed an intention to attack Taiwan. The United States had to remove any ambiguity about what territories it would defend. Leaving the U.S. position unclear, Dulles judged, would now create "greater risk."

Robert Cutler, the President's national security adviser, Treasury Secretary George Humphrey, and Defense Secretary Charles Wilson all vehemently objected to Dulles's view: the United States was going to be drawn directly into war with

China over territory of minimal value. Wilson felt the United States should just hold Taiwan and the Penghus and "let the others go." The president, however, just as vehemently endorsed all of Dulles's recommendations. The Dachens could be given up, he conceded, but unless the United States was prepared "completely to discount Formosa," the NSC had to make up its mind about Jinmen and Mazu, the most important remaining offshore islands. If Chiang lost these, the damage to Nationalist morale might be irreparable. Ever since masses of Chiang's troops had surrendered without a fight in 1949, Washington had doubted the loyalty and determination of his forces. Even a symbolic setback might undermine the entire Nationalist cause. According to Eisenhower, a statement of U.S. resolve would reduce the danger of war with China and correct the current "dangerous drift" in policy. In any case, the president said, it was clear to him that Jinmen and Mazu "were the outposts for the defense of Formosa."

The NSC continued its discussion the following day. Eisenhower remained adamant in his demand that Congress give him broad general authority to defend the islands under Nationalist control. He was "absolutely determined" to avoid at all costs "another Yalu River sanctuary situation in any struggle over Quemoy," he told the NSC. The president wanted no restraints if the United States became involved, and while he wished to avoid being pinned down to a permanent defense of Jinmen and Mazu, he would not abandon them so long as the Communists menaced the islands. Eisenhower said the United States might change its policy in the future after tensions eased, but at present it had to help hold the islands to protect Taiwan. Everyone present should be sure of one thing, he declared: no matter how a congressional resolution was worded, if there was an emergency during this crisis, he would do whatever had to be done to protect the vital interests of the United States, "even if his actions should be interpreted as acts of war." He "would rather be impeached than fail to do his duty."

Three days later Eisenhower sent his special request to Congress, and on January 28, 1955, the Senate, following the House of Representatives, passed what became known as the Formosa Resolution, giving the president a virtual blank check. The president was authorized to employ the armed forces of the United States for the protection of Taiwan and the Penghus and "related positions and territories of that area now in friendly hands." Eisenhower, though, had changed his mind about publicly naming which offshore islands he would defend. None were specified. Eisenhower said that the United States would intervene only if a Communist attack appeared to be preliminary to an assault on Taiwan itself. James Reston of the *New York Times* called the United States line "calculated imprecision." This ambiguity was selective, however: on January 31 Washington directed its ambassador on Taiwan, Karl Rankin, to inform Chiang privately of the U.S. intention to defend Jinmen and Mazu during the present crisis. In exchange for its commitment to Jinmen and Mazu, the United States received Chiang's agreement to withdraw his forces from the Dachens. The islands' 24,000 civilians and soldiers, with the assistance of the U.S. Seventh Fleet, were evacuated a few days later.

Chiang may have agreed to the withdrawal, but he was livid at Washington's actions. His understanding, based on Dulles's talk with Foreign Minister Yeh on January 19, had been that the United States would make a public commitment to defend Jinmen and Mazu. Even though Dulles and Robertson had subsequently informed the Nationalists of the administration's change of mind, Chiang had insisted that Washington live up to its original proposal, or he would not withdraw from the Dachens. Although he felt double-crossed, he finally relented under American pressures. Just before the evacuation of the Dachens, Radford and Dulles's subordinates in the State Department reviewed the confused situation and concluded that Chiang's "misunderstanding" about the U.S. position was legitimate. The officials admitted that even they were unsure of exactly what agreements the administration had reached with the Nationalists about the Dachens. . . .

Chiang would not budge from Jinmen and Mazu, and the United States had committed itself to backing the Nationalists. There was nothing else to do, Eisenhower told the NSC in mid-February, but "to watch the situation as it develops on a day-to-day basis." He reminded the NSC of his belief that the surrender of the offshore islands would result in the collapse of Chiang's government. The president coolly joked that the United States was now in the hands of "a fellow who hasn't anything to lose."

Indeed the United States was backing itself into a corner, helped along by Chiang, who was far from being a simple puppet of Washington. With the war-making discretion granted by the Formosa Revolution, Eisenhower staked his own personal reputation and the prestige of the United States on the defense of the tenuous Nationalist cause, now centered on the offshore islands. Their loss to a Communist assault would have been humiliating and devastating to American credibility. The United States would never have allowed the destruction of one-quarter of Chiang's best troops and the loss of Jinmen and Mazu, even without the secret pledge of Chiang.

During a trip to Taiwan and the Far East at the end of February, Dulles concluded that the situation was even more serious than he had thought. Apparently neither the mutual defense treaty with the Nationalist regime nor the Formosa Resolution had discouraged the Communists. He was now convinced that the Communists intended to take Taiwan by force, reversing his previous estimate that their immediate interest was only the offshore islands. After a meeting in Honolulu with Admiral Felix Stump, commander-in-chief of the Pacific, Dulles cabled Washington that he was disturbed by the considerable increase in Communist forces and activity in the area. Moreover, Dulles warned, "they are skilled at camouflage and may be able to conceal timing." The fanaticism and intransigence of the Communists were even greater than he had feared.

On his return to Washington on March 6, Dulles reported to the president that if the Communists crushed the Nationalists on Jinmen and Mazu, the reaction would be catastrophic not only for the ROC [Republic of China] but also for the rest of Asia. The two reaffirmed their commitment to defending the two island groups and concluded that this would require drastic measures, including "the use of atomic missiles," by which they evidently meant tactical nuclear weapons. Eisenhower had earlier agreed with Admiral Radford that the United States would be unable to destroy the Communist gun emplacements opposite the offshore islands without the use of nuclear weapons. To prepare public opinion Eisenhower directed Dulles to state in a nationally televised speech on March 8 that the administration considered atomic weapons "interchangeable with the conventional weapons" in the American arsenal.

On March 10 Dulles reported to the NSC what he had discussed with the president, stating that the Communists were determined to take Taiwan and the United States had to realize that a fight with them was thus now a matter of "time not fact." He also expressed concern about the loyalty of Chiang's troops. If the Communists succeeded in landing on Taiwan, the KMT [Kuomintang] forces might disintegrate. The United States should try to avoid involvement for the next several weeks during sensitive discussions on strengthening Western European unity, but the administration had to start preparing the American people for hostilities involving U.S. forces in the Taiwan area and for the use of nuclear weapons in the defense of the offshore islands. "The need for such use, to make up for deficiency in conventional forces," said Dulles, "outweighs the repercussive effect of such use upon free world nations in Europe and the Far East. United States and world public opinion must be prepared." Dulles predicted that Communist pressure would continue "until the United States decides to 'shoot off a gun' in the area."

Admiral Radford heartily endorsed Dulles's position on the use of nuclear weapons, noting that the JCS [Joint Chiefs of Staff] had consistently advocated such a view. In fact the JCS had recently ordered the Strategic Air Command to begin, "on an urgent basis," target selection for an "enlarged atomic offensive" against China. The JCS knew Chiang was not averse to the use of atomic weapons against his people on the mainland. As long as "they were warned in advance," Chiang had told Admiral Stump, the Chinese people would accept such attacks "as a war necessity." The other members of the NSC were practically speechless. Dulles made it clear that his conclusions had the support of Eisenhower, who was presiding over the meeting. It was at the president's direction, he noted, that he had included the reference to tactical nuclear weapons in his recent speech. But much more public relations work had to be done if the United States was to use atomic weapons within the "next month or two.". . .

The public relations effort Dulles suggested at the March 10 meeting began immediately. In public statements over the next several days, the administration deliberately introduced specific comments about employing tactical nuclear weapons if war broke out in the Taiwan Strait. Eisenhower caused a furor when, at a news conference on March 16, he said he saw no reason "why they shouldn't be used exactly as you would use a bullet or anything else.". . .

The Chinese Communists took Eisenhower's threats seriously and began to prepare the population for hostilities, possibly including nuclear weapons, with the United States. Mao [Zedong] reportedly told the Finnish ambassador to China that if the United States destroyed Beijing or Shanghai with atomic weapons, American cities would suffer the same fate, and that the present leaders of the United States were bound to be replaced as a result. Mao did not make clear who—Russia or China—was supposed to bomb the American targets.

In moving toward war with China the Eisenhower administration virtually ignored the Soviet Union's potential responses. From the start of the crisis Washington doubted the credibility of Moscow's support for the Communist Chinese position. When Soviet party leader Nikita Khrushchev made a blustery speech in Beijing on China's National Day, October 1, 1954, in which he condemned American interference in China's affairs and supported the liberation of Taiwan, Eisenhower labeled the performance mere "bluffing.". . .

Eisenhower and Dulles in fact believed that Soviet influence over China was not as great as was commonly held in the United States, and that China was acting largely on its own in the crisis. In executive session with the House Committee on Foreign Affairs, Dulles observed, "As far as surface appearances go, the Soviet line has been less violent than the Chinese Communist line, and when judged only by superficial impressions, one would infer that their disposition is to hold back the Chinese Communists. They have, for instance, avoided any formal, explicit endorsement of [the Chinese] position with reference to the conquest and what they call liberation of Formosa." (The Soviet Union's ambassador to the United Nations, Yakov Malik, was spreading the word there that the Soviets were trying to restrain the Chinese but were having a difficult time, since the Chinese were so proud and sensitive about their recent emergence as a world power.) The leadership struggle in the Kremlin [following Josef Stalin's death] also confirmed for Dulles the correctness of the policy of pressure on the Communists. He suspected that the Soviet Union was overextended and having difficulties meeting the demands of the satellite countries, especially China's. He remarked to Foreign Minister George Yeh on February 10 that the strain on the Soviets "must be very great.". . .

Eisenhower was fully prepared, but reluctant, to use nuclear weapons in the Taiwan Strait crisis. Both he and Dulles feared damaging repercussions in Europe if they were used. The secretary of state told the president on March 11 that, for the moment, direct U.S. participation in the defense of the offshore islands, "particularly involving atomic missiles," should be avoided, but after negotiations about forming a European confederation were "buttoned up," they would have more freedom of action in Asia. Later in the day he and the president met with other officials and decided that they had to do everything possible to improve the Nationalists' defense capability to avoid the need for U.S. intervention. If the United States did enter the fight, Eisenhower indicated, it would do so first with conventional weapons; atomic weapons "should only come at the end." The administration considered the remaining days of March critical as the Nationalists completed their fortifications against the ever-growing Communist forces massing opposite the offshore islands. The United States blustered to put off the Communists and give more time to the Nationalists. In a speech on March 21 Dulles accused Beijing of being "dizzy with success" and an "acute and immediate threat." In the short run China might prove "more dangerous and provocative of war" than the Soviet Union. "The aggressive fanaticism of the Chinese Communist leaders," he added ominously, "presents a certain parallel to that of Hitler. Also, it contrasts to the *past* tactics of Soviet Communism." Dulles's emotional words were clearly calculated: he classed the Chinese Communists with the Nazis but explicitly distinguished Moscow from Beijing.

On March 25 Admiral Robert Carney, chief of staff of the Navy, leaked to the press that the United States had plans for an all-out attack on China. Carney said he himself expected that war might break out by April 15, the start of the Afro-Asian Conference in Bandung, Indonesia. Eisenhower was furious with Carney's disclosure and publicly tried to downplay his remarks without explicitly contradicting them. Privately Eisenhower conceded that Carney might be right about the need for the United States to fight, "because the Red Chinese appear to be completely indifferent as to human losses." U.S. military intelligence estimated that the Communists could assemble sufficient air, naval, and land capabilities in just two to three days to take "any or all" of the offshore islands from the Nationalists, barring U.S. intervention.

As Carney had revealed, the U.S. military planning envisaged extensive nuclear attacks on China. On March 31 General Curtis LeMay, commander of the Strategic Air Command, cabled General Nathan Twining, chief of staff of the Air Force. LeMay was personally familiar with China, having directed the firebombing of Japan from the mainland during World War II. His message read in part:

> Plans have been developed and are ready for immed execution by use of B-36 type acft [aircraft] based on Guam to deal with any eventuality involving Communist China. One wg [wing = 30 planes] is in pos at Guam now and two other wgs in the United States are on warning alert for this task. One of these two wgs can move to Guam immed. Guam has capability of supporting sixty B-36 type acft. These will have an immed capability for combat opns [operations]. . . . Target selections have been made, coordinated with other responsible comdrs and asgd [assigned] to B-36 crew.

The following day, according to the Chinese, eighteen U.S. warplanes in four different waves flew over Chinese territory in both the north and the south. The Chinese officially condemned the flights as "military provocations." . . .

In private, . . . the administration was considering extreme measures to end the crisis. Dulles met with his top advisers in the State Department and his brother Allen, director of the CIA, on March 28 to discuss what to do. They began by debating the possibility of again approaching the United Nations, but the idea got nowhere. Talk then centered on the military options open to the United States. The secretary of state proposed blockading the entire China coast to relieve the pressure on the offshore islands. Next, he raised for discussion the possibility of threatening a "generalized" attack with conventional and nuclear weapons, in response to any Chinese assault on Jinmen and Mazu, that would destroy China's "great POL dumps" [petroleum, oil, and lubricants] and the communication and rail lines "across the length and breadth of China." If the Chinese knew that this would be the American reaction, they might not attack, he argued. Robert Bowie, head of the PPS [Policy Planning Staff] and one of the more moderate elements toward China in the administration, suggested that the United States announce it would "from time to time" drop nuclear bombs on Jinmen and Mazu if they were captured by the Communists. Dulles thought this impractical: it would be a "considerable waste" of valuable weapons. The United States could not afford to "splurge" its nuclear arsenal, Dulles cautioned. In any case such a plan would only wind up killing "harmless" fishermen. But Dulles and his colleagues could not come up with any more-attractive idea.

Several days later Eisenhower decided to try one other maneuver. He thought the United States might seek to persuade Chiang to reduce his forces on the offshore islands—to recognize them as "outposts, not citadels"—and de-emphasize their importance to his government. If Chiang's prestige was less involved with the islands, the United States could gradually reduce its own commitment and concentrate on Taiwan and the Penghus. This might well minimize the impact of the loss of the offshore islands on Nationalist morale. Eisenhower presented these ideas to Dulles in a ten-page, single-spaced memo on April 5 and urged the secretary of state to come up with a specific course of action. . . .

Dulles flew to Augusta, Georgia, on April 17 for a private two-hour meeting with the president. The secretary presented the ideas that he, Deputy Secretary of Defense Robert Anderson, Admiral Radford, Under Secretary of State Herbert Hoover, Jr., Assistant Secretary of State [Walter] Robertson, and CIA Director Allen Dulles had developed in response to Eisenhower's April 5 memo. Eisenhower had wanted a way to de-emphasize the offshore islands, to make them into "outposts," but Dulles and his group had concluded that such a path was self-defeating. If the United States was not going to stop onshore Communist preparations for an attack on the islands, they were as good as lost. Even as "outposts" their capture would still be terribly destructive for the Nationalists. It would be better, Dulles argued, for the United States "to encourage a clean break"—get off the islands—and then blockade the China coast along the entire Taiwan Strait, some 500 miles. The position paper Dulles showed Eisenhower read: "Unless and until the Chicoms [Chinese Communists] in good faith renounce their avowed purpose to take Formosa by force, the United States and Chinats [Chinese Nationalists] will, as a measure of self-defense, institute a naval interdiction along the China Coast from and including Swatow in the south to approximately Wenchow in the north." The blockade would aim at stopping the Communists from building up their supplies and facilities for an attack against Taiwan, something they could not easily accomplish overland because of rough terrain. Dulles also proposed stationing nuclear weapons on Taiwan to demonstrate U.S. resolve. His plan thus combined a retreat with a wild counterattack and envisioned the eventual creation of two Chinas effectively separated by the Taiwan Strait.

Eisenhower, after some hesitation, approved Dulles's plan with a few revisions. The United States must not force Chiang into anything he did not want, he insisted; the Nationalists themselves should decide whether they would retain Jinmen and Mazu or give them up. By the end of the discussion, the two men were pleased with themselves, confident that their program "would immeasurably serve to consolidate world opinion" in favor of the United States. After the meeting Dulles spoke to reporters, saying that he and the president discussed questions related to Austria, Vietnam, and the "grave implications" of the offensive buildup of the Chinese Communists in the Taiwan Strait area. The two men, he announced, had concluded that peace "is now in grave jeopardy." Three days later, on April 20, Admiral Radford and Assistant Secretary of State Robertson left for Taipei to present the Dulles-Eisenhower plan to Chiang Kai-shek.

Before meeting with the generalissimo Radford and Robertson conferred with Ambassador Rankin to give him details of the proposal: if the Nationalists withdrew from Jinmen and Mazu, the United States would intercept all seaborne traffic of "a contraband or war-making character" and would "lay mine fields which would force coastwise junk traffic to come out where it also could be intercepted and controlled." Logistically the plan was feasible—the Seventh Fleet and elements of the Fifth Air Force were already in the area, and other naval forces in Okinawa and the Philippines were only twenty-four hours away. Rankin, who usually favored an aggressive policy toward the Chinese Communists and had supported the idea of a Nationalist blockade of the coast, was aghast. This proposal meant war, he told Radford and Robertson. How could the Communists accept a blockade of their coast or the mining of their territorial waters? Radford agreed with Rankin's characterization of the proposal, adding that it would only be a matter of time before Chinese aircraft attacked American ships. He had fully informed Eisenhower of this probable outcome, he said.

While the United States might have extracted itself from the precarious situation in the offshore islands with the evacuation and blockade, it would have doomed itself to a hell on the high seas. The Chinese Communists would never have renounced their claims over Taiwan or their option of using force to bring the island under their suzerainty (Beijing still has not ruled out such a possibility). A naval blockade had military advantages over a static defense of small islands vulnerable to Chinese ground forces, but the United States would have had to maintain a costly act of war indefinitely. China certainly would not have let such an affront go unchallenged.

Fortunately, neither the rest of the world nor the Chinese Communists were ever required to respond to the Dulles-Eisenhower plan. Despite several days of talks Chiang refused to entertain the idea of reducing his forces on the islands, let alone abandoning them to the Communists. Radford and Robertson tried to press Chiang by telling him the United States was withdrawing its secret January 31 pledge to join in the defense of Jinmen and Mazu, though Chiang could still count on U.S. logistical support. Chiang still would not budge. Rankin later surmised that the generalissimo rejected the blockade plan because he distrusted the Americans. After having been betrayed (in his view) by the United States during the evacuation of the Dachens, Chiang could hardly be expected to be receptive to a proposal that depended completely on Washington's reliability.

The initiative that finally ended the crisis came not from Washington but unexpectedly from the Chinese Communists. On April 23, just before Robertson and Radford talked with Chiang, Premier Zhou Enlai dramatically announced at the Bandung Conference that his government wanted no war with the United States. "The Chinese people are friendly to the American people," he said, and China was willing to negotiate with the United States for the reduction of tensions in the Taiwan area. On April 26 Dulles, seizing the chance to extricate the United States from its predicament, indicated that Washington would talk with Beijing about a ceasefire. The shelling soon tapered off, and the area quieted. . . .

In his biography of Eisenhower Stephen Ambrose lauds the president's handling of the crisis as a *"tour de force,"* hailing as the key his "deliberate ambiguity and deception" on the stand he would take if the islands were besieged. Ambrose supports the historian Robert Divine's praise of Eisenhower: "The beauty of Eisenhower's policy is that to this day no one can be sure whether or not he would have responded militarily to an invasion of the offshore islands, and whether he would have used nuclear weapons." Ambrose embellishes this, claiming, "the full truth is that Eisenhower himself did not know." But these conclusions were premature; they are contradicted by the evidence now available. Between January 31 and

April 24, 1955, the United States was formally pledged to support the defense of Jinmen and Mazu. Even before January 31 Eisenhower expressed his belief that the islands were essential to the basic morale and viability of the Nationalist government. His distinction between a Communist attack aimed at taking just Jinmen and Mazu and one that was a prelude to an assault on Taiwan may have seemed real in his own mind, but it was hardly realistic.

Eisenhower, it has been suggested, successfully kept his options open throughout the crisis. But in fact his obdurate attachment to Chiang (Chiang's suspicions of American untrustworthiness notwithstanding) steadily reduced U.S. flexibility. If the Communists had committed sufficient forces to take Jinmen or Mazu in March or April 1955, Eisenhower could not have stood aside and watched: he was clearly pledged to intervene. And he was confident the Communists understood that he would use whatever military means were necessary to stop them. After all, as he told the NSC on March 31, one ought not underestimate their sanity. As far as the president himself was concerned, there was no question in his mind what he would do in the event of an attack in force. The United States would have gone to war. . . .

Eisenhower worked closely with Secretary of State Dulles throughout the crisis and paid close attention to the details of military deployment, as well as the diplomatic problems with nervous allies. And because he was not a detached chief executive, he must bear direct responsibility for leading the country dangerously close to war. U.S.-China hostilities might have occurred in one of two ways. First, the ambiguity of his public stand on the offshore islands (in the apparent absence of any attempt to send secret messages to Beijing) might very well have allowed the Communists to miscalculate American intentions and thus have invited an attack. The result, given Washington's secret commitments to Chiang *and* the administration's own private determination to retain the islands, would have been armed conflict between the United States and China. Second, war would certainly have come if Chiang had accepted the evacuation-blockade plan. It is inconceivable that the Chinese Communists would have acquiesced in such a violation of their sovereignty by the United States.

Finally, it is worth noting that Washington's brandishing of the nuclear cudgel during the crisis provoked a development that would later haunt the United States: Eisenhower's threats apparently helped convince the Chinese Communists that they needed nuclear weapons of their own. In January 1955, in the midst of the offshore crisis and under American pressure, Mao Zedong and other top PRC [People's Republic of China] leaders decided to launch China's nuclear program. The Eisenhower administration's use of nuclear deterrence to protect territory that even Dulles admitted was never considered "essential" to American interests came at great cost.

Several months after the end of the offshore confrontation, John Foster Dulles, in a famous article in *Life* magazine, hailed the administration's handling of the crisis as a successful example of "brinksmanship." His evaluation, obviously, was myopic and much too hasty. That war had been avoided was due more to Chinese Communist caution and to luck than to the diplomatic skills of President Eisenhower and his secretary of state.

✖ *F U R T H E R   R E A D I N G*

Charles C. Alexander, *Holding the Line* (1975)
Stephen E. Ambrose, *Eisenhower: The President* (1984)
Robert Axelrod, *The Evolution of Cooperation* (1984)
Howard Ball, *Justice Downwind: America's Atomic Testing Program in the 1950s* (1986)
Michael R. Beschloss, *Mayday: Eisenhower, Khrushchev, and the U2 Affair* (1986)
H. W. Brands, "The Age of Vulnerability: Eisenhower and the National Insecurity State,"
     American Historical Review, 94 (1989), 963–989
————, *Cold Warriors* (1988)
McGeorge Bundy, *Danger and Survival* (1988)
Blanche Weisen Cook, *The Declassified Eisenhower* (1981)
Robert A. Divine, *Blowing on the Wind: The Nuclear Test Ban Debate* (1978)
————, *The Sputnik Challenge* (1993)
Michael Evangelista, "Cooperation Theory and Disarmament Negotiations in the 1950s,"
     World Politics, 42 (1990), 502–528
————, *Innovation and the Arms Race* (1988)
Lawrence Freedman, *The Evolution of Nuclear Strategy* (1981)
John Lewis Gaddis, *The Long Peace* (1987)
————, *Strategies of Containment* (1982)
Alexander L. George and Richard Smoke, *Deterrence in American Foreign Policy* (1974)
Alexander L. George et al., eds., *U.S.-Soviet Security Cooperation* (1988)
Fred I. Greenstein, *The Hidden-Hand Presidency* (1982)
Morton H. Halperin, *Nuclear Fallacy* (1987)
Greg Herken, *Counsels of War* (1985)
Richard G. Hewlett and Jack M. Holl, *Atoms for Peace and War* (1989)
David Holloway, *The Soviet Union and the Arms Race* (1983)
Townsend Hoopes, *The Devil and John Foster Dulles* (1973)
Samuel P. Huntington, *The Common Defense* (1961)
Richard H. Immerman, "Confessions of an Eisenhower Revisionist," *Diplomatic History,*
     14 (1990), 319–342
————, ed., *John Foster Dulles and the Diplomacy of the Cold War* (1990)
Robert Jervis, *The Meaning of the Nuclear Revolution* (1989)
Fred Kaplan, *The Wizards of Armageddon* (1983)
Milton S. Katz, *Ban the Bomb: A History of SANE* (1986)
Douglas Kinnard, *President Eisenhower and Strategy Management* (1977)
Henry Kissinger, *Nuclear Weapons and Foreign Policy* (1957)
Stewart W. Leslie, *The Cold War and American Science* (1992)
Peter Lyon, *Eisenhower* (1974)
Walter A. McDougall, *The Heavens and the Earth* (1985)
Michael Mandlebaum, *The Nuclear Revolution* (1981)
Frederick W. Marks III, *Power and Peace* (1993)
George T. Mazuzan, "American Nuclear Policy," in John M. Carroll and George C. Her-
     ring, eds., *Modern American Diplomacy* (1986), pp. 147–163
Richard A. Melanson and David Mayer, eds., *Reevaluating Eisenhower* (1987)
Charles R. Morris, *Iron Destinies, Lost Opportunities* (1988)
John Newhouse, *War and Peace in the Nuclear Age* (1988)
Chester J. Pach, Jr., and Elmo Richardson, *The Presidency of Dwight D. Eisenhower* (1991)
Herbert S. Parmet, *Eisenhower and the Great Crusades* (1972)
Richard Pfau, *No Sacrifice Too Great: The Life of Lewis L. Strauss* (1984)
Joseph E. Pilate et al., *Atoms for Peace* (1986)
Ronald E. Powaski, *March to Armageddon* (1987)
Ronald W. Pruessen, *John Foster Dulles* (1982)
David Alan Rosenberg, "The Origins of Overkill," *International Security,* 7 (1983), 3–71
————, "Reality and Responsibility: Power and Process in the Making of United States Nu-
     clear Strategy, 1945–68," *Journal of Strategic Studies,* 9 (1986), 35–52

Walt W. Rostow, *Open Skies* (1982)

Thomas F. Soapes, "A Cold Warrior Seeks Peace: Eisenhower's Strategy for Nuclear Disarmament," *Diplomatic History,* 4 (1980), 55–71

Strobe Talbott, *The Master of the Game: Paul Nitze and the Nuclear Peace* (1988)

Marc Trachtenberg, *History and Strategy* (1991)

———, "A 'Wasting Asset': American Strategy and Shifting Nuclear Balance, 1949–1954," *International Security* (1988–1989), 5–49

Sheldon Ungar, *The Rise and Fall of Nuclearism* (1992)

Samuel F. Wells, "The Origins of Massive Retaliation," *Political Science Quarterly,* 96 (1981), 31–52

Samuel Williamson and Steven L. Rearden, eds., *The Origins of U.S. Nuclear Strategy* (1993)

Cuba and the Missile Crisis

In October 1962 American U-2 reconnaissance planes photographed missile sites installed by the Soviets on the Caribbean island of Cuba. The missiles could carry nuclear weapons, and they could reach the United States. After meeting with his advisers and deciding to announce U.S. policy in a television address, President John F. Kennedy demanded withdrawal of the missiles and imposed a blockade around Cuba. A chilling war scare gripped Moscow, Havana, and Washington—and terrified the world. This was the closest the United States and the Soviet Union had ever come to nuclear war. Exchanges of diplomatic letters, rallying of allies, exhausting meetings, military preparations, and operational accidents soon followed.

In the end, deeply frightened by the prospect of nuclear disaster, Premier Nikita Khrushchev and President Kennedy settled the crisis without consulting Cuban premier Fidel Castro. The United States promised not to invade Cuba (as it had done using Cuban exiles in April 1961, at the Bay of Pigs) and assented to the removal of its Jupiter missiles from Turkey. In return, the Soviet Union agreed to withdraw its missiles from Cuba. The U.S. no-invasion pledge in fact never took effect because Castro refused to permit U.S.-stipulated United Nations follow-up inspections. But the Soviets dismantled their missiles and sent them home, and the Jupiters in Turkey also came down.

Beneath the Cuban missile crisis—or the "Caribbean crisis," as the Russians have called it—lay years of Cuban-American antagonism. On taking power in 1959, Fidel Castro launched a revolution that challenged major U.S. interests on the island, including mob-run casinos, U.S. military missions, and investments worth a billion dollars. Castro decried U.S. hegemony and Cuban dependency, and he vowed a restructuring of economic and political life to reduce U.S. influence that had grown especially since the interventionist Platt Amendment at the start of the century. Washington became alarmed, too, because the Cuban Revolution gained popularity throughout the Western Hemisphere and because Castro declared as one of his missions the spread of revolution across Latin America. In 1960 economic relations deteriorated severely when the United States instituted trade sanctions. The Cubans increasingly turned for help to the Soviet Union, which became the island's economic and military partner. In January 1961 the United States broke diplomatic relations with Havana. In 1961–1962 came the Bay of Pigs expedition, covert operations designed to cripple the Cuban economy through sabotage, Central Intelligence Agency (CIA) assassination plots against Castro, diplomatic efforts to isolate Cuba, and military maneuvers and plans that seemed to portend a U.S. invasion. Because these regional events occurred during a particularly tense time in the Cold War, the U.S.-Cuba contest held international consequences.

In recent years a greater portion of the documentary record on the missile crisis in the archives of the United States, Russia, and Cuba has opened for research, and, using newly released documents, crisis participants have gathered in meetings to reexamine the 1962 confrontation. Several sets of questions remain central to understanding this dangerous episode in world history, beginning with questions about the origins of the crisis. Why did this nuclear showdown occur in Cuba and not somewhere else? Which nation was most responsible for generating the missile crisis? To what extent are the sources of the missile crisis found in the U.S.-Cuba contest? Why did Cuba welcome the Soviet missiles? Was Castro reasonable or off base in his fear that the United States would invade his country? What did the Soviets hope to gain from their installation of nuclear-tipped missiles in Cuba? Did the missiles in Cuba change the strategic balance of power, giving the U.S.S.R. a stronger position?

The second set of questions studies the management of the crisis. How well did the decisionmaking processes in Washington, Moscow, and Havana work? How well did the three belligerents communicate with one another? Why did Kennedy initially shun private negotiations in favor of public confrontation? Why did he choose a naval blockade over an air strike and military invasion? Does Kennedy's handling of the emergency rank as an excellent example of rational crisis management? To what extent should scholars study the personalities of the participants to understand the outcome of the crisis? What role did miscalculations, human error, and operational accidents play in the crisis? Just how dangerous was the episode—how close to nuclear war did the world come?

The third set of issues centers on the settlement of the crisis. Why did Kennedy and Khrushchev compromise in the end? Why did they exclude Castro from their agreement? What reasons did Castro have for rejecting the settlement? Why did all three leaders fail to write a formal agreement? Why did Kennedy promise to dismantle the U.S. Jupiter missiles in Turkey yet insist that this agreement not become public? What if Khrushchev had refused to pull his missiles out of Cuba? What next? Finally: Did anybody win?

The last questions speak to the aftermath: Why did the crisis continue into late November as the three nations squabbled over Soviet bombers and inspections? What lessons did leaders draw from their experience in the Cuban missile crisis? To what extent did the outcome change the Cold War, the nuclear-arms race, or the U.S.-Cuba relationship? Why did the United States enter new crises with Cuba and the Soviet Union in 1970 and 1979?

✖ D O C U M E N T S

The first document is part of a November 1975 report by the U.S. Senate Select Committee to Study Governmental Operations with Respect to Intelligence Activities. Chaired by Senator Frank Church of Idaho, this committee detailed CIA assassination plots against Fidel Castro. The second document presents President Kennedy's hard-hitting views after the failed Bay of Pigs invasion. His April 20, 1961, speech vowed greater toughness. The third selection constitutes the initial guidelines for Operation Mongoose, the CIA's conspiracy to overthrow the Castro government through "indigenous sources" and possibly U.S. military intervention. President Kennedy apparently approved this secret document, and his brother, Attorney General Robert F. Kennedy, became the primary overseer of the spoiling operation.

In the fourth document, General Anatoly I. Gribkov, a member of the Operations Directorate of the Soviet General Staff in 1962 responsible for installing the missiles in Cuba, recalls Soviet motives, calculations, and military preparedness. In his comments at a retrospective conference of scholars and crisis participants in Havana in January 1992, Gribkov revealed that tactical nuclear weapons had arrived in Cuba in 1962 and that the Soviet commander in Cuba had authority to use them if the United States invaded. The fifth selection is a speech by Cuban president Osvaldo Dorticos. In these remarks, delivered to the United Nations on October 18, 1962, just a few days before the crisis publicly erupted, Dorticos defended Cuba's military buildup as necessary to counter U.S. aggression.

The sixth document includes significant parts of the transcribed record of Kennedy's first two meetings with his high-level advisers on October 16, 1962, the day intelligence officials presented him with photographs showing Soviet missile sites under construction in Cuba. In the seventh document, a record of another senior advisers' meeting on October 17 (from the notes of CIA head John A. McCone), Charles E. Bohlen, former ambassador to the Soviet Union and then ambassador to France, unsuccessfully argues the case for private diplomacy to defuse the crisis. The next reading is Kennedy's October 22 television address to the nation and the world. The president insisted on removal of the missiles and announced the U.S. "quarantine" of Cuba. On October 26 Premier Khrushchev replied to a Kennedy letter of the preceding day that had reiterated the U.S. case against the missile bases. The Khrushchev letter, reprinted here as the ninth selection, denounces the blockade and claims that the Soviet weapons had been sent to defend Cuba against a U.S. invasion. The Soviet leader also offered a deal: He would remove the "armaments" from Cuba if the United States pledged not to invade Cuba. That same day, Fidel Castro informed Khrushchev (the tenth document, from Cuban records) that Cuba expected a U.S. attack and urged him to resist it, perhaps with nuclear weapons.

On October 27 Khrushchev sent another letter to Kennedy, included here as the eleventh document. Adding to his earlier request for a no-invasion promise, Khrushchev asked for the removal of American Jupiter missiles from Turkey. President Kennedy again convened his advisers—now called the Executive Committee (ExCom)—to discuss this new request. A record of part of their meeting of October 27 is found in the twelfth document. Kennedy decided to pull the Jupiters out of Turkey; Robert Kennedy soon privately conveyed this concession to the Soviets, and the crisis dissipated. The last selection, from Russian archives, reports conversations between the high-ranking Soviet official Anastas I. Mikoyan and Fidel Castro in Havana on November 3, 4, and 5. Standing out in these intense exchanges are Soviet claims of victory and Cuban protests against both superpowers for their ending the crisis without consulting the Cuban government.

CIA Assassination Plots Against Fidel Castro
(1960–1965), 1975

We have found concrete evidence of at least eight plots involving the CIA to assassinate Fidel Castro from 1960 to 1965. Although some of the assassination plots did not advance beyond the stage of planning and preparation, one plot, involving the use of underworld figures, reportedly twice progressed to the point of sending poison pills to Cuba and dispatching teams to commit the deed. Another plot involved furnishing weapons and other assassination devices to a Cuban dissident.

The proposed assassination devices ran the gamut from high-powered rifles to poison pills, poison pens, deadly bacterial powders, and other devices which strain the imagination. . . .

Efforts against Castro did not begin with assassination attempts.

From March through August 1960, during the last year of the Eisenhower Administration, the CIA considered plans to undermine Castro's charismatic appeal by sabotaging his speeches. According to the 1967 Report of the CIA's Inspector General, an official in the Technical Services Division (TSD) recalled discussing a scheme to spray Castro's broadcasting studio with a chemical which produced effects similar to LSD, but the scheme was rejected because the chemical was unreliable. During this period, TSD impregnated a box of cigars with a chemical which produced temporary disorientation, hoping to induce Castro to smoke one of the cigars before delivering a speech. The Inspector General also reported a plan to destroy Castro's image as "The Beard" by dusting his shoes with thallium salts, a strong depilatory that would cause his beard to fall out. The depilatory was to be administered during a trip outside Cuba, when it was anticipated Castro would leave his shoes outside the door of his hotel room to be shined. TSD procured the chemical and tested it on animals, but apparently abandoned the scheme because Castro cancelled his trip. . . .

A notation in the records of the Operations Division, CIA's Office of Medical Services, indicates that on August 16, 1960, an official was given a box of Castro's favorite cigars with instructions to treat them with lethal poison. The cigars were contaminated with a botulinum toxin so potent that a person would die after putting one in his mouth. The official reported that the cigars were ready on October 7, 1960; TSD notes indicate that they were delivered to an unidentified person on February 13, 1961. The record does not disclose whether an attempt was made to pass the cigars to Castro.

In August 1960, the CIA took steps to enlist members of the criminal underworld with gambling syndicate contacts to aid in assassinating Castro. . . .

The earliest concrete evidence of the operation is a conversation between DDP [Deputy Director for Plans Richard] Bissell and Colonel Sheffield Edwards, Director of the Office of Security. Edwards recalled that Bissell asked him to locate someone who could assassinate Castro. Bissell confirmed that he requested Edwards to find someone to assassinate Castro and believed that Edwards raised the idea of contacting members of a gambling syndicate operating in Cuba.

Edwards assigned the mission to the Chief of the Operational Support Division of the Office of Security. The Support Chief recalled that Edwards had said that he and Bissell were looking for someone to "eliminate" or "assassinate" Castro.

Edwards and the Support Chief decided to rely on Robert A. Maheu to recruit someone "tough enough" to handle the job. Maheu was an ex-FBI agent who had entered into a career as a private investigator in 1954. A former FBI associate of Maheu's was employed in the CIA's Office of Security and had arranged for the CIA to use Maheu in several sensitive covert operations in which "he didn't want to have an Agency person or a government person get caught.". . .

Sometime in late August or early September 1960, the Support Chief approached Maheu about the proposed operation. As Maheu recalls the conversation, the Support Chief asked him to contact John Rosselli, an underworld figure with possible gambling contacts in Las Vegas, to determine if he would participate in a plan to "dispose" of Castro. The Support Chief testified, on the other hand, that it was Maheu who raised the idea of using Rosselli.

Maheu had known Rosselli since the late 1950's. Although Maheu claims not to have been aware of the extent of Rosselli's underworld connections and activities, he recalled that "it was certainly evident to me that he was able to accomplish things in Las Vegas when nobody else seemed to get the same kind of attention.". . .

According to Rosselli, he and Maheu met at the Brown Derby Restaurant in Beverly Hills in early September 1960. Rosselli testified that Maheu told him that "high government officials" needed his cooperation in getting rid of Castro, and that he asked him to help recruit Cubans to do the job. Maheu's recollection of that meeting was that "I informed him that I had been asked by my Government to solicit his cooperation in this particular venture."

Maheu stated that Rosselli "was very hesitant about participating in the project, and he finally said that he felt that he had an obligation to his government, and he finally agreed to participate." Maheu and Rosselli both testified that Rosselli insisted on meeting with a representative of the Government.

A meeting was arranged for Maheu and Rosselli with the Support Chief at the Plaza Hotel in New York. The Inspector General's Report placed the meeting on September 14, 1960. Rosselli testified that he could not recall the precise date of the meeting, but that it had occurred during Castro's visit to the United Nations, which the New York Times Index places from September 18 through September 28, 1960.

The Support Chief testified that he was introduced to Rosselli as a business associate of Maheu. He said that Maheu told Rosselli that Maheu represented international business interests which were pooling money to pay for the assassination of Castro. Rosselli claimed that Maheu told him at that time that the Support Chief was with the CIA.

It was arranged that Rosselli would go to Florida and recruit Cubans for the operation. Edwards informed Bissell that contact had been made with the gambling syndicate.

During the week of September 24, 1960 the Support Chief, Maheu, and Rosselli met in Miami to work out the details of the operation. Rosselli used the cover name "John Rawlston" and represented himself to the Cuban contacts as an agent of ". . . some business interests of Wall Street that had . . . nickel interests and properties around in Cuba, and I was getting financial assistance from them."

Maheu handled the details of setting up the operation and keeping the Support Chief informed of developments. After Rosselli and Maheu had been in Miami for a short time, and certainly prior to October 18, Rosselli introduced Maheu to two individuals on whom Rosselli intended to rely: "Sam Gold," who would serve as a "back-up man," or "key" man and "Joe," whom "Gold" said would serve as a courier to Cuba and make arrangements there. The Support Chief, who was using the name "Jim Olds," said he had met "Sam" and "Joe" once, and then only briefly.

The Support Chief testified that he learned the true identities of his associates one morning when Maheu called and asked him to examine the "Parade" supplement to the *Miami Times*. An article on the Attorney General's ten-most-wanted criminals list revealed that "Sam Gold" was Momo Salvatore Giancana, a Chicago-based gangster, and "Joe" was Santos Trafficante, the Cosa Nostra chieftain in Cuba. The Support Chief reported his discovery to Edwards, but did not know whether Edwards reported this fact to his superiors. The Support Chief testified that this incident occurred after "we were up to our ears in it," a month or so after Giancana had been brought into the operation, but prior to giving the poison pills to Rosselli.

Maheu recalled that it was Giancana's job to locate someone in Castro's entourage who could accomplish the assassination, and that he met almost daily with Giancana over a substantial period of time. Although Maheu described Giancana as playing a "key role," Rosselli claimed that none of the Cubans eventually used in the operation were acquired through Giancana's contacts. . . .

The Inspector General's Report described conversations among Bissell, Edwards, and the Chief of the Technical Services Division (TSD), concerning the most effective method of poisoning Castro. There is some evidence that Giancana or Rosselli originated the idea of depositing a poison pill in Castro's drink to give the "asset" a chance to escape. The Support Chief recalled Rosselli's request for something "nice and clean, without getting into any kind of out and out ambushing," preferably a poison that would disappear without a trace. The Inspector General's Report cited the Support Chief as stating that the Agency had first considered a "gangland-style killing" in which Castro would be gunned down. Giancana reportedly opposed the idea because it would be difficult to recruit someone for such a dangerous operation, and suggested instead the use of poison.

Edwards rejected the first batch of pills prepared by TSD because they would not dissolve in water. A second batch, containing botulinum toxin, "did the job expected of them" when tested on monkeys. The Support Chief received the pills from TSD, probably in February 1961, with assurances that they were lethal, and then gave them to Rosselli.

The record clearly establishes that the pills were given to a Cuban for delivery to the island some time prior to the Bay of Pigs invasion in mid-April 1961. There are discrepancies in the record, however, concerning whether one or two attempts were made during that period, and the precise date on which the passage[s] occurred. The Inspector General's Report states that in late February or March 1961, Rosselli reported to the Support Chief that the pills had been delivered to an official close to Castro who may have received kickbacks from the gambling interests. The Report states that the official returned the pills after a few weeks, perhaps because he had lost his position in the Cuban Government, and thus access to Castro, before he received the pills. The Report concludes that yet another attempt was made in April 1961, with the aid of a leading figure in the Cuban exile movement. . . .

In early April 1962, Harvey, who testified that he was acting on "explicit orders" from [Director of Operations Richard] Helms, requested Edwards to put him in touch with Rosselli. The Support Chief first introduced [Operation Mongoose task force chief William K.] Harvey to Rosselli in Miami, where Harvey told Rosselli to maintain his Cuban contacts, but not to deal with Maheu or Giancana, whom he had decided were "untrustworthy" and "surplus." The Support Chief recalled that initially Rosselli did not trust Harvey although they subsequently developed a close friendship.

Harvey, the Support Chief and Rosselli met for a second time in New York on April 8–9, 1962. A notation made during this time in the files of the Technical Services Division indicates that four poison pills were given to the Support Chief on April 18, 1962. The pills were passed to Harvey, who arrived in Miami on April 21, and found Rosselli already in touch with the same Cuban who had been involved in the pre–Bay of Pigs pill passage. He gave the pills to Rosselli, explaining that "these would work anywhere and at any time with anything." Rosselli testified that he told Harvey that the Cubans intended to use the pills to assassinate Che Guevara as well as Fidel and Raul Castro. According to Rosselli's testimony, Harvey approved of the targets, stating "everything is all right, what they want to do."

The Cuban requested arms and equipment as a *quid pro quo* for carrying out the assassination operation. With the help of the CIA's Miami station which ran covert operations against Cuba (JM/WAVE), Harvey procured explosives, detonators, rifles, handguns, radios, and boat radar costing about $5,000. Harvey and the chief of the JM/WAVE station rented a U-Haul Truck under an assumed name and delivered the equipment to a parking lot. The keys were given to Rosselli, who watched the delivery with the Support Chief from across the street. The truckload of equipment was finally picked up by either the Cuban or Rosselli's agent. Harvey testified that the arms "could" have been for use in the assassination attempt, but that they were not given to the Cuban solely for that purpose.

Rosselli kept Harvey informed of the operation's progress. Sometime in May 1962, he reported that the pills and guns had arrived in Cuba. On June 21, he told Harvey that the Cuban had dispatched a three-man team to Cuba. The Inspector General's report described the team's mission as "vague" and conjectured that the team would kill Castro or recruit others to do the job, using the poison pills if the opportunity arose.

Harvey met Rosselli in Miami on September 7 and 11, 1962. The Cuban was reported to be preparing to send in another three-man team to penetrate Castro's bodyguard. Harvey was told that the pills, referred to as "the medicine," were still "safe" in Cuba.

Harvey testified that by this time he had grave doubts about whether the operation would ever take place, and told Rosselli that "there's not much likelihood that this is going anyplace, or that it should be continued." The second team never left for Cuba, claiming that "conditions" in Cuba were not right. During early January 1963, Harvey paid Rosselli $2,700 to defray the Cuban's expenses. Harvey terminated the operation in mid-February 1963. At a meeting with Rosselli in Los Angeles, it was agreed that Rosselli would taper off his communications with the Cubans. Rosselli testified that he simply broke off contact with the Cubans. However, he never informed them that the offer of $150,000 for Castro's assassination had been withdrawn. . . .

As [for the question of authorization], both Helms and the high Kennedy Administration officials who testified agreed that no direct order was ever given for Castro's assassination and that no senior Administration officials, including McCone, were informed about the assassination activity. Helms testified, however, that he believed the assassination activity was permissible and that it was within the scope of authority given to the Agency. McCone and other Kennedy Administration officials disagreed, testifying that assassination was impermissible without a direct order and that Castro's assassination was not within the bounds of the MONGOOSE operation [the covert U.S. operation designed to undermine the Castro government].

As DDP, Helms was in charge of covert operations when the poison pills were given to Rosselli in Miami in April 1962. Helms had succeeded to this post following Bissell's retirement in February 1962. He testified that after the Bay of Pigs:

> Those of us who were still [in the agency] were enormously anxious to try and be successful at what we were being asked to do by what was then a relatively new Administration. We wanted to earn our spurs with the President and with other officers of the Kennedy Administration.

President John F. Kennedy Vows to "Show Our Will" After the Bay of Pigs, 1961

Any unilateral American intervention, in the absence of an external attack upon ourselves or an ally, would have been contrary to our traditions and to our international obligations. But let the record show that our restraint is not inexhaustible. Should it ever appear that the inter-American doctrine of non-interference merely conceals or excuses a policy of nonaction—if the nations of this Hemisphere should fail to meet their commitments against outside Communist penetration—then I want it clearly understood that this Government will not hesitate in meeting its primary obligations which are to the security of our Nation!

Should that time ever come, we do not intend to be lectured on "intervention" by those whose character was stamped for all time on the bloody streets of Budapest! Nor would we expect or accept the same outcome which this small band of gallant Cuban refugees must have known that they were chancing, determined as they were against heavy odds to pursue their courageous attempts to regain their Island's freedom.

But Cuba is not an island unto itself; and our concern is not ended by mere expressions of nonintervention or regret. This is not the first time in either ancient or recent history that a small band of freedom fighters has engaged the armor of totalitarianism.

It is not the first time that Communist tanks have rolled over gallant men and women fighting to redeem the independence of their homeland. Nor is it by any means the final episode in the eternal struggle of liberty against tyranny, anywhere on the face of the globe, including Cuba itself. . . .

Meanwhile we will not accept Mr. Castro's attempts to blame this nation for the hatred [with] which his onetime supporters now regard his repression. But there are from this sobering episode useful lessons for us all to learn. Some may be still obscure, and await further information. Some are clear today.

First, it is clear that the forces of communism are not to be underestimated, in Cuba or anywhere else in the world. The advantages of a police state—its use of mass terror and arrests to prevent the spread of free dissent—cannot be overlooked by those who expect the fall of every fanatic tyrant. If the self-discipline of the free cannot match the iron discipline of the mailed fist—in economic, political, scientific and all the other kinds of struggles as well as the military—then the peril to freedom will continue to rise.

Secondly, it is clear that this Nation, in concert with all the free nations of this hemisphere, must take an ever closer and more realistic look at the menace of external Communist intervention and domination in Cuba. The American people are not complacent about Iron Curtain tanks and planes less than 90 miles from their shore. But a nation of Cuba's size is less a threat to our survival than it is a base for subverting the survival of other free nations throughout the hemisphere. It is not primarily our interest or our security but theirs which is now, today, in the greater peril. It is for their sake as well as our own that we must show our will.

The evidence is clear—and the hour is late. We and our Latin friends will have to face the fact that we cannot postpone any longer the real issue of survival of freedom in this hemisphere itself. On that issue, unlike perhaps some others, there can be no middle ground. Together we must build a hemisphere where freedom can flourish; and where any free nation under outside attack of any kind can be assured that all of our resources stand ready to respond to any request for assistance.

Third, and finally, it is clearer than ever that we face a relentless struggle in every corner of the globe that goes far beyond the clash of armies or even nuclear armaments. The armies are there, and in large numbers. The nuclear armaments are there. But they serve primarily as the shield behind which subversion, infiltration, and a host of other tactics steadily advance, picking off vulnerable areas one by one in situations which do not permit our own armed intervention. . . .

We dare not fail to see the insidious nature of this new and deeper struggle. We dare not fail to grasp the new concepts, the new tools, the new sense of urgency we will need to combat it—whether in Cuba or South Viet-Nam. And we dare not fail to realize that this struggle is taking place every day, without fanfare, in thousands of villages and markets—day and night—and in classrooms all over the globe.

The message of Cuba, of Laos, of the rising din of Communist voices in Asia and Latin America—these messages are all the same. The complacent, the self-indulgent, the soft societies are about to be swept away with the debris of history. Only the strong, only the industrious, only the determined, only the courageous, only the visionary who determine the real nature of our struggle can possibly survive.

Guidelines for Operation Mongoose, 1962

1. Operation Mongoose will be developed on the following assumptions:
   a. In undertaking to cause the overthrow of the target government, the U.S. will make maximum use of indigenous resources, internal and external, but recognizes that final success will require decisive U.S. military intervention.
   b. Such indigenous resources as are developed will be used to prepare for and justify this intervention, and thereafter to facilitate and support it.
2. The immediate priority objective of U.S. efforts during the coming months will be the acquisition of hard intelligence on the target area. Concurrently, all

other political, economic and covert actions will be undertaken short of those reasonably calculated to inspire a revolt within the target area, or other development which would require armed U.S. intervention. These actions, insofar as possible, will be consistent with overt policies of isolating the [two words illegible on the document but probably are "Cuban leader"] and of neutralizing his influence in the Western Hemisphere.

General Anatoly I. Gribkov Recalls
the Soviet Military Buildup in Cuba (1962), 1992

As you are all well aware, according to our military assessments, a critical situation had developed after the events at Playa Girón, or the Bay of Pigs [17–19 April 1961]. Our problem was to determine how we could help Cuba defend its liberty and its sovereignty. The Soviet government decided to provide Cuba with military assistance, and instructed the High Command, in the middle of May 1962, to prepare a proposal on an operational plan and a force structure to assist the Cuban military in securing the defense of Cuban territory. . . . In the preamble of the agreement [of July 1962], it said—and I would like you to pay attention—"It is necessary and has been decided to take the necessary steps for the joint defense of the legitimate rights of the people of Cuba and the Soviet Union, taking into account the urgent need to adopt measures to guarantee mutual security, in view of the possibility of an imminent attack against the Republic of Cuba and the Soviet Union." As you can see in this draft agreement, there was mention of the defense of the interest of the Soviet Union. This agreement was drafted and examined by the governments of both states. The necessary amendments were made, and the agreement, owing to circumstance, was initialled but not signed by the representatives of Cuba and the Soviet Union.

We presented our government with a proposed plan to deploy troops and equipment in Cuba, but we had to consider how we were going to represent the operation. Our cover was that we were going to carry out a strategic exercise through the deployment of Soviet troops in the north. The troops themselves were later told that they were going to go to Cuba to defend the island's independence. The name of the operation was "Anadyr." That is the name of a river in the northern region of our country, in a very cold region. Well, this story, I would say, allowed us to prepare the troops to be deployed in Cuba.

What was the force that we would have to train in our country in a very short span of time and transport to the other side of the ocean? This was its composition:

• A medium-range missile division. We saw this unit as a means to prevent aggression; I repeat, as a means to deter aggression. This division was made up of five regiments. Three were R-12 [NATO designation SS-4] regiments, with missiles whose range was 2,500 km (24 launchers with a complement of 1½ missiles for each launcher). Two were R-14 [SS-5] missile regiments (sixteen launchers,

James G. Blight, Bruce J. Allyn, and David A. Welch, *Cuba on the Brink: Castro, the Missile Crisis, and the Soviet Collapse*. N.Y.: Pantheon Books, 1993. Pp. 57–62, with deletions.

also 1½ missiles per launcher). Forty launchers were foreseen in all, together with the appropriate number of missiles [sixty]. I would like to add that at the beginning of the crisis—that is, on October 22nd—three R-12 regiments were already in Cuba, and two regiment sites were already laid out in their deployment areas. The third regiment site was under construction. The two R-14 regiments were still en route at sea, and in accordance with the instructions of the Soviet government, returned to the Soviet Union.

• Two air defense missile divisions comprised of twenty-four missile sites: 144 S-75 [NATO designation SA-2] launchers. The Americans are probably familiar with these data, but I can repeat their range (65 km) and altitude (100 m to 30 km).

• Four motorized rifle regiments, reinforced by three tactical nuclear missile batteries—six launchers for *Luna* [NATO designation FROG, or Free Rocket Over Ground] missiles with a 60 km range. We initially considered calling these units brigades, but then we changed our minds and decided to call them regiments that we were going to deploy there to defend the shores and the missile sites, jointly with the Cuban troops.

• The Air Force had a regiment of forty MiG-21 aircraft in Cuba; thirty[-three] tactical aircraft (Il-28s); and a separate naval squadron of nine Il-28 aircraft. At the onset of the crisis, only six planes had been assembled, and only a few flights had been made.

• Two regiments of tactical cruise missiles were also provided. In each regiment there were ten launchers: one for training, and nine for combat. There were eighteen combat launchers in all. Range: 150 km. We brought over eighty conventional cruise missiles for these two regiments.

• We also had an Mi-8 transport helicopter regiment, and a transport air squadron with nine already-obsolete Li-2 planes.

• Now the Navy. We planned to deploy two squadrons to Cuba: one squadron of surface ships, comprising two cruisers and two destroyers; and a squadron of submarines, comprising eleven submarines. These two squadrons never went to Cuba. They were scheduled to be sent out later.

• A missile regiment for coastal defense, with the *Sopka* missile, had eight launchers at four sites on the coast. Thirty-two cruise missiles were brought for these eight launchers. The range of the missiles against targets at sea was 80 km. The Americans are familiar with these data; that's why I merely mention them.

• Finally, there was a brigade of twelve missile-launching *[Komar]* patrol boats, with two P-15 missiles each, with a range of 40 km. . . .

As you can see, this was a very significant group of forces. Much has been written about the missiles, but if you analyze the military structure of what we sent to Cuba, the missile unit was brought only to deter aggression, and that was the only one that was deployed for that purpose. The others—jointly with the Cuban armed forces—were to defend the island of Cuba from attack by air, by land, and by sea.

Before the crisis, we had foreseen bringing in 45,000 men. By the time of the crisis, we had brought in 42,000. Never before in the history of the Soviet Armed Forces and in the history of Russia had we transported so many troops to the other side of the ocean. Consequently, when we were entrusted by the government with the planning of this operation, we said that there were many issues and unknowns to be taken into account. We devoted day and night to these preparations. We made all the necessary calculations, but these had to be done in absolute secrecy. . . .

When the essential planning was completed by the General Staff, and when most of the troops were already aboard the ships and on their way, some units were already being deployed in Cuba. It was then that I was instructed to leave for Cuba by plane, with some other admirals and generals, as a representative of Minister of Defense [Rodion Ya.] Malinovsky, to check on the status of the operation. I would like to quote Malinovsky when he gave me the order to convey Khrushchev's and the defense minister's instructions to [General Issa Alexandrovich] Pliyev: "The missile forces will fire only if authorized by Nikita Sergeievich Khrushchev"—it was repeated—"only if instructed by the Supreme Commander-in-Chief himself." Comrade Pliyev was to remember that the missile division had been sent to Cuba to deter aggression. The tactical nuclear forces—the six *Luna* launchers I've mentioned—could be employed [by Pliyev] with nuclear weapons during a direct invasion by the aggressor. It was said that before arriving at a decision on employing the tactical missiles, the situation had to be very thoroughly and carefully assessed, and, in case of extreme need only, then could the decision be made. That was my mission when I was sent to Cuba.

On October 22nd, the day when Kennedy spoke on the radio and on television, we already had 42,000 troops in Cuba and three missile regiments (one division). The sites were ready for two regiments (not yet for the third). None of the missiles was placed in combat readiness. They had not yet been fueled, nor supplied with oxidating agents. The warheads were some 250 or 300 kilometers from the launch sites, and had not yet been released for use.

All the units—all the necessary units, that is—were in their combat positions covering the missile sites. These units were deployed throughout the territory of Cuba. They were to cover the whole island, together, that is, with the air defense units and the air force, which would work jointly with the Cuban Air Force. The fighter planes were ready for combat. All the planes—forty MiG-21s—had been assembled and were ready for combat. But despite this, no one fired on the American planes that were flying over Cuba. These included high-altitude U-2s, and other low-level reconnaissance planes that flew so low that, in some cases, we could even see the pilots. We later learned that negotiations were taking place between Khrushchev and Kennedy. But, while they were in Cuba, the commanders of our troops were not informed of these secret negotiations.

Now everything is clear. We all know a lot about the Cuban crisis. We know what the situation was like then. But at that time there were many dangers, many things we knew nothing about—not just the Soviets, but also the Cubans. And there were many things that the American command did not know about.

Intelligence provided data on the preparations being made in the United States—that is, strikes that were being prepared. There was the possibility of landings in Cuba. Together with the General Staff of the Cuban Revolutionary Armed Forces, we devised a plan to repel aggression. It was foreseen that if the aggressor were to cut the Cuban territory into sections, we would then have to use fall-back operational command centers in different parts of the country—west, central, and east. That is, the troops stationed in Cuba should be ready to fight in order to thwart aggression against Cuba. I must say that the fighting spirit of the Cuban

Revolutionary Armed Forces and of the Cuban people, and the fighting spirit of the Soviet troops in Cuba, was high. We were all ready and willing to fight to the very last man. We didn't just plan an initial resistance. We even decided that if it proved necessary—if large tracts of the island were occupied—we would form guerrilla units in order to continue defending the interests of revolutionary Cuba. I'm using the very words that we used in 1962. That's the way we were then. We did not have anywhere to withdraw to. . . .

Allow me to say that, considering all the possible options in the event of an attack against Cuba, the aggressor would have suffered great losses, either in the event of an air attack with a subsequent landing, or in a direct assault. An air attack would not have destroyed all the missiles. Even if the three intermediate-range missile regiments had been destroyed, leaving only the six *Luna* launchers (which were very hard to destroy), they would have been made ready with nuclear weapons, and we are all perfectly aware of the fact that losses would have been tremendous.

Allow me to say that the wisdom and common sense of the three leaders— Fidel Castro, Kennedy, and Khrushchev—prevented a catastrophe. But the world was on the brink of a nuclear holocaust.

Cuba Protests U.S. Aggression, October 8, 1962

It was enough for us to promulgate laws which affected the United States monopolistic interests in our country, it was enough to promulgate the land reform act at a period when our revolutionary development was not yet shaped by socialist principles, for aggressive action against our homeland to be undertaken by the United States Government.

That was the start of the insolent diplomatic notes and piratical flights over our territory. Then the Cuban sugar quota was eliminated from the United States market, supplies of petroleum to our country were stopped, and diplomatic measures were taken aimed at isolating Cuba from the continent. Finally there was a whole series of eminently aggressive activities which generated this tension, long before—I repeat—long before we proclaimed that our revolution was a socialist one.

And what has happened since?

It would be unduly tedious, I think, to recapitulate all the acts of aggression committed by the United States against Cuba. Suffice it to mention all the efforts designed to subvert our country from within, the acts of sabotage, the attacks on persons and the espionage activities on our soil. In brief, suffice it to recall the armed invasion of our country by mercenary forces financed, trained in warfare, militarily protected and commanded by the Government of the United States: the invasion of Playa Girón [Bay of Pigs]. And what happened after Playa Girón, that ridiculous fiasco? Did they perchance learn a great lesson of history from it? Did they perchance have sufficient perception and knowledge to realize what immense forces can be marshalled by a nation firmly resolved to preserve its freedom and independence? That is not what happened. We immediately became the victims of further acts of aggression with the infiltration of agents landed on our coasts and trained by the Central Intelligence Agency, new attempts at sabotage, the military training of groups to carry out the hitherto unsuccessful internal subversion of our country and the increase of economic pressure on our homeland—tenaciously and doggedly applied in the hope that it would undermine our revolution and that, as a result, their sole objective would be attained: the downfall of the Revolutionary Government of Cuba. . . .

These aggressive acts continue, like the United States warships that lie near the coast off our harbours. Every day those of us who live in Havana must see with our own eyes these warships lurking around our island, making a show of war or of preparation for war.

This is the situation today but we can also say that it is qualitatively different from the situation which existed before the invasion of our country at Playa Girón, for the following reasons. Before Playa Girón, the Government of the United States had on more than one occasion stated that it had no aggressive intentions towards our country. It is obvious that after Playa Girón even the President of the United States publicly and officially acknowledged his responsibility and his sympathy and support for that invasion.

Today the situation is different, for while it is true that once again it is being asserted—as the Head of the United States delegation has stated here [in the United Nations]—that there are no aggressive designs on our country, on the other hand there are records, and there have been statements and official resolutions which authorize armed aggression against Cuba and seek to justify it in advance. The fact is that the object—as acknowledged recently in a statement by the State Department of the United States—of the foreign policy of the United States Government in regard to Cuba is clearly and obviously the overthrow of the revolutionary Government and the destruction of our glorious revolution. . . .

By way of [further] proof it is sufficient to take a brief look at the operative part of the joint resolution [September 1962] of the United States Congress.

"Resolved by the Senate and House of Representatives of the United States of America in Congress assembled,

"That the United States is determined

"*(a)* To prevent by whatever means may be necessary, including the use of arms"—I repeat, including the use of arms—"the Marxist-Leninist regime in Cuba from extending, by force or the threat of force, its aggressive or subversive activities to any part of this hemisphere.". . .

Of course we should have preferred to devote all those human and material resources, all the energies we have had to employ in strengthening our military defences, to the development of our economy and culture. We have armed ourselves against our wishes and contrary to our aspirations, because we were driven to strengthen our military defences lest we should jeopardize the sovereignty of our nation and the independence of our homeland. We have armed ourselves because the people of Cuba have a legitimate right, sanctioned by history, to defend their sovereign decisions and to steer their country on the historic course which, in the exercise of their sovereignty, they have chosen. . . .

Cuba does not, as has been stated here, represent a problem between the East and the West. Cuba poses a problem of sovereignty and independence. The Cuban problem is a problem involving the sovereign decision of a people and the right of that people to self-determination. Cuba has not wanted to be drawn into the cold war. Cuba merely wants to pursue its economic and cultural development and to shape its own future in peace, and it is ready to demonstrate these intentions at any time. And if it is not true that there is an intention to attack our country—although we consider that such an intention certainly exists—we urge the head of the United States delegation specifically to guarantee before this Assembly that his Government does not intend to attack Cuba. We urge him, however, to back up these guarantees not merely by words, but more especially by deeds. Verbal guarantees were given before Playa Girón, and when the invasion took place, many Members of the Assembly heard the representative of the United States Government state that there was no such invasion and that his Government had not planned one; yet only a few days later, the President of the United States himself publicly and officially assumed the responsibility for that invasion.

Missiles Photographed in Cuba: Kennedy's First Meetings with His Advisers, October 16, 1962

Meeting of 11:50 A.M.–12:57 P.M.

Lundahl*: This is a result of the photography taken Sunday, sir.

JFK: Yeah.

Lundahl: There's a medium-range ballistic missile launch site and two new military encampments on the southern edge of Sierra del Rosario in west central Cuba.

JFK: Where would that be?

Lundahl: Uh, west central, sir. That. . . .

JFK: Yeah. . . .

Lundahl: Well, one site on one of the encampments contains a total of at least fourteen canvas-covered missile trailers measuring 67 feet in length, 9 feet in width. The overall length of the trailers plus the tow-bars is approximately 80 feet. The other encampment contains vehicles and tents but with no missile trailers. . . .

JFK: How far advanced is this? . . . How do you know this is a medium-range ballistic missile?

Lundahl: The length, sir.

JFK: The what? The length?

Lundahl: The length of it. Yes.

JFK: The length of the missile? Which part? I mean which . . .

Lundahl: . . . the missile [word unintelligible] indicates which one is [words unintelligible]. . . .

JFK: Is this ready to be fired?

Graybeal**: No, sir.

JFK: How long have we got. . . . We can't tell, I take it . . .

Graybeal: No, sir.

JFK: . . . how long before it can be fired?

---

*Art Lundahl, National Photographic Interpretation Center.
**Sidney Graybeal.

Graybeal: That depends on how ready the . . .

JFK: But, what does it have to be fired from?

Graybeal: It would have to be fired from a stable hard surface. This could be packed dirt; it could be concrete or, or asphalt. The surface has to be hard, then you put a flame deflect-, a deflector plate on there to direct the missile.

McNamara*: Would you care to comment on the position of nuclear warheads—this is in relation to the question from the president—explain when these can be fired?

Graybeal: Sir, we've looked very hard. We can find nothing that would spell nuclear warhead in terms of any isolated area or unique security in this particular area. The mating of the nuclear warhead to the missile from some of the other short range missiles there would take about, uh, a couple of hours to do this.

McNamara: This is not defensed, I believe, at the moment?

Lundahl: Not yet, sir. . . .

Rusk**: Don't you have to assume these are nuclear? . . .

McNamara: There's no question about that. The question is one of readiness of the, to fire and—and this is highly critical in forming our plans—that the time between today and the time when the readiness to fire capability develops is a very important thing. To estimate that we need to know where these warheads are, and we have not yet found any probable storage of warheads and hence it seems extremely unlikely that they are now ready to fire or may be ready to fire within a matter of hours or even a day or two. . . .

JFK: Secretary Rusk?

Rusk: Yes. [Well?], Mr. President, this is a, of course, a [widely?] serious development. It's one that we, all of us, had not really believed the Soviets could, uh, carry this far. . . . Now, uhm, I do think we have to set in motion a chain of events that will eliminate this base. I don't think we [can?] sit still. The questioning becomes whether we do it by sudden, unannounced strike of some sort, or we, uh, build up the crisis to the point where the other side has to consider very seriously about giving in, or, or even the Cubans themselves, uh, take some, take some action on this. The thing that I'm, of course, very conscious of is that there is no such thing, I think, as unilateral action by the United States. It's so [eminently or heavily?] involved with 2 allies and confrontation in many places, that any action that we take, uh, will greatly increase the risks of direct action involving, uh, our other alliances and our other forces in other parts of the world. Uhm, so I think we, we have to think very hard about two major, uh, courses of action as alternatives. One is the quick strike. The point where we [make or think?], that is the, uh, overwhelming, overriding necessity to take all the risks that are involved doing that. I don't think this in itself would require an invasion of Cuba. I think that with or without such an invasion, in other words if we make it clear that, uh, what we're doing is eliminating this particular base or any other such base that is established. We ourselves are not moved to general war, we're simply doing what we said we

---

*Robert McNamara, secretary of defense.
**Dean Rusk, secretary of state.

would do if they took certain action. Uh, or we're going to decide that this is the time to eliminate the Cuban problem by actually eliminating the island.

The other would be, if we have a few days—from the military point of view, if we have the whole time—uh, then I would think that, uh, there would be another course of action, a combination of things that, uh, we might wish to consider. Uhm, first, uh, that we, uh, stimulate the OAS [Organization of American States] procedure immediately for prompt action to make it quite clear that the entire hemisphere considers that the Rio Pact has been violated [and actually?] what acts should [we take or be taken?] in, under the terms of the Rio Pact. . . .

I think also that we ought to consider getting some word to Castro, perhaps through the Canadian ambassador in Havana or through, uh, his representative at the U.N. Uh, I think perhaps the Canadian ambassador would be best, the better channel to get to Castro [apart?] privately and tell him that, uh, this is no longer support for Cuba, that Cuba is being victimized here, and that, uh, the Soviets are preparing Cuba for destruction or betrayal. . . .

And I think there are certain military, uhm, uh, actions that we could, we might well want to take straight away. First, to, uh, to call up, uh, highly selective units [no more than?] 150,000. Unless we feel that it's better, more desirable to go to a general national emergency so that we have complete freedom of action. If we announce, at the time that we announce this development—and I think we do have to announce this development some time this week—uh, we announce that, uh, we are conducting a surveillance of Cuba, over Cuba, and we will enforce our right to do so. We reject the mission of secrecy in this hemisphere in any matters of this sort. We, we reinforce our forces in Guantánamo. We reinforce our forces in the southeastern part of the United States—whatever is necessary from the military point of view to be able to give, to deliver an overwhelming strike at any of these installations, including the SAM [surface-to-air missile] sites. And, uh, also, to take care of any, uh, MiGs or bombers that might make a pass at Miami or at the United States. Build up heavy forces, uh, if those are not already in position. . . .

I think also that we need a few days, uhm, to alert our other allies, for consultation with NATO [North Atlantic Treaty Organization]. I'll assume that we can move on this line at the same time to interrupt all air traffic from free world countries going into Cuba, insist to the Mexicans, the Dutch, that they stop their planes from coming in. Tell the British, who, and anyone else who's involved at this point, that, uh, if they're interested in peace, that they've got to stop their ships from Cuban trade at this point. Uh, in other words, isolate Cuba completely without at this particular moment a, uh, forceful blockade. . . .

But I think that, by and large, there are, there are these two broad alternatives: one, the quick strike; the other, to alert our allies and Mr. Khrushchev that there is utterly serious crisis in the making here, and that, uh. . . . Mr. Khrushchev may not himself really understand that or believe that at this point. I think we'll be facing a situation that could well lead to general war. . . .

McNamara: Mr. President, there are a number of unknowns in this situation I want to comment upon, and, in relation to them, I would like to outline very briefly some possible military alternatives and ask General Taylor to expand upon them.

But before commenting on either the unknowns or outlining some military alternatives, there are two propositions I would suggest that we ought to accept as, uh, foundations for our further thinking. My first is that if we are to conduct an air strike against these installations, or against any part of Cuba, we must agree now that we will schedule that prior to the time these missile sites become operational. I'm not prepared to say when that will be, but I think it is extremely important that our talk and our discussion be founded on this premise: that any air strike will be planned to take place prior to the time they become operational. Because, if they become operational before the air strike, I do not believe we can state we can knock them out before they can be launched; and if they're launched there is almost certain to be, uh, chaos in part of the east coast or the area, uh, in a radius of six hundred to a thousand miles from Cuba.

Uh, secondly, I, I would submit the proposition that any air strike must be directed not solely against the missile sites, but against the missile sites plus the airfields plus the aircraft which may not be on the airfields but hidden by that time plus all potential nuclear storage sites. Now, this is a fairly extensive air strike. It is not just a strike against the missile sites; and there would be associated with it potential casualties of Cubans. . . .

Taylor*: Uh, we're impressed, Mr. President, with the great importance of getting a, a strike with all the benefits of surprise, uh, which would mean *ideally* that we would have all the missiles that are in Cuba above ground where we can take them out. Uh, that, that desire runs counter to the strong point the secretary made if the other optimum would be to get every missile before it could, becomes operational. Uh, practically, I think the, our knowledge of the timing of the readiness is going to be so, so, uh, difficult that we'll never have the, the exact permanent, uh, the perfect timing. . . . It's a little hard to say in terms of time how much I'm discussing. But we must do a good job the first time we go in there, uh, pushing a 100 percent just as far, as closely as we can with our, with our strike. . . .

I would also mention among the, the military actions we should take that once we have destroyed as many of these offensive weapons as possible, we should, should prevent any more coming in, which means a naval blockade. . . .

JFK: What is the, uh, advant-. . . . Must be some major reason for the Russians to, uh, set this up as a. . . . Must be that they're not satisfied with their ICBMs [Intercontinental Ballistic Missiles]. What'd be the reason that they would, uh. . . .

Taylor: What it'd give 'em is primary, it makes the launching base, uh, for short range missiles against the United States to supplement their rather [deceptive?] ICBM system, for example. . . .

Rusk: Still, about why the Soviets are doing this, uhm, Mr. McCone** suggested some weeks ago that one thing Mr. Khrushchev may have in mind is that, uh, uh, he knows that we have a substantial nuclear superiority, but he also knows that we don't really live under fear of his nuclear weapons to the extent that, uh, he has to live under fear of ours. Also we have nuclear weapons nearby, in Turkey and places like that.

JFK: How many weapons do we have in Turkey?

Taylor?: We have Jupiter missiles. . . .

McNamara?: About fifteen, I believe it is. . . .

---

*General Maxwell Taylor, chairman of the Joint Chiefs of Staff.
**John A. McCone, director of the Central Intelligence Agency.

Rusk: Uhm, and that Mr. McCone expresses the view that Khrushchev may feel that it's important for us to learn about living under medium-range missiles, and he's doing that to sort of balance that, uh, that political, psychological [plank?]. I think also that, uh, Berlin is, uh, very much involved in this. Uhm, for the first time, I'm beginning really to wonder whether maybe Mr. Khrushchev is entirely rational about Berlin. We've [hardly?] talked about his obsession with it. And I think we have to, uh, keep our eye on that element. But, uh, they may be thinking that they can either bargain Berlin and Cuba against each other, or that they could provoke us into a kind of action in Cuba which would give an umbrella for them to take action with respect to Berlin. In other words like the Suez-Hungary combination. If they could provoke us into taking the first overt action, then the world would be confused and they would have, uh, what they would consider to be justification for making a move somewhere else. But, uh, I must say I don't really see the rationality of, uh, the Soviets' pushing it this far unless they grossly misunderstand the importance of Cuba to this country. . . .

JFK: Uh, eh, well, this, which . . . What you're really talking about are two or three different, uh, [tense?] operations. One is the strike just on this, these three bases. One, the second is the broader one that Secretary McNamara was talking about, which is on the airfields and on the SAM sites and on anything else connected with, uh, missiles. Third is doing both of those things and also at the same time launching a blockade, which requires really the, uh, the, uh, third and which is a larger step. And then, as I take it, the fourth question is the, uh, degree of consultation.

RFK*: Mr. President.

JFK: Yes.

RFK: We have the fifth one, really, which is the invasion. I would say that, uh, you're dropping bombs all over Cuba if you do the second, uh, air, the airports, knocking out their planes, dropping it on all their missiles. You're covering most of Cuba. You're going to kill an awful lot of people, and, uh, we're going to take an awful lot of heat on it . . .

JFK: I don't believe it takes us, at least, uh. . . . How long did it take to get in a position where we can invade Cuba? Almost a month? Two months?

McNamara: No, sir. . . .

JFK: I think we ought to, what we ought to do is, is, uh, after this meeting this afternoon, we ought to meet tonight again at six, consider these various, uh, proposals. In the meanwhile, we'll go ahead with this maximum, whatever is needed from the flights, and, in addition, we will. . . . I don't think we got much time on these missiles. They may be. . . . So it may be that we just have to, we can't wait two weeks while we're getting ready to, to roll. Maybe just have to just take *them out,* and continue our other preparations if we decide to do that. That may be where we end up. I think we ought to, beginning right now, be preparing to. . . . Because that's what we're going to do *anyway.* We're certainly going to do number one; we're going to take out these, uh, missiles. Uh, the questions will be whether,

---

*Robert F. Kennedy.

which, what I would describe as number two, which would be a general air strike. That we're not ready to say, but we should be in preparation for it. The third is the, is the, uh, the general invasion. At least we're going to do number one, so it seems to me that we don't have to wait very long. We, we ought to be making *those* preparations.

Bundy*: You want to be clear, Mr. President, whether we have *definitely* decided *against* a political [i.e., diplomatic] track. I, myself, think we ought . . .

Taylor?: Well, we'll have . . .

Bundy: . . . to work out a contingency on that.

Taylor?: We, we'll develop both tracks.

Meeting of 6:30–7:55 P.M.

McNamara: Mr. President, could I outline three courses of action we have considered and speak very briefly on each one? The first is what I would call the political course of action, in which we, uh, follow some of the possibilities that Secretary Rusk mentioned this morning by approaching Castro, by approaching Khrushchev, by discussing with our allies. An overt and open approach politically to the problem [attempting, or in order?] to solve it. This seemed to me likely to lead to no satisfactory result, and it almost stops subsequent military action. . . .

A second course of action we haven't discussed but lies in between the military course we began discussing a moment ago and the political course of action is a course of action that would involve declaration of open surveillance; a statement that we would immediately impose an, uh, a blockade against *offensive* weapons entering Cuba in the future; and an indication that with our open-surveillance reconnaissance which we would plan to maintain indefinitely for the future. . . .

But the third course of action is any one of these variants of military action directed against Cuba, starting with an air attack against the missiles. The Chiefs are strongly opposed to so limited an air attack. But even so limited an air attack is a very extensive air attack. It's not twenty sorties or fifty sorties or a hundred sorties, but probably several hundred sorties. Uh, we haven't worked out the details. It's very difficult to do so when we lack certain intelligence that we hope to have tomorrow or the next day. But it's a substantial air attack. . . . I don't believe we have considered the consequences of any of these actions satisfactorily, and because we haven't considered the consequences, I'm not sure we're taking all the action we ought to take now to minimize those. I, I don't know quite what kind of a world we live in after we've struck Cuba, and we, we've started it. . . .

Taylor: And you'll miss some [missiles].

McNamara: And you'll miss some. That's right. Now after we've launched sorties, what kind of a world do we live in? How, how do we stop at that point? I don't know the answer to this. I think tonight State and we ought to work on the consequences of any one of these courses of actions, consequences which I don't believe are entirely clear. . . .

---

*McGeorge Bundy, assistant for national security affairs.

JFK: If the, uh, it doesn't increase very much their strategic, uh, strength, why is it, uh, can any Russian expert tell us why they. . . . After all Khrushchev demonstrated a sense of caution [thousands?] . . .

Speaker?: Well, there are several, several possible . . .

JFK: . . . Berlin, he's been cautious, I mean, he hasn't been, uh . . .

Ball*: Several possibilities, Mr. President. One of them is that he has given us word now that he's coming over in November to, to the UN. If, he may be proceeding on the assumption, and this lack of a sense of *apparent* urgency would seem to, to support this, that this *isn't* going to be discovered at the moment and that, uh, when he comes over this is something he can do, a ploy. That here is Cuba armed against the United States, or possibly use it to try to trade something in Berlin, saying he'll disarm Cuba, if, uh, if we'll yield some of our interests in Berlin and some arrangement for it. I mean, that this is a, it's a trading ploy.

Bundy: I would think one thing that I would still cling to is that he's not likely to give Fidel Castro nuclear warheads. I don't believe that has happened or is likely to happen.

JFK: Why does he put these in there though?

Bundy: Soviet-controlled nuclear warheads [of the kind?] . . .

JFK: That's right, but what is the advantage of that? It's just as if we suddenly began to put a major number of MRBMs [Medium-Range Ballistic Missiles] in Turkey. Now that'd be goddam dangerous, I would think.

Bundy: Well, we *did,* Mr. President. . . .

JFK: Yeah, but that was five years ago. . . .

Ball: Yes, I think, I think you, you look at this possibility that this is an attempt to, to add to his strategic capabilities. A second consideration is that it is simply a trading ploy, that he, he wants this in so that he could, he could [words unintelligible]. . . .

JFK: Well, it's a goddam mystery to me. I don't know enough about the Soviet Union, but if anybody can tell me any other time since the Berlin blockade where the Russians have given us so clear provocation, I don't know when it's been, because they've been awfully cautious really. The Russians, I never. . . . Now, maybe our mistake was in not saying some time *before* this summer that if they do this we're [word unintelligible] to act.

The Rejection of Ambassador Charles E. Bohlen's Call for Diplomacy, October 17, 1962

Ambassador [Charles E.] Bohlen warned against any action against Cuba, particularly an air strike without warning, stating such would be divisive with all Allies and subject us to criticism throughout the world. He advocated writing both Khrushchev and Castro; if their response was negative or unsatisfactory then we should plan action; advise our principal allies, seek a two-thirds vote from the OAS and then act. The Attorney General [Robert F. Kennedy] and Bohlen ex-

---

*George W. Ball, under secretary of state.

changed views as to just what type of an answer we could expect from Khrushchev and what he might do if we threatened an attack. During this discussion Secretary Rusk seemed to favor asking Congress for a declaration of a state of war against Cuba and then proceed with OAS, NATO, etc., but always preserve flexibility as to the type of action. Bohlen consistently warned that world opinion would be against us if we carried out a military strike. [Under] Secretary Ball emphasized the importance of time, stating that if action was over quickly, the repercussions would not be too serious.

The Attorney General raised the question of the attitude of Turkey, Italy, Western European countries, all of which have been "under the gun" for years, and would take the position that now that the U.S. has a few missiles in their backyard, they become hysterical. This point was discussed back and forth by various people throughout both days of discussion.

Secretary McNamara made the point that missiles in Cuba had no great military consequence because of the stalemate mentioned in my October 18th memorandum. General Taylor supported this view in the early parts of the discussion, but in the later meetings expressed increasing concern over the importance of the missile threat from Cuba. [Under Secretary of Defense Roswell] Gilpatric supported McNamara's position. [CIA director John A.] McCone doubted it, stating that McNamara's facts were not new as they had appeared in estimates months ago (which McNamara questioned). Nevertheless, he and McCone felt that a complex of MRBMs and IRBMs in Cuba would have very important military significance. McNamara took issue claiming that the military equation would not be changed by the appearance of these missiles.

Bohlen and [former ambassador to the Soviet Union Llewellyn] Thompson questioned the real purpose of the Soviets' actions in Cuba and seemed to feel that their acts may be in preparation for a confrontation with President Kennedy at which time they would seek to settle the entire subject of overseas bases as well as the Berlin question. McCone indicated this might be one of several objectives and undoubtedly would be the subject of discussion at the time of confrontation; however, McCone doubted that this was the prime purpose of such an elaborate and expensive installation as the Soviets were going forward with in Cuba. Bohlen seemed to favor precipitating talks, and was supported by Thompson.

SecDef [McNamara] and Taylor both objected to political talks because it would give time for threatening missiles to become operational and also give the Soviets an opportunity to camouflage the missiles. McCone presented most recent photographs and indicated CIA opinion that the first missiles will be operational within one or two weeks.

Bohlen again raised the question of opening up discussions. McNamara agreed that this would be desirable but emphasized the importance of developing [a] sequence of events which would lead to military action. . . .

Dean Acheson then expressed his views as follows:

We should proceed at once with the necessary military actions and should do no talking. The Soviets will react some place. We must expect this; take the consequences and manage the situations as they evolve. We should have no consultations with Khrushchev, Castro, or our allies, but should fully alert our allies in the most persuasive manner by high level people. This would include all NATO partners, and the OAS. The President should forget about the elections and should cancel all future campaign speeches.

As an alternate to military action, a plan was discussed involving a declaration of war and the creation of an all-out blockade. Thompson spoke strongly in favor of a blockade. General Taylor at this point indicated that he favored a blockade although in subsequent meetings he seemed inclined towards a military strike. McCone gave an intelligence estimate on the effects of a blockade, indicating its seriousness would depend upon how "hard" a blockade it turned out to be, and finally stated that the main objective of taking Cuba away from Castro had been lost and we have been overly consumed with the missile problem. McCone stated that we must all bear in mind that we have two objectives, one, disposing of the missile sites, and the other, getting rid of Castro's communism in the Western Hemisphere.

The meeting adjourned for dinner and in the evening Secretary Rusk came forward with the following plan.

The United States cannot accept operational MRBMs in Cuba. There is not much profit in preliminary exchanges with Khrushchev and Castro because the President has said that the establishment of Soviet bases and offensive weapons in the Western Hemisphere would raise serious problems and therefore on September 5th and 13th the President has in effect warned both Khrushchev and Castro.

Rusk continued that more talks with Khrushchev would result in extended parlays and therefore he recommended against such an approach. Rusk then proposed that we hold until the middle of next week and then follow the OD course No. 1 (52 sorties against MRBMs). Prior, we inform key allies probably on Tuesday. . . . On Wednesday, we strike with missiles and simultaneously send a message to Khrushchev, NATO, OAS, etc. We should be alert for an attack on Turkey and be prepared for the consequences in Berlin, Quemoy, Matsu, Korea, etc. Rusk made the estimate that world opinion would go along, 42 allies would go along and some neutrals would be favorable. Latin Americans must be told that we are acting in the interests of the Western Hemisphere. Rusk advocated that the first step—we take out the missiles and thus remove the immediate problem of the establishment of an offensive capability, but that we be prepared for subsequent steps. He emphasized the United States cannot accept missiles in our security interests and in view of statements made by the President and others and our various policy declarations. Bohlen continued to persist for diplomatic approach but Rusk and several others were not at this point persuaded. McNamara raised innumerable questions concerning military operations; the manner in which the strike could be properly covered with protective air and how it might be restricted.

Kennedy's Television Address, October 22, 1962

This urgent transformation of Cuba into an important strategic base—by the presence of these large, long-range, and clearly offensive weapons of sudden mass destruction—constitutes an explicit threat to the peace and security of all the Americas, in flagrant and deliberate defiance of the Rio Pact of 1947, the traditions of this nation and hemisphere, the Joint Resolution of the 87th Congress, the Charter of the United Nations, and my own public warnings to the Soviets on September 4 and 13.

This action also contradicts the repeated assurances of Soviet spokesmen, both publicly and privately delivered, that the arms buildup in Cuba would retain its original defensive character and that the Soviet Union had no need or desire to station strategic missiles on the territory of any other nation.

The size of this undertaking makes clear that it has been planned for some months. Yet only last month, after I had made clear the distinction between any introduction of ground-to-ground missiles and the existence of defensive antiaircraft missiles, the Soviet Government publicly stated on September 11 that, and I quote, "The armaments and military equipment sent to Cuba are designed exclusively for defensive purposes," and, and I quote the Soviet Government, "There is no need for the Soviet Government to shift its weapons for a retaliatory blow to any other country, for instance Cuba," and that, and I quote the Government, "The Soviet Union has no powerful rockets to carry these nuclear warheads that there is no need to search for sites for them beyond the boundaries of the Soviet Union." That statement was false.

Only last Thursday, as evidence of this rapid offensive buildup was already in my hand, Soviet Foreign Minister Gromyko told me in my office that he was instructed to make it clear once again, as he said his Government had already done, that Soviet assistance to Cuba, and I quote, "pursued solely the purpose of contributing to the defense capabilities of Cuba," that, and I quote him, "training by Soviet specialists of Cuban nationals in handling defensive armaments was by no means offensive," and that "if it were otherwise," Mr. Gromyko went on, "the Soviet Government would never become involved in rendering such assistance." That statement also was false.

Neither the United States of America nor the world community of nations can tolerate deliberate deception and offensive threats on the part of any nation, large or small. We no longer live in a world where only the actual firing of weapons represents a sufficient challenge to a nation's security to constitute maximum peril. Nuclear weapons are so destructive and ballistic missiles are so swift that any substantially increased possibility of their use or any sudden change in their deployment may well be regarded as a definite threat to peace.

For many years both the Soviet Union and the United States, recognizing this fact, have deployed strategic nuclear weapons with great care, never upsetting the precarious *status quo* which insured that these weapons would not be used in the absence of some vital challenge. Our own strategic missiles have never been transferred to the territory of any other nation under a cloak of secrecy and deception; and our history, unlike that of the Soviets since the end of World War II, demonstrates that we have no desire to dominate or conquer any other nation or impose our system upon its people. Nevertheless, American citizens have become adjusted to living daily on the bull's eye of Soviet missiles located inside the U.S.S.R. or in submarines.

In that sense missiles in Cuba add to an already clear and present danger—although it should be noted the nations of Latin America have never previously been subjected to a potential nuclear threat.

But this secret, swift, and extraordinary buildup of Communist missiles—in an area well known to have a special and historical relationship to the United States and the nations of the Western Hemisphere, in violation of Soviet assurances, and in defiance of American and hemispheric policy—this sudden, clandestine decision to station strategic weapons for the first time outside of Soviet soil—is a deliberately provocative and unjustified change in the *status quo* which cannot be accepted by this country if our courage and our commitments are ever to be trusted again by either friend or foe.

The 1930's taught us a clear lesson: Aggressive conduct, if allowed to grow unchecked and unchallenged, ultimately leads to war. This nation is opposed to war. We are also true to our word. Our unswerving objective, therefore, must be to prevent the use of these missiles against this or any other country and to secure their withdrawal or elimination from the Western Hemisphere.

Our policy has been one of patience and restraint, as befits a peaceful and powerful nation, which leads a worldwide alliance. We have been determined not to be diverted from our central concerns by mere irritants and fanatics. But now further action is required—and it is underway; and these actions may only be the beginning. We will not prematurely or unnecessarily risk the costs of the worldwide nuclear war in which even the fruits of victory would be ashes in our mouth—but neither will we shrink from that risk at any time it must be faced.

Acting, therefore, in the defense of our own security and of the entire Western Hemisphere, and under the authority entrusted to me by the Constitution as endorsed by the resolution of the Congress, I have directed that the following *initial* steps be taken immediately:

First: To halt this offensive buildup, a strict quarantine on all offensive military equipment under shipment to Cuba is being initiated. All ships of any kind bound for Cuba from whatever nation or port will, if found to contain cargoes of offensive weapons, be turned back. This quarantine will be extended, if needed, to other types of cargo and carriers. We are not at this time, however, denying the necessities of life as the Soviets attempted to do in their Berlin blockade of 1948.

Second: I have directed the continued and increased close surveillance of Cuba and its military buildup. The Foreign Ministers of the OAS in their communiqué of October 3 rejected secrecy on such matters in this hemisphere. Should these offensive military preparations continue, thus increasing the threat to the hemisphere, further action will be justified. I have directed the Armed Forces to prepare for any eventualities; and I trust that, in the interest of both the Cuban people and the Soviet technicians at the sites, the hazards to all concerned of continuing this threat will be recognized.

Third: It shall be the policy of this nation to regard any nuclear missile launched from Cuba against any nation in the Western Hemisphere as an attack by the Soviet Union on the United States, requiring a full retaliatory response upon the Soviet Union.

Fourth: As a necessary military precaution I have reinforced our base at Guantánamo, evacuated today the dependents of our personnel there, and ordered additional military units to be on a standby alert basis.

Fifth: We are calling tonight for an immediate meeting of the Organ of Consultation, under the Organization of American States, to consider this threat to hemispheric security and to invoke articles 6 and 8 of the Rio Treaty in support of all necessary action. The United Nations Charter allows for regional security arrangements—and the nations of this hemisphere decided long ago against the military presence of outside powers. Our other allies around the world have also been alerted.

Sixth: Under the Charter of the United Nations, we are asking tonight that an emergency meeting of the Security Council be convoked without delay to take action against this latest Soviet threat to world peace. Our resolution will call for the prompt dismantling and withdrawal of all offensive weapons in Cuba, under the supervision of U.N. observers, before the quarantine can be lifted.

Seventh and finally: I call upon Chairman Khrushchev to halt and eliminate this clandestine, reckless, and provocative threat to world peace and to stable relations between our two nations. I call upon him further to abandon this course of world domination and to join in an historic effort to end the perilous arms race and transform the history of man. He has an opportunity now to move the world back from the abyss of destruction—by returning to his Government's own words that it had no need to station missiles outside its own territory, and withdrawing these weapons from Cuba—by refraining from any action which will widen or deepen the present crisis—and then by participating in a search for peaceful and permanent solutions.

This nation is prepared to present its case against the Soviet threat to peace, and our own proposals for a peaceful world, at any time and in any forum—in the OAS, in the United Nations, or in any other meeting that could be useful—without limiting our freedom of action. . . .

But it is difficult to settle or even discuss these problems in an atmosphere of intimidation. That is why this latest Soviet threat—or any other threat which is made either independently or in response to our actions this week—must and will be met with determination. Any hostile move anywhere in the world against the safety and freedom of peoples to whom we are committed—including in particular the brave people of West Berlin—will be met by whatever action is needed.

Finally, I want to say a few words to the captive people of Cuba, to whom this speech is being directly carried by special radio facilities. I speak to you as a friend, as one who knows of your deep attachment to your fatherland, as one who shares your aspirations for liberty and justice for all. And I have watched and the American people have watched with deep sorrow how your nationalist revolution was betrayed and how your fatherland fell under foreign domination. Now your leaders are no longer Cuban leaders inspired by Cuban ideals. They are puppets and agents of an international conspiracy which has turned Cuba against your friends and neighbors in the Americas—and turned it into the first Latin American country to become a target for nuclear war, the first Latin American country to have these weapons on its soil.

These new weapons are not in your interest. They contribute nothing to your peace and well-being. They can only undermine it. But this country has no wish to cause you to suffer or to impose any system upon you. We know that your lives and land are being used as pawns by those who deny you freedom.

Many times in the past the Cuban people have risen to throw out tyrants who destroyed their liberty. And I have no doubt that most Cubans today look forward to the time when they will be truly free—free from foreign domination, free to choose their own leaders, free to select their own system, free to own their own land, free to speak and write and worship without fear or degradation. And then shall Cuba be welcomed back to the society of free nations and to the associations of this hemisphere.

My fellow citizens, let no one doubt that this is a difficult and dangerous effort on which we have set out. No one can foresee precisely what course it will take or what costs or casualties will be incurred. Many months of sacrifice and self-discipline lie ahead—months in which both our patience and our will will be tested, months in which many threats and denunciations will keep us aware of our dangers. But the greatest danger of all would be to do nothing.

Premier Nikita Khrushchev Asks for a U.S. No-Invasion Pledge, October 26, 1962

I see, Mr. President, that you too are not devoid of a sense of anxiety for the fate of the world, of understanding, and of what war entails. What would a war give you? You are threatening us with war. But you well know that the very least which you would receive in reply would be that you would experience the same consequences as those which you sent us. And that must be clear to us, people invested with authority, trust, and responsibility. We must not succumb to intoxication and petty passions, regardless of whether elections are impending in this or that country, or not impending. These are all transient things, but if indeed war should break out, then it would not be in our power to stop it, for such is the logic of war. I have participated in two wars and know that war ends when it has rolled through cities and villages, everywhere sowing death and destruction.

In the name of the Soviet Government and the Soviet people, I assure you that your conclusions regarding offensive weapons on Cuba are groundless. It is apparent from what you have written me that our conceptions are different on this score, or rather, we have different estimates of these or those military means. Indeed, in reality, the same forms of weapons can have different interpretations.

You are a military man and, I hope, will understand me. Let us take for example a simple cannon. What sort of means is this: offensive or defensive? A cannon is a defensive means if it is set up to defend boundaries or a fortified area. But if one concentrates artillery, and adds to it the necessary number of troops, then the same cannons do become an offensive means, because they prepare and clear the way for infantry to attack. The same happens with missile-nuclear weapons as well, with any type of this weapon. . . .

You have now proclaimed piratical measures, which were employed in the Middle Ages, when ships proceeding in international waters were attacked, and you have called this "a quarantine" around Cuba. Our vessels, apparently, will soon enter the zone which your Navy is patrolling. I assure you that these vessels, now bound for Cuba, are carrying the most innocent peaceful cargoes. Do you really think that we only occupy ourselves with the carriage of so-called offensive weapons, atomic and hydrogen bombs? Although perhaps your military people imagine that these [cargoes] are some sort of special type of weapon, I assure you that they are the most ordinary peaceful products.

Consequently, Mr. President, let us show good sense. I assure you that on those ships, which are bound for Cuba, there are no weapons at all. The weapons which were necessary for the defense of Cuba are already there. I do not want to say that there were not any shipments of weapons at all. No, there were such shipments. But now Cuba has already received the necessary means of defense. . . .

Let us normalize relations. We have received an appeal from the Acting Secretary General of the UN, U Thant, with his proposals. I have already answered him. His proposals come to this, that our side should not transport armaments of any kind to Cuba during a certain period of time, while negotiations are being conducted—and we are ready to enter such negotiations—and the other side should not undertake any sort of piratical actions against vessels engaged in navigation on the high seas. I consider these proposals reasonable. This would be a way out of the situation which has been created, which would give the peoples the possibility of breathing calmly.

You have asked what happened, what evoked the delivery of weapons to Cuba? You have spoken about this to our Minister of Foreign Affairs. I will tell you frankly, Mr. President, what evoked it.

We were very grieved by the fact—I spoke about it in Vienna [at the 1961 summit meeting]—that a landing took place [Bay of Pigs], that an attack on Cuba was committed, as a result of which many Cubans perished. You yourself told me then that this had been a mistake. . . .

Why have we proceeded to assist Cuba with military and economic aid? The answer is: we have proceeded to do so only for reasons of humanitarianism. At one time, our people itself had a revolution, when Russia was still a backward country. We were attacked then. We were the target of attack by many countries. The USA participated in that adventure. . . .

You once said that the United States was not preparing an invasion. But you also declared that you sympathized with the Cuban counterrevolutionary emigrants, that you support them and would help them to realize their plans against the present government of Cuba. It is also not a secret to anyone that the threat of armed attack, aggression, has constantly hung, and continues to hang over Cuba. It was only this which impelled us to respond to the request of the Cuban government to furnish it aid for the strengthening of the defensive capacity of this country.

If assurance were given by the President and the government of the United States that the USA itself would not participate in an attack on Cuba and would restrain others from actions of this sort, if you would recall your fleet, this would immediately change everything. I am not speaking for Fidel Castro, but I think that he and the government of Cuba, evidently, would declare demobilization and would appeal to the people to get down to peaceful labor. Then, too, the question of armaments would disappear, since, if there is no threat, then armaments are a burden for every people. Then, too, the question of the destruction, not only of the armaments which you call offensive, but of all other armaments as well, would look different. . . .

Let us therefore show statesmanlike wisdom. I propose: we, for our part, will declare that our ships, bound for Cuba, will not carry any kind of armaments. You would declare that the United States will not invade Cuba with its forces and will not support any sort of forces which might intend to carry out an invasion of Cuba. Then the necessity for the presence of our military specialists in Cuba would disappear.

Mr. President, I appeal to you to weigh well what the aggressive, piratical actions, which you have declared the USA intends to carry out in international waters, would lead to. You yourself know that any sensible man simply cannot agree with this, cannot recognize your right to such actions.

If you did this as the first step towards the unleashing of war, well then, it is evident that nothing else is left to us but to accept this challenge of yours. If, however, you have not lost your self-control and sensibly conceive what this might lead to, then, Mr. President, we and you ought not now to pull on the ends of the rope in which you have tied the knot of war, because the more the two of us pull, the tighter that knot will be tied. And a moment may come when that knot will be tied so tight that even he who tied it will not have the strength to untie it, and then it will be necessary to cut that knot. And what that would mean is not for me to explain to you, because you yourself understand perfectly of what terrible forces our countries dispose.

Consequently, if there is no intention to tighten that knot and thereby to doom the world to the catastrophe of thermonuclear war, then let us not only relax the forces pulling on the ends of the rope, let us take measures to untie that knot. We are ready for this.

Fidel Castro Urges Khrushchev to Resist a U.S. Invasion, October 26, 1962

From an analysis of the situation and the reports in our possession, I consider that the aggression is almost imminent within the next 24 or 72 hours.

There are two possible variants: the first and likeliest one is an air attack against certain targets with the limited objective of destroying them; the second, less probable although possible, is invasion. I understand that this variant would call for a large number of forces and it is, in addition, the most repulsive form of aggression, which might inhibit them. . . .

If the second variant is implemented and the imperialists invade Cuba with the goal of occupying it, the danger that that aggressive policy poses for humanity is so great that following the event the Soviet Union must never allow the circumstances in which the imperialists could launch the first nuclear strike against it.

I tell you this because I believe that the imperialists' aggressiveness is extremely dangerous and if they actually carry out the brutal act of invading Cuba in violation of international law and morality, that would be the moment to eliminate such danger forever through an act of clear legitimate defense, however harsh and terrible the solution would be, for there is no other.

Khrushchev Asks for U.S. Removal of Jupiter Missiles from Turkey, October 27, 1962

You are worried over Cuba. You say that it worries you because it lies at a distance of 90 miles across the sea from the shores of the United States. However, Turkey lies next to us. Our sentinels are pacing up and down and watching each other. Do you believe that you have the right to demand security for your country and the removal of such weapons that you qualify as offensive, while not recognizing this right for us?

You have stationed devastating rocket weapons, which you call offensive, in Turkey literally right next to us. How then does recognition of our equal military possibilities tally with such unequal relations between our great states? This does not tally at all. . . .

This is why I make this proposal: We agree to remove those weapons from Cuba which you regard as offensive weapons. We agree to do this and to state this commitment in the United Nations. Your representatives will make a statement to the effect that the United States, on its part, bearing in mind the anxiety and concern of the Soviet state, will evacuate its analogous weapons from Turkey. . . .

The U.S. Government will . . . declare that the United States will respect the integrity of the frontiers of Cuba, its sovereignty, undertakes not to intervene in its domestic affairs, not to invade and not to make its territory available as place d'armes for the invasion of Cuba, and also will restrain those who would think of launching an aggression against Cuba either from U.S. territory or from the territory of other states bordering on Cuba.

Kennedy and ExCom on Trading the Jupiter Missiles in Turkey, October 27, 1962

JFK (reading): "Premier Khrushchev told President Kennedy yesterday he would withdraw offensive missiles from Cuba if the United States withdrew its rockets from Turkey."

Speaker?: He didn't really say that, did he? . . .

JFK: That wasn't in the letter [of October 26] we received, was it?

Speaker?: No. . . .

JFK: We're going to be in an insupportable position on this matter if this becomes his proposal. In the first place, we last year tried to get the [Jupiter] missiles out of there [Turkey] because they're not militarily useful, number one. Number two, it's going to—to any man at the United Nations or any other rational man it will look like a very fair trade. . . .

I think you're going to find it very difficult to explain why we are going to take hostile military action in Cuba, against these [missile] sites—what we've been thinking about—the thing that he's saying is, if you'll get yours out of Turkey, we'll get ours out of Cuba. I think we've got a very tough one here. . . .

He's put this out in a way that's caused maximum tension and embarrassment. It's not as if it was a private proposal, which would give us an opportunity to negotiate with the Turks. He's put it out in a way that the Turks are bound to say they don't agree to this. . . .

They've got a very good card. This one is going to be very tough, I think, for us. It's going to be tough in England, I'm sure—as well as other places on the continent—we're going to be forced to take action, that might seem, in my opinion, not a blank check but a pretty good check to take action in Berlin on the grounds that we were wholly unreasonable. Most think—people think that if you're allowed an even trade you ought to take *advantage* of it. Therefore it makes it much more difficult for us to move with world support. These are all the things that—uh—why this is a pretty good play of his. . . .

I'm just thinking about what—what we're going to have to do in a day or so, which is [deleted] sorties and [deleted] days, and possibly an invasion, all because we wouldn't take missiles out of Turkey, and we all know how quickly everybody's courage goes when the blood starts to flow, and that's what's going to happen in NATO, when they—we start these things, and they grab Berlin, and everybody's going to say, "Well that was a pretty good proposition." Let's not kid ourselves that we've got—that's the difficulty. Today it sounds great to reject it, but it's not going to, after we do something. . . .

Thompson: The important thing for Khrushchev, it seems to me, is to be able to say, I saved Cuba, I stopped an invasion—and he can get away with this, if he wants to, and he's had a go at this Turkey thing, and that we'll discuss later. . . .

*LBJ**: Bob [McNamara], if you're willing to give up your missiles in Turkey, you think you ought to [words unclear] why don't you say that to him and say we're cutting a trade—make the trade there? [mixed voices] save all the invasion, lives and—

Speaker?: The State Department, they invite them—we talked about this, and they said they'd be *delighted* to trade those missiles in Turkey for the things in Cuba.

McNamara: I said I thought it was the realistic solution to the problem.

LBJ: Sure. What we were afraid of was he'd never offer this, but what he'd want to do was trade [mixed voices] *Berlin.* . . .

JFK: We can't very well invade Cuba with all its toil, and long as it's going to be, when we could have gotten them out by making a deal on the same missiles in

---

*Llewellyn E. Thompson, U.S. ambassador to the Soviet Union, July 16, 1957–July 27, 1962; U.S. ambassador-at-large, October 3, 1962–1966.
**Lyndon B. Johnson, vice president.

Turkey. If that's part of the record I don't see how we'll have a very good war. . . .

Well, let's see—uh—let's give him [Khrushchev] an explanation of what we're trying to do. We're trying to get it back on the original proposition of last night, and—because we don't want to get into this trade. If we're unsuccessful, then we—it's *possible* that we may have to get back on the Jupiter thing.

Anastas I. Mikoyan and Castro Debate and Review the Crisis, November 3–5, 1962

Mikoyan-Castro Meeting in Havana, November 3, 1962

[*Castro:*] The Soviet Union's concessions had a depressing effect. Psychologically, our people were unprepared for that. There was a feeling of deep disappointment, bitterness, pain. It was as if we had been deprived not of missiles but of the very symbol of solidarity. The announcement of the dismantling of the missile launchers and the return of the missiles to the Soviet Union was first taken by our people for a shameless lie. After all, the Cuban people knew nothing about the agreement—they didn't know that the missiles still belong to the Soviet side. They had no idea of the legal status of the weapon. They were used to a situation where the Soviet Union supplied us with arms that became our property.

"Why was that decision made unilaterally? Why are the missiles being taken away from us? Will all our arms be taken back?" These questions troubled all Cubans. In a matter of 48 hours, this feeling of bitterness and pain spread to the whole people. Events took place in rapid succession. On October 27, it was proposed to withdraw the weapon[s] from Cuba on condition that the bases in Turkey should be abolished. On October 28, there came orders for dismantling and permission for inspection.

It was unbelievable—everybody thought it was a lie.

Second, the message contained not a line about Cuba's advance consent. One might have thought that our consent is just a formal matter. But Cuba is something more than a small country with a small but courageous people. Our revolution is more important than the destiny of our country, the destiny of our people themselves. We must defend and preserve our revolution for the world. Our people felt that decisions taken without agreement with the Cuban government had caused moral damage to our revolution and told on its prestige in the eyes of Latin American peoples.

After the War of Independence, the Americans imposed the so-called Platt Amendment limiting the validity of the Cuban Constitution. That "amendment" denied our country the right to make its territory available for foreign military bases without the consent of the US government. The Americans took advantage of it to grossly interfere in Cuban affairs. . . .

It seemed to many in those days that the Platt Amendment had come back to life. . . .

Besides, the situation is unchanged from the legal point of view, and so is the status quo after the present crisis.

(1) The blockade established by the US government is still there. The United States continues flouting freedom of the seas.

(2) The Americans are trying to determine what weapons we may possess. They are organising control. The situation now shaping up is similar to the situation—past or present—in Morocco, Guinea, Ghana, Ceylon and Yemen.

(3) The United States continues violating Cuban airspace, expecting us to tolerate it. Besides, inspection has been authorised without asking us.

In the light of current events, we find it difficult to see the reasons for the withdrawal of the Soviet strategic weapon. The question arises: Was the matter considered and studied carefully enough? Or was it assumed from the start that the missiles would be pulled out, except that we didn't know? The information we had on the intentions and plans of the Soviet side was inadequate. When [the Cuban official] Che Guevara went to Moscow, the question of publishing the text of the agreement was raised. No clear answer was given. We had considered that the important thing was to have the missiles in Cuba. This is why we found it so hard to believe that they were being taken back to the Soviet Union.

Had there been a demand for the simultaneous abolition of the US base at Guantánamo, our people would have appreciated the demand. . . .

[Mikoyan:] It so happened that we could not consult you before deciding. Imagine that a moment came when Cuba's—and possibly not only Cuba's—fate hung in the balance. The US government had decided to commit aggression. It had massed warships with troops in the Caribbean and alerted a bomber force. Everything was ready for attack. Had we sent you our proposals, an answer might have come in a day or two—also because coding, decoding and translation would have taken time. We had no time for that. We had to decide the same day. The following day Cuba might have been destroyed if not with atom bombs, then by means of bombers carrying rockets with conventional warheads. So massive an attack could have destroyed the launchers on Cuban territory and provided conditions for a naval landing. It was imperative to solve that complicated problem without delay. At about noon on Sunday, we met after receiving a coded message from Ambassador [to Cuba Aleksandr] Alexeyev. It said that there was information about stepped-up preparations for aggression. Information from other sources confirmed that a US attack on Cuba might come in a matter of hours. We had to make a decision by ourselves on saving Cuba. . . .

We were compelled to decide. The loss of Cuba would have been irreplaceable for the whole international communist movement.

We don't necessarily have to keep missiles in Cuba to strike at the United States in case of need. We can do so from our territory. You know that we have a suitable weapon.

Our missiles in Cuba were detected too early. We had expected to be able to publish a declaration after the elections for the US Congress, that is, by mid-November. . . .

Anastas Mikoyan's explanatory remarks were broken off by news of the death of his wife.

On reading the telegram, Cde. Mikoyan asked that it be interpreted for Cde. Fidel Castro.

Thereupon the conversation was broken off. Fidel Castro and [his advisor] Celia Sánchez, deeply perturbed, saw A. Mikoyan to the car.

Mikoyan-Castro Meeting in Havana, November 4, 1962

[*Mikoyan:*] I remember that after visiting Bulgaria [in May 1962], Nikita Khrushchev told you that all through his stay in that country he had been thinking of Cuba, fearing that the Americans might mount armed intervention with the aid of reactionary Latin American governments or commit outright aggression. They refuse to allow Cuba to grow stronger, Nikita Khrushchev told us, and if Cuba were defeated, the whole world revolutionary movement would suffer a heavy blow. We must thwart the American imperialists' plans, he said. . . .

The only purpose of shipping Soviet troops and strategic arms to Cuba was to strengthen your defences. Ours was a containment plan, a plan intended to discourage the imperialists from playing with fire in regard to Cuba. Had we developed strategic arms in secrecy, with America knowing nothing about those arms' presence in Cuba, they would have served as a strong deterrent. That was the assumption we started from. Our military told us that Cuba's palm forests made it possible to dependably camouflage strategic missiles against detection from the air. . . .

In such a situation [U.S. invasion], we would have been unable to refrain from responding to aggression from the United States. That attack would have amounted to an attack on both you and us because we had Soviet troops and strategic missiles stationed in Cuba. A collision would inevitably have triggered a nuclear war. To be sure, we would have destroyed America and suffered severely for our part, but then our country is larger than America. Cuba would have been destroyed first. The imperialists would have done their utmost to destroy it.

We had 10 to 12 hours to go before the United States attacked Cuba. It was indispensable to use the art of diplomacy. Failure would have led to war. We had to use diplomatic means. . . .

As Kennedy agreed to Soviet troops being left in Cuba and as the Cubans kept powerful weapons and anti-aircraft missiles, we may consider that he made a concession for his part.

Kennedy's statement about nonaggression against Cuba by the United States and Latin American countries is another concession. If we take these reciprocal concessions and all other factors into account, we will see that we've won a big victory. Never before have the Americans made such statements. This is why we came to the conclusion that we were achieving the main goal, which is to preserve Cuba. There will be no attack on Cuba. Nor will there be any war. We are winning more favourable positions.

Of course, we should have sent our draft decision to Cuba, should have consulted you and secured your consent before publishing it. We would actually have done so in a normal situation. Fidel Castro wrote us in his letter [of October 26] that aggression within the next 24 hours was imminent. When we received the letter and discussed the situation, the start of aggression was only 10 to 12 hours away.

Let us compare the situation today with what it was before the crisis. At that time the Americans were planning armed intervention against Cuba. But now they have committed themselves not to attack Cuba. This is a great achievement. . . .

Frankly speaking, we had not at all been thinking about the bases in Turkey. But when discussing the dangerous situation that had developed, we received information from the United States saying that, from what [Walter] Lippmann wrote in his column, the Russians might raise the question of abolishing the US bases in Turkey. The possibility of our putting forward such a demand was discussed among Americans. The idea was debated in the United States. That was how that demand came to be advanced. Subsequently, however, we stopped insisting on it because the US bases in that country are no problem for us. The Turkish bases are of little significance as we see it. They will be destroyed in case of war. Of course, they have some political significance but we don't pay them any particular attention although we plan to press for their elimination.

Mikoyan-Castro Meeting in Havana, November 5, 1962

[*Castro:*] We have no doubt that had the siting of the strategic weapon been completed in secret, we would have obtained in that way a powerful deterrent against American plans for attack on our country. That would have meant achieving goals pursued by both the Soviet government and the government of the Republic of Cuba. We consider, however, that the deployment of Soviet missiles in Cuba was important in that it served the interests of the whole socialist camp. Even assuming that their deployment provided no military advantage, it was important politically and psychologically for the effort to contain imperialism and prevent it from implementing its plans for aggression. It follows that the strategic weapon was deployed in Cuba in the interest of defending not only Cuba but the socialist camp as a whole. It was a move made with our full consent.

We were well aware of the significance of that move and consider that it was the right thing to do.

We fully agree that war is inadmissible. We are not against the fact that the measures adopted had a twofold purpose, namely, preventing an attack on Cuba and staving off a world war. We fully subscribe to these aims pursued by the Soviet Union.

What gave rise to misunderstanding was the form in which the matter was discussed. We realise, however, that there were circumstances demanding prompt action and that the situation was not normal. . . .

The United States could have been told that the Soviet Union was ready to dismantle the facility but wanted to discuss the matter with the Cuban government. We believe you should have decided the question that way rather than issuing instructions at once on the removal of the strategic weapon. Such an approach would have eased international tension and made it possible to discuss the problem with the Americans in a more favourable context. It would have enabled us not only to bring about a lessening of international tension and discuss the matter in more favourable conditions but to secure the signing of a declaration.

※ *E S S A Y S*

In the first essay, Thomas G. Paterson of the University of Connecticut studies the origins of the missile crisis, placing the event in the context of tense Cuban-American relations and the Cold War. Conspicuous, threatening U.S. actions incited Cuban fears of invasion. Cuba's quest for defense joined Soviet objectives to prompt the mid-1962 Cuban-Soviet agreement to place missiles on the island. Paterson next explores the management of the crisis. Noting near misses and accidents, and the Executive Committee's inflated record, Paterson questions the thesis that Kennedy's leadership represents a superb example of calculated crisis management. Rather, fear of events spinning out of control—of a nuclear doomsday—mattered as much as anything else in bringing the crisis to a close, Paterson concludes.

Alexander L. George of Stanford University disagrees. In the second essay, he argues that Kennedy's handling of the Cuban missile crisis satisfied the requirements of successful crisis management, and he doubts the defense-of-Cuba theme. George also speculates on the role of psychological variables—emotions, wishful thinking, and the personalities engaged in the confrontation—and emphasizes Kennedy's political worries. Although George acknowledges the threats to crisis management that might have led to a shooting war, he applauds a prudent Kennedy (and, to some extent, Khrushchev) for not stumbling over the brink.

Spinning Out of Control: John F. Kennedy, the War Against Cuba, and the Missile Crisis

THOMAS G. PATERSON

"My God," muttered Richard Helms of the Central Intelligence Agency, "these Kennedys keep the pressure on about [Fidel] Castro." Another CIA officer heard it straight from John F. and Robert F. Kennedy: "Get off your ass about Cuba." Defense Secretary Robert McNamara remembered that "we were hysterical about Castro at the time of the Bay of Pigs and thereafter." As someone said, *Cuba* became one of the four-letter words of the 1960s.

A knowledgeable and engaged President Kennedy spent as much time on Cuba as on any other foreign-policy problem—or more. Cuba stood at the center of his administration's admitted greatest failure, the Bay of Pigs, and its alleged greatest success, the missile crisis. Why did President Kennedy and his chief advisers indulge such a fixation with Cuba and direct so many U.S. resources to an unrelenting campaign to monitor, harass, isolate, and ultimately destroy Havana's radical regime? One answer springs from a candid remark by Robert F. Kennedy, who later wondered "if we did not pay a very great price for being more energetic than wise about a lot of things, especially Cuba." The Kennedys' famed eagerness for action became exaggerated in the case of Cuba. They always wanted to get moving on Cuba, and Castro dared them to try. The popular, intelligent, but erratic Cuban leader, who in January 1959 overthrew the U.S. ally Fulgencio Batista, hurled harsh words at Washington and defiantly challenged the Kennedy model of evolutionary, capitalist development so evident in the Alliance for Progress. As charismatic figures charting new frontiers, Kennedy and Castro often personalized the Cuban-American contest. To Kennedy's great annoyance, Castro could not be wheedled or beaten.

Kennedy's ardent war against *fidelismo* may also have stemmed from his feeling that Castro had double-crossed him. As a senator, Kennedy had initially joined many other Americans in welcoming the Cuban Revolution as an advancement over the "oppressive" Batista dictatorship. Kennedy had urged a "patient attitude" toward the new government, which he did not see as communist. Castro had in fact denied repeatedly that he was a communist, instead proclaiming his allegiance to democracy and private property. But in the process of legitimizing his revolution and resisting U.S. pressure, Castro turned more and more radical. Americans grew impatient with the regime's highly charged anti-Yankeeism, postponement of elections, jailing of critics, and nationalization of property. The president rejected the idea that intense U.S. hostility toward the Cuban Revolution may have contributed to Castro's tightening political grip and flirtation with the Soviet Union. Nor did Kennedy and other Americans wish to acknowledge the measurable benefits of the revolution—improvements in education, medical care, and housing and the elimination of the island's infamous corruption that once had been the American Mafia's domain. Instead, Kennedy officials concluded that Cuba's was a "betrayed revolution."

Richard N. Goodwin, at the time a young White House and State Department official, provided another explanation for the Kennedy fixation with Cuba. He remarked that "the entire history of the Cold War, its positions and assumptions, converged upon the 'problem of Cuba.' " Indeed, the Cold War dominated international politics, and in the zero-sum accounting of the time, a loss for "us" meant a gain for "them." As Cuban-American relations steadily deteriorated, Cuban-Soviet relations gradually improved. Not only did Americans come to believe that a once loyal ally had jilted them for the tawdry embrace of the Soviets; they also grew alarmed that Castro sneered at the Monroe Doctrine by inviting the Soviet military to the island. When Castro, in late 1961, declared himself a Marxist-Leninist, Americans who had long denounced him as a communist felt vindicated. American leaders began to speak of Cuban membership in the "Sino-Soviet bloc," thus providing communists with a "spearhead" to penetrate the Western Hemisphere. From the moment of victory, Castro had called for Cuban-style revolutions throughout Latin America, and Havana had sent agents and arms to other nations to kindle radical fires. Castro's revolutionary mission happened to coincide with Nikita Khrushchev's alarming statement that the Soviet Union supported wars of national liberation worldwide. Cuba came to represent the Cold War in the Western Hemisphere.

Written especially for this volume, this essay is based on Thomas G. Paterson, "Fixation with Cuba: The Bay of Pigs, Missile Crisis, and Covert War Against Castro," in Thomas G. Paterson, ed., *Kennedy's Quest for Victory: American Foreign Policy, 1961–1963* (New York: Oxford University Press, 1989), pp. 123–155, 343–352; Thomas G. Paterson, "The Defense-of-Cuba Theme and the Missile Crisis," *Diplomatic History,* 14 (Spring 1990), 249–256; and Thomas G. Paterson, *Contesting Castro: The United States and the Triumph of the Cuban Revolution* (New York: Oxford University Press, 1994). Printed with permission of the author.

In addition to the Kennedy style and the Cold War, domestic politics influenced the administration's Cuba policy. In the 1960 presidential campaign, Kennedy had seized the Cuban issue to counter Richard Nixon's charge that the inexperienced Democratic candidate would abandon the Chinese islands of Jinmen (Quemoy) and Mazu (Matsu) to communism and prove no match for the hardnosed Khrushchev. "In 1952 the Republicans ran on a program of rolling back the Iron Curtain in Eastern Europe," Kennedy jabbed. "Today the Iron Curtain is ninety miles off the coast of the United States." He asked in private, "How would *we* have saved Cuba if we had [had] the power?" but he nonetheless valued the political payback from his attack. "What the hell," he informed his aides, "they never told us how they would have saved China." Apparently unaware that President Dwight D. Eisenhower had initiated a clandestine CIA program to train Cuban exiles for an invasion of the island, candidate Kennedy bluntly called for just such a project. After exploiting the Cuban issue, Kennedy, upon becoming president, could not easily have retreated. Partisan politics kept his gaze fixed on the defiant Caribbean leader. Everyone seemed eager to know when Kennedy would knock Castro off his perch, and many expected the president to act before the next election.

Overarching all explanations for Kennedy's obsession with Cuba is a major phenomenon of twentieth-century world history: the steady erosion of the authority of imperial powers, which had built systems of dependent, client, and colonial governments. The strong currents of decolonization, anti-imperialism, revolutionary nationalism, and social revolution, sometimes in combination, undermined the instruments that the imperial nations had used to maintain control and order. The Cuban Revolution exemplified this process of breaking up and breaking away. American leaders reacted especially hostilely to this revolution not simply because Castro and his 26th of July Movement taunted them or because domestic politics and the Cold War swayed them but because Cuba, as symbol and reality, challenged U.S. hegemony in Latin America. The specter of "another Cuba" haunted President Kennedy, not just because it would hurt him politically but because "the game would be up through a good deal of Latin America," as Under Secretary of State George Ball put it. The Monroe Doctrine and the U.S. claim to political, economic, and military leadership in the hemisphere seemed at stake. As Castro once remarked, "The United States *had* to fight his revolution."

The Eisenhower administration bequeathed to its successor an unproductive tit-for-tat process of confrontation with Cuba and a legacy of failure. In November 1959 President Eisenhower decided to encourage anti-Castro groups within Cuba to "check" or "replace" the revolutionary regime, and thus end an anti-Americanism that was "having serious adverse effects on the United States position in Latin America and corresponding advantages for international Communism." In March 1960 Eisenhower ordered the CIA to train Cuban exiles for an invasion of their homeland—this shortly after Cuba had signed a trade treaty with the Soviet Union. The CIA, as well, hatched assassination plots against Castro and staged hit-and-run attacks along the Cuban coast. As Cuba undertook land reform that struck at American interests, and nationalized American-owned industries, the United States suspended Cuba's sugar quota and forbade U.S. exports to the island, drastically cutting a once flourishing commerce. On January 3, 1961, fearing an invasion and certain that the U.S. embassy was a "nest of spies" aligned with counterrevolutionaries who were burning cane fields and sabotaging buildings, Castro heatedly demanded that the embassy staff be reduced to the small size of the Cuban delegation in Washington. The United States promptly severed diplomatic relations with Cuba.

Eisenhower failed to topple Castro, but American pressure accelerated the radicalization of the revolution and helped to open the door to the Soviets. Moscow bought sugar, supplied technicians, armed the militia, and offered generous trade terms. Although the revolution's radicalization, given Cuban conditions, was probably inevitable, it was not preordained that Cuba would end up in the Soviet camp. Hostile U.S. policies helped to ensure that outcome. Revolutionary Cuba needed outside assistance to survive. "Russia came to Castro's rescue," Ambassador Philip Bonsal has concluded, "only after the United States had taken steps designed to overthrow him."

To be sure, Kennedy inherited the Cuban problem from Eisenhower. But he did not simply continue his predecessor's anti-Castro policies. Kennedy greatly exaggerated the Cuban threat, attributing to Castro a capability to export revolution that the Cuban leader never had and lavishing on him an attention he did not deserve. Castro was "an affront to our pride" and a "mischief maker," Walter Lippmann perceptively wrote, but he was not a "mortal threat" to the United States. Kennedy significantly increased the pressures against the upstart island. He inherited the Cuban problem—and made it worse.

The questions of whether and under what conditions to approve an exile expedition dominated the president's discussion of Cuba in his first few months in office. Although Kennedy always reserved the authority to cancel the operation right up to the moment of departure, his choices pointed in one direction: Go. National security affairs adviser McGeorge Bundy later said that the president "really was looking for ways to make it work . . . and allowed himself to be persuaded it would work and the risks were acceptable." Kennedy listened to but rejected the counsel of doubting advisers, and he never revealed moral or legal qualms about violently overthrowing a sovereign government. He never requested a contingency plan to disband the exile brigade. In questioning aides, the president worried most about which methods would deliver success and whether the guiding hand of the United States could be concealed. Kennedy sought deniability of an American role but never the demise of the project.

The Bay of Pigs plan began to unravel from the start. As the brigade's old, slow freighters plowed their way to Cuba, B-26 airplanes took to the skies from Nicaragua. On April 15, D-Day-minus-2, the brigade pilots destroyed several parked planes of Castro's meager air force. That same day, as part of a preinvasion ploy, a lone, artificially damaged B-26 flew directly to Miami, where its pilot claimed that he had defected from the Cuban military and had just bombed his country's airfields. But the cover story soon cracked. Snooping journalists noticed that the nose cone of the B-26 was metal; Cuban planes had plastic noses. They observed, too, that the aircraft's guns had not been fired. The American hand was being exposed. The president, still insistent on hiding U.S. complicity, decided to cancel a second D-Day air strike against the remnants of the Cuban air force.

Shortly after midnight on April 17, more than fourteen hundred commandoes motored in small boats to the beaches at Bahía de Cochinos, where they immediately tangled with Castro's militia. But some commandoes never made it, because their boats broke apart on razor-sharp coral reefs. Castro's marauding airplanes shot down two brigade B-26s and sank ships carrying essential communications equipment and ammunition. Fighting ferociously, the brigade nonetheless failed to establish a beachhead. Would Washington try to salvage the mission? Kennedy turned down CIA appeals to dispatch planes from the nearby USS *Essex,* but he did permit some jets to provide air cover for a new B-26 attack from Nicaragua. Piloted this time by American CIA crews, the B-26s arrived an hour after the jets had come and gone. Cuban aircraft downed the B-26s, killing four Americans. With Castro's boasting that the *mercenarios* had been foiled, the final toll: 114 of the exile brigade dead and 1,189 captured; 150 Cuban defenders dead.

"How could I have been so stupid, to let them go ahead?" Kennedy asked an assistant. Stupid or not, Kennedy knew the answers to his own question. First, he dearly sought to oust Castro and to score a victory in the Cold War. Second, his personality and style encouraged action. Always driven to win, Kennedy believed (as one aide put it) "that his disapproval of the plan would be a show of weakness inconsistent with his general stance." One foreign-policy observer explained "how the President got such bad advice from such good advisers":

> The decision on which they were asked to advise was presented as a choice between action and inaction. . . . None of the President's advisers wants it said of him by his colleagues . . . that he . . . loses his nerve when the going gets hot. The Harvard intellectuals are especially vulnerable, the more so from being new on the scene. They are conscious of the fact that the tough-minded military suspect them of being soft-headed. They have to show that they are he-men too, that they can act as well as lecture.

Third, fear of nasty political repercussions influenced the president. Told to disband, brigade members might have refused to give up their arms or might even have mutinied. In any case, Republicans would have scorned a weak-kneed administration. As CIA director Allen Dulles said, Washington had a "disposal" problem. Kennedy approved the operation, finally, because he felt a sense of urgency. CIA analysts advised that time was on Castro's side. Delay would permit the Soviets to strengthen the Cuban military, perhaps with MiG fighters, and the rainy season was about to begin, during which military maneuvers would be difficult. As well, the Guatemalan president, facing awkward questions about Cuban trainees in his country, beseeched Washington to move the exiles out by late April.

Failures in intelligence, operations, decisionmaking, and judgment doomed the Bay of Pigs undertaking. Arrogant CIA architects knew too little about the landing site and assumed too much about Cuba. The CIA also failed to assassinate Fidel Castro. As one CIA official admitted, the agency intended "that Castro would be dead before the landing."

The most controversial operational question remains the canceled second D-Day air strike. Postcrisis critics have complained that the president lost his nerve and made a decision that condemned the expedition to disaster. Cuban air supremacy did prove important to Cuba's triumph. But was it decisive? A preemptive strike on D-Day against the Cuban air force would not have delivered victory to the invaders. After the first air attack, Castro had dispersed his planes; the brigade's B-26s would have encountered considerable difficulty in locating and destroying them. And even if a D-Day assault had disabled all of Castro's planes, then what? The brigade's 1,400 warriors would have had to face Castro's army of 25,000 and the nation's 200,000 militia. The commandoes most likely would not have survived the Cuban military's overwhelming power.

Kennedy and his advisers believed that the invasion would ignite a popular revolt against an unpopular government. Yet no rebellion erupted. Kennedy also assumed that, should the brigade prove incapable of taking territory, it could melt into the mountains and become a guerrilla army. But the mountains lay eighty miles away, with impassable swamps between. The guerrilla option proved impossible. As well, Kennedy officials nurtured the fiction that American participation could be hidden and plausibly denied. "Trying to mount an operation of this magnitude from the United States," a CIA official later wrote, "is about as covert as walking nude across Times Square without attracting attention." Until his decision to cancel the second strike, Kennedy nonetheless clung to the fiction of deniability.

"Mr. President, it could have been worse," said an aide to Adlai Stevenson. How? "It might have succeeded." Had all gone well with the chain reaction of beachhead, rebellion, and Castro's death or departure, the victory would only have "exchanged a Castro pesthouse for a post-Castro asylum." Tainted as an American stooge, the head of the new government would have struggled to win public favor. Well-armed Castroites would probably have initiated a protracted guerrilla war against the American-created regime. The Soviets might have helped Castro's forces, and volunteers from around the world might have swelled the resistance—as in the Spanish Civil War of the 1930s, as the historian and Kennedy adviser Arthur M. Schlesinger, Jr., had warned. The United States would have had to save its puppet government through military aid, advisers, and maybe even troops. To have sustained a successful Bay of Pigs invasion, then, the Kennedy administration probably would have had to undertake a prolonged and expensive occupation of the island.

Defeat did not chasten the administration. On April 20 the beleaguered president spoke out. "Let the record show," he boomed, "that our restraint is not inexhaustible." Indeed, the United States intended to defend the Monroe Doctrine and carry on a "relentless" struggle with communism in "every corner of the globe." In familiar words, Kennedy declared that "the complacent, the self-indulgent, the soft societies are about to be swept away with the debris of history. Only the strong . . . can possibly survive." Attorney General Robert Kennedy remarked that the Bay of Pigs "insult needed to be redressed rather quickly."

Critical to understanding the missile crisis of fall 1962 is the relationship between post–Bay of Pigs U.S. activities and the Soviet-Cuban decisions to place on the island missiles that could strike the United States. In May 1962 Soviet and Cuban officials first discussed the idea of deploying nuclear-tipped missiles on the island; in July Raúl Castro, in Moscow, initialed an agreement; in late August and early September, during a trip by Che Guevara to Moscow, the two nations put the accord into final form.

After the Bay of Pigs, the Kennedy administration launched a multitrack program of covert, economic, diplomatic, and propagandistic elements calculated to overthrow the Castro government. This multidimensional project prompted the Cuban-Soviet decisions of mid-1962. Secretary of Defense Robert McNamara said later: "If I had been in Moscow or Havana at that time [1961–1962], I would have believed the Americans were preparing for an invasion." Indeed, Havana had to fear a successful Bay of Pigs operation conducted by U.S. forces.

Encouraged by the White House, the CIA created a huge station in Miami called JM/WAVE to recruit and organize Cuban exiles. In Washington, Robert Kennedy became a ramrod for action. At a November 4, 1961, White House meeting, the attorney general made his pitch: "Stir things up on the island with espionage, sabotage, general disorder." The president himself asked Colonel Edward Lansdale to direct Operation Mongoose—"to use our available assets . . . to help Cuba overthrow the Communist regime." Operation Mongoose and JM/WAVE, although failing to unseat Castro, punished Cubans. CIA-handled saboteurs burned cane fields and blew up factories and oil-storage tanks. In a December 1961 raid, for example, a seven-man team blasted a railroad bridge, derailed an approaching train, and torched a sugar warehouse. One group, Agrupacíon Montecristi, attacked a Cuban patrol boat off the northern coast of the island in May 1962. Directorio Revolucionario Estudiantil, another exile organization, used two boats to attack Cuba in August. Alpha 66 attacked Cuba on numerous occasions. CIA agents contaminated goods leaving European ports for Cuba, and they bribed European manufacturers to produce faulty equipment for Cuba—as when a German industrialist shipped off-center ball bearings. British-made Leland buses were sabotaged, too. These spoiling operations compelled the Castro government to divert scarce resources from economic and social programs to coastal defense and internal surveillance. They also pushed Cuba toward greater dependence on the Soviet Union.

By 1962 more than two hundred anti-Castro, Cuban exile organizations operated in the United States. Many of them banded together under the leadership of José Miró Cardona, the former prime minister. Miro Cardona met with President Kennedy in Washington on April 10, 1962, and the Cuban exile left the meeting persuaded that Kennedy intended to use U.S. armed forces against Cuba. Indeed, after Miró Cardona returned to Miami, he and the Revolutionary Council—the government in exile—began to identify possible recruits for a Cuban unit in the U.S. military.

The CIA, meanwhile, devised new plots to kill Castro with poisonous cigars, pills, and needles—to no avail. Did the Kennedys know about these death schemes? Robert Kennedy learned about them in mid-1962, and his biographer Arthur M. Schlesinger, Jr., claims that the attorney general ordered an end to assassination projects. But they did not end. The president apparently never directly ordered the assassination of Castro—at least, no trail of documents leads to the Kennedy White House. But of course, nobody uttered the word *assassination* in the presence of the president or committed the word to paper, thereby honoring the principle of plausible deniability. Advisers instead simply mentioned the need to remove Castro. "And if killing him was one of the things that was to be done in this connection," assassination was attempted because "we felt we were acting within the guidelines." So bespoke the CIA's Richard Helms. President Kennedy may or may not have known about the assassination plots, but he did set the general guidelines.

Intensified economic coercion joined forces with these covert activities. The Kennedy administration banned most imports of Cuban products in February 1962. Washington also pressed its North Atlantic Treaty Organization allies to support the "economic isolation" of Cuba. The embargo hurt. Cuba had to pay higher freight costs, enlarge its foreign debt, and suffer innumerable factory shutdowns because industries could no longer obtain spare parts once bought in the United States. Cuba's economic woes also stemmed from the flight of technicians and managers, a decline in tourism, high workers' absenteeism rates, the drying up of foreign capital investment, hastily conceived policies to diversify the economy, and suffocating government controls. The overall effect on Cuba of U.S. economic measures—greater political centralization, more state management, closer ties to the Soviet Union—did not serve U.S. intentions. By 1962, 82 percent of Cuba's exports flowed to communist countries, and 85 percent of its imports came from them. As with military defense, so with the economy: The Soviet Union became Cuba's lifeline.

The Kennedy administration engineered Cuba's ouster from the Organization of American States in early 1962. The expulsion registered loudly in Havana, which interpreted it as "political preparation for an invasion." By spring 1962, moreover, fifteen Latin American states had answered Washington's call to break relations with Cuba.

At about the same time, American military planning and activities—some public, some secret—demonstrated a determination to cripple the Castro government. Operation Mongoose director Lansdale noted in a top-secret memorandum to the president that he designed his schemes to "help the people of Cuba overthrow the Communist regime from within Cuba and institute a new government." But he asked: "If conditions and assets permitting a revolt [timed for October 1962] are achieved in Cuba, and if U.S. help is required to sustain this condition, will the U.S. respond promptly with military force to aid the Cuban revolt?" Lansdale gave the answer he preferred: "The basic plan requires complete and efficient support of the military." Another contemporary document, this one from the chairman of the Joint Chiefs of Staff, General Maxwell Taylor, noted in the spring of 1962 that the Operation Mongoose plan to overthrow the Cuban government would be undertaken largely by "indigenous resources" but recognized "that final success will require decisive U.S. military intervention." Because the plan also required close cooperation with Cuban exiles, it is likely that Castro's spies picked up from the leaky Cuban community in Miami at least vague suggestions that the U.S. military contemplated military action against Cuba. As CIA agents liked to joke, there were three ways to transmit information rapidly: telegraph, telephone, and tell-a-Cuban.

American military maneuvers heightened Cuban fears. One well-publicized U.S. exercise, staged during April, included 40,000 troops and an amphibious landing on a small island near Puerto Rico. Throughout 1962 some noisy American politicians called for the real thing: an invasion of Cuba. In summer 1962, moreover, the U.S. Army began a program to create Spanish-speaking units; the

Cuban exiles who signed up had as their "primary" goal a "return to Cuba to battle against the Fidel Castro regime."

By the late spring and early summer of 1962, then, when Havana and Moscow discussed defensive measures that included medium-range missiles, Cuba felt besieged from several quarters. The Soviet Union had become its trading partner, and the Soviets, after the Bay of Pigs, had begun military shipments that included small arms, howitzers, machine guns, armored personnel carriers, patrol boats, tanks, MiG jet fighters, and surface-to-air missiles (SAMs). Yet all this weaponry, it seemed, had not deterred the United States. Given the failure, moreover, of Kennedy's multitrack program to unseat Castro, "were we right or wrong to fear direct invasion [next]?" asked Fidel Castro. As he said in July 1962, shortly after striking the missile-deployment agreement with the Soviets: "We must prepare ourselves for that direct invasion."

Had there been no exile expedition at the Bay of Pigs, no destructive covert activities, no assassination plots, no military maneuvers and plans, and no economic and diplomatic steps to harass, isolate, and destroy the Castro government in Havana, the Cuban missile crisis would not have occurred. The origins of the October 1962 crisis derived largely from the concerted U.S. campaign to quash the Cuban Revolution. To stress only the global dimension (Soviet-American competition), as is commonly done, is to slight the local or regional sources of the conflict and thus to miss the central point that Premier Nikita Khrushchev would never have had the opportunity to install dangerous missiles in the Caribbean if the United States had not been attempting to overthrow the Cuban government. This interpretation does not dismiss but incorporates the view, predominant in the scholarly literature, that the emplacement of nuclear missiles in Cuba served the Soviet strategic goal of catching up in the nuclear-arms race. Rather, the interpretation in this essay emphasizes that both Cuba and the Soviet Union calculated that their interests would be served by putting medium- and intermediate-range rockets on the island. Havana hoped to gain deterrent power to thwart an expected American invasion, and Moscow hoped to enhance its deterrent power in the Cold War and save a new ally. From Castro's perspective, the United States would not start a local, conventional war out of fear that it would then have to risk a nuclear war.

"We'd carried out the Bay of Pigs operation, never intending to use American military force—but the Kremlin didn't know that," Defense Secretary Robert McNamara recalled. "We were running covert operations against Castro" and "people in the Pentagon were even talking about a first strike [nuclear policy]. . . . So the Soviets may well have believed we were seeking Castro's overthrow *plus* a first strike capability. This may have led them to do what they did in Cuba."

Cuba's eagerness for Soviet military assistance is well documented in the contemporary record. Castro and other Cuban officials made repeated, consistent, and compelling statements that their nation faced an American onslaught. "Cuba took measures to defend its security against a systematic policy of hostility and aggression," Castro privately explained to United Nations secretary general U Thant during the October crisis. U.S. documents reveal that American decisionmakers knew that the Cuban-Soviet military linkage grew from Cuba's fear of invasion. They did not say so publicly, of course, for this admission would have acknowledged their own responsibility for generating the fear. In September 1962 CIA analysts concluded that "the main purpose of the present military build-up in Cuba is to strengthen the Communist regime there against what the Cubans and Soviets conceive to be a danger that the US may attempt by one means or another to overthrow it." In early October the Department of State concluded that Castro feared a U.S. invasion and that "this crash build-up of military and economic assistance did not represent a Soviet initiative but rather a response to insistent demands from Castro for help." Early in the crisis, a CIA office noted Cuba's numerous "invasion scares" in the summer of 1962, and a postcrisis State Department study indicated that when Soviet "military equipment began arriving in volume in late summer 1962 the US government realized that these chronic [invasion] fears played a part in Castro's motives."

Why did the Cubans and Soviets decide on medium (MRBM) and intermediate (IRBM) missiles, with ranges of 1,020 and 2,200 nautical miles, respectively, instead of on a military pact, nonnuclear, conventional forces, or weapons that might meet the U.S. definition of "defensive"? The answer is that the Cubans sought effective deterrence. One is reminded of similar American thinking, near the end of the Second World War, that the Japanese were so fanatical that only the threat of annihilation from the atomic bomb would persuade them to surrender. The Cubans, in fact, looking for an immediate deterrent effect, had wanted to make the 1962 missile agreement public, but the Soviets, guessing that the deployment could be camouflaged until the missiles became operational, preferred secrecy.

On October 14 an American U-2 plane photographed the missile sites in Cuba, thus providing the first hard evidence, as distinct from the reports of exiles, that the island was becoming a nuclear base. "He can't do that to me!" snapped Kennedy when he saw the pictures two days later. He had warned the Soviets that the United States would not suffer "offensive" weapons in Cuba, although the warnings had come after the Cuban-Soviet decision of early summer. The president convened his top advisers shortly before noon on October 16. His first questions focused on the firing readiness of the missiles and the probability that they carried nuclear warheads. The advisers gave negative, although tentative, answers. All agreed that the missiles could become operational in a brief time. Discussion of military options (invasion? air strike?) dominated this first meeting. Kennedy's immediate preference became clear: "We're certainly going . . . to take out these . . . missiles." Kennedy showed little interest in negotiations.

At a second meeting on October 16, Secretary of State Dean Rusk argued against the surprise air strike that General Taylor had bluntly advocated. Rusk recommended instead "a direct message to Castro." At the close of Rusk's remarks, Kennedy immediately asked: "Can we get a little idea about what the military thing *is*?" Bundy then posed a question now central to the history of the missile crisis: "How gravely does this change the strategic balance?" McNamara thought "not at all," but Taylor disputed him. Although Kennedy himself seemed uncertain, he did complain that the missile emplacement in Cuba "makes them look like they're co-equal with us." And, added Treasury Secretary C. Douglas Dillon, who obviously knew the president's competitive personality, the presence of the missiles made it appear that "we're scared of the Cubans."

Then the rambling discussion turned to Khrushchev's motivation. The Soviet leader had been cautious on Berlin, Kennedy noted. "It's just as if we suddenly began to put a major number of MRBMs in Turkey," the president went on. "Now that'd be goddam dangerous." Bundy jumped in: "Well, we *did,* Mr. President." Not liking the sound of a double standard, Kennedy lamely answered, "Yeah, but that was five years ago." Actually, the American Jupiter missiles in Turkey, under a 1959 agreement with Ankara, had gone into launch position in mid-1961—during the Kennedy administration—and were not turned over to Turkish forces until October 22, 1962, the very day Kennedy informed Moscow that it must withdraw its SS-4 medium-range and SS-5 intermediate-range missiles from Cuba.

For the next several days, Kennedy's advisers, named the Executive Committee (ExCom), met frequently in tight secrecy and discussed four policy options: "talk them out," "squeeze them out," "shoot them out," or "buy them out." In exhausting sessions marked by frank disagreement and changing minds, ExCom members weighed the advantages and disadvantages of invasion, bombing, quarantine, and diplomacy. The president gradually moved with a majority of ExCom advisers toward a quarantine or blockade of Cuba: incoming ships would be stopped and inspected for military cargo. McNamara persistently argued this alternative against the generals, Treasury Secretary Douglas Dillon, CIA director John McCone, and Dean Acheson, all of whom urged an air strike. When queried as to whether an air strike would knock out all of the known missiles, however, Taylor replied: "The best we can offer you is to destroy 90%." In other words, some missiles in Cuba would remain in place for firing against the United States. Robert Kennedy also worried that the Soviets might react unpredictably with military force, "which could be so serious as to lead to general nuclear war." In any case, the attorney general insisted, there would be no "Pearl Harbor type of attack" on *his* brother's record.

By October 22 the president had made two decisions. The first was to quarantine Cuba to prevent further military shipments and to impress the Soviets with U.S. resolve to force the missiles out. If the Soviets kept coming, more drastic measures would be taken. Second, Kennedy decided to inform the Soviets of U.S. policy through a television address rather than through diplomatic channels. ExCom advisers have dubiously argued that a surprise public speech became necessary to rally world opinion behind U.S. policy and to prevent Khrushchev himself from issuing a "blustering ultimatum." But some ExCom participants advised that negotiations be tried first. The former ambassador to the Soviet Union, Charles Bohlen, claimed that Moscow would have to retaliate against the United States if its technicians died from American bombs. A stern letter to Khrushchev should be "tested" as a method to gain withdrawal of the missiles. "I don't see the urgency of military action," Bohlen told the president. And U.N. ambassador Adlai Stevenson grimly appealed to an unreceptive Kennedy: "The existence of nuclear missile bases anywhere is negotiable before we start anything." Going into the crisis, however, Kennedy refused to negotiate with either Khrushchev or Castro.

In his evening televised speech on October 22, Kennedy demanded that the Soviets dismantle the missiles in Cuba, and he announced the Caribbean quarantine as an "initial" step. The missile crisis soon became an international war of nerves. More than sixty American ships began patrols to enforce the blockade. The Strategic Air Command went on nuclear alert, moving upward to Defense Condition (DEFCON) 2 for the first time ever (the next level is deployment for combat). B-52 bombers, loaded with nuclear weapons, stood ready, while men and equipment moved to the southeastern United States to prepare for an invasion. The Soviets did not mobilize or redeploy their huge military, nor did they take measures to make their strategic forces less vulnerable. The Soviets also refrained from testing the quarantine: Their ships turned around and went home. But what next? On October 26 Kennedy and some ExCom members, thinking that the Soviets were stalling, soured on the quarantine. Sentiment for military action strengthened.

The "first real blink" in the crisis came in the afternoon of October 26. A Soviet embassy officer, Aleksander Fomin, met with ABC television correspondent John Scali and urged him to carry a message to the State Department: The Soviet Union would withdraw the missiles if the United States would promise not to invade Cuba. Scali scurried to Rusk, who sent the emissary back to Fomin with the reply that American leaders were interested in discussing the proposal. In the meantime, a rambling private Khrushchev letter arrived with the same offer, claiming that the missiles had been deployed in Cuba only because the United States had been threatening the island.

In the morning of October 27, another Khrushchev message came, upping the stakes: Khrushchev would trade the missiles in Cuba for the American missiles in Turkey. Kennedy felt trapped, because "we are now in the position of risking war in Cuba and in Berlin over missiles in Turkey which are of little military value." At first Kennedy hesitated to accept a swap—because he did not want to appear to be giving up anything in the face of Soviet provocation; because he knew that the proud Turks would recoil from the appearance of being "traded off in order to appease an enemy"; and because acceptance of a missile trade would lend credence to charges that the United States all along had been applying a double standard. Kennedy told ExCom that Khrushchev's offer caused "embarrassment," for most people would think it "a very fair trade." Indeed, Moscow had played "a very good card."

In the afternoon of October 27 more bad news rocked the White House. An American U-2 plane overflew the eastern part of the Soviet Union, probably because its equipment malfunctioned. Soviet fighters scrambled to intercept it, and American jets from Alaska took flight to rescue the errant aircraft. Although the spy plane flew home without having sparked a dogfight, the incident carried the potential of sending the crisis to a more dangerous level. Worse still, a U-2 was shot down over Cuba by a surface-to-air missile (SAM). The shootdown constituted a serious escalation. A distressed McNamara now thought that "invasion had become almost inevitable." But Kennedy hesitated to retaliate, surely scared about taking a step toward a nuclear nightmare. The president decided to ignore Khrushchev's second letter and answer the first. And he dispatched his brother Robert to deliver an ultimatum to Soviet ambassador Anatoly Dobrynin: Start pulling out the missiles within forty-eight hours, or "we would remove them." After Dobrynin asked about the Jupiters in Turkey, Robert Kennedy presented an important American concession: They would be dismantled if the problem in Cuba were resolved. As the president had said in an ExCom meeting, "we can't very well invade Cuba with all its toil . . . when we could have gotten them out by making a deal on the same missiles in Turkey." But should the Soviets leak word of a "deal," Robert Kennedy told the Soviet ambassador, the United States would disavow the offer.

On October 28, faced with an ultimatum and a concession, and fearful that the Cubans might precipitate a greater Soviet-American conflagration, Khrushchev retreated. Washington and Moscow struck an agreement. The Soviet Union promised to dismantle the SS-4s and SS-5s under United Nations supervision, and the United States pledged not to invade Cuba. The crisis had ended just when the nuclear giants seemed about to stumble over the brink. Although an embittered Castro thwarted a United Nations inspection system, U.S. reconnaissance planes monitored the missiles' departure. The Soviets also crated IL-28 bombers and shipped them back to the Soviet Union. In April 1963 the Jupiter missiles came down in Turkey. But Castro remained skeptical of the no-invasion pledge. As he once remarked to U Thant, it was difficult for Cubans to believe a simple American "promise not to commit a crime."

John F. Kennedy's handling of the Cuban missile crisis has received high grades as a stunning success and a model for crisis management. Secretary of State Dean Rusk applauded Kennedy for having "ice water in his veins." Arthur M. Schlesinger, Jr., has effusively written that Kennedy's crisis leadership constituted a "combination of toughness and restraint, of will, nerve, and wisdom, so brilliantly controlled, so matchlessly calibrated." Kennedy's handling of the crisis, as we know from declassified documents today, actually stands less as a supreme display of careful crisis management and more as a case of near misses, close calls, and narrow squeaks that scared officials on both sides into a settlement, because, in the words of McGeorge Bundy, the crisis was "so near to spinning out of control." "We were in luck," Ambassador John Kenneth Galbraith ruminated, "but success in a lottery is no argument for lotteries."

During the hair-trigger days of the crisis, much went wrong, the level of danger constantly rose, and weary and irritable decisionmakers sensed that they were losing their grip. "A high risk of uncontrollable escalation" dogged the crisis, as McNamara recalled. So much came apart; so much could not be reined in. The two U-2 incidents—the shootdown over Cuba and the straying over Soviet territory—rank high on the list. In the first case, a Soviet commander interpreted his orders in such a way as to fire on the U.S. spy plane. At one ExCom meeting, Vice President Lyndon Johnson remarked: "Imagine some crazy Russian captain" shooting another one down. There was also the serious possibility that a "crackpot" exile group would attempt to assassinate Castro or raid the island. Operation Mongoose sabotage teams actually maneuvered inside Cuba during the crisis and could not be reached by their CIA handlers. What if this "half-assed operation," Robert Kennedy worried, ignited trouble? One of these teams did blow up a Cuban factory on November 8.

Not until October 27—to cite another misstep—did the administration think to inform the Soviets that the quarantine line was an arc measured at 500 nautical miles from Cape Maisi, Cuba. What if a Soviet captain inadvertently piloted his ship into the blockade zone? Danger lurked, too, in the way the commander of the Strategic Air Command issued DEFCON 2 alert instructions. He did so in the clear, following the military's standard operating crisis procedures. Alerts serve to prepare American forces for war, but they may also provoke an adversary to think that the United States might launch a first strike. Under such circumstances, the adversary might be tempted to strike first.

The U.S. Navy's antisubmarine warfare activities also carried the potential of escalating the crisis. Soviet submarines prowled near the quarantine line, and, following standing orders, Navy ships forced several of them to surface. In one case, a Navy commander exercised the high-risk option of dropping a depth charge on a Soviet submarine. As in so many of these examples, decisionmakers in Washington lost some control of the crisis to personnel at the operational level.

ExCom members represented considerable intellectual talent and experience, and the policy they urged on the president ultimately forced the Soviets to back down. But a mythology of grandeur, illusion of control, and embellishment of performance have obscured the history of the committee. ExCom debated alternatives under "intense strain," often in a "state of anxiety and emotional exhaustion." Two advisers may have suffered such stress that they became passive and unable to perform their responsibilities. An assistant to Adlai Stevenson recalled that he had had to become an ExCom "backup" for the ambassador because, "while he could speak clearly, his memory wasn't very clear." Asked if failing health produced this condition, Vice Admiral Charles Wellborn answered that the "emotional state and nervous tension that was involved in it [missile crisis] had this effect." Stevenson was feeling "pretty frightened." So apparently was Dean Rusk. Robert Kennedy remembered that the secretary of state "frequently could not attend our meetings," because "he had a virtually complete breakdown mentally and physically." We cannot determine how stress affected the advice ExCom gave Kennedy, but at least we know that the crisis managers struggled against time, sleep, exhaustion, and themselves, and they did not always think clearheadedly at a time when the stakes were very high.

As for the Soviets, they, too, sensed a crisis spinning out of control. Khrushchev's letter of October 26 to Kennedy betrayed desperation, if not disarray, in the Kremlin. "You and I should not now pull on the ends of the rope in which you have tied a knot of war, because the harder you and I pull, the tighter the knot will become," the Soviet premier wrote. When the knot becomes too tight, Khrushchev observed, it will have to be cut, unleashing the "dread forces our two countries possess." Khrushchev also had to worry about *his* field commanders. Soviet forces in Cuba possessed tactical nuclear missiles with warheads. Although the Soviet commander did not have predelegated authority to fire them, the Kremlin had to worry about possible mishap, miscommunication, or panic that might lead to a firing. Given these circumstances and the downing of the U-2 over Cuba, Khrushchev, too, faced a failure of control and the possible ascendancy of accident.

Add to these worries the Soviet premier's troubles with Fidel Castro, who demanded a bold Soviet response to U.S. actions and who might provoke an incident with the United States that could escalate the crisis. Castro pressed the Soviets to use nuclear weapons to save Cuba should the United States attack. "Such adventurists," remarked a Soviet decisionmaker. Khrushchev sternly told his advisers: "You see how far things can go. We've got to get those missiles out of there before a real fire starts." He sensed that time was running out, that events were out-pacing the wits of leaders. The United States might strike Cuba from the air and invade, and then what? Like Kennedy, to head off disaster, he appealed for a settle-ment—and the two men and nations compromised. That Khrushchev had grown nervous and fearful about another dangerous twist in the crisis seems clear, because he took the unusual step of announcing the withdrawal of the missiles in a message on Radio Moscow. He did not want to waste the precious time that would have been required to encode, transmit, decode, and translate a diplomatic message. If the crisis had lasted more than thirteen days, remembered a U.S. adviser, "the whole thing would have begun to unravel."

President Kennedy helped to precipitate the missile crisis by harassing Cuba through his multitrack program. Then he reacted to the crisis by suspending diplo-macy in favor of public confrontation. In the end, with the management of the cri-sis disintegrating, he frightened himself. In order to postpone doomsday, or at least to prevent a high-casualty invasion of Cuba, he moderated the American response and compromised. Khrushchev withdrew his missiles, while gaining what Ambas-sador Llewellyn Thompson thought was the "important thing" all along for the So-viet leader: being able to say "I saved Cuba. I stopped an invasion."

Kennedy's Prudent, Successful Crisis Management

ALEXANDER L. GEORGE

Seven operational principles or "requirements" [of crisis management] have been identified from earlier studies of some past crises.

1. Each side's political authorities must maintain informed control of some kind over military options—alerts, deployments, and low-level actions, as well as the selection and timing of military movements.
2. The tempo and momentum of military movements may have to be deliberately slowed down and pauses created to provide enough time for the two sides to exchange diplomatic signals and communications and to give each side ade-quate time to assess the situation, make decisions, and respond to proposals.
3. Movements of military forces must be carefully coordinated with diplomatic actions as part of an integrated strategy for terminating the crisis acceptably without war or escalation to higher levels of violence.
4. Movements of military forces and threats of force intended to signal resolve must be consistent with limited diplomatic objectives—that is, "noise" must be avoided or minimized.
5. Military moves and threats should be avoided that give the opponent the im-pression that one is about to resort to large-scale warfare, thereby forcing him to consider preemption.

Reprinted from *Avoiding War: Problems of Crisis Management,* by Alexander L. George

6. Diplomatic-military options should be chosen that signal, or are consistent with, a desire to negotiate a way out of the crisis rather than to seek a military solution.

7. Diplomatic proposals and military moves should be selected that leave the opponent a way out of the crisis that is compatible with his fundamental interests. . . .

The Soviet attempt to deploy some 42 medium- and 24 to 32 intermediate-range ballistic missiles (IRBMs) into Cuba during the late summer and early fall of 1962 triggered the most dangerous crisis of the Cold War. Unforeseen and unwanted by either side, this war-threatening confrontation was eventually resolved peacefully through careful crisis management by both Washington and Moscow. In a hastily arranged quid pro quo that Nikita Khrushchev initially proposed, the Soviet leader agreed to remove the missiles in return for a pledge by President John F. Kennedy not to invade Cuba in the future and certain assurances regarding the removal of U.S. Jupiter missiles from Turkey.

This case provides a sobering example of how two leaders can stumble into a war-threatening crisis; it calls attention to the importance of the views and personalities of top-level leaders; it provides a striking example of the fundamental policy dilemma of crisis management; and, most important, it demonstrates the critical importance of adhering to the political and operational "requirements" of crisis management in order to avoid war. At the same time, ironically, the crisis was resolved in part *because* it became difficult to meet some of these requirements and the process of managing the crisis began to break down during the last day of the confrontation, strengthening the incentives of both Kennedy and Khrushchev to end it immediately before it escalated.

To gain his objectives, Khrushchev chose a *fait accompli* strategy for achieving a covert deployment of missiles into Cuba. Before Kennedy discovered that strategic missiles were being deployed into Cuba, and at a time when he regarded such a bold action by Khrushchev as unlikely, the president employed the familiar strategy of "drawing a line." He distinguished between the deployment of "defensive" weapons (after U.S. intelligence reported the presence of Soviet air defense missiles in Cuba), which he regarded as acceptable, and "offensive" weapons that could hit the United States, which the president warned would be unacceptable. After the belated discovery by U.S. intelligence that a large number of strategic missiles were already in Cuba, Kennedy chose a variant of the strategy of coercive diplomacy as a means of persuading Khrushchev to remove them rather than resorting either to military options or a purely diplomatic approach.

Kennedy's initiation of the blockade as the initial move in his strategy of coercive diplomacy triggered a period of intense crisis bargaining between the president and Khrushchev. Both sides improvised tactics that juxtaposed efforts at rational persuasion, threats, and—eventually—offers of accommodation. The risk of escalation cast an ominous pall over the crisis bargaining and played an equivocal role that deserves close scrutiny. Without engaging in a reckless competition in risk-taking, each side attempted to some extent to play upon the other's fear of escalation, but, at the same time, both also acted cautiously to avoid escalation and generally adhered to crisis management principles. . . .

For many years after the Cuban Missile Crisis, Western analysts were forced to infer the motivations and calculations that led Khrushchev to decide upon the missile deployment as best they could without benefit of useful data from well-informed Soviet sources. More recently, several conferences and interviews with Soviet personnel and, later, with Cuban officials, organized since October 1987 by Harvard University's Center for Science and International Affairs of the Kennedy School, and a number of articles by Soviet and Cuban officials, have thrown important new light on various aspects of the Cuban Missile Crisis. However, only limited information has been made available from the Soviet archives, and the recollections and opinions of Soviet participants in these meetings have not settled the question of Khrushchev's motives and objectives. At the same time, these more recent accounts strongly suggest that Khrushchev's motivation included a complex emotional dimension that sprang from frustration at the exposure by the United States of Soviet strategic inferiority and the collapse of his Berlin policy, resentment of the U.S. deployment of Jupiter missiles in Turkey, and concern over mounting foreign policy problems.

While some Soviet participants in these dialogues have argued that fear of a U.S. invasion of Cuba was uppermost in Khrushchev's mind in deciding on the missile deployment, they have not been able to document this claim or to provide a wholly persuasive argument on its behalf. At the same time, other Soviet participants have stated as firmly that the major (or only) purpose of the missile deployment was to redress the strategic imbalance. Given the paucity of hard evidence on this matter and the inherent difficulty of sorting out and assigning weights to different motivations, the question of whether Khrushchev was more interested in deterring a U.S. invasion of Cuba or in redressing the strategic imbalance cannot be resolved. Certainly, Khrushchev did use concern about U.S. intentions to persuade some of his colleagues, and in particular the reluctant Cubans, that installation of Soviet nuclear missiles, and not lesser means, would be necessary to deter a U.S. attack. And, after the crisis, that indeed became the official Soviet rationale for the deployment.

In his memoirs, on the other hand, Khrushchev admitted that his objective in deploying the missiles was not limited to deterring an attack on Cuba but was also aimed at achieving a significant improvement in the strategic nuclear balance. It remains entirely plausible that Khrushchev seized upon the possibility of a threat to Cuba as an opportunity for securing a quick fix of the strategic nuclear imbalance, which the slowly developing Soviet ICBM program could not achieve for a number of years, by deploying medium-range missiles into Cuba. Certainly, no source disagrees that Khrushchev's motivation for finding a way to redress the imbalance was extremely strong following the collapse in late 1961 of his assertive foreign policy of the late 1950s and early 1960s. During these years, it may be recalled, the Soviet leader had attempted to nourish and exploit U.S. fears of a missile gap by repeatedly making dramatic and chilling boasts of a rapid and substantial growth of the Soviet ICBM force. In the autumn of 1961, Khrushchev's boasts were exposed by the Kennedy administration as wholly unfounded.

If the question of Khrushchev's motivation and objectives cannot be fully resolved, what can be said about his calculation of the risks of the missile deployment? . . . There is considerable agreement among Soviet officials and U.S.

analysts that the policy-making procedure Khrushchev employed in this case was seriously flawed and that important components of the decision were so questionable as to raise the possibility that a strong element of wishful thinking on the Soviet leader's part was at work. Still, although the attempt to achieve the missile deployment by means of a covert *fait accompli* was not a well-calculated risk—indeed, it was much more of a gamble than Khrushchev and his supporters believed—the irony is that it almost worked.

That Khrushchev badly miscalculated is evident. It is not clear on what grounds Khrushchev based his confidence that the missile deployment could be completed before the United States became aware of it. Several of his advisers have claimed that they conveyed their doubts on this score to Khrushchev at the time. The risk that the missile deployment would be discovered and trigger a strong U.S. reaction also worried Cuban leaders. Another critical miscalculation was Khrushchev's confident assumption that once Kennedy learned there were missiles in Cuba, he would accept the *fait accompli* without creating a dangerous, war-threatening crisis.

The available record makes amply clear that Khrushchev and some of his key advisers convinced themselves that there was an excellent chance of achieving the *fait accompli* via secrecy and deception. They gave surprisingly little thought to what would happen if the deployment were discovered before it was completed. The available record gives no indication of advance contingency planning for that possibility. It would appear that Khrushchev and his advisers assumed that in the unlikely event the deployment was discovered before it was completed, the initial U.S. response would be at the diplomatic level rather than one of a military character. The graver risk of a shooting war would develop, if at all, only at a later point in the crisis, which would allow Moscow to introduce crisis control measures before a military clash occurred. As [U.S. official] Roger Hilsman put it: "This is not to say that the Soviets thought the Cuban venture was without risk. But it does indicate that they thought of it as an easily manageable risk. As it turned out, the risk was manageable; the error was thinking that it would be easy."

Upon learning of Khrushchev's bold move, President Kennedy quickly perceived multiple dangers and high stakes. Complex motivations were aroused in the president. If the deployment of so many missiles into Cuba, carried out secretly and coupled with deception, were allowed to succeed, he believed it would have a variety of damaging consequences for the U.S. position in the world, for Kennedy's foreign and domestic policies, for his ability to provide leadership during the rest of his term in office, and for his chances for a second term. Not merely his personal prestige and political future but also the prestige and interests of the United States were considered to be at stake.

It is idle to attempt to sort out and weigh separately, as some critics have tried to do, these various dimensions of the president's motivation. A leader's view of his own personal and political stakes does often influence in some way his judgment of his country's interests. And, indeed, Khrushchev could hardly have thought of a better way to arouse Kennedy's personal and political concerns or to ensure that they became so fused with calculations of national interest as to become virtually inseparable from them. It is highly doubtful that Kennedy, however hard he might have tried, could have found a way to accept damage to his personal political stakes without also accepting severe damage to major U.S. interests. One wonders whether the kind of political damage that the covert deployment of missiles would inflict upon the president could have escaped Khrushchev's attention when he decided to undertake it. Indeed, a plausible although necessarily speculative case can be made that the aim of damaging Kennedy's personal and political stature was part of the overall motivation of the Soviet leader, a person noted for his tendency to take the measure of his opponents and to bully them.

The president's domestic political stakes were indeed substantial. Particularly after Soviet military assistance to Cuba began in July 1962, his administration was placed under increasingly severe domestic pressure to take stronger action against Fidel Castro. The Republicans announced that Cuba would be the dominant issue in the midterm Congressional elections in November. The administration mobilized itself to reassure the public that the dangers of the Soviet military buildup in Cuba were being exaggerated and that there was no reason to respond with warlike measures such as a blockade. The administration disclosed considerable intelligence information concerning the character of the Soviet military supplies and personnel flowing into Cuba, hoping thereby to assure the public that it was well-informed as to what the Soviets were and were not doing.

An important development was the discovery in late August of Soviet SA-2 surface-to-air defense missiles in Cuba. Perhaps as much to calm the war psychosis being encouraged by critics such as Senators Kenneth Keating and Barry Goldwater as to deter the Soviets, the president decided to draw the line. On September 4 and again on September 13, Kennedy explicitly warned the Soviets that his administration would not tolerate the introduction of offensive weapons into Cuba. Thereby, it should be noted, the president had publicly committed himself to act if strategic missiles were introduced into Cuba. Such a pledge was relatively easy to make, as Kennedy thought it most unlikely that the Soviets would undertake such a move, a belief buttressed by National Intelligence Estimates. But once he had taken his stand on this issue in the heated domestic political environment, the public pledge to act if challenged was virtually irrevocable. When the missiles were discovered in mid-October, therefore, "The United States might not be in mortal danger but the Administration most certainly was." For the president to have retracted his recent public commitment not to tolerate offensive missiles in Cuba risked eroding other U.S. commitments and inviting Khrushchev and others to question Kennedy's future credibility in ways that could prove to be painful and dangerous.

Even without the impetus of Kennedy's personal and political stakes, Washington considered the need to find a way to remove the missiles compelling, but not because their placement in Cuba would shift the strategic nuclear balance in the Soviet Union's favor. Even now, with additional time and the benefit of hindsight, efforts to assess the real military significance of the 42 MRBMs [Medium-Range Ballistic Missiles] that were already in Cuba or on the way and the additional 24 to 32 IRBMs that were to follow lead to intricate technical calculations. We forgo discussion of this aspect of the issue here, not because it is irrelevant or unimportant but because the president and most of his advisers were swayed less by the military threat posed by the missiles than by the important political-diplomatic advantages they saw accruing to Khrushchev if the missiles remained in Cuba. Administration specialists on the Soviet Union foresaw that Khrushchev would be able to reinvigorate his assertive foreign policy not only to renew pressure on Berlin but in dealing with a variety of other issues as well.

The president's motivation was indeed strong insofar as it was focused on the limited objective of securing the removal of the missiles. His motivation and willingness to accept risks were much more limited, however, for the objective of going beyond removal of the missiles to getting rid of Castro or eliminating Soviet influence from Cuba, as some of his advisers urged. These objectives were significantly more ambitious, and their costs and risks were perceived by Kennedy to be excessive. Even with respect to removal of the missiles, it is uncertain, to say the least, whether the value the president attached to this objective would have been compelling and durable enough to lead him to order an air strike if the pressure he exerted on Khrushchev, coupled with the quid pro quo offer on Saturday, October 27, failed to secure their removal. As we shall note later, Kennedy was not yet committed to the air strike or invasion options when the crisis ended. In fact, Dean Rusk's recent disclosure of new information indicates a propensity on Kennedy's part to make an additional last-minute concession, if his quid pro quo offer did not suffice, to obtain Khrushchev's agreement to remove the missiles.

Kennedy followed prudent crisis management principles in dealing with the situation created by Khrushchev's gambit. The president adhered to the two political requirements for dealing with the policy dilemma of crisis management: He limited both his objectives and the means employed on their behalf. One of the first decisions Kennedy made soon after the discovery of the missiles was to firmly reject the view that the administration should set as its objective in the crisis the overthrow of Castro or, at least, the elimination of all Soviet influence in Cuba. Instinctively grasping that the pursuit of such ambitious objectives would substantially increase the risk of war, the president made it clear at the outset that his objective would be limited to removal of the missiles, no more and no less, and he held firmly to this throughout the crisis.

Although leaning toward an air strike at first, Kennedy soon saw the merits of limiting not only his objective but also the means to achieve it. The president's interest in the blockade option was caught by the possibility that it might rescue him from the policy dilemma confronting him: how to get the missiles out without possibly triggering escalation of the crisis to war. From the beginning, he had rejected acquiescence to the missile deployment; to do nothing seemed to him the worst of all options. A purely diplomatic overture to Khrushchev—that is, words without action—which several of his advisers favored as the opening U.S. move, might be not only ineffectual but dangerous. It could precipitate a crash effort by Khrushchev to capitalize on the situation created by the missile deployment. Further, a purely diplomatic response might have been interpreted by Khrushchev as demonstrating irresolution and could have encouraged the Soviet leader to regard any subsequent threats by the president as mere bluff. An air strike or invasion, on the other hand, would result in heavy casualties; moreover, these military options could trigger a strong Soviet response and lead to war.

The blockade would prevent additional missiles from reaching Cuba, but its inadequacy as a means for obtaining the *withdrawal* of missiles already in Cuba was self-evident. This was argued very cogently by those members of the National

Security Council who advocated an air strike. Adherents of the blockade acknowledged its limitations and conceded, in addition, that they had no specific plan or concept for utilizing the blockade in order to obtain removal of the missiles. Thus, when on October 22 the president disclosed knowledge of the missile deployment and announced a naval quarantine of Cuba, the administration entered the overt phase of the crisis without having resolved critical ambiguities in its strategy. In the end, Kennedy chose the blockade option because it enabled him to postpone and control the risk of a major war better than an air strike would have. In this respect, the blockade offered advantages that an air strike lacked altogether: It enabled the president to initiate a showdown with Khrushchev without immediate resort to force, and, most important, it offered time for an effort to persuade Khrushchev to remove the missiles voluntarily. The president, however, would have to find a way of utilizing the blockade for this purpose, and, as we shall see, this was not an easy matter.

In the interests of crisis management, the president limited both his objective and the means to be employed on its behalf. Limiting the means employed to a blockade required the administration to strengthen its coercive impact on Khrushchev by making sufficiently credible and sufficiently potent threats of further action should he refuse to comply with the demand to remove the missiles. Therefore, the nature of the confrontation, as it was defined by Kennedy's choice of coercive diplomacy, emphasized the critical importance of an essentially psychological variable—the relative motivation of the two sides. The United States clearly enjoyed an asymmetry of power capabilities in the Caribbean as well as a distinct advantage in strategic nuclear weapons. Khrushchev understood this from the beginning, but it had not deterred him from undertaking the deployment. What was more questionable and what Khrushchev doubted was whether the United States—and, in particular President Kennedy—could summon the motivation and will to utilize its assets to prevent Khrushchev from succeeding.

The basic question, of course, was whether Khrushchev could be persuaded to remove the missiles by means other than actual use of force. No one among Kennedy's circle of advisers—even those who favored beginning with a quiet diplomatic effort to persuade the Soviet leader to do so—believed that Khrushchev would lightly forgo the considerable advantages he expected to obtain from the missile deployment or that he would easily accept the considerable domestic costs and, if his retreat became public, the loss of international prestige associated with a conspicuous retreat. Pressure of some kind would be necessary. But what kind of pressure? And would even strong pressure be effective? These questions were of fundamental importance, and the answers that Kennedy and his advisers gave were at the root of the decision to try coercive diplomacy rather than resort immediately to force. Were Khrushchev and his associates coercible on this matter? Were they capable of retreating under pressure, as the old Bolshevik doctrine enjoined Soviet leaders to do when faced with overwhelming danger? Or, had the deployment proceeded so far and were Soviet leaders so committed to the daring venture on which they had embarked that, for them, there could be no turning back?

This was indeed a critical question, but available accounts of policy discussions held by Kennedy and his advisers hardly refer to it. An affirmative, hopeful answer was implicit in their assessment of the calculations that may have led to the

Soviet decision to deploy the missiles. The dominant view was that Khrushchev had miscalculated the risks of his initiative and that if made fully aware of these risks, he would be capable, at least in principle, of retreating and withdrawing them without the necessity of bloodshed. In the end, we are told by Robert Kennedy, the president's image of Khrushchev was decisive: "The President believed from the start that the Soviet Chairman was a rational, intelligent man who, if given sufficient time and shown determination, would alter his position."

What this suggests, of course, . . . is that the image of the opponent plays an important role in crisis management. Just as Khrushchev's defective image of Kennedy—a young, inexperienced, weak leader who could be pushed around and, at the same time, a rational person who would not risk war to get the missiles out— is widely believed, even by some Soviet analysts, to have played a role in his miscalculation of the risks of the missile gambit, so too did Kennedy's correct image of the Soviet leader play a role in his choice of coercive persuasion rather than military means to secure the removal of the missiles. . . .

The question of Kennedy's capacity to act in a resolute manner in dealing with Khrushchev was a central element in the origins of the crisis as well as in its resolution. One would like to believe that fateful questions of war or peace are not influenced by subjective, psychological variables of this kind. However, a fully adequate understanding of the Cuban Missile Crisis is not possible without taking into account the personal aspects of the interaction between the two leaders. There is reason to believe, although it is arguable, that Khrushchev's image of Kennedy as an inexperienced, weak opponent may have played a role in his calculation that the missile deployment was an acceptable, easily controllable risk. (A somewhat different rendition of Khrushchev's image of Kennedy attributed to him by some Soviet officials is that he believed the president to be too rational and prudent to risk war in order to get the missiles out.)

As for Kennedy, from the beginning of the crisis he was deeply concerned—indeed, perhaps haunted—by the feeling that Khrushchev's missile gambit could be adequately understood only in terms of a long-standing problem that had plagued him. Almost from the day he entered office, the president had wrestled with the problem of how to convey his determination to the Soviet leader in order to discourage him from attempting dangerous encroachments on the world position of the United States and, more particularly and urgently, with respect to the unresolved crisis in Berlin. The Bay of Pigs disaster and Khrushchev's behavior at their summit meeting in Vienna severely exacerbated Kennedy's problem and his concern.

As the tension over Berlin mounted once again in the summer of 1961, the president unburdened himself to James Wechsler of the *New York Post:*

> What worried [Kennedy] was that Khrushchev might interpret his reluctance to wage nuclear war as a symptom of an American loss of nerve. Some day, he said, the time might come when he would have to run the supreme risk to convince Khrushchev that conciliation did not mean humiliation. "If Khrushchev wants to rub my nose in the dirt," he told Wechsler, "it's all over." But how to convince Khrushchev short of a showdown? "That son of a bitch won't pay attention to words," the President said bitterly on another occasion. "He has to see you move."

As the prolonged negotiations over Berlin ground to an inconclusive halt during the summer of 1962, the administration readied itself for new Soviet pressure against West Berlin. Many indications pointed to the likelihood that Khrushchev was preparing another major challenge. Some of them were imbedded in his curiously juxtaposed assurances in September and October that Soviet military assistance to Cuba was for purely "defensive" purposes and that he would not embarrass the president by raising the Berlin issue again until after the forthcoming congressional elections in November. In other ways, too, Khrushchev was suggesting a linkage between Cuba and Berlin. This was not lost on the administration, but Kennedy and his advisers failed to penetrate the deception and to guess the linkage—and the trap—that Khrushchev was preparing. Even in September, [presidential assistant Theodore] Sorensen reports, Kennedy was concerned over the possibility that Khrushchev was giving increasing military assistance to Cuba in order to provoke Washington into another invasion of Cuba that would make a martyr out of Castro and wreck U.S. relations with Latin America, while the Soviets moved in on West Berlin. This suspicion was revived briefly after the missiles were discovered and is contained in one of the early theories, the Diverting Trap theory, that ExComm [Executive Committee] entertained when mulling over the motives behind the missile deployment. This, then, was the president's mental set when he learned on October 16 that Khrushchev had been secretly putting missiles into Cuba, even while systematically deceiving him with false assurances.

Some commentators, extremely critical of Kennedy for taking the world to the brink of nuclear war in response to the missile deployment, have attributed the president's desire to demonstrate resolution to personality shortcomings. There is much more reason to support the interpretation that Kennedy's emphasis on the need to demonstrate resolution was a requirement of the situation and that he correctly perceived it as a necessary prerequisite, although certainly not a sufficient one, for the success of his strategy to secure the removal of the missiles without having to resort to an air strike or invasion. Further, we may suppose that this perceived requirement contributed to Kennedy's decision, for which he has also been criticized, not to disclose his knowledge of the missile deployment until he was ready to act and to seize the initiative.

Kennedy's decision to utilize the blockade as a tool of coercive diplomacy initiated a contest in bargaining. The phenomenon of "bargaining" is usefully analyzed in terms of its three components: persuasion, coercive actions and threats, and accommodative gestures and promises. A "bargaining strategy," in turn, is fashioned by employing some mixture of these three elements and determining the sequence of their use over time. Hence, a variety of bargaining strategies is possible depending upon the relative importance given to these three elements and the sequence in which they are employed.

The issue confronting Kennedy was not merely whether he could persuade Khrushchev to remove the missiles but also what price the Soviet leader could exact in return for doing so. Khrushchev had a well-deserved reputation for being a tough bargainer. According to the imperatives of their old operational doctrine, Soviet leaders were expected to strive for optimal gains when embarked on an initiative to advance Soviet interests or when engaged in negotiation. Only through struggle for maximum gains in such situations could it be determined what was objectively possible. One should push to the limit to extract as much as possible, subject only to the caveat of "knowing when to stop" if the risks of continuing seem to be getting out of hand.

There was no basis for assuming that Khrushchev would back off in the event that Kennedy, forgoing mobilization of military forces, confined his response to a stern diplomatic protest, even if it were backed by a verbal threat of action. Had Kennedy chosen this diplomatic option, which several of his advisers favored, the crisis would have entered its bargaining phase under conditions highly favorable to the Soviet leader and severely disadvantageous for Kennedy. When the deployment was discovered, a large number of medium-range missiles were already in Cuba. These provided important bargaining assets for Khrushchev, and his negotiating leverage would increase with every passing day, as preparations for making the missiles operational, already well advanced, were continuing and a large number of additional missiles, including longer-range intermediate missiles, and possibly nuclear warheads were on the way.

It is conceivable that in this disadvantageous bargaining position, the president, forgoing even a blockade, might have bought his way out of the crisis. But in this event, Khrushchev's price tag for removing the missiles, if indeed he would agree to remove all of them, would probably have been extremely high and might well have included demands for a substantial change in the status of West Berlin. In short, in this alternative scenario of the crisis, Khrushchev would have had Kennedy over a barrel.

Almost intuitively, the president saw that in the dangerous situation created by Khrushchev's miscalculation, the only chance of getting the missiles out without war lay in finding a way of impressing the Soviet leader, as never before, with his determination. Kennedy perceived that if he tried to bargain with Khrushchev before correcting the Soviet leader's mistaken view of his resolution, Khrushchev's appetite and expectation of gains to be extracted would remain excessive and unrealistic. In that event, either Kennedy would have to pay too high a price to secure removal of the missiles—a deal that could have had devastating domestic political consequences at home and for the world position of the United States—or else the negotiations would break down and the president in the end would have to take forceful action.

Indeed, this alternative scenario of the crisis—a negotiation without a military buildup and blockade—could have led to a rapidly deteriorating, possibly prolonged bargaining situation for Kennedy in which he could be eventually pressed to employ the air strike or invasion options. That the risk of war might well have become much greater had Kennedy pursued the purely diplomatic option has been ignored by those who have criticized Kennedy for not trying the quiet diplomatic track first before initiating the blockade and the military buildup.

What Kennedy believed he badly needed was action that would counteract Khrushchev's bargaining advantages as much as possible and give the United States the enhanced leverage it would need in order to negotiate an acceptable deal for withdrawal of the missiles. The blockade would not only prevent Khrushchev from deriving additional bargaining leverage from a continuation of the missile deployment, it would also indicate to the Soviet leader that he had miscalculated and, hopefully, signal Kennedy's resolution to secure the removal of the missiles. And backed by the implicit threat of military action against Cuba, Kennedy's demand for removal of the missiles *might* generate sufficient coercive pressure and bargaining leverage to induce Khrushchev to agree to a formula for withdrawing the missiles.

Coercive action embodied in the blockade and the additional coercive threats conveyed by the military buildup of U.S. forces, which lent credibility to the implicit threat of action against Cuba, were one component—and arguably the most important component—of Kennedy's bargaining strategy. As noted earlier, the most useful way to approach the task of devising a bargaining strategy is to view it as a particular mixture, and some pattern or sequencing, of three elements: persuasion, coercion, and accommodation. Kennedy employed all three elements, but he deliberately withheld indicating willingness to accommodate Khrushchev until he felt that the coercion and persuasion components of his bargaining strategy had made an impression on him.

It may come as a surprise even to those who have followed closely the literature on the Cuban Missile Crisis if we assert that from an early stage, the president believed he would probably have to pay a price to get the missiles out. Not only the president himself but others within the ExComm—including his brother and Robert McNamara as well as [Ambassador to the United Nations] Adlai Stevenson—believed this.

At an early stage in the deliberations of the ExComm, the president indicated that a delay in offering a quid pro quo was all-important. In the ExComm planning session on the day after Stevenson outlined his thoughts regarding the need for concessions, the president expressed the belief that such talk of negotiating formulas was "premature." Rather, the president wanted to concentrate in his signaling and communications to Khrushchev "on a single issue—the enormity of the introduction of the missiles and the absolute necessity for their removal."

The president's awareness of the eventual necessity of concessions was conveyed more explicitly by his brother. [The historian] Arthur Schlesinger reports that after the president, Robert Kennedy, Dean Rusk, and others had finished going over the draft of the initial speech on the crisis that Ambassador Stevenson would deliver before the United Nations, "The Attorney General drew me aside to say, 'we're counting on you to watch things in New York. . . . *We will have to make a deal in the end, but we must stand absolutely firm now. Concessions must come at the end of negotiations not at the beginning.*' "

The need to avoid being drawn into serious bargaining until he had impressed Khrushchev with his determination and developed important bargaining assets remained with the president as the crisis unfolded. We see this consideration at work when he and a few advisers were going over a draft of the television address to the nation that the president delivered on October 22. Discussion turned to the question of what the president should say about negotiation in the speech. President Kennedy's answer, Sorensen reports, was in effect, "Nothing that would tie our hands, anything that would strengthen our stand." Furthermore, *"the President deleted from my* [Sorensen's] *original draft a call for a summit meeting,"* preferring to state simply, in the words of the speech as given, that "this nation is prepared to present its case against the Soviet threat to peace, and our own proposals for a peaceful world, at any time and in any forum . . . *without limiting our freedom of action.*"

Later on, when he became depressed and worried by signs that the Russians were about to challenge the quarantine, the president controlled his impulse to rush into negotiations prematurely. On Tuesday evening, October 23, his brother relayed a private conversation with the Soviet ambassador, Anatoly Dobrynin, in which Dobrynin said he knew of no change in instructions to Soviet vessels nearing the blockade line and expected that they would attempt to go through to Cuba. The president, evidently agitated at hearing this, spoke at once about the possibility of arranging an immediate summit with Khrushchev, "but finally dismissed the idea, concluding that *such a meeting would be useless until Khrushchev first accepted, as a result of our deeds as well as our statements, the U.S. determination in this matter.* Before a summit took place, and it should, the president wanted to have some cards in his own hands.". . .

Legitimate questions can be raised concerning the wisdom of Kennedy's decision to withhold any indication of a willingness to offer concessions until late on Friday, October 26. Such a bargaining strategy risks conveying to the opponent that one is unalterably opposed to any modification of one's negotiating position and that escalation of the crisis can be avoided only through unilateral concessions by the opponent. Thus, this tactic violates the seventh operational requirement of crisis management, which emphasizes the desirability of leaving open to the opponent a face-saving way out of the crisis compatible with his basic interests and prestige. Failure to do so may result in an unwanted, unexpected hardening of the opponent's determination. It is possible that Kennedy's bargaining strategy did have this effect for a while on Khrushchev. To be sure, from the beginning of the overt phase of the crisis, the president also relied on efforts to persuade the Soviet leader—both in public as well as in the private letters they exchanged—that he sought a peaceful resolution of the crisis. It is also true that we do not know whether early hints of a willingness to make concessions on Kennedy's part would have been interpreted by Khrushchev, as the president feared, as an indication of weakness and irresolution that would have strengthened the Soviet leader's determination to persist. But in this connection, it has to be noted that Khrushchev also withheld hints of a willingness to negotiate a compromise until he did so on Friday, October 26.

The fact is that for almost four days—from late Monday, October 22, to late Friday, October 26—both sides gave priority to the coercive component of bargaining strategy. Although neither leader initiated a reckless competition in risk-taking, nevertheless the crisis bargaining during these tense days did assume some of the chilling characteristics of the game of "chicken." However, to control and reduce the risks, both sides employed techniques of crisis management that will be discussed later.

Confronted by the unexpected discovery of his missile deployment and surprised by Kennedy's announcement of a blockade, Khrushchev had to improvise a bargaining strategy under unfavorable conditions. Had the Soviet leader anticipated Kennedy's action, he would have had an opportunity to seize the initiative himself. Thus, Khrushchev could have publicly (or privately) disclosed that a missile deployment was in progress, justified it, and asserted a tough negotiating position.

Kennedy's announcement that his crisis objective was the removal of missiles secretly introduced into Cuba and that his opening tactic was a blockade aimed at persuading the Soviet leader to reconsider his move clearly placed Khrushchev on the defensive, as it was indeed intended to do. The important parameters of the initial crisis bargaining having been set for the time being by the United States, Khrushchev now had some difficult policy questions to address. First, he was immediately confronted by the need to decide whether and when he should admit that a missile deployment was underway and how he should attempt to justify it. Second, the Soviet leader had to consider what objectives he should pursue in the crisis bargaining now set into motion and what strategy to adopt.

What, in other words, should Khrushchev bargain for—completion of the missile deployment in defiance of the blockade? Retention of missiles already in Cuba? Maximal concessions from the United States in return for removal of the missiles? Very little information is available to clarify whether these policy choices were clearly identified in Moscow and, if so, how they were evaluated and on what basis they were settled. As already noted, Soviet sources have not revealed whether any contingency plans existed for responding to a premature discovery of the missiles by the United States and, if so, what use, if any, was made of them by Khrushchev. We are forced to rely on what Khrushchev did and did not do, and what he said and did not say, to infer how he addressed difficult policy choices as to objectives and strategy in the following days.

One of the first decisions Khrushchev made after Kennedy's announcement of the blockade—and he made it sooner than U.S. policy makers at the time were aware of and sooner than most analysts of the crisis have noted—was to give orders to Soviet vessels carrying the missiles to immediately turn back. (Other ships carrying nonmilitary cargo en route to Cuba halted but then were allowed by Moscow to continue, and they eventually reached the blockade line.) This order was evidently given sometime late Monday or early Tuesday, appreciably less than 24 hours after Kennedy's announcement of the blockade. Temporarily but perhaps only temporarily, in order to gain more time to assess the situation and to gauge Kennedy's resolution, Khrushchev retreated from the objective of completing the deployment of missiles. At the same time, however, the Soviet leader decided to test and weaken, if possible, Kennedy's resolution to implement the blockade by sending ships carrying nonmilitary cargo into the restricted zone.

Khrushchev relied more on coercive threats and persuasion than on actions to enhance his bargaining leverage. Thus, just as Kennedy had, the Soviet leader operated on the premise that if a retreat and concessions were necessary to terminate the crisis, they should come later, not at the outset, and that he should rely on whatever coercive threats he could prudently muster to convey his own resolution and to weaken Kennedy's. Hence, he would oppose the blockade but in ways that would not risk escalation to a military clash on the high seas or the capture of missiles and warheads intended for Cuba. In addition, Khrushchev placed heavy reliance on efforts to persuade the president and others of the legitimacy of his military assistance to Cuba and his claims that the weapons moved into Cuba were defensive—that is, had no offensive purpose.

Even before Kennedy announced the blockade and, indeed, before he learned of the secret missile deployment, important domestic critics of his policy of allowing the Soviet military buildup of Castro's forces had been calling publicly for a naval blockade of Cuba. No doubt aware of this, Khrushchev attempted to preemptively deter such a move by labeling it a violation of international law that would amount to an act of war, which he would resist by military means. After Kennedy announced the blockade, Khrushchev continued to denounce it as a violation of international law and threatened to defy it at the risk of war. In his private letter to Kennedy on Tuesday evening, Khrushchev objected to the "ultimatum" given him to remove the missiles, and he denounced the blockade as an act of aggression that was in violation of international law. The Soviet leader ended his letter with an ominous threat:

> Our instructions to Soviet mariners are to observe strictly the universally accepted norms of navigation in international waters and not to retreat one step from them. And if the American side violates these rules, it must realize that responsibility will rest upon it in that case. Naturally we will not simply be bystanders with regard to piratical acts by American ships on the high seas. We will then be forced to take the measures we consider necessary and adequate to protect our rights. We have everything necessary to do so.

On the same day, in an interview with U.S. businessman William Knox, Khrushchev was even more explicit: Soviet submarines, he warned, would sink any U.S. naval ship that tried to force a Soviet vessel to stop. In private conversations on October 22 through 24, several Soviet ambassadors, including Dobrynin, soberly predicted that Soviet ships would challenge the blockade.

The coercive component of Khrushchev's bargaining strategy, however, was confined to rhetorical threats. His threat to challenge and to resist the blockade by force, if necessary, was not carried out, and, in fact, in a subsequent letter to Kennedy in the late afternoon of October 26, the Soviet leader assured him "that the vessels which are now headed for Cuba are carrying the most innocuous peacetime cargoes. . . . I assure you that the ships bound for Cuba are carrying no armaments at all." Khrushchev added that there had been shipments of armaments earlier and that Cuba already had the armaments needed for defense. And, indeed, Soviet ships that did approach the blockade line were not carrying military supplies, and they were allowed to pass on to Cuba.

Other ways of exerting coercive pressure on behalf of Khrushchev's objectives in Cuba were conspicuously limited. There was talk but no evidence of Soviet strategic forces being alerted, and there were no threats of counterpressure against Berlin or Turkey, but U.S. intelligence did report that Soviet military leaves and discharges were cancelled and Warsaw Pact forces placed on some degree of alert.

Khrushchev's use of persuasion as part of his bargaining strategy required him to convey a credible, acceptable justification for the missile deployment. But the fact that it was carried out secretly conflicted with his effort to claim legitimacy for the action. Khrushchev's failure to publicly acknowledge the deployment as soon as it was discovered, and denials of it by Soviet officials in the next few days, made the argument that it was legitimate ring hollow. The Soviet position had been further weakened on October 23 when the Organization of American States voted unanimously to condemn the missile deployment.

What remained open for Khrushchev as a means of increasing his bargaining leverage was to rush the missiles already in Cuba to operational status. And this he did, evidently in the hope that he could manage somehow to neutralize U.S. pressure to remove them and to stabilize and terminate the crisis without having to withdraw the missiles. Certainly, it was as obvious to the Soviet leader as it was to Kennedy that while the blockade could prevent additional missiles from reaching Cuba, it could not in itself bring about the removal of missiles already there. If Soviet missiles remained in Cuba, such an outcome of the crisis would be a substantial success for Khrushchev and a substantial defeat for Kennedy.

In the last analysis, however, keeping the missiles in Cuba was not worth the risk of provoking U.S. military action—either a massive air strike against the missile sites or an invasion of Cuba. Khrushchev had to watch closely for signs that U.S. plans for military action were proceeding to the point of action. In the meantime, he made use of several efforts [including one by UN general secretary U Thant], which proved abortive, to neutralize the emerging U.S. military threat via a hastily contrived diplomatic formula designed to draw Kennedy into either negotiations or a summit meeting. . . .

We noted earlier the president's decision to limit both the objectives he would pursue in the crisis and the means he would employ on their behalf. The efficacy of crisis management often depends not only on satisfying these political requirements to some degree but also on governing one's behavior in ways that are sensitive to a number of operational desiderata. The seven operational requirements identified [earlier] deal with different aspects of the need to integrate the military and diplomatic measures that top policy makers choose to employ in managing a crisis. In this respect the president and his advisers were remarkably successful. Although an explicit theory of crisis management was lacking at the outset of the crisis, Kennedy and his advisers displayed an intuitive, common-sense appreciation of the relevance of these operational desiderata and were often guided by them in their choice of what they did and what they said. Let us consider each of these seven operational requirements in turn.

Engaging in remarkably little direct micromanagement of military operations, the president maintained indirect control over most of the military alerts, deployments, and low-level actions that were taken, as well as over the selection and timing of measures to implement the blockade. This first of the operational requirements on our list was achieved largely by Secretary of Defense McNamara's approval of appropriate rules of engagement and consultation with the military chiefs. Contrary to a widespread belief, the president and his top advisers worked through a well-defined chain of command and did not communicate directly with officers commanding the navy ships engaged in blockade operations. Through the chain of command—from midday Wednesday morning, October 24, onward—the president and Secretary of Defense McNamara indicated which ships were to be stopped and boarded.

The president was especially sensitive to the second operational principle. He felt it essential to slow down the tempo and momentum of the implementation of the blockade. Pauses in blockade operations were deliberately introduced in order to give time for Khrushchev to deliberate and for exchange of diplomatic communications. . . .

The third, fourth, and fifth operational criteria emphasize that military moves must be carefully selected, coordinated with, and made consistent with political objectives and diplomatic actions. There is much evidence in reports of the crisis of efforts to develop and apply an integrated diplomatic-military strategy for reaching an acceptable termination of the confrontation that would avoid war. Movements of U.S. military forces and efforts to signal resolve were generally consistent, with some exceptions, with the way in which the president attempted to manage the crisis. "Noise" was largely avoided and minimized. Thorough preparations were undertaken for a possible invasion of Cuba and strikes against the missile sites. These preparations were highly visible, but Washington made it clear that their *immediate* purpose was to provide a credible threat to back up the president's strategy of trying to achieve removal of the missiles peacefully through coercive diplomacy rather than through military action. Toward the end of the week, however, preparations for an invasion reached the stage at which Soviet and Cuban intelligence became concerned that an invasion might be imminent.

The alert of U.S. strategic forces to DefCon-2 [Defense Condition-2] did perhaps risk alarming Soviet leaders that the United States was contemplating initiation of nuclear war and, if so, perhaps forcing Moscow to consider preemption. Whether Soviet leaders were inclined to place this interpretation on the U.S. alert is unlikely; nothing at the time and none of the recent Soviet disclosures have indicated that Soviet leaders misperceived the action. Certainly, the strategic alert had some coercive intent, but its objectives were—as Kennedy indicated in his address of October 22—to deter use of the Cuban-based missiles against the United States or any countries in the Western hemisphere, to discourage escalation by the Soviets, and to provide extended deterrence of possible Soviet moves elsewhere—such as Berlin.

Kennedy's handling of the crisis was also consistent in the main with the sixth operational requirement. Both his choice of diplomatic signals and his restraint in the choice and application of military actions conveyed a strong preference on his part for a peaceful resolution of the crisis rather than a military solution to the problem of the Soviet missiles.

Finally, turning to the very important seventh operational principle, with the exception already noted of his initial unwillingness to offer concessions, Kennedy chose his military actions carefully and eventually coupled them with diplomatic proposals that were intended to leave Khrushchev with a way out of the crisis that would be compatible with his fundamental interests. . . .

Before we turn to the often confused bargaining that occurred, particularly on Saturday, we should make several additional observations. Earlier in the week, tacit cooperation in careful crisis management had developed between Kennedy and Khrushchev. Even while the Soviet leader blustered and exerted pressure of his own in order to undermine Kennedy's resolve and his ability to implement a coercive strategy, Khrushchev nonetheless also went to great lengths to guarantee the avoidance of a clash at sea.

Once the danger of a confrontation on the high seas was safely managed, however, U.S. and Soviet cooperation in managing the crisis began to break down. The tempo of events speeded up on Saturday, and a startling lack of synchronization began to characterize the interaction between the two sides. The context and meaning of certain possibly critical moves and communications that one side was making became confusing to the other. For each side, deciphering the intentions and calculations behind the specific moves of the opponent became difficult. We know that Kennedy experienced this problem acutely and that his adversary felt the same unsettling phenomenon in Moscow. There was real danger in this, but the disturbing sensation that things were getting out of control and the mounting fear that one side or the other might miscalculate were probably not without value in helping to bring the crisis to a sudden halt on early Sunday morning.

United States policy makers and those writing about the crisis thereafter found it difficult to explain the discrepancy between Khrushchev's more personal and more emotional private letter of Friday evening, in which he suggested removal of the missiles in return for Kennedy's pledge not to invade Cuba, and the more formal and composed letter he issued publicly on Saturday morning demanding that the United States remove its missiles from Turkey as well. Members of Kennedy's advisory group speculated that the hawks in the Kremlin, learning of and disapproving Khrushchev's personal initiative of Friday night, overruled him and wrote a new letter that demanded more. This possibility was an additional source of confusion and anxiety among U.S. policy makers on Saturday.

Was it so unlikely that the president would agree to throw in removal of the obsolescent Jupiter bases in Turkey? There was, after all, Walter Lippmann's article of Thursday, October 25, suggesting that the president do so. Soviet leaders might well have thought this was a trial balloon inspired by the more dovish members of the administration, and, additionally, they might have noticed that the administration did not disassociate itself from Lippmann's position.

Even before Lippmann's article appeared, the Soviet government had been preparing the ground for a demand for a "symmetrical" trade of U.S. and Soviet overseas bases. Thus, although the Soviet government had carefully refrained from threatening action in Berlin in response to the blockade, it had been exerting counterpressure with regard to U.S. bases in Turkey. Removal of the Jupiter missiles from Turkey would not constitute the large gain Khrushchev had expected when he deployed missiles into Cuba, but his problem now was to salvage as much as he could. Besides, to force Kennedy into agreeing to remove the bases in Turkey would by no means constitute an insignificant prize—not so much because of the military significance of the Jupiters to either the United States or the Soviet Union but because such a concession would provide Khrushchev political and psychological benefits at home and inflict political-diplomatic consequences for the U.S. position in NATO. We shall note later President Kennedy's attitude toward trading the Jupiters and the role it played in the formula for settling the crisis.

Other disturbing actions took place on Saturday. A U.S. reconnaissance plane wandered over Siberia; a U-2 was shot down over Cuba in midmorning; two other reconnaissance planes were shot at as they swooped low over the missile sites Saturday morning; it was reported that a single Soviet ship outside the quarantine line detached itself from the others and headed for the blockade line. In Washington, these actions were interpreted, not surprisingly, as grim indications that the Soviets had perhaps decided to test U.S. determination. Some ExComm members reasoned that since the Soviets must have realized that shooting down the U-2 would force the United States to take direct action against the surface-to-air missiles (SAMs), "their action seemed to mean that they had decided on a showdown." There was speculation as to whether Khrushchev was still in charge in the Kremlin and contradictory speculation that Khrushchev was trying to extract a higher price. The president would have to decide what to do next under the burden of considerable uncertainty and confusion as to what was going on in the Kremlin.

It now seems reasonable to conclude that the U-2 shoot-down was *not* a calculated part of Khrushchev's bargaining strategy, as had been feared at the time by some of Kennedy's advisers. What impressed itself on the president and his advisers was that a possibly momentous turning point in the crisis had been reached. Contingency plans called for a retaliatory air strike against one of the SAM sites in Cuba. To do so, however, would be to cross a major threshold in the level of violence, which, even if justified by political as well as military considerations, could trigger additional escalation. Kennedy withstood pressure from his advisers to put into effect the contingency plan for retaliation, adding to the mounting internal strains within the advisory group.

But it was clear that the reconnaissance flights over Cuba would have to continue in order to monitor the status of the missile sites and that if another U-2 were shot down, which had to be expected, the president could not easily hold off approving a reprisal attack against the SAM sites. What would happen thereafter, he feared, could lead to uncontrollable escalation.

A new sense of urgency to end the crisis emerged, as it could be only a matter of a few days before another U-2 was shot down. An immediate effort to end the crisis before it went out of control was necessary. Motivated as never before—not merely by a desire to get the missiles removed but by a desperate need to try to end the crisis before it resulted in war—Kennedy was finally ready to exert additional pressure on Khrushchev; at the same time, however, he also saw the need to couple the pressure with concessions to make it easier for Khrushchev to agree to remove the missiles. In other words, the president now improvised a carrot and stick strategy in an effort to bring the crisis to a close before it escalated. Let us consider first the coercive component of his strategy.

Kennedy accepted his advisers' suggestion that he reply to the two contradictory letters from Khrushchev by ignoring the Saturday morning [October 27] demand for exchange of missile bases and accepting the suggestion contained in Khrushchev's first letter [October 26] for a quid pro quo linking removal of the missiles from Cuba with a U.S. pledge not to invade Cuba. (As we shall see, the president decided to deal with the issue of the Jupiters in private discussions his brother would have with Dobrynin.) Kennedy's formal reply to Khrushchev did not hint at an ultimatum, although it did convey a sense of urgency. The equivalent of an ultimatum was conveyed by Robert Kennedy in a private meeting with [Anatoly] Dobrynin in the early evening of October 27, although this has recently been denied by the former Soviet ambassador.

According to the summary provided in Robert Kennedy's posthumous account in *Thirteen Days* [1969], he told Dobrynin, "we had to have a commitment by tomorrow that those bases [missiles in Cuba] would be removed. I was not giving them an ultimatum but a statement of fact. He should understand that if they did not remove those bases, we would remove them. . . . Time was running out. We had only a few more hours—we needed an answer immediately from the Soviet Union. I said we must have it the next day." If Robert Kennedy's account can be taken at face value, it meant that President Kennedy had finally decided to add to his long-standing demand that the missiles be removed the two missing elements of a full-blown ultimatum—a time limit for compliance with the demand and a credible threat of potent punishment for noncompliance—even though, as Robert Kennedy puts it, this was conveyed not as an explicit ultimatum but as "a statement of fact."

Robert Kennedy's account of his conversation with Dobrynin appears to have been contradicted by the former Soviet ambassador at the Harvard-sponsored Moscow conference [of January 1989] on the Cuban crisis. Dobrynin at first denied that any ultimatum was conveyed or, indeed, that any threats were made. Rather, his recollection was that Robert Kennedy had soft-pedaled the danger of imminent U.S. action and that his cable to Moscow summarizing the meeting with the president's brother was similarly low-key on this point. Later in the Moscow conference, however, Dobrynin acknowledged that Robert Kennedy had indeed conveyed acute time pressure for a response; he "persistently asked, it is true, to convey the president's request that if possible he wanted to receive an answer on Sunday. So I conveyed this to Moscow." Continuing, Dobrynin added that he himself had experienced time urgency for a reply and made the telling comment that "[a]ccording to the evidence we had available [in the Soviet embassy], an air strike was considered very likely, perhaps in the coming days. There might have been also an invasion." The former Soviet ambassador to the United States did not disclose or quote from his cable to Moscow, nor did he say he had recently reread it to refresh his memory. If Dobrynin's cable is declassified, it might well help to clarify what Robert Kennedy told him on that occasion.

The possibility that an ultimatum may have been conveyed by another American is suggested and given some weight. . . . At the Moscow conference, Aleksandr Fomin recalled that in his meeting with John Scali on Saturday, October 27, the U.S. newsman angrily threatened that if the missiles were not removed within hours, a U.S. attack would be mounted.

Finally, it should be recognized that the substance of an ultimatum can sometimes be effectively conveyed to an adversary without being fully transmitted in verbal terms. Particularly, the sense of urgency for compliance and the threat of punishment for noncompliance can be effectively conveyed by actions taken that either themselves convey such time-urgent pressure or suggest that the threatener may not be able to maintain control over his side's actions much longer. Thus, before the end of the day on Saturday, October 27, preparations for an invasion of Cuba had reached an advanced stage, and Soviet and Cuban intelligence appears to have reported to Moscow the possibility of imminent U.S. military action. It is possible, therefore, whether or not something like an ultimatum was conveyed by Robert Kennedy, that Khrushchev concluded for other reasons that time was running out and that he had better terminate the crisis immediately.

Including the removal of Jupiters from Turkish bases in the quid pro quo, as we have noted, was a delicate political matter for the president. However, disclosure of new information in recent years establishes that Kennedy felt strongly that the political costs for the U.S. position in NATO should be accepted if including the Jupiters in the deal were necessary for a quick settlement of the crisis. The president's attitude emerges most clearly in his meeting with his advisory group on Saturday, October 27, when he put forward and pressed this view. He was finally persuaded by his Soviet expert, Llewellyn Thompson, to try first to resolve the crisis without including the Jupiters in the quid pro quo. And, as noted earlier, the president made no reference to Khrushchev's demand for removal of the Jupiters in his formal reply to the Soviet leader. But then, as few if any other members of the advisory circle were to know, the president evidently authorized his brother to make a secret deal that explicitly included removal of the Jupiters in the private conversation he had with Dobrynin later that day. . . .

However, these recent disclosures do not challenge the fact that an understanding was reached with the Soviets to keep the missile swap secret. We are now told, too, that the president's determination not to let the matter of the Jupiters prevent a quick settlement of the crisis went further than his authorization of the secret deal for a missile swap. Dean Rusk disclosed at the Hawks Cay Conference in March 1987 that the president quickly followed up the concession for a secret deal his brother made on Saturday evening by creating a fallback option. If the secret deal on the missiles did not suffice, the U.N. secretary-general might then be asked to propose an open missile swap as part of the terms for settling the crisis.

We noted earlier that crisis management began to break down on Saturday, October 27, and that the disturbing sensation that things were getting out of control had a significant impact on Kennedy's policy. These developments had an unsettling effect in Moscow as well and motivated Khrushchev to accept within a matter of hours the formula for settling the crisis that the president proposed toward the end of that day. A few months later, on December 12, 1962, Khrushchev defended his conduct of the Cuban venture in a major speech to the Supreme Soviet. Khrushchev did not allude to having received an ultimatum; however, he did say that he had been placed under urgent pressure to settle the crisis immediately by information that an attack on Cuba would shortly take place: "We received information from our Cuban comrades and from other sources on the morning of October 27 directly stating that this attack would be carried out in the next two or three days. We interpreted these cables as an extremely alarming warning signal. And the alarm was justified. Immediate action was necessary to prevent the attack on Cuba and to preserve the peace." Soviet and Cuban sources have recently added useful details on some of the reasons for Khrushchev's sense of urgency. And we have already alluded to the role played by the shoot-down of the U-2, Scali's statement to Fomin, the advanced military preparations for an invasion of Cuba, the possibility that Cuban air defenses might succeed in their efforts to shoot down U.S. reconnaissance planes, and Robert Kennedy's warning to Dobrynin that time was running out, in heightening Moscow's sense of urgency for ending the crisis.

What would Kennedy have done had Khrushchev not accepted the formula he proposed on Saturday for ending the crisis? Would the president have then ordered an air strike or an invasion, or would he have tried to find still other ways of persuading Khrushchev to remove the missiles? While an answer to this question is necessarily speculative, the available evidence—even before Dean Rusk revealed the fallback option of an open missile swap that the president asked him to prepare—strongly suggests that Kennedy would not have resorted immediately to an air strike or an invasion.

It is useful to recall that during the days when the ExComm was meeting to plan a response to the discovery of the missiles, its members were badly divided on how the general concept of graduated escalation ought to be employed. Some advisers felt that there should be relatively few, if any, steps between the blockade and an air strike (or invasion). Others thought in terms of a series of intervening steps that would permit the president to increase pressure more gradually in the hope that Khrushchev would agree to remove the missiles before either an air strike or invasion became necessary.

Disagreement on this critical issue had not been resolved during the planning sessions. The issue came to the fore again, however, when it became clear that despite the success of the blockade, more pressure would have to be applied to persuade Khrushchev to remove the missiles. On Saturday afternoon, October 27, Sorensen reports, "the Executive Committee was somewhat heatedly discussing plans for the next step. . . . The POL [petroleum products] blockade, air strike and invasion advocates differed over what to do. Consistent with his earlier advocacy of gradual step-by-step escalation McNamara was now in favor of tightening the blockade rather than going immediately to the air strike. The next morning, Sunday, before news arrived of Khrushchev's acceptance of Kennedy's proposal for ending the crisis, McNamara rose early to draw up a list of steps to take short of invasion." At the same time, the Joint Chiefs of Staff and other advisers were pressing the case for an air strike with renewed vigor.

Given the circumstance of a badly divided advisory group and fearing that he was losing control over crisis developments, it is not surprising that the president should bypass the ExComm as a decision-making body and resort to his brother's back-channel meetings with Dobrynin to make additional concessions regarding the Jupiters in order to bring the crisis to a close. Nor is it surprising that he would also secretly prepare the way for an ostensible U.N.-initiated proposal for an open missile swap, should the version of a secret missile swap that his brother had proposed to Dobrynin fail to er.d the crisis. By portraying himself as having no choice but to accept the U.N. secretary-general's proposal—even though it had been privately and indirectly instigated by the president—Kennedy could hope to reduce the political costs of doing so, both among the hawks in his advisory group and in the U.S. public as well as among his NATO allies.

Even though the president had not decided as yet, for he did not have to, whether he would trigger the U.N. initiative, his preparation of this option for possible use later reflects his strong determination not to let the question of the Jupiters stand in the way of a settlement. He was equally determined to end the crisis peacefully, if possible, before additional U-2 shoot-downs might force him to retaliate against the SAM sites, thereby possibly setting into motion further escalation of the crisis. . . .

In brief, war was avoided because the *incentive* to avoid it remained powerful throughout the crisis; because *opportunities* for avoiding escalation were available, were recognized, and were not frittered away; and because the two leaders operated with sufficient *skill* in managing the crisis so as to bring it to a close without being drawn into a shooting war.

✕ FURTHER READING

Graham Allison, *Essence of Decision* (1971)

"Back from the Brink," *Problems of Communism,* 41 (1992), Special Issue

Jules Benjamin, *The United States and the Origins of the Cuban Revolution* (1990)

Barton J. Bernstein, "The Cuban Missile Crisis: Trading the Jupiters in Turkey?" *Political Science Quarterly,* 95 (1980), 97–125

Michael Beschloss, *The Crisis Years* (1991)

Cole Blasier, *The Hovering Giant* (1976)

James G. Blight, *The Shattered Crystal Ball* (1990)

———— and David A. Welch, *On the Brink* (1989)

———— et al., *Cuba on the Brink* (1993)

Philip Brenner, "Cuba and the Missile Crisis," *Journal of Latin American Studies,* 22 (1990), 115–142

Dino Brugioni, *Eyeball to Eyeball* (1991)

McGeorge Bundy, *Danger and Survival* (1988)

Laurence Chang and Peter Kornbluh, eds., *The Cuban Missile Crisis, 1962* (1992)

————, *To Make a World Safe for Revolution* (1989)

Abram Chayes, *The Cuban Missile Crisis: International Crisis and the Role of Law* (1974)

David Detzer, *The Brink* (1979)

Herbert Dinerstein, *The Making of a Missile Crisis: October 1962* (1976)

Jorge I. Domínguez, *Cuba: Order and Revolution* (1978)

Theodore Draper, *Castroism* (1965)

Raymond L. Garthoff, *Reflections on the Cuban Missile Crisis* (1989)

Alexander L. George et al., *The Limits of Coercive Diplomacy* (1971)

James N. Giglio, *The Presidency of John F. Kennedy* (1991)

A. A. Gromyko, "The Caribbean Crisis," *Soviet Law and Government,* 11 (1972), 3–53

Maurice Halperin, *The Rise and Decline of Fidel Castro* (1972)

————, *The Taming of Fidel Castro* (1981)

James G. Hershberg, "Before 'The Missiles of October': Did Kennedy Plan a Military Strike Against Cuba?" *Diplomatic History,* 14 (1990), 163–198

Trumbull Higgins, *The Perfect Failure* (1987) (Bay of Pigs invasion)

Irving L. Janis, *Groupthink* (1982)

Haynes B. Johnson et al., *The Bay of Pigs* (1964)

Montague Kern, Patricia W. Levering, and Ralph B. Levering, *The Kennedy Crises: The Press, the Presidency, and Foreign Policy* (1983)

Richard Ned Lebow, *Between Peace and War* (1981)

———— and Janice Gross Stein, *We All Lost the Cold War* (1993)

Lee Lockwood, *Castro's Cuba, Cuba's Fidel* (1967)

Frank Mankiewicz and Kirby Jones, *With Fidel* (1975)

Morris Morley, *Imperial State and Revolution: The United States and Cuba, 1952–1987* (1987)

James A. Nathan, ed., *The Cuban Missile Crisis Revisited* (1992)

————, "The Missile Crisis," *World Politics,* 27 (1975), 256–281

Henry M. Pachter, *Collision Course* (1963)

Lewis J. Paper, *The Promise and the Performance* (1975)

Herbert S. Parmet, *JFK* (1983)

Thomas G. Paterson, *Contesting Castro* (1994)

————, ed., *Kennedy's Quest for Victory* (1989)

———— and William T. Brophy, "October Missiles and November Elections: The Cuban Missile Crisis and American Politics, 1962," *Journal of American History,* 73 (1986), 87–119

Louis A. Pérez, Jr., *Cuba and the United States* (1990)

Scott Sagan, "Nuclear Alerts and Crisis Management," *International Security,* 9 (1985), 99–139

Arthur M. Schlesinger, Jr., *Robert Kennedy and His Times* (1978)

————, *A Thousand Days* (1965)

Thomas J. Schoenbaum, *Waging Peace and War* (1988) (on Rusk)

Glenn T. Seaborg and Benjamin J. Loeb, *Kennedy, Khrushchev, and the Test Ban* (1981)

Ronald Steel, "Endgame," *New York Review of Books,* March 13, 1969, pp. 15–22

Tad Szulc, *Fidel* (1986)

———— and K. E. Meyer, *The Cuban Invasion* (1962)

Marc Trachtenberg, *History and Strategy* (1991)

Lucien S. Vandenbroucke, "Anatomy of a Failure: The Decision to Land at the Bay of Pigs," *Political Science Quarterly,* 99 (1984), 471–491

————, *Perilous Options* (1993)

Richard E. Welch, Jr., *Response to Revolution* (1985)

Peter Wyden, *Bay of Pigs* (1979)

The Vietnam War

After World War II, the United States' engagement in the Indochinese country of Vietnam deepened over a thirty-year period. In 1945 the Truman administration tolerated the reimposition of French colonialism, and in 1950 Washington began giving massive aid to the French to quell the patriot Ho Chi Minh's nationalist, communist-led insurgency. After the French defeat in 1954, the United States supported the division of Vietnam at the seventeenth parallel, and the Eisenhower administration helped to organize, and to prop up, a noncommunist regime in the South. In 1961 President John F. Kennedy sent U.S. military personnel to fight in Vietnamese jungles; then in 1964, under Kennedy's successor, Lyndon B. Johnson, American bombers launched an air war against North Vietnam. The Johnson administration significantly increased the level of ground forces in South Vietnam in 1965. Following the North Vietnamese–Vietcong Tet offensive in 1968, peace talks began, and in 1973 Washington and Hanoi reached a peace settlement that permitted the United States to continue to support the South Vietnamese regime. But in 1975 communist forces drove Americans pell-mell from Vietnam and seized Saigon, the southern capital, which they renamed Ho Chi Minh City.

With each passing year, the war's costs had mounted. By the end, more than 58,000 American servicemen and women had died in Vietnam, and the United States had spent more than $175 billion in Southeast Asia. Millions of Asians perished, hundreds of thousands of others became refugees, and the countries of Indochina—Vietnam, Cambodia, and Laos—lay in ruins. The war also polarized Americans at home. Peace demonstrations swept the United States during the 1960s and early 1970s. U.S. leaders ultimately responded by withdrawing American forces, but the passionate Vietnam debate nonetheless unhinged a twenty-five-year-old Cold War consensus on foreign policy.

Considering the war's length and historical significance, it is not surprising that scholars vigorously debate all aspects of the conflict. One set of questions probes the causes or motivations for U.S. intervention. Put simply, why did the United States become so deeply entangled in Vietnam and stay so long? Did U.S. security interests, especially the goal of anticommunist containment, lead to intervention? Did Vietnam become a test of the United States' credibility overseas, a place for America to demonstrate its willingness and ability to stand by its allies? To what extent did a misunderstanding of Vietnamese society and politics account for American behavior? Did U.S. officials mistakenly view Vietnamese communism, and Vietnamese nationalism, as Soviet directed? If so, what accounts for their blurred vision: A misguided desire to help Vietnam? Cultural arrogance? A lack of information? Did bureaucratic decisionmaking, which places a premium on consensus, inhibit critical thought on Vietnam? Did the imperial presidency undermine congressional oversight? Or did intervention in Vietnam arise from a determined drive for global hegemony, an urge to secure access to markets and raw materials, military bases, and political influence?

A second set of questions centers on the military conduct of the war and the question of winning. Why did the United States lose the Vietnam War? Did the antiwar movement and an investigative press undermine American resolve? Did civilian authorities err in choosing to fight a "limited war"? To what extent was the military restrained from unleashing all of its firepower, especially airstrikes? Should U.S. troops have invaded North Vietnam? Did the U.S. military wrongly rely on conventional battlefield engagement instead of counterinsurgency and a pacification program better geared to a guerrilla war? Did the U.S. strategy of attrition and massive "search and destroy" campaigns, which measured success through "body counts" of dead Vietnamese, encourage atrocities against civilians and make U.S. officials overconfident of military progress? Would a change in military tactics have brought victory? Or did corruption and instability in, and the lack of popular support for, the South Vietnamese government make victory impossible, especially when combined with the skill and motivation of the Vietnamese communists? Did the United States make a fundamental error by deciding to intervene in an anticolonial struggle in the first place, fighting against people determined to defend their homeland?

✳ D O C U M E N T S

Resistance to foreigners is an enduring theme in Vietnamese history. During World War II, the Vietnamese battled the Japanese. On September 2, 1945, Ho Chi Minh and other nationalists wrote a Declaration of Independence for the Democratic Republic of Vietnam. The document, reprinted here as the first selection, resembled the 1776 American declaration. But the French denied independence and reclaimed their colony, and from 1945 to 1954 an anticolonial rebellion convulsed Vietnam. In the second document, the transcript of a press conference of April 7, 1954, President Dwight D. Eisenhower explains his "domino theory," which posited that a communist takeover of Indochina would lead inexorably to communist domination throughout Asia. The beleaguered French ultimately decided to withdraw from Vietnam, and at the Geneva Conference of May 8–July 21, 1954, the warring parties and their allies, including the United States, prepared peace terms and long-range plans for Indochina. The Geneva Accords that were set down in the final declaration are reprinted here as the third selection. Thereafter, Ho's communists governed North Vietnam, and the United States which refused to accept the Geneva agreements, backed a regime in the south.

Despite U.S. aid, the government of South Vietnam was plagued by rampant corruption, inefficiency, and inadequate popular support. By 1960 a communist-led insurgency, the National Liberation Front (NLF), had gained a widespread following in the South and secured North Vietnamese assistance. In the fourth document, dating from 1961, North Vietnamese general Vo Nguyen Giap explains the strategy of "people's war," whereby a smaller, weaker force could achieve military victory over a stronger, imperialist power. The Tonkin Gulf Resolution, the fifth document, which the U.S. Senate passed on August 10, 1964, with only two dissenting votes, authorized the president to use the force he

Southeast Asia and the Vietnam War

■ Major U.S. bases during the Vietnam War

0   100   200   300
miles

The Tet Offensive January-February 1968

☆ Major battles

deemed necessary in Vietnam. American war managers interpreted this important document as equivalent to a declaration of war. The sixth selection, President Lyndon B. Johnson's passionate speech at The Johns Hopkins University on April 7, 1965, gives the reasons why the United States was fighting in Vietnam. The seventh document, a memorandum to the president from Secretary of Defense Robert S. McNamara on June 26, 1965, recommends military escalation in order to deny the Vietnamese communists a victory and to force a negotiated settlement of the war. The eighth document presents notes of a discussion between President Johnson and Under Secretary of State George Ball on July 21, 1965, when Ball dissented from a policy of military escalation.

J. William Fulbright, chair of the Senate Foreign Relations Committee, became a vocal critic of the Vietnam War. In the ninth selection, a speech on May 5, 1966, he protests an American "arrogance of power." The tenth document is an excerpt from a 1969 article by Clark M. Clifford, McNamara's replacement at the Department of Defense, recalling his disconcerting conferences with military leaders in the bewildering aftermath of the Tet offensive in early 1968. The last selection is a transcript of a November 24, 1969, interview between the news correspondent Mike Wallace of the Columbia Broadcasting System and the Vietnam veteran Private Paul Meadlo, who had participated in the March 1968 massacre of Vietnamese civilians at the village of My Lai.

The Vietnamese Declaration of Independence, 1945

All men are created equal. They are endowed by their Creator with certain inalienable rights, among these are Life, Liberty and the pursuit of Happiness.

This immortal statement was made in the Declaration of Independence of the United States of America in 1776. In a broader sense, this means: All the peoples on the earth are equal from birth, all the peoples have a right to live, to be happy and free.

The Declaration of the French Revolution made in 1791 on the Rights of Man and the Citizen also states: "All men are born free and with equal rights, and must always remain free and have equal rights."

Those are undeniable truths.

Nevertheless, for more than eighty years, the French imperialists, abusing the standard of Liberty, Equality and Fraternity, have violated our Fatherland and oppressed our fellow-citizens. They have acted contrary to the ideals of humanity and justice.

In the field of politics, they have deprived our people of every democratic liberty.

They have enforced inhuman laws; they have set up three distinct political regimes in the North, the Centre and the South of Viet Nam in order to wreck our national unity and prevent our people from being united.

They have built more prisons than schools. They have mercilessly slain our patriots; they have drowned our uprisings in rivers of blood.

They have fettered public opinion; they have practised obscurantism against our people.

To weaken our race they have forced us to use opium and alcohol.

In the field of economics, they have fleeced us to the backbone, impoverished our people and devastated our land.

They have robbed us of our ricefields, our mines, our forests and our raw materials. They have monopolized the issuing of banknotes and the export trade.

They have invented numerous unjustifiable taxes and reduced our people, especially our peasantry, to a state of extreme poverty.

They have hampered the prospering of our national bourgeoisie; they have mercilessly exploited our workers. . . .

For these reasons, we, members of the Provisional Government, representing the whole Vietnamese people, declare that from now on we break off all relations of a colonial character with France; we repeal all the international obligation[s] that France has so far subscribed to on behalf of Viet Nam and we abolish all the special rights the French have unlawfully acquired in our Fatherland.

The whole Vietnamese people, animated by a common purpose, are determined to fight to the bitter end against any attempt by the French colonialists to reconquer their country.

We are convinced that the Allied nations which at Teheran and San Francisco have acknowledged the principles of self-determination and equality of nations, will not refuse to acknowledge the independence of Viet Nam.

A people who have courageously opposed French domination for more than eighty years, a people who have fought side by side with the Allies against the fascists during these last years, such a people must be free and independent.

For these reasons, we, members of the Provisional Government of the Democratic Republic of Vietnam, solemnly declare to the world that Viet Nam has the right to be a free and independent country—and in fact it is so already. The entire Vietnamese people are determined to mobilize all their physical and mental strength, to sacrifice their lives and property in order to safeguard their independence and liberty.

President Dwight D. Eisenhower
Explains the Domino Theory, 1954

Q. Robert Richards, Copley Press: Mr. President, would you mind commenting on the strategic importance of Indochina to the free world? I think there has been, across the country, some lack of understanding on just what it means to us.

The President: You have, of course, both the specific and the general when you talk about such things.

First of all, you have the specific value of a locality in its production of materials that the world needs.

Then you have the possibility that many human beings pass under a dictatorship that is inimical to the free world.

Finally, you have broader considerations that might follow what you would call the "falling domino" principle. You have a row of dominoes set up, you knock over the first one, and what will happen to the last one is the certainty that it will go over very quickly. So you could have a beginning of a disintegration that would have the most profound influences.

Now, with respect to the first one, two of the items from this particular area that the world uses are tin and tungsten. They are very important. There are others, of course, the rubber plantations and so on.

Then with respect to more people passing under this domination, Asia, after all, has already lost some 450 million of its peoples to the Communist dictatorship, and we simply can't afford greater losses.

But when we come to the possible sequence of events, the loss of Indochina, of Burma, of Thailand, of the Peninsula, and Indonesia following, now you begin to talk about areas that not only multiply the disadvantages that you would suffer through loss of materials, sources of materials, but now you are talking about millions and millions and millions of people.

Finally, the geographical position achieved thereby does many things. It turns the so-called island defensive chain of Japan, Formosa, of the Philippines and to the southward; it moves in to threaten Australia and New Zealand.

It takes away, in its economic aspects, that region that Japan must have as a trading area or Japan, in turn, will have only one place in the world to go—that is, toward the Communist areas in order to live.

So, the possible consequences of the loss are just incalculable to the free world.

Final Declaration of the Geneva Conference on Indochina, 1954

1. The Conference takes note of the agreements ending hostilities in Cambodia, Laos and Viet Nam and organising international control and the supervision of the execution of the provisions of these agreements. . . .

4. The Conference takes note of the clauses in the agreement on the cessation of hostilities in Viet Nam prohibiting the introduction into Viet Nam of foreign troops and military personnel as well as of all kinds of arms and munitions. . . .

5. The Conference takes note of the clauses in the agreement on the cessation of hostilities in Viet Nam to the effect that no military base under the control of a foreign State may be established in the regrouping zones of the two parties [above and below the seventeenth parallel], the latter having the obligation to see that the zones allotted to them shall not constitute part of any military alliance and shall not be utilised for the resumption of hostilities or in the service of an aggressive policy. . . .

6. The Conference recognises that the essential purpose of the agreement relating to Viet Nam is to settle military questions with a view to ending hostilities and that the military demarcation line [at the seventeenth parallel] is provisional and should not in any way be interpreted as constituting a political or territorial boundary. The Conference expresses its conviction that the execution of the provisions set out in the present declaration and in the agreement on the cessation of hostilities creates the necessary basis for the achievement in the near future of a political settlement in Viet Nam.

7. The Conference declares that, so far as Viet Nam is concerned, the settlement of political problems, effected on the basis of respect for the principles of independence, unity and territorial integrity, shall permit the Vietnamese people to enjoy the fundamental freedoms, guaranteed by democratic institutions established

as a result of free general elections by secret ballot. In order to ensure that sufficient progress in the restoration of peace has been made, and that all of the necessary conditions obtain for free expression of the national will, general elections shall be held in July 1956, under the supervision of an international commission composed of representatives of the Member States of the International Supervisory Commission, referred to in the agreement on the cessation of hostilities. Consultations will be held on this subject between the competent representative authorities of the two zones from July 20, 1955, onwards. . . .

12. In their relations with Cambodia, Laos and Viet Nam, each member of the Geneva Conference undertakes to respect the sovereignty, the independence, the unity and the territorial integrity of the above-mentioned States, and to refrain from any interference in their internal affairs.

General Vo Nguyen Giap on People's War, 1961

The Vietnamese people's war of liberation was a just war, aiming to win back the independence and unity of the country, to bring land to our peasants and guarantee them the right to it, and to defend the achievements of the August Revolution. That is why it was first and foremost a people's war. To educate, mobilise, organise and arm the whole people in order that they might take part in the Resistance was a crucial question.

The enemy of the Vietnamese nation was aggressive imperialism, which had to be overthrown. But the latter having long since joined up with the feudal landlords, the anti-imperialist struggle could definitely not be separated from antifeudal action. On the other hand, in a backward colonial country such as ours where the peasants make up the majority of the population, a people's war is essentially a peasant's war under the leadership of the working class. Owing to this fact, a general mobilisation of the whole people is neither more nor less than the mobilisation of the rural masses. The problem of land is of decisive importance. From an exhaustive analysis, the Vietnamese people's war of liberation was essentially a people's national democratic revolution carried out under armed form and had [a] twofold fundamental task: the overthrowing of imperialism and the defeat of the feudal landlord class, the anti-imperialist struggle being the primary task.

A backward colonial country which had only just risen up to proclaim its independence and install people's power, Viet Nam only recently possessed armed forces, equipped with still very mediocre arms and having no combat experience. Her enemy, on the other hand, was an imperialist power [France] which has retained a fairly considerable economic and military potentiality despite the recent German occupation [during World War II] and benefited, furthermore, from the active support of the United States. The balance of forces decidedly showed up our weaknesses against the enemy's power. The Vietnamese people's war of liberation had, therefore, to be a hard and long-lasting war in order to succeed in creating conditions for victory. All the conceptions born of impatience and aimed at obtaining speedy victory could only be gross errors. It was necessary to firmly grasp the strategy of a long-term resistance, and to exalt the will to be self-supporting in order to maintain and gradually augment our forces, while nibbling at and progressively destroying those of the enemy; it was necessary to accumulate thousands of small victories to turn them into a great success, thus gradually altering the balance of forces in transforming our weakness into power and carrying off final victory. . . .

From the point of view of directing operations, our *strategy and tactics had to be those of a people's war and of a long-term resistance.*

Our strategy was, as we have stressed, to wage a long-lasting battle. A war of this nature in general entails several phases; in principle, starting from a stage of contention, it goes through a period of equilibrium before arriving at a general counter-offensive. In effect, the way in which it is carried on can be more subtle and more complex, depending on the particular conditions obtaining on both sides during the course of operations. Only a long-term war could enable us to utilise to the maximum our political trump cards, to overcome our material handicap and to transform our weakness into strength. To maintain and increase our forces, was the principle to which we adhered, contenting ourselves with attacking when success was certain, refusing to give battle likely to incur losses to us or to engage in hazardous actions. We had to apply the slogan: to build up our strength during the actual course of fighting.

The forms of fighting had to be completely adapted that is, to raise the fighting spirit to the maximum and rely on heroism of our troops to overcome the enemy's material superiority. In the main, especially at the outset of the war, we had recourse to guerilla fighting. In the Vietnamese theatre of operations, this method carried off great victories: it could be used in the mountains as well as in the delta, it could be waged with good or mediocre material and even without arms, and was to enable us eventually to equip ourselves at the cost of the enemy. Wherever the Expeditionary Corps came, the entire population took part in the fighting; every commune had its fortified village, every district had its regional troops fighting under the command of the local branches of the Party and the people's administration, in liaison with the regular forces in order to wear down and annihilate the enemy forces.

Thereafter, with the development of our forces, guerilla warfare changed into a mobile warfare—a form of mobile warfare still strongly marked by guerilla warfare—which would afterwards become the essential form of operations on the main front, the northern front. In this process of development of guerilla warfare and of accentuation of the mobile warfare, our people's army constantly grew and passed from the stage of combats involving a section or company, to fairly large-scale campaigns bringing into action several divisions. Gradually, its equipment improved, mainly by the seizure of arms from the enemy—the materiel of the French and American imperialists.

From the military point of view, *the Vietnamese people's war of liberation proved that an insufficiently equipped people's army, but an army fighting for a just cause, can, with appropriate strategy and tactics, combine the conditions needed to conquer a modern army of aggressive imperialism.*

The Tonkin Gulf Resolution, 1964

To promote the maintenance of international peace and security in southeast Asia.

Whereas naval units of the Communist regime in Vietnam, in violation of the principles of the Charter of the United Nations and of international law, have deliberately and repeatedly attacked United States naval vessels lawfully present in international waters, and have thereby created a serious threat to international peace; and

Whereas these attacks are part of a deliberate and systematic campaign of aggression that the Communist regime in North Vietnam has been waging against its neighbors and the nations joined with them in the collective defense of their freedom; and

Whereas the United States is assisting the peoples of southeast Asia to protect their freedom and has no territorial, military or political ambitions in that area, but desires only that these peoples should be left in peace to work out their own destinies in their own way: Now, therefore, be it *Resolved by the Senate and House of Representatives of the United States of America in Congress assembled,* That the Congress approves and supports the determination of the President, as Commander in Chief, to take all necessary measures to repel any armed attack against the forces of the United States and to prevent further aggression.

Sec. 2. The United States regards as vital to its national interest and to world peace the maintenance of international peace and security in southeast Asia. Consonant with the Constitution of the United States and the Charter of the United Nations and in accordance with its obligations under the Southeast Asia Collective Defense Treaty, the United States is, therefore, prepared, as the President determines, to take all necessary steps, including the use of armed force, to assist any member or protocol state of the Southeast Asia Collective Defense Treaty requesting assistance in defense of its freedom.

Sec. 3. This resolution shall expire when the President shall determine that the peace and security of the area is reasonably assured by international conditions created by action of the United Nations or otherwise, except that it may be terminated earlier by concurrent resolution of the Congress.

President Lyndon B. Johnson on
Why Americans Fight in Vietnam, 1965

Why must this nation hazard its ease, its interest, and its power for the sake of a people so far away?

We fight because we must fight if we are to live in a world where every country can shape its own destiny, and only in such a world will our own freedom be finally secure.

This kind of world will never be built by bombs or bullets. Yet the infirmities of man are such that force must often precede reason and the waste of war, the works of peace.

We wish that this were not so. But we must deal with the world as it is, if it is ever to be as we wish.

The world as it is in Asia is not a serene or peaceful place.

The first reality is that North Viet-Nam has attacked the independent nation of South Viet-Nam. Its object is total conquest.

Of course, some of the people of South Viet-Nam are participating in attack on their own government. But trained men and supplies, orders and arms, flow in a constant stream from North to South.

This support is the heartbeat of the war.

And it is a war of unparalleled brutality. Simple farmers are the targets of assassination and kidnaping. Women and children are strangled in the night because their men are loyal to their government. And helpless villages are ravaged by sneak attacks. Large-scale raids are conducted on towns, and terror strikes in the heart of cities.

The confused nature of this conflict cannot mask the fact that it is the new face of an old enemy.

Over this war—and all Asia—is another reality: the deepening shadow of Communist China. The rulers in Hanoi are urged on by Peking. This is a regime which has destroyed freedom in Tibet, which has attacked India and has been condemned by the United Nations for aggression in Korea. It is a nation which is helping the forces of violence in almost every continent. The contest in Viet-Nam is part of a wider pattern of aggressive purposes.

Why are these realities our concern? Why are we in South Viet-Nam?

We are there because we have a promise to keep. Since 1954 every American President has offered support to the people of South Viet-Nam. We have helped to build, and we have helped to defend. Thus, over many years, we have made a national pledge to help South Viet-Nam defend its independence.

And I intend to keep that promise.

To dishonor that pledge, to abandon this small and brave nation to its enemies, and to the terror that must follow, would be an unforgivable wrong.

We are also there to strengthen world order. Around the globe from Berlin to Thailand are people whose well being rests in part on the belief that they can count on us if they are attacked. To leave Viet-Nam to its fate would shake the confidence of all these people in the value of an American commitment and in the value of America's word. The result would be increased unrest and instability, and even wider war.

We are also there because there are great stakes in the balance. Let no one think for a moment that retreat from Viet-Nam would bring an end to conflict. The battle would be renewed in one country and then another. The central lesson of our time is that the appetite of aggression is never satisfied. To withdraw from one battlefield means only to prepare for the next. We must say in Southeast Asia—as we did in Europe—in the words of the Bible: "Hitherto shalt thou come, but no further.". . .

In recent months attacks on South Viet-Nam were stepped up. Thus, it became necessary for us to increase our response and to make attacks by air. This is not a change of purpose. It is a change in what we believe that purpose requires.

We do this in order to slow down aggression.

We do this to increase the confidence of the brave people of South Viet-Nam who have bravely borne this brutal battle for so many years with so many casualties.

And we do this to convince the leaders of North Viet-Nam—and all who seek to share their conquest—of a simple fact:

We will not be defeated.

We will not grow tired.

We will not withdraw, either openly or under the cloak of a meaningless agreement. . . .

Stability and peace do not come easily in such a land. Neither independence nor human dignity will ever be won though by arms alone. It also requires the works of peace. The American people have helped generously in times past in these works, and now there must be a much more massive effort to improve the life of man in that conflict-torn corner of our world.

The first step is for the countries of Southeast Asia to associate themselves in a greatly expanded co-operative effort for development. We would hope that North Viet-Nam would take its place in the common effort just as soon as peaceful co-operation is possible.

The United Nations is already actively engaged in development in this area, and as far back as 1961 I conferred with our authorities in Viet-Nam in connection with their work there. And I would hope tonight that the Secretary General of the United Nations could use the prestige of his great office and his deep knowledge of Asia to initiate, as soon as possible, with the countries of that area, a plan for co-operation in increased development.

For our part I will ask the Congress to join in a billion dollar American investment in this effort as soon as it is underway.

And I would hope that all other industrialized countries, including the Soviet Union, will join in this effort to replace despair with hope and terror with progress.

The task is nothing less than to enrich the hopes and existence of more than a hundred million people. And there is much to be done.

The vast Mekong River can provide food and water and power on a scale to dwarf even our own T.V.A. [Tennessee Valley Authority].

The wonders of modern medicine can be spread through villages where thousands die every year from lack of care.

Schools can be established to train people in the skills needed to manage the process of development.

And these objectives, and more, are within the reach of a cooperative and determined effort.

I also intend to expand and speed up a program to make available our farm surpluses to assist in feeding and clothing the needy in Asia. We should not allow people to go hungry and wear rags while our own warehouses overflow with an abundance of wheat and corn and rice and cotton.

So I will very shortly name a special team of outstanding, patriotic, and distinguished Americans to inaugurate our participation in these programs. This team will be headed by Mr. Eugene Black, the very able former president of the World Bank.

This will be a disorderly planet for a long time. In Asia, and elsewhere, the forces of the modern world are shaking old ways and uprooting ancient civilizations. There will be turbulence and struggle and even violence. Great social change—as we see in our own country—does not always come without conflict.

We must also expect that nations will on occasion be in dispute with us. It may be because we are rich, or powerful, or because we have made some mistakes, or because they honestly fear our intentions. However, no nation need ever fear that we desire their land, or to impose our will, or to dictate their institutions.

But we will always oppose the effort of one nation to conquer another nation.

We will do this because our own security is at stake.

But there is more to it than that. For our generation has a dream. It is a very old dream. But we have the power, and now we have the opportunity to make that dream come true.

For centuries nations have struggled among each other. But we dream of a world where disputes are settled by law and reason. And we will try to make it so.

For most of history men have hated and killed one another in battle. But we dream of an end to war. And we will try to make it so.

For all existence most men have lived in poverty, threatened by hunger. But we dream of a world where all are fed and charged with hope. And we will help to make it so.

Secretary of Defense Robert S. McNamara
Recommends Escalation, 1965

Introduction

Our objective is to create conditions for a favorable settlement by demonstrating to the VC/DRV [Vietcong/Democratic Republic of Vietnam (North)] that the odds are against their winning. Under present conditions, however, the chances of achieving this objective are small—and the VC are winning now—largely because the ratio of guerrilla to anti-guerrilla forces is unfavorable to the government. With this in mind, we must choose among three courses of action with respect to South Vietnam: (1) Cut our losses and withdraw under the best conditions that can be arranged; (2) continue at about the present level, with US forces limited to, say, 75,000, holding on and playing for the breaks while recognizing that our position will probably grow weaker; or (3) expand substantially the US military pressure against the Viet Cong in the South and the North Vietnamese in the North and at the same time launch a vigorous effect on the political side to get negotiations started. An outline of the third of these approaches follows.

I. Expanded Military Moves

The following military moves should be taken together with the political initiatives in Part II below.

A. Inside South Vietnam. Increase US/SVN [U.S./South Vietnam] military strength in SVN enough to prove to the VC that they cannot win and thus to turn the tide of the war. . . .

B. Against North Vietnam. While avoiding striking population and industrial targets not closely related to the DRV's supply of war materiel to the VC, we should announce to Hanoi and carry out actions to destroy such supplies and to interdict their flow into and out of North Vietnam. . . .

II. Expanded Political Moves

Together with the above military moves, we should take the following political initiatives in order (a) to open a dialogue with Hanoi, Peking, and the VC looking toward a settlement in Vietnam, (b) to keep the Soviet Union from deepening its military involvement and support of North Vietnam until the time when settlement can be achieved, and (c) to cement the support for US policy by the US public, allies and friends, and to keep international opposition at a manageable level. While our approaches may be rebuffed until the tide begins to turn, they neverthe-less should be made. . . .

III. Evaluation of the Above Program

A. Domestic US Reaction.   Even though casualties will increase and the war will continue for some time, the United States public will support this course of ac-tion because it is a combined military-political program designed and likely to bring about a favorable solution to the Vietnam problem.

B. Communist Reaction to the Expanded Programs

1. *Soviet.* The Soviets can be expected to continue to contribute materiel and advisors to the North Vietnamese. Increased US bombing of Vietnam, including targets in Hanoi and Haiphong, SAM [surface-to-air missile] sites and airfields, and mining of North Vietnamese harbors, might oblige the Soviet Union to enter the contest more actively with volunteers and aircraft. This might result in minor encounters between US and Soviet personnel.

2. *China.* So long as no US or GVN [government of Vietnam (South)] troops invade North Vietnam and so long as no US or GVN aircraft attack Chinese territory, the Chinese probably will not send regular ground forces or aircraft into the war. However, the possibility of a more active Soviet involvement in North Vietnam might precipitate a Chinese introduction of land forces, probably dubbed volunteers, to preclude the Soviets' taking a pre-eminent position in North Vietnam.

3. *North Vietnam.* North Vietnam will not move towards the negotiating table until the tide begins to turn in the south. When that happens, they may seek to counter it by sending large numbers of men into South Vietnam.

4. *Viet Cong.* The VC, especially if they continue to take high losses, can be expected to depend increasingly upon the PAVN [People's Army of Vietnam, regular forces of North Vietnam] forces as the war moves into a more conventional phase; but they may find ways of continuing almost indefinitely their present intensive military, guerrilla and terror activities, particularly if reinforced with some regular PAVN units. A key question on the military side is whether POL [petroleum-oil-lubricants], ammunition, and cadres can be cut off and if they are cut off whether this really renders the Viet Cong impotent. A key question on the political side is whether any arrangement acceptable to us would be acceptable to the VC.

C. Estimate of Success

1. *Militarily.* The success of the above program from a military point of view turns on whether the increased effort stems the tide in the South; that in turn depends on two things—on whether the South Vietnamese hold their own in terms of numbers and fighting spirit, and on whether the US forces can be effective in a quick-reaction reserve role, a role in which they have not been tested. The num-ber of US troops is too small to make a significant difference in the traditional

10–1 government-guerrilla formula, but it is not too small to make a significant difference in the kind of war which seems to be evolving in Vietnam—a "Third Stage" or conventional war in which it is easier to identify, locate and attack the enemy. (South Vietnam has 141 battalions as compared with an estimated equivalent number of VC battalions. The 44 US/3d country battalions mentioned above are the equivalent of 100 South Vietnamese battalions.)

2. *Politically.* It is frequently alleged that such a large expansion of US military personnel, their expanded military role (which would put them in close contact and offer some degree of control over South Vietnamese citizens), and the inevitable expansion of US voice in the operation of the GVN economy and facilities, command and government services will be unpopular; it is said that they could lead to the rejection of the government which supported this American presence, to an irresistible pressure for expulsion of the Americans, and to the greatly increased saleability of Communist propaganda. Whether these allegations are true, we do not know.

The political initiatives are likely to be successful in the early stages only to demonstrate US good faith; they will pay off toward an actual settlement only after the tide begins to turn (unless we lower our sights substantially). The tide almost certainly cannot begin to turn in less than a few months, and may not for a year or more; the war is one of attrition and will be a long one. Since troops once committed as a practical matter cannot be removed, since US casualties will rise, since we should take call-up actions to support the additional forces in Vietnam, the test of endurance may be as much in the United States as in Vietnam.

3. *Generally (CIA estimate).* Over the long term we doubt if the Communists are likely to change their basic strategy in Vietnam (i.e., aggressive and steadily mounting insurgency) unless and until two conditions prevail: (1) they are forced to accept a situation in the war in the South which offers them no prospect of an early victory and no grounds for hope that they can simply outlast the US and (2) North Vietnam itself is under continuing and increasingly damaging punitive attack. So long as the Communists think they scent the possibility of an early victory (which is probably now the case), we believe that they will persevere and accept extremely severe damage to the North. Conversely, if North Vietnam itself is not hurting, Hanoi's doctrinaire leaders will probably be ready to carry on the Southern struggle almost indefinitely. If, however, both of the conditions outlined above should be brought to pass, we believe Hanoi probably would, at least for a period of time, alter its basic strategy and course of action in South Vietnam.

Hanoi might do so in several ways. Going for a conference as a political way of gaining a respite from attack would be one. Alternatively it might reduce the level of insurgent activity in the hopes that this would force the US to stop its punishment of the North but not prevent the US and GVN from remaining subject to wearying harassment in the South. Or, Hanoi might order the VC to suspend operations in the hopes that in a period of temporary tranquility, domestic and international opinion would force the US to disengage without destroying the VC apparatus or the roots of VC strength. Finally, Hanoi might decide that the US/GVN will to fight could still be broken and the tide of war turned back again in favor of the VC by launching a massive PAVN assault on the South. This is a less likely option in the circumstances we have posited, but still a contingency for which the US must be prepared.

Johnson Questions Dissenting Under Secretary of State George Ball, 1965

Morning Meeting of July 21

The President: Is there anyone here of the opinion we should not do what the [Joint Chiefs of Staff] memorandum says [increase U.S. troops in Vietnam by 100,000]? If so, I want to hear from him now, in detail.

Ball: Mr. President, I can foresee a perilous voyage, very dangerous. I have great and grave apprehensions that we can win under these conditions. But let me be clear. If the decision is to go ahead, I am committed.

The President: But, George, is there another course in the national interest, some course that is better than the one McNamara proposes? We know it is dangerous and perilous, but the big question is, can it be avoided?

Ball: There is no course that will allow us to cut our losses. If we get bogged down, our cost might be substantially greater. The pressures to create a larger war would be inevitable. The qualifications I have are not due to the fact that I think we are in a bad moral position.

The President: Tell me then, what other road can I go?

Ball: Take what precautions we can, Mr. President. Take our losses, let their government fall apart, negotiate, discuss, knowing full well there will be a probable take-over by the Communists. This is disagreeable, I know.

The President: I can take disagreeable decisions. But I want to know can we make a case for your thoughts? Can you discuss it fully?

Ball: We have discussed it. I have had my day in court.

The President: I don't think we can have made any full commitment, George. You have pointed out the danger, but you haven't really proposed an alternative course. We haven't always been right. We have no mortgage on victory. Right now, I am concerned that we have very little alternatives to what we are doing. I want another meeting, more meetings, before we take any definitive action. We must look at all other courses of possibility carefully. Right now I feel it would be more dangerous to lose this now, than endanger a great number of troops. But I want this fully discussed.

Afternoon Meeting of July 21

Ball: We cannot win, Mr. President. The war will be long and protracted. The most we can hope for is a messy conclusion. There remains a great danger of intrusion by the Chinese. But the biggest problem is the problem of the long war. The Korean experience was a galling one. The correlation between Korean casualties and public opinion showed support stabilized at 50 percent. As casualties increase,

Reprinted from *Planning a Tragedy: The Americanization of the War in Vietnam,* 107–110, by Larry Berman, with the permission of W.W. Norton & Company, Inc. Copyright © 1982 by Larry Berman.

the pressure to strike at the very jugular of North Vietnam will become very great. I am concerned about world opinion. If we could win in a year's time, and win decisively, world opinion would be alright. However, if the war is long and protracted, as I believe it will be, then we will suffer because the world's greatest power cannot defeat guerrillas. Then there is the problem of national politics. Every great captain in history was not afraid to make a tactical withdrawal if conditions were unfavorable to him. The enemy cannot even be seen in Vietnam. He is indigenous to the country. I truly have serious doubts that an army of Westerners can successfully fight Orientals in an Asian jungle.

The President: This is important. Can Westerners, in the absence of accurate intelligence, successfully fight Asians in jungle rice paddies? I want McNamara and General [Earle] Wheeler [chairman of the Joint Chiefs of Staff] to seriously ponder this question.

Ball: I think we all have underestimated the seriousness of this situation. It is like giving cobalt treatment to a terminal cancer case. I think a long, protracted war will disclose our weakness, not our strength. The least harmful way to cut losses in SVN [South Vietnam] is to let the government decide it doesn't want us to stay there. Therefore, we should put proposals to the GVN [government of Vietnam (South)] that they can't accept. Then, it would move to a neutralist position. I have no illusions that after we were asked to leave South Vietnam, that country would soon come under Hanoi control. . . .

The President: But George, wouldn't all these countries say that Uncle Sam was a paper tiger, wouldn't we lose credibility breaking the word of three presidents, if we did as you have proposed? It would seem to be an irresponsible blow. But I gather you don't think so?

Ball: No sir. The worse blow would be that the mightiest power on earth is unable to defeat a handful of guerrillas.

Senator J. William Fulbright on the "Arrogance of Power," 1966

The attitude above all others which I feel sure is no longer valid is the arrogance of power, the tendency of great nations to equate power with virtue and major responsibilities with a universal mission. The dilemmas involved are preeminently American dilemmas, not because America has weaknesses that others do not have but because America is powerful as no nation has ever been before and the discrepancy between its power and the power of others appears to be increasing. . . .

We are now engaged in a war to "defend freedom" in South Vietnam. Unlike the Republic of Korea, South Vietnam has an army which [is] without notable success and a weak, dictatorial government which does not command the loyalty of the South Vietnamese people. The official war aims of the United States Government, as I understand them, are to defeat what is regarded as North Vietnamese aggression, to demonstrate the futility of what the communists call "wars of national liberation," and to create conditions under which the South Vietnamese people will be able freely to determine their own future. I have not the slightest doubt of the sincerity of the President and the Vice President and the Secretaries of State and

Defense in propounding these aims. What I do doubt—and doubt very much—is the ability of the United States to achieve these aims by the means being used. I do not question the power of our weapons and the efficiency of our logistics; I cannot say these things delight me as they seem to delight some of our officials, but they are certainly impressive. What I do question is the ability of the United States, or France or any other Western nation, to go into a small, alien, undeveloped Asian nation and create stability where there is chaos, the will to fight where there is defeatism, democracy where there is no tradition of it and honest government where corruption is almost a way of life. Our handicap is well expressed in the pungent Chinese proverb: "In shallow waters dragons become the sport of shrimps."

Early last month demonstrators in Saigon burned American jeeps, tried to assault American soldiers, and marched through the streets shouting "Down with the American imperialists," while one of the Buddhist leaders made a speech equating the United States with the communists as a threat to South Vietnamese independence. Most Americans are understandably shocked and angered to encounter such hostility from people who by now would be under the rule of the Viet Cong but for the sacrifice of American lives and money. Why, we may ask, are they so shockingly ungrateful? Surely they must know that their very right to parade and protest and demonstrate depends on the Americans who are defending them.

The answer, I think, is that "fatal impact" of the rich and strong on the poor and weak. Dependent on it though the Vietnamese are, our very strength is a reproach to their weakness, our wealth a mockery of their poverty, our success a reminder of their failures. What they resent is the disruptive effect of our strong culture upon their fragile one, an effect which we can no more avoid than a man can help being bigger than a child. What they fear, I think rightly, is that traditional Vietnamese society cannot survive the American economic and cultural impact. . . .

The cause of our difficulties in southeast Asia is not a deficiency of power but an excess of the wrong kind of power which results in a feeling of impotence when it fails to achieve its desired ends. We are still acting like boy scouts dragging reluctant old ladies across the streets they do not want to cross. We are trying to remake Vietnamese society, a task which certainly cannot be accomplished by force and which probably cannot be accomplished by any means available to outsiders. The objective may be desirable, but it is not feasible. . . .

If America has a service to perform in the world—and I believe it has—it is in large part the service of its own example. In our excessive involvement in the affairs of other countries, we are not only living off our assets and denying our own people the proper enjoyment of their resources; we are also denying the world the example of a free society enjoying its freedom to the fullest. This is regrettable indeed for a nation that aspires to teach democracy to other nations, because, as [Edmund] Burke said, "Example is the school of mankind, and they will learn at no other.". . .

There are many respects in which America, if it can bring itself to act with the magnanimity and the empathy appropriate to its size and power, can be an intelligent example to the world. We have the opportunity to set an example of generous understanding in our relations with China, of practical cooperation for peace in our relations with Russia, of reliable and respectful partnership in our relations with Western Europe, of material helpfulness without moral presumption in our relations with the developing nations, of abstention from the temptations of hegemony in our relations with Latin America, and of the all-around advantages of minding one's own business in our relations with everybody. Most of all, we have the opportunity to serve as an example of democracy to the world by the way in which we run our own society; America, in the words of John Quincy Adams, should be "the well-wisher to the freedom and independence of all" but "the champion and vindicator only of her own.". . .

If we can bring ourselves so to act, we will have overcome the dangers of the arrogance of power. It will involve, no doubt, the loss of certain glories, but that seems a price worth paying for the probable rewards, which are the happiness of America and the peace of the world.

Secretary of Defense Clark M. Clifford
Recalls His Post-Tet Questions (1968), 1969

I took office on March 1, 1968. The enemy's Tet offensive of late January and early February had been beaten back at great cost. The confidence of the American people had been badly shaken. The ability of the South Vietnamese government to restore order and morale in the populace, and discipline and esprit in the armed forces, was being questioned. At the President's direction, General Earle G. Wheeler, Chairman of the Joint Chiefs of Staff, had flown to Viet Nam in late February for an on-the-spot conference with General [William] Westmoreland. He had just returned and presented the military's request that over 200,000 troops be prepared for deployment to Viet Nam. These troops would be in addition to the 525,000 previously authorized. I was directed, as my first assignment, to chair a task force named by the President to determine how this new requirement could be met. We were not instructed to assess the need for substantial increases in men and materiel; we were to devise the means by which they could be provided.

My work was cut out. The task force included Secretary [of State Dean] Rusk, Secretary [of the Treasury] Henry Fowler, Under Secretary of State Nicholas Katzenbach, Deputy Secretary of Defense Paul Nitze, General Wheeler, CIA Director Richard Helms, the President's Special Assistant, Walt Rostow, General Maxwell Taylor and other skilled and highly capable officials. All of them had had long and direct experience with Vietnamese problems. I had not. I had attended various meetings in the past several years and I had been to Viet Nam three times, but it was quickly apparent to me how little one knows if he has been on the periphery of a problem and not truly in it. Until the day-long sessions of early March, I had never had the opportunity of intensive analysis and fact-finding. Now I was thrust into a vigorous, ruthlessly frank assessment of our situation by the men who knew the most about it. Try though we would to stay with the assignment of devising means to meet the military's requests, fundamental questions began to recur over and over.

Clark M. Clifford, "A Viet Nam Reappraisal: The Personal History of One Man's View and How It Evolved," *Foreign Affairs,* 47 (July 1969), pp. 41–43. Copyright 1992 by the Council on Foreign Relations, Inc.

It is, of course, not possible to recall all the questions that were asked nor all of the answers that were given. Had a transcript of our discussions been made—one was not—it would have run to hundreds of closely printed pages. The documents brought to the table by participants would have totalled, if collected in one place—which they were not—many hundreds more. All that is pertinent to this essay are the impressions I formed, and the conclusions I ultimately reached in those days of exhausting scrutiny. In the colloquial style of those meetings, here are some of the principal issues raised and some of the answers as I understood them:

"Will 200,000 more men do the job?" I found no assurance that they would.

"If not, how many more might be needed—and when?" There was no way of knowing.

"What would be involved in committing 200,000 more men to Viet Nam?" A reserve call-up of approximately 280,000, an increased draft call and an extension of tours of duty of most men then in service.

"Can the enemy respond with a build-up of his own?" He could and he probably would.

"What are the estimated costs of the latest requests?" First calculations were on the order of $2 billion for the remaining four months of that fiscal year, and an increase of $10 to $12 billion for the year beginning July 1, 1968.

"What will be the impact on the economy?" So great that we would face the possibility of credit restrictions, a tax increase and even wage and price controls. The balance of payments would be worsened by at least half a billion dollars a year.

"Can bombing stop the war?" Never by itself. It was inflicting heavy personnel and materiel losses, but bombing by itself would not stop the war.

"Will stepping up the bombing decrease American casualties?" Very little, if at all. Our casualties were due to the intensity of the ground fighting in the South. We had already dropped a heavier tonnage of bombs than in all the theaters of World War II. During 1967, an estimated 90,000 North Vietnamese had infiltrated into South Viet Nam. In the opening weeks of 1968, infiltrators were coming in at three to four times the rate of a year earlier, despite the ferocity and intensity of our campaign of aerial interdiction.

"How long must we keep on sending our men and carrying the main burden of combat?" The South Vietnamese were doing better, but they were not ready yet to replace our troops and we did not know when they would be.

When I asked for a presentation of the military plan for attaining victory in Viet Nam, I was told that there was no plan for victory in the historic American sense. Why not? Because our forces were operating under three major political restrictions: The President had forbidden the invasion of North Viet Nam because this could trigger the mutual assistance pact between North Viet Nam and China; the President had forbidden the mining of the harbor at Haiphong, the principal port through which the North received military supplies, because a Soviet vessel might be sunk; the President had forbidden our forces to pursue the enemy into Laos and Cambodia, for to do so would spread the war, politically and geographically, with no discernible advantage. These and other restrictions which precluded an all-out, no-holds-barred military effort were wisely designed to prevent our being drawn into a larger war. We had no inclination to recommend to the President their cancellation.

"Given these circumstances, how can we win?" We would, I was told, continue to evidence our superiority over the enemy; we would continue to attack in the belief that he would reach the stage where he would find it inadvisable to go on with the war. He could not afford the attrition we were inflicting on him. And we were improving our posture all the time.

I then asked, "What is the best estimate as to how long this course of action will take? Six months? One year? Two years?" There was no agreement on an answer. Not only was there no agreement, I could find no one willing to express any confidence in his guesses. Certainly, none of us was willing to assert that he could see "light at the end of the tunnel" or that American troops would be coming home by the end of the year.

After days of this type of analysis, my concern had greatly deepened. I could not find out when the war was going to end; I could not find out the manner in which it was going to end; I could not find out whether the new requests for men and equipment were going to be enough, or whether it would take more and, if more, when and how much; I could not find out how soon the South Vietnamese forces would be ready to take over. All I had was the statement, given with too little self-assurance to be comforting, that if we persisted for an indeterminate length of time, the enemy would choose not to go on.

And so I asked, "Does anyone see any diminution in the will of the enemy after four years of our having been there, after enormous casualties and after massive destruction from our bombing?"

The answer was that there appeared to be no diminution in the will of the enemy. . . .

And so, after these exhausting days, I was convinced that the military course we were pursuing was not only endless, but hopeless. A further substantial increase in American forces could only increase the devastation and the Americanization of the war, and thus leave us even further from our goal of a peace that would permit the people of South Viet Nam to fashion their own political and economic institutions. Henceforth, I was also convinced, our primary goal should be to level off our involvement, and to work toward gradual disengagement.

Private Paul Meadlo Explains the 1968 My Lai Massacre, 1969

Q. And what had you been briefed to do when you got to Pinkville [My Lai]?

A. To search and to make sure that there weren't no N.V.A. [North Vietnamese Army] in the village and expecting to fight—when we got there. . . .

Q. To expect to fight?

A. To expect to fight.

Q. Un-huh. So you took off and—in how many choppers?

A. Well, I'd say the first wave was about four of us—I mean four choppers, and. . . .

New York Times, November 25, 1969. © 1969 by The New York Times Company. Reprinted by permission.

Q. How many men aboard each chopper?

A. Five of us. And we landed next to the village, and we all got in line and we started walking toward the village. And there was one man, one gook in the shelter, and he was all huddled up down in there, and the man called out and said there's a gook over here.

Q. How old a man was this? I mean was this a fighting man or an older man?

A. An older man. And the man hauled out and said that there's a gook over here, and then Sergeant [David] Mitchell hollered back and said shoot him.

Q. Sergeant Mitchell was in charge of the 20 of you?

A. He was in charge of the whole squad. And so then the man shot him. So we moved on into the village, and we started searching up the village and gathering people and running through the center of the village.

Q. How many people did you round up?

A. Well, there was about 40–45 people that we gathered in the center of the village. And we placed them in there, and it was like a little island, right there in the center of the village, I'd say. And—

Q. What kind of people—men, women, children?

A. Men, women, children.

Q. Babies?

A. Babies. And we all huddled them up. We made them squat down, and Lieutenant [William] Calley came over and said you know what to do with them, don't you? And I said yes so I took it for granted that he just wanted us to watch them. And he left, and came back about 10 to 15 minutes later, and said, how come you ain't killed them yet? And I told him that I didn't think you wanted us to kill them, that you just wanted us to guard them. He said, no, I want them dead. So—

Q. He told this to all of you, or to you particularly?

A. Well, I was facing him. So, but, the other three, four guys heard it and so he stepped back about 10, 15 feet, and he started shooting them. And he told me to start shooting. So I started shooting, I poured about four clips into the group.

Q. You fired four clips from your . . .

A. M-16.

Q. And that's about—how many clips—I mean how many—

A. I carried seventeen rounds to each clip.

Q. So you fired something like 67 shots—

A. Right.

Q. And you killed how many? At that time?

A. Well, I fired them on automatic, so you can't—you just spray the area on them and so you can't know how many you killed 'cause they were going fast. So I might have killed ten or fifteen of them.

Q. Men, women and children?

A. Men, women and children.

Q. And babies?

A. And babies.

Q. Okay, then what?

A. So we started to gather them up, more people, and we had about seven or eight people, that we was gonna put into the hootch, and we dropped a hand grenade in there with them.

Q. Now you're rounding up more?

A. We're rounding up more, and we had about seven or eight people. And we was going to throw them in the hootch, and well, we put them in the hootch and then we dropped a hand grenade down there with them. And somebody holed up in the ravine, and told us to bring them over to the ravine, so we took them back out, and led them over to—and by that time, we already had them over there, and they had about 70—75 people all gathered up. So we threw ours in with them and Lieutenant Calley told me, he said, Meadlo, we got another job to do. And so he walked over to the people, and he started pushing them off and started shooting. . . .

Q. Started pushing them off into the ravine?

A. Off into the ravine. It was a ditch. And so we started pushing them off and we started shooting them, so altogether we just pushed them all off, and just started using automatics on them. And then—

Q. Again—men, women, children?

A. Men, women and children.

Q. And babies?

A. And babies. And so we started shooting them and somebody told us to switch off to single shot so that we could save ammo. So we switched off to single shot and shot a few more rounds. And after that, I just—we just—the company started gathering up again. We started moving out, and we had a few gooks that was in—as we started moving out, we had gooks in front of us that was taking point, you know. . . .

Q. Why did you do it?

A. Why did I do it? Because I felt like I was ordered to do it, and it seemed like that, at the time I felt like I was doing the right thing, because like I said I lost buddies. I lost a damn good buddy, Bobby Wilson, and it was on my conscience. So after I done it, I felt good, but later on that day, it was getting to me.

Q. You're married?

A. Right.

Q. Children?

A. Two.

Q. How old?

A. The boy is two and a half, and the little girl is a year and a half.

Q. Obviously, the question comes to my mind . . . the father of two little kids like that . . . how can he shoot babies?

A. I didn't have the little girl. I just had a little boy at the time.

Q. Uh-huh. How do you shoot babies?

A. I don't know. It's just one of them things.

Q. How many people would you imagine were killed that day?

A. I'd say about 370.

Q. How do you arrive at that figure?

A. Just looking.

Q. You say, you think, that many people, and you yourself were responsible for how many of them?

A. I couldn't say.

Q. Twenty-five? Fifty?

A. I couldn't say . . . just too many. . . .

Q. What did these civilians—particularly the women and children, the old men—what did they do? What did they say to you?

A. They weren't much saying to them. They [were] just being pushed and they were doing what they was told to do.

Q. They weren't begging or saying, "No . . . no," or—

A. Right, they were begging and saying, "No, no." And the mothers was hugging their children and, but they kept right on firing. Well, we kept right on firing. They was waving their arms and begging. . . .

Q. Was that your most vivid memory of what you saw?

A. Right.

Q. And nothing went through your mind or heart?

A. Many a times . . . many a times. . . .

Q. While you were doing it?

A. Not while I was doing it. It just seemed like it was the natural thing to do at the time. I don't know . . . I was getting relieved from what I'd seen earlier over there.

Q. What do you mean?

A. Well, I was getting . . . like the . . . my buddies getting killed or wounded or—we weren't getting no satisfaction from it, so what it really was, it was just mostly revenge.

Q. You call the Vietnamese "gooks"?

A. Gooks.

Q. Are they people to you? Were they people to you?

A. Well, they were people. But it was just one of them words that we just picked up over there, you know. Just any word you pick up. That's what you call people, and that's what you been called.

Q. Obviously, the thought that goes through my mind—I spent some time over there, and I killed in the second war, and so forth. But the thought that goes through your mind is, we've raised such a dickens about what the Nazis did, or what the Japanese did, but particularly what the Nazis did in the second world war, the brutalization and so forth, you know. It's hard for a good many Americans to understand that young, capable, American boys could line up old men, women and children and babies and shoot them down in cold blood. How do you explain that?

A. I wouldn't know.

Q. Did you ever dream about all of this that went on in Pinkville?

A. Yes, I did . . . and I still dream about it.

Q. What kind of dreams?

A. About the women and children in my sleep. Some days . . . some nights, I can't even sleep. I just lay there thinking about it.

ESSAYS

In the first essay, Larry Berman of the University of California, Davis, analyzes President Lyndon B. Johnson's decision in July 1965 to escalate U.S. military intervention in Vietnam. Berman argues that cognitive errors and miscalculations, including the administration's misapplication of the containment doctrine to Southeast Asia and Johnson's manipulation of the advisory process, led the administration to fight a war that some doubted could be won. The strategy of gradual escalation, Berman concludes, avoided a full-scale military mobilization and momentarily saved Johnson's domestic reform programs but also set the United States on a perilous course in Vietnam.

Berman's autopsy of the subject differs from the radical perspective of Gabriel Kolko of York University, Canada. In the second essay, Kolko acknowledges the importance of Johnson's decisionmaking process but argues that U.S. intervention grew primarily from a deliberate quest, from 1945 on, to fashion an integrated world capitalist order. In the 1960s, as Vietnam's revolution seemed to weaken America's credibility as a world power, the Johnson administration moved decisively and confidently to intervene militarily and to turn back the challenge. According to Kolko, the Vietnam War became so expensive that it ultimately sapped the nation's economic strength and reduced U.S. power around the world.

In the final essay, Eric M. Bergerud of Lincoln University (California) studies the dynamics of the U.S. military defeat in one province of South Vietnam, Hau Nghia. He disputes those scholars, politicians, and publicists who argue that the United States could have won the Vietnam War. According to Bergerud, the United States confronted a highly motivated and talented communist insurgency whose popular base and guerrilla tactics contrasted sharply with the United States' corrupt, inefficient South Vietnamese allies. Although U.S. forces inflicted heavy damage on the enemy, Bergerud concludes that neither an invasion of North Vietnam nor an intensified pacification program in South Vietnam could have changed the outcome of the conflict.

Lyndon B. Johnson's Tragic Decision to Escalate

LARRY BERMAN

On July 28 [1965] President Johnson announced that U.S. fighting strength in Vietnam would immediately be increased from 75,000 to 125,000 and that additional U.S. forces would be sent as they were requested by field commander Gen. William Westmoreland. This military obligation, taken in response to the rapidly deteriorating political and military situation in South Vietnam, would be achieved through substantial increases in monthly draft calls but, contrary to all previous indications from the White House, no Reserve or National Guard units would be called into service.

The president's decision resulted from extensive deliberations among foreign policy advisors and between these advisors and the president. In his backgrounding of the press, Secretary of Defense Robert McNamara emphasized that "not since the Cuban missile crisis had such care been taken in making a decision. On the average of four hours per day has been spent with the President in discussing the problem. In addition, the President sought the advice of every responsible government official in coming to a decision." These White House deliberations reflected what is generally assumed to be one of the few times that the principal Vietnam advisors focused intensively on fundamental questions of policy and not solely on the technicalities of military strategy. For approximately one month the president and his chief foreign policy advisors faced crucial questions concerning

Reprinted from *Planning a Tragedy: The Americanization of the War in Vietnam* by Larry Berman, pp. xii, 6–7, 130–132, 135–147, 149, 153, with the permission of W. W. Norton & Company, Inc. Copyright © 1982 by Larry Berman.

America's global objectives, vital interests, policy options, and their probable effects. All of those involved understood that to proceed as indicated above would mean a lengthy American military commitment to a land war in Vietnam. . . .

Thirty thousand American troops died in Vietnam between July 28, 1965, and the inauguration of Richard Nixon in January 1969. "How," asked [former U.S. official] James C. Thomson, Jr., "did men of superior ability, sound training and high ideals—American policymakers of the 1960s—create such a costly and divisive policy?" I believe that the primary source documents provide several answers to Thomson's legitimate query—each of these will be explored below. . . .

The primary source documents show that Lyndon Johnson *may* have staged the July deliberations as a smokescreen for buying time to ensure passage of domestic legislation through Congress. What appeared to the press, to attentive publics, and even to some advisors as a month of careful debate during which advisors advised and the president consulted, may have been the president's tactic for building consensus within the administration to legitimize a previously selected policy for political elites in Congress and subsequently to the American public. Lyndon Johnson's personality very probably played the dominant role in the president's undoing—but the reasons are much more complex and interdependent than a personal response to Ho Chi Minh. We need to start at the beginning, however, to understand just how and why the president made such fateful choices. In doing so I accept fully [the historian] C. V. Wedgewood's warning that "history is lived forward but it is written in retrospect. We know the end before we consider the beginning and we can never wholly recapture what it was like to know the beginning only."

[T]he principals [chief policymakers] accepted containment of communism and the domino theory as basic premises for formulating policy and not as hypotheses for analysis. Moreover, the principals approached the problem definition stage with twenty years of intellectual baggage shaped by visions of Soviet-inspired and aggressive communism. There was an almost talmudic adherence to the containment strategy outlined by George Kennan which called for an "unalterable counterforce at every point where they [communists] show signs of encroachment." But in 1965 the principals expanded significantly on the definition of containment and, for that matter, of world communism. Containment of Soviet aggression was originally conceived as limited in both geographical scope and objective. As Vietnam *became* an increasingly important component in U.S. global interests, not losing Vietnam assumed an equally high stature. According to the BDM [Corporation] study, "Early on, American leadership mistakenly believed Vietnam to be vital not only for itself, but for what they thought its 'loss' would mean internationally and domestically. Once the commitment was made, each subsequent president reaffirmed the commitment rather than reassessing the basic rationale as to whether vital US interests were involved or not."

The cognitive error was not Johnson's alone. Six postwar presidents and their advisors refused to think critically about the changing nature of Asian communism. As the BDM study put it:

> All of the presidents had lived through Manchuria, Munich, Poland, Yalta, the "loss" of China, the Korean War, and the McCarthy era. Each drew the lesson that the United States could not afford to be soft on communism, specifically that he could not be the

president who permitted the "loss" of Vietnam to communism. Their close advisers reinforced their own anticommunist orientation. There is no question that the presidents and their advisers were conditioned by such past experiences when considering how to deal with the conflict in Vietnam. . . .

Decision-makers constantly justified their views on the necessity of Communist containment with reference to another "appeasement at Munich" or another "loss of China." These "simplistic adages were often used," according to the BDM study, "in lieu of developing more precise and perhaps more convincing explanations for making a particular policy decision. In addition, they often came to be voiced indiscriminately, leading to generalization, overuse, and misapplication." The BDM study identified a direct cause-and-effect relationship: "The American experience in Vietnam points to the danger of having one fundamental principle— anticommunism—elevated to the status of doctrine for all regions of the world. By elevating a principle to the level of doctrine, further debate of the subject is minimized, thereby reducing the possibility that legitimate dissenting views will receive sufficient attention at the national policy-making level. What tended to happen in Vietnam was that consensus building on the premise of anticommunism was achieved to give coherence to Vietnam policy at the national level, at the sacrifice of a needed closer examination of the accuracy of that premise."

The logical companion to containment was the domino theory. Clark Clifford, for example, referred to the "solid phalanx of advice from [LBJ's] main advisors . . . the unanimous sentiment among his senior advisors that the domino theory was unquestionably so." "The 'domino' theory," according to the BDM study, "saw any conflict with the communists as a test of the US's national resolve and credibility. The communists had threatened to take over 'free world' territory in Berlin, Korea, Iran, Guatemala, Lebanon and the Dominican Republic and actions taken by the US to prevent the loss of these territories were viewed by many as American Cold War successes. Conversely, the communists gaining control over China and Cuba were viewed as Cold War defeats for the U.S. Each successive US president found himself bound, in large measure, by his predecessor's doctrine and thereafter often analyzed issues from the same perspectives, continuing policies long after they had outlived their usefulness." As a result even support for the repressive and authoritarian [Ngo Dinh] Diem was justified as a regrettable means to a nobler end—saving the world from Soviet-inspired Communist aggression. Decision-makers eventually abandoned all of the original preconditions for policy—particularly a stable and meritorious GVN [government of Vietnam (South)]—to pursue the ultimate goal of halting communism in Southeast Asia. Acceptance of the containment legacy led decision-makers to become preoccupied with the question of "how" the government of South Vietnam could be saved, and never with "why" the government was worth saving. . . .

The assumption by McNamara, Westmoreland, and the Joint Chiefs [of Staff] that the Viet Cong were about to abandon their successful guerrilla tactics in favor of more conventional regiment-size confrontations was [also] pivotal to the reasoning of the July 28 decision. According to McNamara, "the enemy clearly was moving into the third phase of revolutionary warfare, committing regiments and subsequently divisions to seize and retain territory and to destroy the government's troops and eliminate all vestiges of government control." In his memoirs Admiral

[U. S. Grant] Sharp wrote, "in early June we had become very concerned that the communists might be about ready to increase the intensity of the conflict. Evidence indicated that the North Vietnamese were now capable of mounting regiment-size operations in many locations throughout the country and battalion-size operations almost anyplace."

Secretary McNamara's forty-four–battalion request [of June–July 1965] was predicated on the assumption that U.S. troops, for the most part, would be engaging main force and not guerrilla units. But the president's advisors were in bitter disagreement over the question of a Third Stage. The case provides an excellent example of how a determined president might have shifted the burden of proof to Westmoreland or McNamara and received answers which were totally incompatible with the preferred option. [Under Secretary of State] George Ball, the CIA, the State Department, [national security adviser] McGeorge Bundy, and [Assistant Secretary of Defense] William Bundy all recorded their *rejection* of Westmoreland's claim that the so-called Third Stage was underway. Unfortunately, little of the correspondence between advisors ever reached the president's desk, especially since Johnson acknowledged its import ("he seemed to agree") when Ball raised the point during the July 21 meeting.

The debate at the staff level is quite revealing. After reading McNamara's June 26 memorandum, William Bundy instructed the State Department Office of Intelligence and Research to examine whether or not the Communists were moving into the Third Stage phase of warfare as predicted by General [Vo Nguyen] Giap. In a July 23, 1965, *Secret—Limited Distribution* report, State Department officials concluded "that their pattern of behavior in Vietnam to date and their probable expectations as to the future argue *against the hypothesis that the communists are preparing to enter the third stage.* . . . We do not believe that the criteria established by Giap for the third stage—size of unit, scale of operation, and nature of attack—have been or are about to be met in South Vietnam. Our examination of Viet Cong capabilities, the campaign against GVN lines of communication, the communist attack pattern, and the content of communist propaganda, persuades us rather that the VC will continue to employ guerrilla tactics with only intermittent recourse to spectacular, multi-battalion attacks against major ARVN [Army of the Republic of Vietnam] reinforcement, and are not now capable of initiating a drastically different phase of warfare.". . .

The report concluded that to accept the assumption of a conventional phase was to be victimized by Communist propaganda: "While both Hanoi and NFLSV [National Front for the Liberation of South Vietnam] propaganda continue to claim 'bigger and bigger' victories for the 'Liberation Armed Forces and Guerrillas' *there are no indications that they have altered their traditional guerrilla strategy and tactics, despite occasional references to the development of conventional warfare in the South."* The State Department cited Ho Chi Minh's remarks that "we are determined to fight till final victory even if we have to go on fighting another 5 years, 10 years, 20 years or even longer" as *"hardly suggesting that the DRV* [Democratic Republic of Vietnam (North)] *is pushing for an early victory by shifting to conventional warfare."* . . .

George Ball also rejected McNamara's "unproven" assumption of a Third Stage. Writing to the president, Ball noted that "implicit in arguments for greatly augmented United States combat forces in South Vietnam is the assumption that the Viet Cong have entered—or are about to enter—their so-called 'third phase' of warfare, having progressed from relatively small-scale hit and run operations to large unit, fixed position conventional warfare. *Yet we have no basis for assuming that the Viet Cong will fight a war on our terms* [McGeorge Bundy's very point to McNamara] when they can continue to fight the kind of war they fought so well against both the French and the GVN." Ball noted that "we can scarcely expect [General Giap] to accommodate us by adopting our preferred method of combat, regardless of how many troops we send. There is every reason to suppose that the Viet Cong will avoid providing good targets for our massive bombing and superior firepower."

In his July 1 memo to the president, William Bundy agreed with Ball's rejection of McNamara's thesis: "As for major additional ground deployments, the first argument is simply whether they would be militarily effective. As the Ball paper points out, Hanoi is by no means committed to a really conventional type of war and they could easily go on making significant gains while giving us precious few opportunities to hit them."

Even after the July 21 NSC meeting, Chester Cooper tried to convince McGeorge Bundy to convince McNamara that "we and the GVN will be faced with the problem of guerrilla rather than positional warfare." But by now reasonable questions of the Third Stage were listened to but not heard. The momentum was simply too great, the reasons perceived as too just, the lessons of history too clear—for erroneous tactics to have thrown things off schedule.

A great deal of uncertainty pervaded the decision process. On July 2 Secretary McNamara asked General [Earle] Wheeler to form a small group of experts to address the question "If we do everything we can, can we have assurance of winning in South Vietnam?" General Wheeler asked General [Andrew] Goodpaster, assistant to the chairman, JCS, to chair the group, and John McNaughton, assistant secretary of defense, provided the staff support. McNaughton, McNamara's closest civilian associate, offered a fascinating perspective on the degree of uncertainty facing decision-makers in early July. He believed that the forty-four–battalion program would be sufficient only through 1965 and urged Goodpaster to "produce a clear articulation of what our strategy is for winning the war in South Vietnam, tough as that articulation will be in the nature of the problem." McNaughton raised several important points: "I think we might avoid some spinning of wheels if we simply assumed that the GVN will not be able to increase its forces in the relevant time period. Indeed, from what Westy [Westmoreland] has reported about the battalions being chewed up and about their showing some signs of reluctance to engage in offensive operations, we might even have to ask the question whether we can expect them to maintain present levels of men—or more accurately, present levels of effectiveness.". . .

With regard to the question "If we do everything we can, can we have assurance of winning in South Vietnam?" [McNaughton wrote]:

One key question, of course, is what we mean by the words "assurance" and "win." My view is that the degree of "assurance" should be fairly high—better than 75% (whatever that means). With respect to the word "win," this I think means that we succeed in demonstrating to the VC that they cannot win; this, of course, is victory for us only if it is, with a high degree of probability, a way station toward a favorable settlement in South Vietnam. I see such a favorable settlement as one in which the VC terrorism is substantially eliminated and, obviously, there are no longer large-scale VC attacks; the central South Vietnamese government (without having taken in the Communists) should be exercising fairly complete sovereignty over most of South Vietnam. I presume that we would rule out the ceding to the VC (either tacitly or explicitly) of large areas of the country. . . .

Challenges to the logic of U.S. involvement continued when McNaughton sent McNamara a "numbers game" scenario of possible options—illustrating that the probability for success and failure increased with each increment [of U.S. forces] and each year. U.S. aims were identified as "70%—to preserve our national honor as a guarantor (and the reciprocal: to avoid a show-case success for Communist 'wars of liberation'); 20%—to keep SVN [South Vietnam] (and then adjacent) territory from hostile expansive hands; 10%—'answer the call of a friend,' to help him enjoy a better life. Also—to emerge from crisis without unacceptable taint from the methods used.". . .

In his concluding prognosis, McNaughton wrote: "even if [we achieve] 'success,' it is not obvious how we will be able to disengage our forces from South Vietnam. It is unlikely that a formal agreement good enough for the purpose could possibly be negotiated—because the arrangement can reflect little more than the power situation. Most likely, in the case of success, is a settling down into a 'compromise'-like situation with a large number—perhaps 2 divisions—of US forces required to stay for a period of years. During that period of time, any number of things can change the picture beyond prediction."

According to the *Pentagon Papers,* "the McNaughton memorandum is of interest because it demonstrates several important items. First, the fact that the question about assurance of winning was asked indicates that *at the Secretary of Defense level there was real awareness that the decision to be made in the next few weeks would commit the US to the possibility of an expanded conflict.* The key question then was whether or not we would become involved more deeply in a war which could not be brought to a satisfactory conclusion. Secondly, the definition of 'win,' i.e., 'succeed in demonstrating to the VC that they cannot win,' indicates the assumption upon which the conduct of the war was to rest—that the VC could be convinced in some meaningful sense that they were not going to win and that they would then rationally choose less violent methods of seeking their goals. But the extent to which this definition would set limits of involvement or affect strategy was not clear. Thirdly, the assumptions on the key variables (the infiltration rates, the strength of GVN forces, the probable usefulness of Third Country forces, the political situation in South Vietnam) were rightfully pessimistic and cautious."

But the expressions of doubt were never to be publicly aired. When Sen. Mike Mansfield wrote with the question "The main perplexity in the Vietnam situation is that even if you win, totally, you still do not come out well. What have you achieved?" McNamara's response reflected just how committed he was to a definition which greatly raised the stakes of losing: "South Vietnam *is vital* to the United States in the significance that a demonstrable defeat would have on the future effectiveness of the United States on the world scene—especially in areas where people are depending upon our guarantee of their independence. It is a *vital US concern* to maintain *our honor* as an ally and our formidability as an opponent. As for how the situation in Vietnam will ultimately come out, we cannot now know. *But there is a range of outcomes—many less than perfect ones—that would satisfy American vital interests.* Our objectives, after all, are quite limited in Vietnam. They are, first, to permit the South Vietnamese to be independent and make a free choice of government and second, to establish for the world that Communist externally inspired and supported wars of liberation will not work." No logic to the contrary would be allowed to disrupt that line of reasoning. . . .

It is not infrequent that one hears the question: If Southeast Asia in general and Vietnam in specific were all that important to U.S. security interests, why didn't the United States (once the Ball scenario had been rejected) just use its power to win and then defend South Vietnam? The primary constraint on U.S. policy was the belief that provocative military measures against the North would bring Chinese troops into the war. President Johnson maintained that it would take only one stray bomb for the cloning of Korea. For that reason he would not risk bombing the dikes [outside Hanoi] or mining Haiphong harbor. According to [the biographer] Doris Kearns, Johnson "lived in constant fear of triggering some imaginary provision of some imaginary treaty" between the Chinese and Hanoi.

There are several different opinions on this important issue. According to Clark Clifford, "the military would have liked to have invaded North Vietnam. President Johnson knew this was wrong because North Vietnam has a mutual assistance pact with Red China and just as soon as we invaded North Vietnam, the North Vietnamese would have triggered that pact and just hordes of Chinese troops would have come over. Every expert that I know in that part of the world agrees to that statement so there he turned the military down." Ambassador [Maxwell] Taylor disagreed with this view, arguing that Washington was unduly apprehensive about possible Chinese reinforcements. In Saigon, "we doubted that either Hanoi or the Vietcong would ever request or accept Chinese combat forces in their country. For centuries the Chinese had been regarded as hated, foreign oppressors by all Vietnamese, North and South, and that historical attitude was not likely to change." In his memoirs Admiral Sharp lamented that the military was never allowed to fight the war "to win" because "political and diplomatic circles in Washington were disproportionately concerned with the possibility of communist and Soviet intervention"—characterized by frequent reference to "mythical hordes" of Chinese streaming into Vietnam should the United States pose a threatening glance. The important point is, however, that President Johnson defined the situation in a way which severely constrained his military options and ultimately undid his political base. In doing so he revealed a fundamental misunderstanding of his adversary's goals and purposes. . . .

Since the U.S. goal was only to deny the Communists a victory and not to gain a military victory for itself, the principals proceeded from the premise that the greatest military power on the planet would eventually destroy the VC in South Vietnam and hit the DRV hard enough in North Vietnam to force a negotiated settlement on Hanoi. This strategy ignored the basic fact that Hanoi's *national* strategy was based on protracted struggle: "The leaders of the DRV had no rigid timetable for the struggle in the South. Rather the regime was confident that *the longer the war lasted, the more serious the 'inherent contradictions' in the US and US-GVN relationship would become.* Thus, while the North Vietnamese communists spoke of winning the decisive victory, *their definition of victory* did not imply the final seizure of power from the Saigon government. Instead, it meant either decisive victory on the battlefield, causing a turning point in the war, or partial annihilation of US and ARVN forces, forcing an American withdrawal. Decisive victory was, therefore, to take place within the context of protracted armed and political struggle."

North Vietnam was involved in a total, not limited war. George Ball recalled that "On his first visit to Vietnam, in 1962, Secretary McNamara reported to the President that 'every quantitative measurement we have shows we are winning the war'—a comment that, as I came to understand, illustrated the Secretary's habitual practice of considering problems in quantitative terms. He was a superb Secretary of Defense—brilliantly skilled in planning, budgeting, devising, and administering efficient procurement policies and controlling all aspects of a great, sprawling part-military, part-civilian Department. But the very quantitative discipline that served him so splendidly as Secretary of Defense tended to interfere with his being a thoroughly successful Secretary of War. . . . What the McNamara approach lacked, of course, was any method of quantifying the quintessential advantage of the North Vietnamese and Viet Cong—the incomparable benefit of superior *élan,* of an intense spirit compounded by the elemental revolutionary drives of nationalism and anti-colonialism. Since anything that could not be quantified tended to be left out of the McNamara equation, the answer never came out right."

We conclude where we started—with questions about the personality of the real principal, Lyndon Johnson. What force did this powerful personality cast over the decision process? Was this the terrifying Caligula whom no one dared challenge? Or was the July 28 decision locked in by events, politics, and human beings unwilling, like most of us, to reject the basis for our political cognitions? Or in a perverse sort of way, was perhaps making a bad military decision in 1965 the best of all available political decisions for a president who still dreamed of increasing his legislative scorecard?

The documents show that the president and his advisors were remarkably consistent in their belief that they had correctly defined the problem and the stakes in Vietnam. Lyndon Johnson was indeed exposed to dissenting views—Ball and Clifford in particular. Ball never held back and neither he nor Clifford was "beaten" into submission—just outnumbered. . . . Ball was also outranked by the major principals. It made a great deal of difference that the paper trail on the president's desk included recommendations for escalation from the secretary of defense, the chairman of the Joint Chiefs of Staff, General Westmoreland, and, most important, Ball's boss, the secretary of state.

In the final analysis the president and not his advisors must accept most of the blame. Johnson was the cause of his ultimate undoing. The president was involved in a delicate exercise of political juggling. . . . Above all else, Johnson wanted to buy time and McNamara's plan allowed the president to hold on in Vietnam and to continue to build a Great Society at home. Johnson believed that to accept Ball's advice would be political suicide and result in political paralysis for the next three years. The domestic repercussion if the United States abandoned its commitment would be too great for a four-year president ever to recoup. Congress, Johnson believed, would turn on the president and the right-wing backlash would be devastating. Television screens would relay the "Communist carnage" into living rooms across the country. The rights of people to live in freedom would be trampled on. Hanoi's propaganda would focus on the United States as a paper tiger; China and the Soviet Union would laugh in the face of U.S. integrity, and there was always the spectre of China's "picking up the pieces at the fringe." Allies would never again trust the seal of the treaty with the United States. Johnson believed that Ball was wrong. There was no way to lose with honor. On the other hand, the Joint Chiefs' option raised the possibility of nuclear confrontation. Besides, how could the most powerful military apparatus in the world not achieve the relatively simple goal of denying Hanoi a victory? The United States sought no military victory of its own, no territory, nothing except the goal of convincing Hanoi it could not unify Vietnam by force. In 1965 Lyndon Johnson believed that with one or two lucky breaks this relatively simple goal could be achieved.

Thus did Lyndon Johnson commit slow political suicide. Once he decided to fight the war, his greatest tactical error as a *political* leader came when he rejected the advice of civilian and military advisors on the question of mobilizing the nation's resources. In deciding *not* to mobilize the Reserves, *not* to seek a congressional resolution or declaration of national emergency, *not* to present the program in a prime-time address to Congress or the nation (rather than an afternoon press conference), and *not* to disclose publicly the full extent of the anticipated military call-up, the president's credibility soon came unraveled. This was not the infamous "Caligula," but rather the soft-selling *Homo politicus*—who believed that losing Vietnam in the summer of 1965 would wreck his plans for a truly Great Society. In doing so he apparently gave very little attention to where he would be six months or one year down the road. But for the moment he pulled it off. On July 28 the country gave a sigh of relief. Lyndon Johnson was acting with restraint. The Reserves were not going to war, the nation was not mobilizing—the soft sell brought Johnson time and support.

Time and support for what? Vietnam was *not* the only important item on the president's agenda the week of July 21. As Johnson explained in [his memoir] *The Vantage Point,* Medicare and the Civil Rights Bill were at crucial stages in conference committee. But even more important, the curtain was closing on a historic era: "In all, thirty six major pieces of legislation had been signed into law, twenty six others were moving through the House and Senate, and eleven more awaiting scheduling." A divisive debate would, in the president's opinion, have ruined his vision of a great America. . . .

In the end Lyndon Johnson was not misled by advisors. He had no reason, no incentive to lead a searching reevaluation of U.S. policy. . . . No one was planning the politics of getting out by December if the July decision was ineffective. It could and should have been done—it was certainly less a threat than Johnson believed. He sought only to hide in the middle of two extremes. He had weighed all the costs and then used his great talents to forge a marginal consensus—enough to get the United States into war, but insufficient for war termination. Moreover,

Johnson did not act indecisively. He chose between short- and long-run risks, and his fatal mistake occurred in that choice. In holding back from total commitment Johnson was juggling the Great Society, the war in Vietnam, and his hopes for the future. He *chose* to avoid a national debate on the war, to keep the Reserves home, and to buy time for a domestic record meriting nothing less than Mount Rushmore (he would later settle for the Johnson Library). . . .

By 1968 the president would run *from* office—his dream of a Great Society ruined by the war. In the end Johnson would fail to make the transition described to him by Vice-President [Hubert] Humphrey: *"President Johnson is personally identified with, and greatly admired for, political ingenuity. He will be expected to put all his great political sense to work now for international political solutions. People will be counting on him to use on the world scene his unrivaled talents as a politician. They will be watching to see how he makes this transition from the domestic to the world stage."*

The personal tragedy was obvious to former President Eisenhower, who on March 31, 1968, following Johnson's announcement that he would not seek reelection, recorded in his diary: "to me it seems obvious that the President is at war with himself and while trying vigorously to defend the actions and decisions he has made in the past, and urging the nation to pursue those purposes regardless of costs, he wants to be excused from the burden of office to which he was elected." Therein rested the legacy of July 1965—a personal and national tragedy.

America's Quest for a Capitalist World Order

GABRIEL KOLKO

The Vietnam War was the United States' longest and most divisive war of the post-1945 epoch, and in many regards its most important conflict in the twentieth century. Obviously, the Vietnamese Communist Party's resiliency made Vietnam distinctive after 1946, but that the United States should have become embroiled with such formidable adversaries was a natural outcome of the logic and objectives of its role in the modern era. . . .

The hallmark of American foreign policy after 1945 was the universality of its intense commitment to create an integrated, essentially capitalist world framework out of the chaos of World War Two and the remnants of the colonial systems. The United States was the major inheritor of the mantle of imperialism in modern history, acting not out of a desire to defend the nation against some tangible threat to its physical welfare but because it sought to create a controllable, responsive order elsewhere, one that would permit the political destinies of distant places to evolve in a manner beneficial to American goals and interests far surpassing the immediate needs of its domestic society. The regulation of the world was at once the luxury and the necessity it believed its power afforded, and even if its might both produced and promised far greater prosperity if successful, its inevitable costs

From Gabriel Kolko, *Anatomy of a War: Vietnam, the United States, and the Modern Historical Experience,* Pantheon, 1985, pp. 72–77, 79, 113, 123–125, 149, 166–168, 283–284, 286, 547–548. Reprinted by permission of Gabriel Kolko.

were justified, as all earlier imperialist powers had also done, as a fulfillment of an international responsibility and mission.

This task in fact far transcended that of dealing with the USSR, which had not produced the world upheaval but was itself an outcome of the first stage of the protracted crisis of the European and colonial system that had begun in 1914, even though the United States always held Moscow culpable to a critical extent for the many obstacles it was to confront. The history of the postwar era is essentially one of the monumental American attempts—and failures—to weave together such a global order and of the essentially vast autonomous social forces and destabilizing dynamics emerging throughout the world to confound its ambitions.

Such ambitions immediately brought the United States face to face with what to this day remains its primary problem: the conflict between its inordinate desires and its finite resources, and the definition of realistic priorities. Although it took years for the limits on American power to become clear to its leaders, most of whom only partly perceived it, it has been this problem of coherent priorities, and of the means to implement them, rather than the ultimate abstract goals themselves that have divided America's leaders and set the context for debates over policy. What was most important for much of the post-1945 era was the overweening belief on the part of American leaders that regulating all the world's political and economic problems was not only desirable but also possible, given skill and power. They would not and could not concede that the economic, political, and social dynamics of a great part of the world exceeded the capacities of any one or even a group of nations to control. At stake were the large and growing strategic and economic interests in those unstable nations experiencing the greatest changes. . . .

By the late 1940s the United States had begun to confront the basic dilemmas it was to encounter for the remainder of the century. The formulation of priorities was an integral part of its reasoning, and so was resistance to communism in whatever form it might appear anywhere in the world. Its own interests had been fully articulated, and these found expression in statements of objectives as well as in the creation of international political, military, and economic organizations and alliances the United States effectively dominated, with American-led "internationalism" becoming one of the hallmarks of its postwar efforts. . . .

The domino theory was to be evoked initially more than any other justification in the Southeast Asian context, and the concept embodied both strategic and economic components which American leaders never separated. "The fall of Indochina would undoubtedly lead to the fall of the other mainland states of Southeast Asia," the Joint Chiefs of Staff argued in April 1950, and with it Russia would control "Asia's war potential. . . . affecting the balance of power." Not only "major sources of certain strategic materials" would be lost, but also communications routes. The State Department maintained a similar line at this time, writing off Thailand and Burma should Indochina fall. Well before the Korean conflict this became the United States' official doctrine, and the war there strengthened this commitment.

The loss of Indochina, Washington formally articulated in June 1952, "would have critical psychological, political and economic consequences. . . . the loss of any single country would probably lead to relatively swift submission to or an alignment with communism by the remaining countries of this group. Furthermore, an alignment with communism of the rest of Southeast Asia and India, and in the longer term, of the Middle East (with the probable exceptions of at least Pakistan and Turkey) would in all probability progressively follow. Such widespread alignment would endanger the stability and security of Europe." It would "render the U.S. position in the Pacific offshore island chain precarious and would seriously jeopardize fundamental U.S. security interests in the Far East." The "principal world source of natural rubber and tin, and a producer of petroleum and other strategically important commodities" would be lost in Malaya and Indonesia. The rice exports of Burma and Thailand would be taken from Malaya, Ceylon, Japan, and India. Eventually, there would be "such economic and political pressures in Japan as to make it extremely difficult to prevent Japan's eventual accommodation to communism." This was the perfect integration of all the elements of the domino theory, involving raw materials, military bases, and the commitment of the United States to protect its many spheres of influence. In principle, even while helping the French to fight for the larger cause which America saw as its own, Washington's leaders prepared for greater intervention when it became necessary to prop up the leading domino—Indochina.

There were neither private nor public illusions regarding the stakes and goals for American power. Early in 1953 the National Security Council reiterated, "The Western countries and Japan need increased supplies of raw materials and foodstuffs and growing markets for their industrial production. Their balance of payments difficulties are in considerable part the result of the failure of production of raw materials and foodstuffs in non-dollar areas to increase as rapidly as industrial production." "Why is the United States spending hundreds of millions of dollars supporting the forces of the French Union in the fight against communism?" Vice-President Richard Nixon explained publicly in December 1953. "If Indo-china falls, Thailand is put in an almost impossible position. The same is true of Malaya with its rubber and tin. The same is true of Indonesia. If this whole part of Southeast Asia goes under Communist domination or Communist influence, Japan, who trades and must trade with this area in order to exist, must inevitably be oriented towards the Communist regime." Both naturally and logically, references to tin, rubber, rice, copra, iron ore, tungsten, and oil were integral to American policy considerations from the inception. As long as he was President, Eisenhower never forgot his country's dependence on the importation of raw materials and the need to control their sources. When he first made public the "falling domino" analogy, in April 1954, he also discussed the dangers of losing the region's tin, tungsten, and rubber and the risk of Japan's being forced into dependence on communist nations for its industrial life—with all that implied. Always implicit in the doctrine was the assumption that the economic riches of the neighbors of the first domino, whether Greece or Indochina, were essential, and when the United States first intervened in those hapless and relatively poor nations, it kept the surrounding region foremost in its calculations. This willingness to accept the immense overhead charges of regional domination was constantly in the minds of the men who made the decisions to intervene.

The problem with the domino theory was, of course, its intrinsic conflict with the desire to impose priorities on U.S. commitments, resources, and actions. If a chain is no stronger than its weakest link, then that link has to be protected even though its very fragility might make the undertaking that much more difficult. But so long as the United States had no realistic sense of the constraints on its power, it was ready to take greater risks. . . .

It was in this larger context of a search for a decisive global strategy and doctrine throughout the 1950s that the emerging Vietnam issue was linked to so many other international questions. Washington always saw the challenge of Indochina as just one part of a much greater problem it confronted throughout the world: the efficacy of limited war, the danger of dominoes, the credibility of American power, the role of France in Europe, and much else. Vietnam became the conjunction of the postwar crisis of U.S. imperialism at a crucial stage of America's much greater effort to resolve its own doubts about its capacity to protect the larger international socioeconomic environment in which its interests could survive and prosper. By 1960 every preceding event required that the credibility of U.S. power be tested soon, lest all of the failures and dilemmas since 1946 undermine the very foundations of the system it was seeking to construct throughout the world. It was mainly chance that designated Vietnam as the primary arena of trial, but it was virtually preordained that America would try somewhere to attain successes—not simply one but many—to reverse the deepening pattern of postwar history. . . .

This perception of Vietnam from 1961 onward gave it a symbolic global significance that far outweighed the specific U.S. interests there, but behind this notion there nonetheless existed more tangible goals, which varied somewhat in importance but always remained a part of a justification of the effort. Raw materials, though less publicly cited than earlier, were still prominent in the decision makers' vision. This included the preservation of existing markets. The retention of South Vietnam was invariably linked to U.S. relations with other nations in the region, particularly with Indonesia, where Washington considered [President] Sukarno the most important threat to its interests.

Credibility rose in importance with the successive failures of each escalation of advisers and resources in Vietnam, reaching 11,000 by the end of 1962 and 23,000 two years later. The domino and the global contexts were incorporated into all justifications of the war. The concepts finally merged late in 1964, when General Maxwell Taylor, a leading limited-war theorist and the ambassador to Saigon, argued typically, "If we leave Vietnam with our tail between our legs, the consequences of this defeat in the rest of Asia, Africa, and Latin America would be disastrous.". . .

The desire in Washington for important new escalations culminated in the National Security Council's March [1964] commitment to make Vietnam a test case of U.S. credibility. In March, too, William Bundy, assistant secretary of state and McGeorge's brother, argued that serious punitive measures against the DRV [Democratic Republic of Vietnam (North)] for the NLF's [National Liberation Front's] action in the south would require congressional approval, and a resolution was drawn up modeled after the Offshore Islands Resolution of January 1955, sanctioning the defense of Formosa. Comparable Cuban and Middle Eastern resolutions also existed for "continuing crises."

The President's advisers debated the exact pressures that would cause the DRV to cease its support of the NLF, fully conscious that they might not work. As William Bundy conceded, "the Viet Cong *do* have a lot of appeal in South Vietnam and *do* rely heavily on captured US weapons," though he nonetheless considered the DRV's role crucial. In any case, McNamara and others could argue, action against the DRV would be good for the otherwise sagging morale and fortunes of the fast-sinking . . . [South Vietnamese] regime. At a conference in Honolulu during the first days of June, the key advisers approved a variety of contingency plans for air strikes against the DRV, including preparation to continue them on a sustained basis, and various options for an increased buildup of U.S. troops and equipment for the beginning of what was clearly going to be a larger, longer war. . . .

It was throughout this June–July period that the United States resumed its OPLAN 34A [Top Secret Operation Plan 34A] operations in the coastal DRV areas, utilizing, as the Pentagon Papers later described it, "South Vietnamese or hired personnel and supported by U.S. training and logistical efforts." OPLAN 34A was in fact always an American project and was active in the DRV coastal region around the nineteenth parallel when the USS *Maddox* on July 31 was sent on a DESOTO patrol, with a special electronic-intelligence crew aboard, planning to electronically simulate an air attack and gather information not closer than four miles off the DRV coast. There is no question it was ordered to draw DRV boats away from 34A operations. It was this combination which caused the forewarned DRV authorities correctly to conclude that the OPLAN 34A and DESOTO boats were collaborating and to attack the *Maddox,* leading to the so-called Tonkin Gulf incident on August 2. George Ball later accurately described the DESOTO missions as serving "primarily for provocation." The U.S. air attack on the patrol boat sites and oil storage facilities was the beginning of the air war against the north, and the passage of the long-prepared Tonkin Gulf Resolution on August 7, with virtually no dissent, authorized the President "to take all necessary steps, including the use of armed force," to aid any Southeast Asian state. . . .

The events leading to the Tonkin Gulf affair had left the United States with no doubt that its alternative to defeat was a much heavier use of military power, and the Tonkin Gulf Resolution had cleared the way for a sustained escalation of the war. . . .

Once the decision to bomb the DRV had been made, the whole paralytic, dangerous logic of credibility extended to it as well. Once initiated, the escalatory process cannot be terminated until it delivers success, lest it, too, appear an implausible and ineffective instrument—thereby depriving military power of its ultimate menace and role as a deterrent. The Tonkin Resolution was in fact the critical threshold regarding the use of U.S. military resources. . . .

While several senior advisers, like Maxwell Taylor, expressed skepticism about phases of this air-ground program, all save George Ball thought persistence essential to the maintaining of credibility. All who counted, their differences notwithstanding, favored some degree of escalation. It is important to stress that there was a continuity in the many steps after summer 1964, some of them quite obscure, leading to the maximum U.S. war effort. No one decision or discussion was a critical turning point, just as the events of 1964 have their antecedents in more fundamental strategic and political commitments. On March 1, 1965, for example, McNamara discussed aid to the RVN [Republic of Vietnam (South)]— whether it should be in the form of goods or of U.S. forces—and informed his service secretaries, "I want it clearly understood that there is an unlimited appropriation available for the financing of aid to Vietnam," a "blank check," as the

Army's chief financial manager later described it, "which military leaders normally expected to receive when preparing for a war." In early April and again in mid-June, troop authorizations increased, and between the end of March and the end of June the actual number of American military personnel in Vietnam doubled to 60,000, with over 10,000 more authorized to go.

By April 1965 both McNamara and the JCS were committed to major escalations of both ground and air war. [Assistant national security affairs adviser] W. W. Rostow at the end of May argued that total victory was now possible—indeed, that it was nearer than anyone could imagine. McNamara thought 200,000 or so men would be the maximum needed to reverse the tide of the war before reducing U.S. forces. By June, Taylor's earlier reticence melted before the desire of the JCS and McNamara to assign 175,000 men to the war immediately, a commitment later climbing to forty-four American battalions. It could keep the NLF from winning, they claimed, and shift the balance of power by the end of the year. McNamara and Westmoreland argued that with yet more troops in 1966 and 1967 the United States could take the initiative—the higher the number of troops, the sooner success. The President prudently decided to pause at thirty-four battalions and 175,000 men for the time being, shrewdly refusing the Pentagon's request to take the politically unpopular step of calling up the Reserves. Nonetheless, convinced that the NLF was winning, the President became increasingly eager to send a massive U.S. force to turn the tide of the war, allowing him to return to his domestic program without being accused of having caused the nation's failure overseas and of having undermined its credibility. By the end of the year, there were 184,000 American military personnel in South Vietnam, and the logic of the vast escalation of American involvement in the war between the summer of 1964 and one year later had yet to reach its climax.

To comprehend the freedom and constraints on Washington's policy choices, one must also compare the events and decisions of the 1964–67 period with those after 1968. Until 1968 the war consisted for America of responding to a series of challenges, above all to the imminent victory of the NLF, and the administration had few institutional or ideological inhibitions on it. After Tet 1968 the very economic and political health of the United States was involved, starkly revealing the ultimate institutional parameters of the system as it approached its economic and social limits. During the three years of escalation, the weaknesses of American foreign policy emerged, proving that however unifying the broad consensus among decision makers on goals and general methods, specific realities eventually could—with growing failure—produce important differences on concrete tactics and unavoidable choices of priorities which acknowledged the limits of power. In this confrontation with a materially far weaker Revolutionary movement, directed by men with a relatively high degree of unity and analytic realism to guide their actions, the importance of the leadership equation on both adversaries in the war began to mount. The degree of combined cohesion and clarity on each side of the war was a possibly decisive factor, if only because the structural limit of the American system was also translated eventually into a prolonged crisis of leadership in which a materially great but increasingly confused and disunited United States found itself outmaneuvered by the physically much poorer Communists.

Precisely because conventional wisdom on the war has stressed the importance of differences among decision makers, it is worth focusing on the nature of leadership in foreign policy, the consensual values shaping it, and the context in which to place normal differences within American foreign policy circles. Whatever the convoluted way command decisions were made after 1946, or the personal chemistry of each set of men of power, in the end the consistency of responses far outweighed any rare deviations from it, and Vietnam was no exception. . . .

President Johnson's often bizarre personal conduct is not unimportant, but the case that his boorish manners were crucial to policy has yet to be made. A shrewd politician who could see the weaknesses of his sycophantic advisers very clearly, a consummate, instinctive fixer, he self-confidently played off people and problems to attain his elusive goals. His commitment to his domestic program was no more his obsession than it had been for other Presidents; the tension between foreign and domestic priorities has repeatedly broken up reform efforts. Whatever the technical differences among key presidential advisers, as a group during 1965–66 they minimized the extent to which earlier dilemmas of the limits of American power and weapons were reappearing. When they acknowledged them, it was only to reinforce the need to redeem prior failures in a new context, with new resources. Few attempted to predict the losses that might arise from the intervention in Vietnam, and they responded to such economic and political costs quite differently until 1968, when external forces and raw facts constrained their choices immeasurably. In this relatively narrow interregnum of 1965–67, the foreign policy consensus did not eliminate real tactical differences. But far more important than the essentially minor eddy of colorful anecdotes and rumor of the sort that makes good journalistic copy, let alone the personal frustrations of those like McNamara who were to lose confidence in themselves or be outmaneuvered by rivals, was the central reality of another massive failure of an essentially consensual system. The drama of this failure, ultimately, was institutional rather than individual, infringing on the very rationality of American imperialism, its postwar foreign policy, its perceptions of the world, itself, and the disparity between its desires and interests on the one hand and the limits of its power on the other. . . .

Imperialism in modern world history has never been an exclusively economic phenomenon, and that reality has been the main source of its demise. Although the economic rationale was crucial at its inception, the justification for imperialism transcended strictly materialist factors to take on geopolitical, cultural, and military dimensions and to form a character and motive too complex and convoluted for simplification. The importance of each element varied among key decision makers. Militarily and politically, Vietnam and, above all, Southeast Asia formed a crucial test for the United States as an imperialist power seeking militarily to impose its geopolitical as well as economic hegemony over major political, economic, and social developments throughout the Third World. By 1965, however, the economic basis for American imperialism in Southeast Asia had created its own fatal contradictions, and these proved to be crucial in inflicting defeat even when, militarily, the United States still appeared capable of success.

Economic factors of imperialism cannot be divorced from the political context in which they operate, and immediate economic consequences may quickly subvert the long-range economic rationality of an action. Economic costs of war always interact with other contemporaneous problems and may undermine a coherent ultimate objective, such as U.S. integration of Third World economies into the world capitalist system. . . .

The massive 1965 intervention in Vietnam began well into the longest sustained period of expansion in the postwar American economy. Starting in 1961, long before outlays for Southeast Asia further stimulated it, it lasted until 1969. The growth of the military budget in this context could only increase inflation. Rather than creating prosperity, it jeopardized it. Internationally, the United States was highly vulnerable. It attempted to play the role of stabilizer of the world economic structure, which was geared to the strength of the dollar, while it simultaneously exported investment funds and goods on the one hand and made costly political and military commitments which undermined its economic role in the world on the other. . . .

The United States' failure to recognize the limits of its economic power and its relation to its military and diplomatic policy was surely not unique in the mid-1960s and remains today a fundamental issue troubling American imperialism. Recognition of one's weaknesses is more difficult for a nation than for an individual, since states have conflicting interests and ample means of procrastinating. In 1965 the United States chose to do so, falling into an economic imbroglio through both naiveté and ignorance, becoming entangled in self-deception and cynical political maneuvering, and eventually reaching a predictable economic impasse, one which only a quick victory could keep from evolving into a prolonged military and political struggle whose economic costs would greatly accelerate America's defeat.

However Washington administered its war effort, its military strategy in limited war by the mid-1960s was certain to be expensive. Nearly half the war's cost arose from its reliance on air activities, not to mention the immense cost of high firepower. Still, the United States took the most expensive way out when McNamara gave a virtual blank check to the generals in March 1965. . . .

The Vietnam War was for the United States the culmination of its frustrating postwar effort to merge its arms and politics to halt and reverse the emergence of states and social systems opposed to the international order Washington sought to establish. It was not the first serious trial of either its military power or its political strategy, only the most disastrous. Despite America's many real successes in imposing its hegemony elsewhere, Vietnam exposed the ultimate constraints on its power in the modern era: its internal tensions, the contradictions between overinvolvement in one nation and its interests and ambitions elsewhere, and its material limits. Precisely because of the unmistakable nature of the defeat after so long and divisive an effort and because of the war's impact on the United States' political structure and aspirations, this conflict takes on a significance greater than that of either of the two world wars. Both of them had only encouraged Washington's ambition to guide and integrate the world's political and economic system—a goal which was surely the most important cause of its intervention in the Vietnam conflict after 1950.

While the strategic implications of the war for the future of American military power in local conflicts was the most obvious dimension of its defeat, it had confronted these issues often since 1946. What was truly distinctive was the collapse of a national consensus on the broad contours of America's role in the world. The trauma was intense; the war ended without glory and with profound remorse for tens of millions of Americans. Successive administrations fought the war so energetically because of these earlier frustrations, of which they were especially conscious in the early 1960s, scarcely suspecting that rather than resolving them, they would only leave the nation with a far larger set of military, political, and economic dilemmas to face for the remainder of this century. But by 1975 the United States was weaker than it had been at the inception of the war in the early 1960s, a lesson hardly any advocate of new interventions could afford to ignore.

The limits of arms and armies in Vietnam were clear by Tet 1968. Although the United States possessed nominally good weapons and tactics, it lacked a military strategy capable of overcoming its enemy's abilities and appropriate to its economic resources, its global priorities, and its political constraints in Vietnam, at home, and in the rest of the world. Although its aims in South Vietnam were never to alter, it was always incapable of coping with the countless political complexities that irrevocably emerge from protracted armed conflict. America's political, military, and ideological leaders remained either oblivious or contemptuous of these until the war was essentially lost. Even today they scarcely dare confront the war's meaning as Washington continues to assert aggressively its classic postwar objectives and interests in Latin America and elsewhere. America's failure was material, of course, but it was also analytic, the result of a myopia whose importance greatly transcended bureaucratic politics or the idiosyncrasies of Presidents and their satraps. The dominating conventional wisdom of American power after 1946 had no effective means of inhibiting a system whose ambitions and needs increasingly transcended its resources for achieving them. They remained unable and unwilling to acknowledge that these objectives were intrinsically unobtainable and irrelevant to the socioeconomic forms much of the Third World is adopting to resolve its economic and human problems, and that the United States' effort to alter this pervasive reality was certain to produce conflict.

An Unwinnable War

ERIC M. BERGERUD

A large number of interesting books and articles have appeared since 1975 concerning the American conduct of the Vietnam War. Some of the authors are former participants in the struggle; others are historians, political scientists, and journalists. Many of the authors argue that a different strategy or method of operation in Vietnam might have led to success. People holding this view do not necessarily believe that success would have been worth the cost, but many do. In general, those believing that the United States lost a war that it could have won fall into three groups.

A first group consists of former policymakers or their apologists, including Richard Nixon, Henry Kissinger, and General Westmoreland. They argue that, even though leaders (never themselves of course) made some strategic mistakes and accepted unwise political constraints, the American effort had been largely successful by 1973. The [National Liberation] Front was crushed, and the NVA [North Vietnamese Army] was contained. The real failure, these men maintain, took place when Congress, stampeded by a shallow and uninformed press and a

From Eric M. Bergerud, *The Dynamics of Defeat: The Vietnam War in Hau Nghia Province,* pp. 323–335, 1991, by permission of Westview Press, Boulder, Colorado.

woefully misguided antiwar movement, abandoned a sovereign ally well on the way to victory. The betrayal resulted from an evil brew of domestic politics, war weariness, and the Watergate scandal. It is further argued that, had Nixon remained in power and had Congress not been so perfidious, a stronger South Vietnam, potentially aided by American air power, would have either deterred attack in 1975 or defeated one if it came. The fact that the NVA fought the final battle singlehandedly is offered as evidence that the United States had been victorious against the Front. These individuals prove their contention that the South could have prevailed by focusing on NVA defeats during the Easter Offensive of 1972.

A second group exemplifies a near-consensus in the American military today. Most notably represented by [Colonel] Harry Summers, these people maintain that once the decision to use force is made (a political decision to be sure) it should be applied quickly and decisively. Pure firepower, sophisticated weaponry, and tactical refinement must never substitute for strategy. Force should never be employed unless the political will exists to support it. Vietnam is cited as a perfect example of how not to fight a war. According to this argument, the political constraints placed on the joint chiefs by President Johnson and other civilians forced General Westmoreland into a "no-win" strategy of attrition. Johnson's decision to raise the level of violence in small increments was a naive, academic, and politically cowardly response. It also allowed the enemy to dictate the tempo of the war. Many officers holding this view are quick to grant that it may have been a mistake to get involved in Vietnam in the first place. However, they contend that, once the decision to intervene was made, a rational conduct of the war would have included a mobilization of the reserves, a declaration of war, unrestricted bombing of the North, a naval blockade of North Vietnam, and a ground campaign aggressive enough to cut the Ho Chi Minh Trail and eject PAVN [People's Army of Vietnam, or the North Vietnamese Army] from South Vietnam. An ideal campaign would have involved ground operations in Cambodia, Laos and across the DMZ [Demilitarized Zone] into North Vietnam. These measures, so this argument goes, should have been implemented as quickly as possible, and this relentless pressure should have stopped only when Hanoi agreed to a genuine, rather than a cosmetic, peace agreement.

A third argument is more popular with many academics and former participants in the village war. . . . This group contends that U.S. policymakers did not understand the "political" nature of the Vietnam War and thus allowed General Westmoreland to follow a futile strategy of attrition. Consequently, Americans neglected the key political and social issues, such as rural poverty, corruption, and administrative inefficiency, that fueled the insurgency. To compound the difficulty, these men maintain, MACV [U.S. Military Assistance Command, Vietnam] created a top-heavy, overly complicated, and unwieldy ARVN [Army of the Republic of Vietnam] in the mirror image of the U.S. Army. Both American forces and their ARVN progeny misused military force by an unnecessary reliance on firepower, which brought politically counterproductive violence in civilian areas. Forces were also poorly deployed to fight the critical "other war." The insurgency was in the hamlets, not in the hinterlands, it is argued; therefore, the bulk of American forces should have been deployed to reflect this reality. Instead of wasting resources on the "big battalion" war, MACV should have concentrated on rebuilding GVN forces and gaining security for the rural population. Furthermore, these men echo the stand of [Colonel] John [Paul] Vann, arguing that the United States could have forced the GVN to "harness the revolution" through sweeping reform. According to this argument, a more sophisticated political strategy could have been created that would have appealed to non-Communist elements within the Front and led to the isolation of the Party.

Advocates of the third group share some common assumptions concerning the insurgency. First of all, they assume that control of the countryside by either player was thin: Most Vietnamese peasants, even in Front areas, were, in truth, neutral. Second, they argue that the problems facing the GVN stemmed from a governmental apparatus that was not responsive to the desires of the rural population—a major problem, no doubt, but one that Americans could have remedied by increasing aid and, more importantly, demanding reform. However, the [Communist] Party's defects, the argument proceeds, were structural and beyond change. Party control was based on cynical propaganda, coercion, and terror. These analysts assume that communism per se was a bad thing for Vietnam, Asia, and the United States. The allies could have countered propaganda with reform, good deeds, and good example, and the Americans and the GVN could have broken the cycle of terror and coercion through proper force deployments and by giving the peasantry the military means to help protect themselves. In other words, if U.S. assistance had provided a credible promise of security and a better life, the people would have turned on their real enemy. The remaining "hard-core" remnant of dedicated Party members then could have been hunted down. Lastly, implicit in this argument is the contention that a more appropriate policy in the countryside, including a redeployment of ground forces to heavily populated areas and a general increase of resources allocated to the pacification campaign, would have led to a less violent war, allowing American participation to continue long enough to obtain victory over the Front. A revitalized GVN, supported by its own people, would then have been strong enough, with continued U.S. aid, to prevail over the long haul. Such arguments should sound familiar by now for they were the "party line" at CORDS [Civil Operations and Revolutionary Development Support].

Hau Nghia province was quite a small political entity, more likely to be of interest to an anthropologist than to a military historian. Yet, the sad history of Hau Nghia illustrates very well the enormous problems facing Americans as they attempted to do battle, physically and psychologically, with a powerful and determined enemy. Both sides, even if sometimes mistaken in strategy or tactics, used all their possible energy to prevail in this strategically important place. Furthermore, although the course of the war differed to some degree from province to province, Hau Nghia had certain characteristics that make possible some important generalizations concerning the wider war in Vietnam. It was quite typical of the entire upper Mekong Delta, the heartland of the insurgency, in terms of ethnic makeup, social structure, and economic base. Densely populated, ethnically Vietnamese, and primarily agricultural, it was exactly the type of province within which the Americans and the GVN had to prevail, within a reasonable amount of time, in order to be victorious. Ultimately, of course, despite an extraordinary military and political effort, victory eluded the allies. And regrettably, the factors that led to failure in Hau Nghia province cast serious doubt on each of the three arguments summarized above that suggest an alternative conduct of war would have led to the continued independence of a non-Communist South Vietnam.

One central conclusion, made clear by the war in Hau Nghia province, bears directly on each of the assertions that a change in policy would have led to success: The Party's analysis of the situation in rural Vietnam in 1965 was correct and ours was wrong. Recall for a moment that Party cadres believed that the GVN never had nor ever could obtain legitimacy because of structural factors that could not be changed. The Party viewed the inefficiency and wholesale corruption that characterized the GVN at every level as the inevitable result of social contradictions. An urban, Westernized, and largely Catholic elite, the Party maintained, could never create a just society—or one viewed as just by the peasantry—in a poor, rural Asian country. The Party argued, with considerable justification, that [GVN Premier Ngo Dinh] Diem and his successors had kept intact the French colonial apparatus, with the Americans assuming the role of protector.

It does not require a Marxist analysis to confirm these assumptions, and a goodly number of Americans, such as John Vann, agreed with most of them. Where Vann and others parted company with the Party was on their belief that the GVN, if pressured sufficiently by the Americans, could have reformed and revitalized itself and attracted non-Communist progressives away from the Front. Such prospects did not worry Party cadres, believing as they did that revolution—a fundamental redistribution of wealth and power—was sought by enough of the peasantry to neutralize any reform efforts by the GVN. In addition, if any reform was identified with the Americans, this could only justify the Party's contention that the GVN was a "puppet" of the foreigners and add fuel to the most widely heralded and supported goal of the Front—expulsion of the United States from Vietnam.

So, it did not really matter whether or not the Front had the support of a majority of the peasantry. It is very possible that Vann and others were right when they claimed that most peasants did not care who ruled in Saigon and just wanted to be left alone. The Party had what it needed, the support of the most politically aware and most determined segment of the peasantry. There can be no doubt that, in Hau Nghia and several other provinces, the Front had a virtual lock on the "best and brightest" of the rural youth. The revolutionary movement that had demolished the GVN in Hau Nghia by 1965, although controlled from the outside, was locally recruited and self-sustaining. To be sure, as charged by the Americans, the Front was ruthless in its tactics, unquestionably more so than the GVN. Yet, no revolutionary movement has ever succeeded on terrorism alone. Enough people in Hau Nghia accepted the ideas of the Front to provide the social and political base for a legitimate government. The situation facing the GVN in Hau Nghia at the time of U.S. intervention was just the opposite—the only support it could find came from a few Catholic hamlets and ARVN artillery. This is not to argue that the Front was more virtuous than the GVN; it was, however, much stronger. These were facts of life in Hau Nghia and several other provinces, and they would have faced the Americans regardless of what course of action was adopted.

Three consequences followed from the fact that the Front and not the GVN possessed legitimacy in much of rural Vietnam. In the first place by 1965 (and probably much earlier), the Front had gained moral ascendancy over the GVN. Once again, this is not to argue that, in absolute terms, the Front was morally superior to the GVN. At present, Vietnam is a sad, oppressed, and destitute country. No doubt, many people in rural Vietnam deeply regret the outcome of the war. However, while the war was on, as confirmed by scores of reports and interrogations received by the Americans at Hau Nghia in every phase of the conflict, peasants perceived the followers of the Front as honest, efficient, and genuinely concerned about the people's welfare. They perceived GVN officials, on the other hand, as aloof and corrupt. The dedication and courage of enemy fighting men, compared with the listless performance that characterized most GVN forces, was widely acknowledged and admired by U.S. troops. No matter how hard and terrifying the war was for American or South Vietnamese soldiers, fighters for the Front led an absolutely hellish existence. They lived in holes, regularly faced hunger and disease, were subjected to air strikes, napalm and artillery bombardment, and lacked decent medical care. Whatever the actual validity of the "body count" figures, there can be no doubt that joining the Front was the most dangerous choice by far that could have been made by young people in Vietnam. Yet, enough Front cadres remained totally convinced that they would prevail to keep the general population's perceptions concerning the outcome of the war very much in doubt. Put another way, the GVN, even with massive American support, could never create the essential foundation for strong and resilient morale—the perception that it could win. The collapse in 1975 is very intelligible in this light.

From this situation follows the second consequence of the lack of legitimacy that faced the GVN: A genuine revival of government support or an actual change in allegiance on the part of the rural population could not have taken place while the war was in progress. As we have seen, any progress the GVN achieved in the countryside was due to measures that weakened the Front, chiefly through military attrition. All efforts to change the fundamental attitudes of the people of Hau Nghia toward the GVN failed, if American records are accurate. An undetermined but substantial number of peasants always either supported the Front or were sympathetic toward it. An even larger number of people were in doubt over the eventual outcome of the struggle, an attitude that encouraged neutrality. To be sure, the GVN did have its supporters in Hau Nghia and many more elsewhere. There were good commanders, good soldiers, good officials, and even a few good policemen—but never enough of them. . . . [T]he Hau Nghia Popular Forces, the units most responsible for hamlet security, were next to worthless, a very good indication that a great many people felt little reason to take major risks to protect the state. In this regard, Americans usually missed the point. When they constructed a political equation for Vietnam, it always resembled a hypothetical public opinion poll that asked whether most people in South Vietnam supported the GVN or the Front. The question they should have asked was which side were more people willing to die for. Had they asked the second question, they would not have liked the answer.

Last, if it is correct to assume that no real possibility existed to change the political allegiance of the rural population to one of genuine support of the GVN, it must follow that the only way for the GVN and the Americans to have prevailed was to have crushed the Front militarily. . . . [T]his very nearly occurred. Indeed, had South Vietnam been an island, the GVN undoubtedly would have survived. But South Vietnam, of course, was not an island. Consequently, considering the geography and terrain of Vietnam and the great strength of the Front in much of the country by 1965 (especially in provinces like Hau Nghia), crushing the Front inevitably would have been a very time-consuming process, regardless of the means chosen to do so.

More specific conclusions drawn from Hau Nghia also bear on the matter of alternative strategies. In the first place, Nixon and Westmoreland are wrong to maintain that Congress sabotaged a basically successful war effort after 1973. On the contrary, if the situation in Hau Nghia province at the time of the cease-fire is any guide, the GVN was in a nearly hopeless situation. Although the insurgency in Hau Nghia and throughout Vietnam had been seriously weakened by 1973, it was still intact, and . . . the Front had halted its downward spiral. At the time of the 1975 NVA offensive, Americans estimated that about 40,000 guerrillas were active in South Vietnam. Some, but not all, were northerners. . . . The continued existence of the insurgency had serious consequences for the GVN. As long as the Front existed, the spell of fear and possible doom continued to blanket the countryside. Weariness generated by years of unending war threatened to bring exhaustion and psychological collapse at any moment. Equally important, the bulk of the military manpower available to the GVN was tied down by the insurgency until the very end. In January 1975, there were nearly 500,000 men in the RF/PF [Revolutionary Forces/Popular Forces] mostly involved with the pacification campaign. In addition, fifteen ARVN regiments were deployed in the Mekong Delta, far from areas of strategic importance. The drain on the South Vietnamese finances from such a military establishment was severe, and, by 1975, the economy had started to collapse and the political system disintegrate. . . .

It is difficult to believe that, had he still been in power, President Nixon would have chosen to reopen hostilities to counter gradual aggression. Even if he had done so, massive air support of the type employed in 1972 would have taken some time to deliver because many of the air assets were no longer in Asia. In addition, the NVA had studied its defeats during 1972 and had instituted several tactical refinements. So, whereas the threat of U.S. air power might have deterred a massive attack in 1975, the North could have responded by finding the threshold at which the Americans would intervene and then exerting pressure just below it. Above all, most ARVN units could match PAVN only through greatly superior firepower. Fighting in Hau Nghia showed that, at every level and despite numerous tactical blunders, PAVN and Front military forces were superior to their GVN counterparts in morale and determination. They were, after all, ultimately able to defeat a sizable army without any friendly air support whatsoever, an impressive military achievement. Unfortunately for the GVN, by 1975, the NVA for the first time had reached at least parity in most fields of land weaponry. There is nothing the United States could have done to prevent the DRV from strengthening its armed forces. Furthermore, it is difficult to believe that a few extra billions of dollars in military aid for the GVN would have made a fundamental difference. Consequently, particularly considering the total and wretched nature of the rout during 1975, more U.S. aid and even the reintroduction of American air power could have, at most, delayed the collapse.

The U.S. military's claim that a rapid and decisive use of force would have led to victory is more plausible, but it, too, has difficulties. As the experience in Hau Nghia province made very clear, the Front was highly dependent upon aid from the DRV once it decided to emphasize main force operations after 1964. Supplies from the DRV, particularly in the field of heavier armament, were required if the Front were to finish off ARVN. They were even more necessary if the Front main force units had any hopes of engaging American units in pitched battle. The sanctuaries in Cambodia offered an excellent place to rest and prepare units. They also frustrated, to a large degree, American efforts in 1966–1967 to trap large enemy units. . . . [T]he temporary loss of the sanctuaries, along with the permanent loss of the Sihanoukville supply line, injured the Front in Hau Nghia quite seriously. Furthermore, there is little doubt that the U.S. Army had the capabilities, especially if reinforced, to have cut the Ho Chi Minh Trail, neutralized the sanctuaries, and isolated Front forces from outside aid.

If the DRV would have been sufficiently frightened by more vigorous bombing, such actions might possibly have led the North to end direct aid to the insurgency and withdraw PAVN. It does not necessarily follow, however, that the North could have or would have tried to end hostilities in South Vietnam. The Front was nominally independent. Had necessity demanded, its political apparatus could have operated without guidance or assistance. It is inconceivable that the Front would have laid down its arms without a fight and yielded the huge portion of rural Vietnam, including Hau Nghia province, that it controlled and administered by 1965. Had the Front chosen to fight on alone, it would have faced serious problems. American units could have operated at squad and company levels at a much earlier date than they, in fact, felt safe to do so, and large offensives would not have been possible. This last point, however, might have been a blessing in disguise for the Front. Had the insurgency been forced to stand on the defensive, the manpower and cadres squandered during the two Tet Offensives would have been saved. It is possible, although not at all certain, that a massive show of force by the Americans might have shaken the conviction held by Front followers that victory was inevitable. However, no increase of military effort against the North in 1965–1966 would have altered the weakness of the GVN in the countryside. The U.S. military still would have had to assist GVN forces in an interminable pacification campaign. Above all, it would have been very difficult to counter a decision by the Front to lower the level of the war, conserve strength, and wait out the Americans no matter how long it took.

Had the United States chosen to go all-out militarily, more serious difficulties would have faced Washington if the DRV had chosen to fight. This would have been a very likely decision (unless vetoed by both Peking and Moscow), particularly if American forces had invaded the North above the DMZ, as urged by the joint chiefs. A land campaign in any part of North Vietnam would have presented daunting problems to the United States. North Vietnamese villages, to varying degrees, were all organized for a "people's war." Front-controlled villages and hamlets in Hau Nghia province were painful and frustrating to deal with for American forces, even with indigenous assistance from the South Vietnamese. In the North, Americans would have faced alone the tactical nightmares created by guerrilla warfare.

Americans would have faced a more serious problem in the strategic realm. The only way U.S. forces could have forced the NVA into a set-piece battle would have been to threaten geographic objectives absolutely vital to the DRV. Yet, not even the most ambitious contingency plans advocated an all-out invasion of the DRV. Consequently, PAVN divisions, unless they chose to fight to the end for the

Ho Chi Minh Trail itself, would have been free to withdraw. As fighting in Hau Nghia province showed time and again, enemy units could be bombed, shelled, and bludgeoned but almost never trapped. Therefore, at some point, both sides would have formed a line, creating a situation similar to that in Korea during 1952–1953. Had such a situation developed, American forces would have faced a war of attrition with a much higher level of casualties than actually were endured. As soon as U.S. divisions stood in place, the tactical initiative would have passed to the NVA. The enemy would not have been compelled to either destroy American forces or seize territorial objectives. Rather, they would have concentrated on killing Americans with selective assaults, sapper attacks, and artillery bombardment. . . . [E]xcept for 1969, the marines facing PAVN near the DMZ suffered the highest level of American casualties by a wide margin. . . .

Of course, NVA losses would have been very painful and perhaps might have led to an acceptable settlement. On the other hand, grim tenacity marked every phase of the enemy's war effort. And North Vietnam would not have lacked moral support from the outside world. As it was, except for some very good clients like South Korea, America's closest friends refused to strongly support the war; the Canadian government even provided sanctuary to young men evading the draft. An all-out "aggressive" war against the DRV would have caused the United States to be treated like an international leper. In addition, it is reasonable to conjecture that a massive American military effort, which would have required higher draft calls, the cancellation of student draft deferments, and mobilization of reserves, could not have been made unless accompanied by political efforts within the United States to justify the action as absolutely vital to national security. In the resulting atmosphere, it would have been extremely difficult for American forces to sit behind a human Maginot Line in the Vietnamese and Laotian jungle, regardless of tactical wisdom. On the contrary, great pressure would have existed to push on ever deeper into North Vietnam in an attempt to break the enemy's will as quickly as possible. Had the United States yielded to this pressure, a very explosive situation would have developed, including the very real possibility of Chinese intervention that, in turn, could have led to general war. Consequently, although a much more vigorous military effort as early as possible would have offered some prospects for eventual success, we must conclude that these prospects were not bright and may well have entailed a debacle far greater than the one suffered.

The American experience in Hau Nghia province also illustrates why a different approach toward fighting the "village war" or the "people's war" would probably not have led to a successful conclusion. If anything, the case that the United States needlessly lost the war in the countryside is more difficult to support than the one that advocated increased military activity as the path to victory. Indeed, the "other war" argument is based upon a major historical distortion and fundamentally wrong assumptions on the nature of U.S. forces available and the nature of revolutionary war in Vietnam.

In the first place, it is often claimed that American leaders, particularly in the military, did not understand the need for a vigorous pacification campaign and were interested only in big battles leading to higher "body counts." This was never true in either practice or theory. . . . [T]he pacification campaign was theoretically crucial for the success of Westmoreland's strategy. And the whole rationale for fighting Front main force and NVA units in their base areas was to provide a "shield" behind which the GVN could rebuild its forces, which had been nearly shattered in 1965, and to allow it to reestablish a basic presence in the countryside. . . .

American arms temporarily rescued the GVN in 1965, but our intervention coincided with a massive intervention on the part of the NVA at a rate initially faster than the U.S. buildup. Immediate operations against the guerrillas in the countryside throughout Vietnam either would have required a far greater number of American troops than anyone envisioned (a number that would have taken a long time to build up anyway) or it would have required spreading American resources very thin—a strategy that MACV, given enemy main force strength, considered much too risky. . . .

Furthermore, even Westmoreland, archvillain in the eyes of the "other warriors," authorized a large number of pacification operations by American units from the very beginning of the war. There was probably not a single month during their entire stay in Hau Nghia that some 25th Division units were not engaged directly in support of the pacification campaign. During the rainy seasons of both 1966 and 1967, such operations were the major effort of the entire division, and, after Tet of 1968, the 25th participated in a furious pacification campaign in Hau Nghia province. To a certain degree, this occurred with every American division. Therefore, it is not true that MACV did not realize the importance of pacification or failed to give it considerable support.

Nor was there ever a shortage of counterinsurgency theory within the U.S. military. Although most officers were trained to fight a large-scale conventional war, scores of others, in tandem with many civilian analysts, had long experience in the various Vietnamese pacification programs before American intervention. These men were well briefed on counterinsurgency theories developed by other countries over the years, which, despite a few differences, were essentially the same: It is no coincidence that a history of the pacification campaign in Hau Nghia province must read the way a broken record sounds. This fact was not at all due to conceptual difficulties for the techniques to defeat an insurgency have been demonstrated time and again in this century alone. The concept of operations in an insurgency was and always has been completely secondary to the balance of forces.

Some people have argued that the formation of CORDS was a major advance and should have been done much sooner. No doubt, CORDS did provide a more rational organizational framework and helped somewhat. Yet, at what point a more efficient arrangement would have made any real difference is not clear. Even the most perfect organizational chart would have been irrelevant in the period of 1965–1966: The GVN had precious little territory to pacify. Indeed, CORDS was formed in May 1967, but the pacification campaign in difficult areas, such as Hau Nghia province, did not begin to show signs of significant progress until 1969. Therefore, we must conclude that the pacification campaign's uneven but undeniable progress in weakening the Front did not result from any major change in operations but reflected a change in the balance of forces. . . .

It is also very difficult to see how a greatly different mode of operation on the part of American ground forces could have been implemented in practice, considering the realities of the battlefield in Vietnam. Advocates of the "village war," during hostilities and since, were very critical of the use of U.S. and ARVN fire-power, contending that it was both wasteful and counterproductive politically. No doubt, this argument has some merit. Certainly, harassing fire by American artillery was used excessively and quite wastefully. Nevertheless, the issue of what one Hau Nghia senior advisor called the "too little–too much violence dilemma" was much more complicated. Critics maintained that American forces should have employed more discriminating small-unit tactics during combat in populated areas. Theoretically, perhaps, they were right. However, the fact remains that a casualty-conscious, conscript force like the U.S. Army in Vietnam was bound to use the maximum amount of force within reason. In Vietnam, as in any other war, it was true that "fire kills," and it would have been disastrous for American morale to have asked "grunts in the grass" to use ground assaults when more effective means were available to deal with the enemy. As it was, the unique frustrations of combat in Vietnam helped lead to the greatest psychological crisis ever faced by the U.S. Army, a trauma that took years to recover from. [The political scientist] Guenter Lewy quotes an American officer as having said, "I'll be damned if I permit the United States Army, its institutions, its doctrine, and its traditions to be destroyed just to win this war." Professor Lewy used this quote as an example of the mental attitude that prevented a more rational conduct of the war. In reality, however, this officer's remark is one of the most perceptive to come from the war. The morale, cohesion, combat skill, and integrity of the U.S. armed forces were indeed more important than whatever we were fighting for in Vietnam. The sad fact remains that a theoretically perfect conduct of the village war would have required a U.S. Army in which every officer was like General [Frederick C.] Weyand, every advisor like John Vann, and every trooper like one of sensitive young volunteers helping with MEDCAPs [Medical Civic Action Programs]. That the army was something else should surprise no one.

Many "other warriors" have criticized the United States for not insisting on American command of all forces, as was done in Korea. Although such an arrangement was never wanted by either the GVN or MACV, it probably could have been obtained. Nevertheless, it is difficult to see the decisive benefit of such an arrangement. In Korea, American command meant operational control. For whatever reason, a stronger will to resist was present on the part of the Koreans than the Vietnamese, and the enemy of that earlier war lacked the determination and skill of the Front and the DRV. The few operations where ARVN units were directly under American command, such as Operation FAIRFAX, were not very successful. In such cases, the Vietnamese often left everything to the Americans. In addition, U.S. command would have given even greater force to the "puppet GVN" propaganda line used by the Front. . . .

Above all, those arguing that a more concentrated effort on the hamlet and village level would have brought success are in error because they implicitly assume that South Vietnamese society was as malleable as clay. As shown over and over again during the war in Hau Nghia province, the best that the GVN could do was attempt to crush the Front. With the aid of U.S. forces, it very nearly succeeded. Yet, all American efforts, as best exemplified by the RD [Revolutionary Development] Cadre Program, failed to bring about a fundamental change in political attitudes in the rural population. The most difficult idea to accept for many Americans in Vietnam was that the GVN was inefficient and corrupt because it was inefficient and corrupt. It is no doubt true that many governments around the world are and have been far more corrupt and repressive than the GVN. It is even probable that many people serving the GVN genuinely believed that they had something of value to offer the people they governed. However, because of the accident of geography, the GVN was faced with an insurgency that could lay claim to a great victory over colonialism, that was extremely strong politically, and that was guided by a determined and powerful ally controlling every inch of land bordering the country. In such circumstances, despite intense effort and great dedication (not to mention the blood and treasure expended), any American hope of "harnessing the revolution" and making a weak society strong was doomed. All that remained was force, coercion, and violence, and, however successfully used, it was not enough.

So we come, at last, full circle. The value of the history of the war in a small place like Hau Nghia province lies in pointing out that the military and political situation facing the United States and the government of South Vietnam in the larger arena was intractable, given the realities existing in those nations and in the world. The United States did not fail in Vietnam because of tactical errors that were open to remedy. The errors made were on a much higher level. The American military seriously underestimated the difficulties involved in dealing with enemy forces. And the civilian leadership, particularly under Johnson, underestimated the strength and tenacity of the enemy and overestimated the willingness of its own people and soldiers to continue the struggle indefinitely. In short, American leaders, both civilian and military, committed a strategic blunder that has brought many a general to grief: They chose the wrong battlefield. Tragically, this error brought violent consequences that Americans must contemplate for a very long time, indeed.

✖ *F U R T H E R   R E A D I N G*

David L. Anderson, ed., *Shadow on the White House* (1993)
———, *Trapped by Success: The Eisenhower Administration and Vietnam, 1953–1961* (1991)
Christian Appy, *Working-Class War* (1993)
Loren Baritz, *Backfire* (1985)
Richard J. Barnet, *Intervention and Revolution* (1972)
David M. Barrett, *Uncertain Warriors* (1993)
Lawrence Bassett and Stephen Pelz, "The Failed Search for Victory," in Thomas G. Paterson, ed., *Kennedy's Quest for Victory* (1989), pp. 223–252, 367–374
Larry Berman, *Lyndon Johnson's War* (1989)
William C. Berman, *William Fulbright and the Vietnam War* (1988)
Melanie Billings-Yun, *Decision Against War: Eisenhower and Dien Bien Phu, 1954* (1988)
Peter Braestrup, *Big Story* (1977)
———, ed., *Vietnam as History* (1984)
Bernard Brodie, *War and Politics* (1973)
Joseph Buttinger, *Vietnam: A Political History* (1970)
Robert Buzzanco, "U.S. Military Opposition to Vietnam, 1950–1954," *Diplomatic History,* 17 (1993), 201–222
Larry Cable, *Unholy Grail* (1991)
Michael Charlton and Anthony Moncrieff, eds., *Many Reasons Why* (1978)
Warren I. Cohen, *Dean Rusk* (1980)

Chester Cooper, *The Lost Crusade* (1970)

Charles DeBenedetti with Charles Chatfield, *An American Ordeal: The Antiwar Movement of the Vietnam Era* (1990)

Robert A. Divine, "Vietnam Reconsidered," *Diplomatic History,* 12 (1988), 79–93

Bernard Fall, *The Two Vietnams* (1967)

———, *Vietnam Witness, 1953–1966* (1966)

Frances FitzGerald, *Fire in the Lake* (1972)

Robert L. Gallucci, *Neither Peace nor Honor* (1975)

Lloyd C. Gardner, *Approaching Vietnam* (1988)

Leslie H. Gelb and Richard K. Betts, *The Irony of Vietnam* (1979)

Philip Geyelin, *Lyndon B. Johnson and the World* (1966)

William C. Gibbons, *The U.S. Government and the Vietnam War* (1986–1987)

James William Gibson, *The Perfect War* (1986)

Allen E. Goodman, *The Lost Peace* (1978)

Daniel P. O'C. Greene, "John Foster Dulles and the End of Franco-American Entente in Indochina," *Diplomatic History,* 16 (1992), 551–572

Fred I. Greenstein and Richard H. Immerman, "What Did Eisenhower Tell Kennedy About Indochina? The Politics of Misperception," *Journal of American History,* 79 (1992), 568–587

David Halberstam, *The Best and the Brightest* (1972)

Daniel C. Hallin, *The "Uncensored War"* (1986)

Ellen J. Hammer, *A Death in November: America in Vietnam, 1963* (1988)

James P. Harrison, ed., *The Endless War* (1989)

Patrick L. Hatcher, *The Suicide of an Elite* (1990)

Kenneth Heineman, *Campus Wars* (1993)

John Hellman, *American Myth and the Legacy of Vietnam* (1986)

Herbert Hendin and Ann P. Haas, *Wounds of War: The Psychological Aftermath of Combat in Vietnam* (1985)

George C. Herring, *America's Longest War* (1986)

———, *LBJ and Vietnam* (1994)

———, "The 'Vietnam Syndrome' and American Foreign Policy," *Virginia Quarterly Review,* 57 (1981), 594–612

Gary R. Hess, *The United States' Emergence as a Southeast Asian Power* (1987)

———, *Vietnam and the United States* (1990)

Townsend Hoopes, *The Limits of Intervention* (1969)

Richard H. Immerman, "The United States and the Geneva Conference of 1954: A New Look," *Diplomatic History,* 14 (1990), 43–66

——— and George Herring, "Eisenhower, Dulles, and Dienbienphu: The Day We Didn't Go to War," *Journal of American History,* 71 (1984), 343–363

Susan Jeffords, *The Remasculinization of America: Gender and the Vietnam War* (1989)

George McT. Kahin, *Intervention* (1986)

——— and John W. Lewis, *The United States in Vietnam* (1969)

David E. Kaiser, "Vietnam, Was the System the Solution?" *International Security,* 4 (1980), 199–218

Lawrence S. Kaplan, Denise Artaud, and Mark R. Rubin, eds., *Dienbienphu and the Crisis in Franco-American Relations, 1954–1955* (1990)

Stanley Karnow, *Vietnam* (1983)

Paul M. Kattenburg, *The Vietnam Trauma in American Foreign Policy, 1945–1975* (1980)

Douglas Kinnard, *The Certain Trumpet: Maxwell Taylor and the American Experience in Vietnam* (1991)

———, *The War Managers* (1977)

Andrew F. Krepinevich, Jr., *The Army and Vietnam* (1986)

Anthony Lake, ed., *The Vietnam Legacy* (1976)

David W. Levy, *The Debate over Vietnam* (1991)

Guenter Lewy, *America in Vietnam* (1978)

William L. Lunch and Peter W. Sperlich, "American Public Opinion and the War in Vietnam," *Western Political Quarterly,* 32 (1979), 21–44

Terry Nardin and Jerome Slater, "Vietnam Revised," *World Politics,* 33 (1981), 436–448
Robert E. Osgood, *Limited War Revisited* (1979)
Bruce Palmer, Jr., *The 25-Year War* (1984)
Thomas G. Paterson, "Historical Memory and Elusive Victories: Vietnam and Central America," *Diplomatic History,* 12 (1988), 1–18
Achimedes L. A. Patti, *Why Viet Nam?* (1980)
Douglas Pike, *History of Vietnamese Communism* (1978)
———, *PAVN: People's Army of Vietnam* (1986)
———, *Viet Cong* (1972)
———, *Vietnam and the Soviet Union* (1987)
Norman Podhoretz, *Why We Were in Vietnam* (1982)
Gareth Porter, *A Peace Denied* (1975)
Jeffrey Race, *War Comes to Long An* (1972)
Earl C. Ravenal, *Never Again* (1978)
Andrew J. Rotter, *The Path to Vietnam* (1987)
William J. Rust, *Kennedy in Vietnam* (1985)
Herbert Y. Schandler, *The Unmaking of a President* (1977) (on Johnson)
Thomas J. Schoenbaum, *Waging Peace and War* (1988) (on Rusk)
Robert Shaplen, *Time Out of Hand* (1970)
———, *A Turning Wheel* (1979)
William Shawcross, *Sideshow: Kissinger, Nixon, and the Destruction of Cambodia* (1979)
Neil Sheehan, *A Bright Shining Lie* (1988)
Anthony Short, *The Origins of the Vietnam War* (1989)
Melvin Small, *Johnson, Nixon, and the Doves* (1988)
——— and William D. Hoover, eds., *Give Peace a Chance* (1992)
Ronald H. Spector, *After Tet* (1992)
———, *The United States Army in Vietnam* (1983)
Shelby L. Stanton, *The Rise and Fall of an American Army* (1985)
Harry G. Summers, *On Strategy* (1981)
James C. Thompson, *Rolling Thunder* (1980)
W. Scott Thompson and Donaldson D. Frizzill, eds., *The Lessons of Vietnam* (1977)
James C. Thomson, "How Could Vietnam Happen? An Autopsy," *Atlantic Monthly,* 221 (1968), 47–53
James W. Trullinger, Jr., *Village at War* (1980)
William S. Turley, *The Second Indochina War* (1986)
Kathleen J. Turner, *Lyndon Johnson's Dual War* (1985) (on the press)
Marilyn B. Young, *The Vietnam Wars* (1991)
Nancy Zaroulis and Gerald Sullivan, *Who Spoke Up?* (1984)

Richard M. Nixon,
Henry A. Kissinger,
the Grand Strategy, and Détente

By the late 1960s the United States no longer dominated global affairs as it had during the two decades immediately following World War II. Defeat in Vietnam, the Soviet Union's achievement of parity in nuclear weapons, and the rise of a multipolar world order—characterized by America's relative decline and a diffusion of global economic and political power—spurred the Nixon administration to reconfigure the nation's foreign policy. President Richard M. Nixon and Henry A. Kissinger designed a grand strategy for achieving stability in the international environment. As self-described realists, they sought to make U.S. diplomacy less ideological and more adaptive to balance-of-power diplomacy. As an influential assistant for national security affairs (1969–1973) and secretary of state (1973–1977), Kissinger worked closely with Nixon to pursue détente with both the People's Republic of China and the Soviet Union. Their management of the Strategic Arms Limitation Talks (SALT) produced major agreements. Secret negotiations helped to extricate the United States from Vietnam. And Kissinger's "shuttle diplomacy" temporarily cooled the Arab-Israeli crisis in the Middle East. Admirers and critics alike applauded the Nixon administration's apparent diplomatic achievements in the 1970s.

But the Nixon-Kissinger team compiled a mixed record, as scholars have shown. Interventions and crises in Indochina, Chile, Cyprus, Bangladesh, Angola, and elsewhere sidetracked détente and undermined global stability. The White House's soft selling of human rights and emphasis on power politics raised doubts about the administration's morality and judgment. The Nixon Doctrine, which tried to reduce U.S. obligations abroad by relying on allies to promote stability, often hinged on U.S. ties to unsavory clients such as the Shah of Iran, Mohammad Reza Pahlavi, and the Philippine dictator Ferdinand Marcos. The international economy meanwhile continued to deteriorate, and, despite SALT, the nuclear-arms race accelerated. Nixon and Kissinger claimed too much for détente, and the public felt disappointed every time the Cold War heated up. Congress, resentful of being shut off from policymaking, increasingly contested Nixon's "imperial presidency." Nixon eventually resigned and the administration fell because of the array of corruptions revealed in the Watergate crisis.

Although scholarship on the Nixon-Kissinger diplomacy remains at an early stage, it has already generated spirited debate. One set of questions centers on the grand design and the policy of détente. Did détente represent a significant departure from traditional Cold War diplomacy? Or did it amount to little more than a change in tactics within the framework of anticommunist containment—a "new Cold War," as some have put it? In other words, how much did Soviet-American relations change during the Nixon era? Did SALT reduce the likelihood of nuclear war? Or did the continued military buildup that SALT allowed actually undermine arms control? Why did the Nixon administration continue to view local and regional conflicts in the Third World through a Cold War prism even as it sought accommodations with the Soviet Union and China? Was the administration's ending of the Vietnam War in 1973 a diplomatic triumph? Or could the war have been concluded earlier, saving tens of thousands of American and Asian lives? Did Nixon and Kissinger understand the limits of American power and successfully adjust to the new international setting of the late 1960s and early 1970s? Or did they continue to make commitments abroad that overstretched the nation's financial and military resources and exacerbated U.S. decline?

A second set of questions focuses on diplomatic style, especially Nixon's and Kissinger's practice of cutting Congress and the State Department out of the policymaking process. Did conservative opposition to détente and popular division over the Vietnam War force Nixon and Kissinger to conceal their controversial tactics and objectives? Or did their penchant for secrecy reflect a paranoia or insecurity deep-seated in each man's personality? Are the achievements of the Nixon-Kissinger years, such as SALT and rapprochement with China, so impressive that we should restrain criticism of the abuses of presidential power evident in Indochina, Chile, and elsewhere? Might a more open relationship with Congress and the public have produced stronger support for détente and made the policy more enduring? In short, could the United States have adjusted more successfully to global change by adhering more consistently to its democratic values and honoring constitutional procedures? And, to which standard, if any, should the administration be held accountable?

As this chapter's selections suggest, Nixon and Kissinger share an ambiguous legacy that invites searching debate.

✖ D O C U M E N T S

Richard M. Nixon, elected president in November 1968, assumed office with a reputation as a hardline Cold Warrior. But the first document, from his memoirs, shows that he recognized new diplomatic opportunities to contain the Soviet Union and to end the war in Vietnam. One method of gaining these objectives was the exploitation of the Sino-Soviet split, sometimes called the "China card." The second selection, a Nixon statement on Asian self-help given during an interview on July 25, 1969, became known as the Nixon Doctrine. Nixon also acknowledged changes in the international economy during his presidency. The third document is an excerpt from a speech he gave in Kansas City, Missouri, on August 2, 1971, in which he discussed the five economic superpowers and America's role in the new global economy. The fourth document, from Henry A. Kissinger's memoirs, recounts the American movement toward détente with the People's Republic of China.

In 1972 the Soviet Union and the United States signed the Strategic Arms Limitation Talks agreement, or SALT-I. The next document is the United States Arms Control and Disarmament Agency's explanation of the two SALT pacts: the Anti-Ballistic Missile (ABM) Treaty and the Interim Agreement on offensive ballistic missile systems. In a September 19, 1974, appearance before the Senate Foreign Relations Committee, Kissinger defined détente and its accomplishments. His statement is reprinted here as the sixth selection.

Chile became a trouble spot from the Nixon-Kissinger perspective in 1970 when a Marxist, Salvador Allende, was elected president of that South American nation. The United States had attempted to block his election through covert operations but had failed. The Nixon administration then plotted to destabilize Allende's government. The seventh document is a 1975 report from the U.S. Senate Select Committee on Intelligence Activities—the Church Committee, named for its chair, Idaho Democrat Frank Church—on covert activities in Chile, 1963–1973. The last document is a January 13, 1977, editorial by Anthony Lewis of the *New York Times,* a writer who sharply indicted Kissinger's diplomatic record.

President Richard M. Nixon Recalls
His Initial Goals (1968), 1978

For twenty-five years, I had watched the changing face of communism. I had seen prewar communism, luring workers and intellectuals with its siren call of equality and justice, reveal itself as an aggressive imperialistic ideology during the postwar period of the Marshall Plan. Despite the most nobly ringing rhetoric, the pattern was tragically the same: as soon as the Communists came to power, they destroyed all opposition. I had watched the Soviets' phenomenal recovery from the devastation of war and their costly but successful struggle to achieve for communism the selling point of potential prosperity. At home I had seen the face of underground subversive communism when it surfaced in the [Alger] Hiss case, reminding people not only that it existed, but that its purpose was deadly serious.

In the late 1940s and during the 1950s I had seen communism spread to China and other parts of Asia, and to Africa and South America, under the camouflage of parties of socialist revolution, or under the guise of wars of national liberation. And, finally, during the 1960s I had watched as Peking and Moscow became rivals for the role of leadership in the Communist world.

Never once in my career have I doubted the Communists mean it when they say that their goal is to bring the world under Communist control. Nor have I ever forgotten [Alger Hiss's accuser] Whittaker Chamber's chilling comment that when he left communism, he had the feeling he was leaving the winning side. But unlike some anticommunists who think we should refuse to recognize or deal with the Communists lest in doing so we imply or extend an ideological respectability to their philosophy and their system, I have always believed that we can and must communicate and, when possible, negotiate with Communist nations. They are too powerful to ignore. We must always remember that they will never act out of altruism, but only out of self-interest. Once this is understood, it is more sensible—and also safer—to communicate with the Communists than it is to live in icy cold-war isolation or confrontation. In fact, in January 1969 I felt that the relationship between the United States and the Soviet Union would probably be the single most important factor in determining whether the world would live at peace during and after my administration.

I felt that we had allowed ourselves to get in a disadvantageous position vis-à-vis the Soviets. They had a major presence in the Arab states of the Middle East, while we had none; they had Castro in Cuba; since the mid-1960s they had supplanted the Chinese as the principal military suppliers of North Vietnam; and except for Tito's Yugoslavia they still totally controlled Eastern Europe and threatened the stability and security of Western Europe.

There were, however, a few things in our favor. The most important and interesting was the Soviet split with China. There was also some evidence of growing, albeit limited, independence in some of the satellite nations. There were indications that the Soviet leaders were becoming interested in reaching an agreement on strategic arms limitation. They also appeared to be ready to hold serious talks on the anomalous situation in Berlin, which, almost a quarter century after the war had ended, was still a divided city and a constant source of tension, not just between the Soviets and the United States, but also between the Soviets and Western Europe. We sensed that they were looking for a face-saving formula that would lessen the risk of confrontation in the Mideast. And we had some solid evidence that they were anxious for an expansion of trade.

It was often said that the key to a Vietnam settlement lay in Moscow and Peking rather than in Hanoi. Without continuous and massive aid from either or both of the Communist giants, the leaders of North Vietnam would not have been able to carry on the war for more than a few months. Thanks to the Sino-Soviet split, however, the North Vietnamese had been extremely successful in playing off the Soviets and the Chinese against each other by turning support for their war effort into a touchstone of Communist orthodoxy and a requisite for keeping North Vietnam from settling into the opposing camp in the struggle for domination within the Communist world. This situation became a strain, particularly for the Soviets. Aside from wanting to keep Hanoi from going over to Peking, Moscow had little stake in the outcome of the North Vietnamese cause, especially as it increasingly worked against Moscow's own major interests vis-à-vis the United States. While I understood that the Soviets were not entirely free agents where their support for North Vietnam was concerned, I nonetheless planned to bring maximum pressure to bear on them in this area. . . .

During the transition period Kissinger and I developed a new policy for dealing with the Soviets. Since U.S.-Soviet interests as the world's two competing nuclear superpowers were so widespread and overlapping, it was unrealistic to separate or compartmentalize areas of concern. Therefore we decided to link progress in such areas of Soviet concern as strategic arms limitation and increased trade with progress in areas that were important to us—Vietnam, the Mideast and Berlin. This concept became known as linkage.

Lest there be any doubt of my seriousness in pursuing this policy, I purposely announced it at my first press conference when asked a question about starting SALT talks. I said, "What I want to do is to see to it that we have strategic arms talks in a way and at a time that will promote, if possible, progress on outstanding political problems at the same time—for example, on the problem of the Mideast and on other outstanding problems in which the United States and the Soviet Union acting together can serve the cause of peace."

Linkage was something uncomfortably new and different for the Soviets, and I was not surprised when they bridled at the restraints it imposed on our relationship. It would take almost two years of patient and hard-nosed determination on our part before they would accept that linkage with what we wanted from them was the price they would have to pay for getting any of the things they wanted from us. . . .

The most pressing foreign problem I would have to deal with as soon as I became President was the war in Vietnam. During the transition Kissinger began a review of all possible policies toward Vietnam, distilling them into specific options that ran the gamut from massive military escalation to immediate unilateral withdrawal. A strong case could be made for each option.

For example, it could be argued that military victory was still possible if I would remove the restrictions [President Lyndon B.] Johnson had placed on our commanders in the field and allow them to use our massive power to defeat the enemy. The most serious of these constraints was the bombing halt; because of it the Communists had been able to regroup their forces and amass supplies for a new offensive. Those who favored the escalation option argued that just the threat of an invasion of North Vietnam would tie down North Vietnamese troops along the DMZ [Demilitarized Zone]; that mining Haiphong Harbor would cripple the enemy's supply lines; and that free pursuit of the Communist forces into Laos and Cambodia would blunt their ability to continue making hit-and-run attacks against our forces in South Vietnam. Renewed bombing would reinforce these other moves. That, in essence, was the escalation option. It was an option we ruled out very early.

The opinion polls showed a significant percentage of the public favored a military victory in Vietnam. But most people thought of a "military victory" in terms of gearing up to administer a knockout blow that would both end the war and win it. The problem was that there were only two such knockout blows available to me. One would have been to bomb the elaborate systems of irrigation dikes in North Vietnam. The resulting floods would have killed hundreds of thousands of civilians. The other possible knockout blow would have involved the use of tactical nuclear weapons. Short of one of these methods, escalation would probably have required up to six months of highly intensified fighting and significantly increased casualties before the Communists would finally be forced to give up and accept a peace settlement. The domestic and international uproar that would have accompanied the use of either of these knockout blows would have got my administration off to the worse possible start. And as far as escalating the conventional fighting was concerned, there was no way that I could hold the country together for that period of time in view of the numbers of casualties we would be sustaining. Resorting to the escalation option would also delay or even destroy any chance we might have to develop a new relationship with the Soviet Union and Communist China.

At the other end of the spectrum from escalation was the case for ending the war simply by announcing a quick and orderly withdrawal of all American forces. If that were done, the argument went, the Communists would probably respond by returning our POWs [Prisoners of War] after the last American had departed. . . .

I began my presidency with three fundamental premises regarding Vietnam. First, I would have to prepare public opinion for the fact that total military victory was no longer possible. Second, I would have to act on what my conscience, my experience, and my analysis told me was true about the need to keep our commitment. To abandon South Vietnam to the Communists now would cost us inestimably in our search for a stable, structured, and lasting peace. Third, I would have to end the war as quickly as was honorably possible. . . .

The Vietnam war was complicated by factors that had never occurred before in America's conduct of a war. Many of the most prominent liberals of both parties in Congress, having supported our involvement in Vietnam under Kennedy and Johnson, were now trying to back off from their commitment. Senators and congressmen, Cabinet members and columnists who had formerly supported the war were now swelling the ranks of the antiwar forces. In 1969 I still had a congressional majority on war-related votes and questions, but it was a bare one at best, and I could not be sure how long it would hold. Another unusual aspect of this war was that the American news media had come to dominate domestic opinion about its purpose and conduct and also about the nature of the enemy. The North Vietnamese were a particularly ruthless and cruel enemy, but the American media concentrated primarily on the failings and frailties of the South Vietnamese or of our own forces. In each night's TV news and in each morning's paper the war was reported battle by battle, but little or no sense of the underlying purpose of the fighting was conveyed. Eventually this contributed to the impression that we were fighting in military and moral quicksand, rather than toward an important and worthwhile objective.

More than ever before, television showed the terrible human suffering and sacrifice of war. Whatever the intention behind such relentless and literal reporting of the war, the result was a serious demoralization of the home front, raising the question whether America would ever again be able to fight an enemy abroad with unity and strength of purpose at home. As *Newsweek* columnist Kenneth Crawford wrote, this was the first war in our history when the media was more friendly to our enemies than to our allies. I felt that by the time I had become President the way the Vietnam war had been conducted and reported had worn down America's spirit and sense of confidence.

As I prepared to enter the presidency, I regarded the antiwar protesters and demonstrators with alternating feelings of appreciation for their concerns, anger at their excesses, and, primarily, frustration at their apparent unwillingness to credit me even with a genuine desire for peace. But whatever my estimation of the demonstrators' motives—and whatever their estimate of mine—I considered that the practical effect of their activity was to give encouragement to the enemy and thus prolong the war. They wanted to end the war in Vietnam. So did I. But they wanted to end it immediately, and in order to do so they were prepared to abandon South Vietnam. That was something I would not permit.

The Nixon Doctrine, 1969

I believe that the time has come when the United States, in our relations with all of our Asian friends, [must] be quite emphatic on two points: One, that we will keep our treaty commitments, our treaty commitments, for example, with Thailand under SEATO [Southeast Asia Treaty Organization]; but, two, that as far as the problems of internal security are concerned, as far as the problems of military defense, except for the threat of a major power involving nuclear weapons, that the United States is going to encourage and has a right to expect that this problem will be increasingly handled by, and the responsibility for it taken by, the Asian nations themselves.

I believe, incidentally, from my preliminary conversations with several Asian leaders over the past few months that they are going to be willing to undertake this responsibility. It will not be easy, but if the United States just continues down the road of responding to requests for assistance, of assuming the primary responsibility for defending these countries when they have internal problems or external problems, they are never going to take care of themselves.

Nixon Explains the Five Power Centers of the New Global Economy, 1971

Many of you, a few of you, are old enough to remember what America was 2[5] years ago.

We were number one in the world militarily, with no one who even challenged us because we had a monopoly on atomic weapons. We also at that point, of course, were number one economically by all odds. In fact, the United States of America was producing more than 50 percent of all the world's goods.

That was just 25 years ago. Now, 25 years having passed, let's look at the situation today and what it may be 5 years from now or 10 years from now. I will not try to limit myself to 5 or 10 years except to say that in the next decade we are going to see changes that may be even greater than what have occurred in the last 25 years, and very great ones have occurred in that respect.

First, instead of just America being number one in the world from an economic standpoint, the preeminent world power, and instead of there being just two super powers, when we think in economic terms and economic potentialities, there are five great power centers in the world today. Let's look at them very briefly.

There is, of course, the United States of America. There is, second, Western Europe—Western Europe with Britain in the Common Market. That means 300 million of the most advanced people in the world, with all the productivity and all the capacity that those people will have and, of course, with the clout that they have when they will act together, as they certainly will. That is a new factor in the world scene that will come, and come very soon, as we all know.

Then in the Pacific, looking also at free world countries, we have a resurgent Japan. I met with steel leaders this morning—leaders of industry and leaders of unions. I pointed out what had happened to Japan in terms of their business: Just 20 years ago Japan produced 5 million tons of steel a year; this year they produced 100 million tons of steel; 2 years from now Japan will produce more steel than the United States of America.

That is what has happened. It has happened in the case of Japan, in the case of Germany, our two major enemies in World War II, partly as a result of our help in getting them on their feet. But it has happened since that time as a result of their own energy and their own ability. . . .

Now we turn to the other two super powers, economic super powers I will say for the moment. The Soviet Union, of course, first comes to mind. Looking at the Soviet Union, we are entering a period which only time will tell may be successful in terms of creating a very new relationship or a very different relationship than we have had previously.

I referred to the need for an era of negotiation rather than confrontation when I made my inaugural speech. . . . I am not suggesting that these negotiations are going to lead to instant peace and instant relationships with the Soviet Union such as we presently have with our friends in Western Europe and with our friends in Asia who may be allied with us, or who may have systems of government that are more closely aligned to ours. What we have to recognize is that even as we limit arms, if we do reach an agreement in that field, and even if we find ways to avoid confrontation in other areas, and perhaps work out negotiated settlements for mutual force reductions in Europe, the problem of Berlin, all the others that come to mind, we must recognize that the Soviet Union will continue to be a very potent, powerful, and aggressive competitor of the United States of America. And, ironically—and this is also true of Mainland China, as I will point out in a moment—as we have more and more success on the negotiation front, as for example the Soviet Union, like the United States, may be able if we have a limitation in nuclear arms, if we are able to turn our eyes more toward our economic development and our economic problems, it simply means that the competition changes and becomes much more challenging in the economic area than it has been previously. . . .

Mainland China is, of course, a very different situation. First in terms of its economic capacity at the present time, a pretty good indication of where it is is that Japan, with 100 million people, produces more than Mainland China, with 800 million people. But that should not mislead us, and it gives us, and should give none of the potential competitors in world markets of Mainland China, any sense of satisfaction that it will always be that way. Because when we see the Chinese as people—and I have seen them all over the world, and some of you have, too, whether in Hong Kong, or whether in Taiwan, or whether they are in Singapore or Bangkok, any of the great cities, Manila, where Chinese are there—they are creative, they are productive, they are one of the most capable people in the world. And 800 million Chinese are going to be, inevitably, an enormous economic power, with all that that means in terms of what they could be in other areas if they move in that direction.

That is the reason why I felt that it was essential that this Administration take the first steps toward ending the isolation of Mainland China from the world community. We had to take those steps because the Soviet Union could not, because of differences that they have that at the present time seem to be irreconcilable. We were the only other power that could take those steps. . . .

Now, I do not suggest, in mentioning these five, that Latin America is not important, that Africa is not important, that South Asia is not important. All nations are important, and all peoples in underdeveloped or less developed countries will play their role. But these are the five that will determine the economic future and, because economic power will be the key to other kinds of power, the future of the world in other ways in the last third of this century.

Now let's see what this means to the United States. It means that the United States, as compared with that position we found ourselves in immediately after World War II, has a challenge such as we did not even dream of. Then we were talking about the dollar gap; then we were talking about the necessity of—putting it in terms of a poker game—that the United States had all the chips and we had to spread a few of the chips around so that others could play.

We did it. One hundred billion dollars worth to Western Europe, for example, to rebuild them, and billions of others to other countries, and it was the correct policy as it turned out. But now when we see the world in which we are about to move, the United States no longer is in the position of complete preeminence or predominance. That is not a bad thing. As a matter of fact, it can be a constructive thing. The United States, let us understand, is still the strongest nation in the world; it is still the richest nation in the world. But now we face a situation where four other potential economic powers have the capacity, have the kind of people—if not the kind of government, but at least the kind of people—who can challenge us on every front.

Secretary of State Henry A. Kissinger on Rapprochement with China (1972), 1979

When we completed drafting the communiqué announcing my secret visit to China in July 1971, Chou En-lai remarked that the announcement would shake the world. He was right. Not only was it a sensation for the media; overnight it transformed the structure of international politics. After twenty bitter years of isolation an American emissary had stepped onto the mysterious soil of Peking; and his President would shortly follow. It was abrupt and astonishing, but behind the climax were thirty months of patient and deliberate preparation as each side felt its way, gingerly, always testing the ground so that a rebuff would not appear humiliating, graduating its steps so that exposure would not demoralize nervous allies or give a new strategic opportunity to those who did not wish them well.

We took even ourselves by surprise. Originally we had not thought reconciliation possible. We were convinced that the Chinese were fanatic and hostile. But even though we could not initially see a way to achieve it, both Nixon and I believed in the importance of an opening to the People's Republic of China.

Events came to our assistance, but I doubt whether the rapprochement could have occurred with the same decisiveness in any other Presidency. Nixon had an extraordinary instinct for the jugular. He was less interested in tactics or the meticulous accumulation of nuance; too much discussion of details of implementation, indeed, made him nervous. Once he had set a policy direction, he almost invariably left it to me to implement the strategy and manage the bureaucracy. But though I had independently come to the same judgment as Nixon, and though I designed many of the moves, I did not have the political strength or bureaucratic clout to pursue such a fundamental shift of policy on my own. Nixon viscerally understood the essence of the opportunity and pushed for it consistently. He had the political base on the right, which protected him from the charge of being "soft on Communism." And his administrative style lent itself to the secretive, solitary tactics the policy required. If the NSC [National Security Council] system of elaborating options interested him for anything, it was for the intelligence it supplied him about the views of a bureaucracy he distrusted and for the opportunity it provided to camouflage his own aims.

There was a marginal difference in our perspectives. Nixon saw in the opening to China a somewhat greater opportunity than I to squeeze the Soviet Union into short-term help on Vietnam; I was more concerned with the policy's impact on the structure of international relations. Nixon tended to believe that ending the isolation of 800 million Chinese itself removed a great threat to peace. To me a China active in foreign policy would call for very skillful diplomacy to calibrate our policies in the more complicated context that would evolve and that would alter all international relationships. But these differences rested on the same fundamental judgment: that if relations could be developed with both the Soviet Union and China the triangular relationship would give us a great strategic opportunity for peace. . . .

Thus by the end of 1969, America's relationship with the Communist world was slowly becoming triangular. We did not consider our opening to China as inherently anti-Soviet. Our objective was to purge our foreign policy of all sentimentality. There was no reason for us to confine our contacts with major Communist countries to the Soviet Union. We moved toward China not to expiate liberal guilt over our China policy of the late 1940s but to shape a global equilibrium. It was not to collude against the Soviet Union but to give us a balancing position to use for constructive ends—to give each Communist power a stake in better relations with us. Such an equilibrium could assure stability among the major powers, and even eventual cooperation, in the Seventies and Eighties. . . .

Nixon was exposed for the first time to the Chinese style of diplomacy. The Soviets tend to be blunt, the Chinese insinuating. The Soviets insist on their prerogatives as a great power. The Chinese establish a claim on the basis of universal principles and a demonstration of self-confidence that attempts to make the issue of power seem irrelevant. The Soviets offer their goodwill as a prize for success in negotiations. The Chinese use friendship as a halter in advance of negotiation; by admitting the interlocutor to at least the appearance of personal intimacy, a subtle restraint is placed on the claims he can put forward. The Soviets, inhabiting a country frequently invaded and more recently expanding its influence largely by force of arms, are too unsure of their moral claims to admit the possibility of error. They move from infallible dogma to unchangeable positions (however often they may modify them). The Chinese, having been culturally preeminent in their part of the world for millennia, can even use self-criticism as a tool. The visitor is asked for advice—a gesture of humility eliciting sympathy and support. This pattern also serves to bring out the visitor's values and aims; he is thereby committed, for the Chinese later can (and often do) refer to his own recommendations. The Soviets, with all of their stormy and occasionally duplicitous behavior, leave an impression of extraordinary psychological insecurity. The Chinese stress, because they believe in it, the uniqueness of Chinese values. Hence they convey an aura of imperviousness to pressure; indeed, they preempt pressure by implying that issues of principle are beyond discussion.

In creating this relationship Chinese diplomats, at least in their encounters with us, proved meticulously reliable. They never stooped to petty maneuvers; they did not haggle; they reached their bottom line quickly, explained it reasonably, and defended it tenaciously. They stuck to the meaning as well as the spirit of their undertakings. As Chou was fond of saying: "*Our* word counts." . . .

The trip [by Richard Nixon to China, February 1972] was increasingly perceived as a great success. As the American public gained hope from the China visit, Vietnam became less an obsession and more a challenge to be mastered. The Administration that had revolutionized international relations could not so easily be accused of neglecting the deepest concern of the American people.

Once more, though, we encountered the curious phenomenon that success seemed to unsettle Nixon more than failure. He seemed obsessed by the fear that he was not receiving adequate credit. He constantly badgered his associates to press a public relations campaign that would call more attention to the China visit. He followed the press carefully, so that any criticism could be immediately countered. He read some commentator's criticism that the Chinese statements of their position in the Shanghai Communiqué were more aggressive than the statements of our position. On March 9, therefore, he sent me a memorandum asking me to make clear to the press the deep thought and analysis that lay behind this "decision" to state our position moderately. His preference for this approach dated back, he said, to a speech he gave in the Soviet Union in 1959, which he urged me to read in his book *Six Crises*. Though Chou En-lai had originally proposed the idea of separate and conflicting statements, though Chou and I had drafted almost all of that part of the text in October 1971 without reference to Washington, and though Nixon had learned of both the approach and the content only after I returned, he wanted me to explain to the press—and I believe had convinced himself—that he had conceived it:

> You could begin by pointing out that I made the decision with regard to the tone of the statement of our position for two basic reasons. First, the more aggressive we stated our position the more aggressive the Chinese would have to be in stating their position. As a result of our presenting our position in a very firm, but non-belligerent manner, their position, while it was also uncompromising on principle, was not nearly as rough in its rhetoric as has been the case in previous statements they have issued over the years. . . .
>
> I was determined that in this document, which would be the first time Chinese leaders, and cadres, and to a certain extent even Chinese masses, would ever hear the American position expressed, I had to make the strongest possible effort to set it in a tone which would not make it totally incredible when they heard it. It would not have been credible, of course, had we set forth our position in more aggressive terms because 22 years of propaganda at the other extreme would have made it impossible for the reader of the communiqué, or those who heard it read on radio, to believe it at all if the tone was too harsh.

Nixon, of course, deserves full credit for the Shanghai Communiqué. A President is always responsible for the policy, no matter who does the technical labors. A less courageous President could have pulled back from the separate statements,

when I presented them to him upon my return in October, in favor of a more ortho-
dox presentation. This trivial incident does not derogate from Nixon's boldness in
his historic opening to China. What it illustrates, however, is the tendency for illusion to become reality, a brooding and involuted streak that, together with starker
character traits, at first flawed, and later destroyed, a Presidency so rich in foreign
policy achievements.

The SALT-I Agreements, 1972

The ABM [Anti-Ballistic Missile] Treaty is a definitive long-term agreement
which contributes in a fundamental way to our security. The possibility of nuclear
war has been dramatically reduced by this Treaty. It sets forth at the outset the joint
commitment not to build a nationwide ABM defense nor provide a base for such
defense. In this undertaking both countries [the United States and the Soviet
Union] have, in effect, agreed not to challenge the credibility of each other's deterrent missile forces by deploying a widespread defense against them. This is the
central consequence of this Treaty, and its importance to avoidance of nuclear war
cannot be overestimated. Both major nuclear powers have agreed that they will not
attempt to build a shield against penetration by the other's missile forces which
serve to deter nuclear attack.

The ABM Treaty limits the United States and the Soviet Union to two ABM
sites each—one for the protection of the national capital, and the other for the defense of an ICBM [Intercontinental Ballistic Missile] complex. At each site, there
can be no more than 100 ABM launchers and 100 associated interceptor missiles.
In addition to numerical limitations on ABM launchers and missiles at each complex, the areas permitted for ABM deployment are limited geographically and
in size. . . .

In order to assure further that there would be adequate restraints on ABM
capabilities, the Treaty provides for significant qualitative limitations on ABM
systems. The two sides agreed not to develop, test, or deploy ABM launchers for
launching more than one interceptor missile at a time, not to modify launchers to
provide them with such a capability, nor to develop, test, or deploy automatic or
semiautomatic or other similar systems for rapid reload of ABM launchers. It was
also agreed that these prohibitions included a ban on more than one independently
guided warhead for an ABM missile.

An additional important qualitative limitation is the prohibition on development and testing, as well as deployment, of sea, air, space-based and land-mobile
ABM systems and components.

Another important element is the agreement that if future types of ABM systems or components based on physical principles different from present technology become feasible, specific limitations thereon will be a subject of discussion
and agreement in accordance with treaty provisions regarding amendments. An example of such a future system would be one depending on the use of laser beams
for destruction of missile reentry vehicles.

To avoid possible circumvention of the ban on a nationwide ABM defense
through developments in non-ABM systems, e.g., antiaircraft surface-to-air missiles, the Parties agreed to prohibit conversion or testing of such other systems, or

components thereof, to perform an ABM role. For much the same reasons, they also agreed to restrict certain categories of large phased-array radars. These provisions deal with what had come to be known in this country as the "SAM-upgrade problem" (upgrading surface-to-air defense missiles for an ABM role).

It has been the position of the United States that a limitation on ABMs alone would not make as great a contribution to stability and security as would limitations on both offensive and defensive strategic systems. However, problems over definition of strategic systems made clear that it would be extremely difficult to negotiate a single comprehensive agreement.

The Interim Agreement is essentially a holding action which freezes existing levels of land and sea-based offensive ballistic missile systems until a more complete agreement, taking into account the complex asymmetries and implications involved, can be reached. Both nations have expressed the belief that a permanent agreement limiting strategic offensive systems can be reached before the 5-year duration of the Interim Agreement has expired.

The May 20, 1971, understanding focused discussions of strategic offensive systems on ICBMs and SLBMs [Submarine-Launched Ballistic Missiles], setting aside consideration of bombers and forward based systems.

The inclusion of ICBMs was never at issue. However, SLBMs became the subject of intense discussions. The Soviet Union was engaged in a very rapid buildup of its nuclear-missile submarine fleet, deploying additional sea-based ballistic missiles at the rate of about 100 per year. In the U.S. view, it was inconsistent with the purpose of the interim offensive freeze to leave the Soviet buildup unconstrained. It was only in late April, 1972, however, that the Soviets agreed in principle to limit SLBMs in some way. The final details were worked out during the 4 weeks leading up to the Moscow Summit Meeting.

The Interim Agreement is limited in duration and scope. The first two Articles deal with ICBM launchers. The Parties commit themselves not to construct additional fixed land-based ICBM launchers or to relocate existing ICBM launchers. In addition, they commit themselves not to convert launchers for light or older ICBMs into launchers for modern heavy ICBMs. This constitutes an important qualitative constraint which prevents the Soviets from replacing older missiles with SS-9s, the largest and most powerful missile in the Soviet inventory. Unrestrained growth in the number of SS-9s has been a concern of U.S. strategic planners.

Under the terms of the agreement, both sides are allowed to continue to modernize their existing ICBM forces. However, an understanding was reached that the dimensions of land-based ICBM silos will not be significantly increased.

The negotiators were unable to reach full agreement on the definition of a "heavy" missile to supplement the prohibition on conversion of existing light missiles to heavy missiles. The United States therefore made a formal unilateral interpretation of this matter, stating that we "would consider any ICBM having a volume significantly greater than that of the largest light ICBM now operational on either side to be a heavy ICBM."

The agreement does not cover land-mobile ICBMs. The Soviet Union did not want them included in the temporary freeze, arguing that neither side presently had such a system. Although no agreement was reached on mobile systems, the United

States served notice to the Soviets in a formal statement that deployment of operational land-mobile ICBMs during the interim period would be considered inconsistent with the objectives of the agreement. . . .

Taking into account current levels of strategic submarine fleets on the two sides, together with other factors in the U.S.-Soviet strategic equation, SLBM limitations were arrived at as follows: For the U.S.S.R., a ceiling of 62 was set on the number of modern, nuclear-powered submarines, and a limit of 950 established for the total number of modern SLBM launchers on either nuclear or diesel-powered submarines. However, for every modern Soviet SLBM launcher over 740 and up to the agreed ceiling of 950, the Soviet Union must, under agreed procedures, retire older land-based launchers (SS-7s and SS-8s) or launchers on older nuclear submarines. In other words, the 741st SLBM launcher on a modern nuclear-powered submarine must be a replacement for a currently deployed launcher. The rapid buildup which, in recent times, had been taking place in the Soviet strategic submarine fleet was thus constrained.

The United States has, under these arrangements, the existing level of 656 SLBM launchers, and the right to have, through replacement of 54 Titan II ICBMs, up to 710 SLBM launchers on 44 modern submarines.

The conversion of U.S. ICBM launchers to handle Minuteman III missiles and the conversion of current Polaris submarines to handle Poseidon missiles are not affected by the freeze.

The undertakings in the ABM Treaty and in the Interim Agreement are to be verified by national technical means of verification. For the types of obligations contained in these agreements, national technical means of verification are practical and effective. Both Parties have made the commitment not to interfere with the national technical means of verification of the other. This would, for example, prohibit interference with a satellite in orbit used for verification purposes. In addition, the Parties have committed themselves not to use deliberate concealment measures to impede the effectiveness of national means of verification. These commitments are landmarks in the joint effort to bring the strategic confrontation under manageable control.

Kissinger on Détente, 1974

There can be no peaceful international order without a constructive relationship between the United States and the Soviet Union. There will be no international stability unless both the Soviet Union and the United States conduct themselves with restraint and unless they use their enormous power for the benefit of mankind.

Thus, we must be clear at the outset on what the term "détente" entails. It is the search for a more constructive relationship with the Soviet Union. It is a continuing process, not a final condition. And it has been pursued by successive American leaders though the means have varied as have world conditions.

Some fundamental principles guide this policy:

The United States does not base its policy solely on Moscow's good intentions. We seek, regardless of Soviet intentions, to serve peace through a systematic resistance to pressure and conciliatory responses to moderate behavior.

We must oppose aggressive actions, but we must not seek confrontations lightly.

We must maintain a strong national defense while recognizing that in the nuclear age the relationship between military strength and politically usable power is the most complex in all history.

Where the age-old antagonism between freedom and tyranny is concerned, we are not neutral. But other imperatives impose limits on our ability to produce internal changes in foreign countries. Consciousness of our limits is a recognition of the necessity of peace—not moral callousness. The preservation of human life and human society are moral values, too.

We must be mature enough to recognize that to be stable a relationship must provide advantages to both sides and that the most constructive international relationships are those in which both parties perceive an element of gain. . . .

To set forth principles of behavior in formal documents is hardly to guarantee their observance. But they are reference points against which to judge actions and set goals.

The first of the series of documents is the Statement of Principles signed in Moscow in 1972. It affirms: (1) the necessity of avoiding confrontation; (2) the imperative of mutual restraint; (3) the rejection of attempts to exploit tensions to gain unilateral advantages; (4) the renunciation of claims of special influence in the world; and (5) the willingness, on this new basis, to coexist peacefully and build a firm long-term relationship.

An Agreement on the Prevention of Nuclear War based on these Principles was signed in 1973. But it emphasizes that this objective presupposes the renunciation of any war or threat of war not only by the two nuclear superpowers against each other, but also against allies or third countries. In other words, the principle of restraint is not confined to relations between the United States and the U.S.S.R. It is explicitly extended to include all countries.

These statements of principles are not an American concession; indeed, we have been affirming them unilaterally for two decades. Nor are they a legal contract; rather, they are an aspiration and a yardstick by which we assess Soviet behavior. We have never intended to rely on Soviet compliance with every principle; we do seek to elaborate standards of conduct which the Soviet Union would violate only to its cost. And if over the long term the more durable relationship takes hold, the basic principles will give it definition, structure, and hope.

One of the features of the current phase of United States–Soviet relations is the unprecedented consultation between leaders either face to face or through diplomatic channels.

It was difficult in the past to speak of a United States–Soviet bilateral relationship in any normal sense of the phrase. Trade was negligible. Contacts between various institutions and between the peoples of the two countries were at best sporadic. Today, by joining our efforts even in such seemingly apolitical fields as medical research or environmental protection, we and the Soviets can benefit not only our two peoples, but all mankind.

Since 1972 we have concluded agreements on a common effort against cancer, on research to protect the environment, on studying the use of the ocean's resources, on the use of atomic energy for peaceful purposes, on studying methods for conserving energy, on examining construction techniques for regions subject to earthquakes, and on devising new transportation methods. . . .

We have approached the question of economic relations with deliberation and circumspection and as an act of policy not primarily of commercial opportunity. As political relations have improved on a broad basis, economic issues have been dealt with on a comparably broad front. A series of interlocking economic agreements with the U.S.S.R. has been negotiated, side by side with the political progress already noted. The 25-year-old lend-lease debt was settled; the reciprocal extension of the most-favored-nation treatment was negotiated, together with safeguards against the possible disruption of our markets and a series of practical arrangements to facilitate the conduct of business; our Government credit facilities were made available for trade with the U.S.S.R.; and a maritime agreement regulating the carriage of goods has been signed. . . .

Over time, trade and investment may leaven the autarkic tendencies of the Soviet system, invite gradual association of the Soviet economy with the world economy, and foster a degree of interdependence that adds an element of stability to the political relationship.

We cannot expect to relax international tensions or achieve a more stable international system should the two strongest nuclear powers conduct an unrestrained strategic arms race. Thus, perhaps the single most important component of our policy toward the Soviet Union is the effort to limit strategic weapons competition.

The competition in which we now find ourselves is historically unique:

Each side has the capacity to destroy civilization as we know it.

Failure to maintain equivalence could jeopardize not only our freedom but our very survival. . . .

The prospect of a decisive military advantage, even if theoretically possible, is politically intolerable; neither side will passively permit a massive shift in the nuclear balance. Therefore, the probable outcome of each succeeding round of competition is the restoration of a strategic equilibrium, but at increasingly higher and more complex levels of forces.

The arms race is driven by political as well as military factors. While a decisive advantage is hard to calculate, the appearance of inferiority—whatever its actual significance—can have serious political consequences. Thus, each side has a high incentive to achieve not only the reality but the appearance of equality. In a very real sense each side shapes the military establishment of the other.

If we are driven to it, the United States will sustain an arms race. But the political or military benefit which would flow from such a situation would remain elusive. Indeed, after such an evolution it might well be that both sides would be worse off than before the race began.

The Soviet Union must realize that the overall relationship with the United States will be less stable if strategic balance is sought through unrestrained competitive programs. Sustaining the buildup requires exhortations by both sides that in time may prove incompatible with restrained international conduct. The very fact of a strategic arms race has a high potential for feeding attitudes of hostility and suspicion on both sides, transforming the fears of those who demand more weapons into self-fulfilling prophecies.

The American people can be asked to bear the cost and political instability of a race which is doomed to stalemate only if it is clear that every effort has been made to prevent it. That is why every President since Eisenhower has pursued negotiations for the limitation of strategic arms while maintaining the military programs essential to strategic balance.

SALT has become one means by which we and the Soviet Union could enhance stability by setting mutual constraints on our respective forces and by gradually reaching an understanding of the doctrinal considerations that underlie the deployment of nuclear weapons. SALT, in the American conception, is a means to achieve strategic stability by methods other than the arms race.

U.S. Covert Action in Chile (1963–1973), 1975

The pattern of United States covert action in Chile is striking but not unique. It arose in the context not only of American foreign policy, but also of covert U.S. involvement in other countries within and outside Latin America. The scale of CIA involvement in Chile was unusual but by no means unprecedented. . . .

The most extensive covert action activity in Chile was propaganda. It was relatively cheap. In Chile, it continued at a low level during "normal" times, then was cranked up to meet particular threats or to counter particular dangers.

The most common form of a propaganda project is simply the development of "assets" in media organizations who can place articles or be asked to write them. The Agency provided to its field Stations several kinds of guidance about what sorts of propaganda were desired. For example, one CIA project in Chile supported from one to five media assets during the seven years it operated (1965–1971). Most of those assets worked for a major Santiago daily which was the key to CIA propaganda efforts. Those assets wrote articles or editorials favorable to U.S. interests in the world (for example, criticizing the Soviet Union in the wake of the Czechoslovakian invasion); suppressed news items harmful to the United States (for instance about Vietnam); and authored articles critical of Chilean leftists.

The covert propaganda efforts in Chile also included "black" propaganda—material falsely purporting to be the product of a particular individual or group. In the 1970 election, for instance, the CIA used "black" propaganda to sow discord between the Communists and the Socialists and between the national labor confederation and the Chilean Communist Party.

Table 1   Techniques of Covert Action: Expenditures in Chile, 1963–73*

TECHNIQUES	AMOUNT
Propaganda for elections and other support for political parties	$8,000,000
Producing and disseminating propaganda and supporting mass media	4,300,000
Influencing Chilean institutions (labor, students, peasants, women) and supporting private sector organizations	900,000
Promoting military coup d'etat	<200,000

*Figures rounded to nearest $100,000.

In some cases, the form of propaganda was still more direct. The Station financed Chilean groups who erected wall posters, passed out political leaflets (at times prepared by the Station) and engaged in other street activities. Most often these activities formed part of larger projects intended to influence the outcomes of Chilean elections . . . but in at least one instance the activities took place in the absence of an election campaign.

Of thirty-odd covert action projects undertaken [in] Chile by the CIA between 1961 and 1974, approximately a half dozen had propaganda as their principal activity. Propaganda was an important subsidiary element of many others, particularly election projects. (See Table 1.) Press placements were attractive because each placement might produce a multiplier effect, being picked up and replayed by media outlets other than the one in which it originally came out.

In addition to buying propaganda piecemeal, the Station often purchased it wholesale by subsidizing Chilean media organizations friendly to the United States. Doing so was propaganda writ large. Instead of placing individual items, the CIA supported—or even founded—friendly media outlets which might not have existed in the absence of Agency support.

From 1953 through 1970 in Chile, the Station subsidized wire services, magazines written for intellectual circles, and a right-wing weekly newspaper. According to the testimony of former officials, support for the newspaper was terminated because it became so inflexibly rightist as to alienate responsible conservatives.

By far, the largest—and probably the most significant—instance of support for a media organization was the money provided to *El Mercurio,* the major Santiago daily, under pressure during the Allende regime. That support grew out of an existing propaganda project. In 1971 the Station judged that *El Mercurio,* the most important opposition publication, could not survive pressure from the Allende government, including intervention in the newsprint market and the withdrawal of government advertising. The 40 Committee [a subcabinet level body of the executive branch which reviewed covert plans] authorized $700,000 for *El Mercurio* on September 9, 1971, and added another $965,000 to that authorization on April 11, 1972. A CIA project renewal memorandum concluded that *El Mercurio* and other media outlets supported by the Agency had played an important role in setting the stage for the September 11, 1973, military coup which overthrew Allende.

Through its covert activities in Chile, the U.S. government sought to influence the actions of a wide variety of institutions and groups in Chilean society. The specific intent of those activities ran the gamut from attempting to influence directly the making of government policy to trying to counter communist or leftist influence among organized groups in the society. That most of these projects included a propaganda component is obvious.

From 1964 through 1968, the CIA developed contacts within the Chilean Socialist Party and at the Cabinet level of the Chilean government.

Projects aimed at organized groups in Chilean society had more diffuse purposes than efforts aimed at government institutions. But the aim was similar: influencing the direction of political events in Chile.

Projects were directed, for example, toward:

- Wresting control of Chilean university student organizations from the communists;
- Supporting a women's group active in Chilean political and intellectual life;
- Combating the communist-dominated *Central Unica de Trabajadores Chilenos* (CUTCh) and supporting democratic labor groups; and
- Exploiting a civic action front group to combat communist influence within cultural and intellectual circles.

Covert American activity was a factor in almost every major election in Chile in the decade between 1963 and 1973. In several instances the United States intervention was massive.

The 1964 presidential election was the most prominent example of a large-scale election project. The Central Intelligence Agency spent more than $2.6 million in support of the election of the Christian Democratic candidate, in part to prevent the accession to the presidency of Marxist Salvador Allende. More than half of the Christian Democratic candidate's campaign was financed by the United States, although he was not informed of this assistance. In addition, the Station furnished support to an array of pro–Christian Democratic student, women's, professional and peasant groups. Two other political parties were funded as well in an attempt to spread the vote.

In Washington, an inter-agency election committee was established, composed of State Department, White House and CIA officials. That committee was paralleled by a group in the embassy in Santiago. No special task force was established within the CIA, but the Station in Santiago was reinforced. The Station assisted the Christian Democrats in running an American-style campaign, which included polling, voter registration and get-out-the-vote drives, in addition to covert propaganda.

The United States was also involved in the 1970 presidential campaign. That effort, however, was smaller and did not include support for any specific candidate. It was directed more at preventing Allende's election than at insuring another candidate's victory. . . .

Most covert American support to Chilean political parties was furnished as part of specific efforts to influence election outcomes. However, in several instances the CIA provided subsidies to parties for more general purposes, when elections were not imminent. Most such support was furnished during the Allende years, 1970–1973, when the U.S. government judged that without its support parties of the center and right might not survive either as opposition elements or as contestants in elections several years away.

In a sequence of decisions in 1971 through 1973, the 40 Committee authorized nearly $4 million for opposition political parties in Chile. Most of this money went to the Christian Democratic Party (PDC), but a substantial portion was earmarked for the National Party (PN), a conservative grouping more stridently opposed to the Allende government than was the PDC. An effort was also made to split the ruling Popular Unity coalition by inducing elements to break away. . . .

As part of its program of support for opposition elements during the Allende government, the CIA provided money to several trade organizations of the Chilean private sector. In September 1972, for instance, the 40 Committee authorized

$24,000 in emergency support for an anti-Allende businessmen's organization. At that time, supporting other private sector organizations was considered but rejected because of the fear that those organizations might be involved in anti-government strikes. . . .

United States covert efforts to affect the course of Chilean politics reached a peak in 1970: the CIA was directed to undertake an effort to promote a military coup in Chile to prevent the accession to power of Salvador Allende [a project known as Track II]. . . . A brief summary here will demonstrate the extreme in American covert intervention in Chilean politics.

On September 15, 1970—after Allende finished first in the election but before the Chilean Congress had chosen between him and the runner-up, [Jorge] Alessandri—President Nixon met with Richard Helms, the Director of Central Intelligence, Assistant to the President for National Security Affairs Henry Kissinger and Attorney General John Mitchell. Helms was directed to prevent Allende from taking power. This effort was to be conducted without the knowledge of the Department of State and Defense or the Ambassador. Track II was never discussed at a 40 Committee meeting.

It quickly became apparent to both White House and CIA officials that a military coup was the only way to prevent Allende's accession to power. To achieve that end, the CIA established contact with several groups of military plotters and eventually passed three weapons and tear gas to one group. The weapons were subsequently returned, apparently unused. The CIA knew that the plans of all groups of plotters began with the abduction of the constitutionalist Chief of Staff of the Chilean Army, General René Schneider. The Committee has received conflicting testimony about the extent of CIA/White House communication and of White House officials' awareness of specific coup plans, but there is no doubt that the U.S. government sought a military coup in Chile.

On October 22, one group of plotters attempted to kidnap Schneider. Schneider resisted, was shot, and subsequently died. The CIA had been in touch with that group of plotters but a week earlier had withdrawn its support for the group's specific plans.

The coup plotting collapsed and Allende was inaugurated President. After his election, the CIA and U.S. military attachés maintained contacts with the Chilean military for the purpose of collecting intelligence. Whether those contacts strayed into encouraging the Chilean military to move against Allende; or whether the Chilean military—having been goaded toward a coup during Track II—took encouragement to act against the President from those contacts even though U.S. officials did not intend to provide it: these are major questions which are inherent in U.S. covert activities in the period of the Allende government. . . .

In addition to providing information and cover to the CIA, multinational corporations also participated in covert attempts to influence Chilean politics. . . .

In 1970, the U.S. government and several multinational corporations were linked in opposition to the candidacy and later the presidency of Salvador Allende. This CIA–multinational corporation connection can be divided into two phases. Phase I comprised actions taken by either the CIA or U.S.-based multinational companies at a time when it was official U.S. policy not to support, even covertly, any candidate or party in Chile. During this phase the Agency was, however, authorized to engage in a covert "spoiling" operation designed to defeat Salvador Allende. Phase II encompassed the relationship between intelligence agencies and multinational corporations after the September 1970 general election. During Phase II, the U.S. government opposed Allende and supported opposition elements. The government sought the cooperation of multinational corporations in this effort.

A number of multinational corporations were apprehensive about the possibility that Allende would be elected President of Chile. Allende's public announcements indicated his intention, if elected, to nationalize basic industries and to bring under Chilean ownership service industries such as the national telephone company, which was at that time a subsidiary of ITT [International Telephone and Telegraph].

In 1964 Allende had been defeated, and it was widely known both in Chile and among American multinational corporations with significant interests in Chile that his opponents had been supported by the United States government. John McCone, a former CIA Director and a member of ITT's Board of Directors in 1970, knew of the significant American government involvement in 1964 and of the offer of assistance made at that time by American companies. Agency documents indicate that McCone informed Harold Geneen, ITT's Board Chairman, of these facts.

In 1970 leaders of American multinational corporations with substantial interests in Chile, together with other American citizens concerned about what might happen to Chile in the event of an Allende victory, contacted U.S. government officials in order to make their views known.

In July 1970, a CIA representative in Santiago met with representatives of ITT and, in a discussion of the upcoming election, indicated that Alessandri could use financial assistance. The Station suggested the name of an individual who could be used as a secure channel for getting these funds to the Alessandri campaign.

Shortly thereafter John McCone telephoned CIA Director Richard Helms. As a result of this call, a meeting was arranged between the Chairman of the Board of ITT and Chief of the Western Hemisphere Division of the CIA. Geneen offered to make available to the CIA a substantial amount of money to be used in support of the Alessandri campaign. In subsequent meetings ITT offered to make $1 million available to the CIA. The CIA rejected the offer. The memorandum indicated further that CIA's advice was sought with respect to an individual who might serve as a conduit of ITT funds to the Alessandri campaign.

The CIA confirmed that the individual in question was a reliable channel which could be used for getting funds to Alessandri. A second channel of funds from ITT to a political party opposing Allende, the National Party, was developed following CIA advice as to a secure funding mechanism utilizing two CIA assets in Chile. These assets were also receiving Agency funds in connection with the "spoiling" operation.

During the period prior to the September election, ITT representatives met frequently with CIA representatives both in Chile and in the United States and CIA advised ITT as to ways in which it might safely channel funds both to the Alessandri campaign and to the National Party. CIA was kept informed of the extent and the mechanism of the funding. Eventually at least $350,000 was passed by ITT to this campaign. A roughly equal amount was passed by other U.S. companies; the CIA learned of this funding but did not assist in it.

The Journalist Anthony Lewis's Critique of Kissinger's Record, 1977

Henry Kissinger is leaving office in a blaze of adulation. The National Press Club produces a belly dancer for him and gives standing applause to his views on world peace. The Harlem Globetrotters make him an honorary member. Senators pay tribute to his wisdom.

Historians of the next generation will find it all very puzzling. Because they will not have seen Mr. Kissinger perform, they will have to rely on the record. And the record of his eight years in Washington is likely to seem thin in diplomatic achievement and shameful in human terms.

The one outstanding accomplishment is Mr. Kissinger's Middle East diplomacy. He restored United States relations with the Arab world, and he set in motion the beginnings of an Arab-Israeli dialogue. Of course, the work is incomplete. But to start something after so many years of total failure was a great breakthrough and it was essentially the work of one man: Henry Kissinger.

The other undoubtedly positive entry on the record is the opening to China, but that was in good part Richard Nixon's doing. Also, the beginnings of a relationship with the People's Republic were not followed up as they might have been, and the failure may prove damaging.

With the Soviet Union, Mr. Kissinger took the familiar idea of easing tensions and glamorized it as détente. The glamor was dangerous. It fostered the illusion that détente could prevent conflict all over the world, and many Americans turned sour on the whole idea when it did not. At times Mr. Kissinger himself seemed to believe the illusion—and became apoplectic when it failed as in Angola. Détente's real achievements are scant; not much more than a halting step toward nuclear arms control.

Ignorance and ineptitude marked his policy in much of the rest of the world. In Cyprus, his blundering led to human tragedy and left America's reputation damaged in both Greece and Turkey. His insensitivity to Japanese feelings had traumatic effects on a most important ally.

In dealing with Portugal and its African territories Mr. Kissinger decided in succession that (1) the Portuguese were in Africa to stay, (2) the U.S. should help Portugal's dictatorship, (3) after the dictatorship's fall the Communists were bound to prevail in Portugal and (4) the U.S. could decide the outcome in Angola by covert aid. That parade of folly was matched in his African policy generally: years of malign neglect, then last-minute intervention for majority rule in Rhodesia.

He often talked about freedom, but his acts show a pre-eminent interest in order. Millions lost their freedom during the Kissinger years, many to dictatorships

Anthony Lewis, "This Way to the Egress," *New York Times,* January 13, 1977, p. 37, © 1977 by the New York Times Company. Reprinted by permission.

that had crucial support from his policies, as in Chile and the Philippines. He expressed little open concern for the victims of Soviet tyranny, and he did little to enforce the human rights clauses of the Helsinki Agreement.

The American constitutional system of checks and balances he treated as an irritating obstacle to power. In his valedictory to the Press Club his only reference to Watergate was an expression of regret at "the disintegration of Executive authority that resulted."

Secrecy and deceit were levers of his power; he had no patience for the democratic virtues of openness and consultation. By keeping all the facts to himself and a few intimates, he centralized control. He practiced deceit with a kind of gusto, from petty personal matters to "peace is at hand."

His conduct in the wiretapping of his own staff gave ugly insight into his character. He provided names for investigation—and then, when the story came out, wriggled and deceived in order to minimize his role. He never expressed regret, even to those who had been closest to him, for the fact that their family conversations had been overheard for months. But when someone ransacked his garbage, he said his wife had suffered "grave anguish."

History will remember him most of all for his policy in Indochina. In the teeth of evidence well known by 1969, this supposed realist pressed obsessively for indefinite maintenance of the status quo. To that end, in his time, 20,492 more Americans died in Vietnam and hundreds of thousands of Vietnamese. The war was expanded into Cambodia, destroying that peaceable land. And all for nothing.

With such a record, how is it that people vie to place laurels on the head of the departing Secretary of State? The answer became clear the other night during an extraordinarily thoughtful Public Broadcasting television program on Mr. Kissinger's career: He has discovered that in our age publicity is power, and he has played the press as Dr. Miracle played his violin. He is intelligent and hard-working and ruthless, but those qualities are common enough. His secret is showmanship.

Henry Kissinger is our P. T. Barnum—a Barnum who plays in a vastly larger tent and whose jokes have about them the air of the grave. That we honor a person who has done such things in our name is a comment on us.

✳ E S S A Y S

In the first essay, John Lewis Gaddis of Ohio University presents a favorable view of the Nixon-Kissinger foreign policy. The Nixon administration, according to Gaddis, responded creatively to the new international realities of the late 1960s, especially the Soviet Union's achievement of parity in nuclear weapons. SALT, the opening to Beijing, and the linkage of improved U.S.-Soviet ties to Moscow's cooperation in the Third World constituted a new kind of containment that, for the most part, effectively regulated superpower competition and safeguarded U.S. interests. Although the Soviet Union at times outmaneuvered Washington, prompting some Americans to champion a more vigorous anticommunism, Gaddis praises the Nixon-Kissinger policy for expanding U.S. freedom of action in the world at a time when America's power relative to that of the Soviet Union had declined.

In the second essay, Raymond L. Garthoff, a former foreign service officer and ambassador who is currently a senior fellow writing works of history at the Brookings Institution in Washington, D.C., advances a much more negative interpretation, finding détente a failure. He criticizes the Nixon-Kissinger team for not defining the meaning of détente more clearly and for not developing with Moscow a viable code of conduct and collaborative measures for managing the superpower rivalry. Each side expected too much from détente and misperceived the other's continued military buildup and interventionism as threatening and destabilizing. The United States, Garthoff argues, maintained a particularly idealized concept of détente that condemned aggressive Soviet behavior but failed to acknowledge that the vigorous foreign policy of the United States itself at times violated the spirit of détente.

The last selection is drawn from Walter Isaacson's lengthy biography of Henry A. Kissinger. In the excerpt, Isaacson, an editor at *Time* magazine, examines Kissinger's foreign policy "realism." Isaacson respects Kissinger's intellectual brilliance and political savvy but emphasizes that Kissinger's concern for U.S. credibility led to imprudent interventions in the Third World. Most important, according to Isaacson, Kissinger's European style of diplomacy clashed with America's democratic traditions and moral values and thus weakened public backing for détente.

The Skill and Wisdom
of the Nixon-Kissinger Détente

JOHN LEWIS GADDIS

Historians have come to regard 1969 as a major turning point in the evolution of the Cold War, for it was in that year that the internal situation in each of the major countries involved simultaneously came to favor détente. The year saw the Soviet Union achieve its long-sought goal of numerical parity with the United States in ICBMs [Intercontinental Ballistic Missiles]; at the same time, however, Moscow's hopes for economic parity receded with the realization that capitalist assistance would be necessary to solve Russia's industrial and agricultural problems. In China, the calculated irrationality known as the "Great Cultural Revolution" was coming to an end, at least insofar as it had been directed against American influences; meanwhile fighting had broken out between Chinese and Soviet forces along the Ussuri River. In the United States, the slow process of disengagement from Vietnam had begun; there had also come to power in Washington an administration that could hardly be accused of "softness" toward communism and that therefore, in the odd logic of American politics, enjoyed greater latitude in negotiating with its ideological adversaries than had been available to its predecessors. This unusual juxtaposition of circumstances produced no overnight disappearance of Soviet-American tensions, but it did make possible, over the next three years, their considerable reduction.

"After a period of confrontation, we are entering an era of negotiation." It was an unexpected tone for Richard M. Nixon to take in his inaugural address, given his long record of hostility toward the communist world. One advantage of protracted ideological rigidity, though, is that by abandoning it one can enhance one's reputation for statesmanship; if this process alienates old supporters, then the influx of new-found and pleasantly surprised allies can more than compensate for them. Another useful trait in a statesman is not to bear grudges: this characteristic (not often applied by Nixon in other situations, one must add) enabled the new president to obtain the services of Henry A. Kissinger as his assistant for national security affairs, despite the fact that the Harvard professor had only months before proclaimed the Republican nominee unfit to occupy the White House. Students of diplomacy, politics, and human behavior will be arguing for years over the precise nature of this remarkable partnership; what is clear now is that Nixon and Kissinger grasped the significance of the moment at which they had come to power and were determined to use it to try to bring about an end to the Cold War.

Their approach, as both men later described it, was to take advantage of uncertainties created by the Soviet achievement of strategic parity, economic difficulties within the USSR, and the fragmentation of the international communist movement to reinforce attitudes on the part of Kremlin leaders conducive to détente. As Nixon put it in 1972:

> There were ambiguous tendencies in Soviet policy; the same factors that might lead the USSR toward greater hostility also suggested the opportunity for a relaxation of tension. The task of American policy was to recognize the persistence of this ambiguity and to take action to strengthen the more positive tendencies.

Kissinger described the same strategy in a slightly different manner two years later: "When Soviet policy moved toward conciliation we sought to turn what may have started as a tactical maneuver into a durable pattern of conduct." It is important to emphasize that neither Nixon or Kissinger contemplated any immediate abandonment of containment: their intent rather was to explore possibilities for altering the Soviet approach to international order for a post–Cold War era; if it succeeded, then containment would have achieved its purpose.

Because there exists no generally agreed-upon standard of strength in this field, it is difficult to say precisely when Soviet strategic power began to approach that of the United States. In numbers of land-based ICBMs the Russians passed the Americans sometime in 1969: by the end of that year they had approximately 1,200 such weapons, as compared to 1,054 for the United States, a figure that had not changed since 1967. The Russians had also deployed by that time an ABM [Anti-Ballistic Missile] system of questionable reliability. The United States retained almost a three-to-one advantage in SLBMs [Submarine-Launched Ballistic Missiles], though (656 versus 230), and an even larger lead in long-range bombers (540 versus 150). The Americans also led the Russians in missile accuracy and in numbers of warheads, an index of increasing significance with the Johnson administration's decision to proceed with the development of MIRV (multiple independently-targetable re-entry vehicle) technology.

In the end, however, numbers and characteristics of weapons are not as significant as the attitudes of political leaders who control their use. In this respect, the turning point in the arms race may well have come with Nixon's first press conference as president, on January 27, 1969. In it, he explicitly renounced the goal of strategic "superiority," which he had strongly advocated during the campaign, in favor of "sufficiency," a concept Kissinger had supported. Nixon thereby served notice that he would not reverse the Johnson administration's tacit acceptance of Soviet numerical parity in ICBMs. The new chief executive had come to his decision for many of the same reasons his predecessor had: studies had shown that further increases in missile strength would provide little additional protection against a Soviet attack; such an effort would cost too much at a time when pressures were intensifying for cuts in the defense budget; and, finally, the Russians appeared capable of matching any new escalation of the arms race weapon for weapon.

Transforming a necessity into a virtue is easier, however, if one can avoid the appearance of having been pushed, and this Nixon and Kissinger skillfully did. The president coupled his blessing of "sufficiency" with the announcement that he would not proceed immediately into talks on the limitation of strategic weapons, stalled the previous year by the Soviet invasion of Czechoslovakia but now eagerly advocated by both the Russians and by former officials of the Johnson administration. He also announced, shortly thereafter, decisions to go ahead with construction of an American ABM system and to deploy MIRVs. The ABM program was almost certainly intended as a bargaining chip in future SALT [Strategic Arms Limitation Talks] negotiations: the costly system was untestable short of nuclear war and so provided little assurance of protection. The MIRVs were far more reliable; moreover, Kissinger doubted whether they would ever be included in a SALT agreement, since verification would require on-site inspection, something the Russians had always resisted. Only after carefully establishing what arms control measures they could accept without violating the standard of "sufficiency" did Nixon and Kissinger, in October, 1969, agree to begin SALT talks with the Russians the following month.

Several things are noteworthy about Kissinger's approach to SALT. He appears to have viewed the early discussions as an opportunity to "educate" the Soviet negotiators, who at times demonstrated a surprising unfamiliarity with their own strategic weapons systems and the intricacies of arms control issues generally. He did all he could to avoid bureaucratic delays—especially useful in this regard were what he called "building blocks," a series of proposals, all cleared in advance, which the American delegation could put before the Russians in various combinations without consulting Washington on each change of position. During the latter stages of the talks Kissinger relied heavily on "back channel" contacts with Moscow, carried on independently of and at times without the knowledge of the SALT negotiators for the purpose of clarifying positions. And, most important, Kissinger sought to circumvent the touchy issue of on-site inspection by focusing the talks on those weapons systems capable of being monitored by "national technical means"—a euphemism for satellite reconnaissance.

It would be difficult to say who came out on top in the strategic arms limitation agreements Nixon and [Soviet party chairman Leonid] Brezhnev signed in Moscow in May, 1972. On the one hand, the Russians, by agreeing to a mutual limitation of ABM deployments to two sites (one defending an ICBM emplacement, the other the national capital), in effect endorsed the long-standing American argument that stability in the nuclear arms race could best be attained by foregoing attempts to defend population centers. Approval of this "mutual assured destruction" concept (MAD) represented a significant change of attitude on the part of the security-conscious Soviet state. On the other hand, the imposition of a freeze on existing numbers of land-based and submarine-launched ballistic missiles constituted not just an acknowledgment of Soviet parity—it actually left the United States with a substantial numerical inferiority in ICBMs (1,618 versus 1,054) and a smaller one in SLBMs (740 versus 656). . . .

The United States could have responded to the Soviet achievement of parity by embarking on a new arms buildup of its own, but such a decision would have required a major escalation of the Cold War in return for only transitory benefits. It could, alternatively, have lapsed into some combination of isolationism and appeasement, but the disadvantages here, too, were obvious. A third option, the one actually followed, was to explore with the Soviet Union opportunities for declaring "off limits" certain areas of strategic weapons competition, to the extent that this could be done without adversely affecting the military balance. There is no reason to believe that the agreements reached at Moscow threatened that equilibrium; in fact, they probably reinforced it by removing the possibility of a race to develop ABMs and by limiting the further deployment of Soviet ICBMs and SLBMs. SALT may well have represented, then, the best of the available possibilities for coming to grips with the undeniable reality of Soviet strategic parity.

But if détente was the product of Soviet self-confidence growing out of the attainment of strategic parity, it also developed in large part from anxieties generated by chronic economic difficulties. Such problems were, of course, nothing new—dislocations stemming from the effort to make economics fit ideology had long been a prominent feature of life in the USSR. What was new was the leadership's awareness that the economic gap between Russia and the West was growing, particularly in the areas of advanced technological and managerial skills, at a time when it confronted the twin necessities of maintaining Soviet military strength while satisfying growing internal demands for consumer goods. Prospects for resolving this dilemma through autarkic means appeared increasingly unpromising; it began to look as though the Soviet Union would not be able to compete with the West without help from the West, in the form of trade, investment, and—most important—technology transfers. . . .

The Soviet leadership's interest in expanding trade with the West stemmed as much from considerations of security as from economics: riots over food prices in Poland the previous December had forced the resignation of Party Secretary Wladyslaw Gomulka and had very nearly provoked Soviet military intervention. This sobering demonstration of how internal discontent could shake the authority of the state was not lost on either Moscow or Washington: it was no accident that, three months later, the Twenty-Fourth Congress of the Soviet Communist Party endorsed a Five-Year Plan which, for the first time, emphasized raising consumer living standards over the needs of heavy industry. Nor was it fortuitous that, soon thereafter, the Nixon administration informed the Russians that it might be willing to loosen export restrictions in return for cooperation on outstanding political and military issues.

Although the overall volume of trade remained relatively small, considerable progress had been made by the end of 1972 in expanding Soviet-American economic ties. The Russians agreed to remedy an old grievance by making at least a token payment ($722 million over the next three decades) on their long-overdue World War II Lend-Lease debt; in return the Nixon administration promised to seek Export-Import Bank credits to finance Soviet purchases in the United States and the restoration by Congress of "most-favored-nation" tariff status to imports from the USSR, which had been withdrawn in 1951. Soviet buyers quietly placed orders for an astonishing 25% of the 1972 United States wheat crop—some 440 million bushels—to meet an unexpected shortfall in their own harvest. Several major American corporations, among them Pepsi-Cola and the Chase Manhattan Bank, made arrangements to open offices or manufacture their products in the Soviet Union; by mid-1973, even the First National City Bank, a prominent fixture of economic life in prerevolutionary Russia, had reopened its Moscow branch after an absence of fifty-one years. And in what may have been the most grandiose project of all, the Soviet government had opened negotiations with the El Paso Natural Gas Company and the Occidental Petroleum Company (the latter headed by Armand Hammer, one of the few successful foreign concessionaires in Russia during the 1920s) for a $10 billion, seven-year plan to build pipelines and tankers with which to transport Siberian natural gas to Japan and the United States.

The Nixon administration encouraged these trends on the assumption that a proliferation of economic relationships would render the Soviet Union dependent on American trade and technology, thereby lessening the danger of war. . . .

Fissures within the international communist movement also provided the Nixon administration with opportunities to encourage movement toward détente. There had been earlier efforts to exploit such fragmentation—Washington had long dealt with Yugoslavia almost as an ally, the Johnson administration had made similar overtures toward Eastern Europe—and throughout the Cold War American officials had known that the Sino-Soviet "alliance" only imperfectly concealed substantial Sino-Soviet differences. There had been no sustained effort to improve relations with the People's Republic of China, though, in part because of that state's unremitting hostility toward the United States and in part because both Kennedy and Johnson feared raising ghosts from the "who lost China" debates of the early 1950s. There is obvious irony in the fact that the president who made the breakthrough to Beijing had himself led the attack on the Democrats' China party two decades earlier. But Nixon's views on the subject had never been as dogmatic as his public rhetoric suggested: he had noted the importance of Sino-Soviet differences as early as 1954, and by 1967 he was arguing publicly against any policy that would seek to keep China indefinitely isolated.

Nixon entered the White House at a delicate moment in the history of Sino-Soviet relations: worried by the border clashes that had taken place along the Ussuri River—and perhaps recalling similar feelers in 1963 from the Kennedy administration—Soviet diplomats during the summer of 1969 began sounding out American officials on what Washington's response would be to a preemptive strike by the USSR on Chinese nuclear installations. In the course of the subsequent SALT talks, the Russians formally proposed what would have been in effect a Soviet-American alliance designed to discourage "provocative" actions by China.

Far from encouraging such cooperation with Moscow against Beijing, Nixon instead initiated a series of gestures aimed at bringing about a Sino-American reconciliation: these concluded with the surprise announcement in July, 1971, that Kissinger had secretly traveled to the Chinese capital to meet with Zhou Enlai, and that the President himself would soon follow. Both Nixon and Kissinger were careful to deny that their China "opening" was directed against the Russians, but there is little doubt that such considerations were present. "The worst thing that could happen for us," Nixon had told his staff in August, 1969, "would be for the Soviet Union to gobble up Red China. . . . We're not doing this because we love the Chinese. We just have to see to it that the U.S. plays both sides." In addition to maintaining the global balance of power, such tactics might induce Soviet cooperation on other issues. "They haven't helped on Vietnam, on the Mideast, on the arms talks," Nixon added. "We've got to give them a reason to help us."

The president's strategy of "linkage"—as this approach came to be known—never produced the results he expected from it, partly because he publicized it too widely and partly because he exaggerated Moscow's ability to shape events in the Middle East and Southeast Asia. But there are convincing indications that the China initiative did cause the Russians to speed up efforts to reach agreements on SALT; certainly it was responsible for the invitation, issued in October, 1971, for Nixon to visit Moscow the following spring after his return from Beijing. Brezhnev, in a speech delivered in March, 1972, described the Sino-American rapprochement as a "natural" development, although he could not help wondering whether Nixon's talks with the Chinese had not gone "beyond the framework of bilateral relations between the USA and China. How else is one to understand, for instance, the statement made during the banquet in Shanghai that 'today our two peoples hold the future of the world in their hands'?" It was the tone of a man resigned to relinquishing at last the luxury of having adversaries who despised each other more than they despised him.

"Linkage" did work in other ways, though. Attempts to solve the perennial German question had received a major boost in September, 1969, with the victory of the Social Democrats in West Germany and the emergence, as chancellor, of Willy Brandt. Three separate series of negotiations with the Russians soon got underway, with progress on each linked to developments in the others: (1) discussions between West Germany, Poland, and the Soviet Union confirming existing boundaries in Eastern Europe, including the controversial Oder-Neisse frontier—Brandt signed treaties to this effect with the Russians in August, 1970, and with the Poles the following December; (2) negotiations among the four powers occupying Berlin aimed at normalizing the position of that divided city—the resulting agreement, recognizing Western access rights there, was signed in September, 1971; and (3) contacts between representatives of NATO and the Warsaw Pact looking toward eventual talks on mutual and balanced force reductions (MBFR) and the Russians' long-sought Conference on Security and Cooperation in Europe (CSCE).

What emerged from these overlapping and interlocking negotiations was the outline of a European settlement based on tacit West German abandonment of reunification, Soviet recognition of the Western position in Berlin, a continued American military presence on the Continent, and a greater reliance than in the past on diplomacy as a means of resolving differences. These agreements by no means removed Europe from the arena of Cold War rivalries, but they did represent an acknowledgment by the major powers of the status quo there. And since postwar Soviet policy in Europe can be explained as much by fear of the Germans as of anyone else, this achievement of at least partial stabilization was no insignificant accomplishment.

"Linkage" also appeared to be an effective tool for "crisis management." Intelligence reports in September, 1970, indicated that the Russians might be building a nuclear submarine base in Cuba. Whatever its purpose, construction at the offending site soon stopped after Kissinger warned that such activity could impair prospects for détente. Another dangerous situation developed that same month in the Middle East, when Syrian tanks crossed into Jordan to aid Palestinian commandos in their struggle with King Hussein. "You and your client started it," Kissinger is said to have told a Soviet diplomat, "and you have to end it." Whether on Moscow's orders or not, the Syrians did turn back, but not before Kissinger had arranged for joint Israeli-Jordanian-American operations against both Syrian and Russian forces, if necessary. Fifteen months later, in December, 1971, war broke out between India and Pakistan over the secession from the latter of Bangladesh (formerly East Pakistan). Concerned over rumors that the Indians, with Soviet encouragement, might dismember West Pakistan as well, Kissinger threatened to cancel the forthcoming Moscow summit unless the Russians induced New Delhi to show restraint.

To what extent these crises actually reflected hostile intent on the part of the Soviet Union—or, alternatively, overreaction by the United States—is still not wholly clear. Certainly Washington appears to have exaggerated Soviet responsibility for the India-Pakistan confrontation (although this may have been done deliberately to impress the pro-Pakistani Chinese). What these incidents do illustrate is the administration's conviction that the Russians needed détente badly enough to pay a substantial price for it: that they would pass up opportunities to exploit specific crises at the expense of the West in order to make progress toward a general relaxation of tensions. . . .

No amount of adroit diplomacy could have produced the results achieved between 1969 and 1972 had not the circumstances been right—had not the Nixon administration had the good fortune to come to power at a time when the internal situations in the United States, the Soviet Union, and the People's Republic of China simultaneously favored détente. But auspicious circumstances are no guarantee of success in and of themselves; clumsy diplomacy has snatched failure from the jaws of triumph more than once. There was undeniably skill, as well as luck, in a foreign policy that expanded American freedom of action in the world at a time when American strategic power, relative to that of the Soviet Union, was declining. There was wisdom, as well as expediency, in a course of action that reverted to the original concept of containment: the conviction that only Soviet expansionism, not international communism, possessed the capacity to threaten American security, and that the United States could effectively weaken the former phenomenon by exploiting strains that existed within the latter. The future of détente would, of course, be at the mercy of both men and circumstances; its prospects for survival, however, would depend in large measure on the extent to which the agreements reached at Moscow matched the interests of the states whose statesmen signed them.

Curiously, few careful efforts were made, in either official or academic circles in the United States, to define "détente" until after that policy had been mutually endorsed by Nixon and Brezhnev at the 1972 Moscow summit. This lapse stemmed partly from the hope that there would be no substantive differences in the way Soviet and American leaders understood the term; partly too, one suspects, from fear that too close an investigation might expose just such contradictions. Once the belated exercise was carried out, it was discovered that while areas of congruence did exist, there were also important discrepancies in the behavior each side expected of the other. Clarification of these by no means destroyed "détente," but it did lead to a gradual scaling-down of expectations—to a realization that despite progress made, much remained to be done before the word could accurately be regarded as a synonym for "rapprochement." . . .

It would, perhaps, have been too much to expect the general secretary of the Soviet Communist Party to disavow the class struggle, even in an era of détente, but there did exist in Washington the expectation that the Kremlin would continue to cooperate in "managing" crises generated by third parties in order to prevent escalation that might involve the superpowers. "The leaders of the Soviet Union are serious men," Nixon noted in May, 1973: "Their willingness to commit themselves to certain principles for the future must be taken as a solemn obligation." Within five months, that assumption would be called into serious question.

There is no evidence that the Soviet Union instigated the October 6, 1973, attack on Israel by Egypt and Syria or the oil embargo against Israel's supporters in the West that the Arab members of the Organization of Petroleum Exporting Countries (OPEC) imposed several days later. But Soviet behavior during this crisis did seem difficult to reconcile with the "code of conduct" Nixon and Brezhnev had agreed upon the previous year. Despite advance knowledge of the attack by at least 48 hours, the Russians made no explicit effort to warn Washington. Nor did they seek to restrain the Egyptians and Syrians from initiating hostilities or make any moves to encourage a cease-fire until it had become clear that the Israelis were going to win. Moscow welcomed the OPEC embargo, a tactic it had been advocating in broadcasts to the Arab world for some time. And, on October 24, angered by Israeli violations of a cease-fire that Kissinger and the Russians had now arranged, Brezhnev in a harsh note to Nixon proposed dispatching a Soviet-American peacekeeping force to the Middle East. "I will say it straight," he added: "If you find it impossible to act jointly with us in this matter, we should be faced with the necessity urgently to consider the question of taking appropriate steps unilaterally."

Alarmed by this development—but also preoccupied to the point of almost total distraction by the rapidly intensifying Watergate crisis—Nixon authorized Kissinger late that evening to order a worldwide Defense Condition 3 military alert (DefCon 1 is war), news of which became public the following morning. The White House coupled this with a note to Brezhnev warning that unilateral action in the Middle East could threaten détente and suggesting instead the dispatch of a United Nations peacekeeping force from which the big powers would be excluded. Brezhnev denied plans for unilateral intervention and accused Nixon of fabricating the crisis, but as the Egyptian-Israeli cease-fire began to take hold, tensions eased and both sides reiterated their commitment to détente. The episode had shown clearly, though, that Moscow's cooperation in managing third-party crises would extend only to preventing escalation to nuclear war, not to foregoing opportunities to exploit such developments at the expense of the West.

This pattern of behavior showed up in other areas as well. Détente proved to be of little value in extricating the United States gracefully from the Vietnam War:

although the Russians may have helped arrange the January, 1973, cease-fire, they were either unwilling or unable to prevent the North Vietnamese from launching the series of offensives that finally overwhelmed South Vietnam and Cambodia two years later, thereby inflicting a humiliating defeat upon the United States. Nor could the Russians resist passing up opportunities created by the April, 1974, revolution in Portugal: they not only funneled aid to Portuguese communists in their unsuccessful bid for power but also sought to fill the vacuum created by the resulting collapse of Portugal's African empire by supporting Marxist factions in Mozambique and Angola. The latter enterprise even involved the dispatch of Cuban mercenaries, a move Secretary of State Kissinger denounced in January, 1976, as "counter to the crucial principles of avoidance of unilateral advantage and scrupulous concern for the interests of others which we have jointly enunciated."

But Soviet officials, too, had reason to complain that détente had not met their expectations. . . . Nixon had regarded Soviet willingness to repay World War II Lend-Lease debts as sufficient compensation for extending Export-Import Bank credits and "most-favored-nation" tariff treatment (MFN), but Congress had to approve these moves and quickly made it clear that it considered the price too low. In October, 1972, Senator Henry M. Jackson of Washington introduced an amendment to the Trade Reform Act denying credits and MFN to "nonmarket economies" that taxed or restricted the emigration of their citizens; Congressman Charles Vanik of Ohio had earlier proposed similar legislation in the House of Representatives. It required little imagination to realize that this obliquely worded measure was aimed at Soviet practices regarding Jewish emigration, or to conclude from its list of seventy-two Senate cosponsors that it had excellent chances of passage. Administration officials spent much of the next two years in parallel negotiations, with the Russians to get them to raise emigration levels and with Jackson to get him to modify his amendment on the grounds that the trade bill was an inappropriate instrument with which to try to reform Soviet society. Jackson was able to claim a major victory on October 18, 1974, when he announced that the Russians had agreed to allow at least 60,000 Jewish emigrants to leave the Soviet Union each year in return for Eximbank credits and MFN.

The Senator spoke too soon, though, for on January 10, 1975, shortly after final Congressional passage of the trade bill, the Russians abruptly rejected the entire economic package that had been under discussion since 1972—tariffs, credits, and Lend-Lease debts. Soviet leaders took this action, one suspects, not so much from fear of relaxing emigration requirements as from reluctance to yield to external pressure on a sensitive internal matter. The dangers of establishing such a precedent apparently outweighed the relatively marginal benefits promised by MFN and Eximbank credits, especially after Congress in December (in a further amendment offered by Senator Adlai E. Stevenson III of Illinois) cut the latter back to $300 million, a figure most experts regarded as unreasonably low. The legislators' effort to tie increased trade to increased emigration raised the price of the first commodity beyond what the Russians were willing to grant in terms of the second, with the result that neither side achieved either. . . .

Congress also intervened—again with Senator Jackson taking the lead—to shape the future course of arms control negotiations. The 1972 SALT I agreements had allowed the Russians a numerical superiority of 564 ICBMs and 84 SLBMs over what would be available to the United States: this imbalance had reflected the number of launchers deployed on each side at that time, together with the assumption that American missiles—many of which now carried multiple war-heads—were more accurate than their Soviet counterparts. Jackson perceived, quite correctly as it turned out, that the Russians would soon catch up in both guid-ance and MIRV technology, and late in 1972 secured passage of a Congressional resolution demanding that future SALT agreements would provide for numerical equality in weapons systems on both sides. This requirement for across-the-board parity created problems in discussions with Moscow because of the quite different characteristics of the two nations' strategic arsenals: neither military establishment was eager to configure its forces according to the other's pattern. Nor was it at all clear how such compliance with such a rule might be verified, since some weapons could be more easily detected from satellites than others. But the domestic political appeal of parity was unquestionable, and it became clear as a consequence that any future SALT II treaty would have to incorporate that principle.

With this constraint in mind, President Gerald R. Ford met with Brezhnev out-side Vladivostok in November, 1974, three months after Nixon's resignation: there they agreed on a general set of guidelines for SALT II that imposed an overall mu-tual limitation of 2,400 strategic delivery systems, including ICBMs, SLBMs, and heavy bombers; within that limit, no more than 1,320 ICBMs and SLBMs could carry multiple warheads. But because this accord provided numerical parity only in aggregate terms, not in individual categories of weapons, it went only part of the way toward meeting Jackson's requirement; moreover, Ford and Brezhnev failed to agree on whether the aggregates would cover such new systems as the American cruise missile, a subsonic but cheap and highly-accurate weapon, or the Soviet Backfire bomber, which Western analysts claimed might have the range to fly intercontinental missions. No further progress would be made on these issues through the remainder of Ford's term.

If détente is looked upon solely as a bargaining process, then evidence from the years 1972–1976 would tend to sustain the argument that the Russians handled themselves more shrewdly than did their American rivals. Détente imposed no sig-nificant limitations on the Soviet Union's ability to intervene by proxy in Third World areas, nor did rejection of the 1972 trade package deny them access to American agriculture or to Western technology. Internally, the Soviet regime be-came less tolerant of dissent than before, with the result that such figures as [the novelist] Alexander Solzhenitsyn and [the physicist] Andrei Sakharov emerged as vigorous critics of détente. That policy produced no reduction in Soviet military expenditures, which continued to rise relative to gross national product while by the same standard American military spending declined. And, at the Conference on Security and Cooperation in Europe, held in Helsinki on July 30–August 1, 1975, the Russians in return for an unenforceable promise to respect human rights suc-cessfully capped a twenty-year campaign by securing the signatures of the United States and its NATO allies on a document affirming the "inviolability" of—and thereby appearing to legitimize—all existing boundaries in Europe.

Meanwhile, American policy seemed paralyzed by indecision and self-doubt, products of the twin traumas of Vietnam and Watergate. Despite Israel's victory in the Middle East war, the United States found itself deferring respectfully to oil-rich sheiks and potentates suddenly possessed of the capacity to wreck havoc with its economy, not to mention those of its European and Japanese allies. . . .

These developments, to be sure, lay more in the realm of symbolism than of substance, but in political campaigns symbolism can have substantive effects. The perception that the Nixon and Ford administrations—and Kissinger in particular— had been too accommodating toward the Soviet Union led California governor Ronald Reagan to challenge Ford for the 1976 Republican presidential nomination. The president, now very much on the defensive, at first defended "détente," but then in March announced his intention to drop the use of the term altogether. At the Republican convention later that summer, Reagan came remarkably close to denying Ford renomination; his forces did succeed in inserting into the party platform language that pointedly praised Solzhenitsyn, condemned "secret agreements," and described the Helsinki agreements as "taking from those who do not have freedom the hope of one day getting it." Ford himself inadvertently sharpened his image of gullibility by claiming, during a televised debate with Democratic presidential candidate Jimmy Carter, in October, that "there is no Soviet domination of Eastern Europe": the gaffe may well have cost Ford the election. . . .

But things are not always what they seem to be in diplomacy. Thanks to Kissinger's efforts, it turned out to have been Soviet and not American influence that declined in the Middle East following the 1973 Arab-Israeli War; similar trends would, in time, emerge in southern Africa and in Southeast Asia as well. Vietnam and Watergate would come to be seen as less than total losses for the United States: the first because it brought an end to indiscriminate globalism in American foreign policy; the second because it demonstrated, in a way few other countries could have managed, the supremacy of constitutional processes over individual leaders, however powerful. The Helsinki declaration came to be remembered less for its implied recognition of Russian hegemony in Eastern Europe than for the standard its human rights provisions established against which to measure the Soviet Union's treatment of its own citizens and those of its satellites. In short, the phenomenon of "unintended consequence," which has shaped so many aspects of Soviet-American relations, should have been enough to give responsible analysts pause before jumping to the conclusion that the Russians had surged far ahead in the great "game" of détente.

For the fact was that détente was not a game from which one side or the other had to emerge victorious: it was rather a process by which the superpowers agreed to *refrain* from competition in certain areas, while continuing it in others. Its durability would depend on the extent to which agreements not to compete could be reconciled with perceived interests on each side and on the ability of the competitors, in areas where competition still persisted, to keep it limited. It was not likely, in and of itself, to alter decisively existing world power relationships: by its very nature it ruled out dramatic coups by one side at the expense of the other. Moreover, to an increasing degree, influence in international affairs was coming to be the product of circumstances only partly within the control of the superpowers. What détente could do was to lessen the danger of war by preventing competition in one area from producing escalation in another, while functioning simultaneously to identify and expand such congruities of interest as existed. As such, it represented progress toward the goal of "graduated reciprocation in tension reduction"; but beyond that it would not have been wise to claim too much.

Why Détente Failed

RAYMOND L. GARTHOFF

The mix of cooperation and competition in American-Soviet relations makes it difficult to define the period of détente precisely. Despite President Nixon's early call for an era of negotiation, a series of confrontations in the ensuing three-and-a-half years made progress toward that goal slow. Then, in mid-1972, the first Nixon-Brezhnev summit meeting took place, and détente suddenly blossomed. During the next few years, a flood of cooperative ventures was inaugurated, culminating symbolically in 1975 in a joint space rendezvous, and accompanied by a great deal of rhetoric about peaceful coexistence and partnership in building a structure of peace.

Although cooperation developed in a number of areas, particularly from 1972 to 1975, it never supplanted ongoing competition nor offered sufficient guarantee against renewed confrontation. From the American perspective, one important cause of the decline of détente was the active Soviet role in Africa and South Asia after 1975. Growing concern over the strategic balance from 1976 on was an equally important source of disenchantment. From the Soviet perspective, successive U.S. administrations were seen as conducting a vigorous policy of containing and curtailing Soviet influence, especially in the Middle East, from the very beginning of détente. Moreover, the U.S. Congress had dashed expectations for economic benefits promised and even granted by the Nixon administration by making them conditional on unacceptable and humiliating concessions concerning internal Soviet affairs, specifically, escalating demands for Jewish emigration. Finally, in the period from 1977 on, the Soviet leaders perceived a growing American attempt to regain strategic superiority.

Was détente a potential solution to the risks and costs of confrontation, a solution undercut by actions of the Soviet Union, or of the United States, or both? Or did détente exacerbate the problem by providing only a disarming illusion of an alternative? Was détente a Soviet snare to lull American sensitivity to a buildup of Soviet military power and political-military expansion? Did the United States and the Soviet Union ever have a common understanding of détente—or did they hold differing conceptions that were incompatible from the start? Did détente fail? Was it ever really tested?. . .

Détente, while the shorthand description for the policies subscribed to by both powers in the 1970s, was not a clearly defined concept held in common. It became increasingly evident, beginning even in the early 1970s when détente was at a high point, that Washington and Moscow had very different conceptions of what a détente policy entailed, and had had from the outset. The expectations of both sides in turn differed greatly. And as their respective expectations were not met, disillusionment with the performance of the other side followed. Moreover, in the United States (although not in the Soviet Union) disillusionment with the very idea of détente itself also followed. . . .

From *Détente and Confrontation: American-Soviet Relations from Nixon to Reagan* by Raymond L. Garthoff, 1994, The Brookings Institution, pp. 2, 24, 25, 1069–1074, 1077–1088. Reprinted by permission of the publisher.

Détente is a French word that actually means a "relaxation of tension" in a literal way—as with the release of a bowstring. Long ago it came to be used in diplomatic parlance to represent an easing of strained or tense relations between states. It is distinguished from another French word, *entente,* which represents a positive development of close and cooperative relations. Much of the confusion in American understanding seems to have stemmed from a tendency to interpret détente as though it meant entente. The Soviets have used a term of their own, *razryadka napryazhennosti,* or simply *razryadka,* also meaning a lessening or relaxation of tension.

The term détente had been used in the 1960s to describe steps aimed at lessening tension in East-West relations. In particular, it had been used by President Charles de Gaulle [of France] in the mid-1960s, and in the North Atlantic Treaty Organization (NATO) in the latter 1960s as one element in an alliance policy calling for balancing defense and détente. The first use of the term to describe the specific efforts launched by President Richard M. Nixon in 1969 (and, in a sense, by the Soviet Union at about the same time) to improve American-Soviet relations is elusive.

Indeed, the Nixon administration went to some lengths to avoid using the word détente. Instead, Nixon and his assistant for national security affairs, Henry A. Kissinger, spoke of "a new era," of substituting negotiations for confrontation, and of pursuing a "structure of peace" through mutual accommodation. By 1973–74, however, détente came to be used in the United States officially as well as popularly as a shorthand term describing the new policy. . . .

Foremost among the causes of the ultimate failure of détente in the 1970s was a fatal difference in the conception of its basic role by the two sides. The American leaders saw it (in Kissinger's words) as a way of "managing the emergence of Soviet power" into world politics in an age of nuclear parity. The Soviet leaders envisaged it as a way of managing the transition of the United States from its former superiority to a more modest role in world politics in an age of nuclear parity. Thus each saw itself as the manager of a transition of the other. Moreover, while the advent of parity ineluctably meant some decrease in the ability of the United States to manage world affairs, this fact was not sufficiently appreciated in Washington. And while it meant a relatively more important role for the Soviet Union, it did not mean acquisition of the kind of power the United States wielded. Finally, both had diverging images of the world order, and although that fact was well enough understood, its implications were not. Thus, underlying the attempts by each of the two powers to manage the adjustment of the other to a changing correlation of forces in the world there were even more basic parallel attempts by both to modify the fundamental world order—in different directions.

The Soviet leaders, conditioned by their Marxist-Leninist ideology, believed that a certain historical movement would ultimately lead to the replacement of capitalism (imperialism) in the world by socialism (communism). But they realized this transition would have to occur in a world made incalculably more dangerous by massive arsenals of nuclear weapons. Peaceful coexistence and détente were seen as offering a path to neutralize this danger by ruling out war between states, permitting historical change to occur, as the Soviets believed it must, through fundamental indigenous social-economic-political processes within states. While

Marxist-Leninists did not shun the use of any other instrument of power if it was expedient, they did not see military power as the fundamental moving force of history. On the contrary, they saw it as a possible ultimate recourse of the doomed capitalist class ruling the imperialist citadels of the West. There was, therefore, no ideological barrier to or reservation about pursuing a policy of détente aimed at preventing nuclear war. Quite the contrary—détente represented a policy aimed at providing stability to a world order that allowed progressive historical change.

The American leadership and the American people, not holding a deterministic ideology, while self-confident, were much less sure of the trend of history. Insofar as they held an ideology for a global order, it was one of pluralism. That ideology did not assume the whole world would choose an American-style democratic and free enterprise system. The world order has been seen as one that should provide stability and at least protect the democratic option for peoples. Occasionally during the Cold War there were crusades to extirpate communism in the world. . . . But the dominant American aim was to contain and deter Soviet or Soviet-controlled communist expansion at the expense of a pluralistic and, in that sense, "free" world order. What varied and periodically was at issue was the relative weight to be placed, on the one hand, on containment achieved by building positions of counterposing power, and on the other, on cooperation, pursued by seeking common ground for mutual efforts to reduce tension and accommodate the differing interests of the two sides. There were varied judgments in both countries about whether objective circumstances permit the latter approach or require the former, and therefore about whether détente was feasible or confrontation was necessary.

When Nixon and Kissinger developed a strategy of détente to replace a strategy of confrontation, the underlying expectation was that as the Soviet Union became more and more extensively engaged in an organic network of relations with the existing world order, it would gradually become reconciled to that order. Ideological expectations of global revolutionary change would become attenuated and merely philosophical rather than actively political. Avoidance of the risks of nuclear war was essential; hence there was acceptance of peaceful coexistence and of efforts at strategic arms limitations and other negotiations to reduce the risks.

The common American and Soviet recognition of the need to avert war was . . . of fundamental significance. But there remained radically different visions of the course world history would follow and, therefore, of the pattern of world politics. This divergence in their worldviews naturally affected the policies of the two powers. The difference was well-known in a general way; its implications for the two superpowers' respective actions, and therefore for their mutual relations and for détente, were not, however, sufficiently understood. And this gap led to unrealistic expectations that were not met and that undermined confidence in détente. . . .

The United States did not analyze critically the underlying postulates of either American or Soviet conceptions—nor, indeed, could that be done before they were more clearly articulated. For example, consider the proposition held by the Soviet leaders until 1986 that "the class struggle" and "national liberation struggle" were not and could not be affected by détente. With the exception of a minuscule minority that accepted the Soviet line uncritically, almost all Americans saw that proposition as communist mumbo jumbo being used as a transparently self-serving argument to excuse pursuit of Soviet interests. In fact, Soviet leaders considered that proposition to be a self-evident truth: détente was a policy, while the class struggle was an objective phenomenon in the historical process that could not be abolished by policy decision, even if the Soviet leaders wanted to do so. While there *was* a self-serving dimension to the Soviet proposition, it was not cynical artifice. To the contrary, it was sincerely believed. On a logical plane, to whatever extent the Soviet premise was true, it was crystal clear that any inevitable historical process could not be stopped by any state's policy or agreement between the two states.

It was not necessary to assume a prior meeting of the minds of the leaders of the two powers on ideological conceptions as a prerequisite to agreements based on calculated mutual advantage. While ideological conditioning and belief did influence policy, they did not determine it. Questions about the historical process can and should be left to history. The critical question was not whether there was a global class struggle or national liberation struggle, as defined by Marxism-Leninism, but what the Soviet leadership was going to do about it. While the Soviet leadership accepted a moral commitment to aid the world revolutionary process, it was also ideologically obliged to do so only in ways that did not weaken or risk the attainments of socialism in the USSR. Moreover, the ideology also held that world revolutionary processes were indigenous. Revolution could not be exported. Neither could counterrevolution. But both could be aided by external forces. . . .

In approaching the question of what was a proper and consistent code of conduct with respect to Soviet—and American—behavior in the third world, each side needed to understand the perspective of the other. Each, naturally, retained its own view of the historical process, as well as its own national interests. Differences of concrete interests remained to be reconciled, but failure to understand each other's viewpoint seriously compounded the problem.

A second cause of the collapse of détente was the failure to turn to greater use of collaborative measures to meet the requirements of security. National military power was bound to remain a foundation of national security in the foreseeable future. But it did not need to be the first, or usual, or sole, recourse. The American-Soviet détente involved efforts to prevent and to manage crises, and to regulate the military balance through arms control and arms limitation. In the final analysis, however, those efforts—while useful and potentially significant—were almost entirely dependent on the political relationship, and in large measure withered with it.

The effort to achieve strategic arms limitations marked the first, and the most daring, attempt to follow a collaborative approach in meeting military security requirements. It involved an unprecedented joint consideration of ways to control the most vital (or fatal) element of national power—the arsenals of strategic nuclear weaponry. Early successes held great promise—but also showed the limits of readiness of both superpowers to take this path. SALT [Strategic Arms Limitation Talks] generated problems of its own and provided a focal point for objection by those who did not wish to see either regulated military parity or political détente. The final lesson of the failure to ratify SALT II was that arms control could not stand alone nor sustain a political détente that did not support itself. Indeed, even the early successes of SALT I, which contributed to an upsurge of détente and were worthwhile on their own merits, became a bone of contention as détente came under fire.

The widely held American view that SALT tried to do too much was a misjudgment: the *real* flaw was the failure of SALT to do enough. There were remarkable initial successes in the agreement on parity as an objective and on stability of the strategic arms relationship as a necessary condition, and the control imposed on strategic defensive competition in ABM [Anti-Ballistic Missile] systems. But there was insufficient political will (and perhaps political authority) to bite the bullet and ban or sharply limit MIRVs [Multiple Independently-targetable Reentry Vehicles]—the key to controlling the strategic offensive arms race. Both sides share the blame for this failure, but especially the United States because it led a new round of the arms competition when it could safely have held back (in view of the ABM Treaty) long enough to make a real effort to ban MIRVs. The failure to control MIRVs was ultimately the key to the essential failure in the 1970s to stabilize the military dimension of parity, and it contributed indirectly to the overall fall of détente.

Too little attention has been paid to the efforts in the 1970s to devise a regime of crisis management and crisis avoidance. Paradoxically, the relatively more successful steps in this direction are rarely remembered because they do not seize attention as do political frictions. The agreements of 1971 on averting war by accident or miscalculation and on upgrading the hot line, the agreement of 1972 on avoiding incidents at sea between the U.S. and Soviet navies, and the agreement of 1973 on prevention of nuclear war played a positive role. (In addition, so did multilateral confidence-building measures in the European security framework.) The one instance sometimes charged to have been a failure of collaboration was in fact, if anything, a success: the defusing of the pseudocrisis between the two superpowers in October 1973 at the climax of the fourth Arab-Israeli war.

A third cause of the failure of American-Soviet détente in the 1970s was the inability of the superpowers to transform the recognition of strategic parity into a common political standard to govern their competitive actions in the world. The divergent conceptions of détente and of the world order underlay this failure, but these were compounded by other factors. One was the unreadiness of the United States, in conceding nominal strategic parity, also to concede political parity. Another was a reciprocated hubris in which each superpower applied a one-sided double standard in perceiving, and judging, the behavior of the other. The basic principles of mutual relations and a code of conduct were never thrashed out with the necessary frank discussion of differing views, a failure that gave rise to a facade of agreement that not only affected public, but to some extent even leadership, expectations. Expectations based on wishful thinking about the effects of the historical process, or based on overconfidence about a country's managerial abilities to discipline the behavior of the other side, were doomed to failure. Paradoxically, these inflated expectations coexisted—on both sides—with underlying excessive and projected fears and imputations of aggressive hostility, which resurfaced when the expectations were not met. That this process influenced wider political constituencies (a much wider body politic in the United States) only compounded a situation that affected the leadership as well. . . .

The consistent failure of each side to sense and recognize the different perspectives and perceptions of the other was strongly detrimental to the development of their relations, compounding their real differences. The dangers of the failure of each side to recognize the effects of its own misperceptions were also too little appreciated, as were the dangers of its failure to perceive the implications of differing perceptions and misperceptions. . . . Rather than recognize a differing perception, judging it to be a valid alternative perception, or misperception, both sides typically ascribed a different and usually malevolent purpose to each other. This tendency, for example, characterized the assessments each made of the military programs of the other, as well as of many of its political moves. Even when attempts were made to take account of different ways of thinking, on each side the usual approach was to apply respective stereotypes of "communist" or "imperialist" modes of calculation to the other side, but in a superficial way that stressed the expansionist or aggressive image of the adversary. The result was usually no more than to provide a self-satisfying illusion that the perceptual factor had been taken into account.

In the United States, many in the 1970s saw a cumulative series of Soviet interventions, involving military means, often with proxies—Angola, Ethiopia, Kampuchea, Afghanistan—that they believed formed a pattern of Soviet expansion and aggrandizement inconsistent with the Basic Principles [a May 1972 Soviet-American agreement to practice restraint in their relations] and détente. Moreover, many believed that these expansionist moves were encouraged by détente, or were at least induced by a weakness of U.S. will and military power. Hence the need to rebuild that power and reassert that will; hence the heightened suspicion of détente.

In fact, the history of diplomatic, political, and interventionist activity during the last decade [1970s] is much more extensive and complex—and much less one-sided. Certainly from the Soviet perspective, not only was the Soviet role more limited and more justified than the United States would concede, but the American role was more active and less benign. . . .

In the Middle East, the United States arranged the defection of Sadat's Egypt—and of the Sudan, Somalia, and to some degree Iraq. It effectively squeezed the Soviet Union out of a role in the Middle East peace process, despite repeated assurances that it would not do so. . . . In Africa, U.S. allies and proxies repeatedly and blatantly intervened with military force—Portugal before 1974; France in numerous cases; France, Belgium, Morocco, and Egypt in Zaire; Zaire, South Africa and others in Angola in 1975–76, albeit unsuccessfully; and so forth. Using covert operations, the United States assisted in the overthrow of an elected Marxist, [Salvador] Allende, in Chile and, with European assistance, of the Marxist-supported [Arelino] Gonçalves in Portugal. . . .

The deterioration of relations during the latter half of the 1970s not only reflected some of these developments but also contributed to them. For the most part the actions of the two powers stemmed not from Soviet or American initiatives, but as responses to local events.

There were, however, also conscious policies of assertive competition by both powers throughout the period of nominal détente. Recall, for example, the U.S. policy initiatives in the immediate aftermath of the first summit meeting in Moscow in 1972, the summit that launched détente. President Nixon flew directly from the Soviet Union to Iran. One purpose of his visit was to establish the shah [of Iran] as, in effect, American proconsul in the region, in keeping with the Nixon

Doctrine. The shah was promised virtually any American arms he wanted. A contributory reason for the shah's deputation that was not apparent was to follow through on some conversations with the Chinese and to signal to them U.S. intention to build regional positions of strength around the Soviet Union, détente notwithstanding. In addition, while in Tehran the president accepted the shah's proposal covertly to arm the Iraqi Kurds. (Iraq had just signed a Treaty of Friendship with the Soviet Union.) Thus the Kurds became proxies of the United States and Iran (and of Israel, which joined in providing support in order to tie the Iraqi army down). And there was a later chapter to this American initiative: the shah persuaded and induced President Mohammad Daoud of Afghanistan in 1975–78 to move away from his previous close alignment with the Soviet Union, to improve relations with Pakistan, and to crack down on Afghan leftists. . . . That led the [pro-Soviet] Khalq military faction to mount a coup and depose him, turning the government over to the People's Democratic Party and setting in train the developments within Afghanistan that culminated in the Soviet intervention.

From Iran President Nixon flew to Poland, where he was greeted by stirring public acclaim, demonstratively showing not only that the United States would support more or less nonaligned communist regimes (Nixon had visited Romania in 1969 and Yugoslavia in 1970, as well as China in 1972), but also that no part of the Soviet alliance was out of bounds to American interest under détente.

As a direct result of the U.S. handling of the Middle East question at the détente summit meeting, [Anwar el-]Sadat [president of Egypt]—who was already secretly in touch with the United States—six weeks later expelled the 20,000 Soviet military advisers (and Soviet reconnaissance aircraft) from Egypt.

Only a few months later, in September 1972, China and Japan—with American encouragement—renewed diplomatic relations. And in December new armed clashes occurred on the Sino-Soviet border.

Further, upon President Nixon's return to Washington from the summit he urged not only ratification of the SALT I agreements, but also an increase in strategic arms. Secretary of Defense [Melvin R.] Laird even conditioned his support for SALT on congressional approval of new military programs, which he justified as necessary so as to be able to negotiate "from a position of strength," wittingly or not invoking a key symbol of the Cold War.

It is not the purpose of this brief recapitulation of some examples of vigorous American competitive activity to argue either that the *Soviet* perception of American responsibility for the decline and fall of détente is justified, or that the United States was wrong to compete with the Soviet Union (individual actions were wise or unwise on their merits, and good or bad in their consequences—as is true of various Soviet actions). But Americans need to recognize that not only the Soviet Union but also the United States was "waging détente" in the 1970s—and that it was not justified in concluding that the Soviet Union was violating some agreed, clear, and impartial standard to which the United States in practice adhered. This same point about the application of a double standard equally needed to be recognized in the Soviet Union, and equally was not.

Both sides in fact sought advantages. Surely Nixon and Kissinger, and Brezhnev and [Soviet foreign minister Andrei] Gromyko, never believed that the other side, or that *either* side, would fail to seek advantages at the expense of the other just because they had agreed, in a document on Basic Principles on Mutual Relations, that "efforts to obtain unilateral advantage at the expense of the other, directly or indirectly, are inconsistent with these objectives" (those objectives being "reciprocity, mutual accommodation and mutual benefit"). . . .

Both the United States and the Soviet Union acted in ways contrary to the spirit and letter of a code of conduct for détente as set forth in the Basic Principles to which both had committed themselves in 1972. Each saw its own actions as compatible with pursuit of a *realistic* policy of détente. Each, however, sought to hold the other side to its own *idealized* view of détente. As a result, each was disappointed in and critical of the actions of the other. The Soviet leaders, however, adjusted their expectations more realistically, seeing no better alternative than to continue an imperfect détente. This was the Soviet judgment even though the United States was seen as taking advantage of détente in the continuing competition, and even though détente proved less of a restraint on the United States than the Soviets had hoped and expected. . . .

The essence of détente, as a practical proposition, was an agreement on mutual accommodation to a political competition in which each side would limit its actions in important (but unfortunately not well-defined) ways in recognition of the common shared interest in avoiding the risks of uncontrolled confrontation. Détente called for political adjustments, both negotiated and unilateral. It did not involve a classical division of the world into spheres of hegemonic geopolitical interests. Rather, it was a compact calling for self-restraint on each side in recognition of the interests of the other to the extent necessary to prevent sharp confrontation. While this general concept and approach were accepted by both sides, regrettably each side had differing conceptions of the proper restraint it—and the other side—should assume. This discrepancy led later to reciprocal feelings of having been let down by the other side. From the outset there was insufficient recognition of the need for more frank exchanges of views and collaboration in dealing with differences of interest. With time, these efforts collapsed. Both sides showed that they were not ready to accommodate the interests of the other. An additional complicating factor was the inability of the U.S. leadership to manage and control its own policy. But more important, on both sides there was a serious gap, even inability, to perceive the viewpoint and interests of the other. This gap grew, rather than lessened, with time and experience. As a consequence, trust—which was never very great—declined. . . .

Many developments during the period under review bear witness to the importance of evaluating correctly the intentions, and not merely the capabilities or ambitions, of the other power. . . . If one side is in fact motivated by an expansionist impulse, then a forceful advance stand in opposition or retaliatory response *is* called for and can sometimes be effective. If, however, the action—no matter how reprehensible and forcible—is motivated by fear of a threat or loss, a vigorous show of strength and threats of counteraction may in fact *contribute* to the perceived threat and hence to the very moves that the other side wants to deter. By contrast, measures to allay the unfounded fears might have been a more effective course. It thus becomes highly important to assess, and assess correctly, the intentions and motivations of the other side.

The importance of assessment is that it not only applies to a specific situation, but also affects the lessons drawn from that experience. The easy conclusion often reached about Soviet moves adverse to American interests (especially by critics but sometimes also by incumbent administrations) was to question whether the United States possessed sufficient strength and had demonstrated clearly enough its readiness to use it. Sometimes that may have been the relevant question. But the record strongly suggests that more often it was not American strength and resolve that Soviet leaders have doubted, but American restraint and recognition of Soviet interests.

If international tension is seen as the product of perceived threats, détente can be characterized as the reduction of threat perceptions. . . .

Both powers also were reluctant to acknowledge, even to recognize, failures of their own political systems. Instead, they were only too ready to project responsibility onto the other side. Thus, for example, Soviet claims of American responsibility for internal opposition in Afghanistan and Poland served (among other purposes) as an alibi for failures of Soviet-style socialism. American charges of Cuban and Soviet responsibility for revolution in Central America were similarly more convenient than acknowledging failures of reactionary regimes to provide for needed peaceful change. In addition to reflecting genuine fears based on perceived vulnerabilities, it was simply easier to project hostile intervention than to admit failures to facilitate or permit peaceful change within respective areas of predominant influence.

Thus, apart from differing conceptions of détente, there were very important differences in perceptions not only of the motivations of the other side, but of the very reality of world politics. Détente should have been recognized as one complex *basis* for a competitive relationship, not as an alternative to competition. That was the reality, and the fact should have been recognized.

During much of the 1970s American perceptions of what was occurring in the world failed to reflect reality. One example was the failure of the United States to see that it was waging a vigorous competition along with the Soviet Union. And the U.S. leadership to varying degrees was more aware of the realities than the public. . . . But even the practitioners of hardheaded détente often failed to recognize the whole reality. Political critics also either did not see, or did not wish to acknowledge, reality. The desire to sustain public support for policy by using a myth of détente (and of conformity with idealistic goals) also inhibited public awareness that the United States was competing as much as the Soviet Union. The result was a shift of public opinion as détente *seemed* not to be safeguarding and serving American interests. Ronald Reagan's challenge to President Ford in 1976 marked the first significant political manifestation of this shift. Although the challenge did not succeed, it did lead Ford to shelve SALT and to jettison the very word détente. By 1980 this shift contributed (along with domestic economic and other concerns, and President Carter's ineptness and plain bad luck) to Reagan's victory and open American renunciation of détente.

Naiveté was charged to the advocates of détente. But while some may have had unrealistic aims and expectations, the American leaders and practitioners of détente . . . were not as naive as were the critics and challengers who preferred to remain blind both to the strength and vigor of U.S. global competition and to the limits on Soviet power and policy. The critics of détente saw both American and Soviet power and its exercise from opposite ends of a telescope—a greatly exaggerated image of relentless Soviet buildup and use of power in a single-minded offensive expansionist policy, and a grossly distorted image of U.S. passivity and impotence in the world.

This U.S. perspective contributed to American-European differences and frictions. The European powers (and most other countries in the world as well) had a much more balanced perception. Although they still exaggerated the Soviet threat, at least they recognized more accurately the active American role in competition—often they were concerned over what they saw as excessive competition. For the Europeans had (and have) a very different view of the cooperative element in détente, valuing more highly than most Americans the potential for economic, political, social, and arms control gains and the realities of cooperation under détente. . . . Even as such key European countries as Britain and West Germany turned to conservative governments in the early 1980s, support for East-West détente (and criticism of American confrontational policies, for example in the Caribbean basin) continued, to the perplexity, dismay and sometimes anger of leaders in Washington.

An additional reason for European satisfaction with détente, and a diverging American view, was that one important but little remarked consequence of détente in Europe from 1969 through 1979 was that the focus of U.S.-Soviet and general East-West competition shifted from Europe to the third world. The Europeans welcomed this shift, which they correctly (if not usually articulately) perceived as a fruit of détente. The United States, with little European support in the third world competition, was less grateful to détente. . . .

A fourth cause of the decline in confidence in détente in the 1970s was the view widely held on both sides that the other side was acquiring military capabilities in excess of what it needed for deterrence and defense, and therefore was not adhering to détente. This is a complex question. For example, the limits under SALT reduced some previously important areas of concern and uncertainties in projecting the military balance—notably with respect to ABMs. But another effect was that the rather complex *real* strategic balance was artificially simplified in the general understanding (and not just of the general public) to certain highlighted indexes, thereby increasing sensitivity to a symbolic arithmetical "balance." And national means of intelligence, which were given high credibility when it came to identifying a threat, were regarded with a more jaundiced eye when called upon to monitor and verify compliance with an arms limitation agreement.

In any event, during the latter half of the 1970s concern mounted in the United States over why the Soviet Union was engaged in what has been termed a relentless continuing arms buildup. At the same time U.S. military programs were justified as meeting that buildup. In turn the Soviet Union saw the American buildup as designed to restore the United States to a position of superiority.

Throughout the preceding two decades of Cold War and cold peace, the United States had maintained a clear strategic nuclear superiority. As the Soviet Union continued to build its strategic forces, despite earlier agreed strategic arms limitations, new fears and suspicions arose in the United States. Unfortunately, the actual consolidation of parity in the latter 1970s was not in synchronization with the political acceptance and public impression of parity in the early 1970s. What the Soviets saw as finally closing the gap through programs of weapons deployment, which they saw as fully consonant both with the terms of the SALT agreement and with achievement of parity, many in the United States saw as a Soviet pursuit of advantages that violated at least the spirit, if not the letter, of SALT and that threatened to go beyond parity to superiority. The real inconsistency was between the continuing Soviet deployments and the American public's *expectation* derived from SALT. The interim freeze of 1972 had set a level with respect to the deployment of forces, including some construction under way that had not yet been completed by the Soviet Union. In addition, it had limited only the level of strategic missile launchers, not of warheads, and the Soviets, who were behind in terms of arming their strategic missile force with MIRVs, sought to catch up in the years following. If the Soviet strategic deployments had occurred more nearly at the time of American deployment, and both countries had agreed to accept parity and stop at the same time (and not merely at the same level), the public perception would have been quite different.

While a desire to influence public opinion played a part in inflating presentations of the military threat posed by the other side, there were real buildups on both sides. In part, then, perceptions on both sides of a hostile arms buildup were genuine. But both sides were unduly alarmist in exaggerating the military capabilities—and imputed intentions—of the other. . . .

In addition to major gaps in mutual understanding of such key elements of détente as behavior in international politics and in managing the arms race, a fifth cause of the decline of détente was a failure to understand its crucial relationship to the internal politics of the two countries. In part this failure was reflected in errors, in particular by the Soviet Union, in comprehending the domestic political processes and dynamics of the other country. There was also some failure by political leaders, especially in the United States, to gauge the degree of their own authority. The Soviet leaders also put too much trust in the ability of an American president to carry out policy. This situation was true in the whole matter of normalization of trade and repeatedly with SALT II from 1975 to 1980. While Nixon, Kissinger, and Ford were careful to relate linkages to foreign policy issues, Congress attempted to make its own linkages with Soviet internal affairs. It failed in the effort, creating in the process new issues in U.S.-Soviet relations and reducing support for détente in the United States. The Soviet leaders also had difficulty understanding the sudden changes and discontinuities between (and occasionally within) administrations. On the other hand, American leaders, especially Presidents Carter and Reagan, have had little understanding of the Soviet political leadership or of Soviet political processes. President Carter was especially insensitive to the necessary limits on détente as a medium for influencing the internal political affairs of the Soviet Union.

Leaders on both sides, especially the Soviet leaders, frequently and seriously underestimated the impact of their own actions on the perceptions and policy of the other side, and the extent to which the actions of one side have been responses to real or perceived challenges. And again, Soviet secrecy, and self-serving justifications on both sides, compounded this problem.

Finally, the failure in the United States to sustain a political consensus in support of détente also ranked as a major cause of its collapse. This conclusion is particularly clear when the role of domestic political factors in the United States in torpedoing the attempt at détente is considered. Most blatant, but far from unique, was the attempt to tie trade, and thus the whole economic dimension of détente, to what amounted to interference in the internal affairs of the Soviet Union. The approach was all the more tragic but no less lethal because of the high moral motivations of many of the supporters of the effort. In this respect, the Soviet leaders were more successful in the less difficult, though not easy, task of maintaining a consensus in their quite different political process.

One reason for the disintegration of the consensus in favor of détente in the United States was the failure of the leadership to explain its limits as well as its promises to the public. To the extent that the leaders themselves failed to gauge the differences in conceptions about détente and were prisoners of their own view of the world order, they could not make this limitation clear to others. But Nixon and Kissinger did understand very well at least that there was a continuing active competition—not only in the Soviet conception, but in their own policy—a competition that was, however, masked by too much talk about a new structure of peace. When the expectations of the public, aroused by the hyperbole about the benefits of peace and détente, were not met, disillusion set in—and so did a natural temptation to blame the other side. This reaction against détente, based on disillusionment (in the pure meaning of the term), was thus in part engendered by both Nixon's and Kissinger's overestimation of their ability to manipulate and manage both international and national affairs. It should also be noted that the public (including the broader congressional and active political constituencies) has been little aware of or prepared to understand the subtleties of international politics, or even the basic idea of a political relationship of mixed cooperation and competition with the Soviet Union. In addition, the political process in the United States not only does not provide a tradition of continuity or cushion against sudden changes in foreign policy, but invites domestic political exploitation of apparent and actual adversities in the course of international relations.

The decade of détente in American-Soviet relations was in fact one of mixed confrontation and détente, of competition and cooperation, with a remarkable if ill-starred attempt to build—too rapidly—a structure for peaceful coexistence between powerful adversaries.

Kissinger's Realism Without Morality

WALTER ISAACSON

"Americans," he [Henry A. Kissinger] once wrote, "are comfortable with an idealistic tradition that espouses great causes, such as making the world safe for democracy, or human rights." But it was not in the country's nature, he often lamented, to sit still for the unedifying work of tending to imperfect alliances or the never-end-

From *Kissinger: A Biography* by Walter Isaacson, pp. 655–657, 764–767. Copyright © 1992 by Walter Isaacson. Reprinted by permission of Simon and Schuster, Inc.

ing meddling necessary to maintain a balance of power. The U.S. has historically been, in [the political scientist] Stanley Hoffmann's words "traditionally hostile to balance of power diplomacy with its closets of partitions, compensations, secret treaties and gunboats."

To Kissinger, this excessive aversion to secret treaties and gunboats, and to all the other trappings of realpolitik and balance-of-power diplomacy, stemmed from the simple, often simplistic, naiveté and decency of most Americans. With a jarring use of the first-person plural that belies the fact that the descriptions scarcely apply to him, Kissinger once wrote that "our native inclination for straightforwardness, our instinct for open, noisy politics, our distrust of European manners and continental elites, all brought about an increasing impatience with the stylized methods of European diplomacy and with its tendency toward ambiguous compromise."

This idealistic streak in the American character, this desire to seek moral perfection rather than messy accommodations, was what caused the nation to lurch over the years between isolationism and interventionism, to embark on crusades (World War I, Vietnam), and then to recoil into self-righteous withdrawal. "Emotional slogans, unleavened by a concept of the national interest, had caused us to oscillate between excesses of isolation and overextension," Kissinger wrote. The way to moderate these pendulum swings, he said, was "by making judgments according to some more permanent conception of national interest."

One key component of Kissinger's brand of realism was his special emphasis on the role of military might. "Throughout history," he once wrote, "the influence of nations has been roughly correlative to their military power." This view led him to favor great displays and pretenses of power: bombings, incursions, aircraft carriers steaming toward trouble spots, nuclear alerts.

Even from a realist perspective, this emphasis on military power was subject to criticism. Other sophisticated realists, such as George Kennan and Hans Morgenthau, emphasized that economic vitality and political stability are equally important elements of national power. Kissinger's best diplomacy came in China, the Middle East, and later Africa, where the direct threat of American force played little role; his greatest failures came in Vietnam, Cambodia, and Pakistan, where displays of force abounded. There was also a political constraint: the brutal and cold application of force was incompatible with America's self-conception and what its citizenry in the 1970s was willing to countenance.

Another component of Kissinger's realism was the stress he put on the role that "credibility" played in determining a nation's influence and power. An emphasis on credibility is why realism in foreign policy is not always the same thing as pragmatism. In dealing with Vietnam, for example, a pragmatist would have come more quickly to the conclusion that the war was simply not worth the effort, that the costs were greater than any potential benefits. Realists such as Kissinger, however, emphasized that America could not abandon its commitments or else it would undermine its influence elsewhere in the world.

From his *Foreign Affairs* piece [on Vietnam negotiations] in 1968, to his analysis of Vietnam options in 1969, to his arguments in early 1975 as Saigon was falling, Kissinger put enormous weight on the credibility argument. The problem with an emphasis on credibility is that it can—and in the case of Vietnam did—result in an inability to discriminate between vital interests and ones that are merely peripheral.

A third aspect of Kissinger's realism was his lack of concern about supporting democratic forces and human rights movements in authoritarian countries. He was more comfortable dealing with strong rulers—Brezhnev, Zhou Enlai, the shah of Iran, [Syrian leader Hafez] Assad, and [Egyptian president Anwar el-]Sadat—than with the messy democracies in Europe and Israel.

In office and after, he opposed the crusades of moral activists who wanted the U.S. to push for domestic reforms in the Soviet Union, China, Pakistan, and the shah's Iran. "Why is it our business how they govern themselves?" an annoyed Kissinger asked at a meeting in 1971 when State Department bureaucrats were recommending pressure on Pakistan. This attitude was later reflected when Kissinger refused to join in the criticism of China after the 1989 crackdown in Tiananmen Square.

Though complex, even ingenious, in its design, Kissinger's realism began with a simple premise: any event should be judged foremost by whether it represented a gain for the Soviets or for the West in the overall global balance. That was the basis of his credibility argument in Vietnam: the war would show the rest of the world whether Washington had the will to stand up to Soviet expansion elsewhere. He embarked on the Middle East peace process partly as a way to undermine Soviet influence there. In the India-Pakistan war, the U.S. became involved on the losing side partly because Kissinger insisted on viewing the regional war as a proxy struggle between a Soviet and an American client.

This tendency to see global disputes through an East-West prism provided his foreign policy with a coherent framework, but it could also be distorting, as he later admitted. "We must outgrow the notion that every setback is a Soviet gain or every problem is caused by Soviet action," he said in May 1975, after setbacks in Vietnam, Cambodia, Portugal, and the Middle East put him on the defensive about his policy of détente with the Soviets. Yet the "we" in his speech fit snugly, for he had spent six years pushing that notion. . . .

At an emotional press conference in Salzburg in 1974, when he brooded about resigning because of stories about the wiretaps [of aides], Kissinger became unusually maudlin. He had been identified, he said, as someone who cared more about stabilizing the balance of power than about moral issues. "I would rather like to think," he added, "that when the record is written, one may remember that perhaps some lives were saved and perhaps some mothers can rest more at ease. But I leave that to history."

This historical judgment is unlikely ever to be a simple one. The structure of peace that Kissinger designed places him with Henry Stimson, George Marshall, and Dean Acheson atop the pantheon of modern American statesmen. In addition, he was the foremost American negotiator of this century and, along with George Kennan, the most influential foreign policy intellectual.

But Kissinger never had an instinctive feel for American values and mores, such as the emphasis that a Stimson would place on honor over intrigue or on idealism over national interests. Nor did he have an appreciation of the strengths to be derived from the healthy raucousness of American politics or from open decisionmaking in a democratic society. "Henry is a balance-of-power thinker," said Lawrence Eagleburger, one of his closest colleagues. "He deeply believes in stability. These kind[s] of objectives are antithetical to the American experience. Americans tend to want to pursue a set of moral principles. Henry does not have an intrinsic feel for the American political system, and he does not start with the same basic values and assumptions."

Kissinger came to power at a perilous moment for the foreign policy of his adoptive nation. America's isolationist reflexes were twitching as a result of its ill-conceived involvement in Vietnam. Congress and the public were in no mood to pay for new weapons or to engage the Soviets in marginal confrontations in the third world.

By ushering in an era of détente, Kissinger helped to assure that the competition with the Soviets would be more manageable and the showdowns less dangerous. And by devising a web of linkages, he provided the U.S. with some diplomatic leverage to compensate for its loss of military resolve. Looking back twenty years later, he could claim with some justification that "we perhaps deserve some credit for holding together the sinews of America at a time of fundamental collapse."

Some of the initiatives that he pursued along the way were enlightened and imaginative, others impulsively brutal and blunt. Some were clever, others too clever by half. As the only European-style realist ever to guide U.S. foreign policy, a power practitioner unencumbered by the sentimental idealism that suffuses American history, he seemed painfully amoral at times. But he was able to take a clear-eyed approach to the creation of a new global balance, one that helped to preserve American influence in the post-Vietnam era and eventually contributed to the end of the cold war.

Although he was too likely to see a Moscow-inspired threat in every regional crisis, Kissinger was correct in resisting the dovish and isolationist forces of the period that sought to abandon the competition with the Soviets. And he was equally correct in resisting the hawkish and neoconservative pressure to abandon cooperation with the Soviets. As Kennan had pointed out in the late 1940s—and Kissinger had reiterated in the early 1970s—the rulers in the Kremlin could prop up their system only by expanding their empire or by invoking foreign threats. If denied these opportunities, the Soviet system would eventually disintegrate, as it did.

In addition, Kissinger and Nixon turned the world's bipolar tug-of-war into a three-dimensional chess game that provided the U.S. with more opportunities for creative diplomacy. The new relationship with China, which previous presidents had barely contemplated, gave both of the world's communist giants an incentive to maintain better relations with the U.S. than they had with one another.

It added up to a fundamental change in America's postwar foreign policy: for the first time since the Potsdam Conference of 1945, cooperation as well as competition with both Moscow and Beijing could be part of a great-power strategy of balance. That alone was a triumph of hard-edged realism worthy of a Metternich [the nineteenth-century Austrian prince Klemens von Metternich].

This new framework incorporated a recognition of America's limits with a belief that the nation still had a major role to play in resisting the spread of Soviet influence. Less ardently anti-Soviet than his conservative critics desired, and more interventionist than most liberals could abide, Kissinger was able to create an American role that kept the pendulum from careening too rapidly in one direction or the other after Vietnam.

The main lines of this policy were followed for the next two decades: a blend of containment and cooperation with Moscow that allowed the internal contradictions of the Soviet system to play out; a step-by-step process in the Middle East that kept the U.S. the dominant player in the region; and a realistic attitude toward China that created a global balance that was more stable and gave Washington more leverage. When the cold war ended, this dose of realism would help the U.S. operate in a new global environment based on multiple power centers and balances.

But Kissinger's power-oriented realism and focus on national interests faltered because it was too dismissive of the role of morality. The secret bombing and then invasion of Cambodia, the Christmas bombing of Hanoi, the destabilization of Chile—these and other brutal actions betrayed a callous attitude toward what Americans like to believe is the historic foundation of their foreign policy: a respect for human rights, international law, democracy, and other idealistic values. The setbacks Kissinger encountered as a statesman, and the antagonism he engendered as a person, stemmed from the perceived amorality of his geopolitical calculations.

Kissinger's approach led to a backlash against détente; the national mood swung toward both the moralism of Jimmy Carter and the ideological fervor of Ronald Reagan. As a result, not unlike Metternich, Kissinger's legacy turned out to be one of brilliance more than solidity, of masterful structures built of bricks that were made without straw.

To Kissinger, an emphasis on realism and national interests—even though it might seem callous in its execution—was not a rejection of moral values. Rather, he saw it as the best way to pursue the stable world order that he believed was the ultimate moral imperative, especially in a nuclear age.

He tried to explain this relationship between realism and morality at a Paris gathering of Nobel Prize laureates in 1988. After being attacked in a closed-door session for his power-oriented and amoral approach—Argentine Adolfo Perez Esquivel, a former Peace Prize winner, accused him of "genocide and collective massacre"—Kissinger began to talk about his childhood. The room hushed.

More than a dozen of his relatives had been killed in the holocaust, he said, so he knew something of the nature of genocide. It was easy for human rights crusaders and peace activists to insist on perfection in this world. But the policymaker who has to deal with reality learns to seek the best that can be achieved rather than the best that can be imagined. It would be wonderful to banish the role of military power from world affairs, but the world is not perfect, as he had learned as a child. Those with true responsibility for peace, unlike those on the sidelines, cannot afford pure idealism. They must have the courage to deal with ambiguities and accommodations, to realize that great goals can be achieved only in imperfect steps. No side has a monopoly on morality.

But Kissinger's realpolitik was ill-suited to an open and democratic society, where it is difficult to invoke distant ends to justify unpalatable means. A belief that America's actions are moral and noble is necessary to rally a naturally isolationist people. Whether marching off to war or rousing itself to counter the spread of communism, America draws its motivation from a desire to defend its values—rather than from a cold calculation of its geopolitical interests. Even when an

American involvement is partly based on economic self-interest, such as the Persian Gulf War of 1991, the more high-minded goals are the ones that tend to be publicly emphasized.

Kissinger considered this idealistic aspect of the American spirit a weakness in terms of sustaining policies in a messy world. To some extent he was right—but it was also a source of strength. The greatest triumph of political influence in the modern age was that of democratic capitalism over communism in the early 1990s. This occurred partly because Kissinger and others helped to create a new global balance during the 1970s, one that preserved American influence in the post-Vietnam era. But the main reason that the United States triumphed in the cold war was not because it won a competition for military power and influence. It was because the values offered by its system—among them a foreign policy that could draw its strength from the ideals of its people—eventually proved more attractive.

✖ *FURTHER READING*

Robert J. Alexander, *The Tragedy of Chile* (1978)
Stephen E. Ambrose, *Nixon* (1987–1991)
Richard J. Barnet, *The Giants* (1977)
———, *The Lean Years* (1980)
Robert L. Beisner, "History and Henry Kissinger," *Diplomatic History,* 14 (1990), 511–527
Coral Bell, *The Diplomacy of Détente* (1977)
Henry Brandon, *The Retreat of American Power* (1973)
Seyom Brown, *The Faces of Power* (1983)
Dan Caldwell, ed., *Henry Kissinger* (1983)
David Calleo, *The Imperious Economy* (1982)
Gregory D. Cleva, *Henry Kissinger and the American Approach to Foreign Policy* (1989)
Thomas M. Franck and Edward Weisband, *Foreign Policy by Congress* (1979)
Edward Friedland et al., *The Great Détente Disaster* (1975)
Michael B. Froman, *The Development of the Idea of Détente* (1992)
John L. Gaddis, *Strategies of Containment* (1982)
Lloyd C. Gardner, ed., *The Great Nixon Turnaround* (1973)
Charles Gati and Toby Trister Gati, *The Debate over Détente* (1977)
Michael Genovese, *The Nixon Presidency* (1990)
Matti Golan, *The Secret Conversations of Henry Kissinger* (1976)
Stephen Graubard, *Kissinger: Portrait of a Mind* (1973)
John Robert Greene, *The Limits of Power* (1992)
Seymour M. Hersh, *The Price of Power: Kissinger in the White House* (1983)
Stanley Hoffmann, "The Case of Dr. Kissinger," *New York Review of Books,* November 2, 1972
———, *Primacy or World Order* (1978)
———, "The Return of Henry Kissinger," *New York Review of Books,* April 29, 1982
Joan Hoff, *Nixon Reconsidered* (1994)
Joan Hoff-Wilson, " 'Nixingerism,' NATO, and Détente," *Diplomatic History,* 13 (1989), 501–526.
William G. Hyland, *Mortal Rivals* (1987)
Robert C. Johansen, *The National Interest and the Human Interest* (1980)
Loch K. Johnson, *A Season of Inquiry: The Senate Intelligence Investigation* (1985)
Bernard Kalb and Marvin Kalb, *Kissinger* (1974)
David Landau, *Kissinger: Uses of Power* (1972)
Thomas B. Larson, *Soviet-American Rivalry* (1978)

Robert S. Litwak, *Détente and the Nixon Doctrine* (1984)
Michael Mandelbaum, *The Nuclear Question* (1979)
Roger Morris, *Richard Milhous Nixon* (1989)
————, *Uncertain Greatness: Henry Kissinger and American Foreign Policy* (1977)
Fred Warner Neal, ed., *Détente or Debacle* (1979)
John Newhouse, *Cold Dawn: The Story of SALT* (1973)
————, *War and Peace in the Nuclear Age* (1988)
Herbert S. Parmet, *Richard Nixon and His America* (1990)
James Petras and Morris Morley, *The United States and Chile* (1975)
Richard Pipes, *U.S.-Soviet Relations in the Era of Détente* (1981)
Walter F. Sater, *Chile and the United States* (1990)
Robert D. Schulzinger, *Henry Kissinger* (1989)
————, "The Naive and Sentimental Diplomat: Henry Kissinger's Memoirs," *Diplomatic History,* 4 (1980), 303–315
Franz Schurmann, *The Foreign Politics of Richard Nixon* (1987)
David Shambaugh, *Beautiful Imperialist* (1991) (Sino-U.S. relations)
Edward R. F. Sheehan, *The Arabs, Israelis, and Kissinger* (1976)
Paul E. Sigmund, *The Overthrow of Allende and the Politics of Chile, 1964–1976* (1977)
————, *The United States and Democracy in Chile* (1993)
Lewis Sorley, *Arms Transfers Under Nixon* (1983)
Harvey Starr, *Henry Kissinger* (1984)
Richard Stevenson, *The Rise and Fall of Détente* (1985)
John G. Stoessinger, *Henry Kissinger: The Anguish of Power* (1976)
Tad Szulc, "How Kissinger Did It: Behind the Vietnam Cease-Fire Agreement," *Foreign Policy,* No. 15 (1974), 21–61
————, *The Illusion of Peace* (1978)
Adam B. Ulam, *Dangerous Relations: The Soviet Union in World Politics, 1970–1982* (1983)
Garry Wills, *Nixon Agonistes* (1970)

CHAPTER
13

Washington and the
Arab-Israeli Peace Process

The Arab-Israeli conflict ranks as one of the most enduring threats to peace since the Second World War. The conflict's roots reach back to biblical times, but the modern crisis can be traced to the postwar decolonization that swept Asia, Africa, and the Middle East. Arab-Israeli tension heightened in 1947, when an exhausted Great Britain, retreating from parts of its empire, surrendered its mandate over Palestine.

For decades, thousands of Jews, inspired by the teachings of Zionism to reestablish a Jewish nation, had migrated to the Holy Land. Following the horror of the Holocaust, in which more than 6 million European Jews had perished, the pace of migration intensified, and settlers increasingly came into conflict with the area's Arab, Palestinian inhabitants. Britain's withdrawal threw the problem into the United Nations, which called for Palestine's division into two states, one Arab and one Jewish. Before partition could be implemented, however, Israel declared its sovereignty in May 1948 and gained diplomatic recognition from the United States and the Soviet Union. Not long after, Egyptian, Jordanian, and Syrian armies entered Palestine and engaged Israeli forces in the first Arab-Israeli war (1948–1949). When a U.N. truce ended the fighting in January 1949, Israel had extended its prepartition borders, Egypt retained the contested Gaza Strip, and Jordan controlled the West Bank of the Jordan River (see maps on pp. 642–643). The ancient city of Jerusalem, moreover, had been carved into Israeli and Jordanian sectors. Hundreds of thousands of Palestinian refugees relocated either to Arab-controlled areas of Palestine or to the neighboring Arab states of Jordan, Lebanon, Syria, Egypt, and Iraq. The events of 1948–1949 foreshadowed a long-lasting pattern of war and terrorism in which both Jews and Arabs, as well as their allies, have participated and suffered.

Numerous factors drew the United States into the Middle East maelstrom. The region's massive oil reserves, especially those of the Persian Gulf states of Saudi Arabia, Kuwait, Iraq, and Iran, carried immense value in both economic and military terms. Throughout the Cold War, Washington also sought military allies in the region and access to strategic and intelligence bases. Egypt's Suez Canal provided an especially vital link joining Asia, the Middle East, and Europe. At the same time, Israel enjoyed a deep reservoir of support in the United States, stemming from American humanitarian sympathy over the Holocaust, effective political lobbying by Jewish Americans, and Israel's strategic position and potential as an ally. Washington struggled to balance competing interests. Support for Israel disturbed American relations with oil-rich Arabs, whereas any U.S. befriending of Arab nationalists alarmed the Israelis and European allies such as Britain and France. Arab nations, moreover, divided into two main groups—moderate, pro-Western monarchies such as Jordan, Saudi Arabia, and Kuwait, and more radical nationalist regimes that emerged in Egypt, Syria, and Iraq.

During the 1950s and 1960s, under Gamel Abdul Nasser's pan-Arabist leadership, Egypt denounced American-sponsored military alliances, spurned negotiations with Israel (which likewise rejected negotiations), and accepted Soviet arms. In 1955 President Dwight D. Eisenhower and Secretary of State John Foster Dulles tried to woo Egypt by promising a World Bank loan for the construction of the High Aswan Dam on the Nile River, but when Cairo went ahead with plans to purchase Soviet-bloc arms, Washington abruptly withdrew the loan offer. Nasser's bold nationalization of the British- and French-run Suez Canal in 1956, from which he hoped to acquire revenue to finance Aswan, and his stout defense against a British-French-Israeli invasion, encouraged Arab nationalists. In July 1958 a coup overthrew the pro-Western monarchy in Iraq, and that same year Egypt and Syria merged to form the United Arab Republic (UAR). Although the Eisenhower administration had exerted economic and diplomatic pressure to help turn back the British-French-Israeli invasion of Suez, it viewed Nasser's popularity with increasing alarm. From Washington's perspective, radical nationalism threatened stability, opened opportunities for Soviet intrigue, and endangered U.S. interests in the region. In 1957 Congress approved the Eisenhower Doctrine, authorizing the president to dispatch U.S. troops to any Middle Eastern nation that requested them to resist international communism. The following year, U.S. Marines landed on Lebanon's shores to bolster a pro-Western regime.

Political alignments, however, rarely remained fixed in the Middle East. Nasser's dream of a Pan-Arab alliance faded when disagreements over domestic policies led to Syria's secession from the UAR in 1961. A series of coups ultimately brought to power in Syria a Baathist Socialist regime that rivaled Nasser's Egypt for leadership in the Arab world. Nasser suffered a devastating setback in the Six-Day War of June 1967, in which Israel won a stunning victory and seized Jordan's West Bank—including the holy city of Jerusalem, Syria's Golan Heights, and Egypt's Sinai Peninsula and Gaza Strip (see maps). Israel cited its need for security from hostile Arab neighbors to justify the continued occupation and settlement of the territories. During 1969–1970, Egypt and Israel fought a limited "war of attrition" across the boundary lines of the occupied Sinai near Suez, but the Israeli occupation stood.

Palestinians living under Israeli rule in the West Bank and Gaza meanwhile looked to Yasir Arafat and the Palestine Liberation Organization (PLO) for leadership. The PLO, formed in 1964, vowed to destroy the Jewish state and retake the captured territories. But in another clash, the Yom Kippur War of October 1973, also known as the October War, Egypt, Syria, and their Arab supporters failed to dislodge the U.S.-backed Israelis. Egyptian president Anwar el-Sadat subsequently maneuvered his country into the U.S. camp and sought normalized relations with Israel. After the October War, President Richard M. Nixon (1969–1974) and Secretary of State Henry A. Kissinger responded to Sadat's overtures by providing Egypt with aid and arranging a cease-fire with Israel.

After the Six-Day War and continuing through the 1970s, U.S. participation in the Arab-Israeli peace process deepened. The United States supported U.N. Resolution 242 (November 22, 1967), which called for Israeli withdrawal from the occupied territories, Arab recognition of Israel's right to exist, and the establishment of well-defined and secure borders for all the belligerents. At the same time, the Nixon administration enlarged the relatively modest economic- and military-aid programs to Israel that the Kennedy and Johnson administrations had initiated. Nixon and Kissinger viewed Israel as a stalwart anticommunist ally capable of standing up to Soviet-backed Syria and Iraq. They also hoped that firm U.S. support would make the Jewish state secure and hence more receptive to negotiations. But the U.S.-Israeli relationship became stormy. Israel proved reluctant to participate in U.S.-sponsored peace talks or to withdraw from the occupied territories. Instead, Tel Aviv (Israel's capital city) undertook an ambitious settlement program in the territories and deployed military forces to quell Palestinian resistance. Evidence also mounted that Israel, much to Washington's disapproval, had transferred fissionable materials from its Dimona nuclear facility to a secret weapons-development program.

As tensions built up in the region, the PLO and other Palestinian groups increasingly resorted to terrorism. Conducted mainly from sanctuaries in Lebanon and Syria (the PLO had been expelled from Jordan by King Hussein in September 1970), Palestinian terrorist attacks often victimized civilians as well as military personnel. The United States condemned the violence and refused to recognize the PLO; Washington thereby alienated the PLO's Arab allies and complicated the peace process. Secretary of State Kissinger nonetheless proceeded on a step-by-step basis to mediate bilateral disputes between Israel, Egypt, and Syria following the October War. President Jimmy Carter's administration (1977–1981) brokered a peace treaty between Sadat and Israel's prime minister Menachem Begin in 1978 at the Camp David summit. In exchange for Israel's withdrawal from Sinai (completed in 1982), Egypt became the first Arab nation to recognize the Jewish state. Carter cemented the deal by promising generous economic- and military-aid packages to both Egypt and Israel. But Camp David left the future of the occupied West Bank, Gaza Strip, and Golan Heights undetermined and did not address the issue of a Palestinian homeland or Palestinian autonomy. Not until a 1994 accord, signed by the PLO and Israel, did Israel withdraw from the Gaza Strip and the West Bank town of Jericho.

The Arab-Israeli peace process during the 1970s provides a revealing study of how the United States attempted to manage a regional Third World conflict during the Cold War. Given the complexities of this subject and the passions it stirs, it is not surprising that scholars have disagreed in their evaluation of U.S. policy. Why did U.S. leaders think it necessary for the United States to participate actively in Mideast affairs? What was at stake? Was U.S. policy driven primarily by economic interests—or by issues of Cold War security? What impact did pro-Israeli Jewish Americans make on policy? What effect did the pro-Arab oil lobby have? To what extent did Soviet support for radical Arab states threaten U.S. interests? Did American policymakers exaggerate Soviet influence?

Scholars also debate the strengths and weaknesses of the U.S. diplomatic strategy once Washington became fully engaged in Middle East negotiations. Did American support for Israel during the 1970s help or hinder the Arab-Israeli peace process? How successfully did Washington accommodate Arab nationalism? Did U.S. policymakers adequately address the issue of Palestinian rights? Would U.S. recognition of the PLO have served the peace process? Should the United States *have sought a comprehensive settlement, perhaps by bringing together all of the parties—Israel, Egypt, Syria, Jordan, and the Palestinians—in a major conference to exchange occupied land for peace and to create a Palestinian state? Or did the step-by-step Nixon-Carter approach, focusing on narrower, bilateral issues, hold greater promise? The answers to these questions vary widely, as this chapter's readings indicate.*

✖ D O C U M E N T S

On November 22, 1967, in the aftermath of the Six-Day War, the United Nations adopted Resolution 242, which asked Israel to withdraw from the territories it had recently occupied but also acknowledged the sovereignty of all of the states in the area—including Israel's. That resolution, reprinted as the first document, became the basis for future peace negotiations. The Palestine Liberation Organization (PLO) issued its National Covenant, the second document, in July 1968. Although the covenant does not mention Israel by name, it denounces a "Zionist invasion" as a tool of Western imperialism and calls for military and political action to regain Palestine for its Arab inhabitants.

The third document, a speech by Egyptian president Gamel Abdul Nasser on July 23, 1968, expresses support for U.N. peace efforts while rejecting direct negotiations with Tel Aviv; criticizes U.S. support for Israel's occupation policies; and applauds the Soviet military aid Egypt received. In the fourth document, dating from October 8, 1968, Israel's foreign minister, Abba Eban, presents his country's nine-point peace plan to the United Nations. Eban describes the Six-Day War as the culmination of twenty years of Arab hostility and criticizes Egyptian president Nasser for refusing to negotiate with Israel. He reaffirms Israel's acceptance of U.N. Resolution 242, calls for bilateral negotiations between Israel and its Arab neighbors to determine political boundaries, and suggests a framework for establishing peace in the region. In the fifth document, an excerpt from Henry A. Kissinger's memoirs, the former national security affairs adviser and secretary of state recalls the Nixon administration's decision in October 1973 to rush large-scale military assistance to Israel during the early stages of the October War. Kissinger reasoned that U.S. supplies would enable the Israelis to turn back Arab advances, undermine Soviet influence, and enhance the United States' role as a mediator.

The sputtering peace process reached a turning point during the Carter administration. The victory of Menachem Begin's right-wing Likud coalition in Israel's national elections in May 1977 ended the domination of the Labor party that had ruled Israel since its founding. At first the Likud triumph seemed to dim chances for Arab-Israeli peace. The platform of the Likud coalition (the sixth document), published in March 1977, did espouse peace as a general goal. But it opposed relinquishing the West Bank (which Begin and his supporters referred to as Judea and Samaria), vigorously defended Israeli settlements in the occupied territories as essential to national security and self-identity, and condemned the PLO as a terrorist organization. Eager to regain the Sinai, Egyptian president Anwar el-Sadat nonetheless traveled to Jerusalem in November 1977 to address the Israeli parliament, the Knesset. His speech of November 20, 1977, the seventh document, argues forthrightly for a comprehensive peace based on Arab recognition of Israel, Israeli withdrawal from occupied territories, and Palestinian self-determination.

In the eighth document, a selection from Jimmy Carter's memoirs, the former president describes the Camp David summit of September 1978 and his delicate negotiations with Sadat and Begin over Sinai, Palestinian self-rule, and Israeli settlement policy. The parties finally signed a framework for peace (excerpted and reprinted as the ninth document) at a White House ceremony on September 17, 1978. This agreement laid the groundwork for normalized Egyptian-Israeli relations but left vague the details of a transition to Palestinian self-rule in the West Bank and Gaza.

United Nations Security Council Resolution 242, 1967

Expressing its continuing concern with the grave situation in the Middle East,

Emphasizing the inadmissibility of the acquisition of territory by war and the need to work for a just and lasting peace in which every State in the area can live in security.

Emphasizing further that all Member States in their acceptance of the Charter of the United Nations have undertaken a commitment to act in accordance with Article 2 of the Charter,

1. *Affirms* that the fulfillment of Charter principles requires the establishment of a just and lasting peace in the Middle East which should include the application of both the following principles:
   (i) Withdrawal of Israel armed forces from territories occupied in the recent conflict;
   (ii) Termination of all claims or states of belligerency and respect for and acknowledgement of the sovereignty, territorial integrity and political independence of every State in the area and their right to live in peace within secure and recognized boundaries free from threats or acts of force;
2. *Affirms further* the necessity
   (a) For guaranteeing freedom of navigation through international waterways in the area;
   (b) For achieving a just settlement of the refugee problem;
   (c) For guaranteeing the territorial inviolability and political independence of every State in the area, through measures including the establishment of demilitarized zones;
3. *Requests* the Secretary-General to designate a Special Representative to proceed to the Middle East to establish and maintain contacts with the States concerned in order to promote agreement and assist efforts to achieve a peaceful and accepted settlement in accordance with the provisions and principles in this resolution;
4. *Requests* the Secretary-General to report to the Security Council on the progress of the efforts of the Special Representative as soon as possible.

The Palestinian National Covenant, 1968

Palestine is the homeland of the Palestinian Arab people and an integral part of the great Arab homeland, and the people of Palestine is a part of the Arab nation.

Palestine with its boundaries that existed at the time of the British mandate is an integral regional unit.

The Palestinian Arab people possesses the legal right to its homeland, and when the liberation of its homeland is completed it will exercise self-determination solely according to its own will and choice.

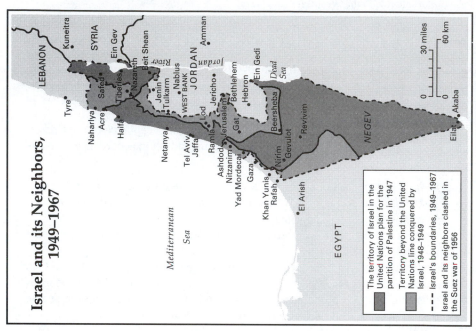

Israel and its Neighbors, 1949–1967

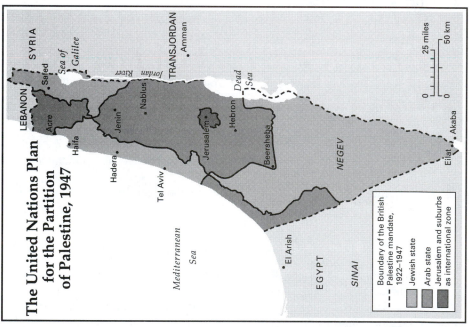

The United Nations Plan for the Partition of Palestine, 1947

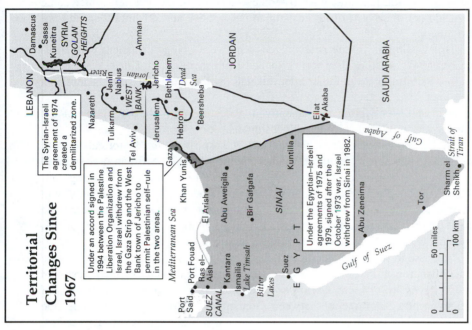

Territorial Changes Since 1967

The Syrian-Israeli agreement of 1974 created a demilitarized zone.

Under an accord signed in 1994 between the Palestine Liberation Organization and Israel, Israel withdrew from the Gaza Strip and the West Bank town of Jericho to permit Palestinian self-rule in the two areas.

Under the Egyptian–Israeli agreements of 1975 and 1979, signed after the October 1973 war, Israel withdrew from Sinai in 1982.

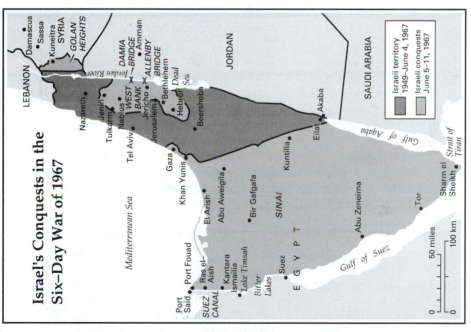

Israel's Conquests in the Six–Day War of 1967

Israeli territory 1949–June 4, 1967

Israeli conquests June 5–11, 1967

The Palestinian personality is an innate, persistent characteristic that does not disappear, and it is transferred from fathers to sons. The Zionist occupation, and the dispersal of the Palestinian Arab people as a result of the disasters which came over it, do not deprive it of its Palestinian personality and affiliation and do not nullify them.

The Palestinians are the Arab citizens who were living permanently in Palestine until 1947, whether they were expelled from there or remained. Whoever is born to a Palestinian Arab father after this date, within Palestine or outside it, is a Palestinian.

Jews who were living permanently in Palestine until the beginning of the Zionist invasion will be considered Palestinians.

The Palestinian affiliation and the material, spiritual and historical tie with Palestine are permanent realities. The upbringing of the Palestinian individual in an Arab and revolutionary fashion, the undertaking of all means of forging consciousness and training the Palestinian, in order to acquaint him profoundly with his homeland, spiritually and materially, and preparing him for the conflict and the armed struggle, as well as for the sacrifice of his property and his life to restore his homeland, until the liberation of all this is a national duty.

The phase in which the people of Palestine is living is that of national struggle for the liberation of Palestine. Therefore, the contradictions among the Palestinian national forces are of secondary order which must be suspended in the interest of the fundamental contradiction between Zionism and colonialism on the one side and the Palestinian Arab people on the other. On this basis, the Palestinian masses, whether in the homeland or in places of exile, organizations and individuals, comprise one national front which acts to restore Palestine and liberate it through armed struggle.

Armed struggle is the only way to liberate Palestine and is therefore a strategy and not tactics. The Palestinian Arab people affirms its absolute resolution and abiding determination to pursue the armed struggle and to march forward towards the armed popular revolution, to liberate its homeland and return to it [to maintain] its right to a natural life in it, and to exercise its right of self-determination in it and sovereignty over it. . . .

The Palestinian Arab people believes in Arab unity. In order to fulfill its role in realizing this, it must preserve, in this phase of its national struggle, its Palestinian personality and the constituents thereof, increase consciousness of its existence and resist any plan that tends to disintegrate or weaken it. . . .

The destiny of the Arab nation, indeed the very Arab existence, depends upon the destiny of the Palestine issue. The endeavour and effort of the Arab nation to liberate Palestine follows from this connection. The people of Palestine assumes its vanguard role in realizing this sacred national aim.

The liberation of Palestine, from an Arab viewpoint, is a national duty to repulse the Zionist, Imperialist invasion from the great Arab homeland and to purge the Zionist presence from Palestine. Its full responsibility falls upon the Arab nation, peoples and governments, with the Palestinian Arab people at their head. For this purpose, the Arab nation must mobilize all its military, human, material and spiritual capacities to participate actively with the people of Palestine in the liberation of Palestine. They must especially in the present stage of armed Palestinian revolution, grant and offer the people of Palestine all possible help and every material and human support, and afford it every sure means and opportunity enabling it to continue to assume its vanguard role in pursuing its armed revolution until the liberation of its homeland.

The liberation of Palestine, from a spiritual viewpoint, will prepare an atmosphere of tranquillity and peace for the Holy Land in the shade of which all the Holy Places will be safeguarded, and freedom of worship and visitation to all will be guaranteed, without distinction or discrimination of race, colour, language or religion. For this reason, the people of Palestine looks to the support of all the spiritual forces in the world.

The liberation of Palestine, from a human viewpoint, will restore to the Palestinian man his dignity, glory and freedom. For this, the Palestinian Arab people looks to the support of those in the world who believe in the dignity and freedom of man.

The liberation of Palestine, from an international viewpoint is a defensive act necessitated by the requirements of self-defence. For this reason the Arab people of Palestine, desiring to befriend all peoples, looks to the support of the states which love freedom, justice and peace in restoring the legal situation to Palestine, establishing security and peace in its territory, and enabling its people to exercise national sovereignty and national freedom. . . .

To realize the aims of this covenant and its principles the Palestine Liberation Organization will undertake its full role in liberating Palestine.

The Palestine Liberation Organization, which represents the forces of the Palestinian revolution, is responsible for the movement of the Palestinian Arab people in its struggle to restore its homeland, liberate it, return to it and exercise the right of self-determination in it. This responsibility extends to all military, political and financial matters, and all else that the Palestine issue requires in the Arab and international spheres.

The Palestine Liberation Organization will cooperate with all Arab States, each according to its capacities, and will maintain neutrality in their mutual relations in the light of and on the basis of, the requirements of the battle of liberation and will not interfere in the internal affairs of any Arab State.

Egypt's Gamel Abdul Nasser Endorses Peace But Denounces Israel and the United States, 1968

I do not want to go back to the circumstances which led to the Middle East crisis. All the details are known, starting with the premeditated aggression against Arab territory, to the imperialist collusion with the Israeli enemy, to the 5th June setback and its serious and sad results for our Arab nation. As you know, we lost the major part of our military power. We accepted the political solution experiment for several reasons. At that time we had no alternative to talking about a political solution; we had no armed forces to depend on. At the same time we are not advocates of war for the sake of war—not at all. If we can obtain our rights through political action, as happened in 1957 [after the Suez crisis], fine; if not, we have no alternative but to struggle for our rights and to liberate our land.

Furthermore, we want world public opinion to be on our side and really to know our position. At the same time, we must consider our present friends and our possible friends before we consider our enemies. A major part of the battle is taking place on an international level and under the eyes of public opinion throughout the entire world, which wants to live in peace.

We realised from the beginning, as we were trying a political solution, that it was a difficult and thorny road because the enemy was drunk with victory. We know that the principle that what has been taken by force cannot be regained by anything but force is a sound and correct principle in all circumstances. But we tried sincerely and are still trying sincerely on a basis from which we do not deviate. This basis is clear and definite in UAR [United Arab Republic] policy: no negotiations with Israel, no peace with Israel, no recognition of Israel, and no deals at the expense of Palestinian soil or the Palestinian people.

These are the foundations on which we proceeded in regard to solving the Middle East crisis peacefully. However, since 23rd November [1967] and until now, give and take has been going on with the UN representative. Have we achieved anything? We have achieved nothing. We co-operated to the maximum with the UN Secretary-General's representative. We accepted the Security Council resolution, but Israel did not.

No projects exist now for a peaceful solution, and it does not seem to me that there will be any in the future. We hear what the representative of the UN Secretary-General says, and we express our opinion on what we hear. So far our opinion has been clear.

With regard to a political solution, we will not in any way agree to give away one inch of Arab territory in any Arab country.

It is clear that Israel, which rejected the Security Council resolution, has many aims. The first is to achieve a political objective, because it won a military victory but did not achieve a political gain. Israel wants direct negotiations and wants a peace treaty signed. We reject this. Israel thus won a military victory but has so far been unable to achieve the political objective—signing a peace treaty with any of the Arab States surrounding it. . . .

Israel continues to refuse the Security Council resolution. Israel refuses to discuss the Security Council resolution. Israel says: We will remain in our places along the cease-fire lines until you agree to negotiate with us and conclude a peace treaty. Naturally we counter this by rebuilding our armed forces. A year ago after the defeat, we had no armed forces. We now have armed forces which may be greater than those existing before the battle. We are working for the development of the armed forces in order to attain supremacy because our enemy is a cunning enemy backed by a force which gives him everything—money and arms. . . .

There exists a basic and principal commitment which is a question of life or death: the liberation of the land inch by inch if necessary even if one martyr must fall on every inch of land. That is clear. A war to regain a right is a legal war. However, we shall allow no one to provoke us. We shall decide, prepare and arrange things. This is a lengthy matter which demands our patience and endurance. We must be patient and stand fast in order to triumph and attain supremacy. Having attained supremacy, we shall triumph. . . .

We do not address ourselves to Israel alone but to the whole world. We have nothing to say as far as Israel is concerned. Israel's role has been exposed. Its role as a stooge of world imperialism and colonialism has been fully exposed. However, our talk today is addressed to the world, which is anxious for peace and adheres to peace. We add that peace in this part of the world will not be achieved by the mere elimination of the consequences of the 5th June aggression. Real peace should take into consideration the legal rights of the Palestinian people. . . .

There is a fact which we must realise and know: Had it not been for the Soviet Union, we would now find ourselves facing the enemy without any weapons and compelled to accept his conditions. The United States would not have given us a single round of ammunition. It has given us and will give us nothing, but it gives Israel everything from guns to aircraft and missiles. . . .

Naturally, I did not pay my recent visit to the Soviet Union to express gratitude only, but to ask for things as well. After expressing my gratitude, I asked for things and after asking, I told them that I was ashamed. Do you not want anything from us? We ask you for things. But they answered: We have nothing to ask of you. I am actually telling this to you and to history so we may know who our friends and enemies are.

We went on asking for hours but they did not make one request of us. Even when I told them I felt ashamed that we were making many demands while they had asked nothing of us—I wish they had a request which we could fulfil—I asked if they had nothing to ask of us. They told us: We take this stand on the basis of our ideology—the ideology of national liberation and the peoples' struggle. We have nothing to ask. . . .

On this occasion, I may make a quick reference to our attitude towards the United States. US policy has failed rapidly in this region. No one other than an obvious agent can openly declare friendship for the United States. The entire Arab world is aware of what the United States has done. We expected something different from the United States, or at least we did not expect all that has happened. However, that is the United States' business.

Giving arms to Israel while it is occupying Arab territory means that the United States supports Israel in the occupation of the Arab territory. Giving aircraft to Israel while it is occupying Arab territory means that the United States supports Israel in the occupation of the Arab territory. The complete US support for Israel at the United Nations and the adoption and defence of the Israeli point of view means that the United States supports Israel's occupation of the Arab territory. The US refusal to make a statement stipulating the need for the withdrawal of the Israeli forces to the positions they occupied before 5th June is proof that the United States supports Israel and, indeed, colludes with Israel in what it has done and is doing. Every member of the Arab nation is aware of this. . . .

The United States, which possesses means of power that no other State has had the chance to possess throughout history or in our era, should really ask itself what the people want of it. The people want the United States to adopt an attitude based on justice, an attitude based on equality, for as a great Power the United States should also have great principles which reject aggression and occupation and in no circumstances agree to support the aggressor and give him arms.

Foreign Minister Abba Eban Presents Israel's Nine-Point Peace Plan, 1968

Israel cannot easily forget the immense loss and burden which it has borne through the implacable hostility directed against it for twenty years, culminating in the unforgettable summer of 1967. For there has not been a Six-Day War. There has been a twenty-year war conducted by the Arab States in varying degrees of intensity with the candid hope of Israel's ruin and destruction. The issue is whether this war is now going to be ended by a final peace or merely interrupted in order to be resumed in conditions more propitious for Arab success.

Our danger in 1967 was the climax and not the whole story of our predicament. No other people has had to live all its days with a mark of interrogation hanging over its collective and individual survival. And behind Israel's quest for secure life, there is a particular and hideous legacy of wholesale death in the European slaughter-house. In May 1967, we found ourselves beset by deadly peril which we faced in utter solitude of action and responsibility. Maritime blockade, murderous incursions, military encirclement, declarations of overt war, a frenzied torrent of violent threats and a formal announcement by President Nasser that the battle was joined for Israel's extinction, all came together in cumulative assault on Israel's life and security. . . .

To prevent the renewal of those dangers is the first law of our policy. The gravest danger is lest through a lassitude of spirit, or imprecision of diplomatic craftsmanship, or collapse of patience, we again revert to fragile, false and ambiguous solutions which carry within them the seed of future wars. Those of us who bear responsibility for our nation's survival and our children's lives cannot have anything to do with vague solutions which fall short of authentic and lasting peace. June 1967 must be the last of the Middle Eastern wars.

This resolve has moved our policy at every stage of the political discussion from the outbreak of hostilities to this very day.

In June and July 1967, the [U.N.] General Assembly rejected all proposals which sought to condemn Israel's resistance or to reconstruct the conditions which had led to the outbreak of war. A new milestone was reached when the Security Council adopted its unanimous Resolution on 22 November 1967. That Resolution was presented to us for our acquiescence, not as a substitute for specific agreement, but as a list of principles on which the parties could base their agreement. It was drafted, as [U.S.] Ambassador George Ball said on 11 September, as "a skeleton of principles on which peace could be erected." It was not meant to be self-executing. As Lord Caradon [Britain's ambassador and principal author of the resolution] said on 22 November, it was not "a call for a temporary truce or a superficial accommodation"; it reflected, as he said, a refusal "to be associated with any so-called settlement which was only a continuation of a false truce." Its author stated that any "action to be taken must be within the framework of a permanent peace, and withdrawal must be to secure boundaries." The term "secure and recognized boundaries" had first appeared in a United States draft, the author of which pointed out that this meant something different from the old armistice demarcation lines. Secure and recognized boundaries, he said, had never existed in the Middle East. They must, therefore, be fixed by the parties in the course of the peacemaking process.

Now these were the understandings on which Israel's cooperation with Ambassador [and U.N. mediator Gunnar] Jarring's mission was sought and obtained. Whatever our views might be on these formulations by other Governments, it has been evident at every stage that the two central issues are the establishment of a permanent peace and an agreement for the first time on the delineation of secure and recognized boundaries. These are the conditions prerequisite for any movement. It is here that the peacemaking process must begin. If these problems are solved, all the other issues mentioned in the Resolution fall into place. To seek a change in the cease-fire dispositions, without the framework of a just and lasting peace and the determination of agreed boundaries, is an irrational course for which there is no international authority or precedent. This would be a short and certain route to renewed war in conditions hostile to Israel's security and existence. . . .

Early in March 1968, Ambassador Jarring sought our reaction on a proposal to convene Israel, the UAR and Jordan in conferences under his auspices to seek an agreed settlement in fulfilment of his mandate under the Security Council's Resolution. We were later informed that the UAR had rejected and that Jordan had not accepted this course. On 1 May, Ambassador [Yosef] Tekoah was empowered to indicate, in the Security Council, Israel's acceptance of the November Resolution for the promotion of agreement on the establishment of a just and lasting peace. The Israeli Representative was authorized to reaffirm that we were willing to seek agreement with each Arab State on all the matters included in the Resolution, and that we accepted the proposal of Dr. Jarring of bringing about meetings between Israel and its neighbours under his auspices in fulfilment of his mandate for the purpose of peaceful and accepted settlement. . . .

During this time, Egyptian policy was authoritatively defined by President Nasser in a formal utterance on 23 June. In that statement, the UAR President expressed willingness to attempt, as in March 1957, "a political solution" on condition that certain principles of Egyptian policy be recognized. He said:

> The following principles of Egyptian policy are immutable:
> 1) No negotiation with Israel
> 2) No peace with Israel
> 3) No recognition of Israel
> 4) No transactions will be made at the expense of Palestinian territories or the Palestinian people.

How one can build peace out of such negative and immutable principles defeats the imagination. . . .

I come to enumerate the nine principles by which peace can be achieved:

1) The establishment of peace.   The situation to follow the cease-fire must be a just and lasting peace, duly negotiated and contractually expressed.

Peace is not a mere absence of fighting. It is a positive and clearly defined relationship with far-reaching political, practical and juridical consequences. We propose that the peace settlement be embodied in treaty form. It would lay down the precise conditions of our co-existence, including a map of the secure and agreed boundary. The essence of peace is that it commits both parties to the proposition that their twenty-year-old conflict is at a permanent end. Peace is much more than what is called "non-belligerency." The elimination of belligerency is one of several conditions which compose the establishment of a just and lasting peace.

2) Secure and Recognized Boundaries.   Within the framework of peace, the cease-fire lines will be replaced by permanent, secure and recognized boundaries between Israel and each of the neighbouring Arab States, and the disposition of forces will be carried out in full accordance with the boundaries under the final peace. We are willing to seek agreement with each Arab State on secure and recognized boundaries within the framework of a permanent peace. . . .

3) Security Agreements.   In addition to the establishment of agreed territorial boundaries, we should discuss other agreed security arrangements designed to avoid the kind of vulnerable situation which caused a breakdown of the peace in the summer of 1967. The instrument establishing peace should contain a pledge of mutual non-aggression.

4) The Open Frontier.   When agreement is reached on the establishment of peace with permanent boundaries, the freedom of movement now existing in the area, especially in the Israel-Jordan sector, should be maintained and developed. It would be incongruous if our peoples were to intermingle in peaceful contact and commerce only when there is a state of war and cease-fire—and to be separated into ghettos when there is peace. We should emulate the open frontier now developing within communities of States, as in parts of Western Europe. Within this concept, we include free port facilities for Jordan on Israel's Mediterranean coast and mutual access to places of religious and historic associations.

5) Navigation.   Interference with navigation in the international waterways in the area has been the symbol of the state of war and, more than once, an immediate cause of hostilities. The arrangements for guaranteeing freedom of navigation should be unreserved, precise, concrete and founded on absolute equality of rights and obligations between Israel and other littoral States.

6) Refugees.   The problem of displaced populations was caused by war and can be solved by peace. On this problem I propose:
One: A conference of Middle Eastern States should be convened, together with the Governments contributing to refugee relief and the specialized agencies of the United Nations, in order to chart a five-year plan for the solution of the refugee problem in the framework of a lasting peace and the integration of refugees into productive life. This conference can be called in advance of peace negotiations.

Two: Under the peace settlement, joint refugee integration and rehabilitation commissions should be established by the signatories in order to approve agreed projects for refugee integration in the Middle East, with regional and international aid.

Three: As an interim measure, my Government has decided, in view of the forthcoming winter, to intensify and accelerate action to widen the uniting of families scheme, and to process "hardship cases" among refugees who had crossed to the East Bank during the June 1967 fighting. Moreover, permits for return which had been granted and not used can be transferred to other refugees who meet the same requirements and criteria as the original recipients.

7) Jerusalem. Israel does not seek to exercise unilateral jurisdiction in the Holy Places of Christianity and Islam. We are willing in each case to work out a status to give effect to their universal character. We would like to discuss appropriate agreements with those traditionally concerned. Our policy is that the Christian and Moslem Holy Places should come under the responsibility of those who hold them in reverence.

8) Acknowledgement and Recognition of Sovereignty, Integrity and Right to National Life. This principle, inherent in the Charter and expressed in the Security Council Resolution of November 1967, is of basic importance. It should be fulfilled through specific contractual engagements to be made by the Governments of Israel and of the Arab States to each other—by name. It follows logically that Arab Governments will withdraw all the reservations which they have expressed on adhering to international conventions, about the non-applicability of their signatures to their relations with Israel.

9) Regional Cooperation. The peace discussion should examine a common approach to some of the resources and means of communication in the region in an effort to lay foundations of a Middle Eastern community of sovereign States.

Former Secretary of State Henry A. Kissinger Defends U.S. Support for Israel in the October War (1973), 1982

[Israeli ambassador Simcha] Dinitz phoned me at 1:45 A.M., [October 9, 1973] shortly after I had gone to sleep, waking me with a puzzling question: What could we do about resupply? I was baffled. By his prognosis of only a few hours earlier, the battle should be turning at about this time toward a decisive victory. What then was the problem? What was needed and why the hurry? The Israeli requests to date had been in the main for special types of ammunition and electronic gear. Almost all the requests had been granted; there had been some bureaucratic foot-dragging by Defense but the Sidewinder missiles had already been picked up. The primary unfulfilled request was for F-4 Phantom jets beyond those in the pipeline whose

From *Years of Upheaval* by Henry A. Kissinger, pp. 491–496, 497–498, 525–526, 535–537, 544, 614.

delivery we had already agreed to accelerate. This presented a special problem in that we had few surplus Phantoms except those coming off the production lines at the rate of about two per month to Israel, and those in our own combat units; to take the latter was bound to raise an outcry both in our armed services and in the Arab world. The unworthy thought crossed my mind that perhaps the Israelis wanted to commit us to a schedule of deliveries now before their probable victory removed the urgency. I told Dinitz that we would talk first thing in the morning, and I went back to bed. . . .

Thus on Tuesday, October 9, we met at 8:20 A.M. in the elegant but little-used Map Room on the ground floor of the White House. Many of my private encounters with Dinitz and his predecessor [Yitzhak] Rabin (and with [Soviet ambassador Anatoly] Dobrynin) had taken place there when I was national security adviser and wanted the meetings kept secret. It is a little dark, as the view from its windows is nearly obscured by rhododendron bushes. Its walls had been covered with battlefield maps when President Roosevelt used it as his military command post and communications center during World War II; hence its name. Dinitz had brought along his Armed Forces Attaché, General Mordechai ("Motta") Gur, to brief me. I was accompanied by [National Security Council staff members Brent] Scowcroft and [Peter W.] Rodman.

Dinitz and Gur wasted no time. Grimly, they explained that Israel's losses to date had been staggering and totally unexpected. Forty-nine airplanes, including fourteen Phantoms, had been destroyed. This figure was high but not completely surprising since both Syria and Egypt possessed large quantities of Soviet surface-to-air missiles. The real shocker was the loss of 500 tanks, 400 on the Egyptian front alone. Dinitz implored me to keep the numbers secret from everyone except the President. If they were known, the Arab countries now standing aloof might join for a knockout blow. Many puzzles cleared up instantly. "So that's why the Egyptians are so cocky," I exclaimed. "How did it happen?" Gur explained that a significant number of Israeli tanks were lost on the way to the battle by being run too fast in the desert after having been inadequately maintained in reserve depots. I was so shocked that I indelicately reminded Dinitz of his prediction two nights before of victory by Wednesday. He admitted that "obviously something went wrong." He did not know what.

Nor did it make any difference. For what Dinitz was reporting would require a fundamental reassessment of strategy. Our entire diplomacy and our resupply policy had been geared to a rapid Israeli victory. These assumptions were now overtaken. But something deeper was involved. I pointed out that the Syrian army, though suffering serious casualties, had not broken. Israel would therefore find it difficult to shift its forces from the Golan to the Sinai. And Israel's equipment losses on the Egyptian front were about equal to Egypt's. Israel stood on the threshold of a bitter war of attrition that it could not possibly win given the disparity of manpower. It had to do something decisive. . . .

At 9:40 A.M. that Tuesday, I urgently convened a special meeting of the WSAG [interdepartmental Washington Special Actions Group] confined to the most senior departmental representatives. Staff was barred to enhance security. I reported the conversation with Dinitz and Gur, omitting the figures for tank losses. My colleagues were skeptical. [CIA director William] Colby reported that Israel was doing well on the Syrian front and holding its own in the Sinai; Israel was simply trying to obtain the maximum military aid from us before victory, as a sign of unrestricted support not so much for the war as for the period afterward. Since I chaired the meeting as Presidential Assistant, Deputy Secretary Kenneth Rush spoke for the State Department. There had been no time to give any instructions; Rush supported Colby. [Secretary of Defense James R.] Schlesinger saw no problem with sending auxiliary equipment not requiring American technicians. But his concern was that meeting Israel's requests and thus turning around a battle that the Arabs were winning might blight our relations with the Arabs. Schlesinger pointed out the distinction between defending Israel's survival within its pre-1967 borders and helping Israel maintain its conquests from the 1967 war. Other participants concurred. . . .

Meanwhile, I was becoming dubious about the Soviets' conduct. They had acquiesced in our stalling tactics because they apparently had better intelligence about the battle than we. Even if that were not so, they must have caught up with events by this time; they were clearly seeking to fish in troubled waters. During a break in the WSAG deliberations I learned from our Ambassador in Amman, Dean Brown, that the Soviet chargé in Jordan had now urged [King] Hussein to enter the battle, promising full Soviet diplomatic support. Later in the day Brezhnev's appeal on similar lines to President Houari Boumedienne of Algeria was made public. "There are two issues," I told the WSAG, "supply and the indication the Soviet Union is stirring up the Arabs. We can't let the Soviet Union get away with this." How different were our prospects now from those of the night before! I adjourned the meeting and requested that various options for resupplying Israel be prepared by noon. I urged Schlesinger to ship straight from the production line to Israel any Phantoms not yet delivered to American units.

Meanwhile, I sought to thwart the Soviet design to turn the conflict into an Arab holy war. King Hussein had so far declined to enter the battle, even refusing King Faisal's request the day before to move a Saudi brigade stationed in Jordan into Syria. I sent a message to Hussein appealing to his statesmanship, promising an active American peace effort as soon as the war was over. He replied by expressing his solidarity with the objectives of his Arab brethren and castigating Israel's refusal since 1967 to make peace. He would exercise self-control for as long as possible, but unless we were able to arrange an early cease-fire he could not hold out. A prolonged war would strengthen the Soviet position in the Arab world.

It was clear to me that there would be no cease-fire unless Israel seemed to be gaining; Israel would have to pull itself together and overcome what was beginning to look like incoherence. To restore confidence, tangible evidence of American assistance was required. At the same time we had to keep the Soviets from seeking to exploit the sudden (at least to us) change in the military situation. During the day I warned Dobrynin against encouraging other nations to enter the conflict. He claimed that the report from Jordan had to be a misunderstanding and that Brezhnev's appeal to Boumedienne was boilerplate Soviet rhetoric. But when a superpower is "misunderstood" the same way in widely separated capitals, it is a pretty good working definition of design. . . .

Dinitz was not idle while we were waiting. Telephone calls descended on me from Capitol Hill urging me to stop dragging my feet on arms supply. Dinitz, of course, professed innocence; many Senators had spontaneously come to the same independent conclusion. My low boiling point was exceeded when Senator Frank Church, our scourge on Vietnam and constant critic of "deceitful" methods, urged us to "slip in" a few Phantoms into Israel, presumably without anyone knowing it. I replied that I would not mind if he went public with his appeal—a reversal of our usual positions. I thought there was some advantage in being seen to be pressed by Congress to do more for Israel; it might deflect some of the Arab resentment.

At 4:45 P.M., [White House chief of staff Alexander] Haig, Scowcroft, [press secretary Ron] Ziegler, and I met with [President Richard] Nixon. I outlined the problem. Diplomatically, we were not badly off. We were the only country in touch with most of the parties, including the Soviet Union. Once diplomacy took over, we would put our central position to good use. But the theoretical advantage would mean nothing if Israel appeared to be losing: "If the Arabs sense that the Israelis have lost more than they have admitted, they might rush in."

Nixon was preoccupied with his domestic scandals [including Watergate]. He had spent much of the day tidying up [Vice President Spiro] Agnew's resignation, to be announced within twenty-four hours. But while this might have deflected him from details, it had not dimmed his eye for essentials. "The Israelis must not be allowed to lose," he said, and acted accordingly. His decision was to speed the delivery of consumables and aircraft. Heavy equipment would not reach Israel before the end of the fighting. We would guarantee to replace Israel's losses; thus Israel would be freed of the need to maintain exorbitant reserve stocks during the battle. At 6:10 P.M. that Tuesday, I conveyed Nixon's crucial decision to Dinitz:

> On your special requests, the President has approved the entire list of consumables, that is, ordnance, electronic equipment—everything on the list except laser bombs. The President has agreed—and let me repeat this formally—that *all* your aircraft and tank losses will be replaced.

On Wednesday morning, October 10, we awoke to the ominous news of a Soviet airlift to Syria. Some twenty transport aircraft were on the way via Hungary and Yugoslavia. An airlift of such magnitude could not have been improvised; it must have been organized for several days. At this stage it seemed confined to consumables, paralleling our decision made the previous Sunday for Israel, though the Soviet effort was on a much larger scale and more overt. Was the purpose to stoke the fire of conflict, or to support a client and keep a Soviet hand in the postwar negotiations? Was it to encourage Arab intransigence, or to establish Soviet bona fides for a peace effort? Were they helping their most hard-pressed associate to keep it from collapsing, or were they encouraging a new onslaught? . . .

Had the Soviets conducted a decisive policy or had the Arab nations not been carried away by euphoria, they might have clinched their gains by pressing for that cease-fire in place on October 10. We would have been hard put to resist. But Egypt and Syria either underestimated Israel's recuperative power or did not know how to end their mutual suspicions—probably a combination of both. What the Soviets hoped to achieve is hard to fathom. Their ambivalence gave us a chance to play for time and recoup. If they hoped to slow down our resupply of Israel, it was a false hope. . . .

Our airlift was proceeding in stunning fashion. Once over its second thoughts, our Defense Department put on the sort of performance no other country can match. Flights of the C-5A began at a rate of four per day, then rose higher. The total of all aircraft—C-5As, C-130s, and C-141s—was twenty flights a day, carrying an average of 1,000 tons of equipment daily, or about 50 tons each hour. In the first full day of the airlift we had more than matched what the Soviet Union had put into all the Arab countries (Egypt, Syria, and Iraq) combined in all of the four previous days. We were bound inexorably to pull ahead of the Soviet resupply effort. Eighteen hundred tons had already landed; three thousand more tons were on the way. I said somewhat cattily to Schlesinger: "I must say when you want to work you are terrific. You are equally awe-inspiring when you don't." . . .

Thus the American airlift resupplying Israel had not impaired—and had perhaps enhanced—Arab conviction that the United States was the key to a peace settlement. The [Arab] ministers seemed determined to refrain from confrontation. On my part, when I met them afterward once again, I urged our visitors not to ask the impossible:

> We know Israel is not prepared to accept any of the present Arab ideas. The Israeli Prime Minister said so yesterday. In any case, and whatever the pressures may be, U.S. influence will have to be used. There is no substitute for U.S. influence. While the Arab armies have done better than expected, these armies cannot attain Arab diplomatic objectives without a long war and the high risk of Great Power involvement.

I cannot say that these observations evoked wild enthusiasm; but neither were they rejected. The four foreign ministers urged me to involve myself despite all my reservations; once you are committed to a medicine man, his sense of reality is interpreted as an act of modesty. I was the deus ex machina—for what, unfortunately, no one could describe.

While I was meeting with the Arab foreign ministers, I asked Scowcroft to have Dinitz obtain his government's reaction to the idea of linking a cease-fire only to some call for implementing Resolution 242. We expected little difficulty; after all, Resolution 242 had been the basis of Mideast negotiations for six years.

The daily WSAG deliberation took place at 3:00 P.M. on October 17 in a relaxed atmosphere. [Deputy Secretary of Defense William] Clements reported that our airlift was meeting the criterion of exceeding the Soviet airlift by 25 percent. I complacently observed that the mood of the Arab ministers seemed to confirm that there would be no immediate oil embargo. Somewhat more accurately, I predicted that diplomacy would be dormant until [Soviet premier Alexei] Kosygin returned to Moscow. "But we have to keep the stuff going into Israel. We have to pour it in until someone quits." . . .

But as the WSAG adjourned, a news ticker spelled out more complications. The Arab oil producers meeting in Kuwait had just announced an immediate production cutback of 5 percent, to be followed by successive monthly cutbacks of 5 percent until Israel withdrew to the 1967 frontiers. Further, in a separate development, the six Persian Gulf members of OPEC [Organization of Petroleum Exporting Countries] unilaterally increased the price of oil by 70 percent, from $3.01 to $5.12 a barrel. We were so focused on the danger of an embargo that we thought the production cutback, which the CIA estimated as initially one million barrels a day, largely a symbolic gesture. This it was—but it had revolutionary implications. As it became progressively evident that the producer cartel could set prices nearly arbitrarily by manipulating production, a new phase of postwar history began. It took some months for all parties to grasp its ramifications. . . .

I have since asked myself whether we accepted the Soviet invitation [for a cease-fire] too quickly. Possibly I could have delayed my departure another twenty-four hours—and strengthened Israel's military position even further. On the other hand, the Soviets would have understood exactly what we were doing, and might have sought to counter our blatant stalling by surfacing a formal resolution at the United Nations or raising the military ante. And Arab frustration would have turned a unified Arab world against the United States. A week earlier I had counseled Israel to delay seeking a cease-fire because I thought the military situation unpromising for postwar diplomacy. But just as it is important not to flinch on the road to strategic success, so it is essential not to press beyond what is sustainable. We had been riding many wild horses simultaneously. We could not now confuse virtuosity with a long-range strategy. We had to avoid risking everything for marginal gains, for we had achieved our fundamental objectives: We had created the conditions for a diplomatic breakthrough. We had vindicated the security of our friends. We had prevented a victory of Soviet arms. We had maintained a relationship with key Arab countries and laid the basis for a dominant role in postwar diplomacy. And we had done all this in the midst of the gravest constitutional crisis of this century.

We held the cards now. Our next challenge was to play our hand. . . .

At the end of October 1973, the war was over, but there was a good deal of high explosive lying around. The Egyptian Third Army was cut off in the Sinai. The Arab oil producers had imposed an embargo and production cuts. The Soviet Union was brooding over its frustrations and loss of influence. We had managed to achieve a cease-fire and were beginning to move into a pivotal position as the arbiter of the peace process. Therefore, what had been conceived of as a visit to Egypt—my first to an Arab country—turned into a journey through several nations of the Middle East.

Platform of Menachem Begin's Likud Coalition, 1977

The right of the Jewish people to the land of Israel is eternal and indisputable and is linked with the right to security and peace; therefore, Judaea and Samaria will not be handed to any foreign administration; between the sea and Jordan there will only be Israeli sovereignty.

A plan which relinquishes parts of western Eretz Israel, undermines our right to the country, unavoidably leads to the establishment of a "Palestinian State," jeopardizes the security of the Jewish population, endangers the existence of the State of Israel, and frustrates any prospect of peace.

The Likud government will place its aspirations for peace at the top of its priorities and will spare no effort to promote peace. The Likud will act as a genuine partner at peace treaty negotiations with our neighbors, as is customary among the nations. The Likud government will attend the Geneva Conference. . . .

The Likud government's peace initiative will be positive. Directly or through a friendly state, Israel will invite her neighbors to hold direct negotiations, in order to sign peace agreements without pre-conditions on either side and without any solution formula invented by outsiders.

At the negotiations each party will be free to make any proposals it deems fit.

Settlement, both urban and rural, in all parts of the Land of Israel is the focal point of the Zionist effort to redeem the country, to maintain vital security areas and serves as a reservoir of strength and inspiration for the renewal of the pioneering spirit. The Likud government will call the younger generation in Israel and the dispersions to settle and help every group and individual in the task of inhabiting and cultivating the wasteland, while taking care not to dispossess anyone.

The PLO is no national liberation organization but an organization of assassins, which the Arab countries use as a political and military tool, while also serving the interests of Soviet imperialism, to stir up the area. Its aim is to liquidate the State of Israel, set up an Arab country instead and make the Land of Israel part of the Arab world. The Likud government will strive to eliminate these murderous organizations in order to prevent them from carrying out their bloody deeds.

Egyptian President Anwar el-Sadat's Plea for Peace Before the Israeli Parliament, 1977

I come to you today on solid ground to shape a new life and to establish peace. We all love this land, the land of God, we all, Moslems, Christians and Jews, all worship God.

Under God, God's teachings and commandments are: love, sincerity, security and peace. . . .

How can we achieve permanent peace based on justice? Well, I have come to you carrying my clear and frank answer to this big question, so that the people in Israel as well as the entire world may hear it. All those devoted prayers ring in my ears, pleading to God Almighty that this historic meeting may eventually lead to the result aspired to by millions.

Before I proclaim my answer, I wish to assure you that in my clear and frank answer I am availing myself of a number of facts which no one can deny.

The first fact is that no one can build his happiness at the expense of the misery of others.

The second fact: never have I spoken, nor will I ever speak, with two tongues; never have I adopted, nor will I ever adopt, two policies. I never deal with anyone except in one tongue, one policy and with one face.

The third fact: direct confrontation is the nearest and most successful method to reach a clear objective.

The fourth fact: the call for permanent and just peace based on respect for United Nations resolutions has now become the call of the entire world. It has become the expression of the will of the international community, whether in official capitals where policies are made and decisions taken, or at the level of world public opinion, which influences policymaking and decision-taking.

The fifth fact, and this is probably the clearest and most prominent, is that the Arab nation, in its drive for permanent peace based on justice, does not proceed from a position of weakness. On the contrary, it has the power and stability for a sincere will for peace. . . .

In the light of these facts which I meant to place before you the way I see them, I would also wish to warn you, in all sincerity I warn you, against some thoughts that could cross your minds. . . .

First, I have not come here for a separate agreement between Egypt and Israel. This is not part of the policy of Egypt. The problem is not that of Egypt and Israel.

An interim peace between Egypt and Israel, or between any Arab confrontation state and Israel, will not bring permanent peace based on justice in the entire region.

Rather, even if peace between all the confrontation states and Israel were achieved in the absence of a just solution of the Palestinian problem, never will there be that durable and just peace upon which the entire world insists.

Second, I have not come to you to seek a partial peace, namely to terminate the state of belligerency at this stage and put off the entire problem to a subsequent stage. This is not the radical solution that would steer us to permanent peace.

Equally, I have not come to you for a third disengagement agreement in Sinai or in Golan or the West Bank.

For this would mean that we are merely delaying the ignition of the fuse. It would also mean that we are lacking the courage to face peace, that we are too weak to shoulder the burdens and responsibilities of a durable peace based upon justice.

I have come to you so that together we should build a durable peace based on justice to avoid the shedding of one single drop of blood by both sides. It is for this reason that I have proclaimed my readiness to go to the farthest corner of the earth.

Here I would go back to the big question:

How can we achieve a durable peace based on justice? In my opinion, and I declare it to the whole world, from this forum, the answer is neither difficult nor is it impossible despite long years of feuds, blood, faction, strife, hatreds and deep-rooted animosity.

The answer is not difficult, nor is it impossible, if we sincerely and faithfully follow a straight line.

You want to live with us, part of the world.

In all sincerity I tell you we welcome you among us with full security and safety. This in itself is a tremendous turning point, one of the landmarks of a decisive historical change. We used to reject you. We had our reasons and our fears, yes.

We refused to meet with you, anywhere, yes.

We were together in international conferences and organizations and our representatives did not, and still do not, exchange greetings with you. Yes. This has happened and is still happening.

It is also true that we used to set as a precondition for any negotiations with you a mediator who would meet separately with each party.

Yes. Through this procedure, the talks of the first and second disengagement agreements took place.

Our delegates met in the first Geneva conference without exchanging direct word, yes, this has happened.

Yet today I tell you, and I declare it to the whole world, that we accept to live with you in permanent peace based on justice. We do not want to encircle you or be encircled ourselves by destructive missiles ready for launching, nor by the shells of grudges and hatreds.

I have announced on more than one occasion that Israel has become a fait accompli, recognized by the world, and that the two superpowers have undertaken the responsibility for its security and the defense of its existence. As we really and truly seek peace we really and truly welcome you to live among us in peace and security.

There was a huge wall between us which you tried to build up over a quarter of a century, but it was destroyed in 1973. It was the wall of an implacable and escalating psychological warfare. . . .

Together we have to admit that that wall fell and collapsed in 1973. Yet, there remains another wall. This wall constitutes a psychological barrier between us, a barrier of suspicion, a barrier of rejection; a barrier of fear, of deception, a barrier of hallucination without any action, deed or decision. . . .

Today, through my visit to you, I ask you why don't we stretch out our hands with faith and sincerity so that together we might destroy this barrier? Why shouldn't our and your will meet with faith and sincerity so that together we might remove all suspicion of fear, betrayal and bad intentions? . . .

Ladies and gentlemen, to tell you the truth, peace cannot be worth its name unless it is based on justice and not on the occupation of the land of others. It would not be right for you to demand for yourselves what you deny to others. With all frankness and in the spirit that has prompted me to come to you today, I tell you you have to give up once and for all the dreams of conquest and give up the belief that force is the best method for dealing with the Arabs.

You should clearly understand the lesson of confrontation between you and us. Expansion does not pay. To speak frankly, our land does not yield itself to bargaining, it is not even open to argument. To us, the nation's soil is equal to the holy valley where God Almighty spoke to Moses. Peace be upon him. . . .

What is peace for Israel? It means that Israel lives in the region with her Arab neighbors in security and safety. Is that logical? I say yes. It means that Israel lives within its borders, secure against any aggression. Is that logical? And I say yes. It means that Israel obtains all kinds of guarantees that will ensure these two factors. To this demand, I say yes. . . .

But, how can this be achieved? How can we reach this conclusion which would lead us to permanent peace based on justice? There are facts that should be faced with courage and clarity. There are Arab territories which Israel has occupied and still occupies by force. We insist on complete withdrawal from these territories, including Arab Jerusalem. . . .

Let me tell you without the slightest hesitation that I have not come to you under this roof to make a request that your troops evacuate the occupied territories. Complete withdrawal from the Arab territories occupied after 1967 is a logical and undisputed fact. Nobody should plead for that. Any talk about permanent peace based on justice and any move to ensure our coexistence in peace and security in this part of the world would become meaningless while you occupy Arab territories by force of arms. . . .

As for the Palestine cause—nobody could deny that it is the crux of the entire problem. Nobody in the world could accept today slogans propagated here in Israel, ignoring the existence of a Palestinian people and questioning even their whereabouts. Because the Palestine people and their legitimate rights are no longer denied today by anybody; that is nobody who has the ability of judgment, can deny or ignore it. . . .

Even the United States of America, your first ally, which is absolutely committed to safeguard Israel's security and existence and which offered and still offers Israel every moral, material and military support—I say, even the United States has opted to face up to reality and admit that the Palestinian people are entitled to legitimate rights and that the Palestine problem is the cause and essence of the conflict and that so long as it continues to be unresolved, the conflict will continue to aggravate, reaching new dimension.

In all sincerity I tell you that there can be no peace without the Palestinians. It is a grave error of unpredictable consequences to overlook or brush aside this cause. . . .

Conceive with me a peace agreement in Geneva that we would herald to a world thirsting for peace. A peace agreement based on the following points:

Ending the occupation of the Arab territories occupied in 1967.

Achievement of the fundamental rights of the Palestinian people and their right to self-determination, including their right to establish their own state.

The right of all states in the area to live in peace within their boundaries, their secure boundaries, which will be secured and guaranteed through procedures to be agreed upon, which will provide appropriate security to international boundaries in addition to appropriate international guarantees.

Commitment of all states in the region to administer the relations among them in accordance with the objectives and principles of the United Nations Charter. Particularly the principles concerning the nonuse of force and a solution of differences among them by peaceful means.

Ending the state of belligerence in the region.

Ladies and gentlemen, peace is not a mere endorsement of written lines. Rather it is a rewriting of history. Peace is not a game of calling for peace to defend certain whims or hide certain admissions. Peace in its essence is a dire struggle against all and every ambition and whim.

Perhaps the example taken and experienced, taken from ancient and modern history, teaches that missiles, warships and nuclear weapons cannot establish security. Instead they destroy what peace and security build. . . .

Allow me to address my call from this rostrum to the people of Israel. I pledge myself with true and sincere words to every man, woman and child in Israel. I tell them, from the Egyptian people who bless this sacred mission of peace, I convey to you the message of peace of the Egyptian people, who do not harbor fanaticism and whose sons, Moslems, Christians and Jews, live together in a state of cordiality, love and tolerance. . . .

Introduce to the entire world the image of the new man in this area so that he might set an example to the man of our age, the man of peace everywhere. Ring the bells for your sons. Tell them that those wars were the last of wars and the end of sorrows. Tell them that we are entering upon a new beginning, a new life, a life of love, prosperity, freedom and peace.

You, sorrowing mother, you, widowed wife, you, the son who lost a brother or a father, all the victims of wars, fill the air and space with recitals of peace, fill bosoms and hearts with the aspirations of peace. Make a reality that blossoms and lives. Make hope a code of conduct and endeavor.

Former President Jimmy Carter Remembers the Highs and Lows of the 1978 Camp David Summit, 1982

I got up earlier than usual and wrote down all the items in the Sinai document with which the Israelis could possibly disagree. I simply listed them, and then went for another long walk with President [Anwar el-]Sadat. When I asked if there was anything I could do for him personally or for his people if we should ever be able to achieve peace, he replied, "I want you and your wife Rosalynn to come to Egypt for a visit." I promised we would.

I then probed very hard for some opening on the Sinai settlements issue, but without success. Sadat was willing to agree not to dismantle the buildings, to allow United Nations forces to be stationed in the area, and to wait three years after the peace treaty was signed for the people to leave. But they had to leave—that was it.

Later I walked over to Holly [the small cottage that served as the conference center], where the Americans and Israelis were talking, and discussed the same issue with [Israeli foreign minister Moshe] Dayan. The best I could get out of him was his personal willingness to have the settlers leave after twenty years. He said that [Menachem] Begin would not agree even to such an extended time period if there had to be an ultimate commitment for them to leave. On the West Bank, Dayan was willing to agree to no *new* settlements—to be specified in an exchange of letters between me and the Prime Minister. He added that Begin was feeling somewhat excluded from the negotiating process, since I had not seen him lately, and suggested that I meet with only him and [Israeli attorney general Aharon] Barak that evening, because [Israeli defense minister Ezer] Weizman had met with Sadat that morning.

I then went to see Weizman, to find out about his meeting with Sadat. As he walked to Aspen [Carter's cabin] with me, he reported that Sadat would be willing to say in the Sinai document that future negotiations would settle the issue of the Israeli settlements. I was startled, because this was not at all what Sadat had just told me. I knew that in general Ezer was an optimist, and that at Camp David, unfortunately, this attitude had rarely been justified. Weizman said he had also predicted to Sadat that the Knesset [Israeli parliament] would vote to remove the settlements; Dayan had told me the opposite.

At this point, as far as the settlements were concerned, we had conflicting reports from the Egyptian President and three levels of opposition in the Israeli delegation; Begin wanted no commitment to withdrawal; Dayan was willing to promise withdrawal after an extended period of time; and Weizman believed that the settlers should leave if the Knesset would agree.

When Sadat and [Egyptian under secretary of foreign affairs Osama] el-Baz came to meet with me and Cy [U.S. Secretary of State Cyrus Vance] in the afternoon, I reported Weizman's impression and asked Sadat to clarify his position on the settlements issue. He responded that Ezer's report was completely erroneous; he had described his attitude accurately to me during our walk that morning.

I listed all the advantages that might come to Egypt with a peace agreement.

We then reviewed the more specific Sinai proposal, and found no significant disagreement except over the Israeli settlements—and no disagreement at all between myself and Sadat.

On the more comprehensive Framework [for Peace], we were also very close. In referring to the Palestinians' authority on the West Bank, I agreed to find a synonym for "self-government." (Sadat thought the word sounded too much like Begin's "self-rule.") With great pressure I induced him to accept the language we had evolved on Jerusalem, provided there would be an exchange of letters reconfirming the historic United States position that East Jerusalem was part of the West Bank. Sadat agreed that the Wailing Wall should always be retained exclusively by the Jews.

I told him that there was no alternative to my handling the question of the settlements directly and personally with Prime Minister Begin, who would be arriving in just a few minutes. Sadat left, having been in an exceptionally sober but nevertheless constructive mood.

Cy and I were very pleased with this meeting, and although we had missed another meal, we considered it well worthwhile.

Begin came with Dayan and Barak, for which we were thankful. If anyone at Camp David had influence on Begin, it was these two men.

Cy and I ate some crackers and cheese as I listed the benefits of the proposed agreement to Israel. Immediately Begin began talking about the blessed settlements, but I insisted that we go through both documents in an orderly fashion, paragraph by paragraph. I wanted the Israelis to realize how few differences remained. In an hour we were finished with the Sinai document, and it was obvious to me that Sadat would be willing to accept almost all the Israeli demands for change. The few others were not very important to Begin, and I felt sure that he would not insist on them.

We then moved to the settlements again, and Begin insisted that he would negotiate with Sadat on all other items for three months in search of a final peace treaty and the resolution of all remaining differences. If this effort was completely successful, he would submit the settlement withdrawal question to the Knesset. I told him again and again that this proposal was totally unacceptable to Sadat, who insisted on a commitment to remove all Israeli settlers from his territory *before* any other negotiations could be conducted.

I thought the discussion would never end. It was obviously very painful for Prime Minister Begin, who was shouting words like "ultimatum," "excessive demands," and "political suicide." However, he finally promised to submit to the

Knesset within two weeks the question: "If agreement is reached on all other Sinai issues, will the settlers be withdrawn?"

I believed this concession would be enough for Sadat. Breakthrough!

I asked Begin if he would maintain a neutral position as the Knesset debated the issue, but he would not promise. He did agree, however, to remove the requirements of party loyalty and let each member of the Knesset vote as an individual. He assured me that the same would apply to cabinet members. I questioned Dayan, but he would not give me a firm commitment of support.

We all agreed that what we had just decided represented a great step forward.

We then had a surprisingly amicable discussion about the Framework for Peace. Barak was a tremendous help as we went over the entire proposed text. Dayan was quite forthcoming on the Palestinian question, and said with some enthusiasm, "We'll let the Palestinians join the Jordanians during the negotiation of the peace treaty with Israel." To accommodate Sadat's request, we searched for a synonym for "self-government for the Palestinians," and came up with "how the Palestinians shall govern themselves." There was no apparent difference, so no harm was done. By this time I had become a master at making insignificant editorial changes to overcome significant objections.

I had a lot of latitude in dealing with the West Bank–Gaza questions. Fortunately, Sadat was not particularly interested in the detailed language of the Framework for Peace, and with the exception of the settlements, Begin was not very interested in the details of the Sinai agreement.

On Jerusalem, I told the Israeli leaders that Sadat had accepted the paragraph as drafted for the Framework text, but he wanted a separate exchange of letters, so that each nation could make public its own different ideas as part of the official record. Israelis would not have to participate in the exchange, but could let their views be known if they preferred to do so.

On the West Bank settlements, we finally worked out language that was satisfactory: that no new Israel settlements would be established after the signing of this Framework for Peace, and that the issue of additional settlements would be resolved by the parties during the negotiations. This would be stated in a letter, to be made public, from Begin to me. (Begin later denied that he had agreed to this, and claimed that he had promised to stop building settlements only for a three-month period. My notes are clear—that the settlement freeze would continue until all negotiations were completed—and Cy Vance confirms my interpretation of what we decided. This was the only serious post–Camp David disagreement about our decisions, so our batting average was good.)

After the Israelis left, Vance and I agreed that we had a settlement, at least for Camp David. There was no doubt that Sadat would accept my recommendations on the issues we had just discussed with Begin. What the Knesset might decide was uncertain, but I was convinced that the people of Israel would be in favor of the overall agreement, including the withdrawal of the settlers from the Sinai. Weizman would be a big help. I intended to try in every way possible to shape world opinion and to get the American Jewish community to support this effort.

[The next day] . . . President Sadat . . . and I quickly went over the proposals for the final language. The few predictable changes that he advocated would, I was sure, be acceptable to the Israelis. The only serious problem was his desire to delete the entire paragraph on Jerusalem. I knew that the Israelis wanted the same thing, but I confess that I did not tell Sadat. I reserved this concession just in case I needed some bargaining points later on. . . .

In the meantime, a serious problem had erupted with the Israelis. Vance had just shown them a copy of our draft letter that would go to Sadat, restating the United States position on Jerusalem, which had been spelled out officially in United Nations debates over the years. There was an absolute furor, and Begin announced that Israel would not sign *any* document if we wrote *any* letter to Egypt about Jerusalem. . . .

Back at Holly, I had a very unpleasant session there, with Dayan, Weizman, Barak, [Vice President Walter] Mondale, Vance, and [Adviser for National Security Affairs Zbigniew] Brzezinski. I asked for a text of our United Nations ambassadors' statements in the debates concerning Jerusalem. Ambassadors Charles Yost, Arthur Goldberg, and William Scranton had spoken on the subject, but I had never read all of what they actually said.

I then asked Barak to walk with me to Aspen to go over the text of our proposed letter, in order to find language which might be acceptable. He was just as adamant as the other Israelis, insisting that the situation was hopeless. However, I proposed that we strike out of our letter all the actual quotations from the United Nations speeches and simply say that the United States position was as it had been expressed by the three ambassadors. Dayan and Barak both agreed to go over this changed text with Begin. It was another tense moment.

Earlier, my secretary, Susan Clough, had brought me some photographs of Begin, Sadat, and me. They had already been signed by President Sadat, and Prime Minister Begin had requested that I autograph them for his grandchildren. Knowing the trouble we were in with the Israelis, Susan suggested that she go and get the actual names of the grandchildren, so that I could personalize each picture. I did this, and walked over to Begin's cabin with them. He was sitting on the front porch, very distraught and nervous because the talks had finally broken down at the last minute.

I handed him the photographs. He took them and thanked me. Then he happened to look down and saw that his granddaughter's name was on the top one. He spoke it aloud, and then looked at each photograph individually, repeating the name of the grandchild I had written on it. His lips trembled, and tears welled up in his eyes. He told me a little about each child, and especially about the one who seemed to be his favorite. We were both emotional as we talked quietly for a few minutes about grandchildren and about war.

Then he asked me to step into his cabin, requesting that everyone else in the room leave. He was quiet, sober, surprisingly friendly. There were no histrionics. He said that the Jerusalem matter was fatal, that he was very sorry but he could not accept our letter to Egypt. I told him I had drafted a new version and submitted it to Dayan and Barak. He had not yet seen it. I suggested he read it over and let me know his decision, but that there was no way that I could go back on my commitment to Sadat to exchange letters. The success of any future peace talks might depend on his and Sadat's assessment of my integrity, and I could not violate a promise once it was made.

I walked back to Aspen, very dejected. Sadat was there with el-Baz, both dressed to go back to Washington. I asked everyone else to leave and told Sadat what was happening. We realized that all of us had done our best, but that prospects were dim indeed.

Then Begin called. He said, "I will accept the letter you have drafted on Jerusalem." I breathed a sigh of relief, because it now seemed that the last obstacle had been removed.

The Camp David Framework for Peace, 1978

The search for peace in the Middle East must be guided by the following:

• The agreed basis for a peaceful settlement of the conflict between Israel and its neighbors is United Nations Security Council Resolution 242, in all its parts.

• After four wars during thirty years, despite intensive human efforts, the Middle East, which is the cradle of civilization and the birthplace of three great religions, does not yet enjoy the blessings of peace. The people of the Middle East yearn for peace so that the vast human and natural resources of the region can be turned to the pursuits of peace and so that this area can become a model for coexistence and cooperation among nations.

• The historic initiative of President Sadat in visiting Jerusalem and the reception accorded to him by the Parliament, government and people of Israel, and the reciprocal visit of Prime Minister Begin to Ismailia [Egypt], the peace proposals made by both leaders, as well as the warm reception of these missions by the people of both countries, have created an unprecedented opportunity for peace which must not be lost if this generation and future generations are to be spared the tragedies of war.

• The provisions of the Charter of the United Nations and the other accepted norms of international law and legitimacy now provide accepted standards for the conduct of relations among the states.

• To achieve a relationship of peace, in the spirit of Article 2 of the United Nations Charter, future negotiations between Israel and any neighbor prepared to negotiate peace and security with it, are necessary for the purpose of carrying out all the provisions and principles of Resolutions 242 and 338. [U.N. Security Council Resolution 338, adopted on October 22, 1973, secured a cease-fire in the October War and called for direct negotiations between the parties on the basis of Resolution 242.]

• Peace requires respect for the sovereignty, territorial integrity and political independence of every state in the area and their right to live in peace within secure and recognized boundaries free from threats or acts of force. Progress toward that goal can accelerate movement toward a new era of reconciliation in the Middle East marked by cooperation in promoting economic development, in maintaining stability, and in assuring security.

• Security is enhanced by a relationship of peace and by cooperation between nations which enjoy normal relations. In addition, under the terms of peace treaties, the parties can, on the basis of reciprocity, agree to special security arrangements such as demilitarized zones, limited armaments areas, early warning stations, the presence of international forces, liaison, agreed measures for monitoring, and other arrangements that they agree are useful.

Taking these factors into account, the parties are determined to reach a just, comprehensive, and durable settlement of the Middle East conflict through the conclusion of peace treaties based on Security Council Resolutions 242 and 338 in all their parts. Their purpose is to achieve peace and good neighborly relations. They recognize that, for peace to endure, it must involve all those who have been most deeply affected by the conflict. They therefore agree that this framework as appropriate is intended by them to constitute a basis for peace not only between Egypt and Israel, but also between Israel and each of its other neighbors which is prepared to negotiate peace with Israel on this basis. With that objective in mind, they have agreed to proceed as follows:

A. West Bank and Gaza

1. Egypt, Israel, Jordan and the representatives of the Palestinian people should participate in negotiations on the resolution of the Palestinian problem in all its aspects. To achieve that objective, negotiations relating to the West Bank and Gaza should proceed in three stages:

   (a) Egypt and Israel agree that, in order to ensure a peaceful and orderly trasfer of authority, and taking into account the security concerns of all the parties, there should be transitional arrangements for the West Bank and Gaza for a period not exceeding five years. In order to provide full autonomy to the inhabitants, under these arrangements the Israeli military government and its civilian administration will be withdrawn as soon as a self-governing authority has been freely elected by the inhabitants of these areas to replace the existing military government. To negotiate the details of a transitional arrangement, the Government of Jordan will be invited to join the negotiations on the basis of this framework. These new arrangements should give due consideration both to the principle of self-government by the inhabitants of these territories and to the legitimate security concerns of the parties involved.

   (b) Egypt, Israel, and Jordan will agree on the modalities for establishing the elected self-governing authority in the West Bank and Gaza. The delegations of Egypt and Jordan may include Palestinians from the West Bank and Gaza or other Palestinians as mutually agreed. The parties will negotiate an agreement which will define the powers and responsibilities of the self-governing authority to be exercised in the West Bank and Gaza. A withdrawal of Israeli armed forces will take place and there will be a redeployment of the remaining Israeli forces into specified security locations. The agreement will also include arrangements for assuring internal and external security and public order. A strong local police force will be established, which may include Jordanian citizens. In addition, Israeli and Jordanian forces will participate in joint patrols and in the manning of control posts to assure the security of the borders.

   (c) When the self-governing authority (administrative council) in the West Bank and Gaza is established and inaugurated, the transitional period of five years will begin. As soon as possible, but not later than the third year after the beginning of the transitional period, negotiations will take place to determine the final status of the West Bank and Gaza and its relationship with its neighbors, and to conclude a peace treaty between Israel and Jordan by the end of the transitional period. These negotiations will be conducted among Egypt, Israel, Jordan, and the elected representatives of the inhabitants of the West Bank and Gaza. . . . The negotiations shall be based on all the provisions and principles of UN Security Council Resolution 242. The negotiations will resolve, among other matters, the location of the boundaries and the nature of the security arrangements. The solution from the negotiations must also recognize the legitimate rights of the Palestinian people and their just requirements. In this way, the Palestinians will participate in the determination of their own future through:

1) The negotiations among Egypt, Israel, Jordan and the representatives of the inhabitants of the West Bank and Gaza to agree on the final status of the West Bank and Gaza and other outstanding issues by the end of the transitional period.
2) Submitting their agreement to a vote by the elected representatives of the inhabitants of the West Bank and Gaza.
3) Providing for the elected representatives of the inhabitants of the West Bank and Gaza to decide how they shall govern themselves consistent with the provisions of their agreement.
4) Participating as stated above in the work of the committee negotiating the peace treaty between Israel and Jordan.

All necessary measures will be taken and provisions made to assure the security of Israel and its neighbors during the transitional period and beyond. To assist in providing such security, a strong local police force will be constituted by the self-governing authority. It will be composed of inhabitants of the West Bank and Gaza. The police will maintain continuing liaison on internal security matters with the designated Israeli, Jordanian, and Egyptian officers.

During the transitional period, representatives of Egypt, Israel, Jordan, and the self-governing authority will constitute a continuing committee to decide by agreement on the modalities of admission of persons displaced from the West Bank and Gaza in 1967, together with necessary measures to prevent disruption and disorder. Other matters of common concern may also be dealt with by this committee.

Egypt and Israel will work with each other and with other interested parties to establish agreed procedures for a prompt, just and permanent implementation of the resolution of the refugee problem.

B. Egypt-Israel

1. Egypt and Israel undertake not to resort to the threat or the use of force to settle disputes. Any disputes shall be settled by peaceful means in accordance with the provisions of Article 33 of the Charter of the United Nations.
2. In order to achieve peace between them, the parties agree to negotiate in good faith with a goal of concluding within three months from the signing of this Framework a peace treaty between them, while inviting the other parties to the conflict to proceed simultaneously to negotiate and conclude similar peace treaties with a view to achieving a comprehensive peace in the area. The Framework for the Conclusion of a Peace Treaty between Egypt and Israel

will govern the peace negotiations between them. The parties will agree on the modalities and the timetable for the implementation of their obligations under the treaty.

C. Associated Principles

1. Egypt and Israel state that the principles and provisions described below should apply to peace treaties between Israel and each of its neighbors— Egypt, Jordan, Syria and Lebanon.
2. Signatories shall establish among themselves relationships normal to states at peace with one another. To this end, they should undertake to abide by all the provisions of the Charter of the United Nations. Steps to be taken in this respect include:
   (a) full recognition;
   (b) abolishing economic boycotts;
   (c) guaranteeing that under their jurisdiction the citizens of other parties shall enjoy the protection of the due process of the law.
3. Signatories should explore possibilities for economic development in the context of final peace treaties, with the objective of contributing to the atmosphere of peace, cooperation and friendship which is their common goal.
4. Claims Commissions may be established for the mutual settlement of all financial claims.
5. The United States shall be invited to participate in the talks on matters related to the modalities of the implementation of the agreements and working out the timetable for the carrying out of the obligations of the parties.
6. The United Nations Security Council shall be requested to endorse the peace treaties and ensure that their provisions shall not be violated. The permanent members of the Security Council shall be requested to underwrite the peace treaties and ensure respect for their provisions. They shall also be requested to conform their policies and actions with the undertakings contained in this Framework. . . .

Framework for the Conclusion of a Peace Treaty Between Egypt and Israel

The following matters are agreed between the parties:
   (a) the full exercise of Egyptian sovereignty up to the internationally recognized border between Egypt and mandated Palestine;
   (b) the withdrawal of Israeli armed forces from the Sinai;
   (c) the use of airfields left by the Israelis near El Arish, Rafah, Ras en Naqb, and Sharm el Sheikh for civilian purposes only, including possible commercial use by all nations;
   (d) the right of free passage by ships of Israel through the Gulf of Suez and the Suez Canal on the basis of the Constantinople Convention of 1888 applying to all nations; the Strait of Tiran and the Gulf of Aqaba are international waterways to be open to all nations for unimpeded and nonsuspendable freedom of navigation and overflight;
   (e) the construction of a highway between the Sinai and Jordan near Elat with guaranteed free and peaceful passage by Egypt and Jordan; and
   (f) the stationing of military forces.

In the first essay, Steven L. Spiegel, a political scientist at the University of California, Los Angeles, praises U.S. policy in the Middle East, especially Washington's strong support for Israel. Spiegel suggests that the Soviet Union posed a significant threat to U.S. interests in the region and that Gamel Abdul Nasser and other Arab nationalists could not be relied upon to cooperate with the West. Israel's impressive victories in the Six-Day War and the October War, according to Spiegel, won wide public approval in the United States and helped U.S. leaders to realize Israel's value as a strategic asset in the Cold War. As Egypt questioned the value of its alliance with the Soviet Union, Spiegel concludes, the United States became the sole external power in the region to which all sides turned for guidance and assistance in deliberating peace.

Cheryl A. Rubenberg, a political scientist at Florida International University, disagrees with those scholars who view Israel as a strategic asset for the United States. Focusing on the Yom Kippur War of October 1973 and its aftermath, Rubenberg argues that President Richard Nixon and Adviser for National Security Affairs Henry A. Kissinger exaggerated Soviet influence in the Middle East, failed to grasp Egypt's willingness to cooperate with Washington, and allowed themselves to be swayed by Jewish American lobbyists. According to Rubenberg, the administration's strong military and diplomatic support for Israel alienated Arab nationalists, precipitated an oil embargo, strained U.S. alliances with Europe and Japan, and nearly provoked a Soviet-American nuclear confrontation. She concludes that the U.S. attachment to Israel also prevented Kissinger from seeking a comprehensive regional settlement after the war and instead encouraged a more limited, step-by-step course of peacemaking.

The third essay, by William B. Quandt, examines the road to Camp David during the Carter years and highlights the importance of U.S. presidential leadership to the Middle East peace process. Quandt served on the National Security Council staff in the Nixon and Carter administrations and is now a senior fellow at the Brookings Institution in Washington, D.C. He emphasizes how fears of regional instability and Carter's lagging domestic political fortunes motivated the administration to assume an active role in the Arab-Israeli dispute. Quandt praises Carter's evenhandedness in dealing with Israel and the Arab states, his sensitivity to Palestinian concerns, and his pragmatic acceptance of a limited Egyptian-Israeli accord. Although Camp David did not achieve a comprehensive regionwide settlement, Quandt concludes that Carter's creative diplomacy helped to normalize relations between two of the major players in the area and provided a basis for broader negotiations in the future.

The Six-Day War and the Benefits of the U.S.-Israeli Alliance

STEVEN L. SPIEGEL

As late as November 1966, the President [Lyndon B. Johnson] told a news conference, "We are increasingly interested in the African continent and the Middle East. Our reports give us a reason to believe that things are going as well as could be expected." By contrast, in a commencement address in May 1968, his earlier compla-

From "America in Middle East Policy Since the Six-Day War," by Steven L. Spiegel in *The Arab-Israeli Conflict: Two Decades of Change,* Yehuda Lukacs and Abdullah M. Battah, eds., Westview Press, 1988, pp. 199–213, by permission of Westview Press, Boulder, Colorado.

cency had vanished. "Today in two areas of danger and conflict—the Middle East and Vietnam—events drive home the difficulty of making peace."

As these contrasting comments by Lyndon Johnson shortly before and after the Six Day War suggest, the dramatic events of May and June 1967 had an immediate impact on American thinking about the Middle East. Previously, it was an area of minor concern, a backwater region only considered a top priority during the first years of the Eisenhower administration. Since the 1967 war, the problems of the area have been almost constantly at the forefront of discussion, from the halls of Congress to the Oval Office to the media. In the perspective of forty years since Israel's establishment, the Six Day War stands as the seminal event which led American policy makers to reassess the importance of the Middle East and, perhaps more importantly, the perils its instability holds for American interests—including the threat to oil supplies, the possibility of Soviet expansion, and the dangers of confrontation with the USSR.

On a wide dimension of American foreign and domestic concerns, the Six Day War can be seen to have led to prime changes in the U.S. approach to the area. In this paper, these changes are viewed from a variety of perspectives: the impact of the Six Day War on the Soviet-American competition, on public attitudes toward the region, on the handling of the Arab-Israeli issue by the Johnson administration and its successors, on the domestic political debate between conservatives and liberals, and on the role of key interest groups, the President, and Congress.

In order to understand the critical importance of the Six Day War to the competition between the United States and the Soviet Union, it is useful to consider briefly the prior history of superpower confrontation in the area. The Truman Doctrine, the basic American declaration of the cold war in 1947, was oriented to two nearby countries, Greece and Turkey. Yet, except for discussion of a Middle East Defense Organization in 1952, U.S. engagement in the region prior to 1953 had largely been economic—the product of American companies seeking expanded involvement, often at the expense of European competitors. From 1945 onward, Americans had progressively become uneasy involved observers in the Palestine question, but the policy had been inconsistent and contradictory. The uncertainties are reflected in alternative support for partition and trusteeship, in recognition of the fledgling State of Israel and the arms embargo which discriminated against the new state, in quiet participation on the United Nations Palestine Conciliation Commission with Turkey and France, and in sponsorship of the Tripartite Declaration [1950] supposedly limiting British, French, and American arms shipments to the area.

[President Dwight D.] Eisenhower and [Secretary of State John Foster] Dulles entered office committed to a more active American policy in order to address the threat of expanded Soviet involvement and influence in the region. In order to block Moscow, they devised a multifaceted strategy: (1) Because the British could no longer be trusted to protect American interests in the area, America would take over; (2) the U.S. would try to encourage a group of states in the area to organize a "mini-NATO" to thwart potential Russian influence (later the Baghdad Pact); (3) arms sales would be stepped up to the Arabs (especially Iraq, hopefully Egypt); (4) the United States would keep its distance from Israel and would try to settle the Arab-Israeli dispute.

Eisenhower and Dulles had correctly identified the threat of Soviet involvement and they had developed a sophisticated strategy, but it did not work. [Soviet premier Nikita] Khrushchev, anxious to develop a strategy for challenging the West in the Third World, simply "jumped over" the Maginot Line the two American leaders had created in the form of the Baghdad Pact when he began selling arms to [Gamel Abdul] Nasser's Egypt and to Syria in 1955. During the Suez crisis the following year, the Russian leader was able to pose as the protector of the Arabs while threatening to punish the British, French, and Israelis. The United States pressured all three to cease their activity and eventually to withdraw; the Russians got the credit. By tying his fate to the nationalist Arab movement led by Nasser, Khrushchev had catapulted the Soviet Union into a central role in the area. When a radical coup overthrew the pro-Western government in Iraq in July 1958, the Russian role appeared to constitute an even wider menace. In response, Eisenhower intervened in Lebanon.

By the end of the 1950's, the Russians were pursuing large programs of arms transfers to Egypt, Iraq, and Syria; they were engaged in demonstrative aid projects like the Aswan Dam; larger numbers of Arab students were travelling to Moscow. The United States, though heavily involved in the region, had no effective means of countering Russian inroads and was attempting to bolster regimes still ready to align with the West.

In the 1960's, the Kennedy administration attempted to improve relations with Nasser, but was thwarted by the Yemen war which seemed to hold the prospect of Russian influence and Egyptian troops at the border of oil-rich Saudi Arabia. The Johnson administration, trying to develop a new program for containing Soviet expansion, began to expand arms sales to several conservative Arab states and Israel. During this period, the Russians had gradually been increasing their involvement in the region, especially through continuing military aid. Yet they too were hindered by quarrelling Arab clients. Particularly after 1966, a new radical Syrian government began calling for a "national liberation campaign" against Israel and complained that Nasser's involvement in the holy campaign was marginal.

In order to resolve these divisions, Moscow began warning Nasser of imminent Israeli plans to attack Syria. This action was consistent with the Soviet pattern of stirring up local conflict in the hopes of gaining political benefits. All parties knew this accusation was false and Nasser at first ignored it. By May 1967, however, with his army bogged down in Yemen and his economy deteriorating, Nasser flirted with the tides of history by ordering a partial withdrawal of the United Nations Emergency Force which had been stationed in the Sinai since 1957. He thus set in place the events which led to the Six Day War three weeks later.

From Moscow's perspective, the consequences of the war were horrifying and indeed it has never fully recovered its former position in the region. The two Arab states most closely associated with the Soviet Union, Egypt and Syria, were roundly defeated. Both lost significant pieces of territory; their armies were decimated. As these defeats occurred, the Russians could do little but fulminate in support of their Arab clients at the United Nations and increase their presence in the Mediterranean. Even their confrontation with the United States in protection of Syria during the last hours of the war appeared to be little more than posturing.

Yet in the immediate aftermath of hostilities, the balance did not appear totally negative from the Kremlin's perspective. Although the Israelis won their victory largely with French rather than American weapons, the United States was blamed. As a consequence, several Arab states broke off diplomatic relations with

Washington and [Charles] de Gaulle's abrupt snub of Israel forced America for the first time into the position of Israel's protector. Moscow's enormous resupply of weaponry to the Arabs compensated for the dismal showing of the USSR and its arms during the war. It forced the United States to step up its arms transfers to Israel in order to maintain the regional balance of power. By 1969, when Nasser started his War of Attrition along the Suez Canal, the Soviets could justifiably argue that the return of Arab power had begun under their sponsorship. They were also heavily engaged in training and support for the Palestine Liberation Organization (PLO), which intensified its terrorist attacks against Israel after 1967.

The Six Day War certainly increased the immediate dependence of key Arab states on Moscow and of Israel on the United States. In more subtle terms, however, the nature of the Soviet-American competition was altered. For the first time the means of Russian involvement in the region had contracted and America's options had expanded. In frustration at the successful Israeli attack and its inability to reverse the outcome of the war, Moscow broke diplomatic relations with Israel. It was to prove a terrible blunder. Henceforth, the United States was the only superpower in close touch with both sides. Since the results of the war necessitated diplomatic discussions on conditions under which Israel might return the territories, a negotiated process of some kind was inevitable. The Soviets, always fearful of losing their Arab support purchased largely with arms transfers, continued to align with the radical ideologues. They thereby proved themselves irrelevant for serious negotiations.

The changed atmosphere could be seen immediately after the war. It was the United States which took the lead in trying to reach some kind of *modus vivendi,* a process that led to UN Security Council Resolution 242 in which an agenda for discussion was set. In 1969 it was the United States which promulgated the first major post-1967 peace plan for the area . . . and the United States which arranged the ceasefire which ended the War of Attrition in August 1970. When Syrian tanks invaded Jordan the following month, the United States and Israel demonstrably maneuvered to strengthen King Hussein [of Jordan]. The Syrians and their Palestinian allies were defeated.

Nasser's successor, Anwar Sadat, was progressively frustrated in his attempts to regain the Sinai through reliance on Moscow. Indeed, in 1972 he expelled the large contingent of Russian advisors who had entered Egypt during the War of Attrition. His countrymen applauded. Following the Yom Kippur war, the supremacy of American diplomacy was epitomized by the Kissinger shuttle [and President Jimmy] Carter's diplomacy. . . .

Thus, the initial outcome of the Six Day War was confusing: America's client had won, but Washington's relations with the Arab world suffered severe setbacks to the advantage of the USSR. Viewed in perspective, however, it was the Six Day War which was the turning point: a consistent tide of frustration for Washington was transformed into a period when opportunities emerged. By contrast, Moscow's fortunes began to decline. While these developments were certainly not inevitable, Russian errors and clever American initiatives concretized advantages that the 1967 war had made possible.

The opportunities created by the Six Day War, and their effect in particular on the Soviet-American competition, can only be seen in retrospect. At the time, Americans greeted the war with a combination of exhilaration, relief, and fear.

There had been earlier Arab-Israeli wars in 1948 and 1956 as well as the U.S. intervention in Lebanon. There had been previous attempts at peace efforts and at blocking the Soviet Union. But the national response to the Six Day War was unusual in its emotion and as an event which seemed to necessitate new policies and attention.

The sudden onset of the crisis made it all the more compelling by comparison with other Mideast crises. The 1948 war had been evolving for years; the Suez Crisis was the culmination of a period of regional tension which began with the Soviet-Czech arms deal in September 1955. Despite its surprise beginning, the Yom Kippur war occurred in a period when Middle East issues were attracting prime attention in the United States. For Americans, easily jolted by shifting tides of mood and fad, the Six Day War struck like a bolt from nowhere.

The shock was intensified by America's preoccupation with Vietnam in 1967. By this time, dissension and self-doubt were emerging from an incubation period into a state of full-scale convulsion. The outbreak of hostilities in the Middle East challenged the administration's concentration on Southeast Asia. The Vietnam war had been sold to Americans by the Johnson administration as crucial to defining America's global role and the future of the conflict with international communism. Yet the events in the Middle East reminded Americans that there was more to the world than Saigon. As several Senatorial critics pointed out, on various scales of determining the national interest, the Middle East appeared more significant than Indochina because of its crucial location astride three continents, the direct threat of Russian expansion, oil, the threat to a democracy (Israel), and the impact on the Suez Canal. By challenging the contemporary dominant worldview, the Six Day War contributed to the disintegration of the Vietnam-centered complex the Johnson administration had propounded.

Americans crave moral clarity in world affairs: good versus evil; democratic versus totalitarian; no grays. By 1967, the distinction between the communist oppressor and the democratic defender was blurring in Vietnam. At a critical moment the Middle East conflict appeared, and seemed to offer the contrast between hero and villain that Americans were losing in Southeast Asia. In the conventional perspective the Israelis were "minding their own business" when Nasser created a crisis, the Arab states encircled the Jewish state, and then threatened to destroy it. The public's impression was that Israel's survival was at stake. Suddenly, the Israelis attacked and vanquished all of their would-be conquerors in six short days.

These events seemed to imitate a Hollywood script, and they were accompanied by an emotional concentration heightened by the impact of television. Except for Vietnam itself and the Cuban missile crisis, the Six Day War was one of the earliest international crises when television operated as a factor in the political equation. It was an equation which aided the Israelis at the Arabs' expense, as suggested by the sudden rise of Israel's popularity in public opinion polls.

Mixed with the public exhilaration were other sentiments, especially within the Johnson administration. First, there was widespread relief that Israel had successfully acted on its own, avoiding the need for American rescue. Second, there was concern at the sudden deterioration of U.S. relations with a large segment of the Arab world. Third, there was fear that the Arab-Israeli dispute could lead to a future Soviet-American confrontation, which made the Middle East even more dangerous than Southeast Asia.

The newfound responsibility for Israel, the search for ways to mend relations with the Arab world, and the danger of Soviet-American confrontation created contradictory requirements for American policy. This is illustrated by the approach to arms sales. Once de Gaulle terminated France's special relationship with Israel, Washington was deprived of flexibility, especially in the wake of Russian resupplies of the Arab belligerents. Since the United States wished to compete by rearming pro-American Arab regimes, especially Jordan, it was forced to assume major responsibility for maintaining the regional arms balance in Israel's favor. In subsequent years administrations attempted to protect the balance of power by selling Israel sufficient weapons to counter British, French, Russian and American arms sold to the Arabs. This policy has been controversial at home and often based on conflicting and inaccurate calculations. The frequent regional wars attest to the difficulty of managing an arms race in which the U.S. is only one of several suppliers and of preventing conflict by arming the participants on both sides to the hilt.

The Six Day War itself was a prominent example of this frustrating task. Although the Johnson administration, like all involved parties, was caught offguard and unprepared, it did work to prevent war. For the first time in a crisis the U.S. and Israel both tried to gain the other's confidence, but their immediate objectives were running at crosspurposes. Israel—mobilized and progressively encircled— wanted quick action. The Johnson administration—overcommitted and uncertain—stalled. The result was a war which could only have been averted by an early major U.S. initiative, at least the contemplated multilateral fleet and perhaps an American or multination expeditionary force sent to the Sinai as a replacement for the recently deposed United Nations Emergency Force. In the light of Vietnam, these steps were unthinkable. Even had the U.S. not been at war, it is unlikely that the Johnson administration would have been prepared to act quickly and effectively.

The events of the war reinforced the need to do something about the Arab-Israeli dispute lest it result in another similar crisis. In comparison with arms sales and crisis diplomacy, there were few contradictions and many potential benefits in attempting to ameliorate the Arab-Israeli dispute. Israel's security would be enhanced, the Arabs could be coaxed into improved relations with Washington, the dangers of Soviet-American confrontation would be reduced.

In their approach to peacemaking, many American leaders, especially Lyndon Johnson, were influenced by the experience of 1957 when Israel had been forced to withdraw from the Sinai and the Gaza Strip on the promise of future Egyptian concessions, which was not fulfilled. When Nasser unilaterally evicted the United Nations Emergency Force from the Sinai, he destroyed the last vestige of the 1957 agreements. Whatever Arab-Israeli compromise individual American officials might advocate after 1967, no principal figures urged unilateral withdrawals by Israel without an Arab commitment to some type of peaceful arrangement. Before the Carter administration, American officials disagreed with Israel's demands for complete normalization of relations with Arab states in return for withdrawals, but they were also not prepared to entertain withdrawals prior to a form of Arab recognition of Israel and commitment to non-aggression.

American officials differed markedly from Israel in their belief that in return for Arab commitments to peace the Jerusalem government should ultimately withdraw totally from the occupied territories with the possible exception of the most minor of adjustments. Within weeks of the Six Day War, they were appalled at Israel's efforts to assume complete control of Jerusalem. They believed that Israel was making unrealistic demands for direct negotiations with Arab representatives and for ultimate normalization of relations as the price of withdrawal. Logically, therefore, it appeared that the occupied territories would become the source of deep division between Jerusalem and Washington. There were certainly frequent tensions between the two governments over the issue, but ironically the occupied territories became a source of agreement as well. The Arab states refused to accept publicly the argument that the Six Day War had altered irretrievably the Mideast balance of political forces. At Khartoum in August 1967 they declared defiantly that there would be no negotiations, no recognition, and no peace with Israel. They were thereby standing firmly in favor of the 1957 formula of unilateral Israeli withdrawals, which the United States would no longer support. Except for Sadat's diplomacy, this stance assured a minimal common Israeli-American perspective toward the peace process. . . .

In American politics, each new administration attempts to set out in new directions, especially in reaction to previous crises. Thus, Richard Nixon came to power determined to address the problems for the United States created by the Six Day War. He therefore sought to reestablish America's shattered image in the Arab world and to resurrect relations broken in 1967; to reduce the Russian role in the area; and to promote America's position by facilitating an Arab-Israeli settlement. He was less certain regarding how he might achieve these goals. During the first term, when the Middle East took a back seat to Vietnam, China, SALT [Strategic Arms Limitation Talks], and détente, Nixon was confronted by two competing strategies represented by his two warring national security aides, Henry Kissinger and William Rogers. The Secretary of State [Rogers], who was at first given the prime responsibility for Mideast policy, favored a region-oriented approach popular at the State Department. The outcome of this strategy was the Rogers Plan of December 1969 which laid out a program by which Israel would withdraw from all but insubstantial territories captured in 1967 in return for the Arabs registering their "binding and specific commitment" to non-belligerency. Kissinger argued that the United States could not press for negotiations until the key Arab parties, particularly Egypt, first made a move toward the United States lest the Soviets receive the credit for any breakthrough which might occur. . . .

After the Yom Kippur war, the incentive to support conflict resolution was even greater. Kissinger's shuttle diplomacy followed by Carter's flirtation with a Geneva conference and then the Camp David accords and the Egyptian-Israeli peace treaty demonstrated that American engagement in the Arab-Israeli peace process had become a consistent pattern of Washington's policy toward the area. This pattern only reinforced the lesson decision makers believed they had learned in 1967—that it was the Arab-Israeli issue which was the perennial source of instability in the region. Zbigniew Brzezinski even suggested at one point that the energy crisis of the 1970s could be solved by a settlement of the Arab-Israeli conflict. . . .

The domestic American reaction to the Six Day War was much deeper than temporary exhilaration. The press and media expanded their coverage of the area—establishing bureaus and stationing correspondents in places where they had not previously been located on a permanent basis. Until 1967, Israel had been pictured in America largely in mythical terms—as suggested by the novel and movie *Exodus* and the oft-repeated description that the Israeli pioneers had turned swamps into orchards. Progressively, with the news media exercising a microscopic examination of the Jewish state, a different picture emerged of a country like any other suffering internal tensions, contradictions, even corruption. The harsh realism conveyed by the intensified news coverage was to have a corrosive impact on Israel's image in America, especially during the 1970s.

Coterminous with a more balanced view of Israel, the Six Day War unleashed the Palestinian question on the American scene. Despite a series of airline hijackings and terrorist incidents in the years following 1967, the Palestinian cause, the PLO and its leader, Yassir Arafat, gained a degree of respectability, especially in liberal intellectual circles. The discovery of the Palestinians was closely tied to Vietnam. A segment of the war's critics argued that Israel, by relying on the military instrument, was demonstrating its identification with American imperialism. The Palestinians, according to this position, were victims suffering oppression analogous to the harm being inflicted on the Vietnamese people by the United States.

Regardless of the accuracy of these attitudes, they had a powerful impact on one segment of American intellectual and political thought. The Palestinian refugees had been a problem for Israel and her supporters since the 1948 war. Now, however, a vibrant moral argument developed to counter the moral claims of Israel represented by the holocaust and the Jewish state's democratic tradition. It was an argument which would come closest to official policy at the outset of the Carter era, by which time the Palestinians had come to symbolize for many American liberals identification with Third World aspirations and concerns.

Support for the Palestinian cause as a moral issue required ignoring or explaining away the PLO's resort to terrorism. This was accomplished by arguing that Israeli actions were either worse or had driven the Palestinians to desperation, or that the Palestinians were comparable to revolutionaries the world over. It was also achieved by the argument that Israel had been transformed from a David to a Goliath, using military means to subjugate the Palestinians. . . .

The crisis preceding the Six Day War conveyed in the most dramatic and emotional of terms to American supporters of Israel that the survival of the Jewish state could be threatened militarily. As liberals gained a reputation for reluctance to use the military option, the argument developed that no liberal administration could be relied upon to protect Israel in a crisis like the Six Day War in which Israel might not be so successful. The surprising support for Richard Nixon over George McGovern in some sections of the Jewish community in the 1972 presidential campaign was directly related to this fear (although McGovern still received a substantial majority of Jewish votes). The faith of Nixon supporters was reinforced by the huge airlift of military supplies to Israel worth $2.2 billion during the Yom Kippur war. Although counterarguments could be made, the Carter administration's diplomatic pressure on Israeli leaders also seemed to confirm a suspicion of liberals which had first emerged after the 1967 war.

Thus, it is not surprising that several dominant members of the neoconservative movement in America are Jewish. Before 1967, Israel received major conservative support, but it was the liberals who took the lead on behalf of the Jewish state. Afterward, liberals, especially in Congress, maintained their backing, but it often appeared that Israel's intense supporters were on the right—militant anti-communists epitomized by Ronald Reagan as well as religious fundamentalists. If some liberals were disillusioned by what they regarded as Israel's overreliance on the military for its survival, many conservatives admired Israel's "moxie" (as Richard Nixon liked to put it), opposition to the Soviet Union, and loyalty to America's anti-communist crusade. Once the Israelis became dependent on American weaponry after 1967, they also acquired the ability to assist the Pentagon and American corporations with the refinement of U.S. equipment. Their reliability and consistency eventually became much admired in Washington. The origins of a new view of Israel's importance can be seen after the Six Day War when the Israelis provided intelligence on Russian equipment used against them, equipment which was also employed by the North Vietnamese against the United States.

The events of 1967 also had a dramatic impact on the way that many conservative Christians interpreted contemporary Middle East history. Many conservatives, especially evangelicals, began to view the continued existence of Israel as a necessary precondition for the Second Coming of Jesus Christ. Since 1967, the American evangelical movement has become a powerful force in support of Israel. From Rev. Billy Graham's friendship with Richard Nixon to Jerry Falwell's significant role in the Reagan coalition to the presidential candidacy of Pat Robertson, the evangelists have become a prime element in the pro-Israeli coalition. In such media as television's electronic church, a link is drawn between support for a theological millennial prophecy based on specific interpretations of the Bible and support for Israeli policies of the moment. . . .

Both before and after the Six Day War, conservatives and liberals have been represented among American supporters of the Arabs and among those who sympathized with Israel. The impact of the war, however, was to alter the balance in favor of Israel even as it increased popular and official attention to Israel. Yet with respect to two very different groups, the international oil companies and the American Jewish community, the war had the effect of reinforcing old patterns.

From the perspective of the international oil companies, the events of mid-1967 were not good news. Nasser had falsely accused the United States and Britain of colluding with Israel in its pre-emptive attack against Egypt. These accusations led several radical Arab states to break off diplomatic relations with the United States. That could have meant attacks against petroleum installations in the area. As a consequence, the companies stepped up their efforts to gain a more "balanced" American policy toward the Middle East. A Senate committee later uncovered briefing papers used by ARAMCO [Arabian-American Oil Company] officials in the late 1960's to greet such dignitaries as visiting businessmen, Congressmen, educators. The papers instructed their readers to call for a more evenhanded policy by the United States, one less disposed toward Israel and more sympathetic to the Arab states.

The increased insecurity of the oil companies after the Six Day War intensified their vulnerability to Arab pressure. This growing leverage led Saudi Arabia to encourage a campaign by company representatives to warn the Nixon administration that the key Arab oil producers, especially Saudi Arabia, might soon employ the oil weapon for political purposes. During the Yom Kippur war, the

ARAMCO chairmen cautioned against sending military supplies to Israel during the war. In 1973 the oilmen performed as they were instructed.

No one, including the Israelis, had to instruct the American Jewish community how to operate in the wake of the Six Day War. No American group was as deeply affected by the events of 1967, which were particularly important in the history of United States Jews. Of all major western Jewish communities, the Americans were the last to embrace the Zionist objective. Only the death of six million European Jews placed American Jewry at the forefront of the international effort outside Palestine to create a Jewish state in at least part of the British mandate.

From 1945 to 1949, in rallies, speeches, articles, and efforts to influence the American government, U.S. Jews became progressively more active in the Zionist enterprise. Following Israel's war of independence, however, such activity lessened, as many Jews turned to charitable contributions and social service organizations as means of expressing their support for Israel. Even the 1956 Suez war failed to change this pattern, because the survival of Israel was not at stake in that war and even many Jewish supporters of Israel had doubts about the wisdom of the Israeli-British-French campaign. Moreover, the 1950's was a period of emerging Jewish suburban life and rising socio-economic status, encouraging a more reserved expression of political action.

The events of May 1967, however, served to re-awaken American Jewry's interest. Israel's apparent vulnerability and the unwillingness of friendly countries such as France and even the United States to come to her aid left an indelible mark. Afterward, American Jewish life would never be the same. Travel to Israel increased dramatically as did the Israel-orientation of Jewish religious, cultural, communal, and political activity. This focus sharpened as a result of increased attention to Israel in the American mass media and the succession of crises that occurred in the Middle East after 1967. These developments created ample opportunities for individuals and organizations to become engaged in political efforts on behalf of Israel. The war thus initiated an era in which much of Jewish life in America was defined by problems confronting the Jewish State. The preoccupation with Israel emerged as an important factor in American politics and a powerful constraint to be confronted whenever presidents sought to deal directly with the Arab-Israeli dispute. In the 1980's the pro-Israel lobby became more active and pro-Israel political action committees intensified contributions to political candidates they viewed as sympathetic. The major impetus for this activity was the defeats the lobby suffered in the Senate in 1978 and 1981, when it did not block major arms sales to Saudi Arabia proposed by the Carter and Reagan administrations.

The intensified attention to the Middle East is reflected in the presidential campaigns which followed the 1967 war. In the two preceding elections of 1960 and 1964, the issue was barely mentioned, of interest only to the most committed partisans of Israel. Afterward, candidates increasingly found it necessary to issue policy statements on such issues as arms sales, the peace process, terrorism, aid to Israel, the Palestine question, even the location of the American embassy in Israel. The heightened priority of Mideast issues and the wider public interest led to pressure on Presidential candidates to reveal their plans and to identify their advisors.

The increased prominence of the problem was reflected each time a new Chief Executive assumed office. After 1967 presidents could no longer afford to leave the Mideast on the back burner, secured safely in the hands of trusted subordinates until occasional decisions might be required. Each president since has deemed it necessary to address the issue as a top priority early in his term. Similarly, Congress has been more engaged in the problem since 1967. Formerly, the majority of legislators made traditional sympathetic statements on behalf of Israel and voted for aid. Symbolism was more significant than substance. Since 1967, however, aid to Israel and the Arab states—especially Egypt—has escalated, and the Mideast has become the central component of the foreign aid package. As part of the intensified involvement of Congress in the formulation of foreign policy, both houses have played a greater role in the determination of arms sales, and prominent legislators have expressed their views on major issues such as the peace process and terrorism. In this sense, Congress has reflected the increased attention by the media, key interest groups, and successive administrations. Major confrontations between the legislative and executive branches have occurred over such issues as the Mideast arms package of 1978 and the sale of AWACS [Airborne Warning and Command System] jets to Saudi Arabia in 1981. . . .

The Six Day War can be seen to have had a major influence on the United States and American policy in the Mideast. Changes have come about in five areas:

1. It created an opportunity for the United States to reverse the adverse direction of its competition with the Soviet Union in the region. Until 1967, the Russians had been on the advance. Although it was not clear at the time, the Six Day War created conditions which led to the emergence of the United States as the preeminent superpower in the area.

2. American policy makers' concerns about the implications of the Six Day War for the competition with the USSR, relations with the Arabs, and the security of Israel led to accelerated American involvement in efforts to resolve the Arab-Israeli conflict. Though the Johnson administration increased America's involvement only gradually, the Nixon administration followed with a more active response to the events of 1967. In turn, the involvement in conflict resolution thrust the United States into the central position in Mideast politics.

3. In relations with Israel, the Six Day War created a new and symbiotic relationship. For the first time, Washington became primarily and directly responsible for Israel's security, leading eventually to the Jewish state's dependence on the United States for both economic and military assistance. The Six Day War also precipitated a cultural interdependence that was subsequently to have a far-reaching impact on Israel politics and society, as the Americanization of Israel began. The United States, as the powerful partner, could have used Israel's new need for support as leverage to press for diplomatic concessions. At times after 1967, American leaders were tempted to exert pressure and even to consider imposing the conditions of peace. Yet Washington invariably retreated because of the difficulties of forcing Israel to undertake policies it rejected, the constraints imposed by domestic favoritism toward Israel, the rejection by the Arabs of most American initiatives, and the belief shared with Jerusalem that territory should be traded only for some form of peace.

4. The territories also created an Arab attraction to the United States. However many arms the Russians might ship to their Arab clients, only diplomacy seemed

capable of dislodging Israel from the territories. The Arabs were largely unsuc-cessful in their military campaigns, but were almost always unprepared to deal directly with Israel. This peculiar combination of requirements brought several key Arab states to rely on Washington, since Moscow had no influence in Jerusalem. Despite America's sponsorship of the Arabs' chief adversary, an enemy which occupied territory they viewed as their own, several Arab states were gradually brought to increased dependence on Washington as the only available avenue for influence on Israel. Thus the results of the Six Day War led the Arabs—like the Israelis—to regard the United States with greater respect and awe.

5. Not only the American role in the Middle East, but domestic attitudes toward the Arab-Israeli dispute were eventually altered by the Six Day War. For Amer-ica's liberals, the Israeli victory exacerbated divisions between supporters and opponents of the Vietnam war and even among opponents of American interven-tion in Southeast Asia. Henceforth, Israeli policy in the occupied territories and the Palestinian claims for independent statehood (non-existent when the Jordani-ans controlled the West Bank and the Egyptians ruled the Gaza Strip before 1967) became a source of concern and controversy on the left of the American political spectrum. Israeli dependence on military instruments and apparent Palestinian deprivations became powerful forces for sympathy with the new Mideast underdog, which Israel's liberal supporters constantly were forced to confront. On the other hand, both political and religious conservatives were fas-cinated with the determination of history in favor of the Israelis. As a beacon of eschatalogical hope or a strategic asset to America's security concerns, the Six Day War opened a period of conservative flirtation with Israel. Meanwhile, oil companies active in the area revived efforts to gain a more evenhanded American policy in the wake of Washington's increased identification with the Jerusalem government, while the American Jewish community emerged from the crisis committed more than ever to engagement with Israel.

The net effect of this increased attention to the region has been a greater prominence for the Arab-Israeli issue in presidential campaigns and in the time and energy devoted to the problem both by Congress and the President. Each president has set the tone, devised policies, and pursued initiatives, while Con-gressional support has contributed to the growth of the American-Israeli relation-ship since 1967.

The October War and the Disadvantages of the U.S.-Israeli Alliance

CHERYL A. RUBENBERG

[Henry A.] Kissinger, . . . was primarily concerned about the global implications of the Arab-Israeli conflict. This preoccupation resulted in his viewing Middle Eastern events almost solely through the prism of Soviet-American competition and in minimizing the internal dynamic of the regional conflict. At the same time, cognizant of public dissatisfaction with American involvement in the Vietnam War, Nixon and Kissinger developed the idea that regional surrogates should be built up that could act to further American interests in the absence of a direct U.S. presence. This policy was specifically formulated with respect to Southeast Asia and became known as the Nixon Doctrine; but it had special ramifications in the Middle East, where Iran and Israel were to be the major surrogate powers (to a lesser extent, Saudi Arabia, although Israeli opposition precluded the military development of Riyadh). For a time (until the fall of the shah in 1979) Iran functioned effectively as an American proxy; Washington provided it with enormous quantities of American weapons and Teheran acted to further American interests. Israel was another matter. While it received unlimited military supplies and massive economic support (Iran paid for its weapons with its oil revenues, while the American government either gave, or loaned at extremely favorable repayment terms, Israel the money it needed to acquire weapons), Israel persistently pursued policies that undermined rather than served American interests. Eventually (in 1974–75) Kissinger became aware of this anomaly, but by then the power of the pro-Israeli constituencies in the domestic political process undercut whatever efforts the administration undertook to modify Israel's behavior. . . .

During the years between 1967 and 1973 the American interest in assuring Israel's security and survival was transformed into a de facto alliance between the two states, predicated on the perception that Israel was a valuable strategic asset to the realization of American interests. The perception was allegedly validated by Israel's powerful military performance in the 1967 war and later its willingness to mobilize in support of the Jordanian regime [against the Palestine Liberation Organization] in 1970. It was also fed by skillful and intensive propaganda disseminated by the Israel lobby. The result was the institutionalization in conventional wisdom and political orthodoxy of the ideas that Israel could contain Soviet expansionism in the Middle East, protect "moderate" Arab regimes from threats by "radical" forces, and maintain regional stability through its military superiority. These mistaken assessments led the Nixon administration to supply Israel with all the sophisticated weapons it desired and to provide full support for Israel's regional political objectives, without any evaluation regarding the compatibility of Israeli and American interests. These misperceptions also resulted in the United States' misreading the signs of impending war in 1973. . . .

Both the American and Israeli governments were taken by complete surprise at the outbreak of hostilities on October 6, 1973. Both countries possessed information on Egyptian and Syrian military buildups but had failed to evaluate and interpret that intelligence adequately. The [initial military] failure of the Israelis can be attributed in large measure to their overall attitude of extreme self-confidence in the post-1967 years. . . .

Kissinger outlined America's contradictory concerns at the outset of the war: (1) assuring the survival and security of Israel; (2) maintaining relations with moderate Arab countries, such as Jordan and Saudi Arabia; (3) preventing Europe and Japan from pursuing a different course than that of the United States; and (4) preserving U.S.-Soviet détente and avoiding a confrontation with the Soviets. While Kissinger does not say explicitly, the oil-energy problem must have been of some concern (at least it should have been) as well as the credibility of the American presidency in the wake of Watergate. Nevertheless, despite all of the obvious potential problems, Kissinger was firmly convinced that "we were in a good position to dominate events," though he discovered that his control was not as absolute as he had imagined. The most striking aspect of American policy during the October War is the extraordinary degree of support Washington provided Israel, including diplomatic and economic measures and military resupply. Indeed, the United States jeopardized—in fact, damaged—its relations with its NATO allies, Japan, the Soviet Union, OPEC [Organization of Petroleum Exporting Countries], and the Arab world to stand "four square" behind the Jewish state, in a situation that resulted from Israel's policies of territorial expansion, militarism, and refusal to participate in a regional diplomatic settlement.

Kissinger's initial decision was to direct the commander of the Sixth Fleet to move four ships—the aircraft carrier *Independence* and three destroyers—from Athens to Crete, 500 miles from the coast of Israel, as a signal to the Soviets not to intervene and of U.S. resolve to support Israel. Kissinger then ordered the U.S. delegation at the United Nations to pursue a "diplomatic maneuver" with the Soviets in the Security Council, involving "joint action" between Moscow and Washington. The secretary of state considered such a maneuver important for several reasons: (1) to keep the Soviets from introducing independent proposals that would be harmful to Israel; (2) to drive a wedge between Moscow and the Arabs; and (3) to delay a call for a cease-fire. Because of the initial Israeli and American view—that Israel would quickly regain the initiative and win a swift and decisive military victory—Kissinger wanted to evade any appeal for an early cease-fire in order to give the Israelis time to reverse the Arab thrust. . . .

Significantly, on the second day of the war, Egypt communicated with Washington and indicated that its military purpose was limited: the objective of the war was to demonstrate to Israel that a defense line along the Suez Canal did not represent security; Israel's security could be based only on mutual respect with its Arab neighbors and withdrawal from Arab territory. Egypt's message reinforced American and Israeli calculations of the limited threat to Israel that the hostilities posed. (The message was a further indication, in addition to the expulsion of the Soviet advisors, of Egypt's strong desire to move firmly and fully into the American sphere.)

On the second day of the war, October 7, the Israelis informed the Americans that they were confident of an early and definitive success. This evaluation, which was shared independently by Kissinger and his staff and by every other major political and military analyst in the government, leads to the issue of military resupply. (By the end of the first day the Israelis had made two separate requests—one for hardware and one for specialized equipment.) Since it was expected that this war would last no longer than the June War, no senior American official believed that a significant arms resupply could reach Israel before the war would end. Moreover, there were two important political calculations from the American perspective. (1) A U.S. resupply might spur the Soviets to similar action, thereby escalating and prolonging the hostilities and risking a potential U.S.-Soviet confrontation. (2) A major resupply in the existing situation (in which the Israelis had all the equipment they needed and expected an early victory) would negate any attempt by the United States to portray itself as impartial. Kissinger expected from the outset (particularly given Sadat's obvious interest in an American-brokered peace with Israel) to use the conditions created by this new war as an opportunity to initiate a peace process between Israel and the Arab states, or at least with Egypt. Thus he was concerned about not unnecessarily antagonizing the Arabs with a resupply to Israel when Israel did not need it.

At the same time, however, Kissinger was concerned, as he discusses in his memoirs, about assuaging the sensitive Israeli psyche, and he believed that it was important for "psychological" reasons to meet Israel's demands for weapons so that the Israelis would not feel they were "standing alone" in their hour of crisis. Kissinger also believed that by meeting the Israeli demands for resupply it would then "affect and perhaps moderate her territorial claims in the negotiations" expected at the conclusion of the war. This seems a highly questionable assumption, considering that the absolute military superiority the United States had provided Israel from 1967 through 1973 had not moderated its negotiating position in the interwar period but rather had hardened it. In fact, Israel's post-1973 negotiating stance was not at all affected by the massive aid the United States gave. Nevertheless, Kissinger continued to subscribe to this thesis and proceeded to oversee a secret resupply of weapons to Israel.

On October 7 Kissinger instructed Secretary of Defense James Schlesinger to make arrangements for ammunition and other high-technology equipment, especially Sidewinder missiles, to be picked up at a naval base in Virginia by Israeli El Al commercial planes that had had their markings painted out. On October 8 the first El Al planes arrived at the Oceana Naval Air Station and took eighty Sidewinder missiles. This secret resupply remained in continuous operation throughout the war. On October 9 President Nixon publicly committed the American government to providing all the armaments the Israelis requested (which in the end included aircraft, tanks, antitank munitions, antitank weapons, laser guided bombs, and "smart" bombs). Nixon also promised that "if it should go very badly and there is an emergency, we will get the tanks in even if we have to do it with American planes." . . .

By October 13 (seven days after the outbreak of hostilities) a massive military airlift of equipment to Israel was underway. . . .

On October 19 the American Congress passed emergency legislation providing Israel $2.2 billion to pay for the new weapons. This financial aid was indeed a watershed in U.S. support for Israel, both quantitatively and qualitatively. Moreover, the dollar amount appears to be unrelated to calculations of weapons cost. The Pentagon had considered $850 million adequate to cover the cost of resupplying Israel. Spokesmen for the administration were unable to tell Congress exactly how $1 billion of the total $2.2 billion would be used, though Congress, in its zeal to demonstrate support for Israel, was apparently not disturbed by this lack of information. Moreover $1.5 billion of the total $2.2 billion was to be an outright grant, entailing no repayment. Kissinger is said to have argued for even more—at least $3 billion and all in outright grants. . . .

The resupply had profound consequences, reverberating far beyond the Middle East. Washington's Western European allies were extremely distressed. No European government was prepared to ignore the fact that on October 9 the Kuwaiti Council of Ministers had announced that it was organizing a meeting of

Arab oil producers to discuss the role of oil in the conflict. By the next day Egyptian and Saudi Arabian officials were publicly discussing ways in which the "oil weapon" might be used. At that time Western Europe obtained over 70 percent of its oil from the Arab states. These factors led to prohibition of U.S. overflights of Europe or landing rights for its airlift to Israel and to serious strains between America and its NATO allies. Thus, the United States had to channel its airlift through the base it leased from Portugal at Lajes in the Azores, not the optimum route. (For permission to use its facilities, Portugal demanded Washington's help in staving off U.N. pressure to force changes in Portugal's colonialist African policies.) Within a week after the start of the resupply, the Saudis denounced the airlift and the $2.2 billion in aid granted by Congress. Led by Riyadh, OPEC imposed an oil embargo on the West, coupled with a price hike for what oil was sold, that threw the Western world into economic turmoil. . . .

The issue of a cease-fire is second only to that of military aid in an analysis of American support for Israel during this war. The Israelis themselves were not always clear about whether they wanted a cease-fire or not. However, until after the joint U.S.-Soviet call for a simple cease-fire in place (with Israel positioned deep inside Egyptian territory on the west bank of the Suez Canal) on October 22, the United States maneuvered in every possible way to accommodate Israel's position on a cease-fire. The initial American view with regard to a cease-fire was to delay it until Israel could reverse the early Egyptian gains. In the end, when Israel held a decisive upper hand militarily, Kissinger insisted on a cease-fire rather than allowing Israel to totally destroy the Egyptian Third Army, as it wanted. For this action, many Israelis and their American friends have never forgiven him. Nevertheless, Kissinger permitted Israel extraordinary latitude in pursuing the Egyptians after a formal cease-fire was to have been implemented.

Israel's policy on the issue of a cease-fire underwent several changes from the beginning of the war. At the outset Israel demanded that there be no cease-fire until there was a return to the status quo ante bellum. Kissinger was in complete agreement and maneuvered the Soviets and the United Nations to delay any vote on a cease-fire. As he explained, "We had to delay the diplomacy until there was a change on the war front." . . . Kissinger states that the Israelis approached him on October 12 asking that the United Nations pass a standstill cease-fire resolution, and he then requested the British to introduce such a resolution. When the British declined because of the Egyptian refusal to go along, Kissinger claims that [Israeli prime minister Golda] Meir asked him to have the United States introduce the resolution, but that he refused. According to Kissinger, he was certain that the Israelis could turn the situation around on the Egyptian front (they already had on the Syrian), and he did not want the Soviets to have even the slightest intimation of American/Israeli "capitulation." Indeed, Kissinger states that "Israel was, if anything, too eager to proceed [with a cease-fire]." . . .

If, however, the Israelis were prepared to accept a cease-fire on October 12, by October 17 they definitely were not (although Prime Minister Meir agreed in principle to the idea), for the tide of battle on the Egyptian front had now also turned decisively in their favor. Indeed, early on October 16 the first paratroopers landed on the west bank of the Suez Canal. Moreover, Meir objected to the suggestion that the cease-fire be linked to Resolution 242; instead, she insisted that a cease-fire be tied to direct negotiations.

On October 20 Kissinger departed secretly to Moscow at the invitation of the Soviet Union to work out cease-fire arrangements. On Kissinger's arrival, the Soviets immediately dropped all their previous demands regarding a cease-fire (undoubtedly because of the severe setbacks sustained by Syria and Egypt) and agreed to go along with the American-Israeli position, including: (1) a cease-fire in place, (2) no Israeli withdrawal to any previous lines, including no call for an implementation of Resolution 242, and (3) immediate negotiations between the parties concerned under appropriate auspices, i.e., the cease-fire would lead to direct negotiations. In addition, both sides agreed that they would serve as co-chairmen of an eventual peace conference and that prisoners should be immediately exchanged by the parties after the cease-fire. (The haste with which the Soviets agreed to the American-Israeli stance made it very difficult for Kissinger to stall for time in order to give the Israelis additional time to push the Egyptians harder.) The text of this American-Soviet agreement became United Nations Resolution 338, which was introduced in the Security Council on October 22. The resolution was adopted unanimously and was to go into effect within twelve hours.

While Kissinger was in Moscow, he received a special message from President Nixon stating that the United States and the Soviet Union should use the end of the war to facilitate a comprehensive peace in the Middle East. "The current Israeli successes at Suez must not deflect us from going all out to achieve a just settlement now," Nixon declared. "We would serve even Israel's best interests if we now used 'whatever pressures may be required in order to gain acceptance of a settlement which is reasonable and which we can ask the Soviets to press on the Arabs.'" Nixon concluded by saying: "United States political considerations [i.e., domestic pro-Israeli pressure] will have absolutely no, repeat no, influence on our decisions in this regard. I want you to know that I am prepared to pressure the Israelis to the extent required, regardless of the domestic political consequences." Thus there existed an extraordinary situation: an American president looking beyond domestic politics, considering the spectrum of American national interests, possessing a clarity of vision with regard to Israel's long-term security interests, and prepared to act on these perceptions; yet Nixon was so crippled by Watergate that his secretary of state was able to treat the message as if he had never seen it and proceed with his own plan. The last thing Kissinger ever envisaged was a comprehensive settlement imposed by the great powers. His desire to check Soviet influence in the Middle East precluded his working with the Soviets in any meaningful sense to obtain an overall agreement. Moreover, his desire to maintain Israel as the dominant regional power, as well as his sensitivity to Israel's interests, precluded even the slightest consideration of "pressuring" Israel into a just settlement. Kissinger simply ignored the president's message.

Despite the fact that the cease-fire agreement favored Israel in every respect, the Israelis were shocked and furious at the joint accord arranged by Kissinger in Moscow. They were particularly outraged that Kissinger had not consulted with them before going to Moscow and claimed that this joint cease-fire call portended future great power solutions that would be imposed on them. They were also unhappy about the timing of the agreement; Meir wrote: "We would have liked the call for a cease-fire to have been postponed for a few more days so that the defeat of the Egyptian and Syrian armies would be even more conclusive."

Kissinger had wired Israel from Moscow, informing government officials of the impending cease-fire call. President Nixon sent Prime Minister Meir a note from Washington urging that the Israeli government make an immediate announcement consenting to the joint agreement. Meir, however, was so enraged over the Moscow "thing" that she demanded that Kissinger come to Israel before returning to Washington; and to assure his appearance, the prime minister indicated that Israel's acceptance of Resolution 338 would be dependent on Kissinger's appearance in Israel. The visit apparently was not easy, and in his great desire to placate the Israelis, Kissinger, by his own admission, indicated that it would be acceptable for Israel to proceed with operations *after* the cease-fire: "I also had a sinking feeling" [after the massive Israeli violations of the cease-fire became known] "that I might have emboldened them. In Israel, to gain their support, I had indicated that I would understand if there was a few hours 'slippage' in the cease-fire deadline."

The "few hours slippage" that Kissinger encouraged amounted to a major Israeli offensive, undertaken after the cease-fire went into effect and lasting some six days. During that time thousands of Israeli troops and hundreds of tanks (emblazoned with the label "Cairo Express") poured across the Suez Canal, cut the main roads from Cairo to Suez, and tightened a huge ring around the Egyptian Third Army, which was trapped on the east side of the Canal. By the end of the operation an Israeli division was on the outskirts of Ismailia threatening its links to Cairo; two divisions had sealed off the Third Army; Israeli forces held a corridor on the west bank of the Canal, with three bridges across it; and Israel occupied an area of 1,600 square kilometers inside Egypt, down to the Port of Adabiyah on the Gulf of Suez. During this massive, illegal offensive the Israelis deliberately lied to Washington, telling Kissinger that the Egyptians had mounted a major attack and that Israel was merely defending itself. Kissinger voiced no public criticism of Israel, despite the fact that in violating a cease-fire arranged by the United States, Israel undermined American credibility with the Arab world (especially Egypt) and precipitated a crisis between Washington and the Soviet Union. . . .

A second cease-fire call, Resolution 339, was passed in the Security Council on October 24. It reaffirmed the October 22 cease-fire and "urged" but did not "demand" the parties to return to the original cease-fire lines (this muting reflected U.S. pressure in the Security Council on Israel's behalf). Sadat accepted Resolution 339 although it still left his Third Army surrounded. Nevertheless, within hours after the new cease-fire was to have gone into effect, the Israelis again resumed their assault on the Third Army. Significantly, even though Kissinger knew in each instance that Israel had initiated the hostilities and while Sadat was pleading for American help to enforce the cease-fire, he refrained from any condemnation of Israel and instead warned the Egyptians not to undertake "offensive" operations. As a result of this obvious American duplicity and because no American pressure was being applied on the Israelis to desist from their strangulation of the Third Army, Sadat turned to the Security Council. He asked that American and

Soviet forces be sent to the Middle East to bring about an end to the fighting and to supervise a cease-fire, a request that triggered a near-confrontation between the United States and the Soviet Union.

Kissinger's response was unequivocal: "We were not prepared to send American troops to Egypt, nor would we accept the dispatch of Soviet forces. We had not worked for years to reduce the Soviet military presence in Egypt only to cooperate in reintroducing it as a result of a United Nations Resolution. Nor would we participate in a joint force with the Soviets, which would legitimize their role in the area and strengthen radical elements." The Soviets, however, saw merit in the idea and informed Washington that they would support such a resolution if it was formally introduced. Washington responded that it would veto any resolution calling for the introduction of Soviet and American forces. The stage was set for a crisis.

Late in the evening of October 24, Soviet Ambassador [Anatoly] Dobrynin phoned Kissinger with a "very urgent" message from Premier Leonid Brezhnev. First, he condemned Israel for drastically violating the cease-fire and suggested that Soviet and American contingents go to Egypt to enforce the truce. Then followed a serious threat: "I will say it straight," Brezhnev cabled, "that if you find it impossible to act together with us in this matter, we should be faced with the necessity urgently to consider the question of taking appropriate steps unilaterally. We cannot allow arbitrariness on the part of Israel." The United States responded with a military alert of ground, sea, and air forces, including both conventional and nuclear units (a DEFCON 3) [Defense Condition 3], and a diplomatic note from Nixon asking the Soviets to cooperate in a U.N. peacekeeping initiative. In the midst of this great power crisis, the Israelis demanded that Washington not ask them to pull back to the line they had occupied when the original cease-fire went into effect on October 22, and Kissinger assured them that no such request would be made. Moreover, the American airlift continued.

Egypt provided the way out of the crisis by changing its request in the Security Council from a Soviet-American contingent to an international force. The Soviets agreed to accept such a force, to be composed of non-permanent members of the Security Council, and the crisis was defused. . . .

On October 27 Sadat signaled that he was prepared for *direct* talks between Egyptian and Israeli officers at the rank of major general, "to discuss the military aspects of the implementation of Security Council Resolution 338 and Resolution 339 of October 22 and 23, 1973." Sadat suggested the talks take place under U.N. supervision at the route marker denoting Kilometer 101 on the Cairo-Suez road. The only conditions he required were a "complete" cease-fire, to go into effect two hours before the meeting, and the passage of one convoy carrying nonmilitary supplies (food, water, and medicine) to the Third Army under U.N. and Red Cross supervision.

The situation could not have been more favorable for Israel. It was about to enter the first direct talks between Israeli and Arab representatives since the independence of the state, and it retained control over the access route to the Third Army even while the United Nations, almost unanimously, was pressing for Israeli withdrawal back from that line to the October 22 line: all this in return for permitting one convoy of nonmilitary supplies to pass. . . .

Despite Israel's bitterness at being denied total victory over Egypt, the secretary of state finally insisted that Israel accept the Egyptian proposal. On October 28 Israeli and Egyptian military representatives met for direct talks under the auspices of U.N. observers, although not until late on October 29 did the convoy reach its destination. The meeting at Kilometer 101 marked the end of the October War.

This third major Arab-Israeli war had profound repercussions for American national interests. Détente with the Soviet Union was severely jeopardized; indeed a near-confrontation between the two great powers occurred. Relations with the European and Japanese allies were severely strained. And the supply of oil, vital to all the Western industrial economies, was interrupted. Even Kissinger acknowledged that the war "had the most drastic consequences" for the United States; he calculated that it "cost us about $3 billion directly, about $10–15 billion indirectly. It increased our unemployment and contributed to the deepest recession we have had in the postwar [World War II] period."

Moreover, the October War challenged virtually every prewar assumption of U.S. Middle East policy. Before the October fighting Nixon and Kissinger had believed that stability in the Middle East could be best ensured by Israeli military predominance; however, the vastly superior Israeli military power did not ensure stability or prevent war. The administration had doubted that Arab oil could be effectively used to pressure the West; the embargo shattered that assumption. It had become almost conventional wisdom that U.S.-Soviet détente would serve to minimize the danger of regional conflicts; the near-confrontation of the superpowers was indeed a sobering lesson. And, finally, the traditional perception of the Arabs as inept both at war-making and cooperating among themselves was severely eroded by their performance in the war. However, of greatest significance in analyzing the October hostilities is that in spite of all the objective contradictions this crisis illustrated with regard to the American perception of Israel as a strategic asset to U.S. interests in the Middle East, the idea was not subject to reevaluation— its merits and drawbacks were not even debated in decision-making circles, while the policies derived from the perception were continued and even intensified.

Indeed, despite the numerous and serious challenges to the conventional wisdom, U.S. policy underwent no fundamental transformation. The only change from the interwar years was a commitment on the part of Kissinger to devote more attention to the Middle East—in fact, the region became a top concern, and Washington made a conscious effort to improve its relations with the major Arab countries, especially Egypt. It is significant, however, that Kissinger expected Washington to be able to better its ties with the Arabs without altering its wholehearted support for Israel or its policy of maintaining Israel as an extension of American power in the region. Kissinger apparently believed that the strength of the U.S.-Israeli tie, with the perceived influence in the Arab world this gave Washington over Israeli policy, would impress the Arabs and convince them that the United States held most of the diplomatic cards. The Soviets could provide them with weapons, but only the United States could get their territory back. Yet, except for Egypt, which simply "fell into the arms" of the United States in spite of its policies, Washington was unable to improve its relations with the Arab regimes—in large measure because Washington did not use its potential leverage with Israel to make progress on issues of concern to the Arabs, and because Kissinger completely acceded to Israel on the Palestinian question.

Washington's unwillingness and/or inability to influence Israel's behavior in the post-1973 period was related both to the absence of any serious reevaluation of the faulty assumptions on which America's Middle East policy was predicated and to the power of the pro-Israeli lobby, acting on behalf of the Israeli government's interests through the domestic political process. Even Kissinger remarked on the constrictions imposed by the lobby: "It's easy to say what we've done is not enough, but . . . they were the *attainable*—given our prevailing domestic situation." In addition, an aide to Kissinger commented that pro-Israeli sentiment in Congress was "the greatest constraint" on Kissinger's efforts to pursue some measure of a Middle East settlement, and "the constraint became the determinant." Indeed, the pro-Israeli groups successfully pressured Congress to resist the administration's efforts to strengthen American ties with Arab states, principally by denying the administration a critical tool—reduced aid—that could have been used to persuade Israel to adopt diplomatic positions more congenial to U.S. interests, and by blocking administration-proposed arms sales to the Arab states.

The eight months that followed the October War saw unprecedented American involvement in the search for a settlement of the Arab-Israeli conflict, although the parameters of that effort were very narrowly defined, conforming to the limitations imposed by Israel. Indeed, no attempt was ever made to raise the core of the Middle East conflict, the Palestinian issue. U.S. policy focused on (1) facilitating a disengagement between Israel and Egypt and between Israel and Syria; (2) laying the groundwork for a separate, bilateral Egyptian-Israeli peace; (3) persuading [Saudi] King Faisal and his OPEC colleagues to lift the oil embargo; and (4) preparing a peace conference. Even the mode of diplomatic activity— a step-by-step approach that avoided linking initial accords to the nature of a final peace agreement—a method that obfuscated the most critical issues, circumventing even a discussion of a comprehensive settlement—was defined by the constraints imposed by Israel.

In fact, step-by-step diplomacy was essentially designed to avoid having to exert pressure on Israel to be forthcoming in a genuine peace settlement, though it also served to divide the Arab world. As [the analyst] John F. Roehm, Jr., aptly described it: "Kissinger's selection of the step-by-step approach to negotiations was partially motivated by his concern that attempts to move Israel too far, too fast, as would be likely in a comprehensive peace plan, would cause the Israeli lobby to activate its 'legions' of supporters in Congress and thereby threaten Kissinger's efforts to transform relations with the Arabs." Regardless of the reasons behind it, the strategy was a failure in terms of American interests in the Middle East.

The problem with Kissinger's belief that America's special relationship with Israel would force the Arabs to deal with the United States in the diplomatic arena was that diplomacy had to hold more promise than war, for in the event of war the Soviet Union could provide more than the United States (though Soviet weapons were repeatedly shown to be inferior to American arms). However, progress toward a settlement, which was essential for maintaining the confidence of the Arab governments, meant at a minimum the return of some territory and eventually at least the appearance of movement toward resolution of the Palestinian issue. For such a policy to be successful Israel would have to make some concessions. The United States might try to extract comparable Arab concessions, but, given the nature of the issues, this would clearly be difficult. Because of this, U.S. diplomacy would have to "compensate" Israel with aid and implicitly threaten Israel with the withholding of such aid if circumstances dictated. In practice, the compensation became endless, and the threat of withholding aid was never entertained. . . .

The end of the 1967 war through the post–October War diplomatic activity in 1973–74 saw extraordinarily strong American support for Israeli interests and policies, in the context of the perception that Israel served as a "strategic asset" to U.S. interests and an extension of American power in the Middle East. The institutionalization of the idea of Israel as a surrogate power and the concomitant growth in U.S. support for Israel resulted both from the faulty assumptions of certain powerful policymakers, especially Henry Kissinger, and from the extensive and effective propaganda disseminated by pro-Israeli groups whose influence with numerous sectors on the American domestic scene expanded greatly in the interwar years. The perception of Israel's surrogate utility was allegedly validated by the Jewish state's stunning military performance in the June War. . . . According to proponents of the surrogate thesis, by providing Israel absolute military superiority the American interests of containing Soviet expansionism, promoting regional stability and preventing war, and assuring Western freedom of access to the area's raw materials, markets, and investment opportunities would be maximized. (In addition, advocates claimed that providing Israel unlimited arms supplies would make it secure, and therefore increasingly flexible with regard to a comprehensive settlement of the Arab-Palestinian-Israeli conflict.) The strategic asset thesis came to be accepted during these years as absolute dogma in the conventional wisdom of American political culture. The most tangible expression of this perception was the provision to Israel by Washington of unlimited quantities of the most sophisticated weapons available as well as increasing economic assistance. Further evidence of Washington's willingness to accommodate Israel in the context of the belief about its surrogate power were Kissinger's relentless and successful efforts to exclude the Palestinian issue from all diplomatic forums and to bar the PLO from participation in the diplomatic process. Indeed, no single American has done more to negate Palestinian interests than Henry Kissinger.

This . . . [essay] has also clearly illustrated the fallaciousness of the strategic asset thesis and the fact that the policies that grew out of it were completely counter to American interests. These policies undermined the entire framework of détente with the Soviet Union; increased Soviet influence and presence in the Middle East: provoked a second U.S.-Soviet confrontation; increased Arab hostility to the United States; produced an Arab oil embargo and a phenomenal spiraling of oil prices; estranged the United States from its Western European and Japanese allies; and led to almost continuous instability in the Middle East. Despite the manifold contradictions between theory and reality, neither the perception nor the policies derived from it were altered to conform to reality. This was due to the convergence between the strength of the thesis in certain powerful elite circles and the power and influence of pro-Israeli constituencies.

Carter's Creative, Pragmatic Summit Diplomacy

WILLIAM B. QUANDT

More than anything else, an analyst studying American policy toward the Arab-Israeli conflict should want to know how the president—and the few key individuals to whom he listens—makes sense of the many arguments, the mountain of "facts," the competing claims he hears whenever his attention turns to the Arab-Israeli conflict. To a large degree he must impose order where none seems to exist; he must make sense out of something he may hardly understand; he must simplify when complexity becomes overwhelming; and he must decide to authorize others to act in his name if he is not interested enough, or competent enough, to formulate the main lines of policy.

What, then, do the president and his top advisers rely on if not generalized views that they bring with them into office? No senior policymaker in American history has ever come to power with a well-developed understanding of the nuances of the Arab-Israeli dispute, the intricacies of its history, or even much knowledge of the protagonists. At best policymakers have general ideas, notions, inclinations, biases, predispositions, fragments of knowledge. To some extent "ideology" plays a part, although there has never really been a neat liberal versus conservative, Democrat versus Republican divide over the Arab-Israeli conflict. Only when it came to dealing with the Soviet Union as a power in the Middle East region—up until 1990—did the cold war ideological divide between conservatives and liberals seem to make a difference, and even then the evidence is not conclusive.

Any account of policymaking would, however, be incomplete if it did nothing more than map the initial predispositions of key decisionmakers. As important as these are in setting the broad policy guidelines for an administration, they are not enough. Policy is not static, set once and forever after unchanged. Nor is policy reassessed every day. But over time views do change, learning takes place, and policies are adjusted. As a result, a process of convergence seems to take place, whereby the views of senior policymakers toward the Arab-Israeli conflict differ most with those of their predecessors when they first take office, and tend to resemble them by the end of their terms. [Gerald] Ford and [Jimmy] Carter disagreed on Middle East policy in 1976–77 but were later to coauthor articles on what should be done to resolve the Arab-Israeli conflict. Even [Ronald] Reagan in his later years seemed closer to his predecessor's outlook than to his own initial approach to Arab-Israeli diplomacy.

It is this process of adjustment, modification, and adaptation to the realities of the Middle East and to the realities of Washington that allows each administration to deal with uncertainty and change. Without this on-the-job learning, American foreign policy would be at best a rigid, brittle affair. . . .

Since most of the American-led peace process has been geared toward procedures, not substance, the ability of top decisionmakers to experiment with various

From *Peace Process: American Diplomacy and the Arab-Israeli Conflict Since 1967* by William B. Quandt, The Brookings Institution and the University of California Press, 1993, pp. 9–11, 255–268, 270–273, 276–283. Reprinted by permission of The Brookings Institution.

approaches as they learn more about the conflict has imparted an almost experimental quality to American foreign policy in the Middle East. Almost every
conceivable tactic is eventually considered, some are tried, and some even work.
And if one administration does not get it right, within a matter of years another
team will be in place, willing to try other approaches. Although American foreign
policy is sometimes maddening in its lack of consistency and short attention
span, this ability to abandon failed policies and move on has often been the hallmark of success.

Foreign-policy making seems to involve an interplay among the initial predispositions of top policymakers, information about the specific issues being considered, the pull of bureaucratic groupings, the weight of domestic political considerations, the management of transitions from one presidency to the next, and the
impact of events in the region of concern. It is often in the midst of crises that new
policies are devised, that the shortcomings of one approach are clearly seen, and
that a new definition of the situation is imposed. And it is in the midst of crises that
presidential powers are at their greatest. . . .

Jimmy Carter came to the presidency with remarkably little experience in foreign affairs. He had served one term as governor of Georgia, and had earned a reputation for his strong commitment to civil rights. But as far as the Middle East was
concerned, he had no known record apart from a few comments made during the
campaign that offered little guide to what his policies might be.

If Carter's specific views on Arab-Israeli issues were difficult to anticipate, he
had displayed certain habits of mind that might be revealing of his basic approach.
Trained as an engineer, Carter seemed to believe complex problems could best be
tackled by careful study, detailed planning, and comprehensive designs. To say the
least, he was a problem solver more than a grand strategist.

Carter also seemed to have an optimistic streak that led him to believe problems could be resolved if leaders would simply reason together and listen to the aspirations of their people. Here he may have been consciously influenced by his
experience with the civil rights movement and by his personal beliefs as a born-
again Christian. None of these attributes ensured that Carter would take a strong
interest in the Arab-Israeli conflict, but they did suggest that he would not be deterred from doing so by the difficulty or complexity of the issue. He might even
sense a challenge in tackling a problem that had for so long defied solution.

Much would depend on his foreign-policy team, and there the evidence suggested that he would rely on mainstream figures from the Democratic party establishment. For secretary of state he selected Cyrus R. Vance, a seasoned negotiator,
international lawyer, and the deputy secretary of defense during the 1967 Arab-
Israeli war. Vance's views on Middle East issues were not widely known, but his
would be a voice for continuity, negotiations, and steady, quiet diplomacy.

As national security adviser, Carter selected the Polish-born academic Zbigniew Brzezinski. Unlike Vance, Brzezinski had left traces, primarily in the form of
numerous articles and books, mostly on Soviet-related topics but a few on the Middle East as well. Brzezinski was an activist who believed in competing for influence with the Soviets, and who saw the Arab-Israeli conflict as a source of
instability and radicalism in a sensitive geostrategic region. He had publicly endorsed the idea of a Palestinian state in the West Bank and Gaza. . . . Brzezinski,
who clearly hoped to achieve the stature of his predecessor and academic rival,

Henry Kissinger, seemed determined to put the Arab-Israeli conflict near the top of the new administration's agenda. . . .

Within days of reaching Washington, President Carter's foreign policy team was beginning to discuss how and whether to launch a new Middle East peace initiative. Both Secretary Vance and National Security Adviser Zbigniew Brzezinski were on record with the president as favoring a strong U.S. role in Middle East peace negotiations. Their assessment, and that of most Middle East specialists at the State Department, was that early 1977 was a good moment for the United States to exercise leadership in a new round of negotiations. The key Arab states seemed to be ready for serious talks. . . .

Israel also seemed to expect the United States to return to the diplomatic arena after the enforced absence of the election year. The cabinet of Prime Minister Yitzhak Rabin was to face elections in the spring, and was on the defensive to an unprecedented degree. But Washington officials felt that preliminary talks could be conducted before Israelis went to the polls, and even if they were not, that any new government would be built around the Labor alignment that had ruled Israel since its birth. And Labor was a known element, likely to adopt a tough stance in negotiations but ultimately prepared to bargain and to coordinate policies with Washington. Three disengagement agreements had been hammered out with Labor governments, and American negotiators had come to respect the skills of leaders like Golda Meir, Yitzhak Rabin, Moshe Dayan, and Shimon Peres. . . .

Having made this initial assessment, the Carter administration spent little time on whether to accord the Arab-Israeli conflict high priority. Most of the early discussion centered on means. It was widely believed that Henry Kissinger's technique of shuttle diplomacy to achieve limited agreements had run its course. . . . The United States had paid a high price for a partial Israeli withdrawal that had not opened the way for any further such agreements. Neither Syria nor Jordan was prepared to follow [Egyptian president Anwar el-]Sadat's lead, and even Sadat was insisting that the next step should move toward an overall settlement. And the Israelis were also disinclined to be edged back from their strategically solid positions in Sinai for less than a peace agreement and direct negotiations with Egypt.

At a meeting on February 4, 1977, the Policy Review Committee of the National Security Council agreed to recommend to the president that the Middle East should be dealt with as a matter of urgent priority and that Secretary Vance should go to the area immediately to begin discussions on procedures and substance. The president's key advisers felt the United States should promote an agreement on broad principles and then seek their staged implementation. From the Arab side the administration should seek a clear definition of peace, and from the Israelis it should try to get an understanding that security could be achieved without significant territorial adjustments in the 1967 lines. At this stage in the internal discussions, there was no sense of urgency about going to Geneva for a formal conference, and the emphasis was on pre-Geneva talks to prepare for more formal negotiations at a later date. It was also agreed at the meeting that the Soviets should be kept informed of the progress of U.S. conversations with the parties but should not be involved in the negotiations at this stage. . . .

In mid-February Vance was already in the Middle East sounding out each of the leaders on how he saw the situation, while making it clear that the United States also had some ideas of its own. Rabin, Sadat, King Hussein of Jordan, and

Saudi Crown Prince Fahd were all invited to come to Washington to meet the new president, and the idea of a meeting between Carter and President [Hafez al-]Asad of Syria was also raised. . . .

In talks with Israeli leaders during his first trip, Secretary Vance had been told that no Israeli government would agree to talk to the PLO so long as it remained committed to the destruction of Israel. Vance had asked Foreign Minister Yigal Allon if it would make any difference if the PLO were to accept UN Resolution 242 and Israel's right to exist as a state. He replied that a PLO which accepted Israel's existence would no longer be the PLO, and Israel's attitude would be different. This answer encouraged the United States to look into the possibility that the PLO might change its formal position on 242. The Egyptians and Saudis both promised to use their influence, and the Egyptians went so far as to say that they would urge the PLO to change its covenant, which called for Israel's destruction.

The next phase of the U.S. strategy included a highly public use of presidential power to try to break the logjam on several substantive issues. Carter and his advisers had little patience with some of the conventional wisdom on how the American role should be played. He had little sympathy for the Arab refusal to make peace with Israel, or to even use the word *peace;* and he strongly believed Israel would in some way have to come to terms with the Palestinians, and probably with the PLO, names he used almost interchangeably in his early months in office. And though he was very sympathetic to Israel's security concerns, he did not feel that territorial aggrandizement was the key to that security.

Carter was willing, even anxious, to speak out in public on all these issues, and to discuss them in private. One of his criticisms of the Kissinger style had been the emphasis on secrecy, which kept the American public in the dark about major foreign problems. Carter's inclination was to talk openly about the foreign-policy initiatives he was considering. At times this openness jangled the nerves of more traditional diplomats, and of foreign leaders, but Carter often seemed to be trying to do so deliberately. He appeared to feel he had a limited period in which to make his mark on Middle East policy and that controversial issues should be tackled early in the administration. This viewpoint led to a profusion of comprehensive plans to settle all sorts of problems, including the Middle East. On occasion, the president spoke with an awareness of the political cycle, the need to stake out strong positions during the early honeymoon phase of the administration, knowing perhaps that he would be obliged to settle for less in the end, but also hoping for a breakthrough here or there.

On March 7–8, 1977, Carter met with Prime Minister Rabin at the White House for very serious substantive discussions. The personal chemistry between the two was not particularly good, but the record of the talks shows that both leaders conducted thoughtful explorations of what might come out of the forthcoming negotiations. In retrospect, these talks stand out as one of the best substantive discussions Carter had with any Middle East leader. Shortly after the talks, however, a misunderstanding arose. Rabin publicly claimed that Carter had supported the Israeli idea of "defensible borders." Carter did not want to leave the false impression that he had offered Rabin a blank check, so the White House issued a clarification. This episode left the false impression that a crisis had broken out in U.S.-Israeli relations, a notion that may have contributed to Labor's defeat at the polls two months later.

Almost immediately after meeting with Rabin, and in part to counter some of the Israeli leaks about what had been discussed, Carter publicly spelled out the three basic principles, as he saw them, of a comprehensive Middle East peace. These entailed the need for concrete manifestations of peace and normal relations, such as trade and the exchange of diplomats; the need for security arrangements for all parties, but without prejudice to the establishment of recognized borders along the 1967 lines; and the need for a solution to the Palestinian problem, which had a political as well as a humanitarian dimension. A few days later, on March 16, in Clinton, Massachusetts, Carter reiterated these points, using for the first time the formulation of a "Palestinian homeland." Needless to say, the Israelis were stunned and apprehensive, and the Arabs were generally encouraged. . . .

Over the next three months Carter met with Sadat, Hussein, Fahd, and Asad. In each meeting the substantive trinity of peace, borders-security, and the Palestinian question was discussed in some depth, along with procedural questions on how to get the Palestinians represented in the upcoming negotiations. The most encouraging sign during this phase was Sadat's willingness to accept the idea that peace would entail normal relations with Israel, including the exchange of diplomats and full recognition. But also, the Israeli government, while insisting that it would never accept an independent Palestinian state on the West Bank, was prepared to discuss withdrawal and was open to the idea that security would not necessarily require significant border changes beyond the 1967 lines. In addition, Rabin, Allon, and Peres all talked of the need to solve the Palestinian problem if there was to be peace in the region. And the Arab leaders were confidently predicting that the PLO would consider softening its position on the recognition of Israel. . . .

Then, on June 21, 1977, the unexpected happened. Menachem Begin, whose Likud bloc had won the Knesset elections the previous month, became prime minister of Israel. Begin was an unknown figure in Washington. Insofar as administration officials knew his views, they were aware that he opposed Labor's approach to "territorial compromise" with Jordan as a means of dealing with the West Bank and the Palestinian question. Begin was known to favor an expansion of Israeli settlements, and one of his first acts that irritated the Carter administration was his visit to Elon Moreh, where he announced he would support many more such settlements. These two issues—Begin's unwillingness to accept the principle of withdrawal from the West Bank under any circumstances, and his commitment to settlements—became the main sources of conflict between the United States and Israel over the next two years.

Somewhat surprisingly, Carter's first meeting with Begin was much more cordial than the one with Rabin. Carter apparently believed Begin would become more rigid if pressured, and some of his advisers were convinced that Begin would respond best to a respectful, polite initial encounter. The personal chemistry between the two men was hardly warm, but the talks were conducted in a friendly manner.

Although Begin came prepared with procedural proposals for negotiations with the Arabs, he showed no sign of wanting to discuss substance with the United States. This, in fact, was one of the initial differences between Begin and Rabin: Begin argued that the United States should not be involved in the substance of Arab-Israeli talks but should limit its role to getting the parties together. He obviously feared that the U.S. stand on many issues would be closer to the

Arab position, and therefore he wanted as little substantive role for Washington as possible. . . .

Unfortunately for Begin, the United States was already rather far down the road of trying to devise draft principles that should be agreed on before a Geneva conference. In discussions held within the administration early in July, five principles had been agreed on, and during Begin's visit these were discussed. The first point set the goal of comprehensive peace; the second reiterated the relevance of UN Resolutions 242 and 338 as the bases of negotiations; the third defined the goal of peace as involving normal relations, not just an end of belligerency; the fourth dealt with the question of borders and withdrawal in stages; and the fifth point concerned the Palestinians and their rights, including means "to permit self-determination by the Palestinians in deciding on their future status."

Vance, and then Carter, reviewed these points with Begin on July 19–20 and found, not surprisingly, that Begin entirely rejected the fifth point on the Palestinians, and was insistent that on point four the United States should not say in public or private that it favored withdrawal to the 1967 lines with only minor modifications. . . .

In early August 1977 Vance left on a very important trip to the Middle East. With him he took a revised set of the five principles to discuss with leaders in Egypt, Israel, Syria, Jordan, Saudi Arabia, and Lebanon. . . .

During Vance's talks in Egypt, Sadat showed considerable anxiety about the shift toward procedural discussions and away from the idea of prior agreement on principles before Geneva. In his view Geneva should be used for signing a pre-agreed document, little more. Sadat had little patience with the idea of negotiating with Israel, preferring that the United States present a plan, to which all the parties could react. To encourage this line of thought, Sadat presented a highly secret document to Vance in Alexandria. It was the draft of a peace treaty that Sadat said he would be prepared to sign, but he did not want any of the other parties to know it existed. Instead he urged Vance to ask the Israelis to put forward a draft treaty of their own; then Vance could unveil the Egyptian draft, which would lead to an eventual U.S. compromise proposal. In a tactic that he was to use repeatedly, Sadat took the Egyptian draft and wrote in the margins in his own handwriting the further concessions he would be prepared to make. These notations were intended, presumably, to convince Vance that Sadat would be flexible on most substantive points, though not on "land and sovereignty," as the Egyptian president repeatedly said. . . .

September 1977 proved to be an eventful month in the evolution of Carter's Middle East strategy. American efforts were concentrated on four parallel, potentially even conflicting, goals. First was the attempt to get each of the parties to provide a written draft of a peace treaty. Israel complied, with a lengthy and legalistic document that left the delicate question of the border and the status of settlements in Sinai obscure. Jordan and even Syria eventually submitted a list of principles that should govern any peace agreement. Although the drafts per se were far from what was needed, they did provide Vance with some building blocks from which to fashion an American compromise proposal, and they had the positive effect of getting the parties to think of committing themselves to concrete positions on paper.

The second strand of policy, largely working through the Syrians, but also pursued in other channels, was an attempt to find a solution to the question of how the Palestinians would be represented in upcoming negotiations at Geneva. Agreement was reached on how the PLO might express its reservation to UN Resolution 242, but the conditions demanded by the PLO for an overt acceptance of 242 were beyond what Washington was prepared to promise. Nonetheless, by early October Sadat had informed Carter that the PLO would agree to be represented in a unified Arab delegation by a Palestinian who was not a PLO official. Since everyone had by then accepted the idea of a unified Arab delegation that would include Palestinians, this issue seemed to be nearly resolved.

The third focus of U.S. efforts was to try to develop some understanding among the negotiating parties about the procedures of the Geneva talks. Sadat was still insistent that Geneva must be "well prepared" in advance; otherwise it could bog down and turn into a hopeless stalemate. He remained wedded to the Kissinger model of highly secret talks at the level of head of government, which would then be finalized and legitimized in a public forum like Geneva. If the actual negotiating was to be done in a semipublic forum like Geneva, he seemed to fear that the other Arabs would try to restrict his freedom to maneuver, and that the United States would be subject to the ever-present pro-Israeli pressures generated by American public opinion and Congress. Israel tended to share this suspicion of Geneva, and Foreign Minister Moshe Dayan warned that a unified Arab delegation was a formula for stalemate. Syria, and to a lesser extent Jordan, favored a single delegation as a way of preventing the much-feared separate Egyptian-Israeli agreement they had come to expect. . . .

The fourth, and probably least carefully thought out, part of the U.S. strategy was aimed at the Soviet Union. As Geneva became more of a real concept, rather than just a symbolic umbrella for a whole series of contacts and talks, the United States had to address the question of the role to be played by the other cochairman. A number of procedures had already been worked out in December 1973, when the Geneva conference had convened in plenary session for the first and last time. To the extent possible, it was useful to adhere to those precedents. But the Soviets were clearly seeking more of a role, and in mid-September they presented a draft of a joint statement to Secretary Vance. For a Soviet document it was remarkably balanced. It did not include calls for a Palestinian state or participation by the PLO. It paid due regard to the need for security and normal peaceful relations among the states of the area. Most of the language was from UN Resolution 242. Practically the only formulation the United States had not itself used was a reference to Palestinian rights, which went a step beyond the standard American reference to Palestinian interests. . . .

Among the potentially controversial elements in the draft were an explicit call for reconvening the Geneva conference by the end of the year; the fact that the Soviet Union would be cochairman; the lack of explicit reference to UN Resolution 242; and a formulation the United States had not previously used referring to Palestinian *rights*. Largely because of these references the Israelis were uncomfortable with the document. But the Carter administration had not picked up any warning signals from Dayan. Thus, when the U.S.-Soviet communiqué was issued on October 1, 1977, few on the American side anticipated the storm of adverse reaction from Israel and Israel's supporters in the United States.

While American efforts were aimed in these various directions, Egypt and Israel were embarking on a round of secret diplomacy. At Sadat's initiative a meeting was held between Dayan and an aide to Sadat, Hassan Touhamy, in Morocco in mid-September. Similar contacts had been held over the years, including that month, between Israeli and Arab leaders, so even when the United States learned of this meeting after the fact, it was not viewed as a vote of no confidence in the ongoing U.S. strategy. In retrospect, one can see that Sadat was beginning to hedge his bets for fear that Geneva would become a straitjacket for his free-wheeling style of diplomacy. It is fair to say that the American side consistently underestimated the degree of distrust between Sadat and Asad, and also tended to take Sadat at his word when he repeatedly said he could never afford to make a separate peace with Israel.

Not surprisingly, with so many initiatives under way during September, something was bound to come unstuck. The proximate cause of the explosion was the U.S.-Soviet communiqué and the firestorm of negative American and Israeli reaction it provoked. Much of the pent-up anxiety and frustration with Carter's Middle East policy now spilled over, finding willing allies in the neoconservative, pro-Israeli, anti-Soviet circles. What was in fact a political error, showing considerable amateurishness, was portrayed as a move of vast significance that would reestablish the Soviets as a major power in the Middle East. To read the text of the communiqué several years later is to wonder what all the fuss was about. The words themselves are innocuous, and even Begin used the phrase "Palestinian rights" at Camp David. Nonetheless, the political reality of early October 1977 was that Carter was under great pressure from the friends of Israel, and the Israelis played on his discomfort with extraordinary skill.

Many analysts believe Sadat went to Jerusalem in November 1977 to escape the dead end of a U.S.-Soviet sponsored Geneva conference. They often emphasize his desire to keep the Soviets out of the diplomatic arena. But the available evidence, including Sadat's own account, does not support this widely held belief. When first informed of the U.S.-Soviet joint communiqué, Sadat termed it a "brilliant maneuver," since he, like some U.S. officials, thought it would soften up the Syrians. In any case, he had ensured against Geneva becoming an Arab-Soviet trap by opening his own direct channel to the Israelis, and from that contact he seemed to be assured that whenever he was ready to sign a separate peace with Israel he would recover most of Sinai. In early October Sadat was still testing to see how much more he could get with U.S. help. It was not the U.S.-Soviet communiqué that disillusioned him; it was Carter's apparent inability to stand up to Israeli pressure, coupled with evidence that Carter was tired of spending so much time on an apparently intractable problem, that seems to have convinced Sadat to strike out on his own. . . .

The initial reaction to Sadat's trip to Jerusalem in official Washington was one of admiration for the personal courage required, and some puzzlement over what Sadat had in mind for an encore. He had often said that 99 percent of the cards were in American hands, but now he seemed to be ready to play his own cards without much help from Carter. No one in Washington proposed that the United States should try to thwart his moves, but there was some concern that negative Arab reactions, coupled with Begin's essential rigidity on the Palestinian issue, would cause the initiative to fall far short of the psychological breakthrough that Sadat sought. Consequently, sooner rather than later the problem would end up back in the American lap. In any case, Sadat's move would not be helped by its appearing to have been made in the United States. These considerations, coupled perhaps with some envy on the part of the politically minded members of the administration for a media-catching move they would have liked to have thought of themselves, led to a fairly reserved public posture, which was strongly criticized at the time by the friends of Israel. . . .

By early December the internal consensus in the administration was that Sadat's initiative should be supported strongly but that the United States should continue to use its influence to try to get as broad agreement as possible. The administration still felt that Sadat would, in the end, not make a separate peace with Israel and that at least some measure of agreement on the Palestinian question would have to serve as a cover for any Egyptian-Israeli deal. Syria would henceforth be ignored for most practical purposes, as would the PLO, but American policy would continue to focus on some form of West Bank–Gaza accord. During the second week of December, Secretary Vance went to the Middle East to consult with the various governments and to begin the process of redefining American strategy.

Just after Vance's return from the area, Begin invited himself to Washington to see President Carter. Vance had seen the prime minister only a few days before, and Begin had not put forward any new ideas, but now he said he had important proposals to discuss with the president before going to a scheduled meeting with Sadat in Ismailia [in Egypt] on Christmas day. Some in Washington were suspicious that Begin's purpose was to try to elicit an American endorsement of his ideas before they were shown to Sadat.

Carter's talks with Begin on December 16–17 confirmed the American suspicion. Begin practically pleaded with the president to say that his proposals were a fair basis for negotiation. In fact, Carter did tell him his Sinai proposal looked promising, adding the caveat that there might be points in it that he did not fully understand yet. (This comment became a source of discord later when the Israelis claimed that Carter had approved of the Sinai proposal, knowing it included a provision that Israeli settlements would not be removed.)

If Begin's Sinai proposal was genuinely seen in positive terms, the same could not be said for his "home rule" proposal for "Judea, Samaria and the Gaza District." In lengthy discussions with Begin, the president, the vice-president [Walter Mondale], Vance, and Brzezinski all tried to encourage Begin to modify his plan. Several points stood out. The home rule proposal was intended as a permanent arrangement, not as a transition to the return of the territory to Arab political control once a peace agreement had been reached. The plan also contained the type of detail that would be bound to irritate Sadat, and Begin was urged to present a simpler set of principles, perhaps only orally. But Begin seemed to be proud of his creation and rather arrogantly told the American side that he did not need their advice on how to negotiate with Sadat. Begin was so eager to win U.S. endorsement, however, that he did imply he would make some improvements in the plan after consulting with his cabinet. With that, he promptly went public with a statement that came very close to saying the president had approved of his plan, which required a clarification from the American side to the effect that the plan was a positive step in the direction of negotiations. . . .

Indicative of the gap between the Egyptian and Israeli positions was the difference in Begin's and Sadat's accounts of their meeting in Ismailia. According to the Israeli version, Sadat was on the verge of accepting the Israeli proposals and issuing a common declaration of principles, but was persuaded not to do so by his hard-line advisers from the Foreign Ministry. Sadat's account, by contrast, said that Begin had not grasped the importance of his Jerusalem visit and that the Israelis were trying to haggle and tread on sovereignty. He was quite caustic in his remarks, suggesting there was little point in going on with direct negotiations. . . .

Discussions within the American negotiating team in January led to a strategy of trying to change two key elements in Begin's position: to achieve a freeze on the construction of new settlements in the occupied territories, an issue of special concern after Begin blatantly allowed new settlements to be started in Sinai within days of his talks in Ismailia with Sadat; and to convince Begin to return to the previous Israeli formula for the West Bank and Gaza by offering to withdraw, at least partially, as the quid pro quo for peace and recognition. This latter point was put in terms of Begin's unwillingness to accept the fact that the withdrawal provision of UN Resolution 242 applied to the West Bank and Gaza. The Labor party in formally accepting 242 in mid-1970 had interpreted the resolution as requiring "peace for withdrawal" on all fronts, and because of this Begin had left the national unity government that existed at the time. . . .

Through the spring and summer of 1978 little substantive progress was made in an endless series of contacts with Egyptian and Israeli leaders. Carter was impatient with the slow pace of diplomacy and seemed to feel a desire to get more directly into the act. During much of July a highly secret planning group began to develop a U.S. proposal under Vance's supervision, and the president followed the progress with interest. On July 20 he discussed with his advisers an idea he had been toying with for some time—a summit meeting at Camp David with both Begin and Sadat. Carter seemed to view a summit as the only way to force decisions to a head, and he doubtless counted on his own role as mediator to bridge the still very large gaps. His view of a summit was psychological and political: once the leaders were committed, they could not afford to fail, and he counted on the special atmosphere of Camp David, away from the press and the burdens of everyday governing, to help produce a positive result. The rest of the foreign-policy team was somewhat more wary of the summit idea, tending to focus on the need for very careful substantive preparations. In early August Vance went to the Middle East to invite Begin and Sadat to Camp David in early September. Both accepted readily, and no doubt Sadat saw this event as the much-awaited moment of truth when he and Carter would corner Begin.

Carter, Sadat, and Begin, along with their top advisers, isolated themselves at the president's mountaintop retreat, Camp David, from September 5 to September 17. Little information reached the outside world of these deliberations at the time, so many were surprised at the news on the last day that agreement had been reached on two frameworks for negotiations. The first dealt with the principles of an Egyptian-Israeli agreement; the second, more complex and less precise, consisted of a formula for an interim period of self-government for Palestinians living in the West Bank and Gaza. The outcome was not quite what anyone had expected at the beginning of the historic summit.

Carter prepared himself meticulously for the talks. His briefing book contained an analytical paper entitled "The Pivotal Issue," which focused on the question of "linkage" between agreements on Sinai and on the West Bank. The point was made that Begin would seek to ensure that any agreement he might reach with Sadat concerning Egyptian-Israeli relations should in no way be dependent on resolving the Palestinian question. Sadat, by contrast, would want some relationship between the two so as to protect himself from the charge that he had abandoned the Palestinians and had accepted a separate peace with Israel. The problem for Carter would be to see if an agreement could be reached at the summit that would make it possible to use the incentive of reaching peace with Egypt to moderate Begin's position on the Palestinian question, without at the same time making Egyptian-Israeli relations entirely subject to whether a solution could be found to the most difficult part of the Arab-Israeli conflict.

The American delegation had identified several specific issues that were likely to be obstacles to a successful agreement at Camp David. First was Begin's unwillingness to accept that the principle of withdrawal from occupied territory, as called for in Resolution 242, should apply to the West Bank and Gaza at the end of a transitional period. Second was the problem of Israeli settlements in Sinai and in the West Bank. Third was the question of how to associate Jordan and the Palestinians with subsequent rounds of negotiations.

The American team felt it was pointless at Camp David to try to resolve the questions of the border between Israel and a Palestinian-Jordanian entity. Not only would Begin be at his most intransigent, but also the Arab parties most directly concerned would not be present. Similarly the Americans felt the question of sovereignty over the West Bank and Gaza, as well as the status of Jerusalem, should be deferred. Instead they thought that Egypt and Israel could make some headway on outlining a transitional regime for the West Bank, building on Dayan's idea of dismantling the military occupation and replacing it with an elected Palestinian body with broad responsibility for day-to-day affairs, perhaps including control over state lands (which would have effectively foreclosed the possibility of extensive new Israeli settlement activity during the transitional period).

No one on the American side anticipated insurmountable problems in reaching a general agreement on principles regarding Sinai. Israel was expected to leave the settlements and the airfields, provided firm security arrangements could be worked out. Sadat was taken seriously when he said that he could not bargain over land or sovereignty, but that everything else could be negotiated.

These assessments led the American team to think in terms of seeking agreement between Begin and Sadat on general principles regarding both Sinai and the West Bank and Gaza. . . .

President Carter's initial reaction to the advice of his team was that it should have aimed higher. Rather than just seek agreement on principles concerning an overall settlement, he wanted to work out the details of an Egyptian-Israeli peace treaty, including specific security arrangements. At Camp David this became his special project, and the first draft of the Egyptian-Israeli accord was done in his hand. Carter, it is fair to say, was less concerned with the so-called linkage problem than were other members of the American team, and he was also more optimistic about the chances of reaching a satisfactory agreement through direct talks with Begin and Sadat.

Those who were somewhat more pessimistic about the prospects of bridging the very large gaps between the two parties were also more inclined to see the Camp David talks as part of an ongoing process. From this perspective, even if the talks fell short of full agreement, negotiations would continue, with the issues, it was hoped, more narrowly focused than before. This somewhat apolitical view stood in sharp contrast to the position taken by the president's domestic affairs advisers, who felt Carter needed to leave Camp David with an apparent success.

Carter's views proved to be partly correct and partly wrong. He was right in sensing that the best avenue for real progress lay in getting a detailed understanding between Begin and Sadat on Sinai and on the basic elements of an Egyptian-Israeli peace treaty. Begin skillfully withheld his final concessions on removal from Sinai of Israeli settlements and return of three airfields to Egypt until the very end, but from the outset it was clear that an agreement was possible. Carter was wrong, however, in believing that the talks could be concluded quickly and that the three leaders could work well together to solve problems. After only two sessions with both Begin and Sadat in the same room, the president realized it would be better to keep them apart.

Sadat arrived at Camp David ready for a fight with Begin. To ensure that it would happen, he presented to Carter and Begin an Egyptian draft of a fairly tough agreement. Begin reacted sharply, and the Israelis began to write a counterdraft. At the same time, however, Sadat privately told Carter that he was prepared to be flexible on most points, except for land and sovereignty, but that Carter should put forward proposals for both delegations to react to. On the Israeli side, Attorney General Aharon Barak had also reached the conclusion that the time had come for the United States to put forward proposals of its own, and that Begin and Sadat should be kept apart. Thus, by the first weekend, the American team began to polish the first of many negotiating drafts.

Over the next ten days a pattern developed whereby the U.S. delegation, and often just the president and Secretary Vance, would meet separately with the Israeli and Egyptian leaders. They would work from nonbinding written drafts, each time trying to elicit concrete reactions to proposals. These would then be discussed within the American team, and a new draft would be produced, often only marginally different than the previous one. By this means the main issues of disagreement surfaced quickly.

On Sinai there were essentially two problems: settlements and airfields. Both were resolved satisfactorily toward the end of the talks, with Begin reserving his position on settlements by saying the issue would have to be put to a vote of the Knesset. Predictably, the final status of the West Bank and Gaza and the question of linkage were the main stumbling blocks. In addition, the Egyptians insisted on including language from Resolution 242 on the nonacquisition of territory by war. The Israelis refused, even though the language was found in 242, which Begin professed to accept. The not-very-elegant solution was to append the full text of 242 to the Camp David Accords, but not to single out that phrase in the text. For Begin this was a minor victory, typical of his tenacious concern for words and principles, and also indicative of Sadat's comparative indifference to precise language.

Two central issues seemed likely to prevent agreement as the days wore on. First was the bedeviling question of what would happen on the West Bank and Gaza after a five-year transitional period. The Egyptians, supported by the Americans, wanted to make it clear that a final agreement would be negotiated during the transitional period which would resolve the questions of borders, sovereignty, security, and recognition according to the same principles of 242 that would govern agreements on other fronts, such as Sinai. In other words, the "peace for withdrawal" formula would remain intact even if the details might be worked out somewhat differently and over a longer period. Begin would have none of it, but instead of fighting the issue head on, he preferred to focus on other matters until the very last days of the negotiations. . . .

The second difficult issue was the question of settlements: the American and Egyptian teams wanted to get a freeze on them during the negotiations over Palestinian self-government. Again, Begin deferred the discussion of this issue until near the end of the talks.

September 16, a Saturday, proved to be the crucial day for addressing the hard issues involving the West Bank and Gaza. Up until that time all of the American drafts contained language on the applicability of 242, including the principle of withdrawal, to the final negotiation on the West Bank and Gaza. And a paragraph calling for a freeze on settlements had always been included. That morning Dayan and Barak met with Vance. The Israelis explained why Begin would never accept the language on 242 and withdrawal. Barak added that he felt a solution could be found, but only if they were all prepared to continue negotiating for another week or so. Prophetically, he said that if agreement had to be reached that day, all they could hope to do was to paper over some very major problems that would come back to haunt them.

Apart from Barak and a few others, however, no one had the stomach for another week in the claustrophobic environment of Camp David. As a result, in the course of the day on Saturday, the American draft was fundamentally changed. The elements of 242, including withdrawal, which had previously been spelled out, were deleted. The language was changed to make it clear that the negotiations, but not necessarily the results of the negotiations, would be based on the principles of 242. And the negotiations about the West Bank and Gaza were artfully obfuscated by creating two tracks, one involving peace-treaty negotiations between Israel and Jordan, and the other involving talks between Israel and representatives of the Palestinians about the West Bank and Gaza.

Israel had no objection to saying that 242 should be the basis for negotiations with Jordan. In Begin's view Jordan had no right to the West Bank, and saying that did not imply a commitment to the "peace for withdrawal" formula. In the Israeli view, 242 did not apply to the talks on the final status of the West Bank and Gaza. A careful reader of paragraph 1(c) of the "Framework for Peace in the Middle East" signed on September 17, 1978, will see language about "two separate but related committees," and "the negotiations shall be based on all the provisions and principles of UN Security Council Resolution 242." It may take a lawyer to explain how, but Begin successfully protected his position of principle that 242 did not apply to the negotiations over the West Bank's future; the Americans accepted the ambiguity; and Sadat may well have wondered what all the verbal gymnastics were about. In any case, Begin won this round as well.

Later on Saturday evening Carter and Vance thought they had finally won a round with Begin. At a late-night session Carter insisted that Begin agree to a freeze on settlement activity in the West Bank and Gaza for the duration of the negotiations over autonomy. Carter agreed to delete the paragraph in the draft text and to substitute a letter from Begin to him, and he dropped his insistence that existing settlements should not be thickened. But he clearly thought a commitment had been made not to construct new settlements during the autonomy talks. Vance also understood Begin to have made such a promise, although he was concerned about Begin's hesitation to accept an open-ended commitment to a freeze.

In any event, the issue should have been settled on Sunday morning, when Begin sent a draft letter on the topic to Carter. By this time Sadat had already been informed that Begin had agreed to a freeze on settlements. But the actual letter did not conform to Carter's understanding, and, without speaking directly to Begin, Carter sent it back. Begin had promised to freeze settlements for three months, a time period he had mentioned the previous evening. Now, however, Begin was linking the freeze to the duration of the Egyptian-Israeli negotiations, not to the autonomy talks, which was an entirely inappropriate and unprecedented step. Alarm bells should have gone off, but so many other issues were on the agenda that day, especially a diversionary argument over Jerusalem which erupted in the afternoon, that both Carter and Vance continued to act as if there had merely been a misunderstanding that would be cleared up as soon as Begin sent back a new draft.

The final version of the letter did not arrive until after the Camp David Accords had been signed, and in it Begin held stubbornly to his position that the freeze would last only through the three-month period of the Egyptian-Israeli talks. Another round went to Begin, and on a position of considerable importance to the skeptical Arab audience that was waiting to see what, if anything, would be offered to the Palestinians as a result of the Egyptian-Israeli separate peace apparently in the making. Carter never got over the feeling that Begin had misled him, and this episode caused deep mutual distrust between the two leaders. . . .

During the lengthy talks that preceded Camp David and at Camp David itself, U.S. policy constantly had to adjust to two realities: events in the Middle East cannot be easily controlled or influenced, so developments there frequently caught the Americans by surprise and obliged them to revise their strategies; and domestic American political realities intrude with particular force on the decisionmaking process regarding the Middle East. A president must simultaneously adjust his plans to the unpredictable twists and turns of Middle East politics and keep an eye on his domestic political base. What seems possible and desirable in the first year of a president's term is likely to be seen as hopelessly ambitious by the third year.

The result of these Middle East and domestic pressures is to move American policy away from grand designs with strong ideological content toward a less controversial, and less ambitious, middle ground that can win bipartisan public support as well as acceptance by Arabs and Israelis. To do so, of course, is not always possible, as much as it might be politically desirable, so American policy toward the Middle East rarely manages to satisfy everyone that has an interest in shaping it. Presidents seem to tire of all the controversy generated by Middle East problems, and the intractability of the issues is a source of much frustration.

The Camp David Accords amply demonstrate the limits of what in fact can be achieved, even with a massive commitment of effort. But they are also a reminder that diplomacy can produce results, if the will, the energy, and the creativity are there. The historical verdict on Camp David cannot be fully rendered, although with each passing year it seems to be more widely accepted as part of the new reality of the Middle East. By any standard, however, this remarkable adventure in summit diplomacy achieved more than most of its detractors have been willing to acknowledge, and less than its most ardent proponents have claimed.

✖ *FURTHER READING*

Isaac Alteras, *Eisenhower and Israel* (1993)

Irvine Anderson, *Aramco, the United States, and Saudi Arabia* (1981)

Geoffrey Aronson, *From Sideshow to Center Stage: U.S. Policy Toward Egypt, 1946–1956* (1986)

George Ball and Douglas Ball, *The Passionate Attachment* (1992) (on U.S.-Israeli relations)

Hashim S. H. Behbehani, *The Soviet Union and Arab Nationalism* (1986)

Abraham Ben-Zvi, *The United States and Israel* (1993)

Ian J. Bickerton and Carla L. Klausner, *A Concise History of the Arab-Israeli Conflict* (1991)

James A. Bill, *The Eagle and the Lion: The Tragedy of American-Iranian Relations* (1988)

H. W. Brands, *The Specter of Neutralism* (1990)

George W. Breslauer et al., *Soviet Strategy in the Middle East* (1990)

Thomas A. Bryson, *Seeds of the Middle East Crisis: The United States Role in the Middle East Crisis During World War II* (1981)

Noam Chomsky, *The Fateful Triangle: The United States, Israel, and the Palestinians* (1983)

Michael J. Cohen, *Truman and Israel* (1990)

Chester L. Cooper, *The Lion's Last Roar: Suez, 1956* (1978)

Alexander DeConde, *Ethnicity, Race, and American Foreign Policy* (1992)

Steven Z. Freiberger, *Dawn over Suez* (1992)

Thomas L. Friedman, *From Beirut to Jerusalem* (1989)

Mark J. Gasiorowski, *U.S. Foreign Policy and the Shah* (1991)

James F. Goode, *The United States and Iran, 1946–1951* (1989)

Stephen Green, *Taking Sides: America's Secret Relations with a Militant Israel* (1984)

Peter Grose, *Israel in the Mind of America* (1983)

Peter L. Hahn, *United States, Great Britain, and Egypt, 1945–1956* (1991)

Robert Kaplan, *The Arabists* (1993)

Gabriel Kolko, *Confronting the Third World* (1988)

Bruce R. Kuniholm, *The Origins of the Cold War in the Near East* (1980)

Diane B. Kunz, *The Economic Diplomacy of the Suez Crisis* (1991)

George Lenczowski, *American Presidents and the Middle East* (1990)

Douglas Little, "From Even-handed to Empty-handed: Seeking Order in the Middle East," in Thomas G. Paterson, ed., *Kennedy's Quest for Victory* (1989), pp. 156–177

———, "Gideon's Band: America and the Middle East Since 1945," *Diplomatic History*, 18 (1994), 513–540

———, "The Making of a Special Relationship: The United States and Israel, 1957–1968," *International Journal of Middle East Studies*, 25 (1993), 563–585

Wm. Roger Louis, *The British Empire in the Middle East, 1945–1951* (1984)

Mark H. Lytle, *The Origins of the Iranian-American Alliance* (1987)

Robert J. McMahon, "Eisenhower and the Third World," *Political Science Quarterly*, 101 (1986), 453–473

Gail E. Meyer, *Egypt and the United States* (1980)

Aaron David Miller, *Search for Security: Saudi Arabian Oil and American Foreign Policy, 1939–1949* (1980)

Benny Morris, *Israel's Border Wars, 1949–1956* (1993)

Donald Neff, "Nixon's Middle East Policy: From Balance to Bias," *Arab Studies Quarterly*, 12 (1990), 121–152
———, *Warriors for Jerusalem* (1984)
———, *Warriors at Suez* (1981)
A. F. K. Organski, *The $36 Billion Bargain* (1990) (on U.S. aid to Israel)
David Painter, *Oil and the American Century* (1986)
Thomas G. Paterson, "Threat to the Middle East? The Eisenhower Doctrine," in Paterson, *Meeting the Communist Threat* (1988), pp. 159–190
Bruce D. Porter, *The USSR in Third World Conflicts* (1984)
Stephen J. Randall, *United States Foreign Oil Policy, 1919–1948* (1985)
Barry Rubin, *Cauldron of Turmoil* (1992)
———, *Paved with Good Intentions: The American Experience and Iran* (1980)
Nadav Safran, *Israel: The Embattled Ally* (1981)
———, *Saudi Arabia* (1988)
Edward W. Said, *Orientalism* (1978)
———, *The Question of Palestine* (1979)
David Schoenbaum, *The United States and the State of Israel* (1993)
Mohammed Shadid, *The United States and the Palestinians* (1981)
Gary Sick, *All Fall Down: America's Tragic Encounter with Iran* (1984)
John Snetsinger, *Truman, the Jewish Vote, and the Creation of Israel* (1974)
Steven L. Spiegel, *The Other Arab-Israeli Conflict* (1985)
Michael Stoff, *Oil, War, and American Security* (1980)
Robert Stookey, *America and the Arab States* (1975)
Seth P. Tillman, *The United States in the Middle East* (1982)
Daniel Yergin, *The Prize: The Epic Quest for Oil, Money, and Power* (1991)

CHAPTER 14

The End of the Cold War

After the tragedy of Vietnam, the Watergate constitutional crisis, and the waning of détente, President Jimmy Carter pledged to revive U.S. prestige and power. Carter initially attempted to reenergize Soviet-American détente, but at the close of his administration (1977–1981), the Cold War had become as contentious as ever: Strategic Arms Limitation Talks (SALT) had reached an impasse; the Soviet Union's invasion of its neighbor Afghanistan had prompted a new version of containment, the Carter Doctrine; Moscow and Washington had exchanged barbs over human-rights violations; and plans had been set in motion to install American Pershing II and cruise missiles in NATO countries in Western Europe to counter Soviet SS-20 missiles, raising the nuclear-arms race to new levels of danger. At the same time, Carter worried that if Americans continued to neglect their mounting domestic problems, including their dependency on foreign energy sources—the "energy crisis"—the United States might lose its preeminent international status.

Contemptuous of the message of decline, and dismissing Carter's display of Cold Warriorism as insufficiently tough, Republican candidate Ronald Reagan charged during the 1980 presidential election that Carter had let American power slip. Ultimately triumphing over Carter, Reagan began his presidency with denunciations of the Soviet Union in raw anticommunist rhetoric. Soon came a huge military buildup to confront the Soviets with superior power. Reagan also issued superpatriotic declarations designed to restore American self-confidence. Blaming most of the world's problems on the Soviets, the Reagan administration (1981–1989) discouraged arms-control talks and, under the Reagan Doctrine, stepped up U.S. aid to anticommunist groups around the world. Reagan sent U.S. troops to Lebanon and Grenada, ordered bombing raids against Libya, financed the contra war against the government in Nicaragua, armed radical Muslim rebels with Stinger missiles in Afghanistan, tolerated death-squad human-rights abuses in El Salvador, announced the Strategic Defense Initiative (SDI, or "Star Wars"), and introduced the largest peacetime military budget in history.

All the while, like President Eisenhower three decades earlier, Reagan disparaged reliance on nuclear weapons for defense in an overarmed world that seemed unlikely to survive a nuclear holocaust. As Reagan wrestled with this question, his most hawkish advisers left the administration toward the end of the 1980s.

Pleased with the hardliners' departure, critics nonetheless argued that the huge budget deficits and rapidly soaring federal debt spelled trouble; that the United States' failure to invest on the home front in education, technology, the urban infrastructure, and the environment condemned the nation to steady decline; and that the country had lost its competitive edge in the international marketplace. Reagan would hear none of it. America, he declared, was "standing tall." Despite his administration's Iran-Contra scandal and few foreign-policy successes (the Intermediate-Range Nuclear Forces, or INF, Treaty signed in late 1987 to disband all American and Soviet intermediate-range missiles ranked as a major exception), Reagan claimed that he had forced the Soviets to retreat from the battlefield in favor of the bargaining table.

While Reagan turned to military solutions for international questions, and as the debate about decline gained intensity in the United States, momentous changes rocked the international system. A new, younger, reform-minded generation of Soviet officials came to power in 1985 under the bold leadership of General Secretary of the Communist Party Mikhail Gorbachev. He launched perestroika ("restructuring") to improve economic performance and glasnost ("openness") to liberalize politics, and he pledged to reduce the military establishment (in 1988 he unilaterally reduced Soviet military forces). Under "new thinking" in the Kremlin, Gorbachev also vowed to settle regional conflicts (all Soviet troops were gone from Afghanistan by early 1989), to stop the nuclear-arms race by eliminating all nuclear weapons (announced in early 1986), and to meet the U.S. president to temper the Cold War (the first summit convened in 1985).

Long simmering protest in the communist-ruled countries of Eastern Europe and East Germany exploded in this new atmosphere of Gorbachev reform. Having reduced Soviet forces in Eastern Europe, Gorbachev made it clear that he would not suppress dissent in the Warsaw Pact nations. When the people rallied against their communist oligarchs, the Red Army stood aside. Communist regimes collapsed one after another in 1989—in Poland, Hungary, East Germany, Czechoslovakia, and Rumania. In November, one of the infamous pillars of the Cold War, the Berlin Wall, came down. Caught in the storm he had unleashed, Gorbachev himself yielded power to more liberal compatriots. The Soviet Communist party disbanded, and the Union of Soviet Socialist Republics dissolved in 1991. Free-market capitalism, it seemed, had defeated statist communism.

The Cold War had ended after almost a half-century. Why and how? And who won? Observers vigorously debate the reasons for this startling turnabout in international history. In explaining the stunning changes in Soviet policies, some point to external factors while others identify internal conditions in the U.S.S.R. Some observers claim that Reagan's huge military expansion, including SDI, and his staunch anti-Sovietism compelled Moscow to change—in short, that the United States won the Cold War by bringing on the Soviet Union's collapse. The patient containment doctrine scored the ultimate victory. Reagan outspent the Soviet Union, which sunk into bankruptcy. Carter, too, earns credit for pressing human-rights issues in a gulag-plagued U.S.S.R. In the end, freedom beat tyranny.

Other analysts who emphasize outside factors argue instead that what counted most in ending the Cold War was not confrontation but engagement and compromise, not a hardline posture but a softening of Cold War positions. Congress placed restraints on Reagan's confrontationism, Reagan advisers such as Secretary of State George Shultz resisted the more confrontation-minded Secretary of Defense Caspar Weinberger, an international antinuclear peace movement gained momentum, and Western Europe's pursuit of détente, often against U.S. wishes, also helped to end the Cold War. Some interpretations particularly applaud the courageous people of Eastern Europe, not U.S. policies, for rolling back the Soviet empire. Still other writers argue that the Cold War ceased because of the decline of both superpowers, *which exhausted themselves waging the long conflict and suffered setbacks in an increasingly interdependent world in which formidable challenges arose from allies and enemies alike. The Soviets, for example, became bogged down in Afghanistan and could neither block nationalism nor stem economic crisis in Poland. The great-power drive to restore faltering international positions generated the Soviet-American cooperation necessary to end a Cold War that neither side was winning.*

Analysts who explain changes in the Soviet Union by emphasizing internal factors spotlight the decay of the Soviet system after years of mismanagement by a corrupt communist bureaucracy. They study the Soviet Union's structural economic problems. They explore the history of anti-Stalinist reformers who waited their turn to lead and finally got it under Gorbachev. In short, a courageous Gorbachev determined to revive his nation, not a Reagan determined to undermine it, ended the Cold War. Even before Reagan became president and beefed up the U.S. military, Gorbachev and the reformers had seen the futility of an endless nuclear-arms race and the dangers of war. And through unusual and long-term self-examination quite independent of American actions, the reformers sought to infuse humane values in a communist ideology that no longer championed them. Reagan rhetoric and policies actually delayed the end of the Cold War by under-cutting the reformers—by emboldening Kremlin hawks who sought to counter U.S. military expansion and to ice arms-control talks.

Such are the outlines of a scholarly debate that will become textured and nuanced as historians learn more from the documentary record as it is gradually declassified, from oral history interviews with participants as they recall the conditions and motives that shaped their decisions, and from interdisciplinary studies as scholars seek answers to the most fundamental question: What makes people and their governments tick in international relations?

✖ D O C U M E N T S

The first document, a speech to the nation on July 15, 1979, represented President Jimmy Carter's anguished reading of what ailed America at a time of concern about high energy costs and economic malaise. In the second document, comprising press-conference comments from January 29, 1981, the newly inaugurated president Ronald Reagan denounces the Soviet Union, setting the Cold War confrontational style of his administration. In a March 23, 1983, speech, Reagan explained U.S. military expansion. Portions of his case are reprinted here as the third document, which also includes Reagan's call for a new defensive system to blunt nuclear weapons (later called the Strategic Defense Initiative, or SDI). The fourth document is a statement by General Secretary Mikhail Gorbachev on November 21, 1985, at a press conference after meeting with Reagan at the Geneva summit conference. In office only a few months, Gorbachev chided the U.S. president for escalating the arms race, seeking world supremacy, and operating under the mistaken notion that the Soviets would fold.

Reagan and Gorbachev met again at Reykjavík, Iceland, in October 1986. They came very close to a major agreement on terminating the nuclear-arms race, but Gorbachev would not accept SDI, which he saw as threatening, and Reagan would not abandon the system, which he saw as defensive. Their opposing positions are presented in the fifth and sixth documents, both televised addresses—Reagan's on October 13 and Gorbachev's on October 22. The seventh document, a concluding part of the Yale University historian Paul

Kennedy's best-selling book *The Rise and Fall of the Great Powers* (1987), discusses the relationship between military spending and the relative economic decline of the United States. Arguing that the United States suffered from "imperial overstretch," Kennedy suggests that U.S. expansion eroded national security. The eighth document, from interviews conducted over 1987–1989 with Georgi Arbatov, one of the reformers who emerged with Gorbachev, provides a glimpse of the "new thinking" in the Soviet Union. A member of the Communist party's Central Committee and his nation's preeminent Americanist scholar, Arbatov headed the USA Institute, a think tank in Moscow. The final document is Zbigniew Brzezinski's explanation for why and how the Cold War ended. As President Carter's national security affairs adviser, the always outspoken, Polish-born Brzezinski constituted the hardline wing of Carter's foreign-policy team. In the statement reprinted here, he lauds Carter more than Reagan for facing the Soviets down. The U.S. human-rights campaign and arms buildup, Brzezinski argues, brought the Cold War to a close.

President Jimmy Carter
Identifies a "Crisis of Confidence," 1979

The erosion of our confidence in the future is threatening to destroy the social and the political fabric of America.

The confidence that we have always had as a people is not simply some romantic dream or a proverb in a dusty book that we read just on the Fourth of July. It is the idea which founded our Nation and has guided our development as a people. Confidence in the future has supported everything else—public institutions and private enterprise, our own families, and the very Constitution of the United States. Confidence has defined our course and has served as a link between generations. We've always believed in something called progress. We've always had a faith that the days of our children would be better than our own.

Our people are losing that faith, not only in government itself but in the ability as citizens to serve as the ultimate rulers and shapers of our democracy. As a people we know our past and we are proud of it. Our progress has been part of the living history of America, even the world. We always believed that we were part of a great movement of humanity itself called democracy, involved in the search for freedom, and that belief has always strengthened us in our purpose. But just as we are losing our confidence in the future, we are also beginning to close the door on our past.

In a nation that was proud of hard work, strong families, close-knit communities, and our faith in God, too many of us now tend to worship self-indulgence and consumption. Human identity is no longer defined by what one does, but by what one owns. But we've discovered that owning things and consuming things does not satisfy our longing for meaning. We've learned that piling up material goods cannot fill the emptiness of lives which have no confidence or purpose.

The symptoms of this crisis of the American spirit are all around us. For the first time in the history of our country a majority of our people believe that the next 5 years will be worse than the past 5 years. Two-thirds of our people do not even vote. The productivity of American workers is actually dropping, and the willingness of Americans to save for the future has fallen below that of all other people in the Western world. . . .

What you see too often in Washington and elsewhere around the country is a system of government that seems incapable of action. You see a Congress twisted and pulled in every direction by hundreds of well-financed and powerful special interests. You see every extreme position defended to the last vote, almost to the last breath by one unyielding group or another. You often see a balanced and a fair approach that demands sacrifice, a little sacrifice from everyone, abandoned like an orphan without support and without friends. . . .

We are at a turning point in our history. There are two paths to choose. One is a path I've warned about tonight, the path that leads to fragmentation and self-interest. Down that road lies a mistaken idea of freedom, the right to grasp for ourselves some advantage over others. That path would be one of constant conflict between narrow interests ending in chaos and immobility. It is a certain route to failure.

All the traditions of our past, all the lessons of our heritage, all the promises of our future point to another path, the path of common purpose and the restoration of American values. That path leads to true freedom for our Nation and ourselves. We can take the first steps down that path as we begin to solve our energy problem.

Energy will be the immediate test of our ability to unite this Nation, and it can also be the standard around which we rally. On the battlefield of energy we can win for our Nation a new confidence, and we can seize control again of our common destiny.

In little more than two decades we've gone from a position of energy independence to one in which almost half the oil we use comes from foreign countries, at prices that are going through the roof. Our excessive dependence on OPEC [Organization of Petroleum Exporting Countries] has already taken a tremendous toll on our economy and our people. This is the direct cause of the long lines which have made millions of you spend aggravating hours waiting for gasoline. It's a cause of the increased inflation and unemployment that we now face. This intolerable dependence on foreign oil threatens our economic independence and the very security of our Nation.

President Ronald Reagan Denounces the Soviet Union, 1981

[S]o far détente's been a one-way street that the Soviet Union has used to pursue its own aims. I don't have to think of an answer as to what I think their intentions are; they have repeated it. I know of no leader of the Soviet Union since the revolution, and including the present leadership, that has not more than once repeated in the various Communist congresses they hold their determination that their goal must be the promotion of world revolution and a one-world Socialist or Communist state, whichever word you want to use.

Now, as long as they do that and as long as they, at the same time, have openly and publicly declared that the only morality they recognize is what will further their cause, meaning they reserve unto themselves the right to commit any crime, to lie, to cheat, in order to attain that, and that is moral, not immoral, and we operate on a different set of standards, I think when you do business with them, even at a détente, you keep that in mind.

Reagan Touts U.S. Military Power and Introduces the Strategic Defense Initiative, 1983

Our efforts to rebuild America's defenses and strengthen the peace began 2 years ago when we requested a major increase in the defense program. Since then, the amount of those increases we first proposed has been reduced by half, through improvements in management and procurement and other savings. . . .

Since the dawn of the atomic age, we've sought to reduce the risk of war by maintaining a strong deterrent and by seeking genuine arms control. "Deterrence" means simply this: making sure any adversary who thinks about attacking the United States, or our allies, or our vital interests, concludes that the risks to him outweigh any potential gains. Once he understands that, he won't attack. We maintain the peace through our strength; weakness only invites aggression.

This strategy of deterrence has not changed. It still works. But what it takes to maintain deterrence has changed. It took one kind of military force to deter an attack when we had far more nuclear weapons than any other power; it takes another kind now that the Soviets, for example, have enough accurate and powerful nuclear weapons to destroy virtually all of our missiles on the ground. . . .

For 20 years the Soviet Union has been accumulating enormous military might. They didn't stop when their forces exceeded all requirements of a legitimate defensive capability. And they haven't stopped now. During the past decade and a half, the Soviets have built up a massive arsenal of new strategic nuclear weapons—weapons that can strike directly at the United States. . . .

Another example of what's happened: In 1978 the Soviets had 600 intermediate-range nuclear missiles based on land and were beginning to add the SS-20—a new, highly accurate, mobile missile with 3 warheads. We had none. Since then the Soviets have strengthened their lead. By the end of 1979, when Soviet leader Brezhnev declared "a balance now exists," the Soviets had over 800 warheads. We still had none. A year ago this month, Mr. Brezhnev pledged a moratorium, or freeze, on SS-20 deployment. But by last August, their 800 warheads had become more than 1,200. We still had none. Some freeze. At this time Soviet Defense Minister [Dmitri] Ustinov announced "approximate parity of forces continues to exist." But the Soviets are still adding an average of 3 new warheads a week, and now have 1,300. These warheads can reach their targets in a matter of a few minutes. We still have none. So far, it seems that the Soviet definition of parity is a box score of 1,300 to nothing, in their favor.

So, together with our NATO allies, we decided in 1979 to deploy new weapons, beginning this year, as a deterrent to their SS-20's and as an incentive to the Soviet Union to meet us in serious arms control negotiations. We will begin that deployment late this year. At the same time, however, we're willing to cancel our program if the Soviets will dismantle theirs. This is what we've called a zero-zero plan. The Soviets are now at the negotiating table—and I think it's fair to say that without our planned deployments, they wouldn't be there. . . .

Some people may still ask: Would the Soviets ever use their formidable military power? Well, again, can we afford to believe they won't? There is Afghanistan. And in Poland, the Soviets denied the will of the people and in so doing demonstrated to the world how their military power could also be used to intimidate.

The final fact is that the Soviet Union is acquiring what can only be considered an offensive military force. They have continued to build far more intercontinental ballistic missiles than they could possibly need simply to deter an attack. Their conventional forces are trained and equipped not so much to defend against an attack as they are to permit sudden, surprise offensives of their own. . . .

When I took office in January 1981, I was appalled by what I found: American planes that couldn't fly and American ships that couldn't sail for lack of spare parts and trained personnel and insufficient fuel and ammunition for essential training. The inevitable result of all this was poor morale in our Armed Forces, difficulty in recruiting the brightest young Americans to wear the uniform, and difficulty in convincing our most experienced military personnel to stay on.

There was a real question then about how well we could meet a crisis. And it was obvious that we had to begin a major modernization program to ensure we could deter aggression and preserve the peace in the years ahead.

We had to move immediately to improve the basic readiness and staying power of our conventional forces, so they could meet—and therefore help deter—a crisis. We had to make up for lost years of investment by moving forward with a long-term plan to prepare our forces to counter the military capabilities our adversaries were developing for the future.

I know that all of you want peace, and so do I. I know too that many of you seriously believe that a nuclear freeze would further the cause of peace. But a freeze now would make us less, not more, secure and would raise, not reduce, the risks of war. It would be largely unverifiable and would seriously undercut our negotiations on arms reduction. It would reward the Soviets for their massive military buildup while preventing us from modernizing our aging and increasingly vulnerable forces. With their present margin of superiority, why should they agree to arms reductions knowing that we were prohibited from catching up?

Believe me, it wasn't pleasant for someone who had come to Washington determined to reduce government spending, but we had to move forward with the task of repairing our defenses or we would lose our ability to deter conflict now and in the future. We had to demonstrate to any adversary that aggression could not succeed, and that the only real solution was substantial, equitable, and effectively verifiable arms reduction—the kind we're working for right now in Geneva. . . .

The calls for cutting back the defense budget come in nice, simple arithmetic. They're the same kind of talk that led the democracies to neglect their defenses in the 1930's and invited the tragedy of World War II. We must not let that grim chapter of history repeat itself through apathy or neglect. . . .

This approach to stability [deterrence] through offensive threat [retaliation] has worked. We and our allies have succeeded in preventing nuclear war for more than three decades. In recent months, however, my advisers, including in particular the Joint Chiefs of Staff, have underscored the necessity to break out of a future that relies solely on offensive retaliation for our security. . . .

If the Soviet Union will join with us in our effort to achieve major arms reduction, we will have succeeded in stabilizing the nuclear balance. Nevertheless, it will still be necessary to rely on the specter of retaliation, on mutual threat. And that's a sad commentary on the human condition. Wouldn't it be better to save lives than to avenge them? Are we not capable of demonstrating our peaceful intentions by applying all our abilities and our ingenuity to achieving a truly lasting stability? I think we are. Indeed, we must.

After careful consultation with my advisers, including the Joint Chiefs of Staff, I believe there is a way. Let me share with you a vision of the future which offers hope. It is that we embark on a program to counter the awesome Soviet missile threat with measures that are defensive. Let us turn to the very strengths in technology that spawned our great industrial base and that have given us the quality of life we enjoy today.

What if free people could live secure in the knowledge that their security did not rest upon the threat of instant U.S. retaliation to deter a Soviet attack, that we could intercept and destroy strategic ballistic missiles before they reached our own soil or that of our allies?

I know this is a formidable, technical task, one that may not be accomplished before the end of this century. Yet, current technology has attained a level of sophistication where it's reasonable for us to begin this effort. It will take years, probably decades of effort on many fronts. There will be failures and setbacks, just as there will be successes and breakthroughs. And as we proceed, we must remain constant in preserving the nuclear deterrent and maintaining a solid capability for flexible response. But isn't it worth every investment necessary to free the world from the threat of nuclear war? We know it is. . . .

I clearly recognize that defensive systems have limitations and raise certain problems and ambiguities. If paired with offensive systems, they can be viewed as fostering an aggressive policy, and no one wants that. But with these considerations firmly in mind, I call upon the scientific community in our country, those who gave us nuclear weapons, to turn their great talents now to the cause of mankind and world peace, to give us the means of rendering these nuclear weapons impotent and obsolete.

Tonight, consistent with our obligations of the ABM [Anti-Ballistic Missile] treaty and recognizing the need for closer consultation with our allies, I'm taking an important first step. I am directing a comprehensive and intensive effort to define a long-term research and development program to begin to achieve our ultimate goal of eliminating the threat posed by strategic nuclear missiles. This could pave the way for arms control measures to eliminate the weapons themselves. We seek neither military superiority nor political advantage. Our only purpose—one all people share—is to search for ways to reduce the danger of nuclear war.

General Secretary Mikhail Gorbachev on U.S. Delusions, 1985

I attempted to explain to the President [Reagan] in a frank and straightforward discussion that, as it seems to me, much in American policy in relation to the USSR is based on delusions. On the one hand, it is hoped that the arms race and its escalation will exhaust the Soviet Union economically, undermine its influence in the world and thus free the hands of the United States. History has put such prophets to shame—even at a time when our society had a far smaller potential than today's, and smaller possibilities in general. Today, however, they are enormous. So delusions on this score only hamper the conduct of a realistic policy.

On the other hand, there were also delusions in the area of military plans. Attempts were made to outstrip us. Intercontinental ballistic missiles were put into regular service. This was followed by a Soviet response. After a slight delay, it is true, but it did follow. Then multiple nuclear warheads came on the scene. A Soviet response followed. We have always been able to meet any challenge.

Today, it seems to me, the illusions lingering in US military circles have been adopted to a certain extent by the political circles; by the President in particular. It is only a likelihood, of course, so I am not positive about it, but we do have such an impression.

It is evidently believed in the United States that it now has a definite edge on the Soviet Union in certain types of technology, computers and electronics. So again a desire has arisen to seize on this "edge" and achieve military superiority. President [Lyndon] Johnson's well known phrase to the effect that the nations that will rule outer space will rule the earth is again in current usage. Someone is evidently itching for a fight and is being consumed by ambition for world supremacy.

It is the old ambition of days of yore. The world has changed very much since then.

Thus, speaking of the so called technological edge which is to be realized through SDI and thus create a predicament for the Soviet Union, I must give this answer: this is just another delusion. We will meet this challenge.

Reagan Defends SDI
After the Reykjavík Summit Meeting, 1986

We proposed the most sweeping and generous arms control proposal in history. We offered the complete elimination of all ballistic missiles—Soviet and American—from the face of the Earth by 1996. While we parted company with this American offer still on the table, we are closer than ever before to agreements that could lead to a safer world without nuclear weapons. . . .

Some years ago, the United States and the Soviet Union agreed to limit any defense against nuclear missile attacks to the emplacement in one location in each country of a small number of missiles capable of intercepting and shooting down incoming nuclear missiles, thus leaving our real defense—a policy called mutual assured destruction, meaning if one side launched a nuclear attack, the other side could retaliate. And this mutual threat of destruction was believed to be a deterrent against either side striking first. So here we sit, with thousands of nuclear warheads targeted on each other and capable of wiping out both our countries. The Soviets deployed the few antiballistic missiles around Moscow as the treaty permitted. Our country didn't bother deploying because the threat of nationwide annihilation made such a limited defense seem useless.

For some years now we've been aware that the Soviets may be developing a nationwide defense. They have installed a large, modern radar at Krasnoyarsk, which we believe is a critical part of a radar system designed to provide radar guidance for antiballistic missiles protecting the entire nation. Now, this is a violation of the ABM treaty. Believing that a policy of mutual destruction and slaughter of their citizens and ours was uncivilized, I asked our military, a few years ago, to study and see if there was a practical way to destroy nuclear missiles after their launch but before they can reach their targets, rather than just destroy people. Well, this is the goal for what we call SDI, and our scientists researching such a system are convinced it is practical and that several years down the road we can have such a system ready to deploy. Now incidentally, we are not violating the ABM treaty, which permits such research. If and when we deploy, the treaty also allows withdrawal from the treaty upon 6 months' notice. SDI, let me make it clear, is a nonnuclear defense. . . .

I offered a proposal that we continue our present [SDI] research. And if and when we reached the stage of testing, we would sign, now, a treaty that would permit Soviet observation of such tests. And if the program was practical, we would both eliminate our offensive missiles, and then we would share the benefits of advanced defenses. I explained that even though we would have done away with our offensive ballistic missiles, having the defense would protect against cheating or the possibility of a madman, sometime, deciding to create nuclear missiles. After all, the world now knows how to make them. I likened it to our keeping our gas masks, even though the nations of the world had outlawed poison gas after World War I. We seemed to be making progress on reducing weaponry, although the General Secretary [Gorbachev] was registering opposition to SDI and proposing a pledge to observe ABM for a number of years. . . .

The Soviets had asked for a 10-year delay in the deployment of SDI programs. In an effort to see how we could satisfy their concerns—while protecting our principles and security—we proposed a 10-year period in which we began with the reduction of all strategic nuclear arms, bombers, air-launched cruise missiles, intercontinental ballistic missiles, submarine-launched ballistic missiles and the weapons they carry. They would be reduced 50 percent in the first 5 years. During the next 5 years, we would continue by eliminating all remaining offensive ballistic missiles, of all ranges. And during that time, we would proceed with research, development, and testing of SDI—all done in conformity with ABM provisions. At the 10-year point, with all ballistic missiles eliminated, we could proceed to deploy advanced defenses, at the same time permitting the Soviets to do likewise.

And here the debate began. The General Secretary wanted wording that, in effect, would have kept us from developing the SDI for the entire 10 years. In effect, he was killing SDI. And unless I agreed, all that work toward eliminating nuclear weapons would go down the drain—canceled. I told him I had pledged to the American people that I would not trade away SDI, there was no way I could tell our people their government would not protect them against nuclear destruction. I went to Reykjavík determined that everything was negotiable except two things: our freedom and our future. I'm still optimistic that a way will be found. The door is open, and the opportunity to begin eliminating the nuclear threat is within reach.

So you can see, we made progress in Iceland. And we will continue to make progress if we pursue a prudent, deliberate, and above all, realistic approach with the Soviets. From the earliest days of our administration this has been our policy.

We made it clear we had no illusions about the Soviets or their ultimate intentions. We were publicly candid about the critical, moral distinctions between totalitarianism and democracy. We declared the principal objective of American foreign policy to be not just the prevention of war, but the extension of freedom. And we stressed our commitment to the growth of democratic government and democratic institutions around the world. And that's why we assisted freedom fighters who are resisting the imposition of totalitarian rule in Afghanistan, Nicaragua, Angola, Cambodia, and elsewhere. And finally, we began work on what I believe most spurred the Soviets to negotiate seriously: rebuilding our military strength, reconstructing our strategic deterrence, and above all, beginning work on the Strategic Defense Initiative. . . .

I realize some Americans may be asking tonight: Why not accept Mr. Gorbachev's demand? Why not give up SDI for this agreement? Well, the answer, my friends, is simple. SDI is America's insurance policy that the Soviet Union would keep the commitments made at Reykjavík. SDI is America's security guarantee if the Soviets should—as they have done too often in the past—fail to comply with their solemn commitments. SDI is what brought the Soviets back to arms control talks at Geneva and Iceland. SDI is the key to a world without nuclear weapons. The Soviets understand this. They have devoted far more resources, for a lot longer time than we, to their own SDI. The world's only operational missile defense today surrounds Moscow, the capital of the Soviet Union.

What Mr. Gorbachev was demanding at Reykjavík was that the United States agree to a new version of a 14-year-old ABM treaty that the Soviet Union has already violated. I told him we don't make those kinds of deals in the United States. And the American people should reflect on these critical questions: How does a defense of the United States threaten the Soviet Union or anyone else? Why are the Soviets so adamant that America remain forever vulnerable to Soviet rocket attack? As of today, all free nations are utterly defenseless against Soviet missiles— fired either by accident or design. Why does the Soviet Union insist that we remain so—forever?

Gorbachev Criticizes SDI
After the Reykjavík Summit Meeting, 1986

Reykjavík generated not hopes alone. Reykjavík also highlighted the hardships on the road to a nuclear-free world. . . .

Quarters linked with militarism and arms race profits are clearly scared. They are doing their utmost to cope with the new situation and, coordinating their actions, are trying in every way to mislead the people, to control the sentiment of broad sections of the world public, to suppress their quest for peace, to hinder governments from taking a clear-cut position at this decisive moment in history.

These quarters have at their disposal political power, economic leverage and powerful mass media. Of course, one should not overestimate their strength, but one should not underrate it, either. All indications are that the battle will be a difficult one. Forces in the camp of the enemies of *détente* and disarmament have begun to regroup. Feverish efforts are being made to put up such obstacles as will check the process set rolling in Reykjavík. . . .

The key elements of the campaign are worth mentioning. Efforts are being made to gloss over the destructive position of a US Administration which came to the meeting unprepared. It came, let me say one more time, with the old baggage. But when there was no avoiding it, in a situation demanding clear answers, it blasted the chance to crown the meeting with accords.

Efforts are being made, in the new post-Reykjavík situation, to compel the Soviet Union to go back to the old approaches, to pull it back to fruitless numbers debates, to walking in circles in conditions of deadlock.

Evidently there is no small number of politicians in the West whom the Geneva talks suit as a screen rather than as a forum for seeking accords.

What was being thoroughly disguised previously is now becoming more clear: among US and West European ruling circles, there are powerful forces which would like to frustrate the process of nuclear disarmament. Some people are again making nuclear weapons out to be a boon. . . .

Far-reaching and interconnected, they [the Soviet proposals presented at the Reykjavík meeting] constitute an integrated package and are based on the program we announced on 15 January for the elimination of nuclear weapons by the year 2000.

The first proposal is to cut by half all strategic arms, without exception.

The second proposal is to fully eliminate Soviet and US medium-range missiles in Europe and immediately set about talks on missiles of this type in Asia, as well as on missiles with a range of less than a thousand kilometres. We suggested freezing the number of such missiles immediately.

The third proposal is to consolidate the ABM Treaty and to start full-scale talks on a total ban on nuclear tests. . . .

The US Administration is now trying in every possible way to convince people that a possible major success with concrete agreements was not achieved owing to Soviet unyieldingness over the program of the so-called Strategic Defence Initiative (SDI).

It is even being asserted that we allegedly lured the President into a trap by putting forward "breathtaking" proposals on cutting down strategic offensive arms and medium-range missiles, and that later on we ostensibly demanded in an ultimatum form that SDI be renounced.

But the essence of our stand and of our proposals is as follows: we are for reduction and then complete elimination of nuclear weapons and are firmly against a new stage in the arms race and against its transfer to outer space.

Hence we are against SDI and are for consolidation of the ABM Treaty.

It is clear to every sober-minded person that if we embark upon the road of deep cuts and then complete elimination of nuclear weapons, it is essential to rule out any opportunity for either the Soviet or US side to gain unilateral military superiority.

We perceive the main danger of SDI precisely in a transfer of the arms race to a new sphere, and in endeavours to go out into space with offensive arms and thereby achieve military superiority.

SDI has become an obstacle to ending the arms race, to getting rid of nuclear weapons, and is the main obstacle to a nuclear-free world.

When Mr. [George] Shultz, US Secretary of State, tells the Americans that SDI is a sort of "insurance policy" for America, that is, to say the least, an attempt to mislead the American people.

In actual fact, SDI does not boost America's security but, by opening up a new stage in the arms race, destabilises the military-political situation and thereby weakens both US and universal security.

The Americans should know this.

They should also know that the US stand on SDI, as stated in Reykjavík, fundamentally contradicts the ABM Treaty. . . .

Many a tale has been invented to raise SDI's prestige. One of them is that the Russians are terribly afraid of it. Another is that it is SDI which brought the Russians to the talks in Geneva and then to Reykjavík. A third is that SDI alone will save America from some "Soviet threat." A fourth is that SDI will give the United States a great technological lead over the Soviet Union and other countries, and so on, and so forth.

Knowing the problem, I can now say only one thing: continuation of the SDI program will sweep the world into a new stage of the arms race and destabilize the strategic situation.

The rest of what is being ascribed to SDI is very dubious in many respects and is being done to gift-wrap a suspect and dangerous commodity.

In upholding the position that thwarted the reaching of agreement in Reykjavík, the President asks rhetorical questions: Why do the Russians so stubbornly demand that America forever remain vulnerable to a Soviet missile strike? Why does the Soviet Union insist that we remain defenceless forever?

I am surprised at such questions, I must say. They have the air of indicating that the American President has an opportunity to make his country invulnerable, to give it secure protection against a nuclear strike.

As long as nuclear weapons exist and the arms race continues, he does not have such an opportunity. The same, naturally, applies to ourselves.

If the President counts on SDI in this respect, he does so in vain. The system would be effective only if all missiles were eliminated. But then, one might ask, why the anti-missile defence altogether? Why build it? I need not mention the money wasted, the cost of the system—according to some estimates, it will run into several trillion dollars.

So far, we have been trying to persuade America to give up that dangerous undertaking. We are urging the American Administration to look for invulnerability and for protection in another way—the way of total elimination of nuclear weapons and the establishment of a comprehensive system of international security that would preclude all war—nuclear and conventional. . . .

It is hard to reconcile oneself to the loss of a unique chance—that of saving mankind from the nuclear threat. Bearing precisely this in mind, I told the press conference in Reykjavík that we did not regard the dialogue as closed and hoped that President Reagan, on returning home, would consult Congress and the American people and adopt decisions logically necessitated by what had been achieved in Reykjavík.

Quite a different thing has happened. Besides distorting the entire picture of the Reykjavík negotiations—I will speak about that later—they have in recent days taken actions that look simply wild in the normal human view after such an important meeting between the two countries' top leaders.

I mean the expulsion of another fifty-five Soviet embassy and consular staff from the United States. We will take measures in response, of course—very tough measures on an equal footing. We are not going to put up with such outrageous practices. But for now let me say the following.

What kind of government is this? What can one expect from it in other affairs in the international arena? To what limits does the unpredictability of its actions go?

It turns out that it has no constructive proposals on key disarmament issues and that it does not even have a desire to maintain the atmosphere essential for a normal continuation of the dialogue. It appears that Washington is not prepared for any of these.

A conclusion suggests itself. It is confirmed by the considerable experience to date. Every time a gleam of hope appears in approaches to the big issues of Soviet-American relations and to a settlement of matters involving the interests of the whole of mankind, provocation is immediately staged with an eye to frustrating any positive solution and poisoning the atmosphere.

Where is the true face of the US Administration? Is it for unravelling and resolving problems or does it want to ultimately destroy all that may serve as a basis for headway and deliberately rule out any normalization?

An unattractive portrait of the Administration of that great country, of an Administration quick to take disruptive actions, is coming into view. Either the President is unable to cope with an entourage which literally breathes hatred for the Soviet Union and for everything that may lead international affairs into a calm channel or he himself wants that. At all events, there is no keeping the "hawks" in the White House in check. And this is very dangerous. . . .

Let me say once again: when SDI is preferred to nuclear disarmament, only one conclusion is possible: it is that through that military program efforts are being made to disprove the axiom of international relations of our epoch expressed in the simple and clear-cut words under which the US President and I put our signatures last year [at the Geneva summit conference]. Here are those words: nuclear war must not be fought and it cannot be won.

Let me say in conclusion: the Soviet Union has put the maximum of goodwill into its proposals. We are not removing these proposals, they still stand! Everything that has been said by the way of their substantiation and development remains in force.

Paul Kennedy on "Imperial Overstretch" and the Relative Decline of the United States, 1987

Although the United States is at present still in a class of its own economically and perhaps even militarily, it cannot avoid confronting the two great tests which challenge the *longevity* of every major power that occupies the "number one" position in world affairs: whether, in the military/strategic realm, it can preserve a reasonable balance between the nation's perceived defense requirements and the means it possesses to maintain those commitments; and whether, as an intimately related

point, it can preserve the technological and economic bases of its power from relative erosion in the face of the ever-shifting patterns of global production. This test
of American abilities will be the greater because it, like Imperial Spain around
1600 or the British Empire around 1900, is the inheritor of a vast array of strategi-
cal commitments which had been made decades earlier, when the nation's political, economic, and military capacity to influence world affairs seemed so much
more assured. In consequence, the United States now runs the risk, so familiar to
historians of the rise and fall of previous Great Powers, of what might roughly be
called "imperial overstretch"; that is to say, decision-makers in Washington must
face the awkward and enduring fact that the sum total of the United States' global
interests and obligations is nowadays far larger than the country's power to defend
them all simultaneously. . . .

This brings us, inevitably, to the delicate relationship between slow economic
growth and high defense spending. The debate upon "the economics of defense
spending" is a highly controversial one, and—bearing in mind the size and variety
of the American economy, the stimulus which can come from large government
contracts, and the technical spin-offs from weapons research—the evidence does
not point simply in one direction. But what is significant for our purposes is the
comparative dimension. Even if (as is often pointed out) defense expenditures
formed 10 percent of GNP under Eisenhower and 9 percent under Kennedy, the
United States' relative share of global production and wealth was at that time
around *twice* what it is today; and, more particularly, the American economy was
not then facing the challenges to either its traditional or its high-technology manufactures. Moreover, if the United States at present continues to devote 7 percent or
more of its GNP to defense spending while its major economic rivals, especially
Japan, allocate a far smaller proportion, then *ipso facto* the latter have potentially
more funds "free" for civilian investment; if the United States continues to invest a
massive amount of its R&D activities into military-related production while the
Japanese and West Germans concentrate upon commercial R&D; and if the Pentagon's spending drains off the majority of the country's scientists and engineers
from the design and production of goods for the world market while similar personnel in other countries are primarily engaged in bringing out better products for
the civilian consumer, then it seems inevitable that the American share of world
manufacturing will steadily decline, and also likely that its economic growth rates
will be slower than in those countries dedicated to the marketplace and less eager
to channel resources into defense.

It is almost superfluous to say that these tendencies place the United States on
the horns of a most acute dilemma over the longer term. Simply because it is *the*
global superpower, with far more extensive military commitments than a regional
Power like Japan or West Germany, it requires much larger defense forces—in
just the same way as imperial Spain felt it needed a far larger army than its contemporaries and Victorian Britain insisted upon a much bigger navy than any other
country. Furthermore, since the USSR is seen to be the major military threat to
American interests across the globe and is clearly devoting a far greater proportion
of *its* GNP to defense, American decision-makers are inevitably worried about
"losing" the arms race with Russia. Yet the more sensible among these decision-
makers can also perceive that the burden of armaments is debilitating the Soviet

economy; and that if the two superpowers continue to allocate ever-larger shares of their national wealth into the unproductive field of armaments, the critical question might soon be: "Whose economy will decline *fastest*, relative to such expanding states as Japan, China, etc.?" A low investment in armaments may, for a globally overstretched Power like the United States, leave it feeling vulnerable everywhere; but a very heavy investment in armament, while bringing greater security in the short term, may so erode the commercial competitiveness of the American economy that the nation will be *less* secure in the long term.

Georgi Arbatov Explains the "New Thinking" in the Soviet Union, 1989

Personally I share the radical view that *perestroika* means building a new model of Soviet socialism. We have to go all the way in democratization, *glasnost,* and economic reforms, not halfway. This bothers some people, but the reasons aren't hard to understand. The Soviet Union is a young country—just over seventy years old. During those years we have lived through so many extraordinary circumstances— the Revolution, the Civil War, Stalinism, the world war, the Cold War—that our structures, psychology, and behavior acquired extraordinary characteristics. It was like growing up under martial law. Even Stalinism was shaped by extraordinary circumstances—the threats of German fascism and Japanese militarism in the 1930s, the burden of the Cold War. So it's not surprising that we haven't yet built the socialist model we intended and believe in.

Now we have to rid ourselves of all those things that arose in those extraordinary times—things in which we used to believe, things we thought were intrinsic to socialism. This isn't easy, partly because many people will believe in all those things but also because the old economic model worked rather well in its time and for certain purposes. If the old economic model had completely failed, if the country had not developed from being a very backward country, it would be easier to change today. It would be easier to give up the obsolete thinking and policies that led the country into a dead end and that had such a negative impact on international relations. I can't think of any other country or government that now is so self-critical and demanding in looking at its own past and learning from the sufferings of the past.

That's why I argue against some of our officials who are guarded or worried about *glasnost.* The anti-*glasnost* tradition was imposed on the country during Stalinism, and it has had very negative effects in our domestic policies—but also in foreign policy. In fact, improvements brought by the Twentieth Party Congress back in the 1950s barely touched foreign policy. I don't mean that everything in our foreign policy stagnated in the years that followed. There were achievements—the beginnings of détente, arms control steps, and other things. But the tradition of secrecy, silence, and the absence of *glasnost* fossilized much of our defense and foreign policy thinking and decision making. When I argue for greater openness, some of our people say that exposing our problems will hurt us abroad. I tell them that the world knew about our problems before *glasnost;* we can't hide them. Moreover, *glasnost* has helped us abroad because more people there understand we are serious about our reforms. If there is an attempt to curtail *glasnost*, it will be harmful and counterproductive. . . .

The main priority of our foreign policy is to create the best international circumstances for the reforms going on inside our country. For us, economic and social progress is the most important thing. Of course, there still are some people here who cling to old ideas about the priority of promoting revolutions abroad—people who still think we can work miracles when foreign Marxists ask us for help. But it doesn't work. The best way to influence other countries is by reforming our own system. *Perestroika* involves a new way of thinking about foreign policy which begins with seeing realities as they are, not as we want them to be. We must face the truth, no matter how bitter it is. Our basic conception of the world has changed. We no longer view it in terms of "we" and "they" but as one humanity that has to live or die together. The nuclear world is too fragile for the use of military force, any kind of serious misbehavior, any geopolitical adventures, or an unlimited arms race. That is a basic principle of our new thinking. . . .

I should say first that we do not claim to have invented all the ideas of the new thinking. Some of them originated years ago outside the Soviet Union with people such as [the scientist] Albert Einstein, [the philosopher] Bertrand Russell, and [the Swedish politician] Olof Palme. We are developing them, along with our own ideas, into a full program for international conduct. To mention just a few of these ideas, we now believe that what unites different countries, their common interests, is more important than the conflicts and differences between them. We also realized that we relied too much on military power for security. Both the Soviet Union and the United States have far more military power than they can use for any reasonable purpose. Militarism on the part of all countries is the real danger. We all must rely for security more on political means—on negotiations, for example. Our mutual task is to reverse the militarization of life. We have no need for all these weapons and huge armies. We also now understand that we cannot obtain national security at the expense of the other side—at your [U.S.] expense—and the same is true for you. This is our concept of mutual security. Our security depends on you feeling secure, and yours depends on us feeling secure. Now we also understand better that the lagging economic development of the Third World is a global problem, and despite our limited resources we have to make our contribution to solving this problem.

More generally, the Soviet Union no longer can live in economic autarchy, isolated from the world economy. Interdependence can only increase. All of these new perceptions make us favor more multilateral efforts, particularly through the United Nations. My own view is that the two superpowers have to be more democratic in their thinking about the world. The Soviet Union and the United States represent only about 10 percent of the world population. We can't and shouldn't try to do everything. And the rest of the world should not be held hostage to U.S.-Soviet relations. . . .

We think [military] sufficiency is enough. Of course, we want some kind of equality, but not in numerical terms. We don't have to have as many airplanes as you have. We don't need them. All we need is enough so that you know it would be folly to start a war.

But we have gone beyond this. We want to create a nonnuclear world or a world with very few nuclear weapons. And we understand that we cannot have these major reductions in nuclear weapons without major reductions in conventional weapons. You can see how serious we are about this from Gorbachev's unilateral reductions in our conventional forces. So far as we are concerned, the door is wide open for even larger reductions through negotiations.

Unfortunately, there is a good deal of hypocrisy on your side. Your authorities complain that we have superiority in conventional weapons. Perhaps we do in some categories and we are prepared to build down in these areas. But you've been complaining about this for forty years, despite the fact that the West's GNP is two and a half times bigger than ours. If you really thought we had such superiority, why didn't you catch up? Your automobile and tractor industries are much stronger than ours. Why didn't they build tanks? No, I think you've used this scare about alleged Soviet superiority to hold your NATO alliance together and to justify building an absolutely irrational number of nuclear weapons.

We are arguing that both sides must adopt a new policy to replace the arms race. The side that is ahead in a weapons category should build down rather than the lagging side build up. This is the reasonable way to solve the problem of imbalances. Unfortunately, the human mind has a tendency to lag behind. Politics and diplomacy do especially. Our task is to bring your perceptions into accord with realities, particularly in foreign and military policy. Since 1985 Gorbachev has proposed getting rid of nuclear weapons. We have liberated ourselves from our own old thinking about nuclear and conventional weapons. President Gorbachev and President Reagan made some important progress on nuclear weapons. But our new thinking seems to have put America in an awkward position. Suddenly we start accepting American proposals and you don't know what to do. We're still getting too many negative responses from you. . . .

I know that some Americans dislike them [Soviet domestic reforms] and I understand why. Since 1945 many American institutions have needed a foreign enemy—an evil empire. Indeed, the general framework of American foreign policy has been constructed on the premise of this enemy. The Cold War was built on a kind of black-and-white, religious fundamentalism. There was the American paradise and the Soviet hell. When hell disappears, when the enemy image erodes, the whole structure becomes shaky. Some Americans fear this. But they will just have to find ways to live without the image of the Soviet enemy. America also needs *perestroika* and new thinking of her own. . . .

But, you know, there is so much ideology about us in America. It's a great irony. You've always accused us of being too ideological, but there's no country in the world more ideological than the Untied States, despite your professed pragmatism. Mr. Reagan's presidency brought this ideological impulse to the fore. We too tended to over-ideologize our foreign policy, but our new thinking is based on realism. For example, that all these weapons are dangerous and useless. Your ideology—or illusions—seem to persist, which is one reason why you can't let go of the enemy image so easily. . . .

The Cold War is a living corpse. It died sometime in the 1960s and has been kept alive by political injections of myths and fantasies about the Soviet threat— like a body kept alive on an artificial heart-and-lung machine. It is time to lay it to rest. Neither of us can any longer afford to squander money on fake problems, false stereotypes, and pointless suspicions. Both of us have plenty of real problems at home. . . .

I'm not confident that you will have new thinking in the United States, but I think your economic problems are going to force a change in your foreign policy anyway. Can you imagine the same amount of military spending and indebtedness over the next eight years? Also, to continue the Cold War you will need a partner. We won't be that partner. So while we may lose valuable time, I think things will be better in the United States.

Zbigniew Brzezinski Lauds Carter for a U.S. Cold War Victory, 1992

The historically dramatic turnabout [end of the Cold War] was precipitated by three critical cases of Soviet overstretch. Geopolitically the Soviet invasion of Afghanistan in December 1979— apparently taken on the assumption that the United States would not react—propelled the United States to adopt, for the first time ever during the entire Cold War, a policy of directly supporting actions aimed at killing Soviet troops. The Carter administration not only undertook immediately to support the Mujahedeen [Afghan forces fighting the Soviets], but it also quietly put together a coalition embracing Pakistan, China, Saudi Arabia, Egypt and Britain on behalf of the Afghan resistance. Equally important was the American public guarantee of Pakistan's security against any major Soviet military attack, thereby creating a sanctuary for the guerillas. The scale and quality of U.S. support steadily expanded during the 1980s under the subsequent Reagan administration. America—along with Pakistan, which played a courageous and decisive role in the effort—thus succeeded in bogging down the Soviet Union in its own equivalent of Vietnam.

Moreover, with the influence of the accommodationist school of thought undercut by Soviet assertiveness, the United States qualitatively expanded its relationship with China. As early as 1980 U.S.-Chinese cooperation assumed a more direct strategic dimension, with sensitive undertakings not only toward Afghanistan but also on other matters. Thus the Soviet Union faced the growing geopolitical menace of a counter encirclement.

In addition, the Carter administration initiated the creation of a Rapid Deployment Force, and, most important, the decision was made together with key NATO allies to match the Soviet SS-20 deployments with new and highly accurate American intermediate-range missiles positioned on European soil. The latter prompted a vigorous Soviet campaign of intimidation directed at Europe, with Europe explicitly warned (in the words of Foreign Minister Andrei Gromyko) that it might suffer the fate of Pompeii unless the Atlantic security link was significantly

Zbigniew Brzezinski, "The Cold War and Its Aftermath" in *Foreign Affairs,* 71 (Fall 1992), pp. 41–43.
Copyright 1992 by the Council on Foreign Relations, Inc.

loosened. However, America's European allies held firm—encouraged by the increasingly assertive tones emanating from Washington and by the acceleration of the U.S. defense buildup adopted by the Reagan administration.

The massive U.S. defense buildup of the early 1980s—including the decision to proceed with the Strategic Defense Initiative—both shocked the Soviets and then strained their resources. Its scale, momentum and technological daring had been totally unexpected in Moscow. By 1983 a genuine war scare began to develop in the Kremlin, with the United States seen as bent perhaps even on a military solution. And then by the middle of the decade it dawned on Soviet leaders that they could neither match nor even keep up with the American efforts.

This realization interacted dynamically with the third reversal, on the ideological and social planes. In the second half of the 1970s President Carter launched his human rights campaign. Within Soviet-controlled Eastern Europe and then within the Soviet Union itself, it first encouraged a few individuals, then larger groups, to pick up the standard of human rights, counting on Western moral and even political support. The struggle for human rights mushroomed, especially in Poland, galvanized by the election of the first Polish pope in Rome. By the late 1970s Solidarity's mass movement was beginning to threaten the communist regime of the Soviet Union's most important European satellite.

The Soviets were poised to intervene militarily in Poland, once in December 1980 and then again in March 1981. In both cases two successive U.S. administrations made clear, through direct and indirect signals, that such intervention would produce grave consequences, a message in the meantime made more credible by U.S. support for the Afghan resistance. Under these circumstances the Kremlin leaders chose to rely on an only partially effective imposition of martial law by the Polish communists themselves. As a result the Polish crisis festered throughout the decade, progressively undermining not only the Polish communist regime but gradually infecting other East European states.

The human rights campaign and the arms buildup thus became the mutually reinforcing central prongs of a U.S. response that not only blunted the Soviet offensive but also intensified the crisis of the Soviet political and socioeconomic system itself. Power and principle combined to reverse the Soviet momentum. Neither one alone would have sufficed.

✷ *E S S A Y S*

In the first essay, Thomas G. Paterson, a historian at the University of Connecticut, probes the external and internal factors that intersected to change both American and Soviet policies. He studies the costs of the long conflict for the United States and the Soviet Union and the changes in the international system that undermined the power of both countries. Moscow and Washington reversed course and ended the Cold War to stem their decline and to recover their sagging international positions. Given their substantial domestic problems by the early 1990s, it can hardly be said that either the United States or the Soviet Union won the Cold War. In the second essay, in a statement representative of the Reagan victory school, the historian John Lewis Gaddis of Ohio University disagrees with Paterson's perspective. Gaddis trumpets Reagan's restoration of national self-confidence, the U.S. military buildup, the bargaining-chip value of SDI, and the United States' negotiation from a position of strength for "spooking" the Soviets. For Gaddis, Reagan stands tall as a skillful visionary whose toughness paid off.

The third essay, by the political scientist Michael MccGwire, the author of studies on Soviet security policy, disputes Gaddis and the victory-through-strength school by emphasizing the generational shift in Soviet leadership epitomized by Mikhail Gorbachev and other reformers. MccGwire claims that Reagan's early "confrontational policies" did not force positive changes on the U.S.S.R. but rather provoked an intransigent Soviet response that delayed Soviet-American accommodation. It took Gorbachev and new leadership— along with a convergence of the antinuclear sentiment harbored by both Gorbachev and Reagan—to effect the turnaround. The final essay, by the political scientists Daniel Deudney of the University of Pennsylvania and G. John Ikenberry of Princeton University, also questions the peace-through-strength argument. These authors, too, note Reagan's distaste for nuclear weapons, and they add that ultimately Reagan's "soft" policies became more influential than his "hard" policies. But they also credit a large peace movement in the West and improving East-West economic relations for tempering the Cold War. Engagement and mutual vulnerability, not containment and strength, drove change. As for the question of victory, Deudney and Ikenberry posit that what triumphed at the end of the Cold War was not Reagan's free-market capitalism but rather the welfare-state ideas of Western European social democracy.

Superpower Decline and Hegemonic Survival

THOMAS G. PATERSON

Simply put, the Cold War ended because of the relative decline of the United States and the Soviet Union in the international system from the 1950s through the 1980s. The Cold War waned because the contest had undermined the power of its two major protagonists. In acts of hegemonic survival in a world of mounting challenges on several fronts, they gradually moved toward a cautious cooperation whose urgent goals were nothing less than the restoration of their economic well-being and the preservation of their diminishing global positions.

At least three sources or trends explain this gradual decline and the consequent attractions of détente. The first was the burgeoning economic costs of the Cold War. Challenges to the leadership of the two major powers from within their spheres of influence constitute the second source. The third was the emergence of the Third World, which brought new players into the international game, further diffused power, and eroded bipolarism. The three elements combined to weaken the standing of the two adversaries and ultimately to persuade Soviet and American leaders to halt their nations' descent by ending the Cold War. The Soviet Union fell much harder than the United States, but the implications of decline became unmistakable for both: The Cold War they made in the 1940s had to be unmade if the two nations were to remain prominent international superintendents.

The first source was the economic burden that the long confrontation inflicted on the United States and the Soviet Union. America's impressive economic standing after the Second World War and into the 1950s went unmatched. The

American economy shifted into high gear during the war while much of the rest of the world was being reduced to rubble. In the postwar years the United States used its abundant economic resources to spur the recovery of its allies and to build an international military network. The costs of maintaining and expanding its global interests climbed dramatically: $12.4 billion for the Marshall Plan, $69.5 billion for the Korean War, $22.3 billion for the Alliance for Progress, $172.2 billion for the Vietnam War. In the years from 1946 through 1987 the United States dispensed more than $382 billion in economic and military foreign aid. International organizations in which the United States was prominent, such as the World Bank, offered another $273 billion in assistance.

The United States also spent billions of dollars for CIA operations such as that at the Bay of Pigs in Cuba (1961) and for invasions like that of the Dominican Republic (1965). Support for factions in civil wars and political contests from Greece to Italy, from Chile to Nicaragua, from Angola to Somalia, from China to the Philippines—and especially in Vietnam—drove up expenses. During 1984 to 1987 Washington sent more than $2 billion in aid just to the government of El Salvador to help that small Central American state combat an insurgency Washington called Communist. The CIA put high-ranking officials from Panama to Bolivia on the agency's payroll. Expenses also mounted for the maintenance of occupying forces in Germany, Japan, and elsewhere. U.S. Information Agency propaganda activities proved expensive, too, as witnessed by the Voice of America's $640 million expenditure in the 1970s.

Security links stretched across the globe. After the Rio Pact (1947) and NATO (1949) came the ANZUS Pact with Australia and New Zealand (1951), the defense treaty with Japan (1952), the South East Asia Treaty Organization (SEATO, 1954), and the Baghdad Pact for the Middle East (1955), which the United States supported but did not join. The rearmament of West Germany began in the early 1950s, and that half nation entered NATO in 1955. In 1959, moreover, one million Americans were stationed overseas; in 1970 the number was nearly nine hundred thousand; and by 1985 the United States still had more than half a million armed forces personnel abroad.

Alliance building, military expansion, clandestine operations, and interventionism spawned galloping defense budgets amounting to trillions of dollars over four decades. U.S. military spending stood at $13.5 billion in 1949, averaged $40 billion a year in the 1950s, rose to $54 billion in 1960 and $90 billion in 1970 (largely because of the Vietnam War), and soared to $155 billion in 1980. By 1988 the military budget alone had reached more than $300 billion. In the mid-1980s the Defense Department was spending an average of $28 million an hour, twenty-four hours a day, seven days a week. Nuclear-arms development and ever more sophisticated technology [also] drove up the cost of waging the Cold War. . . .

America's massive military spending chipped away at the nation's infrastructure, contributing to the relative decline of the United States and stimulating the movement toward Soviet-American détente. Defense spending demanded capital, which the federal government had to borrow, forcing up interest rates, which in turn slowed economic development. Persistent deficit spending by the federal government drove up the federal debt, which stood at $257 billion in 1950, $286 billion in 1960, $371 billion in 1970, and $908 billion in 1980. By 1986 the debt had reached a staggering $2.1 trillion. That year alone 19 percent of the federal budget disappeared just to pay the interest on the debt. In that same year defense gobbled up 28 percent of the budget. By comparison, 11 percent of federal expenditures went to health and Medicare, 3 percent to education, and 1 percent to environmental programs. Analysts noted that in 1984 Japan's per capita military spending came to only $102 and West Germany's to $360. In conspicuous contrast, the figure for the United States was $968.

Military spending constantly drew funds away from other categories so essential to the overall well-being of the nation—what economists call "opportunity costs." Domestic troubles mounted: lower productivity, falling savings rate, sagging agricultural sector, inadequately skilled labor force with an increasing number of functional illiterates, drug abuse, decaying cities, growing high school dropout rates, a health care system that failed to cover large numbers of people, and weak conservation programs that left the U.S. economy vulnerable to sharp swings in prices of imported raw materials. . . .

The United States also became a debtor nation with a serious balance of payments problem and a widening trade deficit. In the late 1950s private overseas investments, U.S. spending for foreign aid and military activities abroad, and the American purchase of more imports than could be matched by the sale of exports precipitated a significant dollar drain. Foreigners came to hold so many U.S. dollars that they threatened the nation's gold reserves. "We're broke, anyone can topple us," Treasury Secretary John Connally told President Richard Nixon in 1971 as Washington scrambled to head off disaster. That year, too, the first trade deficit since 1888 befell the United States. By the 1970s, when American sentiment for détente in the Cold War was growing, *Business Week* magazine concluded that the U.S. "colossus" was "clearly facing a crisis of the decay of power." Henry Kissinger, Nixon's primary foreign policy adviser and a major influence behind détente and withdrawal from Vietnam, explained that "we were becoming like other nations in the need to recognize that our power, while vast, had limits. Our resources were no longer infinite in relation to our problems. . . ."

International economic crises—high oil prices in the 1970s and massive Third World debt in the 1980s—added to America's woes. Debt-ridden nations curbed their purchases of American products and suspended debt payments. By 1985 the U.S. trade deficit had reached a remarkable $148.5 billion. Foreigners used many of the dollars they amassed to buy American companies: Japanese investors owned 7-Eleven, Fotomat, and Columbia Pictures; British buyers acquired Burger King; and German investors purchased RCA Records. Four of California's ten largest banks became Japanese owned. "Did you hear?" went one joke. "The Japanese just bought Pearl Harbor!" Even though such foreign investment represented only a small portion of the American economy, there could be no denying that the United States seemed less able to control its own house and was more susceptible to the decisions of non-Americans.

Americans became increasingly dependent upon foreign capital to pay for their hunger for imports, to fund real estate speculation and corporate buyouts (rather than to upgrade factories, for example), and to finance the federal deficit. Americans were giving to foreigners great amounts of the nation's wealth as debt payments. By 1989 the U.S. foreign debt hit $650 billion. . . .

Although the American economy during the Cold War grew in absolute numbers, the U.S. share of the world's material resources declined relative to other nations. Analysts use different methods of computation, interpret figures differently, and sometimes cite shaky statistics or let political or ideological preferences control the "numbers game," but as somebody has put it, you do not need to be a hydraulic engineer measuring the flow to see that the water runs downhill. The signs of decline and comparative disadvantage became conspicuous. Between 1960 and 1973 the U.S. economic growth rate compared with that of all other countries was 4 percent versus 5.6 percent, and from 1973 to 1980 2 percent versus 3.6 percent. In the decade of the 1970s ninety-eight nations had higher rates of economic growth than the United States. In 1979 and 1980 the U.S. growth rate dropped to minus 0.2 percent; by comparison, Japan's stood at 4.2 percent and West Germany's at 1.8, and the world rate was 2 percent. The U.S. share of gross world product also declined: from approximately 40 percent in 1950 to about 22 percent in 1980. Japan doubled its share in the same period to 9 percent. From the 1950s to the 1980s the American share of world exports slumped while West Germany's and Japan's shares jumped. The American rate for productivity growth (output per worker) also descended; for 1950–1970 the rate was 2.68 percent, then for 1970–1980 it dropped to 1.17 percent, and for 1980–1986 it stood at 1.53 percent. For the same periods Japan's and West Germany's rates ranked higher than the U.S. rate. The American share of world industrial production also fell, and the United States lost its lead in televisions, automobiles, semiconductors, and machine tools. In 1950 the United States produced 46 percent of the world's steel, but by 1987 the American percentage had tumbled to 11 percent, and both Japan (13.7 percent) and the European Economic Community or Common Market (17.8 percent) had surpassed the United States. . . .

The compelling point is that the Cold War was exceedingly costly. With finite resources the U.S. government had to make choices. Money spent on the military and foreign interventions was not spent on building America at home. . . . Defense spending became "Keynesianism on steroids": The short-term effects were stimulating, but like any addiction, it produced long-term ill effects. Perhaps the money, if not devoted to military hardware, would not have been otherwise wisely invested. But it is demonstrably true that "nations that spend heavily on armaments, such as the United States and United Kingdom, have forfeited valuable gains in industrial productivity and economic growth."

Measurable economic decline compelled American policy makers, however reluctantly at times, to take steps toward ending the Cold War. By relieving domestic troubles, détente seemed to offer continuation of America's world-class status. Détente might make expensive interventions and ever-growing arsenals less necessary. It also promised greater trade with both the Soviet Union and the People's Republic of China, the former hungry for American grain and the latter eager for American technology. Overall, détente might move America out of what one journalist called "Sector D"—"depression, decline, depravity, doom, denial, decay, debacle, dementia, . . . dilly-dallying, despair, . . . dysfunction, . . . doubt and disgust."

The Cold War also cost the Soviet Union a great deal—indeed, much more than it cost the United States—and this burden persuaded Moscow to seek détente. . . . The Soviet Union also became a big military spender, in part to catch up in the strategic arms race. . . .

Foreign ventures, too, strained Soviet resources. In the 1950s Moscow began to lend funds to Third World nations—to India for a steel plant, to Egypt for the Aswan Dam. The Warsaw Pact; aid to the People's Republic of China (until halted by Moscow in the early 1960s); support for Egypt (until the Soviets were evicted in 1972), Syria, and other Middle Eastern states; and subsidies to Fidel Castro's Cuba (which averaged close to five billion dollars during the 1980s) also drew heavily on Soviet funds. North Vietnam received more than eight billion dollars in Soviet aid from 1965 to 1975. The Soviet Union subsidized its Eastern European client states, probably spending at least seventeen billion dollars a year by the early 1980s. The invasions of Hungary in 1956 and Czechoslovakia in 1968 and the ten-year war in Afghanistan from 1979 to 1989 cost dearly. In 1980 alone the expense to the Soviet Union of maintaining its empire and worldwide commitments through trade subsidies, military and economic aid, interventions, and covert operations totaled approximately thirty-eight billion dollars. . . .

To pay for its large Red Army encamped in Eastern Europe and along the tense border with China, the considerable expansion of its navy, and its interventions, foreign aid, and nuclear weaponry, the Kremlin shortchanged the nation's domestic development. Under five-year plans, steel, automobile, oil, and electrical production registered gains from the 1940s to the 1980s, and the USSR's raw materials wealth (manganese, chrome, and more) represented fundamental strengths. But a Soviet slide became measurable. The nation's overall industrial and agricultural rates of growth slackened. In the 1950s the rate of Soviet economic growth stood at 5.9; from 1960 to 1973 the rate declined to 4.9 percent; from 1973 to 1980 the rate dropped even more to 2.6 percent; and for 1981 to 1985 the rate plummeted further to 1.9. Actually, there may have been no growth at all in this period, according to some economists. The Soviet share of gross world product also declined.

Low productivity and shoddy craftsmanship stemmed from poor labor morale, alcoholism, high absenteeism, and a stultifying Communist party bureaucracy. "They pretend to pay us and we pretend to work" went the joke. Air and water pollution, crumbling plants, inefficient and hence dismal agricultural output, and declining life expectancy rates also plagued the Soviet Union through the Cold War decades. Shabbily manufactured tractors and trucks required inordinate maintenance; factory breakdowns and lack of spare parts slowed production. The Soviets lagged behind non-Communist nations in key technologies like computers and microcircuits. The Soviet Union had to import foodstuffs, and at times famines afflicted vast areas of the country. "*This* is the political and military regime for fear of which the United States bankrupted itself in the 1980s?" New York Senator Daniel P. Moynihan asked as he thought about why Americans had exaggerated the Soviet threat.

"There are real sources of trouble" in the Soviet Union, admitted Georgi Arbatov, director of Moscow's Institute for United States and Canadian Studies. "The Cold War just prevents us from dealing with them," he explained. "Neither of us can any longer afford to squander money on fake problems, false stereotypes, and pointless suspicions. Both of us have plenty of real problems at home." In 1987, for example, the Chernobyl nuclear plant accident spewed radioactive fallout across Europe and raised anew doubts about Soviet workmanship, management skills, and governmental competence. To Kremlin planners, as Mikhail Gorbachev said in 1986, a year after he came to power, "acceleration of the country's socio-economic development is the key to all our problems. . . ." To save the Soviet economy, the expensive arms race had to be stopped, for military spending was eating up at least a quarter of the nation's budget. Soviet foreign policy, Gorbachev announced, "is more than ever determined by domestic policy. . . . This is why we need lasting peace, predictability, and constructiveness in international relations." Soviet leaders made the point again and again: Urgent needs at home demanded an end to the Cold War.

"Hegemony," one historian has written, "necessarily rests upon both military and economic power, and the dilemma facing a maturing hegemon is that it cannot sustain both." If a major power spends heavily on its military, it hurts its domestic economy; if it bleeds its economy, it is less able to sustain a competitive global position. On the other hand, if it reduces its defense spending to attend to domestic priorities, it endangers its global status, which derives in good part from military superiority. For the United States, the demands of containment compounded the problem. If, as the containment doctrine asserted, the Communist threat was global, American ramparts had to be erected everywhere. Such vigilant monitoring, and the considerable counterforce required to apply the doctrine, strained American resources. Superpower policing of the world and of empire ironically meant "permanent insecurity" for the United States because of the constant fear of falling dominoes and because "empire makes one into a worldwide target." The Soviet Union, with its own brands of containment and imperialism, suffered the same fate. Ending the Cold War, Moscow and Washington officials reasoned, might stop dominoes from falling, enhance security, shield the targets, and make the hegemonic dilemma more manageable.

In addition to the economic burden of the Cold War, another significant source accounted for the great powers' decline and their movement toward détente: challenges to their hegemony from independent-minded client states and allies. Some allies, such as West Germany and France, advanced détente on their own. Others made so much trouble that the hegemonic powers welcomed détente as a means to discipline them—Moscow's eagerness to build Soviet-American cooperation as a counterweight to China, for example. The two great powers also embraced détente as a means to reassert mastery, as in the 1970s, when Moscow hoped that the United States would accept the Soviet Union's preeminent influence in Eastern Europe and Washington hoped that détente would create a great-power "equilibrium" that would help reduce radical revolution in the American sphere. Sometimes détente afforded a great power an apparent opportunity to exploit division within a sphere in order to contain or weaken its adversary. The USSR, for example, attempted to encourage France to spoil U.S. plans for Western Europe, and the United States played its "China card" against the Soviet Union. . . .

The United States, too, faced challenges from within its far-flung sphere of influence, although with less disarray than that experienced by the Soviets [in dealing with Eastern European nationalism and the Sino-Soviet schism]. Europe became for Americans a source not only of friends but also of rivals, who themselves marched in the direction of ending the Cold War. Marshall Plan and NATO allies eagerly sought valuable assistance from the United States and thrived economically, but they chafed under the U.S. influence that accompanied the aid. Many Europeans became alarmed by the American push for German rearmament, by the provocative U.S. march to the Chinese border in Korea, by U.S. strictures on trade with Communist states, and by the extremism of McCarthyism. These developments raised "doubts" in Europe "as to the wisdom of American leadership." Throughout the 1950s and after, America's European partners reached for more independence from the United States as their recovery from the depredation of war progressed. . . .

Such expressions of independence by allies became common during the Vietnam era, when NATO partners failed to support the long U.S. war in Southeast Asia. The British, complained the always pungent President Lyndon B. Johnson, could at least have sent a platoon of bagpipers. . . . Some jittery Europeans also believed that American policy makers preferred to use European territory as a nuclear battleground. Under the weight of such strains the American sphere of influence in Europe progressively frayed.

The nationalism and independent decision making of West Germany also shook the American sphere and advanced détente. Many West Germans scorned Americans when the United States did not knock down the Berlin Wall after it went up in 1961, and Chancellor Konrad Adenauer became suspicious that Moscow and Washington would cut deals at Germany's expense. Soon France and Germany seemed to be competing to see which could first establish détente with the Soviet Union. When Willy Brandt became chancellor in 1969, the Federal Republic of Germany displayed unusual independence by making overtures to Moscow. Brandt's Eastern policy *(Ostpolitik)* led in 1970 to a Soviet-German nonaggression treaty, which especially reduced friction over Berlin. Two years later, in an early gesture toward reunification, the two Germanys opened diplomatic channels. Kissinger bristled at this "new form of classic German nationalism," but he nonetheless endorsed Brandt's efforts because most allies did. "We could best hold the Alliance together," he recalled, "by accepting the principle of détente. . . ."

Greatly expanded Western European trade with and investment in the Soviet sphere of influence beginning in the late 1940s also drew back the "iron curtain" in a seemingly irreversible process of economic détente. After the divisive Suez crisis, for example, America's European allies sought more energy independence from the Middle East—and from the United States. The Soviet Union, to Washington's dismay, became an alternative oil and natural gas source. When Europeans set out in the 1980s to build a natural gas pipeline from Western Europe to Siberia, the United States made a futile and ill-advised attempt to scuttle the project. Tempers flared once again within the Atlantic alliance, leading to further discord and a reduced U.S. position in Europe. At the same time supranational structures, like the European Economic Community (organized in 1959) and the Conference on Security and Cooperation in Europe (formed in 1973), demonstrated the growing initiative of Western European governments. U.S. officials continued to say they welcomed European unity, but they sensed that integration was actually supplanting American supremacy.

The diminution of America's power could be measured even in the most conspicuous arena of its hegemony—Latin America. Pan-Americanism and the Organization of American States had long served as instruments of U.S. influence in the region, much to the regret and annoyance of Mexicans, Argentines, and others who resisted North American paternalistic guidance. . . .

Clear signs of hemispheric independence became evident when Venezuela helped found the Organization of Petroleum Exporting Countries (OPEC) [in 1960] and nationalized American-owned oil companies. American-owned multinational corporations faced higher taxes, terrorism, expropriation, and regulations on the hiring of nationals (Argentina, for example, required that at least 85 percent of management and other high-level personnel in foreign-owned firms be Argentine). During the Vietnam War, when the United States appeared "unreliable as a security partner," Brazil began to import weapons from European suppliers; later it developed its own profitable weapons-exporting business. U.S. hegemony in the Western Hemisphere had rested in part on U.S. dominance in arms production and weapons sales. Washington witnessed another setback in the 1970 election of the Marxist President Salvador Allende in Chile and in Peru's defiant 1970s purchases of Soviet MiGs. The 1979 victory of the radical Sandinistas over the longtime U.S. ally Anastasio Somoza in Nicaragua and Argentina's selling of grain to the Soviet Union in 1980 during a U.S.-imposed embargo against the Soviets provided further evidence of diminished U.S. power in the hemisphere. Although the CIA helped depose Allende in 1973, this American success and the U.S. military interventions in the Dominican Republic (1965), Grenada (1983), and Panama (1989) attested not to U.S. strength but to the loosening of its imperial net. Western Hemispheric nations, overall, boldly questioned the "hegemonic presumption" of the United States.

The most serious defiance to the United States came from Cuba's Fidel Castro. After years of civil war against U.S. ally Fulgencio Batista, Castro's rebel army finally forced the dictator from Havana in January 1959. The emergence of the radical Cuban Revolution rocked Washington while at the same time it buoyed other Latin American nationalists to seek alternatives to their U.S.-backed regimes and capitalist models of economic development. The CIA jumped into action once again. The covert agency's clumsy attempts to depose and assassinate Castro faltered, especially in the disastrous Bay of Pigs operation, but these activities, sabotage, and an economic embargo prompted Cuba to appeal for assistance from a Soviet Union more than willing to exacerbate U.S. woes in its sphere. One result was the Cuban missile crisis of 1962, which seemed to threaten nuclear war after the Soviets had recklessly placed medium-range missiles on the Caribbean island to deter an expected U.S. attack. The United States erected a naval blockade around Cuba and went to the brink of war to get the rockets out. Castro survived the crisis, consolidated his power, and promised revolution all over Latin America. Cuba remained a Soviet ally, although Havana frequently followed an independent foreign policy. Cuban-American hostility persisted despite some steps toward improved relations in the 1970s.

As he cultivated détente in the early 1970s, President Nixon identified five power centers in the world: the United States, the Soviet Union, China, Japan, and the Common Market. Under détente, he declared, each center should maintain order among smaller states in its region of responsibility. Because the "five great economic superpowers will determine the economic future," Nixon explained, "and, because economic power will be the key to other kinds of power, [they will determine] the future of the world. . . ." For the United States, détente seemed to offer opportunities to determine the future—to discipline its Latin American sphere under a global system of great-power management and to deter Soviet inroads or assistance to rebel groups like the insurgent Sandinistas in Nicaragua by threatening to withdraw the economic benefits the Soviets sought from détente. Détente beckoned as a means to reestablish U.S. control of its most traditional sphere. In 1984 the President's Commission on Central America warned that if the United States ever revealed symptoms of decline in its own neighborhood, it would experience the "erosion of our power to influence events worldwide that would flow from the perception that we were unable to influence vital events close to home."

If the erosion of American and Soviet power stemmed from the fracturing of their spheres, so, too, was it due to the rise of the Third World. After the Second World War a cavalcade of colonies broke from their imperial rulers. From 1943 to 1989 no fewer than ninety-six countries gained independence and entered the international system as new states. Many liberations came in the 1950s and 1960s— among them Libya (1951), Sudan, Morocco, and Tunisia (1956), and Ghana (1957). In 1960 alone eighteen new African nations became independent; 1962 and 1975 each saw seven more newborn nations. Diplomats in the early 1960s, Undersecretary of State George W. Ball recalled, necessarily had to focus "on problems involving the bits and pieces of disintegrating empires."

At first analysts tagged them "backward" or "underdeveloped nations," then shifted to less disparaging terms, like "developing" or "emerging states." Soon they became known as the "Third World," a general term applied to those parts of the global community belonging neither to the "First World" of the United States and its allies in the capitalist "West" nor to the "Second World" of the Soviet Union and its allies in the Communist "East." The Third World nations were largely nonwhite, nonindustrialized, poor, and located in the southern half of the globe (thus sometimes called the "South"). Many of them became unstable, plagued by civil wars, dictatorial rulers, tribal, ethnic, and class rivalries, drought, poverty, and economies dependent upon the sale of only one commodity. To the alarm of Washington, some of them launched social revolutions and embraced socialist models of development. On the minds of American leaders, too, was the growth of newly industrialized nations in the Third World, like South Korea and Brazil, that challenged the United States in world markets.

When many Third World nations formed a nonaligned movement to challenge the two Cold Warriors and to press for an end to their dangerous competition, the international system fragmented, bipolarism eroded, and the relative power of the United States and the Soviet Union diminished accordingly. After the 1955 Bandung Conference, many Third World nations in Asia, Africa, and the Middle East declared their neutralism in the Cold War. Third World expressions of alienation from the two superpowers came in many other forms, including Pan-Arabism and Muslim fundamentalism, the Group of 77 in the United Nations, and the movement for a law of the sea treaty to ensure that rich seabed minerals, a "common heritage of mankind," did not become a source of profit for commercial mining companies alone.

By sheer force of numbers Third World states became a formidable bloc in world forums. The United States gradually became isolated in the United Nations. In the Security Council, for example, the United States, losing the majority vote its sphere members had long provided, had to cast its first veto in 1970, and by the 1980s it was averaging four vetoes a year. The United States became the largest caster of nay votes in the General Assembly, where it frequently had to contend with setbacks like the 108–9 vote to condemn its invasion of Grenada. In the 1950s General Assembly members voted 70 percent of the time with the United States; in the 1970s the coincidence rate fell to 30 percent, and by the early 1980s to 20 percent. . . .

The United States and the Soviet Union coveted alignment with Third World states, for they could supply strategic minerals, market and investment opportunities, votes in the United Nations, intelligence posts, and military bases. . . . Populous and neutralist India became a hotly contested prize, not only because it represented a testing ground for competing models of development and political principles but also because India bordered the one nation that Moscow and Washington could agree was threatening both—the People's Republic of China. As much as the Cold War behemoths pressed nonaligned Third World countries like India to abandon their neutralism, they could not halt the movement. "We will not be subjected," boomed Egypt's Gamal Abdul Nasser, "either by West or East."

All of this tugging and pulling jolted the international system. Sometimes U.S. officials felt compelled to compromise with Third World nationalism to retain some influence, as in 1978, when President Carter negotiated canal treaties with Panama that provided for both the return of the waterway to Panama and the endorsement of a continued U.S. security role on the isthmus. The United States, however, never became isolated from the Third World and retained hefty instruments of influence. America did not turn into the "pitiful, helpless giant" that Nixon said it might if the United States lost the Vietnam War. Although the Third World's share of gross world product rose, Third World peoples remained desperately poor, wracked by high infant mortality, unemployment, disease, and illiteracy rates. Third World nations never shed their dependency upon outsiders. Still, developing, neutralist nations presented tenacious challenges to great-power management of the international order. The Third World vigorously, if not always successfully, challenged what Senator J. William Fulbright once called America's "arrogance of power." And U.S. economic problems—high interest rates, indebtedness, and trade imbalances—undercut the American "capacity to lead" the Third World because the United States became less able to provide debt relief and urgently needed development capital. International affairs became more fluid, more unpredictable, less secure, and less manageable.

Détente was born in part as a response to this disorderly, pluralistic world. With the United States suffering Third World setbacks in Vietnam, Iran, Nicaragua, and elsewhere, and the Soviet Union stumbling in Egypt and Afghanistan, among other places, Washington and Moscow looked less and less like superpowers. The declining powers in this transforming international system sought to hold their positions by moving from confrontation to cooperation. Détente seemed to promise a restoration of great-power control, a reassertion of great-power tutelage. If détente was embraced as a means to reduce the costs of the Cold War and to meet challenges from sphere members, it also became attractive as a means to deal with the volatile Third World. As President Jimmy Carter once said, Americans had to put their "inordinate fear of Communism" behind them in order to address long-term Third World crises. For the United States, détente with the Soviet Union also offered a "fulcrum or base from which to exert American diplomatic leverage" in the Third World. In 1990, during the Gulf War, when Soviet-American cooperation marshaled a worldwide condemnation of Iraq after it had invaded neighboring Kuwait, Secretary of State James Baker expressed what leaders before him had been saying about the virtues of détente: "When the United States and the Soviet Union lead, others are likely to follow.". . . .

 The United States and the Soviet Union, bedeviled by Cold War–induced economic problems, independent-minded allies, and contentious Third World nations, gradually moved in fits of truculence and accommodation toward détente and the ultimate end of the Cold War. By the late 1960s, remembered Henry Kissinger, America had to operate "in much more complex conditions than we had ever before faced." That time "marked the end of the period of American predominance based on overwhelming nuclear and economic supremacy." Indeed, he continued, "the Soviet nuclear stockpile was inevitably approaching parity. The economic strength of Europe and Japan was bound to lead them to seek larger political influence. The new, developing nations pressed their claims to greater power and participation." If the world further "tilted against us," he feared, America's strong, if no longer preeminent, position in the international balance of power would falter. In this unsettled environment, détente became even more attractive. Détente did not mean that Soviet-American rivalry would cease, but rather that judicious great-power cooperation, located somewhere between hostile obstructionism and friendly coexistence, would reduce world tensions. Moscow and Washington cautiously endorsed détente as a process to stem the erosion of their power. . . .

 U.S. entry into the Persian Gulf War of 1990 and 1991, following Iraq's brutal invasion and annexation of oil-rich Kuwait, exposed a core feature of the immediate post–Cold War international order: the U.S. drive to recoup lost influence, to reestablish credibility, to reaffirm a counterrevolutionary posture, to reassert the great-power status that the prolonged Cold War had eroded. If President Jimmy Carter had sought a fresh start after the Vietnam War and President Ronald Reagan had called for a "national reawakening," President George Bush claimed that the new war in the Middle East was the first post–Cold War "test of our mettle." The president claimed that "recent events have surely proven that there is no substitute for American leadership" in the world. And "let no one doubt our staying power." The *Wall Street Journal* welcomed the outbreak of war because a U.S. victory "lets America, and above all its elite, recover a sense of self-confidence and self-worth." During Operation Desert Storm proud Americans ballyhooed the destructive power of their high-tech air war, the credibility of their military forces, the skill with which an international coalition was created, and the swiftness of victory. "This is the end of the decline," cheered an official of the conservative American Enterprise Institute. . . .

 Although it became fashionable to say that America had won "the sucker and won it big," and it became evident that democratization and capitalism were ascending, the Cold War actually had no winners. Both the United States and the

Soviet Union had spent themselves into weakened conditions. Both had paid tremendous prices for making and waging the Cold War. That is why President Gorbachev launched his restructuring programs and why President Bush, echoing Carter and Reagan, made the case for American "renewal" and "renewed credibility." Each major power, in groping for an end to the Cold War, was seeking structures of stability at home and abroad to stem the decline—and collapse—that other complex societies had suffered in the past.

Hanging Tough Paid Off

JOHN LEWIS GADDIS

The time has come to acknowledge an astonishing development: during his eight years as president, Ronald Reagan has presided over the most dramatic improvement in U.S.-Soviet relations—and the most solid progress in arms control—since the Cold War began. History has often produced unexpected results, but this one surely sets some kind of record.

Reagan was not an enthusiast for arms control before entering the White House: indeed his 1976 and 1980 campaigns appeared to reject that enterprise altogether in favor of a simpler search for national security through military superiority over the Soviet Union. That arms control has not only survived but prospered under his leadership ought to make us take a fresh look, both at the administration he headed and at the arms control process itself as it has traditionally been understood.

That process had taken on several distinctive characteristics by the end of the 1970s:

Pessimism. It is now almost forgotten (perhaps even by themselves) that Richard Nixon and Henry Kissinger had originally portrayed the SALT I [Strategic Arms Limitation Talks] negotiations as a way to reduce the effects of America's military decline, stemming from a Soviet strategic buildup in the mid-1960s, to which the United States, because of the Vietnam War, had at first been too distracted and then too divided to respond. Arms control carried with it the tacit assumption that, in this situation, SALT was, at best, a way of minimizing the damage. Coincident but unrelated events had reinforced, by the end of the 1970s, the association of arms control with visions of U.S. military inferiority. These developments included the energy crisis and ensuing double-digit inflation; the erosion of presidential authority that began with Watergate and continued under Ford and Carter; the collapse of old allies in Iran and Nicaragua; and, most dramatically, the juxtapostition of American ineffectiveness in the Tehran hostage crisis with apparent Soviet purposefulness in invading Afghanistan.

Complexity. The Partial Test Ban Treaty of 1963 took 10 days to negotiate and fills just over two pages in the Arms Control and Disarmament Agency's published version. SALT I took two-and-a-half years to negotiate; the text is 18

From "Hanging Tough Paid Off," by John Lewis Gaddis in *Bulletin of the Atomic Scientists,* 45 (January–February 1989), 11–14. Copyright © 1989 by the Educational Foundation for Nuclear Science, 6042 South Kimbark, Chicago, Il 60637, USA.

pages. The unratified SALT II Treaty required almost seven years to negotiate; the resulting text and accompanying statements fill 31 pages of text. With arms control agreements becoming so complex that the experts themselves—to say nothing of average citizens—were finding them difficult to understand, it was reasonable to begin to wonder by the end of the 1970s how one would actually know whether they coincided with the national interest, or how to be sure that the Soviets understood them in precisely the same way.

Insularity. As the SALT process became more complex it appeared to take on a life of its own, insulated from outside events. Despite increasingly detailed provisions for verification, arms control still depended to a considerable extent upon trusting the Soviets. But that was becoming harder to do. After 1975 Moscow openly violated the Helsinki Agreement's human rights provisions; indirect military intervention in Angola, Somalia, and Ethiopia suggested at a minimum an unwillingness to cooperate with the West in managing regional conflicts; the Kremlin appeared determined to push the limits of SALT I as far as possible as it continued its buildup of strategic weapons. Yet the SALT II negotiations proceeded, apparently unaffected by these less than reassuring signs.

Illogic. The SALT process seemed to be based on two propositions generally accepted within the arms control community, but that laymen found less and less plausible when tested against the simpler standards of common sense. One was implied in the very term "arms control"; why not "arms reduction"? And why did "strategic arms limitation" agreements seem to do so little actual "limiting"? The other had to do with the assertion that safety could come only through vulnerability, and that defense, therefore, at least in the nuclear realm, was bad. However rational the experts may have found these precepts, they did not appear rational to the average citizen, and as the nuclear standoff showed signs of stretching endlessly into the future, people became uncomfortable with them.

Whether these criticisms of arms control were fair is not the point. What is important is the skill with which Ronald Reagan focused on them during his campaigns for the presidency. And even more important was the way he incorporated them, after January 1981, into a new approach to arms control that would in time, and against conventional wisdom, produce impressive results. The principal means by which he accomplished this were as follows:

Rebuilding self-confidence. There are rare moments in history when public moods reverse themselves almost overnight. One occurred in March 1933, when Franklin Roosevelt replaced Herbert Hoover in the White House; another took place in Great Britain in May 1940, when Winston Churchill became prime minister; still another occurred in Western Europe in June 1947, when Secretary of State George C. Marshall announced the economic recovery plan that came to bear his name. The mood reversal that followed Reagan's January 1981 inauguration was by no means as dramatic as these, but it occurred: long before the new administration had completed its military buildup, before Paul Volcker and the Federal Reserve Board had checked inflation, and before OPEC's disarray had turned the energy crisis into an oil glut, the *perception* had become widespread that events were beginning to break Washington's way. And that made a big difference.

It has since become commonplace to criticize Reagan for having placed greater emphasis on imagery than on substance during his years as president. But leadership begins with the creation of self-confidence, and that—as Roosevelt, Churchill, and Marshall all knew—is a psychological process depending less upon the rational calculation of tangible gains than upon the ability to convince people that however bad things may be at the moment, time is on their side. Reagan managed during his first months in office to project—and therefore to instill—a degree of self-confidence that went well beyond anything his predecessor had achieved. Without that shift from pessimism to optimism, much of what followed could hardly have taken place.

Spooking the Soviets. The second element in the Reagan strategy proceeded logically from the first—to persuade the Kremlin that time was working against it. Nor was it so difficult to do, because events were beginning to demonstrate precisely this: Afghanistan was revealing the costs of what [the historian] Paul Kennedy has called "strategic overstretch"; "Solidarity" had brought Poland to the edge of open rebellion; economic stagnation was becoming a serious problem inside the Soviet Union; and an increasingly sclerotic Kremlin leadership was responding to these difficulties with near catatonic immobility. In one sense, Reagan was lucky to have come into office at a trough in American fortunes and a peak in those of the Soviets. Things could not get much worse, and were likely to get better. But more than luck is involved in the ability to recognize that such trends are under way, and to capitalize upon them. Reagan's leadership proved decidedly superior to Carter's in that respect.

Several subsequent Reagan administration actions sought to reinforce the idea that time no longer favored Moscow. The U.S. military buildup was launched with the intention of so straining an already inefficient economy that the Soviet leadership would have little choice but to make substantial concessions on arms control. Similar intentions lay behind the Strategic Defense Initiative. The vision of a shift from deterrence to a defense based on American technological superiority would, it was thought, shock the Soviets into contemplating for the first time significant reductions in their own long-range strategic forces.

At the same time, the administration was skillfully defusing both the U.S. nuclear freeze movement and opposition to the deployment of Pershing II and cruise missiles in Western Europe by calling for actual *reductions* in nuclear weapons, and by holding out, through SDI, the prospect of ultimately making them obsolete altogether. To the extent that the Soviets had counted on such groups to constrain administration freedom of action—and they almost certainly had—the effect again was to demonstrate that time was no longer on Moscow's side.

Negotiation from strength. A third element in the Reagan strategy was the principle that negotiations should take place only from a position of strength. The idea dates from the Truman administration's military buildup following the outbreak of the Korean War. Over the years it had come to be understood as a way of evading negotiations altogether, since "strength" was so relative a concept that one might never actually attain it and since adversaries would presumably never negotiate from "weakness." There was reason to believe, at the outset of the Reagan years, that this devious approach was alive and well. Presidential subordinates gleefully put forward "killer" proposals for arms control talks, while the Pentagon swallowed huge military appropriations without any indication that "strength" was about to be achieved.

An important characteristic of Reagan's leadership, however, was that he was *not* devious; when he spoke of the possibility that a military buildup might actually lead to reductions in strategic weapons, he appears to have meant precisely what he said. He also understood, perhaps instinctively, a point George Kennan had been arguing: that the arms control process had become too complex while producing too little, and that the only way to rebuild a domestic consensus in support of it was to hold out clear, simple, and sweeping objectives, such as a 50 percent cut in strategic weapons on both sides.

With the 1984 elections coming up and with indications that Congress would resist further defense budget increases, it could be argued that the administration had little choice but to appear to seek negotiations with the Soviets. Certainly some Reagan advisers felt that negotiations so protracted as to produce no results were almost as desirable as having no negotiations at all. But what many of Reagan's subordinates did not understand—and what those who seek to explain what subsequently happened will have to comprehend—is that while the president may have shared their conservatism, he did not share their cynicism. For him the only question was with whom to negotiate.

Responding to Gorbachev. It is difficult to see that much could have been accomplished in this respect until a functional Soviet leadership had been established. That happened in March 1985, and a fourth element in the Reagan strategy soon emerged, which was to acknowledge Mikhail Gorbachev as a new kind of Soviet leader whose chief priority was internal reform, and with whom one could, in the realm of external affairs, find common interests.

The White House was therefore ready to respond when Gorbachev began modifying long-standing Soviet positions on arms control in a way quite consistent with what the Reagan strategy had anticipated. Neither critics on the left, who had favored negotiations for their own sake, nor those on the right, who had sought negotiations from strength, were in any position to object. The long-stalemated arms control process suddenly accelerated, producing by the final year of the Reagan administration not only an Intermediate-range Nuclear Forces (INF) Treaty that contained unprecedented Soviet concessions on asymmetrical reductions and on-site verification, but substantial progress as well toward agreement on deep cuts in long-range strategic systems, and at least the possibility of a grand compromise that would delay if not defer altogether the deployment of SDI.

There were, to be sure, deficiencies in the Reagan strategy. Characteristically, the president found it easier to think of SDI as he had advertised it—as a first step toward abolishing nuclear weapons altogether—than as the successful bargaining chip it turned out to be. This created an opportunity for Gorbachev to endorse nuclear abolition by the year 2000 and thus to align himself with the president against Reagan's own skeptical advisers. There were few signs of progress toward conventional arms limitation, or toward restricting nuclear testing. Little thought had been given to how the United States might respond if the relaxation

of controls that perestroika required were to produce actual rebellions among Soviet nationality groups, or within Eastern Europe. And almost no thought appeared to have been given to the relationship between national security and
national solvency—an issue to which Gorbachev himself seemed keenly attuned.

Still, the [doomsday] clock on the front cover of the *Bulletin* [*of the Atomic
Scientists*] was set back, a year ago, for the first time since 1972. That symbolic act
ought to make us think critically—and without preconceptions—about how we got
to that point. It was not by means of arms control as traditionally practiced: the old
SALT process would never have survived the Reagan administration's insistence
on asymmetrical reductions instead of symmetrical limitations, on intrusive rather
than remote verification, and on the virtues of strategic defense as opposed to mutual vulnerability. Strength this time did lead to negotiations, bargaining chips did
produce bargains, and "hanging tough" did eventually pay off.

The Soviets deserve much of the credit for what happened. They made most of
the concessions, a pattern not likely to be repeated often in the future. It was the
Reagan administration, however, that assessed correctly the potential for Soviet
concessions. And because of the way it came about, this new approach to arms
control has won firmer domestic support within the United States than the SALT
process ever did; witness the caution both sides showed in not making it an issue
during the otherwise hotly contested 1988 presidential election. How valid the approach will be in years to come remains to be seen, but as Reagan leaves office it
would be uncharitable—and historically irresponsible—to begrudge the strategic
vision of an administration once thought by many of us to have had none at all.

Generational Change, Not U.S. Bullying,
Explains the Gorbachev Revolution

MICHAEL MccGWIRE

Mikhail Gorbachev came to power in the wake of Ronald Reagan's first administration. Because of this coincidence there is a tendency to impute a causal relationship between Reagan's confrontational policies and the sharp rise in U.S. defense
budgets, on the one hand, and the changes in Soviet defense and foreign policy
since 1987, on the other. The facts do not support such a relationship. What they do
show is a link between the policies of the first Reagan administration and the Soviet's defense and foreign policy reevaluation in 1983–84. But the findings of that
reappraisal of policy set the Soviet Union on a course that would have been
extremely detrimental to U.S. interests, if Gorbachev had not changed policies
in 1987.

The assumption that it was the confrontational policies of the Reagan administration that led to the Gorbachev revolution is not only wrong, it is dangerous.
It obscures the fact that Soviet perception of the likelihood of war increased
sharply in 1981–84. In itself that was an undesirable state of affairs, but for a variety of reasons, this perception reached a dangerous peak in November 1983, when

From *Perestroika and Soviet National Security* by Michael MccGwire, pp. 381–384, 385–387, 393. The
Brookings Institution, 1991, reprinted by permission of the publisher.

the Soviets evidently misinterpreted a NATO command-post exercise as indicating that the West was actually preparing for nuclear war.

Meanwhile, the assumption that a confrontational stance is productive panders to a bullying strain in U.S. foreign policy that works against the nation's long-term interests. The implication is that if toughness worked when dealing with the Soviet Union during the first Reagan administration, then it is a recipe for action in the future. If it worked with the Soviets, then it will work with other major powers.

The decision to reorient Soviet policy stemmed from a combination of three factors: the bankruptcy of established policies; autonomous new thinking; and concern about the danger of war. To a large extent the failure of established policies, domestic and foreign, can be attributed to deficiencies in the Soviet system and not to Western initiatives. A central problem was the economy's inability to move from extensive to intensive development, which resulted in increasing stagnation. This, combined with the ossification of the party apparatus, corruption in high places, and a general sense of drift, led to growing sociopolitical anomie and a breakdown of work discipline. To be sure, Western containment was a background condition and the arms race imposed a heavy burden, but Soviet economic problems were fundamentally structural. They could not have been solved by rearranging the allocation of resources between defense and the civil economy.

It so happened that during Ronald Reagan's presidency two obstacles to change in the Soviet Union were removed. One was the generation of Soviet citizens who had experienced the fateful events of 1920–60. Its removal by death and disability in 1982–85 resulted in a generational change of leadership. The other obstacle stemmed from the long-standing and perfectly reasonable political-military assumption that world war was inherently possible; the obstacle was the military requirement to cover the contingency. The audacious decision in January 1987 that the Soviet military should develop plans based on the assumption that world war would be prevented by political means signaled the demolition of that obstacle.

That obstacle might have been demolished earlier if the Soviets had not concluded that the danger of world war had increased sharply with the advent of the Reagan administration. The United States showed an explicit disdain for the nuclear arms control process and simultaneously increased its weapons procurement, culminating in the strategic defense initiative announced in March 1983. Furthermore, the first Reagan administration adopted a highly ideological and sharply confrontational policy with its crusade against communism and casual talk of the inevitability of war with the Soviet Union.

It was these U.S. developments that justified the 1983–84 reappraisal of Soviet defense and foreign policy, yielding a series of decisions that were unfavorable to Western interests. In other words, the policies of the first Reagan administration did provoke a Soviet reaction, but it was the opposite of what American advocates of a confrontational policy claim it to be. It did prompt a shift in Soviet policy, but the shift was toward greater intransigence, not in the favorable direction that emerged three years later under Gorbachev. . . .

There was a sharp increase in the allocation of resources to defense. Cuts in weapons production in the 1981–85 five-year plan were reversed, and the plan for 1986–90 provided for a rise of about 40 percent in military expenditure, even though national income was projected to increase by only 22 percent. Production of tanks, which had been cut back to 2,000 in 1981 from the annual rate of about 3,000 in 1976–80, was brought back to the higher rate by 1983. Similarly, the annual production of self-propelled field artillery had been increased by 10 percent by the end of the 1981–85 five-year plan. A further increase in tank production was called for in the 1986–90 five-year plan. Meanwhile, the decision to go ahead with the deferred flight-testing of the fifth-generation intermediate-range and intercontinental ballistic missiles (IRBMs and ICBMs) appears to have been taken in late 1982 or early 1983. Similarly, anti-surface warship programs that had been curtailed following the 1976–77 decisions were reinstated at this period. . . .

While significant in themselves, these increases represented only the most visible tip of defense investment. In 1984 the U.S. Central Intelligence Agency saw these and other Soviet responses as being driven by U.S. developments—"a building defense budget, new initiatives in continental defense, improvements in force readiness and a potentially massive space defense program." The full scope of the Soviet response to Reagan's policies cannot be known because many of the decisions taken in the first half of the 1980s would have been reversed following the reorientation of defense policy in 1987. One can, however, be certain that the response was substantial. . . .

The Soviet reaction to the policies of the first Reagan administration could have been foreseen, for it was the kind of reaction to be expected from any proud and powerful nation. Rather than knuckle under, the Soviets responded in kind. They did not abandon the idea of arms control, but they did go ahead with the flight-testing and development of fifth-generation ICBMs and they subsequently reinstated their plan for deployment of the SS-20 IRBM. In the third world they became more assertive in providing military support to protégés and clients, and they probably embarked on developing the capability for naval interposition. Meanwhile they continued to plan for the possibility of world war and added the contingency of major conflict with the United States in the region north of the Persian Gulf.

None of these developments were in the interest of the United States, the West, or the world at large. Yet they were decided by a leadership headed by Yuri Andropov [General Secretary of the Soviet Communist Party, 1983–1984], mentor of the group of enlightened foreign policy specialists who would come to prominence under Gorbachev. If this damaging response to Reagan's policies emerged when Andropov was general secretary, it is not hard to visualize what the Soviet reaction might be to similar policies in less favorable circumstances.

Rather than prompting the conciliatory style of Soviet foreign policy that emerged in 1987, the crusading rhetoric and confrontational policies of the first Reagan administration made it impossible for that favorable trend to emerge earlier and could easily have prevented it from emerging at all.

In 1981–82 the Soviet succession was not preordained and there was no certainty that Leonid Brezhnev would be followed by Andropov, or that the latter would survive just long enough to move his followers into key positions. Andropov's nonideological approach to foreign policy was not widely supported in the Politburo, and another general secretary would have brought in people with very different views. But even with Andropov as general secretary it was never certain that Gorbachev would succeed Konstantin Chernenko. And it does seem as if Gorbachev was essential to the emergence at this time of democracy in the Soviet Union and of the new political thinking about international relations.

Reagan is said to have been a lucky president, and never more so than in dealing with the Soviet Union. Gorbachev, who was chosen as general secretary because of his competence as a party apparatchik and economic manager, turned out to be a radical in the field of defense and foreign policy. His ideas about national security, dismissed as propaganda or utopian by the Western political-military establishment, allowed him to break the action-reaction cycle and to spurn the U.S. challenge to a new round in the arms race.

But this was despite the assertive policies of the Reagan administration, not because of them. Gorbachev had made it clear that before he could embark on major arms control initiatives, it was essential for him to meet Reagan, to find out whether the president really believed in his administration's rhetoric and bellicose posturing and whether there was any common ground between the two sides. At the November 1985 summit Gorbachev had found a narrow strip of ground that the two leaders posted with their statement that nuclear war could not be won and must never be fought.

In this particular respect, personal credit must go to Reagan. His sincere revulsion against nuclear weapons prompted him to engage in serious negotiations about limiting them, first at Reykjavík in 1986 and subsequently over the Treaty on Intermediate-Range Nuclear Forces (INF) in 1987. He signed the latter despite public objections by the supreme allied commander Europe (a U.S. general), objections that confirmed the claim by Alexander Haig that the "zero option" proposed in 1981 had been designed to be nonnegotiable.

In the circumstances of 1981–83 the zero option was indeed nonnegotiable, despite the Soviet military being in favor of a nonnuclear European theater. But in 1987, Soviet assumptions about world war had changed and so had the Soviet military requirement for INF. A successful arms control agreement and the elimination of a complete category of nuclear weapons were now the priority objectives. It was these changes that enabled agreement on the INF Treaty, with its asymmetrical numbers, and not the intransigence of the first Reagan administration.

In fact, the effects of American intransigence appear to have been quite different from what was imagined or intended. Members of the administration and their right-wing supporters evoked classic Marxist-Leninist images of capitalism in such caricature that in the new reformist atmosphere of the Soviet Union they could be discounted. Their very extremism reinforced the argument that they were not representative of the United States as a whole. This probably helped engender, and certainly lent plausibility to, the inspired idea of outflanking the most intensely committed anti-Soviet zealots in the United States by denying them their lifeblood—the Soviet military threat.

The claim that the democratization of Eastern Europe came about because the West "stood firm" is extraordinarily presumptuous. It is only true in the sense that if the West had succumbed to communism, the change might not have come about. In any other sense, the evidence belies the assertion.

In terms of "standing firm," NATO policy toward the Soviet Union and Eastern Europe did not alter appreciably after the mid-1950s. Before then, the United States talked of "roll back," a dangerous slogan that led to false expectations, notably in Hungary. Thereafter, "standing firm" had had no appreciable effect on Soviet decisions to use force or the threat of force to suppress unrest in Eastern Europe—for example, in 1956 in Hungary, 1968 in Czechoslovakia, or 1981–82 in Poland. Why, therefore, should it suddenly take effect in 1989?

By 1989 there had been a sea change in the Soviet view of Eastern Europe's role in national security. Democratization in Moscow and the policy of nonintervention abroad demanded a new relationship with the countries in the region. And the Soviets judged that the nations of Western Europe would refrain from enlisting the Eastern Europeans in an anti-Soviet bloc. That judgment would have been confirmed in mid-1989 by the evidence that the Bush administration had finally acknowledged the fundamental nature of the rethinking in Moscow and was prepared to support rather than exploit it. It would have been difficult to make such a judgment during the first Reagan administration.

It was these changes that enabled the democratization of Eastern Europe. The democratization was effected by the people in each country. Those who had "stood firm" were the dissidents who had managed to endure and survive despite attempts to eradicate them. In 1989 the West merely watched in amazement, as powerless to influence events (except in a negative way) as it had been in 1956, 1968, and in 1981–82.

Engagement and Anti-Nuclearism, Not Containment, Brought an End to the Cold War

DANIEL DEUDNEY AND G. JOHN IKENBERRY

In thinking about the Cold War's conclusion, it is vital to distinguish between the domestic origins of the crisis in Soviet communism and the external forces that influenced its timing and intensity, as well as the direction of the Soviet response. Undoubtedly, the ultimate cause of the Cold War's outcome lies in the failure of the Soviet system itself. At most, outside forces hastened and intensified the crisis. However, it was not inevitable that the Soviet Union would respond to this crisis as it did in the late 1980s—with domestic liberalization and foreign policy accommodation. After all, many Western experts expected that the USSR would respond to such a crisis with renewed repression at home and aggression abroad, as it had in the past.

At that fluid historic juncture, the complex matrix of pressures, opportunities, and attractions from the outside world influenced the direction of Soviet change, particularly in its foreign policy. The Soviets' field of vision was dominated by the West, the United States, and recent American foreign policy. Having spent more than 45 years attempting to influence the Soviet Union, Americans are now attempting to gauge the weight of their country's impact and, thus, the track record of U.S. policies.

In assessing the rest of the world's impact on Soviet change, a remarkably simplistic and self-serving conventional wisdom has emerged in the United States.

This new conventional wisdom, the "Reagan victory school," holds that President Ronald Reagan's military and ideological assertiveness during the 1980s played the lead role in the collapse of Soviet communism and the "taming" of its foreign policy. In that view the Reagan administration's ideological counter-offensive and military buildup delivered the knock-out punch to a system that was internally bankrupt and on the ropes. The Reagan Right's perspective is an ideologically pointed version of the more broadly held conventional wisdom on the end of the Cold War that emphasizes the success of the "peace-through-strength" strategy manifest in four decades of Western containment. After decades of waging a costly "twilight struggle," the West now celebrates the triumph of its military and ideological resolve.

The Reagan victory school and the broader peace-through-strength perspectives are, however, misleading and incomplete—both in their interpretation of events in the 1980s and in their understanding of deeper forces that led to the end of the Cold War. It is important to reconsider the emerging conventional wisdom before it truly becomes an article of faith on Cold War history and comes to distort the thinking of policymakers in America and elsewhere. . . .

The Cold War's end was a baby that arrived unexpectedly, but a long line of those claiming paternity has quickly formed. A parade of former Reagan administration officials and advocates has forthrightly asserted that Reagan's hard-line policies were the decisive trigger for reorienting Soviet foreign policy and for the demise of communism. As former Pentagon officials like Caspar Weinberger and Richard Perle, columnist George Will, neoconservative thinker Irving Kristol, and other proponents of the Reagan victory school have argued, a combination of military and ideological pressures gave the Soviets little choice but to abandon expansionism abroad and repression at home. In that view, the Reagan military buildup foreclosed Soviet military options while pushing the Soviet economy to the breaking point. Reagan partisans stress that his dramatic "Star Wars" initiative put the Soviets on notice that the next phase of the arms race would be waged in areas where the West held the decisive technological edge.

Reagan and his administration's military initiatives, however, played a far different and more complicated role in inducing Soviet change than the Reagan victory school asserts. For every "hardening" there was a "softening": Reagan's rhetoric of the "Evil Empire" was matched by his vigorous anti-nuclearism; the military buildup in the West matched by the resurgence of a large popular peace movement; and the Reagan Doctrine's toughening of containment was matched by major deviations from containment in East-West economic relations. Moreover, over the longer term, the strength marshaled in containment was matched by mutual weakness in the face of nuclear weapons, and efforts to engage the USSR were as important as efforts to contain it.

Perhaps the greatest anomaly of the Reagan victory school is the "Great Communicator" himself. The Reagan Right ignores that his anti-nuclearism was as strong as his anticommunism. Reagan's personal convictions on nuclear weapons were profoundly at odds with the beliefs of most in his administration. Staffed by officials who considered nuclear weapons a useful instrument of statecraft and who were openly disdainful of the moral critique of nuclear weapons articulated by the arms control community and the peace movement, the administration pursued the hardest line on nuclear policy and the Soviet Union in the postwar era. Then vice president George Bush's observation that nuclear weapons would be fired as a warning shot and Deputy Under Secretary of Defense T. K. Jones's widely quoted view that nuclear war was survivable captured the reigning ethos within the Reagan administration.

In contrast, there is abundant evidence that Reagan himself felt a deep antipathy for nuclear weapons and viewed their abolition to be a realistic and desirable goal. Reagan's call in his famous March 1983 "Star Wars" speech for a program to make nuclear weapons impotent and obsolete was viewed as cynical by many, but actually it expressed Reagan's heartfelt views, views that he came to act upon. As *Washington Post* reporter Lou Cannon's 1991 biography points out, Reagan was deeply disturbed by nuclear deterrence and attracted to abolitionist solutions. "I know I speak for people everywhere when I say our dream is to see the day when nuclear weapons will be banished from the face of the earth," Reagan said in November 1983. . . .

Contrary to the conventional wisdom, the defense buildup did not produce Soviet capitulation. The initial Soviet response to the Reagan administration's buildup and belligerent rhetoric was to accelerate production of offensive weapons, both strategic and conventional. That impasse was broken not by Soviet capitulation but by an extraordinary convergence by Reagan and Mikhail Gorbachev on a vision of mutual nuclear vulnerability and disarmament. On the Soviet side, the dominance of the hardline response to the newly assertive America was thrown into question in early 1985 when Gorbachev became general secretary of the Communist party after the death of Konstantin Chernenko. Without a background in foreign affairs, Gorbachev was eager to assess American intentions directly and put his stamp on Soviet security policy. Reagan's strong antinuclear views expressed at the November 1985 Geneva summit were decisive in convincing Gorbachev that it was possible to work with the West in halting the nuclear arms race. The arms control diplomacy of the later Reagan years was successful because, as *Washington Post* journalist Don Oberdorfer has detailed in *The Turn: From the Cold War to a New Era* (1991), Secretary of State George Shultz picked up on Reagan's strong convictions and deftly side-stepped hardline opposition to agreements. In fact, Shultz's success at linking presidential unease about nuclear weapons to Soviet overtures in the face of right-wing opposition provides a sharp contrast with John Foster Dulles's refusal to act on President Dwight Eisenhower's nuclear doubts and the opportunities presented by Nikita Khrushchev's détente overtures.

Reagan's commitment to anti-nuclearism and its potential for transforming the U.S.-Soviet confrontation was more graphically demonstrated at the October 1986 Reykjavík summit when Reagan and Gorbachev came close to agreeing on a comprehensive program of global denuclearization that was far bolder than any seriously entertained by American strategists since the Baruch Plan of 1946. The sharp contrast between Reagan's and Gorbachev's shared skepticism toward nuclear weapons on the one hand, and the Washington security establishment's consensus on the other, was showcased in former secretary of defense James Schlesinger's scathing accusation that Reagan was engaged in "casual utopianism." But Reagan's anomalous anti-nuclearism provided the crucial signal to

Gorbachev that bold initiatives would be reciprocated rather than exploited. Reagan's anti-nuclearism was more important than his administration's military buildup in catalyzing the end of the Cold War.

Neither anti-nuclearism nor its embrace by Reagan have received the credit they deserve for producing the Soviet-U.S. reconciliation. Reagan's accomplishment in this regard has been met with silence from all sides. Conservatives, not sharing Reagan's anti-nuclearism, have emphasized the role of traditional military strength. The popular peace movement, while holding deeply antinuclear views, was viscerally suspicious of Reagan. The establishment arms control community also found Reagan and his motives suspect, and his attack on deterrence conflicted with their desire to stabilize deterrence and establish their credentials as sober participants in security policy making. Reagan's radical anti-nuclearism should sustain his reputation as the ultimate Washington outsider.

The central role of Reagan's and Gorbachev's anti-nuclearism throws new light on the 1987 Treaty on Intermediate-range Nuclear Forces, the first genuine disarmament treaty of the nuclear era. The conventional wisdom emphasizes that this agreement was the fruit of a hard-line negotiating posture and the U.S. military buildup. Yet the superpowers' settlement on the "zero option" was not a vindication of the hard-line strategy. The zero option was originally fashioned by hardliners for propaganda purposes, and many backed off as its implementation became likely. The impasse the hard line created was transcended by the surprising Reagan-Gorbachev convergence against nuclear arms.

The Reagan victory school also overstates the overall impact of American and Western policy on the Soviet Union during the 1980s. The Reagan administration's posture was both evolving and inconsistent. Though loudly proclaiming its intentions to go beyond the previous containment policies that were deemed too soft, the reality of Reagan's policies fell short. As Sovietologists Gail Lapidus and Alexander Dallin observed in a 1989 *Bulletin of the Atomic Scientists* article, the policies were "marked to the end by numerous zigzags and reversals, bureaucratic conflicts, and incoherence." Although rollback had long been a cherished goal of the Republican party's right wing, Reagan was unwilling and unable to implement it.

The hard-line tendencies of the Reagan administration were offset in two ways. First, and most important, Reagan's tough talk fueled a large peace movement in the United States and Western Europe in the 1980s, a movement that put significant political pressure upon Western governments to pursue far-reaching arms control proposals. That mobilization of Western opinion created a political climate in which the rhetoric and posture of the early Reagan administration was a significant political liability. By the 1984 U.S. presidential election, the administration had embraced arms control goals that it had previously ridiculed. Reagan's own anti-nuclearism matched that rising public concern, and Reagan emerged as the spokesman for comprehensive denuclearization. Paradoxically, Reagan administration policies substantially triggered the popular revolt against the nuclear hardline, and then Reagan came to pursue the popular agenda more successfully than any other postwar president.

Second, the Reagan administration's hardline policies were also undercut by powerful Western interests that favored East-West economic ties. In the early months of Reagan's administration, the grain embargo imposed by President Jimmy Carter after the 1979 Soviet invasion of Afghanistan was lifted in order to keep the Republican party's promises to Midwestern farmers. Likewise, in 1981 the Reagan administration did little to challenge Soviet control of Eastern Europe after Moscow pressured Warsaw to suppress the independent Polish trade union Solidarity, in part because Poland might have defaulted on multibillion dollar loans made by Western banks. Also, despite strenuous opposition by the Reagan administration, the NATO allies pushed ahead with a natural gas pipeline linking the Soviet Union with Western Europe. That a project creating substantial economic interdependence could proceed during the worst period of Soviet-U.S. relations in the 1980s demonstrates the failure of the Reagan administration to present an unambiguous hard line toward the Soviet Union. More generally, NATO allies and the vocal European peace movement moderated and buffered hard-line American tendencies.

In sum, the views of the Reagan victory school are flawed because they neglect powerful crosscurrents in the West during the 1980s. The conventional wisdom simplifies a complex story and ignores those aspects of Reagan administration policy inconsistent with the hard-line rationale. Moreover, the Western "face" toward the Soviet Union did not consist exclusively of Reagan administration policies, but encompassed countervailing tendencies from the Western public, other governments, and economic interest groups.

Whether Reagan is seen as the consummate hardliner or the prophet of antinuclearism, one should not exaggerate the influence of his administration, or of other short-term forces. Within the Washington beltway, debates about postwar military and foreign policy would suggest that Western strategy fluctuated wildly, but in fact the basic thrust of Western policy toward the USSR remained remarkably consistent. Arguments from the New Right notwithstanding, Reagan's containment strategy was not that different from those of his predecessors. Indeed, the broader peace-through-strength perspective sees the Cold War's finale as the product of a long-term policy, applied over the decades.

In any case, although containment certainly played an important role in blocking Soviet expansionism, it cannot explain either the end of the Cold War or the direction of Soviet policy responses. The West's relationship with the Soviet Union was not limited to containment, but included important elements of mutual vulnerability and engagement. The Cold War's end was not simply a result of Western strength but of mutual weakness and intentional engagement as well.

Most dramatically, the mutual vulnerability created by nuclear weapons overshadowed containment. Nuclear weapons forced the United States and the Soviet Union to eschew war and the serious threat of war as tools of diplomacy and created imperatives for the cooperative regulation of nuclear capability. Both countries tried to fashion nuclear explosives into useful instruments of policy, but they came to the realization—as the joint Soviet-American statement issued from the 1985 Geneva summit put it—that "nuclear war cannot be won and must never be fought." Both countries slowly but surely came to view nuclear weapons as a common threat that must be regulated jointly. Not just containment, but also the overwhelming and common nuclear threat brought the Soviets to the negotiating table. In the shadow of nuclear destruction, common purpose defused traditional antagonisms.

A second error of the peace-through-strength perspective is the failure to recognize that the West offered an increasingly benign face to the communist world. Traditionally, the Soviets' Marxist-Leninist doctrine held that the capitalist West was inevitably hostile and aggressive, an expectation reinforced by the aggression of capitalist, fascist Germany. Since World War II, the Soviets' principal adversaries had been democratic capitalist states. Slowly but surely, Soviet doctrine acknowledged that the West's behavior did not follow Leninist expectations, but was instead increasingly pacific and cooperative. The Soviet willingness to abandon the Brezhnev Doctrine in the late 1980s in favor of the "Sinatra Doctrine"—under which any East European country could sing, "I did it my way"—suggests a radical transformation in the prevailing Soviet perception of threat from the West. In 1990, the Soviet acceptance of the de facto absorption of communist East Germany into West Germany involved the same calculation with even higher stakes. In accepting the German reunification, despite that country's past aggression, Gorbachev acted on the assumption that the Western system was fundamentally pacific. As Russian foreign minister Andrei Kozyrev noted subsequently, that Western countries are pluralistic democracies "practically rules out the pursuance of an aggressive foreign policy." Thus the Cold War ended despite the assertiveness of Western hardliners, rather than because of it.

The second front of the Cold War, according to the Reagan victory school, was ideological. Reagan spearheaded a Western ideological offensive that dealt the USSR a death blow. For the Right, driving home the image of the Evil Empire was a decisive stroke rather than a rhetorical flourish. Ideological warfare was such a key front in the Cold War because the Soviet Union was, at its core, an ideological creation. According to the Reagan Right, the supreme vulnerability of the Soviet Union to ideological assault was greatly underappreciated by Western leaders and publics. In that view, the Cold War was won by the West's uncompromising assertion of the superiority of its values and its complete denial of the moral legitimacy of the Soviet system during the 1980s. Western military strength could prevent defeat, but only ideological breakthrough could bring victory.

Underlying that interpretation is a deeply ideological philosophy of politics and history. The Reagan Right tended to view politics as a war of ideas, an orientation that generated a particularly polemical type of politics. As writer Sidney Blumenthal has pointed out, many of the leading figures in the neoconservative movement since the 1960s came to conservatism after having begun their political careers as Marxists or socialists. That perspective sees the Soviet Union as primarily an ideological artifact, and therefore sees struggle with it in particularly ideological terms. The neoconservatives believe, like Lenin, that "ideas are more fatal than guns."

Convinced that Bolshevism was quintessentially an ideological phenomenon, activists of the New Right were contemptuous of Western efforts to accommodate Soviet needs, moderate Soviet aims, and integrate the USSR into the international system as a "normal" great power. In their view, the *realpolitik* strategy urged by George Kennan, Walter Lippmann, and Hans Morgenthau was based on a misunderstanding of the Soviet Union. It provided an incomplete road map for waging the Cold War, and guaranteed that it would never be won. A particular villain for the New Right was Secretary of State Henry Kissinger, whose program of détente implied, in their view, a "moral equivalence" between the West and the Soviet Union that amounted to unilateral ideological disarmament. Even more benighted were liberal attempts to engage and co-opt the Soviet Union in hopes that the two systems could ultimately reconcile. The New Right's view of politics was strikingly globalist in its assumption that the world had shrunk too much for two such different systems to survive, and that the contest was too tightly engaged for containment or Iron Curtains to work. As James Burnham, the ex-communist prophet of New Right anticommunism, insisted in the early postwar years, the smallness of our "one world" demanded a strategy of "rollback" for American survival.

The end of the Cold War indeed marked an ideological triumph for the West, but not of the sort fancied by the Reagan victory school. Ideology played a far different and more complicated role in inducing Soviet change than the Reagan school allows. As with the military sphere, the Reagan school presents an incomplete picture of Western ideological influence, ignoring the emergence of ideological common ground in stimulating Soviet change.

The ideological legitimacy of the Soviet system collapsed in the eyes of its own citizens not because of an assault by Western ex-leftists, but because of the appeal of Western affluence and permissiveness. The puritanical austerity of Bolshevism's "New Soviet Man" held far less appeal than the "bourgeois decadence" of the West. For the peoples of the USSR and Eastern Europe, it was not so much abstract liberal principles but rather the Western way of life—the material and cultural manifestations of the West's freedoms—that subverted the Soviet vision. Western popular culture—exemplified in rock and roll, television, film, and blue jeans—seduced the communist world far more effectively than ideological sermons by anticommunist activists. As journalist William Echikson noted in his 1990 book *Lighting the Night: Revolution in Eastern Europe,* "instead of listening to the liturgy of Marx and Lenin, generations of would-be socialists tuned into the Rolling Stones and the Beatles."

If Western popular culture and permissiveness helped subvert communist legitimacy, it is a development of profound irony. Domestically, the New Right battled precisely those cultural forms that had such global appeal. V. I. Lenin's most potent ideological foils were John Lennon and Paul McCartney, not Adam Smith and Thomas Jefferson. The Right fought a two-front war against communism abroad and hedonism and consumerism at home. Had it not lost the latter struggle, the West may not have won the former. . . .

The Reagan victory school argues that the renewed emphasis on free-market principles championed by Reagan and then British prime minister Margaret Thatcher led to a global move toward market deregulation and privatization that the Soviets desired to follow. By rekindling the beacon of laissez-faire capitalism, Reagan illuminated the path of economic reform, thus vanquishing communism.

That view is misleading in two respects. First, it was West European social democracy rather than America's more free-wheeling capitalism that attracted Soviet reformers. Gorbachev wanted his reforms to emulate the Swedish model. His vision was not of laissez-faire capitalism but of a social democratic welfare state. Second, the Right's triumphalism in the economic sphere is ironic. The West's robust economies owe much of their relative stability and health to two generations of Keynesian intervention and government involvement that the Right opposed at every step. As with Western popular culture, the Right opposed tendencies in the West that proved vital in the West's victory. . . .

Behind the debate over who "won" the Cold War are competing images of the forces shaping recent history. Containment, strength, and confrontation—the trinity enshrined in conventional thinking on Western foreign policy's role in ending the Cold War—obscure the nature of these momentous changes. Engagement and interdependence, rather than containment, are the ruling trends of the age. Mutual vulnerability, not strength, drives security politics. Accommodation and integration, not confrontation, are the motors of change.

That such encouraging trends were established and deepened even as the Cold War raged demonstrates the considerable continuity underlying the West's support today for reform in the post-Soviet transition. Those trends also expose as one-sided and self-serving the New Right's attempt to take credit for the success of forces that, in truth, they opposed. In the end, Reagan partisans have been far more successful in claiming victory in the Cold War than they were in achieving it.

✖ FURTHER READING

David Armstrong and Erik Goldstein, eds., *The End of the Cold War* (1990)

Anders Åslund, *Gorbachev's Struggle for Economic Reform* (1989)

Richard J. Barnet and John Cavanagh, *Global Dreams: Imperial Corporations and the New World Order* (1994)

Donald C. Baucom, *The Origins of SDI, 1944–1983* (1992)

Coral Bell, *The Reagan Paradox* (1989)

C. Fred Bergsten and William R. Cline, *The United States–Japan Economic Problem* (1987)

Larry Berman, ed., *Looking Back on the Reagan Presidency* (1990)

William C. Berman, *America's Right Turn* (1994)

Michael A. Bernstein et al., eds., *Understanding American Economic Decline* (1994)

Michael R. Beschloss and Strobe Talbott, *At the Highest Levels* (1993)

Seweryn Bialer and Michael Mandelbaum, eds., *Gorbachev's Russia and American Foreign Policy* (1988)

Sidney Blumenthal and Thomas B. Edsall, eds., *The Reagan Legacy* (1988)

Paul Boyer, ed., *Reagan as President* (1990)

Roger Buckley, *US-Japan Alliance Diplomacy* (1992)

Dan Caldwell, *The Dynamics of Domestic Politics and Arms Control* (1991)

David P. Calleo, *Beyond American Hegemony* (1987)

Colin Campbell and Bert A. Rockman, *The Bush Presidency* (1991)

Lou Cannon, *President Reagan* (1991)

James Chace, *The Consequences of the Peace* (1992)

Stephen F. Cohen, "Gorbachev and the Soviet Reformation," in Stephen F. Cohen and Katrina Vanden Heuvel, eds., *Voices of Glasnost* (1989), pp. 13–32

Bruce Cumings, " 'Revising Post-Revisionism,' " *Diplomatic History*, 17 (1993), 539–569

Robert Dallek, *Ronald Reagan* (1984)

Dusko Doder and Louise Branson, *Gorbachev* (1990)

Theodore Draper, *A Very Thin Line* (1991) (Iran-Contra)

Michael Duffy and Dan Goodgame, *Marching in Place* (1992)

Matthew Evangelista, "Sources of Moderation in Soviet Security Policy," in Philip E. Tetlock et al., eds., *Behavior, Society, and Nuclear War* (1991), pp. 254–354

Michael A. Freney and Rebecca S. Hartley, *United Germany and the United States* (1991)

John Lewis Gaddis, *The Long Peace* (1987)

———, "The Tragedy of Cold War History," *Diplomatic History,* 17 (1993), 1–16

———, *The United States and the End of the Cold War* (1992)

Jeffrey E. Garten, *A Cold Peace* (1992)

Raymond L. Garthoff, *Détente and Confrontation* (1985)

Charles Gati, *The Bloc That Failed* (1990)

Alexander George et al., eds., *U.S.-Soviet Security Cooperation* (1988)

Fred I. Greenstein, ed., *The Reagan Presidency* (1983)

Fred Halliday, *From Kabul to Managua* (1989)

Jim Hanson, *The Decline of the American Empire* (1993)

Erwin C. Hargrove, *Jimmy Carter as President* (1988)

Jonathan Haslam, *The Soviet Union and the Politics of Nuclear Weapons in Europe, 1969–87* (1990)

Michael J. Hogan, ed., *The End of the Cold War* (1992)

Samuel P. Huntington, "The U.S.—Decline or Renewal?" *Foreign Affairs,* 67 (1988/89), 76–96

William G. Hyland, *The Cold War Is Over* (1990)

Robert Jervis and Seweryn Bialer, eds., *Soviet-American Relations After the Cold War* (1991)

Haynes Johnson, *Sleepwalking Through History* (1991)

Sheila K. Johnson, *The Japanese Through American Eyes* (1990)

Charles O. Jones, *The Trusteeship Presidency* (1988) (Carter)

Robert G. Kaiser, *How Gorbachev Happened* (1991)

Burton I. Kaufman, *The Presidency of James Earl Carter, Jr.* (1993)

William W. Kaufmann, *Glasnost, Perestroika, and U.S. Defense Spending* (1990)

Charles W. Kegley, ed., *The Long Postwar Peace* (1991)

Paul Kennedy, "A Declining Empire Goes to War," *Wall Street Journal,* January 24, 1991

Michael T. Klare and Peter Kornbluh, eds., *Low-Intensity Warfare* (1988)

David E. Kyvig, *Reagan and the World* (1990)

Richard Ned Lebow and Janice Gross Stein, "Reagan and the Russians," *Atlantic Monthly,* 273 (February 1994), 35–37

———, *We All Lost the Cold War* (1994)

Edward T. Linenthal, *Symbolic Defense* (1989) (SDI)

Allen Lynch, *The Cold War Is Over—Again* (1992)

Sean M. Lynn-Jones, ed., *The Cold War and After* (1991)

Michael MccGwire, *Military Objectives in Soviet Foreign Policy* (1987)

Thomas J. McCormick, *America's Half-Century* (1995)

Jeff McMahan, *Reagan and the World* (1986)

Thomas E. Mann, *A Question of Balance* (1990) (Congress)

Walter Mead, *Mortal Splendor* (1987)

Richard A. Melanson, *Reconstructing Consensus* (1991)

Morris Morley, *Crisis and Confrontation* (1988)

Henry R. Nau, *The Myth of America's Decline* (1990)

John Newhouse, *War and Peace in the Nuclear Age* (1989)

Janne E. Nolan, *Guardians of the Arsenal* (1989)

Joseph S. Nye, Jr., *Bound to Lead* (1990)

Kenneth A. Oye et al., eds., *Eagle Defiant* (1983)

———, *Eagle Resurgent?* (1987)

Joseph E. Persico, *Casey* (1990)

Eric F. Petersen, "The End of the Cold War: A Review of Recent Literature," *History Teacher,* 26 (1993), 471–485

John Prados, *Presidents' Secret Wars* (1986)

Thomas Risse-Kappen, "Did 'Peace Through Strength' End the Cold War? Lessons from INF," *International Security*, 16 (1991), 162–188

Nicholas X. Rizopolous, ed., *Sea-Changes* (1990)

Michael Rogin, *Ronald Reagan* (1987)

Richard Rosecrance, *America's Economic Resurgence* (1990)

Michael Schaller, *Reckoning with Reagan* (1992)

Gaddis Smith, *Morality, Reason, and Power* (1986) (Carter)

Steven K. Smith and Douglas A. Wertman, *US–Western European Relations During the Reagan Years* (1992)

Leonard S. Spector, *Nuclear Ambitions* (1990)

"The Strange Death of Soviet Communism," *National Interest,* no. 31 (1993), special issue

Strobe Talbott, *The Russians and Reagan* (1984)

Gregory F. Treverton, *America, Germany, and the Future of Europe* (1992)

Robert W. Tucker and David C. Hendrickson, *The Imperial Temptation* (1992)

Daniel Wirls, *Buildup* (1992)